D1063955

THE
EXPOSITOR'S
BIBLE
COMMENTARY

General Editor:

FRANK E. GAEBELEIN
Former Headmaster, Stony Brook School;
Former Coeditor, *Christianity Today*

Associate Editor:

J. D. DOUGLAS
Editor, *The New International
Dictionary of the Christian Church*

Consulting Editors, Old Testament:

WALTER C. KAISER, JR.
Professor of Semitic Languages
and Old Testament,
Trinity Evangelical Divinity School

BRUCE K. WALTKE
Professor of Old Testament,
Regent College

Consulting Editors, New Testament:

JAMES MONTGOMERY BOICE
Pastor, Tenth Presbyterian Church,
Philadelphia, Pennsylvania

MERRILL C. TENNEY
Professor of Bible and Theology, Emeritus,
Wheaton College

Manuscript Editor:
RICHARD P. POLCYN
Zondervan Publishing House

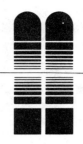

THE
EXPOSITOR'S BIBLE COMMENTARY

with
The New International Version
of
The Holy Bible

IN TWELVE VOLUMES

VOLUME 8

(MATTHEW, MARK, LUKE)

Regency
Reference Library
Zondervan Publishing House
Grand Rapids, Michigan

The Expositor's Bible Commentary
Copyright © 1984 by The Zondervan Corporation
Grand Rapids, Michigan

Regency Reference Library is an imprint of Zondervan Publishing
House, 1415 Lake Drive, S.E., Grand Rapids, Michigan 49506

Library of Congress Cataloging in Publication Data

(Revised for volume 8)
Main entry under title:
The Expositor's Bible commentary.

    Includes bibliographies.
    CONTENTS: v. 1. Introductory articles.—
—v. 8. Matthew-Mark-Luke. —v. 9. John, Acts.
    1. Bible—Commentaries. I. Gaebelein, Frank, Ely,
1899–   .   II. Douglas, James Dixon.   III. Bible.
English.   New International.   1976.
BS491.2.E96   220.6   76-41334
ISBN 0-310-36530-9 (v. 11)

The translation used in The Expositor's Bible Commentary is the New
International Version (North American edition). Copyright © 1978 by
International Bible Society. Used by permission.

Printed in the United States of America

84 85 86 87 88 89 90 — 9 8 7 6 5 4 3 2 1

CONTENTS

CONTRIBUTORS TO VOLUME 8

Matthew: D. A. Carson
B.Sc., McGill University; M.Div., Baptist Seminary in Toronto; Ph.D., Cambridge
    University
Professor of New Testament, Trinity Evangelical Divinity School

Mark: Walter W. Wessel
Th.B., Biola College; M.A., University of California, LA; Ph.D., University of
    Edinburgh, Scotland
Professor of New Testament and Greek, Bethel Theological Seminary, West Campus

Luke: Walter L. Liefeld
Th.B., Shelton College; A.M. Columbia University; Ph.D., Columbia University
    and Union Theological Seminary
Professor of New Testament, Trinity Evangelical Divinity School

By Way of Explanation

The *Expositor's Bible Commentary* allots considerably more space to the first
commentary in this volume than to the other two. Most of the critical problems that
cluster around the Synoptics relate to the Gospel of Matthew; therefore this Gospel
is the logical place for comprehensive interaction with the current views and trends.

In no sense does the length of the first commentary reflect on the other two
commentaries. The writers of these works have accomplished their tasks within the
strict parameters of the word limitation set for them.

Frank E. Gaebelein
General Editor

PREFACE

The title of this work defines its purpose. Written primarily by expositors for expositors, it aims to provide preachers, teachers, and students of the Bible with a new and comprehensive commentary on the books of the Old and New Testaments. Its stance is that of a scholarly evangelicalism committed to the divine inspiration, complete trustworthiness, and full authority of the Bible. Its seventy-eight contributors come from the United States, Canada, England, Scotland, Australia, New Zealand, and Switzerland, and from various religious groups, including Anglican, Baptist, Brethren, Free, Independent, Methodist, Nazarene, Presbyterian, and Reformed churches. Most of them teach at colleges, universities, or theological seminaries.

No book has been more closely studied over a longer period of time than the Bible. From the Midrashic commentaries going back to the period of Ezra, through parts of the Dead Sea Scrolls and the Patristic literature, and on to the present, the Scriptures have been expounded. Indeed, there have been times when, as in the Reformation and on occasions since then, exposition has been at the cutting edge of Christian advance. Luther was a powerful exegete, and Calvin is still called "the prince of expositors."

Their successors have been many. And now, when the outburst of new translations and their unparalleled circulation have expanded the readership of the Bible, the need for exposition takes on fresh urgency.

Not that God's Word can ever become captive to its expositors. Among all other books, it stands first in its combination of perspicuity and profundity. Though a child can be made "wise for salvation" by believing its witness to Christ, the greatest mind cannot plumb the depths of its truth (2 Tim. 3:15; Rom. 11:33). As Gregory the Great said, "Holy Scripture is a stream of running water, where alike the elephant may swim, and the lamb walk." So, because of the inexhaustible nature of Scripture, the task of opening up its meaning is still a perennial obligation of biblical scholarship.

How that task is done inevitably reflects the outlook of those engaged in it. Every biblical scholar has presuppositions. To this neither the editors of these volumes nor the contributors to them are exceptions. They share a common commitment to the supernatural Christianity set forth in the inspired Word. Their purpose is not to supplant the many valuable commentaries that have preceded this work and from which both the editors and contributors have learned. It is rather to draw on the resources of contemporary evangelical scholarship in producing a new reference work for understanding the Scriptures.

A commentary that will continue to be useful through the years should handle contemporary trends in biblical studies in such a way as to avoid becoming outdated when critical fashions change. Biblical criticism is not in itself inadmissible, as some have mistakenly thought. When scholars investigate the authorship, date, literary characteristics, and purpose of a biblical document, they are practicing biblical criticism. So also when, in order to ascertain as nearly as possible the original form of the text, they deal with variant readings, scribal errors, emendations, and other phenomena in the manuscripts. To do these things is essential to responsible exegesis and exposition. And always there is the need to distinguish hypothesis from fact, conjecture from truth.

The chief principle of interpretation followed in this commentary is the grammatico-historical one—namely, that the primary aim of the exegete is to make clear the meaning of the text at the time and in the circumstances of its writing. This endeavor to understand what in the first instance the inspired writers actually said must not be confused with an inflexible literalism. Scripture makes lavish use of symbols and figures of speech; great portions of it are poetical. Yet when it speaks in this way, it speaks no less truly than it does in its historical and doctrinal portions. To understand its message requires attention to matters of grammar and syntax, word meanings, idioms, and literary forms—all in relation to the historical and cultural setting of the text.

The contributors to this work necessarily reflect varying convictions. In certain controversial matters the policy is that of clear statement of the contributors' own views followed by fair presentation of other ones. The treatment of eschatology, though it reflects differences of interpretation, is consistent with a general premillennial position. (Not all contributors, however, are premillennial.) But prophecy is more than prediction, and so this commentary gives due recognition to the major lode of godly social concern in the prophetic writings.

THE EXPOSITOR'S BIBLE COMMENTARY is presented as a scholarly work, though not primarily one of technical criticism. In its main portion, the Exposition, and in Volume 1 (General and Special Articles), all Semitic and Greek words are transliterated and the English equivalents given. As for the Notes, here Semitic and Greek characters are used but always with transliterations and English meanings, so that this portion of the commentary will be as accessible as possible to readers unacquainted with the original languages.

It is the conviction of the general editor, shared by his colleagues in the Zondervan editorial department, that in writing about the Bible, lucidity is not incompatible with scholarship. They are therefore endeavoring to make this a clear and understandable work.

The translation used in it is the New International Version. To the New York International Bible Society thanks are due for permission to use this most recent of the major Bible translations. The editors and publisher have chosen it because of the clarity and beauty of its style and its faithfulness to the original texts.

To the associate editor, Dr. J. D. Douglas, and to the contributing editors—Dr. Walter C. Kaiser, Jr. and Dr. Bruce K. Waltke for the Old Testament, and Dr. James Montgomery Boice and Dr. Merrill C. Tenney for the New Testament—the general editor expresses his gratitude for their unfailing cooperation and their generosity in advising him out of their expert scholarship. And to the many other contributors he is indebted for their invaluable part in this work. Finally, he owes a special debt of gratitude to Dr. Robert K. DeVries, publisher, The Zondervan Corporation; Richard P. Polcyn, manuscript editor; and Miss Elizabeth Brown, secretary, for their continual assistance and encouragement.

Whatever else it is—the greatest and most beautiful of books, the primary source of law and morality, the fountain of wisdom, and the infallible guide to life—the Bible is above all the inspired witness to Jesus Christ. May this work fulfill its function of expounding the Scriptures with grace and clarity, so that its users may find that both Old and New Testaments do indeed lead to our Lord Jesus Christ, who alone could say, "I have come that they may have life, and have it to the full" (John 10:10).

FRANK E. GAEBELEIN

ABBREVIATIONS

A. General Abbreviations

A	Codex Alexandrinus
Akkad.	Akkadian
א	Codex Sinaiticus
Ap. Lit.	Apocalyptic Literature
Apoc.	Apocrypha
Aq.	Aquila's Greek Translation of the Old Testament
Arab.	Arabic
Aram.	Aramaic
b	Babylonian Gemara
B	Codex Vaticanus
C	Codex Ephraemi Syri
c.	*circa*, about
cf.	*confer*, compare
ch., chs.	chapter, chapters
cod., codd.	codex, codices
contra	in contrast to
D	Codex Bezae
DSS	Dead Sea Scrolls (see E.)
ed., edd.	edited, edition, editor; editions
e.g.	*exempli gratia*, for example
Egyp.	Egyptian
et. al.	*et alii*, and others
EV	English Versions of the Bible
fem.	feminine
ff.	following (verses, pages, etc.)
fl.	flourished
ft.	foot, feet
gen.	genitive
Gr.	Greek
Heb.	Hebrew
Hitt.	Hittite
ibid.	*ibidem*, in the same place
id.	*idem*, the same
i.e.	*id est*, that is
impf.	imperfect
infra.	below
in loc.	*in loco*, in the place cited
j	Jerusalem or Palestinian Gemara
Lat.	Latin
LL.	Late Latin
LXX	Septuagint
M	Mishnah
masc.	masculine
mg.	margin
Mid	Midrash
MS(S)	manuscript(s)
MT	Masoretic text
n.	note
n.d.	no date
Nestle	Nestle (ed.) *Novum Testamentum Graece*
no.	number
NT	New Testament
obs.	obsolete
OL	Old Latin
OS	Old Syriac
OT	Old Testament
p., pp.	page, pages
par.	paragraph
Pers.	Persian
Pesh.	Peshitta
Phoen.	Phoenician
pl.	plural
Pseudep.	Pseudepigrapha
Q	Quelle ("Sayings" source in the Gospels)
qt.	quoted by
q.v.	*quod vide*, which see
R	Rabbah
rev.	revised, reviser, revision
Rom.	Roman
RVm	Revised Version margin
Samar.	Samaritan recension
SCM	Student Christian Movement Press
Sem.	Semitic
sing.	singular
SPCK	Society for the Promotion of Christian Knowledge
Sumer.	Sumerian
s.v.	*sub verbo*, under the word
Syr.	Syriac
Symm.	Symmachus
T	Talmud
Targ.	Targum
Theod.	Theodotion
TR	Textus Receptus
tr.	translation, translator, translated
UBS	Tha United Bible Societies' Greek Text
Ugar.	Ugaritic
u.s.	*ut supra*, as above
v., vv.	verse, verses
viz.	*videlicet*, namely
vol.	volume
vs.	versus
Vul.	Vulgate
WH	Westcott and Hort, *The New Testament in Greek*

B. Abbreviations for Modern Translations and Paraphrases

AmT	Smith and Goodspeed, *The Complete Bible, An American Translation*	Mof	J. Moffatt, *A New Translation of the Bible*
ASV	American Standard Version, American Revised Version (1901)	NAB	The New American Bible
		NASB	New American Standard Bible
		NEB	The New English Bible
		NIV	The New International Version
Beck	Beck, *The New Testament in the Language of Today*	Ph	J. B. Phillips *The New Testament in Modern English*
BV	Berkeley Version (The Modern Language Bible)	RSV	Revised Standard Version
		RV	Revised Version — 1881–1885
JB	The Jerusalem Bible	TCNT	Twentieth Century New Testament
JPS	*Jewish Publication Society Version of the Old Testament*		
		TEV	Today's English Version
KJV	King James Version	Wey	*Weymouth's New Testament in Modern Speech*
Knox	R.G. Knox, *The Holy Bible: A Translation from the Latin Vulgate in the Light of the Hebrew and Greek Original*		
		Wms	C. B. Williams, *The New Testament: A Translation in the Language of the People*
LB	The Living Bible		

C. Abbreviations for Periodicals and Reference Works

AASOR	*Annual of the American Schools of Oriental Research*	BASOR	*Bulletin of the American Schools of Oriental Research*
AB	*Anchor Bible*	BC	Foakes-Jackson and Lake: *The Beginnings of Christianity*
AIs	de Vaux: *Ancient Israel*		
AJA	*American Journal of Archaeology*	BDB	Brown, Driver, and Briggs: *Hebrew-English Lexicon of the Old Testament*
AJSL	*American Journal of Semitic Languages and Literatures*	BDF	Blass, Debrunner, and Funk: *A Greek Grammar of the New Testament and Other Early Christian Literature*
AJT	*American Journal of Theology*		
Alf	Alford: *Greek Testament Commentary*	BDT	Harrison: *Baker's Dictionary of Theology*
ANEA	*Ancient Near Eastern Archaeology*	Beng.	Bengel's *Gnomon*
ANET	Pritchard: *Ancient Near Eastern Texts*	BETS	*Bulletin of the Evangelical Theological Society*
ANF	Roberts and Donaldson: *The Ante-Nicene Fathers*	BH	*Biblia Hebraica*
		BHS	*Biblia Hebraica Stuttgartensia*
ANT	M. R. James: *The Apocryphal New Testament*	BJRL	*Bulletin of the John Rylands Library*
A-S	Abbot-Smith: *Manual Greek Lexicon of the New Testament*	BS	*Bibliotheca Sacra*
		BT	*Babylonian Talmud*
AThR	*Anglican Theological Review*	BTh	*Biblical Theology*
BA	*Biblical Archaeologist*	BW	*Biblical World*
BAG	Bauer, Arndt, and Gingrich: *Greek-English Lexicon of the New Testament*	CAH	*Cambridge Ancient History*
		CanJTh	*Canadian Journal of Theology*
		CBQ	*Catholic Biblical Quarterly*
BAGD	Bauer, Arndt, Gingrich, and Danker: *Greek-English Lexicon of the New Testament* 2nd edition	CBSC	*Cambridge Bible for Schools and Colleges*
		CE	*Catholic Encyclopedia*
		CGT	*Cambridge Greek Testament*

MST	McClintock and Strong: *Cyclopedia of Biblical, Theological, and Ecclesiastical Literature*		*Encyclopedia of Religious Knowledge*
		SJT	*Scottish Journal of Theology*
NBC	Davidson, Kevan, and Stibbs: *The New Bible Commentary*, 1st ed.	SOT	Girdlestone: *Synonyms of Old Testament*
		SOTI	Archer: *A Survey of Old Testament Introduction*
NBCrev.	Guthrie and Motyer: *The New Bible Commentary*, rev. ed.	ST	*Studia Theologica*
		TCERK	Loetscher: *The Twentieth Century Encyclopedia of Religious Knowledge*
NBD	J. D. Douglas: *The New Bible Dictionary*		
NCB	*New Century Bible*	TDNT	Kittel: *Theological Dictionary of the New Testament*
NCE	*New Catholic Encyclopedia*		
NIC	*New International Commentary*	TDOT	*Theological Dictionary of the Old Testament*
NIDCC	Douglas: *The New International Dictionary of the Christian Church*	Theol	*Theology*
		ThT	*Theology Today*
NovTest	*Novum Testamentum*	TNTC	*Tyndale New Testament Commentaries*
NSI	Cooke: *Handbook of North Semitic Inscriptions*		
		Trench	Trench: *Synonyms of the New Testament*
NTS	*New Testament Studies*		
ODCC	*The Oxford Dictionary of the Christian Church*, rev. ed.	TWOT	*Theological Wordbook of the Old Testament*
Peake	Black and Rowley: *Peake's Commentary on the Bible*	UBD	*Unger's Bible Dictionary*
		UT	Gordon: *Ugaritic Textbook*
PEQ	*Palestine Exploration Quarterly*	VB	Allmen: *Vocabulary of the Bible*
PNFl	P. Schaff: *The Nicene and Post-Nicene Fathers* (1st series)		
		VetTest	*Vetus Testamentum*
		Vincent	Vincent: *Word-Pictures in the New Testament*
PNF2	P. Schaff and H. Wace: *The Nicene and Post-Nicene Fathers* (2nd series)		
		WBC	*Wycliffe Bible Commentary*
		WBE	*Wycliffe Bible Encyclopedia*
PTR	*Princeton Theological Review*	WC	*Westminster Commentaries*
RB	*Revue Biblique*	WesBC	*Wesleyan Bible Commentaries*
RHG	Robertson's *Grammar of the Greek New Testament in the Light of Historical Research*	WTJ	*Westminster Theological Journal*
		ZAW	*Zeitschrift für die alttestamentliche Wissenschaft*
		ZNW	*Zeitschrift für die neutestamentliche Wissenschaft*
RTWB	Richardson: *A Theological Wordbook of the Bible*		
		ZPBD	*The Zondervan Pictorial Bible Dictionary*
SBK	Strack and Billerbeck: *Kommentar zum Neuen Testament aus Talmud und Midrash*		
		ZPEB	*The Zondervan Pictorial Encyclopedia of the Bible*
		ZWT	*Zeitschrift für wissenschaftliche Theologie*
SHERK	*The New Schaff-Herzog*		

D. Abbreviations for Books of the Bible, the Apocrypha, and the Pseudepigrapha

OLD TESTAMENT

Gen	2 Chron	Dan
Exod	Ezra	Hos
Lev	Neh	Joel
Num	Esth	Amos
Deut	Job	Obad
Josh	Ps(Pss)	Jonah
Judg	Prov	Mic
Ruth	Eccl	Nah
1 Sam	S of Songs	Hab
2 Sam	Isa	Zeph
1 Kings	Jer	Hag
2 Kings	Lam	Zech
1 Chron	Ezek	Mal

NEW TESTAMENT

Matt	1 Tim
Mark	2 Tim
Luke	Titus
John	Philem
Acts	Heb
Rom	James
1 Cor	1 Peter
2 Cor	2 Peter
Gal	1 John
Eph	2 John
Phil	3 John
Col	Jude
1 Thess	Rev
2 Thess	

APOCRYPHA

1 Esd	1 Esdras	Ep Jer	Epistle of Jeremy
2 Esd	2 Esdras	S Th Ch	Song of the Three Child
Tobit	Tobit		(or Young Men)
Jud	Judith	Sus	Susanna
Add Esth	Additions to Esther	Bel	Bel and the Dragon
Wisd Sol	Wisdom of Solomon	Pr Man	Prayer of Manasseh
Ecclus	Ecclesiasticus (Wisdom of	1 Macc	1 Maccabees
	Jesus the Son of Sirach)	2 Macc	2 Maccabees
Baruch	Baruch		

PSEUDEPIGRAPHA

As Moses	Assumption of Moses	Pirke Aboth	Pirke Aboth
2 Baruch	Syriac Apocalypse of Baruch	Ps 151	Psalm 151
3 Baruch	Greek Apocalypse of Baruch	Pss Sol	Psalms of Solomon
1 Enoch	Ethiopic Book of Enoch	Sib Oracles	Sibylline Oracles
2 Enoch	Slavonic Book of Enoch	Story Ah	Story of Ahikar
3 Enoch	Hebrew Book of Enoch	T Abram	Testament of Abraham
4 Ezra	4 Ezra	T Adam	Testament of Adam
JA	Joseph and Asenath	T Benjamin	Testament of Benjamin
Jub	Book of Jubilees	T Dan	Testament of Dan
L Aristeas	Letter of Aristeas	T Gad	Testament of Gad
Life AE	Life of Adam and Eve	T Job	Testament of Job
Liv Proph	Lives of the Prophets	T Jos	Testament of Joseph
MA Isa	Martyrdom and Ascension	T Levi	Testament of Levi
	of Isaiah	T Naph	Testament of Naphtali
3 Macc	3 Maccabees	T 12 Pat	Testaments of the Twe
4 Macc	4 Maccabees		Patriarchs
Odes Sol	Odes of Solomon	Zad Frag	Zadokite Fragments
P Jer	Paralipomena of Jeremiah		

E. Abbreviations of Names of Dead Sea Scrolls and Related Texts

CD	Cairo (Genizah text of the) Damascus (Document)	1QSa	Appendix A (Rule of the Congregation) to 1Qs
DSS	Dead Sea Scrolls	1QSb	Appendix B (Blessings) to 1QS
Hev	Nahal Hever texts	3Q15	Copper Scroll from Qumran Cave 3
Mas	Masada Texts	4QExod a	Exodus Scroll, exemplar "a" from Qumran Cave 4
Mird	Khirbet mird texts		
Mur	Wadi Murabba'at texts	4QFlor	Florilegium (or Eschatological Midrashim) from Qumran Cave 4
P	Pesher (commentary)		
Q	Qumran		
1Q, 2Q, etc.	Numbered caves of Qumran, yielding written material; followed by abbreviation of biblical or apocryphal book.	4Qmess ar	Aramaic "Messianic" text from Qumran Cave 4
		4QpNah	Pesher on portions of Nahum from Qumran Cave 4
QL	Qumran Literature		
1QapGen	Genesis Apocryphon of Qumran Cave 1	4QPrNab	Prayer of Nabonidus from Qumran Cave 4
1QH	*Hodayot* (Thanksgiving Hymns) from Qumran Cave 1	4QpPs37	Pesher on portions of Psalm 37 from Qumran Cave 4
1QIsa a,b	First or second copy of Isaiah from Qumran Cave 1	4QTest	Testimonia text from Qumran Cave 4
1QpHab	Pesher on Habakkuk from Qumran Cave 1	4QTLevi	Testament of Levi from Qumran Cave 4
1QM	*Milhamah* (War Scroll)	4QPhyl	Phylacteries from Qumran Cave 4
1QpMic	Pesher on portions of Micah from Qumran Cave 1	11QMelch	Melchizedek text from Qumran Cave 11
1QS	*Serek Hayyahad* (Rule of the Community, Manual of Discipline)	11QtgJob	Targum of Job from Qumran Cave 11

TRANSLITERATIONS

Hebrew

א	= '	ד	= $\underline{d}$	י	= y	ס	= s	ר	= r
בּ	= b	ה	= h	כּ	= k	ע	= '	שׂ	= $ś$
ב	= $\underline{b}$	ו	= w	כ ך	= $\underline{k}$	פּ	= p	שׁ	= $š$
גּ	= g	ז	= z	ל	= l	פ ף	= $\underline{p}$	תּ	= t
ג	= $\underline{g}$	ח	= $ḥ$	ם מ	= m	צ ץ	= $ṣ$	ת	= $\underline{t}$
ד	= d	ט	= $ṭ$	ן נ	= n	ק	= q		

(ה)ָ	= $â$ (h)	ָ	= $ā$	ַ	= a	ֱ	= ^{a}
ֵי	= $ê$	ֵ	= $ē$	ֶ	= e	ֳ	= ^{e}
ִי	= $î$	ֹ	= $ō$	ִ	= i	ְ	= ^{e} (*if vocal*)
וֹ	= $ô$			ָ	= o	ֳ	= ^{o}
וּ	= $û$			ֻ	= u		

Aramaic

' b g d h w z $ḥ$ $ṭ$ y k l m n s ' p $ṣ$ q r $ś$ $š$ t

Arabic

' b t $\underline{t}$ $ǧ$ $ḥ$ $\underline{h}$ d $\underline{d}$ r z s $š$ $ṣ$ $ḍ$ $ṭ$ $ẓ$ ' $ġ$ f q k l m n h w y

Ugaritic

' b g d $\underline{d}$ h w z $ḥ$ $\underline{h}$ $ṭ$ $ẓ$ y k l m n s $ṡ$ ' $ġ$ $ṗ$ $ṣ$ q r $š$ t $\underline{t}$

xv

Greek

α	—	a	π	—	p	αι	—	ai
β	—	b	ρ	—	r	αὐ	—	au
γ	—	g	σ,ς	—	s	ει	—	ei
δ	—	d	τ	—	t	εὐ	—	eu
ε	—	e	υ	—	y	ηὐ	—	ēu
ζ	—	z	φ	—	ph	οι	—	oi
η	—	ē	χ	—	ch	οὐ	—	ou
θ	—	th	ψ	—	ps	υι	—	hui
ι	—	i	ω	—	ō			
κ	—	k				ῥ	—	rh
λ	—	l	γγ	—	ng	῾	—	h
μ	—	m	γκ	—	nk			
ν	—	n	γξ	—	nx	ᾳ	—	ā
ξ	—	x	γχ	—	nch	ῃ	—	ē
ο	—	o				ῳ	—	ō

MATTHEW

D.A. Carson

MATTHEW

Introduction

1. The Criticism of Matthew

The earliest church fathers to mention this Gospel concur that the author was the apostle Matthew. Papias's famous statement (cf. section 3) was interpreted to mean

"Matthew composed the *Logia* [Gospel?] in the Hebrew [Aramaic?] dialect and every one interpreted them as he was able." In other words the apostle first wrote his Gospel in Hebrew or Aramaic, and it was subsequently translated into Greek. Matthean priority was almost universally upheld; Mark was considered an abbreviation and therefore somewhat inferior. These factors—apostolic authorship (unlike Mark and Luke) and Matthean priority—along with the fact that Matthew preserves much of Jesus' teaching not found elsewhere, combined to give this first Gospel enormous influence and prestige in the church. With few exceptions these perspectives dominated Gospel study till after the Reformation.

The consensus could not last. An indication of its intrinsic frailty came in 1776 and 1778 when, in two posthumously published essays, A.E. Lessing insisted that the only way to account for the parallels and seeming discrepancies among the synoptic Gospels was to assume that they all derived independently from an Aramaic *Gospel of the Nazarenes*. Others (J.A. Eichorn, J.G. Herder) developed this idea; and the supposition of a Primal Gospel, whether oral or literary, began to gain influence. Meanwhile J.J. Griesbach (1745–1812) laid the foundations of the modern debate over the "synoptic problem" (cf. section 3) by arguing with some care for the priority of both Matthew and Luke over Mark, which was taken to be a condensation of the other two. In the middle of the nineteenth century, many in the Tübingen school adopted this view. As a result Matthew as an historical and theological source was elevated above the other Synoptics.

By the end of the nineteenth century, a new tide was running. Owing largely to the meticulous work of H.J. Holtzmann (1834–1910), the "two-source hypothesis" gained substantial acceptance (see EBC, 1:445–47, 510–14). By the beginning of the twentieth century, this theory was almost universally adopted; and subsequent developments were in reality mere modifications of this theory. B.H. Streeter,[1] advocating a "four-source hypothesis" that was essentially a detailed refinement of the two-source theory, argued that Luke's Gospel is made-up of a "Proto-Luke" that was filled out with Mark and Q. This raised the historical reliability of Proto-Luke to the same level as Mark. Streeter's hypothesis still has some followers, and today most scholars adopt some form of the two-source theory or the four-source theory. This consensus has recently been challenged (cf. section 3).

These predominantly literary questions combined with the substantial antisupernaturalism of some critics at the turn of the century to produce various reconstructions of Jesus' life and teaching (see EBC, 1:519–21). During the 1920s and 1930s, the source criticism implicit in these efforts was largely passed by in favor of form criticism (see EBC, 1:447–48). Philologists first applied this method to the "folk literature" of primitive civilizations, especially the Maoris. H. Gunkel and H. Gressmann then used it to classify OT materials according to their "form." New Testament scholars, especially K.L. Schmidt, M. Dibelius, and R. Bultmann (*Synoptic Tradition*), applied the method to the Gospels in an effort to explore the so-called tunnel period between Jesus and the earliest written sources. They began by isolating small sections of the Gospels that they took to be units of oral tradition, classifying them according to form (see EBC, 1:447). Only the passion narrative was taken as a connected account from the beginning. Oral transmission was thought to effect regular modifications common to all such literature (EBC, 1:444–45)—e.g.,

---

[1]*The Four Gospels* (London: Macmillan, 1924).

repetition engenders brevity in pronouncement stories and provides names in legends, rhythm and balance in didactic sayings, and multiple details in miracle stories. The form critics then assigned these forms to various *Sitze im Leben* ("life settings") in the church (see EBC, 1:511–13).

The historical value of any pericope was then assessed against a number of criteria. For instance, the "criterion of dissimilarity" was used to weed out statements attributed to Jesus that were similar to what Palestinian Judaism or early Christianity might have said. Only if a statement was "dissimilar" could it be ascribed with reasonable confidence to Jesus. The net result was a stifling historical skepticism with respect to the canonical Gospels. Many scholars used the same literary methods in a more conservative fashion (e.g., V. Taylor's great commentary on Mark); but the effect of form criticism was to increase the distance between our canonical Gospels and the historical Jesus, a distance increased yet further in Matthew's case because of the continued dominance of the two-source hypothesis. Few any longer believed that Matthew the apostle was the first evangelist.[2]

Following World War II a major change took place. Anticipated by Kilpatrick's study, which focused on the distinctives in Matthew's theology, the age of redaction criticism as applied to Matthew began with a 1948 essay by G. Bornkamm (printed in English as "The Stilling of the Storm in Matthew," *Tradition*, pp. 52–57). He presupposed Mark's priority and then in one pericope sought to explain every change between the two Gospels as a reflection of Matthew's theological interests and biases. Redaction criticism offered one great advantage over form criticism: it saw the evangelists, not as mere compilers of the church's oral traditions and organizers of stories preserved or created in various forms, but as theologians in their own right, shaping and adapting the material in order to make their own points. It became important to distinguish between "traditional" material and "redactional" material, i.e., between what came to the evangelist already formed and the changes and additions he made. In other words, while tradition may preserve authentic historical material, redactional material does not do so. It rather serves as the best way of discerning an evangelist's distinctive ideas. In his meticulous study of one pericope, Bornkamm sought to demonstrate a better method of understanding Matthew's theology—a method that could best be discerned by trying to understand how and why Matthew changed his sources (esp. Mark and Q).

Countless studies have poured forth in Bornkamm's wake, applying the same methods to virtually every pericope in Matthew. The translation of redaction-critical studies by G. Bornkamm, G. Barth, and H.J. Held (*Tradition*) has exercised profound influence in the world of New Testament scholarship; and in 1963 the first full-scale redaction-critical commentary on Matthew appeared (Bonnard). Bonnard handles his tools fairly conservatively. He frequently refuses to comment on historical questions and focuses on Matthew's theology and the reasons (based on reconstructed "life settings") for it. His work, which is immensely valuable, became the forerunner of several later English commentaries (notably Hill's).

Nevertheless a rather naive optimism regarding historical reconstruction has de-

---

[2]For a convenient history of the criticism of Matthew up to this point, see, in addition to some of the major introductions, W.G. Kümmel, *The New Testament: The History of the Investigation of Its Problems* (tr. S.McL. Gilmour and H.C. Kee [Nashville: Abingdon, 1972, and London: SCM, 1973]); Stephen Neill, *The Interpretation of the New Testament 1861–1961* (London and New York: Oxford University Press, 1964).

veloped. Virtually all recent writers on Matthew think they can read off from Matthew's redaction the theological beliefs either of Matthew's community or of the evangelist himself as he sought to correct or defend some part of his community. Kilpatrick argues that the book is catechetical, designed for the church of Matthew's time. Stendahl (*School of Matthew*) thinks the handling of the OT quotations reflects a "school" that stands behind the writing of this Gospel, a disciplined milieu of instruction. The major redaction-critical studies all attempt to define the historical context in which the evangelist writes, the community circumstances that call this Gospel into being (it is thought) between A.D. 80 and A.D. 100, and pay little useful attention to the historical context of Jesus. One need only think of such works as those of Trilling, Strecker (*Weg*), Cope (*Matthew*), Hare, Frankemölle, and the recent books by Thysman and Künzel, to name a few.[3]

Not all redaction critics interpret Matthew's reconstructed community the same way; indeed, the differences among them are often great. Moreover, several recent critics have argued that much more material in the Gospels (including Matthew's) is authentic than was recognized ten years ago.[4] Yet the wide diversity of opinion suggests at least some methodological and presuppositional disarray.

A modern commentary that aims primarily to explain the text must to some extent respond to current questions and the more so if it adopts a fairly independent stance.[5] For many of these questions greatly affect our understanding of what the text says.

2. History and Theology

Few problems are philosophically and theologically more complex than the possible relationships between history and theology. The broader issues in the tension between these two cannot be discussed here: e.g., How does a transcendent God manifest himself in space-time history? Can the study of history allow, in its reconstructions of the past, for authority and influence outside the space-time continuum? To what extent is the supernatural an essential part of Christianity, and what does it mean to approach such matters "historically"? What are the epistemological bases

---

[3]Raymond Thysman, *Communauté et directives ethiques. La catéchèse de Matthieu* (Gembloux: Duculot, 1974); G. Künzel, *Studien zum Gemeindeverständnis des Matthäus-Evangeliums* (Stuttgart: Calwer, 1978); and, for recent surveys of Matthean studies, R.P. Martin, *New Testament Foundations*, 2 vols. (Grand Rapids: Eerdmans, 1975–78), 1:224–43, and esp. the careful essay by Stanton ("Origin and Purpose").

[4]See, for instance, B.F. Meyer; R. Latourelle, *Finding Jesus Through the Gospels*, tr. A. Owen (New York: Alba, 1979); and the recent writings of such scholars as M. Hengel, J. Roloff, H. Schürmann, and P. Stuhlmacher.

[5]The various periods described are not completely sealed off from the other ones, and some did run against the tide of scholarly trends. From rather different perspectives, Schlatter and Stonehouse (*Witness of Matthew*) anticipated the more useful and reliable elements of redaction criticism, pointing out distinctive themes in Matthew's Gospel with deliberate caution and precision. On the other hand, when as recently as 1973 Hendriksen produced his large commentary on Matthew, he took relatively little note of recent developments; yet his work is doubtless of considerable help to pastors. Compare also the independent stances of Maier and of Albright and Mann.

for a system professing to be revealed religion?[6] Even the titles of recent books about Jesus show the chasm that separates scholar from scholar on these points.[7]

This section will therefore ask some preliminary methodological questions.[8] How appropriate and reliable are the various methods of studying the Gospels if we are to determine not only the theological distinctives of each evangelist but also something of the teaching and life of the historical Jesus? We must begin by avoiding many of the historical and theological disjunctions[9] notoriously common among NT scholars. An example is the recent essay by K. Tagama,[10] who arrives at his conclusion that the central theme of Matthew is "people and community" by insisting that all other important themes are mutually contradictory and therefore cancel one another out. But "contradiction" is a slippery category. As most commonly used in NT scholarship, it does not refer to logical contradiction but to situations, ideas, beliefs that on the basis of the modern scholar's reconstruction of early church history are judged to be mutually incompatible.[11]

Such judgments are only as convincing as the historical and theological reconstructions undergirding them; and too often historical reconstructions that in many cases have no other sources than the NT documents depend on illicit disjunctions. Did Jesus preach the nearness of the end of history and of the consummated kingdom? Then he could not have preached that the kingdom had already been inaugurated, and elements apparently denying this conclusion obviously spring from the church. Or did Jesus preach that the kingdom had already dawned? Then the apocalyptic element in the Gospels must be largely assigned to the later church. (On this particular problem, see comments at 3:2; 10:23; and ch. 24.) Was Jesus a proto-rabbi, steeped in OT law and Jewish tradition? Then Paul's emphasis on grace is entirely innovative. Or did Jesus break Jewish Halakah (rules of conduct based on traditional interpretations of the law)? Then clearly Matthew's emphasis on the law (e.g., 5:17–20; 23:1–26) reflects the stance of Matthew's church, or suggests that Matthew wishes to legislate for his church, without helping us come to grips with the historical Jesus. Better yet Matthew's Gospel may even be considered a Jewish-Christian reaction against "Paulinism."

All such disjunctive reconstructions are suspect. Historical "contradictions," as Fischer has shown, too often reside in the eye of the historian. Strange combina-

---

6 On these and similar questions, see, in particular, E.E. Cairns, *God and Man in Time: A Christian Approach to Historiography* (Grand Rapids: Baker, 1979); G.H. Clark, *Historiography: Secular and Religious* (Nutley, N.J.: Craig, 1971); C.T. McIntyre, ed., *God, History and Historians: An Anthology of Modern Christian Views of History* (New York: Oxford University Press, 1977); J.A. Passmore, "The Objectivity of History," *Philosophical Analysis and History*, ed. W.H. Doty (New York: Harper and Row, 1966): 75–94; W.C. Smith, *Belief and History* (Charlottesville: University Press of Virginia, 1977); and A.C. Thiselton, *The Two Horizons* (Grand Rapids: Eerdmans, 1980).

7 Contrast G. Vos, *The Self-Disclosure of Jesus: The Modern Debate About the Messianic Consciousness* (Grand Rapids: Eerdmans, 1954), and G. Vermes, *Jesus the Jew: A Historian's Reading of the Gospels* (London: Collins, 1973).

8 Cf. H. Palmer, *The Logic of Gospel Criticism* (London: Macmillan, 1968), pp. 1ff.; B.F. Meyer, esp. pp. 76–110; Gundry, *Use of OT*, p. 189ff.

9 Cf. Fischer. A fine example is Schweizer's statement (*Matthew*, p. 11) that "the evangelist's intent . . . was theological rather than historical."

10 "People and Community in the Gospel of Matthew," NTS 16 (1969–70): 149–62.

11 This is dealt with at some length in Martin Hengel, *Acts and the History of Earliest Christianity* (London: SCM, 1979), pp. 35–68; Carson, "Historical Tradition," pp. 115–21.

tions of ideas may coexist side by side in one generation, even though a later generation cannot tolerate them and therefore breaks them up. So we need to be cautious about pronouncing what ideas can be "historically" compatible. Acts and the early Pauline Epistles show us considerable diversity in the fast-growing infant church, as a number of NT studies attempt to explain.[12]

Reconstruction is a necessary part of historical inquiry; sometimes meticulous reconstruction from a number of reliable documents shows that some further document is not what it purports to be. But as far as the Gospel of Matthew (or any of the canonical Gospels) is concerned, we must frankly confess we have no access to the alleged "Matthean [or Markan, Lukan, etc.] community" apart from the individual Gospel itself. The numerous studies describing and analyzing Matthew's theology against the background of Christianity and Judaism contemporary with Matthew's "community" in A.D. 80–100 (cf. Stanton, "Origin and Purpose," ch.3) beg a host of methodological questions. This is not to deny that Matthew's Gospel may have been written within a community about A.D. 80, or may have addressed some such community; rather is it to argue the following points.

1. What Matthew aims to write is a Gospel telling us about Jesus, not a church circular addressing an independently known problem.

2. There is substantial evidence that the early church was interested in the historical Jesus and wanted to know what he taught and why. Equally there is strong evidence that the Gospels constitute, at least in part, an essential element of the church's kerygmatic ministry, its evangelistic proclamation (Stanton, *Jesus of Nazareth*), each Gospel having been shaped for particular audiences.

3. It is therefore methodologically wrong to read off some theme attributed by the evangelist to Jesus and conclude that what is actually being discussed is not the teaching of Jesus but an issue of A.D. 80, unless the theme or saying can be shown to be anachronistic.

4. Matthew's reasons for including or excluding this or that tradition, or for shaping his sources, must owe something to the circumstances he found himself in and the concerns of his own theology. But it is notoriously difficult to reconstruct such circumstances and commitments from a Gospel about Jesus of Nazareth.

5. Moreover, virtually all the themes isolated as reflections of A.D. 80 could in fact reflect interests of any decade from A.D. 30 to 100. In the early thirties, for instance, Stephen was martyred because he spoke against the law and the temple. Similar concerns dominated the Jerusalem Council (A.D. 49) and demanded thought both before and after the Jewish War (A.D. 66–70). The truth is that such themes as law and temple, and even many christological formulations (see section 11), offer very little help in identifying a "life-setting" for the church in Matthew's day. Although Matthean scholarship may advance by trying out new theories, no advance that forces a Procrustean synthesis based on methodologically dubious deductions constitutes genuine progress.

Today we are in a position to consider the proper if limited place of redaction criticism. Since this method of study has been scrutinized elsewhere (cf. Carson, "Redaction Criticism," and the literature cited there), only a few points need be made here.

---

[12]Cf. D.A. Carson, "Unity and Diversity: On the Possibility of Systematic Theology," in Carson and Woodbridge.

1. The "criteria of authenticity," as has often been pointed out,[13] are hopelessly inadequate. For instance, the "criterion of dissimilarity," viz., that only if a statement was "dissimilar" from what Palestinian Judaism or early Christianity might have said could it be ascribed with reasonable confidence to Jesus, can only cull out the distinctive or the eccentric, while leaving the characteristic untouched—unless one is prepared to argue that Jesus' teaching characteristically never resembled contemporary Judaism and was never adopted by the church.

2. The analysis of the descent of the tradition, though useful in itself, is marred by four major flaws. First, comparative studies in oral transmission have largely dealt with periods of hundreds of years, not decades. On any dating of the Gospels, some eyewitnesses were still alive when the evangelists published their books. Second, the work of several Scandinavian scholars[14] has drawn attention to the role of memory in Jewish education. Their work has been seriously criticized; but even their most perceptive critics[15] recognize that too little attention has been paid to the power of human memory before Guttenberg—a phenomenon attested in many third-world students today. More impressive yet, the detailed attack on form criticism by Güttgemanns[16] is so compelling that one wonders whether form criticism is of any value as a historical (as opposed to literary) tool. Oral traditions, especially religious oral traditions, are not conducive to tampering and falsification but are remarkably stable. Third, convincing reasons have been advanced for concluding that some written notes were taken even during Jesus' public ministry.[17] *Written* material, of course, necessarily fits into various "forms" or "genres"; but such genres must be considered quite separately from the "forms" of *oral* transmission and the shaping that takes place by this means. If traditions of Jesus' words and deeds were passed on by both oral and written forms, many of the historical conclusions of the form-critical model collapse. Fourth, classic form criticism is intrinsically incapable of dealing historically with several similar sayings of Jesus, since they all tend toward the same form.

3. More broadly, the fact that Jesus was an itinerant preacher (cf. comments at 4:23–25; 9:35–38; 11:21) is passed over too lightly. To attempt a tradition history of somewhat similar sayings, which the evangelists place in quite different contexts, overlooks the repetitive nature of itinerant ministry. Of course each case must be examined on its own merits and depends in some instances on source-critical considerations; but we shall observe how frequently this basic observation is ignored. See especially the introductory discussion on parables at 13:3a.

4. To deduce that all changes in Mark and Q (however Q be defined), including

---

[13]Cf. esp. R.T. France, "The Authenticity of the Sayings of Jesus," *History, Criticism and Faith*, ed. C. Brown (Downers Grove, Ill.: IVP, 1976), pp. 101–43; R.H. Stein, "The 'Criteria' for Authenticity," France and Wenham, 1:225–63; Hengel, *Acts and History*, esp. pp. 3–34.

[14]In particular, cf. H. Riesenfeld, "The Gospel Tradition and its Beginnings," *Studia Evangelica* 1 (1959): 43–65; B. Gerhardsson, *Memory and Manuscript: Oral Tradition and Written Transmission in Rabbinic Judaism and Early Christianity* (Lund: C.W.K. Gleerup, 1961).

[15]Viz., Davies, *Setting*, pp. 464ff.; Peter H. Davids, "The Gospels and Jewish Tradition: Twenty Years After Gerhardsson," France and Wenham, 1:75–99.

[16]E. Güttgemanns, *Candid Questions Concerning Gospel Form Criticism*, tr. W.H. Doty (Pittsburgh: Pickwick, 1979).

[17]Cf. esp. E.E. Ellis, "New Directions in Form Criticism," Strecker, *Jesus Christus*, pp. 299–315, basing itself in large part on the thought-provoking sociological analysis of H. Schürmann, "Die vorösterlichen Anfänge der Logientradition," *Traditionsgeschichtliche Untersuchungen zu den synoptischen Evangelien* (Düsseldorf: Patmos, 1968), pp. 39–65.

omissions and additions, are the result of exclusively theological motives fails to reckon with the extreme likelihood of a multiplicity both of reasons for introducing changes and of sources, oral and written, within the first few decades (cf. Luke 1:1–4) and with the possibility that the author was an apostle (cf. section 5). While apostolic authorship would not give the text more authority than nonapostolic authorship, it must affect our judgment of the role of oral and written sources in the making of this Gospel. These factors—multiplicity of sources and possible apostolic authorship—suggest that in most instances there is no compelling reason for thinking that material judged redactional is for that reason unhistorical.

5. Modern redaction criticism also suffers from dependency on a particular solution to the synoptic problem (cf. section 3).

6. Also, it fails to consider how many changes from Mark to Matthew (assuming Mark's priority) might owe something to stylistic predilections rather than theology. For example, F. Neirynck has clearly shown that Matthew's account of the feeding of the five thousand, often said to reflect more clearly than Mark the institution of the Eucharist, in reality turns out to be entirely consistent with the stylistic changes he introduces elsewhere.[18]

7. Too many redaction-critical studies develop an understanding of the theology of Matthew's Gospel solely on the basis of the changes, instead of giving adequate thought to the document as a whole. Surely what Matthew retains is as important to him as what he modifies. The possibility of distortion becomes acute when on the basis of changes Matthew's distinctive theology is outlined and then anything conflicting with this model is reckoned to be "unassimilated tradition" or the like. It is far wiser to check the "changes" again and determine whether they have been rightly understood and, avoiding a priori disjunctions, to seek to integrate them into all Matthew writes down.

Such considerations do not eliminate the need for redaction criticism. In God's providence we are able to compare the synoptic Gospels with one another, and such study helps us better understand each of them. Matthew's topical treatment of miracles (Matt 8–9), his chiastic arrangement of parables (Matt 13), the differences he exhibits when closely compared with Mark—these all help us identify his distinctives more precisely than would otherwise be possible. Thus no responsible modern commentary on the synoptic Gospels can avoid using redaction criticism. But redaction criticism, trimmed of its excesses and weaned from its radical heritage, throws only a little light on historical questions; and one must always guard against its dethroning what is essential by focusing on what is distinctive and idiosyncratic.

It is possible to approach the question of how much history is found in Matthew by examining the genre of literature—either of the Gospel as a whole or of some section of it. Perhaps a "Gospel" is not meant to convey historical information; perhaps certain stories in Matthew are "midrash" and, like parables, make theological points without pretending to be historical. Anticipating later discussion (section 12), we conclude that the evangelists, including Matthew, intended that their Gospels convey "historical" information. This does not mean they intended to write dispassionate, modern biographies. But advocacy does not necessarily affect truth telling: a Jewish writer on the Holocaust is not necessarily either more or less accurate because his family perished at Auschwitz. Nor is it proper in the study of

---

[18]"La rédaction Matthéenne et la structure du premier évangile," *De Jésus aux Évangiles*, ed. I. de la Potterie (Gembloux: Duculot, 1967), pp. 41–73, esp. p. 51.

any document professedly dealing with history to approach it with a neutral stance that demands proof of authenticity as well as proof of inauthenticity.[19] Goetz and Blomberg, in an adaptation of a Kantian argument, write:

> If the assumption was that no one ever wrote history for the sake of accuracy, then no fraudulent history could ever be written with the expectation that it would be believed. The process of deception is parasitic on the assumption that people normally write history with the intent of historical accuracy. People *must* (a) acknowledge the a priori truth that truth-telling is the logical backdrop to lying, and (b) *actually* assume that people tell the truth in order for a lie to be told with the expectation that it will be believed.[20]

So with any particular historian, including Matthew, the writer of history must be assumed reliable until shown to be otherwise. "The reader must make this a priori commitment if the practice of writing history is to be viable."[21] In other words, other things being equal, the burden of proof rests with the skeptic.

From this perspective harmonization, which currently has a very bad name in NT scholarship, retains a twofold importance: negatively, it is nothing more than one way of applying the coherence test for authenticity; and, positively, once we no longer insist that every Gospel distinctive is the result of theological commitment or that the only possible sources are Mark, Q, and a little undefined oral tradition, harmonization carefully handled may permit the illumination of one source by another, provided legitimate redaction-critical distinctions are not thereby obliterated.

This commentary endeavors to apply these observations and assessments to the Gospel of Matthew. Rigorous application would have trebled the length. Therefore certain sections and pericopes were singled out for more extensive treatment (cf., for instance, at 5:1; 6:9–13; 8:16–17; 13:3; 26:6, 17), in the hope that the positions outlined in this introduction could be grounded in the hard realities of the text. The aim must be to understand as closely as possible the Gospel of Matthew.

3. The Synoptic Problem

The recent return of the synoptic problem to center stage as the focus of much debate (see section 1) necessitates some assessment of the developments that impinge on questions of authorship, date, and interpretation of Matthew. One contributing factor to the debate is the quotation from Papias (c. A.D. 135) recorded by Eusebius (*Ecclesiastical History* 3.39.16). Several of Papias's expressions are ambiguous: "Matthew *synetaxeto* [composed? compiled? arranged?] the *logia* [sayings? Gospel?] in *hebraïdi dialektō* [in the Hebrew (Aramaic?) language? in the Hebrew (Aramaic?) style?]; and everyone *hērmēneusen* [interpreted? translated? transmitted?] them as he was able [contextually, who is 'interpreting' what?]." The early church understood the sentence to mean that the apostle Matthew first wrote his Gospel in Hebrew or Aramaic and then it was translated. But few today accept

---

[19]E.g., see Morna D. Hooker, "Christology and Methodology," NTS 17 (1970–71): 480–87.

[20]Stewart C. Goetz and Craig L. Blomberg, "The Burden of Proof," *Journal for the Study of the New Testament* 11 (1981): 39–63, esp. p. 52, emphasis theirs.

[21]Ibid.

this.[22] Although Matthew has Semitisms, much evidence suggests that it was first composed in Greek.

The most important attempts to understand this sentence from Papias include the following.[23]

1. Manson (*Sayings*, pp. 18ff.) has made popular the view that identifies the *logia* with sayings of Jesus found in Q. That would make Matthew the author of Q (a source or sources including approximately 250 verses common to Matthew and Luke), but not of this Gospel. Papias confused the two. This view falters on two facts. First, it cannot explain how an important apostolic source like the Q this theory requires could have so completely disappeared that there is no other mention of it, let alone a copy. Indeed, the entire Q hypothesis, however reasonable, is still only hypothesis. Second, Papias's two other instances of *logia* (recorded by Eusebius) suggest the word refers to both sayings and deeds of Jesus, while Q is made up almost exclusively of the former. From this perspective *logia* better fits the Gospel of Matthew than a source like Q.

2. This last criticism can also be leveled against the view that *logia* refers to OT "testimonia," a book of OT "proof-texts" compiled by Matthew from the Hebrew canon and now incorporated into the Gospel.[24] Furthermore, it is not certain that such "testimonia" ever existed as separate books; and in any case it would have been unnecessary to compile them in Hebrew and then translate them, since the LXX was already well established. Matthew demonstrably follows the LXX in passages where Mark has parallels (see section 11).

3. If by *logia* Papias meant our canonical Matthew,[25] then in the opinion of many scholars convinced that canonical Matthew was set down in Greek (e.g., Hill), Papias was plainly wrong. Either his testimony must be ignored as valueless or we must suppose that Papias was right as to the language but confused the Gospel with some other Semitic work, perhaps the apocryphal *Gospel According to the Hebrews*.

4. Kürzinger[26] offers a possible way out of the dilemma. He thinks *logia* refers to canonical Matthew but that *hebraïdi dialektō* refers, not to Hebrew or Aramaic language, but to Semitic style or literary form: Matthew arranged his Gospel in Semitic (i.e., Jewish-Christian) literary form dominated by Semitic themes and devices. In this view the last clause of Papias's statement cannot refer to translation, since language is no longer in view. Kürzinger points out that immediately before Papias's sentence about Matthew, he describes how Mark composed his Gospel by

---

[22]For general discussion of this difficult question, see the NT introductions and the literature cited below. For arguments against the view that canonical Matthew uses translation Greek, cf. also Nigel Turner, *Style* in J.H. Moulton, *A Grammar of New Testament Greek*, vol. 4 (Edinburgh: T. & T. Clark, 1976), pp. 37–38.

[23]For discussion, cf. Donald Guthrie, *New Testament Introduction*, 3d ed. (Downers Grove, Ill.: IVP, 1970), pp. 34–37.

[24]Cf. J.R. Harris, *Testimonies*, rev. ed., 2 vols. (Cambridge: University Press, 1920); F.C. Grant, *The Gospels: Their Origin and Their Growth* (New York: Harper, 1957), pp. 65, 144.

[25]So, among others, C.S. Petrie, "The Authorship of 'The Gospel According to Matthew': A Reconsideration of the External Evidence," NTS 14 (1967): 15–32.

[26]J. Kürzinger, "Das Papiaszeugnis und die Erstgestalt des Matthäusevangeliums," *Biblische Zeitschrift* 4 (1960): 19–38; id., "Irenäus und sein Zeugnis zur Sprache des Matthäusevangeliums," NTS 10 (1963): 108–15. The argument above diverges from Kürzinger at one or two minor points.

putting down Peter's testimony; and there Mark is called the *hērmēneutēs* of Peter. This cannot mean Mark was Peter's translator. It means he "interpreted" or "transmitted" (neither English word is ideal) what Peter said. If the same meaning is applied to the cognate verb in Papias's statement about Matthew, then it could be that everyone "passed on" or "interpreted" Matthew's Gospel to the world, as he was able.

It is difficult to decide which interpretation is correct. A few still argue that Matthew's entire Gospel was first written in Aramaic.[27] That view best explains the language of Papias, but it is not easy to reconcile with Matthew's Greek. Why, for instance, does he sometimes use a Greek source like the LXX? It cannot be argued that the alleged translator decided to use the LXX for all OT quotations in order to save himself some work, for only some of them are from the LXX. If this interpretation of Papias's statement does not stand, then Papias offers no support for Matthean priority.

The other two plausible interpretations of Papias are problematic. The view that Papias was referring to Q or some part of it offers the easiest rendering of *hebraïdi dialektō* ("in the Hebrew [Aramaic] language") but provides an implausible rendering for *logia*. Kürzinger's solution provides the most believable rendering of *logia* (viz., canonical Matthew) but a less likely interpretation of *hebraïdi dialektō* ("in the Semitic literary form"). Yet this rendering is possible (cf. LSJ, 1:401) and makes sense of the whole, even though Kürzinger's view has not been well received. The important point is that either of these last two views fits easily with a theory of Markan priority, which may also be hinted at in the fact that, as Eusebius preserves him, Papias discusses Mark at length before turning rather briefly to Matthew.

Quite apart from the testimony of Papias, the NT evidence itself demands some decisions, however tentative, regarding the synoptic problem. Its boundaries are well known. About 90 percent of Mark is found in Matthew, and very frequently Matthew agrees with Mark's ordering of pericopes as well as his wording (see esp. Matt 3–4; 12–28). Matthew's pericopes are often more condensed than Mark's but have a great deal of other material, much of it discourses. Of this material about 250 verses are common to Luke, and again the order is frequently (though by no means always) the same. In both instances the wording is often so similar throughout such lengthy passages that it is impossible to see oral fixation of the tradition as an adequate explanation. Some literary dependence is self-evident. It seems easiest to support the view that Matthew and Luke both depend on Mark rather than vice versa, largely because Matthew and Mark frequently agree against Luke, and Mark and Luke frequently agree against Matthew, but Matthew and Luke seldom agree against Mark. It is not the argument from order itself that is convincing, for all that proves is that Mark stands in the middle between the other two. What is more impressive is that close study finds it easier to explain changes from Mark to Matthew and Luke than the other way around.[28] The two-source hypothesis, despite its weaknesses—what, for instance, is the best explanation for the so-called minor

---

[27]Schlatter; P. Gaechter, both in his commentary, *Matthäus*, and in *Die literarische Kunst im Matthäusevangelium* (Stuttgart: Katholisches Bibelwerk, 1966); J.W. Wenham, "Gospel Origins," *Trinity Journal* 7 (1978): 112–34; and see n. 38, below.

[28]Cf. Christopher M. Tuckett, "The Argument from Order and the Synoptic Problem," *Theologische Zeitschrift* 36 (1980): 338–54.

agreements of Matthew and Luke against Mark if both Matthew and Luke depend on Mark?—is still more defensible than any of its competitors.[29]

Before pointing out a few of the historical and interpretive implications of this view, notice must be taken of the main alternatives.

1. By far the most common alternative is some form of the Griesbach hypothesis.[30] This argues for Matthean priority, dependence of Luke on Matthew (according to some), and Mark as an abbreviation of Matthew and Luke. Despite increasingly sophisticated defenses of this position, it remains implausible. It appears highly unlikely that any writer, let alone a first-century writer like Mark, would take two documents (in this case Matthew and Luke) and analyze them so carefully as to write a condensation virtually every word of which is in the sources—a condensation that is graphic, forceful, and not artificial (so Hill, *Matthew*, p. 28, citing E.A. Abbott's work in EBr 1879). The impressive list of literary analogies compiled by Frye,[31] who argues that Mark must be secondary because it is much shorter than Matthew and Luke and that literary parallels confirm that writers deeply dependent on written sources condense their sources, actually confounds his conclusion; for where he follows Mark, Matthew's account is almost always shorter. His greater total length—and even the occasional longer Matthean pericope—always comes from new material added to that from the Markan source. Frye therefore inadvertently supports the two-source hypothesis. Moreover the Griesbach hypothesis flies in the face of other evidence from Papias, who insists that Mark wrote his Gospel on the basis of material from Peter, not by condensing Matthew and Luke (Eusebius, *Ecclesiastical History* 3.39.15).

2. Gaboury and Léon-Dufour[32] argue that the pericopes preserving the same order in the triple tradition (i.e., in Matthew, Mark, and Luke) constitute a primary source on which all three synoptic Gospels have been built. But it is demonstrable that sometimes the evangelists chose topical arrangements quite different from their parallels (e.g., see at chs. 8–9); so why should it be assumed that all three synoptists conveniently chose to take over this alleged source without any change in topical arrangements?

3. Several British scholars adopt Markan priority but deny the existence of Q.[33]

---

[29]In addition to the standard NT introductions, cf. esp. Stonehouse, *Origins*, pp. 48–77, and the appendix by G.M. Styler in the forthcoming revised edition of Moule, *Birth of NT*.

[30]From the growing bibliography, particular mention may be made of W.R. Farmer, *The Synoptic Problem* (Dillsboro, N.C.: Western North Carolina Press, 1976); David L. Dungan, "Mark—The Abridgement of Matthew and Luke," *Jesus and Man's Hope* (Pittsburgh: Pittsburgh Theological Seminary, 1970), pp. 51–97; H.H. Stoldt, *Geschichte und Kritik des Markushypothese* (Göttingen: Vandenhoeck und Ruprecht, 1977); and several of the essays in *J.J. Griesbach: Synoptic and Text-Critical Studies 1776–1976*, edd. B. Orchard and Thomas R.W. Longstaff (Cambridge: University Press, 1978).

[31]Roland Mushat Frye, "The Synoptic Problems and Analogies in Other Literatures," *The Relationships Among the Gospels: An Interdisciplinary Dialogue*, ed. W.O. Walker, Jr. (San Antonio: Trinity University Press, 1978), pp. 261–302.

[32]A. Gaboury, *La structure des évangiles synoptiques* (SuppNovTest 22; Leiden: Brill, 1970); X. Léon-Dufour, "Redaktionsgeschichte of Matthew and Literary Criticism," *Jesus and Man's Hope* (Pittsburgh: Pittsburgh Theological Seminary, 1970), pp. 9–35.

[33]So Green; A.M. Farrer, "On Dispensing With Q," in Nineham, *Studies*, pp. 55–88; Goulder. This is quite different from B.C. Butler (*The Originality of St Matthew* [Cambridge: University Press, 1951]), who argued that Matthew was prior, Mark abridged Matthew, and Luke was dependent on Matthew for what we call Q material and on Mark for what Matthew and Mark had in common.

Parallels between Matthew and Luke are explained by saying that Luke read Matthew before composing his own Gospel. That is possible; but if so, he has hidden the fact extraordinarily well. Compare, for instance, Matthew 1–2 and Luke 1–2. Gundry (*Matthew*) holds to the existence of a somewhat expanded Q but argues as well that Luke used Matthew—and this explains the "minor agreements" between Matthew and Luke. But this view, though possible, is linked in Gundry's mind with his theory that sources shared by Matthew and Luke include even such matters as the Nativity story; and that is very doubtful.[34]

4. Rist[35] rejects both the two-source hypothesis and the Griesbach hypothesis and argues for the independence of Matthew and Mark. As many others have done, Rist focuses attention on 4:12–13:58, where there are numerous divergences in order between Matthew and Mark. He examines a short list of passages in the triple tradition where there is not only close verbal similarity but identical order and argues that in each case the order is either logical or the result of memory, not literary dependence. But Rist does not adequately weigh the impressive list of instances where Matthew agrees with Mark's order without close verbal similarity. Such order argues strongly for some kind of literary dependence, however the verbal dissimilarities be explained.

5. Others, in the hope of keeping Matthean priority alive, argue that his Gospel was first written in Aramaic; and this became a source for Mark, which in turn influenced the Greek rendering of Matthew.[36] This is possible, but we have already seen that Papias's testimony may not support a Semitic Matthew at all. And it remains linguistically improbable that the whole of Matthew was originally in Aramaic.

There are other proposed solutions to the synoptic problem, generally of much greater complexity.[37] But not only do they suffer from the improbability of some of their details, the theories as a whole are so complex as to be unprovable.

The two-source hypothesis remains the most attractive general solution. This does not mean that it can be proved with mathematical certainty or that all arguments advanced in its favor are convincing.[38] But some small details are very weighty. Gundry (*Use of OT*) has shown that the OT quotations and allusions Matthew and

---

[34]See at chs. 1–2, and D.A. Carson, "Gundry on Matthew: A Critical Review," *Trinity Journal* (1982): 71–91.

[35]J.M. Rist, *On the Independence of Matthew and Mark* (Cambridge: University Press, 1978).

[36]E.g., J.W. Wenham, n. 29; P. Benoit, *L'Evangile selon Saint Matthieu*, 4th ed. (Paris: du Cerf, 1972), pp. 27ff.; Pierson Parker, *The Gospel Before Mark* (Chicago: University of Chicago, 1953); L. Vaganay, *Le problème synoptique—une hypothèse de travail*. (Tournai: Desclée, 1954). Somewhat similar is the view of J.A.T. Robinson (*Redating the New Testament* [Philadelphia: Westminster, 1976], pp. 97–98). Others think the alleged Semitic original was written in Hebrew rather than Aramaic (e.g., Gaechter, *Matthäus;* Carmignac, pp. 33ff.). J. Munck ("Die Tradition über das Mt bei Papias," *Neotestamentica et Semitica* [SuppNovTest 6; Leiden: Brill, 1962], pp. 249ff.) disposes of the entire problem by supposing Papias was in error and that the early assumption of a Semitic source for Matthew developed in connection with the formation of the canon as a way to resolve the synoptic problem. Munck's proposal confuses content and purpose. Even if Papias and others were interested in explaining synoptic differences (a doubtful point), it does not follow that their "facts" are historically incorrect. It would be necessary to show they invented their "facts" in order to offer an explanation.

[37]E.g., J.C. O'Neill, "The Synoptic Problem," NTS 21 (1975): 273–85; P. Benoit, M.E. Boisward, and A. Lamouille, *Synopse des Quatre Evangiles en Français*, 3 vols. (Paris: du Cerf, 1977).

[38]D. Wenham, "Synoptic Problem" (pp. 8–17), exposes some of the weaker arguments—though not all his criticisms are equally telling.

Mark have in common are consistently from the LXX, whereas those found in Matthew alone are drawn from a variety of versions and textual traditions. It is singularly unlikely that Mark was condensing Matthew, for so consistent a collection of Matthew's OT quotations—only those from the LXX—seems too coincidental to be believed. The pattern is easy enough to understand if Matthew depended on Mark.[39]

Yet in itself the two-source hypothesis is almost certainly too simple. Source-critical questions are enormously complex;[40] many facets of the question demand tighter controls.[41] Moreover close study has convinced some careful scholars that the evidence does not warrant the degree of certainty with which many hold the two-source hypothesis.[42] Such uncertainty is unpopular; but it is scarcely more scientific to go beyond the evidence than to admit uncertainty where the evidence does not provide an adequate basis for anything more. Such hesitations are especially anathema to radical redaction critics, for every major redaction-critical study of Matthew rests on the two-source hypothesis. Their aim is to find out how Matthew changed Mark.

In view of the weaknesses inherent in a radical use of redaction criticism and the uncertainties surrounding the two-source hypothesis, this commentary adopts a cautious stance. The two-source hypothesis is sufficiently credible that we do not hesitate to speak of Matthew's changes of, additions to, and omissions from Mark. But such statements say little about historicity or about the relative antiquity of competing traditions (cf. B.F. Meyer, pp. 71–72). In some instances it is apparent that Matthew used not only Mark but Q (however Q is conceived), probably other sources, and perhaps his own memory as well. In some instances an excellent case can be made for Matthew's use of a source earlier than Mark. Any theory of literary dependence must also face subsidiary problems, such as the perplexing features of Luke's "central section" (see comments at Matt 19:1–2). Changes Matthew has introduced may sometimes be motivated by other than theological concerns; but in any case the total content of any pericope in Matthew's Gospel as a whole is a more reliable guide to determine distinct theological bent than the isolated change. As for dramatic diversity (see comments at 16:13–20; 19:16–30), the detailed differences must be treated and plausible reasons for the changes suggested. Rarely, however,

---

[39]Occasionally Gundry's judgment regarding textual affinities may be called in question, especially when he deals with brief allusions to the OT rather than explicit quotations, though the thrust of his argument is not lessened by these few points. D. Wenham ("Synoptic Problem," pp. 3–38) unsuccessfully attempts to reduce the cogency of Gundry's argument. Wenham points out that Mark almost always cites the OT on the lips of participants in his narrative, not in his own descriptions, and that Matthew normally uses the LXX when his participants cite the OT, even though his own use of the OT betrays a much broader array of textual affinities. Therefore it is possible, Wenham reasons, that Mark depended on Matthew; and Mark's consistent appeal to the LXX is explained by his decision to use OT (and therefore LXX) quotations primarily when they are on the lips of participants in his narratives. Wenham's critique, though clever, is not convincing. Not only are there exceptions to his observations, but, more importantly, Wenham deals only with explicit OT quotations, not with OT allusions that, though harder to handle, are more widely distributed.

[40]Cf. Palmer, Gospel Criticism, pp. 112–74.

[41]For instance, we speak of Q with little consensus of what is meant: cf. S. Schulz, Q: Die Spruchquelle der Evangelisten (Zürich: Theologischer Verlag, 1972); M. Devisch, "Le document Q source de Matthieu. Problematique actuelle," in Didier, pp. 71–97. Again, Fitzmyer (Wandering Aramaen, pp. 1ff., 85ff.) offers wise counsel on method in the search for Aramaic substrata underlying sayings of Jesus in the NT.

[42]See esp. E.P. Sanders, The Tendencies of the Synoptic Tradition (Cambridge: University Press, 1969).

are the solutions offered so dependent on the two-source hypothesis that a shift in scholarly opinion on the synoptic problem would irreparably damage them. The aim throughout has been to let Matthew speak as a theologian and historian independent of Mark, even if Mark has been one of his most important sources.

4. Unity

The question of the unity of Matthew's Gospel has little to do with source-critical questions. Instead it deals with how well the evangelist has integrated his material to form cohesive pericopes and a coherent whole. In sections very difficult to interpret (e.g., Matt 24), it is sometimes argued that the evangelist has sewn together diverse traditions that by nature are incapable of genuine coherence. Failing to understand the material, he simply passed it on without recognizing that some of his sources were mutually incompatible.

There are so many signs of high literary craftsmanship in this Gospel that such skepticism is unjustified. It is more likely, not to say more humble, to suppose that in some instances we may not understand enough of the first-century setting to be able to grasp exactly what the text says.

5. Authorship

Nowhere does the first Gospel name its author. The universal testimony of the early church is that the apostle Matthew wrote it, and our earliest textual witnesses attribute it to him (*KATA MATTHAION*). How much of that testimony depends on Papias is uncertain. We have already noted that many today think Papias is referring to some source of canonical Matthew rather than to the finished work or, alternatively, that Papias was wrong (cf. section 3). If Papias is right, the theory of Matthew's authorship may receive gentle support from passages like 10:3, where on this theory the apostle refers to himself in a self-deprecating way not found in Mark or Luke.

Modern literary criticism offers many reasons for rejecting Matthew's authorship. If the two-source hypothesis is correct, then (it is argued) it is unlikely that the eyewitness and apostle Matthew would depend so heavily on a document written by Mark, who was neither an apostle nor (for most events) an eyewitness. Moreover the reconstructions of canonical Matthew's life-setting, fostered by redaction criticism, converge on A.D. 80–100 in some kind of savage Jewish–Christian conflict. This is probably a trifle late to assume Matthew's authorship (though cf. traditions that say the apostle John composed his Gospel c. A.D. 90); and the details of the reconstructed settings discourage the notion. Kümmel (*Introduction*, p. 121) argues further than "the systematic and therefore nonbiographical form of the structure of Mt, the late-apostolic theological position and the Greek language of Mt make this proposal completely impossible." He concludes that the identity of the first evangelist is unknown to us but that he must have been a Greek-speaking Jewish Christian with some rabbinic knowledge, who depended on "a form of the Jesus tradition which potently accommodated the sayings of Jesus to Jewish viewpoints" (ibid.).

These reasons for rejecting Matthew's authorship are widely accepted today. So alternate proposals have sprung up. Kilpatrick (pp. 138–39) suggests that the early patristic tradition connecting the first Gospel with Matthew arose as a conscious community pseudonym by the church that wrote the Gospel, in order to gain acceptance and authority for it. Abel[43] argues that Matthew's extra material is so confused and contradictory that we must assume it represents the efforts of two separate individuals working independently of each other. Several redaction-critical studies have denied that the author was a Jew, feeling that the antipathy exhibited toward Jesus in this Gospel and the ignorance of Jewish life are so deep that the writer must have been a Gentile Christian.[44] Those who think Papias was referring to Q or to some other source used by Matthew are often prepared to say that the apostle composed the source if not the Gospel (e.g., Hill, *Matthew*). There are several other theories.

The objections are not so weighty as they at first seem. If what the modern world calls "plagiarism" (the wholesale takeover, without acknowledgment, of another document) was an acceptable literary practice in the ancient world, it is difficult to see why an apostle might not find it congenial. If Matthew thought Mark's account reliable and generally suited to his purposes (and he may also have known that Peter stood behind it), there can be no objection to the view that an apostle depended on a nonapostolic document. Kümmel's rejection of Matthew's authorship (*Introduction*, p. 121) on the grounds that this Gospel is "systematic and therefore nonbiographical" is a non sequitur because (1) a topically ordered account can yield biographical facts as easily as a strictly chronological account,[45] and (2) Kümmel wrongly supposes that apostolicity is for some reason incapable of choosing anything other than a chronological form. The alleged lateness of the theological position may be disputed at every point (see section 6 and this commentary).

Those who argue that the author could not have been a Jew, let alone an apostle, allege serious ignorance of Jewish life, including inability to distinguish between the doctrines of the Pharisees and the Sadducees (16:12) or, worse, thinking that the Sadducees were still an active force after A.D. 70 (22:23). But the second of these two passages has synoptic parallels (Mark 12:18; Luke 20:27; here Matthew has interpreted Mark's verb as a historical present); and neither Matthean passage denies that there are differences separating Pharisees and Sadducees—differences Matthew elsewhere highlights (22:23–33)—but merely insists that on some things the Pharisees and Sadducees could cooperate. This is scarcely surprising: after all, both groups sat in the same Sanhedrin. Politics and theology make strange bedfellows (see section 11.f). Other "glaring errors" (so Meier, *Vision*, pp. 17–23) prove equally ephemeral (e.g., Matthew's use of Zech 9:9; see comments at 21:4–5). Also Kilpatrick's suggestion of a conscious community pseudonym cannot offer any parallel.

The charge that the Greek of the first Gospel is too good to have come from a Galilean Jew overlooks the trilingual character of Galilee, the possibility that Matthew greatly improved his Greek as the church reached out to more and more Greek speakers (both Jews and Gentiles), and the discussion of Gundry (*Use of OT*, pp. 178–85), who argues that Matthew's training and vocation as a tax gatherer

---

[43]Ernest L. Abel, "Who Wrote Matthew?" NTS 17 (1970–71): 138–52.

[44]E.g., Meier, *Vision*, pp. 17–23; Poul Nepper-Christensen, *Das Matthäusevangelium: Ein judenchristliches Evangelium?* (Aarhus: Universitetsforlaget, 1958); Strecker, *Weg*, p. 34; van Tilborg, p. 171; R. Walker, p. 145.

[45]Not a few contemporary biographies treat certain parts of their subject's life in topical arrangements: e.g., A. Fraser, *Cromwell: Our Chief of Men* (St. Albans: Panther, 1975), esp. pp. 455ff.

(9:9–13; 10:3) would have uniquely equipped him not only with the languages of Galilee but with an orderly mind and the habit of jotting down notes, which may have played a large part in the transmission of the apostolic gospel tradition. Moule[46] wonders whether 13:52, which many take as an oblique self-reference by the evangelist, hides a use of *grammateus* that does not mean "teacher of the law" (NIV) but "clerk, secular scribe." "Is it not conceivable that the Lord really did say to that tax-collector Matthew: 'You have been a "writer" . . . ; you have had plenty to do with the commercial side of just the topics alluded to in the parables—farmer's stock, fields, treasure-trove, fishing revenues; now that you have become a disciple, you can bring all this out again—but with a difference.' "[47]

Moule proposes an apostle who was a secular scribe and note-taker and who wrote primarily in a Semitic language, leaving behind material that was arranged by another scribe, a Greek writer unknown to us. One may wonder if *grammateus*, used so often in the Jewish sense of "teacher of the law," can so easily be assigned a secular sense. But whatever its other merits or demerits, Moule's argument suggests that the link between this first Gospel and the apostle Matthew cannot be dismissed as easily as some have thought.

None of the arguments for Matthew's authorship is conclusive. Thus we cannot be entirely certain who the author of the first Gospel is. But there are solid reasons in support of the early church's unanimous ascription of this book to the apostle Matthew, and on close inspection the objections do not appear substantial. Though Matthew's authorship remains the most defensible position,[48] very little in this commentary depends on it. Where it may have a bearing on the discussion, a cautionary notice is inserted.

6. Date

During the first three centuries of the church, Matthew was the most highly revered and frequently quoted canonical Gospel.[49] The earliest extant documents referring to Matthew are the epistles of Ignatius (esp. *To the Smyrneans* 1.1 [cf. Matt. 3:15], c. A.D. 110–15). So the end of the first century or thereabouts is the latest date for the Gospel of Matthew to have been written.

The earliest possible date is much more difficult to nail down because it depends on so many other disputed points. If Luke depends on Matthew (which seems unlikely), then the date of Luke would establish a new *terminus ad quem* for Matthew; and the date of Luke is bound up with the date of Acts.[50] If the Griesbach hypothesis (cf. sections 1 and 3) is correct, then Matthew would have to be earlier

---

[46]C.F.D. Moule, "St. Matthew's Gospel: Some Neglected Features" *Studia Evangelica* 2 (1964): 91–99.

[47]Ibid., p. 98.

[48]Cf. Gaechter, *Matthäus;* E.J. Goodspeed, *Matthew, Apostle and Evangelist* (Philadelphia: Winston, 1959); Guthrie, *NT Introduction*, pp. 33–44; Maier; very cautiously, E.F. Harrison, *Introduction to the New Testament*, 2d ed. (Grand Rapids: Eerdmans, 1971), pp. 176–77; and esp. Gundry, *Matthew*, pp. 609–22; and Stonehouse, *Origins*, pp. 1–47.

[49]Cf. E. Masseaux, *Influence de l'Evangile de Saint Matthieu sur la littérature chrétienne avant Saint Irénée* (Louvain: Publications Universitaires de Louvain, 1950).

[50]Cf. esp. A.J. Mattill, Jr., "The Date and Purpose of Luke-Acts: Rackham Reconsidered," CBQ 40 (1978): 335–50.

than Mark. Conversely, if the two-source hypothesis is adopted, Matthew is later than Mark; and a *terminus a quo* is theoretically established. Even so there are two difficulties. First, we do not know when Mark was written, but most estimates fall between A.D. 50 and 65. Second, on this basis most critics think Matthew could not have been written till 75 or 80. But even if Mark is as late as 65, there is no reason based on literary dependence why Matthew could not be dated A.D. 66. As soon as a written source is circulated, it is available for copying.

Two other arguments are commonly advanced to support the view now in the ascendancy that Matthew was written between 80 and 100 (between which dates there is great diversity of opinion). First, many scholars detect numerous anachronistic details. Though many of these are discussed in the commentary, one frequently cited instance will serve as an example. It is often argued that Matthew transforms the parable of the great banquet (Luke 14:15–24) into the parable of the wedding banquet (Matt. 22:1–14); and the process of transformation includes an explicit reference to the destruction of Jerusalem in A.D. 70 (22:7). Therefore this Gospel must have been written after that. But the conclusion is much too hasty. Those who deny that Jesus could foretell the future concede that Mark predicts the Fall of Jerusalem (Mark 13:14; Matt 24:15), arguing that if Mark wrote about A.D. 65, he was so close to the events that he could see how political circumstances were shaping up. But on this reasoning Matthew could have done the same thing in 66.

More fundamentally it is at least doubtful that Matthew's parable (22:1–10) is a mere rewriting of Luke 14:15–24; more likely they are separate parables (cf. Stonehouse, *Origins*, pp. 35–42). And on what ground must we insist that Jesus could not foretell the future? That conclusion derives, not from the evidence, but from an antisupernatural presuppositionalism. Moreover the language of 22:7 derives from OT categories of judgment (cf. Reicke, "Synoptic Prophecies," p. 123), not from the description of an observer. One could almost say that the lack of more detailed description of the events of A.D. 70 argues for an earlier date. In any event, if it is legitimate to deduce from 22:7 a post-70 date, it must surely be no less legitimate to deduce from 5:23–24; 12:5–7; 23:16–22; and 26:60–61 a pre-70 date, when the temple was still standing. The absurdity of this contradictory conclusion must warn us against the dangers of basing the date of composition on passages that permit other interpretations.

Second, recent studies have tended to argue that the life-setting presupposed by the theological stance of the Gospel best fits the conditions of A.D. 80–100. It is more difficult to reconstruct a life-setting than is commonly recognized (cf. section 2). Many of the criteria for doing so are doubtful. Explicit references to "church" (16:18; 18:17–18) are taken to reflect an interest in later church order. But the authenticity of 16:18 has been ably defended by B.F. Meyer (see comments at 16:17–20). Moreover 18:17–18 says nothng about the details of order (e.g., elders or deacons are not mentioned) but only of broad principles appropriate to the earliest stages of Christianity. Persecution (24:9) and false prophets (24:11) are often taken to reflect circumstances of 80–100. Yet these circumstances appear as prophecies in Matthew and did not need to wait for 80, as Acts and the early Pauline Epistles make clear.

Though Matthew's Gospel seems to presuppose uneasy relations between church and synagogue, the Gospel is less anti-Jewish than anti-Jewish leaders and their position on Jesus (see section 11.f); and such a stance stretches all the way back to the days of Jesus' ministry. Significantly Matthew records more warnings against the

Sadducees than all other NT writers combined; and after A.D. 70 the Sadducees no longer existed as a center of authority. Other small touches seem to show a definite break with Judaism had not yet occurred;[51] and these agree with Reicke ("Synoptic Prophecies," p. 133), who says, "The situation presupposed by Matthew corresponds to what is known about Christianity in Palestine between A.D. 50 and ca. 64."

We must face the awkward fact that criteria such as Matthew's christology are not very reliable indices of Matthew's date (cf. section 11.a). They might easily allow a range from 40–100. Gundry (*Matthew*, pp. 599ff.) has an excellent discussion; because he believes Luke depends on Matthew and Luke-Acts was completed not later than 63, he argues that Matthew must be still earlier. Clearly this conclusion is only as valid as the hypothesis of Luke's dependence on Matthew, a hypothesis that does not seem well grounded. While surprisingly little in the Gospel conclusively points to a firm date, perhaps the sixties are the most likely decade for its composition.

7. Place of Composition and Destination

Most scholars take Antioch as the place of composition. Antioch was a Greek-speaking city with a substantial Jewish population; and the first clear evidence of anyone using the Gospel of Matthew comes from Ignatius, bishop of Antioch at the beginning of the second century. This is as good a guess as any. Yet we must remember that Ignatius depends more on John's Gospel and the Pauline Epistles than on Matthew. But this does not mean they were all written in Antioch.

Other centers proposed in recent years include Alexandria (van Tilborg, p. 172), Edessa,[52] the province of Syria,[53] and perhaps Tyre (Kilpatrick, pp. 130ff.) or Caesarea Maratima.[54] In each instance the grounds are inadequate (Stanton, "Origin and Purpose," ch. 5; Hill, *Matthew*). More plausible is Slingerland's proposal that Matthew 4:15; 19:1 show that the Gospel was written somewhere east of the Jordan (he specifies Pella, but this is an unnecessary and unprovable refinement); see commentary in loc. If he is right, then Antioch is ruled out.

Actually we cannot be sure of the first Gospel's place of composition. Still more uncertain is its destination. The usual assumption is that the evangelist wrote it to meet the needs of his own center—a not implausible view. But the evangelist may

---

[51]Cf. Robinson, *Redating the NT*, pp. 103–5, esp. p. 103: "Matthew's gospel shows all the signs of being produced for a community (and by a community) that needed to formulate, over against the main body of Pharisaic and Sadducaic Judaism, its own line on such issues as the interpretation of scripture and the place of the law, its attitude to the temple and its sacrifices, the sabbath, fasting, prayer, food laws and purification rites, its rules for admission to the community and the discipline of offenders, for marriage, divorce and celibacy, its policy toward Samaritans and Gentiles in a predominantly Jewish milieu, and so on. These problems reflect a period when the needs of co-existence force a clarification of what is the distinctively Christian line on a number of practical issues which previously could be taken for granted." (See further section 8.) This view differs from that of Hare, Walker et al., who think a decisive break had already come about by the time this Gospel was written.

[52]Bacon, *Studies in Matthew*, pp. 15, 36, 51; R.E. Osborne, "The Provenance of Matthew's Gospel," *Studies in Religion* 3 (1973): 22–25.

[53]E. Schweizer, *Matthäus und seine Gemeinde* (Stuttgart: KBW, 1974), pp. 138–39; Künzel, *Studien*, pp. 252ff.

[54]B.T. Viviano, "Where Was the Gospel According to Matthew Written?" CBQ 41 (1979): 533–46.

have been more itinerant than usually assumed; and out of such a ministry he may have written his Gospel to strengthen and inform a large number of followers and given them an evangelistic and apologetic tool. We do not know. The only reasonably certain conclusion is that the Gospel was written somewhere in the Roman province of Syria (so Bonnard, Filson, Hill, Kümmel [*Introduction*, pp. 119–20], and many others; for the area covered by the designation "Syria," see comment at 4:25).

8. Occasion and Purpose

Unlike many of Paul's epistles or even John's Gospel (20:30–31), Matthew tells his readers nothing about his purpose in writing or its occasion. To some extent the Gospel shows Matthew's purpose in the way it presents certain information about Jesus. But to go much beyond this and specify the kind of group(s) Matthew was addressing, the kind of problems they faced, and his own deep psychological and theological motivations, may verge on speculation. Three restraints are necessary.

1. It is unwise to specify too precise an occasion and purpose, because the possibility of error and distortion increases as one leaves hard evidence behind for supposition.

2. It is unwise to specify only one purpose; reductionism cannot do justice to the diversity of Matthew's themes.

3. Great caution is needed in reconstructing the situation in the church of Matthew's time from material that speaks of the historical Jesus (see sections 1–3). In one sense this may be legitimate, for in all probability Matthew did not compose his Gospel simply out of a dispassionate curiosity about history. He intended to address his contemporaries. But it does not necessarily follow that what he alleges occurred in Jesus' day is immediately transferable to his own day.

Nowhere are these restraints more important than in weighing recent discussion about the diverse emphases on evangelism in this Gospel. On the one hand, the disciples are forbidden to preach to others than Jews (10:5–6); on the other, they are commanded to preach to all nations (28:18–20). Because of this bifurcation, some scholars have suggested that Matthew is preserving the traditions of two distinct communities—one that remained narrowly Jewish and the other that was more outward looking. Others think Matthew had to walk a tightrope between conflicting perspectives within his own community and therefore preserves both viewpoints—a sort of committee report that satisfied neither side. Still others erect a more specific "occasion" for this tension, a conflict between the church and the synagogue over the place of Gentile mission, Matthew taking a mediating (not to say compromised) position whose aim was to avoid cleavage between the two groups.[55] Though such reconstructions cannot be ruled out, they suffer from a serious flaw. They fail to recognize that Matthew himself makes distinctions between what Jesus expects and

---

[55]There are many other reconstructions. For example, K.W. Clark ("The Gentile Bias in Matthew," JBL 66 [1947]: 165–72), followed by Nepper-Christensen (*Matthäusevangelium*) and Strecker (*Weg*, pp. 15–35), argues that the evangelist or final redactor must have been a Gentile addressing a Gentile Christian church. Schuyler Brown ("The Matthean Community and the Gentile Mission," NovTest 22 [1980]: 193–221) locates the Matthean church in a Greek-speaking area of Syria, after A.D. 70, when much Jewish Christianity was forced to move to Syria and therefore new crises in evangelism and conflicts with the Pharisees arose.

demands during his earthly ministry and what he expects and demands after his resurrection.

Matthew 10:5–6 tells us what Jesus required of his disciples in their first-recorded major assignment; it does not necessarily tell us anything about what was going on in Matthew's day. The reason Matthew includes 10:6 as well as 28:18–20, and all the texts akin to one passage or the other, may be to explain how Jesus began with his own people and moved outward from there. One might argue that Jesus' own example is the foundation of Paul's "first for the Jew, then for the Gentile" (Rom. 1:14–17). This change develops not merely on pragmatic grounds but as the outworking of a particular understanding of the OT (see comments at 1:1; 4:12–17; 8:5–13; 12:21; 13:11–17) and of the distinctive role of Jesus the Messiah in salvation history (see comments at 2:1–12; 3:2; 4:12–17; 5:17–20; 8:16–17; 10:16–20; 11:7–15, 20–24; 12:41–42; 13:36–43; 15:21–39; 21:1–11, 42–44; 24:14; 26:26–29, 64; 28:18–20). Matthew thus shows how from the nascent community during Jesus' ministry the present commission of the church developed.

If this is a responsible approach to the evidence, then we are not justified in postulating conflicting strands of tradition within the Matthean community. It may be that by this retelling of the changed perspective effected by Jesus' resurrection Matthew is encouraging Jewish Christians to evangelize beyond their own race. Or it may be that he is justifying before non-Christian Jews what he and his fellow Christian Jews are doing. Or it may be that he is explaining the origins of Christian mission to zealous Jewish-Christian personal evangelists who after the warmth of their initial experience want to learn about the historical developments and teaching of Jesus that made the Jewish remnant of his day the church of their own day. Or it may be that, though such questions have not yet arisen, Matthew forsees that they cannot be long delayed and, like a good pastor, decides to forestall the problem by clear teaching. Or it may be that Matthew has Gentile readers in mind. Or it may be that all these factors were at work because Matthew envisages an extensive and varied readership. Several other possibilities come to mind. But such precise reconstructions outstrip the evidence, fail to consider what other purposes Matthew may have had in mind, and frequently ignore the fact that he purports to talk about Jesus, not a Christian community in the sixth, eighth, or tenth decade of the first century.

Particularly unfortunate are several recent works that define the purpose of this Gospel in categories both reductionistic and improbable. Walker argues that this Gospel does not reflect specific church problems but that it was written as a piece of theological combat, designed to show that Israel has been totally rejected in the history of salvation and had been displaced by the church so completely that the Great Commission must be understood as a command to evangelize Gentiles only (see discussion at 28:18–20). The Jewish leaders are nothing but representative figures, and the Gospel as a whole has no interest in and little accurate information about the historical Jesus. Only rarely is Walker exegetically convincing; nowhere does he adequately struggle with the fact that all the disciples and early converts are Jews.

Frankmölle in his final chapter argues that Matthew's work is so different from Mark's—long discourses, careful structure, prologue, epilogue—that it is meaningless to say it is a "Gospel" in the same sense as Mark (see section 12). Instead, Matthew belongs to the literary *Gattung* (form or genre) to which Deuteronomy and Chronicles belong. Frankmölle (pp. 394ff.) cites several phrases (e.g., cf. Deut 31:1,

24; 32:44–45) used by Matthew to round off his own discourses; and from such evidence he concludes that Matthew's "Gospel" is in reality a "book of history," not of "salvation history" as normally understood, but of the community as it summarized its beliefs. Matthew, Frankmölle maintains, does not distinguish between the life and teaching of the historical Jesus and the present exalted Lord. In his "literary fiction" (p. 351), Matthew fuses the two. Thus Jesus becomes the idealized authority behind Matthew the theologian who here addresses his community. But Frankmölle overemphasizes formal differences between Mark and Matthew and neglects the substantial differences between Matthew and Deuteronomy or Chronicles. His investigation is far from even-handed.

Frankmölle's insistence that Matthew is a unified book is surely right. Yet a book may be theologically unified by appealing to prophecy-fulfillment and other salvation-historical categories. Theological unity does not entail ignoring historical data. Moreover neither Walker nor Frankmölle adequately recognizes that for most of his Gospel Matthew depends heavily on Mark and Q (however Q be understood). Matthew was creative, but not so creative as Walker and Frankmölle think.

Goulder offers a lectionary theory. Arguing somewhat along the lines of Carrington and Kilpatrick,[56] Goulder maintains that Matthew's purpose was to provide a liturgical book. He argues that the evangelist has taken the pattern of lections of the Jewish festal year as his base and developed a series of readings to be used in liturgical worship week by week. Mark, a lectionary book for a half-year cycle, has been expanded by Matthew (not the apostle) to a year-long lectionary; and Mark is Matthew's only source. Luke, dependent on Matthew, has also written a lectionary for a full year but has displaced the festal cycle followed by Matthew with the annual Sabbath cycle of readings. Q does not exist.

Despite Goulder's immense erudition, there is little to commend his thesis. We know very little of the patterns of worship in first-century Judaism.[57] At the end of the second century A.D., triennial cycles were used in some Jewish worship. But the annual cycles Goulder discerns behind Luke are almost certainly later than their triennial counterparts. As for Matthew, we have no evidence of a fixed "festal lectionary" in the first century; and even if it existed, it would have been connected with temple worship, with no evidence that it was ever connected with the synagogue worship Goulder's thesis requires (cf. Stanton, "Origin and Purpose," ch. 4). Not only is our knowledge of first-century *Jewish* liturgical custom very slender, our knowledge of *Christian* worship in the first century is even more slender. Thus we do not know whether Christian lectionary cycles—if they existed—developed out of Jewish lectionary cycles—if those cycles existed! Certainly by the time of Justin Martyr, the churches of which he had knowledge read the "memoirs of the apostles" (i.e., the Gospels) for "as long as time allowed" (*First Apology* 1.67), not according to some lectionary specification. Moreover, to make his pattern fit, Goulder must postulate lections in Matthew that vary enormously in length.[58] Goulder's thesis is unlikely to convince many.

---

[56]P. Carrington, *The Primitive Christian Calendar* (Cambridge: University Press, 1952); id., *According to Mark* (Cambridge: University Press, 1960); Kilpatrick, p. 100.

[57]Cf. Leon Morris, *The New Testament and the Jewish Lectionaries* (London: Tyndale, 1964).

[58]Cf. important critical reviews in Int 30 (1976): 91–94; JBL (1977): 453–55; and J.D.G. Dunn, *Unity and Diversity in the New Testament* (London: SCM, 1977), pp. 141–48.

Numerous studies characterized by more sober judgment have recently contributed to our understanding of Matthew's purposes. Many of these are referred to in the commentary. At the broadest level we may say that Matthew's purpose is to demonstrate (1) that Jesus is the promised Messiah, the Son of David, the Son of God, the Son of Man, Immanuel; (2) that many Jews, and especially the leaders, sinfully failed to perceive this during his ministry; (3) that the messianic kingdom has already dawned, inaugurated by the life, ministry, death, resurrection, and exaltation of Jesus; (4) that this messianic reign, characterized by obedience to Jesus and consummated by his return, is the fulfillment of OT prophetic hopes; (5) that the church, the community of those, both Jew and Gentile, who bow unqualifiedly to Jesus' authority, constitutes the true locus of the people of God and the witness to the world of the "gospel of the kingdom"; (6) that throughout this age Jesus' true disciples must overcome temptation, endure persecution from a hostile world, witness to the truth of the gospel, and live in deeply rooted submission to Jesus' ethical demands, even as they enjoy the new covenant, which is simultaneously the fulfillment of old covenant anticipation and the experience of forgiveness bestowed by the Messiah who came to save his people from their sins and who came to give his life a ransom for many.

Such a complex array of themes was doubtless designed to meet many needs: (1) to instruct and perhaps catechize (something facilitated by the careful arrangement of some topical sections; cf. Moule, *Birth*, p. 91); (2) to provide apologetic and evangelistic material, especially in winning Jews; (3) to encourage believers in their witness before a hostile world; and (4) to inspire deeper faith in Jesus the Messiah, along with a maturing understanding of his person, work, and unique place in the unfolding history of redemption.

9. Canonicity

As far as our sources go, the Gospel of Matthew was promptly and universally received as soon as it was published. It never suffered the debates that divided the Eastern church and the Western church over, for example, the Epistle to the Hebrews but was everywhere regarded as Scripture, at least from Ignatius (died 110) onward.

10. Text

Compared with that of Acts, the text of Matthew is fairly stable. Important variants do occur, however, and some of these are discussed. The most difficult textual questions in Matthew arise because it is a synoptic Gospel. This provides many opportunities for harmonization or disharmonization in the textual tradition (e.g., see comments at 12:47; 16:2–3; 18:10–11). Although harmonization is a secondary feature, this does not necessarily mean that every instance of possible harmonization must be understood as being secondary (e.g., see comments at 12:4, 47; 13:35). Certainly harmonization is more common in the sayings of Jesus than elsewhere. But much work remains to be done in this area, especially in examining the phenomenon of harmonization in conjunction with the synoptic problem (cf. section 3).[59]

11. Themes and Special Problems

We may consider Matthew's principal themes along with the special problems of this Gospel, because so many of Matthew's themes have turned into foci for strenuous debate. To avoid needless repetition, the following paragraphs do not so much summarize the nine themes selected as sketch in the debate and then provide references to the places in the commentary where these things are discussed.

a. Christology

Approaches to the distinctive elements of Matthew's christology usually run along one of three lines, and these are not mutually exclusive.

The first compares Matthew with Mark to detect what differences lie between the two wherever they run parallel. Perhaps the first important study along these lines was an essay by Styler.[60] He argues that Matthew's christology is frequently more explicit than Mark's (he compares, for instance, the two accounts of the Triumphal Entry, 21:1–11). This is surely right, at least in some instances. But it is much less certain that Matthew focuses more attention than Mark on ontology (see comments at 9:1–8; 19:16–17; cf. Hill, *Matthew*, pp. 64–66), at least in those pericopes treated by both evangelists.

The second approach examines the christological titles used in Matthew's Gospel. These are rich and diverse. "Son of David" appears in the first verse, identifying Jesus as the promised Davidic Messiah; and then the title recurs, often on the lips of the needy and the ill, who anticipate relief from him who will bring in the Messianic Age (see comment at 9:27). Matthew uses *kyrios* ("Lord") more often than Mark, and some have taken this to indicate anachronistic ascription of divinity to Jesus. But *kyrios* is a word with a broad semantic range. It often means no more than "sir" (e.g., 13:27). It seems fairer to say that Matthew frequently uses the word because it is vague. During Jesus' ministry before the Cross, it is very doubtful whether it was used as an unqualified confession of Deity. But because it is the most common LXX term for referring to God, the greater insight into Jesus' person and work afforded by the postresurrection perspective made the disciples see a deeper significance to their own use of *kyrios* than they could have intended at first. A somewhat similar but more complex ambiguity surrounds "Son of Man," which is discussed in the Excursus at 8:20. Other titles receive comment where they are used by the evangelist.

The third approach to Matthew's christology is the examination of broad themes, either in exclusively Matthean material (e.g., Nolan's study on Matt 1–2, which focuses on a christology shaped by the Davidic covenant), or throughout the Gospel (e.g., various studies linking messiahship to the Suffering Servant motif).[61] Some

---

[59]Cf. Fee, pp. 154–69; more broadly, cf. C.M. Martini, "La problématique générale du texte de Matthieu," in Didier, pp. 21–36.

[60]G.M. Styler, "Stages in Christology in the Synoptic Gospels," NTS 10 (1963–64): 398–409.

[61]E.g., B. Gerhardsson, "Gottes Sohn als Diener Gottes. Messias, *Agapē* and Himmelherrschaft nach dem Matthäusevangelium," ST 27 (1973): 73–106.

reference is made to these throughout the commentary. Doubtless it is best for these christological titles and themes to emerge from an inductive study of the text, for narrower approaches often issue in substantial distortion. For example, though Kingsbury (*Matthew*) ably demonstrates how important "Son of God" is in Matthew (see comments at 2:15; 3:17; 4:3; 8:29; 16:16; 17:5; 26:63), his insistence that it is the christological category under which, for Matthew's community, all the others are subsumed cannot be sustained.[62] Matthew offers his readers vignettes linked together in diverse ways; the resulting colorful mosaic is reduced to dull gray when we elevate one theme (a christological title or something else) to a preeminent place that suppresses others.

b. Prophecy and fulfillment

Untutored Christians are prone to think of prophecy and fulfillment as something not very different from straightforward propositional prediction and fulfillment. A close reading of the NT reveals that prophecy is more complex than that. The Epistle to the Hebrews, for instance, understands the Levitical sacrificial system to be prophetic of Christ's sacrifice, Melchizedek to point to Jesus as High Priest, and so on. In Matthew we are told that Jesus' return from Egypt fulfills the OT text that refers to the Exodus (2:15); the weeping of the mothers of Bethlehem fulfills Jeremiah's reference to Rachel weeping for her children in Rama; the priests' purchase of a field for thirty pieces of silver fulfills Scriptures describing actions performed by Jeremiah and Zechariah (27:9); and, in one remarkable instance, Jesus' move to Nazareth fulfills "what was said through the prophets" even though no specific text appears to be in mind (2:23). Add to this one other major peculiarity. A number (variously estimated between ten and fourteen) of Matthew's OT quotations are introduced by a fulfillment formula characterized by a passive form of *plēroō* ("to fulfill") and a text form rather more removed from the LXX than other OT quotations. These "formula quotations" are all asides of the evangelist, his own reflections (hence the widely used German word for them, *Reflexionszitate*). What explains these phenomena?

Such problems have been extensively studied with very little agreement.[63] When Matthew cites the OT, this commentary deals with many of these issues. In anticipation of these discussions, four observations may be helpful.

1. From very different perspectives, Gundry and Soarés Prabhu argue that Matthew is responsible for the formula quotations (the difference between them is that Gundry thinks the evangelist was the apostle Matthew, Soarés Prabhu does not). Wherever he follows Mark, Matthew uses the LXX; but he in no case clearly demonstrates a personal preference for the LXX by introducing closer assimilation. There is therefore no good a priori reason for denying that Matthew selected and sometimes translated the non-LXX formula quotations. Doubtless both Hebrew and

---

[62]Cf. the telling critique by D. Hill, "Son and Servant: An Essay on Matthean Christology," *Journal for the Study of the New Testament* 6 (1980): 2–16. Kingsbury maintains, for instance, that "Son of God" dominates the thought of one section of six chapters where the title does not once appear.

[63]See the bibliography in Doeve; Gundry, *Use of OT*; McConnell; Moo, "Use of OT," Rothfuchs; Soarés Prabhu; Stendahl, *School of Matthew*; Strecker, *Weg*. See also the helpful summaries and criticisms of F. Van Sebroeck, "Les citations d'accomplissement dans l'Evangile selon Matthieu d'après trois ouvrages récents," in Didier, pp. 107–30; cf. Longenecker, *Biblical Exegesis*, pp. 140–52; and Stanton, "Origin and Purpose," ch. 4.3.

Greek OT textual traditions were somewhat fluid during the first century (as the DSS attest); and so it is not always possible to tell where the evangelist is using a text form known in his day and where he is providing his own rendering. What does seem certain, however, is that there is no good reason to support the view that the fulfillment quotations arose from a Matthean "school" (Stendahl) or were taken over by the evangelist from a collection of testimonia (Strecker).

2. Though often affirmed, it does not seem very likely that the evangelists, Matthew included, invented their "history" in order to have stories corresponding to their favorite OT proof-texts. The question is most acute in Matthew 1–2 and 27:9 and is raised there. Several points, however, argue against a wholesale creation of traditions. The NT writers do not exploit much of the rich OT potential for messianic prediction.[64] The very difficulty of the links between story and OT text argues against the creation of the stories, because created stories would have eliminated the most embarrassing strains. The parallel of the DSS cannot be overlooked. Even when they treat the OT most tortuously, the Qumran covenanters do not invent "history" (cf. Gundry, *Use of OT*, pp. 193–204).

3. The ways the events surrounding Jesus are said to fulfill the OT varies enormously and cannot be reduced to a single label. Even the Jewish categories commonly applied need certain qualification (on "Midrash," cf. section 12).

Some of Matthew's fulfillment quotations are said to be examples of pesher exegesis (e.g., Stendahl, *School of Matthew*, p. 203; Longenecker, *Biblical Exegesis*, p. 143). Such rabbinical exegesis stresses revelation and authoritatively declares, "This event is the fulfillment of that prophecy" (e.g., Acts 2:16). But even here we must be careful. The clearest examples of pesher exegesis are found in 1QpHab. What is striking about its authoritative pronouncements is that the OT prophecy it refers to, Habakkuk, is interpreted exclusively in terms of the "fulfillments" it is related to, making its original context meaningless.[65] Even the most difficult passages in Matthew, such as 2:15, do not hint that the original OT meaning is void—in this case that the people of Israel were not called by God out of Egypt at the Exodus.

4. What must now be faced is a very difficult question: Even if Matthew does not deny the OT setting of the texts he insists are being fulfilled in Jesus, on what basis does he detect any relationship of prophecy to fulfillment? The verb *plēroō* ("to fulfill") is discussed in the commentary (see comments at 2:15 and esp. 5:17); but when it refers to fulfilling Scripture, it does not lose all teleological force except in rare and well-defined situations. But opinion varies as to exactly how these OT Scriptures point forward. Sometimes the OT passages cited are plainly or at least plausibly messianic. Often the relation between prophecy and fulfillment is typological: Jesus, it is understood, must in some ways recapitulate the experience of Israel or of David. Jesus must undergo wilderness testing and call out twelve sons of Israel as apostles. Even the kind of typology varies considerably. Yet the perception remains constant that the OT was preparing the way for Christ, anticipating him, pointing to him, leading up to him. When we ask how much of this forward-looking or "prophetic" aspect in what they wrote the OT writers themselves recognized, the answer must vary with the particular text. But tentative, nuanced judgments are

---

[64]Cf. C.H. Dodd, *History and the Gospel* (London: Nisbet, 1938), pp. 61–63.

[65]Cf. F.F. Bruce, *Biblical Exegesis in the Qumran Texts* (London: Tyndale; and Grand Rapids: Eerdmans, 1960), pp. 16–17.

possible even in the most difficult cases (e.g., see comments at 1:23; 2:15, 17–18, 23; 4:15–16; 5:17; 8:16–17; 11:10–11; 12:18–21; 13:13–15; 21:4–5, 16, 42; 22:44; 26:31; 27:9). Care in such formulations will help us perceive the deep ties that bind together the Old and New Testaments.

c. Law

Few topics in the study of Matthew's Gospel are more difficult than his attitude to the law. The major studies are discussed elsewhere (cf. esp. Stanton, "Origin and Purpose," ch. 4.4, and this commentary, esp. at 5:17–48); but we may summarize some aspects of the problem here.

The difficulties stem from several factors. First, several passages can be understood as staunch defenses of the law (e.g., 5:18–19; 8:4; 19:17–18) and even of the authority of the Pharisees and teachers of the law in interpreting it (23:2–3). Jesus' disciples are expected to fast, give alms (6:2–4), and pay the temple tax (17:24–27). Second, some passages can be seen as a softening of Mark's dismissal of certain parts of the law. The addition of the "except" clause in 19:9 and the omission of Mark 7:19b ("In saying this, Jesus declared all foods 'clean.'") in Matthew's corresponding pericope (15:1–20) have convinced many that Matthew does not abrogate any OT command. Third, there are some passages where, formally at least, the letter of OT law is superseded (e.g., 5:33–37) or a revered OT institution appears to be depreciated and potentially superseded (e.g., 12:6). Fourth, there is one passage, 5:17–20, that is widely recognized to be programmatic of Matthew's view of the law. However, it embraces interpretive problems of extraordinary difficulty.

In light of these things, various theories have been proposed. Bacon (*Studies in Matthew*), followed by Kilpatrick (pp. 107–9), argues that the Gospel of Matthew presents a "new law" that is to the church what the Torah is to Judaism. The five discourses of Matthew (cf. section 14) became the new Pentateuch. Today few follow this theory; its thematic and formal links are just too tenuous. Some suggest that this Gospel reflects a Matthean church that has not yet broken away from Judaism, while others argue that the church has just broken free and now finds it necessary to define itself over against Judaism (cf. expressions such as "their teachers of the law," "their synagogues," or "your synagogues," when addressing certain Jews [e.g., 7:29; 9:35; 23:34]).

But such arguments are rather finespun. Does "their synagogue" imply a break with Judaism or distinctions within Judaism? The Qumran covenanters used the pronoun "their" of the Pharisees and mainline Judaism. Therefore could not Jesus himself have used such language to distinguish his position from that of his Jewish opponents without implying he was not a Jew? A liberal or high churchman in the Church of England may refer to their colleges, referring to Church of England training colleges reflecting evangelical tradition, without suggesting that any of the three principal groups does not belong to the Anglican communion. And if Jesus spoke in such terms and if Matthew reports this, then Matthew may also be consciously reflecting the circumstances of his own church. But if so, it still remains unclear whether his church (if it is in his mind at all) has actually broken free from Judaism (see further comments at 4:23; 7:29; 9:35; 10:17; 11:1; 12:9–10; 13:35 et al.).

Another example (8:4) is commonly taken to mean that the writer believes Jesus upholds even the ceremonial details of OT law, and that this reflects a conservative view of the continuing validity of the law in Matthew's community. This interpretation, though hard to prove, is logically possible. Alternatively one might also argue that 8:4 reflects a pre-A.D. 70 community, since after that offering temple sacrifices was impossible. Again, if Jesus said something like this, then Matthew's including it may not have been because of his community's conservatism but because it shows how Jesus used even ceremonial law to point to himself (see comment at 8:4).

It is very difficult to narrow down these various possibilities. Clearly they are also related to how one uses redaction criticism (cf. sections 1–3, 5, 7–8). Too frequently these methodological questions are not so much as raised, even when the most astounding conclusions are confidently put forward as established fact. Some argue that Matthew's church had so conservative a view of the OT law that the "evildoers" (lit., "workers of lawlessness") denounced in 7:23 are Pauline Christians (e.g., Bornkamm, *Tradition*, pp. 74–75). Quite apart from the authenticity of Jesus' saying and the danger of anachronism, this view misunderstands both Matthew and Paul. Matthew's attacks are primarily directed against Jewish leaders, especially the Pharisees, whose legal maneuvers blunt the power of the law and who fail to see the true direction in which the law pointed. They are, as the Qumran covenanters bitterly said, "expounders of smooth things" (CD 1:18).[66] As for Paul, doubtless many saw him as being antinomian. But he too spoke strongly about the kind of behavior necessary to enter the kingdom (Rom 8:14; 13:10; Gal 5:14).

Yet if Matthew attacks Pharisees, does this mean the Pharisees of Jesus' day, of Matthew's day, or of both? The least we can say is that Matthew chose to write a Gospel, not a letter. Since he chose to write about Jesus as the Messiah, the presumption must be that he intended to say something about Jesus' life and relationships. This leads us to ask whether some differences between Matthew and Paul are to be explained by the distinctive places in salvation history of their subject matter. Though he writes after Paul wrote Romans, Matthew writes about an earlier period. Undoubtedly he had certain readers and their needs in mind. Yet it is no help in understanding Matthew's treatment of the law to view the needs of his first readers from the viewpoint of his modern readers without first weighing the historical background of his book—viz., the life and teaching of Jesus.

Jesus' teaching about the law, whether gathered from Matthew or from all four Gospels, is not easy to define precisely. Sigal ("Halakah") has recently set forth an iconoclastic theory. He argues that the Pharisees of Jesus' day are not to be linked with the rabbis of the Mishnah (see section 11.f) but were a group of extremists wiped out by the events of A.D. 70. These extremists were opposed both by Jesus and by other teachers who occupied roles similar to his own. After all, ordination was unknown in Jesus' day, so there was no distinction between Jesus and other teachers. Jesus was himself a "proto-rabbi"—Sigal's term for the group that gave rise to the ordained rabbis of the post-Jamnian period (A.D. 85 on). All Jesus' legal decisions, Sigal says, fall within the range of what other proto-rabbis might say. Sigal tests this theory in Matthew's reports of Jesus' handling of the Sabbath (12:1–14) and divorce (19:1–12).

Sigal makes many telling points. His exegesis (cf. the fuller discussion in the commentary) of 5:17–20 and other test passages is not convincing, however, because he eliminates all christological claims (e.g., 12:8) as the church's interpolations into

---

[66]Several have pointed out the pun between $h^a l\bar{a}q\hat{o}t$ ("smooth things") and $h^a l\bar{a}\underline{k}\hat{o}t$ ("legal decisions affecting conduct"), the latter the aim of the Pharisees.

the narrative. He nowhere discusses, on literary or historical grounds, the authenticity of Jesus' christological claims but writes them off merely by referring to similar dismissals by other scholars. Yet the issue is crucial: if Jesus offered judgments concerning the law by making claims, implicit or explicit, concerning his messiahship, the function of the law in Jesus' teaching will certainly be presented differently from the way it would be if Jesus saw himself as no more than a "proto-rabbi." The commentary deals at length with this question (see on 5:17–20; 8:1–4, 16–17; 11:2–13; 12:1–14; 21; 13:35, 52; 15:1–20; 17:5–8; 19:3–12; 22:34–40; 27:51).

Doubtless we may link Matthew's treatment of the law with his handling of the OT (section 11.b). Matthew holds that Jesus taught that the law had a prophetic function pointing to himself. Its valid continuity lies in Jesus' own ministry, teaching, death, and resurrection. The unifying factor is Jesus himself, whose ministry and teaching stand with respect to the OT (including law) as fulfillment does to prophecy. To approach the problem of continuity and discontinuity—what remains unchanged from the Mosaic code—in any other terms is to import categories alien to Matthew's thought and his distinctive witness to Jesus (see esp. comments at 5:17–20; 11:7–15). Within this unifying framework, the problem passages mentioned at the beginning of this discussion can be most fairly explained; by it we may avoid the thesis that makes the double love commandment the sole hermeneutical key to Jesus' understanding of the OT (see comments at 22:34–40).

d. Church

The word *ekklēsia* ("church") occurs twice in Matthew (16:18; 18:17). Partly because it appears in no other Gospel, the "ecclesiasticism" of Matthew has often been overstressed.[67]

Certain things stand out. First, Matthew insists that Jesus predicted the continuation of his small group of disciples in a distinct community, a holy and messianic people, a "church" (see comment at 16:18). This motif rests on numerous passages, not just one or two texts of disputed authenticity. Second, Jesus insists that obeying the ethical demands of the kingdom, far from being optional to those who make up the church, must characterize their lives. Their allegiance proves false wherever they do not do what Jesus teaches (e.g., 7:21–23). Third, a certain discipline must be imposed on the community (see comments at 16:18–19; 18:15–18). But Matthew describes this discipline in principles rather than in details (there is no mention of deacons, elders, presbyteries, or the like), and therefore this discipline is not anachronistic provided we can accept the fact that Jesus foresaw the continuation of his community.

This third theme is much stronger in Matthew than in Mark or Luke. One might speculate on the pressures that prompted Matthew to include this material—apathy in the church, return to a kind of casuistical righteousness, infiltration by those not wholly committed to Jesus Messiah, the failure to discipline lax members. But this is speculation. The essential factor is that Matthew insists that the demand for a disciplined church goes back to Jesus himself.

---

[67]For a convenient summary of recent literature, cf. Stanton, "Origin and Purpose," ch. 4.2. Stanton neglects to mention the extraordinarily important work by B.F. Meyer (see comments at 16:17–19).

e. Eschatology

Matthew consistently distinguishes among four time periods: (1) the period of revelation and history previous to Jesus; (2) the inauguration of something new in his coming and ministry; (3) the period beginning with his exaltation, from which point on all of God's sovereignty is mediated through him, and his followers proclaim the gospel of the kingdom to all nations; (4) the consummation and beyond.

Many features of Matthew's eschatology are still being studied. The seven most important of these (the number may be eschatologically significant!) and the places where they are principally discussed in this commentary are (1) the meaning of peculiarly difficult verses (e.g., 10:23; 16:28); (2) the distinctive flavor of Matthew's dominant "kingdom of heaven" over against "kingdom of God" preferred by the rest of the NT writers (cf. comment at 3:2); (3) the extent to which the kingdom has already been inaugurated and the extent to which it is wholly future, awaiting the consummation (a recurring theme; cf. esp. ch. 13); (4) the bearing of the parables on eschatology (ch. 13, 25); (5) the relation between the kingdom and the church (another recurring theme; cf. esp. 13:37–39); (6) the sense in which Jesus saw the kingdom as imminent (see comments at ch. 24); (7) the Olivet Discourse (chs. 24–25).

f. The Jewish leaders

Two areas need clarification for understanding Matthew's treatment of the Jewish leaders. The first is the identification of the "Pharisees" at the time of Jesus. We may distinguish four viewpoints, each represented by able Jewish scholars.

1. The traditional approach is well defended by Guttmann,[68] who argues that the Pharisees were more effective leaders than the OT prophets. The prophets were uncompromising idealists; the Pharisees, whose views are largely reflected by their successors, the rabbis behind the Mishnah, were adaptable, adjusting the demands of Torah by a finely tuned exegetical procedure issuing in legal enactments designed to make life easier and clarify right conduct.

2. By contrast Neusner[69] insists that a chasm yawns between the rabbinic views reflected in Mishnah and pre-A.D. 70 Pharisaism. The Pharisees shaped the life of pre-70 Judaism by extending the purity rituals of the temple to the daily experience of every Jew.

3. Rivkin[70] argues that the Pharisees—a post-Maccabean and theologically revolutionary group—were men of considerable learning and persuasiveness. They developed the oral law, now largely codified in the Mishnah, and unwittingly departed radically from their OT roots. Rivkin denies that they had separatistic or ritualistic tendencies; their influence was broad and pervasive.

4. Sigal[71] argues for a complete disjunction between the Pharisees, whom he

---

[68]Alexander Guttmann, *Rabbinic Judaism in the Making: A Chapter in the History of the Halakah from Ezra to Judah I* (Detroit: Wayne State University, 1970).

[69]Jacob Neusner, *The Rabbinic Traditions of the Pharisees*, 3 vols. (Leiden: Brill, 1971). For a simplified treatment, cf. his *From Politics to Piety: The Emergence of Pharisaic Judaism* (Englewood Cliffs: Prentice-Hall, 1973).

[70]Ellis Rivkin, *A Hidden Revolution: The Pharisee's Search for the Kingdom Within* (Nashville: Abingdon, 1978).

[71]"Halakah"; id., *The Emergence of Contemporary Judaism*, vols. I.1; I.2, *The Foundations of Judaism*

identifies as the *perushim* ("separatists"), and the rabbis behind Mishnah. In Jesus' day the rabbis were not officially ordained: ordination had not yet been invented. That is why Jesus himself is addressed as "rabbi" in the Gospels (e.g., 26:49; Mark 9:5; 10:51; 11:21; John 1:38, 49; 3:2). He belonged to a class of "proto-rabbis," the forerunners of the ordained rabbis of the Mishnaic period. His opponents, the Pharisees, were extremists who died out after A.D. 70 and left virtually no literary trace.

The tentative assessment adopted in this commentary is that these competing interpretations of the evidence are largely right in what they affirm and wrong in what they deny. Sigal is almost certainly right in arguing that ordination was unknown in Jesus' day (cf. Westerholm, pp. 26–39), though there may have been informal procedures for recognizing a teacher of Scripture. There can be no simple equation of "Pharisee" and Mishnaic rabbi. But against Sigal, it is unlikely that the Pharisees were so separatistic that they did not embrace most if not all "proto-rabbis." The Gospels refer to every other major religious grouping—Sadducees, priests, scribes—and it is almost inconceivable that the evangelists should say almost nothing about the "proto-rabbis," the dominant group after A.D. 70, and vent so much criticism on a group (the Pharisees) so insignificant in Jesus' day that they disappeared from view after A.D. 70. The fairly rapid disappearance of the Sadducees after A.D. 70 is no parallel because much of their life and influence depended on the temple destroyed by the Romans; and in any case the evangelists do give us some description of their theological position.

As for Jesus, he cannot be reduced to a "proto-rabbi," training his followers to repeat his legal decisions. His messianic claims cannot so easily be dismissed. To onlookers he appeared as a prophet (21:11, 46).[72] Guttmann (n. 68) is right in saying that the Pharisees adapted the laws to the times and were effective leaders. The problem is that their minute regulations made ritual distinctions too difficult and morality too easy. The radical holiness demanded by the OT prophets became domesticated, preparing the way for Jesus' preaching that demanded a righteousness greater than that of the Pharisees (5:20). Though Neusner (n. 69) correctly detects the Pharisees' concern with ceremonial purity (cf. 15:1–12), his skepticism concerning the fixity of many oral traditions and the possibility of knowing more about the Pharisees is unwarranted. The evidence from Josephus cannot be so easily dismissed as Neusner would have us think. Even allowing for Josephus's own bias toward the Pharisees, his evidence so consistently demonstrates their wide influence in the nation, not to say their centrality during the Jewish War, that it is very difficult to think of them as a minor separatistic group (Sigal) or as exclusively concerned with ritual purity.

The Mishnah (c. A.D. 200) cannot be read back into A.D. 30 as if Judaism had not faced the growth of Christianity and the shattering destruction of temple and cultus. Nevertheless it preserves more traditional material than is sometimes thought. One suspects that the Pharisees of Jesus' day include the proto-rabbis, ideological forbears of the Mishnaic Tannaim (lit., "repeaters," i.e., the "rabbis" from roughly A.D. 70 to 200). In this view they included men every bit as learned and creative as the

---

from *Biblical Origins to the Sixth Century A.D.* (Pittsburgh: Pickwick, 1980). A somewhat similar dichotomy is adopted by John Bowker, *Jesus and the Pharisees* (Cambridge: University Press, 1973).

[72]Cf. B. Lindars, "Jesus and the Pharisees," *Donum Gentilicium*, edd. E. Bammel, C.K. Barrett, and W.D. Davies (Oxford: Clarendon, 1978), pp. 51–63, esp. pp. 62–63.

second-century rabbis. But they also included many lesser men, morally and intellectually, who were largely purged by the twin effects of the growth of Christianity and the devastation of A.D. 70. These events called forth a "counterreformation," whose legacy is Mishnah. Rivkin (n. 70) is undoubtedly right in seeing the Pharisees as learned scholars whose meticulous application and development of OT law massively influenced Judaism, though his identification of Pharisees with scribes and his handling of the development of oral law are simplistic.

We hold that the Pharisees were a nonpriestly group of uncertain origin, generally learned, committed to the oral law, and concerned with developing Halakah (rules of conduct based on deductions from the law). Most teachers of the law were Pharisees; and the Sanhedrin included men from their number as well (see comment at 21:23), though the leadership of the Sanhedrin belonged to the priestly Sadducees.

The second area needing clarification is the way Matthew refers to Jewish leaders. It is universally agreed that Matthew is quite strongly anti-Pharisaic. Recently, however, more and more scholars have argued that Matthew's picture of the Pharisees reflects the rabbis of the period A.D. 80–100, not the situation around A.D. 30. His grasp of the other Jewish parties, which largely fell away after A.D. 70, is shallow and sometimes wrong. Gaston thinks the depth of Matthew's ignorance, especially of the Sadducees, is "astonishing."[73]

The question is complex.[74] Certain observations, however, will qualify the charge of Matthew's ignorance.

1. If Matthew's sole target had been the rabbis of A.D. 80–100, designated "Pharisees," it is astonishing that they are virtually unmentioned during the Passion Week and the passion narrative when feeling against Jesus reached its height. What we discover is that the chief opponents are priests, elders, members of the Sanhedrin, which is just what we would expect in the vicinity of Jerusalem before A.D. 70. This demonstrates that Matthew is not entirely ignorant of historical distinctions regarding Jewish leaders; it calls in question the thesis that his opponents are exclusively Pharisees and urges caution in making similar judgments.

2. Matthew mentions the Sadducees more often than all the other evangelists combined. If Matthew was so ignorant of them, and if they were irrelevant to his alleged circumstances in A.D. 80–100, why did he multiply references to them?

3. Matthew demonstrates that he was aware of some of the Sadducees' doctrinal distinctives (see comment at 22:23–33). This should make us very cautious in evaluating the most difficult point—viz., that in five places Matthew uses the phrase "Pharisees and Sadducees" in a way that links them closely (3:7; 16:1, 6, 11, 11–12). This linking is peculiar to Matthew. The known antipathy between the two groups was sufficiently robust that many modern commentators have concluded this Gospel was written late enough and by someone far enough removed from the setting of A.D. 30 for this incongruity to slip into the text. But in addition to Matthew's historical awareness, two complementary explanations largely remove the difficulty.

First, the linking of Pharisees and Sadducees under one article in Matthew 3:7 may reflect, not their theological agreement, but their common mission. Just as the

---

[73]L. Gaston, "The Messiah of Israel as Teacher of the Gentiles," Int 29 (1975): 34.

[74]Cf. D.A. Carson, "Jewish Leaders in Matthew's Gospel: A Reappraisal," JETS 25 (1982): 161–74. For a concise presentation of the data, cf. Garland, pp. 218–21.

Sanhedrin raised questions about Jesus' authority, it is intrinsically likely they sent delegates to sound out John the Baptist. The Sanhedrin included both Pharisees and Sadducees (Acts 23:6); and their mutual distrust makes it likely that the delegation was made up of representatives from both parties. The fourth Gospel suggests this. The "Jews of Jerusalem" (who else but the Sanhedrin?) sent "priests and Levites" (John 1:19)—certainly Sadducees—to ask John who he was; but Pharisees were also sent (John 1:24). Matthew's language may therefore preserve accurate historical reminiscence. Something similar may be presupposed in 16:1. We must always remember that though the Pharisees and Sadducees could fight each other fiercely on certain issues, their political circumstances required that they work together at many levels.

Second, though the linking of the Pharisees and Sadducees in the remaining references (16:6, 11–12) appears to make their teaching common, the context demands restraint. In certain circumstances, a Baptist may warn against the "teaching of the Presbyterians and Anglicans," not because he is unaware of fundamental differences between them (or even among them!), but because he wishes to set their pedobaptism against his own views. Quite clearly in 16:5–12 Jesus cannot be denouncing everything the Pharisees and Sadducees teach, for some of what they teach he holds in common with them. The particular point of teaching in this context is their attitude toward Jesus and their desire to domesticate revelation and authenticate it—an attitude so blind it cannot recognize true revelation when it appears (see comment at 16:1–4). It is against this "yeast of the Pharisees and Sadducees" that Jesus warns his disciples; in his view both parties were guilty of the same error.

4. Categories for the Jewish leaders overlap in the Gospels, Matthew included. As far as we know, the Sanhedrin, for instance, was made up of Sadducees, Pharisees, and elders. The Sadducees were mostly priests. The elders were mostly lay nobility and probably primarily Pharisees. Thus "Pharisees" in the Sanhedrin were "laymen" in the sense that they were not priests; but many of them were scribes ("teachers of the law") and thus different from the elders. When 21:23 speaks of the chief priests and elders of the people coming to Jesus, it is probably referring to members of the Sanhedrin described in terms of their clerical status rather than their theological position. The ambiguities are considerable; but we must avoid indefensible disjunctions.

5. Our own ignorance of who the Pharisees were and of the distinctive beliefs of the Sadducees (we know them almost entirely through the writings of their opponents—"almost" because some scholars think that Sirach, for instance, is a proto-Sadducean document) should make us hesitate before ascribing "astonishing" ignorance to the evangelist. The astonishing ignorance may be our own. One suspects that in some instances Matthew's treatment of Jewish leaders is being pressed into a mold to suit a date of A.D. 80–100. The truth is that our knowledge of both Judaism and Christianity during that period has formidable gaps. Though Matthew may have been written then—though in my view this is unlikely—his treatment of Jewish leaders cannot be used to defend the late date view.

But is Matthew's polemic so harsh that he must be considered anti-Semitic (cf. the commentary at 23:1–36; 26:57–59)? The judgment of Légasse is sound.[75] Matthew's

---

[75]S. Légasse, "L' 'antijudaïsme' dans l'Evangile selon Matthieu," in Didier, pp. 417–28.

sternest denunciations are not racially motivated; they are prompted by the response of people to Jesus. These denunciations extend to professing believers whose lives betray the falseness of their profession (7:21–23; 22:11–14) as well as to Jews; the governing motives are concern for the perseverance of the Christian community and for the authoritative proclamation of the "gospel of the kingdom" to "all nations," Jew and Gentile alike (see comments at 28:18–20), to bring all to submission to Jesus Messiah.

g. Mission

It has long been recognized that the closing pericope (28:16–20) is fully intended to be the climax toward which the entire Gospel moves. By tying together some of Matthew's most dominant themes, these verses give them a new depth that reaches back and sheds light on the entire Gospel. For instance, the Great Commission is perceived to be the result of God's providential ordering of history (1:1–17) to bring to a fallen world a Messiah who would save his people from their sins (1:21); but the universal significance of Jesus' birth, hinted at in 1:1 and repeatedly raised in the flow of the narrative (e.g., see comments at 2:1–12; 4:14–16, 25; 8:5–13; 10:18; 13:36–52; 15:21–28; 24:9, 14) is now confirmed by the concluding lines.

We have already observed that the extent of the Great Commission has been limited by some—though on inadequate grounds—to Gentiles only (section 8; see comments at 28:18–20). Matthew does not trace the context of the people of God from a Jewish one to an exclusively Gentile one but from a Jewish context to a racially inclusive one. Unlike Luke (Luke 21:24) and Paul (Rom 11:25–27), Matthew raises no questions about Israel's future as a distinct people.

h. Miracles

The biblical writers do not see miracles as divine interventions in an ordered and closed universe. Rather, God as Lord of the universe and of history sustains everything that takes place under his sovereignty. Sometimes, however, he does extraordinary things; and then we in the modern world call them "miracles." Biblical writers preferred terms like "sign," "wonder," or "power." Parallels between Jesus and Hellenistic miracle workers are not so close as some form critics have thought (cf. Albright and Mann, pp. cxxiv–cxxxi). On the other hand, the value of miracles as proof of Jesus' deity is not so conclusive as some conservative expositors have thought.

Miracles in Matthew share certain characteristics with those in the other Synoptics, and these characteristics must be understood before Matthew's distinctives can be explored. Jesus' miracles are bound up with the inbreaking of the promised kingdom (8:16–17; 12:22–30; cf. Luke 11:14–23). They are part of his messianic work (4:23; 11:4–6) and therefore the dual evidence of the dawning of the kingdom and of the status of Jesus the King Messiah. This does not mean that Jesus did miracles on demand as a kind of spectacular attestation (see comments at 12:38–42; cf. John 4:48). Faith and obedience are not guaranteed by great miracles, though faith and God's mighty power working through Jesus are linked in several ways. Lack of faith may be an impediment to this power (e.g., 17:19–20), not because God's power is curtailed, but because real trust in him submits to his powerful reign and expects mercies from him (e.g., 15:28; cf. Mark 9:24).

"Nature miracles" (the stilling of the storm or the multiplication of loaves and fish) attest, not only the universal sweep of God's power, but may in some cases (calming the storm) provide the creation rebelling against God with a foretaste of restored order—an order to be climaxed by the consummation of the kingdom. In some cases (the multiplication of loaves and fish, the withered fig tree) miracles constitute a "prophetic symbolism" that promises unqualified fruition (the messianic banquet, the certainty of judgment) at the End.

Matthew's miracles are distinctive for the brevity with which they are reported. He condenses introductions and conclusions, omits secondary characters and the like (see comments at 8:1–4). Nevertheless it is too much to say, as Held does, "The miracles are not important for their own sakes, but by reason of the message they contain" (Bornkamm, *Tradition*, p. 210). This might almost suggest that the facticity of the miracles is of no consequence to Matthew provided their message is preserved. Matthew himself specifically disallows this (11:3–6). All the evangelists hold that miracles point beyond the mere factuality of wonderful events: in this Matthew is no different from the others. He simply shifts the balance of event and implication a little in order to stress the latter.

The particular themes most favored by Matthew in connection with Jesus' miracles are worked out in the commentary.

i. The disciples' understanding and faith

Ever since the work of G. Barth (in Bornkamm et al., *Tradition*, pp. 105ff.), many scholars have held that whereas in Mark the disciples do not understand what Jesus says till he explains it to them in secret, Matthew attributes large and instant understanding to the disciples. Indeed, this is what sets them apart from the crowd: the disciples understand, the outsiders do not. Where the disciples falter and must improve is not in their understanding but in their faith.

The thesis can be defended by a careful selection of the data, but it will not withstand close scrutiny. Apart from depending too much on the so-called messianic secret in Mark (see comments in this vol. at Mark 9:9), it does not adequately treat the disciples' request for private instruction (13:36), their failure to understand Jesus' teaching about his passion even after his explanations (e.g., 16:21–26; 17:23; 26:51–56), and the passages that deal with "stumbling" or "falling away." These are not peripheral matters; they are integral to what Jesus and Matthew say about discipleship.

The thesis also errs, not only for the two reasons mentioned above, but also for a third. Adopting a doctrinaire form of redaction criticism, it so stresses what the relevant passages reveal about Matthew's church that it blunts their real thrust. In particular the failure of the disciples to understand the significance of Jesus' passion and resurrection predictions is largely a function of the disciples' unique place in salvation history. They were unprepared before the events to accept the notion of a crucified and resurrected Messiah; not a few of Jesus' christological claims are sufficiently vague (cf. Carson, "Christological Ambiguities") that their full import could be grasped by those with a traditional Jewish mind-set only after Calvary and the empty tomb. To this extent the disciples' experience of coming to deeper understanding and faith was unique because it was locked into a phase of salvation history rendered forever obsolete by the triumph of Jesus' resurrection.

Matthew's readers, whether in the first century or today, may profit from studying the disciples' experience as he records it. But to try subjectively to imitate the disciples' coming to full faith and understanding following Jesus' resurrection is futile. Rather we should look back on this witness to the divine self-disclosure, observing God's wisdom and care as through his Son he progressively revealed himself and his purposes to redeem a fallen and rebellious race. Feeding our faith and understanding on the combined testimony of the earliest witnesses who tell how they arrived by a unique historical sequence at their faith and understanding, we shall learn to focus our attention, not on the disciples, but on their Lord. This is not to say that the disciples have nothing to teach us about personal growth; rather, it is to insist that we shall basically misunderstand this Gospel if we do not see that it deals with a unique coming to faith and understanding. This topic is so important that the commentary refers to it repeatedly (cf. 13:10–13, 23, 36, 43, 51–52; 14:15–17; 15:15–16; 16:21–28; 17:13, 23; 20:17–19, 22; 23:13–36; 24:1; 28:17). Elsewhere it has been comprehensively treated by Trotter.

12. Literary genre

The interpretation of any piece of literature is affected by an understanding of its genre. A sonnet, novel, parable, history, fable, free verse, or an aphorism must be read according to its literary form.

a. Gospel

What, then, is a Gospel? Many theories have been proposed and affinities discovered in other writings (e.g., apocalyptic literature, OT books, Graeco-Roman biographies, etc.). Recently Talbert[76] has argued that the Gospel belongs to the genre of Graeco-Roman biography. In a convincing rejoinder, Aune[77] has shown that Talbert has misunderstood not a few ancient sources and has arrived at his conclusions by adopting ambiguous categories that hide essential differences. Aune rightly insists that the Gospels belong in a class of their own. This does not mean that the Gospels have no relation to other genres. The truth is that " 'new' genres were constantly emerging during the Graeco-Roman period, if by 'new' we mean a recombination of earlier forms and genres into novel configurations."[78]

Thus our Gospels are made up of many pericopes, some belonging to recognized genres, others with close affinities to recognized genres. Each must be weighed, but the result is a flexible form that aims to give a selective account of Jesus, including his teaching and miracles and culminating in his death by crucifixion and his burial and resurrection. The selection includes certain key points in his career (his baptism, ministry, passion, and resurrection) and aims at a credible account of these historical events. At the same time the material is organized so as to stress certain subjects and motifs. The writing is not dispassionate but confessional—something the evangelists considered an advantage. Some of the material is organized along

---

[76]C.H. Talbert, *What is a Gospel? The Genre of the Canonical Gospels* (Philadelphia: Fortress, 1977).

[77]D.E. Aune, "The Problem of the Genre of the Gospels," France and Wenham, pp. 9–60; cf. R.H. Gundry, "Recent Investigations Into the Literary Genre 'Gospel,'" Longenecker and Tenney, pp. 97–114.

[78]Aune, "Problem of Genre," p. 48.

thematic lines, some according to a loose chronology; still other pericopes are linked by some combination of catchwords, themes, OT attestation, genre, and logical coherence. The result is not exactly a history, biography, theology, confession, catechism, tract, homage, or letter—though it is in some respects all these. It is a "Gospel," a presentation of the "good news" of Jesus the Messiah.

b. Midrash

Scholars have increasingly recognized the Jewishness of the NT and have therefore cultivated Jewish literary categories for understanding these documents. Among the most important of these categories is midrash. One application of this work, the lectionary theory of Goulder, has already been discussed (section 8). But the most recent development is the commentary by Gundry. He argues that Q is larger than is customarily recognized, embracing material normally designated "M" (cf. section 3), including the birth narratives in Matthew 1–2. What Matthew does, according to Gundry, is apply "midrashic techniques" to the tradition he takes over, adding nonhistorical touches to historical material, sometimes creating stories, designated "midrashim," to make theological points, even though the stories, like parables, have no historical referent.

Everything depends on definition. Etymologically "midrash" simply means "interpretation." But in this sense, every comment on another text is midrash—including this commentary. Such a definition provides no basis for saying that because Matthew relates midrashic stories in Matthew 1–2 they are not historically true. Most other definitions, however accurate, are not sufficient to yield Gundry's conclusion. Derrett (*NT Studies*, 2:205ff.), for instance, defines midrashic method in terms of its allusiveness to many sources, not in terms of historicity at all. Snodgrass defines midrash, not as a genre, but "as a process in which forms of tradition develop and enrich or intensify later adaptation of Old Testament texts."[79] Many other definitions have been offered.[80]

To compound the difficulty, the term seems to undergo a semantic shift within Jewish literature. By the time of the Babylonian Talmud (fourth century A.D.), midrash had developed a more specialized meaning akin to what Gundry clearly wants. Other Jewish commentaries, mainly the Qumran Pesharim,[81] were characterized by three things: (1) they attempted to deal systematically with every point in the text; (2) they limited themselves almost exclusively to the text; (3) they adopted a revelatory stance toward the text that identified virtually every point in the text with a point of fulfillment in the interpreter's day or later, without any sense of historical context. By contrast the midrashim worked through the text of Scripture more haphazardly, using Scripture as a sort of peg on which to hang discourse, stories, and other pieces to illuminate the theological meaning of the text. This was in conscious distinction from "peshat," the more "literal" meaning of the text. But in the first two centuries, it is very doubtful whether midrash had a

---

[79]Klyne R. Snodgrass, "Streams of Tradition Emerging From Isaiah 40:1–5 and Their Adaptation in the New Testament," *Journal for the Study of the New Testament* 8 (1980): 40.

[80]Cf. D.A. Carson, *Midrash and Matthew* (forthcoming).

[81]Cf. Maurya P. Horgan, *Pesharim: Qumran Interpretation of Biblical Books* (Washington: Catholic Biblical Assoc., 1979).

meaning even this specialized. It referred rather to "an interpretive exposition however derived and irrespective of the type of material under consideration" (Longenecker, *Biblical Exegesis*, p. 32).

In a wide-ranging chapter, Moo ("Use of OT," pp. 8ff.) discusses the various ways in which literature that treats the OT text may be analyzed. He distinguishes literary genre (form and general content), citation procedures (e.g., explicit quotation, allusion, conceptual influence, and the like), appropriation technique (the ways the OT text is applied to the contemporary setting), and the hermeneutical axioms implicitly adopted by the interpreter (e.g., that the Scripture was a closed entity needing to be ingeniously interpreted to elicit answers to questions about conduct not specifically treated in the text).

Now if "midrash" refers to genre, in the first century it is too wide a term to bear the weight Gundry places on it and is inadequate on other grounds (*Matthew*, pp. 63ff.). Attempts to define "midrash" in terms of appropriation techniques have not proved successful, because none of the techniques is restricted to midrash. Moo tentatively suggests that "midrash" be characterized "in terms of the hermeneutical axioms which guide the approach" ("Use of OT," p. 66). There is considerable merit in this; but of course this results in largely limiting midrash to rabbinic Judaism, since the operative hermeneutical axioms include a largely noneschatological perception of itself and a deep preoccupation with enunciating its identity and directing its conduct (corresponding roughly to the two forms haggadic midrash and Halakic midrash).[82] By contrast the stories of Matthew 1–2 are fundamentally eschatological: they are said to fulfill Scripture in the context of a book in which messianic fulfillment and the dawning of the eschatological kingdom constitute fundamental themes. Matthew 1–2 is little concerned with rules of conduct or the identity of the people of God. It bursts with christological concern and a teleological perspective.

When distinctions like these are borne in mind, the modern category "Midrash-Pesher," which some wish to apply to Matthew's treatment of the OT (cf. Moo, "Use of OT," p. 174), is seen as an inadequate label for the Qumran commentaries. Midrash and Pesher are alike in many of their techniques, but the hermeneutical axioms are profoundly different. But if the makeshift Midrash-Pesher is inappropriate for the commentaries of Qumran, it is equally inappropriate for Matthew. And in any case it is definitely not a genre recognized by Jewish readers of the first century.

These conclusions are inevitable:

1. Gundry cannot legitimately appeal to "midrash" as a well-defined and recognized genre of literature in the first century.

2. In particular, if "midrash" reflects genre, as opposed to hermeneutical axioms irrelevant to Matthew, it is being given a sense more or less well-defined only from the fourth century on. This raises the question of what we could expect Matthew's readers to have thought. Gundry argues that the reason the church has failed to recognize the "midrashic" (and therefore nonhistorical) nature of Matthew 1–2 is that this Gospel was quickly taken over by the Gentiles who had little appreciation for Jewish literary genres. This plausible argument is weakened by strong evidence that midrash in any specialized sense relevant to Gundry's thesis is too late in Jewish circles to be useful.

3. Even if we adopt this late narrowing of the term "midrash," it is still inappro-

---

[82]Cf. Daniel Patte, *Early Jewish Hermeneutic in Palestine* (Missoula: SBL, 1975), pp. 49ff.

priate as a description of Matthew's "M" material. Although the Jewish Midrashim are often only loosely connected with the texts they "expound," yet a line of continuity runs through those OT texts. By contrast Matthew's continuity in chapters 1–2, for instance, is established by the story line, not the OT texts, all of which could be removed without affecting the passage's cohesion.

4. Much of the force of Gundry's argument depends on his assessment of the tendencies in Matthew's editing of sources. Gundry feels that demonstrable tendencies in Matthew require appeal to midrashic technique as the only adequate explanation of material that diverges so radically from the sources. But another assessment of the same evidence is often possible. Few will be convinced by his postulation of a common source behind Matthew 1–2 and Luke 1–2. Moreover some of the "tendencies" he detects in Matthew—e.g., he follows the now popular line on the disciples' understanding (see section 11.i)—are better interpreted in other ways. These points depend on details of exegesis and emerge in this commentary. (See also the review of Gundry in Carson, "Gundry on Matthew.")

An important element in Gundry's argument is that the stories cannot be taken as history because, read that way, they include some demonstrable errors. For some of these matters, see the commentary in loc. Here it is sufficient to say that whoever uses "midrash" of any part of Matthew's Gospel should tell his readers precisely what the term means.

c. Miscellaneous

Several other important forms of literature make up the constituent parts of our canonical Gospels: wisdom sayings, genealogies, discourses, parables, and so forth. The most important receive brief treatment in the commentary, the most extensive note being devoted to parables (see at 13:3).

13. Bibliography

a. Selected Commentaries on Matthew

Albright, W.F., and Mann, C.S. *Matthew*. Garden City: Doubleday, 1971.

Alexander, J.A. *The Gospel According to Matthew*. New York: Scribner, 1860.

Allen, Willoughby C. *A Critical and Exegetical Commentary on the Gospel According to S. Matthew*. Edinburgh: T. & T. Clark, 1912.

Barnes, Albert. *Notes on the New Testament*. Grand Rapids: Kregel, repr. 1962.

Benoit, P. *L'Evangile selon Saint Matthieu*. 4th ed. Paris: du Cerf, 1972.

Bonnard, Pierre. *L'Evangile selon Saint Matthieu*. 2d ed. Neuchâtel: Delachaux et Niestlé, 1970.

Box, G. H. *St. Matthew*. Edinburgh: T.C. and E.C. Jack, n.d.

Broadus, John. *Commentary on the Gospel of Matthew*. Valley Forge: American Baptist Publication Society, 1886.

Calvin, John. *Calvin's New Testament Commentaries: Matthew, Mark, and Luke*. 3 vols. Translated by A.W. Morrison and T.H.L. Parker. Edited by D.W. Torrance and T.F. Torrance. Grand Rapids, 1972.

English, E.S. *Studies in the Gospel According to Matthew*. New York: Revell, 1935.

Erdman, Charles R. *The Gospel of Matthew: An Exposition*, 1920. Reprint. Philadelphia: Westminster, 1966.

Fenton, J.C. *Saint Matthew*. Harmondsworth: Penguin, 1963.

Filson, Floyd V. *A Commentary on the Gospel According to St. Matthew*. New York: Harper, 1960.

Gaebelein, Arno C. *The Gospel of Matthew: An Exposition*. 2 vols. New York: Our Hope Publications, 1910.

Gaechter, Paul. *Das Matthäus Evangelium*. Innsbruck: Tyrolia-Verlag, 1963.

Gander, Georges. *L'Evangile de l'Eglise: Commentaire de l'Evangile selon Mattieu*. Aix-en-Provence: Faculte de Theologie Protestante, 1967.

Green, H. Benedict. *The Gospel According to Matthew*. Oxford: University Press, 1975.

Grosheide, F.W. *Het Heilig Evangelie Volgens Mattheus*. Kampen: Kok, 1954.

Grundmann, Walter. *Das Evangelium nach Matthäus*. 4th ed. Berlin: Evangelische Verlagsanstalt, 1975.

Gundry, Robert H. *Matthew: A Commentary on His Literary and Theological Art*. Grand Rapids: Eerdmans, 1981.

Hendriksen, William. *The Gospel of Matthew*. Grand Rapids: Baker, 1973.

Henry, Matthew. *A Commentary on the Holy Bible*. London: Marshall Bros., n.d.

Hill, David. *The Gospel of Matthew*. Grand Rapids: Eerdmans, 1972.

Kingsbury, Jack Dean. *Matthew*. Philadelphia: Fortress, 1977.

Klostermann, Erich. *Das Matthäus-Evangelium*. 2d ed. Tübingen: J.C.B. Mohr, 1927.

Lagrange, M.-J. *Évangile selon Saint Matthieu*. Paris: Lecoffre, 1948.

Lenski, R.C.H. *Interpretation of St. Matthew's Gospel*. Columbus, Ohio: Lutheran Book Concern, 1932.

Lohmeyer, Ernst. *Das Evangelium des Matthäus*. Edited by W. Schmauck. Göttingen: Vandenhoeck und Ruprecht, 1956.

Loisy, A. *Les évangiles synoptiques*. 2 vols. Ceffonds: n.p., 1907.

Luther, Martin. *Works*.

Maier, Gerhard. *Matthäus-Evangelium*. 2 vols. Neuhausen: Hänosler, 1979–.

McKenzie, John L. "The Gospel According to Matthew," *The Jerome Biblical Commentary*. Edited by R.E. Brown, J.A. Fitzmyer, and R.E. Murphy. Englewood Cliffs: Prentice-Hall, 1968.

McNeile, Alan Hugh. *The Gospel According to St. Matthew: The Greek Text with Introduction, Notes, and Indices*. London: Macmillan, 1915.

Merx, Adalbert. *Das Evangelium Matthaeus*. Berlin: Georg Reimer, 1902.

Meyer, Heinrich August Wilhelm. *Critical and Exegetical Commentary on the New Testament*. Part I. *The Gospel of Matthew*. 2 vols. Translated by W.P. Dickson and W. Stewart. Edinburgh: T. & T. Clark, 1877–79.

Micklem, Philip A. *St. Matthew*. London: Methuen and Co., 1917.

Morgan, G. Campbell. *The Gospel According to Matthew*. Old Tappan: Revell, 1929.

Morison, James. *A Practical Commentary on the Gospel According to St. Matthew*. London: Hodder and Stoughton, 1892.

Plummer, Alfred. *An Exegetical Commentary on the Gospel According to S. Matthew*. London: Robert Scott, 1915.

Plumptre, E.H. *The Gospel According to Matthew*. Reprint. Grand Rapids: Zondervan, 1957.

Ridderbos, H.N. *Het Evangelie naar Mattheus*. Kampen: Kok, 1952.

Rienecker, Fritz. *Das Evangelium des Matthäus*. Wuppertal: R. Brockhaus, 1953.

Robinson, Theodore H. *The Gospel of Matthew*. London: Hodder and Stoughton, 1928.

Sabourin, Leopold. *L'Evangile selon Saint Matthiew et ses principaux paralleles*. Rome: BIP, 1978.

Schlatter, Adolf. *Der Evangelist Matthäus: Seine Sprache, sein Ziel, seine Selbständigkeit*. 6th ed. Stuttgart: Calwer, 1963.

Schmid, Josef. *Das Evangelium nach Matthaus*. Regensburg: Friedrich Pustet, 1959.

Schniewind, Julius. *Das Evangelium nach Matthaus*. Gottingen: Vandenhoeck und Ruprecht, 1956.

Schweizer, Eduard. *The Good News According to Matthew*. Atlanta: John Knox, 1975.

Smith, B.T.D. *The Gospel According to S. Matthew*. Cambridge: University Press, 1927.
Spurgeon, C.H. *The Gospel of the Kingdom: A Popular Exposition of Matthew*. London: Passmore and Alabaster, 1893.
Tasker, R.V.G. *The Gospel According to St. Matthew: An Introduction and Commentary*. London: IVP, 1961.
Walvoord, John F. *Matthew: Thy Kingdom Come*. Chicago: Moody, 1974.
Weiss, Bernhard. *Das Matthaus-Evangelium*. Gottingen: Vandenhoeck und Ruprecht, 1898.
Wellhausen, J. *Das Evangelium Matthaei*. Berlin: Georg Reimer, 1904.
Zahn, Theodor. *Das Evangelium des Matthäus*. Leipzig: A. Deichert'sche Buchhandlung, 1903.

b. Other selected works

Arens, Eduardo. *The Ἦλθον-sayings in the Synoptic Tradition: A Historico-Critical Investigation*. Göttingen: Vandenhoeck und Ruprecht, 1976.
Bacon, Benjamin W. *Studies in Matthew*. London: Constable, 1930.
Bammel, E., ed. *The Trial of Jesus*. London: SCM, 1970.
Banks, Robert. *Jesus and the Law in the Synoptic Tradition*. Cambridge: University Press, 1975.
Beasley-Murray, G. R. *Baptism in the New Testament*. London: Macmillan, 1954.
Benoit, P. *Jesus and the Gospel*. New York: Herder and Herder, 1973.
Berger, K. *Die Gesetzesauslegung Jesu*. Neukirchen-Vluyn: Neukirchener Verlag, 1972.
Best, Ernest. *The Temptation and the Passion: The Markan Soteriology*. Cambridge: University Press, 1965.
_____, and Wilson, R. McL., edd. *Text and Interpretation*. Cambridge: University Press, 1979.
Beyer, Klaus. *Semitische Syntax im Neuen Testament*. Göttingen: Vandenhoeck und Ruprecht, 1968.
Black, Matthew. *An Aramaic Approach to the Gospels and Acts*. 3d ed. Oxford: Clarendon, 1967.
Blair, Edward P. *Jesus in the Gospel of Matthew*. New York: Abingdon, 1960.
Blinzler, Josef. *The Trial of Jesus*. Translated by F. McHugh. Cork: Mercier, 1959.
Bonhoeffer, Dietrich. *The Cost of Discipleship*. 6th ed. London: SCM, 1959.
Bornhäuser, Karl. *Die Bergpredigt: Versuch einer Zeitgenössischen Auslegung*. 2d ed. Gütersloh: C. Bertelsmann, 1927.
Bornkamm, Günther. *Jesus of Nazareth*. London: Hodder and Stoughton, 1960.
_____. *Geschichte und Glaube I*. Munchen: Chr. Kaiser, 1968.
_____; Barth, G.; and Held, H.J. *Tradition and Interpretation in Matthew*. Translated by P. Scott. London: SCM, 1963.
Boucher, Madeleine. *The Mysterious Parable: A Literary Study*. Washington: Catholic Biblical Assoc., 1977.
Brown, Raymond E. *The Birth of the Messiah: A Commentary on the Infancy Narratives in Matthew and Luke*. Garden City: Doubleday, 1977.
_____; Donfried, Karl P.; and Reumann, John, edd. *Peter in the New Testament*. Minneapolis: Augsburg, 1973.
Bultmann, Rudolf. *Theology of the New Testament*. 2 vols. Translated by K. Grobel. London: SCM, 1952–55.
_____. *The History of the Synoptic Tradition*. Translated by J. Marsh. Oxford: Blackwells, 1963.
Burger, Christoph. *Jesus als Davidssohn: Eine traditionsgeschichtliche Untersuchung*. Göttingen: Vandenhoeck und Ruprecht, 1970.
Burton, E. de W. *Syntax of the Moods and Tenses in NT Greek*. Edinburgh: T. & T. Clark, 1894.
Carmignac, Jean. *Recherches sur le "Notre Père."* Paris: Letouzey et Aue, 1969.

Carson, D.A. *The Sermon on the Mount*. Grand Rapids: Baker, 1978.

———. *The Farewell Discourse and Final Prayer of Jesus*. Grand Rapids: Baker, 1980.

———. *Divine Sovereignty and Human Responsibility*. Atlanta: John Knox, 1981.

———, ed. *From Sabbath to Lord's Day*. Grand Rapids: Zondervan, 1982.

———, and Woodbridge, J.D., edd. *Scripture and Truth*. Grand Rapids: Zondervan, 1983.

Casey, Maurice. *Son of Man—The Interpretation and Influence of Daniel 7*. London: SPCK, 1980.

Catchpole, David R. *The Trial of Jesus: A Study in the Gospels and Jewish Historiography From 1770 to the Present Day*. Leiden: Brill, 1971.

Chilton, Bruce D. *God in Strength: Jesus' Announcement of the Kingdom.* Freistadt: F. Plöchl, 1977.

Cohn, Haim. *The Trial and Death of Jesus*. New York: Ktav, 1977.

Cope, O. Lamar. *Matthew: A Scribe Trained for the Kingdom of Heaven*. Washington: Catholic Biblical Assoc., 1976.

Cranfield, C.E.B. *The Gospel According to St. Mark*. Cambridge: University Press, 1972.

Cullmann, O. *The Christology of the New Testament*. Translated by Shirley C. Guthrie and Charles A. M. Hall. 2d ed. Philadelphia: Westminster, 1963.

Dahl, N.A. *Jesus in the Memory of the Early Church*. Minneapolis: Augsburg, 1976.

Dalman, A. *Jesus-Jeshua: Studies in the Gospels*. London: SPCK, 1929.

Daube, David. *The New Testament and Rabbinic Judaism*. London: Athlone, 1956.

Davies, W.D. *The Setting of the Sermon on the Mount*. Cambridge: University Press, 1963.

Derrett, J.D.M. *Law in the New Testament*. London: DLT, 1970.

———. *Studies in the New Testament*. 2 vols. Leiden: Brill, 1977–78.

Didier, M., ed. *L'Evangile selon Matthieu: Rédaction et Théologie*. Gembloux: Duculot, 1972.

Dodd, C.H. *The Parables of the Kingdom*. London: Nisbet, 1936.

Doeve, J.W. *Jewish Hermeneutics in the Synoptic Gospels and Acts*. Assen: Van Gorcum, 1954.

Douglas, J.D., ed. *Illustrated Bible Dictionary*. 3 vols. Revised edition. Edited by N. Hillyer. Wheaton: Tyndale, 1980.

Dunn, J.D.G. *Jesus and the Spirit: A Study of the Religious and Charismatic Experience of Jesus and the First Christians as Reflected in the New Testament*. London: SCM, 1975.

———. *Christology in the Making: An Inquiry into the Origins of the Doctrine of the Incarnation*. London: SCM, 1980.

Dupont, Jacques. *Mariage et divorce dans l'évangile, Matthieu 19, 3–12 et parallèles*. Bruges: Descleé de Brouwer, 1959.

Elliott, J.K., ed. *Studies in New Testament Language and Text*. SuppNovTest 44. Leiden: Brill, 1976.

Ellis, E. Earle, and Wilcox, Max, edd. *Neotestamentica et Semitica*. Edinburgh: T. & T. Clark, 1969.

———, and Grässer, E., edd. *Jesus und Paulus*. Göttingen: Vandenhoeck und Ruprecht, 1975.

Fischer, David. *Historians' Fallacies: Toward a Logic of Historical Thought*. New York: Harper and Row, 1970.

Fitzmyer, Joseph A. *Essays on the Semitic Background of the New Testament*. London: Goeffrey Chapman, 1971.

———. *A Wandering Aramaen: Collected Aramaic Essays*. Missoula: Scholars, 1978.

Flender, Helmut. *Die Botschaft Jesu von der Herr-schaft Gottes*. Munchen: Chr. Kaiser, 1968.

France, R.T. *Jesus and the Old Testament: His Application of Old Testament Passages to Himself and His Mission*. London: Tyndale, 1971.

———, and Wenham, D., edd. *Gospel Perspectives*. 2 vols. Sheffield: JSOT, 1980–81.

Frankemölle, Hubert. *Jahwebund und Kirche Christi: Studien zur Form- und Traditionsgeschichte des "Evangeliums" nach Mätthaus*. Münster: Aschendorff, 1974.

Garland, David E. *The Intention of Matthew 23*. Leiden: Brill, 1979.
Gaston, Lloyd. *No Stone on Another: Studies in the Significance of the Fall of Jerusalem in the Synoptic Gospels*. Leiden: Brill, 1970.
Gerhardsson, Birgir. *The Mighty Acts of Jesus According to Matthew*. Lund: C.W.K. Gleerup, 1979.
Gnilka, J., ed. *Neues Testament und Kirche*. Freiburg: Herder, 1974.
Goppelt, Leonhard. *Theologie des Neuen Testaments*. Edited by Jürgen Roloff. Göttingen: Vandenhoeck und Ruprecht, 1976.
Goulder, M.D. *Midrash and Lection in Matthew*. London: SPCK, 1974.
Gundry, Robert H. *The Use of the Old Testament in St. Matthew's Gospel, with Special Reference to the Messianic Hope*. Leiden: Brill, 1975.
Guthrie, Donald. *New Testament Theology*. Downers Grove, Ill.: IVP, 1981.
Hare, Douglas R.A. *The Theme of Jewish Persecution of Christians in the Gospel According to St. Matthew*. Cambridge: University Press, 1967.
Haubeck, W., and Bachmann, M., edd. *Wort in der Zeit*. Leiden: Brill, 1980.
Hawthorne, G.F., ed. *Current Issues in Biblical and Patristic Interpretation*. Grand Rapids: Eerdmans, 1975.
Hennecke, E. *New Testament Apocrypha*. 2 vols. London: Lutterworth, 1965.
Hengstenberg, E.W. *Christology of the Old Testament*. Reprint. 2 vols. Florida: McDonald, n.d.
Hill, David. *Greek Words With Hebrew Meanings*. Cambridge: University Press, 1967.
Hoehner, Harold W. *Herod Antipas*. Cambridge: University Press, 1972.
———. *Chronological Aspects of the Life of Christ*. Grand Rapids: Zondervan, 1977.
Hoekema, A.A. *The Bible and the Future*. Grand Rapids: Eerdmans, 1979.
Hoffmann, Paul et al., edd. *Orientierung an Jesus*. Freiburg: Herder, 1973.
Hooker, Morna D. *Jesus and the Servant*. London: SPCK, 1959.
———. *The Son of Man in Mark*. London: SPCK, 1967.
Hull, John M. *Hellenistic Magic and the Synoptic Tradition*. London: SCM, 1974.
Hummel, Reinhardt. *Die Auseinandersetzung zwischen Kirche und Judentum im Matthäusevangelium*. München: Chr. Kaiser, 1966.
Isaksson, A. *Marriage and Ministry in the New Testament*. Lund: C.W.K. Gleerup, 1965.
Jeremias, J. *Jesus' Promise to the Nations*. Translated by John Bowden. London: SCM, 1958.
———. *Jerusalem in the Time of Jesus*. Translated by F.H. and C.H. Cave. London: SCM, 1962.
———. *The Parables of Jesus*. Translated by S.H. Hooke. London: SCM, 1963.
———. *The Eucharistic Words of Jesus*. Translated by N. Perrin. 3d ed. London: SCM, 1966.
———. *The Prayers of Jesus*. Translated by John Bowden and Christoph Burchard. London: SCM, 1967.
———. *New Testament Theology*. Part I. *The Proclamation of Jesus*. Translated by John Bowden. London: SCM, 1971.
———, and Zimmerli, W. *The Servant of the Lord*. London: SCM, 1965.
Johnson, Marshall D. *The Purpose of the Biblical Geneologies*. Cambridge: University Press, 1969.
Kilpatrick, G.D. *The Origins of the Gospel According to St. Matthew*. Oxford: Clarendon, 1946.
Kingsbury, Jack Dean. *The Parables of Jesus in Matthew 13: A Study in Redaction-Criticism*. London: SPCK, 1969.
———. *Matthew: Structure, Christology, Kingdom*. Philadelphia: Fortress, 1975.
Kistemaker, Simon J. *The Parables of Jesus*. Grand Rapids: Baker, 1980.
Kümmel, W.G. *Jesus' Promise to the Nations*. Translated by S.H. Hooke. London: SCM, 1958.
———. *Introduction to the New Testament*. Translated by Howard Clark Kee. Nashville: Abingdon, 1975.

Ladd, G.E. *The Presence of the Future: The Eschatology of Biblical Realism*. Grand Rapids: Eerdmans, 1974.
_____. *A Theology of the New Testament*. Grand Rapids: Eerdmans, 1974.
Lane, William L. *The Gospel According to Mark*. Grand Rapids: Eerdmans, 1974.
Lindars, Barnabas. *New Testament Apologetic*. London: SCM, 1961.
Livingstone, E.A., ed. *Studia Biblica 1978*. 2 vols. Sheffield: JSOT, 1980.
Longenecker, Richard N. *The Christology of Early Jewish Christianity*. London: SCM, 1970.
_____. *Biblical Exegesis in the Apostolic Period*. Grand Rapids: Eerdmans, 1975.
_____, and Tenney, Merrill C., edd. *New Dimensions in New Testament Study*. Grand Rapids: Zondervan, 1974.
Machen, J. Gresham. *The Virgin Birth of Christ*. New York: Harper and Row, 1930.
Manson, T.W. *The Sayings of Jesus*. London: SCM, 1949.
Marshall, I. Howard. *The Gospel of Luke: A Commentary on the Greek Text*. Grand Rapids: Eerdmans, 1978.
_____. *Last Supper and Lord's Supper*. Exeter: Paternoster, 1980.
_____, ed. *New Testament Interpretation*. Exeter: Paternoster, 1977.
McConnell, Richard S. *Law and Prophecy in Matthew's Gospel*. Basel: Friedrich Reinhardt, 1969.
McHugh, John. *The Mother of Jesus in the New Testament*. Garden City: Doubleday, 1975.
McKay, J.R., and Miller, J.F., edd. *Biblical Studies*. London: Collins, 1976.
Meier, John P. *Law and History in Matthew's Gospel: A Redactional Study of Mt. 5:17–48*. Rome: BIP, 1976.
_____. *The Vision of Matthew: Christ, Church, and Morality in the First Gospel*. New York: Paulist, 1979.
Metzger, Bruce M. *A Textual Commentary on the Greek New Testament*. London: UBS, 1971.
_____. *New Testament Studies: Philological, Versional, and Patristic*. Leiden: Brill, 1980.
Meyer, Ben F. *The Aims of Jesus*. London: SCM, 1979.
Moore, G.F. *Judaism in the First Centuries of the Christian Era*. 3 vols. Cambridge: Harvard University Press, 1927–30.
Morris, Leon. *The Apostolic Preaching of the Cross*. Grand Rapids: Eerdmans, 1955.
_____. *The Gospel According to John*. Grand Rapids: Eerdmans, 1971.
Moule, C.F.D. *An Idiom Book of New Testament Greek*. 2d ed. London: Cambridge University Press, 1959.
_____. *The Birth of the New Testament*. London: A. and C. Black, 1962.
_____. *The Origin of Christology*. Cambridge: University Press, 1977.
Moulton, James Hope. *A Grammar of New Testament Greek*. vol. 1. *Prolegomena*. Edinburgh: T. & T. Clark, 1908.
_____. vol. 2. *Accidence and Word Formation*. Edited by W.F. Howard. Edinburgh: T. & T. Clark, 1920.
Nineham, D.E., ed. *Studies in the Gospels*. Oxford: Blackwell, 1955.
Nolan, Brian M. *The Royal Son of God: The Christology of Matthew 1–2 in the Setting of the Gospel*. Göttingen: Vandenhoeck und Ruprecht, 1979.
Parrot, Andre. *Golgotha and the Church of the Holy Sepulchre*. Translated by E. Hudson. London: SCM, 1957.
Piper, John. *Love Your Enemies*. Cambridge: University Press, 1979.
Przybylski, Benno. *Righteousness in Matthew and His World of Thought*. Cambridge: University Press, 1980.
Ridderbos, Herman. *The Coming of the Kingdom*. Translated by R. Zorn. Philadelphia: Presbyterian and Reformed, 1962.
Riesenfeld, H. *The Gospel Tradition*. Philadelphia: Fortress, 1970.
Robertson, A.T. *Word Pictures in the New Testament*. 6 vols. New York: Harper & Brothers, 1930.

Robinson, John A.T. *Twelve New Testament Studies*. London: SCM, 1962.

Rothfuchs, Wilhelm. *Die Erfüllungszitate des Matthäus-Evangeliums*. Stuttgart: W. Kohlhammer, 1969.

Sand, Alexander. *Das Gesetz und die Propheten: Untersuchungen zur Theologie des Evangeliums nach Matthäus*. Regensburg: Friedrich Pustet, 1976.

Schottroff, Luise et al. *Essays on the Love Commandment*. Philadelphia: Fortress, 1978.

Schweitzer, Albert. *The Quest of the Historical Jesus*. 2d ed. Translated by W. Montgomery. London: A. and C. Black, 1911.

Senior, Donald. *The Passion Narrative According to Matthew: A Redactional Study*. Leuven: Leuven University Press, 1975.

Sherwin-White, A.N. *Roman Society and Roman Law in the New Testament*. Oxford: Clarendon, 1963.

Soarés Prabhu, George M. *The Formula Quotations in the Infancy Narrative of Matthew*. Rome: BIP, 1976.

Stanton, Graham N. *Jesus of Nazareth in New Testament Preaching*. Cambridge: University Press, 1974.

Stendahl, Krister. *The School of St. Matthew and Its Use of the Old Testament*. 2d ed. Lund: C.W.K. Gleerup, n.d.

Stier, Rudolf. *The Words of the Lord Jesus*. Vol. 1. Translated by W.B. Pope. Edinburgh: T. & T. Clark, 1874.

Stonehouse, Ned B. *The Witness of Matthew and Mark to Christ*. Grand Rapids: Eerdmans, 1944.

————. *Origins of the Synoptic Gospels: Some Basic Questions*. Grand Rapids: Eerdmans, 1963.

Stott, John R.W. *Christian Counter-culture*. Downers Grove: IVP, 1978.

Strecker, Georg. *Der Weg der Gerechtigkeit*. Göttingen: Vandenhoeck und Ruprecht, 1962.

————, ed. *Jesus Christus in Historie und Theologie*. Tubingen: J.C.B. Mohr, 1975.

Suggs, M. Jack. *Wisdom, Christology, and Law in Matthew's Gospel*. Cambridge: Harvard University Press, 1970.

Taylor, Vincent. *The Gospel According to St. Mark*. 2d ed. London: Macmillan, 1966.

Thompson, William G. *Matthew's Advice to a Divided Community: Mt. 17, 22–18, 35*. Rome: BIP, 1970.

Thrall, Margaret E. *Greek Particles in the New Testament*. Leiden: Brill, 1962.

Trench, R.C. *Studies in the Gospels*. London: Macmillan, 1878.

Trilling, Wolfgang. *Das wahre Israel: Studien zur Theologie des Matthäus-Evangeliums*. München: Kösel, 1964.

Turner, Nigel. *Syntax*. Vol. 3 of J.H. Moulton. *A Grammar of New Testament Greek*. Edinburgh: T. & T. Clark, 1963.

————. *Grammatical Insights Into the New Testament*. Edinburgh: T. & T. Clark, 1965.

————. *Christian Words*. Edinburgh: T. & T. Clark, 1980.

Urbach, E.E. *The Sages: Their Concepts and Beliefs*. 2 vols. Translated by I. Abrahams. Jerusalem: Magnes, 1975.

van der Loos, H. *The Miracles of Jesus*. Leiden: Brill, 1965.

van Tilborg, Sjef. *The Jewish Leaders in Matthew*. Leiden: Brill, 1972.

Walker, Rolf. *Die Heilsgeschichte im ersten Evangelium*. Göttingen: Vandenhoeck und Ruprecht, 1967.

Warfield, Benjamin B. *Selected Shorter Writings*. 2 vols. Edited by John E. Meeter. Nutley, N.J.: Presbyterian and Reformed, 1970.

Westerholm, Stephen. *Jesus and Scribal Authority*. Lund: C.W.K. Gleerup, 1978.

Winter, Paul. *On the Trial of Jesus*. 2d ed. Berlin: de Gruyter, 1974.

Zerwick, M. *Biblical Greek*. Rome: Scripta Pontificii Instituti Biblici, 1963.

Zumstein, Jean. *La condition du croyant dans l'Evangile selon Matthieu*. Göttingen: Vandenhoeck und Ruprecht, 1977.

c. *Selected articles*

Berger, Klaus. "Die königlichen Messiastraditionen des Neuen Testaments." NTS 20 (1974): 1–44.

Blaising, Craig A. "Gethsemane: A Prayer of Faith." JETS 22 (1979): 333–43.

Brower, Kent. "Mark 9:1 Seeing the Kingdom in Power." *Journal for the Study of the New Testament* 6 (1980): 17–41.

Carson, D.A. "Historical Tradition in the Fourth Gospel—After Dodd, What?" France and Wenham, 2:83–145.

_____. "Jesus and the Sabbath in the Four Gospels." Id. *Sabbath*.

_____. "Jewish Leaders in Matthew's Gospel: A Reappraisal." JETS 25 (1982): 161–74.

_____. "Christological Ambiguities in the Gospel of Matthew." *Christ the Lord: Studies in Christology Presented to Donald Guthrie*. Edited by Harold Rowdon. Downers Grove, Ill.: IVP, 1982, pp. 97–114.

_____. "Redaction Criticism: On the Legitimacy and Illegitimacy of a Literary Tool." Carson and Woodbridge.

_____. "The ὅμοιος Word-Group as Introduction to Some Matthean Parables." NTS, in press.

Dodd, C.H. "New Testament Translation Problems I." *Bible Translator* 27 (1976): 301–11.

Dupont, J. "Le Point de vue de Matthieu dans le chapitre des paraboles." Didier, pp. 221–59.

Ellis, E.E. "New Directions in Form Criticism." Strecker, *Jesus Christus*, pp. 299–315.

Fee, G.D. "Modern Text Criticism and the Synoptic Problem." *J.J. Griesbach: Synoptic and Text-Critical Studies 1776–1976*. Edited by Bernard Orchard and Thomas R.W. Longstaff. Cambridge: University Press, 1978, pp. 154–69.

Fenton, J.C. "Matthew and the Divinity of Jesus: Three Questions Concerning Matthew 1:20–23." Livingston, 2:79–82.

France, R.T. "The Servant of the Lord in the Teaching of Jesus." *Tyndale Bulletin* 19 (1966): 26–52.

_____. "God and Mammon." EQ 51 (1979): 3–21.

_____. "Exegesis in Practice: Two Samples." Marshall, *New Testament Interpretation*, pp. 252–81.

_____. "The Formula Quotations of Matthew 2 and the Problem of Communications." NTS 27 (1980–81): 233–51.

_____. "Scripture, Tradition and History in the Infancy Narratives of Matthew." France and Wenham, 2:239–66.

Gooding, D.W. "Structure littéraire de Matthieu, XIII,53 à XVIII,35." RB 85 (1978): 227–52.

Hartman, L. "Scriptural Exegesis in the Gospel of St. Matthew and the Problem of Communication." Didier, pp. 131–52.

Heil, John Paul. "Significant Aspects of the Healing Miracles in Matthew." CBQ 41 (1979): 274–87.

Hill, David. "Son and Servant: An Essay on Matthean Christology." *Journal of Studies of the New Testament* 6 (1980): 2–16.

Huffmann, Norman A. "Atypical Features in the Parables of Jesus." JBL 97 (1978): 207–20.

Kaiser, W.C. "The Weightier and Lighter Matters of the Law." Hawthorne, pp. 176–92.

Lachs, S.T. "Some Textual Observations on the Sermon on the Mount." JQR 69 (1978): 98–111.

Liefeld, Walter L. "Theological Motifs in the Transfiguration Narrative." Longenecker and Tenney, pp. 162–79.

Neil, Willam. "Five Hard Sayings of Jesus." McKay and Miller, pp. 157–71.

O'Brien, P.T. "The Great Commission of Matthew 28:18–20." *Evangelical Review of Theology* 2 (1978): 254–67.

Ogawa, Akira. "Paraboles de l'Israel véritable? Réconsidération critique de Mt.xxi.28–xxii.14." NovTest 21 (1979): 121–49.

Pamment, Margaret. "The Kingdom of Heaven According to the First Gospel." NTS 27 (1980–81): 211–32.

Payne, Philip Barton. "The Authenticity of the Parable of the Sower and Its Interpretation." France and Wenham, 2:163–207.

Reicke, Bo. "Synoptic Prophecies on the Destruction of Jerusalem." *Studies in New Testament and Early Christian Literature*. Edited by D.E. Aune. Leiden: Brill, 1972, pp. 121–34.

Slingerland, H. Dixon. "The Transjordanian Origin of St. Matthew's Gospel." *Journal of the Study of the New Testament* 3 (1979): 18–28.

Stanton, Graham N. "The Origin and Purpose of Matthew's Gospel: Matthean Scholarship From 1945 to 1980." *Aufstieg und Niedergang der romischen Welt*. Berlin and New York: de Gruyter, 1982, 2:25/2.

Wenham, David. "The Synoptic Problem Revisited: Some New Suggestions About the Composition of Mark 4:1–34." *Tyndale Bulletin* 23 (1972): 3–38.

————. "The Resurrection Narratives in Matthew's Gospel." *Tyndale Bulletin* 24 (1973): 21–54.

————. "The Interpretation of the Parable of the Sower." NTS 20 (1974): 299–319.

————. "The 'Q' Tradition Behind Matthew X." NTS, in press.

d. Unpublished material

Blomberg, Craig. "The Tendencies of the Tradition in the Parables of the Gospel of Thomas." Master's thesis, Trinity Evangelical Divinity School, 1979.

————. "Tradition-History in the Parables Peculiar to Luke's Central Section." Ph.D. dissertation, University of Aberdeen, 1982.

Hulton, D. "The Resurrection of the Holy Ones (Matthew 27:51b–53). A Study of the Theology of the Matthean Passion Narrative." Ph.D. dissertation, Harvard University, 1970.

Martin, Brice L. "Matthew and Paul on Christ and the Law: Compatible or Incompatible Theologies?" Ph.D. dissertation, McMaster University, 1976.

Moo, Douglas J. "The Use of the Old Testament in the Passion Texts of the Gospels." Ph.D. dissertation, University of St. Andrews, 1979.

————. "Jesus Christ's Ethical Use of the Old Testament." Forthcoming in JSNT.

Sigal, Phillip. "The Halakah of Jesus of Nazareth according to the Gospel of Matthew." Ph.D. dissertation, University of Pittsburgh, 1979.

Trotter, Andrew H. "Understanding and Stumbling: A Study of the Disciples' Understanding of Jesus and His Teaching in the Gospel of Matthew." Ph.D. dissertation, Cambridge University, n.d.

14. Structure and Outline

Matthew was a skilled literary craftsman and gave his Gospel structure, form, and rhythm. Two of his larger chiasms are indicated in the outline below. But the structure of the Gospel as a whole is still disputed. With minor variations there are three main views.

First, some (e.g., McNeile) have detected a geographical framework. Matthew 1:1–2:23 is the prologue; 3:1–4:11 is Jesus' preparation for ministry; 4:12–13:58 finds Jesus in Galilee; 14:1–20:34 pictures him around Galilee and heading toward Jerusalem; and 21:1–28:20 finds him at Jerusalem. The divisions are neither precise nor helpful, for the result tells us nothing of Matthew's purposes.

Second, Kingsbury (*Structure*), taking a hint from Lohmeyer (*Matthäus*) and Stonehouse (*Witness of Matthew*, pp. 129–31), argues for three sections. The first he entitles "The Person of Jesus Messiah" (1:1–4:16), the second "The Proclamation of Jesus Messiah" (4:17–16:20), and the third "The Suffering, Death, and Resurrection of Jesus Messiah" (16:21–28:20). Immediately after the two breaks comes the phrase *apo tote* ("from that time on"). Kingsbury further notes that the last two sections each contain three "summary" passages, 4:23–25; 9:35; 11:1 and 16:21; 17:22–23; 20:17–19 respectively;[85] and he suggests that this outline does justice to the centrality of Matthew's christology.

Though this outline has gained adherents, it has serious weaknesses. It is not at all clear that *apo tote* is so redactionally important for Matthew: he also uses it in 26:18 without any suggestion of a break in his outline. One could argue that there are four passion summaries in the third section, not three (add 26:2). Kingsbury's outline not only breaks up the prime Peter passage in an unacceptable way (cf. comments at 16:13–16), but at both transitions Matthew may have been more influenced by the order of Mark than by "structural" considerations. The most important weakness, however, is the artificiality of the topical headings. The person of Jesus (section one) is still a focal point in sections two and three (e.g., 16:13–16; 22:41–46). Why the proclamation of Jesus should be restricted to section two when two of the discourses (chs. 18; 24–25) and several important exchanges (chs. 21–23) await the third section is not clear. The last heading, "The Suffering, Death, and Resurrection of Jesus Messiah," though it accurately summarizes the increasingly dominant theme of 16:21–28:20, seems an inadequate designation of much in those chapters (e.g., most of 18; 21–25).

The third scheme makes the book center on the five main discourses (see outline below). Each begins by placing Jesus in a specific context and ends with a formula found nowhere else in the Gospel (see comment at 7:28–29) and transitional pericope with links pointing forward and backward. Bacon[86] believed the five discourses correspond to the five books of the Pentateuch; but there is little in favor of this refinement (cf. Gundry, *Matthew*), since Moses typology is very weak in this Gospel and the links between the five discourses and the five books of Moses minimal.

Two frequently raised difficulties must be overcome.

1. Why restrict oneself to *five* discourses when chapter 11 could fall into that

---

[85]A slight modification of this scheme has been introduced by Tommy B. Slater, "Notes on Matthew's Structure," JBL 99(1980): 436.

[86]B.W. Bacon, "The 'Five Books' of Moses Against the Jews," Exp 15 (1918): 56–66. The idea is then worked out in detail in his *Studies in Matthew*.

category? This objection misses the mark. The fivefold sequence narrative-discourse does not assume that Jesus is not portrayed as speaking in the narrative sections. He may do so, even extensively (see also on ch. 21). The point is that the five discourses are sufficiently well-defined that it is hard to believe Matthew did not plan them as such.

2. Does this not relegate the birth narrative (chs. 1–2) and the Passion and Resurrection (chs. 26–28) to a sort of secondary status outside the central outline? There is little difficulty in seeing chapters 1–2 as a prologue anticipating the opening of the Gospel, a formal opening common to all the canonical Gospels (see comment at 1:1). But certainly Matthew 26–28 must not be dismissed as an epilogue; it is too much the point toward which the Gospel moves for that. On the other hand, Matthew 26–28 does not constitute an ordinary "conclusion"; for the final verses are purposely open-ended and anticipatory. It seems best to take 26:5–28:20 as constituting an exceptional sixth narrative section with the corresponding teaching section being laid on the shoulders of the disciples (28:18–20).

But no outline should be taken too seriously. The Gospels use vignettes—organized ones, doubtless, but vignettes nonetheless. The following outline organizes Matthew's Gospel and reflects some demonstrable structure. That structure is, however, a guide to its contents, not a comprehensive explanation.

I. Prologue: The Origin and Birth of Jesus the Christ (1:1–2:23)
   A. The Genealogy of Jesus (1:1–17)
   B. The Birth of Jesus (1:18–25)
   C. The Visit of the Magi (2:1–12)
   D. The Escape to Egypt (2:13–15)
   E. The Massacre of Bethlehem's Boys (2:16–18)
   F. The Return to Nazareth (2:19–23)

II. The Gospel of the Kingdom (3:1–7:29)
   A. Narrative (3:1–4:25)
     1. Foundational steps (3:1–4:11)
       a. The ministry of John the Baptist (3:1–12)
       b. The baptism of Jesus (3:13–17)
       c. The temptation of Jesus (4:1–11)
     2. Jesus' early Galilean ministry (4:12–25)
       a. The beginning (4:12–17)
       b. Calling the first disciples (4:18–22)
       c. Spreading the news of the kingdom (4:23–25)
   B. First Discourse: The Sermon on the Mount (5:1–7:29)
     1. Setting (5:1–2)
     2. The kingdom of heaven: its norms and witness (5:3–16)
       a. The norms of the kingdom (5:3–12)
         1) The Beatitudes (5:3–10)
         2) Expansion (5:11–12)
       b. The witness of the kingdom (5:13–16)
         1) Salt (5:13)
         2) Light (5:14–16)
     3. The kingdom of heaven: its demands in relation to the OT (5:17–48)
       a. Jesus and the kingdom as fulfillment of the OT (5:17–20)

2. The condemned and the accepted (11:20–30)
   a. The condemned: woes on unrepentant cities (11:20–24)
   b. The accepted (11:25–30)
      1) Because of the revelation of the Father (11:25–26)
      2) Because of the agency of the Son (11:27)
      3) Because of the Son's gentle invitation (11:28–30)
3. Sabbath conflicts (12:1–14)
   a. Picking heads of grain (12:1–8)
   b. Healing a man with a shriveled hand (12:9–14)
4. Jesus' as the prophesied Servant (12:15–21)
5. Confrontation with the Pharisees (12:22–37)
   a. The setting and accusation (12:22–24)
   b. Jesus' reply (12:25–37)
      1) The divided kingdom (12:25–28)
      2) The strong man's house (12:29)
      3) Blasphemy against the Spirit (12:30–32)
      4) Nature and fruit (12:33–37)
   c. Continued confrontation (12:38–42)
      1) Request for a sign (12:38)
      2) The sign of Jonah (12:39–42)
   d. The return of the evil spirit (12:43–45)
6. Doing the Father's will (12:46–50)
B. Third Discourse: The Parables of the Kingdom (13:1–53)
1. The setting (13:1–3a)
2. To the crowds (13:3b–33)
   a. The parable of the soils (13:3b–9)
   b. Interlude (13:10–23)
      1) On understanding parables (13:10–17)
      2) Interpretation of the parable of the soils (13:18–23)
   c. The parable of the weeds (13:24–30)
   d. The parable of the mustard seed (13:31–32)
   e. The parable of the yeast (13:33)
3. Pause (13:34–43)
   a. Parables as fulfillment of prophecy (13:34–35)
   b. Interpretation of the parable of the weeds (13:36–43)
4. To the disciples (13:44–52)
   a. The parable of the hidden treasure (13:44)
   b. The parable of the expensive pearl (13:45–46)
   c. The parable of the net (13:47–48)
   d. Interlude (13:49–51)
      1) Interpretation of the parable of the net (13:49–50)
      2) On understanding parables (13:51)
   e. The parable of the teacher of the law (13:52)
5. Transitional conclusion: movement toward further opposition (13:53)

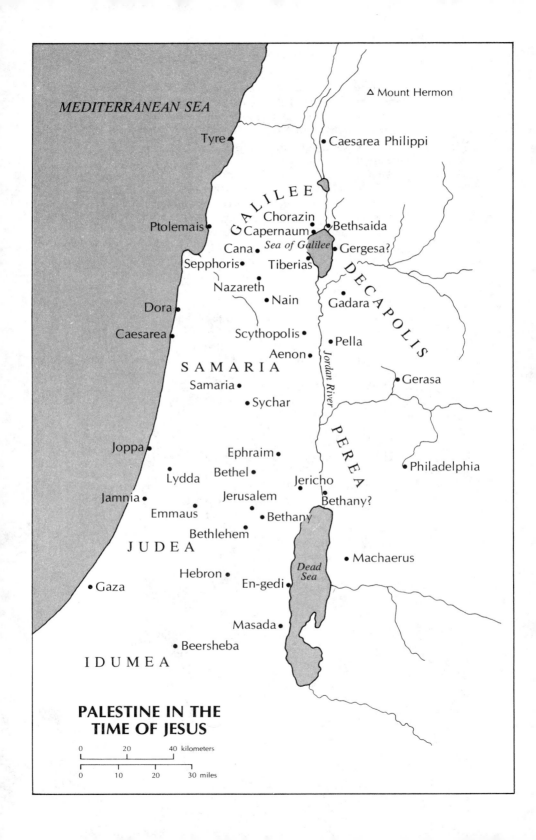

MEDITERRANEAN SEA

△ Mount Hermon

Tyre ●

● Caesarea Philippi

G A L I L E E

Chorazin
Ptolemais ●   Capernaum ● ● Bethsaida

Cana ●   Sea of Galilee   ● Gergesa?

Sepphoris ●   Tiberias ●

Nazareth ●

● Nain   Gadara ●

D E C A P O L I S

Dora ●   Scythopolis ●   ● Pella

Caesarea ●

Aenon ●

S A M A R I A

Samaria ●   ● Gerasa

● Sychar

P E R E A

Joppa ●   Ephraim ●

Lydda ●   Bethel ●   ● Philadelphia

Jamnia ●   Jericho ●

Jerusalem ●   Bethany? ●

Emmaus ●   ● Bethany

Bethlehem ●

J U D E A   ● Machaerus

Hebron ●   Dead Sea

● Gaza   En-gedi ●

Masada ●

I D U M E A

● Beersheba

**PALESTINE IN THE
TIME OF JESUS**

0   20   40 kilometers

0   10   20   30 miles

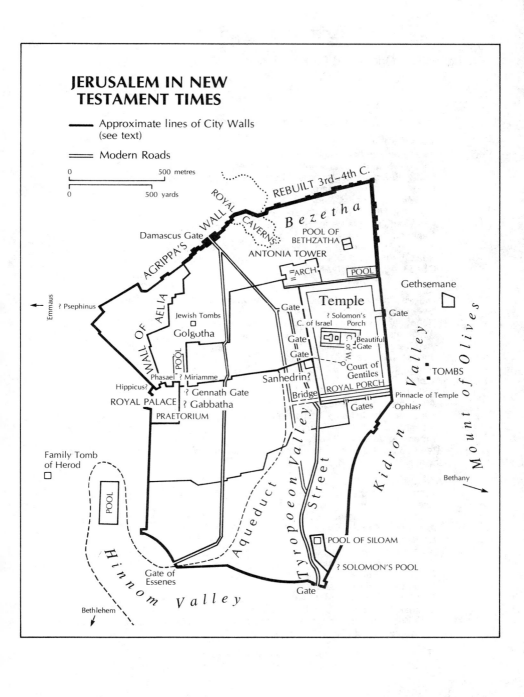

JERUSALEM IN NEW TESTAMENT TIMES

━━━ Approximate lines of City Walls (see text)

═══ Modern Roads

| 0 | | 500 metres |
| 0 | | 500 yards |

Emmaus →

REBUILT 3rd–4th C.

ROYAL CAVERNS

WALL

AGRIPPA'S WALL

Damascus Gate

B e z e t h a

POOL OF BETHZATHA

ANTONIA TOWER

? Psephinus

WALL OF AELIA

ARCH

POOL

Gethsemane

Jewish Tombs

Golgotha

POOL

Phasael ? Miriamme

Hippicus?

ROYAL PALACE

? Gennath Gate

? Gabbatha

PRAETORIUM

Gate

Temple

? Solomon's Porch

C. of Israel

Beautiful Gate

C. of W.

Court of Gentiles

ROYAL PORCH

Gate

Gate

Gate

Sanhedrin?

Bridge

Gates

Gate

K i d r o n   V a l l e y

TOMBS

Pinnacle of Temple

Ophlas?

M o u n t   o f   O l i v e s

Bethany →

Family Tomb of Herod

POOL

A q u e d u c t

T y r o p o e o n   V a l l e y

Street

POOL OF SILOAM

? SOLOMON'S POOL

H i n n o m

Gate of Essenes

V a l l e y

Gate

Bethlehem ↓

Text and Exposition

I. Prologue: The Origin and Birth of Jesus the Christ (1:1–2:23)

A. *The Genealogy of Jesus*

1:1–17

A record of the genealogy of Jesus Christ the son of David, the son of Abraham:

[2]Abraham was the father of Isaac,
Isaac the father of Jacob,
Jacob the father of Judah and his brothers,
[3]Judah the father of Perez and Zerah, whose mother was Tamar,
Perez the father of Hezron,
Hezron the father of Ram,
[4]Ram the father of Amminadab,
Amminadab the father of Nahshon,
Nahshon the father of Salmon,
[5]Salmon the father of Boaz, whose mother was Rahab,
Boaz the father of Obed, whose mother was Ruth,
Obed the father of Jesse,
[6]and Jesse the father of King David.

David was the father of Solomon, whose mother had been Uriah's wife,
[7]Solomon the father of Rehoboam,
Rehoboam the father of Abijah,
Abijah the father of Asa,
[8]Asa the father of Jehoshaphat,
Jehoshaphat the father of Jehoram,
Jehoram the father of Uzziah,
[9]Uzziah the father of Jotham,
Jotham the father of Ahaz,
Ahaz the father of Hezekiah,
[10]Hezekiah the father of Manasseh,
Manasseh the father of Amon,
Amon the father of Josiah,
[11]and Josiah the father of Jeconiah and his brothers at the time of the exile to Babylon.

[12]After the exile to Babylon:
Jeconiah was the father of Shealtiel,
Shealtiel the father of Zerubbabel,
[13]Zerubbabel the father of Abiud,
Abiud the father of Eliakim,
Eliakim the father of Azor,
[14]Azor the father of Zadok,
Zadok the father of Akim,
Akim the father of Eliud,
[15]Eliud the father of Eleazar,
Eleazar the father of Matthan,
Matthan the father of Jacob,
[16]and Jacob the father of Joseph, the husband of Mary, of whom was born Jesus, who is called Christ.

[17]Thus there were fourteen generations in all from Abraham to David, fourteen from David to the exile to Babylon, and fourteen from the exile to the Christ.

In each Gospel Jesus' earthly ministry is preceded by an account of John the Baptist's ministry. This formal similarity does not extend to the introductions to the

Gospels. Mark (1:1) opens with a simple statement. Luke begins with a first-person preface in which he explains his purpose and methods, followed by a detailed and often poetic account of the miraculous births of John and Jesus (1:5–2:20) and brief mention of Jesus' boyhood trip to the temple (2:21–52). Luke reserves Jesus' genealogy for chapter 3. John's prologue (1:1–18) traces Jesus' beginnings to eternity and presents the Incarnation without referring to his conception and birth. In each Gospel the introduction anticipates major themes and emphases. In Matthew the prologue (1:1–2:23) introduces such themes as the son of David, the fulfillment of prophecy, the supernatural origin of Jesus the Messiah, and the Father's sovereign protection of his Son in order to bring him to Nazareth and accomplish the divine plan of salvation from sin (cf. esp. Stonehouse, *Witness of Matthew*, pp. 123–28).

1 The first two words of Matthew, *biblos geneseōs*, may be translated "record of the genealogy" (NIV), "record of the origins," or "record of the history." NIV limits this title to the genealogy (1:1–17), the second could serve as a heading for the prologue (1:1–2:23), and the third as a heading for the entire Gospel. The expression is found only twice in the LXX: in Genesis 2:4 it refers to the creation account (Gen 2:4–25) and in Genesis 5:1 to the ensuing genealogy. From the latter it appears possible to follow NIV (so also Hendriksen; Lohmeyer, *Matthäus*; McNeile); but because the noun *genesis* (NIV, "birth") reappears in 1:18 (one of only four NT occurrences), it seems likely that the heading in 1:1 extends beyond the genealogy. No occurrence of the expression as a heading for a book-length document has come to light. Therefore we must discount the increasingly popular view (Davies, *Setting*; Gaechter, *Matthäus*; Hill, *Matthew*; Maier; Zahn) that Matthew means to refer to his entire Gospel, "A record of the history of Jesus Christ." Matthew rather intends his first two chapters to be a coherent and unified "record of the origins of Jesus Christ."

The designation "Jesus Christ the son of David, the son of Abraham" resonates with biblical nuances. (For comments regarding "Jesus," see on 1:21.) "Christ" is roughly the Greek equivalent to "Messiah" or "Anointed." In the OT the term could refer to a variety of people "anointed" for some special function: priests (Lev 4:3; 6:22), kings (1 Sam 16:13; 24:10; 2 Sam 19:21; Lam 4:20), and, metaphorically, the patriarchs (Ps 105:15) and the pagan king Cyrus (Isa 45:1). Already in Hannah's prayer "Messiah" parallels "king": the Lord "will give strength to his king and exalt the horn of his anointed" (1 Sam 2:10). With the rising number of OT prophecies concerning King David's line (e.g., 2 Sam 7:12–16; cf. Ps 2:2; 105:15), "Messiah," or "Christ," became the designation of a figure representing the people of God and bringing in the promised eschatological reign.

In Jesus' day Palestine was rife with messianic expectation. Not all of it was coherent, and many Jews expected two different "Messiahs." But Matthew's linking of "Christ" and "son of David" leaves no doubt of what he is claiming for Jesus.

In the Gospels "Christ" is relatively rare (as compared with Paul's epistles). More important it almost always appears as a title, strictly equivalent to "the Messiah" (see esp. 16:16). But it was natural for Christians after the Resurrection to use "Christ" as a name not less than as a title; increasingly they spoke of "Jesus Christ" or "Christ Jesus" or simply "Christ." Paul normally treats "Christ," at least in part, as a name; but it is doubtful whether the titular force ever entirely disappears (cf. N.T. Wright, "The Messiah and the People of God: A Study in Pauline Theology with Particular Reference to the Argument of the Epistle to the Romans" [Ph.D.

diss., Oxford University, 1980], p. 19). Of Matthew's approximately eighteen occurrences, all are exclusively titular except this one (1:1), probably 1:16, certainly 1:18, and possibly the variant at 16:21. The three uses of "Christ" in the prologue reflect the confessional stance from which Matthew writes; he is a committed Christian who has long since become familiar with the common way of using the word as both title and name. At the same time it is a mark of Matthew's concern for historical accuracy that Jesus is not so designated by his contemporaries.

"Son of David" is an important designation in Matthew. Not only does David become a turning point in the genealogy (1:6, 17), but the title recurs throughout the Gospel (9:27; 12:23; 15:22; 20:30–31; 21:9, 15; 22:42, 45). God swore covenant love to David (Ps 89:29) and promised that one of his immediate descendants would establish the kingdom—even more, that David's kingdom and throne would endure forever (2 Sam 7:12–16). Isaiah foresaw that a "son" would be given, a son with the most extravagant titles: Wonderful Counselor, Mighty God, Everlasting Father, Prince of Peace: "Of the increase of his government and peace there will be no end. He will reign *on David's throne* and over his kingdom, establishing and upholding it with justice and righteousness from that time on and forever. The zeal of the LORD Almighty will accomplish this" (Isa 9:6–7).

In Jesus' day at least some branches of popular Judaism understood "son of David" to be messianic (cf. Pss Sol 17:21; for a summary of the complex intertestamental evidence, cf. Berger, "Die königlichen Messiastraditionen," esp. pp. 3–9). The theme was important in early Christianity (cf. Luke 1:32, 69; John 7:42; Acts 13:23; Rom 1:3; Rev 22:16). God's promises, though long delayed, had not been forgotten; Jesus and his ministry were perceived as God's fulfillment of covenantal promises now centuries old. The tree of David, hacked off so that only a stump remained, was sprouting a new branch (Isa 11:1).

Jesus is also "son of Abraham." It could not be otherwise, granted that he is son of David. Yet Abraham is mentioned for several important reasons. "Son of Abraham" may have been a recognized messianic title in some branches of Judaism (cf. T Levi 8:15). The covenant with the Jewish people had first been made with Abraham (Gen 12:1–3; 17:7; 22:18), a connection Paul sees as basic to Christianity (Gal 3:16). More important, Genesis 22:18 had promised that through Abraham's offspring "all nations" (*panta ta ethnē*, LXX) would be blessed; so with this allusion to Abraham, Matthew is preparing his readers for the final words of this offspring from Abraham—the commission to make disciples of "all nations" (28:19, *panta ta ethnē*). Jesus the Messiah came in fulfillment of the kingdom promises to David and of the Gentile-blessings promises to Abraham (cf. also Matt 3:9; 8:11).

2–17 Study has shown that genealogies in the Ancient Near East could serve widely diverse functions: economic, tribal, political, domestic (to show family or geographical relationships), and others (see Johnson; also Robert R. Wilson, *Genealogy and History in the Biblical World* [New Haven: Yale University Press, 1977]; R.E. Brown, *Birth of Messiah*, pp. 64–66). The danger in such study is that Matthew's intentions may be overridden by colorful backgrounds of doubtful relevance to the text itself. Johnson sees Matthew's genealogy as a response to Jewish slander. H.V. Wickings ("The Nativity Stories and Docetism," NTS 23 [1977]: 457–60) sees it as an answer to late first-century Docetism that denied the essential humanity of Jesus. One wonders whether a virgin birth would have been the best way to go about correcting the Docetists.

D. E. Nineham ("The Genealogy in St. Matthew's Gospel and Its Significance for the Study of the Gospels," BJRL 58 [1976]: 421–44) finds in this genealogy the assurance that God is in sovereign control. Yet it is unclear how he reconciles this assurance with his conviction that the genealogy is of little historical worth. If Matthew made much of it up, then we may admire his faith that God was in control. But since Matthew's basis was (according to Nineham) faulty, it gives the reader little incentive to share the same faith.

Actually, Matthew's chief aims in including the genealogy are hinted at in the first verse—viz., to show that Jesus Messiah is truly in the kingly line of David, heir to the messianic promises, the one who brings divine blessings to all nations. Therefore the genealogy focuses on King David (1:6) on the one hand, yet on the other hand includes Gentile women (see below). Many entries would touch the hearts and stir the memories of biblically literate readers, though the principal thrust of the genealogy ties together promise and fulfillment. "Christ and the new covenant are securely linked to the age of the old covenant. Marcion, who wished to sever all the links binding Christianity to the Old Testament, knew what he was about when he cut the genealogy out of his edition of Luke" (F.F. Bruce, NBD, p. 459).

For many, whatever its aims, the historical value of Matthew's genealogy is nil. R.E. Brown (*Birth of Messiah*, pp. 505–12) bucks the tide when he cautiously affirms that Jesus sprang from the house of David. Many ancient genealogies are discounted as being of little historical value because they evidently intend to impart more than historical information (cf. esp. Wilson, *Genealogy and History*). To do this, however, is to fall into a false historical disjunction; for many genealogies intend to make more than historical points by referring to historical lines.

Part of the historical evaluation of Matthew 1:2–17 rests on the reliability of Matthew's sources: the names in the first two-thirds of the genealogy are taken from the LXX (1 Chron 1–3, esp. 2:1–15; 3:5–24; Ruth 4:12–22). After Zerubbabel, Matthew relies on extrabiblical sources of which we know nothing. But there is good evidence that records were kept at least till the end of the first century. Josephus (Life 6 [1]) refers to the "public registers" from which he extracts his genealogical information (cf. also Jos. *Contra Apion* I, 28–56 [6–10]). According to Genesis R 98:8, Rabbi Hillel was proved to be a descendant of David because a genealogical scroll was found in Jerusalem. Eusebius (*Ecclesiastical History* 3.19–20) cites Hegesippus to the effect that Emperor Domitian (A.D. 81–96) ordered all descendants of David slain. Nevertheless two of them when summoned, though admitting their Davidic descent, showed their calloused hands to prove they were but poor farmers. So they were let go. But the account shows that genealogical information was still available.

While no twentieth-century Jew could prove he was from the tribe of Judah, let alone from the house of David, that does not appear to have been a problem in the first century, when lineage was important in gaining access to temple worship. Whether Matthew had access to the records himself or gleaned his information from intermediate sources, we cannot know from this distance; but in any case we "have no good reason to doubt that this genealogy was transmitted in good faith" (Albright and Mann).

More difficult is the question of the relation of Matthew's genealogy to Luke's, in particular the part from David on (cf. Luke 3:23–31). There are basic differences between the two: Matthew begins with Abraham and moves forward; Luke begins with Jesus and moves backward to Adam. Matthew traces the line through Jeconiah, Shealtiel, and Zerubbabel; Luke through Neri, Shealtiel, and Zerubbabel. More important, Luke (3:31) traces the line through David's son Nathan (cf. 2 Sam 5:14), and Matthew through the kingly line of Solomon. It is often said that no reconciliation between the two genealogies is possible (e.g., E.L. Abel, "The Genealogies of Jesus Ο ΧΡΙΣΡΟΣ," NTS 20 [1974]: 203–10). Nevertheless two theories are worth weighing.

1. Some have argued that Luke gives Mary's genealogy but substitutes Joseph's name (Luke 3:23) to avoid mentioning a woman. And there is some evidence to support the notion that Mary herself was a descendant of David (cf. Luke 1:32). That Mary was related to Elizabeth, who was married to the Levite Zechariah (Luke 1:5–36), is no problem, since intermarriage between tribes was not uncommon. Indeed, Aaron's wife may well have sprung from Judah (cf. Exod 6:23; Num 2:3) (so Beng., CHS, Luther). H.A.W. Meyer rearranges the punctuation in Luke 3:23 to read "being the son (of Joseph as was supposed) of Heli [i.e., Mary's father], of Matthat." But this is painfully artificial and could not easily be deduced by a reader with a text without punctuation marks or brackets, which is how our NT Greek MSS were first written. Few would guess simply by reading Luke that he is giving Mary's genealogy. The theory stems, not from the text of Luke, but from the need to harmonize the two genealogies. On the face of it, both Matthew and Luke aim to give Joseph's genealogy.

2. Others have argued, more plausibly, that Luke provides Joseph's real genealogy and Matthew the throne succession—a succession that finally jumps to Joseph's line by default. Hill (*Matthew*) offers independent Jewish evidence for a possible double line (Targ. Zech 12:12). This hypothesis has various forms. The oldest goes back to Julius Africanus (c. A.D. 225; cf. Eusebius *Ecclesiastical History* 1.7), who argued that Matthew provides the natural genealogy and Luke the royal—the reverse of the modern theory (so Alf, Farrer, Hill, Taylor, Westcott, Zahn). In its modern form the theory seems reasonable enough: where the purpose is to provide Joseph's actual descent back to David, this could best be done by tracing the family tradition through his real father Heli, to his father Matthat, and thus back to Nathan and David (so Luke); and where the purpose is to provide the throne succession, it is natural to begin with David and work down.

As most frequently presented, this theory has a serious problem (cf. R.E. Brown, *Birth of Messiah*, pp. 503–4). It is normally argued that Joseph's father in Matthew 1:16, Jacob, was a full brother of Joseph's father mentioned in Luke 3:23, Heli; that Jacob, the royal heir, died without offspring; and that Heli married Jacob's widow according to the laws of levirate marriage (Deut 25:5–10). (Though levirate marriages may not have been common in the first century, it is unlikely that they were completely unknown. Otherwise the question of the Sadducees [22:24–28] was phrased in irrelevant terms.) But if Jacob and Heli are to be reckoned as full brothers, then Matthan (Matt) and Matthat (Luke) must be the same man—even though their fathers, Eleazar (Matt) and Levi (Luke) respectively, are different. It seems artificial to appeal to a second levirate marriage. Some have therefore argued that Jacob and Heli were only half-brothers, which entails a further coincidence—viz., that their mother married two men, Matthan and Matthat, with remarkably similar names. We do not know whether levirate marriage was practiced in the case of half-brothers. Moreover since the whole purpose of levirate marriage was to raise up a child in the deceased father's name, why does Luke provide the name of the actual father?

R.E. Brown judges the problems insurmountable but fails to consider the elegant solution suggested by Machen (pp. 207–9) fifty years ago. If we assume that Matthat and Matthan are *not* the same person, there is no need to appeal to levirate marriage. The difficulty regarding the father of Matthat and the father of Matthan disappears; yet their respective sons Levi and Jacob may have been so closely related (e.g., if Levi was an heirless only son whose sister married Jacob or Joseph) that if Levi died, Jacob's son Joseph became his heir. Alternatively, if Matthan and Matthat *are* the same person (presupposing a levirate marriage one generation earlier), we "need only to suppose that Jacob [Joseph's father according to Matthew] died without issue, so that his nephew, the son of his brother Heli [Joseph's father according to Luke] would become his heir" (p. 208).

Other differences between Matthew and Luke are more amenable to obvious solutions. As for the omissions from Matthew's genealogy and the structure of three series of fourteen, see on 1:17.

2 Of the twelve sons of Jacob, Judah is singled out, as his tribe bears the scepter (Gen 49:10; cf. Heb 7:14). The words "and his brothers" are not "an addition which indicates that of the several possible ancestors of the royal line Judah alone was chosen" (Hill, *Matthew*), since that restriction was already achieved by stipulating Judah; and in no other entry (except 1:11; see comment) are the words "and his brothers" added. The point is that, though he comes from the royal line of Judah and David, Messiah emerges within the matrix of the covenant people (cf. the reference to Judah's brothers). Neither the half-siblings of Isaac nor the descendants of Jacob's brother, Esau, qualify as the covenant people in the OT. This allusive mention of the Twelve Tribes as the locus of the people of God becomes important later (cf. 8:11 with 19:28). Even the fact that there were twelve apostles is relevant.

3–5 Probably Perez and Zerah (v.3) are both mentioned because they are twins (Gen 38:27; cf. 1 Chron 2:4); Judah's other sons receive no mention. Ruth 4:12, 18–22 traces the messianic line from Perez to David. There is some evidence that "son of Perez" was a rabbinic designation of Messiah (SBK, 1:18), but the dating of the sources is uncertain.

Tamar, wife of Judah's son Er, is the first of four women mentioned in the genealogy (for comment, see on 1:6). Little is known of Hezron (Gen 46:12; 1 Chron 2:5), Ram (1 Chron 2:9), Amminadab (v.4; Exod 6:23; Num 1:7; 1 Chron 2:10), Nahshon (Num 2:3; 7:12; "the leader of the people of Judah," 1 Chron 2:10), and Salmon (v.5; Ruth 4:18–21; 1 Chron 2:11). Amminadab is associated with the desert wanderings in the time of Moses (Num 1:7). Therefore approximately four hundred years (Gen 15:13; Exod 12:40) are covered by the four generations from Perez to Amminadab. Doubtless several names have been omitted: the Greek verb translated "was the father of" (*gennaō*) does not require immediate relationship but often means something like "was the ancestor of" or "became the progenitor of."

Similarly, the line between Amminadab and David is short: more names may have been omitted. Whether such names properly fit before Boaz, so that Rahab was not the immediate mother of Boaz (just as Eve was not immediately "the mother of all the living," Gen 3:20), or after Boaz, or both, one cannot be sure. It is almost certain, however, that the Rahab mentioned is the prostitute of Joshua 2 and 5 (see further on 1:6). Boaz (1 Chron 2:11–12), who figures so prominently in the Book of Ruth, married the Moabitess (see on 1:6) and sired Obed, who became the father of Jesse (Ruth 4:22; 1 Chron 2:12).

6 The word "King" with "David" would evoke profound nostalgia and arouse eschatological hope in first-century Jews. Matthew thus makes the royal theme explicit: King Messiah has appeared. David's royal authority, lost at the Exile, has now been regained and surpassed by "great David's greater son" (so James Montgomery's hymn "Hail to the Lord's Anointed"; cf Box; Hill, *Matthew*; also cf. 2 Sam 7:12–16; Ps 89:19–29, 35–37; 132:11). David became the father of Solomon; but Solomon's mother "had been Uriah's wife" (cf. 2 Sam 11:27; 12:4). Bathsheba thus becomes the fourth woman to be mentioned in this genealogy.

Inclusion of these four women in the Messiah's genealogy instead of an all-male listing (which was customary)—or at least the names of such great matriarchs as Sarah, Rebekah, and Leah—shows that Matthew is conveying more than merely genealogical data. Tamar enticed her father-in-law into an incestuous relationship (Gen 38). The prostitute Rahab saved the spies and joined the Israelites (Josh 2, 5); Hebrews 11:31 and James 2:25 encourage us to think she abandoned her former way of life. She is certainly prominent in Jewish tradition, some of it fantastic (cf. A.T. Hanson, "Rahab the Harlot in Early Christian Tradition," *Journal for the Study of the New Testament* 1 [1978]: 53–60). Ruth, Tamar, and Rahab were aliens. Bathsheba was taken into an adulterous union with David, who committed murder to cover it up. Matthew's peculiar way of referring to her, "Uriah's wife," may be an attempt to focus on the fact that Uriah was not an Israelite but a Hittite (2 Sam 11:3; 23:39). Bathsheba herself was apparently the daughter of an Israelite (1 Chron 3:5 [variant reading]); but her marriage to Uriah probably led to her being regarded as a Hittite.

Several reasons have been suggested to explain the inclusion of these women. Some have pointed out that three were Gentiles and the fourth probably regarded as such (Lohmeyer, *Matthäus;* Maier; Schweizer, *Matthew*). This goes well with the reference to Abraham (cf. on 1:1); the Jewish Messiah extends his blessings beyond Israel, even as Gentiles are included in his line. Others have noted that three of the four were involved in gross sexual sin; but it is highly doubtful that this charge can be legitimately applied to Ruth. As a Moabitess, however, she had her origins in incest (Gen 19:30–37); and Deuteronomy 23:3 banned the offspring of Moabites from the assembly of the Lord to the tenth generation. R.E. Brown (*Birth of Messiah*, pp. 71–72) discounts this interpretation of the role of the four women, because in first-century Jewish piety they were largely whitewashed and revered. Yet it is not at all certain that Matthew follows his contemporaries in all this. It is important that in this same chapter Matthew introduces Jesus as the one who "will save his people from their sins" (1:21), and this verse may imply a backward glance at some of the better-known sins of his own progenitors.

A third interpretation (favored by Allen, R.E. Brown, Filson, Fenton, Green, Hill, Klostermann, Lohmeyer, Peake) holds that all four reveal something of the strange and unexpected workings of Providence in preparation for the Messiah and that as such they point to Mary's unexpected but providential conception of Jesus.

There is no reason to rule out any of the above interpretations. Matthew, Jew that he is, knows how to write with an allusive touch; and readers steeped in the OT would naturally call to mind a plethora of images associated with many names in this selective genealogy.

7–10 The names in these verses seem to have been taken from 1 Chronicles 3:10–14. Behind "Asa" (v.7) lurks a difficult textual decision (cf. Notes). There is no obvious pattern: wicked Rehoboam was the father of wicked Abijah, the father of the good king Asa. Asa was the father of the good king Jehoshaphat (v.8), who sired the wicked king Joram. Good or evil, they were part of Messiah's line; for though grace does not run in the blood, God's providence cannot be deceived or outmaneuvered.

Three names have been omitted between Joram and Uzziah: Ahaziah, Joash, and Amaziah (2 Kings 8:24; 1 Chron 3:11; 2 Chron 22:1, 11; 24:27). "Uzziah" (vv.8–9) is equivalent to Azariah (1 Chron 3:11; cf. 2 Kings 15:13, 30 with 2 Kings 15:1). The three omissions not only secure fourteen generations in this part of the genealogy (see on 1:17) but are dropped because of their connection with Ahab and Jezebel, renowned for wickedness (2 Kings 8:27), and because of their connection with wicked Athaliah (2 Kings 8:26), the usurper (2 Kings 11:1–20). Two of the three were notoriously evil; all three died violently.

R.E. Brown (*Birth of Messiah*, p. 82) points out that Manasseh was even more wicked, and he is included. Therefore (with Schweizer, *Matthew*), Brown prefers an explanation of the omissions based on a text-critical confusion between "Azariah" and "Uzziah." This conjecture is plausible; but if it is correct, it would have to be pre-Matthean, because Matthew's "fourteens" (see on 1:17) would require this omission or an equivalent. But there is no textual evidence to support the conjecture. Also, Manasseh (v.10), though notoriously evil, repented, unlike the other three.

11 Another name has been dropped: Josiah was the father of Jehoiakim (609–597 B.C.), who was deposed in favor of his son Jehoiachin (some MSS in both OT and NT have "Jeconiah" for the latter). He was deposed after a reign of only three months; and his brother Zedekiah reigned in his stead till the final deportation and destruction of the city in 587 B.C. (cf. 2 Kings 23:34; 24:6, 14–15; 1 Chron 3:16; Jer 27:20; 28:1). The words "and his brothers" are probably added in this instance because one of them, Zedekiah, maintained a caretaker reign until the tragedy of 587 B.C.; but Zedekiah is not mentioned because the royal line does not flow through him but through Jeconiah. The Exile to Babylon marked the end of the reign of David's line, a momentous event in OT history. Alternatively "and his brothers" may refer, not to the royal brothers, but to all the Jews who went into captivity with Jeconiah (Gundry, *Matthew*). The locus of the people of God is thus traced from the patriarchs ("and his brothers," 1:2) to the shame of the Exile, a theme to be developed later (see on 2:16–18).

12 The final list of "fourteen" (see on 1:17) begins with a further mention of the Exile. First Chronicles 3:17 records that Jeconiah (Jehoiachin) was the father of Shealtiel. Matthew goes on to present Shealtiel as the father of Zerubbabel, in accord with Ezra 3:2; 5:2; Nehemiah 12:1; Haggai 1:1; 2:2, 23. The difficulty lies in 1 Chronicles 3:19, which presents Zerubbabel as the son of Pedaiah, a brother of Shealtiel.

Several solutions have been offered, most not very convincing (cf. Machen, pp. 206–7). Some Greek MSS omit Pedaiah in 1 Chronicles 3:19. But the best suggestion is a levirate marriage (Deut 25:5–10; cf. Gen 38:8–9), scarcely an embarrassment to those who have adopted the explanation above (cf. on vv.2–17) and find no other levirate marriage in the genealogy. If Shealtiel were the older brother and died childless, Pedaiah might well have married the widow to "build up his brother's family line" (Deut 25:9). In any case Zerubbabel himself becomes a messianic model (cf. Hag 2:20–23).

13–15 The nine names from Abiud to Jacob are not otherwise known to us today. Possibly names have been omitted from this genealogical section also, but then one wonders why this third section of the genealogy appears to lack one entry (see on 1:17). Gundry's explanations (*Matthew*) of these names is tortured: certain names from Luke's list "catch the evangelist's [Matthew's] eye," as do names from the priestly (nonroyal) list in 1 Chronicles 6:3–14—names that then need abbreviating or changing to mask their priestly connection.

16 The wording in the best reading (cf. Notes), reflected in NIV, is precise. Joseph's royal line has been traced; Joseph is the husband of Mary; Mary is the mother of Jesus. The relation between Joseph and Jesus is so far unstated. But this peculiar form of expression cries out for the explanation provided in the ensuing verses. Legally Jesus stands in line to the throne of David; physically he is born of a woman "found to be with child through the Holy Spirit" (1:18). Her son is Jesus, "who is called Christ." The Greek does not make it clear whether "Christ" is titular or not; but name or title, Jesus' messiahship is affirmed.

17 It was customary among Jewish writers to arrange genealogies according to some convenient scheme, possibly for mnemonic reasons. Strictly speaking the Greek text speaks of "all the generations from Abraham to David . . . to Christ" (cf. KJV, NASB); but since the omissions are obvious to both Matthew and his readers, the expression must mean "all the generations . . . included in this table." So it becomes a hint that the fourteens, here so strongly brought to the reader's attention, are symbolic.

Various arrangements of the three fourteens have been proposed. In one the first set of fourteen runs from Abraham to David, the second from Solomon to Jeconiah, and the third attains fourteen by repeating Jeconiah and running to Jesus. Hendriksen (pp. 125–26) suggests Matthew purposely counts Jeconiah twice: first he presents Jeconiah as cursed, childless, deported (2 Kings 24:8–12; Jer 22:30); the second time he reminds the reader that Jeconiah was subsequently released from prison and restored and became the father of many (2 Kings 25:27–30; 1 Chron 3:17–18; Jer 52:31–34)—a new man as it were. But Matthew does not mention these themes, which do not clearly fit into the main concerns of this chapter. Schweizer prefers to count from Abraham to David. Then, because David is mentioned twice, he passes from David to Josiah, the last free king; and then Jeconiah to Jesus provides a third set of fourteen, at the expense of making the central set one member short and of ignoring the small but distinct literary pause at the end of 1:11. McNeile postulates a possible loss of one name between Jeconiah and Shealtiel owing to homoeoteleuton (identical endings), but there is no textual evidence for it. Gundry (*Matthew*) thinks that Mary as well as Joseph counts for one, pointing to the two kinds of generation, legal (Joseph's) and physical (Mary's). No solution so far proposed seems entirely convincing, and it is difficult to rule any out.

The symbolic value of the fourteens is of more significance than their precise breakdown. Herman C. Waetjen ("The Genealogy as the Key to the Gospel According to Matthew," JBL 95 [1976]: 205–30; cf. Johnson, pp. 193–94) tries to solve both problems by appealing to 2 Baruch 53–74 (usually dated c. A.D. 50–70). This apocalyptic book divides history into a scheme of 12 + 2 = 14 units. Matthew, Waetjen argues, holds that just as David and Jeconiah are transitional figures in the genealogy, so also is Jesus. He is the end of the third period and simultaneously the beginning of the fourth, the inaugurated kingdom. Jesus is therefore the thirteenth and the fourteenth entries, the former a period of gloom in 2 Baruch (corresponding to the Passion in Matthew) and the fourteenth opening into the new age.

But this analysis will not do. Two objections are crucial: (1) it is not at all clear that one may legitimately jump from schematized time periods in apocalyptic literature to names in a genealogy (Is anything less apocalyptic than a genealogy?) just because of a common number; (2) Waetjen has "corrected" the omission in the third set of fourteen by listing Jesus twice, even though the second reference to Jesus, in his scheme, properly belongs to the inaugurated kingdom and not to the third set, which remains deficient.

Schemes like those of Hendriksen and Goodspeed that reduce the 3 × 14 pattern to 6 × 7 and then picture Jesus' coming to inaugurate the seventh seven—the sign of perfection, the dawning of the Messianic Age (cf. 1 Enoch 91:12–17; 93:1–10)—stumble over the fact that Matthew has not presented his genealogy as six sevens but as three fourteens (cf. R.E. Brown, *Birth of Messiah*, p. 75). Other suggestions include those of Johnson (pp. 189–208) and Goulder (pp. 228–33).

The simplest explanation—the one that best fits the context—observes that the numerical value of "David" in Hebrew is fourteen (cf. Notes). By this symbolism Matthew points out that the promised "son of David" (1:1), the Messiah, has come. And if the third set of fourteen is short one member, perhaps it will suggest to some readers that just as God cuts short the time of distress for the sake of his elect (24:22), so also he mercifully shortens the period from the Exile to Jesus the Messiah.

Notes

---

1 For a broader grasp of the place of the Messiah in the OT, cf. Ladd, *NT Theology*, pp. 136ff.; Douglas, *Bible Dictionary*, 2:987–95.

3 Older EV (e.g., KJV) have the names Tamar and Hezron in the OT and Thamar and Esrom in the NT. Because English OT names are roughly transliterated from the Hebrew and English NT names are roughly transliterated from the Greek, which for many names transliterates from the Hebrew, we have these variations. NIV rightly smooths them out.

7–8 In these verses the best textual evidence supports Ἀσάφ (*Asaph*), not Ἀσά (*Asa*). It is transcriptionally more probable that *Asaph* would be changed to *Asa* than vice versa (for the opposite view, cf. Lagrange). Julius Schniewind (*Das Evangelium nach Matthäus* [Göttingen: Vandenhoeck und Ruprecht, 1965]) and Gundry (*Matthew*) suggest *Asaph* is a deliberate change by Matthew to call up images of the psalmist (Pss 50, 73–83), as "Amos" (cf. note on v.10) calls to mind the prophet. This is too cryptic to be believable. Orthography was not so consistent in the ancient world as it is today. Josephus (Antiq. VIII, 290–315 [xii. 1–6]), for instance, uses Ἄσανος (*Asanos*); but in the ancient Latin translation *Asaph* is presupposed. "Mary" varies in the NT between Μαρία (*Maria*) and Μαριάμ (*Mariam*). In 1 Chron 3:10 LXX most MSS read (*Asa*, but one offers Ἀσάβ

(*Asab;* cf. Metzger, *Textual Commentary,* p. 1, n. 1). In short Matthew could well be following a MS with *Asaph* even though *Asa* is quite clearly the person meant.

10 The textual evidence for Ἀμώς (*Amōs*) and Ἀμών (*Amōn*) breaks down much as in vv.7– 8. In this case, however, there is greater diversity in the readings of LXX MSS for 1 Chron 3:14, on which Matt 1:10 depends.

11 The term μετοικεσία (*metoikesia,* "exile") occurs but three times in the NT, all in this chapter (vv.11–12, 17); but it refers (in LXX) to the Babylonian exile in 2 Kings 24:16; 1 Chron 5:22; Ezek 12:11. Βαβυλῶνος (*Babylōnos,* "Babylon") is a genitive "of direction and purpose" (cf. BDF, par. 166).

Schweizer's suggestion (*Matthew*) that Jehoiakim and his son Jehoiachin have been fused into a single figure because in 2 Kings 24:6 (LXX) they are both called "Jehoiakim" explains little, since Matthew betrays a deep knowledge of the OT not likely to be confused by one versional mistransliteration; and in any case Matthew's term is "Jeconiah."

16 The best textual variant, supported by a spread of text types in Greek and versional witnesses and by all but one uncial, stands behind NIV. Several Caesarean and OL witnesses prefer "Joseph, to whom was betrothed the virgin Mary who begot Jesus who is called Christ." This is transcriptionally less likely than the first alternative, in which "the husband" of Mary might well have been thought misleading. No Greek MS supports syr^s in its reading: "Joseph, to whom was betrothed Mary the virgin, begot Jesus who is called the Christ." At first glance it seems to deny the Virgin Birth by ascribing paternity to Joseph; but the "begot" may have merely legal significance, since Mary is still referred to as "the virgin." In any case this last reading is not well attested. The enormously complex problems of textual criticism in this verse are competently treated by Metzger, *NT Studies,* pp. 105–13; Machen, pp. 176–87; R.E. Brown, *Birth of Messiah,* pp. 62–64, 139; and A. Globe, "Some Doctrinal Variants in Matthew 1 and Luke 2, and the Authority of the Neutral Text," CBQ 42 (1980): 55–72, esp. pp. 63–65.

17 In the ancient world letters served not only as the building blocks of words but also as symbols of numbers. Hence any word had a numerical value; and the use of such symbolism is known as gematria. In Hebrew "David" is דָּוִד (*dāwid*); and d = 4, w = 6 (the vowels, a later addition to the text, don't count). Therefore "David" = *dwd* = 4 + 6 + 4 = 14. (This would not work in the DSS, where, with one exception [CD 7:16], the consonantal spelling of "David" is *dwyd* = דָּוִיד.)

B. *The Birth of Jesus*

1:18–25

[18]This is how the birth of Jesus Christ came about: His mother Mary was pledged to be married to Joseph, but before they came together, she was found to be with child through the Holy Spirit. [19]Because Joseph her husband was a righteous man and did not want to expose her to public disgrace, he had in mind to divorce her quietly.

[20]But after he had considered this, an angel of the Lord appeared to him in a dream and said, "Joseph son of David, do not be afraid to take Mary home as your wife, because what is conceived in her is from the Holy Spirit. [21]She will give birth to a son, and you are to give him the name Jesus, because he will save his people from their sins."

[22]All this took place to fulfill what the Lord had said through the prophet: [23]"The virgin will be with child and will give birth to a son, and they will call him Immanuel"—which means, "God with us."

[24]When Joseph woke up, he did what the angel of the Lord had commanded him and took Mary home as his wife. [25]But he had no union with her until she gave birth to a son. And he gave him the name Jesus.

Two matters call for brief remarks: the historicity of the Virgin Birth (more properly, virginal conception), and the theological emphases surrounding this theme in Matthew 1–2 and its relation to the NT.

First, the historicity of the Virgin Birth is questioned for many reasons.

1. The accounts in Matthew and Luke are apparently independent and highly divergent. This argues for creative forces in the church making up all or parts of the stories in order to explain the person of Jesus. But the stories have long been shown to be compatible (Machen), even mutually complementary. Moreover literary independence of Matthew and Luke at this point does not demand the conclusion that the two evangelists were ignorant of the other's content. Yet if they were, their differences suggest to some the strength of mutual compatibility without collusion. Matthew focuses largely on Joseph, Luke on Mary. R.E. Brown (*Birth of Messiah*, p. 35) does not accept this because he finds it inconceivable that Joseph could have told his story without mentioning the Annunciation or that Mary could have passed on her story without mentioning the flight to Egypt. True enough, though it does not follow that the evangelists were bound to include all they knew. It is hard to imagine how the Annunciation would have fit in very well with Matthew's themes. Moreover we have already observed that Matthew was prepared to omit things he knew in order to present his chosen themes coherently and concisely.

2. Some simply discount the supernatural. Goulder (p. 33) says Matthew made the stories up; Schweizer (*Matthew*) contrasts the ancient world in which virgin birth was (allegedly) an accepted notion with modern scientific limitations on what is possible. But the antithesis is greatly exaggerated: thoroughgoing rationalists were not uncommon in the first century (e.g., Lucretius); and millions of modern Christians, scientifically aware, find little difficulty in believing in the Virgin Birth or in a God who is capable of intervening miraculously in what is, after all, his own creation. More important, Matthew's point in these chapters is surely that the Virgin Birth and attendant circumstances were most extraordinary. Only here does he mention Magi; and dreams and visions as a means of guidance are by no means common in the NT (though even here one wonders whether Western Christianity could learn something from Third-World Christianity). Certainly Matthew's account is infinitely more sober than the wildly speculative stories preserved in the apocryphal gospels (e.g., *Protevangelium of James* 12:3–20:4; cf. Hennecke, 1:381–85). R.E. Brown (*Birth of Messiah*) accepts the historicity of the Virgin Birth but discounts the historicity of the visit of the Magi and related events. But if he can swallow the Virgin Birth, it is difficult to see why he strains out the Magi. (See the useful book of Manuel Miguens, *The Virgin Birth: An Evaluation of Scriptual Evidence* [Westminster, Md.: Christian Classics, 1975].)

3. Many point to artificialities in the narrative: e.g., the structure of the genealogy or the delay in mentioning Bethlehem as the place of birth (Hill, *Matthew*). We have noted, however, that though Matthew's arrangement of the genealogy gives us more than a mere table of names and dates, it does not tell us less. More than any of the synoptists, Matthew delights in topical arrangements. But that does not make his accounts less than historical. We are not shut up to the extreme choice historical chronicles or theological invention! Matthew does not mention Bethlehem in 1:18–25 because it does not suit any of his themes. In chapter 2, however, as Tatum has shown (W.B. Tatum, Jr., "The Matthean Infancy Narratives: Their Form, Structure, and Relation to the Theology of the First Evangelist" [Ph.D. dissertation,

Duke University, 1967]), one of the themes unifying Matthew's narrative is Jesus' "geographical origins"; and therefore Bethlehem is introduced.

4. It has become increasingly common to identify the literary genre in Matthew 1-2 as "midrash" or "midrashic haggadah" and to conclude that these stories are not intended to be taken literally (e.g., with widely differing perspectives, Gundry, *Matthew;* Goulder; Davies, *Setting*, pp. 66-67). There is nothing fundamentally objectionable in the suggestion that some stories in the Bible are not meant to be taken as fact; parables are such stories. The problem is the slipperiness of the categories (cf. Introduction, section 12.b; and cf. further on 2:16-18). If the genre has unambiguous formal characteristics, there should be little problem in recognizing them. But this is far from being so; the frequently cited parallels boast as many formal differences (compared with Matt 1-2) as similarities. To cite one obvious example: Jewish Midrashim (in the technical, fourth-century sense) present stories as illustrative material by way of comment on a running OT text. By contrast Matthew 1-2 offers no running OT text: the continuity of the text depends on the story-line; and the OT quotations, taken from a variety of OT books, could be removed without affecting that continuity (cf. esp. M.J. Down, "The Matthean Birth Narratives," ExpT 90 [1978-79]: 51-52; and France, *Jesus;* see on 2:16-18).

R.E. Brown (*Birth of Messiah*, pp. 557-63) argues convincingly that Matthew 1-2 is not midrash. Yet he thinks the sort of person who could invent stories to explain OT texts (midrash) could also invent stories to explain Jesus. Matthew 1-2, though not itself midrash, is at least midrashic. That may be so. Unfortunately, not only does the statement fall short of proof, but the appeal to a known and recognizable literary genre is thus lost. So we have no objective basis for arguing that Matthew's first readers would readily detect his midrashic methods. Of course, if "midrashic" means that Matthew intends to present a panorama of OT allusions and themes, these chapters are certainly midrashic: in that sense the studies of Goulder, Gundry, Davies, and others have served us well, by warning us against a too-rigid pattern of linear thought. But used in this sense, it is not at all clear that "midrashic material" is necessarily unhistorical.

5. A related objection insists that these stories "are not primarily didactic but kerygmatic" (Davies, *Setting* p. 67), that they are intended as proclamations about the truth of the person of Jesus but not as factual information. The rigid dichotomy between proclamation and teaching is not as defensible as when C.H. Dodd first proposed it (see on 3:1). More important, we may ask just what the proclamation intended to proclaim. If the stories express the appreciation of the first Christians for Jesus, precisely what did they appreciate? On the face of it, Matthew in chapters 1-2 is not saying something vague, such as, "Jesus was so wonderful there must be a touch of the divine about him," but rather, "Jesus is the promised Messiah of the line of David, and he is 'Emmanuel,' 'God with us,' because his birth was the result of God's supernatural intervention, making Jesus God's very Son; and his early months were stamped with strange occurrences which, in the light of subsequent events, weave a coherent pattern of theological truths and historical attestation to divine providence in the matter."

6. Some argue that the (to us) artificial way these chapters cite the OT shows a small concern for historicity. The reverse argument is surely more impressive: If the events of Matthew 1-2 do not relate easily to the OT texts, this attests their historical credibility; for no one in his right mind would invent "fulfillment" episodes problematic to the texts being fulfilled. The fulfillment texts, though difficult, do fit

into a coherent pattern (cf. Introduction, section 11.b, and below on 1.22–23). More importantly, their presence shows that Matthew sees Jesus as one who fulfills the OT. This not only sets the stage for some of Matthew's most important themes; it also means that Matthew is working from a perspective on salvation history that depends on before and after, prophecy and fulfillment, type and antitype, relative ignorance and progressive revelation. This has an important bearing on our discussion of midrash, because whatever else Jewish midrash may be, it is not related to salvation history or fulfillment schemes. Add to the foregoing considerations the fact that, wherever in chapters 1–2 he can be tested against the known background of Herod the Great, Matthew proves reliable (some details below). There is a good case for treating chapters 1–2 as both history and theology.

Second, the following theological considerations require mention.

1. Often it is argued, or even assumed (e.g., Dunn, *Christology*, pp. 49–50), that the concepts "virginal conception" and "preexistence" applied to the one person Jesus are mutually exclusive. Certainly it is difficult to see how a divine being could become genuinely human by means of an ordinary birth. Nevertheless there is no logical or theological reason to think that virginal conception and preexistence preclude each other.

2. Related to this is the theory of R.E. Brown (*Birth of Messiah*, pp. 140–41), who proposes a retrojected Christology. The early Christians, he argues, first focused attention on Jesus' resurrection, which they perceived as the moment of his installation into his messianic role. Then with further reflection they pushed back the time of his installation to his baptism, then to his birth, and finally to a theory regarding his preexistence. There may be some truth to the scheme. Just as the first Christians did not come to an instant grasp of the relationship between law and gospel (as the Book of Acts amply demonstrates), so their understanding of Jesus doubtless matured and deepened with time and further revelation. But the theory often depends on a rigid and false reconstruction of early church history (cf. Introduction, section 2) and dates the documents, against other evidence, on the basis of this reconstruction. Worse, in the hands of some it transforms the understanding of the disciples into historical reality: that is, Jesus had no preexistence and was not virgin born, but these things were progressively predicated of him by his followers. Gospel evidence for Jesus' self-perception as preexistent is then facilely dismissed as late and inauthentic. The method is of doubtful worth.

Matthew, despite his strong insistence on Jesus' virginal conception, includes several veiled allusions to Jesus' preexistence; and there is no reason to think he found the two concepts incompatible. Moreover R.H. Fuller ("The Conception/Birth of Jesus as a Christological Moment," *Journal for the Study of the New Testament* 1 [1978]: 37–52) has shown that the virginal conception-birth motif in the NT is not infrequently connected with the "sending of the Son" motif, which (contra Fuller) in many places already presupposes the preexistence of the Son.

3. We are dealing in these chapters with King Messiah who comes to his people in covenant relationship. The point is well established, if occasionally exaggerated, by Nolan, who speaks of the "Royal Covenant Christology."

4. It is remarkable that the title "Son of God," important later in Matthew, is not found in Matthew 1–2. It may lurk behind 2:15. Still it would be false to argue that Matthew does not connect the Virgin Birth with the title "Son of God." Matthew 1–2 serves as a finely wrought prologue for every major theme in the Gospel. We must therefore understand Matthew to be telling us that if Jesus is physically Mary's

son and legally Joseph's son, at an even more fundamental level he is God's Son; and in this Matthew agrees with Luke's statement (Luke 1:35). The dual paternity, one legal and one divine, is unambiguous (cf. Cyrus H. Gordon, "Paternity at Two Levels," JBL 96 [1977]: 101).

18 The word translated "birth" is, in the best MSS (cf. Notes), the word translated "genealogy" in 1:1. Maier prefers "history" of Jesus Christ, taking the phrase to refer to the rest of the Gospel. Yet it is best to take the word to mean "birth" or "origins" in the sense of the beginnings of Jesus Messiah. Even a well-developed christology would not want to read the man "Jesus" and his name back into a preexistent state (cf. on 1:1). The pledge to be married was legally binding. Only a divorce writ could break it, and infidelity at that stage was considered adultery (cf. Deut 22:23–24; Moore, *Judaism*, 2:121–22). The marriage itself took place when the groom (already called "husband," 1:19) ceremoniously took the bride home (see on 25:1–13). Mary is here introduced unobtrusively. Though comparing the Gospel accounts gives us a picture of her, she does not figure largely in Matthew.

"Before they came together" (*prin ē synelthein autous*) occasionally refers in classical Greek to sexual intercourse (LSJ, p. 1712); in the other thirty instances of *synerchomai* in the NT, there is, however, no sexual overtone. But here sexual union is included, occurring at the formal marriage when the "wife" moved in with her "husband." Only then was sexual intercourse proper. The phrase affirms that Mary's pregnancy was discovered while she was still betrothed, and the context presupposes that both Mary and Joseph had been chaste (cf. McHugh, pp. 157–63; and for the customs of the day, M *Kiddushin* ["Betrothals"] and M *Ketuboth* ["Marriage Deeds"]).

That Mary was "found" to be with child does not suggest a surreptitious attempt at concealment ("found out") but only that her pregnancy became obvious. This pregnancy came about through the Holy Spirit (even more prominent in Luke's birth narratives). There is no hint of pagan deity-human coupling in crassly physical terms. Instead, the power of the Lord, manifest in the Holy Spirit who was expected to be active in the Messianic Age, miraculously brought about the conception.

19 The peculiar Greek expression in this verse allows several interpretations. There are three important ones.

1. Because Joseph, knowing about the virginal conception, was a just man and had no desire to bring the matter out in the open (i.e., to divulge this miraculous conception), he felt unworthy to continue his plans to marry one so highly favored and planned to withdraw (so Gundry, *Matthew*; McHugh, pp. 164–72; Schlatter). This assumes that Mary told Joseph about the conception. Nevertheless the natural way to read vv.18–19 is that Joseph learned of his betrothed's condition when it became unmistakable, not when she told him. Moreover the angel's reason for Joseph to proceed with the marriage (v.20) assumes (contra Zerwick, par. 477) that Joseph did not know about the virginal conception.

2. Because Joseph was a just man, and because he did not want to expose Mary to public disgrace, he proposed a quiet divorce. The problem with this is that "just" (NIV, "righteous") is not defined according to OT law but is taken in the sense of "merciful," "not given to passionate vengeance," or even "nice" (cf. 1 Sam 24:17). But this is not its normal sense. Strictly speaking justice conceived in Mosaic prescriptions demanded some sort of action.

3. Because he was a righteous man, Joseph therefore could not in conscience marry Mary who was now thought to be unfaithful. And because such a marriage would have been a tacit admission of his own guilt, and also because he was unwilling to expose her to the disgrace of public divorce, Joseph therefore chose a quieter way, permitted by the law itself. The full rigor of the law might have led to Mary's stoning, though that was rarely carried out in the first century. Still, a public divorce was possible, though Joseph was apparently unwilling to expose Mary to such shame. The law also allowed for private divorce before two witnesses (Num 5:11–31, interpreted as in M *Sotah* 1:1–5; cf. David Hill, "A Note on Matthew i.19," ExpT 76 [1964–65]: 133–34; rather similar, A. Tosato, "Joseph, Being a Just Man (Matt 1:19)," CBQ 41 [1979]: 547–51). That was what Joseph purposed. It would leave both his righteousness (his conformity to the law) and his compassion intact.

20 Joseph tried to solve his dilemma in what seemed to him the best way possible. Only then did God intervene with a dream. Dreams as means of divine communication in the NT are concentrated in Matthew's prologue (1:20; 2:2, 13, 19, 22; elsewhere, possibly 27:19; Acts 2:17). An "angel of the Lord" (four times in the prologue: 1:20, 24; 2:13, 19) calls to mind divine messengers in past ages (e.g., Gen 16:7–14; 22:11–18; Exod 3:2–4:16), in which it was not always clear whether the heavenly "messenger" (the meaning of *angelos*) was a manifestation of Yahweh. They most commonly appeared as men. We must not read medieval paintings into the word "angel" or the stylized cherubim of Revelation 4:6–8. The focus is on God's gracious intervention and the messenger's private communication, not on the details of angelology and their panoramic sweeps of history common in Jewish apocalyptic literature (Bonnard).

The angel's opening words, "Joseph son of David," ties this pericope to the preceding genealogy, maintains interest in the theme of the Davidic Messiah, and, from Joseph's perspective, alerts him to the significance of the role he is to play. The prohibition, "Do not be afraid," confirms that Joseph had already decided on his course when God intervened. He was to "take" Mary home as his wife—an expression primarily reflecting marriage customs of the day but not excluding sexual intercourse (cf. TDNT, 4:11–14, for other uses of the verb)—because Mary's pregnancy was the direct action of the Holy Spirit (a reason that makes nonsense of the attempt by James Lagrand ["How Was the Virgin Mary 'like a man'. . .? A Note on Mt i 18b and Related Syriac Christian Texts," NovTest 22 (1980): 97–107] to make the reference to the Holy Spirit in 1:18, *ek pneumatos hagiou* ["through the Holy Spirit"], mean that Mary brought forth, "as a man, by will").

21 It was no doubt divine grace that solicited Mary's cooperation before the conception and Joseph's cooperation only after it. Here Joseph is drawn into the mystery of the Incarnation. In patriarchal times either a mother (Gen 4:25) or a father (Gen 4:26; 5:3; cf. R.E. Brown, *Birth of Messiah*, p. 130) could name a child. According to Luke 1:31, Mary was told Jesus' name; but Joseph was told both name and reason for it. The Greek is literally "you will call his name Jesus," strange in both English and Greek. This is not only a Semitism (BDF, par. 157 [2]—the expression recurs in 1:23, 25; Luke 1:13, 31) but also uses the future indicative (*kaleseis*, lit., "you will call") with imperatival force—hence NIV, "You are to give him the name Jesus." This construction is very rare in the NT, except where the LXX is being cited; the effect is to give the verse a strong OT nuance.

"Jesus" (*Iēsous*) is the Greek form of "Joshua" (cf. Gr. of Acts 7:45; Heb 4:8), which, whether in the long form *yᵉhôšua'* ("Yahweh is salvation," Exod 24:13) or in one of the short forms, e.g., *yēšûa'* ("Yahweh saves," Neh 7:7), identifies Mary's Son as the one who brings Yahweh's promised eschatological salvation. There are several Joshuas in the OT, at least two of them not very significant (1 Sam 6:14; 2 Kings 23:8). Two others, however, are used in the NT as types of Christ: Joshua, successor to Moses and the one who led the people into the Promised Land (and a type of Christ in Heb 3–4), and Joshua the high priest, contemporary of Zerubbabel (Ezra 2:2; 3:2–9; Neh 7:7), "the Branch" who builds the temple of the Lord (Zech 6:11–13). But instead of referring to either of these, the angel explains the significance of the name by referring to Psalm 130:8: "He [Yahweh] himself will redeem Israel from all their sins" (cf. Gundry, *Use of OT*, pp. 127–28).

There was much Jewish expectation of a Messiah who would "redeem" Israel from Roman tyranny and even purify his people, whether by fiat or appeal to law (e.g., Pss Sol 17). But there was no expectation that the Davidic Messiah would give his own life as a ransom (20:28) to save his people from their sins. The verb "save" can refer to deliverance from physical danger (8:25), disease (9:21–22), or even death (24:22); in the NT it commonly refers to the comprehensive salvation inaugurated by Jesus that will be consummated at his return. Here it focuses on what is central, viz., salvation from sins; for in the biblical perspective sin is the basic (if not always the immediate) cause of all other calamities. This verse therefore orients the reader to the fundamental purpose of Jesus' coming and the essential nature of the reign he inaugurates as King Messiah, heir of David's throne (cf. Ridderbos, pp. 193ff.).

Though to Joseph "his people" would be the Jews, even Joseph would understand from the OT that some Jews fell under God's judgment, while others became a godly remnant. In any event, it is not long before Matthew says that both John the Baptist (3:9) and Jesus (8:11) picture Gentiles joining with the godly remnant to become disciples of the Messiah and members of "his people" (see on 16:18; cf. Gen 49:10; Titus 2:13–14; Rev 14:4). The words "his people" are therefore full of meaning that is progressively unpacked as the Gospel unfolds. They refer to "Messiah's people."

22 Although most EV conclude the angel's remarks at the end of v.21, there is good reason to think that they continue to the end of v.23, or at least to the end of the word "Immanuel." This particular fulfillment formula occurs only three times in Matthew: here; 21:4; 26:56. In the last it is natural to take it as part of Jesus' reported speech (cf. 26:55); and this is possible, though less likely, in 21:4. Matthew's patterns are fairly consistent. So it is not unnatural to extend the quotation to the end of 1:23 as well. (JB recognizes Matthew's consistency by ending Jesus' words in 26:55, making 26:56 Matthew's remark!) This is more convincing when we recall that only these three fulfillment formulas use the perfect *gegonen* (NIV, "took place") instead of the expected aorist. Some take the verb as an instance of a perfect standing for an aorist (so BDF, par. 343, but this is a disputed classification). Others think it means that the event "stands recorded" in the abiding Christian tradition (McNeile; Moule, *Idiom Book*, p. 15); still others take it as a stylistic indicator that Matthew himself introduced the fulfillment passage (Rothfuchs, pp. 33–36). But if we hold that Matthew presents the angel as saying the words, then the perfect may enjoy its normal force: "all this has taken place" (cf. esp. Fenton; cf. also Stendahl, Peake; B. Weiss, *Das Matthäus-Evangelium* [Göttingen: Vandenhoeck und Ruprecht, 1898]; Zahn).

R.E. Brown (*Birth of Messiah*, p. 144, n. 31) objects that nowhere in Scripture does an angel cite Scripture in this fashion; but, equally, nowhere in Scripture is there a virgin birth in this fashion. Matthew knew that Satan can cite Scripture (4:6–7); he may not have thought it strange if an angel does. Broadus's objection, that the angel would in that case be anticipating an event that has not yet occurred, and this is strange when cast in fulfillment language, lacks weight; for the conception has occurred, and the pregnancy has become well advanced, even if the birth has not yet taken place. Joseph needs to know at this stage that "all this took place" to fulfill what the Lord had said through the prophet. The weightiest argument is the perfect tense.

The last clause is phrased with exquisite care, literally, "the word spoken by [*hypo*] the Lord through [*dia*] the prophet." The prepositions make a distinction between the mediate and the intermediate agent (RHG, p. 636), presupposing a view of Scripture like that in 2 Peter 1:21. Matthew uses the verb "to fulfill" (*plēroō*) primarily in his own fulfillment formulas (1:22; 2:15, 17, 23; 4:14; 8:17; 12:17; 13:35; 21:4; 26:56; 27:9; cf. 26:54) but also in a few other contexts (3:15; 5:17; 13:48; 23:32). (On Matthew's understanding of fulfillment and on the origins of his fulfillment texts, cf. 5:17–20 and Introduction, section 11.b.)

Here two observations are in order. First, most of Matthew's OT quotations are easy enough to understand, but the difficult exceptions have sometimes tended to increase the difficulty of the easier ones. Hard cases make bad theology as well as bad law. Second, Matthew is not simply ripping texts out of OT contexts because he needs to find a prophecy in order to generate a fulfillment. Discernible principles govern his choices, the most important being that he finds in the OT not only isolated predictions regarding the Messiah but also OT history and people as paradigms that, to those with eyes to see, point forward to the Messiah (e.g., see on 2:15).

23 This verse, on which the literature is legion, is reasonably clear in its context here in Matthew. Mary is the virgin; Jesus is her son, Immanuel. But because it is a quotation from Isaiah 7:14, complex issues are raised concerning Matthew's use of the OT.

The linguistic evidence is not as determinative as some think. The Hebrew word *'almāh* is not precisely equivalent to the English word "virgin" (NIV), in which all the focus is on the lack of sexual experience; nor is it precisely equivalent to "young woman," in which the focus is on age without reference to sexual experience. Many prefer the translation "young woman of marriageable age." Yet most of the few OT occurrences refer to a young woman of marriageable age who is also a virgin. The most disputed passage is Proverbs 30:19: "The way of a man with a *maiden*." Here the focus of the word is certainly not on virginity. Some claim that here the maiden cannot possibly be a virgin; others (see esp. E.J. Young, *Studies in Isaiah* [London: Tyndale, 1954], pp. 143–98; Richard Niessen, "The Virginity of the עַלְמָה in Isaiah 7:14," BS 137 [1980]: 133–50) insist that Proverbs 30:19 refers to a young man wooing and winning a maiden still a virgin.

Although it is fair to say that most OT occurrences presuppose that the *'almāh* is a virgin, because of Proverbs 30:19, one cannot be certain the word necessarily means that. Linguistics has shown that the etymological arguments (reviewed by Niessen) have little force. Young argues that *'almāh* is chosen by Isaiah because the most likely alternative (*bᵉtûlāh*) can refer to a married woman (Joel 1:8 is commonly cited; Young is supported by Gordon J. Wenham, "*Bethulah*, 'A Girl of

Marriageable Age,'" VetTest 22 [1972]: 326–29). Again, however, the linguistic argument is not as clear-cut as we might like. Tom Wadsworth ("Is There a Hebrew Word for Virgin? *Bethulah* in the Old Testament," *Restoration Quarterly* 23 [1980]: 161–71) insists that every occurrence of *b^etûlāh* in the OT does refer to a virgin: the woman in Joel 1:8, for instance, is betrothed. Again the evidence is a trifle ambiguous. In short there is a presumption in favor of rendering ʿ*almāh* by "young virgin" or the like in Isaiah 7:14. Nevertheless other evidence must be given a hearing.

The LXX renders the word by *parthenos*, which almost always means "virgin." Yet even with this word there are exceptions: Genesis 34:4 refers to Dinah as a *parthenos* even though the previous verse makes it clear she is no longer a virgin. This sort of datum prompts C.H. Dodd ("New Testament Translation Problems I," *The Bible Translator* 27 [1976]: 301–5, published posthumously) to suggest that *parthenos* means "young woman" even in Matthew 1:23 and Luke 1:27. This will not do; the overwhelming majority of the occurrences of *parthenos* in both biblical and profane Greek require the rendering "virgin"; and the unambiguous context of Matthew 1 (cf. vv.16, 18, 20, 25) puts Matthew's intent beyond dispute, as Jean Carmignac ("The Meaning of *parthenos* in Luke 1.27: A reply to C.H. Dodd," *The Bible Translator* 28 [1977]: 327–30) was quick to point out. If, unlike the LXX, the later (second century A.D.) Greek renderings of the Hebrew text of Isaiah 7:14 prefer *neanis* ("young woman") to *parthenos* (so Aq., Symm., Theod.), we may legitimately suspect a conscious effort by the Jewish translators to avoid the Christian interpretation of Isaiah 7:14.

The crucial question is how we are to understand Isaiah 7:14 in its relationship to Matthew 1:23. Of the many suggestions, five deserve mention.

1. Hill, J.B. Taylor (Douglas, *Bible Dictionary*, 3:1625), and others support W.C. van Unnik's argument ("Dominus Vobiscum," *New Testament Essays*, ed. A.J.B. Higgins [Manchester: University Press, 1959], pp. 270–305), who claimed Isaiah meant that a young woman named her child Immanuel as a tribute to God's presence and deliverance and that the passage applies to Jesus because Immanuel fits his mission. This does not take the "sign" (Isa 7:11, 14) seriously; v.11 expects something spectacular. Nor does it adequately consider the time lapse (vv.15–17). Moreover, it assumes a very casual link between Isaiah and Matthew.

2. Many others take Isaiah as saying that a young woman—a virgin at the time of the prophecy (Broadus)—would bear a son and that before he reaches the age of discretion (perhaps less than two years from the time of the prophecy), Ahaz will be delivered from his enemies. Matthew, being an inspired writer, sees a later fulfillment in Jesus; and we must accept it on Matthew's authority. W.S. LaSor thinks this provides canonical support for a *sensus plenior* ("fuller sense") approach to Scripture ("The *Sensus Plenior* and Biblical Interpretation," *Scripture, Tradition, and Interpretation*, edd. W. Ward Gasque and William S. LaSor [Grand Rapids: Eerdmans, 1978], pp. 271–72). In addition to several deficiencies in interpreting Isaiah 7:14–17 (e.g., the supernaturalness of the sign in 7:11 is not continued in 7:14), this position is intrinsically unstable, seeking either a deeper connection between Isaiah and Matthew or less reliance on Matthew's authority. Hendriksen (p. 140) holds that the destruction of Pekah and Rezin was a clear sign that the line of the Messiah was being protected. But this is to postulate, without textual warrant, two signs—the sign of the child and the sign of the deliverance—and it presupposes that Ahaz possessed remarkable theological acumen in recognizing the latter sign.

3. Many (esp. older) commentators (e.g., Alexander, Hengstenberg, Young) reject any notion of double fulfillment and say that Isaiah 7:14 refers exclusively to Jesus Christ. This does justice to the expectation of a miraculous sign, the significance of "Immanuel," and the most likely meaning of 'almāh and parthenos. But it puts more strain on the relation of a sign to Ahaz. It seems weak to say that before a period of time equivalent to the length of time between Jesus' (Immanuel's) conception and his reaching an age of discretion Ahaz's enemies will be destroyed. Most commentators in this group insist on a miraculous element in "sign" (v.11). But though Immanuel's birth is miraculous, how is the "sign" given Ahaz miraculous?

4. A few have argued, most recently Gene Rice ("A Neglected Interpretation of the Immanuel Prophecy," ZAW 90 [1978]: 220–27), that in Isaiah 7:14–17 Immanuel represents the righteous remnant—God is "with them"—and that the mother is Zion. This may be fairly applied to Jesus and Mary in Matthew 1:23, since Jesus' personal history seems to recapitulate something of the Jews' national history (cf. 2:15; 4:1–4). Yet this sounds contrived. Would Ahaz have understood the words so metaphorically? And though Jesus sometimes appears to recapitulate Israel, it is doubtful that NT writers ever thought Mary recapitulates Zion.

5. The most plausible view is that of J.A. Motyer ("Context and Content in the Interpretation of Isaiah 7:14," *Tyndale Bulletin* 21 [1970]: 118–25). It is a modified form of the third interpretation and depends in part on recognizing a crucial feature in Isaiah. Signs in the OT may function as a "present persuader" (e.g., Exod 4:8–9) or as "future confirmation" (e.g., Exod 3:12). Isaiah 7:14 falls in the latter case because Immanuel's birth comes too late to be a "present persuader." The "sign" (v.11) points primarily to threat and foreboding. Ahaz has rejected the Lord's gracious offer (vv.10–12), and Isaiah responds in wrath (v.13). The "curds and honey" Immanuel will eat (v.15) represent the only food left in the land on the day of wrath (vv.18–22). Even the promise of Ephraim's destruction (v.8) must be understood to embrace a warning (v.9b; Motyer, "Isaiah 7:14," pp. 121–22). Isaiah sees a threat, not simply to Ahaz, but to the "house of David" (vv.2, 13) caught up in faithlessness. To this faithless house Isaiah utters his prophecy. Therefore Immanuel's birth follows the coming events (it is a "future confirmation") and will take place when the Davidic dynasty has lost the throne.

Motyer shows the close parallels between the prophetic word to Judah (7:1–9:7) and the prophetic word to Ephraim (9:8–11:16). To both there come the moment of decision as the Lord's word threatens wrath (7:1–17; 9:8–10:4), the time of judgment mediated by the Assyrian invasion (7:18–8:8; 10:5–15), the destruction of God's foes but the salvation of a remnant (8:9–22; 10:16–34), and the promise of a glorious hope as the Davidic monarch reigns and brings prosperity to his people (9:1–7; 11:1–16). The twofold structure argues for the cohesive unity between the prophecy of Judah and that to Ephraim. If this is correct, Isaiah 7:1–9:7 must be read as a unit—i.e., 7:14 must not be treated in isolation. The promised Immanuel (7:14) will possess the land (8:8), thwart all opponents (8:10), appear in Galilee of the Gentiles (9:1) as a great light to those in the land of the shadow of death (9:2). He is the Child and Son called "Wonderful Counselor, Mighty God, Everlasting Father, Prince of Peace" in 9:6, whose government and peace will never end as he reigns on David's throne forever (9:7).

Much of Motyer's work is confirmed by a recent article by Joseph Jensen ("The Age of Immanuel," CBQ 41 [1979]: 220–39; he does not refer to Motyer), who extends the plausibility of this structure by showing that Isaiah 7:15 should be taken in a final sense; i.e., Immanuel will eat the bread of affliction in order to learn (unlike Ahaz!) the lesson of obedience. There is no reference to "age of discretion." Further, Jensen believes that 7:16–25 points to Immanuel's coming only after the destruction of the land (6:9–13 suggests the destruction extends to Judah as well as to Israel); that Immanuel and Maher-Shalal-Hash-Baz, Isaiah's son (8:1), are not the same; and that only Isaiah's son sets a time limit relevant to Ahaz.

The foregoing discussion was unavoidable. For if Motyer's view fairly represents Isaiah's thought, and if Matthew understood him in this way, then much light is shed on the first Gospel. The Immanuel figure of Isaiah 7:14 is a messianic figure, a point Matthew has rightly grasped. Moreover this interpretation turns on an understanding of the place of the Exile in Isaiah 6–12, and Matthew has divided up his genealogy (1:11–12, 17) precisely in order to draw attention to the Exile. In 2:17–18 the theme of the Exile returns. A little later, as Jesus begins his ministry (4:12–16), Matthew quotes Isaiah 9:1–2, which, if the interpretation adopted here is correct, properly belongs to the Immanuel prophecies of Isaiah 7:14, 9:6. Small wonder that after such comments by Matthew, Jesus' next words announced the kingdom (4:17; cf. Isa 9:7). Isaiah's reference to Immanuel's affliction for the sake of learning obedience (cf. on Isa 7:15 above) anticipates Jesus' humiliation, suffering, and obedient sonship, a recurring theme in this Gospel.

This interpretation also partially explains Matthew's interest in the Davidic lineage; and it strengthens a strong interpretation of "Immanuel." Most scholars (e.g., Bonnard) suppose that this name in Isaiah reflects a hope that God would make himself present with his people ("Immanuel" derives from ʿ immānû ʾēl, "God with us"); and they apply the name to Jesus in a similar way, to mean that God is with us, and for us, because of Jesus. But if Immanuel in Isaiah is a messianic figure whose titles include "Mighty God," there is reason to think that "Immanuel" refers to Jesus himself, that he is "God with us." Matthew's use of the preposition "with" at the end of 1:23 favors this (cf. Fenton, "Matthew 1:20–23," p. 81). Though "Immanuel" is not a name in the sense that "Jesus" is Messiah's name (1:21), in the OT Solomon was named "Jedidiah" ("Beloved of Yahweh," 2 Sam 12:25), even though he apparently was not called that. Similarly Immanuel is a "name" in the sense of title or description.

No greater blessing can be conceived than for God to dwell with his people (Isa 60:18–20); Ezek 48:35; Rev 21:23). Jesus is the one called "God with us": the designation evokes John 1:14, 18. As if that were not enough, Jesus promises just before his ascension to be with us to the end of the age (28:20; cf. also 18:20), when he will return to share his messianic banquet with his people (25:10).

If "Immanuel" is rightly interpreted in this sense, then the question must be raised whether "Jesus" (1:21) should receive the same treatment. Does "Jesus" ("Yahweh saves") mean Mary's Son merely brings Yahweh's salvation, or is he himself in some sense the Yahweh who saves? If "Immanuel" entails the higher christology, it is not implausible that Matthew sees the same in "Jesus." The least we can say is that Matthew does not hesitate to apply OT passages descriptive of Yahweh directly to Jesus (cf. on 3:3).

Matthew's quotation of Isaiah 7:14 is very close to the LXX; but he changes "you will call" to "they will call." This may reflect a rendering of the original Hebrew, if 1QIsaᵃ is pointed appropriately (cf. Gundry, *Use of OT*, p. 90). But there is more here: The people whose sins Jesus forgives (1:21) are the ones who will gladly call him "God with us" (cf. Frankmölle, pp. 17–19).

24–25. When Joseph woke up (from his sleep, not his dream), he "took Mary home as his wife" (v.24; same expression as in 1:20). Throughout Matthew 1–2 the pattern of God's sovereign intervention followed by Joseph's or the Magi's response is repeated. While the story is told simply, Joseph's obedience and submission under these circumstances is scarcely less remarkable than Mary's (Luke 1:38).

Matthew wants to make Jesus' virginal conception quite unambiguous, for he adds that Joseph had no sexual union with Mary (lit., he did not "know" her, an OT euphemism) until she gave birth to Jesus (v.25). The "until" clause most naturally means that Mary and Joseph enjoyed normal conjugal relations after Jesus' birth (cf. further on 12:46; 13:55). Contrary to McHugh (p. 204), the imperfect *eginōsken* ("did not know [her]") does not hint at continued celibacy after Jesus' birth but stresses the faithfulness of the celibacy till Jesus' birth.

So the virgin-conceived Immanuel was born. And eight days later, when the time came for him to be circumcised (Luke 2:21), Joseph named him "Jesus."

Notes

18 Some MSS have γέννησις (*gennēsis*, "birth") instead of γένεσις (*genesis*, "birth," "origin," or "history"): the two words are easily confused both orthographically and, in early pronunciation systems, phonetically. The former word is common in the Fathers to refer to the Nativity and is cognate with γεννάω (*gennaō*, "I beget"); so it is transcriptionally less likely to be original.

The δέ (*de*, "but") beginning the verse is doubtless a mild adversative. All the preceding generations have been listed, "but" the birth of Jesus comes into a class of its own.

Οὕτως (*houtōs*, "thus") with the verb ἦν (*ēn*, "was") is rare and is here equivalent to τοιαύτη (*toiautē*, "in this way"; cf. BDF, par. 434 [2]).

"Holy Spirit" is anarthrous, which is not uncommon in the Gospels; and in that case the word order is always πνεῦμα ἅγιον (*pneuma hagion*). When the article is used, there is an approximately even distribution between τὸ ἅγιον πνεῦμα (*to hagion pneuma*, "the Holy Spirit") and τὸ πνεῦμα τὸ ἅγιον (*to pneuma to hagion*, "the Spirit the Holy"); cf. Moule, *Idiom Book*, p. 113.

19 In δίκαιος ὢν καὶ μὴ θέλων (*dikaios ōn kai mē thelōn*, lit., "being just and not willing"; NIV, "a righteous man and did not want"), it does not seem possible to take the first participle concessively (i.e., "although a righteous man") because of the *kai*; the two participles should be taken as coordinate.

20 Ἰδού (*idou*, "behold") appears for the first of sixty-two times in Matthew. It often introduces surprising action (Schlatter), or serves to arouse interest (Hendriksen); but it is so common it seems sometimes to have no force at all (cf. Moulton, *Prolegomena*, p. 11; E.J. Pryke, "IΔE and IΔOY," NTS 14 [1968]: 418–24).

21 The noun ἁμαρτία (*hamartia*, "sin") occurs at 3:6; 9:2, 5–6; 12:31; 26:38; ἁμαρτάνω (*hamartanō*, "I sin") is found at 18:15, 21; 27:4; and ἁμαρτωλός (*hamartōlos*, "sinner") at 9:10–11, 13; 11:19; 26:45.

22 Contrary to Moule (*Idiom Book*, p. 142), the ἵνα (*hina*, "in order to" or "with the result that") clause is not ecbatic (consecutive). Although in NT Greek *hina* is not always telic, yet the very idea of fulfillment presupposes an overarching plan; and if there be such a plan, it is difficult to imagine Matthew saying no more than that such and such took place with the result that the Scriptures were fulfilled, unless the Mind behind the plan has no power to effect it—which is clearly contrary to Matthew's thought. See further on 5:17.

C. The Visit of the Magi

2:1–12

¹After Jesus was born in Bethlehem in Judea, during the time of King Herod, , Magi from the east came to Jerusalem ²and asked, "Where is the one who has been born king of the Jews? We saw his star in the east and have come to worship him."

³When King Herod heard this he was disturbed, and all Jerusalem with him. ⁴When he had called together all the people's chief priests and teachers of the law, he asked them where the Christ was to be born. ⁵"In Bethlehem in Judea," they replied, "for this is what the prophet has written:

⁶" 'But you, Bethlehem, in the land of Judah,
    are by no means least among the rulers of Judah;
for out of you will come a ruler
    who will be the shepherd of my people Israel.' "

⁷Then Herod called the Magi secretly and found out from them the exact time the star had appeared. ⁸He sent them to Bethlehem and said, "Go and make a careful search for the child. As soon as you find him, report to me, so that I too may go and worship him."

⁹After they had heard the king, they went on their way, and the star they had seen in the east went ahead of them until it stopped over the place where the child was. ¹⁰When they saw the star, they were overjoyed. ¹¹On coming to the house, they saw the child with his mother Mary, and they bowed down and worshiped him. Then they opened their treasures and presented him with gifts of gold and of incense and of myrrh. ¹²And having been warned in a dream not to go back to Herod, they returned to their country by another route.

Few passages have received more diverse interpretations than this one (cf. W.A. Schulze, "Zur Geschichte der Auslegung von Matth. 2,1–12," *Theologische Zeitschrift* 31 [1975]: 150–60: M. Hengel and H. Merkel, "Die Magier aus dem Osten und die Flucht nach Ägypten (Mt 2) im Rahmen der antiken Religionsgeschichte und der Theologie des Matthäus," in Hoffmann et al., pp. 139–69). During the last hundred years or so, such diversity has sometimes sprung from a reluctance to accept either the supernatural details or the entire story as historically true. Thus it becomes necessary to find theological motive for creating the pericope. E. Nellessen (*Das Kind und seine Mutter* [Stuttgart: KBW, 1969]), though acute in his theological observations, maintains the evangelist has fused and improved two Palestinian (and probably Galilean) legends (similarly Soarés Prabhu, pp. 261–93).

Many (e.g., Gundry, Hill, Schweizer) suppose that the OT quotations constituted a collection of testimonia to Jesus in their own right, before Matthew (or the church from which he sprang) embellished them with midrashic stories to produce our Matthew 2. The stories have doubtful ties with history. Their real point is theological, to show that the Messiah was born in Bethlehem as predicted, that his appearance provoked Jewish hostility but won Gentile acceptance (the Magi), and above all to set up a contrast between Moses and Jesus.

Jewish tradition is steeped in stories about Pharaoh's astrologers knowing that the mother of Israel's future deliverer was pregnant, that there was a slaughter (by drowning) of all Jewish and Egyptian infants for the next nine months, that the entire house in which Moses was born was filled with great light, etc. Matthew, therefore, may have been trying to show Jesus' significance by ascribing to his birth similar and perhaps greater effects. Full-blown, these stories about Moses are preserved in Midrash Rabbah on Exodus 1, an eighth century A.D. compilation. Their roots, however, stretch at least as far back as the first century (Jos. Antiq. II, 205-7, 15-16[ix.2-3]; cf. also Targ. j on Exod 1:15; and Davies, *Setting*, pp. 78-82, for other veiled hints to Moses in Matt. 1-2).

This reconstruction has numerous weaknesses. The independent existence of collected testimonia is not certain. There is no evidence of Midrashim written on such a diverse collection of texts (if the collection itself ever existed). The presupposed antithesis between theology and history is false; on the face of it, Matthew records history so as to bring out its theological significance and its relation to Scripture. Matthew writes at so early a time that if Jesus had not been born in Bethlehem this claim would have been challenged. We are dealing with decades, not the millennium and a half separating Moses from Josephus.

First-century stories about astrological deductions connected with Augustus Caesar's birth (Suetonius *De Vita Caesarum* 94), about Parthian visits to Nero (Cicero *De Divinatione* 1.47), or about Moses' birth (above) may suggest that Matthew 2:1-12 was fabricated; but they may equally attest the prevalence of astrology and the fact that some such visits undoubtedly occurred in the ancient world. Thus they would establish the verisimilitude of the passage. More important, the stories about Moses' birth (e.g., in Jos.) were almost certainly regarded by most readers as factually true; and there can be little doubt (contra Gundry) that Matthew intends his stories about Jesus to be read the same way. If so, we may conceivably argue that Matthew was himself deceived or else wished to deceive. What we cannot do is to argue that he wrote in a fashion recognized by its form to be divorced from historical reality. In any case, the suggested backdrop—stories about Moses' birth—is not very apt; close study shows the theological matrix of the prologue centering on Jesus as the Davidic King and Son of God (cf. esp. Nolan; Kingsbury, *Matthew*), not on him as the new Moses, to whom the allusions are few and inexplicit.

Of course Matthew did not just chronicle meaningless events. He wrote to develop his theme of fulfillment of Scripture (Had not God promised that nations would be drawn to Messiah's light [Isa 60:3]?); to establish God's providential and supernatural care of this virgin-born Son; to anticipate the hostilities, resentment, and suffering he would face; and to hint at the fact that Gentiles would be drawn into his reign (cf. Isa 60:3; Nellessen, *Das Kind*, p. 120, acutely compares 8:11-12; cf. 28:16-20). The Magi will be like the men of Nineveh who will rise up in judgment and condemn those who, despite their privilege of much greater light, did not receive the promised Messiah and bow to his reign (12:41-42).

1 Bethlehem, the place near which Jacob buried his Rachel (Gen 35:19) and Ruth met Boaz (Ruth 1:22-2:6), was preeminently the town where David was born and reared. For Christians it has become the place where angel hosts broke the silence and announced Messiah's birth (Luke 2). It is distinguished from the Bethlehem in Zebulun (Josh 19:15) by the words "in Judea." Scholars have seen in these two words a preparation for v.6: "Bethlehem, in the land of Judah" (though there the Hebrew form "Judah" is used rather than the Greek "Judea"), or for v.2: "king of the Jews." But "Bethlehem in Judea" may be not much more than a stereotyped phrase (cf. Judg 17:7, 9; 19:1–20; Ruth 1:1–2; 1 Sam 17:12; Matt 2:5). Luke 2:39 makes no mention of an extended stay in Bethlehem and a trip to Egypt before the return to Nazareth; if he knew of these events, Luke found them irrelevant to his purpose.

Unlike Luke, Matthew offers no description of Jesus' birth or the shepherd's visit; he specifies the time of Jesus' birth as having occurred during King Herod's reign (so also Luke 1:5). Herod the Great, as he is now called, was born in 73 B.C. and was named king of Judea by the Roman Senate in 40 B.C. By 37 B.C. he had crushed, with the help of Roman forces, all opposition to his rule. Son of the Idumean Antipater, he was wealthy, politically gifted, intensely loyal, an excellent administrator, and clever enough to remain in the good graces of successive Roman emperors. His famine relief was superb and his building projects (including the temple, begun 20 B.C.) admired even by his foes. But he loved power, inflicted incredibly heavy taxes on the people, and resented the fact that many Jews considered him a usurper. In his last years, suffering an illness that compounded his paranoia, he turned to cruelty and in fits of rage and jealousy killed close associates, his wife Mariamne (of Jewish descent from the Maccabeans), and at least two of his sons (cf. Jos. Antiq. XIV–XVIII; S. Perowne, *The Life and Times of Herod the Great* [London: Hodder and Stoughton, 1956]; and esp. Abraham Schalit, *König Herodes: Der Mann und sein Werk* [Berlin: de Gruyter, 1969]).

Traditionally some have argued that Herod died in 4 B.C.; so Jesus must have been born before that. Josephus (Antiq. XVII, 167[vi.4]) mentions an eclipse of the moon shortly before Herod's death, and this has normally been identified as having occurred on 12–13 March 4 B.C. After Herod's death there was a Passover celebration (Jos. Wars II, 10[i.3]; Antiq. XVII, 213[ix.3]), presumably 11 April 4 B.C.; so the date of his death at first glance seems secure. Recently, however, Ernest L. Martin (*The Birth of Christ Recalculated!* [Pasadena: FBR, 1978], pp. 22–49) has advanced solid reasons for thinking the eclipse occurred 10 January 1 B.C.; and, integrating this information with his interpretation of other relevant data, Martin proposes a birth date for Jesus in September, 2 B.C. (His detailed pinpointing of 1 Sept., based on his understanding of Rev 12:1–5, is too speculative to be considered.) Several lines of evidence stand against this thesis: Josephus dates the length of Herod's reign as thirty-seven years from his accession or thirty-four from the time of his effective reign (Antiq. XVII, 191[viii.1]; Wars I, 665[xxxiii.8], and these favor a death date in 4 B.C. Coins dated at the time of 4 B.C., minted under the reign of Herod's sons, support the traditional date.

Martin answers these objections by supposing that Herod's successors antedated their reigns to 4 B.C. in honor of Herod's sons Alexander and Aristobulus whom he had killed in that year and by arguing that between 4 B.C. and 1 B.C. there was some form of joint rule shared by Herod and his son Antipater. In that case Josephus's figures relating to the length of Herod's rule refer to his unshared reign. This is psychologically unconvincing; the man who murdered two of his sons out of paranoia and jealousy and arranged to have hundreds of Jewish leaders executed on the day of his death was not likely to share his authority, even in a merely formal way. The question remains unresolved. For a more traditional dating of Jesus' birth in late 5 B.C. or early 4 B.C., see Hoehner, *Chronological Aspects*, pp. 11–27 (written before Martin's work).

The "Magi" (*magoi*) are not easily identified with precision. Several centuries earlier the term was used for a priestly caste of Medes who enjoyed special power to interpret dreams. Daniel (1:20; 2:2; 4:7; 5:7) refers to *magoi* in the Babylonian Empire. In later centuries down to NT times, the term loosely covered a wide variety of men interested in dreams, astrology, magic, books thought to contain mysterious references to the future, and the like. Some Magi honestly inquired after truth; many were rogues and charlatans (e.g., Acts 8:9; 13:6, 8; cf. R.E. Brown, *Birth of Messiah*, pp. 167–68, 197–200; TDNT, 4:356–59). Apparently these men came to Bethlehem spurred on by astrological calculations. But they had probably built up their expectation of a kingly figure by working through assorted Jewish books (cf. W.M. Ramsey, *The Bearing of Recent Discovery on the Trustworthiness of the New Testament*, 4th ed. [London: Hodder and Stoughton, 1920], pp. 140–49).

The tradition that the Magi were kings can be traced as far back as Tertullian (died c. 225). It probably developed under the influence of OT passages that say kings will come and worship Messiah (cf. Pss 68:29, 31; 72:10–11; Isa 49:7; 60:1–6). The theory that there were *three* "wise men" is probably a deduction from the *three* gifts (2:11). By the end of the sixth century, the wise men were named: Melkon (later Melchior), Balthasar, and Gasper. Matthew gives no names. His *magoi* come to Jerusalem (which, like Bethlehem, has strong Davidic connections [2 Sam 5:5–9]), arriving, apparently (cf. Note 5), from the east—possibly from Babylon, where a sizable Jewish settlement wielded considerable influence, but possibly from Persia or from the Arabian desert. The more distant Babylon may be supported by the travel time apparently required (see on 2:16).

2 The Magi saw a star "when it rose" (NIV mg.; cf. note at 2:1). What they saw remains uncertain.

1. Kepler (died 1630) pointed out that in the Roman year A.U.C. 747 (7 B.C.), there occurred a conjunction of the planets Jupiter and Saturn in the zodiacal constellation of Pisces, a sign sometimes connected in ancient astrology with the Hebrews. Many details can be fitted to this suggestion (Alf; R.E. Brown, *Birth of Messiah*, pp. 172–73; DNTT, 3:735; Maier), not least that medieval Jews saw messianic significance in the same planetary conjunction. Moreover the conjunction occurred in May, October, and November of 7 B.C.; and one of the latter two appearances could account for 2:9. But there is no solid evidence that the ancients referred to such conjunctions as "stars"; and even at their closest proximity, Jupiter and Saturn would have been about one degree apart—a perceived distance about twice the diameter of the moon—and therefore never fused into one image.

2. Kepler himself preferred the suggestion that this was a supernova—a faint star that violently explodes and gives off enormous amounts of light for a few weeks or months. The suggestion is no more than guess: there is no confirming evidence, and it is difficult on this theory to account for 2:9.

3. Others have suggested comets, what some older writers refer to as "variable stars." The most likely is Halley's Comet (cf. Lagrange), which passed overhead in 12 B.C.; but this seems impossibly early.

4. Martin opts for a number of planetary conjunctions and massings in 3/2 B.C. This suggestion depends on his entire reconstruction and late date for Herod's death (see on 2:1), which is no more than a possibility. The theory also shares some of the difficulties of 1.

5. In the light of 2:9, many commentators insist that astronomical considerations are a waste of time: Matthew presents the "star" as strictly supernatural. This too is possible and obviously impossible to falsify, but 2:9 is not as determinative as is often suggested (cf. on 2:9). The evidence is inconclusive.

Matthew uses language almost certainly alluding to Numbers 24:17: "A star will come out of Jacob; a scepter will rise out of Israel." This oracle, spoken by Balaam, who came "from the eastern mountains" (Num 23:7), was widely regarded as messianic (Targ. Jonathan and Onkelos; CD 7:19–20; 1QM 11:6; 1QSb 5:27; 4QTest 12–13; T Judah 24:1). Both Matthew and Numbers deal with the king of Israel (cf. Num 24:7), though Matthew does not resort to the uncontrolled allegorizing on "star" frequently found in early postapostolic Christian writings (cf. Jean Daniélou, *The Theology of Jewish Christianity* [London: Darton, Longman & Todd, 1964], pp. 214–24).

Granting Matthew's informed devotion to the OT, he surely knew that the OT mocks astrologers (Isa 47:13–15; Dan 1:20; 2:27; 4:7; 5:7) and forbids astrology (Jer 10:1–2). Nevertheless it was widely practiced in the first century, even among Jews (cf. Albright and Mann). Matthew neither condemns nor sanctions it; instead, he contrasts the eagerness of the Magi to worship Jesus, despite their limited knowledge, with the apathy of the Jewish leaders and the hostility of Herod's court—all of whom had the Scriptures to inform them. Formal knowledge of the Scriptures, Matthew implies, does not in itself lead to knowing who Jesus is; just as God sovereignly worked through Caesar's decree that a census be taken (Luke 2:1) to ensure Jesus' birth in Bethlehem to fulfill prophecy, so God sovereignly used the Magi's calculations to bring about the situation this pericope describes.

The question the Magi asked does not tell how their astrology led them to seek a "king of the Jews" and what made them think this particular star was "his." The widely held idea that the ancient world was looking for a Jewish leader of renown (based largely on Jos. War VI, 312–13[v.4]; Suetonius *Vespasian* 4; Tacitus *Histories* v.13; Virgil *Eclogue* 4) cannot stand close scrutiny. The Josephus passage refers to Jewish expectations of Messiah, and the others probably borrowed from Josephus. The Magi may have linked the star to "the king of the Jews" through studying the OT and other Jewish writings—a possibility made plausible by the presence of the large Jewish community in Babylon.

We must not think that the Magi's question meant, Where is the one born to become king of the Jews? but, Where is the one born king of the Jews? (cf. Notes). His kingly status was not conferred on him later on; it was his from birth. Jesus' participation in the Davidic dynasty has already been established by the genealogy. The same title the Magi gave him found its place over the cross (27:37).

"Worship" (cf. Notes) need not imply that the Magi recognized Jesus' divinity; it may simply mean "do homage" (Broadus). Their own statement suggests homage paid royalty rather than the worship of Deity. But Matthew, having already told of the virginal conception, doubtless expected his readers to discern something more —viz., that the Magi "worshiped" better than they knew.

3 In contrast with (*de*, a mild adversative; NIV, "when") the Magi's desire to worship the King of the Jews, Herod is deeply troubled. In this "all Jerusalem" joins him, not because most of the people would have been sorry to see Herod replaced or because they were reluctant to see the coming of King Messiah, but because they well knew that any question like the Magi's would result in more cruelty from the ailing Herod, whose paranoia had led him to murder his favorite wife and two sons.

4 Here "all" modifies "chief priests and teachers of the law," not "the people," and refers to those who were living in Jerusalem and could be quickly consulted. "Chief

priests" refers to the hierarchy, made up of the current high priest and any who had formerly occupied this post (since Herod, contrary to the law, made fairly frequent changes in the high priesthood) and a substantial number of other leading priests (cf. Jos. Antiq. XX, 180[viii.8]; War IV, 159–60[iii.9]; the same Greek word is used for "high priests" and "chief priests"). The "teachers of the law," or "scribes" as other EV call them, were experts in the OT and in its copious oral tradition. Their work was not so much copying out OT MSS (as the word "scribes" suggests) as teaching the OT. Because much civil law was based on the OT and the interpretations of the OT fostered by the leaders, the "scribes" were also "lawyers" (cf. 22:35: "an expert in the law").

The vast majority of the scribes were Pharisees; the priests were Sadducees. The two groups barely got along, and therefore Schweizer (*Matthew*) judges this verse "historically almost inconceivable." But Matthew does not say the two groups came together at the same time; Herod, unloved by either group, may well have called both to guard against being tricked. If the Pharisees and Sadducees barely spoke to one another, there was less likelihood of collusion. "He asked them" (*epynthaneto*, the imperfect tense sometimes connotes tentative requests: Herod may have expected the rebuff of silence; cf. Turner, *Insights*, p. 27) where the Christ (here a title: see on 1:1) would be born, understanding that "the Christ" and "the king of the Jews" (2:2) were titles of the same expected person. (See 26:63; 27:37 for the same equivalence.)

5 The Jewish leaders answered the question by referring to what stands written, which is the force of the perfect passive verb *gegraptai* (NIV, "has written"), suggesting the authoritative and regulative force of the document referred to (Deiss BS, pp. 112–14, 249–50). NIV misses the preposition *dia* (lit., "what stands written *through* the prophet"), which implies that the prophet is not the ultimate source of what stands written (cf. on 1:22). Both in 1:22 and here, some textual witnesses insert the name of the prophet (e.g., Micah or even Isaiah). "Bethlehem in Judea" was introduced into the narrative in 2:1.

6 While expectation that the Messiah must come from Bethlehem occurs elsewhere (e.g., John 7:42; cf. Targ. on Mic 5:1: "Out of you shall come forth before me the Messiah"), here it rests on Micah 5:2(1 MT), to which are appended some words from 2 Samuel 5:2 (1 Chron 11:2). Matthew follows neither the MT nor the LXX, and his changes have provoked considerable speculation.

1. "Bethlehem Ephrathah" (LXX, "house of Ephrathah") becomes "Bethlehem, in the land of Judah." Hill (*Matthew*) says this change was made to exclude "any other Judean city like Jerusalem." But this reads too much into what is a normal LXX way of referring to Bethlehem (cf. Gundry, *Use of OT*, p. 91). "Ephrathah" is archaic and even in the MT primarily restricted to poetical sections like Micah 5:2.

2. The strong negative "by no means" (*oudamōs*) is added in Matthew and formally contradicts Micah 5:2. It is often argued that this change has been made to highlight Bethlehem as the birthplace of the Messiah. Indeed, Gundry's commentary uses this change as an example of Matthew's midrashic use of the OT, a use so free that he does not fear outright contradiction. There are better explanations. Even the MT of Micah implies Bethlehem's greatness: "though you are small among the clans [or rulers, who personify the cities; KJV's 'thousands' is pedantically cor-

rect, but 'thousands' was a way of referring to the great clans into which the tribes were subdivided; cf. Judg 6:15; 1 Sam 10:19; 23:23; Isa 60:22] of Judah" sets the stage for the greatness that follows. Equally, Matthew's formulation assumes that, apart from being Messiah's birthplace, Bethlehem is indeed of little importance (cf. Hengstenberg, 1:475–76, noted by Gundry, *Use of OT*, pp. 91–92). To put it another way, though the second line of Micah 5:2 formally contradicts the second line of Matthew 2:6, a wholistic reading of the verses shows the contradiction to be merely formal. Matthew 2:6 has perhaps slightly greater emphasis on the one factor that makes Bethlehem great.

3. Matthew adds the shepherd language of 2 Samuel 5:2, making it plain that the ruler in Micah 5:2 is none other than the one who fulfills the promises to David.

It is tempting to think that Matthew sees a pair of contrasts (1) between the false shepherds of Israel who have provided sound answers but no leadership (cf. 23:2–7) and Jesus who is the true Shepherd of his people Israel and (2) between a ruler like Herod and the one born to rule. The words "my people Israel" are included, not simply because they are found in 2 Samuel 5:2, but because Matthew, like Paul, faithfully records both the esssential Jewish focus of the OT promises and the OT expectation of broader application to the Gentiles (cf. on 1:1, 5, 21). Jesus is not only the promised Davidic king but also the promised hope of blessing to all the nations, the one who will claim their obeisance (cf. Ps 68:28–35; Isa 18:1–3, 7; 45:14; 60:6; Zeph 3:10). That same duality makes the desires of the Gentile Magi to worship the Messiah stand out against the apathy of the leaders who did not, apparently, take the trouble to go to Bethlehem. Of course, the Jewish leaders may have seen the arrival of the Magi in Jerusalem as one more false alarm.

As far as we can tell, the Sadducees (and therefore the chief priests) had no interest in the question of when the Messiah would come; the Pharisees (and therefore most teachers of the law) expected him to come only somewhat later. The Essenes alone, who were not consulted by Herod, expected the Messiah imminently (cf. R.T. Beckwith, "The Significance of the Calendar for Interpreting Essene Chronology and Eschatology," *Revue de Qumran* 38 [1980]: 167–202). But Matthew plainly says that, though Jesus was the Messiah, born in David's line and certain to be Shepherd and Ruler of Israel, it was the Gentiles who came to worship him.

7–10 The reason Herod wanted to learn, at his secret meeting with the Magi (v.7), the exact time the star appeared was that he had already schemed to kill the small boys of Bethlehem (cf. v.16). The entire story hangs together (see on v.16). Herod's hypocritical humility—"so that I may go and worship him" (v.8)—deceived the Magi. Conscious of his success, Herod sent no escort with them. This was not "absurdly trusting" (Schweizer, *Matthew*), since the deception depended on winning the Magi's confidence. Herod could scarcely have been expected to foresee God's intervention (v.12).

Matthew does not say that the rising star the Magi had seen (cf. on 2:2) led them to Jerusalem. They went first to the capital city because they thought it the natural place for the King of the Jews to be born. But now the star reappeared ahead of them (v.9) as they made their way to Bethlehem (it was not uncommon to travel at night). Taking this as confirming their purposes, the Magi were overjoyed (v.10). The Greek text does not imply that the star pointed out the house where Jesus was; it may simply have hovered over Bethlehem as the Magi approached it. They would then have found the exact house through discreet inquiry since (Luke 2:17–18) the shepherds who came to worship the newborn Jesus did not keep silent about what they saw.

11 This verse plainly alludes to Psalm 72:10–11 and Isaiah 60:6, passages that reinforce the emphasis on the Gentiles (cf. on v.6). Nolan's suggestion (pp. 206–9) that the closest parallel is Isaiah 39:1–2 is linguistically attractive but contextually weak. The evidence that Hezekiah served as an eschatological figure is poor and fails to explain why he should be opening up his treasure store to his visitors. Some time had elapsed since Jesus' birth (vv.7, 16), and the family was settled in a house. While the Magi saw both the child and his mother, their worship (cf. on v.2) was for him alone.

Bringing gifts was particularly important in the ancient East when approaching a superior (cf. Gen 43:11; 1 Sam 9:7–8; 1 Kings 10:2). Usually such gifts were reciprocated (Derrett, *NT Studies*, 2:28). That is not mentioned here, but a first-century reader might have assumed it and seen the Great Commission (28:18–20) as leading to its abundant fruition. Frankincense is a glittering, odorous gum obtained by making incisions in the bark of several trees; myrrh exudes from a tree found in Arabia and a few other places and was a much-valued spice and perfume (Ps 45:8; S of Songs 3:6) used in embalming (John 19:39). Commentators, ancient (Origen, *Contra Celsum* 1.60) and modern (Hendriksen), have found symbolic value in the three gifts—gold suggesting royalty, incense divinity, and myrrh the Passion and burial. This interpretation demands too much insight from the Magi. The three gifts were simply expensive and not uncommon presents and may have helped finance the trip to Egypt. The word "treasures" probably means "coffers" or "treasure-boxes" in this context.

12 This second dream (cf. 1:20) mentions no angel. Perhaps Joseph and the Magi compared notes and saw their danger (cf. P. Gaechter, "Die Magierperikope," *Zeitschrift für Katholische Theologie* 90 [1968]: 257–95); amid their fear and uncertainty, the dreams led them (vv.12–13) to flee. Which way the Magi went is unclear; they might have gone around the north end of the Dead Sea, avoiding Jerusalem, or they might have gone around the south end of the sea.

Notes

1–2 The word ἀνατολή (*anatolē*) can mean "rising" or "east." In v.1 ἀπὸ ἀνατολῶν (*apo anatolōn*, "from the east") is rightly translated by NIV, since the noun normally indicates the point of the compass when it is plural and anarthrous (cf. BDF, 253[5]). By the same token ἐν τῇ ἀνατολῇ (*en tē anatolē*) in vv.2, 9 is less likely to be "in the East" than "at its rising" (the article can have mild possessive force). Other suggestions—e.g., that the expression refers to a particular land in the east or to Anatolia in the west—seem less convincing; but the question is extraordinarily complex (cf. Turner, *Insights*, pp. 25–26; R.E. Brown, *Birth of Messiah*, p. 173).

2 The participle in the construction ὁ τεχθεὶς βασιλεύς (*ho techtheis basileus*, lit., "the born king") is adjectival, not substantival, and is used attributively. Moreover there is no suggestion of "newborn" (cf. C. Burchard, "Fussnoten zum neutestamentlichen Griechisch II," ZNW 29 [1978]: 143–57), which is already ruled out by chronological notes (vv.7, 16).

The verb προσκυνέω (proskyneō, "worship") occurs three times in this pericope (cf. vv.8, 11) and ten other times in Matthew. In the NT the object of this "worship" is almost always God or Jesus, except where someone is acting ignorantly and is rebuked (Acts 10:25–26; Rev 19:10; 22:8–9). But Rev 3:9 is an important exception (NIV, "fall down at your feet"). Secular Greek used the verb for a wide variety of levels of obeisance, and it is precarious to build too much christology on the use of the term in the Gospels.

3 The words πᾶσα Ἱεροσόλυμα (pasa Hierosolyma, "all Jerusalem") betray breach of concord, since pasa is feminine, but this form of "Jerusalem," unlike the alternative Ἱερουσαλήμ (Ierousalēm), is not feminine but neuter plural. Possibly pasa is a precursor of modern Greek's indeclinable pasa (so BDF, par. 56[4]); but it is marginally more likely that the noun is being treated as feminine singular since there are other instances where it is construed as feminine singular even though no pasa is present.

5–6 Matthew uses the singular προφήτου (prophētou, "prophet") even though two different passages, from the latter and former prophets respectively, are cited. Yet it seems a common practice to refer to one author, perhaps the principal one, when citing two or three (cf. 27:9; Mark 1:2–3).

7 Τότε (tote, "then") is very common in Matthew, occurring ninety times as compared with Mark's six and Luke's fourteen; but in Matthean usage only sometimes does it have temporal force (as here), serving more frequently as a loose connective.

10 The words "they were overjoyed" render a cognate accusative, ἐχάρησαν χαράν (echarēsan charan, lit., "they rejoiced with joy"), probably under Semitic influence (cf. Moule, Idiom Book, p. 32; BDF, par. 153[1]).

D. The Escape to Egypt

2:13–15

> 13When they had gone, an angel of the Lord appeared to Joseph in a dream. "Get up," he said, "take the child and his mother and escape to Egypt. Stay there until I tell you, for Herod is going to search for the child to kill him."
> 14So he got up, took the child and his mother during the night and left for Egypt, 15where he stayed until the death of Herod. And so was fulfilled what the Lord had said through the prophet: "Out of Egypt I called my son."

Many commentators think this account has been created to flesh out the OT text said to be "fulfilled" (v.15). On the broader critical questions, see introductory comments at 1:18–25 and 2:1–12. Granted what we know of Herod's final years, there is nothing historically improbable about this account; and precisely because the fulfillment text is difficult, one may assume that the story called forth reflection on the OT text rather than vice versa.

13–14 The verb "had gone" (v.13) is the same as "returned" in the preceding verse, tying the two accounts together. This is the third dream in these two chapters, and for the second time an angel of the Lord is mentioned (cf. 1:20; 2:12). The point is that God took sovereign action to preserve his Messiah, his Son—something well understood by Jesus himself, and a major theme in the Gospel of John. Egypt was a natural place to which to flee. It was nearby, a well-ordered Roman province outside Herod's jurisdiction; and, according to Philo (writing c. A.D. 40), its population included about a million Jews. Earlier generations of Israelites fleeing their homeland (1 Kings 11:40; Jer 26:21–23; 43:7) had sought refuge in Egypt. But if Matthew was thinking of any particular OT parallel, probably Jacob and his family

(Gen 46) fleeing the famine in Canaan was in his mind, since that is the trip that set the stage for the Exodus (cf. 2:15).

The angel's command was explicit. Joseph, Mary, and the Child must remain in Egypt, not only till Herod's death, but till given leave to return (cf. vv.19–20). The command was also urgent. Joseph left at once, setting out by night to begin the seventy-five mile journey to the border. The focus on God's protection of "the child" is unmistakable. Herod was going to try to kill him (v.13), and Joseph took "the child and his mother" (v.14—not the normal order) to Egypt.

15 The death of Herod brought relief to many. Only then, for instance, did the Qumran covenanters return to their center, destroyed in 31 B.C., and rebuild it. In Egypt, Herod's death made possible the return of the Child, Mary, and Joseph, who awaited a word from the Lord. The Greek could be rendered "And so was fulfilled" (NIV) or "[This came about] in order that the word of the Lord . . . might be fulfilled." Either way the notion of fulfillment preserves some telic force in the sentence: Jesus' exodus from Egypt fulfilled Scripture written long before.

The OT quotation (v.15) almost certainly (cf. Notes) comes from Hosea 11:1 and exactly renders the Hebrew, not the LXX, which has "his children," not "my son." (In this Matthew agrees with Aq., Symm., and Theod., but only because all four rely on the Hebrew.) Some commentators (e.g., Beng.; Gundry, *Use of OT*, pp. 93–94) argue that the preposition *ek* ("out of," NIV) should be taken temporally, i.e., "since Egypt" or, better, "from the time [he dwelt] in Egypt." The preposition can have that force; and it is argued that v.15 means God "called" Jesus, in the sense that he specially acknowledged and preserved him, from the time of his Egyptian sojourn on, protecting him against Herod. After all, the exodus itself is not mentioned till vv.21–22.

Some commentators interpret the calling of Israel in Hosea 11:1 in a similar way. But there are convincing arguments against this. The context of Hosea 11:1 mentions Israel's *return* to Egypt (11:5), which presupposes that 11:1 refers to the Exodus. To preserve the temporal force of *ek* in Matthew 2:15, Gundry is reduced to the unconvincing assertion that the preposition in Hosea is both temporal and locative. In support of this view, it is pointed out that Jesus' actual departure *out of* Egypt is not mentioned until v.21. But, although this is so, it is nevertheless implied by vv.13–14. The reason Matthew has introduced the Hosea quotation at this point, instead of after v.21, is probably because he wishes to use the return journey itself to set up the reference to the destination, Nazareth (v.23), rather than the starting-point, Egypt (R.E. Brown, *Birth of Messiah*, p. 220).

If Hosea 11:1 refers to Israel's Exodus from Egypt, in what sense can Matthew mean that Jesus' return to the land of Israel "fulfilled" this text? Four observations clarify the issue.

1. Many have noticed that Jesus is often presented in the NT as the antitype of Israel or, better, the typological recapitulation of Israel. Jesus' temptation after forty days of fasting recapitulated the forty years' trial of Israel (see on 4:1–11). Elsewhere, if Israel is the vine that does not bring forth the expected fruit, Jesus, by contrast, is the True Vine (Isa 5; John 15). The reason Pharaoh must let the people of Israel go is that Israel is the Lord's son (Exod 4:22–23), a theme picked up by Jeremiah (31:9) as well as Hosea (cf. also Ps 2:6, 12). The "son" theme in Matthew (cf. esp. T. de Kruijf, *Der Sohn des lebendigen Gottes: Ein Beitrag zur Christologie des Matthäusevangelium* [Rome: BIP, 1962], pp. 56–58, 109), already present since

Jesus is messianic "son of David" and, by the virginal conception, Son of God, becomes extraordinarily prominent in Matthew (see on 3:17): "This is my Son, whom I love."

2. The verb "to fulfill" has broader significance than mere one-to-one prediction (cf. Introduction, section 11.b; and comments on 5:17). Not only in Matthew but elsewhere in the NT, the history and laws of the OT are perceived to have prophetic significance (cf. on 5:17–20). The Epistle to the Hebrews argues that the laws regarding the tabernacle and the sacrificial system were from the beginning designed to point toward the only Sacrifice that could really remove sin and the only Priest who could serve once and for all as the effective Mediator between God and man. Likewise Paul insists that the Messiah sums up his people in himself. When David was anointed king, the tribes acknowledged him as their bone and flesh (2 Sam 5:1), i.e., David as anointed king summed up Israel, with the result that his sin brought disaster on the people (2 Sam 12, 24). Just as Israel is God's son, so the promised Davidic Son is also Son of God (2 Sam 7:13–14; cf. N.T. Wright, "The Paul of History," *Tyndale Bulletin* 29 [1978]: esp. 66–67). "Fulfillment" must be understood against the background of these interlocking themes and their typological connections.

3. It follows, therefore, that the NT writers do not think they are reading back into the OT things that are not already there germinally. This does not mean that Hosea had the Messiah in mind when he penned Hosea 11:1. This admission prompts W.L. LaSor ("Prophecy, Inspiration, and *Sensus Plenior*," *Tyndale Bulletin* 29 [1978]: 49–60) to see in Matthew's use of Hosea 11:1 an example of *sensus plenior*, by which he means a "fuller sense" than what was in Hosea's mind, but something nevertheless in the mind of God. But so blunt an appeal to what God has absolutely hidden seems a strange background for Matthew's insisting that Jesus' exodus from Egypt in any sense fulfills the Hosea passage. This observation is not trivial; Matthew is reasoning with Jews who could say, "You are not playing fair with the text!" A mediating position is therefore necessary.

Hosea 11 pictures God's love for Israel. Although God threatens judgment and disaster, yet because he is God and not man (11:9), he looks to a time when in compassion he will roar like a lion and his children will return to him (11:10–11). In short Hosea himself looks forward to a saving visitation by the Lord. Therefore his prophecy fits into the larger pattern of OT revelation up to that point, revelation that both explicitly and implicitly points to the Seed of the woman, the Elect Son of Abraham, the Prophet like Moses, the Davidic King, the Messiah. The "son" language is part of this messianic matrix (cf. Willis J. Beecher, *The Prophets and the Promise* [New York: Thomas Y. Crowell, 1905], pp. 331–35); insofar as that matrix points to Jesus the Messiah and insofar as Israel's history looks forward to one who sums it up, then so far also Hosea 11:1 looks forward. To ask whether Hosea thought of Messiah is to ask the wrong question, akin to using a hacksaw when a scalpel is needed. It is better to say that Hosea, building on existing revelation, grasped the messianic nuances of the "son" language already applied to Israel and David's promised heir in previous revelation so that had he been able to see Matthew's use of 11:1, he would not have disapproved, even if messianic nuances were not in his mind when he wrote that verse. He provided one small part of the revelation unfolded during salvation history; but that part he himself understood to be a pictorial representative of divine, redeeming love.

The NT writers insist that the OT can be rightly interpreted only if the entire revelation is kept in perspective as it is historically unfolded (e.g., Gal 3:6–14). Hermeneutically this is not an innovation. OT writers drew lessons out of earlier salvation history, lessons difficult to perceive while that history was being lived, but lessons that retrospect would clarify (e.g., Asaph in Ps 78; cf. on Matt 13:35). Matthew does the same in the context of the fulfillment of OT hopes in Jesus Christ. We may therefore legitimately speak of a "fuller meaning" than any one text provides. But the appeal should be made, not to some hidden divine knowledge, but to the pattern of revelation up to that time—a pattern not yet adequately discerned. The new revelation may therefore be truly new, yet at the same time capable of being checked against the old.

4. If this interpretation of Matthew 2:15 is correct, it follows that for Matthew Jesus himself is the locus of true Israel. This does not necessarily mean that God has no further purpose for racial Israel; but it does mean that the position of God's people in the Messianic Age is determined by reference to Jesus, not race.

Notes

13 The historical present φαίνεται (phainetai, lit., "appears") adds a vivid touch.
15 Because "out of Egypt" occurs in Num 23:22; 24:8, some have suggested a connection between Matt 2:15 and Num 24:7–8 (e.g., Lindars, Hill, Schweizer). In its strongest form this argument depends on the LXX, which reads, "A man shall come forth from his seed," instead of, "Water will flow from their buckets" (Num 24:7), and "him" instead of "them" (Num 24:8). This transforms Num 24:28 into a reference to God bringing Messiah out of Egypt. Apart from the textual question, it must be noted that (1) Matt 2:15 corresponds exactly with MT Hos 11:1 but only approximately with LXX Num 24:8; (2) the LXX rendering makes Num 24 rather incoherent.

E. *The Massacre of Bethlehem's Boys*

2:16–18

> [16]When Herod realized that he had been outwitted by the Magi, he was furious, and he gave orders to kill all the boys in Bethlehem and its vicinity who were two years old and under, in accordance with the time he had learned from the Magi. [17]Then what was said through the prophet Jeremiah was fulfilled:
>
> > [18]"A voice is heard in Ramah,
> >   weeping and great mourning,
> > Rachel weeping for her children
> >   and refusing to be comforted,
> > because they are no more."

Few sections of Matthew 1–2 have been as widely criticized as this one. Most modern scholars think Matthew made the story up (e.g., Goulder, p. 33; E.M. Smallwood, *The Jews Under Roman Rule* [Leiden: Brill, 1976], pp. 103–4), spinning it out of Jeremiah 31:15, cited in Matthew 2:18 (so C.T. Davis, "Tradition and Redaction in Matthew 1:18–2:23," JBL 90 [1971]: 419). In this view, perhaps Matthew invented the tale to draw an analogy between Jesus and Moses or between Jesus and late Jewish traditions about Abraham or Jacob or out of an apologetic need to construct an initial sign of the impending judgment on Israel for rejecting her Messiah (Kingsbury, *Structure*, p. 48). But v. 16 cannot be excised from the chapter without rewriting it all.

The OT citation in v. 18, like other such citations in Matthew 1–2, is itself not strictly necessary to the narrative. These citations illumine the narrative and show its relation to OT Scripture, but they do not create it (cf. on 1:18–25; 2:1–12). It is difficult to see a real parallel with Moses, since Pharaoh's edict was general and before Moses' birth, whereas Herod's edict is specifically for Bethlehem and came after Jesus' birth. At best the parallel is tenuous. Furthermore vv. 16–18 offer a poor sign of the destruction to befall Israel—not least because Jesus escapes rather than suffers, and the children have done Jesus no harm.

Actually, the story is in perfect harmony with what we know of Herod's character in his last years (Schalit, p. 648). That there is no extra-Christian confirmation is not surprising; the same can be said of Jesus' crucifixion. The death of a few children (perhaps a dozen or so; Bethlehem's total population was not large) would hardly have been recorded in such violent times. (See the excellent treatment by R.T. France, "Herod and the Children of Bethlehem," NovTest 21 [1979]: 98–120; id., "The Massacre of the Innocents," Livingstone, pp. 83–94.) "Matthew is not simply meditating on Old Testament texts, but claiming that in what has happened they find fulfillment. If the events are legendary, the argument is futile" (France, "Herod," p. 120).

16 It probably did not take long to carry out Herod's barbarous order. Bethlehem is only five miles from Jerusalem. The Magi set out in the same evening (v. 9) and may have left that same night after their dream (v. 12); the same would be true of Joseph with Jesus and Mary (vv. 13–15). By the next evening Herod's patience would have been exhausted. The two-years age limit was to prevent Jesus' escape; at the time he was between six and twenty months old. Herod, aiming to eliminate a potential king, restricted the massacre to boys. Furious at being deceived (a better translation than "outwitted"), he raged against the Lord and his Anointed One (Ps 2:2). Yet this was no narrow escape. The One enthroned in heaven laughs and scoffs at the Herods of this world (Ps 2:4).

17–18 Jeremiah is named three times in Matthew (cf. 16:14; 27:9) and nowhere else in the NT. The text form of this OT citation in these verses is complex but is probably Matthew's rendering of the Hebrew (cf. Gundry, *Use of OT*, pp. 94–97; R.E. Brown, *Birth of Messiah*, pp. 221–23).

It is uncertain whether Jeremiah 31:15 refers to the deportation of the northern tribes by Assyria in 722–721 B.C. or to the deportation of Judah and Benjamin in 587–586 B.C. (cf. R.E. Brown, *Birth of Messiah*, pp. 205–6). The latter is more likely. Nebuzaradan, commander of Nebuchadnezzar's imperial guard, gathered the captives at Ramah before taking them into exile in Babylon (Jer 40:1–2). Ramah lay north of Jerusalem on the way to Bethel; Rachel's tomb was at Zelzah in the same vicinity (1 Sam 10:2). Jeremiah 31:15 depicts mourning at the prospect of exile; Rachel is seen as crying out from her tomb because her "children," her descendants (Rachel is the idealized mother of the Jews, though Leah gave birth to more tribes than Rachel) "are no more"—i.e., they are being removed from the land and are no longer a nation. But elsewhere we are told that Rachel was buried on the way to Ephrathah, identified as Bethlehem (Gen 35:19; 48:7). Some see a confusion of traditions here and assume that the clan of Ephrathah later settled in Bethlehem and gave it its name, thus starting a false connection Matthew follows. The problem, however, is artificial. Genesis 35:16 makes it clear that Jacob was some distance from Bethlehem-Ephrathah when Rachel died—viz., somewhere between Bethel and Bethlehem (only 1 Sam 10:2 says more exactly where he was). Moreover Matthew does not say Rachel was buried at Bethlehem; the connection between the prophecy and its "fulfillment" is more subtle than that.

Why does Matthew refer to this OT passage? Some think the connection results from word association: the children were killed at Bethlehem, Bethlehem = Ephrathah, Ephrathah is connected with Rachel's death, and Rachel figures in the oracle. Rothfuchs (p. 64) sees a parallel between the condemnation to exile as a result of sin (Jer) and the judgment on Israel as a result of rejecting the Messiah (an interpretation that sees the slaughter at Bethlehem as a sign of the latter). More believable is the observation (Gundry, *Use of OT*, p. 210; Tasker) that Jeremiah 31:15 occurs in a setting of hope. Despite the tears, God says, the exiles will return; and now Matthew, referring to Jeremiah 31:15, likewise says that, despite the tears of the Bethlehem mothers, there is hope because Messiah has escaped Herod and will ultimately reign. The further suggestion that the deep grief in Bethlehem reflected the belief that the Messiah had been massacred and news of his escape should assuage that grief (cf. Broadus) is fanciful.

But there may be a further reason why Matthew quotes this OT passage, a reason discernible once the differences between Matthew and the OT are spelled out. Here Jesus does not, as in v.15, recapitulate an event from Israel's history. The Exile sent Israel into captivity and thereby called forth tears. But here the tears are not for him who goes into "exile" but because of the children who stay behind and are slaughtered. Why, then, refer to the Exile at all? Help comes from observing the broader context of both Jeremiah and Matthew. Jeremiah 31:9, 20 refers to Israel = Ephraim as God's dear son and also introduces the new covenant (31:31–34) the Lord will make with his people. Therefore the tears associated with Exile (31:15) will end. Matthew has already made the Exile a turning point in his thought (1:11–12), for at that time the Davidic line was dethroned. The tears of the Exile are now being "fulfilled"—i.e., the tears begun in Jeremiah's day are climaxed and ended by the tears of the mothers of Bethlehem. The heir to David's throne has come, the Exile is over, the true Son of God has arrived, and he will introduce the new covenant (26:28) promised by Jeremiah.

Notes

16 "He gave orders to kill" is an excellent rendering of the "graphic participle" in ἀπο-στείλας ἀνεῖλεν (*aposteilas aneilen*, lit., "having sent, he killed"; cf. Zerwick, par. 363).

17 Only here and in 27:9 is the fulfillment formula devoid of a ἵνα (*hina*) or a ὅπως (*hopōs*), both of which normally have telic force ("in order that"), though consecutive force is not uncommon in NT Greek (cf. on 2:15). This is probably because in these two passages the action that is fulfilling Scripture is so horrible that there is an instinctive reluctance to use phraseology that might be (mis)-understood to ascribe enormous wickedness to God (cf. Broadus; Rothfuchs, pp. 36–39).

18 The longer reading, reflected in KJV ("lamentation and weeping and great mourning") is most likely an assimilation to some LXX witnesses.

F. *The Return to Nazareth*

2:19–23

> ¹⁹After Herod died, an angel of the Lord appeared in a dream to Joseph in Egypt ²⁰and said, "Get up, take the child and his mother and go to the land of Israel, for those who were trying to take the child's life are dead."
> ²¹So he got up, took the child and his mother and went to the land of Israel. ²²But when he heard that Archelaus was reigning in Judea in place of his father Herod, he was afraid to go there. Having been warned in a dream, he withdrew to the district of Galilee, ²³and he went and lived in a town called Nazareth. So was fulfilled what was said through the prophets: "He will be called a Nazarene."

19–21 This fourth dream and third mention of the angel of the Lord (v.19) continues the divine initiative in preserving and guiding the Child, who is again made prominent ("the child and his mother," v.20). On the date of Herod's death, see on 2:1. (Josephus, Antiq. XVII, 168–69[vi.5], gives a shocking account of Herod's final illness.) The plural ("those who were trying to take the child's life") may owe something to Exodus 4:19 (so Hill, *Matthew*, following Davies, *Setting*). If so, Jesus is being compared with Moses. But that motif is at best weak in Matthew 1–2, and the plural may be accounted for in other ways. H.A.W. Meyer suggests that Herod's father, Antipater, who died a few days before him, may have been associated with Herod in the massacre. More probably the plural is a generalizing or categorical plural (cf. Turner, *Syntax*, pp. 25–26; BDF, par. 141). "Land of Israel" occurs only in vv.20–21 (cf. "cities of Israel," 10:23). Although the whole land was before him and he apparently hoped to settle in Judea (perhaps in Bethlehem, the city of David), Joseph was forced to retire to despised Galilee.

22 Probably Joseph had expected Herod Antipas to reign over the entire kingdom; but Herod the Great made a late change in his will, dividing his kingdom into three parts. Archelaus, known for his ruthlessness, was given Judea, Samaria, and Idumea (see map, p. 58.). Augustus Caesar agreed and gave him the title "ethnarch" (more honorable than "tetrarch") and promised the title "king" if it was earned. But Archelaus proved to be a poor ruler and was banished for misgovernment in A.D. 6. Rome ruled the south through a procurator. But by that time Joseph had settled the family in Galilee. Herod Antipas, who reappears in Matthew 14:1–10, was given the title "tetrarch" and ruled in Galilee and in Perea. Herod Philip (not to be confused with Herodias's first husband, who was not a king) became tetrarch of Iturea, Trachonitis, and some other territories. He was the best of Herod the Great's children; Jesus frequently retired into his territory (14:13; 15:29; 16:13) away from the weak but cruel Antipas. Joseph, guided by the fifth and final dream, settled the family in Galilee.

23 The town Joseph chose was Nazareth, which, according to Luke 1:26–27; 2:39, was his former home and that of Mary (cf. 13:53–58). This final quotation formula, like that of v.15, should probably be construed as telic: this took place "in order to fulfill." But the formula is unique in two respects: only here does Matthew use the plural "prophets"; and only here does he omit the Greek equivalent of "saying" and replace it with the conjunction *hoti*, which can introduce a direct quotation (NIV), but more probably should be rendered "that," making the quotation indirect: "in order to fulfill what was said through the prophets, that he would be called a Nazarene" (cf. W. Barnes Tatum, Jr., "Matthew 2.23," *The Bible Translator* 27 [1976]: 135–37; contra Hartman, "Scriptural Exegesis," pp. 149–50). This suggests that Matthew had no specific OT quotation in mind; indeed, these words are found nowhere in the OT.

The interpretation of this verse has such a long history (for older works, cf. Broadus; for recent studies, cf. Gundry, *Use of OT*, pp. 97–104; R.E. Brown, *Birth of Messiah*, pp. 207–13) that it is not possible to list here all the major options. We may exclude those that see some word-play connection with an OT Hebrew word but have no obvious connection with Nazareth. This eliminates the popular interpretation that makes Jesus a Nazirite or second Samson (cf. esp. Judg 13:5, 7; 16:17, where LXX has *Naziraios* as opposed to Matthew's *Nazōraios;* cf. Luke 1:15). Defenders include Calvin, Loisy, Stendahl, Schweizer, and, more recently, Ernst Zuckschwerdt ("Nazōraîos in Matth.2,23," *Theologische Zeitschrift* 31 [1975]: 65–77). Also to be eliminated are interpretations that try to find in Matthew's term a reference to some kind of pre-Christian sect. But the evidence for this is feeble (cf. Soarés Prabhu, pp. 197–201) and the connection with Nazareth merely verbal. E. Earle Ellis ("How the New Testament Uses the Old," Marshall, *NT Interpretation*, p. 202) sees a pun here as an "implicit midrash," but significantly he then has to put the word "fulfillment" in quotation marks.

Matthew certainly used *Nazōraios* as an adjectival form of *apo Nazaret* ("from Nazareth" or "Nazarene"), even though the more acceptable adjective is *Nazarēnos* (cf. Bonnard, Brown, Albright and Mann, Soarés Prabhu). Possibly *Nazōraios* derives from a Galilean Aramaic form. Nazareth was a despised place (John 7:42, 52), even to other Galileans (cf. John 1:46). Here Jesus grew up, not as "Jesus the Bethlehemite," with its Davidic overtones, but as "Jesus the Nazarene," with all the opprobrium of the sneer. When Christians were referred to in Acts as the "Nazarene sect" (24:5), the expression was meant to hurt. First-century Christian readers of Matthew, who had tasted their share of scorn, would have quickly caught Matthew's point. He is not saying that a particular OT prophet foretold that the Messiah would live in Nazareth; he is saying that the OT prophets foretold that the Messiah would be despised (cf. Pss 22:6–8, 13; 69:8, 20–21; Isa 11:1; 49:7; 53:2–3, 8; Dan 9:26). The theme is repeatedly picked up by Matthew (e.g., 8:20; 11:16–19; 15:7–8). In other words Matthew gives us the substance of several OT passages, not a direct quotation (so also Ezra 9:10–12; cf. SBK, 1:92–93).

It is possible that at the same time there is a discreet allusion to the *neṣer* ("branch") of Isaiah 11:1, which received a messianic interpretation in the Targums, rabbinic literature, and DSS (cf. Gundry, *Use of OT*, p. 104); for here too it is affirmed that David's son would emerge from humble obscurity and low state. Jesus is King Messiah, Son of God, Son of David; but he was a branch from a royal line hacked down to a stump and reared in surroundings guaranteed to win him scorn. Jesus the Messiah, Matthew is telling us, did not introduce his kingdom with outward show or present himself with the pomp of an earthly monarch. In accord with prophecy he came as the despised Servant of the Lord.

Notes

20 The participle οἱ ζητοῦντες (*hoi zētountes*, lit., "those seeking"; NIV, "those who were trying"), quite apart from its being plural, does not because it is present tense signify antecedent action but rather continued, persistent action; the context determines that temporally it is virtually an imperfect (cf. Turner, *Syntax*, pp. 80–81; Moule, *Idiom Book*, p. 206; rightly, NIV).

22 It is uncertain whether the verb χρηματίζω (*chrēmatizō*, "I warn") includes the specification of Nazareth as Joseph's proper destination, or whether he was merely "warned" not to remain in Judea, leaving the choice of town with him.

II. The Gospel of the Kingdom (3:1–7:29)

A. *Narrative* (3:1–4:25)

1. *Foundational steps* (3:1–4:11)

a. *The ministry of John the Baptist*

3:1–12

> [1]In those days John the Baptist came, preaching in the Desert of Judea [2]and saying, "Repent, for the kingdom of heaven is near." [3]This is he who was spoken of through the prophet Isaiah:
>
>> "A voice of one calling in the desert,
>> 'Prepare the way for the Lord,
>>   make straight paths for him.' "
>
> [4]John's clothes were made of camel's hair, and he had a leather belt around his waist. His food was locusts and wild honey. [5]People went out to him from Jerusalem and all Judea and the whole region of the Jordan. [6]Confessing their sins, they were baptized by him in the Jordan River.
> [7]But when he saw many of the Pharisees and Sadducees coming to where he was baptizing, he said to them: "You brood of vipers! Who warned you to flee from the coming wrath? [8]Produce fruit in keeping with repentance. [9]And do not think you can say to yourselves, 'We have Abraham as our father.' I tell you that out of these stones God can raise up children for Abraham. [10]The ax is already at the root of the trees, and every tree that does not produce good fruit will be cut down and thrown into the fire.
> [11]"I baptize you with water for repentance. But after me will come one who is more powerful than I, whose sandals I am not fit to carry. He will baptize you with the Holy Spirit and with fire. [12]His winnowing fork is in his hand, and he will clear his threshing floor, gathering the wheat into the barn and burning up the chaff with unquenchable fire."

For the first time Matthew parallels Mark (1:1–11), Luke (3:1–22), and, more loosely, John (1:19–34). Whatever diversity there is among prologues, the four Gospels unanimously preface the ministry of Jesus with that of John the Baptist. Matthew omits any mention of Jesus' youth (Luke 2:41–52) or of John's birth and background (Luke 1:5–25, 39–45, 57–80). This may imply that Matthew's readers were already familiar with that background (Tasker) or that Matthew wants to plunge dramatically into his account. After four hundred silent years, God was speaking through a new prophet who called people to repentance and promised someone greater to come.

In addition to the implications of this commentary's outline of Matthew, the gospel has many substructures pointing to a writer of great literary skill. Gooding (p. 234) points out interesting parallels between chapters 1–2 and 3–4, too lengthy to be detailed here (cf. also 13:3–53).

1 Matthew's temporal note, "In those days," is vague and reflects a similarly loose expression in the OT (e.g., Gen 38:1; Exod 2:11, 23; Isa 38:1). His phrase may mean "in those crucial days" (Hill, *Matthew*) or even "in the days in which Jesus and his family lived at Nazareth" (Broadus; cf. 4:13). More likely, however, it is a general term that reveals little chronologically but insists that the account is historical (Bonnard). Luke 3:1 offers more chronological help, but its significance is disputed (cf. Hoehner, *Chronological Aspects*, pp. 29–44). The year was A.D. 27, 28, or 29 (less likely 26).

"John," or "Johanan," had been a popular name among the Jews from the time of John Hyrcanus (died 106 B.C.). Four or five "Johns" are mentioned in the NT. The John in Matthew 3:1 was soon designated "the Baptist" (cf. Notes) because baptism was so prominent in his ministry. He began his preaching in the "Desert of Judea," a vaguely defined area including the lower Jordan Valley north of the Dead Sea and the country immediately west of the Dead Sea. It is hot and, apart from the Jordan itself, largely arid, though not unpopulated. It was used for pasturage (Ps 65:12; Joel 2:22; Luke 15:4) and had Essene communities. "Desert" had long had prophetic overtones (the Law was given in the "wilderness"). The Zealots used the desert as a hiding place (cf. Matt 24:26; Acts 21:38; Jos. Antiq. XX, 97–98 [v.1]). Therefore some commentators see more theological than geographical force in Matthew 3:1 (e.g., Bonnard, Maier). The modifying phrase "of Judea" makes the antithesis between geography and theology false. The desert was a particular area (cf. R. Funk, "The Wilderness," JBL 78 [1959]: 205–14) but may also have had prophetic implications for first-century readers.

2 John's preaching had two elements. The first was a call to repent. Though the verb *metanoeō* is often explained etymologically as "to change one's mind," or popularly as "to be sorry for something," neither rendering is adequate. In classical Greek the verb could refer to a purely intellectual change of mind. But the NT usage has been influenced by the Hebrew verbs *nāḥam* ("to be sorry for one's actions") and *šûḇ* ("to turn around to new actions"). The latter is common in the prophets' call to the people to return to the covenant with Yahweh (cf. DNTT, 1:357–59; Turner, *Christian Words*, pp. 374–77). What is meant is not a merely intellectual change of mind or mere grief, still less doing penance (cf. Notes), but a radical transformation of the entire person, a fundamental turnaround involving mind and action and including overtones of grief, which results in "fruit in keeping with repentance." Of course, all this assumes that man's actions are fundamentally off course and need radical change. John applies this repentance to the religious leaders of his day (3:7–8) with particular vehemence. (On the differences between biblical and rabbinic emphases on repentance, cf. Lane, *Mark*, pp. 593–600.)

The second element in John's preaching was the nearness of the kingdom of heaven, and this is given as the ground for repentance. Throughout the OT there was a rising expectation of a divine visitation that would establish justice, crush opposition, and renew the very universe. This hope was couched in many categories: it was presented as the fulfillment of promises to David's heir, as the Day of the Lord (which often had dark overtones of judgment, though there were bright exceptions, e.g., Zeph 3:14–20), as a new heaven and a new earth, as a time of regathering of Israel, as the inauguration of a new and transforming covenant (2 Sam 7:13–14; Isa 1:24–28; 9:6–7; 11:1–10; 64–66; Jer 23:5–6; 31:31–34; Ezek 37:24; Dan 2:44; 7:13–14; cf. esp. Ridderbos, pp. 3–17; Ladd, *Presence*, pp. 45–75).

The predominant meaning of "kingdom" in the OT (Heb. *malkût*; Aram. *malkûta*) is "reign": the term has dynamic force. Similarly in the NT, though *basileia* ("kingdom") can refer to a territory (4:8), the overwhelming majority of instances use the term with dynamic force. This stands over against the prevailing rabbinic terminology in which "kingdom" was increasingly spiritualized or planted in men's hearts (e.g., b *Berakoth* 4a). Contrary to counterclaims (Alva J. McClain, *The Greatness of the Kingdom* [Grand Rapids: Zondervan, 1959], pp. 274ff.), in the first century there was little agreement among Jews as to what the messianic kingdom would be like. One very popular assumption was that the Roman yoke would be shattered and there would be political peace and mounting prosperity.

Except at 12:28; 19:24; 21:31, 43, and in some MSS of 6:33, Matthew always uses "kingdom of heaven" instead of "kingdom of God" (this reckoning excludes references to "my kingdom" and the like), whereas Mark and Luke prefer "kingdom of God." Matthew's preferred expression certainly does not restrict God's reign to the heavens. The biblical goal is the manifest exercise of God's sovereignty, his "reign" on earth and among men. There are enough parallels among the Synoptics to imply that "kingdom of God" and "kingdom of heaven" denote the same thing (e.g., Matt 19:23–24 = Mark 10:23–25); the connotative distinction is less certain.

Dispensationalists (e.g., A.C. Gaebelein, Walvoord) hold that "kingdom of God" is a distinctively spiritual kingdom, a narrower category embracing only true believers, whereas "kingdom of heaven" is the kingdom of millennial splendor, a broader category including (as in the parable, 13:47–50) both good and bad fish. The distinction is unfortunate: it comes perilously close to confusing kingdom and church (see further on ch. 13; 16:17–19), fails to account for passages where the Matthean category is no less restrictive than "kingdom of God" in the other evangelists, and fundamentally misapprehends the dynamic nature of the kingdom. Equally unconvincing is the suggestion of Pamment that "kingdom of heaven" always refers to the future reign following the consummation, whereas in Matthew "kingdom of God" refers to the present manifestation. To arrive at this absolute dichotomy, Pamment must resort to very unlikely interpretations of numerous passages (e.g., 11:12; parables in ch. 13). Many other proposals (e.g., J. Julius Scott, EBC, 1:508) are stated firmly but cannot withstand close scrutiny.

The most common explanation is that Matthew avoided "kingdom of God" to remove unnecessary offense to Jews who often used circumlocutions like "heaven" to refer to God (e.g., Dan 4:26; 1 Macc 3:50, 60; 4:55; Luke 15:18, 21). The suggestion has merit. Yet Matthew is a subtle and allusive writer, and two other factors may also be involved: (1) "kingdom of heaven" may anticipate the extent of Christ's postresurrection authority: God's sovereignty *in heaven* and on earth is now mediated through him (28:18); and (2) "kingdom of God" makes God the King, and though this does not prevent the other Synoptics from ascribing the kingship to Jesus (cf. Luke 22:16, 18, 29–30), there is less room to maneuver. Matthew's "kingdom of heaven" assumes it is God's kingdom and occasionally assigns it specifically to the Father (26:29), though leaving room to ascribe it frequently to Jesus (16:28; 25:31, 34, 40; 27:42; probably 5:35); for Jesus is King Messiah. This inevitably has christological implications. The kingdom of heaven is simultaneously the kingdom of the Father and the kingdom of the Son of Man.

This kingdom, John preached, "is near" (*ēngiken*, lit., "has drawn near"). Jews spoke of the Messiah as "the coming one" (11:3) and the Messianic Age as "the coming age" (Heb 6:5): John says it has now drawn "near," the same message preached by Jesus (4:17) and his disciples (10:7). It is possible, but not certain, that the verb has the same force as *ephthasen* in 12:28. There Jesus unambiguously affirms that the kingdom "has come." That passage makes it clear that it is the exercise of God's saving sovereignty or reign that has dawned. The ambiguous "is near" (3:2; 4:17), coupled with the dynamic sense of "kingdom," prepares us for a constant theme: The kingdom came with Jesus and his preaching and miracles, it came with his death and resurrection, and it will come at the end of the age.

Matthew has already established that Jesus was born King (2:2). Later Jesus declared that his work testified the kingdom had come (12:28), even though he frequently spoke of the kingdom as something to be inherited when the Son of Man comes in his glory. It is false to say that "kingdom" undergoes a radical shift with the mention of "mystery" ("secrets," NIV; see on 13:11). Already in the Sermon on the Mount, entering the kingdom (5:3, 10; 7:21) is equivalent to entering into life (7:13–14; cf. 19:14, 16; and see Mark 9:45, 47).

These and related themes become clearer as the Gospel progresses (cf. esp. Ladd, *NT Theology*, pp. 57–90). But two observations cannot be delayed. First, the Baptist's terminology, though veiled, necessarily roused enormous excitement (3:5). But assorted apocalyptic and political expectations would have brought about a profound misunderstanding of the kingdom being preached. Therefore Jesus himself purposely used veiled terminology when treating themes like this. This becomes increasingly obvious in the Gospel. The second observation relates to the first. Just as the angel's announcement to Joseph declared Jesus' primary purpose to be to save his people from their sins (1:21), so the first announcement of the kingdom is associated with repentance and confession of sin (3:6). These themes are constantly intertwined in Matthew (cf. Goppelt, *Theologie*, pp. 128–88).

3 If the *gar* ("for") has its full force, then NIV should read, "For this is he"; and v.3 becomes the ground for the Baptist's preaching in v.2. This is the one OT citation of Matthew's own eleven direct OT quotations that is not introduced by a fulfillment formula (cf. Introduction, section 11.b). It goes too far, however (contra Gundry), to say that the omission of fulfillment language means that for Matthew, John the Baptist does not fulfill Scripture but serves merely as a "protypical Christian preacher." If Matthew had wanted to say so little, he would have been better off eliminating the OT passage. Instead he introduces it with a Pesher formula (e.g., Acts 2:16; cf. Introduction, section 11.b) that can only be understood as identifying the Baptist in an eschatological, prophecy-and-fulfillment framework with the one of whom Isaiah (40:3) spoke.

The Baptist's role is minimally exemplary. According to John 1:23, the Baptist once applied this passage to himself. Here Matthew does it for him. In the MT the words "in the desert" modify "prepare": "In the desert prepare the way of the LORD." But all three Synoptics here follow the LXX. The immediate effect is to locate in the desert the one who is calling. Some have thought this a deliberate attempt to make the fulfillment extend to geographical details. But Mark consistently follows the LXX, and Matthew often follows Mark. So we must not read too much into the change. There may be an error in the Hebrew accents, which associate "in the desert" with "prepare" (Gundry, *Use of OT*, p. 10). In any case, if one shouts a command in the desert, his intent is that it be spread everywhere; so there is little difference in meaning (Alexander).

In Isaiah 40:3 the way of Yahweh is being "made straight" (a metaphor using road building to refer to repentance); in Matthew 3:3 it is the way of Jesus. This sort of identification of Jesus with Yahweh is common in the NT (e.g., Exod 13:21 and 1 Cor 10:4; Isa 6:1 and John 12:41; Ps 68:18 and Eph 4:8; Ps 102:25–27 and Heb 1:10–12) and confirms the kingdom as being equally the kingdom of God and the kingdom of Jesus. While the deity of Christ is only implicit in such texts, it certainly goes beyond Jesus' being merely a royal envoy. The Qumran covenanters cited the same passage to foster study of the law in preparation for the eschaton (1QS 8:12ff.; 9:19; cf. Fitzmyer, *Semitic Background*, pp. 34–36); but Matthew identifies the Baptist as the voice and the eschatological age as already dawning in Jesus' coming.

4–5 Clothes of camel's hair and a leather belt (v.4, the latter to bind up the loose outer garment) were not only the clothes of poor people but establish links with Elijah (2 Kings 1:8; cf. Mal 4:5). "Locusts" (*akrides*) are large grasshoppers, still eaten in the East, not the fruit of the "locust tree" (BAGD, s.v.). Wild honey is what it purports to be, not gum from a tree (cf. Judg 14:8–9; 1 Sam 14:25–29; Ps 81:16). Both suggest a poor man used to wilderness living, and this suggests a connection with the prophets (cf. 3:1; 11:8–9)—so much so that in Zechariah's day (13:4) some false prophets dressed like prophets to deceive people. Both Elijah and John had stern ministries in which austere garb and diet confirmed their message and condemned the idolatry of physical and spiritual softness. "Even the food and dress of John preached" (Beng.). John's impact was enormous (v.5), and his crowds came from a wide area. In Greek, the places are personified (as in 2:3).

6 Confession of sin was commanded in the law, not only as part of a priest's duties (Lev 16:21), but as an individual responsibility for wrongs done (Lev 5:5; 26:40; Num 5:6–7; Prov 28:13). In Israel's better days this was carried out (Neh. 9:2–3; Ps 32:5). In the NT (cf. Acts 19:18; 1 John 1:9) confession is scarcely less important. Because Matthew does not include "for the forgiveness of sins" (Mark 1:4), some have deduced that he wants to avoid suggesting any possibility of forgiveness until Jesus' death (Matt 26:28). This is too subtle. A first-century reader would hardly hold that sins were not forgiven after being honestly confessed. And since Matthew regularly abbreviates Mark where he uses him, we must be cautious in drawing theological conclusions from such omissions.

The Greek does not make clear whether the confession was individual or corporate, simultaneous with baptism or antecedent to it. Josephus (Antiq. XVIII, 116–17 [v.2] says that John, "surnamed the Baptist," required righteous conduct as a "necessary preliminary if baptism was to be acceptable to God." Since John was urging people to prepare for Messiah's coming by repenting and being baptized, we may surmise that open renunciation of sin was a precondition of his baptism, which was therefore both a confirmation of confession and an eschatological sign.

Since the discovery of the DSS, many have tried to link John's baptism with that of the Qumran covenanters. But their washings, though related to confession, were probably regarded as purifying and were repeated (cf. 1QS 1:24ff.; 5:13–25) to remove ritual uncleanness. John's baptism, probably a once-only rite (contra Albright and Mann), was unrelated to ceremonial impurity. The rabbis used baptism to induct proselytes but never Jews (SBK, 1:102–12). As far as we know, though baptism itself was not uncommon, the pointed but limited associations placed on John's baptism stem from the Baptist himself—not unlike circumcision, which predates Abraham but lacked covenantal significance before his time.

The Jordan River is fast flowing. No doubt John stationed himself at one of the fords, and prepared the way for the Lord.

7 Many have raised the question of the probability of individuals from groups so mutually hostile as Pharisees and Sadducees (cf. Introduction, section 11.f) presenting themselves together (one article governs both nouns) for baptism. But the Greek text need not be taken to mean that they came to be baptized. It may only mean that they were "coming to where he was baptizing" (cf. Notes). If so, it might suggest that representatives of the Sanhedrin (composed of both parties with elders) came to examine what John was doing (cf. John 1:19, 24, which mentions not only priests and Levites [Sadducees] but also Pharisees). Or many Pharisees and Sadducees may have come for baptism with the ostentation that characterized their other religious activities (e.g., 6:2, 5, 16)—i.e., they were showing the world how ready they were for Messiah, though they had not truly repented. Matthew lumps them together because they were leaders; elsewhere he distinguishes them (22:34). The question with which the Baptist confronted them has this sense: "Who suggested to you that you would escape the coming wrath?" Thus John's rhetorical question takes on a sarcastic nuance: "Who warned you to flee the coming wrath and come for baptism—when in fact you show no signs of repentance?" Though the question is the same in Luke 3:7, there Luke relates it to the crowd, whereas Matthew relates it to the Jewish leaders.

John the Baptist stands squarely in the prophetic tradition—a tradition in which the Day of the Lord points much more to darkness than to light for those who think they have no sin (Amos 2:4–8; 6:1–7). "You brood of vipers!" also belongs to the prophetic tradition (cf. Isa 14:29; 30:6; cf. CD 19:22); in Matthew 12:34, Jesus uses these terms to excoriate the Pharisees.

8–9 The coming of God's reign either demands repentance (v.2) or brings judgment. Repentance must be genuine: if we wish to escape the coming wrath (v.7), then our entire lifestyle must be in harmony with our oral repentance (v.8). Mere descent from Abraham is not enough (v.9). In the OT God repeatedly cut off many Israelites and saved a remnant. Yet in the intertestamental period the general use of descent from Abraham, in the context of a rising merit theology, supported the notion that Israel was chosen because it was choice and that the merits of the patriarchs would suffice for their descendants (cf. Carson, *Divine Sovereignty*, pp. 39ff.). But not only may God narrow Israel down to a remnant, he may also raise up authentic children of Israel from "these stones" (perhaps stones lying in the river bed—both Hebrew and Aramaic have a pun on "children" and "stones"). Ordinary stones will suffice; there is no need for the "rocks" of the patriarchs and their merits (cf. S. Schechter, *Some Aspects of Rabbinic Theology* [London: Black, 1903], p. 173; cf. also Rom 4). Verse 9 not only rebukes the self-righteousness of the leaders but implies that participation in the kingdom results from grace and extends the borders of God's people beyond racial frontiers (cf. 8:11).

10 The ax is "already" (emphatic) at the root of the trees (for the idiom, cf. Isa 10:33–34; Jer 46:22). "Not only is there a coming Messianic wrath, but already there is a beginning Messianic discrimination among the descendants of Abraham" (Broadus). Just as the kingdom is dawning already (v.2), so also is the judgment; the two are inseparable. To preach the kingdom is to preach repentance; any tree (not "every tree," NIV; cf. Turner, *Syntax*, p. 199), regardless of its roots, that does not bring forth good fruit will be destroyed.

11 Compare vv.11–12 with Luke 3:15–18 (Q?). Because only Matthew says, "I baptize you with water *for repentance*" (emphasis mine), Hill detects a conscious effort to subordinate John to Jesus. John baptizes as preparation "for repentance"; Jesus baptizes for fulfillment "with the Holy Spirit and fire." But both Mark (1:4) and Luke (3:3) have spoken of John's baptism as one of repentance. And when Jesus begins to preach, he too demands repentance (4:17). If there is an antithesis here between John and Jesus, it is in all three synoptic Gospels. Matthew may be stressing the difference between the baptisms of John and Jesus in order to make a point about eschatology (see below and on 11:7–13).

The phrase "for repentance" (*eis metanoian*) is difficult: *eis* plus the accusative frequently suggests purpose ("I baptize you in order that you will repent"). Contextually (v.6) this is unlikely, even in the peculiar telic sense suggested by Broadus: "I baptize you with a view to continued repentance." But causal *eis*, or something very close to it, is not unknown in the NT (cf. Turner, *Syntax*, pp. 266–67: "I baptize you because of your repentance." The force may, however, be weaker—i.e., "I baptize you with reference to or in connection with repentance." In any case John wants to contrast his baptism with that of the one who comes after him (any allusion here to the messianic title "the one who comes" is doubtful; cf. Arens, pp. 288–90). That one is "more powerful" than John: the same term (*ischyros*) is applied to God in the OT (LXX Jer 32:18; Dan 9:4; cf. also Isa 40:10) and the cognate noun to the Messiah in Psalms of Solomon 17. This is not the normal order: usually the one who follows is the disciple, the lesser one (cf. Matt 16:24; John 13:16; 15:20). But because John's particular ministry is to announce the eschatological figure, he cannot do other than precede him.

Though John was the most sought-after preacher in Israel for centuries, he protested that he was not fit to "carry" (Mark and Luke have "untie") the sandals of the Coming One. Many scholars have argued that this saying must be a late invention of Christians determined to keep the Baptist in his place and exalt Jesus. In fact, such humility as John's is in Christian ethics a virtue, not a weakness. Moreover if he saw his role as that of forerunner to the Messiah, John could not well have set himself on a par with the one to whom he pointed (cf. also John 3:28–31). No doubt the church readily used John's self-depreciation in later conflicts with his followers. But there is no evidence they invented it.

It follows that just as John's purpose was to prepare a way for the Lord by calling people to repentance, so his baptism pointed to the one who would bring the eschatological baptism in spirit and fire. John's baptism was "essentially preparatory" (cf. J.D.G. Dunn, *Baptism in the Holy Spirit* [London: SCM, 1970], pp. 14–17; Bonnard; F. Lang, "Erwägungen zur eschatologischen Verkündigung Johannes des

Täufers," in Strecker, *Jesus Christus*, pp. 459–73); Jesus' baptism inaugurated the Messianic Age.

"Baptism in the Holy Spirit" is not a specialized term in the NT. Its OT background includes Ezekiel 36:25–27; 39:29; Joel 2:28. We need not think that John the Baptist could not have mentioned the Holy Spirit, not least because of somewhat similar references in the literature at Qumran (1QS 3:7–9; 4:21; 1QH 16:12; cf. Dunn, *Baptism*, pp. 8–10). But Matthew and Luke add "and fire." Many see this as a double baptism, one in the Holy Spirit for the righteous and one in fire for the unrepentant (cf. the wheat and chaff in v.12). Fire (Mal 4:1) destroys and consumes.

There are good reasons, however, for taking "fire" as a purifying agent along with the Holy Spirit. The people John is addressing are being baptized by him; presumably they have repented. More important the preposition *en* ("with") is not repeated before fire: the one preposition governs both "Holy Spirit" and "fire," and this normally suggests a unified concept, Spirit-fire or the like (cf. M.J. Harris, DNTT, 3:1178; Dunn, *Baptism*, pp. 10–13). Fire often has a purifying, not destructive, connotation in the OT (e.g., Isa 1:25; Zech 13:9; Mal 3:2–3). John's water baptism relates to repentance; but the one whose way he is preparing will administer a Spirit-fire baptism that will purify and refine. In a time when many Jews felt the Holy Spirit had been withdrawn till the Messianic Age, this announcement could only have been greeted with excited anticipation.

12 Messiah's coming will separate grain from chaff. A winnowing fork tossed both into the air. The wind blew the chaff away, and the heavier grain fell to be gathered up from the ground. The scattered chaff was swept up and burned and the threshing floor cleared (cf. Ps 1:4; Isa 5:24; Dan 2:35; Hos 13:3). The "unquenchable fire" signifies eschatological judgment (cf. Isa 34:10; 66:24; Jer 7:20), hell (cf. 5:29). "Unquenchable fire" is not just metaphor: fearful reality underlies Messiah's separation of grain from chaff. The "nearness" of the kingdom therefore calls for repentance (v.2).

Notes

1 Matthew has ὁ βαπτιστής (*ho baptistēs*, "the baptist"); Mark (1:4) uses the participle [ὁ] βαπτίζων ([*ho*] *baptizōn*, lit., "the baptizer"). It is doubtful whether any distinction is intended since "Baptist" has no sectarian or denominational flavor. It is too much to say with Gundry (*Matthew*) that Matthew consistently uses "the Baptist" instead of "the baptizer" to divert attention from John's practice of baptism to his role as preacher; for the latter is not stressed, and Matthew includes the specific statement of v.6: "they were baptized by" John.

"Preaching" (verb κηρύσσω [*kēryssō*], noun κήρυγμα [*kērygma*]) has often, during the past fifty years, been distinguished from "teaching" (διδαχή [*didachē*]) in such a way that the so-called kerygmatic elements were often robbed of content; and virtually everything in the NT was confidently assigned to one category or the other. More recent study has demonstrated how grossly oversimplified such an antithesis is (J.I.H. McDonald, *Kerygma and Didache* [Cambridge: University Press, 1980]) and has suggested other equally important and sometimes overlapping categories (e.g., A.A. Trites, *The New Testament Concept of Witness* [Cambridge: University Press, 1977]).

2 The verb μετανοέω (*metanoeō*, "I repent") was rendered in Latin *poenitentiam agere* ("to exercise penitence"), the word "penitence" suggesting grief, distress, pain, but not necessarily change. Eventually *poenitentiam agite* ("to do penitence") was preferred; and the contraction to "do penance" completed the slide to a pernicious concept quite alien to the NT.

7 The expression ἐπὶ τὸ βάπτισμα αὐτοῦ (*epi to baptisma autou*) is peculiar (lit., coming "to his baptism"); it could either mean "coming to be baptized" or "coming to the place where he was baptizing" (so NIV).

10 Moule (*Idiom Book*, p. 53) sees πρός (*pros*) plus the accusative here combining linear motion with punctiliar rest on arrival: the ax has taken its first chop, as it were. But it is possible that the verb κεῖται (*keitai*, lit., "lies"; NIV, "is") suggests the ax is merely lying at the root of the tree, ready for action.

---

b. *The baptism of Jesus*

3:13–17

> [13]Then Jesus came from Galilee to the Jordan to be baptized by John. [14]But John tried to deter him, saying, "I need to be baptized by you, and do you come to me?"
> [15]Jesus replied, "Let it be so now; it is proper for us to do this to fulfill all righteousness." Then John consented.
> [16]As soon as Jesus was baptized, he went up out of the water. At that moment heaven was opened, and he saw the Spirit of God descending like a dove and lighting on him. [17]And a voice from heaven said, "This is my Son, whom I love; with him I am well pleased."

Comparing the three synoptic accounts of Jesus' baptism (cf. Mark 1:9–11; Luke 3:21–22) reveals distinctive features (e.g., only Matthew has 3:14–15). But it is easy to exaggerate differences. As is often pointed out, Luke does not say John baptized Jesus; but in view of Luke 3:1–21, there is no doubt of this. As will be shown, some alleged distinctions among the evangelists are artificial; others highlight valuable theological emphases.

13 "Then" (*tote*) is vague in Matthew (see on 2:7); each use needs separate handling. Here *tote* implies that during the time John the Baptist was preaching to the crowds and baptizing them, "then" Jesus came—i.e., it is equivalent to Luke's "When all the people were being baptized, Jesus was baptized too" (3:21). If so, to say that in Luke baptism is a public testimony to Jesus but a private one in Matthew is artificial. This conclusion is especially important to Kingsbury (*Structure*, pp. 13–15) because he wants to avoid any public recognition of Jesus till 4:17. Jeremias (*NT Theology*, p. 51) thinks Luke is closer to historical reality and supposes that Jesus immersed himself along with others in John's presence. Both refinements are too finespun. Any interpretation demanding either privacy or crowds at Jesus' baptism as Matthew or Luke report it reads too much into the texts and probably misses the evangelists' chief points. Jesus came from Galilee (Mark specifies Nazareth) to be baptized by John (though Matthew makes this aim explicit, in Mark and Luke it is implicit), and as a result the Father testified to his Son. This much is common to all three accounts, and it matters little whether only John heard this heavenly witness or whether the crowds heard it as well.

14 Matthew 3:14–15 is peculiar to this Gospel. John tried to deter Jesus (imperfect of attempted action) from his baptism, insisting (the pronouns are emphatic) that he stood in need of baptism by Jesus. Earlier John had difficulty baptizing the Pharisees and Sadducees because they were not worthy of his baptism. Now he has trouble baptizing Jesus because his baptism is not worthy of Jesus.

There are two possible ways of understanding John's reluctance:

1. John recognizes Jesus as the Messiah and wants to receive Jesus' Spirit-and-fire baptism. Despite the rising popularity of this view, it entails serious difficulties. The Spirit theme is not important in Matthew; righteousness is, and it is central to Jesus' response (v.15). Matthew does not present Jesus as bestowing his Spirit-and-fire baptism on anyone: the Cross and Resurrection are focal for him; and, writing after Pentecost (Acts 2), Matthew doubtless believes Jesus' baptism was bestowed on his people later than the time he is writing about. In view of the Baptist's statements about his relation to the Messiah (v.11), if he had recognized Jesus as the Messiah it is doubtful whether Jesus' rebuttal would have convinced him (v.15). Moreover this view brings Matthew into needless conflict with the fourth Gospel (John 1:31–34), which says the Baptist did not "know" Jesus—i.e., recognize him as the Messiah—till after his baptism.

2. But John's baptism did not have purely eschatological significance. It also signified repentance and confession of sin. Whether John knew Jesus well, we do not know. It is, however, inconceivable that his parents had not told him of Mary's visit to Elizabeth some three decades earlier (Luke 1:39–45). At the very least John must have recognized that Jesus, to whom he was related, whose birth was more marvelous than his own, and whose knowledge of Scripture was prodigious even as a child (Luke 2:41–52), outstripped him. John the Baptist was a humble man; conscious of his own sin, he could detect no sin Jesus needed to repent of and confess. So John thought that Jesus should baptize him. Matthew does not tell us when John also perceived that Jesus was the Messiah (though that may be implied by vv.16–17); Matthew focuses on Jesus' sinlessness and the Father's testimony, not on John's testimony (unlike the fourth Gospel, where the Baptist's witness to Jesus is very important).

15 John's consent was won because Jesus told him, "It is proper for us to fulfill all righteousness." Here interpretations are legion. They may be summed up as follows:

1. By undergoing baptism Jesus anticipates his own baptism of death, by which he secures "righteousness" for all. This reads in the Suffering Servant of Isaiah 53:11 ("by his knowledge my righteous servant will justify many"). This view, espoused by many, is well defended by O. Cullmann (*Baptism in the New Testament* [London: SCM, 1950], pp. 15ff.). It presupposes that the significance of Christian baptism should be read back into John's baptism and takes no account of its salvation-historical location. Worse, Cullmann reads Paul's use of "righteousness" back into Matthew, who in fact never uses the term that way but always as meaning "conformity to God's will" or the like (cf. Bonnard's discussion and notes, and esp. Przybylski, pp. 91–94). Moreover the "us" is not a royal "us"; both Jesus *and* John must "fulfill all righteousness," which renders doubtful any theory that ties the righteousness too closely to Jesus' death. G. Barth (Bornkamm, *Tradition*, pp. 140ff.) rejects Cullmann's view but falls into the same weaknesses, holding that Jesus fulfills all right-

eousness by humbly entering the ranks of sinners and acting for them. The same objections apply.

2. Others suggest that Jesus must obey ("fulfill") every divine command ("all righteousness"), and baptism is one such command. Put so crassly this view forgets that the baptism relates to repentance and confession of sins, not to righteousness itself. A slight modification of it says that by being baptized Jesus is acknowledging as valid the righteous life preached by John and demanded of those who accept John's baptism, for Jesus acknowledges (21:32) that John came to show the way of righteousness. But this view forces "fulfill" to become "acknowledge" and neglects the fact that John's baptism relates, not to the standards of righteousness John preached, but to repentance.

3. The strengths of the alternative views may be integrated in a better synthesis. John's baptism, it will be remembered, had two foci: repentance and its eschatological significance. Jesus affirms, in effect, that it is God's will ("all righteousness") that John baptize him; and *both* John *and* Jesus "fulfill" that will, that righteousness, by going through with it ("it is proper for *us*"). The aftermath, as Matthew immediately notes (vv. 16–17), shows that this baptism really did point to Jesus. Within this framework we may recognize other themes. In particular Jesus is indeed seen as the Suffering Servant (Isa 42:1; cf. on 3:17). But the Servant's first mark is obeying God: he "fulfills all righteousness" since he suffers and dies to accomplish redemption in obedience to the will of God. By his baptism Jesus affirms his determination to do his assigned work. Thus the "now" may be significant: Jesus is saying that John's objection (v. 14) is in principle valid. Yet he must "now," at this point in salvation history, baptize Jesus; for at this point Jesus must demonstrate his willingness to take on his servant role, entailing his identification with the people. Contrary to Gundry, "now" does not serve to tell Christian converts they must not delay "this first step on the way of righteousness."

This interpretation assumes that Jesus knew of his Suffering-Servant role from the beginning of his ministry; cf. further at v. 17. This role was hinted at in 2:23; here it makes its first veiled appearance in Jesus' actions. The immediately following temptation narrative confirms it (4:1–11). There Jesus rejects the devil's temptation to pursue messianic glory and power, choosing instead the servant role of obeying every word that comes from the mouth of God.

16 "As soon as" not only suggests that Jesus left the water immediately after his baptism but that the Spirit's witness was equally prompt. Jesus' baptism and its attestation are of a piece and must be interpreted together. "He saw" most naturally refers to Jesus (cf. Mark 1:10), not John, not so much because Matthew excludes John as because he is not the focus of interest. The presence of John (and possibly others) is probably implied by the third-person address "This is my Son" (v. 17), displacing Mark's "You are my Son" (1:11).

"Heaven . . . opened" calls to mind OT visions (e.g., Isa 64:1; Ezek 1:1; cf. Acts 7:56; Rev 4:1; 19:11). "The Spirit of God descending like a dove" simile could mean either that the manner of the Spirit's descent was like a dove's or that the Spirit appeared in a dove's form. Whether or not the latter is visionary, Luke 3:22 specifies it. Because no clear pre-Christian reference links dove and Holy Spirit, some have advanced complex theories: e.g., Mark collected two stories, one mentioning the Holy Spirit's descent and the other the dove's descent, and fused them together (S. Gero, "The Spirit as a Dove at the Baptism of Jesus," NovTest 18 [1976]: 17–35).

But to exclude any new metaphor from the Christian revelation is surely rash. The Spirit's descent cannot be adequately considered apart from v.17; and so resolution of its meaning awaits comment on v.17.

17 Some see in the "voice from heaven" the *baṯ-ḳôl* (lit., "daughter of a voice"), the category used by rabbinic and other writers to refer to divine communication echoing the Spirit of God after the Spirit and the prophets through whom he spoke had been withdrawn. The point, however, is stronger than that. This voice is God's ("from heaven") and testifies that God himself has broken silence and is again revealing himself to men—a clear sign of the dawning of the Messianic Age (cf. 17:5 and John 12:28). What Heaven says in Mark and Luke is "You are my Son"; here it is "This is my Son." The change not only shows Matthew's concern only for the *ipsissima vox* (not generally the *ipsissima verba;* cf. Notes) but also assumes someone besides Jesus heard heaven's witness. There may have been a crowd; if so, that does not interest Matthew. But John needed to hear the Voice confirm his decision (v.15).

Despite arguments to the contrary (e.g., Hooker, *Jesus and the Servant,* pp. 70ff.), the utterance reflects Isaiah 42:1: "Here is my servant, whom I uphold, my chosen one in whom I delight; I will put my Spirit upon him"; and this has been modified by Psalm 2:7: "You are my Son" (cf. Gundry, *Use of OT,* pp. 29–32; and esp. Moo, "Use of OT," pp. 112ff.). The results are extraordinarily important.

1. These words from heaven link Jesus with the Suffering Servant at the very beginning of his ministry and confirm our interpretation of v.15.

2. God here refers to Jesus as "my Son"; implicitly the title "Son of God" is introduced and picked up immediately in the next chapter (4:3, 6). Psalm 2 is Davidic: though it was not regarded in the first century as messianic, the link with David recalls other "son" passages where David or his heir is seen as God's son (e.g., 2 Sam 7:13–14; Ps. 89:26–29).

3. Jesus has already been set forth as the true Israel to which actual Israel was pointing and as such God's Son (see on 2:15); now the heavenly witness confirms the link.

4. At the same time the virginal conception suggests a more than titular or functional sonship: in this context there is the hint of an ontological sonship, made most explicit in the Gospel of John.

5. Jesus is the "beloved" (*agapētos*) Son: the term may mean not only affection but also election, reinforced by the aorist tense that follows (lit., "with him I was well pleased"), suggesting a pretemporal election of the Messiah (cf. John 1:34 [Gr. mg.]).

6. These things are linked in the one utterance: at the very beginning of Jesus' public ministry, his Father presented him, in a veiled way, as at once Davidic Messiah, very Son of God, representative of the people, and Suffering Servant. Matthew has already introduced all these themes and will develop them further. Indeed he definitely cites Isaiah 42:1–4 in 12:18–21, which ends with the assertion (already made clear) that the nations will trust in this Servant.

"Son of God" has particularly rich associations. Therefore it is hard to nail down its precise force at every occurrence. As it is wrong to see ontological sonship in every use, so is it wrong to exclude it prematurely. (For more adequate discussion, see, in addition to the standard dictionaries, Blair, pp. 60ff.; Cullman, *Christology,* pp. 270–305; Kingsbury, *Structure,* pp. 40–83 [though he exaggerates the importance of the theme in Matthew: cf. Hill, "Son and Servant," pp. 2–16]; Ladd, *NT Theology*, pp. 159–72; and Moule, *Christology*, pp. 22ff.)

The Spirit's descent in v.16 needs to be understood in the light of v.17. The Spirit is poured out on the servant in Isaiah 42:1–4, to which v.17 alludes. This outpouring does not change Jesus' status (he was the Son before this) or assign him new rights. Rather it identifies him as the Promised Servant and Son and marks the beginning of his public ministry and direct confrontation with Satan (4:1), the dawning of the Messianic Age (12:28).

Notes

---

14 The καί (*kai*, "and") has adversative force—"and yet" (cf. Zerwick, par. 455; Turner, *Syntax*, p. 334). This may reflect the beginning of an Aramaic apodosis (Lagrange, p. xci).

16 If αὐτῷ (*autō*) is the correct reading, the text says the heavens opened "to him," i.e., to Jesus. But this need not mean that no one else experienced anything (see comment on "This is" in v.17) but only that, in addition to the more public voice, Jesus alone perceived heaven opening. In the NT period the preposition ἀπό (*apo*, "out of") cannot always be distinguished in meaning from ἐκ (*ek*), used in Mark 1:10 (cf. Zerwick, par. 87; Turner, *Syntax*, p. 259).

17 The Latin *vox* simply means "voice" and *verba* "words." *Ipsissima*, from the Latin *ipse* ("self"), basically means "all by oneself" or the like. *Ipsissima vox* and *ipsissima verba* in NT study usually refer to "[Jesus'] own voice" and "[Jesus'] own words" respectively. The first implies that Jesus' teaching is accurately preserved but in the evangelist's own words, style, etc., whereas the latter refers to those places where Jesus' actual words are preserved. In the narrowest sense, however, *ipsissima verba*, since Jesus primarily spoke Aramaic, would be restricted to words like *abba, talitha cum*, etc. Others understand the term to include words of Jesus that are given in precise translation into Greek; but this, too, would be a destructive category to use as the only acceptable reflection of what Jesus taught. In this verse, of course, the words are not those of Jesus but of the Voice from heaven. Even so, Matthew preserves only the general sense, the *ipsissima vox*. For further discussion, see EBC, 1:13–20.

---

c. *The temptation of Jesus*

4:1–11

¹Then Jesus was led by the Spirit into the desert to be tempted by the devil. ²After fasting forty days and forty nights, he was hungry. ³The tempter came to him and said, "If you are the Son of God, tell these stones to become bread."
⁴Jesus answered, "It is written: 'Man does not live on bread alone, but on every word that comes from the mouth of God.' "
⁵Then the devil took him to the holy city and had him stand on the highest point of the temple. ⁶"If you are the Son of God," he said, "throw yourself down. For it is written:

"'He will command his angels concerning you,
and they will lift you up in their hands,
so that you will not strike your foot against a stone.' "

⁷Jesus answered him, "It is also written: 'Do not put the Lord your God to the test.' "

⁸Again, the devil took him to a very high mountain and showed him all the kingdoms of the world and their splendor. ⁹"All this I will give you," he said, "if you will bow down and worship me."
¹⁰Jesus said to him, "Away from me, Satan! For it is written: 'Worship the Lord your God, and serve him only.' "
¹¹Then the devil left him, and angels came and attended him.

In the past many scholars took this pericope and its parallel (Luke 4:1–13) as imaginative embellishments of Mark's much briefer account. But J. Dupont ("L'Arrière-fond Biblique du Récit des Tentations de Jésus," NTS 3 [1956–57]: 287–304) has argued persuasively that Mark's brevity and the ambiguity of such statements as "he was with the wild animals" (Mark 1:13) implies that Mark's readers were familiar with a larger account to which Mark makes brief reference. The account could only have come from Jesus, given to his disciples perhaps after Caesarea Philippi (Dupont). Therefore it gives an important glimpse into Jesus' self-perception as the Son of God (3:17; 4:3, 6), and, judging by the Scripture he quotes, the way he perceived his own relation to Israel (cf. France, *Jesus*, pp. 50–53).

Both Matthew and Mark tie the temptations to Jesus' baptism (see on 4:1). Luke, however, inserts his genealogy between the two, suggesting a contrast between Adam, who though tested in the bliss of Eden yet fell, and Jesus, who was tested in the hardships of the wilderness yet triumphed. Jesus' responses to Satan (all taken from Deut 6–8; i.e., 6:13, 16; 8:3) have led some to argue that this account is a haggadic midrash—i.e., explanatory but minimally historical stories—on the OT text (cf. esp. B. Gerhardsson, *The Testing of God's Son* [Lund: CWK Gleerup, 1966]). But the story line stands independent of the OT background; there are more themes allusively hidden in Matthew's account than first meet the eye (e.g., possible "new Moses" motifs: Davies, *Setting*, pp. 45–48; cf. Bonnard; Petr Pokorny, "The Temptation Stories and Their Intention," NTS 20 [1974]: 115–27); and the repeated reference to Deuteronomy 6–8 is better explained in terms of Israel-Christ typology.

Luke reverses the order of the last two temptations for topographical reasons. Matthew's order is almost certainly original (Schweizer; Walvoord).

It is difficult to be certain exactly what happened or in what form Satan came to Jesus. Standing on a high mountain (v.8) would not itself provide a glimpse of "all the kingdoms of the world"; some supernatural vision is presupposed. Moreover a forty-day fast is scarcely the ideal background for a trek to three separate and rugged sites. When we remember that Paul was not always sure whether his visions were "in the body or out of the body" (2 Cor 12:2), we may be cautious about dogmatizing here. But there is no reason to think the framework of the story is purely symbolic as opposed to visionary, representing Jesus' inward struggles; if the demons could address him directly (e.g., 8:29, 31), it is difficult to say Satan wouldn't or couldn't do this.

1 Jesus' three temptations tie into his baptism, not only by the references to sonship and the Spirit, but by the opening "Then" (*tote*). Jesus' attestation as the Son (3:17) furnishes "the natural occasion for such special temptations as are here depicted" (Broadus). The same Spirit who engendered Jesus (1:20) and attested the Father's acknowledgment of his sonship (3:16–17) now leads him into the desert to be tempted by the devil. The "desert" (cf. on 3:1) is not only the place associated

with demonic activity (Isa 13:21; 34:14; Matt 12:43; Rev 18:2; Trench, pp. 7–8) but, in a context abounding with references to Deuteronomy 6–8, the place where Israel experienced her greatest early testings.

The devil must not be reduced to impersonal "forces" behind racism and pogroms (Schweizer). The Greek word *diabolos* strictly means "slanderer"; but the term is the regular LXX rendering of "Satan" (e.g., 1 Chron 21:1; Job 1:6–13; 2:1–7; Zech 3:1–2), the chief opposer of God, the archenemy who leads all the spiritual hosts of darkness (cf. Gen 3; 2 Sam 19:23; John 8:37–40; 1 Cor 11:10; 2 Cor 11:3; 12:7; Rev 12:3–9; 20:1–4; 7–10; Maier). In a day of rising occultism and open Satanism, it is easier to believe the Bible's plain witness to him than twenty years ago.

That Jesus should be led "by the Spirit" to be tempted "by the devil" is no stranger than Job 1:6–2:7 or 2 Samuel 24:1 (1 Chron 21:1). Recognizing that "to tempt" (*peirazō*) also means "to test" in a good or bad sense somewhat eases the problem. In Scripture "tempting" or "testing" can reveal or develop character (Gen 22:1; Exod 20:20; John 6:6; 2 Cor 13:5; Rev 2:2) as well as solicit to evil (1 Cor 7:5; 1 Thess 3:5). For us to "tempt" or "test" God is wrong because it reflects unbelief or attempted bribery (Exod 17:2, 7 [Ps 95:9]; Deut 6:16 [Matt 4:7]; Isa 7:12; Acts 5:9; 15:10). Moreover God uses means and may bring good out of his agents' evil motives—see Joseph's experience (Gen 50:19–20). In Jesus' "temptations" God clearly purposed to test him just as Israel was tested, and Jesus' responses prove that he understood.

2 The parallels with historic Israel continue. Jesus' fast (doubtless total abstention from food but not from drink; cf. Luke 4:2) of forty days and nights reflected Israel's forty-year wandering (Deut 8:2). Both Israel's and Jesus' hunger taught a lesson (Deut 8:3); both spent time in the desert preparatory to their respective tasks. Other parallels have been noticed (cf. Dupont). The main point is that both "sons" were tested by God's design (Deut 8:3, 5; cf. Exod 4:22; Gerhardsson, *Testing God's Son*, pp. 19–35), the one after being redeemed from Egypt and the other after his baptism, to prove their obedience and loyalty in preparation for their appointed work. The one "son" failed but pointed to the "Son" who would never fail (cf. on 2:15). In this sense the temptations legitimized Jesus as God's true Son (cf. Berger, "Die königlichen Messiastraditionen," pp. 15–18).

At the same time Jesus' hunger introduces us to a number of ironies to which Matthew more or less explicitly alludes: Jesus is hungry (v.2) but feeds others (14:13–21; 15:29–39); he grows weary (8:24) but offers others rest (11:28); he is the King Messiah but pays tribute (17:24–27); he is called the devil but casts out demons (12:22–32); he dies the death of a sinner but comes to save his people from their sins (1:21); he is sold for thirty pieces of silver but gives his life a ransom for many (20:28); he will not turn stones to bread for himself (4:3–4) but gives his own body as bread for people (26:26).

3–4 The tempter came to Jesus—we cannot say in what form—and referred to Jesus' sonship (v.3). The form of the "if" clause in Greek (*ei* + indicative) does not so much challenge his sonship as assume it to build a doubtful imperative. Satan was not inviting Jesus to doubt his sonship but to reflect on its meaning. Sonship of the living God, he suggested, surely means Jesus has the power and right to satisfy his own needs.

Jesus' response is based solely on Scripture: "It is written" (v.4). The Scripture is Deuteronomy 8:3, following the LXX, which reads "every word" instead of a more ambiguous Hebrew expression (unless the non-LXX reading of D be adopted: cf. Gundry, *Use of OT*, p. 67); and it applies initially to Israel. But the statement itself is an aphorism. Even though "man" (*ho anthrōpos*) can specify old Israel (e.g., Ps 80:17), yet it is always true that everyone must recognize his utter dependence on God's word. Jesus' food is to do the will of his Father who sent him (John 4:34).

The point of each temptation must be determined by closely examining both the temptation and Jesus' response. This clearly shows that this first temptation was no simple incitement to use improper means of making bread (Morison), or an attempt to use a miracle to prove to himself that he was really God's Son (J.A.T. Robinson, pp. 55–56) or to act alone without thought of others (Riesenfeld, pp. 87–88); it was a temptation to use his sonship in a way inconsistent with his God-ordained mission. The same taunt, "If you are the Son of God," is hurled at him in 27:40, when for him to have left the cross would have annulled the purpose of his coming. Similarly, though Jesus could have gained the aid of legions of angels, how then could the Scriptures that say Jesus had to suffer and die have been fulfilled (26:53–54)? Israel's hunger had been intended to show them that hearing and obeying the word of God is the most important thing in life (Deut 8:2–3). Likewise Jesus learned obedience through suffering as a son in God's house (Heb 3:5–6; 5:7–8). More necessary than bread for Jesus was obedience to God's Word.

In the light of these parallels, we must conclude that Satan's aim was to entice Jesus to use powers rightly his but which he had voluntarily abandoned to carry out the Father's mission. Reclaiming them for himself would deny the self-abasement implicit in his mission and in the Father's will. Israel demanded its bread but died in the wilderness; Jesus denied himself bread, retained his righteousness, and lived by faithful submission to God's Word. (There may be an allusion to Hab 2:4; cf. J. Andrew Kirk, "The Messianic Role of Jesus and the Temptation Narrative," EQ 44 [1972]: 11–29, 91–102.)

5–7 The second temptation (Luke's third) is set in the "holy city" (v.5), Jerusalem (cf. Neh 11:1; Isa 48:2; Dan 9:24; Matt 21:10; 27:53), on the highest point of the temple complex (*hieron* probably refers to the entire complex, not the sanctuary itself, which Jesus, not being a Levite, would not have approached; but see on 27:5). Josephus (Antiq. XV, 412[xi.v]) testifies to the enormous height from the structure's top to the ravine's bottom. Late Jewish midrash says that Messiah would prove himself by leaping from the temple pinnacle; but apart from its lateness, it mentions no spectators. So it is unlikely that this was a temptation for Jesus to prove himself to the people as a new "David" who will again rid Jerusalem of the "Jebusites" (i.e., Romans—contra Kirk, "Messianic Role," pp. 91–95).

Satan quoted Psalm 91:11–12 (v.6) from the LXX, omitting the words "to guard you in all your ways." The omission itself does not prove he handled the Scriptures deceitfully (contra Walvoord), since the quotation is well within the range of common NT citation patterns. Satan's deceit lay in misapplying his quotation into a temptation that easily traps the devout mind by apparently warranting what might otherwise be thought sinful. Psalm 91:11–12 refers to anyone who trusts God and thus preeminently to Jesus. The angels will lift such a person up in their hands like a nurse a baby (cf. Num 11:12; Deut 1:31; Isa 49:22; Heb 1:14). At the temple, the place where God has particularly manifested himself, Jesus is tempted to test his sonship ("If you are the Son of God") against God's pledge to protect his own. Deuteronomy 6:16 was Jesus' reply.

Jesus' hesitation came, not from wondering whether he or his Father could command the normal forces of nature (cf. 8:26; 14:31), but because Scripture forbids putting God to the test (v.7). The reference alludes to Exodus 17:2–7 (cf. Num 20:1–13), where the Israelites "put the Lord to the test" by demanding water. So Jesus was tempted by Satan to test God; but Jesus recognized Satan's testing as a sort of manipulative bribery expressly forbidden in the Scriptures (cf. esp. J.A.T. Robinson, *Twelve*, pp. 54–56). For both Israel and Jesus, demanding miraculous protection as proof of God's care was wrong; the appropriate attitude is trust and obedience (Deut 6:17). We see then, something of Jesus' handling of Scripture: his "also" shows that he would not allow any interpretation that generates what he knew would contradict some other passage.

8–10 The "very high mountain" (v.8) does not seem much more than a prop for the vision of the world's kingdoms (cf. introduction to this pericope). It is doubtful that there is a conscious reference to Moses' looking at the Promised Land (Deut 34:1–4; contra Dupont, Hill); the parallels are not close. No condition Moses could have met at that point would have let him enter the land.

Satan offers the kingdoms of the world and their "splendor" without showing their sin. Jesus, however, came to remove sin. Here was a temptation "to achieve power by worship of God's rival" (France, *Jesus*, p. 52), a shortcut to fullest messianic authority. Satan was offering an interpretation of the theocratic ideal that sidestepped the Cross and introduced idolatry. At Jesus' baptism the Voice spoke words that united Davidic messiahship and suffering servanthood (cf. on 3:17); here was enticement to enjoy the former without the latter. Small wonder Jesus would later turn on Peter so sharply when the apostle made a similar suggestion (16:23).

Jesus recognized that Satan's suggestion entailed depriving God of his exclusive claim to worship: neither God's "son" Israel nor God's "Son" Jesus may swerve from undivided allegiance to God himself (v.10; cf. Exod 23:20–33; Deut 6:13; cf. esp. McNeile, Bonnard). So Jesus responded with a third "it is written" and banished Satan from his presence. The time would come when Jesus' expanding kingdom would progressively destroy the kingdom Satan had to offer (12:25–28; cf. Luke 10:18). The day still lies ahead when King Messiah's last enemy is destroyed (1 Cor 15:25–26). But Jesus achieves it all without compromising his filial submission to the Father.

In other words Jesus had in mind from the very beginning of his earthly ministry the combination of royal kingship and suffering servanthood attested at his baptism and essential to his mission. Moreover the twin themes of kingly authority and filial submission, developed so clearly in the fourth Gospel (cf. Carson, *Divine Sovereignty*, pp. 146–62), are already present as the complementary poles of the life and self-revelation of Immanuel: "God with us."

11 The devil left Jesus "until an opportune time" (Luke 4:13); and Matthew's present tense (*aphiēsin*) may suggest the same thing (Hill, *Matthew*). Though the conflict has barely begun, the pattern of obedience and trust has been established. He has learned to resist the devil (cf. James 4:7). The angelic help is not some passing blessing but a sustained one (the imperfect tense is probably significant). Jesus had refused to relieve his hunger by miraculously turning stones to bread;

now he is fed supernaturally (*diēkonoun*, "attended," is often used in connection with food; e.g., 8:15; 25:44; 27:55; Acts 6:2; cf. Elijah in 1 Kings 19:6–7). He had refused to throw himself off the temple heights in the hope of angelic help; now angels feed him. He had refused to take a shortcut to inherit the kingdom of the world; now he fulfills Scripture by beginning his ministry and announcing the kingdom in Galilee of the Gentiles (vv. 12–17).

Notes

1–11 The question of the impeccability of Christ is much discussed in older literature but is of doubtful concern to Matthew in this pericope. The problem is partly definitional: to say Christ could not sin does not resolve the nature of the impossibility, and many writers have said he could not sin because he would not (cf. Trench, pp. 25–30). But at a deeper level, the problem concerns the truth of the Incarnation and how to formulate it. The NT documents affirm both Jesus' deity and his humanity, and neither of these affirmations may be permitted to deny the complementary truth. One might argue that Christ's impeccability is a function of his deity but must not be taken to mitigate his humanity, and Christ's temptability is a function of his humanity but must not be taken to mitigate his deity.

2 The aorist participle νηστεύσας (*nēsteusas*, "after fasting") does not prove the hunger began only after the forty days were over, since an aorist participle sometimes indicates action coordinate with the main verb. Luke's more explicit statement has been pushed too hard by some scholars: Luke is saying that Jesus' hunger was caused by the forty-day fast, not that the hunger began then. There is little exegetical warrant for appealing to the supernatural here.

2. *Jesus' early Galilean ministry* (4:12–25)

a. *The beginning*

4:12–17

> [12]When Jesus heard that John had been put in prison, he returned to Galilee. [13]Leaving Nazareth, he went and lived in Capernaum, which was by the lake in the area of Zebulun and Naphtali— [14]to fulfill what was said through the prophet Isaiah:
>
> > [15]"Land of Zebulun and land of Naphtali,
> > the way to the sea, along the Jordan,
> > Galilee of the Gentiles—
> > [16]the people living in darkness
> > have seen a great light;
> > on those living in the land of the shadow of death
> > a light has dawned."
>
> [17]From that time on Jesus began to preach, "Repent, for the kingdom of heaven is near."

12 John the Baptist's imprisonment appears to have prompted Jesus to return (cf. Notes) to Galilee. Though Mark 1:14–15 likewise links the two events, it is saying too much to conclude that Matthew has so strengthened the language to make John's imprisonment the cause of Jesus' withdrawal (*akousas* more likely means "when he heard" than "because he heard"). Equally important is the fact that the language suggests that Jesus remained for some time in Judea—unless we suppose the Baptist's arrest immediately followed Jesus' baptism. The Synoptics make no mention of Jesus' early Judean ministry but imply that his ministry began in Galilee. By contrast the fourth Gospel seems to presuppose an earlier Galilean ministry (John 1:19–2:12), a Judean ministry that overlapped with that of the Baptist (John 2:13–3:21), and then a return to the north via Samaria (John 3:22–4:42). The Johannine chronology has often been dismissed as of little historical worth. Yet there are hints even in the synoptic Gospels that presuppose an early Judean ministry (e.g., Luke 10:38), one such hint being the delay implicit in this verse.

If this approach is valid, we must ask why the synoptists eliminate Jesus' earliest months of ministry. Several reasons are possible.

1. With the Baptist's removal from the scene, Jesus' ministry entered a new phase. The function of the forerunner was over; the one to whom he pointed had come. This transfer might be neatly indicated by beginning the account of Jesus' ministry from the time of John's imprisonment. (Compare years of intercalation among OT kings and their varied treatment by OT writers.)

2. By contrast, when the fourth Gospel was written, the explicit connection between the Baptist and Jesus may have been of more urgent interest if the writer was responding to organized groups of the Baptist's followers (cf. Acts 19:1–4). The synoptists do not seem to be under such pressure.

3. In Matthew, Galilee is of profound significance because it heralds the fulfillment of prophecy (vv.14–16) and points to the gospel's extension to "all nations" (28:19).

According to 1 Maccabees 5:23, the Jewish population in Galilee in 164 B.C. was so small it could be transported to Judea for protection. By Jesus' day, however, though the large population was mixed, owing to both the proximity of Gentile peoples in surrounding areas and the importation of colonists during the Maccabean conquest, the Jewish population was substantial. The many theories concerning the influence of this region on Jesus and thence on Christianity have been neatly summarized and criticized by L. Goppelt (*Christentum und Judentum* [Gütersloh: Bertelsmann, 1954] pp. 32–41). "Galilee" as referring to some part of the northern district has long roots (cf. Josh 20:7; 1 Kings 9:11; 2 Kings 15:29).

13 In Luke, Jesus' move from Nazareth to Capernaum (4:31) follows the violent reaction of the Nazareth townspeople (vv.16–30); and it is uncertain whether Matthew's account (13:54–58) reports the same incident or another one. Capernaum ("village of Nahum"?) lay a little north of the plain of Gennesaret (14:34), on the northwest shore of Lake Galilee. Tell Hum marks the site today, its synagogue ruins dating from the second century. The village enjoyed a fishing industry that probably demanded the presence of a tax collector's booth (9:9). Here, too, was Peter's house (8:14; cf. Mark 1:29; 2:1). But Matthew is interested in pointing out Capernaum's location with reference to the ancient tribal allotments of Zebulun and Naphtali as showing the minute correspondence with the prophecy cited in vv.15–16.

14–16 Jesus' move fulfilled (v.14; cf. Notes) Isaiah 9:1–2. This prophecy is part of a large structure looking to Immanuel's coming (see on 1:23). It is extraordinarily difficult to identify the text form; either this is an independent translation of the Hebrew (Gundry, *Use of OT*, pp. 105–8) or else a modification of divergent LXX MSS (Chilton, *God in Strength*, p. 111). NIV's "the way to the sea" (v.15) is better translated "seawards," i.e., lying by the Sea of Galilee; and "along the Jordan," though convenient, has little lexical warrant and should be replaced by "beyond the Jordan" (cf. Notes).

The point of the quotation is clear enough. In despised Galilee, the place where people live in darkness (i.e., without the religious and cultic advantages of Jerusalem and Judea), the land of the shadow of death (i.e., where the darkness is most dense; cf. Job 10:21; Ps 107:10; Jer 13:16; Amos 5:8), here the light has dawned (v.16). "Dawned" (*aneteilen*) suggests that the light first shone brilliantly here, not that it was shining brightly elsewhere and then moved here (Lindars, *Apologetic*, p. 198). This was God's prophesied plan. Matthew is not interested in the mere fact that some prophecy was fulfilled in Galilee but in this particular prophecy: from of old the Messiah was promised to "Galilee of the Gentiles" (*tōn ethnōn*), a foreshadowing of the commission to "all nations" (*panta ta ethnē*, 28:19). Moreover, if the messianic light dawns on the darkest places, then Messiah's salvation can only be a bestowal of grace—namely, that Jesus came to call, not the righteous, but sinners (9:13).

17 Several have argued that the words "from that time on" (*apo tote*), found only here and in 16:21; 26:16, mark major turning points in this Gospel (Stonehouse, *Witness of Matthew*, pp. 129–31; Kingsbury, *Structure*). In its strong form, this theory divides Matthew into three sections (1:1–4:16; 4:17–16:20; 16:21–28:20) with important interpretive implications. Though there are good reasons for rejecting this structure (cf. Introduction, section 14), the phrase "from that time on" nevertheless marks an important turning point because it ties something new to what has just preceded it.

We best see this when we examine the content of Jesus' preaching. Assuming the soundness of the text preserved in the NIV (cf. Notes), the burden of Jesus' preaching so far is, in itself, identical to that of John the Baptist: "Repent, for the kingdom of heaven is near" (v.17; cf. 3:2). Matthew often shows ties between Jesus and John the Baptist (Klostermann; Chilton, *God in Strength*, p. 117). But when John the Baptist says these words, they are placed in an OT context that highlights his function as the forerunner who looks forward to the Messiah and his kingdom (3:2–12); when Jesus says the same words, they are linked (by "from that time") with an OT context that insists Jesus fulfills the promises of a light rising to shine on the Gentiles (Schweizer).

The longstanding debate that largely discounted C.H. Dodd's theory (that "is near" [3:2; 4:17] equals "has come" [12:28]) rather misses the mark. Neither Dodd nor his critics are subtle enough. The kingdom (see on 3:2) is still future. But the separate contexts of the announcements made by John and by Jesus (3:2; 4:17) show that with Jesus the kingdom has drawn so near that it has actually dawned. Therefore Jesus' hearers must repent—a demand made not only by the Baptist but by Jesus. The structure of the book thus sets up an implicit parallelism: Jesus is not so much a new Moses as a new Joshua (on their names, cf. 1:21); for as Moses did not enter the Promised Land but was succeeded by Joshua who did, so John the Baptist announces the kingdom and is followed by Jesus (Joshua) who leads his people into it (cf. Albright and Mann).

Notes

12 The verb ἀνεχώρησεν (*anechōrēsen*, "he returned") is characteristic of Matthew (2:12, 13, 14, 22; 4:12, 24; 12:15; 14:13; 15:21; 27:5). Only in 9:24 does Jesus use it; elsewhere in the NT it occurs only in Mark 3:7; John 6:15; Acts 23:19; 26:31. On the basis of Matthew's usage, Hill (*Matthew*), following Fenton, suggests the verb means Jesus withdrew strategically—i.e., that the rejection of God's word in one place (here in John's ministry) leads to its proclamation in another place (in Jesus' ministry). But this meaning is possible only in 12:15; 14:13; 15:21; it is impossible in most of the other occurrences in Matthew. More commonly Jesus "withdraws" because of threats or plots. That he then preaches elsewhere is a consequence of his withdrawal for safety's sake, not a sign of judgment on a people who will not hear.

14 The dash separating v.13 and v.14 (NIV) rightly interprets the ἵνα (*hina*, "in order to") as referring to Jesus' move rather than Jesus' motive. In other words, judging by his usage elsewhere (e.g., 1:22; 2:15), Matthew is not saying that Jesus moved in order to fulfill Scripture but that his move fulfilled Scripture.

15 The words ὁδὸν θαλάσσης (*hodon thalassēs*, "the way to the sea") are in LXX Isa 8:23 and may well be a literal rendering of the Hebrew דֶּרֶךְ יָם (*derek yām*), "seawards"; i.e. "by the sea" (cf. "by the way of the sea," NIV, Isa 9:1) rather than the "way *to* the sea" (cf. Turner, *Syntax*, p. 247). The translation "along the Jordan" for πέραν τοῦ Ἰορδάνου (*peran tou Iordanou*) reflects the fact that Zebulun and Naphtali do not extend east of the Jordan. But linguistically the phrase must mean "beyond the Jordan." Normally "beyond the Jordan" refers to the east bank, but the vantage of the speaker must be borne in mind, and sometimes it refers to the west bank (e.g., Num 32:19; Deut 11:30; Josh 5:1; 22:7). The Hebrew is more naturally translated "beyond Jordan." Most likely Isaiah sees the Assyrians coming from the northeast; as they progressively inflict judgment on the nation, they proceed "beyond the Jordan" to the west bank. So Matthew's rendering may simply preserve the same stance—in which case, is there a further reference to the "exile" now ended by Messiah's coming (see on 2:17–18)? The LXX inserts a καί (*kai*, "and") before "beyond the Jordan," eliminating the problem by making two regions. Yet if Matthew is reflecting his own stance, it is possible he is writing from the east bank (so Slingerland), perhaps from the Decapolis. It is hard to be sure of this because of uncertainties in the text form of the quotation and in the meaning of the Hebrew. See further on 19:1.

16 Αὐτοῖς (*autois*, "on them") (is redundant after τοῖς καθημένοις (*tois kathēmenois*, lit., "on those sitting [NIV, 'living']"); but, though not unknown in classical Greek, it is common in Hebrew (cf. BDF, par. 466[4]).

17 The reading omitting μετανοεῖτε (*metanoeite*, "repent") and γάρ (*gar*, "for") is not well attested but is treated seriously because of the possibility of assimilation to 3:2. Nevertheless the longer text stands (cf. esp. Chilton, *God in Strength*, pp. 302–10; Fee, pp. 164f.).

b. *Calling the first disciples*

4:18–22

[18]As Jesus was walking beside the Sea of Galilee, he saw two brothers, Simon called Peter and his brother Andrew. They were casting a net into the lake, for they were fishermen. [19]"Come, follow me," Jesus said, "and I will make you fishers of men." [20]At once they left their nets and followed him.

[21]Going on from there, he saw two other brothers, James son of Zebedee and his brother John. They were in a boat with their father Zebedee, preparing their nets. Jesus called them, [22]and immediately they left the boat and their father and followed him.

Since no temporal expression links this pericope with the last one, there may have been some time lapse. Bultmann's skepticism (*Synoptic Tradition*, p. 28) about the historical worth of these verses is unwarranted (cf. Hill, *Matthew*).

The relation of the various "callings" of the disciples in the Gospel records is obscure. If we take John 1:35–51 as historical, Simon, Andrew, Philip, and Nathaniel first followed Jesus at an earlier date. On returning to Galilee, they again took up their normal work. This is inherently plausible. The disciples' commitment and understanding advanced by degrees; even after the Resurrection, they returned once more to their fishing (John 21). Here (4:20) an earlier commitment may explain their haste in following Jesus. If the miracle of Luke 5:1–11 occurred the night before Matthew 4:18–22 (Mark 1:16–20), that would be another reason for their immediate response to Jesus. In this connection the meaning of *katartizontas* ("preparing," v.21; cf. below) is significant. See further 9:9–13; 10:1–4.

18 In Hebrew "sea," like the German *See*, can refer to lakes. Classical Greek prefers not to use *thalassa* (or *thalatta*—"sea") for lakes; and Luke follows the same pattern by using *limnē* ("lake"), though Matthew, Mark, and John prefer "sea." The Sea of Galilee (named from the district), otherwise known as the "Lake of Gennesaret" (the name "Kinnereth" [Num 34:11; Josh 12:3] comes from a plain on its northwest shore; cf. Matt 14:34), or the "Sea of Tiberias" (a city Herod built on the southwest shore: John 6:1; 21:1), is 12¼ by 8¾ miles at the longest and broadest points respectively. Its surface is 682 feet below sea level. It is subject to violent squalls. In Jesus' day it supported flourishing fisheries; on its west shore were nine towns, and "Bethsaida" may be freely translated "Fishtown." Simon and his brother Andrew came from Bethsaida (John 1:44), though Capernaum was now their home (Mark 1:21, 29).

Simon, Matthew says, was "called Peter"; but he does not tell us how Peter received this name (cf. 10:2; 16:18; Mark 3:16; Luke 6:14). While uncertainties remain, what is quite certain is that *kêpā'*("rock," "stone"), the Aramaic equivalent of "Peter," was already an accepted name in Jesus' day (cf. Joseph A. Fitzmyer, "Aramaic Kepha' and Peter's Name in the New Testament," in Best and Wilson, pp. 121–32)—a fact that has an important bearing on the interpretation of 16:17–18.

Simon and Andrew were casting a "net" (*amphiblestron*, a NT *hapax legomenon* [found only once], with a cognate at Mark 1:16). It refers to a circular "casting-net" and is not to be confused with the more generic term *diktua* in 4:20.

19–20 Greek has several expressions for "follow me" (v.19; cf. at 10:38; Luke 9:23; 14:27), but they all presuppose a physical "following" during Jesus' ministry. His "followers" were not just "hearers"; they actually followed their Master around (as students then did) and became, as it were, trainees. The metaphor "fishers of men" glances back to the work of the two being called. It may also be reminiscent of Jeremiah 16:16. There Yahweh sends "fishermen" to gather his people for the Exile; here Jesus sends "fishermen" to announce the end of the Exile (cf. on 1:11–12; 2:17–18) and the beginning of the messianic reign. But this allusion is uncertain; the danger of "parallelomania" (coined by S. Sandmel, "Parallelomania," JBL 81 [1962]: 2–13) is evident when E.C.B. MacLaurin ("The Divine Fishermen," *St. Mark's Review* 94 [1978]: 26–28) works out many parallels and then opts for Ugaritic mythology a millennium and a half old. In any case there is a straight line from this commission to the Great Commission (28:18–20). Jesus' followers are indeed to catch men.

On the prompt obedience of Simon and Andrew (v.20), see the comments at the introduction to this section. Peter later used this obedience almost as a bartering point (19:27).

21–22 This second pair of brothers were "preparing their nets" (v.21), which sounds as if they were just setting out. The verb *katartizō*, however, connotes "mend" or "restore to a former condition." So James and John may have been making repairs after a night's fishing (cf. Luke 5:1–11 and its possible place in the chronology). Fenton notes that Paul uses *katartizo* for perfecting the church (1 Cor 1:10; 2 Cor 13:11) and sees here an allusion to pastoral ministry. But this is fanciful because the verb is not a technical term. The boat (*ploion* was used of all kinds of boats) was big enough for several men (Mark 1:20). Mark's remark that hired men were left with Zebedee when his sons followed Jesus reminds us that we must not exaggerate the ignorance and poverty of Jesus' first followers. While they were not trained scribes or rabbis, they were not illiterate, stupid, or destitute. Indeed, Peter's protest in 19:27 implies that many or all of the Twelve had given up much to follow Jesus.

Jesus took the initiative and "called" James and John. In the Synoptics, unlike Paul's epistles, Jesus' call is not necessarily effectual. But in this instance it was immediately obeyed.

c. *Spreading the news of the kingdom*

4:23–25

> ²³Jesus went throughout Galilee, teaching in their synagogues, preaching the good news of the kingdom, and healing every disease and sickness among the people. ²⁴News about him spread all over Syria, and people brought to him all who were ill with various diseases, those suffering severe pain, the demon-possessed, those having seizures, and the paralyzed, and he healed them. ²⁵Large crowds from Galilee, the Decapolis, Jerusalem, Judea and the region across the Jordan followed him.

Summaries are common to narrative literature; but the one before us, with its parallel in 9:35–38, has distinctive features.

1. It does not just summarize what has gone before but shows the geographical extent and varied activity of Jesus' ministry.

2. It therefore sets the stage for the particular discourses and stories that follow and implies that the material presented is but a representative sampling of what was available.

3. It is not a mere chronicle but conveys theological substance. Thus it is easy to detect different emphases between this summary and 9:35–38 (see comments in loc.).

Older commentators see in vv.23–25 a first circuit of Galilee and in 9:35–38 a second one. This is possible, but both pericopes may refer to the constant ministry of Jesus rather than to tightly defined circuits.

23 Jesus' ministry included teaching, preaching, and healing. Galilee, the district covered, is small (approximately seventy by forty miles); but according to Josephus (Life 235[45]; War III, 41–43[iii.2]), writing one generation later, Galilee had 204 cities and villages, each with no fewer than fifteen thousand persons. Even if this figure refers only to the walled cities and not to the villages (which is not what Josephus says), a most conservative estimate points to a large population, even if less than Josephus's three million. At the rate of two villages or towns per day, three months would be required to visit all of them, with no time off for the Sabbath. Jesus "went around doing good" (Acts 10:38; cf. Mark 1:39; 6:6). The sheer physical drain must have been enormous. Above all we must recognize that Jesus was an itinerant preacher and teacher who necessarily repeated approximately the same material again and again and faced the same problems, illnesses, and needs again and again.

The connection between "teaching" and "synagogue" recurs at 9:35; 13:54. A visiting Jew might well be asked to teach in the local synagogue (on which cf. Moore, *Judaism*, 1:281–307; Douglas, *Illustrated Dictionary*, 3:1499–503) as part of regular worship (e.g., Luke 4:16). The word "their" may indicate a time when the synagogue and the church had divided. On the other hand, it may simply indicate that the author and his readers viewed these events from outside Galilee (see further on 7:29; 9:35 et al.).

The message Jesus preaches is the "good news [*euangelion*, "gospel"] of the kingdom." The term recurs in 9:35; 24:14, and becomes "this gospel" in 26:13. "Of the kingdom" is an objective genitive: the "good news" concerns the kingdom (cf. Notes), whose "nearness" has already been announced (3:2; 4:17) and which is the central subject of the Sermon on the Mount (5–7). Mark prefers "the gospel" or "the gospel of Christ" or "the gospel of God" (Mark 1:1, 14; 8:35; 10:29; 13:10); but the difference between these expressions and "gospel of the kingdom" is purely linguistic, since the "good news" concerns God and the inbreaking of his saving reign in the person of his Son the Messiah.

The healings of various diseases among the people further attest the kingdom's presence and advance (cf. 11:2–6; Isa 35:5–6). Walvoord (p. 39) relegates these "kingdom blessings . . . due for fulfillment in the future kingdom" to the status of mere "credentials of the King"; but if the kingdom blessings are present, then the kingdom too must have broken in, even if not yet in the splendor of its consummation (cf. Rev 21:3–5).

24 The geographical extent of "Syria" is uncertain. From the perspective of Jesus in Galilee, Syria was to the north. From the Roman viewpoint Syria was a Roman province embracing all Palestine (cf. Luke 2:2; Acts 15:23, 41; Gal 1:21), Galilee excepted, since it was under the independent administration of Herod Antipas at this time. The term "Syria" reflects the extent of the excitement aroused by Jesus' ministry; if the Roman use of the term is here presumed, it shows his effect on people far beyond the borders of Israel. Those "ill with various diseases" and "those suffering severe" pain are divided into three overlapping categories: (1) the demon possessed (cf. 8:28–34; 12:22–29); (2) those having seizures—viz., any kind of insanity or irrational behavior whether or not related to demon possession (17:14–18; on *selēniazomenous* ["epileptics"], which etymologically refers to the "moonstruck" [i.e., "lunatic"], cf. DNTT, 3:734; J.M. Ross, "Epileptic or Moonstruck?" BTh 29 [1978]: 126–28)—and (3) the paralyzed, whose condition also had various causes.

In the NT sickness may result directly from a particular sin (e.g., John 5:14; 1 Cor 11:30) or may not (e.g., John 9:2–3). But both Scripture and Jewish tradition take sickness as resulting directly or indirectly from living in a fallen world (cf. on 8:17).

The Messianic Age would end such grief (Isa 11:1–5; 35:5–6). Therefore Jesus' miracles, dealing with every kind of ailment, not only herald the kingdom but show that God has pledged himself to deal with sin at a basic level (cf. 1:21; 8:17).

25 Jesus' reputation at this point extended far beyond Galilee, even though that is where the light "dawned" (v.16). Two of the named areas, the region across the Jordan (east bank? see on v.15) and the Decapolis, were mostly made up of Gentiles, a fact already emphasized (see on 1:3–5; 2:1–12, 22–23; 3:9; 4:8, 15–16). The Decapolis (lit., "Ten Cities") refers to a region east of Galilee extending from Damascus in the north to Philadelphia in the south, ten cities (under varied reckonings) making up the count (cf. S. Thomas Parker, "The Decapolis Reviewed," JBL 94 [1975]: 437–41). People from all these areas "followed" Jesus. Despite contrary arguments "follow" does not necessarily indicate solid discipleship. It may, as here, refer to those who at some particular time followed Jesus around in his itinerant ministry and thus were loosely considered his disciples.

Notes

23 Further evidence that "preaching the good news of the kingdom" requires taking "of the kingdom" as an objective genitive is suggested by comparing the Greek κηρύσσων τὸ εὐαγγέλιον τῆς βασιλείας (kēryssōn to euangelion tēs basileias, "preaching the good news of the kingdom") with the expression found in Luke 8:1: εὐαγγελιζόμενος τὴν βασιλείαν (euangelizomenos tēn basileian, "proclaiming the good news of the kingdom"), in which "kingdom" is the direct object.
24 The strange expression τοὺς κακῶς ἔχοντας (tous kakōs echontas; NIV, "[those] ill") is idiomatic: elsewhere in the NT, only at 8:16; 9:12; 14:35; Mark 1:32; 2:17; 6:55; Luke 5:31. The only other strictly comparable constructions in the NT are in Acts 24:25; 1 Tim 5:25; 1 Peter 4:5.

B. First Discourse: The Sermon on the Mount

5:1–7:29

The Sermon on the Mount is the first of five major discourses in the Gospel of Matthew. All five follow blocks of narrative material; all five end with the same formula (see on 7:28–29; and Introduction, section 14). Not only because it is first and longest of the five, and therefore helps determine the critical approach toward all of them, but also because it deals with ethical issues of fundamental importance in every age, this "sermon" has called forth thousands of books and articles. Some orientation is necessary.

A useful starting point is Warren S. Kissinger's *The Sermon on the Mount: A History of Interpretation and Bibliography* (Metuchen, N.J.: Scarecrow, 1975). K. Beyschlag ("Zur Geschichte der Bergpredigt in der Alten Kirche," *Zeitschrift für Theologie und Kirche* 74 [1977]: 291–322) and Robert M. Grant ("The Sermon on the Mount in Early Christianity," *Semeia* 12 [1978]: 215–31) unfold the treatment of these chapters in the earliest centuries of Christianity. For clarification of the varied treatment of the sermon during the present century, we are now indebted to Ursula Berner (*Die Bergpredigt: Rezeption und Auslegung im 20. Jahrhundert* [Göttingen:

Vandenhoeck und Ruprecht, 1979]). Popular, recent expositions of use to the working preacher include James M. Boice, *The Sermon on the Mount* (Grand Rapids: Zondervan, 1972); Carson, *Sermon on the Mount;* D. Martyn Lloyd-Jones, *Studies in the Sermon on the Mount,* 2 vols. (London: IVP, 1959–60); F.B. Meyer, *The Sermon on the Mount* (reprint ed., Grand Rapids: Baker, 1959); Stott.

Four introductory matters demand comment:

1. *Unity and authenticity of the discourse.* Since the work of Hans Windisch (*The Meaning of the Sermon on the Mount,* tr. S.M. Gilmour [1929; reprint ed., Philadelphia: Fortress, 1951), few have regarded Matthew 5–7 as thoroughly authentic. The most common proposal today is that these chapters preserve some authentic teaching of Jesus, originally presented at various occasions and collected and shaped by oral tradition. To this the evangelist has added church teaching, taught, perhaps, by an inspired prophet speaking for the exalted Christ; and the discourse has then been further molded by catechetical and liturgical considerations (so, for instance, J. Jeremias, *The Sermon on the Mount* [Philadelphia: Fortress, 1963], and the majesterial study by Davies, *Setting*). According to these critics, at best the so-called Sermon on the Mount preserves no more than isolated sayings of Jesus.

Much of one's judgment in these matters depends on conclusions as to source, form, and redaction criticism (cf. Introduction, sections 1–3). For instance, if one insists that every saying elsewhere in the Gospels similar to any saying in Matthew 5–7 must be traced back to one utterance only (thus ignoring Jesus' role as an itinerant preacher), one may develop a more or less plausible theory of the growth of oral tradition in each case (so, e.g., H.-T. Wrege, *Die Überlieferungsgeschichte der Bergpredigt* [WUNT 9; Tübingen: J.C.B. Mohr, 1968]). This can be done precisely because so many sayings in these chapters do occur elsewhere, either in roughly similar or in identical language (see on 5:13, 15, 18, 25, 29, 32; 6:9, 22, 24–25; 7:2, 7, 17, 23). Moreover, where parallels exist, Matthew's forms are often more stylized or structured.

There is no need to repeat introductory remarks about authenticity. Several observations will, however, focus the approach adopted here.

a. We cannot make much out of Matthew's clear tendency to treat his material topically. Nor can we conclude from his grouping of miracles that he has composed his discourses out of grouped but independent sayings. In the former case Matthew does not pretend to do otherwise, whereas in all his discourses he gives the impression, especially in his concluding formulas (7:28–29; 11:1; 13:53; 19:1; 26:1), that the material is not only authentic but delivered on one occasion.

b. We dare not claim too much on the basis of the unity or its lack in the discourses. Even if the Sermon on the Mount represents material Jesus delivered on one occasion, perhaps over several days, its extreme compression, necessary selection, and problems of translation from Aramaic to Greek (assuming Jesus preached in Aramaic) might all unite to break the flow. If the unity of the discourse be defended (e.g., by A. Farrar, *St Matthew and St Mark* [London: Dacre/A. and C. Black, 1954, 1966], but cf. Davies, *Setting*, pp. 9–13), that unity might be nothing more than the evangelist's editing. He must have seen some coherence in these chapters to leave them in this form. Thus neither unity nor disunity are sufficient criteria for the authenticity of a brief account of extensive discourse.

c. We must suppose that Jesus preached the same thing repeatedly (see on 4:23–25); he was an extremely busy itinerant preacher. The pithier the saying, the more likely it was to be repeated word-perfect. The more common the natural phenomenon behind a metaphor or aphorism, the more likely Jesus repeated it in new situations. Any experienced itinerant preacher will confirm the inescapability of these tendencies. More important, if one distances oneself from the more radical presuppositions of form and tradition criticism, the NT documents themselves confirm this approach (cf. 11:15 with 13:9; 18:3 with 19:14, and cf. 20:26 [and Luke 12:24–31; John 13:13–17]; Matt 17:20 with 21:21; 10:32 with Luke 9:26 and 12:8; 10:24 with Luke 6:40 and John 13:16 and 15:20; 10:38–39 with 16:24–25 and Luke 17:33 and John 12:25). Even longer sections like Jesus' model prayer (6:9–13; see discussion below) are susceptible of such treatment, if for different reasons.

d. Jesus himself was a master teacher. In his sayings, whose authenticity is not greatly disputed, there is evidence of structure, contrast, and assonance. So when some scholars tell us that Matthew's account has more structure (perhaps from catechetical influence) than the other Synoptics, is this a sign of greater nearness to or distance from Jesus? What criteria are there for distinguishing the two possibilities? Surely if we do not pretend to be able to retrieve all the *ipsissima verba* of Jesus but only his *ipsissima vox*, most of the common criteria for testing authenticity evaporate.

e. The assumptions of some form critics make their work more questionable than they think. For if a certain kind of saying tends to take on a certain form in oral tradition, and if the period of oral transmission is long enough to develop that form, then the repetition of the saying on half-a-dozen different occasions in slightly different words would ultimately lead to one common form of the saying. Thus, far from enabling the critic to trace a precise development, form criticism obliterates the richness of the tradition attested by the evangelists themselves.

f. As Matthew's Gospel stands, we must weigh two disparate pieces of evidence: (1) that all five of Matthew's discourses are bracketed by introductory and concluding remarks that cannot fail to give the impression that he presents his discourses as not only authentic but delivered by Jesus on the specified occasions and (2) that many individual bits of each discourse find synoptic parallels in other settings. Many think the second point to be so strong that they conclude that Matthew himself composed the discourses. Conservative writers in this camp say that all of Jesus' sayings are authentic but that Matthew brought them together in their present form. Therefore the first piece of evidence has to be reinterpreted; i.e., the introductory and concluding notes framing each of Matthew's discourses are seen as artistic, compositional devices.

A more subtle approach is to say that Jesus actually did deliver a discourse on each of the five occasions specified but that not all the material Matthew records was from that occasion. In other words the evangelist has added certain "footnotes" of his own, at a time when orthography was much more flexible and there were no convenient ways to indicate what he was doing. While either of these reconstructions is possible, each faces two steep hurdles: (1) the introductory and concluding brackets around the five discourses do not belong to any clear first-century pattern or genre that would show the reader that they are merely artistic devices and not the real settings they manifestly claim to be; and (2) it is remarkable that each conclusion sweeps together all the sayings of the preceding discourse under some such rubric as "when Jesus had finished saying these things" (a possible exception is 11:1). That the introductory and concluding formulas were not recognizable as artistic devices is confirmed by the fact that for the first millennium and a half or so of its existence, the church recognized them as concrete settings. (This is not a surreptitious appeal to return to precritical thinking but a note on the recognizability of a literary genre.)

In view of the above, it seems the wiser course to believe Matthew intended to present real, historical settings for his discourses; and the parallels found elsewhere, though they must be considered individually, do not seem to present insurmountable problems. While many sayings in the Gospels appear in "loose" or in "floating" settings, where an evangelist ostensibly specifies the context, the authenticity of that context must be assumed. This is particularly easy to maintain in Matthew if the date and authorship are as stated in the Introduction (sections 5–6). Thus this commentary takes Matthew's settings seriously. Not that it takes all the discourses as verbatim accounts or unedited reports of Jesus' teaching, it rather assumes that they are condensed notes, largely in Matthew's idiom, selected and presented in accord with his own concerns. But behind them stand the voice and authority of Jesus.

2. *Relation to the Sermon on the Plain (Luke 6:20–49).* Augustine claimed that Matthew 5–7 and the passage in Luke are two separate discourses, and almost all writers agreed with him till the Reformation. Even after it some scholars followed Augustine (e.g., Alexander, Plumptre), and today some are returning to Augustine's view.

Origen, Chrysostom, Calvin, and the majority of recent scholars, however, defend the view (often with appropriate theorizing about Q) that the two accounts represent the same discourse. This has much to commend it. The two sermons begin with beatitudes and end with the same simile. Nearly everything in the Sermon on the Plain is in some form in the Sermon on the Mount and often in identical order. Both are immediately followed by the same events—viz., entrance into Capernaum and healing the centurion's servant. (The point is valid even if it indicates nothing more than a common link in the tradition.) Luke's sermon is much shorter and has its own thematic emphases (e.g., humility); and much of the extra material in Matthew is scattered elsewhere in Luke, especially in his "travel narrative" (Luke 9:51–18:14; discussed at 19:1–2). Moreover Matthew speaks of a mountain, Luke a plain; and Luke's discourse follows the choosing of the Twelve, which does not take place in Matthew till chapter 10.

But these problems can be readily solved.

a. Much of what Luke omits, mostly in Matthew 5:17–37; 6:1–18, is exactly the sort of material that would interest Matthew's Jewish readers more than Luke's readers. Luke has also omitted some material from his "Sermon on the Plain" that he has placed elsewhere (Matt 6:25–34; Luke 12:22–31). It is possible that Jesus gave the sermon more than once. Alternatively, Luke's context is so loose that he may have been responsible for the topical rearrangement. In any case to insist that a writer must include everything he knows or everything in his sources is poor methodology. In the other Matthean discourses, Matthew includes much and Luke includes less; in the Sermon on the Mount, though Matthew's account is much longer than Luke's, in certain places Luke preserves a little more than Matthew (compare Matt 5:12 with Luke 6:23–26; Matt 5:47 with Luke 6:33–35).

b. Of the several solutions to the mountain or plain, the most convincing one takes Matthew's "on a mountainside" to mean "up in the hills" and Luke's "plain" as being some kind of plateau. The linguistic evidence is convincing (see on 5:1–2).

c. Luke's order, placing the sermon after the choosing of the Twelve, is historically believable. But Matthew is clearly topical in his order. Connectives at 5:1; 8:1; 9:35; 11:2; 12:1; 14:1 et al. are loose; his favorite word "then" is general in meaning (see on 2:7). It is unlikely that Matthew intends his readers to think that the Sermon on the Mount succeeded Jesus' circuit (4:23–25). Rather, this sermon was preached during that circuit. Moreover some of Matthew's reasons for placing it here instead of after 10:1–4 are apparent (see below under 4). It seems best, then, to take Matthew 5–7 and Luke 6:20–49 as separate reports of the same occasion, each dependent on some shared tradition (Q?), but not exclusively so. Space limitations prevent tracing all the likely connections; but some attention will be given selected critical problems within this overall approach.

3. *Theological structure and affinities*. Whatever its sources and manner of compilation, the inclusion of the Sermon on the Mount in Matthew must be significant. Some have noted its similarities to Jewish thought. G. Friedlander's classic work, *The Jewish Sources of the Sermon on the Mount* (New York: Ktav, 1911), shows that virtually all the statements in Matthew 5–7 can be paralleled in the Talmud or other Jewish sources. Of course this is right, but it is a little like saying that the parts of a fine automobile can be found in a vast warehouse. Read any fifty pages of the Babylonian Talmud and compare them with Matthew 5–7, and it becomes obvious that they are not saying the same things. Sigal ("Halakhah") argues that the forms of argument in Matthew 5–7 fit into well-accepted patterns of the early rabbis ("proto-rabbis"); Gary A. Tuttle ("The Sermon on the Mount: Its Wisdom Affinities and Their Relation to Its Structure," JETS 20 [1977]: 213–30) draws attention to connections with the forms of argument in wisdom literature. Both are too restrictive: rabbinic and wisdom argumentation overlap much more than is commonly acknowledged, and Jesus (and Matthew) echo both and more—yet they must be interpreted first of all in their own right.

The attempt to do that has not produced consistent results. Schweizer lists seven major interpretive approaches to the Sermon on the Mount; Harvey K. McArthur (*Understanding the Sermon on the Mount* [New York: Harper and Row, 1960], pp. 105–48) lists twelve. Some of the most important are as follows:

a. Lutheran orthodoxy often understands the Sermon on the Mount as an exposition of law designed to drive men to cry for grace. This is Pauline (Rom 3–4; Gal 3), and grace is certainly presupposed in the sermon (e.g., see on 5:3). But though one of Jesus' purposes may have been to puncture self-righteous approaches to God, the sermon cannot be reduced to this. The righteousness envisaged (see on 5:20) is not imputed righteousness. Moreover, Paul himself insists that personal righteousness must characterize one who inherits the kingdom (Gal 5:19–24). Above all, this view fails to grasp the flow of salvation history (see below).

b. Some have argued that Jesus' eschatology is so "realized" that the ethic of the Sermon on the Mount is a sort of moral road map toward social progress. Classic liberalism has been invalidated by two world wars, the Great Depression and repeated recessions, the threat of nuclear holocaust, and post-Watergate, post-Vietnam, post-OPEC malaise. Nor can it be integrated with apocalyptic elements in Jesus' teaching (e.g., Matt 24) or with the vision of a suffering and witnessing community (Matt 10).

c. Today the sermon is commonly interpreted as a set of moral standards used catechetically within Matthew's community. While that may be so if there was a Matthean community, this view is reductionistic. It fails to wrestle with salvation history. The entire Book of Matthew presents itself as *Jesus'* teaching and ministry before the church was called into existence in the full, post-Pentecost sense. This Gospel does not present itself as the catechesis of a church but as a theological portrayal of the one who fulfilled Scripture and introduced the end times.

d. The Anabaptist–Mennonite tradition interprets the ethical demands to apply to all believers in every age and every circumstance. The resulting philosophy of pacifism in the context of a power-loving world demands the conclusion that Christians should not seek to be involved in affairs of state. This tradition rightly perceives the separate status of the believing community, which must not be confused with the world (e.g., 7:13–14, 21–23). But it is insensitive to the place of this sermon in the progress of redemption and absolutizes some of its teaching in a way incompatible with its context and with other Scripture (see on 5:38–42; 6:5–8).

e. Existential interpretation finds in these chapters a summons to personal decision and authentic faith but jettisons the personal and infinite God who makes the summons. Also, by denying the uniqueness of the Jesus who delivers the sermon, it fails to cope with its fulfillment theme and its implications.

f. Still others claim that Jesus is advocating an "interim ethic" to remain in force till the soon-expected consummation. But Jesus, they assume, erred as to the timing of this event; so the "interim ethic" must be toned down accordingly. All this rests on a view of Jesus derived from other passages (not least Matt 24–25 and parallels).

g. It is common among evangelicals and others to interpret the Sermon on the Mount as an intensifying or radicalizing of OT moral law. But this depends largely on a doubtful interpretation of 5:17–20 (cf. below).

h. Classic dispensationalism interprets the Sermon on the Mount as law for the millennial kingdom first offered by Jesus to the Jews. This has faced so many objections (e.g., Can any age be justly described as "millennial" that requires "laws" to govern face slapping?) that the approach has been qualified. J. Dwight Pentecost ("The Purpose of the Sermon on the Mount," BS 115 [1958]: 128ff., 212ff., 313ff.) and Walvoord take the ethical content of the sermon to be binding on any age but continue to drive a wedge between these chapters and the Christian gospel by pointing out that they do not mention the cross, justification by faith, new birth, etc. On that basis the Epistle of James is also non-Christian! Moreover they misinterpret Matthew's fulfillment motif and impose a theological structure on this Gospel demanding improbable exegesis of numerous passages (occasionally identified in this commentary). The disjunction between Matthew 5–7 and the Christian gospel is theologically and historically artificial.

This sketch overlooks many variations of the principal interpretations of the Sermon on the Mount. Recently several scholars have narrowed the focus: C. Burchard ("The Theme of the Sermon on the Mount," in Schottroff, *Command*, pp. 57–75) understands chapters 5–7 to provide rules of conduct for the Matthean church in the light of opposition to its witness; G. Bornkamm ("Der Aufbau der Bergpredigt," NTS 24 [1977–78]: 419–32) interprets the sermon around the Lord's Prayer (6:9–13). Though these perspectives highlight neglected themes, they overlook both the thrust of the sermon as a whole and its place in Matthew.

The unifying theme of the sermon is the kingdom of heaven. This is established, not by counting how many times the expression occurs, but by noting where it occurs. It envelopes the Beatitudes (5:3, 10) and appears in 5:17–20, which details the relation between the OT and the kingdom, a subject that leads to another literary envelope around the body of the sermon (5:17; 7:12). It returns at the heart of the Lord's Prayer (6:10), climaxes the section on kingdom perspectives (6:33), and is presented as what must finally be entered (7:21–23). Matthew places the sermon immediately after two verses insisting that the primary content of Jesus' preaching was the gospel of the kingdom (4:17, 23). It provides ethical guidelines for life in the kingdom, but does so within an explanation of the place of the contemporary setting within redemption history and Jesus' relation to the OT (5:17–20). The community forming around him, his "disciples," is not yet so cohesive and committed a group that exhortations to "enter" (7:13–14) are irrelevant. The glimpse of kingdom life (horizontally and vertically) in these chapters anticipates not only the love commandments (22:34–40) but also grace (5:3; 6:12; 7:7–11; cf. 21:28–46).

4. *Location in Matthew*. Unlike Luke, Matthew does not place the sermon after the calling of the Twelve (10:1–4); for there he puts a second discourse, one concerning mission. This links the call with the commission, a theme of great importance to Matthew (see on 11:11–12; 28:16–20). Not less important is the location of the Sermon on the Mount so early in the Gospel, before any sign of controversies between Jesus and the Jewish leaders as to the law's meaning. This means that, despite the antitheses in 5:17–48 ("You have heard . . . but I tell"), these should not be read as tokens of confrontation but in the light of the fulfillment themes richly set out in chapters 1–4 and made again explicit in 5:17–20: Jesus comes "to fulfill" the Law and the Prophets (i.e., the OT Scriptures). Therefore his announcements concerning the kingdom must be read against that background, not with reference to debates over Halakic details. This framework is Matthew's; by it he tells us that whatever controversies occupied Jesus' attention, the burden of his kingdom proclamation always made the kingdom the goal of the Scriptures, the long-expected messianic reign foretold by the Law and the Prophets alike.

1. Setting

5:1–2

¹Now when he saw the crowds, he went up on a mountainside and sat down. His disciples came to him, ²and he began to teach them, saying:

1 The "crowds" are those referred to in 4:23–25. Here Jesus stands at the height of his popularity. Although his ministry touched the masses, he saw the need to teach his "disciples" (*mathētai*) closely. The word "disciple" must not be restricted to the Twelve, whom Matthew has yet to mention (10:1–4). Nor is it a special word for full-fledged believers, since it can also describe John the Baptist's followers (11:2). In the Lukan parallel we are told of a "large crowd of his disciples" as well as "a great number of people" (6:17). This goes well with Matthew 4:25, which says large crowds "followed" Jesus. Those who especially wanted to attach themselves to him, Jesus takes aside to instruct; but it is anachronistic to suppose that all are fully committed in the later "Christian" sense of Acts 11:26 (cf. Matt 7:13–14, 21–23). Matthew sees the disciples as paradigms for believers in his own day but never loses sight, as we shall repeatedly notice, of the unique, historical place of the first followers (contra U. Luz, "Die Jünger im Matthäusevangelium," ZNW 62 [1971]: 141–71 —though Luz wisely avoids reducing Matthew's disciples to the Twelve. On the importance of the theme of discipleship in this Gospel, cf. Martin H. Franzmann, *Follow Me: Discipleship According to Saint Matthew* [St. Louis: Concordia, 1961]).

At this point in his ministry, Jesus could not escape the mounting crowds; and by the end of his sermon (7:28–29), he was surrounded by yet larger crowds. This suggests that his teaching covered several days, not just an hour or two (cf. the three-day meeting, 15:29–39). The place of retreat Jesus chose was in the hill country (cf. Notes), not "on a mountainside." He "sat down" to teach. Sitting was the accepted posture of synagogue or school teachers (Luke 4:20; cf. Matt 13:2; 23:2; 24:3; cf. DNTT, 3:588–89). The attempt of Lachs (pp. 99–101) to find an anachronism here fails because his sources refer to the position of one who is *learning* Torah, not teaching it. Luke has Jesus standing (6:17) but ministering to the larger crowd from which he could not escape (6:17–19).

2 NIV masks the idiom "he opened his mouth and taught them," found elsewhere in the NT (13:35; Acts 8:35; 10:34; 18:14) and reflecting OT roots (Job 3:1; 33:2; Dan 10:16). It is used in solemn or revelatory contexts. "To teach" (*edidasken*) is imperfect and inceptive: "He began to teach them." Contrary to Davies (*Setting*, pp. 7–8), one must not draw too sharp a distinction between preaching (*kēryssō*, 4:17) and teaching (*didaskō*, 5:2): see on 3:1 and the linking of these categories in 4:23; 9:35. SBK (1:189) notes that teaching was not uncommonly done outdoors as well as in synagogues.

Notes

1 NIV's "on a mountainside" renders εἰς τὸ ὄρος (*eis to oros*). The article does not suggest some well-known mountain (Hendriksen; Turner, *Syntax*, p. 173), still less the mountain where Moses received the law (Loisy). Even Davies (*Setting*, p. 93), after exploring all possibilities, concedes Matthew could have more explicitly delineated a "new Moses" theme. In fact, *to oros* (lit., "the mountain") and the corresponding Hebrew and Aramaic may mean nothing more than "the mountain region" or "the hill country," a point rightly recognized by NIV when it renders *eis to oros* elsewhere in Matthew "into the hills" (14:23; 15:29) or, in the plural, "to the mountains" (24:16). Jesus withdrew to the hill country west of Lake Galilee: the text requires nothing more. Attempts to discern profound symbolic significance (e.g., Gundry; J.B. Livio, "La signification théologique de la 'montagne' dans le premier évangile," *BullCentreProtd'Etud* 30 [1978]: 13–20) are here misguided. Moreover πεδινός (*pedinos*, "plain" or "a level place") in Luke 6:17, a NT *hapax legomenon*, should not conjure up images of American prairie but a relatively flat place in rough, rocky, or hilly terrain—perhaps "plateau" (cf. usage in Jer 21:13 LXX ["rocky plateau" in NIV], or in Isa 13:2 LXX—ἐπ' ὄρους πεδινοῦ [*ep' orous pedinou*, lit., "on a level (flat) mountain"; NIV, "on a bare hilltop"]). There is little difference between Matthew's "mountain" and Luke's "plain."

2. *The kingdom of heaven: its norms and witness* (5:3–16)

a. *The norms of the kingdom* (5:3–12)

1) *The Beatitudes*

    5:3–10

> 3"Blessed are the poor in spirit,
>   for theirs is the kingdom of heaven.
> 4Blessed are those who mourn,
>   for they will be comforted.

> [5]Blessed are the meek,
>   for they will inherit the earth.
> [6]Blessed are those who hunger and thirst for righteousness,
>   for they will be filled.
> [7]Blessed are the merciful,
>   for they will be shown mercy.
> [8]Blessed are the pure in heart,
>   for they will see God.
> [9]Blessed are the peacemakers,
>   for they will be called sons of God.
> [10]Blessed are those who are persecuted because
>   of righteousness
>   for theirs is the kingdom of heaven.

The Beatitudes (Lat. *beatus*, "blessed"), otherwise called macarisms (from Gr. *makarios*, "blessed"), have been the subject of many valuable studies, the most detailed being J. Dupont's *Les Béatitudes*, 3 vols., 2d ed. (Paris: Gabalda, 1969). As to form beatitudes find their roots in wisdom literature and especially the Psalms (for the best discussion of the OT background, cf. W. Zimmerli, "Die Seligpreisungen der Bergpredigt und das Alte Testament," *Donum Gentilicium*, ed. E. Bammel et al. [Oxford: Clarendon, 1978], pp. 8–26; cf. Pss 1:1; 31:1–2; 144:15; Prov 3:13; Dan 12:12). OT beatitudes never bunch more than two together (e.g., Ps 84:4–5; elsewhere, cf. Ecclus 25:7–9).

Comparison of 5:3–12 with Luke 6:20–26 shows that, along with smaller differences, the four Lukan beatitudes stand beside four woes—all in the second person. But Matthew mentions no woes, and his eight beatitudes (vv.3–10) are in the third person, followed by an expansion of the last one in the second person (vv.11–12). Pre-NT beatitudes are only rarely in the second person (e.g., 1 Enoch 58:2) and occur with woes only in the Greek text of Ecclesiasticus 10:16–17; so on formal grounds there is no reason to see Matthew's beatitudes as late adaptations.

No doubt both Matthew and Luke selected and shaped their material. But though this results in differences in the thrust of the two sets of beatitudes, such differences are often overstated (e.g., C.H. Dodd, *More New Testament Studies* [Manchester: University Press, 1968], pp. 7–8). Dupont (*Les Béatitudes*) and Marshall (*Luke*) argue that Luke describes what disciples actually are, Matthew what they ought to be; Luke, the social implications of Jesus' teaching and reversals at the consummation, Matthew, the standards of Christian righteousness to be pursued now for entrance into the kingdom. Similarly, G. Strecker ("Les macarismes du discours sur la montagne," in Didier, pp. 185–208) insists that in Matthew's beatitudes ethics has displaced eschatology: the Beatitudes become ethical entrance requirements rather than eschatological blessings associated with the Messianic Age.

A more nuanced interpretation is presented by R.A. Guelich ("The Matthean Beatitudes: 'Entrance-Requirements' or Eschatological Blessings?" JBL 95 [1973]: 415–34). He notes that Matthew 5:3–5 contains planned echoes of Isaiah 61:1–3, which is certainly eschatological in orientation. Moreover both Isaiah 61:1–3 and the Matthean beatitudes are formally declarative but implicitly hortatory: one must not overlook function for form. The Beatitudes "are but an expression of the fulfillment of Isaiah 61, the OT promise of the *Heilszeit* ['time of salvation'], in the person and proclamation of Jesus. This handling of the Beatitudes is certainly in keeping with Matthew's emphasis throughout the Gospel that Jesus comes in light of the OT promise" (ibid., p. 433). The implicit demands of the Beatitudes are therefore comprehensible only because of the new state of affairs the proclamation of the kingdom initiates (4:17, 23), the insistence that Jesus has come to fulfill the Law and the Prophets (5:17).

3 Two words and their cognates stand behind "blessed" and "blessing" in the NT. The word used in vv.3–11 is *makarios*, which usually corresponds in the LXX to *'ašrê*, a Hebrew term used almost as an interjection: "Oh the blessednesses [pl.] of." Usually *makarios* describes the man who is singularly favored by God and therefore in some sense "happy"; but the word can apply to God (1 Tim 1:11; 6:15). The other word is *eulogētos*, found in the LXX primarily for Hebrew *berākāh*, and used chiefly in connection with God in both OT and NT (e.g., Mark 14:61; Luke 1:68; Rom 1:25; 2 Cor 1:3). *Eulogētos* does not occur in Matthew; but the cognate verb appears five times (14:19; 21:9; 23:39; 25:34; 26:26), in one of which it applies to man (25:34), not God or Christ. Attempts to make *makarios* mean "happy" and *eulogētos* "blessed" (Broadus) are therefore futile; though both appear many times, both can apply to either God or man. It is difficult not to conclude that their common factor is approval: man "blesses" God, approving and praising him; God "blesses" man, approving him in gracious condescension. Applied to man the OT words are certainly synonymous (cf. *Theologische Handwörterbuch zum Alten Testament*, 1:356).

As for "happy" (TEV), it will not do for the Beatitudes, having been devalued in modern usage. The Greek "describes a state not of inner feeling on the part of those to whom it is applied, but of blessedness from an ideal point of view in the judgment of others" (Allen). In the eschatological setting of Matthew, "blessed" can only promise eschatological blessing (cf. DNTT, 1:216–17; TDNT, 4:367–70); and each particular blessing is specified by the second clause of each beatitude.

The "poor in spirit" are the ones who are "blessed." Since Luke speaks simply of "the poor," many have concluded that he preserves the true teaching of the historical Jesus—concern for the economically destitute—while Matthew has "spiritualized" it by adding "in spirit." The issue is not so simple. Already in the OT, "the poor" has religious overtones. The word *ptōchos* ("poor"—in classical Gr., "beggar") has a different force in the LXX and NT. It translates several Hebrew words, most importantly (in the pl.) *'anāwîm* ("the poor"), i.e., those who because of sustained economic privation and social distress have confidence only in God (e.g., Pss 37:14; 40:17; 69:28–29, 32–33; Prov 16:19 [NIV, "the oppressed"; NASB, "the lowly"]; 29:23; Isa 61:1; cf. Pss Sol 5:2, 11; 10:7). Thus it joins with passages affirming God's favor on the lowly and contrite in spirit (e.g., Isa 57:15; 66:2). This does not mean there is lack of concern for the materially poor but that poverty itself is not the chief thing (cf. the Prodigal Son's "self-made" poverty). Far from conferring spiritual advantage, wealth and privilege entail great spiritual peril (see on 6:24; 19:23–24). Yet, though poverty is neither a blessing nor a guarantee of spiritual rewards, it can be turned to advantage if it fosters humility before God.

That this is the way to interpret v.3 is confirmed by similar expressions in the DSS (esp. IQM 11:9; 14:6–7; IQS 4:3; IQH 5:22). "Poor" and "righteous" become almost equivalent in Ecclesiasticus 13:17–21; CD 19:9; 4QpPs (37)2:8–11 (cf. Schweizer; Bonnard; Dodd, "Translation Problems," pp. 307–10). These parallels do not prove literary dependence, but they do show that Matthew's "poor in spirit" rightly interprets Luke's "poor" (cf. Gundry, *Use of OT*, pp. 69–71). In rabbinic circles, too, meekness and poverty of spirit were highly praised (cf. Felix Böhl, "Die Demut als höchste der Tugenden," *Biblische Zeitschrift* 20 [1976]: 217–23).

Yet biblical balance is easy to prostitute. The emperor Julian the Apostate (332–63) is reputed to have said with vicious irony that he wanted to confiscate Christians' property so that they might all become poor and enter the kingdom of heaven. On the other hand, the wealthy too easily dismiss Jesus' teaching about poverty here and elsewhere (see on 6:24) as merely attitudinal and confuse their hoarding with good stewardship. France's "God and Mammon" (pp. 3–21) presents a fine balance in these matters.

To be poor in spirit is not to lack courage but to acknowledge spiritual bankruptcy. It confesses one's unworthiness before God and utter dependence on him. Therefore those who interpret the Sermon on the Mount as law and not gospel—whether by H. Windisch's historical reconstructions or by classical dispensationalism (cf. Carson, *Sermon on the Mount*, pp. 155–57), which calls the sermon "pure law" (though it concedes that its principles have a "beautiful moral application" for the Christian)—stumble at the first sentence (cf. Stott, pp. 36–38). The kingdom of heaven is not given on the basis of race (cf. 3:9), earned merits, the military zeal and prowess of Zealots, or the wealth of a Zacchaeus. It is given to the poor, the despised publicans, the prostitutes, those who are so "poor" they know they can offer nothing and do not try. They cry for mercy and they alone are heard. These themes recur repeatedly in Matthew and present the sermon's ethical demands in a setting that does not treat the resulting conduct as conditions for entrance to the kingdom that people themselves can achieve. All must begin by confessing that by themselves they can achieve nothing. Fuller disclosures of the gospel in the years beyond Jesus' earthly ministry do not change this; in the last book of the canon, an established church must likewise recognize its precarious position when it claims to be rich and fails to see its own poverty (Rev 3:14–22).

The kingdom of heaven (see on 3:2; 4:17) belongs to the poor in spirit; it is they who enjoy Messiah's reign and the blessings he brings. They joyfully accept his rule and participate in the life of the kingdom (7:14). The reward in the last beatitude is the same as in the first; the literary structure, an "inclusio" or envelope, establishes that everything included within it concerns the kingdom: i.e., the blessings of the intervening beatitudes are kingdom blessings, and the beatitudes themselves are kingdom norms.

While the rewards of vv.4–9 are future ("they will be comforted," "will inherit," etc.), the first and last are present ("for theirs is the kingdom of heaven"). Yet one must not make too much of this, for the present tense can function as a future; and the future tense can emphasize certainty, not mere futurity (Tasker). There is little doubt that here the kingdom sense is primarily future, postconsummation, made explicit in v.12. But the present tense "envelope" (vv.3, 10) should not be written off as insignificant or as masking an Aramaic original that did not specify present or future; for Matthew must have meant something when he chose *estin* ("is") instead of *estai* ("will be"). The natural conclusion is that, though the full blessedness of those described in these beatitudes awaits the consummated kingdom, they already share in the kingdom's blessedness so far as it has been inaugurated (see on 4:17; 8:29; 12:28; 19:29).

4 Black (*Aramaic Approach*, p. 157) notes how the Matthean and Lukan (6:21b, 25b) forms of this beatitude could each have been part of a larger parallelism—an observation that goes nicely with the hypothesis that the Sermon on the Mount and the Sermon on the Plain are reports of one discourse, relying somewhat on common sources (cf. introductory comments).

Some commentators deny that this mourning is for sin (e.g., Bonnard). Others (e.g., Schweizer) understand it to be mourning for any kind of misery. The reality is subtler. The godly remnant of Jesus' day weeps because of the humiliation of Israel, but they understand that it comes from personal and corporate sins. The psalmist testified, "Streams of tears flow from my eyes, for your law is not obeyed" (Ps 119:136; cf. Ezek 9:4). When Jesus preached, "The kingdom of heaven is near," he, like John the Baptist before him, expected not jubilation but contrite tears. It is not enough to acknowledge personal spiritual bankruptcy (v.3) with a cold heart. Weeping for sins can be deeply poignant (Ezra 10:6; Ps 51:4; Dan 9:19–20) and can cover a global as well as personal view of sin and our participation in it. Paul understands these matters well (cf. Rom 7:24; 1 Cor 5:2; 2 Cor 12:21; Phil 3:18).

"Comfort, comfort my people" (Isa 40:1) is God's response. These first two beatitudes deliberately allude to the messianic blessing of Isaiah 61:1–3 (cf. also Luke 4:16–19; France, *Jesus*, pp. 134–35), confirming them as eschatological and messianic. The Messiah comes to bestow "the oil of gladness instead of mourning, and a garment of praise instead of a spirit of despair" (Isa 61:3). But these blessings, already realized partially but fully only at the consummation (Rev 7:17), depend on a Messiah who comes to save his people from their sins (1:21; cf. also 11:28–30). Those who claim to experience all its joys without tears mistake the nature of the kingdom. In Charles Wesley's words:

> He speaks, and listening to his voice
> New life the dead receive,
> The mournful, broken hearts rejoice,
> The humble poor believe.

5 This beatitude and those in vv.7–10 have no parallel in Luke. It would be wrong to suppose that Matthew's beatitudes are for different groups of people, or that we have the right to half the blessings if we determine to pursue four out of the eight. They are a unity and describe the norm for Messiah's people.

The word "meek" (*praus*) is hard to define. It can signify absence of pretension (1 Peter 3:4, 14–15) but generally suggests gentleness (cf. 11:29; James 3:13) and the self-control it entails. The Greeks extolled humility in wise men and rulers, but such humility smacked of condescension. In general the Greeks considered meekness a vice because they failed to distinguish it from servility. To be meek toward others implies freedom from malice and a vengeful spirit. Jesus best exemplifies it (11:29; 21:5). Lloyd-Jones (*Sermon on the Mount*, 1:65–69) rightly applies meekness to our attitudes toward others. We may acknowledge our own bankruptcy (v.3) and mourn (v.4). But to respond with meekness when others tell us of our bankruptcy is far harder (cf. also Stott, pp. 43–44). Meekness therefore requires such a true view about ourselves as will express itself even in our attitude toward others.

And the meek—not the strong, aggressive, harsh, tyrannical—will inherit the earth. The verb "inherit" often relates to entrance into the Promised Land (e.g., Deut 4:1; 16:20; cf. Isa 57:13; 60:21). But the specific OT allusion here is Psalm 37:9, 11, 29, a psalm recognized as messianic in Jesus' day (4QpPs 37). There is no need to interpret the land metaphorically, as having no reference to geography or space;

nor is there need to restrict the meaning to "land of Israel" (cf. Notes). Entrance into the Promised Land ultimately became a pointer toward entrance into the new heaven *and the new earth* ("earth" is the same word as "land"; cf. Isa 66:22; Rev 21:1), the consummation of the messianic kingdom. While in Pauline terms believers may now possess all things in principle (2 Cor 6:10) since they belong to Christ, Matthew directs our attention yet further to the "renewal of all things" (19:28).

6 "Hunger and thirst" vividly express desire. The sons of Korah cried, "My soul thirsts for God, for the living God" (Ps 42:2; cf. 63:1) for the deepest spiritual famine is hunger for the word of God (Amos 8:11–14).

The precise nature of the righteousness for which the blessed hunger and thirst is disputed. Some argue that it is the imputed righteousness of God—eschatological salvation or, more narrowly, justification: the blessed hunger for it and receive it (e.g., Grundmann; Lohmeyer; McNeile, Schniewind, Schrenk [TDNT, 2:198], Zahn; Bornkamm, *Tradition* [pp. 123–24]; Bultmann [*Theology*, 1:273]). This is certainly plausible, since the immediate context does arouse hopes for God's eschatological action, and hungering suggests that the righteousness that satisfies will be given as a gift.

The chief objection is that *dikaiosynē* ("righteousness") in Matthew does not have that sense anywhere else (Przybylski, pp. 96–98). So it is better to take this righteousness as simultaneously personal righteousness (cf. Hill, *Greek Words*, pp. 127f.; Strecker, *Weg*, pp. 156–58) and justice in the broadest sense (cf. esp. Ridderbos, pp. 190f.). These people hunger and thirst, not only that they may be righteous (i.e., that they may wholly do God's will from the heart), but that justice may be done everywhere. All unrighteousness grieves them and makes them homesick for the new heaven and earth—the home of righteousness (2 Peter 3:13). Satisfied with neither personal righteousness alone nor social justice alone, they cry for both: in short, they long for the advent of the messianic kingdom. What they taste now whets their appetites for more. Ultimately they will be satisfied (same verb as in 14:20; Phil 4:12; Rev 19:21) without qualification only when the kingdom is consummated (cf. discussion in Gundry, *Matthew*).

7 This beatitude is akin to Psalm 18:25 (reading "merciful" [ASV] instead of "faithful" [NIV]; following MT [v.26], not LXX [17:26]; cf. Prov 14:21). Mercy embraces both forgiveness for the guilty and compassion for the suffering and needy. No particular object of the demanded mercy is specified, because mercy is to be a function of Jesus' disciples, not of the particular situation that calls it forth. The theme is common in Matthew (6:12–15; 9:13; 12:7; 18:33–34). The reward is not mercy shown by others but by God (cf. the saying preserved in 1 Clement 13:2). This does not mean that our mercy is the causal ground of God's mercy but its occasional ground (see on 6:14–15). This beatitude, too, is tied to the context. "It is 'the meek' who are also 'the merciful'. For to be meek is to acknowledge to others that *we* are sinners; to be merciful is to have compassion on others, for they are sinners too" (Stott, p. 48, emphasis his).

8 Commentators are divided on "pure in heart."

1. Some take it to mean inner moral purity as opposed to merely external piety or ceremonial cleanness. This is an important theme in Matthew and elsewhere in the

Scriptures (e.g., Deut 10:16; 30:6; 1 Sam 15:22; Pss 24:3–4 [to which there is direct allusion here]; 51:6, 10; Isa 1:10–17; Jer 4:4; 7:3–7; 9:25–26; Rom 2:9; 1 Tim 1:5; 2 Tim 2:22; cf. Matt 23:25–28).

2. Others take it to mean singlemindedness, a heart "free from the tyranny of a divided self" (Tasker; cf. Bonnard). Several of the passages just cited focus on freedom from deceit (Pss 24:4; 51:4–17; cf. also Gen 50:5–6; Prov 22:11). This interpretation also prepares the way for 6:22. The "pure in heart" are thus "the utterly sincere" (Ph).

The dichotomy between these two options is a false one; it is impossible to have one without the other. The one who is singleminded in commitment to the kingdom and its righteousness (6:33) will also be inwardly pure. Inward sham, deceit, and moral filth cannot coexist with sincere devotion to Christ. Either way this beatitude excoriates hypocrisy (cf. on 6:1–18). The pure in heart will see God—now with the eyes of faith and finally in the dazzling brilliance of the beatific vision in whose light no deceit can exist (cf. Heb 12:14; 1 John 3:1–3; Rev 21:22–27).

9 Jesus' concern in this beatitude is not with the peaceful but with the peacemakers. Peace is of constant concern in both testaments (e.g., Prov 15:1; Isa 52:7; Luke 24:36; Rom 10:15; 12:18; 1 Cor 7:15; Eph 2:11–22; Heb 12:14; 1 Peter 3:11). But as some of these and other passages show, the making of peace can itself have messianic overtones. The Promised Son is called the "Prince of Peace" (Isa 9:6–7); and Isaiah 52:7—"How beautiful on the mountains are the feet of those who bring good news, who proclaim peace, who bring good tidings, who proclaim salvation, who say to Zion, 'Your God reigns!' "—linking as it does peace, salvation, and God's reign, was interpreted messianically in the Judaism of Jesus' day.

Jesus does not limit the peacemaking to only one kind, and neither will his disciples. In the light of the gospel, Jesus himself is the supreme peacemaker, making peace between God and man, and man and man. Our peacemaking will include the promulgation of that gospel. It must also extend to seeking all kinds of reconciliation. Instead of delighting in division, bitterness, strife, or some petty "divide-and-conquer" mentality, disciples of Jesus delight to make peace wherever possible. Making peace is not appeasement: the true model is God's costly peacemaking (Eph 2:15–17; Col 1:20). Those who undertake this work are acknowledged as God's "sons." In the OT, Israel has the title "sons" (Deut 14:1; Hos 1:10; cf. Pss Sol 17:30; Wisd Sol 2:13–18). Now it belongs to the heirs of the kingdom who, meek and poor in spirit, loving righteousness yet merciful, are especially equipped for peacemaking and so reflect something of their heavenly Father's character. "There is no more godlike work to be done in this world than peacemaking" (Broadus). This beatitude must have been shocking to Zealots when Jesus preached it, when political passions were inflamed (Morison).

10 It is no accident that Jesus should pass from peacemaking to persecution, for the world enjoys its cherished hates and prejudices so much that the peacemaker is not always welcome. Opposition is a normal mark of being a disciple of Jesus, as normal as hungering for righteousness or being merciful (cf. also John 15:18–25; Acts 14:22; 2 Tim 3:12; 1 Peter 4:13–14; cf. the woe in Luke 6:26). Lachs (pp. 101–3) cannot believe Christians were ever persecuted because of righteousness; so he repoints an alleged underlying Hebrew text to read "because of the Righteous One"—a reference to Jesus. But he underestimates how offensive genuine righteousness, "proper

conduct before God" (Przybylski, p. 99), really is (cf. Isa 51:7). The reward of these persecuted people is the same as the reward of the poor in spirit—viz., the kingdom of heaven, which terminates the inclusion (see on 5:3).

Notes

3 Most scholars interpret τῷ πνεύματι (tō pneumati, "in spirit") as a dative of respect (e.g., Zerwick, par. 53). Moule (Idiom Book, p. 46) wonders whether it might not border on an instrumental usage, which can often best be rendered by an English adverb: i.e., οἱ πτωχοὶ τῷ πνεύματι (hoi ptōchoi tō pneumati) = "the poor used in its spiritual [i.e., religious] sense," over against "the literally [i.e., materially] poor" of James 2:5. But he acknowledges that Ps 34:18 points in another direction.

5 The word γῆ (gē, "land") occurs forty-three times in Matthew: once for the land of Judah (2:6); twice for the land of Israel (2:20–21); several times for some region (e.g., 4:15; 9:26, 31; 11:24; and possibly 27:45); several times in the expression "heaven and earth" or something similar (5:18, 35; 11:25; 24:35; 28:18); several times to distinguish earth from heaven (6:10; 9:6; 16:19; 18:18 [bis], 19; 23:9); once to refer to the place where sinful people live (5:13); several times to refer to "ground" (e.g., 10:29; 15:35; 25:18, 25; 27:51), "soil" (13:5, 8, 23), or "shore" (14:24); and several times to refer to the whole earth without any of the above connotations (12:40, 42; 17:25; 23:35; 24:30). In Matthew, therefore, gē is used to refer to a specified region or nation (Israel, Judah, Zebulon, Naphtali et al.) only if that region's name is given. The possible exception is 27:45. The most natural way to render this noun in 5:5 is therefore "earth," not "land [of Israel]."

9 Although "son of" can have ontological force, it often means "one who reflects the character of" or the like. Hence a "son of Belial" (= "son of worthlessness") refers to a worthless person, someone of worthless conduct. Similarly, "son of God" may have ontological or purely functional force, depending on the context.

10 The perfect passive participle οἱ δεδιωγμένοι (hoi dediōgmenoi, "those who are persecuted") is rather awkward if the perfect force is retained: "those who have been persecuted." Many see this as a sign of anachronism: persecution had broken out by the time Matthew wrote (e.g., Hill, Matthew). Some older commentators treat it as a more or less Hebraizing "prophetic" perfect; and Broadus adds that the perfect accords "with the fact that the chief rewards of such sufferers do not so much attend on the persecution as follow it." But then we may ask why a future perfect isn't used, or why the same rule isn't applied to those who mourn (5:4). The question must at least be raised whether the perfect occasionally begins to take on aoristic force in the NT and the perfect participle a merely adjectival force (cf. discussion in Burton, par. 88; Moule, Idiom Book, p. 14).

2) Expansion

5:11–12

> 11"Blessed are you when people insult you, persecute you and falsely say all kinds of evil against you because of me. 12Rejoice and be glad, because great is your reward in heaven, for in the same way they persecuted the prophets who were before you.

11–12 These two verses (cf. Luke 6:22–23, 26), switching from third person to second, apply the force of the last beatitude (v.10), not to the church (which would be anachronistic), but to Jesus' disciples. Doubtless Matthew and his contemporaries also applied it to themselves. Verse 11 extends the persecution of v. 10 to include insult, persecution, and slander (Luke 6:22–23 adds hate). The reason for the persecution in v. 10 is "because of righteousness"; now, Jesus says, it is "because of me." "This confirms that the righteousness of life that is in view is in imitation of Jesus. Simultaneously, it so identifies the disciple of Jesus with the practice of Jesus' righteousness that there is no place for professed allegiance to Jesus that is not full of righteousness" (Carson, *Sermon on the Mount*, p. 28). Moreover, it is an implicit christological claim, for the prophets to whom the disciples are likened were persecuted for their faithfulness to God and the disciples for faithfulness to Jesus. Not Jesus but the disciples are likened to the prophets. Jesus places himself on a par with God. The change from "the Son of Man" (Luke) to "me" is probably Matthew's clarification (see excursus at 8:20).

The appropriate response of the disciple is rejoicing. The second verb, *agalliasthe* ("be glad"), Hill (*Matthew*) takes to be "something of a technical term for joy in persecution and martyrdom" (cf. 1 Peter 1:6, 8; 4:13; Rev 19:7). Yet its range of associations seems broader (Luke 1:47; 10:21; John 5:35; 8:56; Acts 2:26; 16:34). The disciples of Jesus are to rejoice under persecution because their heavenly reward (cf. Notes) will be great at the consummation of the kingdom (v. 12). Opposition is sure, for the disciples are aligning themselves with the OT prophets who were persecuted before them (e.g., 2 Chron 24:21; Neh 9:26; Jer 20:2; cf. Matt 21:35; 23:32–37; Acts 7:52; 1 Thess 2:15). This biblical perspective was doubtless part of the historical basis on which Jesus built his own implied prediction that his followers would be persecuted. Treated seriously, it makes ineffective the ground on which some treat the prediction as anachronistic (e.g., Hare, pp. 114–21). Stendahl's suggestion (Peake, par. 678k) that Matthew here refers to Christian prophets is not only needlessly anachronistic but out of step with both Matthew's use of "prophet" and his link between the murder of "prophets" and the sin of the "forefathers" (23:30–32), which shows that the prophets belong to the OT period.

These verses neither encourage seeking persecution nor permit retreating from it, sulking, or retaliation. From the perspective of both redemptive history ("the prophets") and eternity ("reward in heaven"), these verses constitute the reasonable response of faith, one which the early Christians readily understood (cf. Acts 5:41; 2 Cor 4:17; 1 Peter 1:6–9; cf. Dan 3:24–25). "Discipleship means allegiance to the suffering Christ, and it is therefore not at all surprising that Christians should be called upon to suffer. In fact it is a joy and a token of his grace" (Bonhoeffer, pp. 80–81). But in reassuring his disciples that their sufferings are "neither new, nor accidental, nor absurd" (Bonnard), Jesus spoke of principles that will appear again (esp. chs. 10, 24).

Notes

11 Matthew's "falsely say all kinds of evil against you" (cf. Acts 28:21) is an explanation of a Hebrew or Aramaic idiom still preserved in Luke's "reject your name as evil" (6:22; cf. Deut 22:14, 19). The word ψευδόμενοι (*pseudomenoi*, "falsely"), given a D in UBS (3d ed.), is implied whether original or not. External evidence strongly favors inclusion; the internal evidence is equivocal.

12 Morton Smith, *Tannaitic Parallels to the Gospels* (Philadelphia: SBL, 1951), pp. 46–77,

161–84, represents those who hold that the concept of reward in the synoptic Gospels does not differ materially from the concept of reward in early rabbinic literature. His work is essentially a word study and overlooks the substantial conceptual differences (cf. D.A. Carson, "Predestination and Responsibility: Some Elements of Tension Theology Against Jewish Background" [Ph.D. diss., Cambridge University, 1975], pp. 268f.); nor does he mention the balanced treatment of A. Marmorstein, *The Doctrine of Merits in the Old Rabbinical Literature* (London: Jesus' College, 1920). The recent book by E.P. Sanders (*Paul and Palestinian Judaism* [London: SCM, 1977]) rightly warns against reading very late Jewish traditions, steeped in merit theology, back into the NT period; but he seriously oversteps the evidence when he sees no difference at all, on the grace-merit front, between Paul and the "covenantal nomism" of Judaism (cf. Carson, *Divine Sovereignty*, ch. 8). C.S. Lewis (*They Asked For a Paper* [London: Geoffrey Bles, 1962], p. 198; cited in Stott, pp. 131–32) rightly distinguishes various kinds of rewards. A man who marries a woman for her money is "rewarded" by her money, but he is rightly judged mercenary because the reward is not naturally linked with love. On the other hand, marriage is the proper reward of an honest and true lover; and he is not mercenary for desiring it because love and marriage are naturally linked. "The proper rewards are not simply tacked on to the activity for which they are given, but are the activity itself in consummation" (ibid.). The rewards of the NT belong largely to this second category. Life lived under kingdom norms is naturally linked with the bliss of life in the consummated kingdom. Talk of "merit" or of "earning" the reward betrays lack of understanding of Jesus' meaning (cf. further on 11:25; 19:16–26; 20:1–16; 25:31–46).

---

b. *The witness of the kingdom* (5:13–16)

1) *Salt*

5:13

[13]"You are the salt of the earth. But if the salt loses its saltiness, how can it be made salty again? It is no longer good for anything, except to be thrown out and trampled by men.

13 Salt and light are such common substances (cf. Pliny, *Natural History* 31.102: "Nothing is more useful than salt and sunshine") that they doubtless generated many sayings. Therefore it is improper to attempt a tradition history of all Gospel references as if one original stood behind the lot (cf. Mark 4:21; 9:50; Luke 8:16; 11:33; 14:34–35). Salt was used in the ancient world to flavor foods and even in small doses as a fertilizer (cf. Eugene P. Deatrick, "Salt, Soil, Savor," BA 25 [1962]: 44–45, who wants *tēs gēs* to read "for the soil," not "of the earth"; but notice the parallel "of the world" in v.14). Above all, salt was used as a preservative. Rubbed into meat, a little salt would slow decay. Strictly speaking salt cannot lose its saltiness; sodium chloride is a stable compound. But most salt in the ancient world derived from salt marshes or the like, rather than by evaporation of salt water, and therefore contained many impurities. The actual salt, being more soluble than the impurities, could be leached out, leaving a residue so dilute it was of little worth.

In modern Israel savorless salt is still said to be scattered on the soil of flat roofs. This helps harden the soil and prevent leaks; and since the roofs serve as playgrounds and places for public gathering, the salt is still being trodden under foot (Deatrick, "Salt," p. 47). This explanation negates the attempt by some (e.g., Lenski, Schniewind, Grosheide) to suppose that, precisely because pure salt cannot lose its savor, Jesus is saying that true disciples cannot lose their effectiveness. The question "How can it be made salty again?" is not meant to have an answer, as Schweizer rightly says. The rabbinic remark that what makes salt salty is "the after-birth of a mule" (mules are sterile) rather misses the point (cf. Schweizer, *Matthew*). The point is that, if Jesus' disciples are to act as a preservative in the world by conforming to kingdom norms, if they are "called to be a moral disinfectant in a world where moral standards are low, constantly changing, or non-existent . . . they can discharge this function only if they themselves retain their virtue" (Tasker).

Notes

13 The verb $\mu\omega\rho\alpha\nu\theta\widetilde{\eta}$ (*mōranthē*, "loses its saltiness") is used four times in the NT. In Luke 14:34 it again relates to salt, but in Rom 1:22 and 1 Cor 1:20 it has its more common meaning "to make or become foolish" (cf. cognate $\mu\omega\rho\acute{\epsilon}$ [*mōre*, "fool"] in 5:22). It is hard not to conclude that disciples who lose their savor are in fact making fools of themselves. The Greek may hide an Aramaic pun: תפל (*tāpēl*, "foolish") and תבל (tabel, "salted") (Black, *Aramaic Approach*, pp. 166–67).

2) Light

5:14–16

> 14"You are the light of the world. A city on a hill cannot be hidden. 15Neither do people light a lamp and put it under a bowl. Instead they put it on its stand, and it gives light to everyone in the house. 16In the same way, let your light shine before men, that they may see your good deeds and praise your Father in heaven.

14–15 As in v.13, "you" is emphatic—viz., You, my followers and none others, are the light of the world (v.14). Though the Jews saw themselves as the light of the world (Rom 2:19), the true light is the Suffering Servant (Isa 42:6; 49:6), fulfilled in Jesus himself (Matt 4:16; cf. John 8:12; 9:5; 12:35; 1 John 1:7). Derivatively his disciples constitute the new light (cf. Eph 5:8–9; Phil 2:15). Light is a universal religious symbol. In the OT as in the NT, it most frequently symbolizes purity as opposed to filth, truth or knowledge as opposed to error or ignorance, and divine revelation and presence as opposed to reprobation and abandonment by God.

The reference to the "city on a hill" is at one level fairly obvious. Often built of white limestone, ancient towns gleamed in the sun and could not easily be hidden. At night the inhabitants' oil lamps would shed some glow over the surrounding area (cf. Bonnard). As such cities could not be hidden, so also it is unthinkable to light a lamp and hide it under a peck-measure (v.15, NIV, "bowl"). A lamp is put on a lampstand to illuminate all. Attempts to identify "everyone in the house" as a reference to all Jews in contrast with Luke 11:33, referring to Gentiles (so Manson, *Sayings*, p. 93) are probably guilty of making the metaphor run on all fours, especially in view of the Gentile theme so strongly present in Matthew.

But the "city on a hill" saying may also refer to OT prophecies about the time when Jerusalem or the mountain of the Lord's house, or Zion, would be lifted up before the world, the nations streaming to it (e.g., Isa 2:2–5; cf. chs. 42, 49, 54, 60). This allusion has recently been defended by Grundmann, Trilling (p. 142), and especially K.M. Campbell ("The New Jerusalem in Matthew 5.14," SJT 31 [1978]: 335–63). It is not a certain allusion, and the absence of definite articles tells against it; if valid it insists that Jesus' disciples constitute the true locus of the people of God, the outpost of the consummated kingdom, and the means of witness to the world—all themes central to Matthew's thought.

16 Jesus drives the metaphor home. What his disciples must show is their "good works," i.e., all righteousness, everything they are and do that reflects the mind and will of God. And men must see this light. It may provoke persecution (vv.10–12), but that is no reason for hiding the light others may see and by which they may come to glorify the Father—the disciples' only motive (cf. 2 Cor 4:6; 1 Peter 2:12). Witness includes not just words but deeds; as Stier remarks, "The good word without the good walk is of no avail."

Thus the kingdom norms (vv.3–12) so work out in the lives of the kingdom's heirs as to produce the kingdom witness (vv.13–16). If salt (v.13) exercises the negative function of delaying decay and warns disciples of the danger of compromise and conformity to the world, then light (vv.14–16) speaks positively of illuminating a sin-darkened world and warns against a withdrawal from the world that does not lead others to glorify the Father in heaven. "Flight into the invisible is a denial of the call. A community of Jesus which seeks to hide itself has ceased to follow him" (Bonhoeffer, p. 106).

Notes

15 There are several probable Semitisms in this verse (Hill, *Matthew*). The μόδιος (*modios*, "bowl") is a wooden grain measure, usually given as 8¾ liters, i.e., almost exactly one peck (cf. further on 13:33). It is doubtful whether the vessel was used for hiding light, despite various suggestions. A different word is used in Josephus (Antiq. V, 223[vi.5]), and in any case Jesus' point turns on what is *not* done.

3. *The kingdom of heaven: its demands in relation to the OT* (5:17–48)

a. *Jesus and the kingdom as fulfillment of the OT*

5:17–20

17"Do not think that I have come to abolish the Law or the Prophets; I have not come to abolish them but to fulfill them. 18I tell you the truth, until heaven and earth disappear, not the smallest letter, not the least stroke of a pen, will by any means disappear from the Law until everything is accomplished. 19Anyone who breaks one of the least of these commandments and teaches others to do the same will be called least in the kingdom of heaven, but whoever practices and teaches these commands will be called great in the kingdom of heaven. 20For I tell you that unless your righteousness surpasses that of the Pharisees and the teachers of the law, you will certainly not enter the kingdom of heaven.

Three important debates bear on the interpretation of these complex yet programmatic verses.

1. Apart from parallels to v. 18 in Mark 13:31 and Luke 16:17, these verses have no synoptic parallel. Partly because of this, many have argued that these four verses represent four separate sayings from different and even conflicting churches or strata, heavily edited by Matthew (for discussion and recent examples, cf. R.G. Hamerton-Kelly, "Attitudes to the Law in Matthew's Gospel," *Biblical Research* 17 [1972]: 19–32; Arens, pp. 91–116). G. Barth, for instance, insists that the leap from v. 19 to v. 20 is so great that both could not have come from Matthew (Bornkamm, *Tradition*, p. 66). A better synthesis is possible. Yet even if the leap between these verses were as great as Barth imagines, what possessed Matthew (or the "final redactor") to put them together? He must have thought they meant something. And then how does one distinguish methodologically between weak links discerned by a redactor and weak links written up by an author? We shall focus primary attention on the meaning of the text as it stands.

2. The theological and canonical ramifications of one's exegetical conclusions on this pericope are so numerous that discussion becomes freighted with the intricacies of biblical theology. At stake are the relation between the testaments, the place of law in the context of gospel, and the relation of this pericope to other NT passages that unambiguously affirm that certain parts of the law have been abrogated as obsolete (e.g., Mark 7:19; Acts 10–11; Heb 7:1–9:10). Only glancing attention may be given to these issues here.

3. It is often argued that the setting of the pericope is debate in the church, especially among Palestinian Jewish Christians, about the continuation of law. There is no inherent implausibility in this hypothesis if by setting we refer to the circle in which these teachings were preserved because of their immediate relevance. But it must be remembered that Matthew presents these sayings as the teaching of the historical Jesus, not the creation of the church; and we detect no implausibility in his claim.

17 The formula "Do not think that" (or "Never think that," Turner, *Syntax*, p. 77) is repeated by Jesus in 10:34 (cf. 3:9). Jesus' two sayings were designed to set aside potential misunderstandings as to the nature of the kingdom; but neither demonstrably flows out of open confrontation on the issue at stake. Matthew has not yet recorded any charge that Jesus was breaking the law. (On the relation between these verses and the preceding pericopes, cf. W.J. Dumbull, "The Logic of the Role of the Law in Matthew v 1–20," NovTest 23 [1981]: 1–21).

Some have argued that many Jews in Jesus' day believed that law would be set aside and a new law introduced at Messiah's coming (cf. esp. Davies, *Setting*, pp. 109ff., 446ff.). But this view has been decisively qualified by R. Banks ("The Eschatological Role of Law," *Pre- and Post-Christian Jewish Thought*, ed. R. Banks [Exeter: Paternoster, 1982], pp. 173–85; id. *Jesus*, pp. 65ff.), who presents a more nuanced treatment.

The upshot of the debate is that the introductory words "Do not think that" must be understood, not as the refutation of some well-entrenched and clearly defined position, but as a teaching device Jesus used to clarify certain aspects of the kingdom and of his own mission and to remove potential misunderstandings. Moreover, comparison with 10:34 shows that the antithesis may not be absolute. Few would want to argue that there is *no* sense in which Jesus came to bring peace (cf. on 5:9). Why then argue that there is *no* sense in which Jesus abolishes the law?

The words "I have come" do not necessarily prove Jesus' consciousness of his preexistence, for "coming" language can be used of prophets and indeed is used of the Baptist (11:18-19). But it can also speak of coming into the world (common in John; cf. also 1 Tim 1:15) and in the light of Matthew's prologue is probably meant to attest Jesus' divine origins. At very least it shows Jesus was sent on a mission (cf. Maier).

Jesus' mission was not to abolish (a term more frequently connected with the destruction of buildings [24:2; 26:61; 27:40], but not exclusively so [e.g., 2 Macc 2:22]) "the law or the prophets." By these words Matthew forms a new "inclusio" (5:17-7:12), which marks out the body of the sermon and shows that Jesus is taking pains to relate his teaching and place in the history of redemption to the OT Scriptures. For that is what "Law or the Prophets" here means: the Scriptures. The disjunctive "or" makes it clear that neither is to be abolished. The Jews of Jesus' day could refer to the Scriptures as "the Law and the Prophets" (7:12; 11:13; 22:40; Luke 16:16; John 1:45; Acts 13:15; 28:23; Rom 3:21); "the Law. . . , the Prophets, and the Psalms" (Luke 24:44); or just "Law" (5:18; John 10:34; 12:34; 15:25; 1 Cor 14:21); the divisions were not yet stereotyped. Thus even if "or the Prophets" is redactional (Dalman, p. 62, and many after him), the referent does not change when only law is mentioned in v.18, but it may be a small hint that law, too, has a prophetic function (cf. 11:13, and discussion). Yet it is certainly illegitimate to see in "Law and Prophets" some vague reference to the will of God (so G.S. Sloyan, *Is Christ the End of the Law?* [Philadelphia: Westminster, 1978], pp. 49f.; Sand, p. 186; K. Berger, *Die Gesetzesauslegung Jesu* [Neukirchen-Vluyn: Neukirchener Verlag, 1972], p. 224) and not to Scripture, especially in the light of v.18.

The nub of the problem lies in the verb "to fulfill" (*plēroō*). N.J. McEleney ("The Principles of the Sermon on the Mount," JBL 41 [1979]; 552-70) finds the verb so difficult in a context (vv.17-48) dealing with law that he judges it a late addition to the tradition. Not a few writers, especially Jewish scholars, take the verb to reflect the Aramaic verb *qûm* ("establish," "validate," or "confirm" the law). Jesus did not come to abolish the law but to confirm it and establish it (e.g., Dalman, pp. 56-58; Daube, *New Testament,* pp. 60f.; Schlatter, pp. 153f.; and esp. Sigal, "Halakah," pp. 23ff.)

There are several objections.

1. The focus of Matthew 5 is the relation between the OT and Jesus' teaching, not his actions. So any interpretation that says Jesus fulfills the law by doing it misses the point.

2. If it is argued that Jesus confirms the law, even its jot and tittle, by both his life and his teaching (e.g., Hill; Ridderbos, pp. 292ff.; Maier)—the latter understood as setting out his own *Halakah* (rules of conduct) within the framework of the law (Sigal)—one marvels that the early church, as the other NT documents testify, misunderstood Jesus so badly on this point; and even the first Gospel, as we shall see, is rendered inconsistent.

3. The LXX never uses *plēroō* ("fulfill") to render *qûm* or cognates (which prefer *histanai* or *bebaioun* ["establish" or "confirm"]). The verb *plēroō* renders *mālē'* and means "to fulfill." In OT usage this characteristically refers to the "filling up" of volume or time, meanings that also appear in the NT (e.g., Acts 24:27; Rom 15:19). But though the NT uses *plēroō* in a number of ways, we are primarily concerned

with what is meant by "fulfilling" the Scriptures. Included under this head are specific predictions, typological fulfillments, and even the entire eschatological hope epitomized in the OT by God's covenant with his people (cf. C.F.D. Moule, "Fulfilment Words in the New Testament: Use and Abuse," NTS 14 [1967–68]: 293–320; see on 2:15).

The lack of background for *plēroō* ("fulfill") as far as it applies to Scripture requires cautious induction from the NT evidence. In a very few cases, notably James 2:23, the NT writers detect no demonstrable predictive force in the OT passage introduced. Rather, the OT text (in this case Gen 15:6) in some sense remains "empty" until Abraham's action "fulfills" it. But Genesis 15:6 does not predict the action. Most NT uses of *plēroō* in connection with Scripture, however, require some teleological force (see note on 1:22); and even the ambiguous uses presuppose a typology that in its broadest dimensions is teleological, even if not in every detail (see discussion on 2:15). In any case the interchange of *mālē'* ("fulfill") and *qûm* ("establish") in the Targumim is not of sufficient importance to overturn the LXX evidence, not least owing to problems of dating the Targumim (cf. Meier, *Law*, p. 74; Banks, *Jesus*, pp. 208f.).

Other views are not much more convincing. Many argue that Jesus is here referring only to moral law: the civil and ceremonial law are indeed abolished, but Jesus confirms the moral law (e.g., Hendriksen; D. Wenham, "Jesus and the Law: an Exegesis on Matthew 5:17–20," *Themelios* 4 [1979]: 92–96). Although this tripartite distinction is old, its use as a basis for explaining the relationship between the testaments is not demonstrably derived from the NT and probably does not antedate Aquinas (cf. the work of R.J. Bauckham in Carson, *Sabbath*; and Carson, "Jesus"). Also, the interpretation is invalidated by the all-inclusive "not the smallest letter, not the least stroke of a pen" (v.18).

Others understand the verb *plēroō* to mean that Jesus "fills up" the law by providing its full, intended meaning (e.g., Lenski), understood perhaps in terms of the double command to love (so O. Hanssen, "Zum Verständnis der Bergpredigt," *Der Ruf Jesu und die Antwort der Gemeinde*, ed. Edward Lohse [Göttingen: Vandenhoeck und Ruprecht, 1970], pp. 94–111). This, however, requires an extraordinary meaning for *plēroō*, ignores the "jot and tittle" of v.18, and misinterprets 22:34–40.

Still others, in various ways, argue that Jesus "fills up" the OT law by extending its demands to some better or transcendent righteousness (v.20), again possibly understood in terms of the command to love (e.g., Bornhäuser; Lagrange; A. Feuillet, "Morale Ancienne et Morale Chrétienne d'après Mt 5.17–20; Comparaison avec la Doctrine de l'Épître aux Romains," NTS 17 [1970–71]: 123–37, esp. p. 124; Grundmann; Trilling, pp. 174–79). Thus the reference to prophets (v.17) becomes obscure, and the entire structure is shaky in view of the fact that mere extension of law will not abolish any of its stringencies—yet in both Matthew and other NT documents some abolition is everywhere assumed. H. Ljungmann (*Das Gesetz erfüllen: Matth.5, 17ff. und 3, 15 untersucht* [Lund: C.W.K. Gleerup, 1954) takes the "fulfillment" to refer to the fulfillment of Scripture in the self-surrender of the Messiah, which in turn brings forgiveness of sins and the new righteousness the disciples are both to receive and do. But in addition to weaknesses of detail, it is hard to see how all this can be derived from vv.17–20.

The best interpretation of these difficult verses says that Jesus fulfills the Law and the Prophets in that they point to him, and he is their fulfillment. The antithesis is not between "abolish" and "keep" but between "abolish" and "fulfill." "For Matthew, then, it is not the question of Jesus' relation to the Law that is in doubt but rather its relation to him!" (Robert Banks, "Matthew's Understanding of the Law: Authenticity and Interpretation in Matthew 5:17-20," JBL 93 [1974]: 226-42). Therefore we give *plēroō* ("fulfill") exactly the same meaning as in the formula quotations, which in the prologue (Matt 1-2) have already laid great stress on the prophetic nature of the OT and the way it points to Jesus. Even OT events have this prophetic significance (see on 2:15). A little later Jesus insists that "all the Prophets and the Law prophesied" (11:13).

The manner of the prophetic foreshadowing varies. The Exodus, Matthew argues (2:15), foreshadows the calling out of Egypt of God's "son." The writer to the Hebrews argues that many cultic regulations of the OT pointed to Jesus and are now obsolete. In the light of the antitheses (vv.21-48), the passage before us insists that just as Jesus fulfilled OT prophecies by his person and actions, so he fulfilled OT law by his teaching. In no case does this "abolish" the OT as canon, any more than the obsolescence of the Levitical sacrificial system abolishes tabernacle ritual as canon. Instead, the OT's real and abiding authority must be understood through the person and teaching of him to whom it points and who so richly fulfills it.

As in Luke 16:16-17, Jesus is not announcing the termination of the OT's relevance and authority (else Luke 16:17 would be incomprehensible), but that "the period during which men were related to God under its terms ceased with John" (Moo, "Jesus," p. 1); and the nature of its valid continuity is established only with reference to Jesus and the kingdom. The general structure of this interpretation has been well set forth by Banks (*Jesus*), Meier (*Law*), Moo ("Jesus"), Carson ("Jesus"; at a popular level, *Sermon on the Mount*, pp. 33ff.). For a somewhat similar approach, see Zumstein (pp. 119f.) and McConnell (pp. 96-97), who points out that Jesus' implicit authority is also found in the closing verses of the sermon (7:21-23) where as eschatological Judge he exercises the authority of God alone.

The chief objection to this view is that the use of "to fulfill" in the fulfillment quotations is in the passive voice, whereas here the voice is active. But it is doubtful whether much can be made out of this distinction (Meier, *Law*, pp. 80f.).

Three theological conclusions are inevitable.

1. If the antitheses (vv.21-48) are understood in the light of this interpretation of vv.17-20, then Jesus is not primarily engaged there in extending, annulling, or intensifying OT law, but in showing the direction in which it points, on the basis of his own authority (to which, again, the OT points). This may work out in any particular case to have the same practical effect as "intensifying" the law or "annulling" some element; but the reasons for that conclusion are quite different. On the ethical implications of this interpretation, see the competent essay by Moo ("Jesus").

2. If vv.17-20 are essentially authentic (see esp. W.D. Davies, "Matthew 5:17, 18," *Christian Origins and Judaism* [London: DLT, 1962], pp. 31-66; and Banks, "Matthew's Understanding") and the above interpretation is sound, the christological implications are important. Here Jesus presents himself as the eschatological goal of the OT, and thereby its sole authoritative interpreter, the one through whom alone the OT finds its valid continuity and significance.

3. This approach eliminates the need to pit Matthew against Paul, or Palestinian Jewish Christians against Pauline Gentile believers, the first lot adhering to Mosaic stipulations and the second abandoning them. Nor do we need the solution of Brice Martin, who argues that Matthew's approach to law and Paul's approach are non-

complementary but noncontradictory: they simply employ different categories. This fails to wrestle with Matthew's positioning of Jesus within the history of redemption; and Paul well understood that the Law and the Prophets pointed beyond themselves (e.g., Rom 3:21; Gal 3–4; cf. Rom 8:4). The focus returns to Jesus, which is where, on the face of it, both Paul and Matthew intend it to be. The groundwork is laid out in the Gospels for an understanding of Jesus as the one who established the essentially christological and eschatological approach to the OT employed by Paul. But this is made clearer in v.18.

18 "I tell you the truth" signals that the statement to follow is of the utmost importance (cf. Notes). In Greek it is connected to the preceding verse by an explanatory "for" (*gar*): v.18 further explains and confirms the truth of v.17. The "jot" (KJV) has become "the smallest letter" (NIV): this is almost certainly correct, for it refers to the letter ' (*yôḏ*), the smallest letter of the Hebrew alphabet. The "tittle" (*keraia*) has been variously interpreted: it is the Hebrew letter ו (*wāw*) (so G. Schwarz, "ἰῶτα ἓν ἢ μία κεραία [Matthaus 5₁₈]," ZNW 66 [1975]: 268–69); or the small stroke that distinguishes several pairs of Hebrew letters (ב/כ; ד/ר; ד/ך) (so Filson, Lenski, Allen, Zahn); or a purely ornamental stroke, a "crown" (Tasker, Schniewind, Schweizer; but cf. DNTT, 3:182); or it forms a hendiadys with "jot," referring to the smallest part of the smallest letter (Lachs, pp. 106–8). In any event Jesus here upholds the authority of the OT Scriptures right down to the "least stroke of a pen." His is the highest possible view of the OT.

But vv.17–18 do not wrestle abstractly with OT authority but with the nature, extent, and duration of its validity and continuity. The nature of these has been set forth in v.17. The reference to "jot and tittle" establishes its extent: it will not do to reduce the reference to moral law, or the law as a whole but not necessarily its parts, or to God's will in some general sense. "Law" almost certainly refers to the entire OT Scriptures, not just the Pentateuch or moral law (note the parallel in v.17).

That leaves the duration of the OT's authority. The two "until" clauses answer this. The first—"until heaven and earth disappear"—simply means "until the end of the age": i.e., not quite "never" (contra Meier, *Law*, p. 61), but "never, as long as the present world order persists." The second—"until everything is accomplished" —is more difficult. Some take it to be equivalent to the first (cf. Sand, pp. 36–39). But it is more subtle than that. The word *panta* ("all things" or "everything" has no antecedent. Contrary to Sand (p. 38), Hill, Bultmann (*Synoptic Tradition*, pp. 138, 405), Grundmann, and Zahn, the word cannot very easily refer to all the demands of the law that must be "accomplished," because (1) the word "law" almost certainly refers here to all Scripture and not just its commands—but even if that were not so, v.17 has shown that even imperatival law is prophetic; (2) the word *genētai* ("is accomplished") must here be rendered "happen," "come to pass" (i.e., "accomplished" in that sense, not in the sense of obeying a law; cf. Meier, *Law*, pp. 53f.; Banks, *Jesus*, pp. 215ff.).

Hence *panta* ("everything") is best understood to refer to everything in the law, considered under the law's prophetic function—viz., until all these things have taken place as prophesied. This is not simply pointing to the Cross (Davies, "Matthew 5:17, 18," pp. 60ff.; Schlatter), nor simply to the end of the age (Schniewind). The parallel with 24:34–35 is not that close, since in the latter case the events are specified. Verse 18d simply means the entire divine purpose prophesied in Scripture must take place; not one jot or tittle will fail of its fulfillment. A similar point is made in 11:13. Thus the first "until" clause focuses strictly on the duration of OT authority but the second returns to considering its nature; it reveals God's redemptive purposes and points to their fulfillment, their "accomplishment," in Jesus and the eschatological kingdom he is now introducing and will one day consummate.

Meier (*Law*) ably establishes the centrality of the death and resurrection of Jesus as the pivotal event in Matthew's presentation of salvation history. Before it Jesus' disciples are restricted to Israel (10:5–6); after it they are to go everywhere. Similarly, the precise form of the Mosaic law may change with the crucial redemptive events to which it points. For that which prophesies is in some sense taken up in and transcended by the fulfillment of the prophecy. Meier has grasped and explained this redemptive-historical structure better than most commentators. He may, however, have gone too far in interpreting v.18d too narrowly as a reference to the Cross and the Resurrection.

19 The contrast between the least and the greatest in the kingdom probably supports gradation within kingdom ranks (as in 11:11, though the word for "least" is different there; cf. 18:1–4). It is probably not a Semitic way of referring to the exclusion-inclusion duality (contra Bonnard). The one who breaks "one of the least of these commandments" is not excluded from the kingdom—the linguistic usage is against this interpretation (see Meier, *Law*, pp. 92–95)—but is very small or very unimportant in the kingdom (taking *elachistos* in the elative sense). The idea of gradations of privilege or dishonor in the kingdom occurs elsewhere in the synoptic Gospels (20:20–28; cf. Luke 12:47–48). Distinctions are made not only according to the measure by which one keeps "the least of these commandments" but also according to the faithfulness with which one teaches them.

But what are "these commandments"? It is hard to justify restriction of these words to Jesus' teachings (so Banks, *Jesus*, pp. 221–23), even though the verb cognate to "commands" (*entolōn*) is used of Jesus' teachings in 28:20 (*entellomai*); for the noun in Matthew never refers to Jesus' words, and the context argues against it. Restriction to the Ten Commandments (TDNT, 2:548) is equally alien to the concerns of the context. Nor can we say "these commandments" refers to the antitheses that follow, for in Matthew *houtos* ("this," pl. "these") never points forward. It appears, then, that the expression must refer to the commandments of the OT Scriptures. The entire Law and the Prophets are not scrapped by Jesus' coming but fulfilled. Therefore the commandments of these Scriptures—even the least of them (on distinctions in the law, see on 22:36; 23:23)—must be practiced. But the nature of the practicing has already been affected by vv.17–18. The law pointed forward to Jesus and his teaching; so it is properly obeyed by conforming to his word. As it points to him, so he, in fulfilling it, establishes what continuity it has, the true direction to which it points and the way it is to be obeyed. Thus ranking in the kingdom turns on the degree of conformity to Jesus' teaching as that teaching fulfills OT revelation. His teaching, toward which the OT pointed, must be obeyed.

20 And that teaching, far from being more lenient, is nothing less than perfection (see on 5:48). The Pharisees and teachers of the law (see on 2:4; 3:7; and Introduction, section 11.f) were among the most punctilious in the land. Jesus' criticism is "not that they were not good, but that they were not good enough" (Hill, *Matthew*). While their multiplicity of regulations could engender a "good" society, it domesticated the law and lost the radical demand for absolute holiness demanded by the Scriptures.

What Jesus demanded is the righteousness to which the law truly points, exemplified in the antitheses that follow (vv.21–48). Contrary to Flender (pp. 45f.), v.3 (poverty of spirit) and v.20 (demand for radical righteousness) do not stand opposite each other in flat contradiction. Verse 20 does not establish how the righteousness is to be gained, developed, or empowered; it simply lays out the demand. Messiah will develop a people who will be called "oaks of righteousness . . . for the display of [Yahweh's] splendor" (Isa 61:3). The verb "surpasses" suggests that the new righteousness outstrips the old both qualitatively and quantitatively (Bonnard) (see on 25:31–46). Anything less does not enter the kingdom.

Notes

18 "I tell you the truth" is NIV's rendering of two expressions merged together: (1) ἀμήν (*amēn*)—a Greek transliteration of a Hebrew word meaning "faithful," "reliable," often used in the OT as an adverb, "surely," "truly," often at the end of a sentence endorsing or wishing that the sentence is true or may prove true (cf. "Amen" in English at the end of prayers); it also begins some sentences (Jer 28:6; Rev 7:12; 19:4; 22:20) or develops into a response (1 Cor 14:16; Rev 5:14; cf. Deut 27:15–26; cf. also Daube, *New Testament*, pp. 388–93; Jeremias, *Prayers*, pp. 112–15)—and (2) γὰρ λέγω ὑμῖν (*gar legō hymin*, "for I tell you"), which of course would take the order λέγω γὰρ ὑμῖν if it stood on its own.

b. *Application: the antitheses* (5:21–48)

1) *Vilifying anger and reconciliation*

5:21–26

> ²¹"You have heard that it was said to the people long ago, 'Do not murder, and anyone who murders will be subject to judgment,' ²²But I tell you that anyone who is angry with his brother will be subject to judgment. Again, anyone who says to his brother, 'Raca,' is answerable to the Sanhedrin. But anyone who says, 'You fool!' will be in danger of the fire of hell.
> ²³"Therefore, if you are offering your gift at the altar and there remember that your brother has something against you, ²⁴leave your gift there in front of the altar. First go and be reconciled to your brother; then come and offer your gift.
> ²⁵"Settle matters quickly with your adversary who is taking you to court. Do it while you are still with him on the way, or he may hand you over to the judge, and the judge may hand you over to the officer, and you may be thrown into prison. ²⁶I tell you the truth, you will not get out until you have paid the last penny.

Verses 21–48 are often called the six antitheses because all six sections begin with some variation of "you have heard it said . . . but I say." Daube (*New Testament*, pp. 55–62) offers a number of much-cited rabbinic parallels, some of which, in the first part, raise an interpretation as a theoretical possibility only to reject it, and others of which raise a literal interpretation only to circumscribe it with broader considerations. Daube rightly points out that the first part of Matthew's formulas means something like "you have understood" or "you have literally understood." That is, Jesus is not criticizing the OT but the understanding of the OT many of his hearers adopted. This is especially true of vv.22, 43, where part of what was "heard" certainly does not come from the OT.

Beginning with this point, many (e.g., Stendahl [Peake], Hill) hold that Jesus nowhere abrogates the law but merely intensifies it or shows its ultimate meaning. Others (e.g., McConnell) point out that, formally speaking, some OT laws are indeed contravened (e.g., laws on oaths, vv. 33–37). R.A. Guelich ("The Antitheses of Matthew v.21–48: Traditional or Redactional?" NTS 22 [1975–76]: 444–57), in the course of arguing that the first, second, and fourth are traditional, and the third, fifth, and sixth redactional, suggests that the former transcend the law's demands, whereas the latter annul the law—a point contested by G. Strecker ("Die Antithesen der Bergpredigt," ZNW 69 [1978]: 36–72). Apart from the fact that the traditional-redactional bifurcation is not an entirely happy one (cf. Introduction, sections 1–3), a unifying approach to the antitheses is possible in the light of our exegesis of vv.17–20.

The contrast between what the people had heard and what Jesus taught is not based on distinctions like casuistry versus love, outer legalism versus inner commitment, or even false interpretation versus true interpretation, though all of them impinge collaterally on the text. Rather, in every case Jesus contrasts the people's misunderstanding of the law with the true direction in which the law points, according to his own authority as the law's "fulfiller" (in the sense established in v.17). He makes no attempt to fence in the law (contra Przybylski, pp. 80–87) but declares unambiguously the true direction to which it points. Thus if certain antitheses revoke at least the letter of the law (and they do: cf. Meier, Law, pp. 125ff.), they do so, not because they are thereby affirming the law's true spirit, but because Jesus insists that his teaching on these matters is the direction in which the laws actually point.

Likewise Jesus' "you have heard . . . but I say" is not quite analogous to corresponding rabbinic formulas; Jesus is not simply a proto-rabbi (contra Daube, Sigal). The Sermon on the Mount is not set in a context of scholarly dispute over halakic details but in a context of messianic and eschatological fulfillment. Jesus' authority bursts the borders of the relatively "narrow context of legal interpretation and innovation which the rabbis circumscribed for themselves" (Banks, Jesus, p. 85). It is for this reason that the crowds were amazed at his authority (7:28–29).

21–22 Jesus' contemporaries had heard that the law given their forefathers (cf. Notes) forbade murder (not the taking of all life, which could, for instance, be a judicial mandate: cf. Gen 9:6) and that the murderer must be brought to "judgment" (krisis, which here refers to legal proceedings, perhaps the court set up in every town [Deut 16:18; 2 Chron 19:5; cf. Jos. Antiq. IV, 214(vii.14); War II, 570–71 (xx.5)]; or the council of twenty-three persons set up to deal with criminal matters, SBK, 1:275). But Jesus insists—the "I" is emphatic in each of the six antitheses— that the law really points to his own teaching: the root of murder is anger, and anger is murderous in principle (v.22). One has not conformed to the better righteousness of the kingdom simply by refraining from homicide. The angry person will be subject to krisis ("judgment"), but it is presupposed this is God's judgment, "since no human court is competent to try a case of inward anger" (Stott). To stoop to insult exposes one not merely to (God's) council (*synedrion* can mean either "Sanhedrin" [NIV] or simply "council") but to the "fire of hell."

The expression "fire of hell" (*geenna tou pyros*, lit., "gehenna of fire") comes from the Hebrew *gê-hinnōm* ("Valley of Hinnom," a ravine south of Jerusalem once associated with the pagan god Moloch and his disgusting rites [2 Kings 23:10; 2 Chron 28:3; 33:6; Jer 7:31; Ezek 16:20; 23:37], prohibited by God [Lev 18:21; 20:2–5]). When Josiah abolished the practices, he defiled the valley by making it a, dumping ground for filth and the corpses of criminals (2 Kings 23:10). Late traditions suggest that in the first century it may still have been used as a rubbish pit, complete with smoldering fires. The valley came to symbolize the place of eschatological punishment (cf. 1 Enoch 54:12; 2 Bar 85:13; cf. Matt 10:28; 23:15, 33; and 18:9 for the longer expression "gehenna of fire"). Gehenna and Hades (11:23 [NIV mg.]; 16:18) are often thought to refer, respectively, to eternal hell and the abode of the dead in the intermediate state. But the distinction can be maintained in few passages. More commonly the two terms are synonymous and mean "hell" (cf. W.J.P. Boyd, "Gehenna—According to J. Jeremias," in Livingstone, 2:9–12).

"Brother" (*adelphos*) cannot in this case be limited to male siblings. Matthew's Gospel uses the word extensively. Whenever it clearly refers to people beyond physical brothers, it is on the lips of Jesus; and its narrow usage is almost always Matthean. This suggests that the Christian habit of calling one another "brother" goes back to Jesus' instruction, possibly part and parcel of his training them to address God as Father (6:9). Among Christian brothers, anger is to be eliminated.

The passage does not suggest a gradation and climax of punishments (Hendriksen, pp. 297–99), for this would require a similar gradation of offense. There is no clear distinction between the person with seething anger, the one who insultingly calls his brother a fool, and the one who prefers, as his term of abuse, "Raca" (transliteration for Aram. *rēkā'*, "imbecile," "fool," "blockhead"). To a Greek, *mōros* would suggest foolishness, senselessness; but to a speaker of Hebrew, the Greek word might call to mind the Hebrew *mōreh,* which has overtones of moral apostasy, rebellion, and wickedness (cf. Ps 78:8[77:8 LXX]; Jer 5:23).

Many Jewish maxims warn against anger (examples in Bonnard), but this is not just another maxim. Here Jesus offers not just advice but insists that the sixth commandment points prophetically to the kingdom's condemnation of hate.

Jesus' anger, expressed in diverse circumstances (21:12–19; 23:17; Mark 3:1–5), is no personal inconsistency.

1. Jesus is a preacher who gets down to essentials on every point he makes. Thus for a clear understanding of his thought on a particular issue, one must examine the balance of his teaching. Compare, for instance, 6:2–4 with Luke 18:1–8. Similarly, to learn all Jesus says about anger, it is necessary to integrate this passage with others such as 21:12–13 without absolutizing any one text.

2. When suffering, Jesus is proverbial for his gentleness and forbearance (Luke 23:34; 1 Peter 2:23). But if he comes as Suffering Servant, he comes equally as Judge and King. His anger erupts not out of personal pique but out of outrage at injustice, sin, unbelief, and exploitation of others. Unfortunately his followers are more likely to be angered at personal affronts (cf. Carson, *Sermon on the Mount,* pp. 41f.).

23–24 Jesus gives two illustrations exposing the seriousness of anger, the first in a setting of temple worship (vv. 23–24, which implies a pre-70 setting), and the second in a judicial setting (vv.25–26). The first concerns a brother (see on v.22); the second an adversary. Remarkably neither illustration deals with "your" anger but with "your" offense that has prompted the brother's or the adversary's rancor. Some take this as a sign that vv.23–26 represent displaced, independent logia. Yet the connection with vv.21–22 is very powerful. We are more likely to remember when we have something against others than when we have done something to offend others. And if we are truly concerned about our anger and hate, we shall be no less concerned when we engender them in others.

The "altar" (v.23) is the one in the inner court. There amid solemn worship, recollection of a brother with something against one (on the expression, cf. Mark 11:25) should in Christ's disciples prompt immediate efforts to be reconciled (v.24). Only then is formal worship acceptable.

25–26 Compare Luke 12:57–59, where the contextual application warns impenitent Israel to be reconciled to God before it is too late. Many conclude that Matthew has "ethicized" an originally eschatological saying. But the language of the two pericopes is not close, and it is more realistic to postulate two stories from one itinerant preacher. Explanations for one or two of the changes (e.g., McNeile) are not convincing unless they fit a pattern that justifies all the changes.

Jesus again urges haste (v.25). Settle matters with the offended adversary while still "with him on the way" to court, not on "the road to life" (Bonnard). In the ancient world debtors were jailed till the debts were paid. Thus v.26 is part of the narrative fabric and gives no justification for purgatory, universal restoration, or urgent reconciliation to God. It simply insists on immediate action: malicious anger is so evil—and God's judgment so certain (v.22)—that we must do all in our power to end it (cf. Eph 4:26–27).

Notes

---

21 The word ἀρχαίοις (archaiois, "to the people long ago") is translated as an instrumental dative in KJV: "by them of old time," following Beza. The reading is also found in some OL copies: *ab antiquis* (it[a.b.c]) instead of *antiquis* (it[d.f.ff.]), which is as ambiguous as the Greek (similarly in v.33). NIV is almost certainly right: (1) the normal way of expressing agency in Greek is with ὑπό (hypo, "by") plus the genitive (though there are exceptional datives, e.g., 6:1; 23:5); and (2) Jesus' point is not to correct "the people long ago" but the misunderstandings of his contemporaries, for which the NIV rendering is more suitable.

The verb οὐ φονεύσεις (ou phoneuseis, "Do not murder") is future, a not uncommon way for the LXX to express an imperative. Most examples in the NT are in quotations from the LXX (e.g., 5:33, 43, 48). But the construction is not unknown in secular Greek, and some non-LXX instances occur in the NT (e.g., 6:5; 20:26; 21:3, 13; cf. Turner, *Syntax* p. 86).

22 The words "without cause" (NIV mg.) probably reflect an early and widespread softening of Jesus' strong teaching. Their absence does not itself prove there is no exception: see commentary.

23 The change from plural to singular occurs again at 5:29, 36, 39; 6:5, and may reflect the style of a preacher who knows how to bring his lesson home by making it personal.

2) Adultery and purity

5:27–30

27"You have heard that it was said, 'Do not commit adultery.' 28But I tell you that anyone who looks at a woman lustfully has already committed adultery with her in his heart. 29If your right eye causes you to sin, gouge it out and throw it away. It is better for you to lose one part of your body than for your whole body to be thrown into hell. 30And if your right hand causes you to sin, cut it off and throw it away. It is better for you to lose one part of your body than for your whole body to go into hell.

27–28 The OT command not to commit adultery (Exod 20:14; Deut 5:18) is often treated in Jewish sources not so much as a function of purity as of theft: it was to steal another's wife (references in Bonnard). Jesus insisted that the seventh commandment points in another direction—toward purity that refuses to lust (v.28). The tenth commandment had already explicitly made the point; and *gynē* here more likely means "woman" than "wife." "To interpret the law on the side of stringency is not to annul the Law, but to change it in accordance with its own intention" (Davies, *Setting*, p. 102; cf. Job 31:1; Prov 6:25; 2 Peter 2:14).

Klaus Haacker ("Der Rechtsatz Jesu zum Thema Ehebruch," *Biblische Zeitschrift* 21 [1977]: 113–16) has convincingly argued that the second *autēn* ("[committed adultery] with her") is contrary to the common interpretation of this verse. In Greek it is unnecessary, especially if the sin is entirely the man's. But it is explainable if *pros to epithymēsai autēn*, commonly understood to mean "with a view to lusting for her," is translated "so as to get her to lust." The evidence for this interpretation is strong (cf. Notes). The man is therefore looking at the woman with a view to enticing her to lust. Thus, so far as his intention goes, he is committing adultery *with her*, he makes her an adulteress. This does not weaken the force of Jesus' teaching; the heart of the matter is still lust and intent.

29–30 The radical treatment of parts of the body that cause one to sin (cf. Notes) has led some (notoriously Origen) to castrate themselves. But that is not radical enough, since lust is not thereby removed. The "eye" (v.29) is the member of the body most commonly blamed for leading us astray, especially in sexual sins (cf. Num 15:39; Prov 21:4; Ezek 6:9; 18:12; 20:8; cf. Eccl 11:9); the "right eye" refers to one's best eye. But why the "right hand" (v.30) in a context dealing with lust? This may be merely illustrative or a way of saying that even lust is a kind of theft. More likely it is a euphemism for the male sexual organ (cf. *yād*, "hand," most likely used in this way in Isa 57:8 [cf. BDB, s.v., 4.g]; see Lachs, pp. 108f.).

Cutting off or gouging out the offending part is a way of saying that Jesus' disciples must deal radically with sin. Imagination is a God-given gift; but if it is fed dirt by the eye, it will be dirty. All sin, not least sexual sin, begins with the imagination. Therefore what feeds the imagination is of maximum importance in the pursuit of kingdom righteousness (compare Phil 4:8). Not everyone reacts the same way to all objects. But if (vv.28–29) your eye is causing you to sin, gouge it out; or at very least, don't look (cf. the sane exposition of Stott, pp. 88–91)! The alternative is sin and hell, sin's reward. The point is so fundamental that Jesus doubtless repeated it on numerous occasions (cf. 18:8–9).

Notes

28 The verb ἐπιθυμέω (*epithymeō*, "I lust") can have positive force ("I desire"), but more commonly it has a bad sense. It is used explicitly in connection with sexual lust in Rom 1:24.

The expression πρὸς τὸ ἐπιθυμῆσαι αὐτήν (*pros to epithymēsai autēn*) could mean "so as to lust after her," whether with telic or ecbatic force (cf. BDF, par. 402 [5]), here presumably the former. If so, it is the only place where this kind of verb uses the accusative: *autēs* (gen.) rather than the expected *autēn* (cf. BDF, par. 171 [1]). The accusative *autēn* more probably therefore functions as the accusative of reference (i.e., the quasi-subject) of the infinitive (as in the equivalent construction in Luke 18:1) to generate the translation "so that she lusts."

29 The verb σκανδαλίζω (*skandalizō*) can mean (1) "I cause to stumble," "I cause to sin" (as here, 18:6–9; Luke 17:2; Rom 14:21; 1 Cor 8:13; 2 Cor 11:29); (2) "I obstruct another's path," and, hence, "I cause [someone] to disbelieve, reject, forsake" (Matt 11:6; 13:21, 57; 15:12; 24:10; 26:31, 33; John 16:1); (3) "I offend" (Matt 17:27; John 6:61). The cognate noun σκάνδαλον (*skandalon*), originally referring to the trigger of a trap (cf. Rom 11:9), comes to mean, in a similar breakdown, (1) "stumbling block," i.e., "causing another to fall into sin" (Matt 13:41; 18:7; Luke 17:1; Rom 14:13; 1 John 2:10; Rev 2:14); (2) "an obstruction," and, hence, "an occasion of disbelief" (Rom 9:32–33; 16:17; 1 Cor 1:23; 1 Peter 2:8); (3) an object one strikes and which hurts or repels one; hence, "an offense" (Matt 16:23; Gal 5:11). Some texts may appeal to more than one meaning (cf. Broadus; DNTT, 2:707–10).

3) *Divorce and remarriage*

5:31–32

> [31]"It has been said, 'Anyone who divorces his wife must give her a certificate of divorce.' [32]But I tell you that anyone who divorces his wife, except for marital unfaithfulness, causes her to become an adulteress, and anyone who marries the divorced woman commits adultery.

31–32 The introductory formula "It has been said" is shorter than all the others in this chapter and is linked to the preceding by a connective *de* ("and"). Therefore, though these two verses are innately antithetical, they carry further the argument of the preceding pericope. The OT not only points toward insisting that lust is the moral equivalent of adultery (vv. 27–30) but that divorce is as well. This arises out of the fact that the divorced woman will in most circumstances remarry (esp. in first-century Palestine, where this would probably be her means of support). That new marriage, whether from the perspective of the divorcee or the one marrying her, is adulterous.

The OT passage to which Jesus refers (v. 31) is Deuteronomy 24:1–4, whose thrust is that if a man divorces his wife because of "something indecent" (not further defined) in her, he must give her a certificate of divorce, and if she then becomes another man's wife and is divorced again, the first man cannot remarry her. This double restriction—the certificate and the prohibition of remarriage—discouraged hasty divorces. Here Jesus does not go into the force of "something indecent." Instead he insists that the law was pointing to the sanctity of marriage.

The natural way to take the "except" clause is that divorce is wrong because it generates adultery *except* in the case of fornication. In that case, where sexual sin has already been committed, nothing is laid down, though it appears that divorce is then implicitly permitted, even if not mandated (cf. the paraphrase in Stonehouse, *Witness of Matthew*, p. 203).

The numerous points for exegetical dispute (e.g., the meaning of *porneia* ["fornication," or, in NIV, "marital unfaithfulness"], the force of the "except" clause, and the tradition history behind these verses and their relationship to 19:3–9; Mark 10:11–12; Luke 16:18) are treated more fully at 19:3–12. The one theory that must be rejected here (because it has no counterpart in 19:3–12) is that which takes the words "makes her an adulteress" to mean "stigmatizes her as an adulteress (even though it is not so)" (B. Ward Powers, "Divorce and the Bible," *Interchange* 23 [1938]: 159). The Greek uses the verb, not the noun (cf. NIV's "causes her to become an adulteress"). The verbal construction disallows Powers's paraphrase.

4) Oaths and truthfulness

5:33–37

> 33"Again, you have heard that it was said to the people long ago, 'Do not break your oath, but keep the oaths you have made to the Lord.' 34But I tell you, Do not swear at all: either by heaven, for it is God's throne; 35or by the earth, for it is his footstool; or by Jerusalem, for it is the city of the Great King. 36And do not swear by your head, for you cannot make even one hair white or black. 37Simply let your 'Yes' be 'Yes,' and your 'No,' 'No'; anything beyond this comes from the evil one.

33 "Again" probably confirms 5:31–32 as an excursus to the preceding antithesis rather than a new one. Matthew now reports an antithesis on a new theme. What the people have heard is not given as direct OT quotation but as a summary statement accurately condensing the burden of Exodus 20:7; Leviticus 19:12; Numbers 30:2; and Deuteronomy 5:11; 6:3; 22:21–23. The Mosaic law forbade irreverent oaths, light use of the Lord's name, broken vows. Once Yahweh's name was invoked, the vow to which it was attached became a debt that had to be paid to the Lord.

A sophisticated casuistry judged how binding an oath really was by examining how closely it was related to Yahweh's name. Incredible distinctions proliferate under such an approach. Swearing by heaven and earth was not binding, nor was swearing *by* Jerusalem, though swearing *toward* Jerusalem was. That an entire mishnaic tract (M *Shebuoth*) is given over to the subject (cf. also M *Sanhedrin* 3.2; *Tosephta Nedarim* 1; SBK, 1:321–36) shows that such distinctions became important and were widely discussed. Matthew returns to the topic with marvelous examples in the polemical setting of 23:16–22. The context is not overtly polemical here but simply explains how Jesus relates the kingdom and its righteousness to the OT.

34–36 If oaths designed to encourage truthfulness become occasions for clever lies and casuistical deceit, Jesus will abolish oaths (v.34). For the direction in which the OT points is the fundamental importance of thorough and consistent truthfulness. If one does not swear at all, one does not swear falsely. Not dissimilar reasoning was found among the Essenes, who avoided taking oaths, "regarding it as worse than perjury, for they say that one who is not believed without an appeal to God stands condemned already" (Jos. War II, 135[viii.6])—though they did require "tremendous oaths" of neophytes joining the community (ibid., 139[viii.7]; cf. 1QS 5:7–11; CD 15:5).

Jesus insists that whatever a man swears by is related to God in some way, and therefore every oath is implicitly in God's name—heaven, earth, Jerusalem, even the hairs of the head are all under God's sway and ownership (v.36). (There may be allusions here to Ps 48:2; Isa 66:1.) Significantly, Matthew breaks the flow to say (in Gr.) "toward Jerusalem" rather than "by Jerusalem" (on the distinction, cf. on v.33). The "Great King" (v.35) may well be God, but see on 25:34.

37 The Greek might more plausibly be translated "But let your word be, 'Yes, Yes; No, No.'" The doubling has raised questions: according to some rabbinic opinion, a doubled "yes" or "no" constitutes an oath; and Broadus suggests this is an appropriate way to strengthen an assertion. This sounds like casuistry every bit as tortuous as that which Jesus condemns. The doubling is probably no more than preacher's rhetoric, the point made clear by NIV (cf. James 5:12). *Tou ponērou* could be rendered either "of evil" or "of the evil one" ("the father of lies," John 8:44). The same ambiguity recurs at 5:39; 6:13; 13:38.

Many groups (e.g., Anabaptists, Jehovah's Witnesses) have understood these verses absolutely literally and have therefore refused even to take court oaths. Their zeal to conform to Scripture is commendable, but they have probably not interpreted the text very well.

1. The contextual purpose of this passage is to stress the true direction in which the OT points—viz., the importance of truthfulness. Where oaths are not being used evasively and truthfulness is not being threatened, it is not immediately obvious that they require such unqualified abolition.

2. In the Scriptures God himself "swears" (e.g., Gen 9:9–11; Luke 1:68, 73; cf. Ps 16:10 and Acts 2:27–31), not because he sometimes lies, but in order to help men believe (Heb 6:17). The earliest Christians still took oaths, if we may judge from Paul's example (Rom 1:9; 2 Cor 1:23; 1 Thess 2:5, 10; cf. Phil 1:8), for much the same reason. Jesus himself testified under oath (26:63–64).

3. Again we need to remember the antithetical nature of Jesus' preaching (see on 5:27–30; 6:5–8).

It must be frankly admitted that here Jesus formally contravenes OT law: what it permits or commands (Deut 6:13), he forbids. But if his interpretation of the direction in which the law points is authoritative, then his teaching fulfills it.

Notes

34 Ὁμνύναι ἐν or εἰς (*omnynai en* or *eis*, "to swear by" or "by-toward" [Gr. is not entirely unambiguous]) is Hebraic (cf. Moulton, *Accidence*, pp. 463–64); only with "Jerusalem" is *eis* used in the NT. Turner (*Insights*, p. 31) argues that the present prohibition in James 5:12 means "stop swearing," whereas the aorist prohibition here presupposes that the disciples have stopped and now forbids them from starting. This classic distinction based on tenses in prohibitions usually holds but can be too finely spun (cf. Moule, *Idiom Book*,

p. 21). In the strictest sense the aorist is timeless; and linked in v.34 with μή . . . ὅλως (mē . . . holōs, "not . . . at all") it probably simply generates an unconditional negative: "Do not swear at all" (NIV: cf. Schlatter).

---

5) Personal injury and self-sacrifice

5:38–42

> [38]"You have heard that it was said, 'Eye for eye, and tooth for tooth.' [39]But I tell you, Do not resist an evil person. If someone strikes you on the right cheek, turn to him the other also. [40]And if someone wants to sue you and take your tunic, let him have your cloak as well. [41]If someone forces you to go one mile, go with him two miles. [41]Give to the one who asks you, and do not turn away from the one who wants to borrow from you.

The order of the last two antitheses (vv.38–48) is reversed in Luke 6:27–36. While the reasons for this are debatable, if both evangelists are recording the same sermon, the reversal shows that rearranging the order of the materials (preserved in Q and/or other notes) was thought acceptable. Bonnard rightly criticizes the tradition history of Wrege. Parallels repudiating vengeance and vindictiveness are not unknown (T Benjamin 4:1–5:5; 1QS 10:18; CD 8:5–6). The distinctive element in Jesus' teaching is the way he sets it over against the *lex talionis* (the principle of retribution) and the reasons he does this.

38 The OT prescription (Exod 21:24; Lev 24:19–20; Deut 19:21) was not given to foster vengeance; the law explicitly forbade that (Lev 19:18). Rather, it was given, as the OT context shows, to provide the nation's judicial system with a ready formula of punishment, not least because it would decisively terminate vendettas. On occasion payment in money or some other commodity was exacted instead (e.g., Exod 21:26–27); and in Jesus' day the courts seldom imposed *lex talionis*. The trouble is that a law designed to limit retaliation and punish fairly could be appealed to as justification for vindictiveness. But it will not do to argue that Jesus is doing nothing more than combatting a personal as opposed to a judicial use of the *lex talionis*, since in that case the examples would necessarily run differently: e.g., if someone strikes you, don't strike back but let the judiciary administer the just return slap. The argument runs in deeper channels.

39 Jesus' disciple is not to resist "an evil person" (*tō ponērō* could not easily be taken to refer here to the Devil or to evil in the abstract). In the context of the *lex talionis*, the most natural way of understanding the resistance is "do not resist in a court of law." This interpretation is required in the second example (v.40). As in vv.33–37, therefore, Jesus' teaching formally contradicts the OT law. But in the context of vv.17–20, what Jesus is saying is reasonably clear: the OT, including the *lex talionis*, points forward to Jesus and his teaching. But like the OT laws permitting divorce, enacted because of the hardness of men's hearts (19:3–12), the *lex talionis* was instituted to curb evil because of the hardness of men's hearts. "God gives by concession a legal regulation as a dam against the river of violence which flows from man's evil heart" (Piper, p. 90).

As this legal principle is overtaken by that toward which it points, so also is this hardness of heart. The OT prophets foretold a time when there would be a change of heart among God's people, living under a new covenant (Jer 31:31–34; 32:37–41; Ezek 36:26). Not only would the sins of the people be forgiven (Jer 31:34; Ezek 36:25), but obedience to God would spring from the heart (Jer 31:33; Ezek 36:27) as the eschatological age dawned. Thus Jesus' instruction on these matters is grounded in eschatology. In Jesus and the kingdom, fulfillment (even if partial) of the OT promises, the eschatological age that the Law and Prophets had prophesied (11:13) arrives; and the prophecies that curbed evil while pointing forward to the eschaton are now superseded by the new age and the new hearts it brings (cf. Piper, pp. 89–91).

Four illustrations clarify Jesus' point and drive it home. In the first, a man strikes another on the cheek—not only a painful blow, but a gross insult (cf. 2 Cor 11:20). If a right-handed person strikes someone's right cheek, presumably it is a slap by the back of the hand, probably considered more insulting than a slap by the open palm (cf. M *Baba Kamma* 8:6). The verb "strikes" (*rhapizei*) probably refers to a sharp slap. Many commentators contrast Luke's *typtō* ("strikes," Luke 6:29), arguing the latter refers to blows with a rod—i.e., Luke deals not with insult but with pain and damage. The contrast is false; the semantic overlap between the two verbs is substantial, and *typtō* can refer to a slap (e.g., Acts 23:3). But instead of seeking recompense at law under the *lex talionis*, Jesus' disciples will gladly endure the insult again. (There are overtones of Isa 50:6 here, applied in Matt 26:67 to Jesus; cf. Gundry, *Use of OT*, pp. 72–73.)

40 Although under Mosaic law the outer cloak was an inalienable possession (Exod 22:26; Deut 24:13), Jesus' disciples, if sued for their tunics (an inner garment like our suit but worn next to the skin), far from seeking satisfaction, will gladly part with what they may legally keep. Luke 6:29 says nothing about legal action but mentions the garments in reverse order. This has led some to think that Luke had violent robbery in mind because then the outer garment would be snatched off first. But perhaps the order is simply that in which the garments would normally be removed.

41 The third example refers to the Roman practice of commandeering civilians to carry the luggage of military personnel a prescribed distance, one Roman "mile." (On the verb *angareuō*, "I commandeer," cf. W. Hatch, *Essays in Biblical Greek* [Oxford: Clarendon, 1889], pp. 37–38.) Impressment, like a lawsuit, evokes outrage; but the attitude of Jesus' disciples under such circumstances must not be spiteful or vengeful but helpful—willing to go a second mile (exemplars of the Western text say "two more [miles]," making a total of three!). This illustration is also implicitly anti-Zealot.

42 The final illustration requires not only interest-free loans (Exod 22:25; Lev 25:37; Deut 23:19) but a generous spirit (cf. Deut 15:7–11; Pss 37:26; 112:5). The parallel form of this verse (Luke 6:30) does not imply two requests but only one; the repetition reinforces the point. These last two illustrations confirm our interpretation of vv.38–39. The entire pericope deals with the heart's attitude, the better righteousness. For there is actually no legal recourse to the oppression in the third illustration, and in the fourth no harm that might lead to retaliation has been done.

While these four vignettes have powerful shock value, they were not meant to be new legal prescriptions. Verse 42 does not commit Jesus' disciples to giving endless amounts of money to every one who seeks a "soft touch" (cf. Prov 11:15; 17:18;

22:26). Verse 40 is clearly hyperbolic: no first-century Jew would go home wearing only a loin cloth. Nor does this pericope deal with the validity of a state police force. Yet the illustrations must not be diluted by endless equivocations; the only limit to the believer's response in these situations is what love and the Scriptures impose. Paul could "resist" (same Gr. word) Peter to his face (Gal 2) because love demanded it in light of the damage being done to the gospel and to fellow believers. (On the practical outworking of this antithesis, cf. Neil, pp. 160–63; Piper, pp. 92–99; Stott, pp. 104–14.)

6) Hatred and love

5:43–47

> 43"You have heard that it was said, 'Love your neighbor and hate your enemy.' 44But I tell you: Love your enemies and pray for those who persecute you, 45that you may be sons of your Father in heaven. He causes his sun to rise on the evil and the good, and sends rain on the righteous and the unrighteous. 46If you love those who love you, what reward will you get? Are not even the tax collectors doing that? 47And if you greet only your brothers, what are you doing more than others? Do not even pagans do that?

43 The command "Love your neighbor" is found in Leviticus 19:18, but no OT Scripture adds "and hate your enemies." Rabbinic literature as it was later preserved does not usually leap to so bold and negative a conclusion. Thus some commentators have taken this passage as a later Christian mockery of Jewish values. But other considerations question this.

1. The Qumran covenanters explicitly commanded love for those within the community ("those whom God has elected") and hatred for the outsider (cf. 1QS 1:4, 10; 2:4–9; 1QM 4:1–2; 15:6; 1QH 5:4), and they doubtless represent other groups with similar positions. This love-hate antithesis may be mitigated by the covenanters' conviction that they alone were the faithful remnant; at least some of the language anticipates divine eschatological language. But not all of it can be dismissed so easily (cf. Davies, *Setting*, pp. 245ff.).

2. Quite apart from the problems in dating rabbinic literature, we must remember that such literature represents scholarly debate, not common thought. For example, Carl F.H. Henry writes learned tomes read by a few thousand; Hal Lindsey writes popular material read by millions. In a hundred years, if the world lasts that long, some of Henry's work may still be in print, but few will remember Lindsey. Yet today Lindsey is read by far more church people than Henry; and the wise preacher will not forget it. Likewise the popular perversion of Leviticus 19:18 presupposed by Matthew 5:43 was doubtless far more widespread than the rabbinic literature intimates.

The quotation also omits "as yourself," words included in 19:19; 22:39; and the attitude reflected ignores the fact that Leviticus 19:33–34 also commands love of the same depth for the sojourner, the resident alien in the land. The popular reasoning seems to have been that if God commands love for "neighbor," then hatred for "enemies" is implicitly conceded and perhaps even authorized. Luke 10:25–37 shows how far the "neighbor" category extends.

44–47 Jesus allowed no casuistry. The real direction indicated by the law is love, rich and costly, and extended even to enemies. Many take the verb "love" (*agapaō*) and the noun (*agapē*) as always signifying self-giving regardless of emotion. For instance, Hill (*Matthew*) comments on this passage. "The love which is inculcated is not a matter of sentiment and emotion, but, as always in the *OT* and *NT*, of concrete action." If this were so, 1 Corinthians 13:3 could not disavow "love" that gives everything to the poor and suffers even to martyrdom; for these are "concrete actions." The same verb is used when Amnon incestuously loves his half-sister Tamar (2 Sam 13:1 LXX); when Demas, because he loves this world (2 Tim 4:10), forsakes Paul; and when tax collectors love those who love them (Matt 5:46).

The rise of this word group in Greek is well traced by Robert Joly, Ἀγαπᾶν et Φιλεῖν: *Le vocabulaire chrétien de l'amour, est-il original?* (Bruxelles: Presses Universitaires, 1968). Christians doubtless took over the word group and largely filled it with their own content; but the content of that love is not based on a presupposed definition but on Jesus' teaching and example. To love one's enemies, though it must result in doing them good (Luke 6:32–33) and praying for them (Matt 5:44), cannot justly be restricted to activities devoid of any concern, sentiment, or emotion. Like the English verb "to love," *agapaō* ranges widely from debased and selfish actions to generous, warm, costly self-sacrifice for another's good. There is no reason to think the verb here in Matthew does not include emotion as well as action.

Much recent scholarship identifies the "enemies" with the persecutors of Matthew's church. Verses 44–47 are then seen as Matthew's transformation of Luke's more general exhortation (6:32–35) into encouragement for believers in Matthew's day to submit graciously to their persecutors. If Matthew's first readers were being persecuted for their faith, that was doubtless one application they made, though it is unlikely that Matthew himself intends to be quite so restrictive and anachronistic. The words "those who persecute you" introduce one important kind of "enemy" but do not exclude other kinds. Jesus himself repeatedly warns his disciples of impending persecution (e.g., vv.10–12; 10:16–23; 24:9–13); so there is little need to doubt the authenticity of the warning here.

One manifestation of love for enemies will be in prayer; praying for an enemy and loving him will prove mutually reinforcing. The more love, the more prayer; the more prayer, the more love.

> Jesus seems to have prayed for his tormentors actually while the iron spikes were being driven through his hands and feet; indeed the imperfect tense suggests that he kept praying, kept repeating his entreaty, "Father, forgive them; for they know not what they do" (Luke 23:34). If the cruel torture of crucifixion could not silence our Lord's prayer for his enemies, what pain, pride, prejudice or sloth could justify the silencing of ours? (Stott, p. 119).

Jesus' disciples have as their example God himself, who loves so indiscriminately that he sends sun and rain (they are his to bestow) on both the righteous and the unrighteous (cf. Seneca *De Beneficiis* 4.26; b *Taanith* 7b). Yet we must not conclude that God's love toward men is in all respects without distinction, and that therefore all must be saved in the end. The same Jesus teaches otherwise—e.g., in 25:31–46 —and the NT shows that some aspects of God's love are indeed related to his moral character and demands for obedience (e.g., John 15:9–11; Jude 21). Theologians since Calvin have related God's love in vv.44–45 to his "common grace" (i.e., the gracious favor God bestows "commonly," without distinction, on all men). He could with justice condemn all; instead he shows repeated and prolonged favor on all. That is the point here established for our emulation, not that God's love is amoral or without any distinctions whatsoever.

It is equally unsound to conclude that the OT requires harsh terms for an enemy, but that the NT overcomes this dark portrait with new demands for unqualified love. Counter evidence refutes this notion: the OT often mandates love for others (e.g., Exod 23:4–5; Lev 19:18, 33–34; 1 Sam 24:5; Job 31:29; Ps 7:4; Prov 24:17, 29; 25:21–22 [cf. Rom 12:20], and the NT speaks against the reprobate (e.g., Luke 18:7; 1 Cor 16:22; 2 Thess 1:6–10; 2 Tim 4:18; Rev 6:10). Rather, vv.44–45 insist that the OT law cited (v.43) points to the wealth of love exercised by the heirs of the kingdom, a love qualitatively different from that experienced by other people (see on vv.46–47).

God's example provides the incentive for Jesus' disciples to be (*genēsthe*, more likely, "become") sons of their Father (v.45). Ultimately this clause does not mean that the disciples act in a loving way to show what they already are (contra Schniewind, Zahn) but to become what they not yet are (Bonnard, Lagrange)—sons of the Father, in the sense established in v.9. The point of the passage is not to state the means of becoming sons but the necessity of pursuing a certain kind of sonship patterned after the Father's character. "To be persecuted because of righteousness is to align oneself with the prophets (5:12); but to bless and pray for those who persecute us is to align oneself with the character of God" (Carson, *Sermon on the Mount*, p. 53). "To return evil for good is devilish; to return good for good is human; to return good for evil is divine" (Plummer). Both these verses show that Jesus' disciples must live and love in a way superior to the patterns around them. Luke 6:32 uses *charis* ("grace"; NIV, "credit") rather than *misthos* ("reward"), a distinction that has fostered various complex theories concerning the relationship between the two passages. But in the same context, Luke also speaks of *misthos* ("reward," 6:35); and his use of *charis* means no more than thanks or gratitude: "What thanks have you?" (cf. BAGD, p. 878b; hence "credit" in NIV). The two passages are therefore very close, and neither construes "reward" in purely meritorious categories (see on v.12). But the Scriptures do appeal to the hopes and fears of men (e.g., Heb 11:2, 26; cf. Matt 5:12; 6:1) and to greater and lesser felicity in heaven and punishment in hell (Luke 12:47–48; cf. 1 Cor 9:16–18). The verb *echete* ("you have"; NIV, "you get") may be a literal present; but more likely it is future along the line of 6:19–21: i.e., a man "stores up" and therefore "has" various treasure awaiting him in heaven.

The tax collectors in the Synoptics are not the senior holders of the tax-farming contracts (Lat. *publicani*), usually foreigners, but local subordinate collectors (Lat. *portitores*) working under them (BAGD). The latter were despised, not only because the tax-farming scheme encouraged corruption on a massive scale, but also because strict Jews would perceive them as both traitorous (raising taxes for the enslaving power) and potentially unclean (owing to possible contamination from association with Gentiles—a danger for at least the senior ranks of *portitores*, who necessarily had dealings with their Gentile overlords). They are often associated with harlots and other public sinners (cf. Notes). But even these people love those who love them—at least their mothers and other tax collectors!

Proper salutation was a mark of courtesy and respect; but if Jesus' disciples tender such greeting only to their "brothers"—i.e., other like-minded disciples (see on vv.23–24), they do not rise above the standards of *ethnikoi* (strictly speaking, "Gentiles"; but since most Gentiles were pagans, the word came to have more than racial overtones). "In loving his friends a man may in a certain sense be loving only himself—a kind of expanded selfishness" (Broadus). Jesus will not condone this. "The life of the old (fallen) humanity is based on rough justice, avenging injuries and returning favours. The life of the new (redeemed) humanity is based on divine love, refusing to take revenge but overcoming evil with good" (Stott, p. 123).

Notes

43 Zerwick, Par. 279 argues that the future μισήσεις (*miséseis*) may here be used modally: "You shall love your neighbor but you *may hate* your enemy." This is unlikely because (1) the only parallel, 7:4, renders a question; and (2) the command to love in the same sentence is also in the future form (ἀγαπήσεις [*agapéseis*, "you shall love"—see on v.21]). It is therefore best to see the second verb as imperative, as in NIV.

44 The extra words in KJV are assimilations to Luke 6:27–28. They are not only absent from some early representatives of Alexandrian, Western, and Caesarean texts but also "the divergence of reading among the added clauses likewise speaks against their originality" (Metzger, *Textual Commentary*, p. 14).

46 William O. Walker, Jr. ("Jesus and the Tax Collectors," JBL 97 [1978]: 221–38) has recently argued that passages like this and others unflattering to tax collectors suggest that Jesus did not have so warm a relationship with such men as has generally been supposed and that therefore passages supporting the latter (esp. 9:10–13; 11:19; and parallels) must not be accepted as authentic too readily. But Walker creates a false historical disjunction: either this or that, when all the evidence demands both–and. Jesus denounces all sin but befriends both tax collectors and Pharisees (see on 9:9–13).

c. *Conclusion: the demand for perfection*

5:48

⁴⁸Be perfect, therefore, as your heavenly Father is perfect.

48 Some interpret this verse as the conclusion of the last antithesis (vv.43–47; e.g., Allen, Hendriksen). In that case the perfection advocated is perfection in love. But "perfection" has far broader associations, and it is better to understand v.48 as the conclusion to the antitheses.

The word *teleios* ("perfect") usually reflects *tâmîm* ("perfect") in the OT. It can refer to the soundness of sacrificial animals (Exod 12:5) or to thorough commitment to the Lord and therefore uprightness (Gen 6:9; Deut 18:13; 2 Sam 22:26). The Greek word can be rendered "mature" or "full-grown" (1 Cor 14:20; Eph 4:13; Heb 5:14; 6:1). Many judge its force to be nonmoral in v.48, which becomes an exhortation to total commitment to God (e.g., Bonnard; B. Rigaux, "Révélation des Mystères et Perfection à Qumrân et dans le Nouveau Testament," NTS 4 [1957–58]: 237–62). But this makes for a fairly flat conclusion of the antitheses.

A better understanding of the verse does justice to the word *teleios* but also notes that the form of the verse is exactly like Leviticus 19:2, with "holy" displaced by "perfect," possibly due to the influence of Deuteronomy 18:13 (where NIV renders *teleios* by "blameless"; cf. Gundry, *Use of OT*, pp. 73f.). Nowhere is God directly and absolutely called "perfect" in the OT: he is perfect in knowledge (Job 37:16) or in his way (Ps 18:30), and a man's name may be "Yahweh is perfect" (so *yōtām* [Jotham], Judg 9:5; 2 Kings 15:32). But here for the first time perfection is predicated of God (cf. L. Sabourin, "Why Is God Called 'Perfect' in Mt 5, 48?" *Biblische Zeitschrift* 24 [1980]: 266–68).

In the light of the preceding verses (17–47), Jesus is saying that the true direction in which the law has always pointed is not toward mere judicial restraints, concessions arising out of the hardness of men's hearts, still less casuistical perversions, nor even to the "law of love" (contra C. Dietzfelbinger, "Die Antithesen der Bergpredigt im Verständnis des Matthäus," ZNW 70 [1979]: 1–15; cf. further on 22:34–35). No, it pointed rather to all the perfection of God, exemplified by the authoritative interpretation of the law bound up in the preceding antitheses. This perfection Jesus' disciples must emulate if they are truly followers of him who fulfills the Law and the Prophets (v.17).

The Qumran community understood perfection in terms of perfect obedience, as measured exclusively by the teachings of their community (1QS 1:8–9, 13; 2:1–2; 4:22–23; 8:9–10). Jesus has transposed this to a higher key, not by reducing the obedience, but by making the standard the perfect heavenly Father. Ronald A. Ward (*Royal Theology* [London: MMS, 1964], pp. 117–20) points out that in classical and Hellenistic usage *teleios* can have a static and a dynamic force, "the one appropriate to One Who does not develop, and the other suitable for men who can *grow* in grace" (p. 119, emphasis his): "Be perfect, therefore, as your heavenly Father is perfect."

The Gospel writers refer to God as Father only in contexts pertaining to the Messiah or to believers. He is not the Father of all men but the Father of Jesus and the Father of Jesus' disciples (cf. H.F.D. Sparks, "The Doctrine of the Fatherhood of God in the Gospels," in Nineham, *Studies,* pp. 241–62). Just as in the OT it was the distinctive mark of Israel that they were set apart for God to reflect his character (Lev 19:2; cf. 11:44–45; 20:7, 26), so the messianic community carries on this distinctiveness (cf. 1 Peter 1:16) as the true locus of the people of God (cf. France, *Jesus,* pp. 61–62). This must not encourage us to conclude that Jesus teaches that unqualified perfection is already possible for his disciples. He teaches them to acknowledge spiritual bankruptcy (v.3) and to pray "Forgive us our debts" (6:12). But the perfection of the Father, the true eschatological goal of the law, is what all disciples of Jesus pursue.

Notes

48 The future ἔσεσθε (*esesthe*, lit., "you will be") is imperatival as in Lev 19:2 (cf. on 5:21).
Many commentators compare Luke 6:36 ("Be merciful, just as your Father is merciful") and discuss which form of the saying is closer to the original. For instance, Hill (*Matthew*) notes (1) that "merciful" eminently suits Luke's context; (2) Matthew's τέλειοι (*teleioi,* "perfect") may render the Aramaic שְׁלִים (*šᵉlîm,* "perfect"), which could have been part of a pun with שְׁלָם (*šᵉlam,* "greetings") in the greetings of v.47; and (3) concludes that Matthew's version is probably more original. But a good case could be made for the position that there were two sayings:

1. Not only does Matthew have "perfect" and Luke "merciful," the verb is different in the two cases: ἔσεσθε (*esesthe*, "Be") and γίνεσθε, (*ginesthe*, "Be") respectively. Luke also omits "heavenly." In other words, the two sayings have little in common except the comparison between the believer and the Father.

2. Luke's verse indeed fits its context admirably, but so does Matthew's.

3. Matthew may have omitted any reference to mercy in his sixth beatitude because he has already dealt with the theme in v.7 (absent from Luke; and there the word for "mercy" is different).

4. The Aramaic pun is possible (though another Semitic term more commonly stands behind τέλειος [*teleios*, "perfect"]). Strictly speaking, however, such evidence supports the authenticity of v.48 but does not render Luke 6:36 secondary unless it is already assumed they came from the same source—which is the very point in dispute.

---

4. Religious hypocrisy: its description and overthrow (6:1–18)

a. The principle

6:1

> ¹"Be careful not to do your 'acts of righteousness' before men, to be seen by them. If you do, you will have no reward from your Father in heaven.

1 If the text behind NIV is correct (cf. Notes), Jesus, having told his disciples of the superior righteousness expected of them, now warns them of the danger of religious hypocrisy. "Your righteousness," first occurring in 5:20, recurs here, though the focus has changed from "righteousness" in a purely positive sense to "righteousness" in a formal, external sense. Modern translations try to show the distinction by various means: NIV renders the word "acts of righteousness" (in quotation marks); RSV offers "Beware of practicing your piety before men," and NEB, "Be careful not to make a show of your religion before men." Unfortunately they are overstepping the evidence.

"To do righteousness" is an expression found elsewhere (Ps 106:3; Isa 58:2; 1 John 2:29; 3:7, 10). In 1 John 2:29, for instance, it is rendered by NIV "to do what is right"; and that could suffice in Matthew 6:1 as well. Jesus is not so much dealing with a different kind of righteousness or with mere acts of righteousness as with the motives behind righteous living. To attempt to live in accord with the righteousness spelled out in the preceding verses but out of motives eager for men's applause is to prostitute that righteousness. For this there will be no reward (see on 5:12) from the heavenly Father. There is no contradiction with 5:14–16, where disciples are told to let their light shine before men so that they may see their good deeds; there the motive is for men to praise the heavenly Father. Righteous conduct under kingdom norms must be visible so that God may be glorified. Yet it must never be visible in order to win man's acclaim. Better by far to hide any righteous deed that may lead to ostentation. To trade the goal of pleasing the Father for the trivial and idolatrous goal of pleasing man will never do.

This verse introduces the three chief acts of Jewish piety (cf. vv.2–18)—almsgiving, prayer, fasting (C.G. Montefiore and H. Loewe, *A Rabbinic Anthology* [London: Macmillan, 1938], pp. 412–39; Moore, *Judaism*, 2:162–79). In each act the logical structure is the same: (1) a warning not to do the act to be praised by men, (2) a guarantee that those who ignore this warning will get what they want but no more, (3) instruction on how to perform the act of piety secretly, and (4) the assurance that the Father who sees in secret will reward openly (for details of the logical structure, cf. H.D. Betz, "Eine judenchristliche Kult-Didache in Matthäus 6:1–18," in Strecker, *Jesus Christus*, pp. 445–57).

Notes

1 Two variants are of interest.

Ἐλεημοσύνην (*eleēmosynēn*, "alms") was probably an early marginal gloss on δικαιο σύνην (*dikaiosynēn*, "righteousness"), since in the LXX "righteousness" in Hebrew was often rendered "alms." The gloss was then inserted into the text by a copyist. If "alms" were in fact original, then v.1 should be read with vv.2–4, not as the introduction to vv.2–18; and this would break the carefully wrought structure (discussed above). Moreover the external evidence strongly supports *dikaiosynēn*.

The evidence in favor of the connective δέ (*de*, "but") is evenly divided (brackets, UBS; untranslated, NIV). An adversative *de* fits the context very well and therefore may have been inserted.

On εἰ δὲ μή γε (*ei de mē ge*, "otherwise," or "If you do" [NIV]), cf. Thrall, pp. 9–10.

b. *Three examples* (6:2–18)

1) *Alms*

6:2–4

> 2"So when you give to the needy, do not announce it with trumpets, as the hypocrites do in the synagogues and on the streets, to be honored by men. I tell you the truth, they have received their reward in full. 3But when you give to the needy, do not let your left hand know what your right hand is doing, 4so that your giving may be in secret. Then your Father, who sees what is done in secret, will reward you.

Although 6:1–6 has no parallel in the synoptic Gospels, its authenticity is supported by the numerous word plays in Aramaic reconstructions (cf. Black, *Aramaic Approach*, pp. 176–78).

2 The "you" is singular (see on 5:28). While some in Jesus' day believed almsgiving earned merit (Tobit 12:8–9; Ecclus 3:30; 29:11–12; cf. SBK in loc.), ostentation, not merit theology, is the point here. Jesus assumes his disciples will give alms: "*When* you give to the needy," he says, not "*If* you give to the needy" (cf. 10:42; 25:35–45; 2 Cor 9:6–7; Phil 4:18–19; 1 Tim 6:18–19; James 1:27). Rabbinic writers also warn against ostentation in almsgiving (cf. SBK, 1:391ff.): the frequency of the warnings attests the commonness of the practice.

The reference to trumpet announcements is difficult. Many commentators still say this refers to "the practice of blowing trumpets at the time of collecting alms in the Temple for the relief of some signal need" (Hill, *Matthew*, following Bonnard); but no Jewish sources confirm this, and the idea seems to stem only from early Christian expositors who assumed its correctness. Likewise there is no evidence (contra Calvin) that the almsgivers themselves really blew trumpets on their way to the temple. Alfred Edersheim (*The Temple: Its Ministry and Services* [London: Religious Tract Society, n.d.], p. 26), followed by Jeremias (*Jerusalem*, p. 170, n. 73), suggests this is a reference to horn-shaped collection boxes used at the temple to discourage pilfering. Lachs (*Textual Observations*, pp. 103–5), without mentioning Edersheim, has followed up on that idea by postulating a mistranslation from an underlying Semitic source. But unless the trumpet is a metaphorical caricature (like "tooting your own horn")—a poorly attested suggestion—the solution of A. Büchler ("St. Matthew vi 1–6 and Other Allied Passages," JTS 10 [1909]: 266–70) still seems best: public fasts were proclaimed by the sounding of trumpets. At such times prayers for rain were recited in the streets (cf. v.5), and it was widely thought that alms-giving insured the efficacy of the fasts and prayers (e.g., b *Sanhedrin* 35a; P. *Tannith* 2:6; *Leviticus* R 34:14). But these occasions afforded golden opportunities for ostentation.

Lachs objects that this interpretation makes the givers pompous but not hypocrites. In older Greek a *hypokritēs* ("hypocrite") was an actor, but by the first century the term came to be used for those who play roles and see the world as their stage. What Lachs overlooks is that there are different kinds of hypocrisy. In one the hypocrite feigns goodness but is actually evil and knows he is being deceptive (e.g., 22:15–18). In another the hypocrite is carried away by his own acting and deceives himself. Such pious hypocrites (as in 7:1–5), though unaware of their own deceit, do not fool most onlookers; and this *may* be the meaning here. A third kind of hypocrite deceives himself into thinking he is acting for the best interests of God and man and also deceives onlookers. The needy are unlikely to complain when they receive large gifts, and their gratitude may flatter and thus bolster the giver's self-delusion (cf. D.A. Spieler, "Hypocrisy: An Exploration of a Third Type," *Andrews University Seminary Studies* 13 [1975]: 273–79). Perhaps it is best to identify the hypocrisy in 6:2 with this third type.

The Pharisees' great weakness was that they loved men's praise more than God's praise (cf. John 5:44; 12:43). Those who give out of this attitude receive their reward in full (such is the force of *apechousin;* cf. Deiss LAE, pp. 110–11). They win human plaudits, and that is all they get (cf. Ps 17:14).

3–4 The way to avoid hypocrisy is not to cease giving but to do so with such secrecy that we scarcely know what we have given. Jesus' disciples must themselves be so given to God (cf. 2 Cor 8:5) that their giving is prompted by obeying God and having compassion on men. Then their Father, who sees what is done in secret (Heb 4:13), will reward them. The verb "to reward" (*apodidomai*), with God as subject, here and in vv.6, 18, is different from that used in v.2. Bonnard rightly notes it has a sense of "pay back," and this is compatible with "reward" (see on 5:12). "Openly" (KJV), here and in vv.6, 18, is a late gloss designed to complete the antithetic parallelism with "secretly" or "in secret." Jesus does not discuss the locale and nature of the reward; but we will not be far from the NT evidence if we understand it to be "both in time and in eternity, both in character and in felicity" (Broadus).

2) *Prayer* (6:5–15)

a) *Ostentatious prayer*

6:5–6

> [5]"And when you pray, do not be like the hypocrites, for they love to pray standing in the synagogues and on the street corners to be seen by men. I tell you the truth, they have received their reward in full. [6]But when you pray, go into your room, close the door and pray to your Father, who is unseen. Then your Father, who sees what is done in secret, will reward you.

5 Again Jesus assumes that his disciples will pray, but he forbids the prayers of "hypocrites" (see on v.2). Prayer had a prominent place in Jewish life and led to countless rabbinic decisions (cf. M *Berakoth*). In synagogue worship someone from the congregation might be asked to pray publicly, standing in front of the ark. And at certain times prayers could be offered in the streets (M *Taanith* 2:1–2; see on v.2). But the location was not the critical factor. Neither is the "standing" posture in itself significant. In the Bible people pray prostrate (Num 16:22; Josh 5:14; Dan 8:17; Matt 26:39; Rev 11:16), kneeling (2 Chron 6:13; Dan 6:10; Luke 22:41; Acts 7:60; 9:40; 20:36; 21:5), sitting (2 Sam 7:18), and standing (1 Sam 1:26; Mark 11:25; Luke 18:11, 13). Again it is the motive that is crucial: "to be seen by men." And again there is the same reward (cf. v.2 and v.5).

6 If Jesus were forbidding all public prayer, then clearly the early church did not understand him (e.g., 18:19–20; Acts 1:24; 3:1; 4:24–30). The public versus private antithesis is a good test of one's motives; the person who prays more in public than in private reveals that he is less interested in God's approval than in human praise. Not piety but a reputation for piety is his concern. Far better to deal radically with this hypocrisy (cf. 5:29–30) and pray in a private "room"; the word *tameion* can refer to a storeroom (Luke 12:24), some other inner room (Matt 12:26; 24:26; Luke 12:3, 24), or even a bedroom (Isa 26:20 LXX, with which this verse has several common elements; cf. also 2 Kings 4:33). The Father, who sees in secret, will reward the disciple who prays in secret (see on v.4).

Notes

5 UBS and Nestle follow the plural reading, Nestle-Kilpatrick the singular. The former is marginally more probable on external grounds, and many argue that corruption to the singular occurred because of assimilation to the singular in v.4 and v.6. But copyists might equally have noted the recurring pattern of plural to singular changes in these verses (v.1—vv.2–4; v.16—vv.17–18). See on 5:23.

The use of the future οὐκ ἔσεσθε (*ouk esesthe*, "do not be") with imperatival force usually reflects legal language from the OT (BDF, par. 362). But here and in 20:26 it is found in words ascribed to Jesus with no unambiguous OT precedent (Zerwick, par. 443).

On the idiom φιλοῦσιν ... προσεύχεσθαι (*philousin ... proseuchesthai*, "they love ... to pray"), cf. Turner, *Syntax*, p. 226.

b) Repetitious prayer

6:7–8

> [7]And when you pray, do not keep on babbling like pagans, for they think they will be heard because of their many words. [8]Do not be like them, for your Father knows what you need before you ask him.

7–8 Matthew 6:7–15 digresses from the three chief acts of Jewish piety. Yet the content of these verses is certainly relevant to the second of these, which is prayer. Prayer is central to a believer's life. So Jesus gives further warnings and a positive example.

Many argue that whereas vv.5–6 warn against the prayer practices of Jews, vv.7–8 warn against those of Gentiles (pagans; see on 5:47), partly because the parallel in Luke 11:2 (MS D) has "the rest of men." But the distinction is not quite so cut and dried. Every religious group harbors some who pray repetitiously. So with the Jews of Jesus' day. He labeled all such praying—even that of his own people—as pagan! "Pagans" (cf. 1 Kings 18:26) are not so much the target as the negative example of all who pray repetitiously.

The verb *battalogeō* ("keep on babbling") is very rare, apart from writings dependent on the NT (BAGD, p. 137b). It may derive from the Aramaic *battal* ("idle," "useless") or some other Semitic word; or it may be onomatopoeic: if so, "babble" is a fine English equivalent. Jesus is not condemning prayer any more than he is condemning almsgiving (v.2) or fasting (v.16). Nor is he forbidding all long prayers or all repetition. He himself prayed at length (Luke 6:12), repeated himself in prayer (Matt 26:44; unlike Ecclus 7:14!), and told a parable to show his disciples that "they should always pray and not give up" (Luke 18:1). His point is that his disciples should avoid meaningless, repetitive prayers offered under the misconception that mere length will make prayers efficacious. Such thoughtless babble can occur in liturgical and extemporaneous prayers alike. Essentially it is thoroughly pagan, for pagan gods allegedly thrive on incantation and repetition. But the personal Father God to whom believers pray does not require information about our needs (v.8). "As a father knows the needs of his family, yet teaches them to ask in confidence and trust, so does God treat his children" (Hill, *Matthew*).

c) Model prayer

6:9–13

> [9]"This, then, is how you should pray:
>
> > " 'Our Father in heaven,
> > hallowed be your name,
> > [10]your kingdom come,
> > your will be done
> > on earth as it is in heaven.
> > [11]Give us today our daily bread.
> > [12]Forgive us our debts,
> > as we also have forgiven our debtors.
> > [13]And lead us not into temptation,
> > but deliver us from the evil one.'

"The Lord's Prayer," as it is commonly called, is not so much his own prayer

(John 17 is just that) as the model he gave his disciples. Much of the literature has focused on the complex question of the relation between 6:9–13 and Luke 11:2–4. The newer EVs reveal the many differences. KJV does not show the differences so clearly because it preserves the numerous assimilations to Matthew in late MSS of Luke (cf. Metzger, *Textual Commentary*, pp. 154–56). Various theories attempt to account for the differences.

1. Formerly some argued that Matthew's form is the original and Luke's a simplified version of it. This view is no longer popular, largely because of the difficulty of believing that Luke, who was highly interested in Jesus' prayer life, would omit words and clauses from one of his prayers if they were already in a source.

2. Others have argued strongly that Luke's account is original and that Matthew has added to it according to his own theology and linguistic habit (so Jeremias, *Prayers*, pp. 85ff., and Hill). Several reasons for this theory follow.

a) All Luke's content is found in Matthew 6:9–13. But this could support condensation by Luke as easily as expansion by Matthew. More important, mere expansion-condensation theories do not account for the linguistic differences (e.g., tense in the fourth petition, vocabulary and tense in the fifth); and the theory is further weakened when it is argued (e.g., by Hill, *Matthew*) that in the fourth petition the priorities are reversed and Matthew's form is probably more original than Luke's.

b) Matthew's more rhythmical, liturgical formulation may reflect the desire to construct an ecclesiastical equivalent, for Jewish Christians, of the synagogue's main prayer, the *Eighteen Benedictions* (Davies, *Setting*, pp. 310ff.), to which the Lord's Prayer structurally and formally corresponds. But these correspondences have been greatly exaggerated. They are no closer than those found in fine extemporaneous prayers prayed in evangelical churches every Wednesday night (on the differences, cf. Bornkamm, *Jesus*, pp. 136f.). Moreover, Jesus was far removed from innovation for its own sake. Why should he not have expressed himself in current forms of piety?

c) Hill (*Matthew*) argues that the Matthean introduction (v.9) suggests that the prayer is a standardized liturgical form. On the contrary, the text reads "this is *how* [*houtōs*] you should pray," not "this is *what* you should pray." The emphasis is on paradigm or model, not liturgical form.

d) Hill (*Matthew*) also argues that the emphatic "you" (v.9) "sets off the new Christian community from the synagogue (and Gentile usage) whose piety is being contrasted with Christian worship in the surrounding context." But not only is this needlessly anachronistic, it also ignores the constant stress on "you" designating Jesus' disciples as the exclusive messianic community in Jesus' day (see on 6:2).

3. Ernst Lohmeyer (*The Lord's Prayer* [London: Collins, 1965], p. 293) argues that the two prayers do not spring from one source (Q?) but from two separate traditions. In Matthew the prayer reflects the liturgical tradition of the Galilean Christian community and emphasizes a certain eschatological outlook, whereas in Luke the prayer reflects the liturgical tradition of the Jerusalem church and focuses more on daily life. He refuses to be drawn out on what stands behind these two traditions. Lohmeyer's geographical speculations are not convincing, but his emphasis on two separate traditions of the Lord's Prayer is worth careful consideration. Evidence from the *Didache* and the demonstrable tendency for local churches to think of themselves as Christian synagogues (e.g., in the letters of Ignatius) and to adopt some synagogal liturgical patterns combine to suggest that the Lord's Prayer was used in corporate worship from a very early date. If (and this is a big "if") such

church liturgies stretch back to the time when Matthew and Luke were written, it seems unlikely that the evangelists would disregard the liturgical habits of their own communities, unless for overwhelming historical or theological reasons (e.g., correction of heresy within the accepted liturgy). But none such is evident. This reinforces the theory of two separate liturgical traditions. On the other hand, if fixed liturgical patterns had not yet included any form of the Lord's Prayer by the time the evangelists wrote, the differences between the two are not easily explained by a common source.

4. These complexities have generated several mediating theories. To give but one, Marshall (*Luke*, p. 455) suggests that Luke either drew his form of the prayer from Q or from a recension of Q different from that of Matthew, whereas Matthew drew his either from separate tradition and substituted it for what he found in Q (if his recension of Q was the same as Luke's) or else from a separate recension. This is little more than an elegant way of saying that Lohmeyer's two-traditions theory is basically correct. It may be too elegant: many suspect that Q is not a single document (Introduction, section 3), and to speak thus of recensions of Q when our knowledge of Q is so uncertain makes one wonder how to distinguish methodologically between recensions of Q and entirely separate accounts of two historical occasions within Jesus' ministry. Resolving the unknown by appealing to the more unknown is of dubious merit.

5. Though the evidence for two traditions is strong, equally significant is the fact that there are two entirely different historical settings of the prayer. Unless one is prepared to say that one or the other is made up, the reasonable explanation is that Jesus taught this sort of prayer often during his itinerant ministry and that Matthew records one occasion and Luke another. Matthew's setting is not so historically specific as that of Luke only if one interprets the introduction and the conclusion of the entire discourse loosely or if one postulates Matthew's freedom to add "footnotes" to the material he provides (see prefatory remarks for 5:1–7:29). The former is exegetically doubtful, the latter without convincing literary controls; and even in these instances the evidence for two separate traditions for the Lord's Prayer is so strong that the simplest comprehensive explanation is that Jesus himself taught this form of prayer on more than one occasion.

Few have doubted that the prayer is in some form authentic. Goulder (pp. 296–301) argues that Matthew composed it from fragments, most of which were authentic but uttered on other and separate occasions, and that Luke copied and adapted Matthew's work. His theory is unconvincing because it does no more than show parallels between elements of this prayer and other things Jesus said or prayed. The same evidence could equally be read as supporting the prayer's authenticity. It is well worth noting that there is no anachronism in the prayer—no mention of Jesus as high priestly Mediator, no allusion to themes developed only after the Resurrection.

There are signs of Semitic background, whether Aramaic (e.g., Black, *Aramaic Approach*, pp. 203–8) or Hebrew (Carmignac, pp. 29–52). Scholars debate whether Matthew's version has six petitions (Chrysostom, Calvin, and Reformed theologians) or seven, interpreting v.13 as two (Augustine, Luther, most Lutheran theologians). The issue affects the meaning but little. More important, as Bengel remarks, is the division of the petitions: the first three are cast in terms of God's glory ("your . . . your . . . your"); the others in terms of our good ("us . . . us . . . us").

9 By contrast with ostentatious prayer (vv.5–6) or thoughtless prayer (vv.7–8), Jesus gives his disciples a model. But it is only a model: "This is how [not what] you should pray."

The fatherhood of God is not a central theme in the OT. Where "father" does occur with respect to God, it is commonly by way of analogy, not direct address (Deut 32:6; Ps 103:13; Isa 63:16; Mal 2:10). One can also find occasional references to God as father in the Apocrypha and pseudepigrapha (Tobit 13:4; Ecclus 23:1; 51:10; Wisd Sol 2:16; 14:3; Jub 1:24–25, 28; T Levi 18:6; T Judah 24:2—though some of these may be Christian interpolations). There is but one instance in the DSS (1QS 9:35); the assorted rabbinic references are relatively rare and few unambiguously antedate Jesus (b. *Taanith* 25b; the fifth and sixth petitions of the *Eighteen Benedictions*). Pagans likewise on occasion addressed their gods as father: e.g., *Zeu pater* ("Zeus, Father"; Lat. *Jupiter*). But not till Jesus is it characteristic to address God as "Father" (Jeremias, *Prayers*, pp. 11ff.). This can only be understood against the background of customary patterns for addressing God.

The overwhelming tendency in Jewish circles was to multiply titles ascribing sovereignty, lordship, glory, grace, and the like to God (cf. Carson, *Divine Sovereignty*, pp. 45ff.). Against such a background, Jesus' habit of addressing God as his own Father (Mark 14:36) and teaching his disciples to do the same could only appear familiar and presumptuous to opponents, personal and gracious to followers. Unfortunately, many modern Christians find it very difficult to delight in the privilege of addressing the Sovereign of the universe as "Father" because they have lost the heritage that emphasizes God's transcendence.

Jesus' use of *Abba* ("Father" or "my Father"; Mark 14:36; cf. Matt 11:25; 26:39, 42; Luke 23:34; John 11:41; 12:27; 17:1–26) was adopted by early Christians (Rom 8:15; Gal 4:6); and there is no evidence of anyone before Jesus using this term to address God (cf. DNTT, 1:614–15). Throughout the prayer the reference is plural: "Our Father" (which in Aram. would have been 'abînû, not 'abba). In other words this is an example of a prayer to be prayed in fellowship with other disciples (cf. 18:19), not in isolation (cf. John 20:17). Very striking is Jesus' use of pronouns with "Father." When forgiveness of sins is discussed, Jesus speaks of "your Father" (6: 14–15) and excludes himself. When he speaks of his unique sonship and authority, he speaks of "my Father" (e.g., 11:27) and exludes others. The "our Father" at the beginning of this model prayer is plural but does not include Jesus, since it is part of his instruction regarding what his disciples should pray.

This opening designation establishes the kind of God to whom prayer is offered: He is personal (no mere "ground of being") and caring (a Father, not a tyrant or an ogre, but the one who establishes the real nature of fatherhood; cf. Eph 3:14–15). That he is "our Father" establishes the relationship that exists between Jesus' disciples and God. In this sense he is not the Father of all men indiscriminately (see on 5:45). The early church was right to forbid non-Christians from reciting this prayer as vigorously as they forbade them from joining with believers at the Lord's Table. But that he is "our Father in heaven" (the designation occurs twenty times in Matthew, once in Mark [11:25], never in Luke, and in some instances may be a Matthean formulation) reminds us of his transcendence and sovereignty, while preparing us for v.10b. The entire formula is less concerned with the proper protocol in approaching Deity than with the truth of who he is, to establish within the believer the right frame of mind (Stott, p. 146).

God's "name" is a reflection of who he is (cf. DNTT, 2:648ff.). God's "name" is God himself as he is and has revealed himself, and so his name is already holy. Holiness, often thought of as "separateness," is less an attribute than what he is. It has to do with the very godhood of God. Therefore to pray that God's "name" be "hallowed" (the verbal form of "holy," recurring in Matt only at 23:17, 19 [NIV, "makes sacred"]) is not to pray that God may become holy but that he may be treated as holy (cf. Exod 20:8; Lev 19:2, 32; Ezek 36:23; 1 Peter 1:15), that his name should not be despised (Mal 1:6) by the thoughts and conduct of those who have been created in his image.

10 As God is eternally holy, so he eternally reigns in absolute sovereignty. Yet it is appropriate to pray not only "hallowed be your name" but also "your kingdom come." God's "kingdom" or "reign," as we have seen (see on 3:2; 4:17, 23), can refer to that aspect of God's sovereignty under which there is life. That kingdom is breaking in under Christ's ministry, but it is not consummated till the end of the age (28:20). To pray "your kingdom come" is therefore simultaneously to ask that God's saving, royal rule be extended now as people bow in submission to him and already taste the eschatological blessing of salvation and to cry for the consummation of the kingdom (cf. 1 Cor 16:22; Rev 11:17; 22:20). Godly Jews were waiting for the kingdom (Mark 15:43), "the consolation of Israel" (Luke 2:25). They recited "Qaddish" ("Sanctification"), an ancient Aramaic prayer, at the close of each synagogue service. In its oldest extant form, it runs, "Exalted and *hallowed* be his great name in the world which he created according to his will. *May he let his kingdom rule* in your lifetime and in your days and in the lifetime of the whole house of Israel, speedily and soon. And to this, say: amen" (Jeremias, *Prayers*, p. 98, emphasis his). But the Jew looked forward to the kingdom, whereas the reader of Matthew's Gospel, while looking forward to its consummation, perceives that the kingdom has already broken in and prays for its extension as well as for its unqualified manifestation.

To pray that God's will, which is "good, pleasing and perfect" (Rom 12:2), be done on earth as in heaven is to use language broad enough to embrace three requests.

1. The first request is that God's will be done now on earth as it is now accomplished in heaven. The word *thelēma* ("will") includes both God's righteous demands (7:21; 12:50; cf. Ps 40:8) and his determination to bring about certain events in salvation history (18:14; 26:42; cf. Acts 21:14). So for that will to be "done" includes both moral obedience and the bringing to pass of certain events, such as the Cross. This prayer corresponds to asking for the present extension of the messianic kingdom.

2. The second request is that God's will may ultimately be as *fully accomplished* on earth as it is now accomplished in heaven. "Will" has the same range of meanings as before; and this prayer corresponds to asking for the consummation of the messianic kingdom.

3. The third request is that God's will may ultimately be done on the earth *in the same way* as it is now accomplished in heaven. In the consummated kingdom it will not be necessary to discuss superior righteousness (5:20–48) as antithetical to lust, hate, retaliatory face-slapping, divorce, and the like; for then God's will, construed now as his demands for righteousness, will be done as it is now done in heaven: freely, openly, spontaneously, and without the need to set it over against evil (Carson, *Sermon on the Mount*, pp. 66f.).

These first three petitions, though they focus on God's name, God's kingdom, and

God's will, are nevertheless prayers that he may act in such a way that his people will hallow his name, submit to his reign, and do his will. It is therefore impossible to pray this prayer in sincerity without humbly committing oneself to such a course.

11 The last petitions explicitly request things for ourselves. The first is "bread," a term used to cover all food (cf. Prov 30:8; Mark 3:20; Acts 6:1; 2 Thess 3:12; James 2:15). Many early fathers thought it inappropriate to talk about physical food here and interpreted "bread" as a reference to the Lord's Supper or to the Word of God. This depended in part on Jerome's Latin rendering of *epiousios* ("daily," NIV) as *superstantialem:* Give us today our "supersubstantial" bread—a rendering that may have depended in part on the influence of Marius Victorinus (cf. F.F. Bruce, "The Gospel Text of Marius Victorinus," in Best and Wilson, p. 70). There is no linguistic justification for this translation. The bread is real food, and it may further suggest all that we need in the physical realm (Luther).

That does not mean that *epiousios* ("daily") is easy to translate. The term appears only here and in Luke's prayer (11:3); and the two possible extrabiblical references, which could support "daily," have had grave doubt cast on them by B.M. Metzger ("How Many Times Does ἐπιούσιος Occur Outside the Lord's Prayer?" Exp 69 [1957–58]: 52–54). P. Grelot has recently attempted to support the same translation ("daily") by reconstructing an Aramaic original ("La quatrième demande du 'Pater' et son arrièreplan sémitique," NTS 25 [1978–79]: 299–314). But his article deals inadequately with the Greek text, and other Aramaic reconstructions are possible (e.g., Black, *Aramaic Approach*, pp. 203–7).

The prayer is for our needs, not our greeds. It is for one day at a time ("today"), reflecting the precarious lifestyle of many first-century workers who were paid one day at a time and for whom a few days' illness could spell tragedy. Many have suggested a derivation from *epi tēn ousan* [viz., *hēmeran*] ("for today") or *hē epiousa hēmera* ("for the coming day"), referring in the morning to the same day and at night to the next. This meaning is almost certainly right; but it is better supported by deriving the word from the fem. participle *epiousa*, already well established, with the sense of "immediately following," by the time the NT was written (cf. the forthcoming article by C.J. Hemer in JSNT). Whatever the etymological problems, this makes sense of Luke 11:3, where "each day" is part of the text: "Give us each day our bread for the coming day." Equally it makes sense in Matthew, where "today" displaces "each day": "Give us today our bread for the coming day." This may sound redundant to Western readers, but it is a precious and urgent petition to those who live from hand to mouth.

Some derive *epiousios* ("daily") from the verb *epienai*, referring not to the future, still less to the food of the messianic banquet (contra Jeremias, *Prayers*, pp. 100–102), but to the bread that belongs to it, i.e., that is necessary and sufficient for it (cf. R. Ten Kate, "Geef ons heden ons 'dagelijks' brood," *Nederlands Theologisch Tijdschrift* 32 [1978]: 125–39; with similar conclusions but by a different route, H. Bourgoin, "Ἐπιούσιος expliqué par la notion de préfixe vide," *Biblica* 60 [1979]: 91–96; and for literature, BAGD, pp. 296–97; Gundry, *Use of OT*, pp. 74–75). This has the considerable merit of meshing well with both "today" and "each day" (Matthew and Luke respectively), and in Matthew's case it may be loosely rendered "Give us today the food we need." But the derivation is linguistically artificial (cf. C.J. Hemer).

The idea of God "giving" the food in no way diminishes responsibility to work (see further on vv. 25–34) but presupposes not only that Jesus' disciples live one day at a time (cf. v.34) but that all good things, even our ability to work and earn our food, come from God's hand (cf. Deut 8:18; 1 Cor 4:7; James 1:17). It is a lesson easily forgotten when wealth multiplies and absolute self-sufficiency is portrayed as a virtue.

12 The first three petitions stand independently from one another. The last three, however, are linked in Greek by "ands," almost as if to say that life sustained by food is not enough. We also need forgiveness of sin and deliverance from temptation.

In Matthew what we ask to be forgiven for is *ta opheilēmata hēmōn* ("our debts"); in Luke, it is our "sins." Hill (*Matthew*) notes that the crucial word *to opheilēma* ("debt") "means a literal 'debt' in the LXX and *NT*, except at this point." And on this basis S.T. Lachs ("On Matthew vi.12," NovTest 17 [1975]: 6–8) argues that in Matthew this petition of the Lord's Prayer is not really dealing with sins but with loans in the sixth year, one year before the Jubilee. But the linguistic evidence can be read differently. The word *opheilēma* is rather rare in biblical Greek. It occurs only four times in the LXX (Deut 24:10 [*bis*]; 1 Esd 3:20; 1 Macc 15:8); and in Deuteronomy 24:10, where it occurs twice, it renders two different Hebrew words. In the NT it appears only here and in Romans 4:4. On this basis it would be as accurate to say the word always means "sin" in the NT except at Romans 4:4, as to say it always means "debt" except at Matthew 6:12.

More important, the Aramaic word *ḥôḇā* ("debt") is often used (e.g., in the Targums) to mean "sin" or "transgression." Deiss BS (p. 225) notes an instance of the cognate verb *hamartian opheilō* (lit., "I owe sin"). Probably Matthew has provided a literal rendering of the Aramaic Jesus probably most commonly used in preaching; and even Luke (11:4) uses the cognate participle in the second line, *panti opheilonti hēmin* ("everyone who sins against us"). There is therefore no reason to take "debts" to mean anything other than "sins," here conceived as something owed God (whether sins of commission or of omission).

Some have taken the second clause to mean that our forgiveness is the real cause of God's forgiveness, i.e., that God's forgiveness must be earned by our own. The problem is often judged more serious in Matthew than Luke, because the latter has the present "we forgive," the former the aorist (not perfect, as many commentators assume) *aphēkamen* ("we have forgiven"). Many follow the suggestion of Jeremias (*Prayers,* pp. 92–93), who says that Matthew has awkwardly rendered an Aramaic *perfectum praesens* (a "present perfect"): he renders the clause "as we also herewith forgive our debtors."

The real solution is best expounded by C.F.D. Moule (" '. . . As we forgive . . .': a Note on the Distinction between Deserts and Capacity in the Understanding of Forgiveness," *Donum Gentilicium,* edd. E. Bammel et al. [Oxford: Clarendon, 1978], pp. 68–77), who, in addition to detailing the most important relevant Jewish literature, rightly insists on distinguishing "between, on the one hand, earning or meriting forgiveness, and, on the other hand, adopting an attitude which makes forgiveness possible—the distinction, that is, between deserts and capacity. . . . Real repentance, as contrasted with a merely self-regarding remorse, is certainly a *sine qua non* of receiving forgiveness—an indispensable condition" (pp. 71–72). "Once our eyes have been opened to see the enormity of our offence against God, the injuries which others have done to us appear by comparison extremely trifling.

If, on the other hand, we have an exaggerated view of the offences of others, it proves that we have minimized our own" (Stott, pp. 149–50; see on 5:5, 7; 18: 23–35).

13 The word *peirasmos* ("temptation") and its cognate noun rarely if ever before the NT mean "temptation" in the sense of "enticement to sin" (whether from inward lust or outward circumstances) but rather "testing" (cf. also on 4:1–12). But testing can have various purposes (e.g., refinement, ascertaining the strength of character, enticement to sin) and diverse results (greater purity, self-confidence, growth in faith, sin); and as a result the word can slide over into the entirely negative sense of "temptation." See comments on the cognate verb in 4:1. The word sustains the unambiguous meaning in James 1:13–14, which assures us that "God cannot be tempted by evil, nor does he tempt anyone [i.e., with evil]" (cf. also Matt 4:1, 3; 1 Cor 7:5; 1 Thess 3:5; Rev 2:10). In this light *peirasmos* cannot easily mean "temptation" in Matthew 6:13; for that would be to pray God would not do what in fact he cannot do, akin to praying that God would not sin.

But if *peirasmos* in v.13 means "testing," we face another problem. The NT everywhere insists that believers will face testings or trials of many kinds but that they should be faced with joy (James 1:2; cf. 1 Cor 10:13). If this be so, to pray for grace and endurance in trial is understandable; but to pray not to be brought to testings is strange. For detailed probing of the problem and interaction with the sources, see C.F.D. Moule, "An Unsolved Problem in the Temptation-Clause in the Lord's Prayer," *Reformed Theological Review* 33 (1974): 65–75.

Some have argued that the testing is the eschatological tribulation, the period of messianic woes (e.g., Jeremias, *Prayers*, pp. 104–7) characterized by apostasy. The petition becomes a plea to be secured from that final apostasy and is reflected in NEB's "do not bring us to the test." But not only is *peirasmos* ("temptation") never used for this tribulation unless carefully qualified (and therefore Rev 3:10 is no exception, regardless of its interpretation), but one would at least expect to find the article in the Matthean clause. Carmignac (pp. 396, 445) so reconstructs the alleged Hebrew original that he distinguishes "*to* testing" from "*into* testing," interpreting the latter to mean actually succumbing. The prayer then asks to be spared, not from testing, but from failing. Unfortunately his linguistic arguments are not convincing.

Many cite b *Berakoth* 60b as a parallel: "Bring me not into sin, or into iniquity, or into temptation, or into contempt." It is possible that the causative form of the Lord's Prayer is, similarly, not meant to be unmediated but has a permissive nuance: "Let us not be brought into temptation [i.e., by the devil]." This interpretation is greatly strengthened if the word "temptation" can be taken to mean "trial or temptation that results in fall"; and this appears to be required in two NT passages (Mark 14:38; Gal 6:1; cf. J.V. Dahms, "Lead Us Not Into Temptation," JETS 17 [1974]: 229). It also may be that we are forcing this sixth petition into too rigid a mold. The NT tells us that this age will be characterized by wars and rumors of wars (see on 24:6) but does not find it incongruous to urge us to pray for those in authority so "that we may live peaceful and quiet lives" (1 Tim 2:2). While Jesus told his disciples to rejoice when persecuted (5:10–12) he nevertheless exhorted them to flee from it (10:23) and even to pray that their flight should not be too severe (24:20). Similarly, a prayer requesting to be spared testings may not be incongruous when placed beside exhortations to consider such testings, when they come, as pure joy.

"Deliver us" could mean either, on the one hand, "spare us from," "preserve us against" or, on the other hand, "deliver us out of," "save us from" (BAGD, p. 737, s.v. *rhyomai*). Both are spiritually relevant, and which way the verb is taken largely depends on how the preceding clause is understood. The words *tou ponērou* ("the evil one") could be either neuter ("evil"; cf. Luke 6:45; Rom 12:9; 1 Thess 5:22) or masculine ("the evil one," referring to Satan: 13:19, 38; Eph 6:16; 1 John 2:13–14; 3:12; 5:19). In some cases the Greek does not distinguish the gender (see on 5:37). However, a reference to Satan is far more likely here for two reasons: (1) "deliver us" can take either the preposition *ek* ("from") or *apo* ("from"), the former always introducing things from which to be delivered, the latter being used predominantly of persons (cf. J.-B. Bauer, "Libera nos a malo," *Verbum Domini* 34 [1965]: 12–15; Zerwick, par. 89); and (2) Matthew's first mention of temptation (4:1–11) is unambiguously connected with the Devil. Thus the Lord's model prayer ends with a petition that, while implicitly recognizing our own helplessness before the Devil whom Jesus alone could vanquish (4:1–11), delights to trust the heavenly Father for deliverance from the Devil's strength and wiles.

The doxology—"for yours is the kingdom and the power and the glory forever. Amen"—is found in various forms in many MSS. The diversity of what parts are attested is itself suspicious (for full discussion, cf. Metzger, *Textual Commentary*, pp. 16–17; cf. Hendriksen, pp. 337f.); and the MS evidence is overwhelmingly in favor of omission—a point conceded by Davies (*Setting*, pp. 451–53), whose liturgical arguments for inclusion are not convincing. The doxology itself, of course, is theologically profound and contextually suitable and was no doubt judged especially suitable by those who saw in the last three petitions a veiled allusion to the Trinity: the Father's creation and providence provides our bread, the Son's atonement secures our forgiveness, and the Spirit's indwelling power assures our safety and triumph. But "surely it is more important to know what the Bible really contains and really means, than to cling to something not really in the Bible, merely because it gratifies our taste, or even because it has for us some precious associations" (Broadus).

Notes

---

11 Matthew's aorist δὸς ἡμῖν σήμερον (*dos hēmin sēmeron*, "give us today") and Luke's (11:3) present δίδου ἡμῖν τὸ καθ᾽ ἡμέραν (*didou hēmin to kath᾽ hēmeran*, "give us each day") are both contextually appropriate.
12 KJV has the present "we forgive" in both Matthew and Luke and is widely supported. The aorist is attested by ℵ* B Z 1 22 124ᵐᵍ 1365 1582, five MSS of the Latin Vulgate, and several MSS of the Syriac and Coptic versions. This represents a fair spread of text type. But the convincing arguments are the likelihood of assimilation to Luke and the converse implausibility of a copyist changing the present to an aorist.

---

d) *Forgiveness and prayer*

6:14–15

[14]For if you forgive men when they sin against you, your heavenly Father will also forgive you. [15]But if you do not forgive men their sins, your Father will not forgive your sins.

14–15 These verses reinforce the thought of the fifth petition (see on v.12). The repetition serves to stress the deep importance for the community of disciples to be a forgiving community if its prayers are to be effective (cf. Ps 66:18). The thought is repeated elsewhere (18:23–35; Mark 11:25). (On the possible literary relation with Mark 11:25, see Lane, pp. 410–11.)

3) *Fasting*

6:16–18

16"When you fast, do not look somber as the hypocrites do, for they disfigure their faces to show men they are fasting. I tell you the truth, they have received their reward in full. 17But when you fast, put oil on your head and wash your face, 18so that it will not be obvious to men that you are fasting, but only to your Father, who is unseen; and your Father, who sees what is done in secret, will reward you.

16 Under Mosaic legislation, fasting was commanded only on the Day of Atonement (Lev 16:29–31; 23:27–32; Num 29:7); but during the Exile regular fasts of remembrance were instituted (Zech 7:3–5; 8:19). In addition to these national fasts, both OT and NT describe personal or group fasts with a variety of purposes, especially to indicate and foster self-humiliation before God, often in connection with the confession of sins (e.g., Neh 9:1–2; Ps 35:13; Isa 58:3, 5; Dan 9:2–20; 10:2–3; Jonah 3:5; Acts 9:9) or to lay some special petition before the Lord, sometimes out of anguish, danger, or desperation (Exod 24:18; Judg 20:26; 2 Sam 1:12; 2 Chron 20:3; Ezra 8:21–23; Esth 4:16; Matt 4:1–2; Acts 13:1–3; 14:23). It may belong to the realm of normal Christian self-discipline (1 Cor 9:24–27; cf. Phil 3:19; 1 Peter 4:3); but already in the OT it is bitterly excoriated when it is purely formal and largely hypocritical (Isa 58:3–7; Jer 14:12; Zech 7:5–6)—when, for instance, men fasted but did not share their food with the hungry (Isa 58:1–7).

In Jesus' day the Pharisees fasted twice a week (Luke 18:12; cf. SBK, 2:242ff.), probably Monday and Thursday (M *Taanith* 1:4–7). Some devout people, like Anna, fasted often (Luke 2:37). But such voluntary fasts provided marvelous opportunities for religious showmanship to gain a reputation for piety. One could adopt an air that was "somber" (or "downcast," Luke 24:17, the only other place in the NT where the word *skythrōpos* is used) and disfigure oneself, perhaps by not washing and shaving, by sprinkling ashes on one's head to signify deep contrition or self-abnegation, or by omitting normal use of oil to signify deep distress (cf. 2 Sam 14:2; Dan 10:3). The point is not that there was no genuine contrition but that these hypocrites were purposely drawing attention to themselves. They wanted the plaudits of men and got them. And that's all they got.

17–18 Yet Jesus, far from banning fasting, assumes his disciples will fast, even as he assumes they will give alms and pray (vv.3, 6). His disciples may not fast at the moment, for the messianic bridegroom is with them; and it is the time for joy (9:14–17). But the time will come when they will fast (9:15). (Observe in passing that here Jesus assumes the continued existence of his disciples after his departure.) What he condemns is ostentation in fasting. Moreover he forbids any sign at all that a fast has been undertaken, because the human heart is so mixed in its motives that the desire to seek God will be diluted by the desire for human praise, thus vitiating the fast.

Washing and anointing with oil (v.17) were merely normal steps in hygiene. Oil does not here symbolize extravagant joy but normal body care (cf. Ruth 3:3; 2 Sam 12:20; Pss 23:5; 104:15; 133:2; Eccl 9:8; Luke 7:46; cf. DNTT, 1:120). The point of v.18 is not to draw attention to oneself, whether by somber mien or extravagant joy. Jesus desires reticence, not deception. And the Father, who sees in secret, will provide the reward (see on v.4).

The three principal acts of Jewish piety (vv.1–18) are only examples of many practices susceptible of religious hypocrisy. Early in the second century, the Christian document *Didache*, while polemicizing against the Monday and Thursday "fasts of the hypocrites," enjoins Christians to fast on Wednesday and Friday (8:1). Christian copyists added "fasting" glosses at several points in the NT (Matt 17:21; Mark 9:29; Acts 10:30; 1 Cor 7:5). Hypocrisy is not the sole preserve of Pharisees. The solution is not to abolish fasting (cf. Alexander's remark that mortification of the flesh "can be better attained by habitual temperance than by occasional abstinence") but to set it within a biblical framework (references on v.16) and sincerely to covet God's blessing. For if the form of vv.1–18 is negative, the point is positive—viz., to seek first God's kingdom and righteousness (cf. v.33).

5. *Kingdom perspectives* (6:19–34)

Many argue that these verses are made up of four blocks of material that originally had independent settings: (1) Matthew 6:19–21 = Luke 12:33–34; (2) Matthew 6:22–23 = Luke 11:34–36; (3) Matthew 6:24 = Luke 16:13; (4) Matthew 6:25–34 = Luke 12:22–31. But the first pair are very different and should be treated as separate traditions of separate sayings; the third pair are very close (only a one-word difference) and both Matthew and Luke assign it to the same sermon; the second and fourth pairs are fairly close, but exegesis of Luke suggests his settings are topical. The context Matthew establishes should be accepted at face value. Certainly the flow is coherent: having excoriated religious piety that is little more than ostentation, Jesus warns against the opposite sins of greed, materialism, and worry that stem from misplaced and worldly priorities. Instead, he demands unswerving loyalty to kingdom values (vv.19–24) and uncompromised trust (vv.25–34).

a. *Metaphors for unswerving loyalty to kingdom values* (6:19–24)

1) *Treasure*

6:19–21

[19]"Do not store up for yourselves treasures on earth, where moth and rust destroy, and where thieves break in and steal. [20]But store up for yourselves treasures in heaven, where moth and rust do not destroy, and where thieves do not break in and steal. [21]For where your treasure is, there your heart will be also.

Black (*Aramaic Approach*, pp. 178–79) shows the poetical character of vv.19–21, v.19 warning against the wrong way, v.20 prescribing the right way, and v.21 rounding it off with a memorable aphorism. "Such rhythm and balance suggest that these verses contain original dominical teaching" (Hill, *Matthew*). The assessment is fair; one wonders, however, why similar structure and rhythm should elsewhere be judged liturgical, catechetical, and inauthentic (see on 5:1–12).

19 The present tense prohibition *mē thēsaurizete* could well be rendered "Stop storing up treasures" (Turner, *Syntax*, p. 76) rather than "Do not store up"; the time for a decisive break has come (similarly at v.25).

The love of wealth is a great evil (1 Tim 6:10), calling forth frequent warnings. For heirs of the kingdom to hoard riches in the last days (James 5:2-3) is particularly shortsighted. Yet as with many of Jesus' prohibitions in this sermon, it would be foolhardy so to absolutize this one that wealth itself becomes an evil (cf. Luke 14:12; John 4:21; 1 Peter 3:3-4; for other statements that cannot properly be absolutized). Elsewhere the Scriptures require a man to provide for his relatives (1 Tim 5:8), commend work and provision for the future (Prov 6:6-8), and encourage us to enjoy the good things the Creator has given us (1 Tim 4:3-4; 6:17). Jesus is concerned about selfishness in misplaced values. His disciples must not lay up treasure *for themselves;* they must honestly ask where their heart is (vv.20-21).

This verse does not prohibit "being provident (making sensible provision for the future) but being covetous (like misers who hoard and materialists who always want more)" (Stott, p. 155). But it is folly to put oneself in the former category while acting and thinking in the latter (cf. France, "God and Mammon").

The "treasures on earth" might be clothing that could be attacked by moths. Fashions changed little, and garments could be passed on. They could also deteriorate. "Rust" (*brōsis*) refers not only to the corrosion of metals but to the destruction effected by rats, mildew, and the like. Older commentaries often picture a farm being devoured by mice and other vermin. Less corruptible treasures could be stolen: thieves could break in (*dioryssousin*, "dig through," referring to the mud-brick walls of most first-century Palestinian homes) and steal.

20-21 By contrast, the treasures in heaven are forever exempt from decay and theft (v.20; cf. Luke 12:33). The words "treasures in heaven" go back to Jewish literature (M *Peah* 1:1; T Levi 13:5; Pss Sol 9:9). Here it refers to whatever is of good and eternal significance that comes out of what is done on earth. Doing righteous deeds, suffering for Christ's sake, forgiving one another—all these have the promise of "reward" (see on 5:12; cf. 5:30, 46; 6:6, 15; 2 Cor 4:17). Other deeds of kindness also store up treasure in heaven (Matt 10:42; 25:40), including willingness to share (1 Tim 6:13-19).

In the best MSS the final aphorism (v.21) reverts to second person singular (cf. vv.2, 6, 17; see on 5:23). The point is that the things most highly treasured occupy the "heart," the center of the personality, embracing mind, emotions, and will (cf. DNTT, 2:180-84); and thus the most cherished treasure subtly but infallibly controls the whole person's direction and values. "If honour is rated the highest good, then ambition must take complete charge of a man; if money, then forthwith greed takes over the kingdom; if pleasure, then men will certainly degenerate into sheer self-indulgence" (Calvin). Conversely, those who set their minds on things above (Col 3:1-2), determining to live under kingdom norms, discover at last that their deeds follow them (Rev 14:13).

2) *Light*

6:22-23

> [22]"The eye is the lamp of the body. If your eyes are good, your whole body will be full of light. [23]But if your eyes are bad, your whole body will be full of darkness. If then the light within you is darkness, how great is that darkness!

22–23 "The eye is the lamp of the body" (v.22) in the sense that through the eye the body finds its way. The eye lets in light, and so the whole body is illuminated. But bad eyes let in no light, and the body is in darkness (v.23). The "light within you" seems ironic; those with bad eyes, who walk in darkness, think they have light, but this light is in reality darkness. The darkness is all the more terrible for failure to recognize it for what it is (cf. John 9:41).

This fairly straightforward description has metaphorical implications. The "eye" can be equivalent to the "heart." The heart set on God so as to hold to his commands (Ps 119:10) is equivalent to the eye fastened on God's law (Ps 119:18, 148; cf. 119:36–37). Similarly Jesus moves from "heart" (v.21) to "eye" (vv.22–23). Moreover the text moves between physical description and metaphor by the words chosen for "good" and "bad." *Haplous* ("good," v.22) and its cognates can mean either "single" (vs. *diplous*, "double," 1 Tim 5:17) in the sense of "single, undivided loyalty" (cf. 1 Chron 29:17) or in cognate forms "generous," "liberal" (cf. Rom 12:8; James 1:5). Likewise, *poneros* ("bad," v.23) can mean "evil" (e.g., Rom 12:9) or in the Jewish idiomatic expression "the evil eye" can refer to miserliness and selfishness (cf. Prov 28:22). Jesus is therefore saying either (1) that the man who "divides his interest and tries to focus on both God and possessions . . . has no clear vision, and will live without clear orientation or direction" (Filson)—an interpretation nicely compatible with v.24; or (2) that the man who is stingy and selfish cannot really see where he is going; he is morally and spiritually blind—an interpretation compatible with vv.19–21. Either way, the early crossover to metaphor may account for the difficult language of v.22.

At the physical level the "whole body" is just that, a body, of which the eye is the part that provides "light" (cf. R. Gundry, *Soma* [Cambridge: University Press, 1976], pp. 24–25). At the metaphorical level it represents the entire person who is plunged into moral darkness. The "light within you" is therefore the vision that the eye with divided loyalties provides, or the attitude characterized by selfishness; in both cases it is darkness indeed. This approach, which depends on the OT and Jewish usage, is much to be preferred to the one that goes to Hellenistic literature and interprets "the light within you" in a neoplatonic sense (e.g., H.D. Betz, "Matthew vi.22f and ancient Greek theories of vision," in Best and Wilson, pp. 43–56).

3) Slavery

6:24

> 24"No one can serve two masters. Either he will hate the one and love the other, or he will be devoted to the one and despise the other. You cannot serve both God and Money.

24 "Jesus now explains that behind the choice between two treasures (where we lay them up) and two visions (where we fix our eyes) there lies the still more basic choice between two masters (whom we are going to serve)" (Stott, p. 158). "Money" renders Greek *mamona* ("mammon"), itself a transliteration of Aramaic *mamona'* (in the emphatic state; "wealth," "property"). The root in both Aramaic and Hebrew (*'mn*) indicates that in which one has confidence; and the connection with money and wealth, well attested in Jewish literature (e.g., *Peah* 1:1; b *Berakoth* 61b; M *Aboth* 2:7; and not always in a negative sense), is painfully obvious. Here it is personified. Both God and Money are portrayed, not as employers, but as slave-owners. A man may work for two employers; but since "single ownership and full-time service are of the essence of slavery" (Tasker), he cannot serve two slave-owners. Either God is served with a single-eyed devotion, or he is not served at all. Attempts at divided loyalty betray, not partial commitment to discipleship, but deep-seated commitment to idolatry.

b. Uncompromised trust (6:25–34)

1) The principle

6:25

> 25"Therefore I tell you, do not worry about your life, what you will eat or drink; or about your body, what you will wear. Is not life more important than food, and the body more important than clothes?

25 "Therefore," in the light of the alternatives set out (vv.19–24) and assuming his disciples will make the right choices, Jesus goes on to prohibit worry. KJV's "Take no thought" is deceptive in modern English, for Jesus himself demands that we think even about birds and flowers (vv.26–30). "Do not worry" can be falsely absolutized by neglecting the limitations the context imposes and the curses on careless-ness, apathy, indifference, laziness, and self-indulgence expressed elsewhere (cf. Carson, *Sermon on the Mount*, pp. 82–86; Stott, pp. 165–68). The point here is not to worry about the physical necessities, let alone the luxuries implied in the preced-ing verses, because such fretting suggests that our entire existence focuses on and is limited to such things. The argument is *a fortiori* ("how much more") but not (contra Hill, *Matthew*) *a minori ad maius* ("from the lesser to the greater") but the reverse: if God has given us life and a body, both admittedly more important than food and clothing, will he not also give us the latter? Therefore fretting about such things betrays the loss of faith and the perversion of more valuable commitments (cf. Luke 10:41–42; Heb 13:5–6).

Notes

25 Because the subjunctives τί φάγητε ἤ τί πίητε (*ti phagēte ē ti piēte*, "what you will eat or drink") are in indirect discourse, they should be taken as deliberative subjunctives retained with the shift in discourse (cf. the subjunctives in v.31).

2) The examples (6:26–30)

a) Life and food

6:26–27

> 26Look at the birds of the air; they do not sow or reap or store away in barns, and yet your heavenly Father feeds them. Are you not much more valuable than they?
> 27Who of you by worrying can add a single hour to his life?

26 To worry about food and drink is to have learned nothing from the natural creation. If the created order testifies to God's "eternal power and divine nature" (Rom 1:20), it testifies equally to his providence. The point is not that disciples need not work—birds do not simply wait for God to drop food into their beaks—but that they need not fret. Disciples may further strengthen their faith when they remember that God is in a special sense their Father (not the birds' Father), and that they are worth far more than birds ("you" is emphatic). Here the argument is from the lesser to the greater.

This argument presupposes a biblical cosmology without which faith makes no sense. God is so sovereign over the universe that even the feeding of a wren falls within his concern. Because he normally does things in regular ways, there are "scientific laws" to be discovered; but the believer with eyes to see simultaneously discovers something about God and his activity (cf. Carson, *Sermon on the Mount*, pp. 87–90).

27 The word *hēlikia* ("life") can also be rendered "stature" (cf. Luke 19:3; and *pēchys* ("hour") means either "cubit" (about eighteen inches) or "age" (Heb 11:11). No combination fits easily; no one would be tempted to think worrying could add eighteen inches to his stature (KJV), and a linear measure (eighteen inches) does not fit easily with "life." This disparity accounts for the diversity of translations. Most likely the linear measure is being used in a metaphorical sense (cf. "add one cubit to his span of life" [RSV]), akin to "passing a milepost" at one's birthday. Worry is more likely to shorten life than prolong it, and ultimately such matters are in God's hands (cf. Luke 12:13–21). To trust him is enough.

Notes

26 Τὰ πατεινὰ τοῦ οὐρανοῦ (*ta pateina tou ouranou*, lit., "the birds of the heaven") is rightly rendered "birds of the air" (NIV) because "heaven" can refer to the atmosphere around us (cf. Gen 1:26; Matt 8:20; 13:32).

b) *Body and clothes*

6:28–30

> [28]"And why do you worry about clothes? See how the lilies of the field grow. They do not labor or spin. [29]Yet I tell you that not even Solomon in all his splendor was dressed like one of these. [30]If that is how God clothes the grass of the field, which is here today and tomorrow is thrown into the fire, will he not much more clothe you, O you of little faith?

28–30 "Lilies of the field" (v.28) may be any of the wild flowers so abundant in Galilee, and these "flowers of the field" correspond to "birds of the air." The point is a little different from the first illustration, where birds work but do not worry. The flowers neither toil nor spin (cf. Notes). The point is not that Jesus' disciples may opt for laziness but that God's providence and care are so rich that he clothes the grass with wild flowers that are neither productive nor enduring (v.30). Even Solomon, the richest and most extravagant of Israel's monarchs, "in all his splendor" (v.29) was not arrayed like one of these fields. Small wonder that Jesus gently chastises his disciples as *oligopistoi* ("people of little faith"; cf. 8:26; 14:31; 16:8; and the abstract noun at 17:20). The root of anxiety is unbelief.

Notes

28 On the nest of variants, cf. Metzger (*Textual Commentary*, p. 18) and the literature he cites, to which may be added K. Brunner, "Textkritisches zu Mt 6.28: *ou xainousin* statt *auxainousin* vorgeschlagen," *Zeitschrift für Katholische Theologie* 100 (1978): 251–56.

30 The κλίβανος (*klibanos*, "oven") was a pottery oven often fired by burning grass inside, the ashes falling through a hole, and the flat cakes distributed both inside and on top. The term was used metaphorically to refer to the Day of Judgment as early as Hos 7:4 LXX.

3) *Distinctive living*

6:31–32

> ³¹So do not worry, saying, 'What shall we eat?' or 'What shall we drink?' or 'What shall we wear?' ³²For the pagans run after all these things, and your heavenly Father knows that you need them.

31–32 In the light of God's bountiful care ("So"), the questions posed in v.31 (cf. v.25) are unanswerable; and the underlying attitudes are thoughtless and an affront to God who knows the needs of his people (cf. v.8). Worse, they are essentially pagan (v.32); for pagans "run after" (*epizētousin*, a strengthened form of "seek") these things, not God's kingdom and righteousness (v.33). Jesus' disciples must live lives qualitatively different from those of people who have no trust in God's fatherly care and no fundamental goals beyond material things.

4) *The heart of the matter*

6:33

> ³³But seek first his kingdom and his righteousness, and all these things will be given to you as well.

33 In view of vv.31–32, this verse makes it clear that Jesus' disciples are not simply to *refrain* from the *pursuit* of temporal things as their primary goal in order to differentiate themselves from pagans. Instead, they are to *replace* such pursuits with goals of far greater significance. To seek first the kingdom ("of God" in some MSS) is to desire above all to enter into, submit to, and participate in spreading the news of the saving reign of God, the messianic kingdom already inaugurated by Jesus, and to live so as to store up treasures in heaven in the prospect of the kingdom's consummation. It is to pursue the things already prayed for in the first three petitions of the Lord's Prayer (6:9–10).

To seek God's righteousness is not, in this context, to seek justification (contra Filson, McNeile). "Righteousness" must be interpreted as in 5:6, 10, 20; 6:1. It is to pursue righteousness of life in full submission to the will of God, as prescribed by Jesus throughout this discourse (cf. Przybylski, pp. 89–91). Such righteousness will lead to persecution by some (5:10), but others will themselves become disciples and praise the Father in heaven (5:16). Such goals alone are worthy of one's wholehearted allegiance. For any other concern to dominate one's mind is to stoop to pagan fretting. "In the end, just as there are only two kinds of piety, the self-centered and the God-centered, so there are only two kinds of ambition: one can be ambitious either for oneself or for God. There is no third alternative" (Stott, p. 172). Within such a framework of commitment, Jesus' disciples are assured that all the necessary things will be given them by their heavenly Father (see on 5:45; 6:9), who demonstrates his faithfulness by his care even for the birds and his concern even for the grass.

5) Abolishing worry

6:34

> [34]Therefore do not worry about tomorrow, for tomorrow will worry about itself. Each day has enough trouble of its own.

34 In view of God's solemn promise to meet the needs of those committed to his kingdom and righteousness (v.33), "therefore" do not worry about tomorrow. Today has enough *kakia* ("trouble," NIV; what is evil from man's point of view; once applied to crop damage caused by hail [MM]; and frequently translates Heb. *rā'āh* ["evil," "misfortune," "trouble"] in LXX: Eccl 7:14; 12:1; Amos 3:6) of its own. Worry over tomorrow's misfortunes is nonsensical, because today has enough to occupy our attention and because tomorrow's feared misfortunes may never happen (cf. b *Sanhedrin* 100b; b *Berakoth* 9a). It is almost as if Jesus, aware that his disciples are still unsettled and immature, ends his argument by setting the highest ideals and motives aside for a moment and, in a whimsical sally, appeals to common sense. At the same time, he is implicitly teaching that even for his disciples today's grace is sufficient only for today and should not be wasted on tomorrow. If tomorrow does bring new trouble, there will be new grace to meet it.

6. Balance and perfection (7:1–12)

Many argue that these verses have (1) no connection with what precedes, (2) little internal cohesion, and (3) probably find their original context in Luke 6:37–38, 41–42. Only the third assertion is believable.

1. The lack of Greek connectives at vv.1, 7 is not inherently problematic; similar omissions (e.g., 6:19, 24) do not disturb the flow of thought so much as indicate a new "paragraph" or set off an aphorism. The connection with what precedes is internal. The demand for the superior righteousness of the kingdom, in fulfillment of the OT (5:17–20), has called forth warnings against hypocrisy (6:1–18) and the formulation of kingdom perspectives (6:19–34). But there are other dangers. Demands for perfection can breed judgmentalism (vv.1–5), while demands for love can cause chronic shortage of discernment (v.6).

2. Thus the internal connection is in part established by dealing with opposing evils. But such great demands on Jesus' followers must force them to recognize their personal inadequacy and so drive them to prayer (vv. 7–11). The Golden Rule (v. 12) summarizes the body of the sermon (5:17–7:12).

3. The relationship between 7:1–12 and Luke 6:37–38, 41–42 (part of Luke's "sermon") is difficult to assess. After his beatitudes and woes (Luke 6:20–26), Luke adds material (6:27–30) akin to Matthew 5:38–48. He then adds the Golden Rule (Luke 6:31), some material akin to Matthew 5, and then the parallel to Matthew 7:1–5. Thus he omits all of Matthew 6, while Matthew 7:1–5 omits part of what Luke keeps in 6:37–42. One or both of the evangelists have rearranged the order of the material. Both make such good sense in their own context that it seems impossible to decide in favor of either. Though a saying as aphoristic as the Golden Rule may well have been repeated during the course of several days' teaching, there is no sure way of demonstrating this was or was not the case.

a. *The danger of being judgmental* (7:1–5)

1) *The principle*

7:1

> [1]"Do not judge, or you too will be judged.

1 The verb *krinō* ("judge") has a wide semantic range: "judge" (judicially), "condemn," "discern." It cannot here refer to the law courts, any more than 5:33–37 forbids judicial oaths. Still less does this verse forbid all judging of any kind, for the moral distinctions drawn in the Sermon on the Mount require that decisive judgments be made. Jesus himself goes on to speak of some people as dogs and pigs (v. 6) and to warn against false prophets (vv. 15–20). Elsewhere he demands that people "make a right judgment" (John 7:24; cf. 1 Cor 5:5; Gal 1:8–9; Phil 3:2; 1 John 4:1). All this presupposes that some kinds of "judging" are not only legitimate but mandated.

Jesus' demand here is for his disciples not to be judgmental and censorious. The verb *krinō* has the same force in Romans 14:10–13 (cf. James 4:11–12). The rigor of the disciples' commitment to God's kingdom and the righteousness demanded of them do not authorize them to adopt a judgmental attitude. Those who "judge" like this will in turn be "judged," not by men (which would be of little consequence), but by God (which fits the solemn tone of the discourse). The disciple who takes it on himself to be the judge of what another does usurps the place of God (Rom 14:10) and therefore becomes answerable to him. The *hina mē* ("in order that . . . not"; NIV, "or") should therefore be given full telic force: "Do not assume the place of God by deciding you have the right to stand in judgment over all—do not do it, I say, in order to avoid being called to account by the God whose place you usurp" (cf. b *Shabbath* 127b; M *Sotah* 1:7; b *Baba Metzia* 59b).

2) *The theological justification*

7:2

> [2]For in the same way you judge others, you will be judged, and with the measure you use, it will be measured to you.

2 The strong play on words in Greek suggests that this is a proverbial saying. Formally it is very close to M *Sotah* 1:7; but the use made of it is in each case rather distinctive (cf. Dalman, pp. 223f.). Indeed, precisely because it is a proverb, Jesus himself elsewhere turns it to another use (cf. Mark 4:24). The point is akin to that already established (5:7; 6:12, 14–15): the judgmental person by not being forgiving and loving testifies to his own arrogance and impenitence, by which he shuts himself out from God's forgiveness (cf. Manson, *Sayings*, p. 56).

According to some rabbis, God has two "measures"—mercy and justice (Lev R 29.3). Possibly Jesus used this language, adapting it to his own ends. He who poses as a judge cannot plead ignorance of the law (Rom 2:1; cf. James 3:1); he who insists on unalloyed justice for others is scarcely open to mercy himself (James 2:13; 4:12). The problem returns in 18:23–35; here "the command to *judge not* is not a requirement to be blind, but rather a plea to be generous. Jesus does not tell us to cease to be men (by suspending our critical powers which help to distinguish us from animals) but to renounce the presumptuous ambition to be God (by setting ourselves up as judges)" (Stott, p. 177, emphasis his).

3) *An example*

7:3–5

> ³"Why do you look at the speck of sawdust in your brother's eye and pay no attention to the plank in your own eye? ⁴How can you say to your brother, 'Let me take the speck out of your eye,' when all the time there is a plank in your own eye? ⁵You hypocrite, first take the plank out of your own eye, and then you will see clearly to remove the speck from your brother's eye.

3–5 The *karphos* ("speck of sawdust") could be any bit of foreign matter (v.3). The *dokos* ("plank" or "log") is obviously colorful hyperbole. Jesus does not say it is wrong to help your brother (for "brother," see on 5:22; Jesus is apparently referring to the community of his disciples) remove the speck of dust in his eye, but it is wrong for a person with a "plank" in his eye to offer help. That is sheer hypocrisy of the second sort (see on 6:2). Second Samuel 12:1–12 is a dramatic OT example (cf. also Luke 18:9). It will not do to say that Jesus' words in this pericope are "meant to exclude all condemnation of others" (Hill, *Matthew*), for to do that requires not taking v.5 seriously and excluding what v.6 says. In the brotherhood of Jesus' disciples, censorious critics are unhelpful. But when a brother in a meek and self-judging spirit (cf. 1 Cor 11:31; Gal 6:1) removes the log in his own eye, he still has the responsibility of helping his brother remove his speck (cf. 18:15–20).

Notes

4 The future πῶς ἐρεῖς (*pōs ereis*, lit., "how will you say") is an instance in which, under Semitic influence, this tense is sometimes used modally to describe what may be (Zerwick, par. 279). See Luke 6:42: πῶς δύνασαι λέγειν (*pōs dynasai legein*, "how can you say").

b. *The danger of being undiscerning*

7:6

> 6"Do not give dogs what is sacred; do not throw your pearls to pigs. If you do,
> they may trample them under their feet, and then turn and tear you to pieces.

6 Though used later to exclude unbaptized persons from the Eucharist (*Didache* 9.5), that is not the purpose of this saying. Nor is it connected with the previous verses by dealing now with persons who, though properly confronted about their "specks," refuse to deal with them, as in 18:12–20 (so Schlatter). Rather, it warns against the converse danger. Disciples exhorted to love their enemies (5:43–47) and not to judge (v.1) might fail to consider the subtleties of the argument and become undiscerning simpletons. This verse guards against such a possibility.

The "pigs" are not only unclean animals but wild and vicious, capable of savage action against a person. "Dogs" must not be thought of as household pets: in the Scriptures they are normally wild, associated with what is unclean, despised (e.g., 1 Sam 17:43; 24:14; 1 Kings 14:11; 21:19; 2 Kings 8:13; Job 30:1; Prov 26:11; Eccl 9:4; Isa 66:3; Matt 15:27; Phil 3:2; Rev 22:15). The two animals serve together as a picture of what is vicious, unclean, and abominable (cf. 2 Peter 2:22). The four lines of v.6 are an ABBA chiasmus (Turner, *Syntax*, pp. 346–47). The pigs trample the pearls under foot (perhaps out of animal disappointment that they are not morsels of food), and the dogs are so disgusted with "what is sacred" that they turn on the giver.

The problem lies in *to hagion* ("what is sacred"). How is this parallel to "pearls," and what reality is envisaged to make the story "work"?

1. Some suggest *to hagion* refers to "holy food" offered in connection with the temple services (cf. Exod 22:31; Lev 22:14; Jer 11:15; Hag 2:12). But this is a strange way to refer to it, and it is not obvious why the dogs would spurn it.

2. Another suggestion is that *to hagion* is a mistranslation of the Aramaic *qᵉdaša* (Heb. *nezem*, "ring"), referring to Proverbs 11:22 (cf. Black, *Aramaic Approach*, pp. 200ff.). But appeals to mistranslation should not be the first line of approach; and here the parallelism of pearls and pigs, pearls obviously being mistaken for food, is destroyed.

3. P.G. Maxwell-Stuart ("'Do not give what is holy to the dogs.' [Mt 7⁶]," ExpT 90 [1978–79]: 341) offers a textual emendation.

4. However, it seems wiser to recognize that, as in 6:22–23, the interpretation of the metaphor is already hinted at in the metaphor itself. "What is sacred" in Matthew is the gospel of the kingdom; so the aphorism forbids proclaiming the gospel to certain persons designated as dogs and pigs. Instead of trampling the gospel under foot, everything must be "sold" in pursuit of it (13:45–46).

Verse 6 is not a directive against evangelizing the Gentiles, especially in a book full of various supports for this, not least 28:18–20 (10:5, properly understood, is no exception). "Dogs" and "pigs" cannot refer to all Gentiles but, as Calvin rightly perceived, only to persons of any race who have given clear evidences of rejecting the gospel with vicious scorn and hardened contempt. The disciples are later given a similar lesson (10:14; 15:14), and the postresurrection Christians learned it well (cf. Acts 13:44–51; 18:5–6; 28:17–28; Titus 3:10–11). So when taken together vv.1–5 and v.6 become something of a Gospel analogue to the proverb "Do not rebuke a mocker or he will hate you; rebuke a wise man and he will love you" (Prov 9:8).

c. *Source and means of power*

7:7–11

> 7"Ask and it will be given to you; seek and you will find; knock and the door will be opened to you. 8For everyone who asks receives; he who seeks finds; and to him who knocks, the door will be opened.
>
> 9"Which of you, if his son asks for bread, will give him a stone? 10Or if he asks for a fish, will give him a snake? 11If you, then, though you are evil, know how to give good gifts to your children, how much more will your Father in heaven give good gifts to those who ask him!

7–8 Zahn tries to establish a connection between these verses and the preceding ones by saying that Jesus now teaches that it is best to ask God to remove the speck in the other person's eye. Stott understands vv.1–11 in terms of relationships: to believers (vv.1–5), to "pigs" and "dogs" (v.6), and to God (vv.7–11). Bonnard best exemplifies those who say there is no connection at all between vv.7–11 and the preceding verses. Yet there are in fact deep thematic connections. Schlatter perceives one of them when he remarks that Jesus, having told his disciples the difficulties, now exhorts them to prayer. Moreover one of the most pervasive features of Jesus' teaching on prayer is the assurance it will be heard (cf. H.F. von Campenhausen, "Gebetserhörung in den überlieferten Jesusworten und in den Reflexion des Johannes," *Kerygma und Dogma* 23 [1977]: 157–71). But such praying is not for selfish ends but always for the glory of God according to kingdom concerns. So here: the Sermon on the Mount lays down the righteousness, sincerity, humility, purity, and love expected of Jesus' followers; and now it assures them such gifts are theirs if sought through prayer.

The sermon has begun with acknowledgment of personal bankruptcy (5:3) and has already provided a model prayer (6:9–13). Now (v.7) in three imperatives (ask, seek, knock) symmetrically repeated (v.8) and in the present tense to stress the persistence and sincerity required (cf. Jer 29:13), Jesus assures his followers that, far from demanding the impossible, he is providing the means for the otherwise impossible. "One may be a truly industrious man, and yet poor in temporal things; but one cannot be a truly praying man, and yet poor in spiritual things" (Broadus). Far too often Christians do not have the marks of richly textured discipleship because they do not ask, or they ask with selfish motives (James 4:2–3). But the best gifts, those advocated by the Sermon on the Mount, are available to "everyone" (v.8) who persistently asks, seeks, and knocks.

Jesus' disciples will pray ("ask") with earnest sincerity ("seek") and active, diligent pursuit of God's way ("knock"). Like a human father, the heavenly Father uses these means to teach his children courtesy, persistence, and diligence. If the child prevails with a thoughtful father, it is because the father has molded the child to his way. If Jacob prevails with God, it is Jacob who is wounded (Gen 32:22–32).

9–11 Another *a fortiori* argument (see on 6:25) is introduced. In Greek both v.9 and v.10 begin with *ē* ("or"), probably meaning "or to put the matter another way, which of you, etc." No parent would deceive a child asking for bread or fish by giving him a similar looking but inedible stone or a dangerous snake. The point at issue is not merely the parents' willingness to give but their willingness to give good gifts—even though they themselves are evil. Jesus presupposes the sinfulness (v.11) of human nature (himself exempted; "you," he says, not "we") but implicitly acknowledges that does not mean all human beings are as bad as they could be or utterly evil in all they do. People are evil; they are self-centered, not God-centered. This taints all they do. Nevertheless they can give good gifts to their children. How much more, then, will the heavenly Father, who is pure goodness without alloy, give good gifts to those who ask?

Four observations will tie up some loose ends.

1. Lachs ("Textual Observations," pp. 109f.) insists that the "concept that man is evil from birth, born in sin, and similar pronouncements, is a later theological development" and therefore proposes to emend the text of an alleged Semitic original. While it is true that rabbinic literature does not normally portray man as inherently evil, it is false to say that the idea arose only after Jesus, presumably with Paul (cf. Pss 14:1–3; 51; 53:1–3; Eccl 7:20). Jesus regularly assumes the sinfulness of humanity (cf. TDNT, 6:554–55). Therefore the rabbinic parallels to vv.7–11 are of limited value: they stress the analogy of the caring parent, but not on the supposition that the human parent is evil.

2. The fatherhood-of-God language is reserved for God's relationship with Jesus' disciples (see on 5:45). The blessings promised as a result of these prayers are not the blessings of common grace (cf. 5:45) but of the kingdom. And though we must ask for them, it is not because God must be informed (6:8) but because this is the Father's way of training his family.

3. What is fundamentally at stake is man's picture of God. God must not be thought of as a reluctant stranger who can be cajoled or bullied into bestowing his gifts (6:7–8), as a malicious tyrant who takes vicious glee in the tricks he plays (vv.9–10), or even as an indulgent grandfather who provides everything requested of him. He is the heavenly Father, the God of the kingdom, who graciously and willingly bestows the good gifts of the kingdom in answer to prayer.

4. On the "good gifts" as spiritual gifts (cf. Rom 3:8; 10:15; Heb 9:11; 10:1) and the parallel reference to the Holy Spirit (Luke 11:13), see Marshall, *Luke*, pp. 469f.

d. *Balance and perfection*

7:12

> [12]So in everything, do to others what you would have them do to you, for this sums up the Law and the Prophets.

12 The Golden Rule was not invented by Jesus; it is found in many forms in highly diverse settings. About A.D. 20, Rabbi Hillel, challenged by a Gentile to summarize the law in the short time the Gentile could stand on one leg, reportedly responded, "What is hateful to you, do not do to anyone else. This is the whole law; all the rest is commentary. Go and learn it" (b *Shabbath* 31a). Apparently only Jesus phrased the rule positively. Thus stated it is certainly more telling than its negative counterpart, for it speaks against sins of omission as well as sins of commission. The goats in 25:31–46 would be acquitted under the negative form of the rule, but not under the form attributed to Jesus.

The *oun* ("therefore") might refer to vv.7–11 (i.e., because God gives good gifts, therefore Jesus' disciples should live by this rule as a function of gratitude) or to vv.1–6 (i.e., instead of judging others, we should treat them as we ourselves would want to be treated). But more probably it refers to the entire body of the sermon (5:17–7:12), for here there is a second reference to "the Law and the Prophets"; and this appears to form an envelope with 5:17–20. "Therefore," in the light of all I have taught about the true direction in which the OT law points, obey the Golden Rule; for this is (*estin;* NIV, "sums up") the Law and the Prophets (cf. Rom 13:9). This way of putting it provides a powerful yet flexible maxim that helps us decide moral issues in a thousand cases without the need for multiplied case law. The rule is not arbitrary, without rational support, as in radical humanism; in Jesus' mind its rationale ("for") lies in its connection with revealed truth recorded in "the Law and the Prophets." The rule embraces quantity ("in everything") and quality (*houtōs kai,* "[do] even so"). And in the context of fulfilling the Scriptures, the rule provides a handy summary of the righteousness to be displayed in the kingdom.

Above all this verse is not to be understood as a utilitarian maxim like "Honesty pays." We are to do to others what we would have them do to us, not just because we expect the same in return, but because such conduct is the goal of the Law and the Prophets. The verb *estin* (NIV, "sums up") might properly be translated "fulfill," as in Acts 2:16. In the deepest sense, therefore, the rule *is* the Law and the Prophets in the same way the kingdom is the fulfillment of all that the Law and the Prophets foretold.

7. Conclusion: call to decision and commitment (7:13–27)

a. Two ways

7:13–14

> 13"Enter through the narrow gate. For wide is the gate and broad is the road that leads to destruction, and many enter through it. 14But small is the gate and narrow the road that leads to life, and only a few find it.

The Sermon on the Mount ends with four warnings, each offering paired contrasts: two ways (vv.13–14), two trees (vv.15–20), two claims (vv.21–23), and two builders (vv.24–27). They focus on eschatological judgment and so make it plain that the theme is still the kingdom of heaven. But if some will not enter it (vv.13–14, 21–23), the sole basis for such a tragedy is present response to Jesus' words. At the close of the sermon, the messianic claim is implicit and only thinly veiled.

13–14 "Two ways" language is common in Jewish literature, both canonical and extracanonical (e.g., Deut 30:19; Ps 1; Jer 21:8; Ecclus 21:11–14; 2 Esd 7:6–14; T Asher 1:3, 5; 1QS 3:20ff.). The general picture is clear enough: there are two gates, two roads, two crowds, two destinations. The "narrow" gate (KJV's "strait" is from Lat. *strictum,* "narrow"; nothing is said about gate or road being "straight," despite the modern phrase "straight and narrow") is clearly restrictive and does not permit entrance to what Jesus prohibits. The "wide" gate seems far more inviting. The "broad" road (not "easy," RSV) is spacious and accommodates the crowd and their baggage; the other road is "narrow"—but two different words are used: *stenē* ("narrow," v.13) and *tethlimmenē* (v.14), the latter being cognate with *thlipsis* ("tribulation"), which almost always refers to persecution. So this text says that the way of discipleship is "narrow," restricting, because it is the way of persecution and opposition—a major theme in Matthew (see on 5:10–12, 44; 10:16–39; 11:11–12; 24:4–13; cf. esp. A.J. Mattill, Jr., " 'The Way of Tribulation,' " JBL 98 [1979]: 531–46). Compare Acts 14:22: "We must go through many hardships [*dia pollōn thlipseōn*, 'through much persecution'] to enter the kingdom of God."

But the two roads are not ends in themselves. The narrow road leads to life, i.e., to the consummated kingdom (cf. vv.21–23; John's Gospel); but the broad road leads to *apōleia* ("destruction")—"definitive destruction, not merely in the sense of the extinction of physical existence, but rather of an eternal plunge into Hades and a hopeless destiny of death" (A. Opeke, TDNT, 1:396); cf. 25:34, 46; John 17:12; Rom 9:22; Phil 1:28; 3:19; 1 Tim 6:9; Heb 10:39; 2 Peter 2:1, 3; 3:16; Rev 17:8, 11). (On the relative numbers ["many . . . few"], see 22:14; Luke 13:22–30; Rev 7:9.) Democratic decisions do not determine truth and righteousness in the kingdom. That there are only two ways is the inevitable result of the fact that the one that leads to life is exclusively by revelation. But if truth in such matters must not be sought by appealing to majority opinion (Exod 23:2), neither can it be found by each person doing what is right in his own eyes (Prov 14:12; cf. Judg 21:25). God must be true and every man a liar (Rom 3:4).

There remains an important metaphorical difficulty. Granted the correctness of the text (cf. Metzger, *Textual Commentary*, p. 19), are we to think of roads heading up to the gate, so that once through the gate the traveler has arrived at his destination, whether destruction or the consummated kingdom? Or is the gate something entered *in this life*, with the roads, broad and narrow, stretching out before the pilgrim? Tasker and Jeremias (TDNT, 6:922–23) adopt the former alternative, Jeremias appealing to Luke 13:23–24, where a door, not a road, is mentioned. He argues that Jesus originally said something about entering a door or gate and that Matthew's form is a popular *hysteron-proteron* ("later-earlier") way of saying things with the real order reversed (like "thunder and lightning").

Not only is Luke 13:23–24 so far removed from the language of Matthew 7:13–14 (even "door," not "gate") that one may question whether the two spring from the same saying, but even in Luke entrance through the door is not merely eschatological since there comes a time when the door is shut and no more may enter. This suggests that it is the shutting of the door that eliminates further opportunity for entrance, while the entrance itself takes place now—a form of realized eschatology. This conceptual parallel with Matthew, plus the order of gate-road, suggests, not that the gate marks entrance into the consummated kingdom, nor that the gate and road are a hendiadys (Ridderbos), but that entrance through the gate into the narrow way of persecution begins *now* but issues in the consummated kingdom at the other end of that way (Grosheide, Hendriksen). The narrow gate is not thereby rendered superfluous; instead, it confirms that even the beginning of this path to life is restrictive. Here is no funnel that progressively narrows down but a decisive break.

This exegesis entails two conclusions.

1. Jesus is not encouraging committed disciples, "Christians," to press on along the narrow way and be rewarded in the end. He is rather commanding his disciples to enter the way marked by persecution and rewarded in the end. Jesus' "disciples" (see on 5:1) are therefore not full-fledged Christians in the post-Pentecost sense. Jesus is dealing with people more or less committed to him but who have not yet really entered on the "Christian" way. How could they have entered on it? Only

now was it being introduced into the stream of redemptive history as the fulfillment of what had come before. That Matthew should preserve such fine distinctions speaks well of his ability to follow the development of salvation history and thus avoid historical anachronism. Theologian though he is, Matthew is a responsible historian.

2. Implicitly, entrance into the kingdom—or, to preserve the language Matthew uses here but not always elsewhere (e.g., 12:28), entrance into the way to the kingdom—begins here and now in coming through the small gate, onto the narrow way of persecution, and under the authority of Jesus Christ (cf. vv.21, 26).

Notes

13 The phrase δι' αὐτῆς (di' autēs, "through it") could in Greek refer to either the gate or the road (cf. 8:28); but the main lines of exegesis (above) are not affected.
14 Probably τί (ti, normally "what?" or "why?"; "for," KJV; "but," NIV) is the correct reading, carrying the same force as מָה (māh, "how"—e.g., Ps 139:17) in Hebrew (cf. Black, *Aramaic Approach*, p. 123; BDF, Par. 299[4]; Metzger, *Textual Commentary*, p. 19).

b. Two trees

7:15-20

> 15"Watch out for false prophets. They come to you in sheep's clothing, but inwardly they are ferocious wolves. 16By their fruit you will recognize them. Do people pick grapes from thornbushes, or figs from thistles? 17Likewise every good tree bears good fruit, but a bad tree bears bad fruit. 18A good tree cannot bear bad fruit, and a bad tree cannot bear good fruit. 19Every tree that does not bear good fruit is cut down and thrown into the fire. 20Thus, by their fruit you will recognize them.

Much recent debate has focused attention on the identity of these false prophets in the Matthean church. The argument turns in large part on identifying v.15 as Matthew's creation and on attempting to discuss the tradition history of vv.16-20; 12:33-35; Luke 6:43-45. The same evidence is better interpreted to support the thesis that Jesus in his itinerant preaching uses similar metaphors in a wide variety of ways. Verse 15 has no synoptic parallel; but the thought is certainly not foreign to Jesus' other warnings (e.g., 24:4-5, 11, 23-24; Mark 13:22), and Matthew's language is small evidence for inauthenticity (cf. Introduction, section 2). The very diversity of the identifications—the false prophets are Zealots, Gnostics, scribes, antinomians, anti-Paulinists (for a recent survey, cf. D. Hill, "False Prophets and Charismatics: Structure and Interpretation in Matthew 7, 15-23," *Biblica* 57 [1976]: 327-48)—argues that Jesus gave a warning with rather broad limits susceptible to diverse applications. Hill himself sees Pharisees of the A.D. 80 period in vv.15-20 (Were rabbis of A.D. 80 ever called Pharisees?) and Charismatics in vv.21-23. E. Cothenet ("Les prophètes chrétiens dans l'Evangile selon Saint Matthieu," Didier, pp. 281-308) thinks Jesus in vv.15-23 is condemning Zealots, but Matthew reapplies his words to condemn antinomians. And Paul S. Minear ("False Prophecy and Hypocrisy in the Gospel of Matthew," Gnilka, *Neues Testament*, pp. 76–93) criticizes theories that center on antinomians and Pharisees and understands the pericope to warn against hypocrisy and false prophecy entirely within the Christian community.

There is nothing intrinsically unlikely about the notion that Jesus warned against false prophets, provided he foresaw the continued existence of his newly formed community for a sustained period. He was doubtless steeped in the OT reports of earlier false prophets (Jer 6:13–15; 8:8–12; Ezek 13; 22:27; Zeph 3:4). Certainly the first Christians faced the false prophets (cf. v.15) Jesus had predicted (Acts 20:29; 2 Cor 11:11–15; 2 Peter 2:1–3, 17–22; cf. 1 John 2:18, 22; 4:1–6). In view of Matthew's care in preserving historical distinctions (see on 7:13–14), there is little reason to doubt that he is here dealing with the teaching of the historical Jesus. Of course this presupposes that Jesus saw himself as true prophet (cf. 21:11, 46).

15 Warnings against false prophets are necessarily based on the conviction that not all prophets are true, that truth can be violated, and that the gospel's enemies usually conceal their hostility and try to pass themselves off as fellow believers. At first glance they use orthodox language, show biblical piety, and are indistinguishable from true prophets (cf. 10:41). Thus it is vital to know how to distinguish sheep from wolves in sheep's clothing. Jesus does not explicitly say who will have the discernment to protect the community but implies that the community itself, by whatever agency, must somehow protect itself from the wolves.

Neither the damage these false prophets do nor their brand of false teaching is stated; but the flow of the Sermon on the Mount as well as its OT background suggest that they neither acknowledge nor teach the narrow way to life subject to persecution (vv.13–14; cf. Jer 8:11; Ezek 13, where prophets cry "Peace!" when there is no peace). They have never really come under kingdom authority (vv.21–23); and since the only alternative to life is destruction (vv.13–14), they imperil their followers.

16–20 From a distance the little blackberries on the buckthorn could be mistaken for grapes, and the flowers on certain thistles might deceive one into thinking figs were growing (v.16). But no one would be long deceived. So with people! One's "fruit"—not just what one does, but all one says and does—will ultimately reveal what one is (cf. James 3:12). The Semitic way of expression (i.e., both positive and negative—viz., every good tree bears good fruit, no good tree bears bad fruit, etc.) makes the test certain, but not necessarily easy or quick. Living according to kingdom norms can be feigned for a time; but what one is will eventually reveal itself in what one does. However guarded one's words, they will finally betray him (cf. 12:33–37; Luke 6:45). Ultimately false prophets tear down faith (2 Tim 2:18) and promote divisiveness, bitterness (e.g., 1 Tim 6:4–5; 2 Tim 2:23), and various kinds of ungodliness (2 Tim 2:16). Meek discernment and understanding the dire consequences of the false prophets' teachings are needed. But at the same time censoriousness over minutiae must be avoided.

The common wording between 3:10 (spoken by the Baptist) and 7:19 may suggest that v.19 was proverbial or that during the time Jesus and the Baptist were both ministering, various expressions became standard (cf. 3:2; 4:17). Verse 19 is an important example of this, for here we have independent evidence that Jesus

191

preached in this vein (cf. Mark 1:15) so that there is no need to suppose Matthew has transferred a saying of the Baptist to the lips of Jesus.

c. Two claims

7:21–23

> 21"Not everyone who says to me, 'Lord, Lord,' will enter the kingdom of heaven, but only he who does the will of my Father who is in heaven. 22Many will say to me on that day, 'Lord, Lord, did we not prophesy in your name, and in your name drive out demons and perform many miracles?' 23Then I will tell them plainly, 'I never knew you. Away from me, you evildoers!'

21–23 If vv.15–20 deal with false prophets, vv.21–23 deal with false followers. Perhaps some became false because of the false prophets. Their cry of "Lord, Lord" (v.21) reflects fervency. In Jesus' day it is doubtful whether "Lord" when used to address him meant more than "teacher" or "sir." But in the postresurrection period, it becomes an appellation of worship and a confession of Jesus' deity. Therefore some suspect an anachronism here. Two factors support authenticity: (1) the parallel in Luke 6:46 (cf. also John 13:12–16); (2) the fact that throughout Jesus' ministry he referred to himself in relatively veiled categories whose full significance could only be grasped after the Resurrection. The latter point is central to understanding the "Son of Man" title (see on 8:20), recurs in various forms throughout all the Gospels, and is especially focal in John (cf. Carson, "Christological Ambiguities"; id., "Understanding Misunderstandings in the Fourth Gospel," *Tyndale Bulletin* [1982]: 59–91).

On the background of *kyrios* ("Lord") as a christological title, see Fitzmyer, *Wandering Aramaean*, pp. 115–32. Here Jesus' point is made during his ministry, if at that time his disciples understood "Lord" to mean "teacher." But implicitly Jesus is claiming more, since his "name" becomes the focus of kingdom activity; and he alone decrees who does or does not enter the kingdom (vv.22–23). Thus the warning and rebuke would take on added force when early Christians read the passage from their postresurrection perspective.

Indeed, the tables may be turned. Far from providing evidence that virtually every use of *kyrios* ("Lord") in this Gospel is anachronistic because it presupposes a high christology (e.g., Kingsbury, *Matthew*), these verses suggest that Matthew is painfully aware that the title may mean nothing. This explains, for instance, the deep irony of Peter's "Never, Lord" (16:22). Jesus himself is preparing his followers to put the deepest content in the title. For finally obedience, not titles, is decisive.

The determinative factor regarding who enters the kingdom is obedience to the Father's will (v.19; cf. 12:50). This is the first use of "my Father" in Matthew (cf. Luke 2:49; John 2:16); as such it may support the truth, taught throughout the sermon, that Jesus alone claims to be the authoritative Revealer of his Father's will (v.21). It quite misses the point to say that the Father's will is simply the OT law, mildly touched up by Jesus, and that therefore the Matthean church "seems to have been unaware of or uninfluenced by Pauline Christianity" (Hill, *Matthew*), for:

1. If the preceding exegesis of the Sermon on the Mount is correct, Matthew is not saying that Jesus is simply taking over the law but that Jesus *fulfills* the law and thus determines the nature of its continuity.

2. Within this framework Matthew presents Jesus as standing at a different (i.e., earlier) point in salvation-history than any church in Matthew's day, for Jesus is the one who brings about the new dispensation.

3. Paul's alleged antinomian tendencies are implicitly exaggerated by Hill's reconstruction, for it is difficult to think of one thing in the sermon Paul does not say in other words. The differences between Matthew and Paul—and there are major ones—have more to do with differences in interest and in their relative place in the stream of redemptive history. Moreover, Matthew, as we shall see, strongly stresses grace; therefore it is legitimate to wonder whether he is presenting obedience to the will of the Father as the ground or as the requirement for entrance to the kingdom. Paul would deny only the former and insist on the latter no less than Matthew would.

"That day" is the Day of Judgment (cf. Mal 3:17–18; 1 Enoch 45:3; cf. Matt 25:31–46; Luke 10:12; 2 Thess 1:7–10; 2 Tim 1:12; 4:8; Rev 16:14). The false claimants have prophesied in Jesus' name and by that name exorcised demons and performed miracles. There is no reason to judge their claims false; their claims are not false but insufficient. Significantly the miracles Jesus specifies were all done by his disciples during his ministry (cf. 10:1–4): he does not mention a later gift, such as tongues.

Verse 23 presupposes an implicit christology of the highest order. Jesus himself not only decides who enters the kingdom on the last day but also who will be banished from his presence. That he never knew these false claimants strikes a common biblical note, viz., how close to spiritual reality one may come while knowing nothing of its fundamental reality (e.g., Balaam; Judas Iscariot; Mark 9:38–39; 1 Cor 13:2; Heb 3:14; 1 John 2:19). "But not everyone who speaks in a spirit is a prophet, except he have the behavior of the Lord" (*Didache* 11.8).

Two final observations can be made. First, although "I have nothing to do with you" is the mildest of rabbinic bans (SBK, 4:293), the words used here are clearly final and eschatological in a solemn context of "that day" and entrance into the kingdom. Second, "Away from me, you evildoers" is quoted from Psalm 6:8 (cf. Luke 13:27). In the psalm the sufferer, vindicated by Yahweh, tells the evildoers to depart. Again it is difficult to avoid the conclusion that Jesus himself links the authority of the messianic King with the righteous Sufferer, however veiled the allusion may be (see on 3:17).

d. Two builders

7:24–27

> [24]"Therefore everyone who hears these words of mine and puts them into practice is like a wise man who built his house on the rock. [25]The rain came down, the streams rose, and the winds blew and beat against that house; yet it did not fall, because it had its foundation on the rock. [26]But everyone who hears these words of mine and does not put them into practice is like a foolish man who built his house on sand. [27]The rain came down, the streams rose, and the winds blew and beat against that house, and it fell with a great crash."

24–27 Luke's sermon ends on the same note (Luke 6:47–49). Probably the evangelists adapted the parable to the situation of their readers. Verses 21–23 contrast "saying" and "doing"; these verses contrast "hearing" and "doing" (Stott, p. 208), not unlike James 1:22–25; 2:14–20 (cf. Ezek 33:31–32). Moreover the will of the Father (v.21) becomes definitive in what Jesus calls "these words of mine" (v.24): *his* teaching is definitive (see on 5:17–20; 28:18–20).

In the light of the radical choice of vv.21–23, "therefore" (v.24) the two positions can be likened to two builders and their houses. Each house looks secure in good weather. But Palestine is known for torrential rains that can turn dry wadis into raging torrents. Only storms reveal the quality of the work of the two builders. The thought reminds us of the parable of the sower in which the seed sown on rocky ground lasts only a short time, until "trouble or persecution comes because of the word" (13:21). The greatest storm is eschatological (cf. Isa 28:16–17; Ezek 13:10–13; cf. Prov 12:7). But Jesus' words about the two houses need not be thus restricted. The point is that the wise man (a repeated term in Matthew; cf. 10:16; 24:45; 25:2, 4, 8–9) builds to withstand anything.

What wisdom (*phronimos;* the term is absent from Mark and occurs twice in Luke [12:42; 16:8]) consists of is clear. A wise person represents those who put Jesus' words into practice; they too are building to withstand anything. Those who pretend to have faith, who have a merely intellectual commitment, or who enjoy Jesus in small doses are foolish builders. When the storms of life come, their structures fool no one, above all not God (cf. Ezek 13:10–16).

The sermon ends with what has been implicit throughout it—the demand for radical submission to the exclusive lordship of Jesus, who fulfills the Law and the Prophets and warns the disobedient that the alternative to total obedience, true righteousness, and life in the kingdom is rebellion, self-centeredness, and eternal damnation.

Notes

24 The future passive reading ὁμοιωθήσεται (*homoiōthēsetai,* lit., "will become like") is more probable than the active ὁμοιώσω αὐτόν (*homoiōsō auton,* lit., "I will liken him to"), not only on textual grounds, but also because of the possibility of assimilation to the active in Luke 6:47–48: ὑποδείξω ὑμῖν . . . ὅμοιος (*hypodeixō hymin . . . homoios,* "I will show you what he is like"). The future tense is significant: the one who puts Jesus' words into practice will become like the man who, etc.: i.e., on Judgment Day, when the great storm comes, he will stand fast because of his good foundation. See on 13:24.

24–26 The words ἀκούει μου τοὺς λόγους τούτους (*akouei mou tous logous toutous,* "hears these words of mine") could be rendered "hears me, in respect of these sayings"; and Davies (*Setting,* p. 94) argues that "in this sense, the ethical teaching is not detached from the life of him who uttered it and with whom it is congruous." But the verb ἀκούω (*akouō,* "I hear") only once takes the genitive in Matthew, and then it is not a pronoun. The emphatic μου (*mou,* "of mine") is best understood as a way of forcefully identifying Jesus' teaching with the will of his Father (v.21), an important point in light of the exegesis of 5:17–20.

8. Transitional conclusion: Jesus' authority

7:28–29

[28]When Jesus had finished saying these things, the crowds were amazed at his teaching, [29]because he taught as one who had authority, and not as their teachers of the law.

28–29 This is the first of the five formulaic conclusions that terminate the discourses in this Gospel. All five begin with *kai egeneto* (lit., "and it happened") plus a finite verb (7:28; 11:1; 13:53; 19:1; 26:1), a construction common in the LXX (classical Greek preferred *egeneto* plus the infinitive; cf. Zerwick, par. 388; Beyer, pp. 41–60). The only other occurrence in Matthew is of the rather different "Hebrew" construction *kai egeneto . . . kai* (lit., "and it happened . . . and") plus finite verb, which appears once (9:10). Matthew's formula is therefore a self-conscious stylistic device that establishes a structural turning point. (It is not necessary to adopt Bacon's theory of parallelism to the Five Books of Moses; cf. Introduction, section 14.) Moreover, in each case the conclusion is transitional and prepares for the next section. Here (as we shall see below) mention of Jesus' authority leads into his authority in other spheres (8:1–17). In 11:1 Jesus' activity sets the scene for John the Baptist's question (11:2–3). And 13:53 anticipates rejection of Jesus in his hometown, while 19:1–2 points forward to his Judean ministry with new crowds and renewed controversies. Finally, 26:1–5 looks to the Cross, now looming very near.

The crowds—probably a larger group than his disciples—again pressing in on him (see on 5:1–2), are amazed (v.28). Because this is the only conclusion to a discourse that mentions the crowds' amazement, Hill (*Matthew*) suggests that Matthew is returning to Mark 1:22 (Luke 4:32) as his source. This is very tenuous: (1) a closer Matthean parallel is 13:54; (2) the next pericope in Matthew (8:1–4) is paralleled in Mark by 1:40–45, too far on for us to believe Matthew has "returned to his source" at 1:22.

The word *didachē* ("teaching," v.29) can refer to both content and manner (see also on 3:1); and no doubt the crowds were astonished at both. Their astonishment says nothing about their own heart commitment. The cause of their astonishment was Jesus' *exousia* ("authority"). The term embraces power as well as authority, and the theme becomes central (cf. 8:9; 9:6, 8; 10:1; 21:23–24, 27; 28:18). In his authority Jesus differs from the "teachers of the law" (see on 2:4). Many of them limited their teaching to the authorities they cited, and a great part of their training centered on memorizing the received traditions. They spoke by the authority of others; Jesus spoke with his own authority. Yet many teachers of the law did indeed offer new rulings and interpretations; so some have tried to interpret vv.28–29 along other lines.

Daube (pp. 205–16), in arguing that Jesus' lack of official rabbinic authority was an early issue in his ministry, says that some of the crowds' response in Galilee was because they did not often hear ordained rabbis so far north. Sigal ("Halakah"), dating the sources a little differently, insists (probably rightly) that there was no official ordination of rabbis till after Jesus' death. He argues that Jesus himself was not essentially different in his authority from other proto-rabbis. Both these reconstructions miss the central point, which transcends Halakic applications of the law, the formulas used, and the latitude of interpretation permitted.

The central point is this: Jesus' entire approach in the Sermon on the Mount is not only ethical but messianic—i.e., christological and eschatological. Jesus is not an ordinary prophet who says, "Thus says the Lord!" Rather, he speaks in the first person and claims that his teaching fulfills the OT; that he determines who enters the messianic kingdom; that as the Divine Judge he pronounces banishment; that the true heirs of the kingdom would be persecuted for their allegiance to him; and that he alone fully knows the will of his Father. It is methodologically indefensible for Sigal to complain that all such themes are later Christian additions and therefore to focus exclusively on points of Halakic interpretation. Jesus' authority is unique (see on 5:21–48), and the crowds recognized it even if they did not always understand it. This same authority is now to be revealed in powerful, liberating miracles, signs of the kingdom's advance (chs. 8–9; cf. 11:2–5).

Notes

29 The word "their" may indicate a distinction between "Christian" teachers and those of the synagogues. Hummel (pp. 28ff.) and others, following Kilpatrick (*Origins*, p. 40), make much of Matthew's "their" (4:23; 9:35; 10:17; 12:9; 13:54; 23:34) to support a theory that Matthew's life-setting is *just before* the division between church and synagogue (since 6:2, 5; 23:6 make no allusion to Christian synagogues). But "their" may be quite innocuous. It may reflect the geographical stance of a writer not in Galilee (see on 4:23). Better yet, where Jesus' authority is emphasized, "their" may subtly remind the reader that Jesus himself, though a Jew of the line of David (1:1), has his ultimate origin beyond the Jewish race (1:18–25) and so cannot be classed with *their* teachers of the law. Moreover, in two places Matthew is merely following Mark (Mark 1:23, 29) and seems to use "their" in still other, highly unusual places (e.g., 11:1), which caution the reader against reading too much into the word. And some of the preceding debate (e.g., as to the relevance of 6:2, 5; 23:6) is relevant only if anachronism is already assumed, since these references make perfectly good sense under the obvious assumption that the Gospel really is about Jesus. Yet there may well be theological significance in some of the "their" passages (see on 10:17), which gets transferred by association to other occurrences of the pronoun.

III. The Kingdom Extended Under Jesus' Authority (8:1–11:1)

A. *Narrative (8:1–10:4)*

1. *Healing miracles (8:1–17)*

a. *A leper*

8:1–4

> [1]When he came down from the mountainside, large crowds followed him. [2]A man with leprosy came and knelt before him and said, "Lord, if you are willing, you can make me clean."
> [3]Jesus reached out his hand and touched the man. "I am willing," he said. "Be clean!" Immediately he was cured of his leprosy. [4]Then Jesus said to him, "See that you don't tell anyone. But go, show yourself to the priest and offer the gift Moses commanded, as a testimony to them."

Matthew's arrangement of the pericopes in chapters 8–9 is demonstrably topical, not chronological. All these pericopes except 8:5–13, 18–22; 9:32–34 are paralleled in Mark, but not in the same order, and these three are paralleled in Luke. Mark 1:40–2:22 appears to provide the basic framework with numerous exceptions. The events in Matthew 8:18–22 originally occurred not only after the Sermon on the Mount but apparently after the "day of parables" (ch. 13; cf. Luke 8:22–56). On the other hand, 8:2–4; 8:14–17; 9:2–13 almost certainly took place before the Sermon on the Mount (cf. Mark 1:29–34, 40–45; Luke 4:38–41; Hendriksen). Matthew does not purport to follow anything other than a topical arrangement, and most of his "time" indicators are very loose.

This does not mean that Matthew's arrangement is entirely haphazard but that it is governed by themes. Linkage from pericope to pericope is provided by ideas, catchwords, dominant motifs (cf. K. Gatzweiler, "Les récits de miracles dans l'Evangile selon saint Matthieu," in Didier, pp. 209–20). However, it does not follow that all the outlines suggested by various scholars to explain this topical design are equally convincing. Klostermann, for instance, notes the central place of the ten plagues in Jewish thought (e.g., *Pirke Aboth* 5:5, 8) and suggests that the ten miracles in these chapters are planned to picture Jesus as the new Moses or the church as a new Exodus (cf. Grundmann; Davies, *Setting*, pp. 86–93). But this is not convincing: Matthew lays no stress on the number ten, his miracles are not individually parallel to the plagues, and his main themes run on other lines.

J.D. Kingsbury ("Observations on the 'Miracle Chapters' of Matthew 8–9," CBQ 40 [1978]: 559–73) ably discusses and rejects outlines proposed by Burger, Schniewind, Thompson, and others, and opts for a modification of Burger's fourfold division: (1) 8:1–17 treats christology; (2) 8:18–34 concerns discipleship; (3) 9:1–17 focuses on questions pertaining to the separation of Jesus and his followers from Israel; (4) 9:18–34 centers on faith; and over all the "Son of God" christology predominates. But it is hard to avoid the feeling that this outline, like the others, is too simplistic. Christology extends beyond 8:1–17; a new title appears in 8:20 and reappears in 9:6; and Jesus' godlike authority to forgive sins does not appear till chapter 9. Why discipleship should be restricted to 8:18–34 when Matthew is called in 9:9–13 and the distinctive habits of Jesus' disciples are discussed in 9:14–17 is unclear. The distinctions between Jesus' followers and racial Israel can scarcely be said to await 9:1–17 in the light of 8:10, 28–34. Faith, far from awaiting the fourth division, is already central in 8:5–13. And we have already seen that Kingsbury tends to emphasize the Son-of-God theme while minimizing other equally strong christological emphases (see on 3:17).

These chapters cannot legitimately be broken down so simplistically. Though Matthew's pericopes cohere nicely, he intertwines his themes, keeping several going at once like a literary juggler. Thus these chapters are best approached inductively; and one can trace emphases on faith, discipleship, the Gentile mission, a diverse christological pattern, and more. At the same time these chapters prove that Jesus, whose mission in part was to preach, teach, and heal (4:23; 9:35), fulfilled the whole of it. Matthew has shown Jesus preaching the gospel of the kingdom (4:17, 23) and teaching (chs. 5–7). Now he records some examples of his healing ministry.

The first miracle, the healing of a leper, is much shorter in Matthew (vv. 1–4) than in Mark (1:40–45). The omission of Mark 1:41a, 45 and several other bits prompts some to think Matthew is here independent of Mark (Lohmeyer, Schlatter), others to think oral tradition is still having its influence (Bonnard, Hill), still others to offer some theological explanation, e.g, that Matthew suppressed any reference to Jesus' compassion because it did not fit the image the Matthean church members had formed of Christ (e.g., Leopold Sabourin, *L'Evangile selon Saint Matthieu et ses principaux parallèles* [Rome: BIP, 1978], in loc.; cf. Hull, pp. 133f.). But when Matthew follows Mark, he condenses controversy stories by about 20 percent, stories that prove Jesus is the Christ by about 10 percent, actual sayings of Jesus scarcely at all, and miracle stories by about 50 percent (cf. Schweizer).

Matthew, though allusive, is a highly disciplined writer, rigorously eliminating everything unrelated to his immediate concerns. So we must take it as a rule of thumb that Matthew's theology cannot be accurately discovered by studying what he omits—which cannot show more than what is not his immediate concern, and even then some of his omissions are purely stylistic—but primarily by what he includes. This is especially significant in the miracles where Matthew leaves out so much. In the leper's healing, Sabourin's suggestion is especially implausible since Matthew stresses elsewhere Jesus' compassion and draws theological meaning from it (9:35–38).

1 Jesus came down out of the hills (see on 5:1), where the Sermon on the Mount had been delivered; and still the great crowds (4:23–25; 7:28–29) pursued him.

2–3 The introductory *kai idou* (lit., "and behold"; also in Luke, absent from Mark, untranslated in NIV) does not require that this healing immediately follow the sermon. In Matthew *kai idou* has a broad range, sometimes serving as a loose connective, sometimes introducing a startling thought or event, and sometimes, as here, marking the beginning of a new pericope. Whether NT leprosy was actual leprosy ("Hansen's disease"; cf. DNTT, 2:463–66) or a broader category of skin ailments including leprosy is uncertain. But the Jews abhorred it, not only because of the illness itself, but because it rendered the sufferer and all with whom he came in direct contact ceremonially unclean. To be a leper was interpreted as being cursed by God (cf. Num 12:10, 12; Job 18:13). Healings were rare (cf. Num 12:10–15; 2 Kings 5:9–14) and considered as difficult as raising the dead (2 Kings 5:7, 14; cf. SBK, 4:745ff.). In the Messianic Age there would be no leprosy (cf. 11:5).

The man *prosekynei* ("knelt") before Jesus, but the verb can also mean "worshiped." Clearly the former is meant in this historical setting. Yet as with the title "Lord" (see on 7:22–23), Christian readers of Matthew could not help concluding that this leper spoke and acted better than he knew. "If you are willing" reflects the leper's great faith, prompted by Jesus' healing activity throughout the district (4:24): he had no question about Jesus' healing power but feared only that he would be passed by. In affirming his willingness to heal, Jesus proved that his will is decisive. He already had the authority and power and only needed to decide and act. J.D. Kingsbury ("Retelling the 'Old, Old Story,'" *Currents in Theology and Missions* 4 [1976]: 346) suggests that "reached out his hand" symbolizes the exercise of authority (cf. Exod 7:5; 14:21; 15:6; 1 Kings 8:42); but Matthew's use of the same Greek expression elsewhere (12:13 [*bis*], 49; 14:31; 26:51) shows that Kingsbury's interpretation is fanciful. More probably Jesus had to reach to touch the leper because the leper did not dare come close to him.

By touching an unclean leper, Jesus would become ceremonially defiled himself (cf. Lev 13–14). But at Jesus' touch nothing remains defiled. Far from becoming unclean, Jesus makes the unclean clean. Both Jesus' word and touch (8:15; 9:20–21; 29; 14:36) are effective, possibly implying that authority is vested in his message as well as in his person.

4 Despite Held's view (Bornkamm, *Tradition*, p. 256), this verse is not the "entire goal of this story." That is reductionistic and ignores the intertwined themes (cf. comments on 8:1–4; Heil, "Healing Miracles," p. 280, n. 25). While prohibitions against telling of cures and exorcisms are more common in Mark than Matthew, they are not unknown in the latter (8:4; 9:30; 12:16; cf. 16:20; 17:9). They have nothing to do with the so-called messianic secret proposed by Wrede and defended by Bultmann (as Hill rightly holds). Nor does this particular prohibition enjoin silence only till the cured leper has been to Jerusalem to be cleared by the priest (Lenski, Barnes). The synoptic parallels (Mark 1:45; Luke 5:15) as well as other similar occurrences in Matthew demonstrate that these commands to be silent have other functions—to show that Jesus is not presenting himself as a mere wonder-worker (Stonehouse, *Witness of Matthew*, p. 62; Maier) who can be pressured into messiahship by crowds whose messianic views are materialistic and political. Jesus' authority derives from God alone, not the acclaim of men (Bonnard); he came to die, not to trounce the Romans. The people who disobeyed Jesus' injunctions to silence only made his mission more difficult.

Jesus commanded the cured man to follow the Mosaic prescriptions for lepers who claimed healing (cf. Lev 14). This, he said, was *eis martyrion autois* ("as a testimony to them"). Much debate surrounds *autois*. Is the testimony positive, "for them" (Trilling, pp. 128f.), as proof of the healing, or negative, "against them" (Hummel, pp. 81f.), as a sort of denunciation of their unbelief? Such conflicting categories are not helpful. Of the other places where the Synoptics use *eis martyrion* ("for a witness"; 10:18; 24:14; Mark 1:44; 6:11; 13:9; Luke 5:14; 9:5; 21:13), only two require "witness against" (contra Frankmölle, p. 120, n. 193, who insists 10:18 and 24:14 are also negative). Most of the rest are "neutral" and imply division around the "witness" presented.

Better progress can be made by asking why, in this setting, Jesus commands obedience. It cannot be simply to prove that Jesus remains faithful to the law (Calvin) and so encourages Matthew's Jewish Christians to be similarly faithful (Hill, Schniewind, Schweizer). Formally speaking, Jesus has already transcended the law by touching the leper without being defiled, a confirmation of our exegesis of 5:17–20. Furthermore, if around A.D. 85 (when Hill thinks the first Gospel was written) Matthew were simply trying to get his community to adhere (unlike Pauline communities) to the details of OT law, he chose a singularly ill-suited story to make his point, because by that date the destruction of the temple had effectively abolished priests and offerings. It is far easier to deduce from the setting that this material is authentic.

In one sense Jesus does submit to the law. He puts himself under its ordinances. But the result is startling: the law achieves new relevance by pointing to Jesus. In conforming to the law, the cured leper becomes the occasion for the law to confirm Jesus' authority as the healer who needs but to will the deed for it to be done. Thus the supreme function of the "gift" Moses commanded is not as a guilt offering (Lev 14:10–18) but as a witness to men concerning Jesus. In this context "to them" is relatively incidental: it might refer to the priests or the people, but in either case it points to Jesus Christ (see on 5:17–20).

b. *The centurion's servant*

8:5–13

> [5]When Jesus had entered Capernaum, a centurion came to him, asking for help. [6]"Lord," he said, "my servant lies at home paralyzed and in terrible suffering."
> [7]Jesus said to him, "I will go and heal him."
> [8]The centurion replied, "Lord, I do not deserve to have you come under my

roof. But just say the word, and my servant will be healed. ⁹For I myself am a man under authority, with soldiers under me. I tell this one, 'Go,' and he goes; and that one, 'Come,' and he comes. I say to my servant, 'Do this,' and he does it."

¹⁰When Jesus heard this, he was astonished and said to those following him, "I tell you the truth, I have not found anyone in Israel with such great faith. ¹¹I say to you that many will come from the east and the west, and will take their places at the feast with Abraham, Isaac and Jacob in the kingdom of heaven. ¹²But the subjects of the kingdom will be thrown outside, into the darkness, where there will be weeping and gnashing of teeth."

¹³Then Jesus said to the centurion, "Go! It will be done just as you believed it would." And his servant was healed at that very hour.

If this story (cf. Luke 7:1–10) comes from Q, then at least in this instance Q contains more than short sayings of Jesus; or, better, this is evidence against a unitary Q. It is uncertain whether this account is the same as the one in John 4:46–53. The many differences argue against this, though admittedly some of these are overemphasized. In John, Jesus rebukes the centurion and the onlookers for their love of signs; but though there is no mention of that here, Matthew treats that theme elsewhere (12:38–39; 16:1–4). Most modern scholars, unlike those of earlier generations, simply assume that there is but one incident. However, the matter is ably discussed by Edward F. Siegman, "St. John's Use of Synoptic Material," CBQ 30 (1968): 182–98. (On the distinctive theological emphases of Matthew and Luke, cf. R.P. Martin, "The Pericope of the Healing of the 'Centurion's' Servant/Son [Matt 8:5–13 par. Luke 7:1–10]: Some Exegetical Notes," *Unity and Diversity in the New Testament*, ed. R.A. Guelich [Grand Rapids: Eerdmans, 1978], pp. 14–22.)

Form critics find the purpose of the story in the dialogue to which the miracle leads and call it a "pronouncement story" or "apophthegm" rather than a "miracle story." One wonders why it can't be both (cf. Stephen H. Travis, "Form Criticism," Marshall, *NT Interpretation*, esp. pp. 157–60). The chief difference, apart from theological emphases, between vv.5–13 and Luke 7:1–10 is the use of intermediaries in the latter. Probably Matthew, following his tendency to condense, makes no mention of the servants in order to lay the greater emphasis on faith according to the principle *qui facit per alium facit per se* ("he who acts by another acts himself")—a principle the centurion's argument implies (vv.8–9).

5 This is Matthew's second mention of Capernaum (cf. 4:13). In Jesus' day it was an important garrison town. No Roman legions were posted in Palestine, but there were auxiliaries under Herod Antipas, who had the right to levy troops. These were non-Jews, probably recruited from outside Galilee, perhaps from Lebanon and Syria. Centurions were the military backbone throughout the empire, maintaining discipline and executing orders. Luke stresses this centurion's Jewish sympathies and his humility, Matthew his faith and race (vv.10–11). Indeed, one reason Matthew says nothing of the intermediaries may be because they were Jews, and he does not want to blur the racial distinction.

6–7 On "Lord," see on 7:21–23. The word *pais* (v.6) can mean "servant" or "son." Luke's word (*doulos*) means "servant," and many (e.g., Bultmann, *Synoptic Tradition*, p. 38, n. 4) insist Matthew's *pais* means "son." But fair examination of NT usage (cf. France, "Exegesis," p. 256) reveals that only one of twenty-four NT occurrences requires "son," viz., John 4:51. This further supports the view that John 4 records a different healing on a separate occasion. Conceivably it was the earlier healing of an official's son (John 4) that strengthened the centurion's faith in this instance. Though paralysis coupled with severe pain is attested elsewhere (e.g., 1 Macc 9:55–56), the nature of the servant's malady is unknown. Derrett's psychosomatic speculations (*NT Studies*, 1:156–57, 166–68) are fanciful.

Jewish rabbis, like ministers today, were often invited to pray for the sick (cf. SBK, 1:475); but the parallels are not close, for the centurion is implicitly asking for healing, not prayers. Many (Zahn; Klostermann; Turner [*Insights*, pp. 50f.]; Held [Bornkamm, *Tradition*, p. 194]) interpret Jesus' response (v.7) as a question: "Shall I [*egō*, emphatic; i.e., I, a Jew] come and heal him?" This is probably right. The parallel with the Canaanite woman (15:21–28) is compelling, and otherwise it is difficult to explain the emphatic "I." Jesus' response was not based on fears of ritual defilement—vv.1–4 set that to rest—or even on his general restriction of his ministry to Israel (see on 10:5–6; 15:24; but even in Matthew there are significant exceptions, e.g., 8:28–34). It was based on a desire to find out exactly what the centurion was after and what degree of faith stood behind his ambiguous request (v.6).

8–9 Both here and in the story of the Canaanite woman (15:21–28), faith triumphs over the obstacle Jesus erects. Luke records neither Jesus' question (see on v.7) nor the story of the Canaanite woman; his treatment of faith is not quite so pointed. The centurion's reply opens with "Lord" (v.8), implying tenacity and deference (cf. v.6; 7:21–23). As John the Baptist felt unworthy to baptize Jesus, so this centurion felt unworthy to entertain him in his home. The feeling of unworthiness did not arise from an awareness that the centurion might render Jesus ceremonially defiled (contra Bonnard); race had nothing to do with it. *Hikanos* ("sufficient," "worthy") here as elsewhere (3:11; 1 Cor 15:9; 2 Cor 2:16) reveals the man's sense of unworthiness (NIV, "do not deserve") in the face of Jesus' authority (cf. TDNT, 3:294; France. "Exegesis," p. 258). "Here was one who was in the state described in the first clauses of the 'Beatitudes,' and to whom came the promise of the second clauses; because Christ *is* the connecting link between the two" (LTJM 1:549; emphasis his).

The centurion believed that Jesus' word was sufficient to heal his servant. It is significant that we have no recorded evidence that up to this point Jesus had performed a healing miracle at a distance and by word alone (unless John 4:46–53 is an exception). The centurion's thinking (v.9) is profound. There is no need to take the first clause as implying that the *only* parallel between his authority and that of Jesus was in their ability to order things to be done: "I, although I am a man under orders, can effect things by my word" (Hill, *Matthew*). That is a barely possible rendering of the opening *kai gar egō;* the more natural translation is that of NIV ("for I myself"), which applies the words to the entire verse. This means that the centurion's words presuppose an understanding of the Roman military system. All "authority" (*exousia*, as in 7:29) belonged to the emperor and was delegated. Therefore, because he was under the emperor's authority, when the centurion spoke, he spoke with the emperor's authority, and so his command was obeyed. A footsoldier who disobeyed would not be defying a mere centurion but the emperor, Rome itself, with all its imperial majesty and might (cf. Derrett, *NT Studies*, 1:159f.). This self-understanding the centurion applied to Jesus. Precisely because Jesus was under God's authority, he was vested with God's authority, so that when Jesus spoke, God spoke. To defy Jesus was to defy God; and Jesus' word must therefore be vested with God's authority that is able to heal sickness. This analogy, though not perfect, reveals an astonishing faith that recognizes that Jesus needed neither ritual, magic, nor any other help; his authority was God's authority, and his word was effective because it was God's word.

10 In Mark 6:6 Jesus is astonished at deeply rooted unbelief. Here he is astonished (same verb) at the faith of the centurion. "Though amazement is not appropriate for God, seeing it must arise from new and unexpected happenings, yet it could occur in Christ, inasmuch as he had taken on our human emotions, along with our flesh" (Calvin). Jesus spoke to those following him (not necessarily his disciples; cf. 4:25; 8:1) with the prefatory notice ("I tell you"; cf. on 5:22) that warns of the solemn remark to follow.

Jesus commended the man's faith (cf. also v.13). The greatness of his faith did not rest in the mere fact that he believed Jesus could heal from a distance but in the degree to which he had penetrated the secret of Jesus' authority. That faith was the more surprising since the centurion was a Gentile and lacked the heritage of OT revelation to help him understand Jesus. But this Gentile penetrated more deeply into the nature of Jesus' person and authority than any Jew of his time. Matthew's words stress even more than Luke's the uniqueness of the centurion's faith and underline the movement of the gospel from the Jews to the Gentiles, or rather from the Jews to all people regardless of race—a movement prophesied in the OT, developed in Jesus' ministry (see on 1:1, 3–5; 2:1–12; 3:9–10; 4:15–16), and commanded by the Great Commission (28:18–20). "This incident is a preview of the great insight which came later through another centurion's faith, 'Then to the Gentiles God has granted repentance unto life' (Acts 11:18)" (France, "Exegesis," p. 260).

11–12 Again "I say to you" (v.11) solemnizes what follows (cf. v.10). Most interpreters assume that Matthew has added these two verses (not in Luke) to the narrative, taking them from an entirely different setting (viz., Luke 13:28–29; e.g., Chilton, *God in Strength*, pp. 179–201). But this is problematic apart from clear criteria distinguishing it from the obvious alternative—that Jesus said similar things more than once. The words of the saying are not very close in the two passages; but the imagery is so colorful that an itinerant preacher could have used it repeatedly, especially if warnings to the Jews and the prospect of Gentile admission to the fellowship of God's people were two of his major themes.

The picture is that of the "messianic banquet," derived from such OT passages as Isaiah 25:6–9 (cf. 65:13–14) and embellished in later Judaism (cf. TDNT, 2:34–35). These embellishments did not usually anticipate the presence of Gentiles at the banquet, which symbolized the consummation of the messianic kingdom (cf. 22:1–14; 25:10; 26:29). But Jesus here insists that many will come from the four points of the compass and join the patriarchs at the banquet. These "many" can only be Gentiles, contrasted as they are (v.12) with "subjects of the kingdom" (*hoi huioi tēs basileias*, lit., "the sons of the kingdom").

"Son of" or "sons of" can mean "belonging to" or "destined for" (cf. "sons of the bridal chamber" [9:15; NIV, "guests of the bridegroom"] and "son of hell" [23:15; cf. SBK, 1:476–78; 1QS 17:3; and comments on 5:9]). So the "subjects of the kingdom" are the Jews, who see themselves as sons of Abraham (cf. 3:9–10), belonging to the kingdom by right. Some Jews (e.g., those at Qumran) restricted the elect to a smaller group of the pious within Israel. But Jesus reverses roles (cf. 21:43); and the sons of the kingdom are thrown aside, left out of the future messianic banquet, consigned to darkness where there are tears and gnashing of teeth—elements common to descriptions of gehenna, hell (cf. 4 Ezra 7:93; 1 Enoch 63:10; Pss Sol 14:9; 15:10; Wisd Sol 17:21; cf. Matt 22:13; comments on 5:29).

The definite articles with "weeping" and "gnashing" (cf. Gr.) emphasize the horror of the scene: *the* weeping and *the* gnashing (Turner, *Syntax*, p. 173). Weeping suggests suffering and gnashing of teeth despair (McNeile). The reversal is not absolute. The patriarchs themselves are Jews, as were the earliest disciples (Rom 11:1–5). But these verses affirm, in a way that could only shock Jesus' hearers, that the locus of the people of God would not always be the Jewish race. If these verses do not quite authorize the Gentile mission, they open the door to it and prepare for the Great Commission (28:18–20) and Ephesians 3.

There may be a still deeper implication in these words of Jesus. OT passages that may be reflected in vv.11–12 can be divided into three groups: (1) those that desribe a gathering of Israel from all quarters of the earth (Ps 107:3; Isa 43:5–6; 49:12); (2) those that predict the worship of God by Gentiles in all parts of the earth (Isa 45:6; 59:19; Mal 1:11); (3) those that predict the coming of Gentiles to Jerusalem (Isa 2:2–3; 60:3–4; Mic 4:1–2; Zech 8:20–23). The closest literary parallels lie between vv.11–12 and the first group (cf. Gundry, *Use of OT*, pp. 76f.); and on this basis France (*Jesus*, p. 63; id., "Exegesis," pp. 261–63) proposes that a typology is assumed—the true "Israel" is now being gathered from the four corners of the earth, i.e., from the Gentiles. This is possible, for we have already seen several ways Matthew treats OT history as prophetic. But because he is not using fulfillment language here, Jesus may be using OT language without affirming that the relationship between OT and NT at this point is typological.

13 The *hōs* ("just as," NIV) must be rightly understood: Jesus performed a miracle, not *in proportion to* the centurion's faith, nor *because of* the centurion's faith, but in content what was *expected by* the centurion's faith (cf. 15:28, where the emphasis is also on faith).

Notes

9 The three commands are aorist, present, and aorist respectively. Sometimes "the tense appears to be determined more by the meaning of the verb or by some obscure habit than by the 'rules' of *Aktionsart*" (Moule, *Idiom Book*, p. 135).

11 The verb ἀνακλιθήσονται (*anaklithēsontai*, lit., "will recline") describes the normal posture when eating; people lay on low couches or pallets (cf. John 13:23; 21:20). In the NT reclining is not restricted to banquets (e.g., Mark 6:39; Luke 7:36), and there is no theological or symbolic significance in the act itself (contra Schlatter; Lohmeyer, *Matthäus*). Hence NIV's paraphrastic "take their places."

12 Stonehouse (*Witness of Matthew*, pp. 231f.), to avoid saying that the "subjects of the kingdom" are such only in appearance and self-estimation, understands "kingdom" to refer to the "theocratic kingdom" as opposed to the "kingdom of heaven." But strictly speaking the theocratic kingdom was no longer in existence; and it is difficult to see how "kingdom" in the phrase "subjects of the kingdom" may properly be taken as anything other than the kingdom just mentioned (v.11).

c. Peter's mother-in-law

8:14–15

> ¹⁴When Jesus came into Peter's house, he saw Peter's mother-in-law lying in bed with a fever. ¹⁵He touched her hand and the fever left her, and she got up and began to wait on him.

14–15 In Mark 1:29–31; Luke 4:38–39, this incident follows the casting out of a demon on a Sabbath from a man in the synagogue at Capernaum. Presumably this healing takes place on that same Sabbath. Matthew, however, condenses the account by omitting what does not bear on his immediate theme—Jesus' authority.

Peter was married (1 Cor 9:5) and had moved with his brother Andrew from their home in Bethsaida (John 1:44) to Capernaum, possibly to remain near Jesus (Matt 4:13). His mother-in-law's fever (v.14) may have been malarial; fever itself was considered a disease, not a symptom, at that time (cf. John 4:52; Acts 28:8). Jewish Halakah forbade touching persons with many kinds of fever (SBK, 1:479f.). But Jesus healed with a touch (v.15). As in v.3, the touch did not defile the healer but healed the defiled. The imperfect *diēkonei* is best taken as conative: "began to serve," almost certainly a reference to waiting on him. Matthew mentions her service, not to tell his readers that those touched by Jesus become his servants (contra P. Lamarche, "La guérison de la belle-mère de Pierre et le genre littéraire des évangiles," *Nouvelle Revue Théologique* 87 [1965]: 515–26), but to make it clear that the miracle was effective and instantaneous (cf. v.26, where the result of Jesus' stilling the storm is complete calm). Jesus' authority instantly accomplishes what he wills.

d. Many at evening

8:16–17

> ¹⁶When evening came, many who were demon-possessed were brought to him, and he drove out the spirits with a word and healed all the sick. ¹⁷This was to fulfill what was spoken through the prophet Isaiah:
>
> > "He took up our infirmities
> > and carried our diseases."

16 Because the context is still the Sabbath in Mark 1:32–34; Luke 4:40–41, mention of the evening there suggests that the people waited till Sabbath was over at sundown before again flocking to Jesus with their sick. Here in Matthew, where there is no indication this is a Sabbath, mention of the evening simply shows the pace of Jesus' ministry (cf. also other summaries—4:23–24; 9:35; 11:4–5; 12:15; 14:35; 15:30; 19:2).

With the exception of the quotation from Isaiah 53 (v.17), most of Matthew's other changes are not very significant. The addition of "a word" is neither typical (vv.3, 8) nor atypical (v.15) of Matthew's healing reports. The change from "many" (Mark) to "all" (Matthew) is less significant than is often claimed, for Mark does not say Jesus healed many but not all the sick; rather, when "the whole town gathered at the door," he healed "many" of the people (Mark 1:33–34). Matthew does not say that Jesus forbade the demons to tell who he was; he prefers to focus attention on Jesus' power and on the Scripture witness to his person and ministry. Other differences are even more minor. (Omission of Luke 4:41 may tell against Kingsbury's view of the centrality of the "Son of God" theme.)

Jesus drives out *ta pneumata* ("the spirits" ["demons" in Mark and Luke]), often recognized in intertestamental literature as agents of disease. They are normally qualified by the adjective "evil" in the NT. On the idiom for "the sick," see on 4:24.

17 (On the fulfillment formulas, see on 1:23; 2:5, 15, 23; 4:14; Introduction, section 11.b.) This quotation is Isaiah 53:4. Matthew's rendering does not follow LXX or Targum, both of which spiritualize the Hebrew. Most likely v.17 is Matthew's own translation of the Hebrew (Stendahl, *School*, pp. 106f.). Because Isaiah 52:13–53:12, the fourth "Servant Song," pictures the Servant suffering vicariously for others, whereas, on the face of it, Matthew renders the Hebrew in such a way as to speak of "taking" and "carrying" physical infirmities and physical diseases but not in terms of suffering vicariously for sin, many detect in this passage strong evidence that Matthew cites the OT in an indefensible and idiosyncratic fashion. McConnell (p. 120) sees this as another instance of Matthew's using an OT passage out of context for his own ends (cf. also Rothfuchs, pp. 70–72). McNeile suggests Isaiah 53:4 had already become detached from its context when Matthew used it.

There are, however, better ways of interpreting this passage:

1. It is generally understood since the work of C.H. Dodd (*According to the Scriptures* [London: Nisbet, 1952]) that when the NT quotes a brief OT passage, it often refers implicitly to the entire context of the quotation. This is very likely here, for Matthew has a profound understanding of the OT. Moreover, Isaiah 53:7 is probably alluded to in Matthew 27:12, Isaiah 53:9 in Matthew 27:57, and Isaiah 53:10–12 in Matthew 20:28, the latter in a context affirming vicarious atonement theology. Any interpretation of v.17 that does not take into account the thrust of the entire Servant Song is therefore dubious.

2. Both Scripture and Jewish tradition understand that all sickness is caused, directly or indirectly, by sin (see on 4:24; cf. Gundry, *Use of OT*, pp. 230f.). This encourages us to look for a deeper connection between v.17 and Isaiah 53:4.

3. Isaiah is thinking of the servant's "taking the diseases of others upon himself through his suffering and death for their sin" (Gundry, *Use of OT*, p. 230). The two verbs he uses are *nāśā'* ("took up [our infirmities]") and *sebālām* ("carried [our sorrows]"), which do not themselves necessarily have the force of substitution, though they can be interpreted that way. The LXX spiritualizes "infirmities" to "sins"; and in this sense the verse is referred to in 1 Peter 2:24 in defense of substitutionary atonement. That interpretation of the verse is legitimate because the flow of the Servant Song supports it. But strictly speaking Isaiah 53:4 simply speaks of the Servant's bearing infirmities and carrying sicknesses; and it is only the context, plus the connection between sickness and sin, that shows that the *way* he bears the sickness of others is through his suffering and death.

4. Isaiah 53, as we have seen, is important among NT writers for understanding the significance of Jesus' death (e.g., Acts 8:32–33; 1 Peter 2:24); but when Matthew here cites Isaiah 53:4, at first glance he applies it only to Jesus' healing ministry, not to his death. But in the light of the three preceding points, the discrepancy is resolved if Matthew holds that *Jesus' healing ministry is itself a function of his substitutionary death*, by which he lays the foundation for destroying sickness. Matthew's two verbs, contrary to some opinion, exactly render the Hebrew: the Servant "took up" (*elaben*) our infirmities and "carried" (*ebastasen*) our diseases (Gundry,

Use of OT, pp. 109, 111). Matthew could not have used the LXX and still referred to physical disease. Yet his own rendering of the Hebrew, far from wrenching Isaiah 53:4 out of context, indicates his profound grasp of the theological connection between Jesus' healing ministry and the Cross.

5. That connection is supported by various collateral arguments. The prologue insists Jesus came to save his people from their sin, and this within the context of the coming of the kingdom. When Jesus began his ministry, he not only proclaimed the kingdom but healed the sick (see on 4:24). Healing and forgiveness are tied together, not only in a pericope like 9:1–8, but by the fact that the consummated kingdom, in which there is no sickness, is made possible by Jesus' death and the new covenant that his death enacted (26:27–29). Thus the healings during Jesus' ministry can be understood not only as the foretaste of the kingdom but also as the fruit of Jesus' death. It could be that Matthew also judges Isaiah 53:4 appropriate because it seems to form a transition from the Servant's being despised to his suffering and death. Certainly at least some rabbinic tradition understood Isaiah 53:4 to refer to physical disease (cf. SBK, 1:481–82).

6. This means that for Matthew, Jesus' healing miracles pointed beyond themselves to the Cross. In this he is like the evangelist John, whose "signs" similarly point beyond themselves.

7. But even here there is a deeper connection than first meets the eye. These miracles (ch. 8) have been framed to emphasize Jesus' authority. This authority was never used to satisfy himself (cf. 4:1–10). He healed the despised leper (vv.1–4), a Gentile centurion's servant who was hopelessly ill (vv.5–13), other sick (vv.14–15), no matter how many (vv.16–17). Thus when he gave his life a ransom for many (20:28), it was nothing less than an extension of the same authority directed toward the good of others (cf. Hill, "Son and Servant," pp. 9, 11, who also points out how reductionistic Kingsbury's "Son of God" christology is in light of such intertwining themes). Jesus' death reflected the intermingling of authority and servanthood already noted (e.g., 3:17) and now progressively developed. After all, following the momentous miracles of vv.1–17, the Son of Man had nowhere to lay his head (v.20).

Despite the stupendous signs of kingdom advance, the royal King and Suffering Servant faced increasingly bitter opposition. The Father had committed everything to him, but he was gentle and humble in heart (11:27, 29). This moving theme needs to be traced out inductively (cf. B. Gerhardsson, "Gottes Sohn als Diener Gottes: Messias, *Agapē* und Himmelherrschaft nach dem Matthäus-evangelium," ST 27 [1973]: 73–106). If the Davidic Messiah of Jewish expectation (Pss Sol 17:6) purifies his people by annihilating sinners, Matthew's Davidic Messiah–Suffering Servant purifies his people with his death, takes on himself their diseases, and opens fellowship to sinners (cf. Hummel, pp. 124–25).

This discussion does not resolve two related questions.

1. Did Jews in Jesus' day understand Isaiah 53 messianically? Most scholars say no. Jeremias answers more cautiously—viz., many Jews did so interpret Isaiah's "Servant" but ignored references to his suffering (cf. Jeremias and Zimmerli).

2. Did Jesus interpret his own ministry in terms of the Suffering Servant? Matthew 8:17 does not help us because it gives us no more than Matthew's understanding of the significance of Jesus' healing miracles. (See further on 20:28; cf. Hooker, *Jesus and the Servant*; T.W. Manson, *The Servant Messiah* [Cambridge: University Press, 1953], pp. 57–58, 73.)

It should be stated that this discussion cannot be used to justify healing on demand. This text and others clearly teach that there is healing in the Atonement; but similarly there is the promise of a resurrection body in the Atonement, even if believers do not inherit it until the Parousia. From the perspective of the NT writers, the Cross is the basis for all the benefits that accrue to believers; but this does not mean that all such benefits can be secured at the present time on demand, any more than we have the right and power to demand our resurrection bodies. The availability of any specific blessing can be determined only by appealing to the overall teaching of Scripture. Modern Christians should avoid the principal danger of Corinth, viz., an over-realized eschatology (cf. A.C. Thistleton, "Realized Eschatology at Corinth," NTS 24 [1977]: 510–26), which demands blessings that may not be ours till the end of the age.

2. The cost of following Jesus

8:18–22

> 18When Jesus saw the crowd around him, he gave orders to cross to the other side of the lake. 19Then a teacher of the law came to him and said, "Teacher, I will follow you wherever you go."
> 20Jesus replied, "Foxes have holes and birds of the air have nests, but the Son of Man has no place to lay his head."
> 21Another disciple said to him, "Lord, first let me go and bury my father."
> 22But Jesus told him, "Follow me, and let the dead bury their own dead."

Compare Luke 9:57–62, in a later but detached setting, with three inquirers, not two. The stilling-of-the-storm incident (vv.23–27; Mark 4:35–41), following the "day of parables," shows that Matthew 8:18 parallels Mark 4:35. Matthew does not specify the time of this pericope (vv.18–22) beyond saying that it was one of many occasions when crowds pressed Jesus. Apparently Matthew chose to insert these two vignettes here because they help show the nature of Jesus' ministry and the disciples he was seeking. Hengel's attempt to limit to a few selected individuals Jesus' call to discipleship (M. Hengel, *Nachfolge und Charisma* [Berlin: Töpelmann, 1968], pp. 68–70) is insensitive to Jesus' place in the history of redemption and the ambiguity of what it meant at that time to be his disciple (see further, below).

18–19 Perhaps Jesus' imminent departure to the east side of the lake (v.18) prompted certain people to beg him to include them in the circle of disciples going with him. Discipleship in the strict sense required close attachment to the master's person. The fact that the first candidate was "a [*heis*, "one," can have the force of *tis*, "a certain," in NT Gr.: cf. Zerwick, par. 155; Moule, *Idiom Book*, p. 125] teacher of the law" (see on 2:4) has led to no little controversy; for it is often argued that the opponents in Matthew are Pharisees and scribes ("teachers of the law"), yet here a scribe appears as a candidate for discipleship. R. Walker (pp. 26–27) and others therefore say Jesus rejected this teacher of the law (v.19). By comparison with the next inquirer, he is neither called a disciple nor told to follow Jesus (vv.21–22). But this reasoning will not stand up.

1. "Disciple" does not necessarily refer to a fully committed follower and cannot have that force in v.21 (see on 5:1). Albright and Mann dislike this fact so much that they are reduced to emending the text. It is difficult to see why a wedge should be drawn between the two inquirers, both "disciples" in this loose sense.

2. Verse 21 does not say, "Another man, one of his disciples" (NIV), but, "Another of his disciples," implying that the teacher of the law was also a disciple in this loose sense. Moreover *heteros* ("another," sometimes "another of a different kind") cannot normally be distinguished in the NT from *allos* ("another," sometimes "another of the same kind"), and certainly not in Matthew (cf. BAGD, p. 315).

3. Judged by their respective approaches to Jesus, if either of the two approaches Jesus with no hesitation, it is the teacher of the law, not the "other disciple." Significantly, the scribe, a teacher of the law, addressed Jesus as "teacher" and simply promised to follow him anywhere.

4. In this light Jesus' response to the second man—"Follow me"—does not mean he is preferred but is necessary precisely because the inquirer was not at this time planning to follow Jesus.

Scholars who reject the reconstruction of Walker and others argue that Matthew, far from being opposed to teachers of the law, has positive things to say about them (v. 19; 13:52; 23:8–10, 34), some of which even suggest that Matthew's church had leaders who called themselves "teachers of the law" (cf. Grundmann; Hummel, p. 27; Kilpatrick, pp. 110ff.).

But this reverse argument is too strong. What other categories could Jesus have used for his church's future leaders than those already established (13:52; 23:34)? A great deal of the reconstructed Matthean church hangs by the thread of overdrawn exegesis. But they have correctly pointed out that vv. 19–20 and similar passages show that Matthew is not in principle antiscribe or anti-anyone else: rather, in Matthew's view, all people, scribes or not, divide around the absolute claims of Jesus and must be weighed according to their response to him (cf. van Tilborg, pp. 128–31). This is the fruit, not of anti-Semitism (see further on 26:57–68), but of claims to truth and, like other matters judged offensive by both Jews and Gentiles (1 Cor 1:21–23), cannot be eliminated without relativizing truth and him who is the truth.

20 Jesus' response shows that he identifies the scribe's request as less the commitment of an Ittai (2 Sam 15:21) than the overconfidence of a Peter (Luke 22:33). "Nothing has done more harm to Christianity than the practice of filling the ranks of Christ's army with every volunteer who is willing to make a little profession, and talk fluently of experience" (Ryle). "Nothing was less aimed at by our Lord than to have *followers*, unless they were genuine and sound; he is as far from desiring this as it would have been easy to attain it" (Stier, emphasis his). Jesus' reply says nothing about the inquirer's response. Strictly speaking it was neither invitation nor rebuke but a pointed way of saying that true discipleship to the "Son of Man" (see excursus, below) is not comfortable and should not be undertaken without counting the cost (cf. Luke 14:25–33). In the immediate context of Jesus' ministry, the saying does not mean that Jesus was penniless but homeless; the nature of his mission kept him on the move (cf. 4:23–25; 9:35–38) and would keep his followers on the move.

21–22 For the significance of the reference to "disciples," see on vv. 19–20. If the scribe was too quick in promising, this "disciple" was too slow in performing (v. 21). Palestinian piety, basing itself on the fifth commandment (Exod 20:12; cf. Deut 27:16), expected sons to attend to the burial of their parents (cf. Tobit 4:3; 14:10–11; M Berakoth 3:1; cf. Gen 25:9; 35:29; 50:13). Jesus' reply used paradoxical language (as in 16:25): Let the (spiritually) dead bury the (physically) dead (cf. Notes). Yet the response seems harsh to many interpreters; so they understand the inquirer to be requesting a delay to wait for an aged parent to die rather than a delay to bury a father who has died. Hebrew or Aramaic could mean that, Greek only with difficulty; and it is difficult to see how it makes Jesus' answer (v.22) more compassionate. Though in the OT certain people were not permitted to come in contact with corpses (Lev 21:1–12; Num 6:7), it is doubtful that Jesus saw his followers as priests or Nazirites needing special ceremonial safeguards (contra Trench, *Studies*, p. 169). More likely vv.21–22 are a powerful way of expressing the thought in 10:37—even closest family ties must not be set above allegiance to Jesus and the proclamation of the kingdom (Luke 9:60).

In actuality we may well question whether Jesus was really forbidding attendance at the father's funeral, any more than he was really advocating self-castration in 5:27–30. In this inquirer he detected insincerity, a qualified acceptance of Jesus' lordship. And that was not good enough. Commitment to Jesus must be without reservation. Such is the importance Jesus himself attached to his own person and mission.

Excursus: "The Son of Man" as a christological title

During the last twenty-five years, more than a dozen books and scores of important articles on the Son of Man have appeared. This excursus on the Son of Man as a christological title will provide some of the evidence and its interpretation in the recent debate and will sketch in the approach adopted for the commentary. Good summaries of earlier treatments are found in the work of A.J.B. Higgins (*Jesus and the Son of Man* [London: Lutterworth, 1964]), J. Neville Birdsall ("Who Is This Son of Man?" EQ 42 [1970]: 7–17), and I. Howard Marshall ("The Son of Man in Contemporary Debate," EQ 42 [1970]: 67–87). More recent treatments of the term and its major theological implications may be found in the works and bibliographies of C. Colpe (TDNT, 8:400–477), C.F.D. Moule (*Christology*, pp. 11–22), I. Howard Marshall (*The Origins of Christology* [Downers Grove, Ill.: IVP, 1976], pp. 63–82), the essays edited by R. Pesch and R. Schnackenburg (*Jesus und der Menschensohn* [Freiburg: Herder, 1975]), Goppelt (*NT Theologie*, pp. 226–53), Ladd (*NT Theology*, pp. 145–58), Dunn (*Christology*, pp. 65–97), Guthrie (*NT Theology*, pp. 270–82), Matthew Black ("Jesus and the Son of Man," *Journal for the Study of the New Testament* 1 [1978]: 4–18), and Stanton (*Jesus of Nazareth*, pp. 156ff.). To this can be added the recent work by Maurice Casey and that of A.J.B. Higgins (*The Son of Man in the Teaching of Jesus* [Cambridge: University Press, 1980]).

The expression Son of Man occurs eighty-one times in the Gospels, sixty-nine in the Synoptics. In every instance it is found either on Jesus' lips or, in two instances, on the lips of those quoting Jesus (viz., Luke 24:7; John 12:34). Outside the Gospels it is found in the NT as a christological title only in Acts 7:56; Revelation 1:13; 14:14 (Heb 2:6–8 is not relevant). The Gospel occurrences are usually classified according to the themes associated with the title: (1) the apocalyptic Son of Man who comes at the end of the age; (2) the suffering and dying Son of Man; and (3) the earthly Son of Man, engaged in a number of present ministries (in this context the title many serve as a circumlocution for "I"). Ladd (*NT Theology*, pp. 149–51) offers a typical breakdown of all the passages. There is some overlap of these categories and room for differences of interpretation. But of the thirty occurrences of "Son of Man" in Matthew, approximately thirteen belong to the first category (13:41; 16:27; 19:28; 24:27, 30 [bis], 37, 44; 25:31; 26:64; probably 24:39; and possibly 10:23; 16:28), ten to the second (12:40; 17:9, 12, 22; 20:18, 28; 26:2, 24 [bis], 45), and seven to the third (8:20; 9:6; 11:19; 12:8, 32; 13:37; probably 16:13; cf. also the variant at 18:11).

The meaning of any term or title depends at least in part on the way it has been used before. Much of the debate surrounding the precise significance of "Son of Man" in the Gospels turns on the influence ascribed to one or the other of the following backgrounds.

1. Daniel 7:13–14 pictures "one like a son of man" who approaches the Ancient of Days and is given "authority, glory and sovereign power" and "an everlasting dominion that will not pass away" in which "all peoples, nations and men of every language" worship him.

2. In Psalm 8:4 it is used generically for man.

3. In Ezekiel it appears repeatedly in the vocative as God's favorite way of addressing the prophet.

4. Psalm 80:17 places "son of man" in the context of vine imagery in such a way that it clearly refers to the nation Israel.

5. In 1QapGen 21:13 it appears as a Semitism for man generically ("I will make your descendants as the dust of the earth, which no son of man can number"). According to Vermes, "son of man" or "the son of man" in Aramaic was used in Jesus' day to refer generically to man or as a circumlocution by which a speaker might refer to himself (cf. G. Vermes in Black, *Aramaic Approach*, Appendix E; id., "The 'Son of Man' Debate," *Journal for the Study of the New Testament* [1978]: 19–32). But some of his claims must be tempered by the more sober dating and philology of Joseph A. Fitzmyer ("Another View of the 'Son of Man' Debate," *Journal for the Study of the New Testament* 4 [1979]: 58–68).

6. Many detect a background in the Similitudes of Enoch (1 Enoch 37–71) or other apocalyptic literature. Some have raised grave doubts that such literature is pre-Christian, based largely on the fact that the Similitudes are not found in the DSS copy of 1 Enoch; and if they are right, clearly the use of "Son of Man" in 1 Enoch 37–71 cannot have influenced Jesus' use of the term (cf. Longenecker, *Christology*, pp. 82–88; Dunn, *Christology*, pp. 67–82). The consensus among specialists of 1 Enoch, however, is that the Similitudes were in fact written before Christ's ministry, but that the "Son of Man" in these writings unambiguously refers to Enoch. The famous but unsupported emendation by R. H. Charles ("This is the Son of Man who was born unto Righteousness," 1 Enoch 71:14) is without warrant: the text reads "Thou, O Enoch, art the Son of Man" (cf. further James H. Charlesworth, *The Pseudepigrapha and the New Testament* [Cambridge: University Press, forthcoming]). We thus reach an ironic conclusion: the similitudes are pre-Christian and therefore must be considered a possible influence on Jesus' usage of "the Son of Man"; but they narrowly identify the figure with Enoch, and so whatever influence they exercised cannot be more than that of model or pattern, if that.

Against such diverse backgrounds, then, how are we to understand "the Son of Man" in the NT? Numerous proposals have been made, many of which fail to explain the evidence. The following are the most important.

1. Bultmann (*NT Theology*, 1:29–31, 49) made popular the view, later espoused by P. Vielhauer, H. Conzelmann, and H.M. Teeple, that Jesus never used the title "Son of Man" of himself but only of another figure coming in the future; and this future figure was based in Jesus' mind on the apocalyptic redeemer figure in 1 Enoch. This idea has been developed by other scholars who say that Jesus originally justified his authority by referring to a future apocalyptic figure who would come and vindicate him but that the church connected that

figure with Jesus himself. This will not do, for even if the Similitudes are not a late addition to 1 Enoch, the "Son of Man" figure there *may* not be an apocalyptic figure (cf. Casey, pp. 99–112) and in any case refers primarily to Enoch. Moreover the NT evidence connects Jesus with the Son of Man (e.g., Mark 14:62 and parallels); and, more important yet, any interpretation is called in question that flies in the face of the fact that the Gospel writers never use the term to describe Jesus but always report it as being on Jesus' lips. On the face of it, this shows that it was Jesus' favorite self-designation and that the early church respected this, even when it did not always know what to make of it (cf. further Jeremias, *NT Theology*, pp. 267f.).

2. Jeremias (*NT Theology*, pp. 257–76) has argued that some of the Son-of-Man sayings in all three classifications are authentic; but where in synoptic parallels one Gospel includes the reference to the Son of Man and another omits it (e.g., Matt 24:39–Luke 17:27; Matt 10:32–Luke 12:8), the latter is authentic. On the last point, some have argued just the reverse (e.g., F.H. Borsch, *The Son of Man in Myth and History* [London: SCM, 1967]). The weakness of Jeremias's view lies primarily in the consistency with which the expression occurs on Jesus' lips alone: if evangelists were adding the title to displace "I," it is at least strange they never use the title to refer to Jesus in contexts where there is no synoptic parallel. Here it seems best to side with Borsch, though we cannot be sure. Moreover Jeremias's chosen background runs from Daniel 7:13–14 in a straight line through the Similitudes of Enoch to the NT. Thus he depends on an established apocalyptic Son-of-Man figure that the sources do not support.

3. By appealing to Aramaic background, Vermes (Black, *Aramaic Approach*, Appendix E) argues that only those passages are authentic in which "Son of Man" is no more than a circumlocution for "I," by which the speaker refers to himself obliquely out of modesty or humility; the other uses in the Gospels are the creation of an apocalyptically minded church. Somewhat similar stances are adopted by Casey, who deems authentic the sayings that refer to mankind generally, and Barnabas Lindars ("Jesus as Advocate: A Contribution to the Christology Debate," BJRL 62 [1980]: 476–97; id., "The New Look on the Son of Man," BJRL 63 [1981]: 437–62), who argues that the use of the article (*ho*) in Greek, making the expression *"that* Son of Man" or "the [known] Son of Man" or "the [expected] Son of Man," shows that it was the translation of the tradition from Aramaic to Greek that gave messianic or Danielic meaning to the term. Therefore usages reflecting such meaning cannot be authentic. Quite apart from problems surrounding the dating of the linguistic evidence (cf. Fitzmyer, above), this theory postulates a creative church and a comparatively dull Jesus even though the evangelists consistently restrict the creative use of "Son of Man" to Jesus. The more it is argued that the church exercised a creative role in the theological development of this title, the stranger it is that the evangelists themselves do not apply the term to Jesus.

4. In his most recent book (*Son of Man*), Higgins reiterates and polishes his thesis that the "kernel" (i.e., authentic) sayings are all from Q and refer without exception to some of the future activities of the Son of Man, but not to his "coming" or "coming in glory," based on the "reasonable assumption of the existence of a Son of man concept in Judaism" (p. 124), and on a strange appeal to multiple attestation even though all his "kernel" sayings originally spring from Q (p. 125). Higgins says Jesus does not so much identify himself as the Son of Man (counterevidence, such as Mark 14:62, he ascribes to the church) as confine the term "to Jesus' clothing of his message of his anticipated judicial function in the judgment in symbolic imagery" (ibid.). The theory therefore falls under the strictures raised against 1 and 2.

5. C.F.D. Moule ("Neglected Features in the Problem of 'the Son of Man,'" in Gnilka, *Neues Testament*, pp. 413ff.; id., *Christology*, pp. 11–22), in contrast to Vermes, insists that the definite article (used everywhere except John 5:27) proves the designation to be titular, and thus whatever Semitic construction lay behind it, it must have referred to a particular, known "Son of Man." The only candidate is the figure in Daniel 7:13–14, possibly expounded in Judaism. This figure was understood to refer in a corporate way to "the saints of the Most High" (Dan 7:18); and, applied to Jesus, the title simultaneously affirms that he represents those saints and is a part of them. "Son of Man" is less a title than "a symbol of a vocation to be utterly loyal, even to death, in the confidence of ultimate vindication in the heavenly court. . . . Jesus is thus referring to the authority (whether in heaven or on earth) of true Israel, and so, of authentic Man, obedient, through thick and thin, to God's design" (*Christology*, p. 14).

Despite attractive features of this reconstruction, some reservations must be voiced. There appears to be more titular (indeed, messianic) force in some passages than Moule allows (e.g., Matt 16:13–20; 26:63–64); yet ironically he may be overemphasizing the significance of the definite article, since there is evidence in the Gospels that the people of Jesus' day did not always understand the designation to refer to the "well-known" Son of Man (e.g., Matt 16:13–30; John 12:34).

The best explanation attempts to avoid the reductionism that is implicit in most of the previous approaches, which too quickly rules out certain kinds of evidence or takes them as late creations of the church. Apart from the fact that in the Gospels "Son of Man" is always found on Jesus' lips, the authenticity of the Son-of-Man sayings sums up well under the criteria of redaction criticism (R.N. Longenecker, "'Son of Man' Imagery," JETS 18 [1975]:8–9).

But what did Jesus mean by the expression? The simplest answer is that he used the term precisely because it was ambiguous: it could conceal as well as reveal (cf. E. Schweizer, "The Son of Man," JBL 79 [1960]: 128; Longenecker, "'Son of Man' Imagery," pp. 10–12; Hendriksen; Marshall, *Origins*, pp. 76–78). When Jesus vested the term with its full messianic significance, it could only refer to Daniel 7:13–14. He did this most often toward the end of his ministry, when alone with his disciples and talking about eschatological events (esp. 24:27, 30 and parallels), or when under oath at his trial (26:63–64). Despite the fact that the Danielic figure is often said to be a symbol for the saints of the Most High (Dan 7:18), this is not certain. A good case can be made for the hypothesis that "one like a son of man" is not a symbol for the saints (7:18, 27). *He* is in the presence of the Ancient of Days; *they* are on earth during the time of the "little horn" (v.21). Perhaps "one like a son of man" secures the everlasting kingdom for the saints of the Most High (cf. W.J. Dumbrell, "Daniel 7 and the Function of Old Testament Apocalyptic," *Reformed Theological Review* 34 [1975]: 16ff.; and esp. Christopher Rowland, "The Influence of the First Chapter of Ezekiel on Jewish and Early Christian Literature," [Ph.D. dissertation, Cambridge University, 1974], p. 95). One "like a son of man" is a representative figure, not a corporate one; and the use of the symbol of the cloud rider favors a personal rather than a corporate interpretation.

Be that as it may, the messianic import of the title in some NT passages can scarcely be doubted. But Daniel 7:13–14 did not wield such large influence on first-century Judaism that simple reference to "the Son of Man," even with the article, would be instantly taken to refer to the Messiah. John Bowker ("The Son of Man," JTS 28 [1977]: 19–48) has decisively shown how many Semitic passages —in Ezekiel, Psalm 8, the Targums—use the term to contrast the chasm between frail, mortal man and God himself. This admirably suits a host of NT references, not only the suffering and passion texts, but others like Matthew

8:20. Jesus combined the two, Danielic Messiah and frail mortal, precisely because his own understanding of messiahship was laced with both themes.

We have already detected in Matthew the intermingling of Davidic Messiah and Suffering Servant. While "Son of Man" captures both authority and suffering, it is ambiguous enough that people who did not think of the Messiah in this dual way would have been mystified till after the Cross. It may well have been an acceptable way for a speaker to refer to himself, in which case the titular usage could only have been discerned from the context. Moreover it would have been extremely difficult for Jews expecting a purely political and glorious Messiah to know what the title meant, because just when they thought they had discerned its messianic significance, Jesus inserted something about the Son of Man's sufferings. That explains the perplexed question, "Who is this 'Son of Man'?" (John 12:34; cf. Luke 22:69–70). Even the disciples who had at some level begun to recognize Jesus the Son of Man as Messiah (Matt 16:13–16) could not accept or comprehend Jesus' repeated assertions that the Son of Man was destined to suffer and die (Matt 16:21–23; 17:9–12, 22, and parallels). Only when under oath and when it no longer mattered whether his enemies heard his clear claim to messiahship did Jesus reveal without any ambiguity at all that he, the Son of Man, was the messianic figure of Daniel 7:13–14 (Matt 26:63–64 and parallels); and then his opponents did not realize that an essential part of his messiahship was suffering and death. In Jesus' ministry "Son of Man" both reveals and conceals. Therefore he chose it as the ideal expression for progressively, and to some extent retrospectively, revealing the nature of his person and work.

After the Passion, Jesus' disciples could not help but find in his frequent earlier use of the term a messianic claim. Indeed, it is a mark of their fidelity to the separate historical stages of the unfolding history of redemption that in describing Jesus' prepassion ministry they confine the designation to the lips of Jesus alone. Thus no reader of Matthew who through the prologue knows that Jesus though a man is more than a man and through 16:13–20; 26:63–64 knows that the Son of Man is the Messiah could fail to see irony in 9:1–8. Jesus forgives sins and performs a miracle so that the onlookers may know that the "Son of Man" has authority on earth to forgive sins; but the people praise God because he has given such authority "to men." They are right (Jesus, the Son of Man, is mortal, a man born of woman, and heading for suffering and death), and they are wrong (they do not yet recognize him as more than a man, virgin born, and the messianic figure who appeared "as a son of man"—i.e., in human form—in one of Daniel's visions). So the interpretation that prevailed from the second century on—that "Son of Man" designates Jesus' humanity and "Son of God" his divinity —is not so much wrong as simplistic.

In Matthew 8:20, "the Son of Man" could easily be replaced by "I." Moreover it occurs in a setting that stresses Jesus' humanity and may foreshadow his sufferings. For postpassion Christian readers, it could only speak of the Messiah's wonderful self-humiliation. For the teacher of the law (vv. 18–19), it was a great challenge—just how great a one could only be known after the Resurrection.

Notes

22 Black (*Aramaic Approach*, pp. 207–8) suggests that the original Aramaic may have read, "Let the מְתַנְיִין [*mᵉṭiniyn*, 'waverers'] bury their מִיתִיהוּן [*mitihûn*, 'dead']"—and the first of the two Aramaic words has been mistakenly translated as if it were from מִיתִין (*mîṯîn*,

"corpses"). But like many of Black's suggestions, though philologically plausible, these hardly help explain the text and are hampered by the implausible thesis that Matthew (or some unknown person in the process of the oral tradition) was rather incompetent in Hebrew and Aramaic.

---

3. Calming a storm

8:23–27

23Then he got into the boat and his disciples followed him. 24Without warning, a furious storm came up on the lake, so that the waves swept over the boat. But Jesus was sleeping. 25The disciples went and woke him, saying, "Lord, save us! We're going to drown!"

26He replied, "You of little faith, why are you so afraid?" Then he got up and rebuked the winds and the waves, and it was completely calm.

27The men were amazed and asked, "What kind of man is this? Even the winds and the waves obey him!"

Jesus' authority over nature is now displayed. He may have less shelter than the beasts and birds of nature (v.20); yet he is nature's master (cf. parallels in Mark 4:35–41; Luke 8:22–25). Cope's attempt (*Matthew*, pp. 96–98) to argue that the pericope, at a pre-Matthean level, has been structured on Jonah is far from convincing. His parallels are either painfully forced ("a miraculous stilling related to the main character") or so general that it is difficult to conceive of any miraculous stilling-of-the-sea story that would not fit in his list of parallels.

23–25 The narrative moves forward from v.18; the order to cross the lake to escape the crowd is now carried out. A *ploion* ("boat") was a vessel of almost any size and description (v.23). Here it is doubtless a fishing boat, big enough for a dozen or more men and a good catch of fish, but not large, and without sails.

Bornkamm's insight—viz., that this pericope faces Matthew's readers with the demand for greater faith (v.26) in a setting requiring total discipleship (vv.18–22; cf. Bornkamm, *Tradition*, pp. 52–57)—has been distorted to make discipleship the exclusive concern. Because the disciples "followed" Jesus into the boat, Matthew, it is alleged (e.g., Bonnard, Hill), is using a characteristic theme, almost a technical term, to describe discipleship: those who follow Jesus need not fear, for they will be safe in any storm. But in Matthew *akoloutheō* ("to follow"), though it can refer to true followers (e.g., 4:20, 22; 9:9), often describes the action of the crowd as opposed to the disciples (e.g., 4:25; 8:1, 10; 12:15). When someone is physically following another, it is risky to invest the term with deep notions of discipleship; in 9:19 Jesus and his disciples "follow" (Gr.) the ruler but were certainly not his disciples! And if "follow" is so crucial a category for Matthew, why in 8:28–34 does he omit the parallel reference to following Jesus (Mark 5:18–20)?

Tertullian (*De Baptismo* 12) saw in the boat a picture of the church. Therefore some conclude that the storm "is a threat to the boat, rather than to the disciples" because it stands for the church, "and, in particular, the Church facing the upheaval of persecution (perhaps under Domitian, A.D. 81–96)" (Hill, *Mathew*; cf. Bonnard). But aside from the anachronistic nature of this appeal to Domitian, it is historically very doubtful whether there was widespread persecution under his reign (cf. John

Sweet, *Revelation* [London: SCM, 1979], esp. pp. 25-27). And is Matthew's story greatly helped by seeing danger for the boat but not the disciples? One wonders what would happen to them if the boat were destroyed.

While Matthew may have seen some kind of valid application of the principles in this pericope to his own situation, the story was for him primarily a miracle story with christological implications (see on vv.26-27). Some redaction critics, in their desire to interpret the Gospels exclusively in terms of reconstructed church life-settings instead of hearing the church's thoughtful witness to the historical Jesus, come close to undisciplined allegorizing.

It is well known that violent squalls (the term *seismos* can refer to an earthquake or a sea storm) develop quickly on Lake Galilee (v.24). The surface is more than six hundred feet below sea level, and the rapidly rising hot air draws from the south-eastern tablelands violent winds whose cold air churns up the water. Those among Jesus' contemporaries who really knew the OT would remember that in it God is presented as the one who controls and stills the seas (cf. Job 38:8-11; Pss 29:3-4, 10-11; 65:5-7; 89:9; 107:23-32).

The form of the cry, *Kyrie, sōson* (lit., "Lord, save!" v.25), is often thought to reflect liturgical influence (cf. Mark 4:38; Luke 8:24). But it is doubtful that the disciples all used the same words; and the verbal differences among the Synoptics may reflect, not theological motivation, but historical recollection of various cries (esp. if Matthew was present). This event almost certainly occurs later chronologically than Matthew's call (9:9-13; cf. Luke 5:27-32). The words of later liturgy took on this form. Yet we know almost nothing about first-century liturgy, and it is more likely that the Bible influenced the shape of liturgy than vice versa. Significantly, later textual tradition adds "us" (cf. Metzger, *Textual Commentary*, p. 22). The verb *akoloutheō* ("follow") does not require a direct object, though it is difficult to see why "us" should have been eliminated if it had been there originally. The later liturgical form prefers to abandon the "us." If that form was not strong enough to control the textual tradition, is it likely that it was strong enough (let alone early enough) to control the shape of the cry in the transfer from Mark to Matthew?

26-27 "He does not chide them for disturbing him with their prayers, but for disturbing themselves with their fears" (Matthew Henry). The word *oligopistoi* ("you of little faith," v.26) occurs five times in the NT (6:30; here; 14:31; 16:8; Luke 12:28; cf. the cognate noun at Matt 17:20) and always with reference to disciples. Lack of faith among those for whom faith must be central is especially disappointing. Mark (4:40) has "Do you still have no faith?" and Matthew's "little faith" is therefore taken by many as a conscious toning down of the rebuke, perhaps because he cannot envisage discipleship apart from *some* faith (Gundry, *Matthew*). But there are reasons for thinking this conclusion is somewhat hasty.

1. It may be pushing Mark's question too hard to understand it as meaning that the disciples were utterly without faith. An exasperated preacher might well berate those he regards as believing disciples with words like those in Mark precisely because he believes their conduct in the face of some crisis belies their profession of faith. The large change in meaning ascribed to Matthew may therefore rest on too pedantic an understanding of Mark. This is confirmed by Mark's not developing the notion of "disciples" who have no faith.

2. *Both* Matthew (17:17) *and* Mark (9:19) preserve sayings about the unbelieving generation that must in context be applied to Jesus' disciples.

3. The word *oligopistoi* ("you of little faith") probably does not refer merely to quantity of faith but to its poor quality (see on 17:20). If so, Matthew may be credited with a little more theological precision than Mark but scarcely a radically new meaning. The change from a question (Mark) to the one word epithet *oligopistoi* (Matthew) is quite within the range of reportage in the Gospels. What Jesus' exact words were, we cannot know; nor can we be certain that Matthew's only access to the event was Mark's report.

4. If Matthew were so eager to insist that true discipleship involves *some* faith and changes Mark's expression for this reason, it is strange that he would insert a verse like 17:20 (contrast Mark 9:29). It is more likely that Matthew favors *oligopistoi* as part of his working vocabulary, but without heavy, theological implications; the demonstrable redactional tendencies of an author do not necessarily bear on questions of authenticity (cf. Introduction, section 2).

5. What is clear is that both Mark and Matthew set faith over against fear. Faith chases out fear, or fear chases out faith.

That the disciples could cry to Jesus for help reveals that they believed, or hoped, he could do something. More than others they had witnessed his miracles and apparently believed he could rescue them. Jesus' rebuke is therefore not against skepticism of his ability, nor against the fear that the disciples like others might drown. Rather they failed to see that the one so obviously raised up by God to accomplish the messianic work could not possibly have died in a storm while that work remained undone. They lacked faith, not so much in his ability to save them, as in Jesus as Messiah, whose life could not be lost in a storm, as if the elements were out of control and Jesus himself the pawn of chance. This aspect of their unbelief is hinted at in Mark and Luke; in Matthew it is rendered more explicit with the disciples' cry to save them, for here they cannot be thought to be awakening Jesus because of pique at his still being asleep. Jesus' sleep stems not only from his exhaustion (see on v.16) or from the Son of Man having nowhere to lay his head (v.20) but from his confidence that, to use John's language, his hour had not yet come.

The disciples' response to the miracle (v.27) does not weaken this interpretation, as if their surprise shows they were not expecting Jesus to intervene. Just as a crowd expects a magician to do his trick, yet marvels when it is done, so the disciples turn to Jesus for help, yet are amazed when he stills the storm so that there is complete calm. What kind of man is this? Readers of this Gospel know the answer—he is the virgin-born Messiah who has come to redeem his people from their sins and whose mission is to fulfill God's redemptive purposes. But the disciples did not yet understand these things. They saw that his authority extended over nature and were thus helped in their faith. Yet they did not grasp the profundity of his rebuke. Indeed, wherever *oligopistos* is used in Matthew, a root cause of the "little faith" is the failure to see beyond the mere surface of things. Thus the pericope is deeply christological: themes of faith and discipleship are of secondary importance and point to the "kind of man" (cf. BDF, par. 298[3]) Jesus is.

It may also be that Matthew is again juxtaposing Jesus with man's limitations and Jesus with God's authority, a device he so effectively uses in this Gospel. As Jesus is tempted but rebukes Satan (4:1–11), as he is called the devil but casts out demons (12:22–32); so he sleeps from weariness but muzzles nature (see further at 4:2).

4. *Further demonstration of Jesus' authority* (8:28–9:8)

a. *Exorcising two men*

8:28–34

> 28When he arrived at the other side in the region of the Gadarenes, two demon-possessed men coming from the tombs met him. They were so violent that no one could pass that way. 29"What do you want with us, Son of God?" they shouted. "Have you come here to torture us before the appointed time?"
>
> 30Some distance from them a large herd of pigs was feeding. 31The demons begged Jesus, "If you drive us out, send us into the herd of pigs."
>
> 32He said to them, "Go!" So they came out and went into the pigs, and the whole herd rushed down the steep bank into the lake and died in the water. 33Those tending the pigs ran off, went into the town and reported all this, including what had happened to the demon-possessed men. 34Then the whole town went out to meet Jesus. And when they saw him, they pleaded with him to leave their region.

All three synoptists (cf. Mark 5:1–20; Luke 8:26–39) place this event after the boat landed, after the storm had been stilled. Matthew's account is much shorter than the other two; and he does not refer to "Legion," or to the desire of the liberated men to follow Jesus. The central motif, Jesus' authority over the evil spirits, is accented and only lightly interwoven with other themes.

28 The locale seems to have been in the district controlled by the town of Gadara, near the village of Gerasa (cf. Notes), which lay about midpoint on the lake's eastern shore. On the adjacent hillside are ancient tombs. Probably small antechambers or caves provided some protection from the weather; and a graveyard would, apparently, prove a congenial environment for demons and render the man ceremonially defiled. This region lay in the predominantly Gentile territory of the Decapolis (see on 4:25); the presence of the pigs (v.30), inconceivable in a Jewish milieu, points to its Gentile background. Jesus has withdrawn here, not for ministry, but to avoid the crowds (v.18). Yet there can be no rest as long as the hosts of darkness oppose him.

On differences between Jewish and NT views of demon possession, see Edersheim (LTJM, Appendix XVI; cf. SBK, 1:491–92). Matthew mentions two men; Mark and Luke only one. This pattern occurs elsewhere (20:30), making it very unlikely that Matthew changed the number because he saw an implication of more than one man in Mark's "Legion" (applied to the demons). It is even less likely that Matthew introduced the extra person to make up the legally acceptable minimum of two witnesses, since not only is the witness theme not found in either of the two Matthean pericopes (vv.28–34; 20:29–34), but here Matthew has eliminated the witness theme (cf. Mark 5:18–20). While the disciples could have served as witnesses, the best explanation is that Matthew had independent knowledge of the second man. Mention of only one by the other Gospel writers is not problematic. Not only was one sufficient for the purpose at hand, but where one person is more remarkable or prominent, it is not uncommon for the Gospels to mention only that one (cf. "I saw John Smith in town today. I hadn't seen him in years"—even though both John and Mary Smith were in fact seen).

The violence of these demoniacs is more fully described by Mark and Luke.

29 "While the men in the boat are doubting what manner of man this is, that even the winds and the sea obey him, the demons come to tell them" (Theophylact, cited in Broadus). They knew who Jesus was and yet remained demons; to know Jesus yet hate him is demonic. The question the demoniacs hurled at Jesus could be either harsh or gentle, depending on context (2 Sam 16:10; Mark 1:24; John 2:4). Here it is hateful and tinged with fear. The title "Son of God" is probably to be taken in its richest sense: Jesus was recognized, not solely in terms of his power but in terms of his person. He was the Messiah, God's Son (see on 3:17). Even if Jesus had already begun to confront them when they reacted so venomously (cf. Mark 5:7–8), there was nothing in Jesus' command in itself to betray his identity. We must suppose that the demons enjoyed some independent knowledge of Jesus' identity (cf. Acts 19:15; Ladd, *NT Theology*, p. 165).

The second question shows that there will be a time for demonic hosts to be tortured and rejected forever (cf. Jude 6; Rev 20:10; cf. 1 Enoch 16:1; Jub 10:8–9; T Levi 18:12; 1QS 3:24–25; 4:18–20). As the question is phrased, it recognizes that Jesus is the one who will discharge that judicial function at the "appointed time"; therefore it confirms the fullest meaning of "Son of God." That Jesus was in any sense circumscribing their activity before the appointed time (Matthew only) already shows that Jesus' casting out of demons was an eschatological function, a sign that the kingdom was dawning (cf. 12:28).

The significance of "here" is disputed. It can mean either (1) "here in this Gentile territory," reflecting "the difficulty of the Church's mission in those regions of Palestine" (Hill, *Matthew*)—but surely demon possession was not restricted to Gentile territory (cf. 10:5, 8; 12:22–24), and "the appointed time" makes little sense in such an interpretation—or (2) "here on earth, here where we have been given some freedom to trouble men before the end." This obvious sense of the text presupposes that Jesus has come to the earth before the End. It is difficult to avoid the conclusion that Jesus' preexistence is presupposed.

30–31 Mark (5:13) puts the number of the herd at two thousand and says it was "there." Matthew says it was "some distance from them" (v.30), the sort of detail an eyewitness might well remember. This detail also weakens the suggestion that the pigs stampeded because of the men's convulsions. J.D.M. Derrett's proposed reconstruction ("Legend and Event: The Gerasene Demoniac: An Inquest into History and Liturgical Projection," in Livingstone, 2:63–73), based on the Romans' sacrificing of pigs and on Jewish myths connecting Gentiles with bestiality, has no textual support. There are other reasons why the demons may have pled (v.31) to be sent into the herd of pigs: (1) desire for a bodily "home"; (2) hatred of God's creatures; (3) desire to stir up animosity against Jesus. The first does not seem likely because the first thing the demons do is precipitate the death of their new "home." The second and third are more plausible, because the Gospels elsewhere show that exorcized evil spirits sometimes expressed their rage by visible acts of violence or mischief (e.g., 17:14–20 = Mark 9:14–32; cf. Jos Antiq. VIII, 48[ii.5], often cited, but of doubtful relevance because the exorcist there commands the demon to manifest himself).

Gundry (*Matthew*) observes that the herd rushes down the slope but that in Matthew "they" (pl.) die; i.e., Matthew has transformed Mark to make the demons die. Thus Jesus "tortures" the demons "before the appointed time" by sending them to the torments of hell, and Matthew thus "deals in a bit of realized eschatology." This reconstruction is far from convincing.

1. There is no hint that the drowning of the pigs sends the demons to hell.

2. Mark also shifts from the singular—the herd rushing down the slope—to the plural—"were drowning." The only difference is that Matthew has omitted reference to the number "two thousand."

3. But if Matthew's plural verb cannot refer back to "two thousand," its most natural subject is the word "pigs," found in this same verse (32). The reason Matthew does not use a singular verb for died is because it would be awkward to speak of a herd's dying. Matthew has therefore preserved Mark's pattern—single verb followed by plural verb.

32–34 The question as to why Jesus would grant the demons their desire and let them destroy the herd of pigs (v.32), the livelihood of their owners, is part of larger questions as to why human beings are possessed or why disease, misfortune, or calamity overtake us—questions only to be answered within the context of a broad theodicy outside the scope of this commentary. But the context offers some hints. He who is master of nature (vv.23–27) is also its ultimate owner (vv.28–34; cf. Ps 50:10). The "appointed time" (v.29) for full destruction of the demons' power has not yet arrived. The pigs' stampede dramatically proved that the former demoniacs had indeed been freed (v.33). But in the light of vv.33–34, the loss of the herd became a way of exposing the real values of the people in the vicinity. They preferred pigs to persons, swine to the Savior.

This ending of the pericope bears significantly on its total meaning. If the story shows once more that Jesus' ministry was not restricted to the Jews but foreshadowed the mission to the Gentiles, it likewise shows that opposition to Jesus is not exclusively Jewish. To this extent it confirms earlier exegesis (see on 8:11–12) that showed that opponents in Matthew are not selected on the basis of race but according to their response to Jesus.

Notes

28 The textual evidence in all three synoptic Gospels, though highly complex, has been well summarized by Metzger (*Textual Commentary*, pp. 23–24). The three options are Gadara, Gerasa, and Gergesa. In Mark and Luke the textual evidence is strongest for Gerasa, probably in reference to a little village (modern Kersa or Koursi) on the eastern shore. However, there was a city of the Decapolis named Gerasa (modern Jerash) some thirty miles southeast of Galilee. Clearly that is geographically incompatible with v.32; so early copyists made emendations.

Gadara (modern Um Qeis), also a Decapolis city, was five miles southeast. Origen (*In Ioannes* 6.41) objected to both Gerasa (as commonly understood to refer to the city thirty miles off) and Gadara for similar reasons of distance. But Josephus (Life 42[9]) says Gadara had territory and villages on the border of the lake, and probably this included the little village of Gerasa. Indeed coins of Gadara sometimes display a ship (cf. HJP, 2:132–36). Gadara was thus the regional or toparchic capital (cf. Sherwin-White, p. 128, n. 3). The external evidence in Matthew favors Gadara: for some reason the name of the toparchic capital was preferred to Gerasa (which in Matthew enjoys only versional support).

Origen, rejecting Gerasa and Gadara, proposed Gergesa, but on entirely inadequate grounds, including doubtful etymology (cf. Metzger, above; Tj. Baarda, "Gadarenes, Gerasenes, Gergesenes, and the 'Diatessaron' Traditions," in Ellis and Wilcox, pp. 181–97). Gergesa could also be suggested by a very guttural "r" in Gerasa. Other variants doubtless resulted from later attempts at "correction" and from mutual assimilation (cf. further Lane, p. 181, n. 6, and Franz Annen, *Heil für die Heiden* [Frankfurt: Josef Knecht, 1976], pp. 201–4).

32 The phrase κατὰ τοῦ κρημνοῦ (*kata tou krēmnou*, "down the steep bank") is a very rare instance of this preposition plus genitive in a local sense and here means "down and over" (BDF, par. 225) or "down along" (Moule, *Idiom Book*, p. 60).

---

b. Healing a paralytic and forgiving his sins

9:1–8

[1]Jesus stepped into a boat, crossed over and came to his own town. [2]Some men brought to him a paralytic, lying on a mat. When Jesus saw their faith, he said to the paralytic, "Take heart, son; your sins are forgiven."

[3]At this, some of the teachers of the law said to themselves, "This fellow is blaspheming!"

[4]Knowing their thoughts, Jesus said, "Why do you entertain evil thoughts in your hearts? [5]Which is easier: to say, 'Your sins are forgiven,' or to say, 'Get up and walk'? [6]But so that you may know that the Son of Man has authority on earth to forgive sins...." Then he said to the paralytic, "Get up, take your mat and go home." [7]And the man got up and went home. [8]When the crowd saw this, they were filled with awe; and they praised God, who had given such authority to men.

Again Matthew's account is shortened (cf. Mark 2:2–12; Luke 5:17–26), the entrance through the roof having been eliminated. The interrelationships among the Synoptics in this pericope are complex. It has been shown, as Bo Reicke says, that the various narrative elements "cannot be derived from any source that did not include the essentials of the quotation elements represented by three gospels together" ("The Synoptic Reports on the Healing of the Paralytic: Matt. 9:1–8 with Parallels," in Elliott, p. 325; though it is doubtful that Reicke has disproved the two-source hypothesis, as he seems to think).

The shortened opening does not change this from a "miracle story" to a "controversial story" (contra Held, in Bornkamm, *Tradition,* pp. 176f.). Heil ("Healing Miracles," pp. 276–78) has shown that the form-critical marks of a miracle story are retained. Still less is this a miracle story into which a controversy about forgiving sin has been inserted, sparked by the church's attempt to tie its own forgiving function to Jesus' ministry (so Bultmann, *Synoptic Tradition,* pp. 14–16). The pericope is exclusively christological and has nothing to do with the disciples. Form-critical categories are handled mechanically if taken a priori to require that no controversy triggered by the way Jesus performed a healing *could* have been passed on! Moreover the close connections between sin and sickness (see on v. 17) and this extension of Jesus' authority beyond healing, nature, and the demonic realm to the forgiveness of sins make the narrative internally coherent and contextually suitable.

1 It is unclear whether this verse ties in more closely with 8:28–34 or with 9:2–8. The problem is not just academic, for the preceding pericope is almost certainly chronologically later (cf. Mark 5:1–20) than this one (cf. Mark 2:2–12); and a break more easily fits between 9:1 and 9:2 than between 8:34 and 9:1. Begged to leave (8:34), Jesus embarked in the boat he had so recently left and returned to "his own town," viz., Capernaum (4:13), on the western shore of the lake.

A larger problem concerning synoptic interrelationships now faces us. Matthew 9:14 and Luke 5:33 show that the questions about fasting sprang from the dinner Matthew sponsored. And 9:18 shows that the healing of Jairus's daughter and of the hemorrhaging woman immediately followed. Mark 5:21–23 and Luke 8:40–44 place the raising of Jairus's daughter after Jesus returned from Gadara (as in Matthew) but the healing of the paralytic (Mark 2:2–12; Luke 5:17–26) much earlier—even though Matthew places it after Gadara and seems to tie it to the pericopes that follow in his account.

Harmonization should be avoided where details are obscure, but refusal to attempt harmonization of documents treating the same events is methodologically irresponsible. Here a fairly straightforward solution is possible. There is a significant time lapse between Matthew's calling and the dinner he gives his friends. All three synoptists put these two personally related events side by side. But significantly no synoptist makes a temporal connection between the two. The following shows the arrangement.

| Time A: before Gadara | { healing of a paralytic
{ calling of Matthew
[TIME LAPSE: Gadara incident and others] | } All Synoptics put these two events together | } Mark and Luke place these three together at Time A | } Matthew places all four together at Time B |
| Time B: after Gadara | { dinner given by Matthew
{ raising of Jairus's daughter | | | |

Thus all the Synoptics put the raising of Jairus's daughter in the correct chronological order. Mark and Luke report the healing of the paralytic and the calling of Matthew at the earlier time, when they occurred, but then link to this Matthew's dinner—a topical arrangement. Matthew links all four together, placing them later, though there is a chronological break at vv. 1–2 (see above) and again between Matthew's call and Matthew's dinner. The first evangelist has introduced the first chronological break in order to preserve the topical arrangement of his presentation of Jesus' authority and the second break (vv. 9–10), along with Mark and Luke, because of the personal connection (Matthew's call and Matthew's dinner). This rather obvious solution is invalid only if Matthew's (and Luke's) sole source of information in this pericope is Mark. But despite some critics, this is most unlikely (cf. Introduction, sections 1–5).

2 Many (e.g., Weiss, Hill) insist that though in Mark and Luke the paralytic is lowered through a roof, here the imperfect *prosepheron* ("they were bringing," NASB) means the paralytic and his bearers met Jesus in the street. But the imperfect tense often adds color to action (cf. the imperfect even in Luke), and little is gained by manufacturing discrepancies.

Jesus "saw" *their* faith—presumably that of the paralytic and those carrying him— exemplified in their coming. But he spoke only to the paralytic. "Son" (*teknon*) is no more than an affectionate term from one's senior (cf. 1 John 2:1, 28 et al.). What Jesus went on to say implies a close link between sin and sickness (see on 8:17)— perhaps in this case a direct one (cf. John 5:14; 1 Cor 11:29–30). It implies that of the two, paralysis and sin, sin is the more basic problem. The best MSS read *aphientai* ("Your sins are forgiven"), not the perfect *apheōntai* ("Your sins have been forgiven"): see Notes. The latter might imply that the man's sins were forgiven at some time in the past and now remain forgiven.

3 Some teachers of the law (see on 2:4; 8:18–22) muttered among themselves that Jesus was blaspheming. It is God alone who forgives sin (Isa 43:25; 44:22), since it is against him only that men commit sin (Ps 51:4). The verb *blasphēmeō* often means "slander"; and when something is said that slanders God, the modern meaning of "blaspheme" is not far away. Though among Jews in Jesus' day the precise definition of blasphemy was hotly disputed (cf. SBK, 1:1019f.), the consensus seemed to be that using the divine name was an essential element. Here the teachers of the law, in their whispered consultation, expanded blasphemy to include Jesus' claim to do something only God could do.

4 Jesus had seen the faith of the paralytic and his friends; now he saw the evil thoughts of some of the teachers of the law (cf. Notes). Such discernment may have been supernatural, though not necessarily so. In this situation it would not have been difficult to surmise what the teachers of the law were whispering about. Jesus' charge probed beyond their talk of blasphemy to what they were thinking in their hearts. And what they were thinking was untrue, unbelieving, and blind to what was being revealed before their eyes.

5–7 Jesus did not respond to his opponents' thoughts according to the skeptical view—viz., that to say "your sins are forgiven" is easier to say than "Get up and walk" (v.5). On the contrary, he responded according to the perspective of the teachers of the law—viz., that to say "Get up and walk" is easier since only God can forgive sins. Jesus claimed to do the more difficult thing. Thus v.6 is ironical—"All right, I'll also do the lesser deed." Yet if Jesus had blasphemed in pronouncing forgiveness, how could he now perform a miracle (cf. John 9:31)? But so that they might know that he had authority to forgive sin, he proceeded to the easier task. The healing therefore showed that Jesus truly had authority to forgive sins. To do this is the prerogative of the "Son of Man." This expression goes beyond self-reference and, seen in the light of the postresurrection period, surely indicates that the eschatological Judge had already come "on earth" (cf. "here" in 8:29) with the authority to forgive sin (cf. Hooker, *Son of Man*, pp. 81–93). This is the authority of Emmanuel, "God with us" (1:23), sent to "save his people from their sins" (1:21). Jesus did not finish the sentence: the broken syntax (BDF, par. 483) is followed by Jesus' word of power and his command to the paralytic to go home (*hypage*, "go," is here gentle as in 8:13, not rough as in 4:10). To sum up, the healing not only cured the paralytic (v.7), it also assured him that his sins were forgiven and refuted the charge of blasphemy.

8 The external evidence for "were afraid" is early and in three text types (Alexandrian, Western, Caesarean). Copyists, failing to see the profundity of the verb, softened it to "were amazed." NIV's "were filled with awe" implies fear but is too paraphrastic. Men *should* fear the one who has the authority to forgive sins. Indeed, they should fear whenever they are confronted by an open manifestation of God (cf. 17:6; 28:5, 10). Such fear breeds praise.

Matthew alone adds the clause "who had given such authority to men." Many argue that "to men" refers to the church and cite 16:19; 18:18 in support (e.g., Benoit, Held, Hill, Hummel). But this is unlikely. If "Son of Man" (v.6) refers to the eschatological Judge, then it is unlikely that this function is to be shared with the church, at least in the same way (cf. Colpe, TDNT, 8:405). The pericope has christological, not ecclesiastical, concerns, compatible with the prologue (1:21, 23; see on vv.5–7). The onlookers simply saw a man exercising the authority of God, but readers recognize him as "God with us" and eschatological "Son of Man." God's gracious reign has come "on earth" (v.6); the kingdom of David's Son, who came to save his people from their sins, has dawned.

Notes

---

2 The reasons the perfect displaced the present in many MSS are clear enough: the present in Greek is often durative, which here makes little sense ("your sins are being forgiven"); and there is assimilation to Luke 5:20, where the text is firm (Mark 2:5 has a similar difficulty). In any case, the Greek present can have a punctiliar force (cf. Burton, *Syntax*, p. 9; Turner, *Syntax*, p. 64).

4 "Seeing their thoughts," not "knowing their thoughts," is almost certainly the correct reading, not least because the change from the former to the latter is comprehensible, but the reverse is highly unlikely. But "seeing" is obviously metaphorical, a point recognized by KJV and NIV in their periphrastic rendering "knowing."

---

5. *Calling Matthew*

9:9

> 9As Jesus went on from there, he saw a man named Matthew sitting at the tax collector's booth. "Follow me," he told him, and Matthew got up and followed him.

9 The locale is probably the outskirts of Capernaum. Matthew was sitting "at the tax collector's booth," a customs and excise booth at the border between the territories of Philip and Herod Antipas. On attitudes toward tax collectors, see on 5:46 (cf. also SBK, 1:377–80). Having demonstrated his authority to forgive sins (vv.1–8), Jesus now called to himself a man whose occupation made him a pariah—a sinner and an associate of sinners (cf. 1 Tim 1:15).

The name "Matthew" may derive from the Hebrew behind "Mattaniah" (1 Chron 9:15), meaning "gift of God," or, in another etymology, from a word meaning "the faithful" (Heb. 'emet). In Mark the name is "Levi" (though in Mark there are difficult textual variants), and the change to "Matthew" in the first Gospel has prompted much speculation. The most radical theory is that of R. Pesch ("Levi-Matthäus," ZNW 59 [1968]: 40–56), who says that the first evangelist purposely substituted a name from the apostolic band because he habitually uses "disciple" for the Twelve and therefore could not allow an outsider to stand. The evangelist then made a "sinner" out of him to represent the "sinners" among the apostles. "Matthew" in the first Gospel is thus reduced entirely to a redactional product. But

Pesch's understanding of "disciple" is questionable (see on 5:1–2; 8:18–22), and his skepticism is vast.

Since Jews not uncommonly had two or more names, the simple equation of Levi and Matthew is the most obvious course to take. Matthew may have been a Levite. Such a heritage would have assumed intimate acquaintance with Jewish tradition. Mark and Luke have "Matthew" in their lists of apostles (Mark 3:18; Luke 6:15; Pesch has to say Mark 3:18 is also redactional). See for another example of a prominent NT figure with two names the apostle Paul. Acts has both "Saul" and "Paul," but in his own writings Paul always refers to himself by the latter name.'So Mark and Luke use both "Levi" and "Matthew," but Matthew uses only the latter. (There is no evidence that either "Paul" or "Matthew" are Christian names, and the parallel is inexact because "Paul," unlike "Matthew," is a Gentile name.)

Gundry (*Use of OT*, pp. 181–83) suggests that Matthew's work as a tax collector assured his fluency in Aramaic and Greek and that his accuracy in keeping records fitted him for note taking and later writing his Gospel. Hill (*Matthew*), following Stendahl (Peake, p. 673j), thinks it unlikely that a person living on "the despised outskirts of Jewish life" could be responsible for this Gospel. But does it not also seem unlikely that "a son of thunder" should become the apostle of love, or that the arch-persecutor of the church should become its greatest missionary and theologian? If Matthew wrote 9:9 regarding his own call, it is significant that it is more self-deprecating than Luke's account, which says that Matthew "left everything" and followed Jesus.

6. Eating with sinners

9:10–13

> ¹⁰While Jesus was having dinner at Matthew's house, many tax collectors and "sinners" came and ate with him and his disciples. ¹¹When the Pharisees saw this, they asked his disciples, "Why does your teacher eat with tax collectors and 'sinners'?"
>
> ¹²On hearing this, Jesus said, "It is not the healthy who need a doctor, but the sick. ¹³But go and learn what this means: 'I desire mercy, not sacrifice.' For I have not come to call the righteous, but sinners."

On the chronological relation between v.9 and vv.10–13, see on 9:1. Matthew abbreviates the account of Jesus' eating with tax collectors and sinners, excluding descriptive elements that do not contribute to the confrontation, but adding an OT quotation (v.13).

10–11 For comment on the opening words *kai egeneto* ("and it came to pass"; NIV, "while"), see on 7:28–29. The Greek text does not mention "Matthew's" house, though v.9 implies it is Matthew's and both Mark and Luke specify it (so NIV). Jesus himself had said that even a tax collector has his friends (5:46), and Matthew's dinner substantiates this. "Sinners" may include common folk who did not share all the scruples of the Pharisees (cf. TDNT, 1:324–25); hence the quotation marks in NIV. But almost certainly it groups together those who broke Pharisaic Halakoth (rules of conduct)—harlots, tax collectors, and other disreputable people (cf. Hummel, pp. 22ff.). Though eating with them entailed dangers of ceremonial defilement, Jesus and his disciples did so. The Pharisees' question, put not to Jesus but to his disciples, was less a request for information than a charge; and contemptuously it lumped together "tax collectors and sinners" under one article (cf. 11:19; Luke 15:1–2 for the same attitude).

There can be little doubt that Jesus was known as a friend to tax collectors and sinners (Matt 11:19; cf. M. Völkel, " 'Freund der Zöllner und Sünder,' " ZNW 69 [1978]: 1–10; and see note on 5:46).

12–13 These verses again connect Jesus' healing ministry with his "healing" of sinners (see on 8:17). The sick need a doctor (v.12), and Jesus healed them; likewise the sinful need mercy, forgiveness, restoration, and Jesus healed them (v.13). The Pharisees were not so healthy as they thought (cf. 7:1–5); more important they did not understand the purpose of Jesus' mission. Expecting a Messiah who would crush the sinful and support the righteous, they had little place for one who accepted and transformed the sinner and dismissed the "righteous" as hypocrites. Jesus explained his mission in terms reminiscent of 1:21. There is no suggestion here that he went to sinners because they gladly received him; rather, he went to them because they were sinners, just as a doctor goes to the sick because they are sick.

The quotation (v.13) is from Hosea 6:6 and is introduced by the rabbinic formula "go and learn," used of those who needed to study the text further. Use of the formula may be slightly sardonic: those who prided themselves in their knowledge of and conformity to Scripture needed to "go and learn" what it means. The quotation, possibly translated from the Hebrew by Matthew himself, is cast in Semitic antithesis: "not A but B" often means "B is of more basic importance than A."

The Hebrew word for "mercy" (*ḥesed*) is close in meaning to "covenant love," which, according to Hosea, is more important than "sacrifice." Through Hosea, God said that the apostates of Hosea's day, though continuing the formal ritual of temple worship, had lost its center. As applied to the Pharisees by Jesus, therefore, the Hosea quotation was not simply telling them that they should be more sympathetic to outcasts and less concerned about ceremonial purity, but that they were aligned with the apostates of ancient Israel in that they too preserved the shell while losing the heart of the matter, as exemplified by their attitude to tax collectors and sinners (cf. France, *Jesus*, p. 70). Jesus' final statement (v.13b) therefore cannot mean that he viewed the Pharisees as righteous people who did not need him, who were already perfectly acceptable to God by virtue of their obedience to his laws so that their only fault was the exclusion of others (contra Hill, *Greek Words*, pp. 130f.). If the Pharisees were so righteous, the demand for righteousness surpassing that of the Pharisees and teachers of the law (5:20) would be incoherent.

On the other hand, it may not be exactly right to say that "righteous" is ironic here. The saying simply defines the essential nature of Jesus' messianic mission as he himself saw it. If pushed he would doubtless have affirmed the universal sinfulness of man (cf. 7:11). Therefore he is not dividing men into two groups but disavowing one image of what Messiah should be and do, replacing it with the correct one. His mission was characterized by grace, a pursuit of the lost, of sinners. The verb *kalesai* ("to call") means "to invite" (unlike Paul's usage, where the call is always efficacious). By implication those who do not see themselves in the light of Jesus' mission not only fail to grasp the purpose of his coming but exclude themselves from the kingdom's blessings.

If Matthew does not add "to repentance" after "sinners" (as Luke 5:32), it is not because he is disinterested in repentance (cf. 3:2; 4:17). Rather, the words are not in his principal source (Mark) and do not in any case contribute to his present theme.

Hosea 6:6 is also quoted in 12:7, again in a context challenging the Pharisees' legal scruples. Cope (*Matthew*, pp. 68–70) suggests that the verse reveals a contrast between the substantial demands of mercy and merely legal and ceremonial piety, a contrast traceable in the following pericopes (vv. 14–17, 18–26, 27–34, 35–38). But his evidence is slightly overdrawn. In 9:27–34, for instance, vv.27–31 raise no overt hints of ceremonial defilement.

7. *Fasting and the dawning of the messianic joy*

9:14–17

14Then John's disciples came and asked him, "How is it that we and the Pharisees fast, but your disciples do not fast?"

15Jesus answered, "How can the guests of the bridegroom mourn while he is with them? The time will come when the bridegroom will be taken from them; then they will fast.

16"No one sews a patch of unshrunk cloth on an old garment, for the patch will pull away from the garment, making the tear worse. 17Neither do men pour new wine into old wineskins. If they do, the skins will burst, the wine will run out and the wineskins will be ruined. No, they pour new wine into new wineskins, and both are preserved."

14 Mark (2:18–22; cf. Luke 5:33–39) says that both the Pharisees and the disciples of John were fasting—probably on one of the regularly observed but voluntary fast days (see on 4:2; 6:16–18)—and that "some people" asked this question. Luke makes it the Pharisees, Matthew the disciples of John. On the face of it (see Luke), the setting is the same as for the previous pericope, and regarding fasting the disciples of John are in accord with the Pharisees. The Baptist himself showed a noble freedom from jealousy when Jesus' ministry began to supersede his own (cf. esp. John 3:26–31). But some of John's disciples felt differently now that he was in prison (4:12); and because they kept up their leader's asceticism (11:18), not heeding his strong witness to Jesus, they saw an occasion for criticism.

Most modern commentators believe that here Matthew is referring to the Baptist's followers who never accepted Jesus' supremacy and who by the end of the first century had developed their own sect. Doubtless Matthew would have cheerfully applied Jesus' response to them also. But there is no reason to deny that this incident happened during Jesus' ministry. Moreover, after the bridegroom was taken away (v.15), Jesus' disciples often fasted (e.g., Acts 13:3; 14:23; 27:9), making it less likely that these Baptist sectarians would have leveled their charge after the Passion and Resurrection than before it. Just as the "questioners" (accusers?) had approached Jesus' disciples about his conduct (v.11), so now questioners approached Jesus about his disciples' conduct.

15 For his response Jesus used three illustrations (Luke 5:39 adds a fourth), all given in the same order by the Synoptics. There seems little to be gained by supposing that the sayings were at one time separate.

The first illustration about the "guests of the bridegroom" (lit., "the sons of the brideschamber"; see on 5:9; 8:12) picks up a metaphor from the Baptist, who saw himself as the "best man" and Jesus as the groom (John 3:29). This similar metaphor would therefore be the more effective to this audience—Jesus is the groom and the disciples his "guests" who are so overjoyed at being with him that for them to fast is inappropriate.

In exonerating his disciples' eating, Jesus used messianic-eschatological terms. In the OT the bridegroom metaphor was repeatedly applied to God (Isa 54:5–6; 62:4–5; Hos 2:16–20); and Jews sometimes used it of marriage in connection with Messiah's coming or with the messianic banquet (cf. SBK, 1:500–518; and in the NT, cf. Matt 22:2; 25:1; 2 Cor 11:2; Eph 5:23–32; Rev 19:7, 9; 21:2). Thus Jesus' answer was implicitly christological: he himself is the messianic bridegroom, and the Messianic Age has dawned.

The objection is often made that the second part of Jesus' answer, regarding the disciples' mourning once the groom is taken (*aparthē*, "taken," may bear overtones of Isa 53:8 LXX) from them, is not authentic on two chief grounds.

1. Such an obvious reference to the Passion (and Ascension?) comes too early in Jesus' ministry. Some try to avoid this objection by supposing that Jesus was saying no more than that he like other men must die sometime. Neither the objection nor its proposed solution is relevant to one who has already revealed so formidable a messianic self-consciousness.

2. Matthew has allegorized the original parable—a sign of late accretion or adaptation. Yet this simplistic view of "parable" will not withstand scrutiny (cf. further on 13:3a). Above all the language is so cryptic that it is doubtful whether even Jesus' disciples grasped the messianic implications of these words till the early weeks of the postresurrection church.

16–17 Luke 5:36 labels these illustrations "parables." In general terms the first of this pair is clear enough: a piece of unshrunk cloth tightly sewed to old and well-shrunk cloth in order to repair a tear will cause a bigger tear (v.16). Admittedly the grammar is difficult (cf. Notes). The second (v.17) is also a "slice of life" in the ancient world. Skin bottles for carrying various fluids were made by killing the chosen animal, cutting off its head and feet, skinning the carcass, and sewing up the skin, fur side out, to seal off all orifices but one (usually the neck). The skin was tanned with special care to minimize disagreeable taste. In time the skin became hard and brittle. If new wine, still fermenting, were put into such an old skin, the buildup of fermenting gases would split the brittle container and ruin both bottle and wine. New wine was placed only in new wineskins still pliable and elastic enough to accommodate the pressure.

These illustrations show that the new situation introduced by Jesus could not simply be patched onto old Judaism or poured into the old wineskins of Judaism. New forms would have to accompany the kingdom Jesus was now inaugurating; to try to domesticate him and incorporate him into the matrix of established Jewish religion would only succeed in ruining both Judaism and Jesus' teaching.

Two extreme interpretations must be avoided.

1. Some, noticing that the words "and both are preserved" (v.17) are found only in Matthew, conclude that this first Gospel, unlike Mark, envisages the renewal and preservation of Judaism, not its abolition. This will not do: the "both" that are preserved refers to the new wine and the new wineskins, not the old wineskins. Jesus' teaching and the kingdom now dawning must be poured into new forms. Matthew makes it at least as clear as does Mark that the new wine can only be

preserved in new forms. Is it any surprise that Matthew includes explicit mention of the church (16:18; 18:17)?

2. Dispensationalists are inclined to make this wine so new that there is no connection whatever with what has come before. Walvoord (p. 70) cites Ironside: "He had not come to add something to the legal dispensation but to supersede it with that which was entirely new. . . . The new wine of grace was not to be poured into the skin-bottles of legality." So sharp an antithesis is suspect on three grounds: (1) the grace–legality disjunction is greatly exaggerated; (2) it is not very obviously a set of Matthean categories; and (3) Matthew, as we have seen, repeatedly connects the OT with his own message in terms of prophecy and fulfillment.

The two parables of vv.16–17 are frequently said to be independent sayings tacked on here, since they go beyond the question of fasting. That may be, but all three synoptists put them in the same place. Moreover they go beyond the question of fasting only to lay the groundwork for the coherence of Jesus' answer about fasting. The newness Jesus brings cannot be reduced to or contained by traditions of Jewish piety. The messianic bridegroom has come. These parables bring unavoidable and radical implications for the entire structure of Jewish religion as its leaders then conceived it. Scholars who understand the first Gospel to reflect a Jewish Christian community that preserves all the old forms of piety not only misinterpret 5:17–20 but do not adequately weigh this pericope.

Notes

---

16 The verb αἴρει (airei, "takes," "draws," or "pulls") is consistently transitive in the active voice (BAGD, s.v.), and therefore τὸ πλήρωμα αὐτοῦ (to plērōma autou, lit., "its fullness"; NIV, "patch") must be construed as the direct object, perhaps referring to the overlapping section of the patch. See the rendering of Michael G. Steinhauser ("The Patch of Unshrunk Cloth [Mt 9:16]," ExpT 87 [1975–76]: 312f.): "No one puts a patch of unshrunk cloth to an old cloak; because the patch of unshrunk cloth draws the overlapping section of the unshrunk cloth from the cloak and the tear becomes worse."

---

8. A resurrection and more healings (9:18–34)

a. Raising a girl and healing a woman

9:18–26

> [18]While he was saying this, a ruler came and knelt before him and said, "My daughter has just died. But come and put your hand on her, and she will live." [19]Jesus got up and went with him, and so did his disciples.
>
> [20]Just then a woman who had been subject to bleeding for twelve years came up behind him and touched the edge of his cloak. [21]She said to herself, "If I only touch his cloak, I will be healed."
>
> [22]Jesus turned and saw her. "Take heart, daughter," he said, "your faith has healed you." And the woman was healed from that moment.
>
> [23]When Jesus entered the ruler's house and saw the flute players and the noisy crowd, [24]he said, "Go away. The girl is not dead but asleep." But they laughed at him. [25]After the crowd had been put outside, he went in and took the girl by the hand, and she got up. [26]News of this spread through all that region.

For the chronology, see on v.1. Matthew abbreviates Mark (5:21–43; cf. Luke 8:40–46) by almost one-third. Again, the three synoptists are very close in reporting the words of Jesus.

Gérard Rochais (*Les récits de résurrection des morts dans le Nouveau Testament* [Cambridge: University Press, 1980], pp. 88–99) reduces the point of Matthew's account to the importance of faith. Faith is indeed an important theme (v.22), but scarcely exclusive of others. While these are best discovered inductively, we may note that in vv. 18–34 Jesus performs three new kinds of miracles: raising the dead (the healing of the hemorrhaging woman is already an integral part of this account in the Markan source) and healing the blind and the dumb. The latter two appear in Matthew much earlier than in the closest parallels in Mark and Luke (see on vv. 27–31), because his topical concerns demand it. He includes at this point these final examples of spheres over which Jesus has authority because they figure in his defense to the disciples of John the Baptist (11:2–5): the blind receive sight, the lame walk, those who have leprosy are cured, the deaf hear (usually also associated with muteness), the dead are raised. Jesus' messianic credentials are thus being grouped together.

18–19 Matthew tightly links this narrative to the dinner in his house. Mark 5:21 provides another setting: while Jesus was by the lake, etc. This anomaly has called forth numerous explanations, mostly unsatisfactory. Some have postulated that Matthew here follows another source (a desperate expedient that does not explain why he chooses to contradict Mark); others that Matthew simplifies Mark in the interests of catechesis (How is catechesis helped by a different setting almost as long as the first?); others by supposing the dinner party in v.10 took place in a house by the lake (barely possible but artificial); others that vv.14–17 should be detached from the dinner (barely possible, but artificial in light of Luke 5:33).

The best solution accepts the connection between Matthew's dinner (vv.9–13), the discussion about fasting (vv.14–17), and this miracle (vv.18–26). But the NIV rendering of Mark 5:21–22 links Jesus by the lake with the approach of the synagogue ruler ("While he was by the lake, one of the synagogue rulers . . . "). The Greek does not suggest this; syntactically Jesus' presence by the lake terminates the thought of Mark 5:21: Jesus crossed back after the Gadara episode, a large crowd again gathered, and he was by the lake. Verse 22 then begins a new pericope without a necessary transition—which is exactly what Mark does elsewhere (e.g., 3:20, 31; 8:22; 10:46; 14:66). In some instances like this one (Mark 5:22; cf. 1:40), the precise division is ambiguous. But Mark's practice elsewhere encourages us to think this interpretation is right, and the NIV translation wrong.

Further, the words *kai idou* in Luke 8:41 should not be rendered "Just then" (NIV). This suggests that Jairus approached Jesus almost immediately on disembarking from the boat. In fact, *kai idou* in Luke very often either does not or cannot mean "just then" (e.g., Luke 5:18; 7:37, 9:30, 39 et al.) and is not so rendered by NIV. Though the words can fix a chronological connection, they may simply suggest a new or surprising development or even serve as a loose connective. There seems little merit in translating them so as to exclude the possibility of an obvious harmonization.

"A ruler" (cf. Notes) in the context of Capernaum almost certainly refers to a synagogue ruler (v.18), a point made explicit by Mark 5:22, which also tells us his name was Jairus. He must therefore have been a Jew and a man of considerable influence in the lives of the people. He "knelt before" Jesus: the verb here does not suggest "worship" (contra KJV) but deep courtesy, a pleading homage before someone in a position to grant a favor (see on 2:2; 8:2). His daughter "has just died": attempts to make *arti eteleutēsen* mean "is now dying" (NIV mg.) stem not from Greek syntax but from too simplistic a desire to harmonize this account with Mark and Luke. Better to recognize that Matthew, having eliminated the messengers as extraneous to his purposes, condenses "so as to present at the outset what was actually true before Jesus reached the house" (Broadus): such is Matthew's condensed style elsewhere (see on 8:5).

The synagogue ruler felt Jesus' touch had special efficacy, but his faith was not as great as that of the centurion who believed that Jesus could heal by his word (8:5–13). Jesus did not refuse him but responded to faith, small or great. He "got up" (v.19; the word *egeirō* most likely means, in this context, "rose from reclining at table" [cf. v.10]; see on harmonization problem, above) and "went with [*akoloutheō*, an evidence that this verb does not necessarily imply discipleship; see on 8:23] him."

20–21 The nature of the woman's hemorrhage (v.20) is uncertain; if, as seems probable, it was chronic bleeding from the womb, then she was perpetually unclean (cf. Lev 15:25–33). The regulation of such a woman's life was considered so important that the Mishnah devotes an entire tractate to the subject (*Zabim*) and gives some of the "remedies" for staunching the flow. Having heard of others who had been healed at Jesus' touch, this woman decided to touch even a tassel of Jesus' cloak (v.21). Moved in part by a superstitious view of Jesus, she struggled through the crowd, which, because of her "unclean" condition, she should have avoided.

The word *kraspedon* can mean either "edge" or "tassel." The former may be the meaning here (so NIV); but the latter is certainly the meaning in 23:5. Tassels (Heb. *ṣîṣit*) were sewn on the four corners of every Israelite's cloak (Num 15:37–41; Deut 22:12) as reminders to obey God's commands. While the tassels could easily become mere showpieces (23:5), Jesus himself, like any male Jew, doubtless wore them.

22 Though Matthew's account is again abbreviated, various explanations of this—e.g., short accounts are easier to memorize (Hill, *Matthew*), or Matthew eliminates magical elements (Hull, pp. 136f.)—are less convincing than the obvious one: viz., Matthew keeps only what is of most interest to him. The account is so short that it is not entirely clear whether Jesus turned and saw the woman before or after she touched him. The parallel accounts say the latter, and this may well be reflected in the perfect tense "your faith *has healed* you." The woman was healed on touching Jesus' cloak. He said that it was her faith that was effective, not the superstition mingled with it.

This seems better than the view that holds that Jesus first encouraged the woman ("Take heart, daughter") and then healed her without any reference to touching. Matthew 9:2; 14:27 are cited as parallels for this order. In fact, the three incidents differ somewhat; 9:2 according to the best variant says, in effect, "Take heart, for I now forgive you"; 9:22 says, "Take heart, for you have now been healed"; and 14:27 is quite different, since "Take heart" logically relates to "It is I," and the miracle of the stilling of the tempest is yet future. The final clauses of v.22 should therefore be interpreted to mean, not that the woman was healed from the "moment" Jesus spoke, but that she was healed from the *hōra* (lit., "hour") of this encounter with Jesus.

23–26 Flute players (v.23) were employed both on festive occasions (Rev 18:22) and at funerals. Matthew alone mentions them, not so much because he had special knowledge of Jewish funeral customs (cf. M *Ketuboth* 4:4, which required even a poor family to hire two flute players and one professional wailing woman), but out of personal recollection. Jesus was about to reverse funeral symbolism of the finality of death. The "noisy crowd" was made up of friends mourning, not in the hushed whispers characteristic of our Western funerals, but in loud outbursts of grief and wailing augmented by cries of hired mourners. Jesus' miracle not only brought a corpse to life (v.24) but hope to despair.

"Laughed" (*katagelaō*) occurs only here (v.24) and in the synoptic parallels. The crowd mocked Jesus, not just because he had said, "The girl is not dead but asleep," but even more because they thought that this great healer had arrived too late. Now he was going too far; carried away by his own success, he would try his skill on a corpse and make a fool of himself. In such a situation Jesus' words became, in retrospect, all the more profound. They not only denied that death—confronted by his power—was final, they also assumed that contrary to the Sadducean view (22:23) "sleep" better described the girl's condition. In the Bible "sleep" often denotes "death" but never "nonexistence" (cf. Dan 12:2; John 11:11; Acts 7:60; 1 Cor 15:6, 18; 1 Thess 4:13–15; 2 Peter 3:4).

The mocking crowd was ejected from the house (v.25). Matthew does not tell us, as Mark does, that the five witnesses remained; nor does he give us Jesus' words. But Matthew says that Jesus touched the corpse; and the body, far from defiling him, came to life. By itself the miracle did not prove Jesus to be more than a prophet or an apostle (cf. 1 Kings 17:17–24; 2 Kings 4:17–37; Acts 9:36–42). But prophets and apostles never claimed to be more than their office indicated. Jesus made vastly greater claims; so for Matthew the miracle showed that Jesus' authority as the Christ extended even over the dead.

Notes

---

18 Ἄρχων εἷς (*archōn heis*) is a relatively rare but not unknown way of saying "a ruler" or "a certain ruler," *heis*, (lit., "one") functioning more or less like the enclitic τις (*tis*, "a certain"; cf. Gr. 8:19). Interpretation is compounded by complex variants, probably generated not only by the rarity of the construction but the ambiguity of uncial texts: ΕΙΣΕΛΘΩΝ could be read εἷς ἐλθών (*heis elthōn*, lit., "one having come") or εἰσελθών (*eiselthōn*, lit., "having entered"), the latter presupposing the house of v.10. For a defense of the text behind NIV, cf. J. O'Callaghan, "La variante εισ/ελθων en Mt 9, 18," *Biblica* 62 (1981): 104–6.

20 "Tassel" or "edge" in Matthew and Luke makes this one of the most important "minor agreements" of Matthew and Luke against Mark, one that has generated many theories. Some take it with other "minor agreements" as sufficient evidence to defend the Griesbach hypothesis (Introduction, section 3); others postulate a shared source, a coincidence, a textual emendation, or (most recently) the influence of Mark 6:56 (J.T. Cummings, "The Tassel of His Cloak: Mark, Luke, Matthew—and Zechariah," in Livingstone, 2:47–61). However explained—and perhaps some theory of common information is best—it is scarcely enough to threaten the two-source hypothesis. Why Matthew should include such a descriptive detail when he eliminates so much is hard to say. Yet Matthew's narrative is not unpolished: he includes the piquant touch and occasional small detail, while eliminating characters and scenes not germane to his purpose.

---

b. *Healing two blind men*

9:27–31

27As Jesus went on from there, two blind men followed him, calling out, "Have mercy on us, Son of David!"
28When he had gone indoors, the blind men came to him, and he asked them, "Do you believe that I am able to do this?"
"Yes, Lord," they replied.
29Then he touched their eyes and said, "According to your faith will it be done to you"; 30and their sight was restored. Jesus warned them sternly, "See that no one knows about this." 31But they went out and spread the news about him all over that region.

This pericope is usually taken as a doublet of the Bartimaeus miracle (20:29–34; Mark 10:46–52; Luke 18:35–43). But close examination shows little verbal correspondence between the Synoptics; and such correspondence as exists is considerably less than that between two pericopes in Matthew telling of entirely different miracles (cf. Bornkamm, *Tradition*, pp. 219–20). Blindness was and still is common in the Mideast. Jesus performed many such miracles (see on 4:23; 8:16–17; 9:35). The most striking parallel is the cry "Have mercy on us, Son of David" (v.27). But this also occurs in 15:22 in a story having nothing to do with blindness; so the title "Son of David" may well have another explanation (see below). Certainly the point of 20:29–34 is quite different from this pericope. Here the focus is on Jesus' authority and the blind men's faith; there it is on the compassion of Jesus the King as he interrupts his journey to Jerusalem to respond to their cries. Moreover Matthew, we have repeatedly observed, condenses his narratives. Proposals that similar stories are doublets (a form of lengthening) must therefore be treated with suspicion. Likewise the supposition that Matthew has two blind men because Mark (his source) has two stories (8:22–26; 10:46–52), each describing the healing of one blind man, and that Matthew has simply added the number of the men and put them into one story is fanciful. Mark does have two stories of separate healings, one of which Matthew takes over (Mark 10:46–52; Matt 20:29–34). And Matthew and Mark each add another healing-of-the-blind miracle (Matt 9:27–31; Mark 8:22–26). This is scarcely surprising, in view of the prevalence of blindness and the extent of Jesus' healing ministry.

27–28 Apparently Jesus was returning from the ruler's house (v.23) either to his own house (4:13) or to that of Matthew (vv.10, 28—the article in Greek implies it was either his own dwelling or the one previously mentioned). We should probably envisage a large crowd after the dramatic raising of the ruler's daughter. Attached to the crowd were two blind men who had faith enough to follow him indoors.

This is the first time Jesus is called "Son of David" (v.27), and there can be no doubt that the blind men were confessing Jesus as Messiah (see on 1:1). They may have been physically blind, but they really "saw" better than many others—further evidence that Jesus came to those who needed a doctor (vv.12–13; see on 15:22). "The use of the Davidic title [cf. 15:22; 20:30; 21:9, 15; 22:42] in address to Jesus is less extraordinary than some think: in Palestine, in the time of Jesus, there was an intense Messianic expectation" (Hill, *Matthew*). The Messianic Age was to be characterized as a time when "the eyes of the blind [would be] opened and the ears of the deaf unstopped," when "the lame [would] leap like a deer, and the tongue of the dumb shout for joy" (Isa 35:5–6). If Jesus was really the Messiah, the blind reasoned, then he would have mercy on them; and they would have their sight. So their need drove them to faith. Perhaps this is what lies behind the fact in the Synoptics that "Son of David" is so often associated with the needy—those possessed by demons or, as here, in need of healing (cf. C. Burger, *Jesus als Davidssohn* [Göttingen: Vandenhoeck und Ruprecht, 1970]; Dennis C. Duling, "The Therapeutic Son of David: An Element in Matthew's Christological Apologetic," NTS 24 [1978]: 392–410).

Jesus did not deal with the blind men until they were indoors (v.28). This may have been to dampen messianic expectations (see on v.30) on a day marked by two highly public and dramatic miracles (v.26). It may also have been a device to increase their faith. The latter is suggested by his question (v.28), which accomplished two other things: (1) it revealed that their cries were not merely those of desperation only but of faith; and (2) it showed that their faith was directed not to God alone but to Jesus' person and to his power and authority. Their title for Jesus was therefore right; he is truly the messianic Son of David. Thus we return to the first reason for delaying the healing—its being done within the house prevented the excited crowd from witnessing an implicit christological claim.

29–31 Jesus' touching the blind men's eyes (v.29)—perhaps no more than a compassionate gesture to encourage faith—was not the sole means of this healing: it also depended on Jesus' authoritative word. "According to your faith" does not mean "in proportion to your faith" (so much faith, so much sight) but rather "since you believe, your request is granted"—cf. "your faith has healed you" (v.22). The miracle accomplished (v.30), Jesus "warned them sternly" to tell no one: *embrimaomai* ("I sternly warn") occurs only five times in the NT and always in connection with deep emotion (cf. Mark 1:43; 14:5; John 11:33, 38). This rather violent verb reveals Jesus' intense desire to avoid a falsely based and ill-conceived acclaim that would not only impede but also endanger his true mission (see on 8:4). But the men whose faith brought them to Christ for healing did not stay with him to learn obedience. So the news spread like wildfire throughout the region (cf. v.26).

Notes

27 Instead of the vocative υἱέ (*huie*, "son"), the text offers nominative υἱὸς Δαυίδ (*huios David*, "son of David"). What is surprising is that the nominative noun in such a construction is anarthrous. This may well reflect Hebrew construction (cf. BDF, par. 147[3]).

c. *Exorcising a dumb man*

9:32-34

> [32]While they were going out, a man who was demon-possessed and could not talk was brought to Jesus. [33]And when the demon was driven out, the man who had been mute spoke. The crowd was amazed and said, "Nothing like this has ever been seen in Israel."
> [34]But the Pharisees said, "It is by the prince of demons that he drives out demons."

Again many see in these verses a "partial doublet," this time with 12:22-24; and again the verbal parallels are minimal. Hill (*Matthew*) says that 9:32-34 has been formed out of 12:22-24 "in order to complete the cases of miraculous healing presupposed in 11.5 and 10.1." But Matthew 4:24 shows that Jesus performed many exorcisms. Was Matthew so pressed for another example that he had to tell the same story twice? If so, why is the demon-possessed man in Matthew 12 both blind and mute and this one only mute? Moreover, if v.34 is genuine (see below), it is surely not surprising that the charge of being in league with Beelzebub (12:24) should begin on a private scale and take some time to explode into the open (12:24). In any case the charge is presupposed by 10:25.

32-33 The word *kōphos* ("could not talk") in classical, Hellenistic, and biblical Greek means "deaf" or "dumb" or "deaf mute"; the two ailments are commonly linked, especially if deafness is congenital. Perhaps the man here (v.32) was not only mute but a deaf mute. (On demon possession, see on 4:24, 8:28, 31.) The NT frequently attributes various diseases to demonic activity; but since the same ailment appears elsewhere without any suggestion of demonic activity (e.g., Mark 7:32-33), the frequent connection between the two is not based on primitive superstition but presupposes a real ability to distinguish between natural and demonic causes. The crowd's amazement (v.33) climaxes the earlier excitement (vv.26, 31). Nothing has ever been seen like this in Israel—and, by implication, if not among God's chosen people, then nowhere. But the same amazement ominously sets the stage for the Pharisees' cynical response (v.34).

34 This verse is missing from the Western textual tradition; and Allen, Klostermann, Zahn, and others follow suit, detecting an intrusion from 12:24. But the external evidence is strong; and the verse seems presupposed in 10:25. This is not the first intimation of direct opposition to Jesus in Matthew (vv.3, 11, 14, 24; cf. 5:10-12, 44); and even here the imperfect *elegon* (lit., "they were saying"; NIV, "said") may imply that the ferment was constantly in the background. But the tide of opposition, which later brought Jesus to the cross, now becomes an essential part of the background to the next discourse (cf. esp. 10:16-28).

9. *Spreading the news of the kingdom* (9:35-10:4)

a. *Praying for workers*

9:35-38

> [35]Jesus went through all the towns and villages, teaching in their synagogues, preaching the good news of the kingdom and healing every disease and sickness.

36When he saw the crowds, he had compassion on them, because they were harassed and helpless, like sheep without a shepherd. 37Then he said to his disciples, "The harvest is plentiful but the workers are few. 38Ask the Lord of the harvest, therefore, to send out workers into his harvest field."

As 4:23–25 prepares for the first discourse (5–7), so vv.35–38 provide a report and summary that prepares for the second (10:5–42). A new note is added; not only are we told again of the extensiveness of Jesus' labors, but we now learn that the work was so great that many workers were needed. This leads to the commissioning of 10:1–4 and to the related discourse of 10:5–42.

Mark 6:6b has few affinities with this passage. Verse 35 is close to 4:23. Verse 36 is akin to Mark 6:34, and vv.37–38 to Luke 10:2 (cf. also John 4:35).

35 The setting is the same as in Mark 6:6b. For the exegesis, see on 4:23. The principal difference is the omission of any mention of Galilee, though doubtless that is the region in view. It is possible, as older commentaries suggest, that this represents a second circuit through Galilee; but in view of Matthew's highly topical arrangement, it is precarious to deduce so much from it. Verse 35 summarizes the heart of Jesus' Galilean ministry and prepares us for the new phase of mission via the Twelve. (On "their" synagogues, see also on 7:29 and 10:17.)

36 Like Yahweh in the OT (cf. Ezek 34), Jesus showed compassion on the shepherdless crowds and judgment on the false leaders. The "sheep" Jesus sees are "harassed" (not "fainted" [KJV], which has poor attestation), i.e., bullied, oppressed; and in the face of such problems, they are "helpless," unable to rescue themselves or escape their tormentors. The language of the verse is close to Numbers 27:17 (which could almost make Joshua a "type" of Jesus); but other parallels (e.g., 1 Kings 22:17; 2 Chron 18:16; Isa 53:6; Ezek 34:23–24; 37:24) remind us not only of the theme's rich background but also that the shepherd can refer either to God or to the Davidic Messiah God will send (cf. 2:6; 10:6, 16; 15:24; 25:31–46; 26:31).

37–38 The metaphor changed from sheep farming to harvest (v.37), as Jesus sought to awaken similar compassion in his disciples. Later on the harvest is the end of the age (13:49) and the judgment it brings—a common symbol (cf. Isa 17:11; Joel 3:13). Many commentators see this verse as a warning to Israel that judgment time is near. The word "plentiful" stands in the way of this interpretation; it makes sense only if here *therismos* does not mean "harvest-time" but "harvest-crop" (cf. BAGD, s.v.), as in Luke 10:2; John 4:35b. In that case the crop will be plentiful; many people will be ready to be "reaped" into the kingdom.

Jesus is speaking here to "his disciples," which many take to refer to the Twelve. More likely "his disciples" designates a larger group exhorted to ask (v.38) that the Lord of the harvest (possibly "Lord who is harvesting," if this is a verbal genitive; cf. G.H. Waterman, "The Greek 'Verbal Genitive,'" in Hawthorne, p. 292) will thrust laborers into his *therismou* (here in the sense "harvest field"). By contrast the Twelve are immediately commissioned as workers (10:1–4). This interpretation best fits 10:1: Jesus "called his twelve disciples to him." The clause is clumsy if they are the same as the "disciples" of 9:37–38 and natural only if they are part of the larger group.

b. *Commissioning the Twelve*

10:1–4

> ¹He called his twelve disciples to him and gave them authority to drive out evil spirits and to cure every kind of disease and sickness.
> ²These are the names of the twelve apostles: first, Simon (who is called Peter) and his brother Andrew; James son of Zebedee, and his brother John; ³Philip and Bartholomew; Thomas and Matthew the tax collector; James son of Alphaeus, and Thaddaeus; ⁴Simon the Zealot and Judas Iscariot, who betrayed him.

1 He whose word (chs. 5–7) and deed (chs. 8–9) were characterized by authority now delegates something of that authority to twelve men. This is the first time Matthew has explicitly mentioned the Twelve (cf. v.2; 11:1; 20:17; 26:14, 20, 47), who are introduced a little earlier in Mark (3:13–16). This commission appears to be the culmination of several previous steps (John 1:35–51; see on Matt 4:18–22). Indeed, Matthew's language suggests that the Twelve became a recognized group somewhat earlier. At the same time this commission was a stage in the training and preparation of those who, after Pentecost, would lead the earliest thrust of the fledgling church. Twelve were chosen, probably on an analogy to the twelve tribes of Israel (cf. also the council of twelve at Qumran, 1QS 8:1ff.), and they point to the eschatological renewal of the people of God (see on 19:28–30).

The authority the Twelve received enabled them to heal and drive out "evil [lit., 'unclean'] spirits"—spirits in rebellion against God, hostile to man, and capable of inflicting mental, moral, and physical harm, directly or indirectly. This is the first time in Matthew that demons are so described, and only again at 12:43 (but see on 8:16). "Every kind of disease and sickness" is exactly the expression in 4:23; 9:35. The authority granted the Twelve is in sharp contrast to the charismatic "gifts [pl.] of healing" at Corinth (1 Cor 12:9, 28), which apparently were individually more restricted in what diseases each could cure.

2–4 For the first and only time in Matthew, the Twelve are called "apostles." *Apostolos* ("apostle"), cognate with *apostellō* ("I send"), is not a technical term in the background literature. This largely accounts for the fact that as used in NT documents it has narrower and wider meanings (cf. DNTT, 1:126–37). Luke 6:13 explicitly affirms that Jesus himself called the Twelve "apostles"; and certainly Luke shows more interest in this question than the other three, partly in preparation for his work on the Acts of the Apostles. But in the NT the term can mean merely "messenger" (John 13:16) or refer to Jesus ("the apostle and high priest whom we confess," Heb 3:1) or elsewhere (esp. in Paul) denote "missionaries" or "representatives"—i.e., a group larger than the Twelve and Paul (Rom 16:7; 2 Cor 8:23). Nevertheless, the most natural reading of 1 Corinthians 9:1–5; 15:7; Galatians 1:17, 19 et al. is that even Paul could use the term in a narrow sense to refer to the Twelve plus himself (by special dispensation, 1 Cor 15:8–10).

Lists of the Twelve are found here and in three other places in the NT:

Matthew 10:2–4	Mark 3:16–19	Luke 6:13–16	Acts 1:13
Simon Peter	Simon Peter	Simon Peter	Simon Peter
Andrew	James	Andrew	John
James	John	James	James
John	Andrew	John	Andrew
Philip	Philip	Philip	Philip
Bartholomew	Bartholomew	Bartholomew	Thomas
Thomas	Matthew	Matthew	Bartholomew
Matthew	Thomas	Thomas	Matthew
James son of Alphaeus	James son of Alphaeus	James son of Alphaeus	James son of Alphaeus
Thaddaeus	Thaddaeus	Simon the Zealot	Simon the Zealot
Simon the Cananaean	Simon the Cananaean	Judas brother of James	Judas brother of James
Judas Iscariot	Judas Iscariot	Judas Iscariot	[Vacant]

Many significant things arise from comparing these lists.

1. Peter is always first, Judas Iscariot always last. Matthew uses "first" in connection with Peter; the word cannot mean he was the first convert (Andrew or perhaps John was) and probably does not simply mean "first on the list," which would be a trifling comment (cf. 1 Cor 12:28). More likely it means *primus inter pares* ("first among equals"; cf. further on 16:13–20).

2. The first four names of all four lists are those of two pairs of brothers whose call is mentioned first (cf. 4:18–22).

3. In each list there are three groups of four, each group headed by Peter, Philip (not to be confused with the evangelist), and James the son of Alphaeus respectively. But within each group the order varies (even from Luke to Acts!) except that Judas is always last. This suggests, if it does not prove, that the Twelve were organizationally divided into smaller groups, each with a leader.

4. The commission in Mark 6:7 sent the men out two by two; perhaps this accounts for the pairing in the Greek text of Matthew 10:2–4.

5. Some variations in order can be accounted for with a high degree of probability. For the first four names, Mark lists Peter, James, John, and appends Andrew, doubtless because the first three were an inner core privileged to witness the raising of Jairus's daughter and the Transfiguration and invited to be close to Jesus in his Gethsemane agony. Matthew preserves the order suggested by sibling relationships. He not only puts himself last in his group but mentions his less-than-savory past. Is this a sign of Christian humility?

6. Apparently Simon the Canaanite (Matt, Mark) is the same person as Simon the Zealot (Luke, Acts). If so, then apparently Thaddaeus is another name for Judas the brother of (or son of) James (see further below).

Not much is known concerning most of these men. For interesting but mostly incredible legends about them, see Hennecke (pp. 167–531).

Simon Peter. "Simon" is probably a contraction of "Simeon" (cf. Gen. 29:33). Natives of Bethsaida on Galilee (John 1:44), he and his brother Andrew were fishermen (Matt 4:18–20) and possibly disciples of John the Baptist before they became disciples of Jesus (John 1:35–42). Jesus gave Simon the name Cephas (in Aram.; "Peter" in Gr. [John 1:43]; see on 4:18). Impulsive and ardent, Peter's great strengths were his great weaknesses. New Testament evidence about him is abundant. Tracing Peter's movements after the Jerusalem Council (Acts 15) is very difficult.

Andrew. Peter's brother is not nearly so prominent in the NT. He appears again only in Mark 13:3; John 1:35–44; 6:8; 12:22, and in late and unreliable traditions. The Johannine evidence shows him to have been quietly committed to bringing others to Jesus.

James and John. James was probably the older (he almost always appears first). But as he became the first apostolic martyr (Acts 12:2), he never achieved his brother's prominence. The brothers were sons of Zebedee the fisherman, whose business was successful enough to employ others (Mark 1:20) while his wife was able to support Jesus' ministry (Matt 27:55–56; Luke 8:3). His wealth may help account for the family's link with the house of the high priest (John 18:15–16), as well as for the fact that he alone of the Twelve stood by the cross. The brothers' mother was probably Salome (cf. Matt 27:56; Mark 15:40; 16:1), and her motives were not unmixed (see on Matt 20:20–21). Perhaps the sons inherited something of her aggressive nature; whatever its source, the nickname "sons of thunder" (Mark 3:17; cf. also Mark 9:38–41; Luke 9:54–56) reveals something of their temperament. John may have been a disciple of John the Baptist (John 1:35–41). Of James we know nothing until Matthew 4:21–22. John was undoubtedly a special friend of Peter (Luke 22:8; John 18:15; 20:2–8; Acts 3:1–4:21; 8:14; Gal 2:9). Reasonably reliable tradition places him after the Fall of Jerusalem in Ephesus, where he ministered long and usefully into old age, taking a hand in the nurture of leaders like Polycarp, Papias, and Ignatius. Broadus's summary does not seem too fanciful: "[The] vaulting ambition which once aspired to be next to royalty in a worldly kingdom (20:20ff.], now seeks to overcome the world, to bear testimony to the truth, to purify the churches, and glorify God."

Philip. Like Peter and Andrew, Philip's home was Bethsaida (John 1:44); he too left the Baptist to follow Jesus. For incidents about him, see John 6:5–7; 12:21–22; 14:8–14. In the lists he invariably appears first in the second group of four. Polycrates, a second-century bishop, says Philip ministered in the Roman province of Asia and was buried at Hierapolis.

Bartholomew. The name means "son of Tolmai" or "son of Tholami" (cf. LXX Josh 15:14) or "son of Tholomaeus" (cf. Jos. Antiq. XX, 5[i.1]). Many have identified him with Nathanael on the grounds that (1) the latter is apparently associated with the Twelve (John 21:2; cf. 1:43–51), (2) Philip brought Nathanael to Jesus (John 1:43–46), and (3) Philip and Batholomew are always associated in the lists of apostles. The evidence is not strong; but if it is solid, we also know he came from Cana (John 21:2). He is remembered for Jesus' tribute to him (John 1:47).

Thomas. Also named "Didymus" (John 11:16; 21:2), which in Aramaic means "Twin," Thomas appears in Gospel narratives only in John 11:16; 14:5; 20:24–29. Known for his doubt, he should also be known for his courage (John 11:16) and his profound confession (John 20:28). Some traditions claim he went to India as a missionary and was martyred there; others place his later ministry in Persia.

Matthew. See on 9:9; Introduction, section 5.

James the son of Alphaeus. The extra phrase distinguishes him from James the son of Zebedee. If we assume (and this is highly likely) that this James is not the same as "James the brother" of Jesus (see on 13:55), we know almost nothing about him. Assuming Matthew = Levi (see on 9:9), then Matthew's father was also called Alphaeus (Mark 2:14); and if this is the same Alphaeus, then James and Matthew are another pair of brothers among the Twelve. Some have argued that Alphaeus is an alternative form of Cleophas (Clopas), which would mean that "James son of Alphaeus" is the same person as "James the younger" (Mark 15:40) and that his mother's name was Mary (Matt 27:56; Mark 15:40; 16:1; John 19:25). But such connections are by no means certain.

Thaddaeus. The textual variants are difficult. The longer ones (e.g., KJV, "Lebbaeus, whose surname was Thaddaeus") are almost certainly conflations. "Thaddaeus" has the support of early representatives from Alexandrian, Western, and Caesarean witnesses (cf. Metzger, *Textual Commentary*, p. 26). Through elimination he appears to be identified with (lit.) "Judas of James"—which could mean either "Judas son of James" or "Judas brother of James." The former is perhaps the more normal meaning; but the author of the Epistle of Jude designates himself as "Jude [Gr. *Ioudas*] . . . a brother of James" (Jude 1, where *adelphos* ["brother"] is actually used). If Jude is the apostolic "Judas of James," then the meaning of the latter expression is fixed. On the other hand, if canonical Jude is the half-brother of Jesus and full brother of Jesus' half-brother James (see on 13:55), then "Judas of James" most likely means "Judas son of James." "Thaddaeus" comes from a root roughly signifying "the beloved." Perhaps this apostle was called "Judas the beloved" = "Judas Thaddaeus," and "Thaddaeus" was progressively used to distinguish him from the other Judas in the apostolic band. Only John 14:22 provides us with information about him. Later traditions are worthless.

Simon the Zealot. Matthew and Mark have "Simon the Cananaean" (not "Canaanite," which would suggest a pagan Gentile; cf. the different Gr. word in 15:22). "Cananaean" (*qan'ân*) is the Aramaic form of "Zealot" specified in Luke–Acts. The Zealots were nationalists, strong upholders of Jewish traditions and religion; and some decades later they became a principal cause of the Jewish War in which Rome sacked Jerusalem. The Zealots were probably not so influential in Jesus' time. The nickname may reveal Simon's past political and religious associations; it also distinguishes him from Simon Peter.

Judas Iscariot. Judas's father is called "Simon Iscariot" in John 6:71; 13:26. Scholarly interest has spent enormous energy and much ingenuity on the name "Iscariot." Explanations include (1) "man of Kerioth" (there are two eligible villages of that name (cf. ZPEB, 3:785; IBD, 2:830); (2) transliteration of Latin *sicarius*, used to refer to a Zealot-like movement; (3) "man of Jericho," an explanation depending on a Greek corruption; (4) a transliteration of the Aramaic *šᵉqāryaᶜ* ("falsehood," "betrayal"; cf. C.C. Torrey, "The Name 'Iscariot,'" HTR 36 [1943]: 51–62), which could therefore become a nickname for Judas only after his ignominy and not at this point in his life; (5) "Judas the dyer," reflecting his occupation (cf. A. Ehrman, "Judas Iscariot and Abba Saqqara," JBL 97 [1978]: 572f.; Y. Arbeitman, "The Suffix of Iscariot," JBL 99 [1980]: 122–24); (6) as an adaptation of the last, "Judas the redhead" (Albright and Mann). The first and fifth seem most likely; the second is currently most popular. Judas was treasurer for the Twelve, but not an honest one

(John 12:6; 13:29; see also on 26:14–16; 27:3–10). Matthew and Mark add the damning indictment—"who betrayed him." Luke 6:16 labels him a traitor.

Notes

1 The construction ὥστε (*hōste*, "so that") plus an infinitive to indicate purpose is extraordinary (cf. BDF, par. 390[3]; Zerwick, par. 352) but cannot easily be taken any other way.

B. *Second Discourse: Mission and Martyrdom* (10:5–11:1)

1. Setting

10:5a

⁵These twelve Jesus sent out with the following instructions:

5 For a general introduction to the discourses and their problems, see comments at 5:1. On the face of it, this discourse is as tightly bracketed as the others (v.5a; 11:1), giving at least the impression that all the material of vv.5b–42 was delivered on one occasion. It is also peculiarly difficult. Two separate but related questions need careful attention before a judgment is formed.

The literary question. Roughly speaking, vv.5–15 have some parallels with Mark 6:8–11; Luke 9:3–5; 10:5–15. The last of these references, however, concerns the mission of the Seventy-two, not found in Matthew or Mark. Matthew 10:16a is close to Luke 10:3. But Matthew 10:17–25, concerning the disciples' persecution and their arraignment before tribunals, finds its closest parallel in the Olivet Discourse (Mark 13:9–13; Luke 21:12–19; cf. Matt 24:9–14). The final section (vv.26–42), setting out conditions for discipleship in more general terms, resembles material in Mark 9 and Luke 12:2–12. With the exception of only a few places (vv.5–6, 8, 16b), little in vv.5–42 is peculiar to the first Gospel, though admittedly some parallels are not as close as others.

The most common literary theory is that Matthew composed this address from segments of his two principal sources, Mark and Q. Those who reject Mark's priority and insist on Matthew's priority do not need Q and have an easier time defending the unity of this chapter. But Mark's priority still has best credentials (cf. Introduction, section 3), and so the problems remain. David Wenham ("The 'Q' Tradition") has followed Schürmann and Lambrecht in arguing that almost this entire discourse comes from various strands of the Q tradition (this does not necessarily mean Q is a single, written document). Mark's parallels are thereby judged secondary and condensations of earlier sources.

The historical and theological question. How do such source theories affect the context Matthew establishes? Here there is little agreement. F.W. Beare ("The Mission of the Disciples and the Mission Charge: Matthew 10 and Parallels," JBL 89 [1970]: 1–13) does not think there ever was a mission of the Twelve. The setting is a fabrication designed to enhance the discourse, itself an edited collection of sayings, few of them authentic. Many scholars, including conservative ones, suppose the discourse to be an amalgam of authentic material given on at least two separate occasions (Allen, Grosheide, Ridderbos). Tasker leaves the question open. R. Morosco ("Redaction Criticism and the Evangelical: Matthew 10 a Test Case," JETS 22 [1979]: 323–31) resurrects the old theory of B.W. Bacon, assuming not only five discourses in Matthew, but also their having been modeled on the five books of the Pentateuch (cf. Introduction, section 14). Morosco does not make clear, however, whether he thinks (1) that there is some historical commissioning of the Twelve to which a collage of material has been attached, (2) that a discourse was delivered on that occasion and this is an expanded adaptation of it, or (3) that the setting itself is fictitious.

Related to the historical question are several observations about the content of Matthew 10. In vv.5–16, all Jesus' instructions neatly fit the situation of the Twelve during Jesus' public ministry. This includes Jesus' prohibition of ministry to others than Jews (vv.5–6). But vv.17–22 clearly envisage a far more extensive ministry— even to kings and Gentiles. The persecution described does not fit the period of the first apostolic ministry but looks beyond it to times of major conflict long after Pentecost. As a result the great majority of modern commentators take this to be what Schuyler Brown describes as a literary means for Jesus to instruct "the Matthean community through the transparency of the twelve missionary disciples" ("The Mission to Israel in Matthew's Central Section," ZNW 69 [1978]: 73–90)— though, of course, many of the sayings are not thought to be dominical.

The historical and especially the literary issues are complex and intertwined, as is clear from the diversity of proposed solutions. The evidence can be weighed variously. Most solutions mask some unproved presuppositions and embrace a succession of judgments that could go another way.

The setting Matthew gives must be accepted. Although he arranges much of his material topically, uses loose time-connectives, condenses his sources and sometimes paraphrases them, there is no convincing evidence that Matthew *invents* settings. Nor will appeal to some elusive genre suffice. If Matthew is a coherent writer, such nonhistorical material must be reasonably and readily separable from his historical material, if the alleged "genre" was recognizable to the first readers. Verse 5a could scarcely be clearer: "These twelve Jesus sent out with the following instructions."

Since Luke records both the commission of the Twelve and that of the Seventy-two (9:1–6; 10:1–16), we must assume that these were separate events. But probably the Twelve were part of the Seventy-two; instructions given the latter were therefore given the former. Although v.5a is historically specific about the fact of Jesus' instructing the Twelve and commissioning them, it does not pinpoint the exact time in his ministry when this took place. We have already found that Matthew, in condensing the account of the raising of Jairus's daughter and omitting the messengers, effectively collapses the first approach of Jairus and the news from the messengers, with the result that the daughter is presented as dead a little earlier than in the synoptic parallels (see on 9:18–26). Similarly, if Jesus instructed the Twelve both at their own first commissioning and later as part of the commissioning of the Seventy-two, the omission of the latter might well be motive enough to combine elements of the two sets of instructions. Both v.5a and 11:1 would still be strictly true.

David Wenham ("The 'Q' Tradition") would go further: he notes that 11:1 is the only ending to a Matthean discourse that omits "these words" or "these parables" or the like and wonders whether the omission might be a hint that this second discourse, unlike the others, is meant to be taken as a Matthean collection of Jesus' sayings. Such an argument from silence seems a slender thread on which to hang so much, not least because, apart from the opening words *kai egeneto* (lit., "and it happened"—see on 7:28–29), the fivefold formula at the end of each discourse varies considerably. But it is difficult simply to discount the possibility; and the suggestion that Matthew has collapsed the two commissionings is not implausible, even if not demonstrable.

Careful study of vv.5–42 suggests that the discourse is more unified than often recognized. Many of the alleged discrepancies are artificial. There is no conflict, for instance, between the ready harvest of 9:37–38 and the resistance in 10:16–22 (contra Morosco, *Redaction Criticism*, p. 325). "The blood of the martyrs is the seed of the church" is a valid principle; and many great awakenings, including the Whitefield and Wesleyan revivals, have shown afresh that the harvest is most plentiful when the workers reap in the teeth of opposition. If Matthew omits the account of the Twelve's actual departure and return (kept in Mark 6:12–13; Luke 9:6, 10), it cannot mean that he does not know of the event or does not believe it happened; otherwise 10:1, 5; 11:1 are incoherent. Matthew is less interested in the details of many events he relates than in Jesus' words; but "less interested" does not mean "not interested," which seems to be the favorite disjunction of many redaction critics.

Certainly vv.17–23 go beyond the immediate mission of the Twelve, and in at least two ways the latter verses envisage a mission to the Gentiles, unlike vv.5b–6, and far severer opposition than anything the Twelve faced during Jesus' ministry. Yet these are not new themes; we have already found Jesus predicting severe persecution (5:10–12 et al.), seeing a time of prolonged witness to the "world" (5:13–14; 7:13–14) after his departure (9:15), and many Gentiles participating in the messianic banquet (8:11–12). Therefore it is surely not unnatural for Jesus to treat this commission of the Twelve as both an explicit short-term itinerary and a paradigm of the longer mission stretching into the years ahead. For the latter, the Twelve need further instruction beyond those needed for the immediate tour, which they must see as in part an exercise anticipating something more. In this sense the Twelve become a paradigm for other disciples in their post-Pentecost witness, a point Matthew understands (cf. 28:18–20); and in this sense he intends that Matthew 10 should also speak to his readers.

The very fact that Matthew includes both what is historically specific in the first, short-term commission (e.g., restriction to Jews, certain clothing) and what is historically relevant only to the post-Pentecost church strongly supports his material's authenticity. If he were simply addressing his own community, much of chapter 10 would be irrelevant. Attempts to get around this by envisaging a divided Matthean community of people for or against a Gentile mission (e.g., S. Brown, "The Two-fold Representation of the Mission in Matthew's Gospel," ST 31 [1977]: 21–32 are extremely speculative. Such a theory depends not only on a selective reading of the Gospels that judges inauthentic all evidence that refutes it, but also on an evangelist abysmally incapable of editing his sources into a coherent whole. Yet Schuyler Brown ("Matthean Community," p. 194) writes: "The fact that contradictory missionary mandates are placed on Jesus' lips is evidence enough that he himself took no position on this matter, one way or the other, and this is not surprising. Jesus took for granted that he and his disciples were sent to Israel."

The presuppositions here are (1) that Jesus did not envisage a racially mixed church and (2) that the Gospels must be read as church documents that do not distinguish between Jesus' day and the time of writing. The first point is repeatedly denied by all four Gospels; the second is called in question by explicit "before–after" passages (e.g., John 2:20–22) and themes or titles (see excursus at 8:20). Jesus says and does many things in the Gospels before the Cross and Resurrection that are fully comprehensible only after these events. The real contrast between vv. 5–16 and vv. 17–42 is salvation-historical. There is implicit recognition that the two situations are not the same, but the first prepares for the second. This distinction is ascribed to Jesus and thus confirms that he saw a continuing community that would grow under fire. Moreover there is evidence elsewhere that Jesus was prepared to discuss widely separate events within the same framework if those separate events are internally connected in some way (see on chs. 24–25).

If this second discourse is coherent, some account must be given of parallels scattered elsewhere in the Synoptics. Earlier discussion (see on chs. 5–7) is still relevant: Jesus was an itinerant preacher who said the same things many times in similar words; the evangelists rarely claim to present *ipsissima verba* but only *ipsissima vox* (see on 3:17); their discourses are very substantial condensations in line with their own interests; they do not hesitate to rearrange the order of presentation of some material within a discourse in order to highlight topical interests. But the sad fact is that there are few methodologically reliable tools for distinguishing between, say, two forms of one aphoristic saying, two reports of the same saying uttered on two occasions, or one report of one such saying often repeated in various forms but preserved in the tradition in one form (surely not problematic if only the *ipsissima vox* is usually what is at stake).

Suppose, for instance, that David Wenham ("The 'Q' Tradition") is essentially right, and most of vv. 5–42 comes from Q, conceived as a variety of sources, oral and written, of Jesus' words: what historical conclusions does such a theory entail? The surprising answer is "Not much." For it is possible that some sayings of Jesus, repeated by him often and on diverse occasions, were jotted down in a sort of amalgam form encapsulating their substance and then used by the evangelists in different contexts and adapted accordingly. Those contexts may well include the historical settings in which the teaching was first uttered. That would be easy to believe if the apostle Matthew really did compose the first Gospel (cf. Introduction, section 5). Authorship does not necessarily affect the authority of any NT book. But it does affect the way the tradition descended and thereby limits the wildest form-critical speculation (cf. Introduction, section 2).

Although Wenham's Q hypothesis may be challenged at many points on the ground that his argument turns on debatable judgments, yet the chief point is that the notion of Q sources behind vv. 5–42 does not itself preclude the authenticity or unity of this discourse. A dozen variations could be shown to produce the same equivocal result. Problems arise only when theories regarding the contributing factors (authors, sources, context, redaction, historical reconstruction of Jesus' life and of the early church) are so aligned as to produce a synthesis that quite unnecessarily contradicts the text or some part of it. This is extremely unfortunate when in fact the text is the only hard evidence we have.

It is not possible in small compass to demonstrate the many factors contributing to scholars' diverse decisions in each passage of the mission discourse and how such factors may, taking full account of the hard evidence, come together in a way justifying Matthew's presentation of this material as a discourse to the Twelve. While the following exposition focuses on the meaning of the text as it stands, a few hints are given as to how difficult source critical and historical problems may be most profitably probed.

2. The commission

10:5b–16

"Do not go among the Gentiles or enter any town of the Samaritans. [6]Go rather to the lost sheep of Israel. [7]As you go, preach this message: 'The kingdom of heaven is near.' [8]Heal the sick, raise the dead, cleanse those who have leprosy,[a] drive out demons. Freely you have received, freely give. [9]Do not take along any gold or silver or copper in your belts; [10]take no bag for the journey, or extra tunic, or sandals or a staff; for the worker is worth his keep.

[11]"Whatever town or village you enter, search for some worthy person there and stay at his house until you leave. [12]As you enter the home, give it your greeting. [13]If the home is deserving, let your peace rest on it; if it is not, let your peace return to you. [14]If anyone will not welcome you or listen to your words, shake the dust off your feet when you leave that home or town. [15]I tell you the truth, it will be more bearable for Sodom and Gomorrah on the day of judgment than for that town. [16]I am sending you out like sheep among wolves. Therefore be as shrewd as snakes and as innocent as doves."

5b–6 Jesus forbade the Twelve (v.5b) from taking "the road to the Gentiles" (cf. Notes)—presumably toward Tyre and Sidon in the north or the Decapolis in the east—and from visiting Samaritan towns in the south. They were to remain in Galilee, ministering to the people of Israel (v.6). Jews despised Samaritans, not only because they preserved a separate cult (cf. John 4:20), but also because they were a mixed race, made up partly of the poorest Jews who had been left in the land at the time of the Exile and partly of Gentile peoples transported into the territory and with whom the remaining Jews had intermingled, thereby succumbing to some syncretism (cf. 2 Kings 17:24–28; cf. ISBE, 4:2673–74). The Twelve were to restrict themselves to "the lost sheep of Israel." This designation does not refer to a certain segment of the Jews (so Stendahl, Peake, 683–84), since in the OT background (esp. Ezek 34; see on Matt 9:36; cf. Isa 53:6; Jer 50:6) the term refers to all the people (Hill, *Matthew*).

Why this restriction? In part it was probably because of pragmatic considerations. That Jesus felt it necessary to mention the Samaritans at all presupposes John 4. The disciples, happy in the exercise of their ability to perform miracles, might have been tempted to evangelize the Samaritans because they remembered Jesus' success there. Judging by Luke 9:52–56, however, the Twelve were still temperamentally ill-equipped to minister to Samaritans. And even after Pentecost, despite an explicit command from the risen Lord (Acts 1:8), the church moved only hesitantly toward the Samaritans (Acts 8).

The most important consideration, however, was not pragmatic but theological. Jesus stood at the nexus in salvation history where as a Jew and the Son of David he came in fulfillment of his people's history as their King and Redeemer. Yet his personal claims would offend so many of his own people that he would be rejected by all but a faithful remnant. Why increase their opposition by devoting time to Gentile ministry? His mission, as predicted, was worldwide in its ultimate aims (see on 1:1; 2:1; 3:9–10; 4:15–16; 5:13–16; 8:1–13; 10:18; 21:43; 24:14; 28:16–20); and all along he had warned that being a Jew was not enough. But his own people must not be excluded because premature offense could be taken at such broad perspectives. Therefore Jesus restricted his own ministry primarily (15:24), though not exclusively (8:1–13; 15:21–39), to Jews. He himself was sent as their Messiah. The messianic people of God developed out of the Jewish remnant and expanded to include Gentiles. The restriction of vv.5–6, therefore, depends on a particular understanding of salvation history (cf. Meier, *Law*, pp. 27–30), which ultimately goes back to Jesus. This Paul well understood: both salvation and judgment were for the Jew first, then for the Gentile (Rom 1:16); and this conviction governed his own early missionary efforts (e.g., Acts 13:5, 44–48; 14:1 et al.).

On modern theories of the significance of vv.5–6, see on v.5a.

7–8 The content of the disciples' message was very like that in 3:2; 4:17. "Repent" is not mentioned but is presupposed. The long-awaited kingdom was now "near" enough (see on 4:17) to be attested by miracles directed at demonism and malady. The "authority" in v.1 cannot be limited to the list of powers mentioned there, for here (v.8) two more are added: raising the dead (textually well attested, if not quite certain) and cleansing lepers (see on 9:18–26; 8:1–4, respectively).

Jesus expected the Twelve to be supported by those to whom they were to minister (cf. vv.9–13; 1 Cor 9:14), but they needed to understand that what they had received—the good news of the kingdom, Jesus' authority, and this commission—they had received "freely" (not "in large bounty"—though that was true—but gratis). Therefore it would have been mercenary to charge others (NEB: "You have received without cost; give without charge"; cf. *Didache* 11–13; *Pirke Aboth* 1:13). The danger of profiteering is still among us (cf. Micah 3:11).

9–10 The imperative *mē ktēsesthe* ("Do not take along," v.9) more likely means "Do not procure" (as in Acts 1:18; 8:20; 22:28). Even then the longer expression *mē ktēsesthe . . . eis* ("Do not procure . . . with a view to [filling your belts]") could mean either "Do not accept money [i.e., fill your moneybelt] for your ministry" or "Do not provide your belt with money when you start out." The parallel in Mark 6:9 obviously means the latter. Gold, silver, and copper refer either to money or to a supply of the metals that could be exchanged for goods or money.

Mark permits "taking" (*airō*) sandals and a staff (a walking stick) and forbids everything else (6:8); Matthew's account forbids "procuring" (*ktaomai*) even sandals or a walking stick (v.10). It may be that Mark's account clarifies what the disciples are permitted to bring, whereas Matthew's assumes that the disciples already have certain things (one cloak, sandals, a walking stick) and forbids them from "procuring" anything more. Two cloaks (cf. on 5:40) might seem too much but would be comforting if sleeping out. The disciples needed to learn the principle that "the worker is worth his keep" (cf. 1 Cor 9:14; 1 Tim 5:17–18) and to shun luxury while learning to rely on God's providence through the hospitality of those who would take them in overnight, thus obviating the need for a second cloak. See further discussion in the Notes.

What is clear is that the Twelve must travel unencumbered, relying on hospitality and God's providence. The details ensure that the instructions were for that mission alone (cf. Luke 22:35–38) and confirm Matthew's consciousness of the historicity of this part of the discourse.

11–15 To settle into the house of a "worthy" person (v.11) implies that the disciples were not to shop around for the most comfortable quarters. In this place "worthy" probably does not refer to a morally upright, honorable, or religious person but to one willing and able to receive an apostle of Jesus and the gospel of the kingdom (cf. discussion in Bonnard)—the opposite of "dogs" and "pigs" (7:6). As the disciples entered the house, they were to give it their "greeting." Luke (10:5) gives us the actual words: "Peace to this house." Neither Matthew nor Luke is introducing post-resurrection notions of *šālôm* ("peace"), even though later Christians would be reminded of the peace Jesus achieved for them (Luke 24:36; John 14:27 et al.). Instead the greeting prepares for v. 13: "As you enter the home" (NIV; same word as "house" in v. 12, probably with the meaning "household"), you are to give the normal greeting; but if the home turns out to be "unworthy" (as defined above), contrary to what you had been led to believe, then let your greeting of peace return to you (v. 13); i.e., don't stay. The Twelve were emissaries of Jesus. Those who received them received him (cf. v. 40). Their greeting was of real value because of their relationship to him. Loss of their greeting was loss of their presence and therefore loss of Jesus. Potiphar's household was blessed because of Joseph's presence (Gen 39:3–5). How much more those homes that harbored the apostles of the Messiah!

What was true for the home applied equally to the town (v. 14). A pious Jew, on leaving Gentile territory, might remove from his feet and clothes all dust of the pagan land now being left behind (SBK, 1:571), thus dissociating himself from the pollution of those lands and the judgment in store for them. For the disciples to do this to Jewish homes and towns would be a symbolic way of saying that the emissaries of Messiah now view those places as pagan, polluted, and liable to judgment (cf. Acts 13:51; 18:6). The actions, while outrageously shocking, accord with Matthew 8:11–12; 11:20–24. Sodom and Gomorrah faced catastrophic destruction because of their sin (Gen 19) and became bywords of loathsome corruption (Isa 1:9; Matt 11:22–24; Luke 17:29; Rom 9:29; 2 Peter 2:6; Jude 7; cf. Jub 36:10). Although there is still worse to come for them on the Day of Judgment, there is yet more awful judgment for those who reject the word and the messengers of the Messiah (cf. Heb 2:1–3).

Once again the christological claim, though implicit, is unambiguous. As in 7:21–23, Jesus here insists that one's eternal destiny turns on relationship to him or even to his emissaries. At the same time, even in this early ministry, Jesus' apostles were to face the certainty of opposition—as did Jesus himself, rejected at Nazareth (13:53–58) and in Samaria (Luke 9:52–53), and not believed in the towns of Galilee (11:20–24). That early opposition pointed to the greater suffering still to come (vv. 17ff.) and also aligned the disciples of Jesus with the prophets of old (5:10–12) and with Jesus himself (10:24–25). Thus the disciples began to learn that the advance of the kingdom was divisive (vv. 34–35; cf. 2 Cor 2:15–16) and would meet with violent opposition (see on 11:11–12).

16 The first part of v. 16 has a close parallel in Luke 10:3, part of the commission to the Seventy-two. Because it is short and aphoristic, it is impossible to be certain how many times Jesus said it. Here it links the preceding pericope with the following warnings about persecution. The verse goes as well with what succeeds as what precedes.

Jesus pictured his disciples, defenseless in themselves, located in a dangerous environment. This is where he himself was sending them. The shepherd in this metaphor sends his sheep into the wolf pack (cf. 7:15; John 10:12; Acts 20:29). Therefore they must be *phronimoi* ("shrewd") as serpents, which in several ancient Near Eastern cultures were proverbial for prudence. But prudence can easily degenerate into cheap cunning unless it goes with simplicity. The disciples must prove not only "shrewd" but *akeraioi* ("innocent"; used elsewhere in the NT only in Rom

16:19; Phil 2:15). Yet innocence becomes ignorance, even naiveté, unless combined with prudence.

The dove was not an established symbol. In Hosea 7:11 a dove is pictured as "easily deceived and senseless." In a late Midrash the serpent–dove contrast appears ("God saith to the Israelites: 'Towards me they are sincere as doves, but toward the Gentiles they are cunning as serpents'" [Cant.R.2:14]). Yet not only is this Midrash late, the contrast is not at all what Jesus had in mind. His followers were to be, not prudent toward outsiders and innocent toward God, but both prudent and innocent in their mission to outsiders. In this light the dove image becomes clear. Doves are retiring but not astute; they are easily ensnared by the fowler. So Jesus' disciples, in their mission as sheep among wolves, must be "shrewd," avoiding conflicts and attacks where possible; but they must also be "innocent," i.e., not so cautious, suspicious, and cunning that circumspection degenerates into fear or elusiveness. The balance is difficult, but not a little of Jesus' teaching combines such poles of meaning (see on 7:1–6).

Notes

---

5 The prohibition εἰς ὁδὸν ἐθνῶν μὴ ἀπέλθητε (eis hodon ethnōn mē apelthēte) means literally "Do not go away on the road of the Gentiles"—i.e., Do not go in the direction of (Aram. לְאֹרַח leʾōraḥ) the Gentiles; "Do not take the road to Gentile lands" (NEB).

9–10 Though the distinction between κτάομαι (ktaomai, "procure") and αἴρω (airō, "take") may work in Matthew and Mark, it fails in Luke, who uses airō (as in Mark) but forbids a staff in 9:3 and sandals in 10:4. This suggests to Marshall (Luke, pp. 352f.) that Matthew and Luke depend on Q as opposed to Mark. That is possible. But the fact that Luke's verb (airō) is the same as Mark's calls it in question. Many solutions have been proposed, none altogether convincing (cf. E. Power, "The Staff of the Apostles: A Problem in Gospel Harmony," Biblica 4 [1923]: 241–66; Lagrange; Schniewind; Lane, pp. 207f.). Perhaps the simplest is that Luke has not changed Mark but in both passages (Luke 9:3; 10:4) draws from Q, like Matthew; but in 9:3 Luke changes ktaomai ("I procure") to airō ("I take"), which has a semantic range large enough to mean the former, and in 10:4 changes ktaomai to βαστάζω (bastazō, "bear," "carry"), the latter perhaps suggesting carrying some luggage: no "purse" ("no money"), no "bag" (no "luggage"), and no "sandals" (none carried). This suggestion is supported by the fact that the two verbs in Luke and the one in Matthew are all imperatives, unlike Mark's subordinate construction and subjunctive mood. In other words Matthew and Luke agree not only on what is permitted but on the grammatical construction. Luke's only agreement with Mark is in one of his two verbs.

16 The pronoun ἐγώ (egō, "I") is probably not emphatic, as ἰδοὺ ἐγώ (idou egō, lit., "behold I") reflects a Semitic parallel that is unemphatic (cf. Turner, Syntax, p. 38).

---

3. Warnings of future sufferings (10:17–25)

a. The Spirit's help

10:17–20

> [17]Be on your guard against men; they will hand you over to the local councils and flog you in their synagogues. [18]On my account you will be brought before governors and kings as witnesses to them and to the Gentiles. [19]But when they arrest

you, do not worry about what to say or how to say it. At that time you will be given what to say, [20]for it will not be you speaking, but the Spirit of your Father speaking through you.

There are parallels in vv.17–25 both to 24:9, 13 and to Luke 6:40; 12:11–12; 21:12. Although it has often been affirmed, it is doubtful that Matthew has simply pulled back some material from the Olivet Discourse (see on 10:5a). But there may be substantial reliance on Q (cf. D. Wenham, "The 'Q' Tradition"). The language is demonstrably Palestinian. Even if Matthew applies some of these things to his own readers (cf. Hare, pp. 96–114), there is no reason to doubt the authenticity of these warnings. What this means is that Jesus envisaged an extended time of witness in the midst of persecution—in short, a witnessing and suffering church.

17 The *de* ("But," NIV) does not have adversative force. It merely connects this warning with the aphorism in v.16, showing how it is to be applied. The men who will hand the disciples over must be Jews, as the context is the synagogue; and so the persecution here envisaged is Jewish persecution of Christians (unlike v.18). The *synedria* ("local councils," pl. only here in the NT), which could be civic or synagogal, were charged with preserving the peace. That flogging is used for punishment, rather than the broader term "beating," implies that the opposition is not mob violence but the result of judicial action (Hare, p. 104). Moreover Jesus is envisaging a time before the absolute separation of church and synagogue has taken place, for synagogue floggings (cf. 23:34; Mark 13:9; Acts 22:19; cf. 2 Cor 11:24–25) were most easily inflicted on synagogue members. At a later period the worshipers would sometimes sing a psalm while the flogging took place. But there is no evidence this was practiced in NT times. In any case we are reminded of the slowness with which Jewish Christians withdrew from broader Jewish worship in the post-Pentecost period.

The reference to "their" synagogues is often interpreted as an anachronism, reflecting the church–synagogue polarity (see on 4:23; 7:29; 9:35; 11:1; 12:9; 13:54). Normally the word "their" is explicitly Matthean, but here Jesus uses it. This may suggest redactional phrasing. Significantly, however, the OT prophets in speaking for God commonly used "their" and "them" language when referring to apostate Israel. Here it is very likely that the OT background explains the usage. And because Matthew makes much of the failure of most Jews to receive their own Messiah, it is likely that the OT has affected his phrasing elsewhere. Certainly Christian readers, understanding themselves to be recipients of the revelation most Jews had refused, would see the "their" within this polarized context. Nevertheless the term itself is no proof of anachronism unless it was similarly anachronistic in its OT setting, which is absurd. Indeed, if this OT background is determinative, then both Jesus and Matthew self-consciously spoke of Israel from the perspective of a divine revelatory stance that warned Israel afresh against apostasy, a theme elsewhere made explicit (e.g., 8:11–12).

18 As the witness would extend at some future time beyond Galilee and the Jewish race, so also the opposition: "governors" (*hēgemonas*, rulers and magistrates at various levels) and "kings" make this clear. As in 8:4 and 24:14, the "witness" is not against people but to them; it becomes either the means by which they accept the truth or, when they reject it, a condemnation. The disciples would be harassed and persecuted, not on account of who they are but on account of who Christ is (see on 5:10-12). For his sake their witness would extend "to them and to the Gentiles"— probably not a reference "to Jews [or Jewish magistrates] and to the Gentiles," but "to governors and kings and to [other] Gentiles." Overlapping between the paired elements is not uncommon in such constructions (e.g., Mark 16:7; Gr. of Acts 5:29; 9:16; cf. Hare, pp. 108-9).

19-20 The translation of *paradidōmi* (lit., "I hand over," as in v.17) as "arrest" (v.19) is doubtful. The subject is ambiguous: "people," "opponents," or "Jewish leaders" could be "handing over" the disciples to the Gentile authorities. Later on this happened to Paul and other Christians, who at first witnessed to their faith with relative impunity under the Roman laws granting exemptions from emperor worship to Jews, but fell victim to increasing Roman wrath as the Jews progressively denied any link between themselves and Christians.

Confronting a high Roman official would be far more terrifying to Jewish believers than confronting a synagogue council. High officials, even when hated, were accorded far greater respect than in modern democracies; and they used professional orator-lawyers in legal matters (e.g., Tertullus, Acts 24:1). But if Jesus warned his disciples of dangers, he also promised them help: the Spirit would speak through them when the time came; so they should not fret about their response. This promise is neither a sop for lazy preachers nor equivalent to the promises given the Twelve in the farewell discourse (John 14-16) that the Spirit would recall to their memory all they had heard from Jesus (John 14:16, 26). It is a pledge to believers who have been brought before tribunals because of their witness. The promised assistance does not assume an absolute disjunction between "you" and the "Spirit" (v.20), for the underlying Semitic disjunction is rarely absolute (e.g., Gen 45:8; Exod 16:8; cf. Zerwick, par. 445). The history of Christian martyrs is studded with examples of the fulfillment of this promise.

Unlike Luke, Matthew does not often mention the Spirit. But from other passages in his Gospel, it is clear that he associates the Spirit with the kingdom's dramatic coming (3:11; 12:28, 31) and the church's witness (28:18-20). That same Spirit, "the Spirit of your Father," would provide Jesus' followers with the help they needed under persecution when facing hostile officials.

b. *Endurance*

10:21-23

> 21"Brother will betray brother to death, and a father his child; children will rebel against their parents and have them put to death. 22All men will hate you because of me, but he who stands firm to the end will be saved. 23When you are persecuted in one place, flee to another. I tell you the truth, you will not finish going through the cities of Israel before the Son of Man comes.

21-22 It is not enough for Jesus' disciples to be opposed by Jewish and Gentile officialdom; they will be hounded and betrayed by their own family members (v.21; see further vv.34-39). The theme of division between persons as a sign of the End is not unknown in Jewish apocalyptic literature (4 Ezra 5:9; Jub 23:19; 2 Baruch 70:3—though none of these refers explicitly to family divisions). Here the allusion is to Micah 7:6, quoted in vv.35-36. "All men" (v.22) does not mean "all men without exception," for then there would be no converts, but "all men without distinction" —all men irrespective of race, color, or creed. That the good news of the kingdom of God and his righteousness should elicit such intense and widespread hostility is a sad commentary on "all men." The hatred erupts, Jesus says, *dia to onoma mou* (lit., "on account of my name")—either because one bears the name "Christian" (cf. 1 Peter 4:14) or, less anachronistically and more likely, "on account of me" (see on 5:10–12.

The one who "stands firm"—the verb *hypomenō* does not signify active resistance so much as patient endurance (cf. LXX Dan 12:12; Mark 13:13; Rom 12:12; 1 Peter 2:20)—will be saved; but he must stand firm *eis telos* ("to the end"). Though this anarthrous expression could be taken adverbially to mean "without breaking down," it is far more likely purposely ambiguous to mean either "to the end of one's life" or, because of the frequent association of *telos* ("end") and cognates with the eschatological end, "to the end of the age." This is not to say that only martyrs will be saved; but if the opposition one of Jesus' disciples faces calls for the sacrifice of life itself, commitment to him must be so strong that the sacrifice is willingly made. Otherwise there is no salvation. Thus from earliest times Christians have been crucified, burned, impaled, drowned, starved, racked—for no other reason than that they belonged to him. As with martyrs among God's people before the coming of Christ, so now: the world was not worthy of them (Heb 11:38).

23 This verse is among the most difficult in the NT canon. The textual variants (cf. Metzger, *Textual Commentary*, p. 28) are complex but affect the main interpretive questions little.

1. Some have understood the coming of the Son of Man to refer to a coming of the historical Jesus in the wake of the mission of the Twelve as in the mission of the Seventy-two (Luke 10:1). The focus of attention has thus reverted back to the immediate commission (vv.5b–16). Jesus is telling the Twelve to "get a move on," because they will not have visited the cities of Israel before he "comes" to them— i.e., catches up with them. This view has been elegantly defended by J. Dupont (" 'Vous n'aurez pas achevé les villes d'Israël...' [Mat. X²³]," NovTest 2 [1958]: 228–44), who points out that elsewhere Matthew can bring the title "Son of Man" back (from 16:21 to 16:13) to a new location where it is equivalent to no more than a sonorous "I" (assuming his source is Mark 8:27, 31). Dupont suggests that in Matthew's source 10:23 was read after 10:5–6, which would confirm his interpretation. This view therefore turns in part on finding a source common to Matthew 10:23 and Luke 10:1—presumably a Q tradition—and this possibility has been strengthened somewhat by the source-critical arguments of H. Schürmann ("Zur Traditions- und Redaktionsgeschichte von Mt 10, 23," *Biblische Zeitschrift* 3 [1959]: 82–88) and David Wenham ("The 'Q' Tradition"), who try to show that v.23 springs from Q. The arguments are unconvincing. In Wenham's case they hinge on the assertion that v.23 is awkward because the literary parallel wth vv.19–20 is inexact (v.23 uses the verb "to persecute" instead of the verb "to hand over"). But it is not at all clear why Matthew should use the same verb: most Semitic parallelism depends on small verbal changes.

David Wenham ("The 'Q' Tradition") argues that v.23 "seems something of an afterthought in its present position following the climactic 'he who endures to the end shall be saved.' " But v.23 is anticlimactic only if the coming of the Son of Man refers exclusively to Jesus' follow-up ministry. If instead Jesus in v.22 is enjoining perseverance amid suffering witness, in clear reference to a post-Pentecost setting, then the persecution in v.23 should be similarly interpreted. The disciples' perseverance to the end does not mean withdrawal but moving on from city to city until the Son of Man comes. In this light v.23 is still difficult but certainly not anticlimactic. Indeed, this first interpretation fails to come to grips with two major hurdles. It fails to explain adequately why Matthew should move a comprehensible saying from a location following vv.5–6 (or even v.14) and place it here, where (we must implausibly suppose) the verse has nothing to do with its immediate context. Moreover, the geographical territory to be covered (see on 4:23–25) embraces enough towns and villages that, under this interpretation, the urgent call for haste seems inept. And Luke 10:1, the alleged parallel, does not speak of ministry to all the cities of Israel but only to the towns to which Jesus was about to go. Above all there is no evidence in any Gospel that the Twelve were actively persecuted during their first mission but only on occasion rebuffed (as in vv.11–15).

2. Some take "the Son of Man's coming" to refer to the public identification of Jesus as the Messiah, presumably at the Resurrection (Sabourin) or shortly after. Not only would this be an odd use of the expression, but the interpretation fails to show how the disciples were actually persecuted up to that time, or how there could be any urgency in such a deadline. Older commentators follow a similar line, exchanging the coming of the Spirit (John 14:23) for the Resurrection (e.g., Chrysostom, Calvin, Beza). But we have noted that the Spirit is not a major theme in Matthew (see on v.20); and in any case never in the NT is the Son of Man completely identified with him. A better modification of this view is offered by Stonehouse (*Witness of Matthew*, pp. 139f.) and Gaechter (*Matthäus*), who argue that this is the lesser inbreaking of the kingdom in the events succeeding Pentecost, the most probable meaning of 16:28 (below). But in v.23 this interpretation fails to account for the note of urgency. One might almost make a case for delaying witness until such an inbreaking.

3. Others take the verse to refer to the Second Coming, equivalent to 24:30; 25:31; 26:64. Although some would argue the point (see on Matt 24–25), the language of the Son of Man's coming most easily fits that interpretation. The problem then is the words "of Israel," so difficult in this interpretation that they are wrongly omitted by B (Alexandrian) and D (Western). Various expedients are appealed to in order to mitigate the problem: "Israel" is a symbol for the world or for the church, or there is some kind of double fulfillment (on the latter, cf. Hendriksen, who speaks of "prophetic foreshortening"; and A. Feuillet, "Les origines et la signification de Mt 10, 23b," CBQ 23 (1961): 197f.—though the article as a whole, pp. 182–90, supports 7 below). That "Israel" represents church or world is almost impossible in the context of Matthew's theology, and that there is some kind of double fulfillment is not much more than a surreptitious appeal for double incoherence: in the first fulfillment the difficulties of 1 remain, and in the second the problem words "of Israel" are still not explained. Whatever one thinks of multiple fulfillment in the Scriptures, this is not a clear instance of it. Bonnard sees a reference to Jesus' second coming in v.23b but sees no urgency. The verse simply insists on all the possibilities of witness given in Israel until the End and closely ties together Israel with that end (as in Rom 11:25). This view has its attractions. Nevertheless the note of urgency linking v.23a and v.23b cannot be disposed of so easily. Gundry has a similar view and also argues that the verse is redactional and therefore not authentic.

4. At the turn of the century, Schweitzer (pp. 358ff.) used this text to develop his "thoroughgoing eschatology." He argued that v.23b shows that Jesus believed the end of time would take place so soon that he did not expect to see the disciples return before the End arrived. Jesus was wrong, of course, and therefore had to readjust his own theology. This was the first "delay of the Parousia." Unfortunately Jesus was also wrong in expecting God to exonerate him before he died. Therefore the church was forced to adjust its theology to accommodate these errors; and only a few traces of Jesus' earliest teachings, like this passage, still peep unambiguously through the text. This view is well criticized by Kümmel (*Jesus' Promise*, pp. 61ff.).

5. A combination of the last two views is now espoused by several scholars (e.g., Fenton, Hill) who think v.23b refers to the Second Coming and that Jesus expected it within one generation or so (see also on 24:34; Hill specifies forty or fifty years). But there are so many hints of a much longer delay before the Second Coming (e.g., 13:24–33; 18:15–35; 19:28; 21:43; 23:32, 39 et al.; cf. Maier) that there seems little to be gained by this interpretation and much to be lost.

6. Dispensationalists are inclined to see v.23b as a reference to the Second Coming that "views the entire present church age as a parenthesis not taken into account in this prophecy" (Walvoord; cf. A.C. Gaebelein). Quite apart from the correctness or otherwise of the entire theological structure presupposed by this interpretation, it detaches v.23 from its context (if vv.16–22 refer to post-Pentecost *Christian* experience—so Walvoord) or else detaches vv.16–23 from their context (if the verses do not apply to any of Jesus' disciples but to believers living during the Tribulation after the church has been raptured away). There is no exegetical warrant for either detachment; and both would be incomprehensible, not only to Jesus' hearers, but also to the first readers of Matthew's Gospel.

7. The "coming of the Son of Man" here refers to his coming in judgment against the Jews, culminating in the sack of Jerusalem and the destruction of the temple (so France, *Jesus*, p. 140; Feuillet, "Les origines," pp. 182–98; Moule, *Birth*, p. 90; J.A.T. Robinson, *Jesus and His Coming* [London: SCM, 1957], pp. 80, 91–92; and others). Calvin thinks this interpretation farfetched, Hill that it is improbable. In fact a powerful case can be made for it. The coming of the Son of Man refers to the same event as the coming of the kingdom, even though the two expressions are conceptually complementary. Thus *the* coming of the Son of Man brings in the consummated kingdom (see on 24:30–31; 25:31). But the kingdom, as we have seen, comes in stages (see on 4:17; 12:28). In one sense Jesus was born a king (see on 2:2); in another he has all authority as a result of his passion and resurrection (28:18); and in yet another his kingdom awaits the end. Mingled with this theme of the coming of the kingdom are Jesus' repeated warnings to the Jews concerning the disaster they are courting by failing to recognize and receive him (cf. esp. Feuillet). In this he stands on the shoulders of the OT prophets; but his warnings are unique because he himself is the eschatological judge and because the messianic reign is now dawning in both blessing and wrath (8:11–12; 21:31–32).

Against this background the coming of the Son of Man in v.23 marks that stage in the coming of the kingdom in which the judgment repeatedly foretold falls on the Jews. With it the temple cultus disappears, and the new wine necessarily takes to new wineskins (see on 9:16–17). The age of the kingdom comes into its own, precisely because so many of the structured foreshadowings of the OT, bound up with the cultus and nation, now disappear (see on 5:17–48). The Son of Man comes.

Above all this interpretation makes contextual sense of v.23. The connection is not with v.22 alone but with vv.17–22, which picture the suffering witness of the church in the post-Pentecost period *during a time when many of Jesus' disciples are still bound up with the synagogue*. During that period, Jesus says in v.23, his disciples must not use the opposition to justify quitting or bravado. Far from it. When they face persecution, they must take it as no more than a signal for strategic withdrawal to the next city (W. Barclay, *The Gospel of Matthew*, 2 vols. [Philadelphia: Westminster, 1975], 1:378–80) where witness must continue, for the time is short. They will not have finished evangelizing the cities of Israel before the Son of Man comes in judgment on Israel.

Interpreted in this way the "Son of Man" saying of v.23 belongs to the eschatological category (see excursus on 8:20), but the eschatology is somewhat realized. The strength of this interpretation is sometimes diluted by applying it unchanged to 16:28; 24:31 (so France, *Jesus*). In fact there are important differences disallowing the view that all these texts refer to the Fall of Jerusalem in A.D. 70. Nevertheless they confirm the view that "the coming of the Son of Man" bears in Matthew the same rich semantic field as "the coming of the kingdom" (see on 6:10; 12:28).

c. Inspiration

10:24–25

> 24"A student is not above his teacher, nor a servant above his master. 25It is enough for the student to be like his teacher, and the servant like his master. If the head of the house has been called Beelzebub, how much more the members of his household!

24–25 The two brief analogies in vv.24–25a occur in various forms elsewhere in the NT (Luke 6:40; John 13:16; 15:20) and in Jewish literature (b *Berakoth* 58b); and like many good proverbs, they could be applied variously by capable preachers. Here Jesus forbids the disciples from being surprised when they suffer persecution. If they follow him, they should expect no less. The statement reveals something of Jesus' perception of the nature of his own ministry and of the way the "gospel of the kingdom" will advance in the world.

Those who deny the authenticity of vv.24–25a and other passages in which Jesus speaks implicitly of his sufferings do so not on literary evidence but on the basis of a priori decisions about what Jesus could and could not have known.

The insult "Beelzebub" (or, to preserve the best orthography, *Beelzeboul*) has an uncertain derivation. In the NT the term occurs only here and at 12:24, 27; Mark 3:22; Luke 11:15, 18–19. It may have come from OT Hebrew *ba'alzebûb* ("lord of flies"), a mocking takeoff of *ba'al z*ᵉ*bûl* ("Prince Baal"), a pagan deity (2 Kings 1:2–3, 16). But in that case one wonders why the final syllable has been changed in NT Greek to *boul*. Other derivations include a mocking "lord of dung" and "lord of the heights" (heaven). One of the best suggestions is that of E.C.B. MacLaurin ("Beelzeboul," NovTest 20 [1978]: 156–60), who shows it may well be a straightforward translation of *oikodespotēs* ("head of the house," NIV). Beelzeboul is recognized in the NT as the prince of the demons and identified with Satan (12:24–27; Mark 3:22–26; Luke 11:18–19). Thus the real head of the house, Jesus, who heads the household of God, is being wilfully confused with the head of the house of demons. The charge is shockingly vile—the Messiah himself rejected as Satan! If so, why should his disciples expect less?

This verse has not been constructed by the evangelist out of bits from 12:22–32, as if the charge were leveled at Jesus only the once. On the contrary, 9:34 suggests that it was a frequent slur.

4. Prohibition of fear (10:26–31)

a. The emergence of truth

10:26–27

> 26"So do not be afraid of them. There is nothing concealed that will not be disclosed, or hidden that will not be made known. 27What I tell you in the dark, speak in the daylight; what is whispered in your ear, proclaim from the roofs.

Probably vv.26–27 are also transitional, like v.16. Consideration of how disciples must expect to face persecution and opprobrium makes it necessary to say something about how to handle fear (vv.26–31) and about the high standards of discipleship such a perspective presupposes. There are similar sayings elsewhere (cf. Luke 12:2–9; see also Mark 4:22; 8:38; Luke 9:26; 21:18). Yet there is no easy source pattern (cf. Hill); and most of the individual sayings are brief, easily memorized, and usable again and again.

26–27 "Them" refers to the persecutors (v.23). The connective *oun* ("So") may simply begin a new exhortation based on the preceding (Bonnard), or it may offer a tighter connection: in view of a master who suffers ahead of his disciples, *therefore* do not fear, etc. The truth must emerge; the gospel and its outworkings in the disciples may not now be visible to all, but nothing will remain hidden forever. And if the truth will emerge at the End, how wise to declare it fully and boldly now. Flat rooftops of Palestinian houses provided excellent places for speakers (cf. Jos. War II, 611 [xxi. 5]). In a sense the apostles were to have more of a public ministry than Jesus himself. He told them things in private, some of which they did not even understand till after the Resurrection (see excursus on 8:20; cf. John 14:26; 16:12–15). But they were to teach them fully and publicly.

b. The nonfinality of death

10:28

> 28Do not be afraid of those who kill the body but cannot kill the soul. Rather, be afraid of the One who can destroy both soul and body in hell.

28 The second reason for learning not to fear men emerges from the fact that the worst they can do does not match the worst God can do. Though Satan may have great power (6:13; 24:22), only God can destroy soul and body in hell. "The fear of the LORD is" therefore "the beginning of wisdom" (Prov 9:10); for if God be truly feared, none other need be. Fear of men proves to be a snare (Prov 29:25). The same thought is found in extracanonical Jewish literature (e.g., Wisd Sol 16:13–14; 2 Macc 6:26; 4 Macc 13:14–15).

For "hell," see on 5:22. The force of *psychē* ("soul") in the NT is closely related to *nepeš* ("soul") and *lēb* ("heart," "inner man") in the OT (for full discussion, cf. DNTT, 3:676–89). The thought is not so much of an ontological part utterly distinct from body as of the inner man destined for salvation or damnation (cf. 1 Peter 1:9; 2:11, 25; 4:19). Unavoidable in this context is the thought that hell is a place of torment for the whole person: there will be a resurrection of the unjust as well as of the just.

c. Continuing providence

10:29–31

> ²⁹Are not two sparrows sold for a penny? Yet not one of them will fall to the ground apart from the will of your Father. ³⁰And even the very hairs of your head are all numbered. ³¹So don't be afraid; you are worth more than many sparrows.

29–31 The third reason for not being afraid is an a fortiori argument: If God's providence is so all embracing that not even a sparrow drops from the sky apart from the will of God, cannot that same God be trusted to extend his providence over Jesus' disciples? The sparrow was used for food by very poor people. Two might be sold for "a penny" (one-sixteenth of a denarius, which was about a day's wage; cf. Deiss LAE, pp. 272–75). "Your Father" adds a piquant touch: this God of all providence is the disciples' Father. God's sovereignty is not limited only to life-and-death issues; even the hairs of our heads are counted. Jesus' third argument against fear is thus the very opposite of what is commonly advanced. People say that God cares about the big things but not about little details. But Jesus says that God's sovereignty over the tiniest detail should give us confidence that he also superintends the larger matters.

5. Characteristics of discipleship (10:32–39)

a. Acknowledging Jesus

10:32–33

> ³²"Whoever acknowledges me before men, I will also acknowledge him before my Father in heaven. ³³But whoever disowns me before men, I will disown him before my Father in heaven.

32–33 Many assume that Matthew here edits Mark 8:38, which was addressed to a crowd (cf. also Luke 12:8–9). But Mark's words have a structure that has led to much of the debate over the "Son of Man" question.

> Whoever confesses me . . .
> The Son of Man will confess . . .
> Whoever disowns (or is ashamed of) me . . .
> The Son of Man will disown (or be ashamed of) . . . .

This ABAB parallelism has induced many, especially since Bultmann (*Synoptic Tradition*, pp. 112, 128), to argue that the historical Jesus distinguished the Son of Man from himself (cf. excursus on 8:20), and that Matthew's editing, by eliminating the "Son of Man" elements and substituting the first person personal pronoun, has identified Jesus with the Son of Man. The explanation of Hooker (*Son of Man*, pp. 120–21, 189) is generally satisfying. The "I" clauses in Mark picture Jesus speaking to those thinking of following him in his earthly life; the "Son of Man" clauses picture Jesus in the future, and at this point some of his claims are still veiled. It is difficult to see how Jesus could have proclaimed another Son of Man and still have left room for himself. Elsewhere he explicitly identifies the two (Mark 14:61–62). But we may take Hooker's argument one step further. Obviously vv.32–33 are not addressed to indiscriminate crowds but to the Twelve. The reason for the clarity of Matthew's form of the saying may therefore turn, not on a development in the church's theology, but on the distinction in the audience. This was one of the things Jesus said clearly to his disciples in secret and which they would one day shout from the housetops (v.27).

Though addressed to the Twelve (vv.1–5), like much of vv.17–42, this saying looks beyond the apostles to disciples at large. The point is made clear by "Whoever" (v.32). A necessary criterion for being a disciple of Jesus is to acknowledge him publicly (cf. Rom 1:16; 10:9). This will vary in boldness, fluency, wisdom, sensitivity, and frequency from believer to believer (cf. Calvin); but consistently to disown Christ (same verb as in 26:69–75) is to be disowned by Christ. Jesus now speaks not of "your Father" (as in v.29) but of "my Father." In view is his special filial relationship with the Father, by which the final destiny of all humanity depends solely on his word (see on 7:21–23; cf. 25:12). The christological implications of Jesus' words are unavoidable. "Jesus makes the entire position of men in the world to come, whether for weal or woe, to depend upon their relationship to and attitude toward him in this present world. Is this a claim which any mere man might have made? Do we not encounter here essentially the exclusiveness of Acts 4:12?" (Stonehouse, *Origins*, p. 190).

Notes

32 The rather strange Greek ὁμολογεῖν ἐν ἐμοί (*homologein en emoi*, "to acknowledge me") is perfectly natural Aramaic (but not Heb.); cf. Moulton, *Accidence*, p. 463; Moule, *Idiom Book*, p. 183.

b. *Recognizing the gospel*

10:34–36

34"Do not suppose that I have come to bring peace to the earth. I did not come to bring peace, but a sword. 35For I have come to turn

" 'a man against his father,
a daughter against her mother,
a daughter-in-law against her mother-in-law—
36 a man's enemies will be the members of his own household.'

34–36 As many Jews in Jesus' day thought the coming of Messiah would bring them political peace and material prosperity, so today many in the church think that Jesus' presence will bring them a kind of tranquility. But Jesus insisted that his mission entailed strife and division (v.34). Prince of Peace though he is (see on 5:9), the world will so violently reject him and his reign that men and women will divide over him (vv.35–36); cf. Luke 12:49–53; cf. Neil, pp. 157–60). Before the consummation of the kingdom, even the peace Jesus bequeaths his disciples will have its setting in the midst of a hostile world (John 14:27; 16:33; cf. James 4:4).

The repeated statement "I have come" shows Jesus' christological and eschatological awareness (contra Arens, pp. 63–90 who uses the same evidence to argue that such elements must be church creations). Earlier he warned his disciples of the world's hatred of his followers, a hatred extending even to close relatives (vv.21–22); now he ties this perspective to an OT analogy (Mic 7:6; on the text form, cf. Stendahl, *School*, pp. 90f.; Gundry, *Use of OT*, pp. 78f.). Micah describes the sinfulness and rebellion in the days of King Ahaz; but insofar as Jesus' disciples by following him align themselves with the prophets (5:10–12), then the situation in Micah's time points to the greater division at Messiah's coming. Many critics think these verses apply solely to Christians in Matthew's day, and doubtless they caused Matthew's readers to think of their own sufferings. But some older commentators (e.g., Plumptre) wonder whether the Twelve, even during Jesus' earthly ministry, did not face some opposition from family and friends—as did Jesus himself (13:53–58; John 7:3–5). Even today the situation has not greatly eased. In the "liberal" West people who have become Christians have occasionally been disowned and disinherited by their families and have lost their jobs. And under totalitarian regimes of the right or the left there has been and still is untold suffering for Christ—witness Christians in the Gulag Archipelago.

c. *Preferring Jesus*

10:37–39

> [37]"Anyone who loves his father or mother more than me is not worthy of me; anyone who loves his son or daughter more than me is not worthy of me; [38]and anyone who does not take his cross and follow me is not worthy of me. [39]Whoever finds his life will lose it, and whoever loses his life for my sake will find it.

37–39 The absolutism of the Semitic idiom (Luke 14:26) is rightly interpreted by Matthew: a man must love (for comments on this verb, see on 5:43) his wife, family, friends, and even his enemies; but he must love Jesus supremely (v.37). Again the saying is either that of the Messiah or of a maniac. The rabbinic parallels of the master–disciple relationship (cf. M *Baba Metzia* 2:11) are not very close; though they place the master above the father, they allow the disciple's personal interest to stand above his allegiance to his master. Jesus demanded death to self (vv.38–39). "Taking one's cross" does not mean putting up with some awkward or tragic situation in one's life but painfully dying to self. In that sense every disciple of Jesus bears the same cross. After Jesus' death and resurrection, the emotional impact of these sayings must have been greatly heightened; but even before those events, the reference to Crucifixion would vividly call to mind the shame and pain of such a sacrifice. For "worthy," see on v.11.

The appeal is not to gloom but to discipleship. There is a strong paradox here. Those who lose their *psychē* ("soul," "life"—see on vv.28–30), whether in actual martyrdom or disciplined self-denial, will "find" it in the age to come. Those who "find" it now (the expression in classical Greek means "to win or preserve" life) by living for themselves and refusing to submit to the demands of Christian disciple-ship lose it in the age to come (cf. 16:25; Mark 8:35; Luke 9:24; 17:33).

6. Encouragement: response to the disciples and to Jesus

10:40–42

> [40]"He who receives you receives me, and he who receives me receives the one who sent me. [41]Anyone who receives a prophet because he is a prophet will receive a prophet's reward, and anyone who receives a righteous man because he is a righteous man will receive a righteous man's reward. [42]And if anyone gives even a cup of cold water to one of these little ones because he is my disciple, I tell you the truth, he will certainly not lose his reward."

The foregoing teaching about what it means to be a disciple of Jesus has its darker side. This final section of the discourse is more encouraging—it reverts again to the ultimate tie between the treatment of Jesus and that of his followers (see on vv.24–25); it turns our eyes to the future (see on v.28) and shows us that God is indebted to no one.

40–42 It is commonly understood in the NT that a man's agent must be received as the man himself (v.40; cf. Luke 10:16; John 12:44–45; 13:20; Acts 9:4). And as this section closes the discourse that opens with instructions to the Twelve, many inter-pret "prophet" and "righteous man" (v.41) as alternative designations of the apostles in v.40, and v.42 as an extension to all disciples (e.g., Bonnard; Allen; Manson, *Sayings*, p. 183). By contrast David Hill ("Δίκαιοι as a Quasi-Technical Term," NTS 11 [1964–65]: 296–303; cf. also Cothenet) has advanced another interpretation. He suggests that both "prophets" and "righteous men" refer to distinguishable classes within Christianity. "Prophets" are distinguishable from "apostles," and "righteous men" refers to some other distinguishable group of teachers (cf. also 13:17; 23:29; and on 7:15–23). Hill further suggests (*Matthew*) that v.42, derived from Mark 9:41, is given this setting "to suggest that travelling and persecuted missionaries [the "little ones"] are dependent on the hospitality and help of non-Christians." E. Schweizer ("Observance of the Law and Charismatic Activity in Matthew," NTS 16 [1969–70]: 213–30) says the colocation of "prophet" and "righteous man" in v.41 means that Matthew urges his community to imitate the ideal of a charismatic ("prophet") still bound by the law as interpreted by Jesus ("righteous man"). E. Käsemann (*New Testament Questions of Today* [London: SCM, 1969], pp. 90–91) sees in "prophets" the leaders of Matthew's community and in "righteous men" the general body of believers.

A better synthesis is possible. As the discourse, viewed as a whole, moves from the Twelve to all believers, so also does its conclusion. Verse 40 probably refers primarily to the apostles, and vv.41–42 move through "prophets" and "righteous men" down to "these little ones"—viz., the least in the kingdom, seen as persecuted witnesses in the latter part of the discourse. The order "descends" only according to prominence. But the classes mentioned are not mutually exclusive, since "these little ones" surely includes the apostles, prophets, and righteous men; they are all "little ones" because they are all targets of the world's enmity. To give a cup of cold, freshly drawn water, the least courtesy demands, to the least disciple just because he is a disciple does not go unrewarded. Thus the "little ones" are not portrayed as a special class of "travelling missionaries" (contra Hill, *Matthew*) but as disciples. "Prophets" are referred to, not because Christian prophets are in view, but because this is an already accepted category for God's spokesmen and for those with whom Jesus' followers are aligned (5:10–12).

"Righteous men" is more difficult. But in two of the three passages where the term occurs in connection with "prophets" (13:17; 23:29), it must refer to righteous men of earlier generations—OT and perhaps Maccabean figures, not Christian contemporaries of Matthew, and not traveling teachers. It seems best to take the term here from the same perspective. None of Hill's evidence points unambiguously to a class of teachers known as "righteous men." Most of his DSS evidence (1QS 3:20, 22; 5:2, 9; 9:14; 1QSa 1:2, 24; 2:3) clearly demonstrates that the sectarians perceived themselves as "the righteous" over against other men. Moreover it is far from certain that Daniel 12:3 refers to a part of the people of God with a special assignment to teach righteousness: even there it is easy to detect a reference to all of God's people. After all, "righteousness" is a category already used in Matthew to describe all of Jesus' disciples (5:20).

Some scholars have been too eager to read anachronisms into the text and detect special groups on the basis of slender evidence. In reality v.40, though very general, applies in the first instance to the Twelve; v.41 repeats the aphorism twice more using OT categories familiar to Jesus but extending the application from prophets to all of God's righteous people. Verse 42 groups the previous aphorisms together to make it quite clear that the sole reason for rewarding those who treat Jesus' disciples well is not because they are prophets or righteous people—they are in fact but "little ones"—but because they are Jesus' disciples. The prophet's reward and the righteous man's reward are therefore not disparate but kingdom rewards (see on 5:12) that are the fruit of discipleship. To receive a prophet because he is a prophet (as in 1 Kings 17:9–24; 2 Kings 4:8–37) presupposes, in the context of v.40, that he is Christ's prophet—so also for the "righteous man." Thus the person who receives a prophet receives Christ, his word, his ways, and his gospel, and expresses solidarity with the people of God, these little ones, by receiving them for Jesus' sake (cf. 2 John 10–11; 3 John 8). No such person will lose his reward. While the applications to Matthew's churches, as to our own, are many, the text itself does not venture so far.

Notes

41–42 The expression εἰς ὄνομα προφήτου (*eis onoma prophētou*, "because he is a prophet"), with its parallels, is an instance of the causal use of *eis* (cf. Zerwick, pars. 98, 106; contra M.J. Harris, DNTT, 3:1187). Some hold this is important in understanding Matthew's baptismal formula, but see on 28:18–20.

7. *Transitional conclusion: expanding ministry*

11:1

[1]After Jesus had finished instructing his twelve disciples, he went on from there to teach and preach in the towns of Galilee.

1 For the significance of the formulas that end Jesus' discourses, see on 7:28–29. This one omits "these things" or the like (see on 10:5a). Unlike Mark 6:30; Luke 9:10, there is no mention of the return of the Twelve, since their early successes are of less concern to Matthew than is Jesus' teaching. Attention returns to Jesus' ministry, for he did not send out the apostles in order to relieve himself of work but in order to expand the proclamation of the kingdom (9:35–10:4).

Notes

1 The pronoun αὐτῶν (autōn, "their," NIV mg.) is exceptionally awkward here. It cannot refer to the apostles but to the Galileans, not mentioned in the context. Nor can this easily be taken as an anachronistic distinction between church and synagogue. Most likely it is an instance of pronominal sense-construction not uncommon in then contemporary secular Greek and found throughout the NT (cf. Turner, *Insights*, pp. 149–50). If so, it is especially important not to be hasty in reading church–synagogue anachronisms into other similar passages (see on 4:23; 7:29; 9:35; 10:17).

IV. Teaching and Preaching the Gospel of the Kingdom: Rising Opposition (11:2–13:53)

A. *Narrative* (11:2–12:50)

1. *Jesus and John the Baptist* (11:2–19)

a. *John's question and Jesus' response*

   11:2–6

> 2When John heard in prison what Christ was doing, he sent his disciples 3to ask him, "Are you the one who was to come, or should we expect someone else?"
>
> 4Jesus replied, "Go back and report to John what you hear and see: 5The blind receive sight, the lame walk, those who have leprosy are cured, the deaf hear, the dead are raised, and the good news is preached to the poor. 6Blessed is the man who does not fall away on account of me."

Matthew 12–13 depends in large part on Mark 2:23–3:12; 3:20–4:34. Before this comes 11:2–30, most of which is paralleled in various parts of Luke. Thematically the three chapters (11–13) are held together by the rising tide of disappointment in and opposition to the kingdom of God that was resulting from Jesus' ministry. He was not turning out to be the kind of Messiah the people had expected. Even John the Baptist had doubts (vv.2–19), and the Galilean cities that were sites of most of Jesus' miracles hardened themselves in unbelief (vv.20–24). The nature of Jesus' person and ministry were "hidden" (an important word) from the wise, despite the most open and compassionate of invitations (vv.28–30). Conflicts with Jewish leaders began to intensify (12:1–45), while people still misunderstood the most basic elements of Jesus' teaching and authority (12:46–50). But does this mean that he had been checkmated or that the kingdom had not come after all? Matthew 13 is the answer—the kingdom of God was continuing its advance even though it was often contested and ignored.

Matthew 11:2–19 is closely paralleled by Luke 7:18–35. Occasional divergences are noted below (see esp. on v.19).

2–3 According to Josephus (Antiq. XVIII, 119[v.2]), Herod imprisoned John the Baptist in the fortress of Machaerus, east of the Dead Sea. The bare fact is recorded in Matthew 4:12, the circumstances in 14:3–5. Apparently John had been in prison during Jesus' extensive Galilean ministry, perhaps as long as a year. The one to whom he had pointed, the one who would come in blessing and judgment (3:11–12), had brought healing to many but, it would seem, judgment to none—not even to those who had immorally and unlawfully confined the Baptist in a cruel prison, doubtless made the more unbearable for its contrast with his accustomed freedom (cf. Luke 1:80).

John heard "what Christ was doing" (v.2). The clause hides two subtle points. First, the use of (lit.) "the Christ" is peculiar, for at this stage in Jesus' ministry there was but little thoughtful ascription of this title to Jesus; and Matthew normally avoids it. Some have thought that at this point Matthew was somewhat careless about consistency in his narrative. Precisely the opposite is the case. The entire Gospel is written from the perspective of faith. The very first verse affirms Jesus as the Messiah, and the prologue (chs. 1–2) seeks to prove it. So at this point Matthew somewhat unusually refers to Jesus as "the Christ" in order to remind his readers who it was that John the Baptist was doubting. Though John doubted, from Matthew's perspective the time for doubt had passed. Far from being an anachronism, this use of "the Christ" is Matthew's own designation of Jesus. Indeed, Matthew's fidelity is attested by the way he distinguishes between his own understanding and insight, drawn from his postresurrection perspective, and the gradual development of that understanding historically, including the Baptist's doubts.

The second point is that *ta erga tou Christou* (lit., "the works of Christ"; NIV, "what Christ was doing") is suitably vague to embrace a triple allusion, not only to Jesus' miracles (chs. 8–9), but also to his teaching (5–7) and growing mission (10).

As a result of these reports, John sent a pointed question "by" (reading *dia* as in RSV, not *duo* ["two"] as in KJV) his disciples. This use of "disciples" shows that the term is a nontechnical one for "Christians" or "the Twelve" in Matthew (see on 5:1–6; 9:37). The objection, probably first raised by D.F. Strauss (*The Life of Jesus Critically Examined* [1846; reprint ed., London: SCM, 1973], pp. 219–30, esp. p. 229), that John was in no position to send messengers presumes to know more about security arrangements at Machaerus than we do—the more so since the Gospels show that Herod himself was ambivalent toward the prophet (Mark 6:17–26). John's question was whether Jesus was *ho erchomenos* ("the coming one," v.3), exactly the same expression ascribed to John at 3:11 (cf. also 21:9; 23:39; John 6:14; 11:27; Heb 10:37). The expression is not a common messianic title in intertestamental literature. It probably was drawn from such passages as Psalm 118:26; Isaiah 59:20. The description of the actions of "the coming one" in 3:11 nullifies the old theory (Schweitzer) that the Baptist merely expected Elijah *redivivus* ("come to life again") to follow him. John was asking Jesus whether he was the Messiah.

The question at first glance seems so out of character for what we know of the Baptist that many of the Fathers and Reformers, and even Bengel, suggest that John asked it, not for his own sake, but for the sake of his followers. Not a shred of exegetical evidence supports this view. Not only may the Baptist have become demoralized, like his namesake Elijah, but the Baptist had preached in terms of imminent blessing and judgment. By contrast Jesus was preaching in veiled fulfillment terms and bringing much blessing but no real judgment (cf. Dunn, *Jesus*, pp. 55–62), and as a result the Baptist was having second thoughts.

4–6 Jesus' answer briefly summarized his own miracles and preaching, but in the language of Isaiah 35:5–6; 61:1, with possible further allusions to 26:19; 29:18–19. At one level the answer was straightforward: Isaiah 61:1 is an explicit messianic passage, and Isaiah 35:5–6, though it has no messianic figure, describes the return of God's people to Zion with accompanying blessings (e.g., restoration of sight). Jesus definitely claimed that these messianic visions were being fulfilled in the miracles he was performing and that his preaching the Good News to the poor (see on 5:3) was as explicit a fulfillment of the messianic promises of Isaiah 61:1–2 as Luke 4:17–21. The powers of darkness were being undermined; the kingdom was advancing (cf. v.12).

But there is a second, more subtle level to Jesus' response. All four of the Isaiah passages refer to judgment in their immediate context: e.g., "your God will come . . . with vengeance; with divine retribution" (35:4); "the day of vengeance of our God" (Isa 61:2). Thus Jesus was allusively responding to the Baptist's question: the blessings promised for the end time have broken out and prove it is here, even though the judgments are delayed (cf. Jeremias, *Promise*, p. 46; Dunn, *Jesus*, p. 60). Verse 6, which may include an allusion to Isaiah 8:13–14 (in which case Jesus is set in the place of Yahweh: see on 11:10), is then a gentle warning, applicable both to John and his disciples: Blessed (see on 5:3) is the "man who does not fall away" (for this verb, see on 5:29) on account of Jesus, i.e., who does not find in him and his ministry an obstacle to belief and therefore reject him. The miracles themselves were not irrefutable proof of who Jesus was (cf. Mark 8:11–12 and parallels); faith was still required to read the evidence against the background of Scripture and to hear in Jesus' claim the ring of truth. But the beatitude in this form assumes the questioner has begun well and now must avoid stumbling. It is therefore an implicit challenge to reexamine one's presuppositions about what the Messiah should be and do in the light of Jesus and his fulfillment of Scripture and to bring one's understanding and faith into line with him.

b. *Jesus' testimony to John* (11:7–19)

1) *John in redemptive history*

11:7–15

> [7]As John's disciples were leaving, Jesus began to speak to the crowd about John: "What did you go out into the desert to see? A reed swayed by the wind? [8]If not, what did you go out to see? A man dressed in fine clothes? No, those who wear fine clothes are in kings' palaces. [9]Then what did you go out to see? A prophet? Yes, I tell you, and more than a prophet. [10]This is the one about whom it is written:
>
> > " 'I will send my messenger ahead of you,
> > who will prepare your way before you.'[d]
>
> [11]I tell you the truth: Among those born of women there has not risen anyone greater than John the Baptist; yet he who is least in the kingdom of heaven is

greater than he. ¹²From the days of John the Baptist until now, the kingdom of heaven has been forcefully advancing, and forceful men lay hold of it. ¹³For all the Prophets and the Law prophesied until John. ¹⁴And if you are willing to accept it, he is the Elijah who was to come. ¹⁵He who has ears, let him hear.

John had often borne witness to Jesus; now Jesus bears witness to John. But, as we will see, the effect is to point back to himself as the sole figure who brings in the kingdom. Historically it was almost inevitable for Jesus to define the position of John the Baptist with respect to himself. Most scholars doubt he did so consecutively as set forth here. Nevertheless the passage holds together well, and there is little literary or historical evidence to suggest that this is a composite of words spoken on other occasions. The parallel in Luke 7:24–35 preserves the same themes and movement. It omits Matthew 11:12–13 and adds Luke 7:29–30. The extra verses in Matthew are usually said to derive from Mark 9:11–13. But the two passages are linguistically and thematically rather distinct, and it is easy to imagine that Jesus had to take some position on John more than once and very definitely so for his disciples. Moreover the tone of this passage reflects no personal conflict between John and Jesus. And this, contrary to much recent discussion, is typical of the NT witness of the relationship between the two men (cf. esp. J.A.T. Robinson, *Twelve*, pp. 28–52).

7–8 "Began" (v.7) does not imply that Jesus commences his remarks while the Baptist's disciples were leaving and completed them only after they had gone (Broadus); as in v.20, it means that he took the opportunity to speak to the crowd about John. The rhetorical questions are a gently ironic way of eliminating obviously false answers in order to give the truth in vv.10–11. "A reed [probably a collective singular referring to cane grass, found in abundance along the Jordan] swayed by the wind" suggests a fickle person, tossed about in his judgment by the winds of public opinion or private misfortune (Lucian uses a similar metaphor, BAGD, p. 398). Certainly the people did not go out to witness such an ordinary spectacle. Nor did they go out into the desert to find a man dressed "in fine clothes" (v.8). "Fine" (*malakos*), used elsewhere in the NT only at Luke 7:25 and 1 Corinthians 6:9, connotes "softness" or even "effeminacy" and may be ironic. Contrast the rugged garb the prophet actually wore (see on 3:4–6). Those who are "in kings' palaces" is a sly cut at the man who was keeping John in prison.

It appears, then, that Jesus spoke in this way to disarm suspicion among the people that John's question (v.3) might betray signs of fickleness (v.7) or undisciplined weakness (v.8). Not so, responds Jesus; the man the people went out to see was neither unstable nor faithless. His question arose not from personal weakness or failure but from misunderstanding about the nature of the Messiah, owing to John's place in salvation history (see on v.11). Hence Jesus addressed the crowd, not to defend himself following the Baptist's question, but to defend the Baptist.

9–11 What the people had flocked to the desert to see was a prophet (v.9), since it was commonly agreed that a true prophet had not appeared for centuries but only the *bat̲-k̲ôl* (lit., "daughter of a voice"; see on 3:17). Small wonder there was such excitement. Jesus confirms the crowd's judgment but goes beyond it—John was not only a prophet but more than a prophet. In what respect? In this: Not only was he, like other OT prophets, a direct spokesman for God to call the nation to repentance, but he himself was also the subject of prophecy—the one who, according to Scripture, would announce the Day of Yahweh (v.10).

The form of the quotation shows influence from Exodus 23:20 (LXX) in the first clause (cf. Gundry, *Use of OT*, pp. 11f.). Yet there is no doubt that the primary passage being cited is Malachi 3:1. The messenger in Malachi 3:1 (Elijah in Mal 4:5–6) prepares the way for the great and dreadful Day of Yahweh. The form of the text, adding "ahead of you" (probably by using Exod 23:20) in the first line, changing "before me" to "before you" in the second line, and adding "your," has the effect of making Yahweh address Messiah. On any reading of Malachi 3:1 (on which see France, *Jesus*, pp. 91f., n. 31), Yahweh does not address Messiah; but inasmuch as the messenger prepares the way for Yahweh (Mal 4:5–6), with whom Jesus is constantly identified in the NT (see on 2:6; and esp. 3:3), this periphrastic rendering makes Jesus' identity unambiguous (cf. France, *Jesus*, p. 155). Even if Malachi 3:1 had been exactly quoted, the flow of the argument in Matthew demands that if John the Baptist is the prophesied Elijah who prepares the way for Yahweh (3:3; cf. Luke 1:76) or for the Day of Yahweh (Mal 4:5–6), and John the Baptist is Jesus' forerunner, then Jesus himself is the manifestation of Yahweh and brings in the eschatological Day of Yahweh.

Hill (*Matthew*) comments: "It is probable that the quotation has been inserted by the evangelist; it breaks the logical connection between verses 9 and 11, and anticipates the mysterious announcement in verse 14." It seems difficult to have it both ways: if the quotation anticipates v.14, then it must be left in place unless v.14 is also judged inauthentic. More important, v.10, far from breaking them up, ties v.9 and v.11 together. By citing Malachi, Jesus (v.10) has shown in what way John the Baptist is greater than a prophet: he is greater in that he alone of all the prophets was the forerunner who prepared the way for Yahweh-Jesus and personally pointed him out. While the OT prophets doubtless contributed to the corpus of revelation that pointed to Messiah, they did not serve as immediate forerunners. This is what makes John greater than a prophet (v.9)—indeed the greatest born of women (v.11; i.e., the greatest human being; cf. Job 14:1).

Thus far the argument flows coherently. But who is the "least in the kingdom of heaven," and how is he greater than John the Baptist? Many have found this comparison so difficult that some fanciful suggestions have been made. McNeile holds the kingdom to be entirely future: the least in the kingdom will *then* be greater than John *now* is. But will not John also be in the kingdom then? And how will this contribute to the argument? Others argue that *ho mikroteros* means not "the least" but "the younger," the "lesser" in a purely temporal sense. In this view it refers to Jesus: Jesus, though lesser through being younger, is greater than John the Baptist (so Chrysostom; Augustine; cf. Fenton; BDF par. 61 [2]; O. Cullmann, "Ὁ ὀπίσω μου ἐρχόμενος," *Coniectanea Neotestamentica* 11 [1947]: 30; Zerwick, par. 149; M. Brunec, "De Legàtioni Ioannis Baptistae (Mt 11:2–24)," *Verbum Domini* 35 [1957]: 262–70). This implies that John the Baptist is himself, according to Matthew, in the kingdom—a conclusion widely defended, largely on the grounds of comparing the ministries of John and Jesus (e.g., 3:2; 4:17; so, for instance, Walter Wink, *John the Baptist in the Gospel Tradition* [Cambridge: University Press, 1968], pp. 33–35).

It must be admitted, however, that *ho mikroteros* is made to mean "the younger" chiefly because v.11 is so difficult. In view of the fact that a comparison establishing

John as greater than the prophets immediately precedes this text, it is most natural to take *ho mikroteros* as meaning "the least" in the kingdom. This entails the view that John the Baptist was not himself in the kingdom. Parallels between John's and Jesus' preaching are readily explained (see on 4:17), and v. 12 can best be taken that way as well (see below).

In what way, then, is the least in the kingdom greater than John the Baptist? The answer must not be in terms of mere privilege—viz., the least are greater because they live to see the kingdom actually inaugurated—but in terms of the greatness already established for John. He was the greatest of the prophets because he pointed most unambiguously to Jesus. Nevertheless even the least in the kingdom is greater yet because, living after the crucial revelatory and eschatological events have occurred, he or she points to Jesus still more unambiguously than John the Baptist. This interpretation entirely suits the context and accomplishes three things.

1. It continues a defense of John by showing that his question (v. 3), which springs neither from fickleness nor weakness (vv. 7–8), does not make him forfeit his primacy among the prophets because of his being the forerunner of Jesus (vv. 9–10), but that the question owes its origin to his still-veiled place in the redemptive history now unfolding.

2. By contrast it continues the theme of discipleship whose essential function is to acknowledge Jesus before people (10:32–33) and establishes that function as the disciples' essential greatness. Even the least in the kingdom points to Jesus Christ more clearly than all his predecessors, not excluding John. For they either live through the tumultuous events of the ministry, Passion, and beyond, after which things are much clearer; or they enter the kingdom after these events, with the same clear understanding. Thus the ground is being laid for the Great Commission: clear witness to Christ before men is not only a requirement of the kingdom (10:32–33) and a command of the resurrected Lord (28:18–20) but the true greatness of the disciple (11:11).

3. At the same time, by explaining John's greatness and his place in salvation history, this verse points back to the preeminence of Jesus himself.

12 This enigmatic saying has called forth a host of interpretations. These depend on several alternatives related to several exegetical turning points that can be combined variously. A complete list of the possibilities (for bibliography, see Chilton, *God in Strength*, pp. 203ff.) must be passed over in favor of an interpretation that does justice both to the context and to the language. The turning points are three.

1. "From the days of John the Baptist until now." As already pointed out (vv. 10–11), most commentators understand "until" in v. 13 to be an exclusive usage, putting John within the kingdom (though most scholars hold that Luke 16:16 is an inclusive usage of "until"). Indeed, John P. Meier ("John the Baptist in Matthew's Gospel," *JBL* 99 [1980]: 383–405) makes it the crux of his interpretation of Matthew's treatment of the Baptist. The phrase "from the days of John the Baptist" is almost certainly a Semitic way of saying "from the time of the activity of John the Baptist" (cf. Jeremias, *NT Theology*, pp. 46f.). John's ministry provides the *terminus a quo*, the phrase "until now" the *terminus ad quem*. But many argue that "until now" means "up until" Matthew's time of writing, not "up until" Jesus' time of speaking (e.g., Cope, *Matthew*, pp. 75f.; Albright and Mann). This interpretation is rendered plausible (Albright and Mann) because the rest of the verse seems to picture violent

men ransacking the kingdom (see discussion below); and this certainly did not happen in the short time between the Baptist's death and this saying by Jesus during his earthly ministry.

A better synthesis emerges by taking the text strictly. The idiom "from . . ." in Matthew *includes* the following term (cf. 1:17; 2:16; 23:35; 27:45; Schweizer). But the entire expression "from the days of John the Baptist" does not say that John inaugurates the kingdom but only that during his time of ministry it was inaugurated and (or) attacked. The expression does not even assume John's death; it only assumes that the crucial period of his ministry during which the kingdom was inaugurated lies in the past. Now that kingdom has begun, in however preliminary a way, with Jesus' preaching and powerful works during "the days of John the Baptist." Thus there is no reason why the Prophets and the Law should not prophesy "until John" in an inclusive sense (v.13)—an interpretation that not only agrees with Luke 16:16 but goes best with Matthew 11:9–11.

Whether the kingdom has been "forcefully advancing" (NIV) or attacked (see below), this has been going on from its inception under Jesus' ministry during the days of John the Baptist (there had to be temporal overlap if the forerunner was to prepare his way and point him out) "until now"—viz., till this point in Jesus' ministry. This does not mean that the activity (whether of forceful advance or of being attacked) stops at that point, any more than the same expression in John 2:10 (the only other place it occurs in the NT) means that everybody at the wedding instantly stopped drinking the best wine. The continuation is not the focus of interest.

2. "The kingdom of heaven has been forcefully advancing." The crux of the problem is the verb *biazetai* ("has been forcefully advancing"). The form is either middle or passive. If the former, the NIV rendering, or something like it, is right; if the latter, it means that the kingdom is being attacked (in a negative sense) or is being forcefully advanced (by God?) (cf. TDNT, 1:610f.). In Greek sources relevant to the NT, *biazetai* is considerably more common in the deponent middle than in the active or passive voices (in the NT the verb is found only here and in Luke 16:16); and this supports the NIV rendering of the clause (cf. BAGD, pp. 140–41; DNTT, 3:711–12) as Ridderbos, NEB (mg.), Hendriksen, Chilton, and others do. But many object to this rendering on one of two grounds: (1) it brings a notion of "force" to the kingdom contrary to the Gospels' emphases; and (2) it deals poorly with the last clause of the text, since *biastēs* really must not be rendered "forceful man" (in a positive sense) but "violent man" (see discussion, below). The first objection is insubstantial. The kingdom has come with holy power and magnificent energy that has been pushing back the frontiers of darkness. This is especially manifest in Jesus' miracles and ties in with Jesus' response to the Baptist (v.5). Some kind of compulsion even of people is presupposed elsewhere (Luke 14:23). Moreover the force implied by the middle deponent verb is not always violent or cruel (cf. BAGD). The second objection is important and brings us to the third part of the verse.

3. "And forceful men lay hold of it." Hendriksen, for instance, thinks the cognate noun *biastēs* ("forceful man") finds its meaning now established by the considerations discussed above for the meaning of the verb *biazetai* ("has been forcefully advancing"). The kingdom is making great strides; now is the time for courageous souls, forceful people, to take hold of it. This is no challenge for the timorous or fainthearted. This interpretation is possible but not convincing. The noun *biastēs* is rare in Greek literature (only here in the NT), but where it occurs it always has the negative connotations of violence and rapacity. Moreover the verb *harpazousin* ("lay

hold of "), a fairly common verb, almost always has the same evil connotations (a rare exception is Acts 8:39). For these reasons most commentators see a reference to violent men and then read the verb in the preceding clause as a passive: "the kingdom of heaven is suffering violence and violent men are seizing it"—so, more or less, KJV, NASB, Wey, NEB (text), Hill, Gaechter, Maier, Hobbs, E. Moore ("Βιάζω, ἁρπάζω and Cognates in Josephus," NTS 21 [1975]: 519–43), C. Spicq (*Notes de lexicographie néo-testamentaire*, 2 vols. [Göttingen: Vandenhoeck und Ruprecht, 1978], s.v.), and many others. There are many conflicting views about who the violent men are—Zealots, Pharisees, evil spirits and their human hosts, Herod Antipas, Jewish antagonists in general. But the thrust is the same in any case.

Not satisfied with this, others have made suggestions, none convincing. The kingdom of heaven "has been taken by storm and eager men are forcing their way into it" (offered by Ph and Wms and defended by McNeile) is a rendering that combines the unlikelihood of a passive verb with the unlikelihood of a positive-connotative noun. James Swetnam, in a review of Spicq (*Biblica* 61 [1980]: 440–42), wants the verse to mean that from the time of John the kingdom has been suffering violence (passive verb) *of interpretation;* and those who are of like-minded violence—i.e., who understand the kingdom in the same way—are the ones who snatch it away. To the weaknesses of the last suggestion, this one adds an unparalleled meaning ("to suffer violence of interpretation") to the verb.

The best solution is to take the verb in its most likely voice, middle deponent, and the noun and verb of the last clause with their normal evil connotations: viz., from the time of John the Baptist (as explained above) until now, the kingdom of heaven has been forcefully advancing; and violent or rapacious men have been trying (conative present) to plunder it—so Pamment (pp. 227f.), though she then makes the rendering nearly incoherent by saying the kingdom of heaven is exclusively future (see also on 5:3). Furthermore, the verbs in the last two clauses are both in the present tense. If they are rendered as presents in English, the syntax is wrong: "From the time of John until now the kingdom is forcefully advancing, and violent men are pillaging it." But that acceptable Greek syntax calls in question Pamment's views on the futurity of the kingdom of heaven and sets up the picture of a tremendous, violent struggle being waged even as Jesus speaks. Certainly "Jesus considers his ministry to be a time when the Kingdom can be attacked as being present" (Hill, *Matthew;* cf. Kümmel, *Jesus' Promise,* pp. 121ff.).

If this is a form of antanclasis (a figure of speech in which the same word is repeated in a different or even contradictory sense), based in this instance not on exactly the same word but on a cognate, the verse admirably suits the context. The argument up to v.11 has established John the Baptist's greatness, grounded in his ministry of preparing for and pointing out Christ; and it has anticipated the witness of those in the kingdom who are even greater than John because the least of them testifies to Christ yet more clearly. Now, Jesus goes on to say, from the days of the Baptist—i.e., from the beginning of Jesus' ministry—the kingdom has been forcefully advancing (the point also made in Luke 16:16). But it has not swept all opposition away, as John expected (see on vv.2–4).

Simultaneous with the kingdom's advance have been the attacks of violent men on it. That is the very point John could not grasp. Now Jesus expressly affirms it. The statement is general because it does not refer to just one kind of opposition. It includes Herod's imprisonment of John (cf. J.A.T. Robinson, *Twelve,* pp. 44–45), the attacks by Jewish leaders now intensifying (9:34; 12:22–24), the materialism that craved a political Messiah and the prosperity he would bring but not his righteousness (11:20–24). Already Jesus has warned his disciples of persecution and suffering (10:16–42); the opposition was rising and would get worse. Meanwhile, not the aggressive zealots will find rest for their souls, but the weary, the burdened, the children to whom the Father has revealed the truth (vv.25–30). The last-mentioned passage is the death-knell of those who think the *biastai* are "forceful men" (in a positive sense): that is exactly what the chapter, taken as a whole, rules out. Instead, we are hearing the sound of divine grace, a note that becomes a symphony later in this Gospel.

If this interpretation is sound, there seems little reason either for thinking that v.12 is out of place or for seeing in it the later creation of the church.

13 In view of the preceding, "until John" means up to and including John. The Baptist belongs to the last stage of the divine economy before the inauguration of the kingdom (as in Luke 16:16). Sigal ("Halakah," pp. 68f.) mishandles this verse because he treats it as if the Prophets and the Law must prophesy about John rather than until John. Some of what the OT says about John has been set out in v.10; here the point is to set out the redemptive-historical turning point that has brought about the transformation of perspectives explained in vv.11–12. The two anomalies in the verse are (1) "the Prophets" precedes "the Law," an unusual order (cf. 5:17; 7:12), and (2) both "Prophets" and "Law" prophesy—and both anomalies serve the same purpose: a powerful way of saying that the entire OT has a prophetic function, a function it maintained up until, and including, John the Baptist.

In the twin settings of Matthew's "fulfillment" theme (see on 2:15; 5:17–20) and the role of John the Baptist (11:10), it is understood that now, after John the Baptist, that which Prophets and Law prophesied has come to pass—the kingdom has dawned and Messiah has come. This establishes the primary function of the OT in Matthew's Gospel: it points to Jesus and the kingdom. This confirms our interpretation of 5:17–20. The *gar* ("For") therefore ties v.13, not to v.11, but to v.12 (confirming v.12 as an integral part of the argument). Verse 13 further explains that "from the days of John the Baptist"—i.e., from the beginning of Jesus' ministry—the kingdom has been forcefully advancing. The Prophets and the Law prophesied until then and, implicitly, prophesied of this new era. And from that time on, the fulfillment of the prophecy, the kingdom itself, has been forcefully advancing.

14–15 The argument returns to vv.9–10, stating explicitly what Jesus said there: John the Baptist was the prophesied "Elijah" (v.14). This locates his place and function in the history of redemption and affirms again that what Jesus was doing was eschatological—he was bringing in the Day of Yahweh. The clause "if you are willing to accept it" does not cast doubt on the truth of the identification; but, like v.15, it acknowledges how difficult it was to grasp it, especially before the Cross and the Resurrection. For if the people had truly understood, they would necessarily have seen Jesus' place in salvation history as the fulfillment of OT hopes and prophecy. That is why the sonorous formula of v.15 is added (cf. 13:9, 43; 24:15; Rev 2:7, 11 et al.): the identification of John with prophesied Elijah has messianic implications that "those with ears" would hear. The formula is both a metaphorical description of and a challenge to spiritual sensitivity to the claims of the gospel.

Notes

8 Here and in v.9, ἀλλά (alla, "but") is used after a rhetorical question, with the answer implied but suppressed. In other words the Greek conjunction here adopts the force of Aramaic אֶלָּא ('ellā', "if not"). But this meaning of alla is also a feature of classical Greek; and NIV, following McNeile, translates it "if not."

9 The meaning of τί (ti) affects punctuation: if "what," read τί ἐξήλθατε ἰδεῖν; προφήτην (ti exēlthate idein; prophētēn) as "What did you go out to see? A prophet?" if "why," read "Why did you go out to see a prophet?" The problem is compounded by an important variant that reverses the last two Greek words and makes impossible the former punctuation. But the textual evidence is strongest for the order given above, and the parallel use of ti in vv.7–8 likewise favors "what." It is doubtful whether Gospel of Thomas 78, which prefers "why," is authentic.

12 Obviously related to the interpretation of this verse is the interpretation of the parallel in Luke 16:16. The clause "the good news of the kingdom of God is being preached" is an acceptable parallel to Matthew's "the kingdom of heaven has been forcefully advancing" and eliminates the perplexing verb βιάζεται (biazetai, "is forcefully advancing"). The problem lies in the last clause of Luke 16:16: καὶ πᾶς εἰς αὐτὴν βιάζεται (kai pas eis autēn biazetai), which might mean (1) "and everyone is forced into it" or (2), more plausibly, "and everyone is forcing his way into it" (NIV). The latter might be taken in a positive sense, in which case it is not parallel to Matt 11:12 as we have interpreted it (above); or in a negative sense dealing with opponents manifesting hostile intent, in which case the clause is parallel to Matt 11:12 as we have interpreted it, but the verb is being used in a different sense than in Matthew, where the negative part of the verse depends only on the cognate noun, not the verb. The question remains a very difficult one (cf. discussion in Marshall, Luke, pp. 626–30).

14 It is difficult to know why, according to John 1:21, the Baptist should deny that he was Elijah. Modern scholarship for the most part assumes independent and mutually contradictory traditions about the Baptist that reached the separate evangelists, who passed them on without recognizing the problem. But other suggestions include (1) John denied he was Elijah because his questioners expected a literal fulfillment—if he had answered in the affirmative, they would therefore have heard an untruth—and (2) John the Baptist saw himself as the voice of one crying in the wilderness (cf. John 1:23) but did not himself recognize that he was also fulfilling the Malachi prophecy. The second alternative may have support from Matt 11:7–15; for according to it, John's knowledge did not extend to the nuanced dimensions of Christian "already–not yet" eschatology, and he may well have been in the dark on other points.

2) *The unsatisfied generation*

11:16–19

16"To what can I compare this generation? They are like children sitting in the marketplaces and calling out to others:

17" 'We played the flute for you,
and you did not dance;
we sang a dirge,
and you did not mourn.'

18For John came neither eating nor drinking, and they say, 'He has a demon.' 19The Son of Man came eating and drinking, and they say, 'Here is a glutton and a drunkard, a friend of tax collectors and "sinners." ' But wisdom is proved right by her actions."

16-17 See the close parallel in Luke 7:31-35. "Comparison" stands at the heart of Jesus' parables (see on 13:24). Here Jesus uses an analogy to show his view of "this generation" (v.16), a designation recurring in Matthew 12:41-42, 45; 23:36; 24:34 (cf. 12:39; 16:4; 17:17) and used of Jesus' generation in connection with their general rejection of himself as Messiah. This identification of "this generation" is confirmed here by the next pericope (vv.20-24). "It cannot but be noted that the Lord, *nihil humani a se alienum putans* ['judging nothing human to be without interest to himself'], as he took notice of the rending of mended garments (9:16), and the domestic concerns of the children in their beds (Luke 11:7), so also observes the children's play in the market place, and finds in everything the material for the analogies of his wise teaching" (Stier). There are either two kinds of games (v.17), a wedding game and a funeral game, or, less likely, two cries within one game; but the children cannot be satisfied with either.

18-19 "For" shows that Jesus now gives the reason the behavior of "this generation" suggests the comparison he has drawn. John the Baptist lived ascetically, "neither eating nor drinking" (v.18), i.e., neither indulging in dinner parties (cf. 3:4) nor drinking alcohol (cf. Luke 1:15). Although he drew crowds (vv.7-8) and many were willing to enjoy his light for a time (John 5:35), yet the people as a whole rejected him, even charging him with demon possession. Jesus came eating and drinking (9:10-11; Luke 15:1-2; cf. John 2:1-11) and was charged with gluttony, drunkenness, and bad associations (v.19; cf. Prov 23:20). Like disgruntled children, "this generation" found it easier to whine their criticisms and voice their discontent than to "play the game." Jesus says in effect: "But all you do is to give orders and criticize. For you the Baptist is a madman because he fasts, while you want to make merry; me you reproach because I eat with publicans, while you insist on strict separation from sinners. You hate the preaching of repentance, and you hate the proclamation of the Gospel. So you play your childish game with God's messengers while Rome burns!" (Jeremias, *Parables*, pp. 161-62).

But the criticism runs at a still deeper level. If they had understood John, they would have understood Jesus, and vice versa; the thought has links with vv.7-15 (Bonnard).

Here Jesus uses "Son of Man" not only as a self-reference but as a veiled messianic allusion (see on 8:20). For tax collectors and sinners, see on 5:46.

The closing proverb has provoked much debate because Luke has "all her children" and Matthew "her actions." This proved so difficult that copyists in many MSS assimilated Matthew to Luke, where the text is relatively firm (cf. Metzger, *Textual Criticism*, p. 30; and esp. O. Linton, "The Parable of the Children's Game," NTS 22 [1975-76]: 165-71). But the problem cannot be so easily evaded. Aramaic reconstructions are not convincing.

Luke's form is probably original. It is commonly interpreted to mean that the claims of widsom are proved true by all her children—all who accept the message of widsom's envoys, John and Jesus (cf. Luke 7:29-30; some do accept it: cf. Marshall, *Luke*, pp. 303f.). Why the change to "actions" in Matthew? Suggs (pp. 36-58) argues that the proverb should not be read as the conclusion to the immediately preceding parable but to vv.2-18 and notes the use of *erga* ("actions") in v.2 (NIV, "what Christ was doing"). On this basis he argues that the proverb in Matthew reflects Son-of-Man "wisdom" christology: Wisdom is proved right by her actions, and those actions are the actions of Christ (vv.2–5). Jesus is therefore widsom incarnate (similarly, but more cautiously, David R. Catchpole, "Tradition History," in Marshall, *NT Interpretation*, pp. 167–71; Dunn, *Christology*, pp. 197f.; and many others).

Certainly wisdom, already personified in the OT (e.g., Job 28; Prov 1; 8) and developed in Jewish tradition into a quasi-personal hypostasis in heaven, an agent who (or which) expresses the mind of God (cf. TDNT, 7:465–526; F. Christ, *Jesus Sophia* [Zürich: Zwingli, 1970], pp. 13–60, 156–63), sometimes serves in the NT as a vehicle for christology. Yet here wisdom is best understood in its more traditional association with God. God's wisdom is vindicated by her (wisdom's) actions. The wisdom-christology theory must be rejected here. The theme of chapter 11 is not christology but the place of John the Baptist (and therefore of Jesus) in salvation history. The addition of such a christology in v.19b adds little to the argument, and Suggs's detailed reasons for defending this view entail reconstructions of church history fundamentally questionable on other grounds.

The proverb should be read in the light of the preceding parable: God's wisdom has been vindicated (*edikaiōthē;* NIV, "is proved right"—but the aorist, contra Jeremias [*Parables*, p. 162, n. 42] and Turner [*Syntax*, p. 73], should not be taken as gnomic in this highly specific context) by her actions—i.e., by the lifestyles of both John and Jesus, referred to in the previous verses. Wisdom in the OT is much concerned with right living. John and Jesus have both been criticized and rejected for the way they live. But wisdom, preeminently concerned about right living, has been vindicated by her actions: their respective lifestyles are both acknowledged as hers (for questions of authenticity, cf. TDNT, 8:431–32).

A similar approach best interprets Luke. The phrase "all her children" does not refer to all those who accept John and Jesus as wisdom's envoys: vv.29–30 do not picture the masses accepting them but, unlike the Pharisees and other leaders, merely hearing them gladly. The parable follows in which "this generation" is denounced for not truly understanding and participating. Wisdom's "children" are therefore John and Jesus, not the crowds. "All her children" does not militate against this, because the form is proverbial and meant to include all God's messengers, even those so radically different as John and Jesus. The two forms of the saying are therefore not very far apart. Luke focuses on the lifestyles of John and Jesus as wisdom's children, thus concentrating on their persons; Matthew on their actions. Not only is this interpretation coherent and contextually suitable, but it wraps up the preceding section in which Jesus has been exonerating the Baptist by explaining his role in redemptive history and simultaneously castigating the people for their spiritual dullness.

Notes

16 KJV's "friends" is explained by minor textual support for ἑταίροις (*hetairois*, "friends") instead of ἑτέροις (*heterois*, "others").

19 Several have argued (most recently Linton ["Children's Game," pp. 177f.], following Wellhausen) that the preposition ἀπό (*apo;* "by," NIV) could be rendered "over against," reflecting מִן קֳדָם (*min qʰdām*). In that case "children" is required: i.e., wisdom is proved right over against her children—the Pharisees and others who think they are right. But it is doubtful whether Greek readers would naturally think of *apo* in this way, and such a meaning is nonsensical in Matthew.

---

2. The condemned and the accepted (11:20–30)

a. The condemned: woes on unrepentant cities

11:20–24

> 20Then Jesus began to denounce the cities in which most of his miracles had been performed, because they did not repent. 21"Woe to you, Korazin! Woe to you, Bethsaida! If the miracles that were performed in you had been performed in Tyre and Sidon, they would have repented long ago in sackcloth and ashes. 22But I tell you, it will be more bearable for Tyre and Sidon on the day of judgment than for you. 23And you, Capernaum, will you be lifted up to the skies? No, you will go down to the depths. If the miracles that were performed in you had been performed in Sodom, it would have remained to this day. 24But I tell you that it will be more bearable for Sodom on the day of judgment than for you."

See Luke 10:12–15, in the context of the commission to the Seventy-two. The structure of the two passages is not close, the language moderately so. There is no particular reason to think that Matthew 11:20–24 is the original: "then" is a loose expression in this Gospel (see on 3:13) and "began" (see on v.7) not much tighter. Luke's context is not clearly original; the second person in 10:13–15 may argue against it (but see on v.24, below). But there is no way to rule out the possibility Jesus uttered these "woes" repeatedly as warnings.

The denunciation in the last pericope (vv.16–19) now becomes sharper. Structurally there are two series of warnings, each with the same sequence of warning (vv.21a, 23a), explanation (vv.21b, 23b), and comparison (vv.22, 24) (cf. Joseph A. Comber, "The Composition and Literary Characteristics of Matt 11:20–24," CBQ 39 [1977]: 497–504).

---

20 The verb *oneidizein* ("to denounce"), used only here and in 5:11; 27:44 in Matthew, is a strong verb, conveying indignation along with either insults (as in 5:11) or justifiable reproach (as here; cf. BAGD, s.v.). The expression *hai pleistai dynameis autou* (lit., "his very many miracles," elative superlative; cf. Turner, *Insights*, p. 34; id., *Syntax*, p. 31) is rightly rendered "most of his miracles." Jesus did not denounce these cities for vicious opposition but because, despite the fact that most of his miracles took place there—miracles that attested his messianic mission (vv.5–6)—they had not repented (see on 3:2; 4:17). The many miracles again remind us of the extent of Jesus' ministry (cf. 4:23; 8:16; 9:35; John 20:30; 21:25) and of the depth of responsibility imposed on those with more light. "Every hearer of the New Testament is either much happier (v.11), or much more wretched than them of old time" (Beng.)—those who lived before Christ.

21–22 *Ouai* can mean doom or solemn warning ("woe") or pity ("alas"); both are mingled here (v.21). Warnings have been given before; now woes are pronounced. Korazin is mentioned in the NT only here and in Luke 10:13. Its ruins may probably be identified with Kirbet Keraze, about two miles northwest of Capernaum. The Bethsaida in question was probably the home of Andrew, Peter, and Philip (John 1:44; 12:21) on the west side of Galilee, not Bethsaida Julius on the northeast shores near the Jordan inlet. Tyre and Sidon were large Phoenician cities on the Mediterranean, not far away, and often denounced by OT prophets for their Baal worship (Isa 23; Ezek 26–28; Joel 3:4; Amos 1:9–10; Zech 9:2–4). "Sackcloth" is a rough fabric made from the short hairs of camels and usually worn next to the skin to express grief or sorrow (2 Sam 3:31; 1 Kings 21:27; 2 Kings 6:30; Joel 1:8; Jonah 3:5–8). Ashes were added in cases of deep emotion (cf. Job 42:6; Dan 9:3), whether one put them on the head (2 Sam 13:19; Lam 2:10), sat in them (Jonah 3:6), lay on them (Esth 4:3), or even rolled in them (Jer 6:26; Mic 1:10). For "But I tell you" (v.22), properly "Indeed I tell you" (here and in v.24), see on 26:64.

Three large theological propositions are presupposed by Jesus' insistence that on the Day of Judgment (see on 10:15; cf. 12:36; Acts 17:31; 2 Peter 2:9; 3:7; 1 John 4:17; Jude 6), when he will judge (7:22; 25:34), things will go worse for the cities that have received so much light than for the pagan cities. The first is that the Judge has contingent knowledge: he knows what Tyre and Sidon would have done under such-and-such circumstances. The second is that God does not owe revelation to anyone, or else there is injustice in withholding it. The third is that punishment on the Day of Judgment takes into account opportunity. There are degrees of felicity in paradise and degrees of torment in hell (12:41; 23:13; cf. Luke 12:47–48), a point Paul well understood (Rom 1:20–2:16). The implications for Western, English-speaking Christendom today are sobering.

23–24 For Capernaum, see on 4:13. The city was not only Jesus' base (4:13), but he performed many specific miracles there (8:5–17; 9:2–8, 18–33; Mark 1:23–28; John 4:46–54). For the difficult textual variants, see Metzger (*Textual Commentary*, pp. 30f.) and France (*Jesus*, p. 243): the question, kept in the NIV (v.23), is probably right. Whether "go down" (conforming to Isa 14:15) or "will be brought down" (conforming to Luke 10:15) is correct, the thrust is clear; and the allusion to Isaiah 14:15 is unmistakable. The favored city of Capernaum, like self-exalting Babylon, will be brought down to Hades (see on 5:22). The OT passage is a taunt against the wicked and arrogant city, personified in its king; and Capernaum is lumped together with Babylon, which all Jews regarded as the epitome of evil (cf. Rev 17:5). The heaven–hades contrast can be metaphorical for exaltation–humiliation or the like (cf. Job 11:8; Ps 139:8; Amos 9:2; Rom 10:6–7). But in view of the surrounding references to "day of judgment," Hades must be given more sinister overtones. Similarly, though Sodom (Gen 19) was proverbial for wickedness (cf. Ezek 16:48), it will be easier on the Day of Judgment for "the land of Sodom" (so Gr., recalling that several cities were involved in the sin and the destruction) than for Capernaum (see on vv. 21–22).

In the words "I tell you" (v.22), "you" is plural, probably implying the crowd (v.7), since the singular "you" is used for the city (vv.23–24, Gr.). This means that using the second person to address the cities is no more than a rhetorical device of Jesus' preaching.

b. *The accepted* (11:25–30)

1) *Because of the revelation of the Father*

11:25–26

> [25]At that time Jesus said, "I praise you, Father, Lord of heaven and earth, because you have hidden these things from the wise and learned, and revealed them to little children. [26]Yes, Father, for this was your good pleasure.

If vv.20–24 describe the condemned, vv.25–30 describe the accepted. Verses 25–30 can be broken into three parts: vv.25–26, 27, 28–30. The first two are paralleled by Luke 10:21–22. The unity of the three parts and the authenticity of each has been hotly debated. Contrary to earlier opinion (esp. E. Norden, *Agnostos Theos* [Stuttgart: Teubner, 1913]), the language is not that of Hellenistic mysticism (Norden proposed Ecclus 51 as the closest parallel, following Strauss) but is thoroughly Semitic (cf. W.D. Davies, "'Knowledge' in the Dead Sea Scrolls and Matthew 11:25–30," *Christian Origins and Judaism* [London: Darton, Longman and Todd, 1962], pp. 119–44; Manson, *Sayings*, p. 79; Jeremias, *NT Theology*, pp. 24, 57f.), which means that the provenance is Palestinian. Further aspects of the authenticity question are discussed below (see esp. A.M. Hunter, *Gospel and Apostle* [London: SCM, 1975], pp. 60–67). Jesus' prayer builds on his rejection (vv.16–24) while still recognizing his mission (cf. 10:5–42).

25 The Greek *en ekeinō tō kairō* ("At that time") is a loose connective in Matthew (cf. 12:1; 14:1), loosely historical (it was about that time) and tightly thematic (this pericope must be read in terms of the preceding denunciation). Luke 10:21 has Jesus saying these words "at that hour" (*en autē tē hōra;* NIV, "At that time") when the Seventy-two joyfully returned from their mission, an event Matthew does not record. Luke's connective relates to the success of the mission; Matthew's assumes that there has been some success (God has revealed these things to little children) but draws a sharper antithesis between the recipients of such revelation and the "wise and learned" who, like the inhabitants of the cities just denounced, understand nothing.

While *exomologoumai soi* ("I praise you") can be used in the sense of "I confess my sins" (cf. 3:6), the basic meaning is acknowledgment. Sins truly acknowledged are sins confessed. When this verb is used with respect to God, the person praying "acknowledges" who God is, the propriety of his ways, and the excellence of his character. At that point acknowledgment is scarcely distinguishable from praise (as in Rom 14:11; 15:9; Phil 2:11; cf. LXX of Ps 6:6; 7:18; 17:50 et al.).

Here Jesus addresses God as "Father" and "Lord of heaven and earth" (cf. Ecclus 51:10; Tobit 7:18). These are particularly appropriate titles, because the former indicates Jesus' sense of sonship (see on 6:9) and prepares for v.27, while the latter recognizes God's sovereignty over the universe and prepares for vv.25–26. God is sovereign, free to conceal or reveal as he wills. God has revealed "these things"— the significance of Jesus' miracles (cf. vv.20–24), the Messianic Age unfolding largely unnoticed, the content of Jesus' teaching—to *nēpiois* ("little children," "childlike disciples," "simple ones"; Jeremias, *NT Theology*, p. 111; see further on 18:1–5; cf. John 7:48–49; 1 Cor 1:26–29; 3:18); and he has hidden them from the "wise and learned."

Many restrict the "wise and learned" to the Pharisees and teachers of the law, but the context implies something broader. Jesus has just finished pronouncing woes on "this generation" (v. 16) and denouncing entire cities (vv. 20–24). These are "the wise and learned" (better: "the wise and understanding") from whom the real significance of Jesus' ministry is concealed. The point of interest is not their education, any more than the point of interest in the "little children" is their age or size. The contrast is between those who are self-sufficient and deem themselves wise and those who are dependent and love to be taught.

For revealing the riches of the good news of the kingdom to the one and hiding it from the other, Jesus uttered his praise to his Father. Zerwick (par. 452) argues that though the construction formally puts God's concealing and his revealing on the same level, in reality it masks a Semitic construction (cf. Rom 6:17, which reads, literally, "But thanks be to God that you were servants of sin, you obeyed from the heart the form of teaching with which you were entrusted."). But this example does not greatly help here; for even when rendered concessively ("I praise you . . . because, *though* you have hidden these things from the wise and learned, you have revealed them to little children"), God remains the one who reveals and conceals.

Yet we must not think that God's concealing and revealing are symmetrical activities arbitrarily exercised toward neutral human beings who are both innocent and helpless in the face of the divine decree. God is dealing with a race of sinners (cf. 1:21; 7:11) whom he owes nothing. Thus to conceal "these things" is not an act of injustice but of judgment—the very judgment John the Baptist was looking for and failed to find in Jesus (see on 11:2–6). The astonishing thing about God's activity is not that God acts in both mercy and judgment but who the recipients of that mercy and judgment are: those who pride themselves in understanding divine things are judged, those who understand nothing are taught. The predestination pattern is the counterpoint of grace.

26 Far from bemoaning or finding fault with his Father's revealing and concealing, Jesus delighted in it. The conjunction *hoti* is best understood as "because" or "for" (NIV): I thank you *because* this was your good pleasure; and that is what Jesus "acknowledges" or "praises." Whatever pleases his Father pleases him. "It is often in a person's prayers that his truest thoughts about himself come to the surface. For this reason the thanksgiving of Jesus here recorded is one of the most precious pieces of spiritual autobiography found in the Synoptic Gospels" (Tasker). Jesus' balance mirrored the balance of Scripture: he could simultaneously denounce the cities that did not repent and praise the God who does not reveal; for God's sovereignty in election is not mitigated by man's stubbornness and sin, while man's responsibility is in no way diminished by God's "good pleasure" that sovereignly reveals and conceals (cf. Carson, *Divine Sovereignty*, pp. 205ff.).

Notes

25 The Greek has ἀποκριθεὶς ὁ Ἰησοῦς εἶπεν (apokritheis ho Iēsous eipen, "Jesus answered and said"), not just ὁ Ἰησοῦς εἶπεν (ho Iēsous eipen, "Jesus said," NIV); similarly 12:38; 17:4; 26:63 (mg.); 28:5, where there is no "question" to "answer." This simply reflects Hebrew idiom (Zerwick, par. 366).

2) *Because of the agency of the Son*

11:27

27"All things have been committed to me by my Father. No one knows the Son except the Father, and no one knows the Father except the Son and those to whom the Son chooses to reveal him.

27 Despite contrary opinions, the arguments for the authenticity of this saying are very strong. Long rejected because it was thought to reflect Johannine theology, which was judged to be the product of late Hellenization, this verse has by and large gained the recognition of scholarship that the "knowledge" categories here are Jewish and the structure of the verse Semitic (cf. Jeremias, *Prayers*, pp. 45ff.). Dunn (*Christology*, pp. 199–200) has shown that the closest parallels to v.27 are in the election language of the OT, a strong argument for the unity of vv.25–27.

Hill (*Matthew*) denies the authenticity of the saying but candidly admits, "The greatest barrier to the acceptance of the genuineness of the verse is the supposition that Jesus could not have made such an absolute claim for himself." This turns in part on the observation that, apart from the fourth Gospel, the absolute expression "the Son" is exceedingly rare. But significantly it does occur twice more in Matthew, at 24:36 (cf. Mark 13:32) and 28:19 (elsewhere, cf. 1 Cor 15:28; Heb 1:8). Jeremias (*Prayers*) argues that Jesus' habit of addressing God as "Father" could well have contributed to such a self-understanding on the part of Jesus; but even he thinks v.27 should be understood generically: "Just as only a father really knows his son, so only a son really knows his father" (p. 50). But even if he is right, in a context where (1) Jesus has just addressed God as "Father" (vv.25–26), (2) makes himself a son in an exclusive sense, (3) with the sole power to mediate knowledge of God, one must conclude that the "generic" statement Jeremias finds could *only* be applied to Jesus, and that in such a way as to make his sonship exclusive.

Past interpreters often said that "the Son" is never used in pre-Christian sources as a title for the Messiah. With the discovery of 4QFlor 10–14, citing 2 Samuel 7:14 and applying to "the Branch" of David the words "I will be his Father and he shall be my Son," this judgment must be reconsidered. Though it may not be a direct messianic title, it was certainly used to refer to an apocalyptic figure who was the son of a king, presumably David and thus picks up OT uses of "Son" (cf. Ps 2; see on 2:15; 3:17; 16:13–16; cf. Fitzmyer, *Wandering Aramaen*, pp. 102–7; M. Hengel, *The Son of God* [Philadelphia: Fortress, 1976]; Guthrie, *NT Theology*, 301ff.). As with "Son of Man" (see excursus on 8:20), so with "Son of God": it appears that Jesus used a designation not firmly defined and open to several interpretations as part of his gradual self-disclosure, a revelation that could be fully grasped only after the Cross and the Resurrection. Thus for Matthew there is no doubt of what Jesus is saying, because Matthew's "Son" or "Son of God" categories must be seen against the backdrop, not only of the prologue, but also of 3:17.

The latter passage raises a still more basic point. Cannot Jesus himself be thought to originate some things? Was the church so rich in imagination and Jesus so imaginatively poor that all new developments in titles and theology must be ascribed only to the church? If 3:17 is historical, why should not Jesus think of himself as the Son in 11:27? Is it necessary to conclude, with Hill, that 11:27 cannot be authentic because it sounds like the authority of the postresurrection Jesus in 28:18?

And if the two do sound alike, why should we not therefore conclude that there is more continuity between the earthly ministry of Jesus and the resurrected Lord than most scholars are prepared to admit?

Verse 27 is a christological claim of prime importance, fitting easily into the context. After declaring that the Father gives true understanding of "these things" to "little children" (vv.25–26), Jesus now adds that he is the exclusive agent of that revelation. "All things" may have reference not to "all authority" (as in 28:18) but to "all divine knowledge," all knowledge of "these things" (in v.25). But because the Son has not only knowledge but the authority to choose those to whom he will reveal God, probably "all things" includes authority. The reciprocal knowledge of Son and Father where the Father is God presupposes a special sonship indeed. And this unique mutual knowledge guarantees that the revelation the Son gives is true. Not least astonishing about this reciprocity is the clause "No one knows the Son except the Father." Even if it is rendered in Jeremias's way (above), in this exclusivistic context it makes a claim no mere mortal could honestly make. There is a self-enclosed world of Father and Son that is opened to others only by the revelation provided by the Son. "It is one thing to know by equality of nature, and another by the condescension of him who reveals" (Jerome, cited in Broadus). This revelation is not only factual (the Son reveals "these things") but personal (the Son reveals "him"—the Father).

The Son reveals the Father to those whom he, from time to time, wills (present subjunctive: cf. Turner, *Syntax*, p. 107). Just as the Son praises the Father for revealing and concealing according to his good pleasure (v.26), so the Father has authorized the Son to reveal or not according to his will. The text places enormous emphasis on Jesus' person and authority. The thought is closely echoed both in John (3:35; 8:19; 10:15; 14:9; 16:15) and in the Synoptics (Matt 13:11; Mark 4:11—Jesus makes known the secrets of the kingdom; cf. Matt 10:37–39; 11:25; Luke 10:23–24; ch. 15 et al.). What is made clear in this passage is that sonship and messiahship are not quite the same. "Sonship precedes messiahship and is in fact the ground for the messianic mission" (Ladd, *NT Theology*, pp. 165–67, esp. p. 167).

3) *Because of the Son's gentle invitation*

11:28–30

> [28]"Come to me, all you who are weary and burdened, and I will give you rest. [29]Take my yoke upon you and learn from me, for I am gentle and humble in heart, and you will find rest for your souls. [30]For my yoke is easy and my burden is light."

These verses are only in Matthew. Jesus is the one who alone reveals the Father (v.27). Jesus it is who invites, not "the wise and learned" (v.25), but "the weary and burdened" (v.28). The Son reveals the Father, not to gratify learned curiosity or to reinforce the self-sufficiency of the arrogant, but to bring "the little children" (v.25) to know the Father (v.27), to introduce the weary to eschatological rest (v.28)—or, as the angel once said to Joseph, so that Jesus Messiah might save his people from their sins (1:21).

Partly because these verses have some links with Ecclesiasticus 51:23–27, where wisdom invites men to her yoke, several have argued that Matthew here identifies Jesus with hypostasized wisdom (e.g., Zumstein, pp. 140ff.; Dunn, *Christology*, pp.

200f.). But the contrasts between Ecclesiasticus 51 and this passage are more impressive than the similarities. In the former, Sirach is in fact inviting men to take on the yoke of studying Torah as the means of gaining acceptance and rest; in the latter, Jesus offers eschatological rest, not to the scholar who studies Torah, but to the weary. Jesus' teaching must be adopted, not Torah; and this stands, as the next pericopes show (12:1–8, 9–14), in welcome relief to legalistic understanding of the OT.

28 The "me" is grammatically unemphatic but in the wake of v.27 extremely important. Jesus invites the "weary" (the participle suggests those who have become weary through heavy struggling or toil) and the "burdened" (the passive side of weariness, overloaded like beasts of burden) to come to him; and he (not the Father) will give them rest. There is an echo of Jeremiah 31:25, where Yahweh refreshes his people through the new covenant.

While there is no need to restrict the "burdens," it is impossible not to be reminded of the "heavy loads" the Pharisees put on men's shoulders (23:4; cf. 12:1–14; cf. Schlatter; Klostermann; M. Maher, " 'Take my yoke upon you' [Matt.xi.29]," NTS 22 [1976]: 97–103). The "rest" (cf. use of cognate term in Heb 3–4) is eschatological (cf. Rev 6:11; 14:13) but also a present reality.

29–30 The "yoke" (v.29), put on animals for pulling heavy loads, is a metaphor for the discipline of discipleship. If Jesus is not offering the yoke of the law (*Pirke Aboth* 3:6; cf. Ecclus 51:26), neither is he offering freedom from all constraints. The "yoke" is Jesus' yoke, not the yoke of the law; discipleship must be *to him*. In view of v.27, "learn from me" cannot mean "imitate me" or "learn from my experience" (contra Stauffer, TDNT, 2:348f.) but "learn from the revelation that I alone impart" (cf. Schmid).

The marvelous feature of this invitation is that out of his overwhelming authority (v.27) Jesus encourages the burdened to come to him because he is "gentle and humble in heart." Matthew stresses Jesus' gentleness (18:1–10; 19:13–15). Apparently the theme is connected with the messianic servant language (Isa 42:2–3; 53:1–2; cf. Zech 9:9, cited in Matt 21:5) that recurs in 12:15–21. Authoritative revealer that he is, Jesus approaches us with a true servant's gentleness. For the present his messianic reign must not be understood as exclusively royal. On "rest," see v.28; but here the words "and you will find rest for your souls" are directly quoted from Jeremiah 6:16 (MT, not LXX). The entire verse is steeped in OT language (cf. Gundry, *Use of OT,* p. 136); but if this is intended to be not just an allusion but a fulfillment passage, then Jesus is saying that "the ancient paths" and "the good way" (Jer 6:16) lie in taking on his yoke because he is the one to whom the OT Scriptures point. That yoke is "easy" (good, comfortable) and his burden is light (v.30). The "rest" he promises is not only for the world to come but also for this one as well.

The implicit contrast between Jesus' yoke and that of others is not between antinomianism and legalism, for in a deep sense his demands (5:21–48) are far more radical than theirs; nor between salvation by law and salvation by grace (contra Bornkamm, *Tradition* p. 148, n. 2); nor between harsh attitudes among Jewish teachers of the law and Jesus' humane and humble approach (Klostermann). No, the contrast is between the burden of submission to the OT in terms of Pharisaic regulation and the relief of coming under Jesus' tutelage as under the authority of gentle

Revealer to whom the OT, the ancient paths, truly pointed (cf. H.D. Betz, "The Logion of the Easy Yoke and of Rest [Matt 11:28–30]," JBL 86 [1967]: 10–24).

3. *Sabbath conflicts* (12:1–14)

a. *Picking heads of grain*

12:1–8

> ¹At that time Jesus went through the grainfields on the Sabbath. His disciples were hungry and began to pick some heads of grain and eat them. ²When the Pharisees saw this, they said to him, "Look! Your disciples are doing what is unlawful on the Sabbath."
> ³He answered, "Haven't you read what David did when he and his companions were hungry? ⁴He entered the house of God, and he and his companions ate the consecrated bread—which was not lawful for them to do, but only for the priests. ⁵Or haven't you read in the Law that on the Sabbath the priests in the temple desecrate the day and yet are innocent? ⁶I tell you that one greater than the temple is here. ⁷If you had known what these words mean, 'I desire mercy, not sacrifice,' you would not have condemned the innocent. ⁸For the Son of Man is Lord of the Sabbath."

Opposition to Jesus had already surfaced (9:3, 11, 14, 34; 10:25; 11:19). Now it erupts in a concrete issue that generates enough hatred to lead Jesus' enemies to contemplate murder (v.14).

Matthew now picks up the narrative from Mark 2:23 (cf. Mark 2:23–28; Luke 6:1–5) at the point where he had left the source as far back as Matthew 9:18. Only here does he speak of conflicts over the Sabbath (though cf. 13:54–58; 24:20).

The Jewish rules of conduct about Sabbath were extremely detailed; and it was wryly admitted that "the rules about the Sabbath . . . are as mountains hanging by a hair, for [teaching of] Scripture [thereon] is scanty and the rules many" (M *Hagigah* 1:8). Yet for many Jews of Jesus' day the Sabbath was a joyful festival, a sign of the covenant, a reminder of divine creation in six days, and, provided the rules were obeyed, a means of gaining merit for Israel (Mek Exod 20:16; 23:15; 26:13; b *Shabbath* 10b). At many points there were diverse interpretations; and though the Pharisees were strict, the Qumran covenanters were stricter yet (CD 10:14–11:8). (For detailed study and bibliography of vv.1–14 in the context of the canonical question of the relation between Sabbath and Lord's Day, cf. Carson, "Sabbath.")

1 "At that time" need not mean the same day as the events of chapter 11 but "at about that time" (see on 3:1; 11:25; cf. 13:1). Here it introduces an *example* of burdensome Pharisaic regulation (arising out of 11:28–30) along with the theme of rising opposition to Jesus that ties much of this section (11:2–13:53) together.

Various explanations for what Jesus' disciples (presumably the Twelve) did have been advanced. Some scholars have noted that only Matthew mentions their hunger and have suggested that they ate the grain out of necessity (Kilpatrick, p. 116; Willy Rordorf, *Sunday*, tr. A.A.K Graham [London: SCM, 1968]). But there is no necessity unless one has not eaten for days. The reference to hunger is simply part of the story: why else would the disciples pick a little grain? Samuele Bacchiocchi's suggestion (*From Sabbath to Sunday* [Rome: Pontifical Gregorian University Press, 1977], p. 50) that Jesus' rebuke (v.7) implies that the Pharisees should have taken Jesus and his disciples home for lunch after the synagogue service instead of criticizing them for picking heads of grain is fanciful.

Manson (*Sayings*, p. 190) remarks that Jesus and his disciples were going from place to place on missionary work and so invests their act with kingdom significance. But why, then, were they not charged with exceeding a Sabbath day's journey (about eleven hundred meters; cf. M *Sotah* 5:3)? And what were the Pharisees doing there? The scene is reminiscent of a Sabbath afternoon stroll within the permitted distance. P.K. Jewett (*The Lord's Day* [Grand Rapids: Eerdmans, 1971], p. 37) suggests the disciples were making a path for Jesus, an idea based on Mark's "began to make their way." This will not do in Matthew and wrongly interprets Mark. A path cannot be made merely by picking heads of grain. At the time fields were not separated by fences but by landmark stones (cf. Deut 19:14). Paths went right across fields or closely skirted them, the grain being sown to the field's very edge and sometimes beyond (cf. 13:4); and the right to pluck grain casually (though not necessarily on the Sabbath) was established by Deuteronomy 23:25.

2 The Pharisees' charge that the disciples were breaking the law was based, not on their picking grain in someone else's field, but on the fact that picking grain—i.e., "reaping" (cf. j. *Shabbath* 7.2,9.c)—was one of thirty-nine kinds of work forbidden on the Sabbath (M *Shabbath* 7:2) under prevailing Halakah. Though exceptions to these were granted in the case of temple service and where life was at stake, neither exception applied here. Sigal ("Halakah," p. 160) argues that not all authorities prohibited what the disciples were doing; but M *Shabbath* 10:2, to which he refers, does not deal with casually picking grain in an open field and so is in any case irrelevant. At a much later period, the Gemara expressly permits picking grain by hand and eating it on the Sabbath but merely forbids the use of a tool (b *Shabbath* 128a, b; cf. Bonnard). But this refinement is much later and may even owe something to Christian influence.

3–4 The use of counterquestion and appeal to Scripture was common, though not exclusively so, in rabbinic debates (cf. v.5; 19:4; 21:16, 42; 22:31). The account to which Jesus refers is from the "former prophets," as the Jews called these books (1 Sam 21:1–6). (On the regulations regarding the consecrated bread [lit., "bread of the presentation"], see Exod 25:30; Lev 24:5–9.)

The "house of God" that David entered was the tabernacle (cf. Exod 23:19; Judg 18:31; 1 Sam 1:7, 24; 3:15; 2 Sam 12:20; Ps 5:7), at that time at Nob, just south of Jerusalem. Both David and his companions ate what should only have been eaten by the priests and did so after lying to the priest about their mission. It is possible that this event took place on a Sabbath, since 1 Samuel 21:5–6 sounds as if the consecrated bread had just been changed. Many Jews understood the text that way (cf. SBK, 1:618f.; TDNT, 7:22). But Jesus makes nothing of David's deceit nor depends on any supposition regarding the day on which it occurred. If it was on a Sabbath, others than the priests should not have eaten that bread; and if it was not a Sabbath, the bread should not have been changed, let alone eaten by nonpriests.

The argument takes a common rabbinical form (cf. Sigal, "Halakah," pp. 162f.): viz; the juxtaposition of two apparently contradictory statements from Scripture in order to draw a Halakic conclusion (a conclusion regarding regulations for conduct). On the one hand, David ate; on the other, it was unlawful for him to do so. Jesus' point is not simply that rules admit of exceptions but that the Scriptures themselves do not condemn David for his action; therefore the rigidity of the Pharisees' interpretation of the law is not in accord with Scripture itself (cf. Cranfield, *Mark*, pp. 11f.; Lane, *Mark*, p. 117). The point is not "The Sabbath is delivered unto you, you are not delivered unto the Sabbath" (Mek Exod 26:13; cf. 2 Macc 5:19) but that the Pharisees' approach to the OT was wrong and could not explain the incident of David.

How, then, does this apply to Jesus and his disciples? They were not desperate and famished, unlike David and his men. It is not even clear how they were breaking any OT law, where commandments about the Sabbath were aimed primarily at regular work. The disciples were not farmers trying to do some illicit work, but they were itinerant preachers casually picking some heads of grain. Indeed, apart from Halakic interpretations, it is not at all obvious that any commandment of Scripture was being broken. It seems, then, that Jesus used the David incident not merely to question the Pharisees' view of the Sabbath, for the David incident was not directly relevant. Rather he was questioning their approach to the law itself.

There is more. In the incident to which Jesus referred, regulations (even of the written law) were set aside for David "and his companions." Is there not therefore a case for setting aside regulations (which had no clear base in the written law) for Jesus and those with him (so Hooker, *Son of Man*, pp. 97f.)? This analogy holds good only if Jesus is at least as special as David, and it is to this conclusion that the argument builds in the following verses.

5–6 Jesus' second appeal, preserved only in Matthew (doubtless because it was of interest to his Jewish-Christian readers), is from Torah in the narrow sense of Pentateuch (cf. Num 28:9–10). Formally speaking the Levitical priests "broke" the Sabbath every week (v.5), since the right worship of God in the temple required them to do some work (changing the consecrated bread [Lev 24:8] and offering the doubled burnt offering [Num 28:9–10]). In reality, of course, the priests were guiltless; the law that established the Sabbath also established the right of the priests, formally speaking, to "break" it (for a similar argument, cf. John 7:21–23).

But how does this apply to Jesus and his disciples? The form of the argument is *qal waḥômer* (lit., "the light and the weighty," an *a fortiori* argument [see on 5:25–30]), a recognized procedure for establishing a Halakic regulation (Daube, *New Testament*, pp. 67ff.). But this is valid only if the "one greater than the temple" (v.6) is truly greater. The "one greater" is neuter (the masculine variant is poorly attested) as in vv.41–42—i.e., "something greater" (NIV mg.). The neuter, however, can refer to persons when some quality is being stressed rather than the individual per se (Turner, *Syntax*, p. 21).

So the question remains, Who or what is greater than the temple? B. Gerhardsson ("Sacrificial Service and Atonement in the Gospel of Matthew," *Reconciliation and Hope*, ed. R. Banks [Exeter: Paternoster, 1974], p. 28), followed by David Hill ("On the Use and Meaning of Hosea vi.6 in Matthew's Gospel," NTS 24 [1978]: 115), argues that this refers to the service or worship of God in which Jesus was engaged. This is greater than the service of the temple performed by the priests. But Jesus and his disciples were not really "engaged" in such service while plucking heads of grain, the way the priests were engaged in worship on the Sabbath. Moreover the comparison in the text is not with the service of the temple but with the temple itself.

Others have argued that what is greater than the temple is the love command

(Sigal, "Halakah," pp. 163–66; cf. D.M. Cohn-Sherbok, "An Analysis of Jesus' Arguments Concerning the Plucking of Grain on the Sabbath," *Journal for the Study of the New Testament* 2 [1979]: 31–41; cf. Sand, pp. 43–45), finding support for this in the plea for mercy in v.7. But the supremacy of the love command has not yet been introduced (cf. 22:34–40). More importantly the argument neglects the sequential–eschatological "is here." This refutes Sigal's insistence that Jesus is answering purely on the level of dispute over Halakah. Instead, he is insisting that a new and greater development–thing–person has arrived at this point in history, something not there before. And the reference to "mercy" (v.7) is open to a better interpretation.

There are still other suggestions. But the most likely is that the "something greater" is either Jesus himself (Bornkamm, *Tradition*, p. 35; Georges Gander, *L'Evangile de l'Englise: Commentaire de l'Evangile selon Matthieu* [Aix-en-Provence: Faculté Libre de Théologie Protestante, 1967]) or the kingdom (Lohmeyer, *Matthäus*). And in fact the two merge into one. If the kingdom, it is the kingdom Jesus is inaugurating; if Jesus, it is not only Jesus as a man but as Messiah, Son of David (vv.3–4), Son of Man (v.8), the one who ushers in the Messianic Age. Yet "Jesus" is perhaps marginally more plausible, not only because of the christological connections just alluded to, but also because of the parallel drawn by Jesus himself between his own body and the temple (26:61; cf. John 2:20–21).

Jesus' argument, then, provides an instance from the law itself in which the Sabbath restrictions were superseded by the priests because their cultic responsibilities took precedence: the temple, as it were, was greater than the Sabbath. But now, Jesus claims, "something" greater than the temple is here. And that, too, takes precedence over the Sabbath. This solution is entirely consistent with what we have perceived to be Jesus' attitude to the law in this Gospel. The law points to him and finds its fulfillment in him (see on 5:17–48). Not only, then, have the Pharisees mishandled the law by their Halakah (vv.3–4), but they have failed to perceive who Jesus is. The authority of the temple laws shielded the priests from guilt; the authority of Jesus shields his disciples from guilt. It is not a matter of comparing Jesus' action with the action of the priests; nor is it likely that Jesus is suggesting that all his disciples are priests (contra Lohmeyer). "Rather, it is a question of *contrasting* [new emphasis] His authority with the authority of priests" (Carson, "Sabbath," p. 67).

7–8 Again (cf. v.3) Jesus rebuked the Pharisees for their failure to understand the Scriptures (cf. John 5:39), and this time (v.7) he quoted Hosea 6:6 as he had once before (see on 9:13). The relevance of this quotation from the "latter prophets" depends on the Pharisees' attitude to the law being as worthy of condemnation as the attitude of those who relied superficially and hypocritically on mere ritual in Hosea's day. Jesus claims, in effect, that the Pharisees had not really grasped the significance of the law, and this was demonstrated by their Halakah. The accusers stand accused; the disciples are explicitly declared "innocent." Their innocence was not (contra Rordorf) established on their being hungry but on the ground that something greater than the temple was present. In other words the Son of Man is Lord of the Sabbath. Whether "For" (v.8) relates to v.6 or v.7 is unclear and of little consequence. If the former, it sums up Messiah's supremacy over the temple; if the latter, it does the same but also serves as explicit ground for the innocence of the disciples.

Some have argued that "Son of Man" here has corporate significance: the community of Jesus' disciples together is "Lord" of the Sabbath (e.g., T.W. Manson, "The Son of Man in Daniel, Enoch and the Gospels," BJRL 32 [1949–50]: 191). But this is based on a disputed understanding of "Son of Man" (see excursus on 8:20) and on a misunderstood connection with Mark 2:27 (on which cf. Carson, "Sabbath," pp. 62–65). In all three Synoptics the Son of Man is David's son, Jesus the Messiah (Hill). But the title is ambiguous enough that few would grasp the point till after the Resurrection, at which time few could miss it. The claim (v.8) is implicitly messianic, a claim that goes beyond the mere right to tamper with Halakah. It places the Son of Man in a position to handle the Sabbath law any way he wills, or to supersede it in the same way that the temple requirements superseded the normal Sabbath restrictions (cf. Hooker, *Son of Man*, pp. 100ff.).

Notes

4 Moule (*Idiom Book*, p. 27) points out that ὃ οὐκ ἐξὸν ἦν αὐτῷ φαγεῖν (*ho ouk exon ēn autō phagein*, "which was not lawful for him to eat") is a mixed construction: the relative pronoun *ho*, which refers to the eating of the bread in the preceding clause, seems to serve simultaneously as subject of *ouk exon ēn* and object of *phagein*. Moule suggests the clause is being treated as if it had begun with ἀλλά (*alla*, "but") or καίπερ (*kaiper*, "although").

The reading ἔφαγεν (*ephagen*, "he ate") has very strong attestation but is rejected by Metzger (*Textual Commentary*, p. 31) and UBS 3d ed. in favor of ἔφαγον (*ephagon*, "they ate"), supported only by ℵ B and one miniscule, on the grounds that it represents the nonparallel reading (cf. Mark 2:26; Luke 6:4). But the change may have gone the other way, in order to make it unambiguous that not only David but all his men ate—a fact clearly relevant to Jesus and his disciples. "He ate and his companions" is an acceptable but ambiguous way of saying in Greek "he and his companions ate."

b. *Healing a man with a shriveled hand*

12:9–14

> ⁹Going on from that place, he went into their synagogue, ¹⁰and a man with a shriveled hand was there. Looking for a reason to accuse Jesus, they asked him, "Is it lawful to heal on the Sabbath?"
>
> ¹¹He said to them, "If any of you has a sheep and it falls into a pit on the Sabbath, will you not take hold of it and lift it out? ¹²How much more valuable is a man than a sheep! Therefore it is lawful to do good on the Sabbath."
>
> ¹³Then he said to the man, "Stretch out your hand." So he stretched it out and it was completely restored, just as sound as the other. ¹⁴But the Pharisees went out and plotted how they might kill Jesus.

Luke (6:6–11) specifies that this event took place on another Sabbath (cf. Mark 3:1–6). Unlike the previous pericope, Jesus does not refer to Scripture. This time it is *his* activity that is in question, not that of his disciples; and his argument, at first glance a stinging *ad hominem*, holds deeper implications.

The first-century Jews discussed at length what was permitted in caring for the sick on the Sabbath (e.g., M *Eduyoth* 2:5; M *Shabbath* 6:3; Mek Exod 22:2; 23:13). Jesus' attitude was more fundamental: it is lawful to do good on the Sabbath.

9–10 "Going on from that place" (v.9) is a Matthean connective to move the action from the field to the synagogue without reference to time. Regarding "their" synagogue, see on 10:17; 11:1. All three synoptists make plain the malice in the Pharisees' watching (Mark) and question (Matthew). In Mark and Luke, Jesus precipitates the action by calling forward the man with the shriveled hand; in Matthew that is omitted.

The form of the Pharisees' question in Matthew (v.10) is general. The customary Jewish ruling was that healing was permitted on the Sabbath when life was in danger (cf. M *Yoma* 8:6; Mek Exod 22:2; 23:13), which of course did not apply here. Even so, what rabbinic discussion had in view was medical help by family members or professionals, not miraculous healings. But Jesus did not reply on that level.

11–13 For the third time in this Gospel, Jesus' argument depends on a contrast between animals and men (cf. 6:26; 10:31) and presupposes the greater value of human beings based on their special creation: man alone was made in the image of God (Gen 1–2). This particular argument occurs only in Matthew; but a similar analogy is drawn in Luke 13:15; 14:5. In all three instances Jesus assumed that the Pharisees would lift an animal out of a pit on the Sabbath—though the most that was allowed at Qumran was to do something that would enable the animal to help itself (CD 11:13–14). Sigal ("Halakah," pp. 169f.), in support of his too rigid theory that the Pharisees are to be identified as *perushim* (see Introduction, section 11.f), is reduced to thinking that *probaton hen* (v.11) should be taken literally to mean "one sheep," viz., the last one. But the expression probably means no more than "a sheep" (see on 8:19).

Jesus' argument is again *qal wahomer* (see on vv.5–6): If a sheep, how much more a man (v.12)? Neither the sheep in the pit nor the man in Jesus' presence is in mortal danger. The question is simply one of doing good. This does not mean Jesus is saying that failure to do good is itself an evil thing (e.g., Klostermann; Cranfield, *Mark*, p. 120). Jesus is talking about what is "lawful," not what is required; and if it were absolutely true that failure to do good is *always* evil, there would be no possibility of any rest at all. Jesus' rhetorical question therefore has a narrower focus: Was the Sabbath a day for maleficent activity—like their evil intentions in questioning him—or for beneficent action, like the healing about to be done?

The healing (v.13), like that in 9:1–8, comes after the shocking word (in all three Synoptics) and therefore serves to confirm that word. The miracle itself says nothing of the cripple's faith, since the focus is not on him but on the Pharisees. Yet in light of the preceding interchange, it also confirms Jesus' claim to lordship over the Sabbath, as his healing in 9:1–8 confirmed his authority to forgive sins.

14 A great deal has been made of the fact that Matthew omits mention of the Herodians (Mark 3:6), as if that proves that the point of reference is now after A.D. 70, when the Herodians no longer existed and the sole opponents were the Pharisees (e.g., Hummel, pp. 12ff.; Hill, *Matthew*). But giving reasons for *omissions* in Matthew is extremely hazardous (see on 8:1–4). And in this instance it is noteworthy that Matthew mentions the Herodians in 22:16 and refers often to the Sadducees.

Sigal ("Halakah," p. 175) wants *apolesōsin* ("destroy") to mean, not "kill," but "put under the synagogue ban," because no Pharisee would consider executing another Jew merely over a Halakic dispute. While he is correct in the latter supposition, the point is that these Sabbath confrontations are *not* mere disputes over Halakah. They have to do with Jesus' fundamental messianic claims, a point vigorously denied by Sigal, who generally assigns passages like v.8 to later Christian theology and reduces the remainder to purely Halakic categories. But it is very doubtful (contra Sigal) that Jesus tolerated the oral tradition implicit in much Jewish Halakah (cf. Jeremias, *NT Theology*, pp. 208–11). Moreover the Sabbath-controversy pericopes cohere as they stand: this first mention of a plot to kill Jesus springs not from disputes over the legality of various Sabbath activities but over Jesus' authority. The Sabbath conflicts are not the cause of the plotting but its occasion. Therefore Sabbath disputes were not mentioned at Jesus' trials; in themselves they were never as much an issue as Jesus' claim to be Sabbath's Lord.

4. *Jesus the prophesied Servant*

12:15–21

¹⁵Aware of this, Jesus withdrew from that place. Many followed him, and he healed all their sick, ¹⁶warning them not to tell who he was. ¹⁷This was to fulfill what was spoken through the prophet Isaiah:

> ¹⁸"Here is my servant whom I have chosen,
> the one I love, in whom I delight;
> I will put my Spirit on him,
> and he will proclaim justice to the nations.
> ¹⁹He will not quarrel or cry out;
> no one will hear his voice in the streets.
> ²⁰A bruised reed he will not break,
> and a smoldering wick he will not snuff out,
> till he leads justice to victory.
> ²¹ In his name the nations will put their hope."

Verses 15–16 constitute a brief summary of Mark 3:7–12, omitting, among other things, a "Son of God" title. To this summary Matthew adds a fulfillment passage, citing Isaiah 42:1–4. Thus he interprets Jesus' healing ministry, not so much in terms of "Son of God" or even royal "Son of David" christology, but in terms of Yahweh's Suffering Servant (see also on 8:17). This section simultaneously contrasts the hatred of the Pharisees (v.14) with Jesus' tranquility (v.19) and gentleness (v.20) and prepares the way for themes in the rest of the chapter (discussed below).

15–17 Jesus often withdrew when opposition became intense (cf. 4:12; 14:13; 15:21; 16:5); at least that was his custom until the appointed hour arrived (26:45; cf. John 7:8). This practice becomes for his disciples an example of moving from place to place (10:23). Thus his extensive ministry continued (cf. 4:23; 8:16; 9:35). Warnings to those healed to keep silence increased for the same reasons as before and with as little effect (cf. 8:4; 9:30). But Jesus' conduct under these pressures, Matthew perceives, was nothing less than the fulfillment of the Scriptures. Though the Pharisees might plot to kill him (v.14), he would not quarrel or cry out (v.19). Despite all Matthew has done to show Jesus to be the messianic Son of David and unique Son of God, he wants to separate himself from exclusively royal and militaristic interpretations of Messiah's role. He knows that the ministry of Jesus Messiah must also be understood as the fulfillment of the prophecies of the Suffering Servant.

18–21 This quotation (Isa 42:1–4), the longest in Matthew, is remarkable for its text

285

form. The changes have been variously assigned to Matthew's "school" (Stendahl, *School*, pp. 107ff.), to a developing Christian apologetic (Lindars, *Apologetic*, pp. 147–52), to the evangelist's redactional interests (Hill, *Matthew*). Certainly there is a mixed text-character here (for details, cf. Gundry, *Use of OT*, pp. 110–16), and the reason for each change is not easy to discern.

The noun *pais* ("servant," v.18) can also mean "son," though the Hebrew is unambiguously "servant." Cope (*Matthew*, pp. 44f.), in line with his generally plausible view that this quotation anticipates the major themes of the rest of Matthew 12, suggests that Matthew exploits the Son–Servant ambiguity to anticipate vv.46–50—his disciples are brothers and sisters, but he is the unique Son of the Father. This seems tenuous, for elsewhere in Matthew God is the Father of the disciples (e.g., 6:9, 26; 10:29) as well as of Jesus (though in a somewhat different sense). The link between this quotation and vv.46–50 is on a different level, a christological one: viz., Jesus cannot be understood in terms of the normal family relationships that bind humanity. He is God's chosen Servant, the one on whom God has poured out his Spirit with a specific mission in view. Therefore his disciples, not his family, must be reckoned closest to him.

The words "whom I have chosen" (Heb. "whom I uphold") may have been borrowed by Matthew from the second line of Isaiah 42:1, or from Isaiah 43:10; 44:1 (thus making the quotation composite); and "the one I love" carries overtones of Matthew 3:17; 17:5, because love and election are closely connected. God's "delight" in his servant and the mention of the Spirit God puts on him to a special degree (cf. John 3:34) remind us of both Jesus' baptism and his transfiguration (3:16–17; 17:5), where Jesus was called God's Son. Yet far from subsuming Jesus' servant role under his sonship (Kingsbury), Matthew omits Mark's mention of "Son of God" (Mark 3:11) and here makes the servant motif preeminent (cf. Hill, "Son and Servant," pp. 4–12).

This "servant" will proclaim "justice" to the nations: neither the Hebrew *mišpaṭ* nor Greek *krisis* easily suggests "the true faith" (JB). But the suggestion is not entirely without merit, since what is in view is "justice"—i.e., righteousness broadly conceived as the self-revelation of God's character for the good of the nations (cf. Isa 51:4), yet at the same time calling them to account. Concern for the Gentiles thus emerges again (cf. 1:1; 2:1–12; 3:9; 4:15–16; 8:5–13 et al.) in anticipation of the Great Commission (28:18–20).

But even within this chapter, the twin themes of Spirit and Gentiles are programmatic (Cope, *Matthew*, pp. 32ff.; Hill, "Son and Servant," pp. 10f.). God has poured out his Spirit on his Servant; so the exorcisms he performs by the Spirit constitute proof of the kingdom's inauguration (v.28). Therefore blasphemy against that Spirit cannot be forgiven (see on v.32). Moreover the pericope about the sign of Jonah (vv.38–41) returns to the theme of the place of the Gentiles in the merciful salvation of God and warns "this wicked generation" (v.45) once more.

The servant "will not quarrel or cry out" or raise his voice in the streets (v.19). The picture is not one of utter silence (else how could he "proclaim" justice [v.18]? cf. John 7:37) but of gentleness and humility (11:29), of quiet withdrawal (see on vv.15–17) and a presentation of his messiahship that is neither arrogant nor brash.

The first two lines of v.20 are very close to both LXX and MT. The double metaphor breathes compassion: the servant does not advance his ministry with such callousness to the weak that he breaks the bruised reed or snuffs out the smoldering wick (smoldering either because it is poorly trimmed or low on oil). This may include reference to Jesus' attitude to the sick (v. 15). But the last clause of v. 20 ("till he leads justice to victory"), apparently a paraphrase of Isaiah 42:3 ("in faithfulness he will bring forth justice") and Isaiah 42:4 ("till he establishes justice on earth") under influence of Habakkuk 1:4 (cf. Gundry, *Use of OT*, pp. 114f.), suggests something more—namely that he brings eschatological salvation to the "harassed and helpless" (9:36), the "weary and burdened" (11:28).

"Leads" is a trifle weak for *ekbalē:* though the verb can have a wide semantic range, it requires something like "thrusts forth" in this context (used elsewhere in this chapter in vv. 24, 26, 27 [*bis*], 28, 35 [*bis*]). What is pictured is a ministry so gentle and compassionate that the weak are not trampled on and crushed till justice, the full righteousness of God, triumphs. And for such a Messiah most Jews were little prepared (cf. Pss Sol 17:21). Small wonder that the Gentiles put their hope in his name (v. 21; cf. Isa 11:10; Rom 15:12). The Hebrew reads literally "the coastlands wait for his laws," but the word "coastlands" often signifies Gentiles (*ethnē;* NIV, "nations"); and "will put their hope" is idiomatic for "look forward to" or "expect."

"Name" follows the LXX, even though MT has "law" (*torāh*, "teaching"). In view of the mixed text-character, which testifies to Matthew's ability and willingness to use the MT or to set it aside (unless, with Gundry [*Use of OT*, pp. 115f.], we postulate that LXX here renders a lost Hebrew original), this must be thought strange if certain recent reconstructions of the importance of the law in Matthew are correct (cf. Introduction, section 11.c). However, if, as we have maintained, the law in this Gospel serves primarily to point to Jesus, then it is not surprising that Matthew prefers the LXX term. For "in his name," see on 5:10–12.

5. *Confrontation with the Pharisees* (12:22–37)

a. *The setting and accusation*

12:22–24

> [22]Then they brought him a demon-possessed man who was blind and mute, and Jesus healed him, so that he could both talk and see. [23]All the people were astonished and said, "Could this be the Son of David?"
> [24]But when the Pharisees heard this, they said, "It is only by Beelzebub, the prince of demons, that this fellow drives out demons."

For a convenient summary of the parallels, see Albright and Mann. The analogous incident in 9:32–34 is not a doublet but a sample of the same outrageous charge that is raised in v. 24.

22 The *tote* ("then") is very loose (see on 2:7; 11:20), and probably this event took place a good deal later (compare Mark and Luke). NIV sounds as if the man suffered from three distinct ailments; the Greek, very condensed, puts blind and mute (*kō-phos*, as in 9:32) in opposition to "demon-possessed," suggesting the latter is the cause of the other two. The healing itself is told with admirable brevity, for it is not so much the miracle itself that captures the attention of the synoptists as the confrontation that follows.

23–24 The acute astonishment of the crowd (the verb *existanto*, "were astonished," is used only here in Matthew, though it is common in Mark and Luke) prompted the question (v.23). Its form in Greek suggests the crowds were none too sure: "This couldn't be the Son of David, could it?" The question does not ask whether Jesus is a magician of the kind attributed by popular superstition to David's son Solomon (contra Loren L. Fisher, "'Can This Be the Son of David?'" *Jesus and the Historian*, ed. F.T. Trotter [Philadelphia: Westminster, 1968], pp. 82–97) but whether Jesus is the Messiah (see on 1:1; 9:27; 15:22). The Messiah was expected to perform miracles (cf. v.38); so the exorcism-healing stood in Jesus' favor. But perhaps his reticence, his nonregal sayings, and his servant ministry engendered doubt. Matthew's readers can see the connection between the Suffering Servant (vv.18–21) and the Son of David (vv.22–23), but those who witnessed Jesus' ministry could not view it in the light of the Resurrection.

On "Beelzebub" (v.24), see on 10:25.

b. Jesus' reply (12:25–37)

1) The divided kingdom

12:25–28

> 25Jesus knew their thoughts and said to them, "Every kingdom divided against itself will be ruined, and every city or household divided against itself will not stand. 26If Satan drives out Satan, he is divided against himself. How then can his kingdom stand? 27And if I drive out demons by Beelzebub, by whom do your people drive them out? So then, they will be your judges. 28But if I drive out demons by the Spirit of God, then the kingdom of God has come upon you.

While the structure of vv.25–37 is parallel to that of Mark 3:23–30, Matthew's length is surprising. Some but not all of Matthew's "response" section is closer to Luke than to Mark. Most likely Matthew used both Mark and a "Q" source for this narrative. Part of Jesus' response in Matthew is scattered in Luke (cf. Luke 6:43–45; 11:17–23; 12:10), prompting some to think this passage to be a composite of a number of independent sayings. That is possible; the transitions are loose, and, unlike the five major discourses, the end of the response is not decisive. But it is also possible that one of the two Lukan parallels (Luke 6:43–45) has been placed elsewhere for topical reasons and that the other (12:10) is simply a report of a similar saying. At any rate the argument in Matthew 12:25–37 is unified and coherent.

25–26 Jesus "knew their thoughts" (v.25; cf. 9:4). The narrative is condensed (cf. Mark 3:20, 23), and the "house" is not mentioned. The argument is clear: any kingdom, city, or household that develops internal strife will destroy itself. The same holds true for Satan's *basileia* ("kingdom," v.26), his exercise of authority among his minions (cf. H. Kruse, "Das Reich Satans," *Biblica* 58 [1977]: 29–61). "For the prince of the demons to cast out his subjects would be virtually casting out himself, since they were doing his work" (Broadus).

27 Whether the words *hoi huioi hymōn* (lit., "your sons") mean no more than "your people" (the Jews) or those instructed by the Pharisees (cf. 22:15–16; 23:9–15) is uncertain. Jesus' argument is ad hominem: he is saying "your sons" cast out demons on occasion (a not uncommon practice linked to some bizarre notions; cf. Jos. Antiq. VIII, 45–48[ii.5]; id., Wars VII, 185[vi.3]; Tobit 8:2–3; Justin Martyr *Dialogue* 85;

cf. Acts 19:13), and I do this so powerfully that great damage is done to Satan's kingdom. So if I who do so much damage to his kingdom by my exorcisms perform them by Satan's power, by whom do your sons drive out demons?

28 Luke 11:20 has "the finger of God" instead of "the Spirit of God." Possibly the latter is original (cf. Dunn, *Jesus*, pp. 44–46), but the matter is of little consequence since they both refer to the same thing (cf. Exod 8:19; Deut 9:10; Ps 8:3). Matthew's phrase makes a clearer connection with 12:18 (Isa 42:1) and a more specific contrast with Beelzebub (cf. Gundry, *Matthew*). Only here and in Matthew 19:24; 21:31, 43 does Matthew have "kingdom of God" instead of "kingdom of heaven" (see on 3:2); and this may reflect his source, common to Luke (though elsewhere, when following a source, Matthew changes to "kingdom of heaven" except at 19:24), or he may use "kingdom of God" stylistically to go with "Spirit of God." What is certain is that Jesus knows that his exorcisms, performed by the Spirit of God, prove that the "kingdom of God" to go stylistically with "Spirit of God." What is certain is that the kingdom age has already dawned.

Of course this also implies that Jesus is King Messiah without explicitly affirming it. Dunn (*Jesus*, pp. 46–49) rightly emphasizes the realized eschatology but overstates his Spirit christology when he adds, "The eschatological kingdom was present for Jesus only because the eschatological Spirit was present in and through him. In other words, it was not so much a case of 'Where *I* am there is the kingdom,' as, 'Where the *Spirit* is there is the kingdom' " (emphasis his).

Four considerations argue strongly against this view.

1. Dunn has introduced a disjunction alien to the text ("only because the eschatological Spirit was present," he says) and maintains the disjunction by interpreting Jesus' messianic claims in non-Spirit dress as anachronistic. Jesus knew *both* that he was unique, the promised Messiah, *and* that the eschatological Spirit was on him.

2. If Jesus' self-recognition turned exclusively on his ability to exorcise demons by the Spirit's power, then on what basis could he deny similar self-recognition to the "your people" (v.27) who also drove out demons? In other words, Spirit-prompted phenomena were not sufficient in themselves for Jesus' self-understanding, especially in the light of his own warnings in this respect (cf. 7:21–23).

3. Dunn has too quickly turned this pericope into a question of Jesus' self-understanding ("The eschatological kingdom was present for Jesus," he says), whereas on the face of it Jesus is arguing, not to convince himself, but manifestly to convince the Pharisees that the kingdom had come on them.

4. In his Gospel's structure Matthew is less interested in Jesus' self-understanding than in his apologetics and fulfillment of OT prophecies (see the reference to "Spirit" in v.18).

Notes

26 The first clause is an excellent instance of a "real" condition, εἰ (*ei*, "if ") plus the indicative, in which the "reality" need not be admitted by the speaker but only assumed for the sake of argument (cf. RHG, p. 1008; Zerwick, par. 306).

2) *The strong man's house*

12:29

> 29"Or again, how can anyone enter a strong man's house and carry off his possessions unless he first ties up the strong man? Then he can rob his house.

29 The opening *ē* (lit., "or"; cf. 7:9; 12:5; 20:15) here means "Or look at it another way." Some Jewish expectation looked forward to the binding of Satan in the Messianic Age (As Moses 10:1; cf. Rev 20:2); and under this metaphor Jesus is the one who ties up the strong man (Satan) and carries off his "possessions" (*ta skeuē;* "vessels" preserves the metaphor of the house and has no relation to [demonic] possession except metaphorically). The argument has thus advanced: if Jesus' exorcisms cannot be attributed to Satan (vv.25–26), then they reflect authority greater than that of Satan. By this greater power Jesus is binding "the strong man" and plundering his "house." So the kingdom of heaven is forcefully advancing (see on 11:12).

3) *Blasphemy against the Spirit*

12:30–32

> 30"He who is not with me is against me, and he who does not gather with me scatters. 31And so I tell you, every sin and blasphemy will be forgiven men, but the blasphemy against the Spirit will not be forgiven. 32Anyone who speaks a word against the Son of Man will be forgiven, but anyone who speaks against the Holy Spirit will not be forgiven, either in this age or in the age to come.

30 Here several of Jesus' sayings are aphoristic. Their relation to the pericope is internal, not grammatical; and the relation to what precedes goes back to the tradition itself and cannot be ascribed to Matthew (cf. Luke 11:23).

The general thrust of v.30 is straightforward: in our relationship to Jesus there can be no neutrality. As to some issues and persons, neutrality is possible and may even be wise. But in the great struggle (vv.25–29), neutrality is impossible. The claims of the kingdom and the demands of Jesus are so exclusivistic that to be indifferent or apathetic to him is to be on the side of those who do not confess that he is the Messiah who brings in the kingdom of God (cf. 11:16–24). Jesus' claim implies a high christology, which is underlined by the harvest figure in v.30b (cf. 3:12; 6:26; John 4:36). Jesus is the one who will harvest in the last days, a function the OT regularly assigns to God. Hill (*Matthew*) objects to the authenticity of the setting of this saying on the grounds that an affirmation about the impossibility of neutrality with respect to Jesus "is hardly likely to have been addressed to implacable opponents such as the Pharisees." But crowds were also present (v.23). And this form of statement could serve as both a rebuke to the Pharisees and a warning to the questioning crowd (v.23) that failure to follow Jesus wholeheartedly is as dangerous as outright opposition.

The inverted saying—"whoever is not against us is for us" (Mark 9:40; Luke 9:50) —and this one "are not contradictory if the one was spoken to the indifferent about themselves and the other to the disciples about someone else" (McNeile).

31–32 "And so"—*dia touto* (lit., "on account of this")—ties the statements about blasphemy against the Spirit (v.31) to the preceding verse. But the transition cannot easily be readily grasped till vv.31–32 are understood. Introduced by the solemn "I tell you" (see on 5:18), these statements constitute a pair, one from Mark (v.31 = Mark 3:28), one from Q (v.32 = Luke 12:10, in a different context; cf. comment, above). "Blasphemy" is extreme slander (see on 9:3), equivalent to "speaking against" (cf. v.32). Blasphemy against God was viewed by Jews with utmost gravity (26:65); but here Jesus makes a sharp distinction between blasphemy against the Son of Man, which is forgivable, and blasphemy against the Spirit, which is not.

His statement is remarkable because one of the glories of the biblical faith is the great emphasis Scripture lays on the graciousness and wideness of God's forgiveness (e.g., Pss 65:3; 86:5; 130:3–4; Isa 1:18; Mic 7:19; 1 John 1:7). A common interpretation of vv.31–32 is that they originated with a Christian prophet speaking for the exalted Jesus and are here read back into the life of the earthly Jesus. The blasphemy against the Son of Man is rejection of him by nonbelievers, and this is clearly forgivable when a person becomes a Christian. But blasphemy against the Holy Spirit is committed by a Christian (Christians after Pentecost would understand that only believers enjoy the Spirit) and is equivalent either to apostasy or to rejection of a Christian prophet's inspired message. For this there is no forgiveness (so Stendahl, Peake, 684q; and in a highly structured scheme, M.E. Boring, "The Unforgivable Sin Logion Mark III 28–29/Matt XII 31–32/Luke XII 10: Formal Analysis and History of the Tradition," NovTest 18 [1976]: 258–79).

But there is strong and consistent evidence that the writers of the NT did *not* read words of Christian prophets back into the life of the historical Jesus (cf. esp. Bonnard; J.D.G. Dunn, "Prophetic 'I'-Sayings and the Jesus Tradition: The Importance of Testing Prophetic Utterances within Early Christianity," NTS 24 [1978]: 175–98). It is highly unlikely that "Son of Man" would be used as an object of blasphemy without some qualifications about "Son of Man" (i.e., as "earthly Jesus only," etc.), which do not appear until Origen. Moreover this does not explain what these sayings are doing in their Gospel contexts (esp. Mark and Matthew).

The views of many older conservative scholars are also unhelpful. Broadus, for instance, ties blasphemy against the Holy Spirit to the "age of miracles" when the Spirit's power could be directly perceived—and rejected. But apart from the question of whether miracles take place now, Jesus elsewhere warned that miracles are not *necessarily* the criterion of true discipleship (7:21–23), i.e., they do not *necessarily* reveal the Spirit's presence and power.

Among the many other interpretations of this difficult incident, the best treats it in its setting during Jesus' life. The Pharisees have been attributing to Satan the work of the Spirit and have been doing so, as Jesus makes plain, in such a way as to reveal that they speak, not out of ignorance or unbelief, but out of a "conscious disputing of the indisputable" (the phrase is from G.C. Berkouwer, *Sin* [Grand Rapids: Eerdmans, 1971], p. 340; cf. pp. 323–53, to which this exposition is indebted).

The distinction between blasphemy against the Son of Man and blasphemy against the Spirit is not that the Son of Man is less important than the Spirit, or that the first sin is prebaptismal and the second postbaptismal, still less that the first is against the Son of Man and the second rejects the authority of Christian prophets. Instead, within the context of the larger argument the first sin is rejection of the truth of the gospel (but there may be repentance and forgiveness for that), whereas the second sin is rejection of the same truth in full awareness that that is exactly what one is doing—thoughtfully, willfully, and self-consciously rejecting the work of the Spirit even though there can be no other explanation of Jesus' exorcisms than that. For such a sin there is no forgiveness, "either in this age or the age to come" (cf. 13:22; 25:46)—a dramatic way of saying "never" (as in Mark 3:29).

If this interpretation is correct, the distinction between Son of Man and Spirit is relatively incidental. After all, blasphemy against the Spirit is also a rejection of Jesus' own claims: the christological implications of the sin are not diminished but increased in moving from "blasphemy against the Son of Man" to "blasphemy against the Spirit." This provides a clue for understanding how the unforgivable sin of which Jesus here speaks compares with the sins referred to in Hebrews 6:4-6; 10:26-31; and possibly 1 John 5:16. In each instance there is self-conscious perception of where the truth lies and the light shines—and a willful turning away from it. This is very different from Paul's persecution of the church (1 Cor 15:9), which was not unforgivable (1 Tim 1:13).

C.K. Barrett (*The Holy Spirit and the Gospel Tradition* [London: SPCK, 1966], pp. 106-7) discusses this matter wisely, except for his assumption that the sin is committed within the church and "because it denies the root and spring of the Church's life, cannot rediscover the forgiveness by which the sinner first entered the community of the forgiven." But the biblical texts are more subtle than that. The author of Hebrews says, with a surprising combination of tenses, "We have come [perfect] to share in Christ if we hold firmly [aorist subjunctive] to the end the confidence we had at first" (Heb 3:14). In other words our past participation in the blessings of the gospel is valid only if we continue in it. John presupposes the same thing—that those who leave the church show that they never really belonged in it (1 John 2:19; 2 John 9). Even Hebrews 6:4-6; 10:26-31 shows how much of the truth may be grasped, how much of the life of the age to come may be sampled, without coming to the place from which there is no turning back (cf. Philip E. Hughes, *A Commentary on the Epistle to the Hebrews* [Grand Rapids: Eerdmans, 1977], in loc.). This is apostasy, and it involves a break with what one has formally adhered to.

The universal witness of the NT is that apostasy if persisted in not only damns but shows that salvation was never real in the first place. The NT reveals how close one may come to the kingdom—tasting, touching, perceiving, understanding. And it also shows that to come this far and reject the truth is unforgivable. So it is here. Jesus charges that those who perceive that his ministry is empowered by the Spirit and then, for whatever reason—whether spite, jealousy, or arrogance—ascribe it to Satan, have put themselves beyond the pale. For them there is no forgiveness, and that is the verdict of the one who has authority to forgive sins (9:5-8).

The significance of the transitional words "And so" now becomes plain. Neutrality to Jesus is actually opposition to him (v.30); and therefore Jesus gives this warning regarding those who blaspheme against the Spirit, since the self-professedly neutral person may not recognize the inherent danger of his position.

4) *Nature and fruit*

12:33-37

33"Make a tree good and its fruit will be good, or make a tree bad and its fruit will be bad, for a tree is recognized by its fruit. 34You brood of vipers, how can you who are evil say anything good? For out of the overflow of the heart the mouth speaks. 35The good man brings good things out of the good stored up in him, and the evil man brings evil things out of the evil stored up in him. 36But I tell you that men will have to give account on the day of judgment for every careless word they have spoken. ³⁷For by your words you will be acquitted, and by your words you will be condemned."

This section has no parallel in Mark, but it fits well into Matthew. A similar metaphor occurs in 7:16–19; but there the point is that Jesus' disciples must test character by conduct, whereas here it is that conduct, especially speech, reveals character. Therefore the only remedy is a radical change of heart. Parts of vv.33–34 are also reflected in Luke 6:43–45.

33 It is possible to construe the expression "make a tree good . . . bad" to mean "suppose a tree is good . . . bad." But in that case the word "and" fits badly, and the final "for" clause relates poorly to what precedes. Jesus is rather telling his hearers to make the tree good or bad, knowing that its fruit will be correspondingly good or bad, because a tree is recognized by its fruit (cf. Ecclus 27:6). To speculate on the means—pruning, grafting, watering, fertilizing—is to go beyond the metaphor.

34–35 Then Jesus drives the point home. "You brood of vipers" (v.34; see on 3:7; 23:33) was most likely addressed to the Pharisees in the crowd (cf. vv.23–24), though this is not certain (cf. 7:11). Verse 35 makes a tight connection with v.33: what a person truly is determines what he says and does. Out of the *perisseuma* ("overflow," v.34—what remains, the excess) the "mouth speaks." *Perisseuma* is used in the NT only here and in Mark 8:8; Luke 6:45; 2 Corinthians 8:14 (*bis*) of the heart, the center of human personality (see on 5:8). It is the mouth that reveals what is in the heart. How, then, can those who are evil say anything good? What is needed is a change of heart.

36–37 These two verses occur only in Matthew. That Jesus describes the evil of the "brood of vipers" in terms of their hearts or natures does not thereby excuse them. Far from it! A person will be held accountable on the Day of Judgment for "every careless word" (v.36). The Greek *argos* ("careless") does not refer here to "unfounded" words (JB) but to words that might be thought "insignificant" (Stendahl, Peake) except for their revealing what is in the heart. Jesus is saying that every spoken word reflects the heart's overflow and is known to God. Therefore words are of critical importance (cf. Eph 5:3–4, 12; Col 3:17; James 1:19; 3:1–12).

The change to the second person (v.37) implies that the saying may be proverbial. Here it heightens the warning that what one says about Jesus and his miracles reveals what one is and that he will be judged accordingly. Jesus' authority in saying this is staggering. It is not he who is being assessed when men ask, "Could this be the Son of David?" (v.23), or utter blasphemies (v.24); it is they who are being assessed, and by their words they will be judged.

Notes

36 The syntax is difficult. If πᾶν ῥῆμα ἀργόν (*pan rhēma argon*, "every careless word") is construed as nominative, there is an awkward anacolouthon (. . . περὶ αὐτοῦ λόγον [*peri* *autou logon*, lit., "concerning his (or its) word"]; cf. 13:19); but this may be accusative by attraction to the relative ŏ (*ho*, "which").

---

c. *Continued confrontation* (12:38–42)

1) *Request for a sign*

12:38

> **38**Then some of the Pharisees and teachers of the law said to him, "Teacher, we want to see a miraculous sign from you."

38 One might take *apekrithēsan* ("answered"; NIV, "said") as meaning that the Pharisees and teachers of the law were continuing the controversy. That is possible, and the parallel in Luke 11:29–32 is sufficiently detached from its context to permit this interpretation. But *apekrithēsan* does not always have its full strength in Matthew (see on 11:25); so it seems best not to insist on the continuance of the controversy.

In 9:11 Matthew mentions only Pharisees, whereas the parallel in Mark 2:16 has Pharisees and teachers of the law. On that basis many say Matthew has pruned the expression because in his day, unlike the days of Jesus' ministry, only the Pharisees, understood to represent the rabbis (cf. Introduction, section 11.f), constituted any real opposition. Here, however, the roles are reversed: Mark (8:11) has "Pharisees"; Matthew (12:38) mentions "Pharisees and teachers of the law." Such changes are of little use in establishing Matthew's life-setting.

The Jewish leaders phrased their question respectfully ("Teacher"; see on 8:19) and asked for a "sign" (*sēmeion*), not just for another miracle. Jesus had already done many miracles. Old Testament and intertestamental Jewish literature shed light on the request (cf. K.H. Rengstorf, TDNT, 7:208–21, 225–29; F.J. Helfmeyer, TDOT, 1:167–88; and 1 Sam 2:30–33; 1 Kings 20:1–14; Isa 7:10–25; b *Sanhedrin* 98a; b *Baba Metzia* 59b; cf. O. Linton, "The Demand for a Sign from Heaven [Mk.8,11–12 and Parallels]," ST 19 [1965]: esp. 123ff.). A "sign" was usually some miraculous token to be fulfilled quickly, or at once, to confirm a prophecy. The Jews were not asking for just another miracle, since they had already persuaded themselves that at least some of those Jesus had performed were of demonic agency (12:24); they were asking for a "sign" performed on command to remove what seemed to them to be the ambiguity of Jesus' miracles. (In John "sign" is not so much something people ask for as the evangelist's standard label for what the synoptists call "powers" or "wonders." The "signs" Jesus performs under John's pen bear implicit and explicit symbolic weight.)

2) *The sign of Jonah*

12:39–42

> **39**He answered, "A wicked and adulterous generation asks for a miraculous sign! But none will be given it except the sign of the prophet Jonah. **40**For as Jonah was three days and three nights in the belly of a huge fish, so the Son of Man will be three days and three nights in the heart of the earth. **41**The men of Nineveh will stand up at the judgment with this generation and condemn it; for they repented at the preaching of Jonah, and now one greater than Jonah is here.

42The Queen of the South will rise at the judgment with this generation and condemn it; for she came from the ends of the earth to listen to Solomon's wisdom, and now one greater than Solomon is here.

39-40 The Pharisees and teachers of the law did not, in Jesus' view, stand alone: they represented this "wicked and adulterous generation" (v.39; cf. 11:16-24). "Adultery" was frequently used by OT prophets to describe the spiritual prostitution and wanton apostasy of Israel (Isa 50:1; 57:3; Jer 3:8; 13:27; 31:32; Ezek 16:15, 32, 35-42; Hos 2:1-7; 3:1 et al.). Here Jesus applies it to his contemporaries as did his brother James later on (James 4:4). Israel had largely abandoned her idolatry and syncretism after the Exile. But now Jesus insists that she was still adulterous in heart. In the past God had graciously granted "signs" to strengthen the faith of the timid (e.g., Abraham [Gen 15]; Gideon [Judg 6:17-24]; Joshua [Josh 10]). Here, however, Jesus says that signs are denied "this wicked and adulterous generation," because they are never to be performed on demand or as a sop to unbelief (cf. 1 Cor 1:22).

In Mark 8:11-12, Jesus refuses to give any sign; but in Matthew and Luke (Q) the sign of Jonah is expected. This has led many to conclude that the reference to Jonah is an unauthentic, late addition (Stendahl, Peake; G. Schmitt, "Das Zeichen Jona," ZNW [1978]: 123-29, suggests that the addition was made in the seventh decade A.D. through the influence of *Lives of the Prophets*). On the other hand, Taylor (*Mark*, p. 363), quoted by Hill (*Matthew*), suggests Mark has abbreviated the original in the interests of his messianic-secret theme so as to produce a flat refusal to provide a sign. But the difference between Mark and the other two synoptists may be more subtle. Rightly understood the sign, which is the exception in Matthew and Luke, is not a sign at all as Jesus' opponents understood the word. It becomes a sign only for those with eyes to see. In that sense there is no exception: Jesus offers no miraculous token on demand. That is Mark's point, a point not contradicted by the "exception" the other synoptists record.

But what is "the sign of Jonah"? This question is tied to the absence of 12:40 from the parallel in Luke and its being regarded as a late addition. The argument, it is said, must therefore run from 12:39 to 12:41; and the sign of Jonah must be his preaching of repentance, a ministry in which Jesus has likewise been engaged. Verse 40 is, then, a late typological addition.

Nevertheless a good case can be made for the authenticity of v.40 (cf. especially France, *Jesus*, pp. 80-82). Luke does not simply "drop out" Matthew 12:40. Rather, following the reference to the "sign of Jonah," Luke writes (11:30): "For as Jonah was a sign to the Ninevites, so also will the Son of Man be to this generation." He then includes the visit of the queen of the South before returning to the men of Nineveh, who will rise up and condemn Jesus' contemporaries (cf. Matt 12:41). In other words Luke, for whom Jonah's preaching is not a sign, does not support the alleged continuity between Matthew 12:39 and 12:41. If this is correct, then either Matthew 12:40 is an enlargement of an original but cryptic Luke 11:30, or else Luke 11:30 is an effort to veil the specificity of an original Matthew 12:40. The latter view is more credible, for Luke has an obvious reason for making the saying more cryptic —viz., the reference to three days and three nights, so readily understood in Matthew's Jewish environment (see below), would be problematic to Luke's readers who would see a conflict with the length of time Jesus was actually in the tomb. The same concern doubtless accounts for Justin Martyr's quoting (*Dialogue* 107:1) Matthew 12:39 and saying that Jesus was speaking cryptically of the Resurrection, though Justin does not actually quote v.40.

The rejection of v.40 is tied to the interpretation of the "sign of Jonah." If v.40 is removed, the "sign" is most likely the preaching. But this is intrinsically unlikely: in both Matthew and Luke the sign is future to Jesus' utterance (Matt 12:39; Luke 11:30), which suits Jesus' death and resurrection but not his preaching. Verse 40 therefore becomes an integral part of Matthew's pericope. And the contention of R.A. Edwards (*The Sign of Jonah* [London: SCM, 1971], pp. 25ff.), that the sayings of this pericope are in the form of a new *Gattung*, a Christian invention after Jesus' time, has been disproved by lists of much older examples of the same form (cf. Daryl Schmidt, "The LXX Gattung 'Prophetic Correlative,'" JBL 96 [1977]: 517–22).

In "the sign of Jonah," then, "of Jonah" must be construed as an epexegetic genitive (Zerwick, par. 45; Turner, *Syntax*, p. 214). It is the sign that Jonah himself was, not the sign given him or presented by him. This interpretation commonly accepts the view that the Ninevites learned what had happened to Jonah and how he got to their city. Jonah himself thus served as a "sign" to the Ninevites, for he appeared to them as one who had been delivered from certain death (cf. J. Jeremias, TDNT, 3:409; Eugene H. Merrill, "The Sign of Jonah," JETS 23 [1980]: 23–30). As Jonah was three days and three nights in the belly of the fish, so the Son of Man— seen here in his suffering role (see on 8:20)—will be three days and three nights in the "heart [perhaps an echo of Jonah 2:3; cf. Ps 46:2] of the earth"—a reference to Jesus' burial, not his descent into Hades. That is to say, Jesus' preaching will be attested by a deliverance like Jonah's only still greater; therefore there will be greater condemnation for those who reject the significance of Jonah's deliverance.

Some scholars perceive the strength of the argument for the authenticity of this pericope but interpret v.40 as if it were referring to the "sign" of the coming Son of Man (24:30), or to Jesus' vague awareness that he must die sometime, or that Jesus by his suffering will carry the truth of God to the Gentiles as Jonah did. But this overlooks the connection between Jonah and Jesus established by the text. Grant the authenticity of v.40, and the only legitimate conclusion is that Jesus knew long in advance about his death, burial, and resurrection, and saw his life moving toward that climax; and the christological implications must not be avoided.

Jonah spent "three days and three nights" in the fish (Jonah 1:17). But if the normal sequence of Passion Week is correct (see on 26:17–30), Jesus was in the tomb only about thirty-six hours. Since they included parts of three days, by Jewish reckoning Jesus was buried "three days" or, to put it another way, he rose "on the third day" (16:21). But this does not cover more than two nights. Some advocate a Wednesday crucifixion date (see on 26:17); but though that allows for "three days and three nights," it runs into difficulty with "on the third day." In rabbinical thought a day and a night make an *ōnâh*, and a part of an *ōnâh* is as the whole (cf. SBK, 1:649, for references; cf. further 1 Sam 30:12–13; 2 Chron 10:5, 12; Esth 4:16; 5:1). Thus according to Jewish tradition, "three days and three nights" need mean no more than "three days" or the combination of any part of three separate days.

41 The first point of comparison between Jonah and Jesus is that they were both delivered from death—a deliverance that attested the trustworthiness of their preaching. The second point of comparison is the different responses of the hearers. The men of Nineveh repented. But even though "something [neuter, as in 11:19;

12:6; NIV, 'one'] greater than Jonah is here"—the reference is to Jesus, not his deliverance, because the comparison is with Jonah, not his deliverance—the people of Jesus' day—"this generation" (cf. v.39)—did not repent. Therefore men of Nineveh (the nouns are anarthrous) "will stand up with" this generation at the final judgment—i.e., they will rise to bear witness against them (see on 11:20–24; and on the Semitic legal idiom, cf. Mark 14:57; Black, *Aramaic Approach,* p. 134). Thus Jesus' "sign" does not meet the Jews' demand for a special token (see on v.38). Yet it is the only one he will provide. For his own followers, his authority will be grounded in his death and resurrection. And as for those who do not believe, they will only prove themselves more wicked than the Ninevites.

42 Jonah and Solomon are linked in other Jewish literature (cf. D. Correns, "Jona und Salomo," in Haubeck and Bachmann, pp. 86–94). The nature of the link—Jonah and the queen with "this generation" rising at the Judgment—strongly supports the view that for Jesus, Jonah was a historical person. The queen of the South (the Arabian peninsula, which for the Jews was "at the ends of the earth"; cf. Jer 6:20; Joel 3:8, NASB) was the queen of Sheba (1 Kings 10:1–13), who came to Jerusalem because of reports of Solomon's wisdom. But Jesus is "something greater" (see on v.41) than Solomon; Jesus is the Messiah, who will introduce the promised eschatological age. Therefore the queen of Sheba will rise at the Judgment to join the Ninevites in condemning the unbelieving generation of Jesus' time.

Notes

41 The phrase εἰς τὸ κήρυγμα Ἰωνᾶ (*eis to kērygma Iōna,* "at the preaching of Jonah") cannot be final but establishes the ground for the Ninevites' repentance. On this rather rare use of *eis,* cf. Turner, *Syntax,* p. 255; Zerwick, par. 106; BDF, par. 207(1). See note on 10:41.

d. *The return of the evil spirit*

12:43–45

> ⁴³"When an evil spirit comes out of a man, it goes through arid places seeking rest and does not find it. ⁴⁴Then it says, 'I will return to the house I left.' When it arrives, it finds the house unoccupied, swept clean and put in order. ⁴⁵Then it goes and takes with it seven other spirits more wicked than itself, and they go in and live there. And the final condition of that man is worse than the first. That is how it will be with this wicked generation."

The parallel in Luke 11:24–26 is, as here, tied to the Beelzebub controversy, though the preceding verse is different (Luke 11:23 = Matt 12:30). Though many think Luke applies the parable to the individual and Matthew to the nation, this contrast is too facile. Luke omits (according to the best texts) the connective *de* ("and" or "but"). This suggests an independent saying that fits the movement of the chapter but is not meant to be tied too tightly to the verse preceding it. The warning in both Matthew and Luke is not (contra Marshall, *Luke,* p. 479) aimed at "those who exorcise demons without giving a positive substitute to their patients." In both Matthew (12:27) and Luke (11:19) the comparison Jesus draws between himself and other exorcists is not meant to prove his superiority but to show that even Jewish exorcists achieve some success in their work by virtue, not of Beelzebub, but of God's power.

This story about the unclean spirit who after being driven out returns with seven wicked spirits goes beyond Jesus' comparison; for Luke (11:21–22) has shown Jesus' authority in binding Satan, and Matthew (12:38–42) has insisted that Jesus is greater than Jonah and Solomon. In other words, in both Gospels this pericope is set in a milieu of veiled messianic claims. The point here and in Luke is that those who through the kingdom power of God experience exorcisms must beware of neutrality toward Jesus the Messiah, for neutrality opens the door to seven demons worse than the one driven out. Commitment to Jesus is essential. Thus the pericope supports Luke 11:23, which, like Matthew 12:30, rules out neutrality.

Against the broader background in Matthew of the Beelzebub controversy and the sign of Jonah, in sweeping out the house and ridding it of its demons, Jesus has been testifying to the presence of the kingdom (12:28). Yet many of that "wicked and adulterous generation" are so neutral toward him they require signs (12:38) and fail to see that one greater than Jonah and Solomon has come. Luke 11:23 does not mean that Matthew 12:43–45 and Luke 11:24–26 refer to individual demon possession in contrast to the national rejection of Jesus Messiah portrayed in Matthew; on the contrary, both evangelists deal with the same issue, the extreme danger of being neutral toward Jesus (see further on v.45).

43 When an evil spirit (see on 8:28; 10:1) leaves a man (lit., "the man," but the article presents a typical case), it goes "through arid places" in search of rest. This conforms to the view that demons have an affinity for such places (Tobit 8:3; cf. Rev 18:2). Ultimately, however, they seek another body in order to do even more harm.

44 Verse 43 implies the possibility of repossession. While v.44 may be theoretically interpreted as a universal fact of experience, that would make Jesus' exorcisms an invitation to catastrophe. So it is better to take the language of the text as a Semitic paratactic conditional protasis to v.45 (i.e., "If the demon on his arrival finds the house unoccupied, etc."; cf. H.S. Nyberg, "Zum grammatischen Verständnis von Matth.12,44f.," *Coniectanea Neotestamentica* 13 [1949]: 1–11; Jeremias, *Parables*, pp. 197f.) or to take the details of the story as representing a dangerous contingency (Beyer, 1:281–86).

45 Though the seven evil spirits may have been harder to drive out than just one (cf. Mark 5:9; 9:29), the text only mentions their greater wickedness. The man from whom the demon had been driven out is now in a far worse condition than before. Jesus' final statement in this pericope—"That is how it will be with this wicked generation" (omitted by Luke)—does not change the point of the story from one of demon possession to the nation's failure to recognize Jesus, for both Matthew and Luke understand the story to demand recognition of Jesus Messiah. But what Matthew adds (1) closes off the main part of the pericope by referring again to "this wicked generation" (cf. 12:39)—a common but overlooked Matthean device (see on 15:20)—and (2) makes the warning less cryptic than Luke (cf. v.40; Luke 11:30).

Though Luke knows the danger into which the Jews' rejection of Jesus (Luke 21:20–24) will place them, this is not for him, as it is for Matthew, a major theme.

6. *Doing the Father's will*

12:46–50

> [46]While Jesus was still talking to the crowd, his mother and brothers stood outside, wanting to speak to him. [47]Someone told him, "Your mother and brothers are standing outside, wanting to speak to you."
>
> [48]He replied to him, "Who is my mother, and who are my brothers?" [49]Pointing to his disciples, he said, "Here are my mother and my brothers. [50]For whoever does the will of my Father in heaven is my brother and sister and mother."

Here Matthew basically follows Mark 3:31–35 (cf. Luke 8:19–21; John 7:3–5), though he omits the background in Mark 3:20–21. As a result these verses are not so much a confrontation between Jesus and his family as a statement about what it really means to be a disciple of Jesus and to be totally committed to him. The way for us to be as close to Jesus as his nearest and dearest is to do the will of his Father.

46–47 The obvious implication is that Jesus is inside the house (cf. Mark 3:20, 31). Though v.47 is omitted in many MSS, probably by homoeoteleuton (words, clauses, or sentences with similar endings being dropped by oversight: both v.46 and v.47 end in *lalēsai* ["to speak"]), it was likely in the original text and clearly helps the sense of the pericope. While the verse might represent assimilation to Mark 3:32, this would not explain *tō legonti autō* ("to the one who had spoken to him," omitted from v.48 in NIV), which presupposes v.47.

The most natural way to understand "brothers" (v.46) is that the term refers to sons of Mary and Joseph and thus to brothers of Jesus on his mother's side. To support the dogma of Mary's perpetual virginity, a notion foreign to the NT and to the earliest church fathers, Roman Catholic scholars have suggested that "brothers" refers either to Joseph's sons by an earlier marriage or to sons of Mary's sister, who had the same name (cf. Lagrange; McHugh, pp. 200ff.). Certainly "brothers" can have a wider meaning than male relatives (Acts 22:1). Yet it is very doubtful whether such a meaning is valid here for it raises insuperable problems. For instance, if "brothers" refers to Joseph's sons by an earlier marriage, not Jesus but Joseph's firstborn would have been legal heir to David's throne. The second theory —that "brothers" refers to sons of a sister of Mary also named "Mary"—faces the unlikelihood of two sisters having the same name. All things considered, the attempts to extend the meaning of "brothers" in this pericope, despite McHugh's best efforts, are nothing less than farfetched exegesis in support of a dogma that originated much later than the NT (see on 1:25; Luke 2:7; cf. Broadus on 13:55–56).

48–50 Jesus' searching question (v.48) and its remarkable answer (vv.49–50) in no way diminish his mother and brothers but simply give the priority to his Father and doing his will. "For, had He not entered into earthly kinship solely for the sake of the higher spiritual relationship which He was about to found . . . ? Thus, it was not that Christ set lightly by His Mother, but that He confounded not the means with the end" (LTJM, 1:577). Henceforth the disciples are the only "family" Jesus recognizes.

The metaphorical nature of v.49 is shown by the "ands" (v.50): "my brother and sister [Jesus had physical sisters; cf. 13:56] and mother" instead of ". . . or . . . or." We do not make ourselves Jesus' close relatives by doing the will of his heavenly Father. Rather, doing the Father's will *identifies* us as his mother and sisters and brothers (cf. 7:21). The doing of that will turns on obedience to Jesus and his teaching, according to Matthew, for it was Jesus who preeminently revealed the will of the Father (cf. 11:27). This means that Jesus' words in this pericope are full of christological implications, but they also establish the basic importance of the community now beginning to form around him, God's chosen Servant who, despite rising opposition, will lead justice to victory (12:18, 20).

B. *Third Discourse: The Parables of the Kingdom* (13:1–53)

1. *The setting*

13:1–3a

> ¹That same day Jesus went out of the house and sat by the lake. ²Such large crowds gathered around him that he got into a boat and sat in it, while all the people stood on the shore. ³Then he told them many things in parables, saying:

1 Doubtless *en tē hēmera ekeinē* must be rendered "that same day," but NIV introduces an insurmountable problem by translating *palin* in Mark 4:1 "on another occasion." *Palin* does not mean that; indeed, it can often be translated "furthermore" or "thereupon" (BAGD, s.v.). At any rate Matthew links the parabolic discourse in chapter 13 to the preceding controversies (either 12:38–50 or 12:22–37) and ends it with a formulaic conclusion (13:53), which implies that all these parables were given on this occasion. The statement "Jesus went out of the house" implies the same thing by setting a specific scene carried forward by 13:36.

Jesus "sat by the lake," taking the normal position of a teacher (see on 5:1–2). The explanation that Jesus' posture was a symbol drawn from apocalyptic literature representing God sitting in judgment (cf. Rev 7:9–12; Kingsbury, *Parables*, pp. 23f.) is not only overly subtle and needlessly anachronistic but misunderstands the parables. Although in some parables Jesus portrayed himself as the Judge coming at the end of the age (esp. vv.40–43), such a judicial session is future. During his ministry Jesus' chosen role was that of a teacher who taught others about the kingdom so that they might teach others (see on vv.51–52).

2 This is the only one of the five major discourses in Matthew that is addressed, not to the "disciples" (in the broad sense of 5:1–2), but to the crowds. Therefore Matthew includes in it two major digressions (vv.10–23, 36–43) to explain to his disciples the significance of parables and to interpret two of them. While these digressions doubtless took place after the public discourse, Matthew moves them back as parentheses so that the significance of the parables will not be lost to the reader. Some scholars contend that the crowds, unlike the Jewish leaders, are portrayed favorably, since they are the group Matthew wants immediately to reach. But that is farfetched. In Matthew, Jesus has already criticized "this generation" (11:16–24) and can treat the Jewish leaders as typical of it (12:38–39). Here the crowds are not given "the secrets of the kingdom" (v.11).

Matthew changes Mark's "taught" (4:2) to "told" (v.3a)—a change that has encouraged many to suppose that he is turning the parables into "proclamation narratives" (e.g., W. Wilkens, "Die Redaktion des Gleichniskapitels Mark.4 durch Matth.," *Theologische Zeitschrift* 20 [1964]: 305–27). On the other hand, Kingsbury (*Parables*, pp. 28–31) holds that the change from "taught" to "told" owes everything to the structure of Matthew's Gospel. After Matthew 12 Jesus never teaches or preaches to the Jews. So Matthew looks on this chapter as a sort of "apology." To base such large theological implications on the change of a single verb is not convincing, because Matthew often shows considerable independence in verbal expression. What he understands Jesus to be doing in the parables must be based on the exegesis of the whole chapter, and especially on that of Matthew 13:10–17, which purports to answer that very question. Kingsbury's view that Jesus does not teach or preach to the crowd after Matthew 12 is in any case manifestly wrong. Little of such teaching occurs before Matthew 12; most references to it are general (e.g., 4:23; 9:35); and after Matthew 12 we find similar remarks (13:54; 15:10; 21:23; cf. 22:16; 26:55; and implicitly 14:13–36; 15:29–31). These and similar reconstructions attempt to see in the antithesis between the "crowds" and the "disciples" a covert disjunction between the church and the synagogue. J. Dupont ("Point de vue," pp. 221–59) analyzes these efforts in detail and shows that the language is simply not specific enough to draw such far-reaching conclusions. In particular he shows that the disciples-crowds contrast relates to what is just or unjust and with either doing or not doing the will of the Father.

3a Jesus told the crowd "many things in parables." Before we examine them, however, three comments are needed.

1. The history of the interpretation of parables is very complex, and the number of new developments in parable scholarship has accelerated in recent years. This has been set forth concisely by J.G. Little ("Parable Research in the Twentieth Century," ExpT 87 [1975–76]: 356–60; 88 [1976–77]: 40–44, 71–75) and comprehensively by W.S. Kissinger (*The Parables of Jesus: A History of Interpretation and Bibliography* [Metuchen, N.J.: Scarecrow, 1979]).

Commentators tended to interpret the parables more or less by appeal to allegory (with notable exceptions such as Augustine and, to a lesser extent, Calvin) till Adolph Jülicher's huge study (*Die Gleichnisreden Jesu*, 2 vols. [Tübingen: J.C.B. Mohr, 1910]), which contends that Jesus told not allegories but parables—simple stories with a single point. Traces of allegorical interpretation of parables in the Gospels must therefore be assigned to the postapostolic church. Studies by Dodd (*Parables*) and Jeremias (*Parables*) have proceeded along similar lines. Dodd has tried to show that some parables demonstrate the eschatological orientation of Jesus' preaching and the "presentness" of the kingdom, while Jeremias has established "laws" of parable transmission to determine how Jesus' simple stories were progressively changed in the process of oral and written retelling and application. Using these "laws," Jeremias has argued that we can strip off later accretions and discover what the historical Jesus really taught.

Two essays challenge Jeremias's view. Both Matthew Black ("The Parables as Allegory," BJRL 42 [1959–60]: 273–87) and Raymond E. Brown ("Parable and Allegory Reconsidered," NovTest 5 [1962]: 36–45) convincingly demonstrate that the allegory-parable distinction is too facile, that Jesus himself occasionally derived more than one or two points from certain of his parables, and that all "allegorizing" of the parables cannot be automatically assigned to the postapostolic church. Two things follow: (1) what Jeremias calls allegorization does not by itself prove secondary accretion; (2) as McNeile (p. 186) observed long ago, a certain unavoidable ambiguity is built into the parables. For it is not always easy to distinguish illustrative details and details that are merely part of the story structure. While there is room for difference of opinion here, the slight loss in certainty of meaning is more than compensated for by the greater flexibility in understanding the parables.

More recent developments in parable scholarship have moved in different directions. Hans Weder (*Die Gleichnisse Jesu als Metaphern* [Göttingen: Vandenhoeck und Ruprecht, 1978], pp. 69–75) distinguishes parabolic (as opposed to allegorical) elements as those tied to the narrative flow and lacking independent existence both in the narrative and its interpretation. His work largely follows the studies of Eta Linnemann (*Parables of Jesus* [London: SPCK, 1966]), D.O. Via (*The Parables* [Philadelphia: Fortress, 1967]), and J.D. Crossan (*In Parables* [New York: Harper and Row, 1973]), who say that what distinguishes parable from allegory is not that only the former has one central point but that the former alone ties all its elements to one another within the parable's framework. These interconnections are determined not so much by a one-to-one link with the historical or theological situation to which the parable refers but by the demands of the story—viz., the parable itself. Therefore some parabolic elements may have a historical referent; others none. But where such "outside" connections are made, they are subsidiary to the connections "inside" the parable, the point of which is contained within the story's internal movement.

These are important insights. Yet those who have developed them unfortunately tend to think deeply on the literary level but naively on the historical one. Many recent interpreters tend to be far less conservative than Jeremias in what they ascribe to the historical Jesus. And it is astonishing how often, once they have finished their interpretations, they exhort their readers to choose authentic existence, trust the benevolence of the universe, or the like. Whatever else Jesus was, he was no twentieth-century existentialist! Coupling these literary studies with insights from "the new hermeneutic," Mary Ann Tolbert (*Perspectives on the Parables: An Approach to Multiple Interpretations* [Philadelphia: Fortress, 1979]) tries to establish the legitimacy of interpreting the parables in different ways that depend largely on the stance of the interpreter, and argues that the parables' "dynamic indeterminacy" (p. 115) requires such an approach. Questions raised by such studies and the German works on which many of them are based cannot be handled here. For a responsible treatment of the issues involved, see A.C. Thiselton, *The Two Horizons* (Grand Rapids: Eerdmans, 1980).

Suffice it to say that historical doubts are not always tied as intimately to the genuine literary insights of these writers as they seem to think. Jesus, though he did indeed confront people and demand existential choices, did so within a message that was, and can still be, defined and defended propositionally. Moreover the criteria for distinguishing between Jesus' parables and church accretions to them are becoming less and less justifiable. Although there are many *kinds* of parables (see below), Thiselton is right in pointing out how many of them are designed to capture the listener and make him a participant, overturning his world view and leading him to call in question his most basic values (cf. esp. pp. 12–15, 344–47). These convictions undergird the following exposition.

2. Some areas of disagreement might be eliminated if more attention were paid to the word "parable" itself. Behind it stands the Hebrew *māšāl* (twenty-eight of

thirty-three instances in the OT are rendered *parabolē* [parable] in the LXX), a word referring to proverbs, maxims, similes, allegories, fables, comparisons, riddles, taunts, stories embodying some truth (Num 23:7, 18; 1 Sam 10:12; 24:13; Job 27:1; Pss 49:4; 78:2; Prov 1:6; Eccl 12:9; Isa 14:4; Ezek 12:2; 17:2; 24:3; 13; Mic 2:4; Hab 2:6). And the word "parable" in the NT comes close to duplicating this range (cf. esp. DNTT, 2:743–60). Thus a parable can be a proverb (Luke 4:23; something John calls a *paroimia* ["figure of speech," John 10:6; 16:25, 29; cf. Job 27:1 LXX]); a profound or obscure saying (Matt 13:35); a nonverbal symbol or image (Heb 9:9; 11:19); an illustrative comparison, whether without the form of a story (Matt 15:15; 24:32) or with (in the most familiar kind of "parable"—e.g., 13:3–9); an illustrative story not involving comparison of unlikes (e.g., the rich fool, Luke 12:16–21); and more. So it becomes obvious that much learned discussion actually focuses on only one or two kinds of NT "parables." Most, though not all, parables are extended metaphors or similes. Yet even so broad a definition as this eliminates some of the material listed above that NT writers label "parable." Most generalized conclusions about parables require painful exceptions; and on the whole it is best to deal inductively with parables, while at the same time being aware of the questions posed by recent studies and the scholarly analyses of some parable material.

One of the most responsible of these is Boucher's recent work, some of whose conclusions are adopted later (see on vv. 10–17). But even Boucher narrows down parable to "a *narrative* having two levels of meaning" (p. 23) and confusingly defines allegory as merely "a device of meaning, and not in itself a literary form or genre" (p. 20), while insisting that allegory must extend a metaphor over a whole story, thus tying it inescapably to a form. By this definition some parables are allegories. Yet it is useful, for instance, to be able to distinguish allegories that are types from those that are not. Progress in understanding parables depends, it seems, in greater scholarly agreement over the semantics of the labels and in greater willingness to recognize the diversity of kinds of parables in the NT. (On this point, cf. G.B. Caird, *The Language and Imagery of the Bible* [London: Duckworth, 1980], pp. 161–67; Robert H. Stein, *The Method and Message of Jesus' Teachings* [Philadelphia: Westminster, 1978], pp. 34–39.)

3. The structure of the third discourse (13:3–52) bears directly on its interpretation. Certain things are obvious. Two of the parables are also found in Mark and Luke: viz., the sower and its interpretation (13:3–9, 18–23; Mark 4:3–9, 13–20; Luke 8:5–15) and the mustard seed (13:31–32; Mark 4:30–32; Luke 13:18–19). One is paralleled in Luke but not Mark (the yeast [13:33; Luke 13:20–21]), and the other four (or five; see below) are found only in Matthew. Mark 4:26–29 adds still another to this discourse; and both Mark 4:33 and Matthew 13:3 suggest there was a great deal more left unreported.

These are the agreed facts, but the structure of the discourse as it stands is more disputed (cf. Dupont, "Point de vue," pp. 231f.; Kingsbury, *Parables*, pp. 12–15). The best analysis has been provided by David Wenham ("Structure," pp. 516–22), who argues, with Lohmeyer and Kingsbury (*Parables*), that v.52 is a parable (note the form "is like [plus dative]" and the opening words of v.53). The discourse may then be broken down into two parts of four parables each (vv. 3–33, 44–52). The first four are addressed to the crowds, the last four to the disciples. Wenham's distinctive contribution lies in identifying the emergent chiastic structure. Of the first four parables, the first stands apart from the other three, separated by discussion about the purpose of parables (vv. 10–17) and the interpretation of the parable (vv. 18–23).

It has a formally different introduction (the other three begin "Jesus told them another parable, 'The kingdom of heaven is like . . .' "). The matching chiastic four in the second half begin with three parables with the same opening ("The kingdom of heaven is like . . ."), separated from the fourth, which has a different beginning, by the explanation in vv.49–50 and the question and answer about the disciples' understanding of parables. The central section separating the two sets of parables (vv.34–43) divides the chiasm and further explains the function of parables while expounding one of them. (See outline, Introduction, section 14.) The implications are important.

1. Matthew reports two rationales for parables, one related to their function for outsiders and one related to their function for disciples.

2. The detailed structure reveals Matthew's skill as an author; and the alleged dislocations (esp. vv.12, 34–35), often taken to support Markan priority, turn out to be, not aporias (i.e., a break that demands explanation), but an integral part of the outline (see below). This does not of course disprove Mark's priority here; but if Matthew is indeed prior or independent for all or part of this chapter (as Wenham argues in "The Synoptic Problem Revisited"), it supports an important point—viz., that it is methodologically doubtful to think that the only access to information Matthew has when following Mark is Mark itself.

3. This structure also calls in question the traditional dispensational interpretation of the parables in this chapter. Typical is Walvoord: "Jesus deliberately adopted the parabolic method of teaching at a particular stage in His ministry for the purpose of withholding further truth about Himself and the kingdom of heaven from the crowds, who had proved themselves to be deaf to His claims and irresponsive to His demands. . . . From now onwards, when addressing the unbelieving multitude, He speaks only in parables which He interprets to His disciples in private."

There is insight here: Walvoord rightly detects the note of judgment bound up with some parables. Walvoord's position, however, is too cut and dried. First, remembering the broad definition of "parables" in the NT, it is doubtful that we are to think that chapter 13 contains Jesus' first use of parables in Matthew (cf. 7:24–27; 9:15–17; 11:16–19). Second, if Walvoord were to respond that such passages are not labeled "parables," the historical problem recurs when any synoptic harmony is attempted (a procedure he would approve). Historically Jesus does not use parables for the first time at this stage in his ministry (cf. Luke 5:36; 6:39). What does seem likely is that rising opposition to Jesus encouraged his greater and greater use of parables (see on vv.10–17, 34–35). But there is little ground for the sudden switch in method Walvoord sees. Third, parables are not restricted to Jesus' ministry to outsiders: he also uses them positively for his disciples (cf. structure, above). Fourth, there has been no extensive teaching to outsiders before this third discourse and there is none after it to test Walvoord's claim that Jesus' use of parables is a new departure here. We have only the fact that Jesus' preaching to outsiders is repeatedly mentioned but no extended samples of it (see on 13:11).

2. To the crowds (13:3b–33)

a. The parable of the soils

13:3b–9

3b"A farmer went out to sow his seed. 4As he was scattering the seed, some fell along the path, and the birds came and ate it up. 5Some fell on rocky places, where it did not have much soil. It sprang up quickly, because the soil was shallow. ⁶But when the sun came up, the plants were scorched, and they withered because they had no root. ⁷Other seed fell among thorns, which grew up and choked the plants. ⁸Still other seed fell on good soil, where it produced a crop—a hundred, sixty or thirty times what was sown. ⁹He who has ears, let him hear."

3b–7 The focus of the parable is not the sower (the article is used in v.3 to designate a class; cf. 12:43) but the soils. The farmer scatters the seed (v.3b), which falls in various places. Paths run through and around the unfenced fields (see on 12:1); and the earth paths are too hard to receive the seed, which is eaten by birds (v.4). "Rocky places" (v.5) are those in which the limestone bedrock lies close to the surface: there is little depth of soil. As the rainy season ends and the sun's heat increases, the shallow soil heats up quickly (v.6). The seeds sprout and promise to be the best of the crop (on the appropriateness of these details to the Palestinian setting, cf. P.B. Payne, "The Order of Sowing and Ploughing in the Parable of the Sower," NTS 25 [1978–79]: 123–29). But the unrelenting summer heat demands that plants send deep roots down for water, and the bedrock prevents this. Like grass on rooftops, the young plants wither before they can grow (Ps 129:6). Other seed falls into hedges of thorns that deprive the plants of sun and nourishment (v.7).

8–9 But some seed falls on good soil and produces crops of various yields (v.8), which, contrary to what many think, are not extremely high, symbolic of the fertility of the Messianic Age, but well within ordinary expectations (cf. Payne, "Authenticity," pp. 181–86). The same seed produces no crop, some crop, or much crop according to the soil's character. The final exhortation (v.9; see on 11:15) warns Jesus' hearers and Matthew's readers that the parable needs careful interpretation.

At this point many commentators, believing vv.18–23 to be unauthentic, attempt to interpret vv.3b–9 without reference to vv.18–23. Their efforts fail to produce interpretations more believable than the one Matthew ascribes to Jesus. Typical is that of Hill (*Matthew*), who says the parable means that just as every (Palestinian) sower does his work in spite of many frustrations, so the kingdom makes its way in spite of many difficulties. It will be established in time, with a sure and glorious harvest, but only after much loss. The parable has little to do with how to hear the word of God. But Hill's interpretation depends on treating the parable serially— i.e., the sower sows seed in all the bad places first! On the face of it, the differences lie in the soils, not in the order of sowing: i.e., the kingdom, while advancing now by the promulgation of the good news about the kingdom (4:23), is meeting many different responses.

b. *Interlude* (13:10–23)

1) *On understanding parables*

13:10—17

¹⁰The disciples came to him and asked, "Why do you speak to the people in parables?"

¹¹He replied, "The knowledge of the secrets of the kingdom of heaven has been given to you, but not to them. ¹²Whoever has will be given more, and he will have an abundance. Whoever does not have, even what he has will be taken from him. ¹³This is why I speak to them in parables:

"Though seeing, they do not see;
    though hearing, they do not hear or understand.

¹⁴In them is fulfilled the prophecy of Isaiah:

    " 'You will be ever hearing but never understanding;
      you will be ever seeing but never perceiving.
¹⁵For this people's heart has become calloused;
    they hardly hear with their ears,
    and they have closed their eyes.
Otherwise they might see with their eyes,
    hear with their ears,
    understand with their hearts
and turn, and I would heal them.' "

¹⁶But blessed are your eyes because they see, and your ears because they hear.
¹⁷For I tell you the truth, many prophets and righteous men longed to see what you see but did not see it, and to hear what you hear but did not hear it.

Matthew's treatment is not only longer than Mark's (4:10–12) and Luke's (8:9–10; 10:23–24), but it includes more OT Scripture and is structured with great care. The disciples' question (v.10) evokes Jesus' basic answer (vv.11–12), which is then applied in greater detail first to "them" (vv.13–15) and then to the disciples (vv.16–18). The latter two sections are a well-ordered chiasm whose inversion echoes OT form (e.g., Ps 89:28–37) and emphasizes the climax of judgment and mercy (so K.E. Bailey, *Poet and Peasant* [Grand Rapids: Eerdmans, 1976], pp. 61f.):

Therefore I speak to them in parables,
1 because seeing *they see not* and hearing *they hear not*, nor understand.
  2 And *it is fulfilled to them* the *prophecy* of Isaiah which says,
    3 "Hearing *you shall hear* and shall *not understand,*
      4 and seeing you *shall see* and shall *not perceive.*
        5 For this people's *heart* is become dull
          6 and the *ears* are dull of hearing
            7 and their *eyes* they have closed,
            7' lest they should perceive with the *eyes*
          6' and hear with the *ear*
        5' and understand with the *heart*, and should turn again and I should heal them."
    4' But blessed are *your eyes*, for they see,
    3' and your *ears*, for they *hear.*
  2' For truly *I say unto you* that many *prophets* and righteous men
1' desired to see what *you see*, and *did not see*, and to hear what *you hear*, and *did not hear.*

10 "The disciples" (Mark: "the Twelve and the others around him") approached Jesus, apparently in private (cf. Mark 4:10). If this occurred at the end of the discourse, the plural "parables" would be well accounted for. Kingsbury (*Parables*, pp. 40–41) detects in the verb *proselthontes* ("came to him") a "cultic connotation": the disciples approached Jesus "with the same reverence that would be due to a king or deity." He defends this doubtful view with a prejudicial selection of the evidence that could in some cases be taken that way, while ignoring contrary evidence regarding Matthew's use of the verb (cf. 4:3; 8:19; 9:14; 15:1, 30; 16:1; 17:24; 22:23 et al.).

Recent scholarship rightly sees in this chapter the distinction between the disciples and the crowds, presupposed by the above outline. But there has been a regrettable tendency to think Matthew has absolutized the distinction, idealized the disciples, and played down their lack of understanding (Bornkamm, *Tradition*, pp. 105ff.; Kingsbury, *Parables*, pp. 42ff.; Schmid; Grundmann). This idealization, it is alleged, is very strong in vv.10–17 and emerges in v.10. The disciples ask why Jesus speaks to the crowds in parables, not what the parables mean—and this presupposes they already know. But Mark's question is ambiguous (Mark 4:10); Matthew typically has merely clarified the point. The critics' contention is based on an argument from silence. But if the disciples did understand the parable of the sower, why does Jesus proceed in a few verses to give them an explanation (vv.18–23)? And why do they ask for an explanation to a later parable (v.36)? The focus of Jesus' reply (vv.11–17) is not so much on the disciples' understanding as on the fact that the revelation is given to some and not to others and why. (On this recurring question, cf. Trotter.)

11–12 Jesus' answer cannot legitimately be softened: at least one of the functions of parables is to conceal the truth, or at least *to present it in a veiled way*. This point is strengthened if the *hoti* is not "recitative" (equivalent to the quotation marks in NIV) but fully causal, "because." The disciples ask, "Why do you speak, etc.?" and Jesus replies, "Because the secrets of the kingdom have been given to the disciples but not to others." The strength of this translation turns not only on its suitability after "Why?" but also on the fact that *hoti* is nowhere else in the NT "recitative" after the particular formula used: *ho de apokritheis eipen* ("he replied," v.11; cf. D. Wenham, "Structure," p. 519, n. 5, and literature there cited). The pronoun *autois* ("to them") does not refer first to the Jews in Matthew's day but to "the people" mentioned by the disciples in the previous verse.

Ta mysteria tēs basileias ("the secrets of the kingdom") is not explained; its meaning may be deduced by the context and by the use of *mysterion* ("secret") elsewhere. *Mysterion* has no obvious connections with pagan mystery religions but reflects a thoroughly Semitic background (cf. R.E. Brown, *The Semitic Background of the Term "Mystery" in the New Testament* [Philadelphia: Fortress, 1968]). It appears in the OT in Daniel (Aram. *rāz*), which refers to some eschatological secret, some portent of what God has decreed will take place in the future. The Greek term can also reflect the Hebrew *sôd* ("secret," "confidential speech"), taken from the heavenly council (cf. Brown, *Mystery*, pp. 2–6; DNTT, 3:502). The same range of meanings is found in the DSS. "Mysteries" are divine plans or decrees, often passed on in veiled language, known only to the elect, and usually relating to eschatological events.

For the "secrets of the kingdom" to be "given" the disciples suggests that to them certain eschatological realities are being revealed. What is revealed is not who Jesus is, the nature of God, or the power of love (all of which have been suggested); rather, the "mystery of the Kingdom is the coming of the Kingdom into history in advance of its apocalyptic manifestation" (Ladd, *Presence*, pp. 218–42, esp. p. 222). That God would bring in his kingdom was no secret. All Jews looked forward to it. "The new truth, now given to men by revelation in the person and mission of Jesus, is that *the Kingdom which is to come finally in apocalyptic power, as foreseen by Daniel, has in fact entered into the world in advance in a hidden form to work secretly within and among men*" (ibid., p. 225, emphasis his).

It is unlikely that the plural "secrets," as opposed to Mark's "secret," refers to everything Jesus has taught (so Kingsbury, *Parables*, pp. 44f.). The strongest reason for the latter view is that some of the parables deal with ethical matters, not eschatology, reflecting, it is argued, the full gamut of Jesus' teaching (e.g., parables of the hidden treasure, of the pearl, of the unforgiving servant). But in reality all such parables, as we shall see, necessarily presuppose some form of realized eschatology to make their ethical demands meaningful. The plural "secrets" is best accounted for as a typical Matthean preference for the plural (cf. Matt 4:3–Luke 4:3; Matt 8:26–Mark 4:39; Matt 26:15–Mark 14:11; and a regular changing of "crowd" to "crowds" at Matt 12:46; 13:2; 14:22; 15:36; 21:46; 23:1; 27:20), or as a reflection of a non-Markan source (there are several Matt–Luke "minor agreements" against Mark here; for details cf. D. Wenham, "Synoptic Problem"), or perhaps as a reference to the multiple elements bound up with the basic eschatological truth that the age to come has already dawned.

The antithesis of v.12 is proverbial and repeated elsewhere (25:29; cf. Mark 4:25; Luke 8:18). It warns against taking spiritual blessings for granted and serves to increase gratitude and a sense of privilege among those who continue to enjoy them. What is lost in the second part of the antithesis is not the law but one's standing as the expected subject of the kingdom (cf. 8:11–12).

13 Jesus now explicitly applies his answer (vv. 11–12) to those who are not disciples. Discussion of this verse turns on Matthew's change of *hina* plus subjunctive in Mark 4:12 ("in order that, etc.")—which implies that the parables' blinding outsiders is a function of divine election—to *hoti* ("because"), which means that Jesus speaks in parables because the people are spiritually insensitive. Though they "see," they do not *really* "see." There are four possible approaches to the above data.

1. Some argue that Matthew's change of *hina* to *hoti* is motivated by his editorial desire to blame the Jews or to establish a moral basis for their being rejected (e.g., Kingsbury, *Parables*, pp. 48–49; Dupont, "Point de vue," pp. 233f.). But this badly oversimplifies the matter because of the strong note on election in the best rendering of v.11 (above).

2. Others suggest a sort of additive harmonization: "because" (*hoti*, Matt) the willful rejectors refused to see and hear, Jesus spoke to them in parables "in order that" (*hina*, Mark–Luke) they might not (truly) see and hear (Hendriksen). This may be theologically sound, but it is doubtful whether simple addition best explains what Matthew has done.

3. Many attempt to soften the *hina* in Mark to lose its telic force ("in order that") and take on a consecutive force ("with the result that"; cf. NIV's ambiguous "so that"). Mark and Matthew would then be very close in thought in this verse. Certainly *hina* can have consecutive force in Hellenistic Greek, a distinct departure from the classical; but Mark has *hina . . . mēpote* (lit., "in order that . . . lest"; NIV, "otherwise"), and it is very difficult to give such an expression anything else than full telic force. Moule (*Idiom Book*, p. 143) recognizes the strength of this argument; but because he judges the notion of parables told to prevent any who are not predestined for salvation from hearing "too incongruous with any part of the N.T. period to be plausible," he is forced to appeal to Semitic idiom or even the much later linguistic development of causal *hina*. But attempts to ground Mark's *hina* in a Semitic mistranslation (cf. esp. T.W. Manson, *The Teachings of Jesus*, 2d ed. [Cambridge: University Press, 1935], pp. 76ff.) have proved futile (cf. Gundry, *Use of OT*, pp. 34–35, n. 1; Boucher, pp. 43–44; J. Gnilka, *Die Verstockung Israels* [Mün-

chen: Kösel-Verlag, 1961]). And appeals to rabbinic parables and their function have turned out to support the telic view, since rabbis did indeed use parables to mask truth: the rabbinic parable "is not a universalistic form" (D. Daube, "Public Pronouncement and Private Explanation in the Gospels," ExpT 57 [1945-46]: 177).

4. Though the last two approaches are not convincing, the first can become plausible if presented with greater awareness of the relationship v.12 enjoys with v.11 and v.13. Verse 11 most likely embraces a strictly predestinarian viewpoint, more strongly than Mark 4:11 and doctrinally, though not verbally, like Mark 4:12. The reply to the disciples' question (Matt 13:10) is thus given in terms of election in v.11, which is further explained in v.12. Verse 13 recapitulates the reason for speaking in parables but now frames the reason, not in terms of election, but in terms of spiritual dullness. Matthew has already given Jesus' answer in terms of divine election (v.11); now he gives the human reason. While this brings him into formal conflict with Mark 4:12, he has already sounded the predestinarian note of Mark 4:12. Here Matthew includes much more material than Mark; and in the ordered structure (see parallelisms, above) that results from the inclusion of such new material, verbal parallels are lost in favor of conceptual ones.

Three broader reflections help resolve the problem.

1. Biblical writers in both the OT and the NT have, on the whole, fewer problems about the tension between God's sovereignty and man's responsibility than do many moderns. This is not because they fail to distinguish purpose and consequence, as many affirm (e.g., Moule, *Idiom Book*, p. 142), but because they do not see divine sovereignty and human responsibility as antitheses. In short they are compatibilists and therefore juxtapose the two themes with little self-conscious awareness of any problem (cf. Gen 50:19-20; Judg 14:4; Isa 10:5-7; Hag 1:12-14; John 11:49-52; cf. Carson, *Divine Sovereignty*).

2. Thus, even though he records Jesus' answer in terms of election, Mark does not thereby mean to absolve the outsiders of all responsibility. How could he, in the light of the interpretation of the parable of the sower he records (4:13-20), his record of John's demand for repentance (1:4), and much more? Matthew has taken up these themes in greater detail because he wishes simultaneously to affirm that what is taking place in the ministry of Jesus is, on the one hand, the decreed will of God and the result of biblical prophecy and, on the other hand, a terrible rebellion, gross spiritual dullness, and chronic unbelief. This places the responsibility for the divine rejection of those who fail to become disciples on their own shoulders while guaranteeing that none of what is taking place stands outside God's control and plan. The same sort of pairing has already been expressed in 11:25-30.

3. This sheds much light on the parables. It is naive to say Jesus spoke them so that everyone might more easily grasp the truth, and it is simplistic to say that the sole function of parables to outsiders was to condemn them. If Jesus simply wished to hide the truth from the outsiders, he need never have spoken to them. His concern for mission (9:35-38; 10:1-10; 28:16-20) excludes that idea. So he must preach without casting his pearls before pigs (7:6). He does so in parables: i.e., in such a way as to harden and reject those who are hard of heart and to enlighten—often with further explanation—his disciples. His disciples, it must be remembered, are not just the Twelve but those who were following him (see on 5:1-12) and who, it is hoped, go on to do the will of the Father (12:50) and do not end up blaspheming the Spirit (12:30-32) or being ensnared by evil more thoroughly than before (12:43-45). Thus the parables spoken to the crowds do not simply convey information, nor

mask it, but challenge the hearers. They do not convey esoteric content only the initiated can fathom but present the claims of the inaugurated kingdom and the prospects of its apocalyptic culmination in such a way that its implications are spelled out for those in the audience with eyes to see (overstated but rightly defended by Boucher, pp. 83–84).

The parables of the soils not only says that the kingdom advances slowly and with varied responses to the proclamation of that kingdom but implicitly challenges hearers to ask themselves what kinds of soil they are. Those whose hearts are hardened and who lose what little they have do not participate in the messianic kingdom they have been looking for, and for them the parable is a sentence of doom. Those who have ears to hear, to whom more is given, perceive and experience the dawning of the Messianic Age; and for them the parable conveys the mysteries of the kingdom. In the varied responses given to the challenge of the parables, God's act of judgment and his self-disclosure in Jesus are both seen to be taking place in exactly the same way that various "soils" respond to the "seed," which is the message about the kingdom. (See further on 15:10–13.)

14–15 Stendahl and others advance several reasons for taking this quotation as a late gloss on the Gospel, including an anomalous introductory formula, and insist that the quotation is tautologous after v. 13. But parallels to this introductory formula are common in the LXX and other Greek-Jewish literature with which Matthew is familiar, and vv. 14–15 are not strictly tautologous since they go on to stress the theme of fulfillment. Moreover, if Matthew follows Mark (4:12) in v. 13, it is unlikely that he abridged his source by omitting the entire last clause of Mark 4:12 ("otherwise they might turn and be forgiven"). The one area where Matthew almost invariably gives more material than the other synoptists is in OT quotations and allusions. "We must rather assume that verse 13 leads up to the formal quotation in verses 14, 15" (Gundry, *Use of OT*, pp. 116–18). These two verses thus become the rough equivalent of Mark 4:12–13.

The text form is LXX (as also in Acts 28:26–27), which follows the MT of Isaiah 6:9–10 pretty closely, except that the LXX is a description of the people, whereas MT makes this a command to the prophet ("Be ever hearing, but never understanding. . . . Make the heart of this people calloused"). But this is not as significant a change as some have thought; for judging by the prophet's later messages, the words in Isaiah 6:9–10 are steeped in bitter irony. After all, Isaiah was not given this charge because the result was desirable but because it inevitably came on people who were calloused. So also in Jesus' day! The Messiah who comes to reveal the Father (11:25–27) succeeds only in dulling what little spiritual sense many of the people have, for they do not want to turn and be healed. Indeed, the context of Isaiah 6:9–10 reveals that their dullness will continue "until the cities lie ruined . . . and the fields ruined and ravaged . . . and the land is utterly forsaken. And though a tenth remains in the land, it will again be laid waste" (Isa 6:11–13). The reference is to the Exile; but the events surrounding the Exile are seen as a paradigm, the classic case of rejection of God and resulting judgment, repeated in Jesus' generation on a new level and so fulfilling the words of the prophecy. It is unclear whether any claim that Isaiah 6:9–10 has predictive force is implied (if so, see on 2:15). What is certain is the racial connection (cf. also Acts 28:26–27; cf. John 12:38–40): the failure of most Jews to discern spiritual realities was no new thing. Moreover, if the context of Isaiah 6:9–10 goes with the quotation, a strong hint of judgment accompanies the description.

The first two lines of the quotation are in the second person plural: the people are directly addressed. But v.15 gives us God's description of the people in the third person. This makes it at least possible to interpret the "otherwise" clauses (*mēpote*, "lest"), not as the people's purpose (they have closed their eyes lest they see and turn and be healed), but as God's judgment (they have closed their eyes as the result of divine judicial action, otherwise they might see and turn, etc.). The thought then becomes similar to 2 Thessalonians 2:11. Again, of course, neither Jesus nor Matthew would see anything incongruous in God's judicial hardening (see on v.13).

16–17 (For "blessed," see on 5:3; and cf. Luke 10:23–24.) The disciples were blessed by God and privileged above the crowd because they saw and heard (v.16) what "many prophets and righteous men" (v.17; see on 10:40–42) longed to see but did not. The reference is to OT prophets and others who were just before God—people who looked forward to the coming of the kingdom. Here one cannot help but include Simeon (Luke 2:25–35) and Anna (Luke 2:36–38). Implicitly there is in Jesus' saying a rich christological and eschatological claim: no mere prophet could say as much as he did.

Those who think Matthew idealizes the disciples (see on v.10) observe that the parallel in Luke 10:23–24 contrasts Jesus' generation with earlier generations but argue that Matthew contrasts the disciples ("your" is emphatic) with the hard people of that same generation (Bornkamm, *Tradition*, p. 107). In fact Matthew does something of both. Verse 16, in connection with the preceding verses, contrasts the disciples with the calloused crowd; but v.17 contrasts them with prophets and righteous men of past generations. So the crowd in Jesus' day stands in the line of the willfully blind in the OT (vv.14–15), and Jesus' disciples stand in the line of the prophets (as in 5:11–12). The fulfillment motif is operating, showing that the division taking place in Jesus' time with the coming of the kingdom stands in succession to the divisions already spelled out in the Scriptures. The disciples are not idealized; they will later have to ask for an explanation (v.36). But by contrast with the crowds, they really did follow Jesus and gradually grasped the critical turning point in redemption history Jesus was even then introducing.

Notes

14 The addition of a cognate participle or a cognate dative to a verb in order to strengthen the verb is a customary way for the LXX to render the Hebrew infinitive absolute (cf. BDF, par. 422; Zerwick, par. 369). Both are found here in this LXX quotation: ἀκοῇ ἀκούσετε (*akoē akousete*, lit., "in hearing you will hear"), βλέποντες βλέψετε (*blepontes blepsete*, lit., "seeing you will see"). In English these are confusing tautologies, and their meaning is rightly rendered by NIV: "You will be ever hearing," or "you will be hearing acutely," etc.

2) Interpretation of the parable of the soils

13:18–23

18"Listen then to what the parable of the sower means: 19When anyone hears the message about the kingdom and does not understand it, the evil one comes and snatches away what was sown in his heart. This is the seed sown along the path. 20The one who received the seed that fell on rocky places is the man who hears the word and at once receives it with joy. 21But since he has no root, he lasts only a short time. When trouble or persecution comes because of the word, he quickly falls away. 22The one who received the seed that fell among the thorns is the man who hears the word, but the worries of this life and the deceitfulness of wealth choke it, making it unfruitful. 23But the one who received the seed that fell on good soil is the man who hears the word and understands it. He produces a crop, yielding a hundred, sixty or thirty times what was sown."

Jeremias (*Parables,* p. 62) thinks the interpretation provided in all three Gospels (cf. Mark 4:14–20; Luke 8:11–15) is a later church creation, but we have already questioned the cogency of some of his criteria. Payne ("Authenticity") has taken up the points in question and offered comprehensive rejoinders, some of which will be noted below. Here it is enough to say that (contra Jeremias, *Parables,* p. 79) not every point in the parable is interpreted allegorically: no explanation is given of the sower, the path, the rocky ground, or the diverse yield. What "allegorical" points are scored emerge naturally from the story (even the identification of the birds: see on v.19), once the main point of the extended metaphor is established.

The general point is that the "message about the kingdom" (v.19) receives a varied reception among various people, and that during this time of difficulty and frustration there is an implied delay while the seed produces in some soils its various yields. The interpretation therefore demands that each person look to himself as to how he "hears" the message. Broadus cites Chrysostom: "Mark this, I pray thee, that the way of destruction is not one only, but there are differing ones, and wide apart from one another. Let us not soothe ourselves upon our not perishing in all these ways, but let it be our grief in whichever way we are perishing."

18 The *hymeis* ("you") is probably emphatic: in light of the great privilege extended to you, which prophets and righteous men wanted to enjoy and the calloused spurn, *you* listen.

19 Matthew omits "The farmer sows the word" (Mark 4:14) and plunges right into the significance of the various soils. This does not mean that he is concerned with the ecclesiastical implications at the expense of the christological ones (so Kingsbury, *Parables,* p. 72), since Mark himself does not identify the sower as Jesus. If he here depends on Mark, Matthew simplifies to get to the point. But D. Wenham ("Interpretation") has provided a plausible source reconstruction that would invalidate redaction-critical conclusions in this pericope that depend on Markan priority. Possibly Matthew and Mark share a common source.

Neither "word" (Mark) nor "word of the kingdom" (Matt; NIV, "message about the kingdom") indicates later ecclesiastical tradition (cf. Payne, "Authenticity," pp. 178–79; contra Jeremias, *Parables,* pp. 77f.; Hill, *Matthew*). On the change from "word" to "word of the kingdom," compare Matthew's "gospel of the kingdom" (4:23; 9:35; 24:14). More difficult is the mixed metaphor: the seed appears to be "the message about the kingdom," but in the last sentence of the verse it is *ho para tēn hodon spareis* (lit., "he who was sown along the path"; NIV has smoothed out the difficulty by treating the masculine participle as if it were neuter).

A similar problem occurs in Mark's parallel. Several ways for resolving the problem have been suggested. Box and McNeile are among those who take the text literally but think there is a purposeful link between the seed and human character, which grows from the seed. But surely the point of this part of the parable is that the seed is taken away before it has time to grow. Others have suggested some sort of ellipsis: "This is [the situation of] the seed sown along the path," understanding "This" to refer to the situation, not the seed or the person, which would also explain vv.20–23, though the masculine *houtos* ("this"), instead of the neuter, is somewhat surprising. Alexander and Hendriksen therefore opt for a fairly complex ellipsis: "He is the one that [in his reaction to the message resembles the reaction of the ground to the seed that] was sown along the path"—which is possible but rather finely drawn.

D. Wenham ("Interpretation") offers a complex but plausible source-critical solution; Payne ("Authenticity," pp. 172–77) proposes an underlying Aramaic too literally translated and observes that the Greek can be understood to mean, not "this is he who was sown along the path," but "this is the man who received the seed along the edge of the path" (JB; cf. NASB), understanding the passive participle *ho spareis* to mean, not "the one [seed] sown," but "the one [*soil*] sown." C.F.D. Moule ("Mark 4:1–20 Yet Once More," in Ellis and Wilcox, p. 112) has shown that the ambiguity is no indication that the interpretation is secondary; the same thing occurs in Colossians 1:6, 10, where the metaphor of growing and bearing fruit is applied first to the seed sown and then to the ground in which it is sown.

Two further features of this verse require explanation.

1. The words "in his heart" make the heart the place of decision, the center of personality (see on 5:8). Kingsbury (*Parables*, p. 55) is wrong to conclude from this that the person in view actually becomes a Christian and church member and then rejects the message. He argues that the words "when anyone hears the message about the kingdom" is "tantamount to saying that he becomes a Christian." The conclusion is untenable if one considers the next words: "and does not understand it" (cf. the same verbs in vv.13–14). The hunt for anachronisms can distort scholarly judgment.

2. The evil one (cf. 6:13; 12:45; 13:38–39), called "Satan" in Mark 4:15 and "the devil" in Luke 8:12, has been symbolized by the birds, a point Via (*Parables*, p. 8) uses to argue that this interpretation goes beyond the range of the natural and understandable symbolism inherent in the parable and must therefore be judged guilty of falling into allegorizing. In fact, close study of birds as symbols in the OT and especially in the literature of later Judaism shows that birds regularly symbolize evil and even demons or Satan (cf. b. *Sanhedrin* 107a; cf. Rev 18:2).

Jesus' interpretation is clear. Some people hear the message about the kingdom; but like hardened paths, they do not let the truth penetrate, and before they really understand it the devil has snatched it away.

20–21 The language of these verses is often taken to reflect the apostolic age, not Jesus (cf. Jeremias, *Parables*). But "root" (v.21) is appropriate to the extended agricultural metaphor, and "persecution" is amply treated by Jesus elsewhere in nonparabolic settings (e.g., 5:10–12, 43–44; 10:16–25; 24:9; see further Payne, "Authenticity," pp. 177–80). Jesus' interpretation is coherent. The person who receives "the word" (same Gr. word as "message" in v.19) in a thoughtless way may show immediate signs of life and promise to be the best of the crop: he receives the truth "with joy" (v.20). But without real root, there is no fruit; and external pressures, trouble, and persecution (cf. 24:9, 21, 29), like sun beating on a rootless plant, soon reveal the shallowness of this soil. "At once" (*euthys*) he receives the word with joy, and as "quickly" (*euthys*) "falls away" (for *skandalizetai*, see on 5:29). Such temporary disciples are always numerous in times of revival and were so in Jesus' ministry (cf. comments on 12:32).

22 This person does not hear the word "with joy" (as in v.20) but simply never permits the message about the kingdom to control him: life has too many other commitments that slowly choke the struggling plant, which never matures and bears fruit. The competing "thorns" are summed up under two headings—the worries of this life (lit., this "age," as opposed to the age to come; see on 6:25–34) and "the deceitfulness of wealth." The latter category, *hē apatē tou ploutou*, may possibly be rendered "the delight in wealth," since in late Greek *apatē*, which earlier meant "deceitfulness," came to mean "pleasure" or "delight," usually involving sin (e.g., 2 Peter 2:13; cf. BAGD, s.v.). The idea is clear: worries about worldly things or devotion to wealth (cf. 1 Tim 6:9) snuff out spiritual life. If "deceit" is understood, there is an added warning that these "thorns" are so subtle that one may not be aware of the choking that is going on. The warning is timeless. Moreover it is as unconvincing to deduce from this verse that Matthew's church was wealthy (contra Kilpatrick, *Origins*, pp. 124ff.; Kingsbury, *Parables*, p. 61) as to deduce from 6:28–32 that his church was poverty-stricken. What must be avoided is unfruitfulness, for only fruitfulness, not its opposite, indicates spiritual life (cf. John 15:1–8). This person finds "all the seeming good effect is gone, leaving the soul a very thicket of thorns" (Broadus).

23 By contrast with the negative results of the preceding verses, we now come to the person who hears the word and understands it (thus reverting to the categories of Isa 6:9–10 used in vv.13–15, 19). The use of *synienai* ("to understand") in vv.19, 23, a verb not found in the Markan parallels, has led some to say that "understanding" is a fundamental characteristic of discipleship in Matthew, and that his disciples have again become idealized (see on v.10): they are made to "understand" more than the disciples really did at this point in their pilgrimage (cf. Bornkamm, *Tradition*, p. 107; Schniewind; Kingsbury, *Parables*, pp. 61f.). But this may be premature. Certainly *synienai* with its nine occurrences is an important part of Matthew's vocabulary. But Mark uses *synienai* six times, in a book about two-thirds the length of Matthew.

David Wenham has shown that granted Matthew's syntax in v.19, he could not very well have omitted *synienai* ("to understand") there ("Interpretation," pp. 308f., n. 5). Its use in v.23 picks up the Isaiah quotation given more briefly in Mark. Moreover v.23 does not apply the verb directly to the disciples but interprets the parable aphoristically; and in so doing it is merely in line with Mark's "hear the word, *accept it*" (4:20). In this chapter the disciples are distinguished from the crowd; but their understanding is only relatively better (v.36), and they are not idealized. Misunderstanding of this point springs from too ready a willingness to read the later church into every phrase of the parable and from a failure to recognize the absolute categories that any competent preacher, including Jesus, uses (see on 6:5–8).

The interpretation, like the parable itself, ends positively. And we must not fail to notice that the soil that produces only a small crop is nevertheless called "good" (cf. 25:22–23).

Notes

23 The particle δή (*dē*, used for various kinds of emphasis) is normally employed in the NT in sentences of command or exhortation. This is the sole NT exception (though there are good classical parallels): "he is just the man who, etc." (cf. BDF, par. 451[4]). The anomaly has prompted a variant reading in the Western textual tradition.

c. The parable of the weeds

13:24–30

24Jesus told them another parable: "The kingdom of heaven is like a man who sowed good seed in his field. 25But while everyone was sleeping, his enemy came and sowed weeds among the wheat, and went away. 26When the wheat sprouted and formed heads, then the weeds also appeared.

27"The owner's servants came to him and said, 'Sir, didn't you sow good seed in your field? Where then did the weeds come from?'

28" 'An enemy did this,' he replied.

"The servants asked him, 'Do you want us to go and pull them up?'

29" 'No,' he answered, 'because while you are pulling the weeds, you may root up the wheat with them. 30Let both grow together until the harvest. At that time I will tell the harvesters: First collect the weeds and tie them in bundles to be burned; then gather the wheat and bring it into my barn.' "

This parable occurs only in Matthew. For the reasons why its interpretation (vv.36–43) is separated from it, see above on 13:3a regarding the structure of the chapter. A few (e.g., Manson, *Sayings*, p. 143) have argued that this parable is not authentic but a creation of Matthew, constructed out of the parable of the seed growing quietly (Mark 4:26–29). But the similar language on which this theory is based owes more to the common agricultural setting than to borrowing. Though many affirm the authenticity of the parable but deny the authenticity of the interpretation (Dodd, *Parables*, pp. 183–84; Jeremias, *Parables*, pp. 81ff.; Kingsbury, *Parables*, pp. 65–66), the criteria for such distinctions are faulty (see on v.3a); and specific arguments can be advanced to defend their joint integrity in this case (see on vv.36–43). David R. Catchpole ("John the Baptist, Jesus and the Parable of the Tares," SJT 31 [1978]: 557–70) unwittingly supports the view that the parable and its interpretation stand or fall together when, in the course of defending his reconstruction of a much shorter parable (vv.24b, 26b, 30b) that Matthew allegedly expanded, he expresses dissatisfaction with this parable because it includes elements that invite the "allegorizing" interpretations of vv.36–43.

The parable of the sower shows that though the kingdom will now make its way amid hard hearts, competing pressures, and even failure, it will produce an abundant crop. But one might ask whether Messiah's people should immediately separate the crop from the weeds; and this next parable answers the question negatively: there will be a delay in separation until the harvest.

24 Jesus *paretheken* ("told") the people another parable (lit., "he set another before them"). This verb is used in the NT only here and in v.31 in the sense of teaching, though that meaning is attested elsewhere. "Them" must be the crowd, not the disciples (cf. vv.34, 36).

The kingdom of heaven is not "like a man" but "like the situation of a man who . . .": the "is like" formula reflects an Aramaic idiom meaning "It is the case with X as with Y" (cf. Jeremias, *Parables*, pp. 100f.; Zerwick, par. 65). But the peculiar tense used here (cf. Notes) also implies that the kingdom *has become* like the situation of a man who, etc. The thought is intriguing; for whereas Judaism was accustomed to delays in waiting for the coming of Messiah (cf. R.J. Bauckham, "The Delay of the Parousia," *Tyndale Bulletin* 31 [1980]: 3–36), what Jesus argues is both that the kingdom has come (see 4:17; 12:28) and that the Parousia is still delayed (i.e., the kingdom has become like . . . —a parable dealing with the *delay* of the kingdom's arrival).

25–26 "Sleeping" (v.25) does not imply that the servants were neglectful but that the enemy was stealthy and malicious. What he sowed was *zizania* ("weeds"— almost certainly bearded darnel (*lolium temulentum*), which is botanically close to wheat and difficult to distinguish from it when the plants are young. The roots of the two plants entangle themselves around each other; but when the heads of grain appear on the wheat, there is no doubt which plant is which (v.26). This weed the enemy sowed "among the wheat"; the Greek suggests thorough distribution. The growing plants gradually become identifiable, and the servants tell their master about the weeds.

27 For *oikodespotes* ("owner"), see on 10:25; 13:52. The servants are not identified; their function in the parable is to elicit information from the owner. In v.27 *kyrios* ("sir") has no special significance; but later Christian readers doubtless saw in it further evidence that the owner is the "Lord" Jesus. The interrogative pronoun *pothen* ("where") can refer to a person as well as to a location (cf. use in 13:54, 56; 21:25), as Jesus' answer (v.28) presupposes.

28–30 The owner blames (v.28) an enemy (lit., "a man [who is] an enemy": the construction occurs again in v.52). But the owner forbids his servants from attempting to separate weed from wheat till the harvest (v.29). Then, as the workers reap the field, only the wheat will be gathered; the weeds, apparently so plentiful they must first be gathered up and burned (v.30—though nothing is made of this point in vv.40–42), contaminate the wheat no longer. "Harvest" is a common metaphor for the final judgment (see on 9:37–38). In this light the "good seed" (v.24) cannot be the "word" or "message" of vv.19–23 but people who must face final judgment.

An astonishing number of scholars treat this parable as if there were behind it a Matthean church riddled with problem people, perhaps even apostates. So Jesus' answer in Matthew becomes, in effect, advice not to try to have a pure church, because the Lord will make the right distinctions at the end (most recently, G. Barth, "Auseinandersetzungen um die Kirchenzucht im Umkreis des Matthäusevangeliums," ZNW 69 [1978]: 158–77). But this is a major error in category. Nowhere in Matthew does "kingdom" (or "reign"—see on 3:2) become "church" (see on 16:18; and esp. 13:37–39). The parable does not address the church situation at all but explains how the kingdom can be present in the world while not yet wiping out all opposition. That must await the harvest. The parable deals with eschatological expectation, not ecclesiological deterioration.

Notes

24 The normal way for synoptic parables of the sort "the kingdom is like" to express "is like" consists of ὁμοία ἐστίν (homoia estin, "is like") plus dative. In Matthew, however, this pattern sometimes changes to aorist passive ὁμοιώθη (homoiōthē, "has become like," here and in 18:23; 22:2) or to future passive ὁμοιωθήσεται (homoiōthēsetai, "will become like," 7:24, 26; 25:1). The future passive usages of the verb focus on the kingdom at its consummation and the aorist passive on the kingdom as it has already been inaugurated (cf. Strecker, Weg, pp. 214f.; Kingsbury, Parables, p. 67; and esp. Carson, "Word-Group"). If so, Pamment's view (see on 5:3; 11:12), that "kingdom of heaven" is always future, referring to the consummated kingdom, receives a fatal blow.

29 Only here in the NT does the adverb ἅμα (hama, "at the same time"; NIV, "when") function as an improper preposition "with," "along with" (plus dative; cf. Moule, Idiom Book, p. 81; BDF, par. 194[3]).

d. The parable of the mustard seed

13:31–32

> [31]He told them another parable: "The kingdom of heaven is like a mustard seed, which a man took and planted in his field. [32]Though it is the smallest of all your seeds, yet when it grows, it is the largest of garden plants and becomes a tree, so that the birds of the air come and perch in its branches."

31–32 Close comparison with Mark 4:30–32 and Luke 13:18 suggests that Matthew may have slightly modified the Q form of this parable under Mark's influence. Yet it is easy to exaggerate the differences. (See discussion and chart at 19:1–2.) Many have held that in Mark the contrast in size is of greatest importance, in Luke the process of growth, and that Matthew has conflated the two ideas. Such distinctions are too finely drawn: if size were for Mark the most important factor, one wonders why Mark's Jesus would choose a plant that reaches a height of only ten to twelve feet.

There is a better interpretation. In all three Gospels the parable begins with a mustard seed (for the introductory formula and the verb parethēken ["he told"], see on v.24). This seed is designated "the smallest of all your seeds," but it becomes "the largest of garden plants" (meizon tōn lachanōn, v.32; cf. Notes). In rabbinical thought the mustard seed was proverbial for smallness (cf. M Niddah 5:2; cf. SBK, 1:669). It becomes a tree, large in comparison with the tiny seed, large enough for birds to perch in its branches (Matt; Luke) or in its shade (Mark). The image recalls OT passages that picture a great kingdom as a large tree with birds flocking to its branches (Judg 9:15; Ezek 17:22–24; 31:3–14; Dan 4:7–23).

But if the greatness of the kingdom is in view, why a mustard plant? The contrast in size between seed and plant does not itself establish the greatness of the kingdom; and, contrary to Kingsbury (*Parables*, p. 81) and Huffmann (p. 211), it is doubtful whether Jesus' point is that the kingdom grows supernaturally. Instead, the point is the organic unity of small beginning and mature end (cf. Dahl, *Jesus in Memory*, pp. 155–56). No pious Jew doubted that the kingdom would come and that it would be vast and glorious. What Jesus is teaching goes beyond that: he is saying that there is a basic connection between the small beginnings taking place under his ministry and the kingdom in its future glory. Though the initial appearance of the kingdom may seem inconsequential, the tiny seed leads to the mature plant.

We can now see why Jesus chose the mustard seed. For him it was not essential to stress the greatness of the future kingdom; few would dispute that. It was more important for him to find a metaphor emphasizing the kingdom's tiny beginning. Jacques Dupont ("Le couple parabolique du séneré et du levain: Mt 13, 31–33; Le 13, 18–21," in Strecker, *Jesus Christus*, pp. 331–45) has suggested another reason for this metaphor. He convincingly shows that the parables of the mustard seed and of the yeast, linked in Matthew and Luke but only the first occurring in Mark, actually belonged together from the beginning. He argues that Mark has structural reasons for dropping the parable of the yeast, and so his silence is scarcely determinative. But one of the links he finds between the two parables is the incongruity of both metaphors. He quotes authors who find the mustard plant an incongruous or even bizarre symbol for the kingdom, while everyone knows that yeast normally symbolizes evil (see further on v.33). But that, Dupont says (pp. 344–45), is just the point. In both parables the strange choice of images evokes surprise, encourages the reader to penetrate the parable's meaning, and accords with other parables designed to jar the unthinking (e.g., the coming of the kingdom is like the coming of a thief in the night [24:43]).

Notes

31 The construction ὅν λαβὼν ἄνθρωπος ἔσπειρεν (*hon labōn anthrōpos espeiren*, lit., "which having taken a man sowed") represents a Semitic auxiliary construction and occurs only here in the NT and at 13:33, 44; Luke 12:37; 13:19, 21.

32 The word μεῖζον (*meizon*, "the largest") is neuter and is therefore in agreement with τὸ σίναπι (*to sinapi*, "mustard," "mustard plant") rather than ὁ κόκκος (*ho kokkos*, "seed"). There is no smooth way of translating the anomaly.

e. The parable of the yeast

13:33

33He told them still another parable: "The kingdom of heaven is like yeast that a woman took and mixed into a large amount of flour until it worked all through the dough."

33 The general thrust of this parable is the same as that of the mustard seed. The kingdom produces ultimate consequences out of all proportion to its insignificant beginnings. Efforts by most dispensationalists (e.g., Walvoord) to interpret the yeast as a symbol for evil are not very convincing in this setting because they require the introduction of anachronistic ideas like "the professing church." Moreover, though yeast is *normally* associated with evil in the OT, this is *not always* so (cf. Lev 7:13; 23:15–18). Metaphors may have diverse uses: the lion at different times symbolizes both Satan and Jesus. In any case the anomalous metaphor is here best explained along the lines suggested by Dupont (on vv.31–32).

If there is a distinction between this parable and the last one, it is that the mustard seed suggests extensive growth and the yeast intensive transformation. The yeast doesn't grow, it permeates; and its inevitable effect, despite the small quantity used, recalls Jesus' words in 5:13. In both parables it is clear that at present the kingdom of heaven operates, not apocalyptically, but quietly and from small beginnings.

There seems little merit in trying to identify the woman, any more than the man in v.31. Some have thought that *enekrypsen* ("hid," RSV) resonates with "hidden" (*kekrymmai*) in vv.35, 44: "The Kingdom was inaugurated without display or pomp; its silent, secret character must have surprised those who were zealously impatient for its expected manifestation in power and glory" (Hill, *Matthew*). These comments, while relevant to the parable as a whole, read too much into the verb itself. It simply means "put something into something," even in nonbiblical Greek (cf. BAGD, p. 216); NIV's "mixed" is therefore not bad. Usage of *enekrypsen* in later verses of this chapter (vv.35, 44) is best interpreted in other ways.

Notes

33 The phrase εἰς ἀλεύρου σάτα τρία (*eis aleurou sata tria*, "into three satas of flour") is anomalous (an anarthrous noun that depends on a preposition is normally placed before a case governed by it) but not unprecedented (cf. BDF, par. 474[4]).

Far more difficult is the expression σάτα τρία (*sata tria*, "three satas"). NIV has "a large amount of flour," which is true enough; but it is not an unreasonable amount of flour, adopted for parabolic purpose, since the same amount was mixed by Sarah in Genesis 18:6. It probably represents the largest amount of flour a woman might make up into bread at one time. But how much is it? The NIV margin specifies "about ½ bushel or 22 liters." In fact, the standard reference works (including ISBE; EBC, 1:609–10 et al.) adopt an unrecognized and conflicting pair of computations leading to mutually exclusive results. If one follows OT ratios and equivalences, τὸ σάτον (*to saton*) = Aram. סָאתָא (*sāˀtā*) = Heb. סְאָה (*seˀāh*) = 1/3 of an ephah or bath. Therefore three satas, as here, equal 1 ephah, known to be 1/10 of a homer.

Now an ephah (or bath) is normally reckoned at about 22 liters. Measurements were imprecise in the ancient world, ranging substantially in place and time (cf. Jeremias, *Jerusalem*, p. 32). That this estimate is approximately correct has been confirmed by an archaeological find that has measured what is almost certainly a "bath" jar and found it to have the capacity of about 21 liters (David Ussishkin, "Excavations at Tel Lachish—1973–1977," *Tel Aviv* 5 [1978]: 87, n. 9. I am indebted to Hugh G.M. Williamson for this reference.). This agrees with the NIV margin. But Josephus (Antiq. IX, 85 [iv. 5]) and other Jewish sources (cf. SBK, 1:669–70) establish that one *saton* = 1½ *modii*, where 1 *modius* = 16 sextarii = approx. 8.75 liters (confirmed by Jos. Antiq. VIII, 57 [ii. 9], which says a bath contains 72 sextarii); and in that case 3 *sata* (as in Matt 13:33) = 1.5 ×

3×8.75 = approx. 39.4 liters—a long way from the 22 suggested by the alternative computation. Both approaches are unwittingly juxtaposed in the standard reference works (cf. Douglas, *Illustrated Dictionary*, 3:1637–39; IDB, 4:833–35), though the writer in the former mentions in passing that "the bath is variously calculated between 20.92 and 46.6 litres." The matter has not been finally resolved. D.J. Wiseman, in a private communication (2 December 1980), suggests that the solution may be analogous to the "greater" and "lesser" (half) weights measures (cf. the approximately double "royal bath").

---

3. *Pause (13:34–43)*

a. *Parables as fulfillment of prophecy*

13:34–35

> [34]Jesus spoke all these things to the crowd in parables; he did not say anything to them without using a parable. [35]So was fulfilled what was spoken through the prophet:
>
> > "I will open my mouth in parables,
> > I will utter things hidden since the creation of
> > the world."

Mark 4:33–34 concludes Mark's report of Jesus' parables on this occasion. But Matthew has already departed from Mark at 13:16–17 and 13:24–30 and by omitting Mark 4:21–29. Now he continues on his own. To believe that he has simply modified Mark in this section is difficult because of the great differences between the two accounts. Speculating about Matthew's dependence on an earlier form of Mark (Schniewind) seems too uncontrolled. It is better to assume that Matthew had independent information (Lohmeyer).

34 The Greek's chiasm puts the emphasis on parables: Jesus did not speak to the crowds without using them. The first verb is aorist (*elalēsen*, "spoke"), referring to the situation at hand; the second is imperfect (*elalei*, "used to say"), implying that this was Jesus' constant custom. But *chōris parabolēs* ("without a parable") does not mean that he told nothing but parables to the crowd but that he said nothing to them without using parables. In short parables were an essential part of his spoken ministry.

35 The quotation is from Psalm 78 (LXX 77):2, a psalm of Asaph. In addition to two difficult textual variants (cf. Notes), the text form is notoriously difficult to resolve. The first line follows the LXX exactly; hence it uses the plural *en parabolais* ("in parables") to translate the Hebrew *bᵉmāšāl* ("in a parable" or "in a wise saying"; for the meaning of these words, see on 13:3a). But the singular is probably generic; so LXX has caught the main point. The second line means roughly the same thing as both LXX and MT but is quite independent. The verb *ereuxomai* (lit., "I belch forth," "I utter") is an etymological rendering of the MT and may have been chosen above the LXX's *phthenxomai* ("I will utter") simply because it is stronger (Goulder, *Midrash*, p. 371) and may indicate the richness of the revelation: "I will pour forth things hidden" (as in Ps 19:2 [LXX 18:3]). Matthew's *kekrymmena* ("things hidden") is likewise closer to the Hebrew *ḥîḏôṯ* ("enigmas," "dark sayings") than LXX's *problēmata* ("tasks," "problems").

But in what sense can Jesus' ministry in parables be said to be a fulfillment of Asaph's psalm? The problem does not arise just because the quotation is from a psalm: in 22:43–44 another psalm is quoted as prophecy. Matthew 11:11–13 has already established that the entire OT is in some sense prophetic (see on 2:15, 17–18; 5:17–20); and 2 Chronicles 29:30 attests that Asaph is a "seer." The problem arises rather in the way Psalm 78:2 is applied to Jesus. Contemporary NT scholars almost universally agree that Matthew has taken Psalm 78:2 badly out of context. Psalm 78 repeats Israel's well-known history, none of which is "mysterious" or "hidden." But Matthew presents Jesus as uttering hidden things. He speaks to the people in parables, in a hidden way, whereas his disciples are enlightened and understand all things. Thus, though Mark 4:33 presents Jesus using the parables to communicate as much truth to the crowds as they could understand, Matthew sees parables as a means of hiding the truth from the outsiders (so, more or less, Lindars, *Apologetic*, pp. 156–57; Kingsbury, *Parables*, pp. 88–90; Rothfuchs, pp. 78–80; Hill, *Matthew;* and others).

Despite its popularity, this approach misunderstands both Psalm 78 and Matthew 13. It is true that Psalm 78 recounts the known history of Israel; but there is no escaping the fact that Psalm 78:2 nevertheless finds the psalmist declaring that he will open his mouth "in parables, wise sayings," and pour forth *ḥîḏôṯ* ("enigmas," "dark sayings"). The point is that though the history of the Jews, which Asaph relates, is well known, the psalmist selects the historical events he treats and brings them together in such a way as to bring out things that have been riddles and enigmas "from of old." The pattern of history is not self-evident; but the psalmist will show what it is really all about. He enlarges on God's might at the time of the Exodus and at other major turning points, a might exercised on behalf of his people. With these events the psalmist juxtaposes the people's persistent rebellion, the result being a vivid portrayal of God's justice and mercy and the people's obtuseness, need, and privilege.

The psalmist teaches all this by opening his mouth "in parables" (i.e., by comparing various things) and in so doing utters "things hidden from of old" (NIV)—"things we have heard and known, things our fathers have told us" (v.3), yet enigmatic and hidden. They are "deep and hidden teachings, which the events of the past embrace" (Louis Jacquet, *Les Psaumes*, 3 vols. [Bruxelles: Duculot, 1975–81], 2:522). Thus the psalmist makes his deep points, as does Stephen in Acts 7, by comparing events in redemptive history.

We turn to Matthew 13:35 and discover a similar pattern. If Jesus pours forth things hidden from the beginning, does this mean that those things remain hidden, i.e., that Jesus pours forth teaching in so hidden a form that outsiders cannot understand them? That is what the popular interpretation of the passage requires; but its death knell is the final phrase: "from the beginning." Whatever that phrase means—NIV has "since the creation of the world" (cf. Notes)—it modifies *kekrymmena* ("things hidden"), the unavoidable implication being that those hidden things are no longer hidden since Jesus has revealed them. Otherwise Jesus is saying no more than this: "I will reveal things that have always been hidden so that they will remain hidden"—an unnatural way to take the sentence.

Apparently, then, as applied to Jesus the second line of the quotation pictures him as revealing things formerly hidden. This does not necessarily mean that he is teaching entirely new things any more than the psalmist was teaching such things. In both cases the patterns of redemptive history may be so stressed that when rightly interpreted they point toward new revelation—viz., they are fulfilled (see on 2:15; 5:17–20). This admirably suits v.52: the "teacher of the law . . . instructed about the kingdom of heaven is like the owner of a house who brings out of his storeroom new treasures as well as old." But Jesus teaches these hitherto hidden things "in parables," i.e., by comparing various things. The parables of this chapter are not exactly like the comparisons and wise sayings offered in Psalm 78. Yet the term "parable" can embrace both kinds of utterance. So we must be careful not to impose on the text too narrow an understanding of what a parable is.

It follows that vv.34–35 are much closer in thought to Mark 4:33–34 than is commonly believed. Jesus does teach the crowds, in parables, revealing new things. How much they understand is a different matter. Yet we have already seen that even Matthew 13:11–13 must not be taken to mean that in Matthew the parables for nondisciples are designed only to conceal. Actually they have a dual role; and here Matthew, rightly understanding the psalmist and reverting to the Hebrew from the LXX so as not to miss his desired nuance, insists that Jesus reveals new truth to the crowds.

But what are these "hidden things" Jesus is now uttering? In Psalm 78 they are "the righteous acts of God in redemption" (Lindars, *Apologetic*, p. 157). Likewise that is what Jesus is now revealing—the righteous acts of God in redemption taking place in his teaching, miracles, death, and resurrection. Matthew insists that the OT Scriptures prophesied these things. They are not novel. If in one sense they have not been known before, it is because they have not all been brought together in the same pattern before. Jesus' kingdom parables to the crowds declare new things, secrets (v.11), hidden things (v.35). Yet they are secret and new chiefly because they depend on an approach to Scripture not unlike Asaph's—bringing together various pieces of previous revelation into new perspectives. Thus Messiah is Son of David but also Suffering Servant. Jesus is the royal King and Son of David foreseen in Scripture (21:4–11) but also the stricken Shepherd equally foreseen in Scripture (26:31). Who clearly foresaw that both streams would merge in one person?

Taken as a whole, Jesus' parables preserve the expectation of the apocalyptic coming of Messiah. They also introduce a new pattern of an inaugurated kingdom that anticipates the Parousia. Moreover this pattern rests on Jesus' self-understanding as the Messiah who unites in himself streams of revelation from the old covenant that had not been so clearly united before.

The connection between Matthew 13:35 and Psalm 78:2 is thus very close. But what does Matthew mean when he says that Jesus' ministry of parables "fulfilled" the word spoken through the prophet? Elsewhere when psalms are treated as prophecies, there is normally a Davidic typology, but not so here. A number of things probably led Matthew to this psalm. The phrase "in parables" may have drawn his attention to Psalm 78 but in itself that does not account for the notion of "fulfillment." But a second connection presents itself: it is possible that, as Psalm 78 recounts Israel's history, so Jesus is presented as the one who is the supreme embodiment of Israel and her history, the one who fulfills all the patterns of the OT regarding Israel. We have noticed this theme before in Matthew, though it is stronger in the fourth Gospel.

But there may be a third and more subtle factor. Matthew understands that "prophecy" does not necessarily predict the future; it may reveal hidden things (cf. 26:68 with parallels in Mark and Luke). This sense of "prophecy" and its predictive sense "converge" in a passage like 11:13, where, as we have seen, the entire OT Scripture, both Law and Prophets "prophesy"—i.e., they comprehend certain patterns, types, predictions, declarations, which cumulatively look forward to him who "fulfills" them. Now in Psalm 78 Asaph claims to be explaining such earlier patterns in redemptive history; but in so doing, from a NT perspective he is also himself becoming a constituent element of the recorded redemptive history the NT explains. As such Psalm 78 becomes part of the "Law and Prophets" that prophesy. If part of this sacred record interprets and brings new truth out of an earlier part, it establishes a pattern that looks to one who will interpret and bring new truth out of the whole. Jesus, Matthew claims, fulfills that role and is exercising it in his own parabolic teaching.

Notes

---

35 There are two important and extremely difficult variants in this verse.

1. Most MSS read διὰ τοῦ προφήτου (*dia tou prophētou*, "through the prophet"). A few witnesses in Jerome's day read διὰ Ἀσάφ τοῦ προφήτου (*dia Asaph tou prophētou*, "through Asaph the prophet"); but none have come down to us, and "Asaph" is certainly an interpolation. But an impressive group of witnesses (א* H f¹ f¹³ 33 ethᵐˢ et al.) read διὰ Ἡσαΐου τοῦ προφήτου (*dia Esaiou tou prophētou*, "through Isaiah the prophet"); and precisely because the quotation does not come from Isaiah, the reading could lay claim to being the *lectio difficilior* that scribes would want to correct. On the other hand, transcriptional evidence favors the probability of adding a prophet's name where none is mentioned (e.g., 1:22; 2:5; 21:4; Acts 7:48). This factor is even more compelling in Matthew than elsewhere since the first evangelist tends not to name the prophet except when quoting Isaiah or Jeremiah, a habit that makes it less likely that he would falsely ascribe to Isaiah, a book with which he was intimately familiar, something extraneous to Isaiah. Scribal misascription is therefore more likely than misascription by Matthew.

2. A majority of the witnesses support the reading ἀπὸ καταβολῆς κόσμου (*apo katabolēs kosmou*, "from the foundation of the world"); but a second reading, ἀπὸ καταβολῆς (*apo katabolēs*, "from the foundation"), is attested by a small but diversified number of Alexandrian, Western, and Eastern text types (אᵇ B f¹ itᵉ,ᵏ syr ᶜ,ˢ eth et al.). Although the preponderance of external evidence supports inclusion of *kosmou*, yet the phrase "the foundation of the world" is so stereotyped in the NT (25:34; Luke 11:50; John 17:24; Eph 1:4; Heb 4:3; 9:26; 1 Peter 1:20; Rev 13:8; 17:8) that there is far greater transcriptional probability that the word was added rather than omitted.

There is another reason for thinking the shorter text is original. While we have already seen that in the second line of the quotation Matthew stops following the LXX and apparently offers his own rendering of the MT, I did not discuss this closing phrase of the second line. The Hebrew here reads מִנִּי-קֶדֶם (*minnî-qedem*, "from of old"), which the LXX renders ἀπ' ἀρχῆς (*ap' archēs*, "from the beginning"). Now MT's "from of old" can mean "from the beginning" or "from eternity" (cf. parallelism in Prov 8:23; cf. also Deut 33:27; Ps 55:19). Yet the expression itself is indefinite and in the context of Psalm 78 may only refer to the beginning of the nation, since God's dealings with Israel constitute the focus of discussion. If so, then LXX's "from the beginning" might sound too absolute; and this could account for Matthew's "from the foundation [i.e., of the nation]." Certainly καταβολή (*katabolē*, "foundation") does not have to be taken to refer to the foundation of the world: cf. ἡ καταβολὴ τῆς ἀποστάσεως (hē katabolē tēs apostaseōs, "the beginning of the insurrection") in Jos. War II, 260 (xiii. 4) (other examples in BAGD, s.v.). The shorter expression in Matthew might then easily have been lengthened by later scribes. If this reasoning is right, then "since the creation of the world" (NIV) is wrong; and the probability that Matthew is treating his OT text thoughtfully and with profound theological understanding is all the more increased. For fuller discussion of the technical questions of translation and related bibliography, see Gundry (*Use of OT*, pp. 118f.) and Rothfuchs (pp. 78–80).

---

b. Interpretation of the parable of the weeds

13:36–43

36Then he left the crowd and went into the house. His disciples came to him and said, "Explain to us the parable of the weeds in the field."
37He answered, "The one who sowed the good seed is the Son of Man. 38The field is the world, and the good seed stands for the sons of the kingdom. The weeds are the sons of the evil one, 39and the enemy who sows them is the devil. The harvest is the end of the age, and the harvesters are angels.
40"As the weeds are pulled up and burned in the fire, so it will be at the end of the age. 41The Son of Man will send out his angels, and they will weed out of his kingdom everything that causes sin and all who do evil. 42They will throw them into the fiery furnace, where there will be weeping and gnashing of teeth. 43Then the righteous will shine like the sun in the kingdom of their Father. He who has ears, let him hear.

For comments on the authenticity of this interpretation, see on 13:3a, 24. The reasons for separating the parable from its interpretation relate to Matthew's plan for this chapter (see on vv.3a, 10–17) and on the need for a setting for this explanation to disciples only (cf. Bonnard).

Those who see more of Matthew's church than of Jesus in the Gospel commonly identify the kingdom in vv.41, 43 with Matthew's church. There is, they argue, a double level of meaning. At one level the passage tells the church not to excommunicate its members because there will be a mixture of "wheat" and "weeds" in the church till the end of the age. For Hill (*Matthew*) this leads to an anomaly: 18:8–9, which he applies to church government, suggests excommunication. But it is doubtful whether Matthew ever confuses kingdom and church: these are two quite distinct categories (see further on vv.37–39).

Hendriksen recognizes the distinction in principle but then ignores it, arguing (1) if tares are "sown *among* the wheat, not alongside of it or on some other field," then it is "natural to think of the intermingling of true and false members within the church"; (2) that the parables shed light on "mysteries" (13:11), and there is no "mystery" in both kinds of people living on the same earth, but it is "far more of a mystery . . . that *within the church visible* God allows both the true and the merely nominal Christians to dwell side by side"; and (3) that the gathering "out of his kingdom" (v.41) assumes the weeds were inside, "in this case inside the church visible" (emphasis his).

We make this reply.

1. Jesus explicitly says the "field is the world" (v.38), not the church; so how could there be "some other field"? The intermingling is adequately explained if it takes place on the field of the world. See further on v.38.

2. The "mysteries" of 13:11 are bound up, not with the intermingling of good and evil per se, in church or world, but in a preliminary or inaugurated form of the kingdom that is not yet the apocalyptic and totally transforming kingdom belonging to the end of the age.

3. The gathering "out of his kingdom" (v.41) is perfectly clear on a synoptic understanding of "kingdom" (see on 3:2; 5:3; 13:41). But to say that "in this case" the expression refers to the church visible is to assume the very thing that must be proved (see esp. Bonnard).

36 The Greek *apheis tous ochlous* could mean either that Jesus sent the crowds away (KJV) or that he left them (NIV). The house referred to is the one Jesus left in order to preach to the crowds (13:1) and was located, presumably, in Capernaum. In Matthew's narrative the house provides the setting both for Jesus' private explanations (vv.37–43; cf. vv.10–23) and for the parables aimed at his disciples (vv.44–52).

Whether the verb "explain" is *diasaphēson* (used elsewhere in the NT only in 18:31) or *phrason* (used elsewhere in the NT only in 15:15) is uncertain but of little consequence. More important is the fact that the disciples need explanations (cf. also 15:15–16). They are not distinguished from the crowds by their instant and intuitive understanding but by their persistence in seeking explanations. Jesus' disciples come to him and ask, and therefore a full explanation is given them (see on vv.10–13).

37–39 On "Son of Man," see on 8:20. The title recurs at v.41: Jesus is the one who both sows the good seed (v.37) and directs the harvest. One of the most significant details in Jesus' parables is the way key images that in the OT apply exclusively to God, or occasionally to God's Messiah, now stand for Jesus himself. These images include sower, director of the harvest, rock, shepherd, bridegroom, father, giver of forgiveness, vineyard owner, lord, and king (cf. Philip B. Payne, "Jesus' Implicit Claim to Deity in His Parables," *Trinity Journal* [1981]: 3–23).

"The field is the world" (v.38). This brief statement presupposes a mission beyond Israel (cf. 10:16–18; 28:18–20) and confirms that the narrower command of 10:5–6 is related exclusively to the mission of the Twelve during the period of Jesus' earthly ministry. Of greater importance in the history of the church has been the view that this actually means that the field is the church. The view was largely assumed by the early church fathers, and the tendency to interpret the parable that way was reinforced by the Constantinian settlement. Augustine made the interpretation official: struggling against the Donatists, who were overzealous in their excommunication practices, he went so far as to say that a mixture of good and evil in the church is a necessary "sign" of the church (cf. esp. his *Breviculus Collationis cum Donatistis* and his *Ad Donatistas post Collationem*). Most Reformers followed the same line: Calvin went so far as to say that the "world" here represents the church by synecdoche.

Ironically some modern redaction criticism has returned to this interpretation because it sees more of Matthew's church than of Jesus in this Gospel. Nevertheless this interpretation is without exegetical foundation. The kingdom is a category flexible enough to be used simultaneously for the saving reign of God (so that "sons of the kingdom" can refer to those who are truly God's people, v.38) and for his reign more broadly considered (so that the kingdom in this sense might well embrace wheat and tares; see on 3:2; 5:3; 28:18); but it is not demonstrable that "church" ever has such semantic flexibility, or that "church" is ever confused with "kingdom" (cf. Ladd, *NT Theology*, pp. 105ff.; Guthrie, *NT Theology*, pp. 702–6).

In this parable and its interpretation, unlike the parable of the sower, the good seed stands for the sons of the kingdom—a healthy reminder that images can symbolize different things in different contexts (see on v.33). But "sons of the kingdom" has also changed its meaning from its use in 8:12. There it refers to those who by birth into the Jewish race have a covenant right to look forward to the messianic kingdom but who, by and large, are forfeiting that right. Here it refers to those who truly are the objects of messianic favor and participants in the messianic kingdom. For their sake the "weeds" are now preserved, and at the "harvest" for their sake the "weeds" will be destroyed. These weeds are "the sons of the evil one." (On "sons of," see on 5:9; and with the entire expression compare John 8:44; 1 John 5:19). The devil himself is the enemy (v.39); the harvest is the end of the age (see on 9:37; cf. Jer 51:33; Hos 6:11; Joel 3:13; 4 Ezra 4:28–29; 2 Bar 70:2); and the harvesters are angels (24:30–31; 25:31; cf. 18:10; Luke 15:7; Heb 1:14; 1 Peter 1:12; also cf. 1 Enoch 63:1).

What must also be pointed out is how many features in the parable are not given nonsymbolic equivalents. These include the conversation between the man and his servants, the servants' sleep, and the fact that the wheat was sown before the tares. This selective use of elements in the story is not atypical of parables (see on v.3a), and the other elements should not be allegorized.

40–42 The identification of the actors is over, and the description of the action begins. As the weeds are "pulled up" (v.40; same verb as "collect" in v.30b) and burned, so it is at the end. The kingdom we have known as the kingdom of heaven or the kingdom of God is also seen as the kingdom of the Son of Man, Jesus' kingdom (cf. 20:21; 25:31; cf. Dan 2:35; Rev 11:15). This is not the church (contra Bornkamm, *Tradition*, p. 44: see above), for Jesus' reign after the Resurrection extends to the farthest reaches of the universe (28:18). In that sense "everything that causes sin and all who do evil" may be weeded out of his kingdom (v.41). For the meaning of *panta ta skandala* ("everything that causes sin"), see on 5:29; with "all who do evil" (lit., "those who do lawlessness") compare 7:23.

The entire expression "everything that causes sin and all who do evil" appears to be a periphrastic rendering of the Hebrew of Zephaniah 1:3; *hammakšēlôt 'et-hārᵉš āᵉîm* (lit., "the stumbling blocks with the wicked"), a phrase so difficult in its context that emendations have been suggested and the best MSS of LXX omit it. The first of the two Hebrew words occurs elsewhere only at Isaiah 3:6, where it means "ruins." Hence NIV translates the phrase in Zephaniah 1:3 as "The wicked will have only heaps of rubble." If this is correct, Matthew is either not referring to Zephaniah 1:3 or else is freely adapting it. But the Hebrew word may well mean "stumbling-blocks," "offenses." For what it is worth, etymology supports it; and the Targum understands it that way. Thus in Zephaniah 1:3 the word may refer to idols, or, better yet, in a figurative manner to people seen as "things that cause offense." If so, Matthew's rendering is appropriate.

The "sons of the evil one" (v.38) may be metaphorically considered as "everything that causes sin," or, without any metaphor, "all who do evil." They, like the weeds, are thrown into the fiery furnace (v.42; see on 3:11; 5:22; cf. Jer 29:22; Dan 3:6; Rev 20:15), where there will be weeping and gnashing of teeth (see on 8:12; cf. 4 Ezra 7:36)—viz., eschatological doom. Nothing is made of the word "first" in v.30, and here the order is reversed. What is clear is that Jesus ascribes to himself the role of eschatological Judge that Yahweh assigns himself in the OT, including Zephaniah 1:3 (cf. France, *Jesus*, pp. 156f.; Payne, "Jesus' Claim").

43 In contrast to the evil-doers, "the righteous will shine like the sun in the kingdom of their Father." The allusion is to Daniel 12:3 LXX, somewhat shortened by omitting *hoi synientes* (= Heb. *hammaśkîlîm*, "those who are wise" or "those who understand"), further evidence that Matthew has not idealized the disciples as those who have understanding (see on 13:10–13, 19, 23, 36). Hill (*Matthew*) remarks that early in the tradition there may have been a word-play on *maśkîlîm* (Aram. *maśkîlîn*) ("wise" or "understanding") in v.43 and *makśēlōt* (Aram. *makśelān*) ("stumbling blocks" or "things that cause offense") in v.41. These righteous people (see on 5:20, 45; 9:13; 10:41; 13:17; 25:37, 46), once the light of the world (5:13–16), now radiate perfections and experience bliss in the consummation of their hopes.

The "kingdom of their Father" must not, as is commonly done, be set over against the kingdom of the Son of Man (v.41) on the supposed ground that the former alone is eternal, or that the Son of Man hands over the elect to him (1 Cor 15:24). The Son's postascension reign is a mediated reign. All God's kingly authority is given Jesus (28:18) and mediated through him; and for all that time the kingdom can be called the kingdom of God or the kingdom of the Son of Man or, more generally, the kingdom of heaven. But even when that mediation ceases, halted by the destruction of the last enemy (1 Cor 15:24–26), in Matthew's terminology it is still appropriate to call Jesus Messiah the King (20:31; 25:34; cf. 26:64), for the kingdom remains no less his.

Notes

39 In the final two identifications of the list in vv.37–39, the subjective complement precedes the copula verb and becomes anarthrous, in conformity with the rules developed by E.C. Colwell and extended by Lane C. McGaughy (*Toward a Descriptive Analysis of EINAI* [Missoula, Mont.: SBL, 1972]). The absence of articles in συντέλεια αἰῶνος (*synteleia aiōnos*, "the end of the age") is therefore no evidence for a construction built on analogy to the Hebrew construct state (contra Hill), not least because the construction is very common in the NT (706 occurrences) and widely distributed.

4. *To the disciples* (13:44–52)

a. *The parable of the hidden treasure*

13:44

> ⁴⁴"The kingdom of heaven is like treasure hidden in a field. When a man found it, he hid it again, and then in his joy went and sold all he had and bought that field.

For the way these parables relate to the structure of the chapter, see on vv.10–17. The parables of the hidden treasure and the pearl are a pair; and pairing is not uncommon in Matthew (e.g., 5:14b–16; 6:26–30; 7:6; 9:16–17; 10:24–25; 12:25; 13:31 –33; 24:43–51), an excellent way of reinforcing a point. Like the paired parables with which these two are chiastically coordinated (mustard seed and yeast, vv.31–33), these two make the same general point but have significant individual emphases.

Unlike the parables earlier in the chapter, these two do not deal so much with the hidden, inaugurated form of the kingdom and the concomitant delay of the Parousia as with the superlative worth of the kingdom of heaven. Yet even here the previous eschatological structure underlies them; for in traditional Jewish apocalyptic, one could scarcely liken the kingdom to a man finding a treasure or buying a pearl: the kingdom was to come apocalyptically at the end of the age by an act of God alone. In contrast to this, some kind of realized or inaugurated eschatology is here presupposed.

44 On the "is like" language, see on v.24. The kingdom is not simply like a treasure, but its situation is like the situation of a treasure hidden in a field. The Greek articles are generic (cf. Turner, *Syntax*, p. 179). Finding the treasure appears to be by chance. In a land as frequently ravaged as Palestine, many people doubtless buried their treasures; but, as Huffman (p. 213) points out, actually to find a treasure would happen once in a thousand lifetimes. Thus the extravagance of the parable dramatizes the supreme importance of the kingdom.

Derrett (*Law*, pp. 1–16) has pointed out that under rabbinic law if a workman came on a treasure in a field and lifted it out, it would belong to his master, the field's owner; but here the man is careful not to lift the treasure out till he has bought the field. So the parable deals with neither the legality nor the morality of the situation (as with the parable of the thief in the night) but with the value of the treasure, which is worth every sacrifice. When the man buys the field at such sacrifice, he possesses far more than the price paid (cf. 10:39). The kingdom of heaven is worth infinitely more than the cost of discipleship, and those who know where the treasure lies joyfully abandon everything else to secure it.

Two alternative interpretations must be dismissed.

1. The first, represented by Walvoord, understands the treasure to represent Israel and Jesus as the man who sold everything to purchase her. He rejects the above view by making the parable mean that "a believer in Christ has nothing to offer and the treasure is not for sale" and proposes his own interpretation by noting that in Exodus 19:5 Israel is called God's treasure. But any view, including Walvoord's, can be made to look foolish by pressing a parable into a detailed allegory: for instance one could rebut his view by showing that it entails Israel's being worth far more than the price paid. But would Walvoord be comfortable with this implicit depreciation of Christ's sacrifice? He must come to grips with the nature of parables (see on 13:3a). And "treasure" has a vast range of associations in the OT and NT; on what basis does he select Exodus 19:5? Above all, his interpretation does not adequately handle the opening clause.

2. J.D. Crossan (*Finding Is the First Act* [Philadelphia: Fortress, 1979], esp. pp. 93ff.) argues that "sold all he had" must be taken so absolutely that "all" includes the parable itself. One must give up the parable itself and, in abandoning all, abandon even abandonment. The parable is therefore a paradox, like the sign that reads "Do not read this sign." Crossan's interpretation is unacceptable for exegetical, literary, historical, and theological reasons: exegetical, in that this parable does not speak of "abandoning" or "giving up" things but of "selling," and one cannot imagine giving the parable away by selling it; literary, in that Crossan, like Walvoord, fastens on one word and rides it so hard that the nature of parables is overlooked; historical, in

that ascription of such existentialist results to Jesus or to Matthew is so anachronistic as to make a historian wince; theological, in that his interpretation of "paradox" is defective and is used in undifferentiated ways. Crossan oscillates between paradox construed as a merely formal contradiction and paradox construed as antinomy or even incoherence.

b. *The parable of the expensive pearl*

13:45–46

> 45"Again, the kingdom of heaven is like a merchant looking for fine pearls. 46When he found one of great value, he went away and sold everything he had and bought it.

45–46 The word *palin* ("again") ties this parable fairly closely to the preceding one (cf. 5:33). Walvoord recognizes that this parable is roughly equivalent to the last. But here, he says, the pearl represents not Israel but the church. The church, like the pearl, is formed organically; and "there is a sense in which the church was formed out of the wounds of Christ." This does not take us much beyond patristic allegorizing. The real connection with the last parable is the supreme worth of the kingdom. But here we deal with a merchant whose business it is to seek pearls, and who chances on one of supreme value. Derrett (*Law*, p. 15) sees a rabbinic parallel: "One wins eternal life after a struggle of years, another finds it in one hour" (b *Abodah Zarah* 17a): contrast the conversions of Saul and the Ethiopian eunuch.

Unlike the man in the last parable, the merchant, though he sells everything he has to purchase the pearl, apparently pays a full price. Although he is an expert in pearls, this single find so far surpasses any other pearl the merchant has ever seen that he considers it a fair exchange for everything else he owns. Thus Jesus is not interested in religious efforts or in affirming that one can "buy" the kingdom; on the contrary, he is saying that the person whose whole life has been bound up with "pearls"—the entire religious heritage of the Jews?—will, on comprehending the true value of the kingdom as Jesus presents it, gladly exchange all else to follow him.

Notes

45–46 There is no obvious explanation for the change from present tense (v.44) to aorist (vv. 45–46, but the latter are not gnomic but narrative (Moule, *Idiom Book*, p. 13). The perfect πέπρακεν (*pepraken*, "sold") with obvious aorist force is probably not an early instance of the later use of the perfect in narrative but a tense chosen because there is no aorist active form for this verb. For discussion, cf. Zerwick, par. 289; Moulton, *Prolegomena*, pp. 142–46; Turner, *Syntax*, p. 70; RHG, p. 897; BDF, pars. 343–44.

c. *The parable of the net*

13:47–48

> 47"Once again, the kingdom of heaven is like a net that was let down into the lake and caught all kinds of fish. 48When it was full, the fishermen pulled it up on

the shore. Then they sat down and collected the good fish in baskets, but threw
the bad away.

47–48 This parable, like the last two, is peculiar to Matthew. In the chiastic structure of the chapter (see on v.3b), it is parallel to the parable of the weeds and has a
somewhat similar meaning. But whereas the parable of the weeds focuses on the
long period of the reign of God during which tares coexist with wheat and the
enemy has large powers, the parable of the net simply describes the situation that
exists when the Last Judgment takes place: the kingdom embraces "good" fish and
"bad" fish, and only the final sweep of the net sorts them out. That is why the
introductory formula uses the present tense (cf. further on v.24; Carson, "Word-
Group"). The chief concern of the parable is neither the consummated kingdom
(which in Matthew would call forth a future tense—"the kingdom of heaven will
become like") nor the inaugurated kingdom ("the kingdom of heaven has become
like") but the situation that exists at the End. And, once again, kingdom and church
must not be equated.

A *sagēnē* (lit., "drag net," used only here in the NT) was drawn along between
two boats or tied on shore at one end and put out by a boat at the other end, which
was then drawn to land by ropes. "All kinds of fish" (v.47) might hint at the multi-
racial character of the subjects of the kingdom, but more probably this refers to
"good" and "bad" fish (v.48). In the parable itself, "good" and "bad" fish have no
moral overtones but refer simply to fish ceremonially suitable and large enough for
eating and those for some reason unacceptable, respectively. The word *sapron*
("bad") can mean "decayed," but here it simply means "worthless."

d. Interlude (13:49–51)

1) Interpretation of the parable of the net

13:49–50

> [49]This is how it will be at the end of the age. The angels will come and separate
> the wicked from the righteous [50]and throw them into the fiery furnace, where there
> will be weeping and gnashing of teeth."

49–50 Many separate the parable (vv.47–48), supposedly about the disciples on
mission as "fishers of men," and the interpretation (vv.49–50), which transforms the
parable into a last judgment scene. Hill (*Matthew*) insists that this is "not a suitable
ending, for the furnace is hardly the place for bad fish." But that is to confuse
symbol with what is symbolized; the furnace is not for the fish but for the wicked.
To be consistent, Hill (and many others; e.g., Jeremias, *Parables*, p. 85; Strecker,
Weg, pp. 160f.) would also have to object that the tares, when burned (v.42), do not
weep and gnash their teeth (Kingsbury, *Parables*, pp. 165f., n. 143). The parable
itself cannot easily be made to refer to the missionary activity of the church; for it
describes a separation *when the net is full*, not a continuous separation. Nor may
one attach some deep significance to the distinction between catching all the fish
(v.47) and separating them (v.48)—as if the original parable referred to both the
church's witness in catching men and the final separation (so Kingsbury, *Parables*,
p. 120)—any more than it is legitimate in interpreting the tares to divide the har-

vesting from the final separation of weeds and wheat. Both the parable and its interpretation point to the Last Judgment. On the angels and the image of the fiery furnace, see on vv.41–42.

But this does not mean that the parable and its interpretation are about the Last Judgment in the same way 25:1–13 (the ten virgins) and 25:31–46 (the sheep and the goats) are, the one warning of the need for readiness and the other establishing a basis for judgment. The focus here is on the state of the kingdom when the Judgment occurs. Though it includes both the righteous and the wicked, a thorough sorting out will certainly take place.

2) On understanding parables

13:51

> 51"Have you understood all these things?" Jesus asked. "Yes," they replied.

51 Both "Jesus says to them" and "Lord" (KJV) are late additions to the text; it is difficult to explain why they were dropped if part of the original text.

Jesus' question picks up the disciples' request for an explanation (v.36) but goes beyond it, since the question is introduced, not after v.43, but after three additional parables. The words "all these things" have been taken to refer to what Jesus means by his parables (Filson, Plummer, Schweizer, Schmid) or to the unexplained parables (Robinson) or to the "secrets of the kingdom" in v.11 (Grundmann, Bonnard, Hill, Fenton). In fact, all these are so tightly linked that it is hard to imagine how one could understand one of these areas and not the other two.

This is the only place in this chapter where the disciples themselves are explicitly said to understand, and they say it by themselves. It is as wrong to say that Matthew has portrayed them as understanding everything as it is to say that they understood nothing. The truth lies between the extremes. The disciples certainly understood more than the crowds; on the other hand, they are shortly to be rebuked for their dullness (15:16). Like another positive response in this Gospel (see on 20:22–23), this one cannot be simply dismissed as presumptuous enthusiasm (as if they think they know everything when in fact they know nothing) nor taken at face value (as if their understanding were in fact mature). In any event the disciples' *claim* is not as important as the last parable to which it leads (for the structure of this section, see on v.3a).

e. The parable of the teacher of the law

13:52

> 52He said to them, "Therefore every teacher of the law who has been instructed about the kingdom of heaven is like the owner of a house who brings out of his storeroom new treasures as well as old."

52 Interpretations of this difficult verse are legion. It has been variously held that it refers to scribes who become disciples of the kingdom (Jeremias, *Parables*, p. 216) or join the Christian community (Hummel, pp. 17ff.); that Matthew here refers to the way he himself functions within the community (C.F.D. Moule, "St. Matthew's

331

Gospel," *Studia Evangelica* 2 [1964]: 98f.); that the verse demonstrates the existence of Christian "scribes" or "teachers of the law" in Matthew's church, men who exercise much the same role as scribes in Judaism (Kilpatrick, *Origins*, p. 111; Strecker, *Weg*, pp. 37–38; Grundmann), or even that disciples within Christianity are more important than scribes within Judaism (Manson, *Sayings*, pp. 198f.); that each disciple who is able to qualify may present himself as a "teacher of the law" (Lagrange); that any scribe who understands what has been taught about the kingdom is like the lord of a house "who handles everything in a carefree manner, who does not save anything and even uses what is old" (van Tilborg, p. 132; R. Walker, pp. 27–29).

The verse's parabolic structure must be noted and a number of exegetical details explored before its meaning can be grasped or the significance of the introductory "therefore" rightly perceived. The "is like" formula (see on v.24) means "it is with a teacher of the law who has been instructed about the kingdom as it is with the owner of a house." The problem is to discern the point of the comparison. The *oikodespotēs* ("owner of a house") is a frequent figure in Jesus' parables and can stand for God (21:33), Jesus (10:25), or disciples (24:43). Very often he is a figure who dispenses wealth in some way (20:1–16; 21:33–43). So here he brings out of his "storeroom" (same word as "treasure" in 2:11; 6:19–21; 12:35[*bis*]; 13:44, 19:21) new things and old things. Why would an owner of a house do this? Presumably it is not simply to ogle his wealth but for some useful purpose. The point is that his treasure *includes* both the new and the old, and that he can use both.

The point of comparison becomes clearer when we remember that a *grammateus* ("scribe") in Jesus' day was not simply a theological interpreter of the Scriptures capable of rendering Halakic decisions (rules for conduct) but a teacher (hence NIV's "teacher of the law"; see on 2:4; 8:19). From this he derived much of his prestige and power (HJP, 2:332–34; Trotter); indeed, he was seen as having esoteric knowledge that could only be passed on to committed initiates (cf. Jeremias, *Jerusalem*, pp. 237–40). But Jesus adds a qualifying factor: the scribe with whom he is concerned *mathēteutheis tē basileia tōn ouranōn* ("has been instructed about the kingdom of heaven"). Whether the verbal form is construed as deponent ("has become a disciple") or strictly passive ("has been made a disciple"), it is not at all clear that the dative expression means "*about* the kingdom of heaven"; and in the one NT passage with similar construction (27:57), Joseph of Arimathea had become a disciple *of* Jesus, not *about* Jesus. By analogy the scribes in this verse have become disciples *of the kingdom of heaven*.

If the preceding exegetical observations are correct, the points of comparison in the parable are two. The emphasis in the first part of the verse rests, not on the supposition that the scribe has been instructed *about* the kingdom and therefore understands, but that he has become a disciple *of* the kingdom and therefore his allegiance has been transformed. It is with such a person as with "the owner of a house"—a discipled scribe brings out of his storeroom new things and old.

The *thēsauros* ("storeroom") so regularly stands for a man's "heart," its wealth and cherished values (see above; esp. on 12:35), that we must understand the discipled scribe to be bringing things out of his heart—out of his understanding, personality, and very being. What he brings out are *kaina kai palaia*, not "new things as well as old" (NIV), which suggests the new things have been added to the old, but "new things and old things"—a subtle touch that reminds the alert reader that in Matthew the gospel of the kingdom, though new, takes precedence over the old revelation and is its fulfillment (cf. 5:17–20). The new is not added to the old; there is but one revelation, and its focus is the "new" that has fulfilled and thereby renewed the old, which has thereby become new (Bonnard). Thus the OT promises of Messiah and kingdom, as well as OT law and piety, have found their fulfillment in Jesus' person, teaching, and kingdom; and the scribe who has become a disciple of the kingdom now brings out of himself deep understanding of these things and their transformed perspective affecting all life.

But the order is of great importance. The parable shows that a discipled scribe has this understanding, *not* that understanding generates discipleship. This conforms perfectly to the chapter's structure: the disciples are not defined as having understanding but are described as having been given revelation and understanding (vv.11–12). When the disciples ask for an explanation, they are given it (vv.36–43) and thus claim some measure of understanding (v.51). "Therefore" (v.52) a *discipled* scribe is like, etc. Discipleship to Jesus, recognition of the revelation he is and brings, and submission to the reign he inaugurates and promises are necessary prerequisites to understanding and bringing out from oneself the rich treasures of the kingdom (see further on 25:31–46).

But there is a second point of comparison in the parable. The last one could have been made by stressing discipleship but omitting any reference to scribes. Scribes were "teachers of the Scriptures." If they are likened to the owner of a house who brings treasures out of his storeroom, the further implication is unavoidable—they are not bringing forth things new and old for purely private or personal reasons *but in their capacity as teachers*. Jesus' disciples claim they have understood what he has been teaching. "Therefore," he responds, discipled teachers of the Scriptures, if they have understood, must themselves bring out of their storeroom the treasures now theirs so as to teach others (cf. Trotter).

This interpretation admirably fits in with three other Matthean themes.

1. The disciples have a major responsibility in evangelizing and making disciples, both during Jesus' ministry (ch. 10) and after his departure (28:18–20).

2. In the latter instance they are told to "disciple" the nations and teach them all Jesus has commanded them: i.e., the focus of their mission is Jesus and the revelation—the new "fulfillment" revelation—he has brought.

3. This interpretation, which places some teaching responsibility on the disciples, also fits the purpose of the parables described in the comments on vv.12–17, 34–35. Indeed, part of the reason for private instruction may again be linked to the place of Jesus' earthly ministry in redemptive history; for what he tells his disciples in secret they are to proclaim from the rooftops (10:27). Jesus explains the parables to his disciples in private; they are to bring out of their treasure rooms "new things and old."

If this interpretation of v.52 is correct, then though "disciples" in this chapter most probably refers to the Twelve, they epitomize the church to come. In that event "disciples" does not refer to a special group of "teachers of the law" within Matthew's community (see further on 23:34) but to those who by Matthew's day were called Christians. Just as they have been aligned with prophets and righteous men from past ages (e.g., 5:11–12; 10:41), so are they aligned with "teachers of the law." In fact, only Jesus' "disciples" are able to bring forth new things and old: the Jewish teachers of the law could bring forth only the old.

5. Transitional conclusion: movement toward further opposition

13:53

53When Jesus had finished these parables, he moved on from there.

53 On the Greek preliminary formula, see on 7:28–29. The common view that v.53 properly introduces the following pericope fits neither that beginning nor the structure of Matthew. Gooding's claim (p. 229) that v.24 is syntactically tied to v.53 is incorrect: compare the same openings at 8:14; 9:23, where new pericopes are introduced. This verse, as Hill (*Matthew*) points out, "suggests that Jesus spoke all the preceding parables at once"—though he thinks this "is unlikely" (cf. further on 5:1–12; 13:3a). What is clear is that Jesus' movement from Capernaum to "his home town" (vv.53–54) turns out to be a further fulfillment of vv.14–15: these people will be ever hearing but never understanding.

Notes

53 The verb μετῆρεν (*metēren*, "he moved on"), found in the NT only here and at 19:1 (again in a formulaic discourse ending), is normally transitive and probably owes its present intransitive force to Semitic influence (Moisés Silva, "New Lexical Semitisms?" ZNW 69 [1978]: 256).

V. The Glory and the Shadow: Progressive Polarization (13:54–19:2)

A. Narrative (13:54–17:27)

The danger of outlines is oversimplification. Even genuine insight in outline form may eliminate or minimize various themes that occur in sections where the discovered "structure" does not allow for them. Matthew, as we have seen, can use structure most effectively; and several complex structures have been found in, or imposed on, these chapters (cf. J. Murphy-O'Conner, "The Structure of Matthew XIV–XVII," RB 82 [1975]: 360–84; Gooding, pp. 248ff.). No detailed and comprehensive outline of these chapters is quite convincing; so it seems best to deal with them pericope by pericope.

The principal themes of these chapters are clear. There is a progressive polarization along several axes. As Jesus extends his ministry, the opposition sharpens (15:1–9; 16:1–14). When he reveals himself to his disciples, they perceive some truth clearly and entirely reject other truth (16:13–22; 17:1–13). As Jesus is increasingly opposed by Jewish leaders, so his own disciples become increasingly important (18:1–10). Over it all is the contrast between Christ's glory, goodness, and grace, and the blind misunderstanding of the disciples (15:15–16, 33; 16:22; 17:4, 19; 18:21) and Jewish leaders (15:2, 8; 16:6, 12; 17:24) alike. And rising less ambiguously now is the shadow of the Cross (16:21–22; 17:22–23).

In the narrative section (13:54–17:27), Matthew follows Mark 6–9 fairly closely until Mark 9:33. Of course Matthew leaves out all the material between Mark's parables and the rejection at Nazareth (viz., Mark 4:35–5:43) because he has presented it earlier (chs. 8–9).

1. *Rejected at Nazareth*

13:54–58

> [54]Coming to his hometown, he began teaching the people in their synagogue, and they were amazed. "Where did this man get this wisdom and these miraculous powers?" they asked. [55]"Isn't this the carpenter's son? Isn't his mother's name Mary, and aren't his brothers James, Joseph, Simon and Judas? [56]Aren't all his sisters with us? Where then did this man get all these things?" [57]And they took offense at him.
>
> But Jesus said to them, "Only in his hometown and in his own house is a prophet without honor."
>
> [58]And he did not do many miracles there because of their lack of faith.

Placing this pericope immediately after the discourse on parables extends the hostility and rejection of the scribes and Pharisees even to Jesus' hometown (cf. Mark 6:1–6). It is almost universally assumed that this is the same rejection recorded in Luke 4:16–31, which ties the event to OT prophecy. Though not unlikely, this is not certain. Unlike Luke, Mark and Matthew mention no hostility so great as to lead people to kill Jesus. If there were two incidents, the one recorded by the first two evangelists may reflect an abating of instinctive rage as the village's most famous son has grown in reputation in the area.

54 On the formal connection between this verse and the preceding one, see on v.53. Jesus' *patris* ("home town") is here understood to be Nazareth, explicitly named only by Luke (4:16; cf. Matt 2:23; 4:13). That Jesus taught extensively in the synagogues is certain (cf. 4:23; 12:9); but he did not limit himself to this environment. (On "their" synagogue, see on 4:23; 7:29; 9:35; 10:17; 11:1; 12:9–10.) The imperfect *edidasken* (lit., "he was teaching") could suggest that Jesus taught here on more than one occasion (Filson, Schweizer) but is more probably inceptive (cf. NIV's "began teaching").

The interrogative *pothen* ("Where"; repeated in v.56) is not so much concerned with location as with source of authority (cf. also v.27; Bonnard). Do Jesus' wisdom and powers—his teaching and miracles, both evidences of his authority—reflect God's authority or something else (cf. 12:24)?

55–57a Obviously some of the questioners' motivation springs less from a serious desire to know whence Jesus derives his authority than from personal pique that a hometown boy has outstripped them. The questions (vv.55–56) do not call for answers but merely reveal that there has already been a denial of who Jesus is. Mark 6:3 has "the carpenter," not Matthew's "the carpenter's son" (v.55); but in a day when most lads followed their father's trade, both are correct. *Tektōn* can mean "carpenter"—one who works with wood—or perhaps even "builder," in a time and place when most homes were made of mud brick. Justin Martyr (*Dialogue* 88.8, c. A.D. 150) says Jesus was a maker of plows and yokes. The definite article ("*the* carpenter's son") suggests there was only one in town. On the question of Jesus' brothers and sisters, see on 12:46–50. The four names listed (cf. Notes) are typically Jewish.

In one sense, of course, the questions of the people are understandable, if not justifiable. Here was a young artisan from a rough town, with no special breeding or education. Whence, then, his wisdom and miracles? (Incidentally, their questions render impossible the fanciful miracles ascribed to Jesus' childhood by the apocryphal gospels.) But by their questions the people merely condemn themselves: they cannot doubt the fact of his wisdom and miracles (v.56) yet reject his claims (v.57). "They took offense at him" (*eskandalizonto en autō*), i.e., found in him obstacles to faith (see on 5:29; 11:6), even though the biggest obstacles were in their own hearts. It is sad that every time in the NT somebody is "scandalized" by someone, that someone is Jesus (cf. Bonnard, citing G. Stählen, TDNT, 7:349; cf. Matt 11:6; 26:31, 33; Mark 6:3; Luke 7:23).

57b–58 The proverb in v.57b recurs at Mark 6:4; Luke 4:24; John 4:44 (cf. Hennecke, 1:109). Most often a person is better received at home than anywhere else; but if he enjoys an elevated position, the reverse is true.

Many say that v.58 softens Mark's "He could not do any miracles there, except lay his hands on a few sick people and heal them. And he was amazed at their lack of faith" (Mark 6:5–6). But two factors must be borne in mind: (1) Mark mentions some miracles, and Matthew, typically condensing, may be referring to these rather than commenting on Jesus' ability to do miracles; and (2) it is doubtful whether Mark's "could not" is ontological or absolute, for Mark records other miracles in which the beneficiaries exhibit no faith (feeding the five thousand, stilling the storm, healing the Gadarene demoniac). The "could not" is related to Jesus' mission: just as Jesus could not turn stones to bread without violating his mission (4:1–4), so he could not do miracles indiscriminately without turning his mission into a sideshow. The "lack of faith" (*apistia*, used only here in Matthew) of the people was doubtless a source of profound grief and frustration for Jesus (cf. *apistos*, "unbelieving," in 17:17), rather than something that stripped him of power.

Notes

55 Many MSS read Ἰωσῆς (*Iōsēs*, "Joses," KJV), instead of Ἰωσήφ (*Iōsēph*, "Joseph," NIV), doubtless following the Galilean pronunciation יוֹסֵי (*yôsê*) of the correct Hebrew יוֹסֵף (*yôsēp*).

56 The phrase πρὸς ἡμᾶς (*pros hēmas*, "with us") with the sense of position instead of motion (i.e., having the force of παρ' ἡμῖν [*par' hēmin*, "with us"]) represents a Hellenistic Greek far more fluid than its Attic forbear (cf. Moule, *Idiom Book*, p. 52).

2. Herod and Jesus (14:1–12)

a. Herod's understanding of Jesus

14:1–2

> [1]At that time Herod the tetrarch heard the reports about Jesus, [2]and he said to his attendants, "This is John the Baptist; he has risen from the dead! That is why miraculous powers are at work in him."

1–2 Of the two parallels (Mark 6:14–16; Luke 9:7–9), only Mark (6:17–29) goes on to give the story of John's death; and Matthew follows this account (vv.3–12). On the chronological problem raised by a comparison of vv.1–2 and v.13, see on v.13.

The phrase "At that time" is very loose (see on 11:25; 12:1) and should not be tied to the previous pericope. Mark sets the scene after the mission of the Twelve; and certainly the multiplication of Jesus' influence through his disciples would upset Herod, one of whose motives in imprisoning the Baptist had been to thwart any threat to political stability (cf. Jos. Antiq. XVIII, 116–19[v.2]).

Herod Antipas, son of Herod the Great (see on 2:1), was tetrarch (v.1; see on 2:22), not king—though doubtless "king" was used popularly (Mark 6:14). His tetrarchy included Galilee (4:12) and Perea (19:1). Because John the Baptist's ministry had been exercised in Perea (John 1:28), he had come under Herod's power. Herod had been ruling more than thirty years, and at this time he lived primarily at Tiberias on the southwest shore of Galilee. Thus Jesus' ministry was taking place largely within Herod's jurisdiction.

How the reports of Jesus' ministry reached Herod is unknown; it may have been through Cuza (Luke 8:3). So extensive a ministry could not have been kept from Herod for long. His conclusion, that this was John the Baptist risen from the dead (v.2), is of great interest. It reflects an eclectic set of beliefs, one of them the Pharisaic understanding of resurrection. During his ministry John had performed no miracles (John 10:41); therefore Herod ascribes the miracles in Jesus' ministry, not to John, but to John "risen from the dead." Herod's guilty conscience apparently combined with a superstitious view of miracles to generate this theory.

b. Background: Herod's execution of John the Baptist

14:3–12

> [3]Now Herod had arrested John and bound him and put him in prison because of Herodias, his brother Philip's wife, [4]for John had been saying to him: "It is not lawful for you to have her." [5]Herod wanted to kill John, but he was afraid of the people, because they considered him a prophet.
> [6]On Herod's birthday the daughter of Herodias danced for them and pleased Herod so much [7]that he promised with an oath to give her whatever she asked. [8]Prompted by her mother, she said, "Give me here on a platter the head of John the Baptist." [9]The king was distressed, but because of his oaths and his dinner guests, he ordered that her request be granted [10]and had John beheaded in the prison. [11]His head was brought in on a platter and given to the girl, who carried it to her mother. [12]John's disciples came and took his body and buried it. Then they went and told Jesus.

3–5 Both Mark (6:16–29; cf. Luke 3:19–20) and Matthew insert this story as an excursus, a bit of explanatory background (see further on v.13). Typically Matthew is more condensed than Mark, yet does add one detail (see on v.12); but in this case it is doubtful whether Matthew is a condensation of Mark. More likely Matthew follows independent information (cf. Hoehner, *Herod Antipas*, pp. 114–17). Many scholars have insisted the Gospel reports of John's death and the report of Josephus (Ant. XVIII, 116–19[v.2]) cannot be reconciled, especially because Josephus assigns a political motive to the execution of the Baptist and the synoptists a moral and religious one. Hoehner (*Herod Antipas*, pp. 124–49) has exhaustively treated these problems and points out that the two motives are not as far apart as some have thought.

Herod's first wife was the daughter of Aretas (cf. 2 Cor 11:32), Arabian king of the Nabateans, whose land adjoined Perea on the south. To divorce her in favor of Herodias was politically explosive. Indeed, some years later border fighting broke out, and Antipas was defeated, but saved by Roman intervention. John's rebuke would be like a spark on tinder; and his powerful preaching about the nearness of the messianic kingdom fueled the expectations of the populace, not least for the reestablishment of the law by which John was rebuking Herod. Religious fanaticism with messianic overtones is more politically dangerous than mere political extremism. This Herod well knew. Josephus and the Gospel writers blend together.

Herodias was married to Herod Philip (not Philip the tetrarch, Luke 3:1), son of Herod the Great and Mariamne II (for this identification, cf. Hoehner, *Herod Antipas*, pp. 131–36), and therefore half-brother to Herod Antipas. John probably did not denounce Antipas for divorcing his former wife, an action probably judged allowable (cf. b *Ketuboth* 57b; Jeremias, *Jerusalem*, p. 371, n. 60), but for incestuously marrying his half-brother's wife (Lev 18:16; 20:21); and John probably kept on repeating his rebuke (imperfect *elegen* means "he used to say [repeatedly]"; so McNeile). John's courage in denouncing Herod distinguishes him from the Essenes (with whom many scholars associate him), for they tended to refuse to meddle in political life, no matter how evil it became (Bonnard). Herodias was not only Antipas's sister-in-law but also his niece, the daughter of his half-brother Aristobulus; but for most Jews there was no bar to marrying a niece (cf. Hoehner, *Herod Antipas*, pp. 137–39, n. 4, for the literature).

Some think Matthew's statement that "Herod wanted to kill John, but he was afraid of the people" (v.5) conflicts with Mark's picture of a Herod who wants to spare John but is pushed into killing him by Herodias (cf. esp. Mark 6:19–21). The total situation is psychologically convincing. Like Ahab, Antipas was wicked but weak; and Herodias, like Jezebel, wicked and ruthless. Herod's grief (not mere distress) in v.9 shows his ambivalence. Moreover if he was "afraid of the people" because they held John to be a prophet (cf. 21:26, 46), then Matthew confirms Josephus's view that Herod's actions were largely motivated by politics.

6–8 "On Herod's birthday"—or, better, "At Herod's birthday feast" (cf. Notes)— Herodias's daughter by her former marriage, Salome, a girl between twelve and fourteen yeas of age (Hoehner, *Herod Antipas*, pp. 151–56), danced before the king and his lords (v.6). The dance may have been very sensual, but the text does not say so. The outrageous morals of the Herodians suggest it, as does the low status of dancing girls. At any rate, Salome pleased Herod Antipas enough for him to put on the airs of a lavish and powerful emperor; petty ruler though he was, he imitated the grandiloquence of ancient Persian monarchs (Esth 5:3, 6; 7:2)—the story also has certain parallels with a later oath made by the Roman emperor Gaius to Herod Agrippa (cf. Hoehner, *Herod Antipas*, pp. 165–67)—and with drunken dignity made a fool of himself. Salome, still young enough to ask her mother's advice, became the means for accomplishing Herodias's darkest desire—the death of the man whose offense had been telling the truth.

9–11 Though grieving because of his oath (the Greek is plural but refers to the single oath Herod had made: see on 2:20; Turner, *Insights*, p. 27, n.; BDF, par.

142) and his loss of face before his guests if he were to renege on his vow (cf. Notes), Herod gave the order (v.9). "Like most weak men, Herod feared to be thought weak" (Plumptre). His oath should neither have been made nor kept. Decapitation (v.10) though sanctioned by Greeks and Romans was contrary to Jewish law, which also forbade execution without trial.

The Gospel writers have been charged with fabrication on the ground that the prompt execution of John would have quenched the merriment. But hardened men are unlikely to let a little gore spoil their merriment. While Alexander Jannaeus feasted with his concubines in a public place, he ordered eight hundred rebels to die by crucifixion, their wives and children being slaughtered before the eyes of the victims (Jos. Antiq. XIII, 380[XIV. 2]). When Cicero's head was brought to Fulvia, the wife of Antony, she spat on it and pierced its tongue with a pin in spite against the man who had opposed Antony. Jerome says Herodias did the same thing to the head of John. We do not know where Jerome got his information, and it may not be historical; but it would not have been out of character for a cruel and ruthless woman intent on aping the imperial court. So John died, the last of the OT prophets (11:9, 13) who through persecution became models for Jesus' disciples (5:11–12).

For the significance of *korasion* ("girl," v.11), see Hoehner (*Herod Antipas*, pp. 154–56).

12 Though both Mark and Matthew tell of the burial of John the Baptist's body by his disciples, only Matthew mentions the report to Jesus. This report does not become the reason why Jesus withdraws (see on v.13) but serves other purposes: (1) it draws John and Jesus together against the opposition; (2) it suggests, though it does not prove, a positive response to Jesus by John and his disciples following 11:2–6; and (3) it supports the view that Matthew often finishes his longer narrative pericopes by returning to the opening theme (see on 12:45; 15:20)—Herod hears reports of Jesus (14:1); Jesus hears reports of Herod (v.12). The frequency of this device gains importance in interpreting Matthew's later chapters.

Notes

6 The Greek γενεσίοις δὲ γενομένοις (*genesiois de genomenois*, "at the birthday feast") is so difficult that it has generated a nest of variant readings. It appears to be a dative absolute, which, though apparently common in Plutarch, has no other certain example in the NT (cf. further Moule, *Idiom Book*, pp. 44f.).

9 There are two principal readings: (1) λυπηθεὶς ὁ βασιλεὺς διά (*lypētheis ho basileus dia*) attested by B D Θ f[1] f[13] 700 it[a,b,d] et al.; (2) ἐλυπήθη ὁ βασιλεύς; διὰ δέ (*elypēthē ho basileus; dia de*) attested by ℵ C K (L omit *de*) L[c] W X Byz et al. The first, adopted here, is supported by witnesses of Alexandrian, Western, and Caesarean text types but has an ambiguity: does the *dia* phrase qualify *lypētheis* ("grieving")—i.e., "the king, grieving because of his oath and his dinner guests, ordered, etc."—or ἐκέλευσεν (*ekeleusen*, "he ordered")—i.e., "the king was grieved; but because of his oath and his dinner guests, he ordered, etc."? The second reading, most likely secondary, removes the ambiguity (usually evidence of being secondary) and requires the second interpretation. The difference is one of emphasis only; but the harder reading may be taken to support the more nuanced interpretation of Herod's motives given above.

3. *The feeding of the five thousand*

14:13–21

[13]When Jesus heard what had happened, he withdrew by boat privately to a solitary place. Hearing of this, the crowds followed him on foot from the towns. [14]When Jesus landed and saw a large crowd, he had compassion on them and healed their sick.

[15]As evening approached, the disciples came to him and said, "This is a remote place, and it's already getting late. Send the crowds away, so they can go to the villages and buy themselves some food."

[16]Jesus replied, "They do not need to go away. You give them something to eat."

[17]"We have here only five loaves of bread and two fish," they answered.

[18]"Bring them here to me," he said. [19]And he directed the people to sit down on the grass. Taking the five loaves and the two fish and looking up to heaven, he gave thanks and broke the loaves. Then he gave them to the disciples, and the disciples gave them to the people. [20]They all ate and were satisfied, and the disciples picked up twelve basketfuls of broken pieces that were left over. [21]The number of those who ate was about five thousand men, besides women and children.

The feeding of the five thousand is found in all four Gospels (cf. Mark 6:30–44; Luke 9:10–17; John 6:1–14; cf. further on Matt 15:32–39 = Mark 8:1–10). Comprehensive interpretations are too numerous to list. There is probably an implicit anticipation of the messianic banquet (see on 8:11); but the text focuses more on Jesus' compassion (v.14), on the responsibility of the disciples to minister to the crowds (v.16), and on this miracle of creation. Suggestions that what "really happened" was that the people started sharing their lunches have much more in common with late nineteenth-century liberalism than with the text. Those who see Eucharistic significance in the event (Benoit, Gundry) make it meaningless at the time it occurred; the most that can be said is that after the institution of the Lord's Supper and after the Passion and Resurrection, some Christians may have seen parallels to the Eucharist. John 6, often taken to support this, is not as convincing as is commonly thought (cf. Carson, "Historical Tradition," pp. 125–26).

Possible OT allusions to Exodus 16 or 2 Kings 4:42–44 cannot be more than allusions, for the differences between this story and those are more significant than the similarities. Hence, as Davies notes (*Setting*, pp. 48f.), that Matthew here develops a "new Moses" theme based on a manna typology (Exod 16) is unlikely since (1) none of the synoptists stresses the desert setting; (2) in the OT the manna was not to be kept, but here the fragments are to be kept; (3) Jesus ministers to a crowd from which he has tried to escape, and Exodus has no parallel to this. It is far more likely that this pericope shows that Jesus himself cannot be reduced to one of the readymade categories of the day—prophet, rabbi, teacher of the law (cf. van der Loos, esp. pp. 634–37).

13–14 If "what had happened" (v.13) refers to John's death, then the chronology is either contradictory (so Bultmann, *Synoptic Tradition*, pp. 351f.) or a return to a much earlier time, since the beginning of the chapter presupposes the Baptist's death (v.2). But vv.3–12 must be seen as an excursus: the section opens with *gar* ("for"), commonly used to introduce excursuses, and the *de* ("and") in v.13 is resumptive (cf. L. Cope, "The Death of John the Baptist in the Gospel of Matthew, or, The Case of the Confusing Conjunction," CBQ 38 [1976]: 515–19). Therefore v.13 picks up from vv.1–2: when Jesus heard, viz. Herod's response to his preaching and miracles, he decided to withdraw. He had done so previously to escape the animus of the Pharisees (12:15); he now does so to avoid Antipas. But as elsewhere (e.g., Mark 7:24–25), it was often not possible for Jesus to escape the crowds even when it was possible for him to leave a place.

Luke (9:10) specifies that the "solitary place" was in the region belonging to Bethsaida—i.e., Bethsaida Julius (see on 11:21) on the northeast shore of Galilee. The crowds ran "on foot" around the top of the lake, presumably crossing the upper Jordan at a ford two miles north of where the river enters Galilee. They "followed" Jesus, seeing where he was going and setting out after him; but arriving first, they were already there when he landed with his tired disciples (v.14). Lohmeyer (*Matthäus*) finds profound symbolism—Jesus "withdraws" from the presence of God in prayer, like a high priest leaving the Holy of Holies, and presents himself to the people. But this is as uncontrolled a piece of allegorizing as any church father ever thought of. (On Jesus' neverfailing compassion, see 9:36.)

15–17 "Evening" (*opsios*) is a flexible word, referring to any period from mid-afternoon to just after sunset. The later period is in view in v.23; here (v.15) the earlier one.

On the face of it, the conversation between Jesus and his disciples is straightforward, though very condensed compared with the other Gospels. The "villages" to which the disciples wished to send the crowds were small, unwalled hamlets. Bread and fish were staples in Galilee, especially for the poor. John 6:9, 13 specifies *barley* loaves—the cheaper, coarser bread. The numbers "five" and "two" (v.17) are simply accurate details: efforts to explain them (e.g., as referring to the Pentateuch and two tables of the law) are as fanciful as Christian frescoes making them Eucharistic symbols, which would turn fish into wine!

But in recent years the influence of Held (Bornkamm, *Tradition*, pp. 181–83) has convinced many that Matthew's changes of Mark (assuming absolute dependence in this pericope) demonstrate two other themes operating: (1) the disciples take part in the miracle, and so discipleship is prominent; (2) the omission of Mark 6:37b shows that though in Mark the disciples do not understand Jesus' words—"You [emphatic] give them something to eat" (v.16; i.e., they do not understand that they themselves should perform a miracle)—in Matthew they do understand but lack the requisite faith. This will not do.

1. Held is establishing a great deal on the basis of an omission in a book characterized by condensations and omissions, and he does not even raise the question whether Mark 6:37b was omitted for nontheological reasons.

2. Similarly, would a first-century reader of Matthew perusing this Gospel without critically comparing it with Mark at every turn suspect that Matthew was any easier on the disciples than Mark was at this point?

3. Neither "understanding" nor "faith" is explicitly raised in this pericope.

4. Jesus' words "you give them something to eat" are not easy to understand; but whatever they mean, it is possible that the disciples do not understand them, even in Matthew. If (and this is doubtful, though Held seems to assume it) Jesus means that they should perform such a miracle, then their response (v.17) betrays their complete misunderstanding; for miracles of creation cannot be thought to require something first. If on the other hand Jesus is simply making them responsible to

find out what is needed, buy food, or pray—if they remembered the miracle of the wine in Cana (John 2:1–11), they should have asked Jesus to meet the need, not send the people away—then their answer not only reveals limited vision but an approach to the problem betraying a lack of both understanding and faith.

5. The disciples' role in the miracle is limited to the organization and distribution needed for a crowd of thousands. This can scarcely mean that the disciples contribute to the miracle. Indeed, the story could more easily be taken as contrasting Jesus with his disciples in this miracle rather than elevating them to major roles.

18–21 Jesus alone multiplies the loaves and fishes. He gives the orders, gives thanks, and breaks the loaves (vv. 18–19). The actions—looking up to heaven, thanking God, and breaking the loaves—are normal for any head of a Jewish household (cf. Moore, *Judaism*, 2:216f.; SBK, 1:685f.; M *Berakoth* 6–8) and have no special Eucharistic significance. A common form of prayer before eating was "Blessed art thou, O Lord our God, King of the Universe, who bringest forth bread from the earth."

Matthew omits many details—the green grass, the groups of fifty and one hundred—but points out that all ate and were satisfied (v. 20), perhaps an anticipation of the messianic banquet, and at least evidence that there was lots to eat! The twelve baskets (*kophinos,* a stiff wicker basket) of leftovers and the size of the crowd (which might have been fifteen or twenty thousand total, if there were five thousand "men," v. 21) also support the latter point. But the "twelve basketfuls" may be significant: that there were twelve tribes and twelve apostles—emphasized in 19:28 —cannot be coincidence. Yet the precise significance is uncertain. The best suggestion may be that Messiah's supply is so lavish that even the scraps of his provision are enough to supply the needs of Israel, represented by the Twelve.

4. The walk on the water

14:22–33

> [22]Immediately Jesus made the disciples get into the boat and go on ahead of him to the other side, while he dismissed the crowd. [23]After he had dismissed them, he went up on a mountainside by himself to pray. When evening came, he was there alone, [24]but the boat was already a considerable distance from land, buffeted by the waves because the wind was against it.
>
> [25]During the fourth watch of the night Jesus went out to them, walking on the lake. [26]When the disciples saw him walking on the lake, they were terrified. "It's a ghost," they said, and cried out in fear.
>
> [27]But Jesus immediately said to them: "Take courage! It is I. Don't be afraid."
>
> [28]"Lord, if it's you," Peter replied, "tell me to come to you on the water."
>
> [29]"Come," he said.
>
> Then Peter got down out of the boat, walked on the water and came toward Jesus. [30]But when he saw the wind, he was afraid and, beginning to sink, cried out, "Lord, save me!"
>
> [31]Immediately Jesus reached out his hand and caught him. "You of little faith," he said, "why did you doubt?"
>
> [32]And when they climbed into the boat, the wind died down. [33]Then those who were in the boat worshiped him, saying, "Truly you are the Son of God."

Many scholars since Bultmann (*Synoptic Tradition,* p. 216) have surmised that two stories are woven together in Mark's account (6:45–52; cf. John 6:16–21)—an account of walking on the water and a later storm-calming miracle. But Scot

McKnight ("The Role of the Disciples in Matthew and Mark: A Redactional Study" [Master's thesis, Trinity Evangelical Divinity School, 1980], pp. 153–56) has shown the two to be integrally related. Some of the points arising from the differences between Mark and Matthew are briefly treated below. On the theological thrust of the passage, see John P. Heil, *Jesus Walking on the Sea* (Rome: Biblical Institute Press, 1981), who notes the association in the OT between chaos and sea. The stilling of the sea is therefore not only christological in orientation but also eschatological: Jesus is even now stilling the deep.

22 Why Jesus "made" (the verb is very strong and might be translated "compelled") the disciples go on ahead of him may be deduced from these bits of information: (1) he wanted to be alone to pray (v.23); (2) he wanted to escape the crowd with his disciples to get some rest (Mark 6:31–32); and (3) he may have dismissed the disciples forcefully to help tame a messianic uproar (John 6:15).

The omission of "Bethsaida" (Mark 6:45) in Matthew raises a difficult geographical problem. From the perspective of the site where the feeding took place, "to the other side" means the west shore; and that is where the boat ultimately landed, at Gennesaret (Mark 6:53 = Matt 14:34), a small triangular plain on the northwest shore of the lake (Kinnereth in the OT, 1 Kings 15:20). John 6:17 specifies the town of Capernaum. But Mark (6:45) says Jesus sent his disciples "on ahead of him to the other side [in the best MSS] to Bethsaida, while he dismissed the crowd." This was most likely Bethsaida Julius, just up the coast to the north, on the same side of the lake. The apparent discrepancy has prompted some MSS of Mark to omit "to the other side." The explanation that the boat was blown off course and landed on the west side does not explain the reference to Bethsaida, if this be Bethsaida Julius.

The problem is knotty. The simplest solution is that defended by Westcott and also by Morris on John—viz., Jesus sent the disciples off to cross the lake, with the command to wait for him on the eastern shore near Bethsaida Julius, but not beyond a certain time. The delay in waiting for Jesus would then account for the actual walking on the water not occurring till the fourth watch (v.25), i.e., after 3:00 A.M. A bit of syntax may support this view. Matthew's *heōs hou* plus the aorist subjunctive verb should normally be rendered "until" (as in 13:33; 17:9; 18:34; though cf. 26:36)—i.e., the disciples were "to go on ahead" (*proagein*) of him *until*, not *while*, he was free of the crowds, after which he hoped to join them, after some time alone in prayer; and they would then cross "to the other side." Mark (6:45) specifies Bethsaida but has *heōs* plus the indicative [in the best MSS]: the disciples were to go "to Bethsaida while," not "until," he sent the crowds away.

23–24 If this interpretation is correct, then it is the length of Jesus' prayer time that delays his coming and sends the disciples across the lake on their own. On the phrase "into the hills" (v.23), see on 5:1–2. The burden of Jesus' prayer is not revealed; but it is possible that the crowd's attempts to make him king (John 6:15) prompted him to seek his Father's face. If so, it is not a Matthean concern here (as is a similar crisis at 26:39).

NIV's "a considerable distance" (v.24) masks a considerable textual difficulty. The most likely reading is "many *stadia* [one *stadion* was about two hundred yards] from land" (Metzger, *Textual Commentary*, p. 37). In any event the boat was out towards the middle of the lake. If *enantios* is taken literally to mean "against," and not metaphorically to mean "hostile to," then the clause "the wind was against it," on the basis of the movements suggested above, refers to a strong wind from the west—a regular feature during the rainy season (Mark's "green grass" [6:39] confirms the season).

Many eager to find signs of the Matthean church take the boat as a symbol of that church—a community of disciples in stormy times (e.g., Bonnard, Schweizer). But if so, why did Peter want to step "out of the boat"?

25–27 The ancient Hebrew world divided the night from sunset to sunrise into three watches (Judg 7:19; Lam 2:19), but the Romans used four (v.25); and their influence prevailed in the evangelists' chronologies. Jesus' approach to the boat therefore occurred between 3:00 A.M. and 6:00 A.M. Matthew omits the difficult words "He was about to pass by them" (Mark 6:48), on which see Lane (*Mark*, pp. 235–36). The disciples were terrified (v.26), thinking they were seeing a *phantasma* ("apparition"; NIV, "ghost"; used in the NT only here and in Mark 6:49). There is no merit in the supposition that this is a transposed resurrection appearance. Jesus' "Take courage!" (v.27, as in 9:2, 22) and his "Don't be afraid" bracket the central reason for these calming exhortations: "It is I." Although the Greek *egō eimi* can have no more force than that, any Christian after the Resurrection and Ascension would also detect echoes of "I am," the decisive self-disclosure of God (Exod 3:14; Isa 43:10; 51:12). Once again we find Jesus revealing himself in a veiled way that will prove especially rich to Christians after his resurrection (see on 8:20; cf. Carson, "Christological Ambiguities").

28 Verses 28–32 have no parallel in the other Gospels; and two of the verbs ("to sink" and "to doubt") are used elsewhere in this Gospel only in exclusively Matthean sections (18:6 and 28:17 respectively). Perhaps Matthew was the first to commit this part of the story to writing, though the evidence from two verbs each used but once elsewhere is not commanding. This is the first of three scenes in which Peter receives special treatment, all in chapters 14–17 (cf. 16:13–23; 17:24–27). Benoit thinks that already in this story Peter gains primacy over the rest of the Twelve; but "if so, it is a primacy which reveals weakness in faith" (Hill, *Matthew*; similarly Bonnard). See further on v.31.

Peter's protasis ("if it's you") is a real condition, almost "since it's you." The request is bold, but the disciples had been trained for some time and given power to do exactly the sort of miracles Jesus was doing (10:1). What is more natural than for a fisherman who knew and respected the dangers of Galilee to want to follow Jesus in this new demonstration of supernatural power?

29–31 How far Peter got is unclear (cf. Notes), but at Jesus' command (v.29) he walked on the water (the plural "waters" in Greek may be in imitation of Hebrew, which uses "water" only in the plural; cf. Mark 9:22; John 3:23). But his outlook changed: when he saw the wind (synecdoche for the storm), he began to sink (v.30). It was not that he lost faith in himself (so Schniewind), but that his faith in Jesus, strong enough to get him out of the boat and walking on the water, was not strong enough to stand up to the storm. Therefore Jesus calls him a man "of little faith" (v.31; see on 6:30; 8:26; and esp. on 17:20); and his rhetorical question—"Why [cf. Notes] did you doubt?"—helps both Peter and the reader recognize that doubts and fears quickly disappear before a strict inquiry into their cause. Thus Peter in this pericope is both a good example and a bad example (cf. R.E. Brown, K.P. Donfried, and J. Reumann, edd., *Peter in the New Testament* [Minneapolis: Augsburg, 1973]. p. 83). His cry for help is natural, not a liturgical creation—Did not liturgy have to choose some formulas on which to build?—and Jesus' rescuing him is akin to God's salvation in the OT (Pss 18:16; 69:1–3; 144:7).

32–33 The climax of the story is not the stilling of the storm (v.32) but the confession and worship of the disciples: "Truly you are the Son of God" (v.33). This is the first time Jesus has been addressed by the disciples with this full title (cf. 16:16; 26:63; 27:40, 43, 54). But it already lurks behind 3:17 ("my Son"), and the devil has used it of Jesus (4:3, 6). It is most likely abbreviated to "the Son" in Jesus' self-references in 11:25–27. In the earlier passage (cf. also 3:17) we have seen how the title would most likely have been understood by the disciples at the time and how it would have been fleshed out in light of the Resurrection. On the absence of the Greek articles, see on 13:39.

The objection that v.33 so anticipates 16:16 as to make the latter anticlimactic is psychologically unconvincing. Similar reasoning would make the rebuke of Peter (16:21–23) following his grand confession (16:13–20) impossible or preclude defection from Jesus at his passion. The synoptic Gospels show us that the disciples understand only by degrees. Therefore their confessions of Christ must not be interpreted as if they had postresurrection understanding of him. One of the marks of the evangelists' fidelity to the historical development of the disciples' understanding of Christ lies precisely in this—that they show the disciples coming around to the same points again and again, each time at a deeper level of comprehension, but always with a mixture of misapprehension.

Exactly what the disciples meant by "Son of God" is uncertain. It is very doubtful that at this point they understood the title in a genuine ontological sense (though they would later). It is even less likely that they thought of Jesus as a *theios anēr* ("divine man"), allegedly an understood category in Hellenistic Judaism for various miracle workers. Carl Holladay (*Theios Anēr in Hellenistic Judaism: A Critique of the Use of This Category in New Testament Christology* [Missoula, Mont.: SP, 1977]) has shown the category was not well defined, that it had no fixed content in our period, and that it was not that common (contra Cullmann, *Christology*, p. 277; E. Lövestam, "Wunder und Symbolhandlung: Eine Studie über Matthäus 14, 28–31," *Kerygma und Dogma* 9 [1962], esp. p. 135; and many others). Probably they used the title in a messianic way (see on 3:17; 11:25–30), but still with superficial comprehension.

Many feel that vv.32–33 decisively alter Mark 6:51–52 (cf. esp. Bornkamm, *Tradition*, pp. 204ff.). Mark, it is alleged, leaves a final impression of confusion: no mention is made of the disciples' worship; instead they are amazed, they do not understand the previous miracle of the loaves, and their hearts are hardened. But Matthew portrays them worshiping, uttering an important christological confession, with no mention of amazement, hard hearts, or failure to understand. These are indeed undeniable differences; but the two evangelists are not so far apart as one might think.

1. Mark says they are "amazed"; but the verb used is often associated, not with fear, but with joyful worship (Lev 9:24 LXX; similarly the cognate noun, Luke 5:26). When used in Mark, the word usually, but not always, denotes amazement in response to some divine self-disclosure, but without fear. Why should they be afraid? The storm had ceased!

2. The comment in Mark 6:52 that the disciples' hearts were hardened does not refer to their amazement but to an underlying attitude that could allow for amazement after having seen so much of Jesus' work. The same point could be deduced from Matthew, even though it is not spelled out there.

3. Matthew may have omitted the censure in Mark 6:52 because he thought it would be repetitive: he had already shown the fear and lack of faith of the disciples (vv. 26–27). (On these points, cf. Meyer, Gaechter, and esp. Trotter.)

This is not to deny differences in emphasis between Matthew and Mark but to deny that the historical reality behind the two accounts is too small to sustain both emphases. Mark focuses on the disciples' "hardness" that continued despite another miracle like a previous one (cf. 8:23–27; Mark 4:35–41) by someone who could multiply loaves. Matthew hints at such unbelief through his narrative—he is capable of much more subtle characterization than Mark—and by the example of Peter (if he is a man of little faith, what about the rest of them?) but focuses explicitly on the disciples' confession of Jesus as God's Son. But even there, in view of later developments in Matthew, a reader might think that the disciples' confessions are much greater than their actual comprehension (see on 16:21–28).

Notes

29 The principal textual options are (1) καὶ ἦλθεν (kai ēlthen, "he came *or* went [to Jesus]") and (2) ἐλθεῖν (elthein, "to come," "to go"). The latter signifies intent, the former accomplishment. (NIV does not translate the word.) The external evidence is neatly divided. Metzger's argument (*Textual Commentary*, p. 37) that "he went" was changed to "to go" because the former seemed to say too much may be right; but one might argue instead that "to go" seems to say too little, since the text claims that Peter actually walked on the water; yet, when Peter began to sink, Jesus needed only reach out his hand to seize him, which implies Peter had walked almost all the way.

31 Εἰς τί (eis ti; "Why," NIV), probably equivalent to לָמָה (lemâh, "why"), is extraordinary: the customary form is διὰ τί (dia ti, "why"), as in 9:14. Turner (*Syntax*, pp. 266f.) detects a subtle difference: the latter means "because of what" = "why," whereas the former means "in order to what" = "why"; and in this instance the latter nuance in "why" makes good sense. Jesus does not ask "because of what" Peter doubted (any fool could see that!) but for what purpose, to what end: what was the point of his doubt, having come so far?

5. Transitional summary of constant and unavoidable ministry

14:34–36

34When they had crossed over, they landed at Gennesaret. 35And when the men of that place recognized Jesus, they sent word to all the surrounding country. People brought all their sick to him 36and begged him to let the sick just touch the edge of his cloak, and all who touched him were healed.

34–36 Gennesaret (v. 34) was the fertile plain on the northwest side of the lake (see on v. 22), vividly described by Josephus (War III, 516–21[x.8]). The crowds' instant recognition of Jesus (v. 35) showed the extent of his ministry; again, word-of-mouth reports led to crowds (cf. 3:5; 4:24). Like the woman with the hemorrhage (9:20–22), the people were satisfied if only they could touch the edge of his cloak (v.36); and even that degree of faith brought thorough healing (the preposition compounded with the verb in *diesōthēsan* ["were healed"] is perfective).

This little pericope does three things: (1) it again stresses the sweeping extent of Jesus' public ministry (cf. 4:23–25; 8:16; 9:35–36); (2) it also shows that Jesus' ministry extended to all the people, though his close disciples had special access to him and his more intimate instruction; and (3) because the stricter groups, such as the Pharisees and the Essenes, counted it an abomination to rub shoulders in a crowd— one never knew what ceremonial uncleanness one might contract—Jesus' unconcern about such things neatly sets the stage for the confrontation over clean and unclean (15:1–20). As in 8:1–4; 9:20–22, he himself cannot become unclean: instead, he makes clean.

6. *Jesus and the tradition of the elders*

15:1–20

¹Then some Pharisees and teachers of the law came to Jesus from Jerusalem and asked, ²"Why do your disciples break the tradition of the elders? They don't wash their hands before they eat!"

³Jesus replied, "And why do you break the command of God for the sake of your tradition? ⁴For God said, 'Honor your father and mother' and 'Anyone who curses his father or mother must be put to death.' ⁵But you say that if a man says to his father or mother, 'Whatever help you might otherwise have received from me is a gift devoted to God,' ⁶he is not to 'honor his father' with it. Thus you nullify the word of God for the sake of your tradition. ⁷You hypocrites! Isaiah was right when he prophesied about you:

⁸" 'These people honor me with their lips,
    but their hearts are far from me.
⁹They worship me in vain;
    their teachings are but rules taught by men.' "

¹⁰Jesus called the crowd to him and said, "Listen and understand. ¹¹What goes into a man's mouth does not make him 'unclean,' but what comes out of his mouth, that is what makes him 'unclean.' "

¹²Then the disciples came to him and asked, "Do you know that the Pharisees were offended when they heard this?"

¹³He replied, "Every plant that my heavenly Father has not planted will be pulled up by the roots. ¹⁴Leave them; they are blind guides. If a blind man leads a blind man, both will fall into a pit."

¹⁵Peter said, "Explain the parable to us."

¹⁶"Are you still so dull?" Jesus asked them. ¹⁷"Don't you see that whatever enters the mouth goes into the stomach and then out of the body? ¹⁸But the things that come out of the mouth come from the heart, and these make a man 'unclean.' ¹⁹For out of the heart come evil thoughts, murder, adultery, sexual immorality, theft, false testimony, slander. ²⁰These are what make a man 'unclean'; but eating with unwashed hands does not make him 'unclean.' "

Controversies become sharper and more theological as Matthew's narrative moves on. This controversy is of great importance in grasping Jesus' understanding of the law. Some have tended to draw radical conclusions as to Matthew's distinctive emphases by comparing this pericope with Mark 7:1–23 (e.g., Bornkamm, *Tradition,* pp. 86–89). The most prominent differences between Matthew and Mark are these: Matthew omits Mark 7:3–4, adds Matthew 15:12–14, omits Mark's interpretation

(7:19) that Jesus made all foods clean, and adds Matthew 15:20b to keep the focus on food eaten with washed or unwashed hands. Thus many argue that whereas in Mark Jesus annuls the law, in Matthew he does not do more than annul one small bit of Halakah (rabbinic interpretation affecting conduct). These issues must be kept in mind in interpreting the text more closely. (See esp. Bank's balanced study, *Jesus*, pp. 132–46.)

1 "Then" (see on 2:7) certain Pharisees (see on 3:7, and Introduction, section 11.f) and teachers of the law (see on 2:3) came to Jesus "from Jerusalem." These did not belong to the many such leaders scattered throughout the land but came from Jerusalem. They would probably therefore be held in special esteem (cf. SBK, 1:-691). But from Matthew's perspective, they were probably a quasi-official deputation (cf. John 1:19) and a source of Jesus' most virulent opposition.

2 As in 9:14, the attack on Jesus comes through the behavior of his disciples, though elsewhere we learn that the disciples reflected his own practices (Luke 11:37–41). Matthew is much more condensed than Mark, for two reasons: (1) unlike Mark, Matthew does not need to explain Jewish customs to his readers; and (2) Mark deals with an array of Pharisaic Halakic regulations (Mark 7:1–3), whereas Matthew stresses the one issue of eating food with unwashed hands. It must be emphasized that this distinction says nothing about the sharpness of the Pharisees' attack on Jesus' response but only about the concentration of issues (see on v.20). (For other differences between Matthew and Mark, cf. Banks, *Jesus*, pp. 132–34.)

The "tradition of the elders," the "tradition of men" (Mark 7:8; Col 2:8), "your tradition" (Matt 15:3, 6; Mark 7:9, 13), and the "traditions of the fathers" (Gal 1:14) refer to the great corpus of oral teaching that commented on the law and interpreted it in detailed rules of conduct, often recording the diverse opinions of competing rabbis. This tradition in Jesus' time was largely oral and orally transmitted; but the Pharisees, though not the Sadducees, viewed it as having authority very nearly equal to the canon. It was later codified under Rabbi Judah the Prince (c. A.D. 135–200) to form the Mishnah (cf. SBK, 1:691–95; TDNT, 6:661f.; Moore, *Judaism*, 1:251–62). One entire tractate, *Yadaim*, deals with "hands" (i.e., *yāḏayim*), specifying such details as how much water must be used for effective ceremonial purification: e.g., "If a man poured water over the one hand with a single rinsing, his hand is clean; but if over both hands with a single rinsing, R. Meir declares them unclean unless he pours over them a quarter-log or more" (M *Yadaim* 2:1).

3–6 Jesus' words, in slightly different order in Mark, are less a response than a counterattack. He made a fundamental distinction between the authority of "the command of God" (as found in Scripture) and the Halakic tradition; and he insisted that the Pharisees and teachers of the law were guilty of breaking the former for the sake of (lit., "on account of") the latter (v.3). The two texts cited are Exodus 20:12 and 21:17 (cf. also Deut 27:16; Prov 1:8; 20:20; 30:17; 1 Tim 5:3), and their point is clear enough. The English verb "curses" (v.4) is too narrow: *kakologeō* means "to insult," "to speak evil of," "to revile" (used in the NT only here and at Mark 7:10; 9:39; Acts 19:9). The one who speaks evil of his parents must surely be put to death (on the construction of the latter clause, cf. Zerwick, par. 60).

"But you" (v.5)—the "you" is emphatic—have evaded through your traditions God's command (v.6), broadly interpreted by Jesus to lay responsibility on children to take responsibility for their parents. Greed could keep a son from discharging this duty by simply declaring the goods or money that might have gone to support his parents *korbān*, a gift devoted to God (cf. Lev 27:9, 16), set aside for the temple treasury (cf. M *Nedarim*, esp. 1, 9, 11; cf. SBK, 1:711–17). Such a vow could be annulled in various ways. It would not mean that one could use the goods or money in question but that he could withhold it from his parents (for legal questions, cf. Derrett, *NT Studies*, 1:112–17). Thus Halakic tradition was nullifying the word of God (the textual variants "law of God" or "command of God" are not critical).

A further observation may be important, though it should not be overstressed. For Jesus and the kingdom, a man must be willing to put aside family loyalties and love Jesus supremely (10:37–39). Yet here Jesus accuses the Pharisees and teachers of the law of breaking God's command when they use similar arguments to support vows devoting certain gifts to God. Apparently neither Jesus nor Matthew sees any inconsistency here, because in their view Jewish Halakah cannot take precedence over the law, whereas Jesus and the kingdom may do so because they "fulfill" it. Other factors are also relevant. The Halakic regulations Jesus opposed permitted a son sometimes to act against his parents, whereas 10:37–39 presupposes family opposition against disciples. Not only is the rule different, but the victim is also different.

7–9 This is the first recorded instance of Jesus' calling the Pharisees and teachers of the law hypocrites (v.7; see on 6:2): Luke 11–12 probably refers to a later time. The charge was that, while they made a show of devotion to God, their religious traditions took precedence over God's will. In referring to Isaiah 29:13, Jesus did not say, Isaiah was right when he said . . . and now I make a secondary application, but, "Isaiah was right when he prophesied about you." Yet Isaiah 29:13 is addressed to men of Isaiah's day. What then did Jesus mean? There are three points of contact: (1) in each case those warned were Jews, (2) from Jerusalem, (3) with a religion characterized by externals that sometimes vitiated principle. Moreover the Jews of Jesus' day thought of themselves as preserving ancient traditions; but Jesus said that what they were actually preserving was the spirit of those whom Isaiah criticized long before. The thought is close to, though different in categories from, 23:29–32.

The quotation essentially follows the shorter form of the Septuagint (for details, cf. Gundry, *Use of OT*, pp. 14–16). The burden of the Scripture Jesus quotes is that the Pharisees and teachers of the law have displaced the true religion of the heart (v.8), of the entire personality and will, with a religion of form. Therefore their worship is vain (v.9) and their teachings their own with nothing of God's authority behind them.

The judgment is so sweeping that it calls in question not only the Jews' Halakah but their entire worship and teaching.

10–11 Jesus' sharpest barb against the Pharisees and teachers of the law had been private. Now he teaches the crowd the same things (v.10). These two verses also answer the Pharisees' question (v.2) directly, not just by countercharge (vv.3–9).

What Jesus now says, the disciples call a "parable" (v.15; so also Mark 7:17; see on 13:3a). In presenting it to the crowd (v.10), Jesus exhorts them to understand; for the parable was not meant to be cryptic, though only few seemed to have grasped it at the time, and the disciples had trouble with it (vv.15–16). This confirms our earlier comments on Jesus' parables (13:10–17, 34–35).

The verb *koinoi* ("makes [him] 'unclean' "), here used (v.11) for the first of thirteen times in the NT, literally means "to render common"; but because participation in what was common was for a practicing Jew to become ceremonially unclean, the customary NT meaning is very similar.

Perhaps Mark 7:15 is a shade more generalized than Matthew's form of the "parable" (v.11), but the differences are slight. "[If] Matthew really wished to exclude the kind of laxity represented by his Markan source, it is hard to see why he kept the potentially dangerous parable around which this whole controversy is constructed" (C.E. Carlston, "The Things That Defile (Mk 7.14) and the Law in Matthew and Mark," NTS 15 [1968–69]: 77). The language is so general it lets in everything Mark allows, even though the final application is to food eaten with unwashed hands (v.20). The form of the argument is from this principle to that application, the former being broader than the latter. Thus, though Matthew omits Mark's parenthetical interpretation—"(In saying this, Jesus declared all foods 'clean')" (Mark 7:19b)—yet retention of the "parable" and its interpretation (vv.17–20) lead precisely to that conclusion.

12–14 These verses are peculiar to Matthew and reflect what took place after Jesus and his disciples had retired from the crowd and entered the house (cf. Mark 7:17). The disciples' question shows that the Pharisees understood enough of Jesus' parable to take offense (v.12). The disciples' request to have the parable explained (v.15) does not reveal them as being more obtuse than the Pharisees but shows that, in common with most Jews at the time, they held the Pharisees in high regard and therefore wanted to be certain of exactly what Jesus had said that had offended them so badly. Therefore vv.12–14 are not out of place. Jesus must disillusion his disciples as to the reliability of the Pharisees and teachers of the law as spiritual guides, as well as explain the parable. This is not to say that these verses turn the entire section (vv.1–20) into a personal attack on the Pharisees rather than on their use of the law (so Kilpatrick, *Origins*, p. 180); for the chief point for which they are blamed relates to their misunderstanding of the law.

Jesus uses two images. The first (v.13) predicts the rooting up of any plant the heavenly Father has not planted. Israel often saw herself as a plant God had planted (Ps 1:3; Isa 60:21; cf. 1QS 8:5; CD 1:7; 1 Enoch 10:16; Pss Sol 14:2), and the prophets turned the image against them (Isa 5:1–7). Thus Jesus is not saying that every false doctrine will be rooted up (so Broadus) but that the Pharisees, the leaders of the Jewish people, are not truly part of God's planting. This shocking idea has already been hinted at in Matthew (3:9; 8:11–12) and will recur.

The second image (v.14) may depend on a title some Jewish leaders apparently took on themselves. They had the law, they reasoned, and therefore were fit to serve as "guides of the blind" (Rom 2:19; cf. Luke 6:39). This Jesus disputes. In his view they were "blind guides of the blind" (NIV mg., so the most likely variant; cf. Metzger, *Textual Commentary*, p. 39); and "both will fall into a pit" (cf. also Luke 6:39). Though the Pharisees and teachers of the law had the scrolls and interpreted them in the synagogues, this does not mean that they really understood them. On the contrary, they were blind and failed to comprehend the Scriptures they claimed to follow. Jesus' denunciation presupposes that anyone who truly understands the "word of God" (v.6) will discern who he is and follow him (cf. John 5:39–40). The Pharisees did not follow Jesus; so they did not understand and follow the Scriptures.

15–16 Peter speaks on behalf of the other disciples (v. 15): Jesus' answer shows that the "parable" to which Peter refers is v. 11. The disciples' failure to understand shocks Jesus. (1) *Kai* ("also")—are you, too, "still so dull?" Dullness might be understandable in others, but in you disciples? (2) *Akmēn* ("still," used only here in Matthew) may mean either "Are you *still* without understanding?" (NIV; Hill, McNeile) or "Are you still—*but not for long*—without understanding?" (Schlatter). The context strongly favors the former; and therefore the question, far from toning down the disciples' failure to grasp Jesus' teaching (so Schweizer), magnifies its enormity.

17–20 Verse 17 explains that "what goes into a man's mouth" (v. 11) is merely food, which passes through the body and is excreted (lit., "is cast into a latrine"). On the sanitary conditions of the time, cf. Edward Neufeld, "Hygiene Conditions in Ancient Israel," *Biblical Archaeologist* 34 (1971): 42–66. Verses 18–20 explain that "what comes out of a man's mouth" (v. 11), and what makes him unclean, comes from his heart (see on 12:34–35). Matthew's list of the heart's products (v. 19) is shorter than Mark's. After the first, "evil thoughts," the list follows the same order as the sixth and seventh commandments, followed by *porneia* ("sexual immorality"; see on 19:3–12), the order of the eighth and ninth commandments, and finally "slander," which probably includes blasphemy (cf. 12:31). The list itself negates (as Banks [*Jesus*, pp. 143–44] points out) Kilpatrick's suggestion that Matthew has transformed Mark's principle of morals into a precept of law (*Origins*, p. 38).

It would be puerile to ask how every item on the list results directly in defiling speech. The point, as in 12:34–35, is that what a man truly *is* affects what he says and does. Jesus presupposes that the heart is essentially evil (cf. 7:11). But the burden of this pericope is not to be pure on the inside and forget the externals but that what ultimately defiles a man is what he really is. Jesus is not spiritualizing the OT but insisting that true religion must deal with the nature of man and not with mere externals.

Because v. 20b does not occur in Mark, many have thought it to be Matthew's way of limiting the application of the controversy to the single question of eating food with unwashed hands. Two things militate against this view: (1) Jesus deals with a broad principle touching *all* foods and applies it to this situation, but the application can be no more valid than the broader principle on which it is based; and (2) Matthew frequently ends his pericopes by referring back to the questions that precipitate them (see on 12:45; 14:12; 16:11–12; 17:13); so v. 20b requires no more explanation than that.

The way one interprets this pericope relates to a larger understanding of how Matthew deals with Jesus' attitude to the law and the situation in his own church.

1. It goes beyond the evidence to argue, as does Ernst Käsemann (*Essays on New Testament Themes* [London: SCM, 1964], p. 101), that Jesus now abrogates the distinction between the sacred and the profane; or, as Lohmeyer (*Matthäus*) does, that Jesus now distinguishes "word of God" from "word of man" even within Scripture itself; or, as McNeile and R. Walker (p. 142) do, that Jesus now undermines, as in Mark, *all* Mosaic distinctions between clean and unclean. He deals, principially, with the clean-unclean distinctions as to foods and applies this principle to foods eaten with unwashed hands.

2. On the other hand, it does not go as far as the exegetical evidence to pit

Matthew against Mark so that the former, unlike the latter, is seen as absolutely restricting Jesus' words to the single problem of foods eaten with unwashed hands. Verses 3, 7–9, 11, 14, 17–19 cannot be taken so narrowly.

3. The approach that sees a Jewish-Christian church behind this pericope—whether still related to the synagogue or recently separated from it—is exegetically unsatisfying. Matthew is slightly more cautious than Mark and perhaps a shade less explicit, but that is not solid enough evidence to support Barth's reconstruction of the Matthean church (in Bornkamm, *Tradition*). Though Ebionite groups doubtless flourished, Matthew neither belonged to one, nor anything like one; for no Ebionite could write vv. 11, 17–20.

4. Banks (*Jesus*, pp. 140–41) contends that if Jesus explicitly repudiated the food laws contained in Leviticus 11 and Deuteronomy 14 (Dan 1:8–16; cf. Jud 10:5; Tobit 1:10–11), then the hesitations of the primitive church on the issue (Acts 10:14–15; 15:28–29; Rom 14:14; Gal 2:11–13) are inexplicable. But he avoids falling into the trap of thinking that Jesus' original teaching on this matter was no more than Semitic hyperbole, with the meaning that "pollutions from within are more serious than pollutions from without" (Banks, *Jesus*, p. 141; cf. Hos 6:6). Rather, he holds that Jesus' approach neither attacked nor affirmed the law but moved on a different level, expressing "an entirely new understanding of what does and does not constitute defilement" (Banks, *Jesus*, p. 141). Abrogation was latent within the saying, but not more. This is a shade too timid.

The hesitations of the early church regarding the food laws are not inexplicable: a great deal of what Jesus taught became *progressively* clear to the church after the Resurrection and did not immediately gain universal assent. The same is true of Jesus' words on Gentile conversion, on the Great Commission, on the delay of the Parousia. What can be said is that Jesus' teaching in this pericope (and in its Markan parallel) opens up an entirely fresh approach to the question of the law. It does not simply subordinate the ritual to the moral (these are not the categories appealed to); instead it discounts the Pharisees' oral tradition while defending the law (vv. 3–6) and yet insists that real "cleanness" is of the heart, so discounting some of the law's formal requirements.

The only way to explain these phenomena is the one Matthew has already developed (see esp. 5:21–48): Jesus insists that the true direction in which the OT law points is precisely what he teaches, what he is, and what he inaugurates. He has fulfilled the law; therefore whatever prescriptive force it continues to have is determined by its relationship to him, not vice versa. It is within this framework that Jesus' teaching in this pericope theologically anticipates Romans 14:14–18; 1 Corinthians 10:31; 1 Timothy 4:4; Titus 1:15, and that historically it took some time for the ramifications of Jesus' teaching to be thoroughly grasped, even by his own disciples. Once again it is a mark of Matthew's fidelity to the historical facts that he does not overstate Jesus' teaching, and a mark of his literary skill that he does not find it necessary to draw Mark's parenthetical conclusion (Mark 7:19b), even though he obviously shares it.

5. It follows that Jesus not only rejected the Pharisees and teachers of the law as authentic interpreters of Scripture (esp. vv. 12–14) but assigned that role finally and absolutely to himself (cf. 5:21–48). Historically the conflict between Jesus and the traditional interpreters of Scripture would wax fierce and would ultimately bring him to the Cross; theologically the fundamental distinctions between a Christian and a Jewish reading of Scripture must be traced to Jesus himself.

6. What concerned Jesus was not so much the form of religion as human nature. He wanted to see people transformed and their hearts renewed (cf. 6:1–33; 12:34–35; comments on 25:31–46) because he came to save his people from their sins (1:21).

7. More healings (15:21–31)

a. The Canaanite woman

15:21–28

> ²¹Leaving that place, Jesus withdrew to the region of Tyre and Sidon. ²²A Canaanite woman from that vicinity came to him, crying out, "Lord, Son of David, have mercy on me! My daughter is suffering terribly from demon-possession."
> ²³Jesus did not answer a word. So his disciples came to him and urged him, "Send her away, for she keeps crying out after us."
> ²⁴He answered, "I was sent only to the lost sheep of Israel."
> ²⁵The woman came and knelt before him. "Lord, help me!" she said.
> ²⁶He replied, "It is not right to take the children's bread and toss it to their dogs."
> ²⁷"Yes, Lord," she said, "but even the dogs eat the crumbs that fall from their masters' table."
> ²⁸Then Jesus answered, "Woman, you have great faith! Your request is granted." And her daughter was healed from that very hour.

It is by no means clear which way—if at all—the literary dependency of this pericope on Mark (cf. 7:24–30) runs. (For the most recent analysis, see E.A. Russell, "The Canaanite Woman and the Gospels," in Livingston, 2:263ff.) Of greater interest is the placing of this pericope in both Gospels. It not only records Jesus' withdrawal from the opposition of the Pharisees and teachers of the law (cf. 14:13) but contrasts their approach to the Messiah with that of this woman. They belong to the covenant people but take offense at the conduct of Jesus' disciples, challenge his authority, and are so defective in understanding the Scriptures that they show themselves not to be plants the heavenly Father has planted. But this woman is a pagan, a descendant of ancient enemies, and with no claim on the God of the covenant. Yet in the end she approaches the Jewish Messiah and with great faith asks only for grace; and her request is granted (cf. 8:5–13).

This essentially christological approach to the pericope is more defensible than the one that sees in these verses guidance for Matthew's Jewish church in its relations to Gentiles: they could not claim immediate access to salvation, but exceptions would be made where there was deep faith (Hill, *Matthew*). This begs too many issues. Would they, or would they not, then have to conform to all Jewish law? How do we know so much of Matthew's church (cf. Introduction, section 2)? What this explains to Matthew's readers (Matthew's "church," though this designation may give the wrong impression of a group hermetically sealed off from other churches) is not what attitude they ought to adopt toward Gentile evangelism, whether opposition or occasional acquiescence, but rather "how we got from there to here"—i.e., how the development of redemptive history changed the position of God's people from late OT concepts to the full Christian concept. This story is a step along the way, focused on the self-disclosure of the Messiah and his attitudes to his own mission, his pivotal role in salvation history. But if Matthew's Jewish-Christian readers want to learn more about what their attitude should be toward Gentile evangelism, they must also read the words of the resurrected and glorified Jesus after the climax of his self-disclosure (28:18-20).

The worst feature of many redaction-critical attempts to reconstruct Matthew's church and its problems is the implicit elimination of the salvation history insisted on by the Gospels themselves, a persistent refusal to believe that the evangelists are interested in writing about Jesus to explain him, and therefore "how we got from there to here," rather than to address their "churches" from the perspective of a theology infinitely flexible and shaped by contemporary problems alone. Once the perspective of redemptive history is granted, we may cheerfully acknowledge that the evangelists include material and write it down in such a way that it will prove of interest and/or use (not necessarily both) to their readers. But the loss of the historical perspective from which the evangelists claim to write leads to an unnecessary and basic distortion of their Gospels.

21 Jesus "withdraws" (as in 2:12, 22; 4:12; 12:15; 14:13) to the region of Tyre and Sidon, cities on the Mediterranean coast lying about thirty and fifty miles respectively from Galilee. Kilpatrick (*Origins*, pp. 130ff.) notes Matthew's interest in them (cf. 11:21-24) and suggests that Matthew and his church were there—a possibility, but without much supporting evidence. "The vicinity of Tyre" (Mark 7:24) leads us to ask whether Jesus actually entered the region of Tyre and Sidon or went only to the border—which would mean the woman came out to meet him. But v.21 and Mark 7:31 make it clear that Jesus left Galilee and entered pagan territory. According to Mark 3:8 and Luke 6:17, some crowds had come from Tyre and Sidon to be helped by him; but there he would hardly be known.

22 The introductory *idou* (lit., "behold," untranslated in NIV) probably points to the extraordinary nature of the story. Mark (7:26) calls the woman "a Greek [i.e., a non-Jewess], born in Syrian Phoenicia." Matthew's use of the old term "Canaanite" shows that he cannot forget her ancestry: now a descendant of Israel's ancient enemies comes to the Jewish Messiah for blessing. *Exelthousa* (lit., "coming out") does not mean that she came out of that pagan region to meet Jesus (see on v.21) but either that her ancestry was there or that she had left her home (Lohmeyer, Bonnard). Her calling Jesus "Son of David" shows some recognition of Jesus as the Messiah who would heal the people (see discussion at 9:27; 12:23); "Lord" is ambiguous (see on 8:2). For other instances of demon possession in this Gospel, see on 4:24; 8:16, 28, 33; 9:32; 12:22.

23-24 That these verses are peculiar to Matthew is not surprising. Matthew's Jewish readers would be intensely interested in Jesus' doing a miracle to aid a Gentile, on Gentile territory. Mark's Gentile readers would, however, have needed much explanation had this saying been included in his Gospel. Jesus had healed Gentiles before (4:24-25; 8:5-13), but always in Jewish territory.

Jesus' silence does not quiet the woman; so his disciples beg him to stop her persistent cries (v.23). If they mean "Send her away without helping her," either they suppose she is annoying him or they themselves are being annoyed. But their words could also be taken to mean "Send her away with her request granted" (so Meyer, Benoit). Indeed only this interpretation makes sense, because v.24 gives a reason for Jesus' not helping her rather than for not sending her away.

Bultmann (*Synoptic Tradition*, p. 155), Arens (pp. 315-19), and others judge

Jesus' answer (v.24) to be inauthentic, largely on the grounds that "I was sent" sounds Johannine and thus for them is late and inauthentic. Regardless of this similarity the particularism of the thought supports its authenticity, since the church, even before Paul, engaged in Gentile evangelism and could therefore hardly be thought to have created the saying (cf. Jeremias, *Promise*, pp. 26–28; Bonnard; Hill). The thought echoes 10:6, where the same language is used (lit., "the lost sheep of the house of Israel"). But even chapter 10 recognizes that one day the mission of the disciples will take them to Gentiles (10:18). But that time was not yet. Meanwhile Jesus, doing the Father's will (cf. 11:27), recognized that his own mission was to Israel; and he delighted to do the will of him who sent him.

Either "the lost sheep of the house of Israel" means "the lost sheep *among* the house of Israel"—i.e., some in the house of Israel are not lost—or "the lost sheep *who are* the house of Israel"—i.e., all Israel, regarded as lost sheep. The latter is correct, for in the identical expression at 10:6 the contrast is, not between these lost sheep and others in Israel who are not lost, but between these lost sheep and Gentiles or Samaritans. Flender (pp. 23ff.) errs in the opposite direction, holding that Jesus sees himself gathering *all* Israel, not just a remnant. But Jesus is not so naive (cf. 7:13–14; 10:17–22, 34–37), for there is a categorical distinction between a target people and a converted people.

It appears, then, that Jesus wanted his disciples and the Canaanite woman to recognize "that His activities were circumscribed not only by the inevitable limitations of His manhood, but by the specific part that He had been called to play during His brief earthly life" (Tasker). True, he was "Son of David," as the woman said; but that did not give her the right to enjoy the benefits covenanted to the Jews. The kingdom must first be offered to them. The thought is like John 4:22: "Salvation is from the Jews." The Samaritan woman, like this Canaanite woman, had to recognize this—even if a time was coming when true worship would transcend such categories (John 4:23–26).

25 The woman knelt (see on 2:2; 8:2) before Jesus (probably the imperfect is used to make the action more vivid) and cried, as only the mother of an afflicted child could, "Lord, help me!"

26 Still Jesus made certain that she grasped the historic distinction between Jew and Gentile. Jesus' short aphorism supposes that the "children" are the people of Israel and the "dogs" are Gentiles. The "crumbs" (v.27) do not designate the quantity of blessing bestowed; and still less does the table refer to the Eucharist (rightly Bonnard). The question is one of precedence: the children get fed *first*.

27 The woman's answer is masterly. "Yes, Lord," she agrees, "for even [not 'but even,' NIV; cf. Notes] the dogs eat the crumbs that fall from their masters' table." Those two words "for even" reveal immense wisdom and faith. She does not phrase her answer as a counterstroke but as a profound acquiescence with the further implications of "dogs." She does not argue that her needs make her an exception, or that she has a right to Israel's covenanted mercies, or that the mysterious ways of divine election and justice are unfair. She abandons mention of Jesus as "Son of David" and simply asks for help; "and she is confident that even if she is not entitled to sit down as a guest at Messiah's table, Gentile 'dog' that she is, yet at least she may be allowed to receive a crumb of the uncovenanted mercies of God" (Tasker; cf.

Schlatter). There may be no significance to the use of the diminutive "dogs" (*kynaria*) in vv.26–27, because in Hellenistic Greek the diminutive force is often entirely lacking; but if there is such force here, it does not make the dogs more acceptable—i.e., "pet dogs" or "house dogs" as opposed to "wild dogs"—but more dependent: i.e., little, helpless dogs eat little scraps of food (*psichiōn*—equally diminutive in form). As does Paul in Romans 9–11, the woman preserves Israel's historical privilege over against all radical idealization or spiritualization of Christ's work, yet perceives that grace is freely given to the Gentiles.

28 The faith that simply seeks mercy is honored. Again Jesus speaks, this time with emotion (cf. Notes); and the woman's daughter is healed "from that very hour" (cf. 8:13; 9:22). The Clementine homilies (end of the second century) call the woman Justa and her daughter Berenice, but the names may have been invented.

Notes

27 The words καὶ γάρ (*kai gar;* "but even") are used approximately thirty-nine times in the NT. In no other place does NIV render them adversatively ("but even"); and there is no justification for doing so here. The natural translation is "for even." The Markan parallel (Mark 7:28) exhibits far more variants; but the correct reading almost certainly omits both γάρ (*gar,* "for") and ἀλλά (*alla,* "but") in favor of a simple "Lord, even the dogs," whose precise nuance is a shade more ambiguous.

28 The ejaculation ὦ (*ō,* "O [woman]," omitted in D) has emotional force (cf. BDF, par. 146 [1*b*], which contrasts with use of the vocative "woman" without the word in Luke 22:57; John 2:4; 4:21 et al.), as seems usual in the Hellenistic Greek of the NT, with the exception of Acts, which prefers the classical usage (cf. Zerwick, par. 35).

b. *The many*

15:29–31

> [29]Jesus left there and went along the Sea of Galilee. Then he went up on a mountainside and sat down. [30]Great crowds came to him, bringing the lame, the blind, the crippled, the mute and many others, and laid them at his feet; and he healed them. [31]The people were amazed when they saw the mute speaking, the crippled made well, the lame walking and the blind seeing. And they praised the God of Israel.

Mark 7:31–37 here tells of the healing of a deaf mute; Matthew provides a summary of more extensive healings (cf. T.J. Ryan, "Matthew 15:29–31: An Overlooked Summary," *Horizons* 5 [1978]: 31–42; for other summaries, cf. 4:23–25; 9:35–38; 12:15–21; 14:14–36). Ryan points out the echoes of Isaiah 29:18–19; 35:5–6. Of greater consequence is the geographical location. Contrary to Bonnard, these healings and the subsequent feeding of the four thousand take place in Gentile territory —viz., in the Decapolis (see below). Jesus had already displayed the power of the kingdom here (8:28–34). His reluctance to respond to the request of the Canaanite woman (vv.21–28) must therefore turn not just on her being a Gentile, or on this being Gentile territory (cf. 8:28–34), but more on her appealing to him as Son of

David and on his being conscious of his primary aims during his earthly ministry. Because of her faith, making appeal to his mercy, the woman receives the "crumbs." Then lest anyone think the crumbs betray a restricted blessing for Gentiles, Matthew immediately tells us of the feeding of four thousand Gentiles. If Jesus' aphorism about the children and the dogs merely reveals *priority* in feeding, then it is hard to resist the conclusion that in the feeding of the four thousand Jesus is showing that blessing for the Gentiles is beginning to dawn.

29–31 "Jesus left there" (v.29) refers to the region of Tyre and Sidon (v.21). But to which (not "along" which, as in NIV; cf. Moule, *Idiom Book*, pp. 50f.) side of the Sea of Galilee did he go? If to the west, he was in Jewish Galilee; if to the east, in predominantly Gentile Decapolis (on which see on 4:25). Mark 7:31 has Jesus traveling north from the vicinity of Tyre to Sidon, and then south and east to the Decapolis on the southeastern side of the lake, still outside Herod's jurisdiction (cf. Matt 14:13). This places him not far from where he had healed the demoniacs and may account for the growing crowds.

But all this depends on reading Mark into Matthew. Could it be that Matthew simply does not care about where Jesus was at this point? No; the evidence suggests rather that he assumes it: (1) the clause "they praised the God of Israel." (v.31) could be naturally said only by Gentiles; (2) the remoteness of the place (v.33) suggests the eastern side of the lake; and (3) the number of "basketfuls of broken pieces" (v.37) left over avoids the symbolic "twelve" (cf. 14:20). More incidental bits of information point in the same direction (see below).

Jesus did many miracles over the course of several days (cf. vv.30–32). The order of the ailments varies in the MSS, possibly owing in part to homoeoteleuton (cf. further Metzger, *Textual Commentary*, p. 40). (For "into the hills" [v.29], see on 5:1–2.)

8. *The feeding of the four thousand*

15:32–39

> [32]Jesus called his disciples to him and said, "I have compassion for these people; they have already been with me three days and have nothing to eat. I do not want to send them away hungry, or they may collapse on the way."
>
> [33]His disciples answered, "Where could we get enough bread in this remote place to feed such a crowd?"
>
> [34]"How many loaves do you have?" Jesus asked.
>
> "Seven," they replied, "and a few small fish."
>
> [35]He told the crowd to sit down on the ground. [36]Then he took the seven loaves and the fish, and when he had given thanks, he broke them and gave them to the disciples, and they in turn to the people. [37]They all ate and were satisfied. Afterward the disciples picked up seven basketfuls of broken pieces that were left over. [38]The number of those who ate was four thousand, besides women and children. [39]After Jesus had sent the crowd away, he got into the boat and went to the vicinity of Magadan.

Many scholars hold that this miracle, reported here and in Mark 8:1–10, is a doublet of the feeding of the five thousand, though there is little agreement about why Matthew should include a doublet here. A few have thought the requirements of a liturgical calendar led him to do this—a theory lacking in substantial evidence. More common is the view that Mark put in the doublet to affirm that Gentiles as well as Jews will enjoy the messianic banquet. "The repetition of the story therefore serves theology, not history" (Hill, *Matthew*).

This is not very satisfactory; for if even one of Mark's or Matthew's readers knew there was only one miraculous feeding, *and that of Jews,* the point about the Gentiles would be lost and the credibility of the two evangelists impugned. The events were within the lifetime of many of Matthew's readers: we are dealing with a few decades, not centuries. Thus the validity of the theological point depends here on the credibility of the historical record. Moreover both Mark 8:17–19 and Matthew 16:9–11 report that Jesus referred to the two feedings as separate occasions. Even if one rejects the authenticity of what Jesus said, it argues that the evangelists themselves believed in two miraculous feedings.

Close comparison of the two miracles shows similarities only where there could scarcely be anything else: (1) they both take place in the country; (2) bread and fish appear in both, but this was the common food of the area; (3) Jesus gives thanks and breaks the bread, as one would expect him to (see on 14:19); (4) both portray the disciples distributing the food, a necessity because of the many thousands; and (5) both end in a boat trip, but so do many other stories located near Galilee, especially when Jesus desires to escape the crowds.

On the other hand, the differences between the two miracles are impressive (cf. esp. Maier): (1) the different numbers, five thousand and four thousand; (2) the different locales, northeast shore and southeast shore of Galilee (clearest in Mark); (3) no mention of grass in the second story, implying a different season of the year; (4) a different supply of food at the beginning; (5) a different number of basketfuls of leftovers and even different words for "basket"; and (6) the longer stay of the people in the second miracle (15:32).

It might be wise to remember that two feeding miracles by Moses (Exod 16; Num 11) and Elisha are reported (2 Kings 4:1–7, 38–44). The only impressive reason for taking this account as a doublet is the disciples' response in v.33, and this is best accounted for in other ways (below).

32–33 On Jesus' compassion, see on 9:36. It appears that Jesus' preaching and miracles so captivated the people (cf. their exuberant praise, v.31) that they refused to leave him till he hesitated to dismiss them, fearing that many of them would collapse for hunger on their way home (v.32). Some had come a long distance (Mark 8:3). The response of the disciples is not surprising and not sufficient to prove this pericope a doublet of the feeding of the five thousand, for:

1. The disciples may have understood the feeding of the five thousand Jews as anticipating the messianic banquet. But, though they might have been prepared for Jesus to perform miracles of healing and exorcism on Gentiles as expressions of his mercy and compassion, they might still have been a long way from admitting that Gentiles could share in any anticipation of the messianic banquet.

2. According to John 6:26, after the feeding of the five thousand, Jesus rebuked the crowds for just wanting food; and the disciples may therefore have thought better of bringing the subject up again.

3. More important, we must never lose sight of a human being's vast capacity for unbelief. After this healing, whether a doublet of the feeding of the five thousand or not, Jesus' disciples completely misinterpreted one of his enigmatic sayings because even then they did not understand that those with Jesus could never starve (16: 5–12).

34–39 Here in v.36 the verb *eucharisteō* ("I give thanks") is used, not *eulogeō* (lit., "I bless"), as in 14:19, though there is no substantial difference in meaning. The *spyridas* ("baskets") were woven of rushes and used for fish or other food (cf. *kophinous* ["baskets"] in 14:20). A. E. J. Rawlinson (*The Gospel According to St. Mark*, 5th ed. [London: Methuen, 1942], p. 87) cites Juvenal to the effect that, at least in Rome, Jews commonly used *kophinous* to carry kosher food. If so, the use of *spyridas* in this setting may imply that the locale and its people were non-Jewish.

If the number of baskets of leftovers in 14:20 is symbolic, it is hard to see why the seven baskets here (v.37) are not symbolic (see on vv.29–31). The number seven may be significant because it is not twelve and therefore not allusive to the twelve apostles or twelve tribes. This seems more sensible than seeing an allusion to the seven deacons (Acts 6:1–6; so Lohmeyer)—an anachronistic view that ignores that: (1) the seven in Acts 6 are not explicitly called deacons; (2) the church was then entirely Jewish; and (3) the twelve apostles exercised general oversight. It is barely possible that the seven baskets represent the fullness of the people of God now being touched by Jesus' power, as the twelve baskets bore an allusion to Israel; but what is surprising on this view is that the audience here was not apparently comprised of both Jew and Gentile but only the latter.

As before, *hoi esthiontes* ("those who ate," v.38; on the tense, cf. Zerwick, par. 291) are all satisfied, and the men only are numbered. The whole crowd may have exceeded ten thousand.

The site of Magadan (v.39; cf. Notes) is unknown. Both Mark and Matthew now speak of a conflict with the Pharisees and Sadducees (16:1–4). If this occurred when Jesus and the disciples landed, it must have been on Jewish territory, probably on the western shores of Galilee.

Notes

39 Mark 8:10 has τὰ μέρη Δαλμανουθά (*ta merē Dalmanoutha*, "the region of Dalmanoutha"); but we do not know where that is. The uncertainty of the site of Μαγαδάν (*Magadan*) has prompted several textual variants, including Μαγδαλάν (*Magdalan*) and Μαγδαλά (*Magdala*), which may have been influenced by a Semitic word for "tower" (Heb. מִגְדָל [*migdāl*]; Aram. מִגְדְּלָא [*migdᵉlā'*]).

9. *Another demand for a sign*

16:1–4

> [1]The Pharisees and Sadducees came to Jesus and tested him by asking him to show them a sign from heaven.
> [2]He replied, "When evening comes, you say, 'It will be fair weather, for the sky is red,' [3]and in the morning, 'Today it will be stormy, for the sky is red and overcast.' You know how to interpret the appearance of the sky, but you cannot interpret the signs of the times. [4]A wicked and adulterous generation looks for a miraculous sign, but none will be given it except the sign of Jonah." Jesus then left them and went away.

Doubtless there were many requests for signs (see on 12:38–40), as there continued to be after Jesus' resurrection and ascension (1 Cor 1:22–24). Moreover itinerant preachers develop standard responses to standard questions. But this pericope (cf. Mark 8:11–13) has a crucial place in the narrative. Jesus has barely returned to Jewish territory when the opposition of Jewish leaders again surfaces, prompting him to leave the area once more, cross the lake, and head far north to Caesarea Philippi (v.13), where in God's providence and in the heart of Gentile territory, Peter makes the great confession that Jesus is the Messiah (v.16).

1 The single article in *hoi Pharisaioi kai Saddoukaioi* ("the Pharisees and Sadducees") implies that they acted together. Because the two groups were so frequently at odds theologically and politically, many think such united action improbable. Moreover critical orthodoxy dates this Gospel at about A.D. 85, a time when the Sadducees, closely connected with Jerusalem and the temple, destroyed in A.D. 70, no longer existed as a coherent force. Therefore many feel that since only Pharisaism was dominant in Judaism at that time, this reference to the Sadducees implies no more than that Matthew vaguely remembered all official Judaism being opposed to Jesus.

A better approach is possible.

1. It is precarious to identify, without remainder, the Pharisees of Jesus' day and the rabbis of A.D. 85 (cf. Introduction, section 11.f); and the Sadducees did not continue as a group with genuine influence after A.D. 70. Matthew's use of these terms might therefore be taken as evidence for historical accuracy in the pre–A.D. 70 setting and not as an anachronism.

2. The Introduction has already questioned critical orthodoxy regarding the date and setting of Matthew's Gospel. A date in the ninth decade should not be lightly assumed. Overcoming that barrier, references to the Sadducees in the synoptic Gospels can be taken to support the evangelists' accuracy. Would not failure to mention the Sadducees have raised questions about how close the evangelists were to what they were writing about? Why then should mention of them not argue for the evangelists' fidelity? If the Sadducees do not appear more often than they do, it is because they were a small group, and closely tied to Jerusalem—a long way from Galilee where Jesus exercised so much of his ministry. Indeed the controversy between Jesus and the Sadducees, recorded in 22:23–34; Mark 12:18; Luke 20:27, occurs in the south, where, too, there is much more frequent mention of "priests" and "chief priests," exactly as one would expect from an accurate historian.

3. The other references to the Sadducees in the Gospels are all in Matthew (3:7; 16:1, 6, 11, 12), exactly as might be expected of a writer who often relies on the understanding of his Jewish readers.

4. Pharisees and Sadducees may here be lumped together because they represent the Sanhedrin, which included both groups (cf. Acts 23:6), or because a common opponent transforms enemies into friends (cf. Luke 23:12; cf. Ps 2:2). Also Matthew elsewhere distinguishes between the two groups (22:33–34; see Introduction, section 11.f).

These men came to Jesus to "test" him (see on 4:1, 7; cf. 19:3; 22:18, 35), asking for "a sign from heaven" (see on 12:38).

2–3 Jesus' words in vv.2–3 are omitted by a small but important group of witnesses. Jerome reports that most MSS known to him omit the words; and many scholars consider them an assimilation to Luke 12:54–56. But if that were so, one wonders why the wording is not closer. Lagrange, Metzger (*Textual Commentary*, p. 41), and others have postulated that the words are original but were dropped from some MSS by scribes living in climates such as Egypt, where a red sky in the morning (v.3) does not presage rain. The evidence is rather finely balanced, and it is probably best to include the words. If so, Jesus' point is clear enough: the Pharisees and Sadducees can read the "signs" that predict weather, but they remain oblivious to the "signs of the times" already happening. Here these "signs of the times" neither point to the future, nor (contra Hoekema, p. 133) to what God has done in the past. Instead, they testify to Jesus and the kingdom now dawning (cf. 11:4–6; 12:28). The proof that they cannot discern the "signs" is that they ask for a sign (v.1)! For those with eyes to see, the "signs of the times," if not the kind of "sign" the Pharisees and Sadducees demanded, were already abundant.

4 But if a definitive sign is demanded, none but the sign of Jonah will be given (see on 12:39). Mark 8:12 is no exception. In one sense both evangelists are right, for the Jews would not have recognized Jonah as the kind of sign they were after (so there was no exception, Mark), even though that was the only definitive sign Jesus would allow (so there was an exception, Matthew). For exposition, see on 12:38–42.

Mark also says that Jesus sighed: the controversies were wearying. Jesus leaves his opponents and withdraws by boat to the other side of the lake (v.5) and points north (v.13). But his withdrawal is emotional and judicial as well as geographical.

10. The yeast of the Pharisees and Sadducees

16:5–12

> 5When they went across the lake, the disciples forgot to take bread. 6"Be careful," Jesus said to them. "Be on your guard against the yeast of the Pharisees and Sadducees."
>
> 7They discussed this among themselves and said, "It is because we didn't bring any bread."
>
> 8Aware of their discussion, Jesus asked, "You of little faith, why are you talking among yourselves about having no bread? 9Do you still not understand? Don't you remember the five loaves for the five thousand, and how many basketfuls you gathered? 10Or the seven loaves for the four thousand, and how many basketfuls you gathered? 11How is it you don't understand that I was not talking to you about bread? But be on your guard against the yeast of the Pharisees and Sadducees."
>
> 12Then they understood that he was not telling them to guard against the yeast used in bread, but against the teaching of the Pharisees and Sadducees.

This is Jesus' last and most important withdrawal from Galilee before his final trip south (19:1), and it continues to 17:20. Close comparison of these verses with Mark 8:13–21 shows significant differences. In particular, (1) Matthew omits Mark 8:17b–18; (2) Matthew 16:9–11a shortens and rearranges Mark 8:19–21; (3) Matthew adds 16:11b–12; and (4) Matthew refers to the yeast of the Pharisees and Sadducees, but Mark to the yeast of the Pharisees and of Herod.

What do we make of these differences? Some writers (Barth, in Bornkamm [*Tradition*, pp. 114–16]; Strecker [*Weg*, p. 193]; Zumstein [p. 203]) argue that Matthew minimizes the disciples' lack of understanding, so pronounced in Mark, and separates understanding from faith (see on 13:10–15). Though the differences must not be minimized, the question is, What prompts them?

The single-strand theological motivation advanced by many is reductionistic, when on the face of it numerous factors must be weighed.

1. Commentators on Mark complain that Mark 8:13–21 lacks cohesion or is verbose. In part Matthew, as usual, is simply tightening things up and condensing his source.

2. Matthew 16:9 is still very negative: the disciples do not understand (a verb no weaker than the one used in Mark 8:17–18).

3. When they finally do understand (v.12), it is as a result of Jesus' explanation—as in the case of the parables (13:36–43; 15:15–16). The disciples are *beginning* to understand (Trotter), exactly as we might expect from their position in salvation history.

4. Far from driving a wedge between faith and understanding, the charge in vv.8–9a links them. Yet faith in Christ is made the prerequisite to understanding Jesus' remark (cf. comments on 13:34–35). This makes explicit what is merely implicit in Mark.

5. Matthew's distinctive emphases, as compared with Mark, are two: first, he takes the story to the point where the disciples do achieve some understanding, whereas Mark leaves the outcome hanging. This rounded-off conclusion is typical of Matthew (see on 15:20). Second, in Matthew Jesus specifies that the "yeast" metaphor refers to the "teaching" of the Pharisees and Sadducees, whereas in Mark it extends to Herod but is not explained. From the context of Mark we may deduce that yeast refers to "the disposition to believe only if signs which compel faith are produced" (Lane, *Mark*, p. 281), evidenced by the Pharisees in the preceding pericope and by Herod a short while before (Matt 14:1–2; Mark 6:14). Matthew may not be very different. Jesus is surely not telling his disciples to beware of *all* the teaching of the Pharisees and Sadducees. These two groups did not always agree; and Jesus can stand with the Sadducees against the Pharisees on the authority of Halakah (rules of conduct derived from interpretations of Scripture, preserved in oral tradition) and with the Pharisees against the Sadducees on the Resurrection (22:23–33). The "teaching of the Pharisees and Sadducees" to which Jesus refers (vv.5–12), therefore, is an attitude of unbelief toward divine revelation that could not perceive Jesus to be the Messiah (vv.1–4) but that tried to control and tame the Messiah they claimed to await. The disciples are to avoid that. That is why the next pericope (vv.13–20) is so important: Peter makes the confession that Jesus is the Messiah, not on the basis of manipulative signs, but by revelation from the Father.

5–7 The setting may be the boat in which Jesus and his disciples cross the lake (v.5; Notes). The conversation reveals the contrasting attitudes of Jesus and his disciples: he is still thinking about the malignity of the Pharisees and Sadducees (vv.1–4), and the disciples are thinking about food (15:29–38), which they forgot to bring. Mark 8:14 says they were down to one loaf. (For "Pharisees and Sadducees" governed by one article, see on v.1.)

"Yeast" (v.6) was a common symbol for evil (see on 13:33) and could therefore be applied to different kinds of wickedness (e.g., Luke 12:1; cf. Exod 34:25; Lev 2:11; 1 Cor 5:6–8), but always with the idea that a little of it could have a far-reaching and insidious effect. The disciples do not understand what Jesus is saying but find his words enigmatic and discuss them (v.7).

8–12 Because they were men of little faith (v.8; cf. 6:30; 8:26; 14:31), they came to an unimaginative conclusion (v.7; cf. Notes). Jesus could not have been talking about bread because he had already shown his power to provide all the bread they needed (vv.9–10; cf. 14:13–21; 15:32–39). He had performed two "food" miracles, and there had been basketfuls of leftovers each time.

Jesus' charge (v.11) against the disciples ran deep. Jesus had already denounced the Pharisees and Sadducees for their particular "teaching" that demanded manipulative signs instead of believing in the bountiful evidence already supplied. And now the disciples are perilously close to the same unbelief in Jesus' person and miracles. The miracles Jesus performs, unlike the signs the Pharisees demand, do not compel faith; but those with faith will perceive their significance. Moreover, it is just possible that Jesus was asking his disciples to recognize symbolic meaning in the numbers of leftover baskets, here reiterated (see on 14:20; 15:37). Jesus is the Messiah who spreads bounty and invites both the twelve tribes of Israel and the Gentiles to his messianic banquet. But whether or not this thought is valid, Jesus' criticism of his disciples was sharp.

Instead of explaining the meaning of his metaphor of the yeast, Jesus repeats it in both Matthew and Mark. This suggests that, great teacher that he is, he is trying to train his disciples to think deeply about the revelation he is giving and is not content to keep on spoonfeeding them. Only Matthew provides the interpretation (v.12); Mark leaves it to the reader to discern (but cf. Matt 15:19–20 and Mark 7:19).

Notes

5 NASB (et al.) handles the tenses awkwardly: "The disciples came to the other side and had forgotten to take bread." Ἔρχομαι (erchomai) can mean "I come" as well as "I go," and its aorist participle ἐλθόντες (elthontes) can indicate either action antecedent to ("having come," "having gone") or coordinate with ("coming," "going") the main verb. NIV's "When they went . . . , the disciples forgot" is coherent and renders the verbs accurately.

7 The ὅτι (hoti) could be (1) recitative: the disciples said, "We didn't bring any bread"; (2) causal: the disciples said, "[It is] because we didn't bring any bread"; or (3) an abbreviated form of τί ἐστιν ὅτι (ti estin hoti), introducing a question, "Why did we bring no bread?" In light of v.7a, where the disciples discuss Jesus' enigmatic saying among themselves, the second option is to be preferred.

11. *Peter's confession of Jesus and its aftermath (16:13–23)*

a. *The confession*

16:13–20

> 13When Jesus came to the region of Caesarea Philippi, he asked his disciples, "Who do people say the Son of Man is?"
> 14They replied, "Some say John the Baptist; others say Elijah; and still others, Jeremiah or one of the prophets."
> 15"But what about you?" he asked. "Who do you say I am?"
> 16Simon Peter answered, "You are the Christ, the Son of the living God."
> 17Jesus replied, "Blessed are you, Simon son of Jonah, for this was not revealed to you by man, but by my Father in heaven. 18And I tell you that you are Peter, and on this rock I will build my church, and the gates of Hades will not overcome it. 19I will give you the keys of the kingdom of heaven; whatever you

bind on earth will be bound in heaven, and whatever you loose on earth will be loosed in heaven." [20]Then he warned his disciples not to tell anyone that he was the Christ.

Broadly speaking Matthew and Mark treat Peter's confession similarly. All three Synoptics (cf. Mark 8:27–30; Luke 9:18–21) immediately follow it by Jesus' prediction of his sufferings, a theme Matthew develops (17:12, 22–23; 20:17–19). (For questions of structure, see on v.21 and Introduction, section 14.)

The connections between this key passage and the rest of Matthew are intricate. Some have already been dealt with (cf. on vv.5–12). Peter recognizes Jesus as the Messiah by revelation, not by signs Peter dictates and thus uses to manipulate the Messiah. That Jesus is the Messiah leads inexorably to his self-disclosure as the suffering Messiah (vv.21–23), a theme anticipated earlier (see on 8:17; 10:24–25; 12:15–21). Moreover the suffering of the Servant is not only redemptive (20:28) but exemplary (16:24–26). Therefore the fourth discourse (18:3–35) is grounded in christology.

Peter's role in this passage has been analyzed hundreds of times and is further discussed below. At the risk of oversimplification, we may classify the positions defended in this century into two classes. The first thinks of Peter as a "typical" disciple who speaks for the other disciples, who in turn represent all believers. Thus everything said about Peter becomes a lesson for all Christians (e.g., R. Walker, p. 118; Strecker, *Weg*, p. 205). The second sees Peter as in some way unique: he becomes a kind of supreme rabbi on whom Jesus builds his church, a rabbi who guarantees and transmits the traditions of Jesus in Matthew's church (cf. esp. Hummel, pp. 59ff.; Paul Hoffmann, "Der Petrus-Primat im Matthäusevangelium" in Gnilka, *Neues Testament*, pp. 94–114; C. Kähler, "Zur Form- und Traditionsgeschichte von Matth.xvi.17–19," NTS 23 [1977]: 36–58).

In a balanced essay J.D. Kingsbury ("The Figure of Peter in Matthew's Gospel as a Theological Problem," JBL 98 [1979]: 67–83) has shown how both alternatives distort the text. The second will not stand: Matthew's Gospel insists that only Jesus is to be called rabbi (23:8, 10) and that after his resurrection he himself will remain with his disciples to the end of the age (28:20; cf. 18:20). Moreover, if Peter is given power to bind and loose, so also is the church (18:18); and all of Jesus' followers are to be involved in discipling and teaching the nations (28:18–19). Yet the first view is also simplistic. Matthew 16:16–17 is intensely personal, not merely representative. Whatever the precise meaning of these verses, Matthew presents Peter as the "first" disciple to be called (4:18–20; 10:2–4) and now the first one truly to understand that Jesus is the promised Messiah, the Son of God. So these passages honor his "salvation-historical primacy" (Kingsbury's expression), and we must not do less.

For brief comments on problems connected with the authenticity of vv.17–19, see below.

13 Caesarea Philippi was built by Herod Philip the tetrarch (cf. 2:20, 22), who enlarged a small town on a plane 1150 feet above sea level at the base of Mount Hermon, renaming it in honor of Caesar, "Philippi" being added to distinguish it from the coastal city of the same name. It lies twenty-five miles north of Galilee; snow-capped Mount Hermon can be seen on a clear day from as far away as Nazareth, where Jesus grew up. The inhabitants were largely Gentile. Though Jesus exercised some broader ministry here (17:14; cf. Mark 8:34), primarily he gave himself to the Twelve. Matthew omits Mark's casual details (Mark 8:27).

In Mark and Luke, Jesus' question leaves out the "Son of Man": "Who do people say I am?" (For the title, see excursus on 8:20.) This clear self-designation must have been somewhat ambiguous or else Jesus' question would have been fatuous. Which form of the question is original is not certain. But that only Jesus uses the title in the Gospels, and that it can serve as a self-designation with some ambiguous messianic significance, favors the view that Matthew is original, while Mark and Luke preserve the self-designation ("I") but delete the title for fear that their non-Jewish readers, who have learned to see messianic significance in it but not Jesus' self-designation, might think the question odd.

14 Opinion on Jesus' identity was divided. Some thought he was John the Baptist risen from the dead—Herod Antipas's view (14:2). Those who thought he was Elijah saw him as forerunner to a Messiah still to come (see on 3:1–3; 11:9–10; 17:10–13; Mal 4:5–6). Only Matthew mentions Jeremiah, the first of the so-called latter prophets in the Hebrew canon (cf. on 27:9). There may have been late Jewish traditions about Jeremiah's death that supported this identification (cf. 2 Macc 2:1–12; 15:14–15); and it is possible that some onlookers had been struck by the mixture of authority and suffering characteristic of Jesus' ministry and well exemplified by Jeremiah (Bonnard). J. Carmignac ("Pourquoi Jérémie est-il mentionné en Matthieu 16,14?" *Tradition und Glaube*, edd. G. Jeremias et al. [Göttingen: Vandenhoeck und Ruprecht, 1971], pp. 283–98) suggests that Jesus, like Jeremiah, must have seemed to many like a prophet of doom because of his negative prognosis for Israel.

"One of the prophets" testifies to the diversity of eschatological expectations in Jesus' day, some of the people expecting a long series of prophetic forerunners. But no group was openly and thoughtfully confessing Jesus as Messiah. Probably aberrations such as 9:27; 15:22 were considered extravagant devices used by desperate people, not maliciously, but in deep hope that their own needs might be met. What we must recognize is that christological confession was not cut and dried, black or white. It was possible to address Jesus with some messianic title without complete conviction, or while still holding some major misconceptions about the nature of his messiahship, and therefore stopping short of unqualified allegiance or outright confession. If Peter had some misconception (vv.21–23), how much more misconception would there be in disciples outside the Twelve? Thus confessions like those in 9:27; 15:22 may not be so surprising.

15–16 The "you" is emphatic and plural (v.15). Therefore, at least in part, Peter serves as spokesman for the Twelve (as he often does: cf. 15:15–16; 19:25–28; 26:40; Mark 11:20–22; Luke 12:41; John 6:67–70; cf. Acts 2:37–38; 5:29). Peter's confession (v.16) is direct: "You are the Christ" (Mark); "The Christ of God" (Luke); "You are the Christ, the Son of the living God" (Matthew). (For comments regarding Messiah = Christ, see on 1:1.)

Majority opinion assigns "the Son of the living God" to Matthean redaction, a sort of explanatory gloss. Yet this may be premature. Ben F. Meyer (pp. 189–91) has given good reason for accepting Matthew's form as authentic: (1) it better explains the genesis of the other forms, not only in Mark and Luke, but also "the Holy One of God" in John 6:69, than does Mark's "You are the Christ"; (2) "Son of God" may well have had purely messianic significance in Peter's mind (see on 3:17; 11:27; 14:33), even though it came to indicate divinity (Bonnard; cf. excursus on "Son of Man" at 8:20); and (3) other details in this pericope support Matthew's priority (see on vv.17–19). Guthrie (*NT Theology*, pp. 305f.) reminds us that since the other synoptists record the application of "Son of God" to Jesus in other contexts, it is not intrinsically unlikely here.

17–19 Many scholars doubt the authenticity of these verses because they are missing in Mark and Luke. We may note that in addition to positions that simply deny that these words are authentic (e.g., Bultmann, *NT Theology*, 1:45; J. Kahmann, "Die Verheissung an Petrus," in Didier, pp. 261–80), there are more sophisticated options. O. Cullmann (*Peter: Disciple-Apostle-Martyr* [London: SCM, 1953], pp. 158–70) holds that the *saying* is authentic, but not the *setting*, which originally lay during the passion period, in some such place as Luke 22:31–38. R.E. Brown et al. (*Peter*, pp. 85ff.) argue that the origin of this saying lies in some tradition on the Resurrection. And recently Max Wilcox ("Peter and the Rock: A Fresh Look at Matthew xvi.17–19," NTS 22 [1976]: 73–88) has held that these verses spring from some ecclesiastical linking of Jesus as the Son with the "rejected stone" and related testimonia (Ps 118:22–23; Isa 8:14; 28:16), and that the possibility of linking "stone" with Peter's name prompted the transfer of this category from Jesus to Peter. Critical orthodoxy largely concurs that "church" is an anachronism; that the omission of the word "this" in the Greek text of v.17 suggests that the words did not originally stand here (Cullmann); and that words such as "blessed," "my Father," and "in heaven" are characteristically Matthean and are therefore probably inauthentic.

But B.F. Meyer (pp. 185–97) has recently mounted a detailed defense of the authenticity of vv.17–19. Some of his points, plus one or two others, are included below.

1. "Blessed" is not exclusively Matthean; and "my Father in heaven" no more vitiates the authenticity of this saying than it does of the opening line of the Lord's prayer (6:9). This is so of any view of the relation between 6:9–13 and Luke 11:2–4, since a redactional formulation says nothing about authenticity unless we are thinking in terms only of *ipsissima verba*, not *ipsissima vox*.

2. The omission of "this" from the Greek in v.17 does not prove the saying was moved from some other place. Greek transitive verbs often omit the direct object where it is obvious. The verb in question, *apokalyptō* ("I reveal"), is used transitively seven other times in the NT. Three of these require for clarity inclusion of the direct object. Of the remaining four (11:27; Luke 10:22; 1 Cor 2:10; Phil 3:15), where the meaning is so clear that no direct object must be included, only one of the four has it (viz., Phil 3:15). Matthew 16:17 fits the majority usage.

3. The use of "church" is not anachronistic: see on v.18.

4. B.F. Meyer (pp. 189f.) advances good reasons for doubting Mark's priority in this pericope but rightly points out that even if Matthew depends on Mark, this says nothing at all about the historical value of Matthew's redaction (pp. 71f.; cf. Introduction, sections 1–3).

5. The verb "reveal" has its closest links, not with any resurrection text, but with 11:25, where, as in 16:17, "the Father's revealing is correlative to the insight of faith, and the correlation 'revelation/faith' is placed in the present of the ministry" (B.F. Meyer, p. 192). Similar things can be said for the next closest parallel, viz., 11:27.

Though the history of the interpretation of these verses is even more tortuous than the recent history of critical opinion about them, part of it has been well chronicled by Joseph A. Burgess (*A History of the Exegesis of Matthew 16:17-19 from 1781 to 1965* [Ann Arbor: Edwards Brothers, 1976]).

17 For "Blessed," see on 5:3. Jesus is the "Son of the living God" (v. 16); Peter is the "son of Jonah" (cf. Notes). Yet Jesus' Father has revealed to Peter the truth he has just confessed. Indeed, no one knows the Son except the Father (11:27; cf. John 6:44), who has now graciously revealed his identity to Peter. Such knowledge could not have originated in "flesh and blood"—a common Jewish expression referring to man as a mortal being (cf. 1 Cor 15:50; Gal 1:16; Eph 6:12; Heb 2:14; cf. Ecclus 14:18; 17:31.) We must neither minimize nor exaggerate this revelation of the Father to Peter. Similar confessions by others do not necessarily evoke similar theological conclusions (e.g., 21:9; 27:54); so Peter's confession assumes a God-given insight deeper than these.

On the other hand we need not suppose that the idea that Jesus was Messiah was here entering the apostles' minds for the first time. If so, Jesus' closest disciples were remarkably obtuse (e.g., see on 5:17-48; 7:21-23; 11:2-6). John's witness is surely sound: the disciples began following Jesus in the hope that he was the Messiah (John 1:41, 45, 49). But their understanding of the nature of Jesus' messiahship was hindered by their own expectations (see on 16:21-23); and they did not come into a full "Christian" understanding till after Easter. This verse marks a crucial stage along that growth in understanding and faith. Partial as it was (16:21-23), Peter's firm grasp of the fact that Jesus is the Messiah set him apart from the uncertainty and confusion of the crowd and could only be the result of the Father's disclosure. Indeed, the depth of Peter's conviction was the very thing that simultaneously made talk of Jesus' suffering and death difficult to integrate and prevented more serious defection when the one confessed as Messiah went to his death on a Roman cross.

18 *And I tell you . . . :* Weiss sees a contrast between Jesus and his Father, as if Jesus were saying, "Just as the *Father* revealed something to you and thereby honored you, so now *I* do the same." But the formula is common enough in places without such a contrast, and this may be an unwarranted refinement. The words simply point to what is coming.

that you are Peter . . . : The underlying Aramaic *kêpāʾ* ("Cephas" in John 1:42; 1 Cor 15:5; Gal 1:18 et al.) was an accepted name in Jesus' day (see on 4:18). Though B.F. Meyer (pp. 186-87) insists that Jesus gave the name Cephas to Simon at this point, Jesus merely made a pun on the name (4:18; 10:2; Mark 3:16; John 1:42). Yet Meyer is right to draw attention to the "rock" motifs on which the name Cephas is based (pp. 185-86, 194-95), motifs related to the netherworld and the temple (and so connoting images of "gates of Hades" and "church": see below.) The Greek *Kēphas* (Eng. "Cephas") transliterates the Aramaic, and *Petros* ("Peter") is the closest Greek translation. P. Lampe's argument ("Das Spiel mit dem Petrusnamen— Matt.xvi.18," NTS 25 [1979]: 227-45) that both *kêpāʾ* and *petros* originally referred to a small "stone," but not a "rock" (on which something could be built), until Christians extended the term to explain the riddle of Simon's name is baseless. True, the Greek *petros* commonly means "stone" in pre-Christian literature; but the Aramaic *kêpāʾ*, which underlies the Greek, means "(massive) rock" (cf. H. Clavier,

"Πέτρος καὶ πέτρα," *Neutestamentliche Studien,* ed. W. Eltester [Berlin: Alfred Töpelmann, 1957], pp. 101–3).

and on this rock . . . "Rock" now becomes *petra* (feminine); and on the basis of the distinction between *petros* (above) and *petra* (here), many have attempted to avoid identifying Peter as the rock on which Jesus builds his church. Peter is a mere "stone," it is alleged; but Jesus himself is the "rock," as Peter himself attests (1 Peter 2:5–8) (so, among others, Lenski, Gander, Walvoord). Others adopt some other distinction: e.g., "upon this rock of revealed truth—the truth you have just confessed—I will build my church" (Allen). Yet if it were not for Protestant reactions against extremes of Roman Catholic interpretation, it is doubtful whether many would have taken "rock" to be anything or anyone other than Peter.

1. Although it is true that *petros* and *petra* can mean "stone" and "rock" respectively in earlier Greek, the distinction is largely confined to poetry. Moreover the underlying Aramaic is in this case unquestionable; and most probably *kêpāʾ* was used in both clauses ("you are *kêpāʾ* and on this *kêpāʾ*"), since the word was used both for a name and for a "rock." The Peshitta (written in Syriac, a language cognate with Aramaic) makes no distinction between the words in the two clauses. The Greek makes the distinction between *petros* and *petra* simply because it is trying to preserve the pun, and in Greek the feminine *petra* could not very well serve as a masculine name.

2. Paronomasia of various kinds is very common in the Bible and should not be belittled (cf. Barry J. Beitzel, "Exodus 3:14 and the Divine Name: A Case of Biblical Paronomasia," *Trinity Journal* [1980]: 5–20; BDF, par. 488).

3. Had Matthew wanted to say no more than that Peter was a stone in contrast with Jesus the Rock, the more common word would have been *lithos* ("stone" of almost any size). Then there would have been no pun—and that is just the point!

4. The objection that Peter considers Jesus the rock is insubstantial because metaphors are commonly used variously, till they become stereotyped, and sometimes even then. Here Jesus builds his church; in 1 Corinthians 3:10, Paul is "an expert builder." In 1 Corinthians 3:11, Jesus is the church's foundation; in Ephesians 2:19–20, the apostles and prophets are the foundation (cf. also Rev 21:14), and Jesus is the "cornerstone." Here Peter has the keys; in Revelation 1:18; 3:7, Jesus has the keys. In John 9:5, Jesus is "the light of the world"; in Matthew 5:14, his disciples are. None of these pairs threatens Jesus' uniqueness. They simply show how metaphors must be interpreted primarily with reference to their immediate contexts.

5. In this passage Jesus is the builder of the church and it would be a strange mixture of metaphors that also sees him within the same clauses as its foundation.

None of this requires that conservative Roman Catholic views be endorsed (for examples of such views, cf. Lagrange, Sabourin). The text says nothing about Peter's successors, infallibility, or exclusive authority. These late interpretations entail insuperable exegetical and historical problems—e.g., after Peter's death, his "successor" would have authority over a surviving apostle, John. What the NT does show is that Peter is the first to make this formal confession and that his prominence continues in the earliest years of the church (Acts 1–12). But he, along with John, can be sent by other apostles (Acts 8:14); and he is held accountable for his actions by the Jerusalem church (Acts 11:1–18) and rebuked by Paul (Gal 2:11–14). He is, in short, *primus inter pares* ("first among equals"); and on the foundation of such men (Eph 2:20), Jesus built his church. That is precisely why Jesus, toward the close of his earthly ministry, spent so much time with them. The honor was not earned but stemmed from divine revelation (v.17) and Jesus' building work (v.18).

I will build my church . . . : *Ekklēsia* ("church") occurs only here and at 18:17 in the Gospels. Etymologically it springs from the verb *ekkaleō* ("call out from") and refers to those who are "called out"; but usage is far more important than etymology in determining meaning. In the NT *ekklēsia* can refer to assemblies of people in a nonreligious setting (Acts 19:39); and once it refers to God's OT people, the "church" in the desert at the giving of the law (Acts 7:38; cf. Heb 2:12). But in Acts and in the Epistles it usually refers to Christian congregations or to all God's people redeemed by Christ. Therefore R. Bultmann ("Die Frage nach der Echtheit von Mt 16, 17–19," *Theologische Blätter* 20 [1941]: col. 265–79) argues that the use of *ekklēsia* in Matthew 16:18; 18:17 cannot be authentic. It refers to a practicing group of Christians, a separate community, or a Christian synagogue in contrast to the Jewish synagogues, and is presided over by Peter.

K.L. Schmidt (TDNT, 3:525) suggests that the Aramaic term behind *ekklēsia* in Matthew is a late term, *kᵉništāʾ*, which could mean either "the people [of God]" or "a [separate] synagogue." In fact the strongest linguistic evidence runs in another direction. Whenever *ekklēsia* in the LXX is translating Hebrew, the Hebrew word is *qāhāl* ("assembly," "meeting," "gathering"), with reference to various kinds of "assemblies" (cf. E. Jenni and C. Westermann, eds., *Theologisches Handwörterbuch zum Alten Testament*, 2 vols., 3d ed. [München: Chr. Kaiser Verlag, 1978–79], 2:610–19), but increasingly used to refer to God's people, the assembly of Yahweh.

The Hebrew *qāhāl* has a broad semantic range and is not always rendered *ekklēsia;* sometimes in the LXX it is translated "synagogue" or "crowd." "Synagogue" customarily translates an entirely different Hebrew word (*ʿēdâh*, "corporate congregation"), which the LXX never translates *ekklēsia* (on these words, see DNTT, 1:291ff.). Thus *ekklēsia* ("church") is entirely appropriate in Matthew 16:18; 18:17, where there is no emphasis on institution, organization, form of worship, or separate synagogue. Even the idea of "building" a people springs from the OT (Ruth 4:11; 2 Sam 7:13–14; 1 Chron 17:12–13; Pss 28:5; 118:22; Jer 1:10; 24:6; 31:4; 33:7; Amos 9:11). "Jesus' announcement of his purpose to build his *ekklēsia* suggests . . . that the fellowship established by Jesus stands in direct continuity with the Old Testament Israel" (Ladd, *NT Theology,* p. 110), construed as the faithful remnant with the eyes of faith to come to terms with the new revelation. Acknowledged as Messiah, Jesus responds that he will build his *ekklēsia,* his people, his church— which is classic messianism. "It is hard to know what kind of thinking, other than confessional presupposition, justifies the tendency of some commentators to dismiss this verse as not authentic. A Messiah without a Messianic Community would have been unthinkable to any Jew" (Albright and Mann).

Implicitly, then, the verse also embraces a claim to messiahship. The "people of Yahweh" become the people of Messiah (cf. also 13:41). If the Qumran community thinks of itself as the "people of the covenant," Jesus speaks of his followers as *his* people—*his* church—who come in time to see themselves as people of the new covenant established by Messiah's blood (26:28).

Jesus' "church" is not the same as his "kingdom" (contra Hill, *Matthew*): the two words belong to different concepts, the one to "people" and the other to "rule" or "reign" (see on 13:28–30, 36–43). But neither must they be opposed to each other, as if both cannot occupy the same place in time (contra Walvoord). The messianic reign is calling out the messianic people. The kingdom has been inaugurated; the people are being gathered. So far as the kingdom has been inaugurated in advance of its consummation, so far also is Jesus' church an outpost in history of the final eschatological community. "The implication is inescapable that, in the establishment of the church, there was to be a manifestation of the kingdom or rule of God" (Stonehouse, *Witness of Matthew,* p. 235). When the kingdom is consummated, then Messiah's "assembly" shall also attain the richest blessings Messiah's reign can give. Nothing, therefore, can eliminate Messiah's church or prevent it from reaching that consummation.

The gates of Hades will not overcome it (On Hades, see DNTT, 2:206–8; SBK, 4:1016–29; comments on 5:22; 11:23.): The "gates of Hades" have been taken to represent the strength of Satan and his cohorts (since "gates" can refer to "fortifications," Gen 22:17; Ps 127:5): the church, because Jesus is building it, cannot be defeated by the hosts of darkness. Other scholars focus, not on "gates," but on "Hades" and, turning to Revelation 1:18, think this means that death will not prevent Messiah's people from rising at the last day. But "gates of Hades" or very similar expressions are found in canonical literature (Job 17:16; 38:17; Pss 9:13; 107:18; Isa 38:10), noncanonical Jewish literature (Wisd Sol 16:13; 3 Macc 5:51; Pss Sol 16:2), and pagan literature (Homer *Iliad* 9. 312; *Odyssey* 11.277; Aeschylus *Agam.* 1291; Euripedes *Hecuba* 1), and seem to refer to death and dying. Hence RSV: "The powers of death shall not prevail against it." Because the church is the assembly of people Jesus Messiah is building, it cannot die. This claim is ridiculous if Jesus is nothing but an overconfident popular preacher in an unimportant vassal state of first-century Rome. It is the basis of all hope for those who see Jesus as the Messiah who builds his people.

19 *I will give you the keys of the kingdom of heaven:* As in v.18, the promise goes beyond the days of Jesus' earthly ministry. What Jesus' disciples thought this meant at the time is uncertain. Perhaps they hoped that when Jesus established his earthly reign and defeated the Romans, they would hold major posts under his reign (cf. Bonnard). In the postresurrection period, the nature of this inaugurated kingdom became progressively clearer.

Here, as in 7:21, the "kingdom" (see on 3:2; 5:3) is to be entered. The metaphor therefore changes: from being the rock-foundation of the church, Peter now becomes the one who wields the keys of the kingdom (as Alexander points out, the metaphor would be equally mixed if Jesus–rock–foundation "gives" the keys). The person with the keys has power to exclude or permit entrance (cf. Rev 9:1–6; 20:1–3). There may be an allusion here to the chief stewards of monarchs (Isa 22:15, 22). But we cannot go on without understanding the binding and loosing (v.19b) to which the keys are related.

whatever you bind . . . loosed in heaven . . . : Five separate and difficult questions must be considered to understand the force of this verse, and some answers must be tentative.

1. How are the future periphrastic perfects to be translated? In 1938, J.R. Mantey ("The Mistranslation of the Perfect Tense in John 20:23, Matthew 16:19, and Matthew 18:18," JBL 58 [1939]: 243–49) argued that the perfects in all three instances must have their normal force. The finite perfect in John 20:23 must be rendered "If you forgive anyone his sins, they have already been forgiven"; and when the perfect participle is given its full force in the Matthean passages, the periphrastic future perfect in 16:19 becomes "whatever you bind on earth *shall have been* bound in heaven, and whatever you loose on earth *shall have been loosed* in

heaven" (similarly for 18:18). Thus, as Mantey insisted, there is no evidence for "sacerdotalism or priestly absolution" in the NT.

In the same issue of JBL, H.J. Cadbury ("The Meaning of John 20:23, Matthew 16:19, and Matthew 18:18," pp. 251–54) noted that the six perfects or future perfects in the three passages all occur in the apodosis of a general condition. The question, then, is "whether a perfect in the apodosis indicates an action or condition prior to the time of the apodosis" (p. 251); and, citing 1 John 2:5; James 2:10; Romans 13:8; 14:23, along with certain grammarians (BDF, par. 344; Moulton, *Prolegomena*, p. 271; RHG, pp. 897–98, 908), he denied that this must be so. Although he thought the future an acceptable translation here, he suggested that in Matthew the perfects have the force "shall be once for all" (cf. Allen's "Whatsoever thou bindest *shall remain bound*, etc.").

The matter was picked up by W.T. Dayton ("The Greek Perfect Tense in Relation to John 20:23, Matthew 16:19, and Matthew 18:18" [Th.D. dissertation, Northern Baptist Theological Seminary, 1945]) and once more by J.R. Mantey ("Evidence that the Perfect Tense in John 20:23 and Matthew 16:19 is Mistranslated," JETS 16 [1973]: 129–38). Both works are marred by the tendency to cite quotations from grammarians in their favor without a fair handling of counterarguments. Of more use are Dayton's short lists of periphrastic future perfects in Strabo, Lucian, and some papyri; for all these retain perfect force, even when used in the apodosis of a general condition. This is valuable comparative material, since periphrastic future perfects in the NT are very rare; and there are no finite future perfects at all.

While the question is partly grammatical, it must be noted that, regardless of whether v. 19 is translated as an English future perfect or as an English future, there are difficulties in interpretation. If the tense is translated as a future ("shall be bound"), the passage can be taken to justify some form of extreme sacerdotalism without unambiguous defense elsewhere in the NT. But if it is translated as a future perfect ("shall have been bound"), it can be taken to support the notion that the disciple must therefore enjoy infallible communication from God in every question of "binding and loosing," a communication that is the role of the so-called charismatic gifts. Paul Elbert ("The Perfect Tense in Matthew 16:19 and Three Charismata," JETS 17 [1974]: 149–55) introduces them here with no sensitivity to broader questions of context, awareness of anachronism, or consciousness that the gifts do not provide infallible guidance (cf. 1 Cor 14:29). But in neither case do these conclusions *necessarily* follow. More moderate interpretations of both grammatical options are possible. But the extremes must be noted, especially because some give the impression that if the Greek is rendered as an English future perfect, we have eliminated sacerdotalism. The truth is that sacerdotalism will neither stand nor fall by these texts alone, though it may be helped or hindered by them. Meanwhile a future perfect rendering is itself not without theological problems.

Recent commentators and grammarians are divided on this question. Hendriksen, who finds Mantey's way of taking the perfects "artificial," opts for "shall be and shall definitely remain bound/loosed," a variation of Allen; and Hendriksen can scarcely be called a sacerdotalist. Many grammarians treat the perfect participle in this construction as little more than an adjective, with little perfect sense remaining (K.L. McKay, "On the Perfect and Other Aspects in New Testament Greek," unpublished, graciously sent me by the author; Moule, *Idiom Book*, p. 18; cf. esp. Luke 12:52, where it is very difficult to find any perfect force at all ["there will be . . . divided": the parallel future passive in the next verse makes this clear]). But Turner (*Insights*, pp. 80–82; id., *Syntax*, p. 82) challenges these views. In disagreeing with

Allen and Hendriksen, he points out that the future force is restricted to the auxiliary verb *estai* ("will be") and is not found in the participle, which must retain its perfect sense, thereby agreeing with Mantey. Turner further argues that this is even clearer in John 20:23, where the finite perfect, not the future periphrastic future, is used. Similarly Albright and Mann say, "The church on earth carries out heaven's decisions, not heaven ratifying the church's decisions," which is something of a caricature of the options.

What Turner (*Syntax*, pp. 82–83) and Zerwick (pars. 288f.) point out, however, is that where finite perfects have some force other than the normal perfect in the NT, they tend to be in well-known stereotyped forms: *oida* ("I know," not "I have known"); *pepoitha* ("I am persuaded"); *hestēka* ("I stand"). Similar is the periphrastic future perfect in Hebrews 2:13: although *esomai pepoithōs* means "I will put my trust" (NIV), not "I will have put my trust," this participle commonly takes on perfect form with present meaning. Likewise, when the perfect has an aorist force (Zerwick, pars. 288–89; as at 13:46), there are normally good reasons for it, as when the verb is defective and has no aorist form (cf. further discussion in BDF, pars. 340ff.).

This leads us to the following conclusion: Where questions dealing strictly with Greek syntax are asked, it seems impossible to reach a firm decision, because there are too many clear instances where perfects, whether finite or participial, have something other than perfect force. But where paradigmatic questions are asked— Why was this word or syntax used instead of something else?—we can make some progress. In John 20:23 the Greek perfects must be taken as retaining their normal force as perfects, because both verbs have acceptable present and future tenses used elsewhere: neither verb exhibits a preferential pattern for the perfect. The perfect participles in the periphrastic constructions of Matthew 16:19; 18:18 are based on the two verbs *lyō* ("I loose") and *deō* ("I bind"). Evidence regarding the latter is ambiguous; it often occurs as a perfect participle in the NT, sometimes as an aorist participle, never as a present participle; so one might hold that its perfect-participle form has purely adjectival or present force in some instances—a debatable point. But the former is unambiguous. *Lyō* has a full range of forms, and it is difficult to see why Matthew did not use either the future or the present participle in a periphrastic future if that was all he meant. This result spills over onto *deō* ("I bind"), since the two verbs are so tightly linked in these verses. But though they must therefore be rendered "shall have been bound/loosed," what that means here awaits the rest of the argument.

2. Does the "whatever" (*ho*) refer to things or people? Formally *ho* is neuter, and "things" might be expected. Moreover the rabbis spoke of "binding" and "loosing" in terms of laying down Halakah (rules of conduct): Shammai is strict and "binds" many things on the people, while Hillel allows greater laxity and "looses" them. It might be argued, then, that in Acts 15:10 Peter looses what certain Judaizers want to bind. Yet despite this, it is better to take the binding and loosing in Matthew 16:19 to refer to persons, not rules. The neuter *hosa* ("whatever") occurs in 18:18, where the context demands that persons are meant. Indeed, Greek often uses the neuter of people for classes or categories rather than for individuals. The context of v.19 supports this; for the keys in the preceding clause speak of permission for entering the kingdom or being excluded from it, not rules of conduct under heaven's rule. Acts 15:10 is scarcely an example of the opposite viewpoint, for there Peter does not proceed by legislative fiat. The church in Acts 15 seeks spiritually

minded consensus, not imposed Halakoth; and James is more prominent than Peter.

3. But exactly what is meant by this "binding and loosing" of persons, and is it absolute? And how is it related to the power of the keys? Substantial help comes from comparing Jesus' denunciation of the teachers of the law in Luke 11:52. There they are told that they "have taken away the key to knowledge" and have not only failed to enter [the kingdom] themselves but have "hindered those who were entering." Clearly, then, by their approach to the Scriptures, Jesus says, they are making it impossible for those who fall under the malign influences of their teaching to accept the new revelation in Jesus and enter the kingdom. They take away "the key to knowledge."

In contrast, Peter, on confessing Jesus as Messiah, is told he has received this confession by the Father's revelation and will be given the keys of the kingdom: i.e., by proclaiming "the good news of the kingdom" (4:23), which, by revelation he is increasingly understanding, he will open the kingdom to many and shut it against many. Fulfillments of this in Acts are not found in passages like 15:10 but in those like 2:14–39; 3:11–26, so that by this means the Lord added to the church those who were being saved (2:45), or, otherwise put, Jesus was building his church (Matt 16:18). But the same gospel proclamation alienates and excludes men; so we also find Peter shutting up the kingdom from men (Acts 4:11–12; 8:20–23). The periphrastic future perfects are then perfectly natural: Peter accomplishes this binding and loosing by proclaiming a gospel that has already been given and by making personal application on that basis (Simon Magus). Whatever he binds or looses will have been bound or loosed, so long as he adheres to that divinely disclosed gospel. He has no direct pipeline to heaven, still less do his decisions force heaven to comply; but he may be authoritative in binding and loosing because heaven has acted first (cf. Acts 18:9–10). Those he ushers in or excludes have already been bound or loosed by God according to the gospel already revealed and which Peter, by confessing Jesus as the Messiah, has most clearly grasped.

4. Does this promise apply to Peter only, to the apostolic band, or to the church at large? The interpretation given so far broadly fits a major theme of Matthew's Gospel: the disciples were called to be fishers of men (4:19), to be salt (5:13) and light (5:14–16), to preach the good news of the kingdom (10:6–42), and, after the Resurrection, to disciple the nations and teach them all that Jesus commanded (28:18–20). Within this framework Matthew 16:18–19 fits very well. Unlike the messianic kingdom expected by so many Jews, which would come climactically without any agreement or action taken by men, Jesus announces something different. In full Christian perspective the kingdom will be consummated in sudden, apocalyptic fashion at the Parousia, when God's actions are final and quite independent of human means. But now the keys of the kingdom are confided to men. They must proclaim the Good News, forbid entrance, urge conversion. They constitute a small minority in a big world; their mission will be to function as the eschatological *ekklēsia*, the people of God Jesus is building within this world. Inevitably the assignment involves them in using the keys to bind and lose. These verses are therefore the result of the partially realized—and one day to be consummated —eschatology implicit in the NT.

Understanding the text thus largely answers the question as to how far the promise applies; for the focus is no longer on the individual and what he does or does not represent but on his place in salvation-history. In one sense Peter stands with the other disciples as fishers of men, as recipients of the Great Commission (notice in v.20 that Jesus warns *all* his disciples, not just Peter, to tell no one). In that sense the disciples stand as paradigms for all believers during this period of redemptive history. But this does not exclude a special role for Peter or the apostles (see on v.18). Peter was the foundation, the first stone laid: he enjoys this "salvation historical primacy," and on him others are laid. This results in certain special roles in the earliest years of the Christian church. But notions of hierarchy or sacerdotalism are simply irrelevant to the text.

Confirmation that this is the way 16:19 is to be taken comes at 18:18. If the church, Messiah's eschatological people already gathered now, has to exercise the ministry of the keys, if it must bind and loose, then clearly one aspect of that will be the discipline of those who profess to constitute it. Thus the two passages are tightly joined: 18:18 is a special application of 16:19. Again, if we may judge from Paul's ministry, this discipline is a special function of apostles, but also of elders and even of the whole church (1 Cor 5:1–13; 2 Cor 13:10; Titus 2:15; 3:10–11)—an inescapable part of following Jesus during this age of the inaugurated kingdom and of the proleptic gathering of Messiah's people. The church of Jesus the Christ is more than an audience. It is a group with confessional standards, one of which (viz., "Jesus is the Christ") here precipitates Jesus' remarks regarding the keys. The continuity of the church depends as much on discipline as on truth. Indeed, faithful promulgation of the latter both entails and presupposes the former.

It appears, then, that the text is not interested in whether Peter's (or the church's) decisions are infallible. Its concern is with the role Jesus' disciples must play within this new phase of redemptive history. To press the "whatever" absolutely not only misunderstands the context but fails to reckon with Jesus' tendency to use absolutist language even when he cannot possibly mean to be taken that way (see on 5:33–37).

5. How is the contrast between "heaven" and "earth" to be understood? Our exegesis determines the answer. Some have understood the contrast temporally: what is bound or loosed now on earth will be bound or loosed then in heaven. But if our remarks on the periphrastic future perfect are correct, then such an interpretation is impossible. Rather, "heaven" (= "God," as in "kingdom of heaven") has revealed the gospel in the person of Jesus the Messiah, and heaven's rule has thereby broken in. Thus Jesus' disciples, in accordance with his gospel of the kingdom, take up the ministry of the keys and bind and loose on earth what has with the coming of the kingdom been bound and loosed in heaven. The thought is akin to, though more comprehensive than, Acts 18:9–10.

20 Jesus' warning his disciples not to tell anyone that he was the Christ does not stem from personal reluctance to accept the title, nor from merely qualified acceptance subject to teaching that he was a suffering Messiah (vv.21–26), still less because all the commands to keep silence are church constructions designed to create a "messianic secret" to explain why Jesus failed openly to present himself to the people as Messiah. The categories are wrong. "Contrary to common misappropriation of the messianic secret, it was not Jesus' purpose to conceal his messianic identity. It was his purpose to set before Israel symbol-charged acts and words implying a persistent question: Who do you say that I am?" (B.F. Meyer, p. 305, n. 59; see also pp. 250; 309–10, nn. 119–20). Jesus steadily refuses to make an explicit messianic claim, refusing to bow to demands for a definitive sign (12:38–39; 16:4) and insisting that the "step into messianic faith would be taken only under the combined impact of his densely symbolic career and of a divine illumination disclosing its sense" (ibid., p. 250; cf. 11:4, 25–26; 16:17).

The disciples are now charged with the same reticence. Having come to faith, they must not go beyond the Master himself in the means and limitations of his self-disclosure. The aim must not be to hide Jesus' identity from Israel or to keep it an esoteric secret but to guarantee (1) that the decisive factors in the conversion of men are not nationalistic fervor and impenitent messianic expectation but faith, obedience, and submission to Jesus; and (2) that the events leading to the Cross are not to be short-circuited by premature disclosure. After the Resurrection there could be unqualified proclamation (cf. 10:27), but not yet. The disciples were beginning to comprehend the first of these two aims; but the second, as the next pericope shows, completely eluded them (cf. comments on 13:10–17, 34–35, 51–52).

Notes

14 On the anomalous mixing of ἄλλοι (alloi, "others") and ἕτεροι (heteroi, "others"), see BDF, par. 306(2).

17 Βαριωνᾶ (Bariōna) is a Greek transliteration of בַּר יוֹנָה (bar yônāh), where bar means "son of" (cf. English John*son*, Robin*son* et al.). In John 1:42 Peter is called "son of John" (in Gr.; there is no transliteration from the Aram.). Probably Peter was called בַּר יוֹחָנָן (bar yôḥān*e*n, "son of Johanan"), and "Jonah" is a shortened form of "Johanan" whereas Ἰωάννης (Iōannēs, "John") is the closest Greek translation of the name.

18 Often cited as a parallel to Peter as a rock is Isaiah 51:1–2. But the analogy is not close: the point of the Isaiah passage is that Israel should remember her poor beginnings and be conscious of Yahweh's goodness toward her. Still less relevant, though formally closer, is the Jewish Midrash on Isaiah 51:1–2, where God before creating the world looks ahead till he finds Abraham and says, "Behold, I have found a rock on which I can build and found the world"; but there the point concerns Abraham's merits and worth, quite clearly not paralleled by Peter in Matthew 16. For rabbinic references and some of the impact of the exegesis on the Targums, see N.A. van Uchelen, "The Targumic Versions of Deuteronomy 33:15: Some remarks on the origin of a traditional exegesis," JSS 31 (1980): 199–209.

---

b. *The first passion prediction*

16:21–23

[21]From that time on Jesus began to explain to his disciples that he must go to Jerusalem and suffer many things at the hands of the elders, chief priests and teachers of the law, and that he must be killed and on the third day be raised to life.

[22]Peter took him aside and began to rebuke him. "Never, Lord!" he said. "This shall never happen to you!"

[23]Jesus turned and said to Peter, "Get behind me, Satan! You are a stumbling block to me; you do not have in mind the things of God, but the things of men."

21 Kingsbury (Matthew, pp. 7ff.), following Lohmeyer (*Matthäus*) and Stonehouse (*Witness of Matthew*, pp. 129–31), argues strongly that *apo tote* ("From that time"),

both here and at 4:17, marks a major turning point in Matthew. Turning point there is, but it is not at all clear that the structure of the entire Gospel is dominated by these twin foci. The same expression is found in 26:16, which marks a turning point in Judas Iscariot's pilgrimage but scarcely a major turning point in the book. On the contrary, the very nature of the expression links what follows with what precedes (cf. Introduction, section 14).

For the meaning of "began," see on 11:7, 20, and compare 16:22. At the very least the verb implies that Jesus gave this explanation again and again. This is not the first time he alludes to his death (cf. 9:15; 10:38; 12:40; cf. also John 2:19; 3:14), but it is the first time he discusses it openly with his disciples. The time for symbols and veiled language was largely over now that they had recognized him as Messiah. That is probably the significance of the change from Mark's *didaskō* ("I teach") to Matthew's *deiknyō* ("I point out," "I show"—not, as in NIV, "I explain"). Jesus had taught the Passion earlier but in symbolic language. Now he shows these things to his disciples clearly. Matthew's verb (*deiknyō*) is equivalent to Mark's clause: "He spoke plainly about this" (8:32).

The prediction is remarkably detailed. Jesus must go to Jerusalem (cf. Luke 13:33); but the "must" of Jesus' suffering lies, not in unqualified determinism, nor in heroic determination (though some of both is present), but in willing submission to his Father's will. At Jerusalem, the killer of prophets (23:37), he will suffer many things (more details specified in 20:19) at the hands of the elders, chief priests, and teachers of the law—the three groups that largely constituted the Sanhedrin (see on 3:7; 26:59; one governing article, as in 16:1, 6; Pharisees would overlap with the first and third groups). There he would be killed and rise again the third day (see on 12:40).

The parallel in Mark 8:31 uses "Son of Man" language (see on 8:20; 16:13). The authenticity of this and other passion predictions has been widely discussed. Bultmann (*Synoptic Tradition*, p. 151) flatly denies it. Jeremias and Zimmerli (pp. 57ff.) approach the question by examining whether there are any Jewish antecedents to the notion of a suffering Messiah. Hill (*Matthew*) thinks Jesus foresaw confrontation in Jerusalem, typical of the prophets, and the possibility of suffering and death, but doubts that he could have spoken so explicitly. C.F.D. Moule ("From Defendant to Judge—and Deliverer: An Inquiry into the Use and Limitations of the Theme of Vindication in the New Testament," NTS 3 [1952–53]: 40–53) argues that the "Son of Man" (Mark 8:31), related to the "saints of the Most High" in Daniel 7, is vindicated after trial and suffering; so if Jesus takes this title and role to himself, he might well perceive the need to suffer before being exalted (cf. 26:64).

Lindars (*Apologetic*, pp. 60ff.) turns to Hosea 6:2 and suggests that historically Jesus spoke of resurrection, of being "raised to life," in a metaphor, as referring to the restoration of God's people. If so, what is surprising, especially in a book as studded with OT quotations as Matthew, is that Hosea is not mentioned nor his words clearly referred to, even allusively. On the face of it, our texts speak of Jesus' resurrection after being killed, not of Jesus' death followed by the restoration of God's people. Others have suggested that Jesus is thinking of Isaiah 53.

These approaches seek to make some part of Jesus' passion predictions historically credible through some historical antecedent on which Jesus allegedly based his predictions. While this is not wrong, it is too restrictive for dealing with one who claims exclusive and intimate knowledge of the Father (11:27). Is it reasonable to think that Jesus could have predicted the details of his passion only if he read about them somewhere? This is not to question the applicability of some of the OT allusions to him; it is rather to question the historical reductionism of some Gospel research.

How much of Jesus' sayings about his death did the disciples understand before the event? The Gospel evidence points in two complementary directions. On the one hand the disciples understand perfectly well: otherwise, for instance, Peter could not possibly have rebuked Jesus (v.22). On the other hand they cannot believe that Messiah will really be killed because their conceptions of the Messiah do not allow for a Suffering Servant. Therefore Peter dares to rebuke Jesus, and the disciples begin to think Jesus' predictions of his sufferings must be in some way nonliteral (Mark 9:10; Luke 9:45; see on Matt 17:4).

22 Peter's rebuke reveals how little he understands the kind of messiahship Jesus has in mind. "Began" (cf. v.21) suggests that Peter gets only so far before Jesus cuts him off (v.23). Peter uses very strong language. "Never, Lord!" (cf. Notes) is a vehement Septuagintalism. "This shall never happen to you!" renders *ou mē* ("never") plus a future indicative, instead of the expected aorist subjunctive. The future indicative after *ou mē*, which makes a strong expression even stronger, is comparatively rare in the NT (only here and in 15:6; 26:35; Mark 13:31; 14:31; Luke 21:33; John 4:14; 6:35; 10:5; Heb 10:17; Rev 9:6; 18:14), and most of these occurrences have textual variants. Peter's strong will and warm heart linked to his ignorance produce a shocking bit of arrogance. He confesses that Jesus is the Messiah and then speaks in a way implying that he knows more of God's will than the Messiah himself.

23 That "Jesus turned" means "Jesus turned away from Peter" or "turned his back on Peter" (B.F. Meyer) is doubtful: the connection with what follows is too awkward. If Jesus told Peter to get out of his way, even metaphorically, it must have been that Jesus was confronting him face to face, not turning away from him. It is better to assume that Jesus turned toward Peter to speak to him, the detail implying an indelible historical reminiscence. The sharp rebuke is made up of three parts.

1. *Hypage opisō mou, Satana* (lit., "Go behind me, Satan") could, by itself, be a call to discipleship (cf. the same adverb in Mark 1:17, 20; 8:34) and therefore be a sharp reminder for Peter to remember that as a disciple he must follow, not lead. But this ill suits the vocative "Satan." The verb *hypagō* is therefore best taken in the way it is used in Matthew 4:10 ("Away from me, Satan"). It is not simply that Peter should get out of Jesus' sight (so NIV) but, as a stumbling block, out of Jesus' way.

2. A few moments earlier Jesus had called Peter a rock. Now he calls him a different kind of "rock," a *skandalon* ("a stumbling block"; see on 5:29). This is one of several striking parallels between vv.13–20 and vv.21–23 (cf. A. Vögtle, "Messiasbekenntnis und Petrusverheissung: Zur Komposition Mt 16,13–23 Par.," *Biblische Zeitschrift* 1 [1957]: 269). As Satan offered Jesus kingship without suffering (4:8–9), so Peter does the same, adopting current expectations of victorious messianic conquest (Pss Sol 17; cf. HJP, 2:517–25, and bibliography, pp. 488–92). Jesus recognizes the same diabolical source behind the same temptation. For him to acquiesce would be to rebel against the will of his Father. The notion of a suffering Messiah, misunderstood by Peter so that he became a stumbling block to Jesus, itself becomes, after the Resurrection, a stumbling block to other Jews (1 Cor 1:23).

3. Peter was not thinking (the verb *phroneō* ["have in mind," NIV], common in Paul, is used elsewhere in the NT only here, in Mark 8:33, and in Acts 28:22) God's

thoughts (viz., that Jesus must go to Jerusalem and die, v.21), but men's thoughts (viz., that he must *not* go). In vv.13–17 Peter, unlike other men, did think God's thoughts because divine revelation was given him. Here, however, he has switched sides, aligning himself not only with men but with Satan.

Many scholars have thought the contrast between Peter in vv:13–20 and vv.21–23 so remarkable that they have worked out elaborate explanations of it. The most common view is that Peter is a stumbling block during Jesus' earthly ministry but becomes a foundation stone after the Resurrection (Brown et al., *Peter*, p. 94). There is an element of truth in this because Jesus' promise to Peter (vv. 17–19) does look to the future. But it looks to the future on the basis of the revelation Peter has *already* grasped (vv.16–17). This means that historically Peter did and did not understand. Along with the other disciples, he understood much more than the crowds; yet even so he did not reach full understanding till after the Resurrection. The juxtaposition of vv.13–20 and vv.21–23 clearly shows the (at best) qualified understanding of Jesus' disciples at this point in salvation history (Trotter).

Notes

21 The variants are very difficult. Most witnesses support ὁ Ἰησοῦς (*ho Iēsous*, "Jesus"); אᐟ B* cop^sa mss, bo offer Ἰησοῦς Χριστός (*Iēsous Christos*, "Jesus Christ"). The latter has early and important but very limited attestation. Its strength is that it admirably fits the context, after Jesus has just been confessed as being the Christ. By the same token a copyist might well think the same. The title in the second reading is very rare, which makes it the *lectio difficilior* ("the harder reading"). Internal evidence is therefore ambivalent. On external grounds alone the first reading is to be preferred. A few witnesses omit both, probably due to accidental deletion, something easily done in uncial scripts where the names were regularly abbreviated to IC and XC respectively.

22 Ἵλεώς σοι, κύριε (*Hileōs soi, kyrie*, "Never, Lord") has been understood two ways.

1. The word *hileōs*, used in the NT only here and in Heb 8:12, is taken to mean "propitious," "merciful," "gracious"; and the entire expression is an abbreviation of something longer, either ἵλεως εἴη σοι ὁ θεός (*hileōs eiē soi ho theos*, "May God be merciful to you") or ἵλεως ἔσται σοι ὁ θεός (*hileōs estai soi ho theos*, "God will be merciful to you"). Coupled with what Peter next says, the rebuke is still there but in rather soft language: "This won't happen to you, Lord, for God will be merciful to you" or "may God be merciful to you" (cf. Moulton, *Prolegomena*, p. 240; TDNT, 3:300–301).

2. It is far more likely that *hileōs* is merely a homonymic rendering of the Hebrew חָלִילָה (*ḥālîlāh*, "far be it from"). This is a common Septuagintalism and has the force in confrontational situations of a very strong "Never!" or "Be it far from you!" or "God forbid!" For references and discussion, see Turner, *Syntax*, p. 309; P. Katz, *Theologische Literaturzeitung* 82 (1957): 113f.; H.St.J. Thackeray, *A Grammar of the Old Testament in Greek According to the Septuagint* (Cambridge: University Press, 1909), 1:38; BDF, par. 128(5).

12. *The way of discipleship*

16:24–28

24Then Jesus said to his disciples, "If anyone would come after me, he must deny himself and take up his cross and follow me. 25For whoever wants to save his life will lose it, but whoever loses his life for me will find it. 26What good will it be for a man if he gains the whole world, yet forfeits his soul? Or what can a man give in exchange for his soul? [27]For the Son of Man is going to come in his Father's glory with his angels, and then he will reward each person according to what he has done. [28]I tell you the truth, some who are standing here will not taste death before they see the Son of Man coming in his kingdom."

Matthew omits mention of the crowds (cf. Mark 8:34) and omits Mark 8:38 because he has provided a parallel thought elsewhere (10:33). In v.27 Matthew adds some words from Psalm 62:12. This pericope does two things: (1) after the passion prediction in vv.21–23, it demands the disciples' willingness to deny themselves absolutely, a kind of death to self; (2) yet it assures us that the consummated kingdom will at last come. For the pericope's structure, see on v.28.

24 Though addressed to Jesus' "disciples" (see on 5:1–2), the thought is expressed in widest terms—"if anyone." As in 10:33, Jesus speaks of "disowning" or "renouncing" oneself. The Jews renounced the Messiah (Acts 3:14); his followers renounce themselves (cf. Rom 14:7–9; 15:2–3). They "take up their cross" (cf. 10:38): any Jew in Palestine would know that the man condemned to crucifixion was often forced to carry part of his own cross (see on 27:32)—a burden and a sign of death. Though Jesus does not explicitly mention the mode of his death till a few days before it takes place (20:19), the impact of this saying must have multiplied after Golgotha. Death to self is not so much a prerequisite of discipleship to Jesus as a continuing characteristic of it (see on 4:19; cf. John 12:23–26). (On the differences between discipleship to Jesus and discipleship to first-century rabbis, see Bornkamm, *Jesus*, pp. 144f.)

25–26 The logic is relentless: *gar* ("for") begins vv.25, 26, 27. For the sense of v.25, see on 10:39. The orientation is eschatological: saving one's *psychē* ("life," NIV; see on 10:28) *now* will result in losing it *at the end*, and losing it *now* will result in finding it *at the end*. Verse 26 (compare 2 Bar 51:15) furthers the argument by asking twin rhetorical questions, showing the folly of possessing all created abundance and wealth at the expense of one's *psychē*. NIV here changes its rendering "life" (v.25) to "soul" (v.26). This is not necessarily wrong. The abrupt change from the physical to the spiritual is amply attested elsewhere (cf. 8:22; John 4:10; 6:27); but the change in English is perhaps too sharp (cf. Luke 9:25: "his very self"). The focus is still eschatological, and the loss is the eternal loss of one's soul = life = self (on the afterlife, see on 22:23–33). Terminology aside, the bargain is a bad one.

27 Not only Jesus' example (v.24; cf. 10:24–25), but the judgment he will exercise is an incentive to take up one's cross and follow him. The Son of Man (see on 8:20; 16:13) will come "in his Father's glory"—the same glory God his Father enjoys (cf. 26:64; John 17:1–5), another implicit claim to the status of deity—along with his angels, who both enhance his glory and serve as his agents for the eschatological ingathering (13:41; 24:31; 25:31–32; Luke 9:26). They are *his* angels: he stands so far above them that he owns them and uses them. At that time he will reward each person *kata tēn praxin auton* ("according to what he has done"). The language is that of Psalm 62:12, where Yahweh rewards his people; and the Yahweh–Jesus exchange is not uncommon. The use of *praxis* ("conduct," "deeds") is Matthew's rendering of the Hebrew collective singular by a corresponding singular in Greek (Gundry, *Use of OT*, p. 138). For the concept of rewards, see on 5:12.

28 Many of the possible interpretations and difficult issues bound up with this verse have been treated at 10:23 and need not be repeated. Martin Künzi (*Das Naherwartungslogion Markus 9, 1 par: Geschichte seiner Auslegung* [Tübingen: J.C.B. Mohr, 1977]) has an excellent history of interpretation.

The parallel in Mark 9:1 has a somewhat different "before" clause: "before they see the kingdom of God come with power." But this and Matthew's "before they see the Son of Man coming in his kingdom" may mean much the same thing, when it is remembered that "kingdom" is a dynamic concept (see on 3:2), and that "the coming of the Son of Man" also has a wide range of possible meanings (see on 10:23). The principal explanations of this verse may be briefly listed.

1. C.H. Dodd (*Parables*, pp. 53–54) interprets Mark's form of the saying as meaning "there are some who stand here who will never taste death until they have seen that the kingdom of God has come with power." In other words, the kingdom *had come* when Jesus was speaking (perfect participle *elēlythuian*) and the disciples "see"—i.e., perceive—that this is so. But, as many have shown, this is an unnatural way of taking the verb "to see"; and it introduces an insurmountable problem in Matthew, where the participle is *erchomenon* ("the kingdom of God *coming*").

2. Many have held that this verse refers to the Transfiguration, the very next pericope in both Matthew and Mark. The problem is twofold. First, "some who are standing here will not taste death before they see" is an extraordinary way to refer to Peter, James, and John, who witness the Transfiguration a mere six days later (17:1). Second, as magnificent as the Transfiguration was, it is not entirely clear how the Son of Man comes in his kingdom (Matt) or the kingdom comes in power (Mark) through this event.

3. Others take this to refer to the Resurrection or to Pentecost. This view has been strenuously defended, but again it faces the difficulty that even these events are not far enough off to warrant the phrasing "some standing here who will not taste death."

4. Still others (Plummer, Gaechter) think the saying refers to the Fall of Jerusalem (a view this commentary defends for 10:23). The chief problem is that the context does not encourage this interpretation here, as it does in 10:23: there is no mention of the cities of Israel, of persecution in synagogue settings, etc. Indeed, the preceding verse (16:27) appears to refer to the Parousia.

5. Others interpret this verse as referring to the Parousia but draw divergent conclusions. Some think the saying shows that Jesus expected history to end within a few years but was clearly wrong; others that "some who are standing here" refers, not to those then standing there, but to the final generation, prophetically foreseen. If Matthew believed that the former was what Jesus meant, we would expect a Gospel full of the Thessalonian heresy, loaded with expectation of the Second Coming because few of the first generation would still be alive. Instead, the disciples' mission is to continue to the end of the age (28:20). The second alternative means that the words were calculated to be misunderstood by "those who [were] standing here."

6. Recently Bruce Chilton has offered a novel interpretation (*God in Strength*, pp. 251–74; id., "An Evangelical and Critical Approach to the Sayings of Jesus," *Themelios* 3 [1977–78]: 78–85). He argues that "those not tasting death" is a technical reference to "immortals" like Elijah and Enoch (cf. Gen R 9:6; 4 Ezra 6:26); that what Jesus actually said was that the immortals, like Elijah and Moses in the Trans-

figuration scene that immediately follows, do indeed witness the reality of the king-dom, understood as God's revelation on behalf of his people. If this is correct, then the problem of trying to find a suitable period to explain Jesus' prediction in Matthew 16:28 and Mark 9:1 is resolved: there is no prediction left. But Chilton's argument depends on adopting a doubtful reading in Mark 9:1 (cf. Brower, pp. 30–31) and on reasoning that maintains that both Mark and Matthew so completely misinterpreted Jesus that they make him say something quite different from what he really said. The word "here," despite Chilton's contention that it contrasts those not tasting death with Jesus' hearers, is most naturally understood to refer to them.

Moreover, most of Chilton's sources for nailing down "those not tasting death" ("taste death" itself simply means "die"; cf. Heb 2:9) as a special phrase for "immortals" are either certainly or probably late. Whereas some elements of Jewish tradition did treat Moses, along with Elijah, as a "deathless figure," the OT firmly insists that "Moses the servant of the LORD died" (Deut 34:5). Furthermore, what "those who are standing here" will see is, in Mark, the kingdom "coming with power" or "having come with power"—i.e., they see evidence of the kingdom's powerful operation. This is interpreted by Matthew to be the equivalent of "the Son of Man coming in [or perhaps 'with'; cf. BDF, par. 198(2)] his reign"—i.e., they see evidence of the Son of Man's reigning authority. But Chilton's interpretation allows for none of this. In his view the "deathless figures" merely perceive the reality of God's reign; and thus Chilton confuses the kingdom with evidence for the coming of the kingdom.

Jesus refers to those who "will not taste death," but Chilton treats them as if they are generically "those not tasting death." He does this by rightly pointing out that the words do not necessarily mean that those "standing" there will necessarily taste death *after* they have seen the kingdom coming in power. The words *ou mē . . . heōs an* ("not . . . until") reflect a Semitic construction, used in Genesis 28:15, where God says to Jacob, "I will not leave you until I have done what I have promised you," which does not mean God will leave him afterwards. From this Chilton deduces that "will not taste death until ['before,' NIV]" refers to "immortals," or "deathless figures," because the "until" does not necessarily mark the end of something. But this, though correct, misses two crucial points.

First, whether "those standing" must one day die or not, with this expression the part of the sentence *before* the "until" clause always expresses something new or the ending or changing of something. The main clause always demands sequence and change. For example, in the Genesis passage just quoted, "until" may not mean that God will then leave Jacob; but the main clause does mean that God will keep every word of his promises and remain with Jacob, *at least* "until" all the promises have been fulfilled. Likewise in Mark 9:1 and Matthew 16:28, the "until" clause ("before," NIV) does not necessarily mean those "standing" must die; but the verse as a whole does mean they will at some future time witness the powerful operation of the reign of God (Mark), the coming of the Son of Man with his reign (Matthew), and that *at least* until then they will not die. Thus even Chilton's reconstruction does not eliminate the difficulty of determining what time period within salvation is in view. He has sidestepped the problem but not resolved it.

Second, the *ou mē . . . heōs an* ("not . . . until") construction *can* mean that at the "until" the action or state of the first clause will cease (as in 23:39). There are numerous NT occurrences of this construction (5:18, 26; 10:23; 16:28; 23:39; 24:34;

Mark 9:1; 14:25; Luke 9:27; 12:59; 13:35; 21:32); and in addition there are important variations with the same meaning, none more so than Luke 2:26, where it had been revealed to Simeon that he would not see death *until* (*prin an* or *prin ē an* or *heōs an*) he saw the Lord's Christ, after which, apparently, he died. Many of these references give evidence of the termination of the action of the first clause when the time of the "until" clause has passed. Along with comments on the natural force of "here," these data suggest that the best way to take "some who are standing *here* will not taste death *until* they see the Son of Man coming with his reign" therefore depends solely on the meaning of "the Son of Man coming with his reign." If this is a reference to the Parousia, then the "some who are standing here" will not die even then; but in that case Jesus' chronology would be very wrong. If it is a reference to the demonstrable evidences of powerful kingship, then "some who are standing here" will die at some point after seeing those evidences. Moreover it must be said that Chilton's redaction-critical methods, though done with rigor, are so procrustean in distinguishing between the "traditional" and the "redactional" that they can only produce suspect results.

7. It seems best to take 16:28 as having a more general reference—viz., not referring simply to the Resurrection, to Pentecost, or the like, but to the manifestation of Christ's kingly reign exhibited after the Resurrection in a host of ways, not the least of them being the rapid multiplication of disciples and the mission to the Gentiles. Some of those standing there would live to see Jesus' Gospel proclaimed throughout the Roman Empire and a rich "harvest" (cf. 9:37–38) of converts reaped for Jesus Messiah. This best suits the flexibility of the "kingdom" concept in the synoptic Gospels (see on 3:2; 10:23; 12:28) and the present context. Thus 16:28 does not refer to the same thing as 10:23. But the distinction is made, not on the basis that consistency is "the hobgoblin of little minds," but on the basis of context.

This pericope contains an important chiasm:

> v.24: challenge to take up the cross and follow Christ in the immediate future
>> v.25: incentive—reward and punishment at the Parousia
>>> v.26: central weighing of values
>> v.27: incentive—reward and punishment at the Parousia
> v.28: promise of witnessing the kingdom power of Jesus in the immediate future

The setting is quite different from that in 10:23. But if the evidence of the kingdom is seen in the church, this does not mean that the church and the kingdom are to be identified. Rather, at this point in salvation history it is the power of the kingdom working through Jesus' disciples that calls the church into being (see further on 13:36–43). Moreover, as Brower (pp. 32ff.) points out, the larger context also offers important insights. Though the Transfiguration is not the fulfillment of v.28, it is related to it in an important way. Sections that stress suffering and the Cross (16:21–28; 17:9–13) envelop the Transfiguration and bracket this clearest manifestation of divine glory by suffering. The way to glory is the way of the Cross; and the reign of the Son of Man, which "some standing here" will see before they "taste death," will be inaugurated by the Cross.

13. The Transfiguration (17:1–13)

a. Jesus transfigured

17:1–8

> [1]After six days Jesus took with him Peter, James and John the brother of James, and led them up a high mountain by themselves. [2]There he was transfigured before them. His face shone like the sun, and his clothes became as white as the light. [3]Just then there appeared before them Moses and Elijah, talking with Jesus.
> [4]Peter said to Jesus, "Lord, it is good for us to be here. If you wish, I will put up three shelters—one for you, one for Moses and one for Elijah."
> [5]While he was still speaking, a bright cloud enveloped them, and a voice from the cloud said, "This is my Son, whom I love; with him I am well pleased. Listen to him!"
> [6]When the disciples heard this, they fell facedown to the ground, terrified. [7]But Jesus came and touched them. "Get up," he said. "Don't be afraid." [8]When they looked up, they saw no one except Jesus.

This passage raises difficult literary, historical, and theological questions. The *literary* questions arise largely from the several important "minor agreements" of Matthew and Luke (9:28–36) against Mark (9:2–8), raising doubts about the adequacy of the two-source hypothesis (cf. Introduction, section 3). These have recently been scrutinized by F. Neirynck ("Minor Agreements of Matthew-Luke in the Transfiguration Story," in Hoffmann et al., pp. 253–66) and judged to be of greater relevance to the tendencies of Matthew and Luke than to source-critical relationships.

The *historical* questions arise because there have been numerous attempts to explain the origin of this story in some setting other than what the evangelists present. Schweitzer (pp. 380ff.) holds that when Jesus' dreams were shattered following the mission of the Twelve (he thought that mission would usher in the kingdom), he experienced an ecstatic, perhaps glossalalic, vision later reinterpreted by his disciples. This historical reconstruction depends on Schweitzer's broader theories, now long discredited (see on 10:23). More influential is Bultmann's view that this story is a misplaced resurrection narrative (*Synoptic Tradition*, p. 259). But this has been decisively rebutted by Robert H. Stein ("Is the Transfiguration [Mark 9:2–8] a Misplaced Resurrection-Account?" JBL 95 [1976]: 79–96), who shows that in language and form the theory of Bultmann and many others will not work.

More recently B.D. Chilton ("The Transfiguration: Dominical Assurance and Apostolic Vision," NTS 27 [1980]: 115–24) has followed up his interpretation of v.28 (details above) by positing that the genesis of the transfiguration narrative is his reconstruction of Jesus' saying behind v.28—viz., Jesus swears by "deathless witnesses" that the "kingdom," the revelation of "God in strength," continues in forceful operation. These "deathless witnesses" were understood by the disciples to be Moses and Elijah, a step not dominical but consistent with it. Then Peter, James, and John, who saw themselves as Aaron, Nadab, and Abihu with reference to the new Moses (i.e., Jesus), emphasized the continuity of Jesus' disclosure with the prophetic revelation of old in this "visio-literary fashion." Chilton's first and essential step we have seriously questioned (see on v.28), and the rest is little more than mere assertion without further supporting evidence. Even if his understanding of v.28 were correct, it is difficult to see on what evidential grounds he holds that 17:1-8 is meant by the evangelist to be nonhistorical.

The *theological* questions arise because the story has so many nuances—allusions to Moses, his experience of glory and his role in redemptive history, Elijah and his role as eschatological forerunner, Jesus' baptism (the Voice from heaven saying much the same thing, cf. 3:17), the Parousia, perhaps the shekinah glory, and others. The narrative is clearly a major turning point in Jesus' self-disclosure, and some attempt must be made to weave these themes together without merely allegorizing the passage. The best recent exposition is that of Liefeld. Also, G.H. Boobyer (*St. Mark and the Transfiguration Story* [Edinburgh: T. & T. Clark, 1942], pp. 1–47) provides a useful survey of theological options.

1 Precise time indicators like "after six days" are rare in the Synoptics apart from in the passion narrative. Luke's "about eight days after Jesus said this" (9:28) is based on a Greek way of speaking and means "about a week later." Numerous suggestions have been made as to why "six days" should be mentioned. Bonnard, following H. Baltensweiler (*Die Verklärung Jesu* [Zürich: Zwingli, 1959]), sees an allusion to the six days separating the Day of Atonement from the Feast of Tabernacles. In this view the first explicit mention of Jesus' passion (16:21–23) occurs on the former day and the Transfiguration, with its "shelters" (v.4) or "tabernacles," on the latter. But it seems highly unlikely that Jesus and his disciples would travel from Caesarea Philippi to this mountain during the feast. Nor is there any direct evidence of its being that time of year. Others see a reference to Exodus 24:16 ("For six days the cloud covered the mountain, and on the seventh day the Lord called to Moses from within the cloud"). Such views are probably too subtle—especially for Luke! The "six days" may simply indicate the time it took to travel from one place (16:13) to another (17:1) and thus establish the fact, noted by all three synoptists, that the Transfiguration took place within a few days of the prediction that Jesus must go to Jerusalem and be killed. The two passages must therefore be read together.

Mount Tabor, the traditional "high mountain," lies south of Galilee; but it is not at all "high" (about 1,900 feet), and going to it would have been a roundabout way of traveling from Caesarea Philippi to Capernaum (vv.22, 24; Mark 9:30, 33). Moreover, according to Josephus it had a walled fortress at its summit (War II, 573 [xx.6]; IV, 54–55 [i.8]). Mount Hermon, rising above Caesarea Philippi, is the most popular alternative (9,232 feet); but it is so high and cold at its summit—if indeed they went to the top—it seems a strange place to pass the night (Luke specifies they descended the next day). Immediately after their descent Jesus and the inner three faced crowds that included "teachers of the law" (Mark 9:14). This is almost inconceivable at Mount Hermon in Gentile territory. Liefeld (p. 167, n. 27) has plausibly suggested Mount Miron (3,926 feet), the highest mountain within Israel and on the way from Caesarea Philippi to Capernaum. The "mountain" calls to mind Moses and Elijah, both of whom received revelation on a mountain (Exod 19; 24; 1 Kings 19), though here part of the purpose was to ensure privacy ("by themselves," Matt 17:1; "all alone," Mark 9:2).

Those Jesus "took with him" (the verb, contrary to some recent expositions, has no obvious connection with master–disciple relations; cf. its use in 2:13; 4:5; 12:45) were Peter, James, and John, the inner circle of the Twelve (see on 10:2; 20:20; 26:37; cf. Mark 5:37, and the continued friendship of Peter and John, Acts 8:14; Gal 2:9 [with a different James]).

2 Moses' face shone because it reflected something of God's glory (Exod 34:29–30). But as for Jesus, he himself was transfigured. The verb *metamorphoō* ("transfigure," "transform," "change in form") suggests a change of inmost nature that may be outwardly visible (as here; cf. Exod 34:29; 2 Bar 51:3, 5) or quite invisible (Rom 12:2; 2 Cor 3:18). That Jesus was transfigured "before them" implies that it was largely for their sakes: whatever confirmation the experience may have given Jesus, for the disciples it was revelatory. As they would come to realize, they were being privileged to glimpse something of his preincarnate glory (John 1:14; 17:5; Phil 2:6–7) and anticipate his coming exaltation (2 Peter 1:16–18; Rev 1:16). Their confession of Jesus as Messiah and his insistence that he would be a suffering Messiah (16:13–21; 17:9) were confirmed. Therefore they had reason to hope that they would yet see the Son of Man coming in his kingdom (16:28). The contrast between what Jesus had just predicted would be his fate (16:21) and this glorious sight would one day prompt Jesus' disciples to marvel at the self-humiliation that brought him to the cross and to glimpse a little of the height to which he had been raised by his vindicating resurrection and ascension.

3 The word *idou* should not be pressed to mean "Just then" (NIV): it is used twice more in v.5 where it stresses the marvel of the experience (see on 1:20). Unlike Mark, Matthew puts Moses before Elijah, giving him slightly greater status; and only Matthew mentions the brightness of the cloud (v.5), reminiscent of the shekinah glory (cf. Davies, *Setting*, pp. 50–56). Both Moses and Elijah had eschatological roles: Moses was the model for the eschatological Prophet (Deut 18:18) and Elijah for the forerunner (Mal 4:5–6; Matt 3:1–3; 11:7–10; 17:9–13). Both had strange ends; both were men of God in times of transition, the first to introduce the covenant and the second to work for renewed adherence to it. Both experienced a vision of God's glory, one at Sinai (Exod 31:18) and the other at Horeb (1 Kings 19:8). Now, however, the glory is Jesus' glory, for it is he who is transfigured and who radiates the glory of Deity. Both suffered rejection of various kinds (for Moses, cf. Stephen's summary, Acts 7:35, 37; and for Elijah, cf. 1 Kings 19:1–9; Matt 17:12). Together they may well summarize the Law and the Prophets. This is the more plausible when we recall that these two figures very rarely appear together in Judaism or in the NT (possibly Rev 11:3; cf. Zech 4:14; J. Jeremias, TDNT, 4:863–64). All these associations gain importance as the narrative moves on and Jesus is perceived to be superior to Moses and Elijah and, indeed, to supersede them (vv.5, 8).

The verb *ōphthē* ("appeared"), sometimes used in connection with Jesus' resurrection, does not in itself suggest a resurrection setting, since Moses and Elijah are the ones who "appear," not Jesus.

4 Peter "answered" Jesus (NIV, "said"): the peculiar verb form (*apokritheis*) may mean that his suggestion was called forth by the circumstances, but more likely it has no force of "response" (see on 11:25). Peter, speaking for the three ("it is good for *us* to be here"), sensing something of the greatness of what he, James, and John are seeing, suggests building three *skēnas* ("tabernacles"; NIV, "shelters"). While the word looks back to the tabernacle in the wilderness, forerunner of the temple, the idea of building "tabernacles" also reflects the Feast of Tabernacles, when Jews built shelters for themselves and lived in them for seven days (cf. Lev 23:42–43). The feast had eschatological overtones. So Peter may have been saying that in gratitude for witnessing Jesus' transfiguration and recognizing the imminent dawn of the Messianic Age, he would build three "tabernacles"—one for Jesus, one for Moses, and one for Elijah.

The rebuke that follows does not offer criticism of Peter's eschatology, nor even of its timing, but is administered solely because what Peter blurted out compromised Jesus' uniqueness. *Jesus* was transfigured; they must bear witness concerning *him* (v.5). Mark says Peter spoke out of fear; Luke that he made his suggestion as Moses and Elijah were about to leave. Mark and Luke point out the foolishness of Peter's remark. Matthew simplifies and so highlights the christological error of Peter.

Mark (9:5) has "Rabbi," Luke (9:33) "Master," and Matthew "Lord." Mark is probably original; Luke translates "Rabbi" by "Master" for his non-Jewish readers; and Matthew probably uses "Lord" in its general sense (see on 7:21), connoting no more respect than "rabbi." But why Matthew's different form of address? Perhaps it is to stress what Peter is doing. Earlier Peter confessed Jesus as Christ and yet rebuked him because Peter did not understand the full meaning of "Christ." Here he again treats Jesus with respect ("Lord") but suggests something that compromises his identity. Matthew's readers know very well that "Christ" means more than messianic political conqueror and that "Lord" would in time include unqualified supremacy. But Peter does not yet know these things.

5 The "cloud" is associated, in both the OT and intertestamental Judaism, with eschatology (Ps 97:2; Isa 4:5; Ezek 30:3; Dan 7:13; Zeph 1:15; cf. 2 Baruch 53:1–12; 4 Ezra 13:3; 2 Macc 2:8; b *Sanhedrin* 98a; cf. Luke 21:27; 1 Thess 4:17) and with the Exodus (Exod 13:21–22; 16:10; 19:16; 24:15–18; 40:34–38). Of the synoptists only Matthew says that the cloud was "bright," a detail that recalls the shekinah glory. The latter eschatological associations (Luke 21:27; 1 Thess 4:17) show Jesus in his role as the one who succeeds Moses the eschatological prophet; the former associations (Ps 97:2 et al.) assure us that Jesus is the messianic King whose kingdom is dawning. But as Liefeld (p. 170) points out, common to both sets of passages and to others as well is the more fundamental idea of the presence of God.

It is uncertain whether *epeskiasen* means "enveloped" (NIV) or "overshadowed" (cf. Exod 40:35). What the Voice from the cloud says is largely a repetition of 3:17, an apparent mingling of Psalm 2:7 and Isaiah 42:1, stressing that Jesus is both Son and Suffering Servant. This is the high point of the narrative (cf. S. Pedersen, "Die Proklamation Jesu als des eschatologischen Offenbarungsträgers," NovTest 17 [1975]: 241–64). (Mark omits the allusion to Isa 42:1; but both Matthew and Luke, not to mention 2 Peter 1:17, attest the connection in different ways: cf. Gundry, *Use of OT*, pp. 36–37.) But if Matthew 3:17 identifies Jesus, this verse in its context goes further and places him above Moses and Elijah.

The additional words "Listen to him"—an allusion to Deuteronomy 18:15—confirm Jesus is the Prophet like Moses (Deut 18:15–18; cf. Acts 3:22–23; 7:37). This does not mean Jesus is another prophet of Moses' stature but the eschatological Prophet patterned on Moses as a type; for, as Liefeld has suggested (p. 173), Moses' primary role here is typological, whereas Elijah's, not explained till vv.9–13, is eschatological. As Moses' antitype, Jesus so far outstrips him that when Moses is put next to him, men must "listen" to Jesus, as Moses himself said. The climax of biblical revelation is Jesus, the Son and Servant God loves and with whom God is well pleased. Even Moses and Elijah (the Law and the Prophets) assume supporting roles where he is concerned. This confirms our interpretation of 5:17–48; 11:11–15.

6–8 The effect of the Transfiguration on the disciples reminds us of Daniel (Dan 10:7–9; cf. also Deut 5:25–26; Heb 12:19). The visible glory of Deity brings terror, but Jesus calms his disciples' fears (cf. 14:26–27; cf. Dan 8:18; 10:18). Mark relates fear to Peter's foolish words; Matthew, to the disciples' response to the Voice from the cloud. Both are psychologically convincing; both make different points in the narrative. In Mark fear helps explain Peter's folly. In Matthew it magnifies the greatness of the Transfiguration. Matthew alone tells us that at the divine splendor the disciples "fell facedown to the ground" (v.6), a prelude to their seeing no one "except Jesus" (v.8). These words are pregnant with meaning. Compared with God's revelation through him, all other revelations pale. Supporting, pointing, prophetic roles such revelation may enjoy; but that Jesus is God's Son (and here Matthew's readers must have remembered chs. 1–2) is primary. Therefore all must "listen to him!" (v.7).

The Transfiguration was largely for the disciples (Jesus brought the inner three to it; he was transfigured before "them"; the Voice spoke to "them": cf. Allison A. Trites, "The Transfiguration of Jesus: The Gospel in Microcosm," EQ 51 [1979]: 77f.). This does not mean that they understood it fully; but it was a crucial step in the symbol-charged self-disclosure of Jesus that would be much better understood (2 Peter 1:16–19) following the Resurrection. For the present, it indelibly confirmed the disciples' conviction that Jesus was the Messiah.

Notes

4 BDF, par. 372(2c), suggests that "If you wish," found only in Matthew, is Hellenistic for "please" (cf. French *s'il vous plaît*).
5 There have been many attempts to relate the words of the Voice from heaven to the story of the near sacrifice of Isaac in Genesis 22, as that story is developed in late Judaism into vicarious atonement motifs. But P.R. Davies and B.D. Chilton ("The Aqedah: A Revised Tradition History," CBQ 40 [1978]: 514–46) have clearly shown that such Jewish traditions did not develop until after A.D. 70.

b. *The place of Elijah*

17:9–13

> [9]As they were coming down the mountain, Jesus instructed them, "Don't tell anyone what you have seen, until the Son of Man has been raised from the dead."
> [10]The disciples asked him, "Why then do the teachers of the law say that Elijah must come first?"
> [11]Jesus replied, "To be sure, Elijah comes and will restore all things. [12]But I tell you, Elijah has already come, and they did not recognize him, but have done to him everything they wished. In the same way the Son of Man is going to suffer at their hands." [13]Then the disciples understood that he was talking to them about John the Baptist.

Luke has no parallel, but see Mark 9:9–13. Matthew omits Mark 9:10; and his handling of Mark 9:12–13 in 17:11–13 is so independent, though complementary, that some scholars think Matthew here draws on an independent source (e.g., Schlatter, Lohmeyer).

9 In Matthew this is Jesus' fifth and last command for the disciples to be silent (see on 8:4). This time Jesus permits his disciples to tell everything after the Son of Man (see excursus on 8:20) "has been raised from the dead." Jesus could scarcely have attached this permission to earlier warnings to keep silent (16:20), since he had not yet spoken clearly about his sufferings and death. Nevertheless the same salvation-historical change—first silence, then proclamation—occurs as early as 10:27.

The command must have been in some ways disappointing and its lifting a delight. Why did Jesus impose it? Probably for two principal and complementary reasons:

1. The story would only stir up superficial political messianism, already a menace. If Jesus' closest disciples found it hard to understand a suffering and dying Messiah, how would the crowds fare—till after the Resurrection?

2. The strongest evidence for Jesus' messiahship would be his resurrection, by which he "was declared with power to be the Son of God" (Rom 1:4). Premature self-disclosure in a direct fashion, without the supreme "sign of Jonah," the Resurrection (see on 12:40), would not only foster false expectations but would also quickly disillusion those who held them. Thus with his prospective converts in mind, Jesus knew it was better for their sakes to wait till after the Resurrection before allowing Peter, James, and John to tell what they had seen.

This does not mean that Jesus' full glory could be known only through the Resurrection. On the contrary, it means that though his true glory antedated the Resurrection and was revealed to three intimates before the Passion, it could be made known to others only after the Resurrection.

10 Why did the disciples ask this question, connecting it (in Matthew) with *oun* (normally a logical connective, "therefore," "then")? There are two false solutions:

1. If Jesus was the Messiah, how were the disciples to answer the objection of the scribes that Elijah must *precede* Messiah's coming (Mal 4:5–6; see on 11:7–15; M *Eduyoth* 8:7; M *Baba Metzia* 3:5; SBK, 4:764–98)? In this view the *oun* follows the fact of Jesus' messiahship and the disciples' acceptance of Jesus' reiteration of his death and resurrection: *because* the disciples understand who Jesus is, they ask why, therefore, the scribes insist Elijah precedes Messiah, since apparently Elijah has not yet appeared. This interpretation is intrinsically unlikely, as Mark's account shows: the disciples are there pictured "discussing what 'rising from the dead' meant" (Mark 9:10), thereby showing they did *not* truly understand what Jesus was talking about; and as a result of this discussion, they ask the question in Mark 9:11 and Matthew 17:10. Commentators on Mark assume this is a second relevant question but do not show how it ties in with the disciples' discussion. Trench (*Studies*, p. 222) goes so far as to say that the disciples do not venture to raise the first subject and so move on to this one; Lagrange says Matthew omits Mark 9:10 because that text leads nowhere. Yet a tight connection can be established.

2. A few scholars have suggested that the disciples' question was prompted by an assumption that Elijah's appearance during the Transfiguration was itself the fulfillment of Malachi 4:5; and then the question becomes, Why did Messiah (Jesus) appear before Elijah did, when the scribes say the order should be reversed (B.F. Meyer; Robertson, 1:141)? But this interpretation suffers from the weakness of the

former view (viz., that the disciples properly understand Jesus' teaching of 17:9 and par.), while resting on the dubious assumption that the disciples would interpret this brief vision of Elijah as the fulfillment of a prophecy that promised that Elijah would "turn the hearts of the fathers to their children, and the hearts of the children to their fathers" (Mal 4:6).

The real connection is deeper. Elijah was expected to restore all things—to bring about a state of justice and true worship. If that were so, how could it be that Messiah would be killed in such a restored environment—killed, Jesus had told them only a week before, by elders, chief priests, and teachers of the law (16:21)? This interpretation makes sense both of Matthew's *own* ("therefore") and of Mark 9:10. If Jesus as Messiah (whose messiahship the disciples do not now doubt) must *suffer*, then how could it be said that Elijah must first come *to restore all things?* Their confusion is not merely chronological, though that may be involved; it is their inability to find a framework in which they can believe that the Messiah could die.

11–12 Jesus' answer confirms this interpretation. He approves the teaching of the scribes but insists that another fact must be taken into account. NIV's "To be sure, . . . But" structure accurately reflects this duality (Gr. *men*, . . . *de*). On the one hand, Elijah comes "first" (*prōton*, in some MSS) and "will restore all things" (v.11; the combination of present and future tenses is less consistent than Mark 9:12 but reflects the OT prophecy: see Zerwick, par. 281). John's mission was a success (3:5–6; 14:5); but, on the other hand, "restore all things" must not be taken absolutely. The Baptist stood in succession of the OT prophets who were persecuted and even killed. The unrecognized fact is that although the scribes' *interpretation* is right—Elijah must precede the Messiah—their grasp of recent *history* is wrong, for Elijah has already come (v.12; cf. 11:14; Luke 1:17); but the people in general and the scribes and leaders in particular did not recognize him and did to him "everything they wished"—a vague expression hinting at John's rejection by most Jewish leaders (cf. 21:24–27) and his death, for which the Jewish leaders were not directly responsible.

Jesus' point is general: the Baptist (Elijah) did fulfill his mission, but he was killed doing it. "In the same way the Son of Man is going to suffer [cf. BDF, par. 315] at their hands" (v.12b). If the Baptist's restoration of "all things" did not prevent his own death, why should Messiah be any better received?

13 Matthew's conclusion, not found in Mark, has provoked much speculation. G. Barth (Bornkamm, *Tradition*, p. 106) takes it as further evidence for his idea that in Matthew "understanding" is essential to discipleship. Others think it a turning point in Matthew's narrative—the disciples now arrive at true understanding (Klostermann; Trilling, p. 92). Still others hold that this introduces a split between what the disciples understand and the teachers of the law don't (McNeile; Schweizer; Frankmölle, p. 151; Meier, *Vision*, p. 123). Though this has some validity, there are two other factors: (1) Matthew again rounds off a pericope by returning to the question first raised (see on 15:20); and (2) what the disciples understand is that John the Baptist is Elijah. It is not at all clear, however, that they have understood much more about the death and resurrection of the Son of Man, and it becomes very obvious during the passion narrative that they have not understood (cf. esp. 26:50–56). In short, this pericope marks another small step in the understanding of Jesus' disciples.

Notes

---

9 Because Matthew has τὸ ὅραμα (*to horama*, lit., "the vision"; NIV, "what you have seen") for Mark's ἃ εἶδον (*ha eidon*, "what they had seen," NIV), many suggest that Matthew is seeking to explain the Transfiguration in acceptable terms to his readers. But *horama* does not necessarily mean "vision" as a result of a dream or a trance; it can simply refer to what is seen (BAGD, s.v.). Therefore too much should not be made of the difference between the two expressions.

---

14. *The healing of an epileptic boy*

17:14–20[21]

¹⁴When they came to the crowd, a man aproached Jesus and knelt before him. ¹⁵"Lord, have mercy on my son," he said. "He has seizures and is suffering greatly. He often falls into the fire or into the water. ¹⁶I brought him to your disciples, but they could not heal him."

¹⁷"O unbelieving and perverse generation," Jesus replied, "how long shall I stay with you? How long shall I put up with you? Bring the boy here to me." ¹⁸Jesus rebuked the demon, and it came out of the boy, and he was healed from that moment.

¹⁹Then the disciples came to Jesus in private and asked, "Why couldn't we drive it out?"

²⁰He replied, "Because you have so little faith. I tell you the truth, if you have faith as small as a mustard seed, you can say to this mountain, 'Move from here to there' and it will move. Nothing will be impossible for you."

All three synoptists (cf. Mark 9:14–29; Luke 9:37–43) put this miracle right after the descent from the Mount of Transfiguration. Matthew's account is much shorter than Mark's, which has led some to think Matthew used independent information here. It introduces v.20 (the thrust of which occurs again at 21:21) and thus makes faith pivotal in the narrative. The contrast between the glory of the Transfiguration and Jesus' disciples' tawdry unbelief (see v.17) is part of the mounting tension that magnifies Jesus' uniqueness as he moves closer to his passion and resurrection.

14–16 Matthew's account, with its sudden introduction of the crowd (v.14), clearly presupposes some fuller narrative (cf. Mark). The word for "knelt" (*gonypeteō*, used in the NT only here and at 27:29; Mark 1:40; 10:17) has no overtones of worship but suggests humility and entreaty. For "Lord" (v.15; Mark has "Teacher"), see on 8:2; 17:4. *Selēniazetai* ("is an epileptic") occurs only twice in the NT (see on 4:24). Mark 9:18–20 describes the boy's symptoms more vividly. "Epilepsy" in this instance is associated with demon possession (see on 8:28). The "disciples" who are unable to heal him are presumably the nine left behind when Jesus took Peter, James, and John with him when he was transfigured.

The disciples' failures are a recurring theme throughout this section (14:16–21, 26–27, 28–31; 15:16, 23, 33; 16:5, 22; 17:4, 10–11). This failure in their healing ministry at first seems strange, since Jesus had clearly given them power to heal and exorcise demons (10:1, 8). Yet it is part of the pattern of the disciples' advance and failure. In other situations they had shown lack of faith (14:26–27, 31; 15:5, 8)—a reminder that their power to do kingdom miracles was not their own but, unlike magic, was entirely derivative and related to their own walk of faith.

17–18 Jesus' response is reminiscent of Deuteronomy 32:5, 20. *Apistos* (v.17) can mean either "untrustworthy" or "unbelieving." The latter is dominant here (cf. v.20); yet it does not mean "this generation" has no faith whatsoever but that unbelief is characteristic of "this generation." The perfect passive participle *diestrammenē* ("perverse") probably has adjectival force, rather than denoting a state consequent on some previous action (see on 16:19). Juxtaposing "perverse" and "unbelieving" implies that the failure to believe stems from moral failure to recognize the truth, not from want of evidence, but from willful neglect or distortion of the evidence. *Diastrephō* ("to pervert") is used seven times in the NT (cf. Luke 9:41; 23:2; Acts 13:8, 10; 20:30; Phil 2:15). In the last of these, Paul applies to the entire world the same words Jesus uses here.

But what does "generation" (*genea*) cover? Assuredly it extends Jesus' excoriation beyond the disciples (cf. also 11:16; 12:39–42; 16:4; 23:36; 24:34). But it goes past the evidence to hold with R. Walker (pp. 35ff.) that the word here means "race," and therefore that the Jews are henceforth excluded from salvation, or to say with Frankmölle (pp. 21ff.) that Israel alone is being addressed. That the disciples' unbelief is central to Jesus' exasperation is made clear by Matthew's omitting Mark 9:23–24; if his description extends beyond them to the entire contemporary generation, it must principally extend also to all guilty of the same unbelief, regardless of their race.

The rhetorical questions—"How long shall I stay with you? How long shall I put up with you?"—express not only personal disappointment but also Jesus' consciousness of his heavenly origin and destiny. His disciples' perverse unbelief is actually painful to him. He must endure ("put up with," NIV) it, though this theme is stronger in Mark than in Matthew (cf. Mark 8:12 and Matt 16:4; Mark 3:5 and Matt 12:13). As for the miracle, Matthew describes it succinctly, leaving no doubt of Jesus' power to heal and exorcise demons (v.18). The boy is healed "from that moment" (lit., "from that hour"; cf. 9:22; 15:28).

19–20 [21] The disciples, presumably the nine who had tried and failed (v.16), ask Jesus, in private (cf. also Mark 9:28), why "we" (emphatic) could not drive out the demon (v.19). The reason, Jesus says, is because of their *oligopistia* ("little faith," v.20; cf. Notes). Despite the etymology of the word, it probably does not refer so much to the littleness of their faith as to its poverty (Bonnard). Little faith, like a little mustard seed, can be effectual; poor faith, like that of the disciples' here, is ineffectual. The noun occurs only here in Matthew, but the cognate adjective occurs at 6:30; 8:26; 14:31; 16:8, and always refers to disciples. Removal of mountains was proverbial for overcoming great difficulties (cf. Isa 40:4; 49:11; 54:10; Matt 21:21–22; Mark 11:23; Luke 17:6; 1 Cor 13:2). Nothing would be impossible for them—a promise that, like its analogue in Philippians 4:13, is limited by context, not by unbelief. Here it refers to the accomplishment of the works of the kingdom for which they had been given authority.

Jesus' answer in Matthew is not the same as the one in Mark 9:29 ("This kind can come out only by prayer"); but if the comment on *oligopistia* ("poverty of faith") is correct, then at least the two answers are complementary, each shedding light on the other. At a superficial level the disciples did have faith: they expected to be able to exorcise the demon. They had long been successful in this work, and now they are surprised by their failure. But their faith is poor and shoddy. They are treating the authority given them (10:1, 8) like a gift of magic, a bestowed power that works *ex opere operato*. In Mark, Jesus tells them that this case requires prayer—not a form or an approved rite, but an entire life bathed in prayer and its concomitant faith. In Matthew, Jesus tells his disciples that what they need is not giant faith (tiny faith will do) but true faith—faith that, out of a deep, personal trust, expects God to work.

Notes

14 The genitive absolute here, in v.26, and in Acts 17:14 is defective—a participle without a substantive (cf. Zerwick, par. 50; Moule, *Idiom Book*, p. 203). This evokes the introduction of a pronoun in many later MSS, or a change in the participle to the nominative singular in a few of them.

17 In exclamations expressing very strong emotion, ὦ (*ō*, "O") is not restricted to the vocative but may color an entire sentence, which is often, as here, a question (cf. BDF, par. 146[2]).

18 For the confusion between the prepositions ἀπό (*apo*, "from," "away from") and ἐκ (*ek*, "from," "out from") in Hellenistic Greek, see on 3:16.

20 Ὀλιγοπιστίαν (*oligopistian*, "little faith," or, better, "poor faith") is read by א B H f¹ f¹³ 33 700 892 et al., and ἀπιστίαν (*apistian*, "faithless," as in v.17) by the rest. But the first reading has strong witnesses; it is a NT *hapax legomenon* (single occurrence); its cognate is distinctively, if not exclusively, Matthean (6:30; 8:26; 14:31; 16:8); and the change to the second reading may well have been prompted by v.17, where the text is firm.

21 "But this kind does not go out except by prayer and fasting" is omitted by a powerful combination of witnesses. It is obviously an assimilation to the synoptic parallel in Mark 9:29. There is no obvious reason why, if original, it should have been omitted; and textual harmonization is quite demonstrably a secondary process.

15. *The second major passion prediction*

17:22–23

> ²²When they came together in Galilee, he said to them, "The Son of Man is going to be betrayed into the hands of men. ²³They will kill him, and on the third day he will be raised to life." And the disciples were filled with grief.

This is the second major passion prediction (see on 16:21–24), though there are earlier allusions to Jesus' death (9:15; 10:38; 12:40) and one intervening specific reference (17:12b). Jesus not only foresees the inevitability of his death but, precisely because he knows this to be the Father's will (26:39), recognizes it as an essential part of the divine plan. But that death issues in the Resurrection.

22 Thompson (pp. 13ff.) finds here the beginning of a new literary unit, ending at 18:35, based partly on the references to Galilee here and at 19:1. But the departure from Galilee (19:1) not only ends this brief stay but also this entire period of Jesus' northern ministry (4:23–25). From 19:1 on, Jesus moves toward Jerusalem and

Judea. "When they came together" (the best reading) does not necessarily suggest new activities but the general time when Jesus and the inner circle of disciples joined the other nine in Galilee (see on vv.1, 14–20). No sooner are they all together after the Transfiguration than Jesus again takes up the theme he introduced to them earlier (16:21–23). The verb *paradidosthai* ("to be betrayed") is doubly ambiguous. First, it can have either a weak meaning ("to hand over") or a strong meaning ("to betray"), depending on context; second, the passive ("to be handed over") is perhaps a studied ambiguity leaving it unclear whether God or Judas Iscariot is the one who hands Jesus over or betrays him respectively.

23 Mark and Luke say the disciples do not understand. Matthew, adept at fine characterization, establishes the same point by noting the disciples' grief. They are beginning to absorb the announcement of Jesus' death, but of his resurrection they have no comprehension.

16. *The temple tax*

17:24–27

> 24After Jesus and his disciples arrived in Capernaum, the collectors of the two-drachma tax came to Peter and asked, "Doesn't your teacher pay the temple tax?"
> 25"Yes, he does," he replied.
> When Peter came into the house, Jesus was the first to speak. "What do you think, Simon?" he asked. "From whom do the kings of the earth collect duty and taxes—from their own sons or from others?"
> 26"From others," Peter answered.
> "Then the sons are exempt," Jesus said to him. 27"But so that we may not offend them, go to the lake and throw out your line. Take the first fish you catch; open its mouth and you will find a four-drachma coin. Take it and give it to them for my tax and yours."

This incident is peculiar to Matthew (cf. Mark 9:33 for geographical detail). Its significance in Matthew depends heavily on its interpretation at several critical points.

24 Although the point is disputed (see on v.25), the *didrachma* (lit., "two drachmas") was probably not a civil tax in support of Rome (cf. on 22:15–22) but a Jewish "tax" levied on every male Jew between the ages of twenty and fifty in support of the temple and its services. The *didrachma*, worth one-half a *statēr* or shekel, was seldom minted at this time; and probably two people joined to pay a *tetradrachma* ("a four-drachma coin," v.27) or shekel. Originally half a shekel was levied on each Jew at every census (Exod 30:11–16), the money going to support the tabernacle; after the Exile one-third of a shekel was gathered annually. In Jesus' day the amount was two drachmas (half a shekel) annually. This is well attested in both Josephus (*Antiq.* III, 193–96 [viii.2]; XVIII, 312 [ix.1]) and Mishnah (*Shekalim*). The imposition of this "tax" lacked the sanction of Roman law, but it was understood that the Jews would pay it.

25–26 Peter's defense of Jesus (v.25) is misguided. Once they are alone in the house (perhaps Peter's; cf. 4:13; 8:14), Jesus takes the initiative—whether he overheard

Peter's response or knew it supernaturally is unclear—and asks Peter a provocative question. The vast literature on this pericope stems largely from Jesus' question being cast in *civil* terms: "kings of the earth," "duty," "taxes." The majority view today (e.g., Kilpatrick, *Origins*, pp. 41f.; Walker, pp. 101–3; Bonnard; Hill, *Matthew*) holds that the original question was recast in the period after A.D. 70 (when Matthew is alleged to have been writing) to address questions faced by Christians about taxes paid to Rome. The effect of the pericope, then, is like that of 22:15–22, though Jesus' reported answer here is anachronistic. Jesus is made to say that the Son of God, and therefore Christians, *need* not pay taxes to Rome because of their allegiance to God but *should* do so in order not to cause offense. This will not do, for in Jesus' reply the "king" who collects the tax is Jesus' "Father." Therefore this cannot refer to Rome.

Others (Thompson, pp. 50–68) suggest that this is the tax paid the post-Jamnia patriarchate and that the question Matthew is facing is whether Christians at his time of writing should bow to Jewish religious authority. This means not only that Jesus' question and Peter's answer are anachronistic but that the redaction here is inept. Would Jews at the end of the first century think of the Jamnia rabbis as kings or of Jesus Messiah as their son? The suggestion that the tax is the one imposed by Vespasian in support of the temple of *Jupiter Capitolinus* after the Fall of Jerusalem (Jos. War VII, 218 [vi.6]—so H.W. Montefiore [cf. Hill, *Matthew*] and others) is incredible. No Christian willingly advocated direct subsidy of pagan idolatry in order not to offend Rome, and on this reading Jesus' question becomes even more obscure.

Because of such difficulties, Richard J. Cassidy ("Matthew 17:24–27—A Word on Civil Taxes," CBQ 41 [1979]: 571–80) argues that the entire pericope deals, not with the temple tax, but with civil taxes. The terminology of v.25 supports him; but again it is less than clear how sonship to an imperial "king" fits Jesus.

It is better to allow the most likely interpretations of both v.24 and v.25 to stand —temple tax and civil tax respectively—but to recognize that, whereas v.24 establishes the topic of the entire pericope, v.25 is parabolic. This is suggested by the generalized "kings of the earth"—scarcely an adequate way to refer to Caesar. The point is that, just as royal sons are exempt from the taxes imposed by their fathers, so too Jesus is exempt from the "tax" imposed by his Father. In other words Jesus acknowledges the temple tax to be an obligation to God; but since he is uniquely God's Son, therefore he is exempt (v.26). The focus of the pericope is thus supremely christological and, unlike 22:15–22, says nothing about responsibilities to Caesar.

27 Exempt though he is, Jesus will pay the tax so as not to offend (for the verb, see on 5:29). Thus he sets an example later followed by Paul (1 Cor 8:13; 9:12, 22). The plural "we" and the four-drachma coin to pay for Jesus and Peter at first sight makes the above interpretation seem difficult. In what sense are we to suppose that Peter's reason for paying the tax is akin to Jesus'? Part of the explanation may lie in the freedom Jesus extends to his disciples: e.g., he alone is Lord of the Sabbath, and this has implications for his disciples (see on 12:1–8). More important, Jesus here implicitly frees his followers from the temple tax on the grounds that they, too, will belong to the category of "sons," though derivatively.

Both the christological implication and the relevance to Peter and the disciples are made clear in the course of the narrative. Jesus has just been declared God's unique Son (v.5); yet his glory is veiled as he moves toward betrayal and death, thus establishing a pattern of humility for his followers (18:1–5). At the same time Jesus' death and resurrection have again been introduced (vv.22–23), a foretaste of the lengthy passion and resurrection narratives about to begin and the means by which the Son of Man, in giving his life "a ransom for many" (20:28), completes the redemptive act inaugurating the gathering of his "church" (16:18; 28:18–20). At that point the redemptive-historical significance of the temple will end. Its claims for the two-drachma tax may continue till its destruction forty years later; the sons of God (cf. 5:9) are exempt. But that time is not yet. Like so many of Jesus' actions at this turning point, the full significance of what Jesus was saying could not be grasped even by Peter till after the Resurrection.

The miracle itself has no close canonical parallel. This is the only place in the NT where a fish is caught with a hook (nets were normally used). Extravagant symbolism for "fish" and "lake" (e.g., Neil J. McEleney, "Mt 17:24–27—Who Paid the Temple Tax?" CBQ 38 [1976]: 189–92) is fanciful. This miraculous way of paying the tax is something only Jesus could do; it therefore suggests that though Jesus as the unique Son is free from the law's demands, he not only submits to them but makes provision, as only he can, for the demands on his disciples (cf. Gal 4:4–5)—and this right after a passion prediction (17:22–23)! Perhaps, too, we are reminded again of Jesus' humility: he who so controls nature and its powers that he stills storms and multiplies food now reminds Peter of that power by this miracle, while nevertheless remaining so humble that he would not needlessly cause offense (cf. 11:28–30; 12:20). The lesson in humility is for Peter and the other disciples. We have no evidence that the tax collectors witnessed it. (The nonhealing miracles in Matthew are almost always for the sake of the disciples: see Gerhardsson, *Mighty Acts*). But humility is about to be explained to the disciples in some detail (18:1–35).

Notes

26 As in v.14, the genitive absolute is defective and has led to many variants (cf. Metzger, *Textual Commentary*, p. 46).

27 Although some (e.g., Zerwick, par. 93) suggest ἀντί (*anti*, "instead of," "in substitution for") here has the force of ὑπέρ (*hyper*, "on behalf of"), it is perhaps better to think of Exod 30:11–16 as the background, remembering that this tax was perceived as a ransom payment *instead* of the person (cf. Turner, *Insights*, p. 173).

B. *Fourth Discourse: Life Under Kingdom Authority* (18:1–19:2)

1. *Setting*

18:1–2

¹At that time the disciples came to Jesus and asked, "Who is the greatest in the kingdom of heaven?"
²He called a little child and had him stand among them.

This fourth discourse, like the previous three, is bracketed by remarks suggesting that it was delivered on the one occasion specified (see on 5:1; 7:28–29). The chapter parallels Mark 9:33–50 to some extent but omits Mark 9:38–41 (cf. Matt 10:42). The differences between Mark and Matthew are so great that some scholars assume separate sources (Lohmeyer) or wisely advocate cautious agnosticism (Thompson, pp. 147–51).

Many writers compare Matthew 18 with 1QS, the "Manual of Discipline" at Qumran, and interpret it as regulation for the life of the Christian community. But two major reservations forbid too easy a comparison.

1. There is very little in Matthew 18 that has the flavor of regulation and much that deals with principles. The contrasts with 1QS are far more noticeable than the similarities. Even vv.15–17, the closest approximation to "regulation," is far less concerned with mechanical details than with the importance and means of reconciliation. And the whole chapter shows up the carnality of the opening question (v.1) and establishes a radical set of values for greatness in the kingdom.

2. The Qumran covenanters had little doubt about their identity or place in God's eschatological scheme. But here we are dealing with disciples at a critical turning-point in salvation history, men of seriously defective understanding who remain such till after the Cross.

1–2 Mark (9:33–38) says that the disciples were disputing along the way, and when challenged they fell silent. Luke (9:46–48) says Jesus discerned their thoughts. It is not difficult or unnatural to suppose that Jesus detected their rivalry (Luke), challenged them, and thereby silenced them (Mark), and that they then blurted out their question (Matthew). Alternatively Matthew uses this brief question to summarize what was truly on their minds.

"At that time" (lit., "hour," v.1) may only mean "in that general phase of the ministry" (cf. 10:19; 26:45), but it alerts the reader to the transition from what precedes. "At that time," when Jesus has again spoken of his suffering and death, the disciples' grief (17:23) proves short lived; and they busy themselves with arguing about who is greatest in the kingdom. Jesus has already said that there will be distinctions in the kingdom (5:19; cf. also 1QS 3:19–25; 6:9–13); and recently three of them have been specially favored (17:1–3), while Peter has been repeatedly singled out (14:28–29; 15:15; 16:16–18, 22–23; 17:4, 24–27)—though sometimes for rebuke! Perhaps these things set off the dispute, which continues in the ambition of James, John, and their mother to the period right before the Cross (20:20–23) and which embraces the jealousy of the other ten (20:24). Substantial misunderstanding of Jesus by his disciples is presupposed throughout Jesus' entire earthly ministry.

The "disciples" are probably the Twelve but may include others (cf. Thompson, pp. 83–84; see on 5:1–2). The child (v.2) may have been Peter's, if the house is his (17:25; Mark 9:33).

2. Humility and greatness

18:3–4

> ³And he said: "I tell you the truth, unless you change and become like little children, you will never enter the kingdom of heaven. ⁴Therefore, whoever humbles himself like this child is the greatest in the kingdom of heaven.

3–4 With the solemn introductory formula "I tell you the truth" (v.3; see on 5:18), Jesus warns his disciples that they must "change and become like little children"; for unless they do, they will "never enter the kingdom of heaven." Clearly, the consummated kingdom is in view. The child is held up as an ideal, not of innocence, purity, or faith, but of humility and unconcern for social status. Jesus advocates humility of mind (v.4), not childishness of thought (cf. 10:16). With such humility comes childlike trust (cf. TDNT, 8:16–17). The disciples must "change" (lit., "turn," probably not to be taken as a Semitic auxiliary to "become," i.e., "become again a little child"; cf. J. Dupont, "Matthieu 18, 3," in Ellis, and Wilcox, pp. 50–60) from their present conduct and attitudes and adopt this new norm or be excluded from the kingdom. Conversely, the person who truly humbles himself (cf. Notes) like this child is "the greatest in the kingdom of heaven": the expression completes a link with v.1, and the present tense may suggest that the disciple's greatness, doubtless made obvious in the consummated kingdom in the future, has already begun here as far as kingdom norms are concerned.

The thought is not far removed from 5:3 and vitiates any thought that the kingdom can be gained by personal merit or violent force (see on 11:12). It is to "little children" that the Lord of heaven and earth reveals his truth (11:25).

Notes

4 The verb ταπεινώσει (tapeinōsei, lit., "will humble") is one of the few instances in which the distinction between a future indicative and an aorist subjunctive plus ἄν (an, untranslatable particle used to suggest some kind of contingency) is obliterated (cf. BDF, par. 380[2]).

3. The heinousness of causing believers to sin

18:5–9

> 5"And whoever welcomes a little child like this in my name welcomes me. 6But if anyone causes one of these little ones who believe in me to sin, it would be better for him to have a large millstone hung around his neck and to be drowned in the depths of the sea. 7Woe to the world because of the things that cause people to sin! Such things must come, but woe to the man through whom they come! 8If your hand or your foot causes you to sin, cut it off and throw it away. It is better for you to enter life maimed or crippled than to have two hands or two feet and be thrown into eternal fire. 9And if your eye causes you to sin, gouge it out and throw it away. It is better for you to enter life with one eye than to have two eyes and be thrown into the fire of hell.

Although some read v.5 with vv.3–4, it is better to link it with vv.6–9, because (1) v.4 already rounds off 18:1–4 with a summary, and (2) vv.5–6 taken together constitute a neat promise-warning proverb (cf. esp. Thompson, pp. 101–7). This pericope is held tightly together by its repeated *skandalon* ("stumbling block") language (see on 5:29), what Paul calls a *proskomma* ("obstacle," "cause of stumbling"; cf. Rom 14:13; 1 Cor 8:9). Rabbinic literature contains denunciations of the evil of causing others to sin (cf. Bonnard), but never with reference to "little ones."

5–6 This promise-warning couplet (like 12:32 in structure) advances the thought by turning attention from the self-humiliation of the true disciple (vv.3–4) to the way others receive such "little ones." The opening clauses of v.5 and v.6 are roughly parallel. The one who welcomes "a little child like this *in my name*" is not welcoming literal children but "children" defined in the previous verses—those who humble themselves to become like children, i.e., Jesus' true disciples. They are not welcomed because they are great, wise, or mighty, but because they come in Jesus' name (v.5)—i.e., they belong to him. "In my name" (v.5), the parallel clause "who believe in me" (v.6), and the necessity of becoming childlike even to enter the kingdom (v.3) all confirm the view that those referred to in vv.5–6 are simply Jesus' disciples—Christians (to use a later term), not literal children or some smaller group of especially humble disciples (see Warfield, 1:234–52; Trotter). These "little ones" (cf. 25:40, 45) can stumble, even the greatest of them (14:28–31; 26:30–35); but whoever causes them to stumble (NIV, "to sin") stands in grave peril.

It is no objection to this identification of "little ones" with believers that Jesus is here addressing his disciples and not the world that is most in need of the warning, for (1) the "whoever" takes in everybody; (2) despite the fact that Jesus is speaking to disciples (v.1), he utters a woe on the world in v.7; (3) this suggests that the passage aims at encouraging the disciples who are going to have to face the world's opprobrium (as also 10:40–42); and (4) the warnings against the world, though not at this moment directed to the world, will in due course become part of the disciples' arsenal in their preaching.

The person who welcomes one of these "little ones," these disciples of Jesus, simply because they are his, welcomes Jesus himself (cf. 10:42). Presupposed is the world's animosity. Mere hospitality is not in view but hospitality given because of the "little ones' " link with Jesus; and it is probably presupposed that hospitality motivated in this way would be shown only if the benefactor were already well disposed toward Jesus, or at least moving in that direction. The antithetic alternative, causing the "little ones" to stumble, does not mean that the "little ones" are led into apostasy. Rather, they are not welcomed but are rejected, ignored. This causes them to stumble in their discipleship. It may lead to serious sin; but, as in 10:40–42 and 25:31–46, the really grave aspect of the rejection is that it signifies rejection of Jesus.

Implicitly, the offense is gravely magnified when with particular perversity some wicked people self-consciously try to entice Christ's "little ones" into sin; but the evil is broader than that. Because it signals a rejection of Jesus as well as damaging his people, drowning at sea before the evil was committed is much preferable to eschatological judgment, the eternal fire of hell (vv.8–9) that awaits the perpetrators. Drowning was a not uncommon punishment in Greek and Roman society. Though rare in Jewish circles, it was done at least once in Galilee (Jos. Antiq. XIV, 450[xv.10]). Most millstones were hand tools for domestic use (see on 24:41); here it is the heavy stone pulled around by a donkey. The picture is more graphic than in Mark, the horror of the judgment sharpened.

7 The Greek text proclaims a "woe" (here, clearly, a proclamation of judgment, not of "sympathetic sorrow" [McNeile], since Matthew heightens the judgment language; see further on 23:13–32) on the "world," understood not merely as the neutral "setting for the struggle between belief and unbelief " (Thompson, pp. 109–10), but the source of all stumbling. Jesus pronounces this woe *apo tōn skandalōn*, which, contrary to NIV, should not be rendered "because of the things that cause *people* to sin," as if the discussion had progressed from Jesus' "little ones" to "people" in general, but "because of stumbling blocks," i.e., because of the things that cause the stumbling already referred to in v.6. Such things must come; but this inevitably does not mitigate the responsibility of those through whom they come (cf. Isa 10:5–12; Acts 4:27–28; see on Matt 13:13). The necessity does not spring from divine compulsion but, like all things, falls nonetheless within the sphere of his sovereignty so that he may use those very things to accomplish his plan and perfect his people (cf. 24:10–13; 1 Cor 11:19). Thus on the one hand the disciples are not to think such opposition strange, for Jesus himself has declared it must occur; on the other hand they are assured that justice will be done in the end (cf. 26:24).

8–9 Jesus now abandons denunciation of the world's causing his disciples to stumble and tells his disciples they may prove to be not only victims but aggressors. The adversative *de* is given its full force: "*But*, beyond all this, if *your* hand" (v.8). This does not mean that the church, pictured as a body in anticipation of Paul's language (e.g., 1 Cor 12:12–27), is here exhorted to excommunicate offending members. The word "body" is not used, and the language is akin to that in 5:29–30 (q.v.). Certain attitudes nurtured by Jesus' disciples toward other believers could also be sinful; thus, instead of being enticed to sin by outsiders, they would cause their own stumbling. Perhaps the particular believer-to-believer attitude that most needs rooting out is pride; so vv.8–9 prepare for v.10.

The argument is clear. Jesus' followers must become like children in humility if they are to enter the kingdom (vv.3–4). Those who receive such "little ones" because they belong to him in effect receive Jesus; those who reject them, causing them to stumble, are threatened with condemnation (vv.5–6). Things causing Jesus' people to stumble are inevitable yet damning (v.7). But the disciples themselves must beware: failure to deal radically with similar sin in their own lives betrays their allegiance to the world and threatens them with the eternal fire of hell (vv.8–9; see on 5:22). Jesus' disciples must deal as radically with pride as they were earlier commanded to deal with lust (5:29–30).

Notes

7 The γάρ (*gar*, "for") retains its normal causal force but applies to the next clause, here introduced by πλήν (*plēn*, "but"). The content of the *gar* itself is parenthetical so far as the force of *gar* is concerned. The same construction is found elsewhere (cf. 22:14; 24:6; cf. Zerwick, pars. 474–75).

4. *The parable of the lost sheep*

18:10–14

> ¹⁰"See that you do not look down on one of these little ones. For I tell you that their angels in heaven always see the face of my Father in heaven.
> ¹²"What do you think? If a man owns a hundred sheep, and one of them wanders away, will he not leave the ninety-nine on the hills and go to look for the

one that wandered off? ¹³And if he finds it, I tell you the truth, he is happier about that one sheep than about the ninety-nine that did not wander off. ¹⁴In the same way your Father in heaven is not willing that any of these little ones should be lost.

Verse 10 clearly follows vv.5–9; but because it also forms a neat inclusion with v.14, vv.10–14 must be read together in the light of the preceding pericope. This link raises important questions concerning the relation between this parable and the parable of the lost sheep in Luke 15:3–7, where it is addressed, not to disciples, but to Pharisees and teachers of the law, in defense of Jesus' attitude to sinners. Almost all scholars hold that one parable stands behind both Gospels, and then they debate over which form and setting are most primitive (for discussion, cf. Jeremias, *Parables*, pp. 38ff.; Marshall, *Luke*, pp. 600–601; Hill, *Matthew*), some arguing in favor of the form in Gospel of Thomas 107 (most recently W.L. Petersen, "The Parable of the Lost Sheep in the Gospel of Thomas and the Synoptics," NovTest 23 [1981]: 128–47; but cf. Blomberg, "Tendencies," pp. 29–63, 96–100). All these views presuppose that at least one of the two settings defined by Matthew and Luke is a late creation by the church or by one of the evangelists to apply the parable to some new problem.

But if the original parable was "simple enough and rich enough to be applied to more than one situation" (Hill, *Matthew*), why did not Jesus apply it to more than one situation? What methodological reasons are advanced for distinguishing between multiple usage by Jesus and multiple usage by the church? It is remarkable how different Matthew's and Luke's forms of the parable are when closely compared in the Greek text. Almost every relevant term is not the same as in the parallel, and the few that are the same are well within the bounds of repetition expected in an itinerant ministry (see on 5:1–2). The evidence suggests that these are two similar parables, both taught by Jesus, but with very different aims: see on 19:1–2 for the bearing of the problems of "Luke's central section" on this discussion. Matthew is not concerned with "faithful pastorship in the community" (Hill, *Matthew*) but, following the preceding pericope, with the importance in Messiah's community of harming no member, of sharing the Father's concern that none of "these little ones" be lost.

10[11] Verse 10 continues the note of humility struck at the discourse's beginning (vv.3–4) and the concern for "these little ones" (vv.5–9). There is no conflict between "you" and "these little ones." At this stage of their pilgrimage, even the disciples must change and become like little children (v.3). Jesus is discussing what will be normative when his passion and resurrection fully inaugurate the messianic community. Its members will be poor in spirit (5:3), humble (18:3–4), and none will be admitted to it without these graces. If his disciples become like that, they will belong to the "little children"; if they look down on them, they will share in the woes (vv.8–9). The warning was not irrelevant: at least one disciple left Jesus.

Jesus says that the "little ones"—believers in him—must be treated with respect because "their angels in heaven" always see the face of the heavenly Father. Many believe this supports the idea of a guardian for each "little one." That these angels are "in heaven" is thought to mean that they are of highest rank and that their seeing the Father's face means they always have access to his presence. This is based largely on Jewish sources (cf. SBK, 1:781ff.; 3:48ff., 437ff.; TDNT, 1:82, 86; see esp. Tobit 12:14–15). Yet the idea will not bear close scrutiny.

It is true that angels are sent to minister to those who will inherit salvation (Heb 1:14). But nowhere in Scripture or Jewish tradition of the NT period is there any suggestion that there is one angel for one person. Daniel and Zechariah imply one angel for each nation. Appeal to Acts 12:15 does not help. Why should Peter's supposed guardian angel sound like Peter? And if ministering angels are sent to help believers, what are the angels in Matthew 18:10 doing around the divine throne, instead of guarding those people to whom they are assigned? References in the DSS to angels who share in the community's worship (1QSa 2:9–10) or minister to the Lord (1QH 5:20–22) are even less relevant, for this context does not deal with corporate worship.

The most likely explanation is the one Warfield (1:253–66) defends. The "angels" of the "little ones" are their spirits after death, and they always see the heavenly Father's face. Do not despise these little ones, Jesus says, for their destiny is the unshielded glory of the Father's presence. The present tense (they "always see") raises no difficulty because Jesus is dealing with a class, not individuals. The same interpretation admirably suits Acts 12:15: what the assembled group thinks is standing outside is Peter's "spirit" (angel), which accounts for Rhoda's recognition of his voice.

But can the word "angel" be pressed into this interpretation? Certainly Jesus teaches that God's people in the Resurrection "will be like the angels in heaven" as to marriage (22:30) and immortality (Luke 20:36). Similar language is also used in 2 Baruch 51:5, 12 (cf. also 1 Enoch 51:4): the righteous will become angels in heaven, will be transformed into the splendor of angels, and will even surpass the excellency of angels. The evidence, though not overwhelming, is substantial enough to suppose that "their angels" simply refers to their continued existence in the heavenly Father's presence.

12–13 Here is another reason not to despise these "little ones": the shepherd—the Father (v. 14)—is concerned for each sheep in his flock and seeks the one who strays (v. 12). His concern for the one wandering sheep is so great that he rejoices more over its restoration than over the ninety-nine that do not stray (v. 13). With a God like that, how dare anyone cause even one of these sheep to go astray?

14 Jesus drives the lesson home: the heavenly Father is unwilling for any of "these little ones" (see on vv. 3–6) to be lost. If that is his will, it is shocking that anyone else would seek to lead one of "these little ones" astray. This love for the *individual* sheep is not at the expense of the entire flock but so that the flock as a whole may not lose a single one of its members. On God's preservation of his own, see comments on 12:32; 13:3–9, 18–23.

Notes

11 This verse is omitted by the earliest witnesses of the Alexandrian, pre-Caesarean, Egyptian, and Antiochene text types. Inclusion in various forms appears to be an assimilation to Luke 19:10.

12 Some commentators argue that the verb πλανηθῇ (*planēthē*, "wanders away") signifies for Matthew apostasy from the Christian community (cf. 24:4–5, 11, 24). Two of these references (24:4–5) are taken from Mark 13:5–6, but Matthew ignores two other good references (Mark 12:24, 27). *Planēthē* has for Matthew no technical force and in 22:29 cannot possibly refer to such apostasy. It is general and suits the pastoral setting of the parable. Doubtless Jesus' teaching looks forward to the established church, but there is no evidence here to support theories about Matthew's anachronisms.

---

5. *Treatment of a sinning brother*

18:15–20

> [15]"If your brother sins against you, go and show him his fault, just between the two of you. If he listens to you, you have won your brother over. [16]But if he will not listen, take one or two others along, so that 'every matter may be established by the testimony of two or three witnesses.' [17]If he refuses to listen to them, tell it to the church; and if he refuses to listen even to the church, treat him as you would a pagan or a tax collector.
>
> [18]"I tell you the truth, whatever you bind on earth will be bound in heaven, and whatever you loose on earth will be loosed in heaven.
>
> [19]"Again, I tell you that if two of you on earth agree about anything you ask for, it will be done for you by my Father in heaven. [20]For where two or three come together in my name, there am I with them."

15 Jesus has just spoken to his disciples to warn them not to cause one of these "little ones" to stumble. Now the thought shifts. What the shift is depends on the variant reading chosen. If the words "against you" are included, Jesus is looking at offenses within the messianic community from the opposite perspective—from the viewpoint of the brother against whom the sin is committed. If "against you" is omitted (cf. Notes), Jesus is telling the community as a whole how to handle the situation when a brother sins; and in the immediate context, the sin is that of despising another brother.

Either way the proper thing is to confront the brother privately and "show him his fault." The verb *elenchō* probably suggests "convict" the brother, not by passing judgment, but by convicting him of his sin. The aim is not to score points over him but to win him over (same verb as in 1 Cor 9:19–22; 1 Peter 3:1) because all discipline, even this private kind, must begin with redemptive purposes (cf. Luke 17:3–4; 2 Thess 3:14–15; James 5:19–20; cf. Ecclus 19:13–17). Jesus assumes that the individual (second person singular) who personally confronts his brother will do so with true humility (vv.3–4; cf. Gal 6:1): if it is hard to accept a rebuke, even a private one, it is harder still to administer one in loving humility. Behind this verse stands Leviticus 19:17: "Do not hate your brother in your heart. Rebuke your neighbor frankly so you will not share in his guilt."

16 If private confrontation does not work, the next step (backed by Deut 19:15) is to take two or three witnesses (though the text form of the quotation is much disputed: cf. Gundry, *Use of OT*, p. 139). Doubtless this Deuteronomic law was designed for what we would call "secular" cases. But the distinction is artificial and should not be pressed for the Israelite nation understood itself to be not a nation like others but a theocratic nation, God's chosen people. In conformity with his customary interpretation of the Scriptures, Jesus perceives the link joining his messianic community with ancient Israel.

It is not at first clear whether the function of the witnesses is to support the one who confronts his erring brother by bringing additional testimony about the sin committed (which would require at least three people to have observed the offense) or to provide witnesses to the confrontation if the case were to go before the whole church. The latter is a bit more likely, because Deuteronomy 19:15 deals with judicial condemnation (a step taken only by the entire assembly), not with attempts to convince a brother of his fault. By the united testimony of two or three witnesses, every matter "may be established" (*stathē*, lit., "may be made to stand"—though the rise of deponents in Hellenistic Greek, including the use of *stathē*, implies that "may stand" is a superior rendering; cf. Zerwick, par. 231; Turner, *Syntax*, p. 57).

17 The same three-step procedure is known elsewhere (1QS 5:25–6:1; cf. CD 9:2–3; cf. Davies, *Setting*, pp. 221ff.). Refusal to submit to the considered judgment of Messiah's people means that they are to treat the offender as "a pagan or a tax collector." It is poor exegesis to turn to 8:1–11; 9:9–13; 15:21–28 and say that such people should be treated compassionately. The argument and the NT parallels (Rom 16:17; 2 Thess 3:14) show that Jesus has excommunication in mind. That his words should be preserved in this form, with the mention of "pagan and tax collector," suggests that the people for whom Matthew is writing are predominantly Jewish Christians. NIV's "treat him as you would" catches the idea; but in the Greek expression, "let him be to you as," the "you" is singular. This suggests that each member of the church is to abide by the corporate judgment and reminds the reader of the individual responsibility each believer has toward the others, already presupposed by the singular "your brother" in v.15.

18 For comments on the grammar and theology of this verse, see on 16:19.

19–20 These two verses should not in this setting be taken as a promise regarding any prayer on which two or three believers agree (v.20). Scripture is rich in prayer promises (21:22; John 14:13–14; 15:7–8, 16); but if this passage deals with prayer at all, it is restricted by the context and by the phrase *peri pantos pragmatos* (NIV, "about anything"), which should here be rendered "about any judicial matter": the word *pragma* often has that sense (cf. 1 Cor 6:1; BAGD, s.v.), a sense nicely fitting the argument in Matthew 18.

Recently, however, J. Duncan M. Derrett (" 'Where two or three are convened in my name . . .': a sad misunderstanding," ExpT 91 [1979–80]: 83–86) has argued that vv.19–20 do not deal with prayer at all. The two who agree are the offender and the one against whom the offense has been committed. They come to agreement on earth about any judicial matter they have been pursuing: the verb *aiteisthai* can refer to "pursuing a claim," as well as asking in prayer (cf. F. Preisigke, *Wörterbuch der griechischen Papyrusurkunden, mit Einschluss der griechischen Inschriften, Aufschriften, Ostraka, Mumienschilder, usw. aus Ägypten*, ed. E. Kiessling, 4 vols. [Berlin: 1927–31], s.v.). The promise, then, is that if two individuals in the church come to agreement concerning any claim they are pursuing (presumably on the basis of the church's judgment, v.18), "it will be allowed, ratified (literally it shall succeed, 'come off') on the part of my heavenly Father" (Derrett, "Two or three," p. 84). This is because God's will and purpose stand behind the binding and loosing of v.18 and also because ("for," v.20) the presence of Jesus is assured with the two or three who are (lit.) "brought together"—judges solemnly convened before the church and by the church to render a decision (cf. Notes). It is a truism of the biblical revelation that God's presence stands with the judges of his people (Ps. 82:1).

Here as elsewhere, Jesus takes God's place: Jesus will be with the judges. As he has identified himself with God before (cf. on 2:6; 3:3; 11:4–6, 7–8), so he does again, and thus anticipates the broader promise of 28:20: he will be with his people "to the very end of the age." Jesus thereby implicitly points forward to a time when, as "God with us" (1:23), he will be spiritually present with the "two or three" and with all his followers; and he presupposes that this time will be of considerable duration (see on 24:1–3).

Notes

15 Eἰς σέ (*eis se*, "against you") is omitted by ℵ B f [1] cop[sa, bo mss] Origen Basil [3/6] Cyril. If the omission was original, the words were added very early, perhaps to make the general case (suggested by the omission) apply more tightly to the sins of the immediate context. But one might equally argue that omission was an early change designed to generalize the passage. Moreover, because η (*ē*), ῃ (*ē*), and ει (*ei*) were all pronounced the same way in NT times, it is very easy to see how ἁμαρτήσῃ [εἰς σέ] (*hamartēsē* [*eis se*], "sins against you") could foster errors in writing down dictation. UBS (3d ed.) and Nestle (26th ed.) include the words with square brackets, indicating considerable doubt.

The aorist indicative, ἐκέρδησας (*ekerdēsas*, "you have won over") after a future condition is to some extent futuristic itself (cf. BDF, par. 333[2]).

19 The word οὗ (*hou*, "which") is one of only three instances in Matthew in which the relative is attracted to the case of its antecedent (cf. 24:50; 25:24; cf. Zerwick, par. 16).

20 Derrett ("Two or three") suggests that the "two or three" [judges] reflect known Jewish legal practice. Each of the disputing parties would nominate his own "judge," a layman known to be impartial; and these two would try to settle the problem. If this effort failed, they would approach a third, unconnected with the disputants, who worked with the others either along the lines of arbitration or adjudication. The parallel is very neat and nicely accounts for Jesus' "two or three." My chief hesitation comes from the fact that Jesus has just told the complainant to "tell it to the church" (v.17), not to judges appointed by the disputants. Here the DSS (referred to above) may offer a closer parallel. Moreover Derrett assumes that the "two" in v.19 and the "two or three" in v.20 are not the same individuals but disputants and judges respectively. But these points are not decisive. We have as parallels not only 1 Cor 5, where the entire church meets on an issue, but also 1 Cor 6:4, where the church becomes involved *through appointed judges*. Verses 19–20 remain difficult; at this point we must be content with a balance of probabilities.

6. Forgiveness (18:21–35)

a. Repeated forgiveness

18:21–22

> [21]Then Peter came to Jesus and asked, "Lord, how many times shall I forgive my brother when he sins against me? Up to seven times?"
> [22]Jesus answered, "I tell you, not seven times, but seventy-seven times.

21–22 "Then" (v.21) is probably to be taken strictly (see on 3:13). The issue is not the adjudication of the church, still less the absolute granting of forgiveness by the church (only God and Jesus can forgive sins in so absolute a fashion), but personal forgiveness (cf. 6:14–15). In rabbinic discussion the consensus was that a brother might be forgiven a repeated sin three times; on the fourth, there is no forgiveness. Peter, thinking himself big-hearted, volunteers "seven times" in answer to his own question—a larger figure often used, among other things, as a "round number" (cf. Lev 26:21; Deut 28:25; Ps 79:12; Prov 24:16; Luke 17:4).

Jesus' response (v.22) alludes to Genesis 4:24 (cf. Notes): Lamech's revenge is transformed into a principle of forgiveness. In this context Jesus is not saying that seventy-seven times is the upper limit, nor that the forgiveness is so unqualified it vitiates the discipline and procedural steps just taught (vv.15–20). Rather he teaches that forgiveness of fellow members in his community of "little ones" (brothers) cannot possibly be limited by frequency or quantity; for, as the ensuing parable shows (vv.23–35), all of them have been forgiven far more than they will ever forgive.

Notes

---

21 The Greek is literally "How many times will my brother sin against me and I will forgive him?"—an excellent example of parataxis under Semitic influence, especially in interrogative sentences (cf. BDF, par. 471[2]; Zerwick, par. 453, who compares Isa 50:2).
22 The Greek could just barely be taken to mean 70×7 (490) instead of $70 + 7$ (77); but it follows the LXX of Gen 4:24 exactly, which is a rendering of the Hebrew 77. For discussion and bibliography, cf. Gundry, *Use of OT*, p. 140.

---

b. *The parable of the unmerciful servant*

18:23–35

23"Therefore, the kingdom of heaven is like a king who wanted to settle accounts with his servants. 24As he began the settlement, a man who owed him ten thousand talents was brought to him. 25Since he was not able to pay, the master ordered that he and his wife and his children and all that he had be sold to repay the debt.

26"The servant fell on his knees before him. 'Be patient with me,' he begged, 'and I will pay back everything.' 27The servant's master took pity on him, canceled the debt and let him go.

28"But when that servant went out, he found one of his fellow servants who owed him a hundred denarii. He grabbed him and began to choke him. 'Pay back what you owe me!' he demanded.

29"His fellow servant fell to his knees and begged him, 'Be patient with me, and I will pay you back.'

30"But he refused. Instead, he went off and had the man thrown into prison until he could pay the debt. 31When the other servants saw what had happened, they were greatly distressed and went and told their master everything that had happened.

32"Then the master called the servant in. 'You wicked servant,' he said, 'I canceled all that debt of yours because you begged me to. 33Shouldn't you have had mercy on your fellow servant just as I had on you?' [34]In anger his master turned him over to the jailers to be tortured, until he should pay back all he owed.

[35]"This is how my heavenly Father will treat each of you unless you forgive your brother from your heart."

23 "Therefore," since Jesus requires his followers to forgive, the kingdom of heaven has become like (not "is like"; see on 13:24) a king who . . . : the reference is to the kingdom already being inaugurated. The reign of God establishes certain kinds of personal relationships, portrayed by this parable, whose point is spelled out in v.35. It quite misses the point to identify kingdom and church and argue that just as the king, though merciful, must be severe in judging the unforgiving, so the church must follow a similar pattern (so Hill, *Matthew*). "Kingdom" and "church" are distinct categories (see esp. on 13:37–39), and the immediate context has returned to the question of *repeated, personal* forgiveness (vv.21–22) and the reasons for it. Those in the kingdom serve a great king who has invariably forgiven far more than they can ever forgive one another. Therefore failure to forgive excludes one from the kingdom, whose pattern is to forgive.

The "servants" (*douloi*, lit., "slaves") may include high-ranking civil servants in a huge colonial empire, for the amount of indebtedness is astronomical (v.24). Yet Jesus may simply be using hyperbole to make clear how much the heirs of the kingdom have really been forgiven.

24–27 We glimpse some idea of the size of the indebtedness when we recall that David donated three thousand talents of gold and seven thousand talents of silver for the construction of the temple, and the princes provided five thousand talents of gold and ten thousand talents of silver (1 Chron 29:4, 7). Some recent estimates suggest a dollar value of twelve million; but with inflation and fluctuating precious metal prices, this could be over a billion dollars in today's currency. (For "talent," see on 25:15.)

Such indebtedness could not possibly be covered by selling the family into slavery (v.25): top price for a slave fetched about one talent, and one-tenth that amount or less was more common. The practice of being sold for debt was sanctioned by the OT (Lev 25:39; 2 Kings 4:1), but such slaves had to be freed in the year of Jubilee (every fiftieth year). (For Jewish and Gentile slavery in Jesus' day, cf. EBC, 1:489; SBK, 4:697–716; Jeremias, *Jerusalem*, pp. 312ff., 345ff.)

In this parable selling the slave and his family does not mean the debt is canceled but rather highlights the servant's desperate plight. With neither resources nor hope, he begs for time and promises to pay everything back (v.26)—an impossibility. So the master takes pity on him and cancels the indebtedness (v.27). The word *daneion* ("loan," a *hapax legomenon*) suggests that the king mercifully decides to look on the loss as a bad loan rather than embezzlement; but by v.32 he abandons that terminology and calls it a "debt."

28–31 The servant's attitude is appalling. The amount owed him is not insignificant: though worth but a few dollars in terms of metal currency, a hundred denarii (v.28) represented a hundred days' wages for a foot soldier or common laborer. Yet the amount is utterly trivial compared with what has already been forgiven him. The similarity of his fellow servant's plea (v.29) to his own (v.26) does not move this unforgiving man. He has him thrown into a debtor's prison (v.30). Even an inexpensive slave sold for five hundred denarii, and it was illegal to sell a man for a sum greater than his debt. But the other servants (v.31), deeply distressed by the inequity, tell the master everything (*diesaphēsan* is a strong verb meaning "explained in detail," not merely "told" [NIV]; it occurs in the NT only here and at 13:36).

32–34 When the servant owes ten thousand talents, the king forgives him; but when the servant shows himself unforgiving toward a fellow servant, the king calls him wicked (v.32) and, foregoing selling him, turns him over to the "torturers" (*basanistais*, not merely "jailers," NIV); the word reminds us of earlier warnings in this chapter (18:6, 8–9). The servant is to be tortured till he pays back all he owes (v.34), which he can never do.

35 Jesus sees no incongruity in the actions of a heavenly Father who forgives so bountifully and punishes so ruthlessly, and neither should we. Indeed, it is precisely because he is a God of such compassion and mercy that he cannot possibly accept as his those devoid of compassion and mercy. This is not to say that the king's compassion can be earned: far from it, the servant is granted freedom only by virtue of the king's forgiveness. As in 6:12, 14–15, those who are forgiven must forgive, lest they show themselves incapable of receiving forgiveness.

Notes

28 Ἀπόδος εἴ τι ὀφείλεις (*apodos ei ti opheileis*, lit., "pay back, if you owe anything") is not an expression of pitiless logic (B.F. Meyer) but the Hellenistic equivalent of ἀπόδος ὅ τι ἂν ὀφείλῃς (*apodos ho ti an opheilēs*, "pay back what you owe," NIV; cf. BDF, par. 376).
30 In negations the aorist is normally used, "because usually the action as a whole is negated" (BDF, par. 327). When the imperfect is used in negations, the durative or iterative force is usually clear—e.g., Mark 14:55; οὐχ ηὕρισκον (*ouk hēuriskon*, "they did not find any [in spite of repeated attempts]"). In this light οὐκ ἤθελεν (*ouk ēthelen*, "he refused") is very telling: he repeatedly refused, maintained a sustained unwillingness (as in 22:3).
32 BDF (par. 328) points out that—especially in verbs to command, order, request, or send —if an action is complete in itself but the accomplishment of a second action toward which the first points is represented as unaccomplished or still outside the scope of the assertion, then the first verb takes the imperfect, not the aorist. Hence the use of aorist παρεκάλεσάς με (*parekalesas me*, "you begged me to"), pointing toward the forgiveness (ἀφῆκά σοι [*aphēka soi*, "I canceled . . . yours"]) means that "the simple request sufficed" (similarly at 26:53).

7. Transitional conclusion: introduction to the Judean ministry

19:1–2

[1]When Jesus had finished saying these things, he left Galilee and went into the region of Judea to the other side of the Jordan. [2]Large crowds followed him, and he healed them there.

1–2 For the formula used in this transition and the manner in which it points ahead, see on 7:28–29. Jesus "left" (*metairō;* for the verb, see on 13:53) Galilee and began to make his way toward Jerusalem, traveling by way of Perea, on the east side of the Jordan, thus avoiding Samaria—at least that is the customary explanation (v.1). But it is possible that *peran tou Iordanou* (lit., "across the Jordan") modifies "Judea" on the west bank. This implies that the writer describes the movements from a stance on the *east* bank (so Slingerland; see on 4:15). The parallel in Mark 10:1 is difficult because of the textual uncertainty concerning *kai* ("and [across the Jordan]"): if the *kai* is original, Mark is thinking of *two* areas—Judea *and* Perea ("across the Jordan"). But Matthew's expression "the other side of Jordan" could be taken as an awkward adverbial modifier of "went": Jesus "went across the Jordan [by that route] into the region of Judea."

The large crowds (v.2) and the many healings show that Jesus did in Judea what he had already done in Galilee. But the many summaries of Jesus' ministry in this Gospel (cf. 4:23; 9:35; 14:14; 16:30), along with showing how busy Jesus was, have another function. Because this Gospel contains so many discourses, "the picture of Jesus might easily become that of a *prophet*, attended by certain signs and wonders but with one single main task: to speak." These summaries help maintain balance and declare the full-orbed ministry of the Messiah (Gerhardsson, *Mighty Acts,* p. 36, emphasis his).

Behind these two verses lurks a very complex problem in synoptic harmony. Although Matthew and Mark are roughly parallel from Matthew 14 to the end, here Luke goes his own way. He pictures Jesus going through Samaria (Luke 9:51–56) and then begins a lengthy series of accounts, some having no synoptic parallel and others appearing to be parallel to earlier material in Mark and Matthew, material Matthew has omitted (e.g., cf. Luke 11:14–36 with Matt 12:22–45; Mark 3:19–30; and Luke 12:22–31 with Matt 6:25–34). Not till 18:15 does Luke rejoin Matthew (19:13) and Mark (10:13), thereafter running roughly parallel with them. The long section, Luke 9:51–18:14 (though the precise ending is disputed), formerly called Luke's "travel narrative" but now commonly referred to as his "central section," is a problem for commentators on Luke, not Matthew; but it cannot be ignored by any synoptic commentator, because the way we perceive Luke's "central section" bears directly on the question of how many of the pericopes in Luke 9:51–18:14 are taken as real parallels to similar ones in the other Synoptics.

Because in Luke's "central section" Jesus is regularly portrayed as heading for Jerusalem (Luke 9:51–53; 13:22; 17:11), some have argued that there is a direct route to Jerusalem, with various side trips; but the chronology and topography become so tortuous as to render this unbelievable. Others see the three chief references to Jerusalem as parallels to (1) Jesus' journey to Jerusalem at the Feast of Tabernacles (John 7:2–10), (2) Jesus' journey south at the time of the raising of Lazarus (John 11:17–18), and (3) the journey terminating in the final Passover and the Cross. Therefore the entire "travel narrative" stands under the shadow of the Cross. This is possible, but it raises more questions of Gospel chronology and harmony than can be discussed here; and, in particular, it means that none of the apparent parallels to similar synoptic material can possibly spring from the same historical event. That too is just possible and is defended by many older commentators (e.g., Broadus). But it is unlikely that an evangelist like Luke—whose "orderly account" (1:3) clearly organizes much material in topical, not chronological or geographical, order—abandons this in 9:51–18:14.

Therefore even if (as I am willing to assume) Luke's central section is framed by certain historical journeys to Jerusalem, used theologically to point to the final journey, it is only to be expected that topical material is also incorporated, because many of Luke's transitions between pericopes (when he uses them at all) are chronologically imprecise. What this means for a commentator on Matthew is that each apparent parallel between a pericope in Matthew and one in Luke's "central section" must be assessed on its own merits. In some cases they probably refer to the same event, in others not; and in some instances the evidence may be such that a convincing decision is impossible.

Craig Blomberg ("Tradition-history") has made some of the careful comparisons that are necessary. In the following chart of parables found in Luke's central section, prepared by Blomberg, column a lists the total number of words in Luke's account that appear in identical form in the synoptic parallel, b lists the number of words common to both texts but in different lexical or grammatical forms, and c the number of words in Luke that are clear synonyms for corresponding words in the other text. Column d provides the percentage of words in Luke falling into category a, and column e the percentage falling into a, b, or c.

Lukan parable	Synoptic parallel	No. of words in Luke	a	b	c	d	e
12:39–40	Matt 24:43–44	34	29	2	3	85.3	100.0
13:20–21	Matt 13:33	21	15	4	1	71.4	95.2
12:42–46	Matt 24:45–51	102	83	5	4	81.4	90.2
8:5–8	Mark 4:3–9	76	44	11	7	57.9	81.5
7:31–35	Matt 11:16–19	76	45	14	2	59.2	80.3
11:11–13	Matt 7:9–11	48	34	2	2	70.8	79.2
13:18–19	Matt 13:31–32	38	19	5	4	50.0	73.7
20:9a–16a	Mark 12:1–9	120	64	11	6	53.3	67.5
14:5	Matt 12:11	17	2	6	1	11.7	52.9
6:47–49	Matt 7:24–27	83	21	16	3	25.3	48.2
19:12–27	Matt 25:14–30	253	54	23	28	21.3	41.5
15:4–7	Matt 18:12–14	81	15	12	2	18.5	35.8
14:16–24	Matt 22:2–10	159	10	14	4	6.3	17.6
12:35–38	Mark 13:33–37	67	2	4	3	3.0	13.4

The chart reveals three groups of parables: (1) those with considerable verbal similarity, 53.3%–85.3% in column d, and 67.5%–100% in column e; (2) those with very little verbal similarity, 3.0%–6.3% in column d, and 13.4%–17.6% in column e; and, bunched between these two extremes, (3) those with a significant but not high verbal similarity, 18.5%–25.3% in column d, and 35.8%–52.9% in column e. As far as these statistics alone are concerned, one might be tempted to think that parables in group (1) probably have a common source, parables in group (2) are distinct, and parables in group (3) have to be handled one by one. This is largely the way they have worked out in this commentary.

Yet other mitigating factors must be kept in mind. For instance, if a parable is brief and aphoristic, then high verbal similarity is less likely to indicate a common source: the parable may have been repeated many times. Again, contrary to Jeremias (*Parables*, pp. 33ff.), P.B. Payne ("Metaphor as a Model for Interpretation of the Parable of the Sower" [Ph.D. diss., Cambridge University, 1975], pp. 308–11) has shown in detail that in almost all instances the audience claimed by the evangelist for any parable found in two or more synoptic Gospels does not contradict the audience claimed by another synoptic evangelist for what appears to be the same parable. If the Gospel writers are careful to preserve the correct audience in all but two cases, one suspects that, if there is independent reason in those two cases to think the parallels may not be parallels but *independent* parables, that is reasonable evidence to believe the alleged parables were separate stories with similar plot lines and vocabularies from the beginning. One such case is the parable of the lost sheep (see on Matt 18:10–14), which falls at the bottom of the intermediate group on the accompanying chart (cf. further Blomberg, "Tradition-history," ch. 2).

While the work of Blomberg and Payne is largely restricted to the parables in Luke's central section (or in Payne's case to synoptic parables), their methods and general observations are applicable to other materials in that section that are paralleled in Matthew. (See comments on 18:10–14; 22:2–10; 24:43–44; 25:14–30.)

VI. Opposition and Eschatology: The Triumph of Grace (19:3–26:5)

A. *Narrative* (19:3–23:39)

1. *Marriage and divorce*

19:3–12

> ³Some Pharisees came to him to test him. They asked, "Is it lawful for a man to divorce his wife for any and every reason?"
>
> ⁴"Haven't you read," he replied, "that at the beginning the Creator 'made them male and female,' ⁵and said, 'For this reason a man will leave his father and mother and be united to his wife, and the two will become one flesh'? ⁶So they are no longer two, but one. Therefore what God has joined together, let man not separate."
>
> ⁷"Why then," they asked, "did Moses command that a man give his wife a certificate of divorce and send her away?"
>
> ⁸Jesus replied, "Moses permitted you to divorce your wives because your hearts were hard. But it was not this way from the beginning. ⁹I tell you that anyone who divorces his wife, except for marital unfaithfulness, and marries another woman commits adultery."
>
> ¹⁰The disciples said to him, "If this is the situation between a husband and wife, it is better not to marry."
>
> ¹¹Jesus replied, "Not everyone can accept this word, but only those to whom it has been given. ¹²For some are eunuchs because they were born that way; others were made that way by men; and others have renounced marriage because of the kingdom of heaven. The one who can accept this should accept it."

On the dangers and difficulties of constructing detailed outlines, see on 13:54–58. Yet certain themes in these chapters (19:3–26:5) are crystalized. The opposition to Jesus becomes more heated and focused: the stances of Jesus and the Jewish leaders become more irreconcilable. Jesus not only reveals more of himself and his mission to his disciples but centers more attention on the End, the ultimate eschatological hope, the consummation of the kingdom. Within these two poles, opposition and eschatology, the grace of God toward those under the kingdom becomes an increasingly dominant theme. Without ever using the word "grace," Matthew returns to this theme repeatedly (e.g., 19:21–22; 20:1–16). But grace does not mean there is no judgment (23:1–39). Rather, it means that despite the gross rejection of Jesus, the chronic unbelief of opponents, crowds, and disciples alike, and the judgment that threatens both within history and at the End, grace triumphs and calls out a messianic people who bow to Jesus' lordship and eagerly await his return.

By and large 19:3–26:5 follows the structure of Mark; but there are substantial additions (20:1–16; 21:28–32; 22:1–14), expansions (esp. 23:1–39; cf. Mark 12:38–44), alterations (esp. 21:10–17), and additional parables after the Olivet Discourse (ch. 25).

For three reasons the first pericope in this section of Matthew has called forth an enormous quantity of comment and exposition: (1) it deals with a perennially burning pastoral issue in society and in the church; (2) it includes some notoriously difficult words and phrases (see esp. v.9); and (3) its relation to the parallel in Mark 10:2–12 is hotly disputed. Only some of these issues can be directly addressed here. (For the cultural background to marriage in the Bible, see Edwin M. Yamauchi, "Cultural Aspects of Marriage in the Ancient World," BS 135 [1978]: 241–52; and for post-Pentateuchal developments on divorce, canonical and other, see Sigal, "Halakah," pp. 130–42.)

3 Pharisees (see on 3:7) are often found in Matthew's Gospel testing or opposing Jesus in some way (12:2, 14, 24, 38; 15:1; 16:1; 19:3; 22:15, 34–35). Their "test," here, is probably delivered in the hope that Jesus would say something to damage his reputation with the people or even seem to contradict Moses. Perhaps, too, they hoped that Jesus would say something that would entangle him in the Herod–Herodias affair so that he might meet the Baptist's fate. Machaerus was not far away (see on 14:3–12).

The question whether it is right for a man to divorce his wife "for any and every reason" (NIV has rightly rendered a difficult phrase: cf. Turner, *Insights*, p. 61) hides an enormous diversity of Jewish opinion. Among the Qumran covenanters, divorce was judged illicit under all circumstances (CD 4:21; and esp. 11QTemple 57:17–19; on which see J.R. Mueller, "The Temple Scroll and the Gospel Divorce Texts," *Revue de Qumran* 38 [1980]: 247ff.).

In mainstream Palestinian Judaism, opinion was divided roughly into two opposing camps: both the school of Hillel and the school of Shammai permitted divorce (of the woman by the man: the reverse was not considered) on the grounds of *'erwat dābār* ("something indecent," Deut 24:1), but they disagreed on what "indecent" might include. Shammai and his followers interpreted the expression to refer to gross indecency, though not necessarily adultery; Hillel extended the meaning beyond sin to all kinds of real or imagined offenses, including an improperly cooked meal. The Hillelite R. Akiba permitted divorce in the case of a roving eye for prettier women (M *Gittin* 9:10).

On any understanding of what Jesus says in the following verses, he agrees with neither Shammai nor Hillel; for even though the school of Shammai was stricter than Hillel, it permitted remarriage when the divorce was not in accordance with its own Halakah (rules of conduct) (M *Eduyoth* 4:7–10); and if Jesus restricts grounds for divorce to sexual indecency (see on v.9), then he differs fundamentally from Shammai. Jesus cuts his own swath in these verses, as Sigal ("Halakah," pp. 104ff.) rightly points out; and he does so in an age when in many Pharisaic circles "the frequency of divorce was an open scandal" (Hill, *Matthew*). Josephus, for instance, himself a divorcé, was a Pharisee; and in his view divorce was permitted "for any causes whatsoever" (Jos. Antiq. IV, 253[viii.23]).

Thus the setting of the divorce question in this pericope is different from 5:31–32. There divorce is set in a discourse that gives the norms of the kingdom and the sanctity of marriage; here it is set in a theological disputation that raises the question of what divorces are allowed.

4–6 Jesus aligns himself with the prophet Malachi, who quotes Yahweh as saying, "I hate divorce" (2:16), and also refers to creation (2:14–15). Jesus cites first Genesis 1:27 and then Genesis 2:24. The Creator made the race "male and female" (v.4): the implication is that the two sexes should be united in marriage. But lest the implication be missed, the Creator then said that "for this reason" (v.5)—because God made them so—a man will leave father and mother, be united to his wife, and become one flesh (cf. Ecclus 25:26; Eph 5:28–31).

The words "for this reason" in Genesis 2:24 refer to Adam's perception that the woman was "bone of his bone and flesh of his flesh" because she had been made from him and for him—i.e., the man and the woman were in the deepest sense "related." The same thing is implied by Genesis 1:27—i.e., the "one flesh" in every marriage between a man and a woman is a reenactment of and testimony to the very structure of humanity as God created it.

"So" (*hōste* here is "simply an inferential particle" [Moule, *Idiom Book*, p. 144]), Jesus concludes, the husband and wife are no longer two but one, and that by God's doing (v.6). If God has joined them together, according to the structure of his own creation, divorce is not only "unnatural" but rebellion against God. God and man are so far apart on this issue that what God unites, man divides.

Jesus' response cuts through a great deal of casuistry and sets forth a dominant perspective that must not be lost in the exegetical tangles of v.9. Two profound insights must be grasped.

1. Although Jewish leaders tended to analyze adultery in terms, not of infidelity to one's spouse, but of taking someone else's wife (cf. M *Ketuboth* and M *Kiddushin*), Jesus dealt with the sanctity of marriage by focusing on the God-ordained unity of the couple.

2. Jesus essentially appealed to the principle, "The more original, the weightier," an accepted form of argument in Jewish exegesis (cf. Paul in Gal 3:15–18); and it is impossible to go further back than creation for the responsibilities of mankind. If marriage is grounded in *creation*, in the way God has made us, then it cannot be reduced to a merely covenantal relationship that breaks down when the covenantal promises are broken (contra David Atkinson, *To Have and to Hold: The Marriage Covenant and the Discipline of Divorce* [London: Collins, 1979], esp. pp. 114ff.). But the argument in this instance leaves unanswered the question of how the Mosaic law is to be taken; and therefore the stage is set for the Pharisees' next question.

7–8 The Pharisees refer to Deuteronomy 24:1–4, which they interpret to mean something like this: "If a man takes a wife . . . and she does not find favor in his eyes . . . he shall write a bill of divorce . . . and shall send her away from his house" (so also Vul.). But the Hebrew more naturally means something like this: "If a man takes a wife . . . and she does not find favor in his eyes . . . and he writes a bill of divorce . . . and he sends her away from his house . . . and her second husband does the same thing, then her first husband must not marry her again" (presumably because that would be a kind of incest; cf. Zerwick, par. 458; G.J. Wenham, "The

Restoration of Marriage Reconsidered," *Journal of Jewish Studies* 30 [1979]: 36–40). In other words Moses did not *command* divorce but permitted it for ʿ*erwaṯ dāḇār* ("something indecent"); and the text is less concerned with explaining the nature of that indecency (the precise expression is found in only one other place in the OT—Deut 23:14, with reference to human excrement) than with prohibiting remarriage of the twice-divorced woman to her first husband. Divorce and remarriage are therefore presupposed by Moses: i.e., he "permitted" them (v.8).

The general thrust of Mark 10:2–9 is the same as in Matthew 19:3–8. But there (1) the Pharisees ask their test question without "for any and every reason"; (2) Jesus mentions Moses' command; (3) the Pharisees reply in terms of what Moses permitted; and (4) only then does Jesus offer his basic perspective in terms of the creation ordinance. The net effect of the two passages this far is the same. But it is not easy to reconstruct the historical details. Matthew seems more concerned about the thrust of the exchange than about who said what first.

Both Matthew and Mark show that Jesus taught that Moses' concession reflected not the true creation ordinance but the hardness of men's hearts. Divorce is not part of the Creator's perfect design. If Moses permitted it, he did so because sin can be so vile that divorce is to be preferred to continued "indecency." This is not to say that the person who, according to what Moses said, divorced his spouse was actually committing sin in so doing; but that divorce could even be considered testified that there had already been sin in the marriage. Therefore any view of divorce and remarriage (taught in either Testament) that sees the problem only in terms of what may or may not be done has already overlooked a basic fact—divorce is never to be thought of as a God-ordained, morally neutral option but as evidence of sin, of hardness of heart. The fundamental attitude of the Pharisees to the question was wrong.

It should be noted also that Jesus, when speaking of the sin of the people, invariably refers to *their* sin, *your* sin, never *our* sin (cf. 6:14–15).

But what was the "indecency" in Moses' day that allowed for divorce? "Something indecent" could not be equated with adultery, for the normal punishment for that was death, not divorce (Deut 22:22)—though it is not at all clear that the death penalty was in fact regularly imposed for adultery (cf. Henry McKeating, "Sanctions Against Adultery in Ancient Israelite Society," JSOT 11 [1979]: 57–72). Nor could the indecency be suspicion of adultery, for which the prescribed procedure was the bitter-water rite (Num 5:5–31). Yet the indecency must have been shocking: ancient Israel took marriage seriously. The best assumption is that the indecency was any lewd, immoral behavior, sometimes including, but not restricted to, adultery—e.g., lesbianism or sexual misconduct that fell short of intercourse.

9 Four problems contribute to the difficulty of understanding this verse. The first is textual. The "except" clause appears in several forms, doubtless owing to assimilation to 5:32; but there can be no doubt that an except clause is original. Though some MSS add a few more words (e.g., "and the divorcée who marries another commits adultery"), the diversity of the MS additions and the likelihood of assimilation to 5:32, not to mention the weight of external evidence, support the shorter text (cf. Metzger, *Textual Commentary*, pp. 47–48).

The second problem concerns the meaning of *porneia* ("marital unfaithfulness," NIV; "fornication," KJV). H. Baltensweiler (*Die Ehe im Neuen Testament* [Zürich: Zwingli, 1967], p. 93) thinks that it refers to marriage within prohibited degrees

(Lev 18), i.e., to incest. Many others, especially Roman Catholic scholars, have defended that view in some detail (cf. J.A. Fitzmyer, "The Matthean Divorce Texts and Some New Palestinian Evidence," *Theological Studies*, 37 [1976]: 208–11). Appeal is often made to 1 Corinthians 5:1, where "a man has his father's wife" (his stepmother). But it should be noted that even here Paul gives no indication he is dealing with an incestuous marriage but only an incestuous affair. It is very doubtful whether Paul or any other Jew would have regarded an incestuous relationship as marriage: Paul would not have told the couple to get a divorce but to stop what they were doing. And in the next chapter Paul uses the same word (*porneia*) to describe prostitution (1 Cor 6:13, 16).

Others have argued that *porneia* refers to premarital unchastity (Isaksson, pp. 135ff.; Mark Geldard, "Jesus' Teaching on Divorce," *Churchman* 92 [1978]: 134–43): if a man discovers his bride is not a virgin, he may divorce her. This has the advantage (it is argued) of being no *real* exception to Jesus' prohibition of divorce, making it easier to reconcile Matthew and Mark, who omits the "except" clause. Moreover it provides a neat background for the disciples' shock (v. 10); for if *porneia* refers to every sexual sin, Jesus is saying no more than what many rabbis taught. The latter objection is best treated at v. 10. The former is a possible way of reconciling Matthew and Mark, but there are many other possibilities; and there is no reason to adopt this one if *porneia* is being squeezed into too narrow a semantic range.

Still others hold that *porneia* here means "adultery," no more and no less (e.g., T.V. Fleming, "Christ and Divorce," *Theological Studies* 24 [1963]: 109; Sigal, "Halakah," pp. 116ff.). Certainly the word can include that meaning (Jer 3:8–9; cf. MT and LXX; cf. Ecclus 23:23). Yet in Greek the normal word for adultery is *moicheia*. Matthew has already used *moicheia* and *porneia* in the same context (15:19), suggesting some distinction between the words, even if there is considerable overlap. A. Mahoney ("A New Look at the Divorce Clauses in Mt 5, 32 and 19, 9," CBQ 30 [1968]: 29–38) suggests *porneia* refers to spiritual harlotry, a metaphor often adopted by the OT prophets. Jesus then prohibits divorce except where one spouse is not a Christian. But it is almost impossible to conceive how such a response, couched in such language, could have any relevance (let alone intelligibility) to the disputants here. Moreover Paul knows no dominical word on the subject of mixed marriages (1 Cor 7:12), and the answer he provides (1 Cor 7:12–16) seems somewhat stricter.

The reason these and many other creative suggestions have been advanced lies in the difficulty of the verse as a whole, both in its immediate context and as a parallel to Mark–Luke. But it must be admitted that the word *porneia* itself is very broad. In unambiguous contexts it can on occasion refer to a specific kind of sexual sin. Yet even then this is possible only because the specific sexual sin belongs to the larger category of sexual immorality. *Porneia* covers the entire range of such sins (cf. TDNT, 6:579–95; BAGD, s.v.; Joseph Jensen, "Does *porneia* Mean Fornication? A Critique of Bruce Malina," NovTest 20 [1978]: 161–84) and should not be restricted unless the context requires it.

The third problem is why Matthew alone of the synoptic Gospels includes the except clause; and the fourth is just what that clause means. These may be handled together. Proposed solutions are legion; but there are seven important ones.

1. Some hold that the except clause here and in 5:32 is really no exception at all. The preposition *epi* plus the dative can have the sense of addition: "in addition to"

or even "apart from" (cf. Luke 3:20; Col 3:14; Zerwick, par. 128). In this verse the words should be rendered "not apart from sexual promiscuity" in v.9; and similar reasoning applies to the slightly different construction in 5:31: "whoever repudiates his wife, in addition to the *porneia* [for which he repudiates her], causes her to be defiled by adultery." There is then no exception to Jesus' prohibition of divorce as reported in Mark–Luke. But all this requires almost impossible Greek. When *epi* has this "additive" force, it is nowhere preceded by *mē* ("not"), which most naturally introduces an exception. Dupont (*Mariage et divorce*, pp. 102–6) has clearly shown that a real exception is meant.

2. The majority of recent commentators hold that Matthew has simply taken over Mark's pericope but liberalized it. The absolute prohibition was no longer possible in the Matthean church, and so the except clause was introduced (so David R. Catchpole, "The Synoptic Divorce Material as a Traditio-Historical Problem," BJRL 57 [1974–75]: 92–127; R.H. Stein, " 'Is It Harmful for a Man to Divorce His Wife?' " JETS 22 [1979]: 115–21; H. Reisser, DNTT, 1:500). The particular reason for adding the exception is variously put: (1) Jesus' absolute prohibition was only meant to be a guideline, which the evangelists felt free to adapt—after all, "Jesus was not a legalist" (Stein); (2) Matthew felt it necessary to align Jesus with the school of Shammai in the context of rabbinic debates in his day (Bornkamm, *Tradition*, pp. 25–26); and (3) *porneia* refers to incestuous marriages, not uncommon among Gentiles; so Matthew added the except clause because an increasing number of Gentile converts were entering his predominantly Jewish church, and Jesus' prohibition of divorce must not be thought to apply to their illicit marriages (Mahoney, "New Look"; cf. also Benoit, Bonnard).

But all these views have serious problems.

a. There is serious debate about whether Matthew has actually *added* something to the tradition or whether he is independent of Mark at this point.

b. To stigmatize an absolute prohibition by suggesting it would make Jesus a "legalist" is to beg a number of questions. Could not any absolute prohibition be subjected to the same cavalier labeling? The word "legalist" is a loaded word that can refer either to someone who sets up absolutes or to someone who thinks he is accepted by God on the basis of his obedience. In the first sense Jesus *is* a "legalist" (e.g., 22:37–38); in the second sense he is not. But only the first sense is relevant to this verse.

c. It is not clear why Matthew would feel it necessary to align his Gospel with a particular rabbinic school that, as he knew, already existed in Jesus' day. There is no new situation, in this respect, in A.D. 85.

d. The new situation suggested by Mahoney ("New Look") is not very plausible because it requires an unnatural reading of *porneia*, it assumes that Matthew would see an incestuous "marriage" as a genuine marriage subject to divorce (instead of a sinful affair that must be terminated), and it introduces an unsupported major anachronism.

e. Moreover simple alignment with the school of Shammai is implausible in a book demanding a righteousness surpassing that of the Pharisees (5:20) and in a context where Jesus' teaching on divorce evokes a cynical response from the disciples (19:10).

3. Hill, Sigal, and others argue that *porneia* simply means "adultery" in this context and that Jesus is interpreting the *'erwat dābār* ("something indecent") of Deuteronomy 24:1 in this way. This does not necessarily mean that Matthew softens

Mark: as Hill (*Matthew*) points out, in Jewish circles of the first century, Jewish law *required* a man to divorce an adulterous wife (M *Sotah* 5:1); and this may well be assumed by the other Gospels "as an understood and accepted part of any teaching on the subject of divorce" but spelled out only in Matthew. This interpretation probably narrows down the meaning of *porneia* too far; but apart from that, the objections against it can be satisfactorily answered (cf. below on 7).

4. Bruce Vawter, in two articles ("The Divorce Clauses in Mt 5, 32 and 19, 9," CBQ 16 [1954]: 155–67; and "Divorce and the New Testament," CBQ 39 [1977]: 528–48), argues strongly that the except clauses have been misunderstood: they are preteritions, i.e., exceptions to the proposition itself, not simply to the verb. The except clause in 19:9 therefore "means that *porneia* [which he takes to be equivalent to the 'something indecent' of Deut 24:1] is not involved"—i.e., "I say to you, whoever dismisses his wife—the permission in Deut 24:1 notwithstanding—and marries another, commits adultery." Similarly, in 5:32 he understands the crucial phrase to mean "quite apart from the matter of *porneia*." Vawter is followed by Banks (*Jesus*, pp. 156–57). The effect of this interpretation is similar to 1: Matthew allows no more of an exception than Mark, and Jesus specifically abrogates the Mosaic permission. It makes good sense of the disciples' next remarks (v.10)—though Jesus' rejoinder (vv.11–12) seems a bit of a letdown, in a book in which the redactional pattern is *not* to have Jesus agree with his misunderstanding disciples but to reemphasize the point just made (cf. Q. Quesnell, " 'Made Themselves Eunuchs for the Kingdom of Heaven' (Mt 19, 12)," CBQ 30 [1968]: 340ff.). Moreover it is not at all obvious that the except clauses are preteritions: certainly the earliest Greek commentators did not take them that way, as Quesnell (p. 348) points out.

5. What Quesnell himself argues is that Jesus by using the verb *apolyō* (v.9) permits, in the case of the wife's marital infidelity, separation but not divorce (similarly G.J. Wenham, "May Divorced Christians Remarry?" *Churchman* 95 [1981]: 150–61; Dupont, *Mariage et divorce*, pp. 93–157), and therefore no remarriage under any circumstances. Such separation without possibility of remarriage was unheard of in Jewish circles and, of course, would have been much stricter than the school of Shammai; and this prompts the disciples' reaction (v.10). But two considerations stand against this view. First, *apolyō* has already been used in v.3 with the undoubted meaning "to divorce." It is unwarranted to understand the same verb a few verses later in some other way, unless there is some compelling contextual reason for the change. Again, though it is formally true that the except clause is syntactically linked to the divorce clause, not the remarriage clause, this is scarcely decisive. Locating the except clause anywhere else would breed even more ambiguity. For instance, if it is placed before the verb *moichatai* ("commits adultery"), the verse might be paraphrased as follows: "Whoever divorces his wife and marries another, if it is not for fornication that he divorces one and marries another, commits adultery." But this wording suggests that fornication is being advanced as the actual *reason* for marrying another, and not only for the divorce—an interpretation that borders on the ridiculous. Moreover, if the remarriage clause is excluded, the thought becomes nonsensical: "Anyone who divorces his wife, except for *porneia*, commits adultery"—surely untrue unless he remarries. The except clause must therefore be understood to govern the entire protasis. We may paraphrase as follows: "Anyone who divorces his wife and marries another woman commits adultery—though this principle does not hold in the case of *porneia*."

6. John J. Kilgallen ("To What Are the Matthean Exception-Texts [5, 32 and 19, 9] an Exception?" *Biblica* 61 [1980]: 102–5) suggests that the except clauses need only mean that in some cases divorce is not adulterous, rather than that in some cases divorce is not morally wrong. He renders 5:32: "Everyone who divorces his wife (except in the case of *porneia*) makes her adulterous." But in the case of *porneia*, he does not *make* her adulterous; she is *already* adulterous (similarly Westerholm [pp. 118f.] and the literature he cites). This is not convincing; for the Greek does not read "makes her adulterous" or "makes her an adulteress," but "makes her commit adultery" (the passive infinitive does not mean "to become an adulter[ess]" but "to commit adultery"; cf. BAGD, s.v., 2.b). If the woman has already committed *porneia*, doubtless divorce (and the remarriage that would ensue) could scarcely be said to make her an adulteress; but such divorce and remarriage would make her commit adultery. And this approach does not work in v.9, where the result is not that the man makes his wife commit adultery but that he commits adultery.

7. It seems best, then, to permit both *porneia* and the except clause to retain their normal force. Jesus is then saying that divorce and remarriage always involve evil; but as Moses permitted it because of the hardness of men's hearts, so also does he—but now on the sole grounds of *porneia* (sexual sin of any sort). The principal exegetical difficulties surrounding this view may be treated as follows:

a. Formally Jesus is abrogating something of the Mosaic prescription; for whatever the *'erwat dābār* ("something indecent") refers to (Deut 24:1), it cannot easily be thought to refer to adultery, for which the prescribed punishment was death. That this was rarely carried out (McKeating, "Sanctions Against Adultery"; cf. Joseph in 1:19–20) is beside the point: as a legal system, irrespective of whether it was enforced, the Deuteronomic permission for divorce and remarriage could scarcely have adultery primarily in view. But *porneia* includes adultery even if not restricted to it. Jesus' judgments on the matter are therefore both lighter (no capital punishment for adultery) and heavier (the sole exception being sexual sin).

b. This exception is not in contradiction with Jesus' strong words in vv.4–8, despite frequent insistence on the contrary. In vv.4–8 Jesus lays out the true direction in which Scripture points (cf. Jesus' treatment of oaths, 5:33–37, where there is also formal abrogation of a Mosaic command). Even here Jesus acknowledges that the Mosaic concession springs not from divine desire but human hardheartedness. Would Jesus say human hearts were any less hard in his own day? Might there not therefore be some exception to the principle he lays out, precisely because *porneia* was not on the Creator's mind in Genesis 1–2? More importantly sexual sin has a peculiar relation to Jesus' treatment of Genesis 1:27; 2:24 (in Matt 19:4–6), because the indissolubility of marriage he defends by appealing to those verses from the creation accounts is predicated on sexual union ("one flesh"). Sexual promiscuity is therefore a de facto exception. It may not necessitate divorce; but permission for divorce and remarriage under such circumstances, far from being inconsistent with Jesus' thought, is in perfect harmony with it.

c. Although it is commonly held that the except clauses are secondary and bring Matthew into a clash with Mark, the issue is not so simple. Not a few scholars hold that, at least on this point, Matthew 19:9 is authentic and that Mark omits the obvious exception (e.g., Schlatter; Isaksson, pp. 75–92; D.L. Dungan, *The Sayings of Jesus in the Churches of Paul* [Philadelphia: Fortress, 1971], pp. 122–25).

Catchpole ("Synoptic Material"), on the other hand, argues for Markan priority on the ground that the aporias he finds in Matthew 19:3–12 can all be explained by recognizing that they have been introduced precisely where Matthew has changed Mark. His argument has some weight only if the aporias are real; but the four he mentions are either imagined or explainable in other ways. For instance, Catchpole holds that v.9 does not cohere with vv.4–8, and this problem can be remedied only by the removal of the except clause in v.9—which is precisely the new bit Matthew has added. But we have shown above at b that v.9 *does* cohere with vv.4–8. This does not prove Matthew did not depend on Mark, but it forbids claiming he *did*. And even if Mark's priority prevails in this pericope, Matthew's redactional additions cannot be assumed to be nonhistorical unless we have evidence that Matthew had access to no other information (cf. Introduction, sections 1–3). We conclude, therefore, that there is no decisive evidence for literary dependence either way, and that there is no overwhelming reason why the except clauses, both here and in 5:32, should not be authentic.

Certainly, on the interpretation adopted here, Matthew and Mark–Luke have this in common—they abrogate any permission for divorce in Deuteronomy 24:1 if that permission extends, or is thought to extend, beyond sexual sin. If Mark has priority, the except clause in Matthew seems best explained along the line suggested by Hill above at 3; if the reverse, or if the two Gospels preserve independent accounts of the same incident, Mark may think the exception so obvious (because it concerns sexual infidelity, the heart of the union according to Genesis) as not worth mentioning. Moreover the exception is particularly appropriate to Jesus' day and to Matthew's Jewish readers; for though Jesus had formally dismissed the Mosaic divorce provisions and substituted marital unfaithfulness as the sole basis of a rupture of the "one flesh," this exception collided with the Mosaic sentence of stoning in such cases—a fact of which Jewish audiences were doubtlessly aware. With the death penalty for marital *porneia* effectively abolished, "the termination of the relationship might appropriately be effected by divorce" (James B. Hurley, *Man and Woman in Biblical Perspective* [Leicester: IVP, 1981], p. 104; cf. further John Murray, *Divorce* [Philadelphia: Presbyterian and Reformed, 1953], pp. 51ff.).

d. The final problem is whether this interpretation adequately accounts for the disciples' reaction (v.10). Before turning to this, we may observe that Mark 10:12 makes the same responsibilities and privileges concerning divorce and remarriage extend to the woman as well as the man—probably a pointed rebuke of Herodias (cf. Lane, *Mark*, p. 358). Mark omits the except clause and retains the remark about women, Matthew the reverse. (The related question of the so-called Pauline privilege [1 Cor 7:15] must be left to commentaries on 1 Corinthians.)

10–12 Dupont (*Mariage et divorce*, pp. 161–222) argues that these verses deal, not with celibacy, but with continence after divorce. Believing that no remarriage is legitimate, Dupont argues that the divorced believer must remain continent "for the sake of the kingdom"—i.e., in order to enter it—because remarriage would be adulterous. Somewhat similar is Francis J. Moloney's position ("Matthew 19, 3–12 and Celibacy. A Redactional and Form-Critical Study." *Journal of the Study of the New Testament* 2 (1979): 42–60, esp. 47ff.). But in addition to the difficulties entailed by holding that no remarriage is permitted (see on v.9), "eunuch" is a strange figure for continence after marriage, especially since if the divorced spouse died, the survivor could remarry (Dupont's view).

There is a better way to look at these verses. First, the disciples' reaction (v.10) must not be exaggerated. Unlike v.25, there is no mention of astonishment. Jesus, though not forbidding *all* divorce and remarriage, has come close to the school of Shammai on the grounds for exceptions, while taking a far more conservative stance than Shammai on who may remarry. In the light of the position, tacitly adopted by most Jews, that marriage was a duty, the disciples rather cynically conclude that such strictures surely make marriage unattractive. This virtually makes the appeal of marriage contingent on liberal divorce and remarriage rights—a stance that fails miserably to understand what Jesus has said about the creation ordinance.

Verse 11 can then be understood in one of two ways. Either *ton logon touton* (lit., "this word"—regardless of whether *touton* is original, since *ton* can be a mild demonstrative) refers to Jesus' teaching in vv.4–9 or to the disciples' misguided remark in v.10. NIV's "this teaching" (v.11) favors the former; but this is unlikely, for it makes Jesus contradict himself. After a strong prohibition, it is highly unlikely that Jesus' moral teaching dwindles into a pathetic "But of course, not everyone can accept this."

It helps little to say with Bonnard that those to whom the teaching is given are Christians who must follow Jesus' moral standards but that others cannot accept what he says, for Jesus' appeal has been to the creation ordinance, not to kingdom morality. It is better to take "this word" to refer to the disciples' conclusion in v.10: "it is better not to marry." Jesus responds that not everyone can live by such a verdict, such abstinence from marriage. But some do, namely those to whom it is given—those born eunuchs, those made eunuchs by men (possibly in groups like the Essenes, but more likely a reflection of the rabbinic distinction between two types of eunuch: the impotent and the castrated—the latter very often for some high court position where there were royal women (cf. Acts 8:26–39; SBK, 1:805–7)—and those who have made themselves eunuchs because of the kingdom of God. The latter is not a commendation of self-castration but of renunciation of marriage in light of the disciples' remark, "it is better not to marry."

Jesus, like Paul after him (1 Cor 7:7–9), is prepared to commend celibacy "because of the kingdom" (not "for the sake of attaining it," but "because of its claims and interests": cf. J. Blinzler, "Εἰσὶν εὐνοῦχοι: Zur Auslegung von Mt 19, 12," ZNW 28 [1957]: 254–70). Thus, far from backing down at the disciples' surliness, Jesus freely concedes that for those to whom it is given "it *is* better not to marry"; and "The one who can accept this should accept it." But it is important to recognize that neither Jesus nor the apostles see celibacy as an intrinsically holier state than marriage (cf. 1 Tim 4:1–3; Heb 13:4), nor as a condition for the top levels of ministry (Matt 8:14; 1 Cor 9:5), but as a special calling granted for greater usefulness in the kingdom. Those who impose this discipline on themselves must remember Paul's conclusion: it is better to marry than to burn with passion (1 Cor 7:9).

Two final observations: (1) The authenticity of v.12 has been admirably defended by T. Matura ("Le célibat dans le Nouveau Testament," *Nouvelle Revue Théologique* 107 [1975]: 481–500); and (2) Jesus' remarks betray a certain self-conscious independence of the OT law, which excluded eunuchs from the assembly of Yahweh (Deut 23:1; cf. Lev 22:24; SBK, 1:806–7; Schweizer). One cannot forget the conversion of the Ethiopian eunuch (Acts 8:26–40) who, though he would have been excluded from the assembly of Yahweh, was joyfully welcomed to the assembly of Messiah.

Notes

5 On the use of εἰς σάρκα μίαν (*eis sarka mian*, "one flesh") instead of a predicative nominative, see Moule, *Idiom Book*, pp. 183, 208; Zerwick, par. 32.

10 Οὕτως (*houtōs*, lit., "thus") here takes on a relatively rare adjectival function (NIV, "this"; cf. BDF, par. 434[1]).

Contrary to B.F. Meyer, αἰτία (*aitia*) here means not "cause" but "case" or "situation" (NIV; cf. BDF, par. 5[3*b*]).

2. Blessing little children

19:13–15

> [13]Then little children were brought to Jesus for him to place his hands on them and pray for them. But the disciples rebuked those who brought them.
> [14]Jesus said, "Let the little children come to me, and do not hinder them, for the kingdom of heaven belongs to such as these." [15]When he had placed his hands on them, he went on from there.

13 "Then" is ambiguous (see on 2:7). Children in Jesus' day were often brought to rabbis and elders to be blessed, customarily by placing hands on them (cf. Gen 48:14; Num 27:18; Acts 6:6; 13:3; cf. Matt 9:18, 20; Mark 10:16). The disciples "rebuked them" (lit.): both the context and the synoptic parallels show that "them" refers, not to the children, but to "those who brought them" (NIV).

Why did the disciples stoop to this rebuke? Perhaps they were annoyed that Jesus was being delayed on his journey to Jerusalem; perhaps they felt they were being interrupted in their important discussion. Although children in Judaism of the time were deeply cherished, they were thought in some ways to be negligible members of society: their place was to learn, to be respectful, to listen. But two deeper insights suggest themselves: (1) the preceding pericope (vv.3–12) implicitly stresses the sanctity of the family, and vv.13–15 continue by saying something important about children; and (2) in 18:1–9 children serve as models for humility, patterns for Jesus' "little ones"; yet Jesus' disciples, his "little ones," show little humility here.

14–15 Jesus does not want the little children prevented from coming to him (v.14), not because the kingdom of heaven belongs to them, but because the kingdom of heaven belongs to those like them (so also Mark and Luke, stressing childlike faith): Jesus receives them because they are an excellent object lesson in the kind of humility and faith he finds acceptable.

Notes

14 O. Cullmann (*Baptism in the New Testament* [London: SCM, 1950], pp. 71–80) finds in μὴ κωλύετε (*mē kōluete*, "do not hinder") an echo of a primitive baptismal formula, because this verb refers to baptism elsewhere (3:14; Acts 8:36; 10:47; 11:17). He does not argue that here Jesus teaches infant baptism but that the church transmitted the story in

a way Christians would remember an event in Jesus' ministry "by which they might be led to a solution of the question of infant Baptism" (p. 78). Apart from the propriety of finding a solution to a later problem in a story all agree does not address it, the suggestion that *mē kōluete* was a technical term that connoted baptism is very doubtful. The verb occurs twenty-three times in the NT, and only five of these relate to baptism. The four (outside this passage) allegedly referring to baptism fail to establish a clear baptismal formula: at 3:14 John tries "to deter" Jesus; in Acts 8:36 the Ethiopian eunuch asks what "prevents" him from being baptized; and the remaining two occurrences (Acts 10:47; 11:17) justify the baptism of the Gentile Cornelius on the grounds that the Spirit had fallen on him.

---

3. *Wealth and the kingdom* (19:16–30)

a. *The rich young man*

19:16–22

> [16]Now a man came up to Jesus and asked, "Teacher, what good thing must I do to get eternal life?"
>
> [17]"Why do you ask me about what is good?" Jesus replied. "There is only One who is good. If you want to enter life, obey the commandments."
>
> [18]"Which ones?" the man inquired.
>
> Jesus replied, " 'Do not murder, do not commit adultery, do not steal, do not give false testimony, [19]honor your father and mother,' and 'love your neighbor as yourself.' "
>
> [20]"All these I have kept," the young man said. "What do I still lack?"
>
> [21]Jesus answered, "If you want to be perfect, go, sell your possessions and give to the poor, and you will have treasure in heaven. Then come, follow me."
>
> [22]When the young man heard this, he went away sad, because he had great wealth.

Some of the differences between Matthew and Mark–Luke (cf. Mark 10:17–31; Luke 18:18–30) are so sharp (cf. vv.16–17) that they have frequently served as tests for redaction criticism. Many, of course, are of little significance. Matthew introduces the central figure as "a man" and later says he was "young" (v.20). Mark (10:17) says nothing about his age but provides more details of the initial meeting: it was "as Jesus started on his way" that a man "ran up" to him and "fell on his knees before him." These and many similar differences have been treated elsewhere (cf. Carson, "Redaction Criticism"). The nub of the problem turns on vv.16–17 and parallels.

16–17 A certain man—identified by all three evangelists as rich, by Matthew (v.20) as young, and by Luke (18:18) as a ruler—asks Jesus what he must do to inherit "eternal life" (v.16). The latter expression refers to a life "approved by God and to which access to the kingdom (present and eschatological) is promised (cf. the rabbinic 'life of the age to come')" (Hill, *Matthew*; cf. 7:14; 25:46; Hill, *Greek Words*, pp. 163–201).

The problem arises when Matthew is compared with Mark and Luke. In the latter, the questioner asks, "Good teacher, what must I do to inherit eternal life?" (Luke 18:18). Jesus replies, "Why do you call me good? No one is good—except

God alone" (v. 19). In Matthew, however, the questioner asks, "Teacher, what good thing must I do to inherit eternal life?" (v. 16). "Good" no longer modifies "teacher"; and therefore Jesus' response is correspondingly adapted: "Why do you ask me about what is good? There is only One who is good" (v. 17). A majority of modern scholars hold that Matthew has transformed the exchange because, at his later time of writing, the church can no longer live with the suggestion that Jesus himself is not sinless.

It is logically possible to achieve harmonization by mere addition ("*Good* teacher, what *good* thing?" followed by Jesus giving both answers); indeed, later copyists of NT MSS sometimes opted for such an approach (hence KJV). But the procedure is notoriously implausible. The evangelists, as we have often witnessed, are far more concerned with Jesus' *ipsissima vox* than his *ipsissima verba* (see note on 3:17); and we do the Scriptures disservice when we fail to consider the implications. Nevertheless the christological explanation ventured by many is equally implausible. A better understanding of the text is gained from the following observations.

1. Stonehouse (*Origins*, pp. 93–112) has convincingly demonstrated that christological concerns do not stand at the heart of *any* of the three synoptic accounts. The argument of G. M. Styler ("Stages in Christology in the Synoptic Gospels," NTS 10 [1963–64]: esp. pp. 404–6), that Matthew reflects a growing interest in ontology, is especially weak. Styler argues that, unlike Mark, Matthew believes Jesus is divine. But Hill (*Matthew*) rightly points out that Matthew still preserves the words "There is only One who is good," a clear reference to God; and the alteration says nothing about Jesus' status in relation to God. Moreover Styler has adopted a historical reconstruction of the development of doctrine that not all find convincing (cf. D. A. Carson, "Unity and Diversity: On the Possibility of Systematic Theology," in Carson and Woodbridge), especially here where Luke, probably writing after Matthew or at least very close to him, senses no embarrassment in Mark's words but records them verbatim—and this despite the fact that Luke elsewhere feels free to drop bits that could be taken as detrimental to Jesus. We must therefore look for nonchristological explanations for Matthew's alteration.

2. The thrust of the passage in both Mark and Matthew must be grasped. Irrespective of what "good" refers to, the man approaches Jesus with a question showing how far he is from the humble faith that, as Jesus has just finished saying, characterizes all who belong to the kingdom (vv. 13–15). He wants to earn eternal life; and in the light of v. 20, he apparently thinks there are good things he can do, beyond the demands of the law, by which he can assure his salvation. Many Jews believed that a specific act of goodness could win eternal life (SBK, 1: 808ff.); and this young man, assuming this opinion is correct, seeks Jesus' view as to what that act might be. Whatever differences exist between Matthew and Luke, Jesus' response is not designed either to confess personal sin (Mark) nor to call in question his own competence to discuss what is good (Matthew), for such topics are not in view (see esp. B. B. Warfield, "Jesus' Alleged Confession of Sin," PTR 12 [1914]: 127–228). Instead Jesus calls in question his interlocutor's inadequate understanding of goodness. In the absolute sense of goodness required to gain eternal life, only God is good (cf. Ps 106:1; 118:1, 29; 1 Chron 16:34; 2 Chron 5:13; and there is no discussion of whether Jesus shares that goodness). Jesus will not allow anything other than God's will to determine what is good. By approaching Jesus in this way (esp. vv. 16, 20), the young man reveals simultaneously that he wants something beyond God's will (v. 20) and that he misconstrues the absoluteness of God's goodness.

3. In this light Matthew's phrasing of the initial exchange between Jesus and the young man focuses on the issue central for both Matthew and Mark more clearly than Mark does. To that extent it also ties this pericope more closely to the preceding one than Mark does. This young man stands in stunning contrast to those to whom, according to Jesus, the kingdom belongs. This may help explain Matthew's wording.

4. Within this framework Mark 10:18 no more calls in question Jesus' sinlessness than Matthew 19:17 calls in question Jesus' competence to judge what is good. Apart from the assumption of Mark's priority without either evangelist having access to other traditions, it is difficult to see why, if we charge Matthew with eliminating the possibility that readers might think Jesus could sin, we should not charge Mark with eliminating the possibility that some readers might think Jesus could not pronounce on what was good. Both charges would miss the central point of both Matthew and Mark.

5. "If you want to enter life, obey the commandments" (v.17) does not mean that Matthew, unlike Mark, thinks eternal life is *earned* by keeping the commandments. After all, Mark himself is about to report Jesus' exhortation to keep specific commandments. The entire debate has been bedevilled by a false split between grace and obedience to the will of God. No less staunch a supporter of grace than Paul can insist that without certain purity a man cannot inherit the kingdom (1 Cor 6:9–10). Jesus tells this young man, in similar vein, what good things he must do if he is to gain eternal life, precisely because he perceives his questioner has little understanding of such things. But that is still far from telling him that by doing these things he will *earn* eternal life.

6. But why, then, has either Matthew or Mark edited the exchange? Or, if the two reports are independent, or if Matthew depends on Mark but has eyewitness knowledge of the events, how is it possible that both accounts can be accepted as trustworthy representations of the same incident? Lohmeyer (*Matthäus*) suggests that the variations stem from different translations of an Aramaic report of the incident. Better yet is a reconstruction of the incident that, though not simple additive harmonization, provides a historical basis broad enough to support reports of both Matthew and Mark–Luke and fits well within the normal latitude the evangelists show in their reportage. This reconstruction is worked out in more detail elsewhere (Carson, "Redaction Crticism"). Briefly, it suggests the young ruler's question was "Good teacher, what must I do to inherit eternal life?" and that Jesus' reply was "Why do you ask *me* questions regarding the good? There is only one who is good, namely God."

18–20 Jesus lists the sixth, seventh, eighth, ninth, and fifth commandments of Exodus 20 in that order. He omits "do not defraud" (Mark 10:19, apparently an application of the eighth and ninth) and adds "love your neighbor as yourself" (Lev 19:18; cf. Matt 22:34–40). On the text form, compare Gundry (*Use of OT*, pp. 17–19) and K.J. Thomas ("Liturgical Citations in the Synoptics," NTS 22 [1975–76]: 205–14). The man's impulsive reply is reflected by Paul (Phil 3:6; cf. SBK, 1:814) on a certain understanding of the law; but the man's further words, "What do I still lack?" show his uncertainty and lack of assurance of ever being good enough for salvation, as well as his notion that certain "good works" are over and above the law (cf. SBK, 4:536ff., 559ff.). Wealth he enjoyed (v.22), while suffering barrenness of soul.

21–22 Many have taken these verses to indicate a two-tier ethic: some disciples find eternal life, and others go further and become perfect by adopting a more compassionate stance (e.g., Klostermann; DNTT, 2:63). But G. Barth (Bornkamm, *Tradition* pp. 95ff.) convincingly disproves this exegesis. In particular the young man's question in v.20, "What do I still lack?" clearly refers to gaining eternal life (v.17); and Jesus' answer in v.21 must be understood as answering the question. A two-tier Christianity is implicitly contradicted by 23:8–12; and the same word "perfect" is applied to all of Jesus' disciples in 5:48. Matthew shows no strong tendency toward asceticism. Therefore the basic thrust of v.21 is not "Sell your possessions and give to the poor" but "Come, follow me."

What the word "perfection" suggests here is what it commonly means in the OT: undivided loyalty and full-hearted obedience. This young man could not face that. He was willing to discipline himself to observe all the outward stipulations and even perform supererogatory works; but because of his wealth, he had a divided heart. His money was competing with God; and what Jesus everywhere demands as a condition for eternal life is absolute, radical discipleship. This entails the surrender of *self*. "Keeping the individual commandments is no substitute for the readiness for self-surrender to the absolute claim of God imposed through the call of the gospel. Jesus' summons in this context means that true obedience to the Law is rendered ultimately in discipleship" (Lane, *Mark*, p. 367).

Formally, of course, Jesus' demand goes beyond anything in OT law (cf. Banks, *Jesus*, p. 163): no OT passage stipulates v.21. Equally remarkable is the fact that the focus on *God's will* (vv.17–19) should culminate in following *Jesus*. The explanation of this is that Jesus is prophesied by the OT. The will of God, as revealed in Scripture, looks forward to the coming of Messiah (see on 2:15; 5:17–20; 11:11–13). Absolute allegiance to him, with the humility of a child, is essential to salvation. The condition Jesus now imposes not only reveals the man's attachment to money but shows that all his formal compliance with the law is worthless because none of it entails absolute self-surrender. What the man needs is the triumph of grace; for as the next verses show, for him entering the kingdom of heaven is impossible (v.26). God, with whom all things are possible, must work. The parable in 20:1–16 directly speaks to this issue. But the young man is deaf to it: he leaves because, if a choice must be made between money and Jesus, money wins (cf. 6:24).

Notes

20 Here and elsewhere (Allen, p. xxiii), Matthew uses the aorist active verb—this time ἐφύλαξα (*ephylaxa*, "I have kept")—rather than the middle Mark uses—but the distinction is hardly worth mentioning (cf. Moule, *Idiom Book*, p. 24).

b. *Grace and reward in the kingdom*

19:23–30

> [23]Then Jesus said to his disciples, "I tell you the truth, it is hard for a rich man to enter the kingdom of heaven. [24]Again I tell you, it is easier for a camel to go through the eye of a needle than for a rich man to enter the kingdom of God."

25When the disciples heard this, they were greatly astonished and asked, "Who then can be saved?"

26Jesus looked at them and said, "With man this is impossible, but with God all things are possible."

27Peter answered him, "We have left everything to follow you! What then will there be for us?"

28Jesus said to them, "I tell you the truth, at the renewal of all things, when the Son of Man sits on his glorious throne, you who have followed me will also sit on twelve thrones, judging the twelve tribes of Israel. 29And everyone who has left houses or brothers or sisters or father or mother or children or fields for my sake will receive a hundred times as much and will inherit eternal life. 30But many who are first will be last, and many who are last will be first.

23–24 Jesus is not saying that all poor people and none of the wealthy enter the kingdom of heaven (v.23; see on 3:2). That would exclude Abraham, Isaac, and Jacob, to say nothing of David, Solomon, and Joseph of Arimathea. The point of Jesus' teaching lies elsewhere. Most Jews expected the rich to inherit eternal life, not because their wealth could buy their way in, but because their wealth testified to the blessing of the Lord on their lives. Jesus' view is a different and more sober one. (On "I tell you the truth," see on 5:18). The proverbial saying of v.24 refers to the absolutely impossible. The camel was the biggest animal in Palestine (a similar proverb in BT [B *Berakoth* 55b] prefers "elephant" to "camel" because elephants were not uncommon in Babylon). Attempts to weaken this hyperbole by taking "needle," not as a sewing needle, but as a small gate through which an unladen camel could just squeeze—and only on his knees—are misguided. This conjecture may come from some of Jerome's allegorizing (cf. Broadus).

25–26 "Saved" (v.25) is equivalent to entering the kingdom of God (v.24) or obtaining eternal life (v.16). The disciples, reflecting the common Jewish view of the rich, are astonished and ask that if rich men, blessed of God, cannot be saved, then who *can* be? Jesus agrees: "With man this [the salvation of anyone] is impossible, but with God all things are possible" (v.26; cf. Gen 18:14; Job 42:2; Luke 1:37).

27–28 Peter, impressed by "impossible" and speaking for his fellow disciples, thinks Jesus' words are unfair to the Twelve (v.27). Peter emphatically replies, "We have left everything to follow you" (cf. 4:20). Even here he and the others are thinking in terms of deserving or earning God's favor. Yet Jesus does not castigate his disciples for being mercenary: they have made sacrifices and deserve an answer. But what he says—that the blessing to come, whether belonging exclusively to the Twelve at the renewal (v.28) or to all believers now (vv.29–30), far surpasses any sacrifice they might make—implies that it is a gentle rebuke.

Verse 28 has no parallel in Mark and only a loose one in Luke 22:28–30. The solemn "I tell you the truth" points to something important. Jesus looks forward to the session of the Son of Man (see on 8:20). He will sit on his "glorious throne" (lit., "throne of glory"; cf. Zerwick, par. 41; Turner, *Syntax,* p. 214; cf. 7:22; 16:27; 25:31, 34) at the *palingenesia* ("renewal" of all things), a word used only twice in the NT, the other occurrence dealing with "rebirth . . . by the Holy Spirit" (Titus 3:5). Here it has to do with the consummation of the kingdom (RSV, "in the new world"). (For its use elsewhere, cf. TDNT, 1:686–89; DNTT, 1:184–85; and cf. 13:32; Acts 3:21; Rom 8:18–23; 2 Peter 3:13; Rev 21:1, 5; 1QS 4:25.)

Contrary to Schweizer (*Matthew*), there is no allusion to the endless Stoic cycles of conflagration and "renewal": the idea moves strictly within Jewish teleological and apocalyptic expectation. But the remarkable feature of this verse is that the Twelve will "sit on twelve thrones," sharing judgment with the Son of Man. The idea that believers will at the consummation have a part in judging is not uncommon in the NT (Luke 22:30; 1 Cor 6:2). What is less clear is whether (1) the twelve apostles exercise judgment over the twelve tribes of Israel physically and racially conceived, or whether (2) the twelve apostles will exercise some kind of judgment over the entire church, symbolized by "Israel" (cf. Rev 21:12–14), or whether (3) the Twelve represent the entire assembly of Messiah, who will exercise a juridical role over racial Israel. The third supposition has no scriptural parallel; the second is possible but an unnatural way of taking "Israel" in a book that, though applying OT promises to Gentiles and Jews alike—viz., the "church" of Messiah—distinguishes between the two. The most plausible interpretation is the first one. At the consummation the Twelve will judge the nation of Israel, presumably for its general rejection of Jesus Messiah. (On the symbolism, cf. Joseph M. Baumgarten, "The Duodecimal Courts of Qumran, Revelation, and the Sanhedrin," JBL 95 [1976]: 59–78, esp. pp. 70–72; France, *Jesus*, pp. 65f.)

29–30 Jesus now extends his encouragement to all his self-sacrificing disciples (cf. Mark 10:30). The promise is not literal (one cannot have one hundred mothers). God is no man's debtor: if one of Jesus' disciples has, for Jesus' sake, left, say, a father, he will find within the messianic community a hundred who will be as a father to him—in addition to inheriting eternal life (v.29).

The proverbial saying (v.30) is one Jesus repeats on various occasions. Here he immediately illustrates it by a parable (20:1–16), climaxed by the proverb in reverse form (20:16) as a closing bracket. It indicates something of the reversals under the king's reign. Attempts to restrict the application of this parable to one setting are not successful.

1. Some say the rich become poor at the consummation and the poor rich (cf. vv.16–29), as in Luke 16:19–31: the story of Lazarus and the beggar. But such reversals are not absolute: Zacchaeus (Luke 19:1–10) was a rich man to whose house salvation came; and Abraham, to whose "bosom" the beggar went, had great wealth.

2. Many of the Fathers hold that the first-last idea refers to Jews and Gentiles respectively. Doubtless it may, but this theme is not dominant in these chapters.

3. Some think the proverb assumes that the disciples had been arguing about priority on the basis of who was first called, to which Jesus responds that "the last will be first, etc." But this better suits the situation in Matthew 18 than in Matthew 19.

4. It seems preferable, therefore, to take the proverb as a way of setting forth God's grace over against *all* notions that the rich, powerful, great, and prominent will continue so in the kingdom. Those who approach God in childlike trust (vv.13–15) will be received and advanced in the kingdom beyond those who, from the world's perspective, enjoy prominence now.

4. The parable of the workers

20:1–16

> 1"The kingdom of heaven is like a landowner who went out early in the morning to hire men to work in his vineyard. 2He agreed to pay them a denarius for the day and sent them into his vineyard.

3"About the third hour he went out and saw others standing in the marketplace doing nothing. 4He told them, 'You also go and work in my vineyard, and I will pay you whatever is right.' 5So they went.

"He went out again about the sixth hour and the ninth hour and did the same thing. 6About the eleventh hour he went out and found still others standing around. He asked them, 'Why have you been standing here all day long doing nothing?'

7" 'Because no one has hired us,' they answered.

"He said to them, 'You also go and work in my vineyard.'

8"When evening came, the owner of the vineyard said to his foreman, 'Call the workers and pay them their wages, beginning with the last ones hired and going on to the first.'

9"The workers who were hired about the eleventh hour came and each received a denarius. 10So when those came who were hired first, they expected to receive more. But each one of them also received a denarius. 11When they received it, they began to grumble against the landowner. 12'These men who were hired last worked only one hour,' they said, 'and you have made them equal to us who have borne the burden of the work and the heat of the day.'

13"But he answered one of them, 'Friend, I am not being unfair to you. Didn't you agree to work for a denarius? 14Take your pay and go. I want to give the man who was hired last the same as I gave you. 15Don't I have the right to do what I want with my own money? Or are you envious because I am generous?'

16"So the last will be first, and the first will be last."

On parables generally, see on 13:3a. From this one, found only in Matthew, we learn how "the last" person can become "first" (19:30)—by free grace (Schlatter; see esp. v.15). The point is not that those who work just an hour do as much as those who work all day (unlike a Jewish parable c. A.D. 325 that tells of a man who on those grounds is paid a month's wages for a few hours' discussion), nor that the willingness of the latecomers matches that of the all-day workers (contra Preisker, TDNT, 4:717 and n. 91), nor that Gentiles are the latecomers in contrast to the Jews (the context knows no such distinctions), nor that all men are equal before God or that all kingdom work is equal. Still less acceptable is Derrett's lengthy explanation (*NT Studies*, 1:48–75). He rightly holds that the entire parable portrays working conditions in the first century; but the eleventh-hour men, entitled to a certain minimum wage, actually get more. But Derrett's view depends on late sources for minimum wage laws; and he assumes that the grapes were urgently in need of harvesting and that it must have been Friday afternoon—none of which the text implies.

Huffmann (pp. 209–10) is right. The parable begins with a typical scene and introduces atypical elements to surprise the reader and make a powerful point. "Jesus deliberately and cleverly led the listeners along by degrees until they understood that if God's generosity was to be represented by a man, such a man would be different from any man ever encountered" (p. 209).

1–2 On "the kingdom of heaven is like" formula (v.1), see on 13:24. The normal working day was ten hours or so, not counting breaks. The landowner in the parable finds his first set of men at about 6 A.M. (*hama prōi* means "at dawn"; NIV, "early in the morning": on the construction, see Moule, *Idiom Book*, p. 82) and agrees to pay each worker a denarius (v.2)—the normal wage for a foot soldier or day laborer (Tobit 5:14; Tacitus *Annales*, 1.17; Pliny 33.3).

3–7 There were twelve "hours" from dawn to sundown. The third hour (v.3) would be about 9:00 A.M., the sixth about 12:00 M., and the eleventh about 5:00 P.M. The marketplace would be the central square, where all kinds of business was done and casual labor hired. Why the landowner kept returning to hire more men—lack of foresight, not finding enough workers earlier in the day at the marketplace, the poor work of the first laborers—is not spelled out and therefore cannot be the key to the parable. The third-hour men are promised "whatever is right" (v.4); and, trusting the landowner's integrity, they work on that basis (v.5). The last group (v.6) were standing around ("idle" [KJV] is a late addition) because no one had hired them (v.7).

8–12 Some take "when evening came" (v.8) as an allusion to the judgment, but this is doubtful. It is essential to the story in a time when laborers were customarily paid at the end of each day (cf. Lev 19:13). The foreman is told to pay each man (lit.) "the wage"—the standard day-laborer's wage. Who gets paid first is crucial: it is only because the last hired receive a day's wage (v.9) that those first hired expect to get more than they bargained for (v.10). They "grumble against" (v.11) the owner because he has been generous to others and merely just to them. They have borne "the heat of the day" (v.12, either direct sunlight or hot wind [BAGD, s.v. *kausōn*], which could drive workers from the field; and, though fairly paid, they feel unfairly treated because others who worked much less received what they did. Nothing in the parable implies that Jews have borne the burden of the law and now Gentile outcasts are made equal to them.

13–15 "Friend" (v.13) suggests that this rebuke is only a mild one. "I am not being unfair to you"—I am not cheating you, defrauding you (cf. M. Black, "Some Greek Words with 'Hebrew' Meanings in the Epistles and Apocalypse," in McKay and Miller, pp. 142ff.). The owner has paid the agreed wage (v.14). Should he want to pay others more, that is his business. Provided he has been just in all his dealings, does he not have the right to do what he wants with his money (v.15)? NIV translates "is your eye evil" (lit. Gk.) by "are you envious," because the "evil eye" was an idiom used to refer to jealousy (cf. Deut 15:9; 1 Sam 18:9; see on Matt 6:22–23).

These rhetorical questions (vv.13b–15) show that God's great gifts, simply because they *are* God's, are distributed, not because they are earned, but because he is gracious (cf. W. Haubeck, "Zum Verständnis der Parabel von den Arbeitern im Weinberg [Mt. 20, 1–15]," in Haubeck and Bachmann, pp. 95–107, esp. pp. 106f.). Jesus is not laying down principles for resolving union-management disputes. On the contrary, "the principle in the world is that he who works the longest receives the most pay. That is just. But in the kingdom of God the principles of merit and ability may be set aside so that grace can prevail" (Kistemaker, pp. 77f.). (See note on 5:12 and G. de Ru's article "The Conception of Reward in the Teaching of Jesus," NovTest 8 [1966]: 202–22.)

16 God's grace makes some who are last first. The point of the parable is not that all in the kingdom will receive the same reward but that kingdom rewards depend on God's sovereign grace (cf. v.23). For the inclusion around the parable, see on 19:30.

Notes

10 The article in τὸ ἀνὰ δηνάριον (*to ana dēnarion*) is anaphoric, i.e., "a denarius to each man *as to the others who preceded*": cf. BDF, par. 266(2).

15 "Or" is omitted by some MSS, with the evidence rather evenly divided (cf. Metzger, *Textual Commentary*, pp. 50f.).

16 Many MSS add to the end of the verse "for many are invited, but few are chosen." The shorter reading is Alexandrian and Western. The longer reading, if original, might have been dropped by homoeoteleuton; but it is equally possible the extra words are an assimilation to 22:14 (so Metzger, *Textual Commentary*, p. 5).

5. *Third major passion prediction*

20:17–19

> ¹⁷Now as Jesus was going up to Jerusalem, he took the twelve disciples aside and said to them, ¹⁸"We are going up to Jerusalem, and the Son of Man will be betrayed to the chief priests and the teachers of the law. They will condemn him to death ¹⁹and will turn him over to the Gentiles to be mocked and flogged and crucified. On the third day he will be raised to life!"

See on 16:21–23; 17:9, 22–23; and for the synoptic parallels, see Mark 10:32–34; Luke 18:31–34. Here there is the first mention of the mode of Jesus' death and of the Gentiles' part in it (only the Romans could crucify people). These three verses may look back to the preceding parable by implying the grounds of God's grace—viz., what his Son did on the cross. Also, just as 19:13–15 sets the stage for 19:16–30, so 20:17–19 sets it for 20:20–28. While Jesus faces crucifixion, his disciples, still blind to the nature of his messiahship, squabble over their places in the kingdom.

17 "Going up" does not necessarily mean that Jesus has left Perea, crossed the Jordan, passed through Jericho, and begun the ascent to Jerusalem; for it had become customary to speak of "going up" to Jerusalem regardless of where one was in Palestine, as in England one "goes up" to London from every place except Oxford or Cambridge. We should therefore not be surprised to find Jesus still in Jericho (20:29). Before setting out for Jerusalem, doubtless to attend the festival, Jesus took the Twelve aside from the throngs of pilgrims choking the roads to Jerusalem at such times (see on 21:9). Only the Twelve were even remotely ready to hear this passion prediction.

18–19 Jerusalem was the focal point of Jewish worship. We are going there, Jesus says, because there the Son of Man will be betrayed and crucified. He will be "condemned"—his death will result from legal proceedings (v.18). Mention of the Resurrection is brief (v.19) and apparently not understood (cf. Luke 18:34)—though in Matthew the disciples' misunderstanding is not spelled out as in Luke but exemplified by the succeeding story (vv.20–28), which Luke omits.

6. Suffering and service

20:20–28

²⁰Then the mother of Zebedee's sons came to Jesus with her sons and, kneeling down, asked a favor of him.

²¹"What is it you want?" he asked.

She said, "Grant that one of these two sons of mine may sit at your right and the other at your left in your kingdom."

²²"You don't know what you are asking," Jesus said to them. "Can you drink the cup I am going to drink?"

"We can," they answered.

²³Jesus said to them, "You will indeed drink from my cup, but to sit at my right or left is not for me to grant. These places belong to those for whom they have been prepared by my Father."

²⁴When the ten heard about this, they were indignant with the two brothers. ²⁵Jesus called them together and said, "You know that the rulers of the Gentiles lord it over them, and their high officials exercise authority over them. ²⁶Not so with you. Instead, whoever wants to become great among you must be your servant, ²⁷and whoever wants to be first must be your slave— ²⁸just as the Son of Man did not come to be served, but to serve, and to give his life as a ransom for many."

Luke parallels Matthew both before and after this pericope but omits it (cf. Mark 10:35–45). He has a somewhat similar account (Luke 22:24–30), but it is probably a different occasion.

Again the question of rank returns (cf. 18:1–5). Despite Jesus' repeated predictions of his passion, two disciples and their mother are still thinking about privilege, status, and power.

S. Légasse ("Approche de l'Épisode préévangélique des Fils de Zébédée [Mark x.35–40 par.]," NTS 20 [1974]: pp. 161–77) represents those who discount the historicity of this narrative largely on the hypothesis that "cup" and "baptism" are theological symbols around which a fictional episode was woven to convey certain theological truths. Bultmann (*Synoptic Tradition*, p. 24) goes farther and says that even the "prospect" of James's and John's death could not have been implied till after their martyrdom. The grounds for such theorizing are slender indeed. Why cannot theologically loaded terms be used in a historical narrative? Bultmann's critique reflects presuppositional antisupernaturalism in its most naive form. Jesus predicts his death (vv.17–19); and, when two of his disciples ask for preferential treatment, it is entirely natural that he should ask them if they are prepared to face similar suffering and death (cf. 5:10–12; 10:37–39). Moreover it is highly unlikely the church would invent a story so damaging to two of its leading apostles.

20 In Mark, John and James approach Jesus themselves; here, it is through *their mother*. Many find this historically improbable because in v.22 Jesus responds to her sons only. But the following points make the obvious synthesis plausible:

1. According to v.20, the mother *and her sons* approach Jesus, the implication being that all three are asking this favor, with the mother as the speaker.

2. This is confirmed by the other apostles' indignation (v.24), showing that James and John as well as their mother were involved.

3. That the mother should be the one to approach Jesus becomes the more plausible if she is Jesus' aunt on his mother's side—not certain, but not unlikely (see on 10:2; 27:56).

4. By adding the mother, Matthew cannot be shielding James and John: they still get the same response as in Mark. Matthew has no obvious theological motive for introducing their mother; he is simply recording a historical detail.

5. That the request should come from James and John, whether through their mother or not, accords with what we know of their aggressiveness (cf. Mark 9:38; Luke 9:54).

The "kneeling down" is not "worship" of Deity but may imply homage to the one increasingly recognized as King Messiah (see on 2:2).

21 The "right hand" and "left hand" suggest proximity to the King's person and so a share in his prestige and power. Such positions increase as the King is esteemed and has absolute power (cf. Pss 16:11; 45:9; 110:1; Matt 27:64; Acts 7:55–56; cf. Jos. Antiq. VI, 235 [xi. 9]). Mark has "in your glory," Matthew "in your kingdom." Mark's phrase clearly points to the Parousia, "when Jesus is enthroned as eschatological judge" (Lane, *Mark*, p. 379). Hill (*Matthew*) proposes that the "kingdom" in Matthew is the kingdom of Christ (13:41–43; 25:31–46), identified as the church; and the change from "glory" to "kingdom" therefore means that the original story is now being applied to competition for leadership in the church. But we have already seen that "kingdom" is never identified with "church" in Matthew (see on 13:37–39); and Christ's kingdom is equivalent to the kingdom of heaven (13:41; 20:21; 25:31). Because the "kingdom" comes in stages, there is no substantial difference between Matthew and Mark: the kingdom here is the reign of Messiah at the consummation. The link with 19:28—a verse that speaks (cf. Gk.) of both "throne" and "glory"—is unmistakable. What the sons of Zebedee want and their mother asks for is that they might share in the authority and preeminence of Jesus Messiah when his kingdom is fully consummated—something they think to be near at hand without the Cross or any interadvent period.

22 The additional words "or be baptized with the baptism I am baptized with" (cf. KJV)—and similarly in v.23—are almost certainly an assimilation to Mark 10:38–39. Jesus' answer is not severe but mingles firmness with probing. It is often ignorance that seeks leadership, power, and glory: the brothers do not know what they are asking. To ask to reign with Jesus is to ask to suffer with him; and not only do they not know what they are asking for (cf. 10:37–39; Rom 8:17; 2 Tim 2:12; Rev 3:21), they have as yet no clear perceptions of *Jesus'* sufferings. To ask for worldly wealth and much honor is often to ask for anxiety, temptation, disappointment, and envy; and in the spiritual arena to ask for great usefulness and reward is often to ask for great suffering (cf. 2 Cor 11:23–33; Col 1:24; Rev 1:9). "We know not what we ask, when we ask for the glory of wearing the crown, and ask not for grace to bear the cross in our way to it" (Henry).

The "cup" (cf. 26:39) characteristically refers, in OT imagery, to judgment or retribution (cf. Ps 75:8; Isa 51:17–18; Jer 25:15–28). If the disciples grasped anything of Jesus' passion predictions, they probably thought the language partly hyperbolic (Jesus did use hyperbole elsewhere [e.g., 19:24]) and referred to the eschatological conflict during which Messiah's side would suffer losses; but these could scarcely be too severe for one who could still storms and raise the dead. Thus by their bold response, James and John betray their misunderstandings of the timing of the dawn of the kingdom in all its glory (cf. Luke 19:11), and equally of the uniqueness and redemptive significance of Jesus' sufferings (cf. v.28) now imminent.

23 Jesus answers them first on their own terms before speaking of his own death as a ransom (v.28). In a sense they can and will drink from his cup of suffering. James would become the first apostolic martyr (Acts 12:2); and John (if it is the same one) would suffer exile (Rev 1:9). But it is not Jesus' role to determine who sits on his right hand and his left. Here, as elsewhere (see on 11:27; 24:36; 28:18; cf. John 14:28), Jesus makes it clear that his authority is a derived authority. These positions have already been assigned by the Father: Jesus cannot assign them at a mother's request.

24–27 The indignation of the ten (v.24) doubtless sprang less from humility than jealousy plus the fear that they might lose out. If these verses scarcely support egalitarianism—choice positions, after all, will be allotted—they demonstrate that interest in egalitarianism may mask a jealousy whose deepest wellsprings are not concern for justice but "enlightened self-interest." The disciples revert to the squabbling of an earlier period (Mark 9:33–37; cf. Matt 18:1). Jesus calls them together and draws a contrast between greatness among *ta ethnē* ("pagans" or "Gentiles," v.25) and greatness among heirs of the kingdom. The "pagans" or "Gentiles" who would spring to mind were Romans: power and authority characterized their empire. NIV's "lord it over" gives a false impression. Jesus is not criticizing abuse of power in political structures—the verb never has that meaning (cf. K.W. Clark, "The Meaning of [$\kappa\alpha\tau\alpha$] $\kappa\upsilon\rho\iota\epsilon\dot{\upsilon}\epsilon\iota\nu$" in Elliott, pp. 100–105) and should be translated "exercise lordship over," parallel to "exercise authority over" in the next line—but insists that the very structures themselves cannot be transferred to relationships among his followers.

Greatness among Jesus' disciples is based on service. Anyone who wants to be great must become the *diakonos* ("servant," v.26) of all. Here *diakonos* does not mean "deacon" or "minister" (KJV) in the modern church use. One of the ironies of language is that a word like "minister," which in its roots refers to a helper, one who "ministers," has become a badge of honor and power in religion and politics. But lest the full force of his teaching be lost, Jesus repeats it in v.27 with the stronger word *doulos* ("slave"; cf. 1 Cor 9:19; 2 Cor 4:5; 1 Peter 1:22; 5:1–3). In the pagan world humility was regarded, not so much as a virtue, but as a vice. Imagine a slave being given leadership! Jesus' ethics of the leadership and power in his community of disciples are revolutionary.

28 At this point Jesus presents himself—the Son of Man (see on 8:20)—as the supreme example of service to others. The verse is clearly important to our understanding of Jesus' view of his death. Three related questions call for discussion.

1. *Authenticity.* Many reject the authenticity of v.28, or at least of v.28a (and, correspondingly, Mark 10:45), on the grounds that it ill suits the context, since Jesus' atoning death cannot be imitated by his disciples, that nowhere else is he reported as speaking of his death in this way, and that the language reflects the influence of the Hellenistic church. On the contrary, the language has been shown to be Palestinian (Jeremias, *Eucharistic Words*, pp. 179–82); and Jesus speaks of his death in not dissimilar terms when instituting the Lord's Supper (26:26–29) and also in Luke 22:37, assuming that it relates to a different occasion. It is quite common in the NT, both in words ascribed to Jesus and elsewhere, to begin with the disciples' need to die to self and end up with Jesus' unique, atoning death as an ethical example—or, conversely to begin with Jesus' unique death and find it applied as an

example to the disciples (John 12:23–25; Phil 2:5–11; 1 Peter 2:18–25). There are no substantial reasons for denying the authenticity of this saying (cf. esp. S.H.T. Page, "The Authenticity of the Ransom Logion [Mark 10:45b]," in France and Wenham, 1:137–61); and its nuances seem much more in keeping with the way Jesus progressively revealed himself (cf. Carson, "Christological Ambiguities") than with a clear-cut, postresurrection, apostolic confession.

2. *Meaning*. It is natural to take "did not come" as presupposing at least a hint of Jesus' preexistence, though the language does not absolutely require it. He came not to be served, like a king dependent on countless courtiers and attendants, but to serve others. Stonehouse (*Witness of Matthew*, pp. 251ff.; id. *Origins*, p. 187) rightly points out that the verse assumes that the Son of Man had every right to expect to be served but served instead. Implicit is a self-conscious awareness that the Son of Man who, because of his heavenly origin, possessed divine authority was the one who humbled himself even to the point of undergoing an atoning death. The tripartite breakdown of the Son of Man references (see excursus on 8:20) is to this extent artificial. The display of divine glory shines most brightly when it is set aside for the sake of redeeming man by a shameful death. This stands at the very heart of Jesus' self-disclosure and of the primitive gospel (1 Cor 1:23: "We preach Christ [Messiah] crucified").

The Son of Man came "to give his life a ransom for many." Deissmann (LAE, pp. 331f.) points out that *lytron* ("ransom") was most commonly used as the purchase price for freeing slaves; and there is good evidence that the notion of "purchase price" is always implied in the NT use of *lytron* (cf. esp. Morris, *Apostolic Preaching*, pp. 11ff.). Others, however, by examining the word in the LXX conclude that, especially when the subject is God, the word means "deliverance" and the cognate verb "to deliver," without reference to a "price paid" (see esp. Hill, *Greek Words*, pp. 58–80). The matter may be difficult to decide in a passage like Titus 2:14. Is wickedness a chain from which Jesus by his death *delivers* us or a slave owner from whom Jesus by his death *ransoms* us? The parallel in 1 Peter 1:18 suggests the latter, even though (as Turner, *Christian Words*, pp. 105–7, insists) there is never any mention in the NT of the one to whom the price is paid; and in Matthew 20:28 this meaning is virtually assured by the use of *anti* ("for"). The normal force of this preposition denotes substitution, equivalence, exchange (cf. esp. M.J. Harris, DNTT, 3:1179f.). "The life of Jesus, surrendered in a sacrificial death, brought about the release of forfeited lives. He acted on behalf of the many by taking their place" (ibid., p. 1180).

"The many" underlines the immeasurable effects of Jesus' solitary death: the one dies, the many find their lives "ransomed, healed, restored, forgiven," a great host no man can number (cf. J. Jeremias, "Das Lösegeld für Viele," *Judaica* 3 [1948]: 263). But it should be remembered that "the many" can refer, in the DSS and the rabbinic literature, to the elect community (cf. Ralph Marcus, "'Mebaqqer' and 'Rabbim' in the Manual of Discipline vi, 11–13," JBL 75 [1956]: 298–302). This suggests Jesus' substitutionary death is payment for and results in the eschatological people of God. This well suits "the many" of Isaiah 52:13–53:12.

3. *Dependence on Isaiah 53*. C.K. Barrett ("The Background of Mark 10.45," *New Testament Essays*, ed. A.J.B. Higgins [Manchester: University Press, 1959], pp. 1–18; id., "Mark 10.45: A Ransom for Many," *New Testament Essays* [London: SPCK, 1972], pp. 20–26), Hooker (*Son of Man*, pp. 140–47), and others have argued that there is no allusion to Isaiah in Mark 10:45 and Matthew 20:28. They argue this

on two grounds: linguistic and conceptual. Linguistically, they point out that the Greek verb *diakonein* ("to serve," v.28) and its cognates are never used in the LXX to render *'ebed* ("servant" of Isaiah's "Servant Songs") and its cognates. But the evidence is slight and the conceptual parallels close—Isaiah's Servant benefits men by his suffering, and so does Jesus. Hooker is certainly incorrect in restricting *diakonein* to *domestic* service (cf. France, "Servant of the Lord," p. 34). Both France and Moo ("Use of OT," pp. 122ff.) have also shown that "to give his life" springs from Isaiah 53:10, 12, and that *lytron* ("ransom") is not as impossible a rendering of *'āšām* ("a guilt offering") as some allege. The Hebrew word *'āšām* includes the notion of substitution, at least of an equivalent. The guilty sinner offers an *'āšām* to remove his own guilt; and in Leviticus 5 *'āšām* refers to compensatory payment. Thus, though *'āšām* has more sacrificial overtones than *lytron*, both include the idea of payment or compensation. Most scholars have also recognized in "the many" a clear reference to Isaiah (cf. esp. Dalman, pp. 171–72). The implication of the cumulative evidence is that Jesus explicitly referred to himself as Isaiah's Suffering Servant (see on 26:17–30) and interpreted his own death in that light—an interpretation in which Matthew has followed his Lord (see on 3:17; 12:15–21).

Notes

21 Compare this use of εἰπὲ ἵνα (*eipe hina*, "Grant that") with the use in 4:3. "Command that" is the idea common to both. The mother believes Jesus need only say the word for it to be done.

28 For an interesting and extended gloss on this verse, see Metzger, *Textual Commentary*, p. 53.

7. Healing two blind men

20:29–34

[29]As Jesus and his disciples were leaving Jericho, a large crowd followed him. [30]Two blind men were sitting by the roadside, and when they heard that Jesus was going by, they shouted, "Lord, Son of David, have mercy on us!"

[31]The crowd rebuked them and told them to be quiet, but they shouted all the louder, "Lord, Son of David, have mercy on us!"

[32]Jesus stopped and called them. "What do you want me to do for you?" he asked.

[33]"Lord," they answered, "we want our sight."

[34]Jesus had compassion on them and touched their eyes. Immediately they received their sight and followed him.

Mark (10:44–52) and Luke (18:35–43) mention only one blind man, and Mark names him (Bartimaeus, Mark 10:46); but Matthew habitually gives fuller details on numbers of persons (cf. 8:28). This story is not a doublet of 9:27–31, which stresses faith and ends with a command to be silent. It lacks those twin foci but has other purposes. It pictures Jesus still serving and again links his healing ministry with his death (v.28; see on 8:17). Moreover it reminds us that the one going up to Jerusalem to give his life a ransom for many is the Messiah, the Son of David, whose great power, used mercifully (v.30) and compassionately (v.34), is not used to save himself.

29 Matthew and Mark say that Jesus was "leaving," Luke that he was "entering" Jericho. While there are several possible reasons for this, none is certain. Many "explanations" are inadequate: that Jesus healed one blind man on entering the town and two on leaving; that the healings occurred while Jesus was going "in and out"; that Jesus went through Jericho (Luke 19:1) without finding lodging and on his way out healed the blind men, met Zacchaeus, and returned to his place—so that Jesus' "leaving" was really his "entering." Calvin's "conjecture," followed by many, is that Jesus on his way into the city did not respond to the petitions of the blind men (perhaps in order to increase their faith: cf. 15:21–28) but healed them on his way out. Marshall (*Luke*, pp. 692f.) offers a literary explanation—viz., Luke made the change to accommodate the ensuing Zacchaeus story that takes place in Jericho and which Luke wants to place as a climax. One might have thought that Luke's simpler course would have been to drop any mention of Jericho in this healing, since he gains nothing by it and his alteration brings him into conflict with Mark.

Many avoid geographical contradiction by noting that in this period there were *two* Jerichos—an older town on the hill, largely in ruins, and the new Herodian town about one mile away (cf. Jos. War IV, 459 [viii. 3]). In this view Matthew and Mark, under Jewish influence, mention the old town Jesus was leaving; Luke the Hellenist refers to the new one, which Jesus is entering. This may well be the explanation. But there is no certain evidence that the old town was still inhabited at this time, and we do not know the local names of the two sites.

Jericho was not only the home of Jesus' ancestor Rahab (1:5) but was also a day's journey from Jerusalem. The "large crowd" implies more than messianic excitement; it also reflects the multitudes of pilgrims from Galilee and elsewhere heading to Jerusalem for the feast.

30 The rather common suggestion that Matthew increases the number of blind men to two because two was the minimum number of witnesses for attesting Jesus' messiahship is misguided. To *experience* the healings would not prove Jesus was the Messiah. He might simply be a prophet. On the other hand, if the miracle confirmed or promoted belief in Jesus' messiahship, it might do so as easily for *those who witnessed the miracle* as for those who experienced it. The "large crowd" would have provided witnesses aplenty. The "two" therefore has no theological motivation, but shows personal knowledge of the events. There may have been many blind people in the Jericho area; for the region produced large quantities of balsam, believed to be very beneficial for many eye defects (cf. Strabo 16.2.41). These two were sitting by the roadside, doubtless begging (Mark–Luke), and, hearing that Jesus was passing, cried out, "Lord, Son of David, have mercy on us!" (in the most likely text; cf. Metzger, *Textual Commentary*, pp. 53–54). On the title "Son of David" in relation to healing, see on 9:27.

31–34 Matthew's account is simple but stresses that Jesus mercifully healed the men despite the opposition of the crowds (v.31) that, like the disciples (cf. 19:13–15), wanted to bask in his glory but not practice his compassion. After this healing, unlike 9:30, there is no command to be silent. That point in Jesus' ministry has been reached when more public self-disclosure could not change the course of events. The two healed men joined the crowds following Jesus (v.34), pressing on to the Passover they expected and the Cross they did not.

8. Opening events of Passion Week (21:1–23:39)

a. The Triumphal Entry

21:1–11

> [1]As they approached Jerusalem and came to Bethphage on the Mount of Olives, Jesus sent two disciples, [2]saying to them, "Go to the village ahead of you, and at once you will find a donkey tied there, with her colt by her. Untie them and bring them to me. [3]If anyone says anything to you, tell him that the Lord needs them, and he will send them right away."
> [4]This took place to fulfill what was spoken through the prophet:
>
> > [5]"Say to the Daughter of Zion,
> > 'See, your king comes to you,
> > gentle and riding on a donkey,
> > on a colt, the foal of a donkey.' "
>
> [6]The disciples went and did as Jesus had instructed them. [7]They brought the donkey and the colt, placed their cloaks on them, and Jesus sat on them. [8]A very large crowd spread their cloaks on the road, while others cut branches from the trees and spread them on the road. [9]The crowds that went ahead of him and those that followed shouted,
>
> "Hosanna to the Son of David!"
> "Blessed is he who comes in the name of the Lord!"
> "Hosanna in the highest!"
>
> [10]When Jesus entered Jerusalem, the whole city was stirred and asked, "Who is this?"
> [11]The crowds answered, "This is Jesus, the prophet from Nazareth in Galilee."

T.W. Manson ("The Cleansing of the Temple," BJRL 33 [1951]: 271–82) suggests the feast in question is Tabernacles (autumn), not Dedication (winter) or Passover (spring). Because Jesus died at Passover, Manson spreads Matthew 21–28 (and parallels) over six months, instead of six days. His view rests largely on the observation that figs do not usually appear on the trees around Jerusalem till June and September, which seems to rule out Passover (usually April) as the right period for 21:18–21. But figs are regularly found in Jericho much earlier—and sometimes also in Jerusalem—and Manson's view introduces some difficult problems in the passion chronology.

For the moment we shall assume that this trip to Jerusalem occurred a few days before the Passover on which Jesus was crucified. Matthew does not mention the stay at Bethany (John 12:1–10) where Jesus arrived "six days before Passover," probably Friday evening (at the beginning of the Sabbath) before the Passion Week, and stayed there for Sabbath, entering Jerusalem on Sunday. Apparently Jesus went back and forth to Bethany throughout the week (21:17). (For the most recent detailed chronology of Passion Week, cf. Hoehner, *Chronological Aspects;* for close study of the question of authenticity, cf. Dhyanchand Carr, "Jesus, the king of Zion: A Traditio-Historical Enquiry into the So-called 'Triumphal' Entry of Jesus" [Ph.D. diss., University of London, 1980], pp. 128–218, 350–92.)

1–2 The Roman military road from Jericho to Jerusalem was about seventeen miles long and climbed three thousand feet. It passed through Bethany and nearby Bethphage ("house of figs"), which lay on the southeast slope of the Mount of Olives, then crossed over the mount and the Kidron Valley and entered Jerusalem (v.1). The mount itself stands about three hundred feet higher than the temple hill and about one hundred feet higher than the hill of Zion, affording a spectacular, panoramic view of the city.

Jesus sent two disciples (unnamed, but cf. Luke 22:8) ahead to Bethphage (for the grammar, cf. RHG, pp. 643–44) to fetch the animals (v.2). The distinguishing feature of the synoptic accounts, as opposed to John 12, is that Jesus arranged for the ride. The applause and the crowds were not manipulated; they would have occurred in any case. But the ride on a colt, because it was planned, could only be an acted parable, a deliberate act of symbolic self-disclosure for those with eyes to see or, after the Resurrection, with memories by which to remember and integrate the events of the preceding weeks and years. Secrecy was being lifted.

3 "Lord" (also Mark–Luke) might mean "owner"; but then the disciples' response would be untrue, unless Jesus owned the animals, which is extremely unlikely. The title might refer to Yahweh—the animals are needed in Yahweh's service. But the most natural way to take "Lord" is Jesus' way of referring to himself. This step is not out of keeping with the authority he has already claimed for himself and fits this late period of his ministry, when he revealed himself with increasing clarity. J. Gresham Machen (*The Origin of Paul's Religion* [New York: Macmillan, 1928, 1947], pp. 296–97) notes that even the church's ascription of "Lord" to Jesus in a full christological sense finds its roots in Jesus' self-references.

4–5 It is possible that Matthew presents these verses as having been spoken by Jesus. The perfect *gegonen* should then be translated "This has taken place" (v.4), spoken somewhat proleptically because the order had been given (see discussion on 1:22). The alternative is to take the verses as Matthew's comment. This requires taking the perfect as either having aoristic force or meaning "This stands as something that happened." John's statement that the disciples did not understand all this at the time (12:16) does not necessarily support the alternative, since Jesus said many things they did not understand at the time (cf. John 2:20–22).

A few MSS add "Zechariah" or "Isaiah" to "prophet," doubtless because the quotation comes from both. The introductory words of the quotation are from Isaiah 62:11 and the rest from Zechariah 9:9. The omitted words "righteous and having salvation" (Zech 9:9) may be understood as implicitly included, or omitted because the chief stress is on Jesus' humility (Stendahl, *School*, pp. 118–20).

The text form of the quotation (v.5) is disputed, but at least the latter parts depend directly on the MT (cf. Gundry, *Use of OT*, pp. 120–21; Moo; "Use of OT," pp. 178f.). The last word, *hypozygion*, means a "beast of burden," which in Palestine was usually a donkey. Such an animal was sometimes ridden by rulers in times of peace (Judg 5:10; 1 Kings 1:33; cf. Rev 19:11). Jews certainly understood Zechariah 9:9 to refer to the Messiah, often in terms of the Son of David (SBK, 1:842–44). Therefore for those with eyes to see, Jesus was not only proclaiming his messiahship and his fulfillment of Scripture but showing the kind of peace-loving approach he was now making to the city.

Many scholars find difficulty with the fact that Matthew alone of the four evangelists mentions *two* animals: a donkey and her colt (vv.2, 7); and only he cites the Hebrew text so fully that the unwary might think there *were* two animals. The Hebrew, of course, refers to only one beast: the last line is in parallelism with the next-to-the-last line and merely identifies the "donkey" (line 3) as a colt (a young, male donkey). But it is quite unreasonable to suggest that Matthew, who demonstrably had a good command of Hebrew (cf. Gundry, *Use of OT*, p. 198), added the extra animal to fit a text he radically misunderstood (contra McNeile, Schniewind). Nor is it more reasonable to assume that Matthew knows there actually were two animals and quotes Zechariah because the prophet's words might barely refer to two; for his Jewish readers would not likely be convinced. Still less likely is the appeal to unassimilated sources (cf. R. Bartnicki, "Das Zitat von Zach IX, 9–10 und die Tiere im Bericht von Matthäus über dem Einzug Jesu in Jerusalem (Mt XXI, 1–11)," NovTest 18 [1976]: 161–66).

The most reasonable suggestion is that Mark's "which no one has ever ridden" prompted Matthew to mention both animals (cf. Stendahl, *School*, pp. 118–20; Lindars, *Apologetic*, p. 114; Longenecker, *Biblical Exegesis*, pp. 148–49). Gundry (*Use of OT*, pp. 198–99) holds that Matthew witnessed the scene. Matthew's reference to both animals is his way of highlighting what the other synoptists affirm—the animal Jesus rode on *was* "a colt." If we assume that Matthew understood Hebrew, the full quotation affirms that Jesus rode on the "colt," not its mother. Mark and Luke say the animal was so young that it had never been ridden. In the midst, then, of this excited crowd, an unbroken animal remains calm under the hands of the Messiah who controls nature (8:23–27; 14:22–32). Thus the event points to the peace of the consummated kingdom (cf. Isa 11:1–10). Though Matthew may have something of the same thing in mind, in addition he stresses that Jesus fulfills Scripture even in this detail—that the animal he rode was a colt. Without warrant is the appeal to Midrash, at least in its technical, fourth-century sense (cf. Introduction, section 12.b). Although Jewish midrashic writers occasionally give a separate meaning to each part of Hebrew parallelism (cf. examples in Carr), the continuity of the Midrash lies in the passage being expounded, not in the narrative explanations. But here the continuity lies in the narrative. Still less credible is the allegorizing of many of the Fathers, and even of Lange: the donkey symbolizes Jews accustomed to the yoke of the law and the colt hitherto untamed Gentiles ("The old theocracy runs idly and instinctively by the side of the young Church, which has become the true bearer of the divinity of Christ," CHS).

6–8 The two disciples returned from their errand (v.6) and put their cloaks (their outer garments; see on 5:40) on the beasts—both animals were in the procession (v.7). Jesus sat "on them." Not a few critics take the antecedent of "them" to be the animals and ridicule the statement. But as Plummer remarks, "The Evangelist credits his readers with common sense." The antecedent of "them" may be the cloaks; or the plural may be a "plural of category" (cf. "He sprang from the horses"; cf. Turner, *Insights*, p. 41; see on 2:20). Less convincing is appeal to very weak textual traditions: "he sat on *it*" or "they sat him on *it*" ("thereon," KJV; cf. Broadus; BDF, par. 141).

A "very large crowd" (v.8, the Gr. superlative is merely elative; cf. Moule, *Idiom Book*, p. 98) spread their cloaks on the road, acknowledging Jesus' kingship (cf. 2 Kings 9:13). Still others "cut branches" and "spread them" (the Gr. imperfects make the action vivid) on the road. It has been argued that cutting down tree branches well suits the activities of the Feast of Tabernacles, when the people built "booths" to live in for the week (cf. Lev 23:41–42). But those "branches" were substantial boughs, big enough to support a lean-to; these "branches," thrown before the animals, were not more than twigs. The somewhat parallel entrance of Simon Maccabeus into Jerusalem (1 Macc 13:51; 2 Macc 10:7) does not depend on the season of the year but on the man.

9 Crowds ahead and behind may be incidental confirmation of two other details. First, John 12:12 speaks of crowds coming out of Jerusalem to meet Jesus. Apparently the Galilean pilgrims accompanying Jesus and the Jerusalem crowd coming out to greet him formed a procession of praise. Second, that the Jerusalem crowds knew he was approaching supports the stopover in Bethany, which allows time for the news to spread. Messianic fervor was high, and perhaps this contributed to Jesus' desire to present himself as Prince of Peace.

The words of praise come primarily from Psalm 118:25–26. "Hosanna" transliterates the Hebrew expression that originally was a cry for help: "Save!" (cf. 2 Sam 14:4; 2 Kings 6:26). In time it became an invocation of blessing and even an acclamation, the latter being the meaning here (cf. Gundry, *Use of OT*, pp. 41–43). "Son of David" is messianic and stresses the kingly role Messiah was to play (cf. Mark, Luke, and John for explicit references to "kingdom" or "king"). "He who comes in the name of the Lord" is cited by Jesus himself a little later (23:39; cf. 3:11; 11:3), but some scholars object that if this phrase had been a messianic acclamation by the people, the authorities would have stepped in. The words, they say, must be a formula of greeting to pilgrims on the way to the temple.

Such an assessment betrays too stark an "either-or" mentality to weigh the evidence plausibly. "Son of David" in the previous line is unavoidably messianic, and the authorities *do* raise objections (v.16). But crowd sentiments are fickle. On the one hand, acclamation can rapidly dissipate; so instant action by the authorities was scarcely necessary. On the other hand, it is foolish to antagonize the crowd at the height of excitement (cf. 26:4–5, 16). "Hosanna in the highest" is probably equivalent to "Glory to God in the highest" (Luke 2:14). The people praise God in the highest heavens for sending the Messiah and, if "Hosanna" retains some of its original force, also cry to him for deliverance.

Two final reflections on this verse are necessary: first, Psalm 118 was not only used at the Feast of Tabernacles (M *Succoth* 4:5) but also at the other two major feasts, Dedication and Passover—at the latter as part of "the great Hallel" (Pss 113–18). The use of Psalm 118 is therefore no support for Manson's suggestion. Second, Walvoord's interpretation stumbles badly: "They recognized that He was in the kingly line, although they do not seem to have entered into the concept that He was coming into Jerusalem as its King." On the contrary, it is hard to think of the crowd's making fine distinctions between "kingly line" and "king." Moreover one growing thrust of this Gospel is, as we have seen, that even where Jesus was perceived, however dimly, as King Messiah, he was not perceived as Suffering Servant. In the expectations of the day, it was fairly easy for the crowd, after hearing Jesus' preaching and seeing his miracles, to ascribe messiahship to him as much in their hope as in conviction. But it was far harder for them to grasp the inevitability of his suffering and death and the expansion of the "people of God" beyond the Jewish race.

10–11 Only Luke (19:41–44) pictures Jesus weeping over the city as he approaches it. Mark 11:11 establishes chronology; Matthew's information stands alone. Jesus probably entered Jerusalem through what some now call Saint Stephen's gate, near the north entrance to the outer court of the temple. As the city was stirred earlier (2:3), so here (v.10): news of Jesus' presence is inevitably disturbing. "Who is this?" does not mean that Jesus was virtually unknown in Jerusalem, and so needed to be identified (Bonnard), but "Who really is this about whom there is so much excitement?" The answer of the crowds accurately reflects the historical setting: many of his contemporaries saw him as a prophet (cf. 16:14; 21:46) "from Nazareth in Galilee"—his hometown and primary field of ministry respectively. The phrase probably also connotes surprise that a prophet should come from so unlikely a place (see on 2:23). In the light of the messianic acclamation (v.9), some may well have seen Jesus as the eschatological Prophet (Deut 18:15–18; cf. John 7:40, 52; Acts 3:22; 7:37), though there is no more than a hint of that here. Yet there is also no evidence that Matthew deprecates the people's understanding as faulty, preferring "Son of God" (contra Kingsbury, *Matthew*, pp. 22, 88–89).

Notes

3 Zerwick (par. 280) rightly points out that the verb ἐρεῖτε (*ereite*, lit., "you will say"; NIV, "tell") is one of the rare instances when a future indicative in the NT has imperatival force (apart from passages where the NT cites the LXX).
11 Note this use of ἀπό (*apo*, "from," "away from") to denote place of origin instead of ἐκ (*ek*, "from," "out from"; cf. BDF, par. 209[3]).

b. *Jesus at the temple*

21:12–17

12Jesus entered the temple area and drove out all who were buying and selling there. He overturned the tables of the money changers and the benches of those selling doves. 13"It is written," he said to them, " 'My house will be called a house of prayer,' but you are making it a 'den of robbers.' "
14The blind and the lame came to him at the temple, and he healed them. 15But when the chief priests and the teachers of the law saw the wonderful things he did and the children shouting in the temple area, "Hosanna to the Son of David," they were indignant.
16"Do you hear what these children are saying?" they asked him.
"Yes," replied Jesus, "have you never read,

" 'From the lips of children and infants
you have ordained praise'?"

17And he left them and went out of the city to Bethany, where he spent the night.

Matthew is considerably more condensed than Mark (11:11–19; cf. Luke 19:45–48; John 2:13–22). Matthew omits, among other things, Mark's more precise chronology, all mention of the habit of carrying merchandise through the temple courts, and reference to the Gentiles in the quotation from Isaiah 56:7. It is doubtful whether

Matthew's silence in any of these things reflects major theological motivation, but see on v.13. Matthew focuses on the cleansing of the temple as the work of the Son of David (vv.9, 15) and as of as much messianic significance as any of Jesus' miracles.

The great majority of contemporary scholars believe there was only one cleansing of the temple and debate about whether the synoptists or John put it at the right time in Jesus' ministry. Although some argue that the event occurred early in Jesus' ministry (John), more side with the Synoptics in placing it late. Certainly we have ample evidence that the evangelists arranged some materials topically; yet there are, in this instance, numerous reasons for the possibility, indeed the likelihood, of two separate cleansings—something most commentators never seriously consider.

1. Leon Morris (*John*, pp. 288ff.) has shown the striking differences between the details John provides and those the Synoptics provide. If there was but one cleansing, some of these differences became surprising; if two cleansings, they became quite reasonable.

2. Those who hold that John's placing of the cleansing is topical usually assume that he does so to lead up to the saying, "Destroy this temple, and I will raise it again in three days" (John 2:19), part of his "replacement" theme—viz., that Jesus himself replaces much of the Jewish cultic milieu. But this view fails to provide any reason for shifting the temple's cleansing so as to make it an *early* theme in Jesus' ministry. Moreover in this particular case the temple-replacement theme is reflected in the trial of Jesus in two of the Synoptics (Matt 26:61; Mark 14:58).

3. If the Synoptics fail to mention the earlier cleansing, this may go back to their omission of Jesus' entire early Judean ministry.

4. Some hold that if Jesus had inaugurated his ministry by cleansing the temple, the authorities would not have let him do it a second time. But two or three years have elapsed. The money changers and merchants, protected by the temple police, doubtless returned the day after the first cleansing. But it is doubtful that tight security would have been kept up for months and years. This second cleansing took a few dramatic minutes and could not have been prevented, and its prophetic symbolism quickly spread throughout Jerusalem.

5. It is difficult to tell from the Gospels how much the cleansing(s) of the temple contributed to official action against Jesus, and to overstate the evidence is easy (cf. E. Trocmé, "L'expulsion des marchands du Temple," NTS 15 [1968–69]: 1–22). But a second cleansing as Passover drew near was far more likely to have led to the authorities' violent reaction than the first one.

12 Jesus entered the *hieron* ("temple area"). Temple service required provision to be made for getting what was needed for the sacrifices—animals, wood, oil, etc.— especially for pilgrims from afar. The money changers converted the standard Greek and Roman currency into temple currency, in which the half-shekel temple tax had to be paid (cf. 17:24–27). (For some of the customs and regulations, cf. M *Shekalim*; LTJM, 1:367–74.) But letting these things go on at the temple site transformed a place of solemn worship into a market where the hum of trade mingled with the bleating and cooing of animals and birds. Moreover, especially on the great feasts, opportunities for extortion abounded. Jesus drove the lot out.

13 Jesus here refers to Scripture, much as he did when confronted by the devil (4:1–10). His first words are from Isaiah 56:7. Isaiah looked forward to a time when the temple would be called a house of prayer. But now, at the dawn of the Messianic Age, Jesus finds a "den of robbers." The words come from Jeremiah 7:11, which warns against the futility of superstitious reverence for the temple compounded with wickedness that dishonors it. This suggests that the Greek *lēstai* ("robbers") should be given its normal meaning of "nationalist rebel" (see on 27:16). The temple was meant to be a house of prayer, but they had made it "a nationalist stronghold" (cf. C.K. Barrett, "The House of Prayer and the Den of Thieves," in Ellis and Grässer, p. 16).

The point is even clearer in Mark, who retains "house of prayer for all nations" (Isa 56:7 uses the longer form once and the shorter one once). The temple was not fulfilling its God-ordained role as witness to the nations but had become, like the first temple, the premier symbol of a superstitious belief that God would protect and rally his people irrespective of their conformity to his will. The temple would therefore be destroyed (vv. 18–22; 24:2). Matthew does not omit "for all nations" because he writes after the temple has been destroyed and therefore recognizes the promise in Isaiah no longer capable of fulfillment. Even Mark knows the temple cannot stand and that this temple could never become a rallying place "for all nations." The omission may simply be for conciseness; but it shifts the contrast from "temple mission—nationalist stronghold" (Mark) to "house of prayer—nationalist stronghold" (Matthew)—a shift that focuses attention more on spiritual neglect and mistaken political priorities than on neglect of what the temple was really for. These are the things Jesus denounces.

The Lord whom the people see now comes to his temple (Mal 3:1). Purification of Jerusalem and the temple was part of Jewish expectation (cf. Pss Sol 17:30). So for those with eyes to see, Jesus' action was one of self-disclosure and an implicit claim to eschatological authority over the Holy Place. That the purification would entail destruction and building a new temple (John 2:19–22) none but Jesus could yet foresee.

14 Verses 14–15 are found only in Matthew. Not only is v.14 the last mention of Jesus' healing ministry, but it takes place *en tō hierō* ("at the temple [site]") and probably within the temple precincts in the Court of the Gentiles. It was not uncommon for the chronically ill to beg at the approaches to the temple (Acts 3:2); but where the lame, blind, deaf, or otherwise handicapped could go in the temple area was restricted. The Court of the Gentiles was open to them all, and there were even crippled priests. But restrictions were imposed when the handicap required certain kinds of cushions, pads, or supports that might introduce "uncleanness" (cf. Jeremias, *Jerusalem*, pp. 117f.).

Most Jewish authorities forbade any person lame, blind, deaf, or mute from offering a sacrifice, from "appearing before Yahweh in his temple." The Qumran covenanters wanted to go further and exclude all cripples from the congregation, the messianic battle, and the messianic banquet (1QSa 2:5–22; 1QM 7:4–5). But Jesus heals them, thus showing that "one greater than the temple is here" (12:6). He himself cannot be contaminated, and he heals and makes clean those who come into contact with him. These two actions—cleansing the temple and the healing miracles —jointly declare his superiority over the temple (Heil, "Healing Miracles," pp. 283f.) and raise the question of the source of his authority (v.23).

15–16 The "chief priests and teachers of the law" (v.15; see on 2:4; 26:59) express indignation, not so much at what he has done, as at the acclamation he is receiving for it. The children cry out, "Hosanna to the Son of David" (see on v.9); and if Jesus is prepared to accept such praise, then "the wonderful things" he is doing must have messianic significance. When challenged, Jesus supports the children by quoting Psalm 8:2, introducing it with his "have you never read" (v.16), which exposes the theological ignorance of the Scripture experts (cf. 12:3; 19:4; 21:42; 22:31). God *has* ordained praise for himself from "children and infants" (lit., "infants and sucklings" —nursing sometimes continued among the Jews to the age of three: cf. 2 Macc 7:27). Jesus' answer is a masterstroke and simultaneously accomplishes three things.

1. It provides some kind of biblical basis for letting the children go on with their exuberant praise and thus stifles, for the moment, the objections of the temple leaders.

2. At the same time thoughtful persons, reflecting on the incident later (especially after the Resurrection), perceive that Jesus was saying much more. The children's "Hosannas" are not being directed to God but to the Son of David, the Messiah. Jesus is therefore not only acknowledging his messiahship but justifying the praise of the children by applying to himself a passage of Scripture applicable only to God (cf. Notes).

3. The quotation confirms that the humble perceive spiritual truths more readily than the sophisticated (cf. 19:13–15). The children have picked up the cry of the earlier procession and, lacking inhibitions and skepticism, enthusiastically repeat the chant, arriving at the truth more quickly than those who think themselves wise and knowledgeable.

17 During the festivals Jerusalem was crowded. So Jesus spent his last nights at Bethany, on a spur of the eastern slopes of the Mount of Olives (cf. Mark 11:19; Luke 21:37). The home where he stayed was probably that of Mary, Martha, and Lazarus.

Notes

16 Part of the interpretation of this verse given above depends on the view that Ps 8 is not messianic. This is almost certainly the case; and even application of Ps 8:5–7 to Jesus in 1 Cor 15:27; Heb 2:6 is due, not to the Psalm's messianic character, but to Jesus' role in introducing humanity to the heights God designed for it, as most expositors now acknowledge. The treatment of Ps 8 as messianic by ancient Jewish authorities in the Targum on Ps 8 (cf. F.J. Maloney, "The Targum on Ps. 8 and the New Testament," *Salesianum* 37 [1975]: 326–36) almost certainly postdates the NT.

c. The fig tree

21:18–22

> [18]Early in the morning, as he was on his way back to the city, he was hungry. [19]Seeing a fig tree by the road, he went up to it but found nothing on it except leaves. Then he said to it, "May you never bear fruit again!" Immediately the tree withered.
> [20]When the disciples saw this, they were amazed. "How did the fig tree wither so quickly?" they asked.

> [21] Jesus replied, "I tell you the truth, if you have faith and do not doubt, not only can you do what was done to the fig tree, but also you can say to this mountain, 'Go, throw yourself into the sea,' and it will be done. [22] If you believe, you will receive whatever you ask for in prayer."

This story is found only here and in Mark, where it is split into two parts (11:12–14, 20–26), with the temple's cleansing in between. Chronologically Mark is more detailed. If the Triumphal Entry was on Sunday, then, according to Mark, the cursing of the fig tree was on Monday; and the disciples' surprise at the tree's quick withering, along with Jesus' words about faith, were on Tuesday. Matthew has simply put the two parts together in a typical topical arrangement. He leaves indistinct (v.20) the time when the disciples see the withered fig tree, though he implies it was the same day. Compare the condensation in 9:18–25.

The most recent major study on this passage is by William R. Telford (*The Barren Temple and the Withered Tree* [Sheffield: JSOT, 1980]). Though he admirably surveys earlier studies, his own is less convincing (cf. review by D. Wenham, EQ 72 [1980]: 245–48). The idea that "this mountain" (v.21) refers to the temple, thus making the cursing of the fig tree a sign of the temple's doom, is unlikely. More probably it refers to the Mount of Olives as a sample of any mountain. Telford's exhaustive examination of the uses of "fig tree" as a metaphor does no more than show that "fig tree" could be applied metaphorically to many different things; but only the context of the metaphor is determinative. Still less convincing is the view that this story is a mere dramatization of the parable in Luke 13:6–9 (so van der Loos, pp. 692–96); for, apart from the question of whether such "historicization" of parabolic material ever occurs, the latter treats *delay* in judgment, whereas the present passage is concerned with *imminent* judgment.

It is commonly held that 21:20–22 and the corresponding Markan material is a separate tradition unrelated to the original. Preferable is the view that the awkward transition reflects the historical chronology, which Mark preserved. Cursing the fig tree is, then, an acted parable related to cleansing the temple and conveying a message about Israel. But when the next day the disciples see how quickly the fig tree has withered, their initial—and shallow—response is to wonder how it was done; and this leads to Jesus' remarks on faith. So this single historical event teaches two theological lessons.

18–19 Somewhere on the road between Bethany and Jerusalem, Jesus approached a fig tree in the hope of staunching his hunger (v.18). Mark tells us that though it was not the season for figs, the tree was in leaf. Fig leaves appear about the same time as the fruit or a little after. The green figs are edible, though sufficiently disagreeable as not usually to be eaten till June. Thus the leaves normally point to every prospect of fruit, even if not fully ripe. Sometimes, however, the green figs fall off and leave nothing but leaves. All this Matthew's succinct remark—"He . . . found nothing on it except leaves" (v.19)—implies; his Jewish readers would infer the rest. This understanding of the text confirms the chronology established at 21:1–11. If these events took place at Dedication, when figs were plentiful, not only would Mark's explicit statement be incorrect (11:13), but in both Matthew and Mark Jesus' cursing of the tree would be harder to understand, for if he was hungry, he could simply go to the next tree.

Many commentators think otherwise and suppose that by omitting Mark's statement "it was not the season for figs," Matthew has eliminated a moral difficulty. Why should Jesus curse a tree for not bearing fruit when it was not the season for fruit? But this theory misses the point. That it was not the season for figs explains why Jesus went to this particular tree, which stood out because it was in leaf. Its leaves advertised that it was bearing, but the advertisement was false. Jesus, unable to satisfy his hunger, saw the opportunity of teaching a memorable object lesson and cursed the tree, not because it was not bearing fruit, whether in season or out, but because it made a show of life that promised fruit yet was bearing none.

Most scholars interpret the cursing of the fig tree as a symbolic cursing of the people of Israel for failing to produce faith and righteousness, as evidenced primarily in their attitude to Jesus. The fig tree then becomes akin to the imagery of the vine in Isaiah 5:1–7 or the figs in Jeremiah 8:13; 24:1–8: sterility, the absence of fruit, or bad fruit—all lead to judgment. Walvoord objects, insisting that there is no place in the Bible where a fig tree serves as a type of Israel (Jer 24:1–8 is dismissed because the good and bad figs refer to captives versus those who remain in the land). The Gospel pericope is a lesson on faith and the miraculous, no more. But if the common interpretation will not stand, Walvoord's reductionism will not withstand close scrutiny either.

1. Mark's arrangement of the material, with the temple's cleansing sandwiched between the two parts, must be taken into account. Even Matthew, who condenses Mark's arrangement and eliminates the division of the pericope into two, places this immediately after the cleansing of the temple and right before the questioning of Jesus' authority. We have learned to respect Matthew's arrangement of pericopes enough to see them linked; and therefore to read vv.18–22 as nothing more than a lesson on faith forfeits the obvious links.

2. Jeremiah 24:1–8 may provide a closer parallel than Walvoord thinks, for even in the Gospels Jesus is not saying that all Jews fall under whatever curse this may be; after all, his disciples at this point in history were all Jews. In the Synoptics, as in Jeremiah, there is a division between Jew and Jew.

3. Yet even if Jeremiah 24:1–8 is not too close a parallel, one cannot make too much of the fig tree's not being a type of Israel; for one could similarly argue that there is no other example in the Bible of Jesus' performing a miracle *simply* to teach faith, without there being some organic connection with the narrative.

This does not mean the common interpretation—that the fig tree represents Israel, cursed for not bearing fruit—is correct. In light of the discussion on the relation between leaves and fruit, Jesus is cursing those who make a show of bearing much fruit but are spiritually barren. This has four advantages.

1. It deftly handles both Mark and Matthew on the fig tree and its leaves.

2. It directs the attack against the hypocrites among the Jewish people, a constant target in all four Gospels, but especially in Matthew (e.g., 6:2, 5, 16; 7:5; 15:7; 22:18; and we now approach 23:1–39!).

3. It is compatible with the cleansing of the temple, which criticizes, not the Jewish children and their praise, or the Jewish blind and lame who came to be healed (vv.14–15), but those who used the temple to make a large profit, and those who stifled the children's praises of Messiah. These, like this leafy fig tree, Jesus finds full of advertised piety without any fruit; and them he curses.

4. Unlike other passages (3:9; 8:11–12), there is no mention of something being taken from the Jews and given to Gentiles. The cursing of the fig tree is an acted parable cursing hypocrites, not Jews or Judaism.

The cursing of the fig tree is not so far out of character for Jesus as some would have us believe. The same Jesus exorcised demons so that two thousand pigs were drowned (8:28–34), drove the animals and money changers out of the temple precincts with a whip, and says not a little about the torments of hell. Perhaps the fact that the two punitive miracles—the swine and the fig tree—are not directed against men should teach us something of Jesus' compassion. He who is to save his people from their sin and its consequences resorts to prophetic actions not directed against his people, in order to warn them of the binding power of the devil (the destruction of the swine) and of God's enmity against all hypocritical piety (the cursing of the fig tree).

20–22 Though it is uncertain whether v.20 is a question or an exclamation (cf. Moule, *Idiom Book*, p. 207), the effect is the same. The substance of Jesus' response has already been given in 17:20, which implies that the figure of a mountain cast into the sea was common in Jesus' teaching. Here, however, attention shifts "from the smallest effective amount of faith to the opposition of faith to doubt" (Hill, *Matthew*). The miracle Jesus selects to teach the power of faith—throwing a mountain into the sea (v.21)—is no more than a hyperbolic example of a miracle. But because the Dead Sea can be seen from the Mount of Olives, some have suggested an allusion to Zechariah 14:4 (Lane, *Mark*, p. 410)—viz., what the disciples must pray for is the coming eschatological reign. This seems unlikely, for Zechariah speaks of the splitting of the Mount of Olives rather than its removal into the sea.

Jesus used the fig tree to teach the power of *believing* prayer, an extrapolation on the theme of faith, the lesson just taught by the immediate withering of the fig tree. But belief in the NT is never reduced to forcing oneself to "believe" what he does not really believe. Instead, it is related to genuine trust in God and obedience to and discernment of his will (see on 19:20; cf. Carson, *Farewell Discourse*, pp. 43, 108–11). Though exercised by the believer, such faith reposes on the will of God who acts.

Notes

19 Μίαν (*mian*, lit., "one") here has the force of enclitic τις (*tis*, "a certain," "a"): see on 8:19; 9:18; cf. 19:16; 21:24; BDF, par. 247(2).

d. *Controversies in the temple court* (21:23–22:46)

1) *The question of authority*

21:23–27

23Jesus entered the temple courts, and, while he was teaching, the chief priests and the elders of the people came to him. "By what authority are you doing these things?" they asked. "And who gave you this authority?"

24Jesus replied, "I will also ask you one question. If you answer me, I will tell you by what authority I am doing these things. 25John's baptism—where did it come from? Was it from heaven, or from men?"

They discussed it among themselves and said, "If we say, 'From heaven,' he will ask, 'Then why didn't you believe him?' ²⁶But if we say, 'From men'—we are afraid of the people, for they all hold that John was a prophet."

²⁷So they answered Jesus, "We don't know."

Then he said, "Neither will I tell you by what authority I am doing these things.

This long section (21:23–22:46) is characterized by a number of controversies with various Jewish leaders, along with several parables that must be interpreted in the light of such controversies. In Mark's chronology these controversies apparently took place on Tuesday, the third day of Passion Week. It was customary to stop well-known teachers and ask them questions (cf. 22:16, 23, 35), and the crowds delighted in these exchanges. Eventually Jesus turned primarily to the crowds and addressed them without excluding the Pharisees and teachers of the law (ch. 23); and then, as evening fell, he retired to the Mount of Olives and gave his last "discourse" to his disciples (chs. 24–25).

In the first exchange (vv.23–27), Matthew follows Mark (11:27–33) fairly closely (cf. Luke 20:1–8).

23 Jesus' teaching takes place in the "temple courts," probably in one of the porticos surrounding the Court of the Gentiles. The chief priests were high temple functionaries, elevated members of the priestly aristocracy who were part of the Sanhedrin (see on 2:4); the elders were in this case probably nonpriestly members of the Sanhedrin, heads of the most influential lay families (cf. Jeremias, *Jerusalem*, pp. 222ff.). In other words, representative members of the Sanhedrin, described in terms of their clerical status rather than their theological positions (e.g., Sadducees and Pharisees), approached Jesus and challenged his authority to do "these things" —viz., the cleansing of the temple, the miraculous healings, and perhaps also his teaching (v.23). Their first question was therefore not narrowly theological but concerned Jesus' authority; yet their concern in asking who gave him this authority (cf. Acts 4:7) sprang less from a desire to identify him than from a desire to stifle and perhaps ensnare him.

24–26 Jesus' reply is masterful. He responds to their question with a question of his own (v.24), a common enough procedure in rabbinic debate. "John's baptism" (v.25) is a way of referring to the Baptist's entire ministry (cf. v.25b and the reference to *believing* John, not simply being *baptized* by him). Jesus asks whether that ministry was from heaven or from men. He does not raise this question as a simple rebuke— as if to say that if the authorities cannot make up their minds about John, neither will they be able to do so about him. His question is far more profound. If the religious authorities rightly answer it, they will already have the correct answer to their own question. If they respond, "From heaven," then they are morally bound to believe John—and John pointed to Jesus (see on 11:7–10; cf. John 1:19, 26–27; 3:25–30). They would therefore have their answer about Jesus and his authority. If they respond, "From men" (v.26), they offer the wrong answer; but they will not dare utter it for fear of the people. The religious authorities share Herod's timidity (14:5).

Far from avoiding the religious leaders' question, Jesus answers it so that the honest seeker of truth, unswayed by public opinion, will not fail to see who he is, while those interested only in snaring him with a captious question are blocked by a hurdle their own shallow pragmatism forbids them to cross. At the same time

Jesus' question rather strongly hints to the rulers that their false step goes back to broader issues than Jesus' identity. It they cannot discern Jesus' authority, it is because their previous unbelief has blinded their minds to God's revelation.

27 "We don't know," they said—which is not so much a lie as a misrepresentation of the categories that bound them in public indecision. Their equivocation gave Jesus a reason for refusing to answer their question. Rejection of revelation already given is indeed a slender basis on which to ask for more. In one sense the Sanhedrin enjoyed not only the right but the duty to check the credentials of those who claimed to be spokesmen for God. But because they misunderstood the revelation already given in the Scriptures and rejected the witness of the Baptist, the leaders proved unequal to their responsibility. They raised the question of Jesus' authority; he raised the question of their competence to judge such an issue.

2) The parable of the two sons

21:28–32

> 28"What do you think? There was a man who had two sons. He went to the first and said, 'Son, go and work today in the vineyard.'
> 29" 'I will not,' he answered, but later he changed his mind and went.
> 30"Then the father went to the other son and said the same thing. He answered, 'I will, sir,' but he did not go.
> 31"Which of the two did what his father wanted?"
> "The first," they answered.
> Jesus said to them, "I tell you the truth, the tax collectors and the prostitutes are entering the kingdom of God ahead of you. 32For John came to you to show you the way of righteousness, and you did not believe him, but the tax collectors and the prostitutes did. And even after you saw this, you did not repent and believe him.

This is the first of three parables by which Jesus rebukes the Jewish leaders (vv.28–32, 33–46; 22:1–14). The first and third of these are peculiar to Matthew. There is no convincing evidence that this first parable is only a variation of Luke 15:11–32. Helmut Merkel ("Das Gleichnis von den 'ungleichen Söhnen' [Matth. xxi.28–32]," NTS 20 [1974]: 254–61) argues that the entire parable is inauthentic; but his approach—isolating, sometimes on doubtful grounds, Matthew's redaction and wondering if enough of the parable is left for us to posit an authentic core—is so one-sided that few follow it. It is much more common to deny the authenticity of v.32 (e.g., Strecker, *Weg*, p. 153; Ogawa, pp. 121ff.), or of the last clause of v.32 (van Tilborg, pp. 52–54). Jeremias (*Parables*, pp. 80f.) argues for the authenticity of the whole.

That the verb *metamelomai* ("I change my mind") occurs in the Synoptics only in Matthew (21:29, 32; 27:3) is scarcely evidence against authenticity (so Strecker) because (1) the figures are so low (three occurrences) as to be statistically useless—one might as cogently argue that the verse is Pauline since Paul uses the verb once; (2) its use in this parable (v.29) might as easily suggest the entire parable is traditional; and (3) even if the language is Matthean—and the evidence is not conclusive either way—such considerations are not themselves conclusive concerning content (cf. Introduction, section 2). As we shall see, the entire parable makes excellent sense in context; indeed, van Tilborg (pp. 47–52) has convincingly argued that all three parables belong together as a block, even if Matthew has tightened the connections. This supports the view that 21:23–22:46 constitutes a block of confrontations and warnings that took place on the one occasion (see on 21:23).

28 The particular wording "What do you think?" is distinctively Matthean (17:25; 18:12; 22:17). The parable is introduced without any preamble other than the question. The normal way to take *prōteros* ("first") and *deuteros* ("second") in this context is "older" and "younger" son respectively (Derrett, *NT Studies*, 1:78).

29–31 The last point has a useful bearing on the complex textual problem in these verses. The evidence is neatly set out by Metzger (*Textual Commentary*, pp. 55–56) along with some useful bibliography (cf. also Derrett, *NT Studies*, 1:76ff.). When the textual evidence is sifted, three choices remain.

1. The older son says no, but repents and goes; the second son says yes, but does nothing. Who performs the Father's will? The first.
2. The older son says yes, but does nothing; the second son says no, but repents and goes. Who performs the Father's will? The younger, or the last, or the second.
3. The older son says no, but repents and goes; the second son says yes, but does nothing. Who performs the Father's will? The last.

Clearly 3 is the hardest reading; and from the time of Jerome, some have defended it for precisely that reason (Merx, Wellhausen). But not only is this reading weakly attested (Jerome knew of some Greek MSS supporting it, but only versional evidence remains today), it is either nonsensical, or else we must say the Jews are represented as perversely giving a farcical answer to avoid the application to themselves. This is not very convincing. If we do not adopt the position of WH, who suggest that a primitive textual error lies behind all extant copies, we must choose between 1 and 2. Many choose 1—as NIV—largely on the grounds that it has somewhat better external attestation than 2 and that the change from 1 to 2 can easily be envisaged. For one thing, if the first son actually went, the second might not be necessary. Also, it was natural to identify the older son with the disobedient one and the younger son with the obedient one, once the interpretation of the Fathers was widely adopted—viz., that the disobedient son stands for the Jew (who chronologically came first) and the obedient son stands for Gentile sinners. The first of these two arguments is irrelevant: there is nothing whatsoever to suggest that only one son was needed in the vineyard. The second argument is, by itself, more convincing; but it needs to face another possibility.

Derrett (*NT Studies*, 1:76ff.) has shown that in the world of Jesus' day option 2 is psychologically far more natural. The older son is somewhat pampered and favored because he is the heir, whereas the younger son is sullen and resentful but has to go out of his way to prove himself to his father. The change from 2 to 1 may have occurred if copyists supposed that in this context the father stands for John the Baptist (so, for instance, Jülicher, Jeremias), whom tax-gatherers and prostitutes, open sinners, first denied and then believed. The evidence does not admit of certain resolution, but perhaps the balance of probabilities slightly favors NASB (option 2) rather than NIV.

Either way the story is fairly straightforward. *Metamelomai* ("he changed his mind," v.29) may or may not be followed by change of purpose in the NT, unlike *metanoeō* ("I repent"). For the first time Jesus openly makes a personal application of one of his parables to the Jewish leaders. "I tell you the truth" (v.31; see on 5:16), he solemnly begins, "the tax collectors and the prostitutes enter the kingdom of God—and you do not"—for so the verb *proagō* must be translated here, rather than "are entering . . . ahead of you" (NIV; cf. Bonnard; Jeremias, *Parables*, p. 101, n. 54; TDNT, 8:105, n. 158; BDF, par. 245a[3]).

The shock value of Jesus' statement can only be appreciated when the low esteem in which tax collectors (see on 5:46) were held, not to mention prostitutes, is taken into account. In our day of soft pornography on TV, we are not shocked by "prostitutes." But Jesus is saying that the scum of society, though it says no to God, repents, performs the Father's will, and enters the kingdom, whereas the religious authorities loudly say yes to God but never do what he says, and therefore they fail to enter. Their righteousness is not enough (cf. 5:20). Thus the parable makes no distinction between Jew and Gentile but between religious leader and public sinner.

32 This verse links the parable to the preceding pericope, where the importance of believing John has already been established (vv.23–27). John pointed the way to the kingdom (11:12), which sinners are now entering (21:31). NIV interprets 21:32 in much the same way; but strictly speaking the Greek text says, "John came to you in the way of righteousness," not "John came to show you the way of righteousness." This probably means that John came preaching God's will about what was right (cf. "the way of God" in 22:16; cf. Przybylski, pp. 94–96). But in Matthew's thought John's preaching includes the demand for ethical reformation in light of the imminent coming of the kingdom (cf. 3:2–3). In this way John pointed to Jesus and the kingdom's superior righteousness (5:20). But the religious leaders did not believe John's witness, even after seeing society's vilest sinners repenting and believing him and his message.

Notes

32 Hill (*Greek Words*, pp. 124f.), Przybylski (pp. 94–96), and others rightly insist that δικαιοσύνη (*dikaiosynē*, "righteousness") in Matthew means "righteousness that is practiced," "performing the will of God." But this does not necessarily mean that practicing righteousness *in itself* gains entrance into the kingdom; for if Matthew says that John taught men to repent, he equally makes clear that John's ministry pointed to Jesus and the kingdom. If John is believed, men are led to Jesus. "Righteousness," or, better, "doing what is right, in accordance with the Father's will," includes not merely ethics, narrowly conceived, but believing Jesus and welcoming him as Messiah: the Father's will focuses on Jesus (11:25–27), who comes not only to set an example but to give his life as a ransom for many (20:28) and to inaugurate the new covenant in his blood (26:27–28). Word studies on "righteousness" by Hill and Przybylski, sound as they are, must not blind us to the larger themes in Matthew with which "righteousness" is inextricably connected.

3) *The parable of the tenants*

21:33–46

33"Listen to another parable: There was a landowner who planted a vineyard. He put a wall around it, dug a winepress in it and built a watchtower. Then he rented the vineyard to some farmers and went away on a journey. ³⁴When the harvest time approached, he sent his servants to the tenants to collect his fruit.

³⁵"The tenants seized his servants; they beat one, killed another, and stoned a third. ³⁶Then he sent other servants to them, more than the first time, and the tenants treated them the same way. ³⁷Last of all, he sent his son to them. 'They will respect my son,' he said.

³⁸"But when the tenants saw the son, they said to each other, 'This is the heir. Come, let's kill him and take his inheritance.' ³⁹So they took him and threw him out of the vineyard and killed him.

⁴⁰"Therefore, when the owner of the vineyard comes, what will he do to those tenants?"

⁴¹"He will bring those wretches to a wretched end," they replied, "and he will rent the vineyard to other tenants, who will give him his share of the crop at harvest time."

⁴²Jesus said to them, "Have you never read in the Scriptures:

" 'The stone the builders rejected
has become the capstone;
the Lord has done this,
and it is marvelous in our eyes'?

⁴³"Therefore I tell you that the kingdom of God will be taken away from you and given to a people who will produce its fruit. ⁴⁴He who falls on this stone will be broken to pieces, but he on whom it falls will be crushed."

⁴⁵When the chief priests and the Pharisees heard Jesus' parables, they knew he was talking about them. ⁴⁶They looked for a way to arrest him, but they were afraid of the crowd because the people held that he was a prophet.

This parable has long been a battleground for complex debate. It is marginally easier to account for synoptic differences (cf. Mark 12:1–12; Luke 20:9–19) postulating both a Markan and a Q recension; but this is by no means certain (cf. chart and discussion at 19:1–2).

On the face of it, the parable continues to make a statement against the Jewish religious authorities. The metaphorical equivalences are obvious: the landowner is God, the vineyard Israel, the tenants the leaders of the nation, the servants the prophets, and the son is Jesus Messiah. Such obvious metaphors have troubled many scholars, who detect late "allegorizing," which, they judge, could not have been part of the original parable but belongs only to the church's interpretation of it.

The reconstructed parable is therefore given other interpretations (cf. Jeremias, *Parables*, p. 76; Dodd, *Parables*, pp. 124–32) so far removed from the texts as we have them that others have despaired of reconstructing the original. W.G. Kümmel ("Das Gleichnis von den bösen Weingärtnern [Mark.12.1–9]," *Aux Sources de la Tradition Chrétienne*, edd. O. Cullmann and P. Menoud [Neuchâtel: Delachaux et Niestlé, 1950], pp. 120–38) argues that the creative milieu from which this parable springs is neither Galilee, nor the ministry of Jesus, but the first-century church influenced by its own interpretation of Isaiah 5. The following observations, however, point in a different direction.

1. We have already noted (see on 13:3a) that to draw a rigid line between "parable" and "allegory" or "parable" and "interpretation" has no methodological base.

2. Certainly Jesus himself faced opposition from the religious leaders of his people and day. There is no historical reason to think he could not himself have referred to Isaiah 5 in this connection and substantial formal literary reason for thinking that the parable, as the Synoptics preserve it, fits in with some of Jesus'

established patterns of teaching (cf. E.E. Ellis, "New Directions," in Strecker, *Jesus Christus*, pp. 299–315, esp. pp. 312–14).

3. Recognizing these things, some scholars have argued that the "son" motif in the parable itself depends on the logic of the story and therefore must not be judged inauthentic (Hill, *Matthew;* cf. J. Blank, "Die Sendung des Sohnes," in Gnilka, *Neues Testament*, pp. 11–41). This is surely right. But to assign the identification of this "son" as Jesus only to the church seems a rather artificial expedient. Even the most skeptical approach to the Gospels acknowledges that Jesus enjoyed a sense of special sonship to the Father. It is almost inconceivable, therefore, that Jesus could use this "son" language in defending his mission and not be thinking of himself. It is far more natural to read the "son" language of the parable as yet another veiled messianic self-reference, especially in light of the use of "Son of God" as a messianic title in 4QFlor (see on 2:15; 3:17; 11:27).

4. As far as source criticism is concerned, it will no longer do to postulate that the Gospel of Thomas 65–66 preserves the original form of the parable. K.R. Snodgrass ("The Parable of the Wicked Husbandmen: Is the Gospel of Thomas Version the Original?" NTS 21 [1975]: 142–44), along with reviewing the evidence that argues that the omissions in Thomas owe something to Gnostic influence, shows the dependence of this version on the Syriac Gospels.

33–34 This parable is probably addressed not only to Jewish rulers (v.23) but to the crowds in the temple courts, not excluding the rulers (cf. Luke 20:9). "Another" (v.33) links this parable with the last one (cf. pl. "parables" in v.45). Verses 33–34 clearly allude to Isaiah 5:1–7 and Psalm 80:6–16: Jesus' parable is an old theme with new variations. The pains the landowner takes show his care for the vineyard. He builds a wall to keep out animals, a watchtower to guard against thieves and fire, and digs a winepress to squeeze the grapes right there. All this shows his confidence that his vineyard will bear fruit. The tenant farmers take care of the vineyard during the owner's absence and pay rent in kind.

The "servants" are the owner's agents sent "to collect his fruit." Mark stipulates merely "some of the fruit of the vineyard"; and some over-zealous critics think *tous karpous autou* ("his fruit," NIV; but possibly "its fruit" [i.e., the vineyard's] as in v.43, where the "its" refers to the kingdom) in Matthew represents the *whole* crop. That any first-century reader would take words referring to rent this way is very doubtful (v.33). Mark mentions one servant at a time but says that many others were sent (cf. v.36); again, it is very doubtful that any profound theological issue hangs on the differences.

35–37 The verb *derō* ("beat," v.35) can also mean "flay" or "flog" and stands for general bodily ill-treatment (cf. Jer 20:1–2; 37:15; for Micaiah, cf. 1 Kings 22:24). Killing the prophets is attested in the OT (1 Kings 18:4, 13; Jer 26:20–23), as is stoning (2 Chron 24:21–22; cf. Matt 23:37; Heb 11:37). The landowner sends more servants (some commentators detect an allusion to the Jewish distinction between "former" and "latter" prophets) who are treated in the same brutal way (v.36). "Last of all" (v.37) he sends his son—there is a note of pathos here—hoping the tenants will respect him. This is not as implausible as it might seem to a Western reader (cf. Derrett, *NT Studies*, 2:97–98); here it shows the landowner's forbearance with his wicked tenant farmers (cf. Rom 2:4) and motivates the ultimate implacability of his wrath.

38-41 The action of the tenants is consistently callous. Precisely how it applies to Jesus is not entirely clear. Many object that the Jewish leaders did not recognize Jesus and did not desire to kill Messiah and usurp his place (v.38). But these objections miss the mark; they run into the danger of making the details of the parable run on all fours. Matthew does not take so tolerant a view as some modern scholars do of the way the Jewish leaders discharged their responsibility. Elsewhere he shows (23:37) their fundamental unwillingness to come to terms with Jesus' identity and claims (see also on 21:23-27) because they did not want to bow to his authority. True, their attitude was not, according to the synoptic record, "This is the Messiah: come, let us kill him"; yet, in the light of the Scriptures, their rejection of him was no less culpable than if it had been that. Therefore, though all the parable's details may not be pressed, rejection of the son (v.39) by the leaders *is* the final straw that brings divine wrath on them.

For six months Jesus has been telling his disciples that the rulers at Jerusalem would kill him (16:21; 17:23; 20:18). Now he tells the rulers themselves, albeit in a parable form, which, at some level, the leaders understand (vv.45-46). Undoubtedly some who heard Peter a few weeks later (Acts 2:23-37; 3:14-15) were the more convicted when they remembered these words of Jesus.

Many take the order of events—"threw him out of the vineyard and killed him" (Matthew and Luke in the best texts), the reverse of Mark (12:8)—as the result of an attempt to align the parable a little more closely with Jesus' passion: he was taken outside the city wall and then crucified (a point made by all four Gospels). This is possible. But if Matthew and Luke here depend on Q, it is at least equally possible that they preserve the original order; and Mark has a climactic arrangement: the tenants kill the son and throw him out of the vineyard. Nothing in the parable suggests that the vineyard stands for Jerusalem.

In Matthew alone Jesus elicits the self-condemning response (vv.40-41) of the hearers of the parable, thus concluding his teaching in this parable, instead of simply presenting it. Of course the conclusion remains his, regardless of how he gets it across. NIV nicely preserves the verbal assonance in the Greek ("wretches . . . wretched end").

42 In the NT, only Jesus asks, "Have you never read?" (12:3; 19:4; 21:16; Mark 12:10); and in each case he is saying, in effect, that the Scriptures point to him (John 5:39-40). The quotation is from Psalm 118:22-23 (LXX, which faithfully renders MT; cf. Notes). Luke adds a free translation of Isaiah 8:14 (cf. Isa 28:16), which appears in Matthew 21:44. "Stone" symbolism was important in the early church (Acts 4:11; Rom 9:33; 1 Peter 2:6) to help Christians understand why Jesus was rejected by so many of his own people; and doubtless its effectiveness was enhanced by Jesus' use of it.

Jesus now turns to the image of a building. The "capstone" (lit., "head of the corner") is most probably the top stone of roof parapets, exterior staircases, and city walls (cf. Derrett, *NT Studies*, 1:61). Psalm 118 may have been written about David, the type of his greater Son. All the "builders"—Goliath, David's own family, even Samuel—overlooked or rejected David, but God chose him. So in Jesus' day the builders (leaders of the people) rejected David's antitype, Jesus. But God makes him the Capstone. Alternatively, and more probably, the psalm concerns Israel. The nation was despised and threatened on all sides, but God made it the capstone. Jesus, who recapitulates Israel (see on 2:15) and is the true center of Israel, receives similar treatment from his opponents, but God vindicates him (cf. 23:39).

The building metaphor makes no explicit allusion to the church: the point is christological, not ecclesiastical. The reversal of what man holds dear, the elevation of what he rejects, can only be the Lord's doing; "and it is marvelous in our eyes."

43 This verse, found only in Matthew (cf. van Tilborg, pp. 54–58), further explains the parable. Up to this time the Jewish religious leaders were the principal means by which God exercised his reign over his people. But the leaders failed so badly in handling God's "vineyard" and rejecting God's Son that God gave the responsibility to another people who would produce the kingdom's fruit (cf. 7:16–20). For a somewhat similar explanation, see Stonehouse (*Witness of Matthew*, p. 230). Strictly speaking, then, v.43 does not speak of transferring the locus of the people of God from Jews to Gentiles, though it may hint at this insofar as that locus now extends far beyond the authority of the Jewish rulers (cf. Acts 13:46; 18:5–6; 1 Peter 2:9); instead, it speaks of the ending of the role the Jewish religious leaders played in mediating God's authority (see further on 23:2–3; so also Ogawa, pp. 127–39, though he unsuccessfully questions the authenticity of v.43).

44–46 Jesus' words are confirmed by what "the chief priests [mostly Sadducees] and the Pharisees" (v.45)—the two principal voices of authority in the Judaism of Jesus' day—understood this parable to mean: "they knew he was talking about them." Verse 44 is inserted in many MSS. It is certainly dominical but may be an assimilation to Luke 20:18. A "capstone," if too low, could be tripped over by an unwary person, sending him over the parapet; if too light or insecurely fastened, leaning against it could dislodge it and send it crashing onto the head of some passerby (v.44). There is probably an allusion to both Isaiah 8:14–15 and Daniel 2:35. This despised stone (v.42) is not only chosen by God and promoted to the premier place, it is also dangerous.

The pericope ends with magnificent yet tragic irony (v.46). The religious leaders are told they will reject Jesus and be crushed. But instead of taking the warning, they hunt for ways to arrest him, hindered only by fear of the people who accept Jesus as a prophet (see on v.11), and so trigger the very situation they have been warned about—a dramatic example of God's poetic justice. God in the Scriptures foretells this very event; and these men, prompted by hatred, rush to bring it to pass.

Notes

42 The words αὕτη (*hautē*, "this") and θαυμαστή (*thaumastē*, "marvelous") are feminine and could be construed with κεφαλή (*kephalē*, "head," as in "head of the corner" = "capstone"); but more likely this LXX feminine is a slavish rendering of the Hebrew, which has no neuter and often uses feminine for general ideas; i.e., זאת (*zō't*, "this") = *hautē*, and so forth (cf. BDF, par. 138[2]). The case of λίθον (*lithon*, "stone") has been determined by inverse relative attraction (cf. BDF, par. 295; Zerwick, par. 19).

On εἰς (*eis*, "for") plus an accusative as a substitute for the predicate nominative, see Zerwick, par. 32.

46 On εἰς (eis, "for") as substitute for the predicate accusative—an unmistakable trace of Semitic influence—see BDF, par. 157(5); Turner, *Syntax*, p. 266; Zerwick, par. 70.

---

4) The parable of the wedding banquet

22:1–14

[1]Jesus spoke to them again in parables, saying: [2]"The kingdom of heaven is like a king who prepared a wedding banquet for his son. [3]He sent his servants to those who had been invited to the banquet to tell them to come, but they refused to come.

[4]"Then he sent some more servants and said, 'Tell those who have been invited that I have prepared my dinner: My oxen and fattened cattle have been butchered, and everything is ready. Come to the wedding banquet.'

[5]"But they paid no attention and went off—one to his field, another to his business. [6]The rest seized his servants, mistreated them and killed them. [7]The king was enraged. He sent his army and destroyed those murderers and burned their city.

[8]"Then he said to his servants, 'The wedding banquet is ready, but those I invited did not deserve to come. [9]Go to the street corners and invite to the banquet anyone you find.' [10]So the servants went out into the streets and gathered all the people they could find, both good and bad, and the wedding hall was filled with guests.

[11]"But when the king came in to see the guests, he noticed a man there who was not wearing wedding clothes. [12]'Friend,' he asked, 'how did you get in here without wedding clothes?' The man was speechless.

[13]"Then the king told the attendants, 'Tie him hand and foot, and throw him outside, into the darkness, where there will be weeping and gnashing of teeth.'

[14]"For many are invited, but few are chosen."

The similarities between this parable and the one in Luke 14:16–24 lead most commentators to take them as separate developments of the same tradition, found also in the Gospel of Thomas (64). This almost inevitably leads to the view that Matthew is later on the grounds that it is more "allegorizing" (but cf. discussion on 13:3a) and that vv.6–7, 11–13 are secondary (e.g., Ogawa, p. 140), vv.11–13 perhaps representing another parable. Some go so far as to argue that the Thomas version is the most primitive of the three (but cf. Blomberg, "Tendencies of Tradition," esp. pp. 81ff.). Even when there is perfunctory recognition that Jesus may have repeated the same parable on many different occasions and applied it in quite different ways, the text is subjected to ingenious theories that "explain" all the differences without any attempt to explain the methodological grounds on which one may distinguish two historical accounts of the same or similar parables from one account considerably modified in the tradition and placed in an entirely different setting. (To cite one of many examples, cf. Robert W. Funk, *Language, Hermeneutic, and the Word of God* [New York: Harper and Row, 1966], pp. 163–87. For more recent literature, see van Tilborg, pp. 58–63; Ogawa, pp. 139–49; and for discussion on the general problem, see Introduction, section 6, and comments on 5:1–12.)

Until we have unambiguous criteria, it seems wiser to accept Matthew's setting and report and Luke's setting and report (for detailed discussion, cf. Stonehouse, *Origins*, pp. 35–42). This is especially so here because of the very small degree of verbal similarity between Matthew and Luke (see chart and discussion at 19:1–2).

In this instance the differences between Matthew and Luke are striking. In Luke the story concerns "a certain man," in Matthew "a king"; in Luke a great supper, in Matthew a wedding banquet for the king's son; in Luke one invitation, in Matthew two; in Luke the invited guests make excuses, in Matthew they refuse and turn violent; in Luke the invited guests are passed by, in Matthew they are destroyed. Each parable makes admirable sense in its own setting; and whereas the skeptical may judge such suitability to be due to editorial tampering, one might equally conclude from the evidence itself that the suitability of the two parables in their respective settings stems from two historical situations.

Moreover the alleged evidence for later "allegorizing" in Matthew, in addition to being of doubtful worth as an index of later editorial activity, since more and more scholars recognize that parables and allegorizing are not mutually exclusive, must be set against the view that Luke's very simplicity may argue for the lateness of his account. Both criteria—allegorizing and simplicity—are well-nigh useless for determining historical settings. And if Matthew's parable is much harsher than Luke's, may this not owe something to the historical situation—open confrontation with the Jewish leaders during Passion Week, which sets it considerably later than in Luke?

If the parable of the tenants exposes Israel's leaders' neglect of their covenanted duty, this one condemns the contempt with which Israel as a whole treats God's grace. The parable of the wedding banquet is therefore not redundant.

1 *Apokritheis* ("answered," NASB; untr. in NIV) may reflect Jesus' response to the Jewish leaders' desires (21:45–46), but it is probably merely formulaic (see on 11:25).

2–3 For "kingdom of heaven," see on 3:2. This kingdom has become like the following story (cf. Carson, "Word-Group"). The kingdom has already dawned; invitations to the banquet have gone out and are being refused. The son's wedding banquet doubtless hints at the messianic banquet; but this must not be pressed too hard, for when that banquet comes, there is no possibility of acceptance or refusal.

The king's son is clearly Messiah, not uncommonly represented as a bridegroom (9:15; 25:1; John 3:29; Eph 5:25–32; Rev 21:2, 9). Prospective guests to a major feast were invited in advance and then notified when the feast was ready, but these guests persistently refuse (imperfect tense).

4–5 The king not only graciously repeats his invitation but describes the feast's greatness in order to provide an incentive to attend it (v.4). *Ariston* ("dinner") properly means "breakfast." It refers to the first of two meals, usually taken about mid-morning (unlike Luke 14:16, where the word *deipnon* refers to the evening meal). But large wedding feasts went on for days in the ancient world. This *ariston* is therefore just the beginning of prolonged festivity. By v.13 the celebration is continuing at night. Those invited stay away for mundane and selfish reasons (v.5). They slight the king, whose invitation is both an honor and a command, and the marriage of whose son is a time for special joy.

6–7 The scene turns violent. Some of those invited treat the king's messengers outrageously (*hybrizō* is stronger than "mistreat," v.6). Enraged, the king sends his army (cf. Notes), destroys the murderers, and burns their city (v.7). Many object that vv.6–7 introduce an unexpectedly violent tone; but it is unexpected *only* if Luke 14:16–24 is presupposed to be the more primitive form of the story. Matthew's readers, who have just finished 21:38–41, would not find 22:6–7 out of place. Nor is there a veiled allusion to A.D. 70 (contra Hummel, pp. 85f., and many others): Reicke ("Synoptic Prophecies," p. 123) has shown how implausible this is because the language belongs to the general OT categories of judgment (cf. Introduction, section 6).

8–10 The situation having gone beyond that at normal wedding banquets, these shocking developments make their points that much more effectively. The king sends his servants to *tas diexodous tōn hodōn* ("street corners," v.9)—probably the forks of the roads, where they would find many people. They extend the king's invitation to all and succeed in drawing in all kinds of people, "both good and bad" (v.10). That Jesus is reported as saying this in Matthew clearly shows that the superior righteousness (5:20) believers must attain to enter the kingdom is not merely rigorous obedience to law. After all, this Gospel promises a Messiah who saves his people from their sins (1:21; 20:28).

11–13 Whether one is good or bad, there is an appropriate attire for this wedding feast (v.11). Evidence that the host in first-century Palestinian weddings furnished appropriate attire is inadequate and probably irrelevant to what Matthew is saying. The guest's speechlessness proves he knows he is guilty, even though the king gently calls him "friend" (v.12; cf. 20:13). In view of "good or bad" (v.10), it is difficult to believe that the wedding clothes symbolize righteousness, unless we construe it as a righteousness essential not to enter but to remain there. It is better to leave the symbolism a little vague and say no more than that the man, though invited, did not prepare acceptably for the feast. Thus, though the invitation is very broad, it does not follow that all who respond positively actually remain for the banquet. Some are tied (presumably so they can't get back in) and thrown outside into the darkness, where final judgment awaits (v.13).

.14 The *gar* ("for") introduces a general, pithy conclusion explaining the parable (see on 18:7; Zerwick, pars. 474–75). Many are invited; but some refuse to come, and others who do come refuse to submit to the norms of the kingdom and are therefore rejected. Those who remain are called "chosen" (*eklektoi*), a word implicitly denying that the reversals in the parable in any way catch God unawares or remove sovereign grace from his control. At the same time it is clear from all three parables (21:28–22:14) that not the beginning but the end is crucial.

Notes

2 The plural γάμους (*gamous*, lit., "wedding feasts"), as in vv.3–4 (though sing. in vv.8, 11–12), may suggest a feast with successive stages (cf. English "nuptials"; TDNT, 1:648–57).

7 The words τὰ στρατεύματα αὐτοῦ (*ta strateumata autou*, lit., "his armies") might lead the English reader to think of vast numbers of soldiers but is probably no more specific than the English idiom "sending in the army" or "police."

5) *Paying taxes to Caesar*

22:15–22

¹⁵Then the Pharisees went out and laid plans to trap him in his words. ¹⁶They sent their disciples to him along with the Herodians. "Teacher," they said, "we know you are a man of integrity and that you teach the way of God in accordance with the truth. You aren't swayed by men, because you pay no attention to who they are. ¹⁷Tell us then, what is your opinion? Is it right to pay taxes to Caesar or not?"

¹⁸But Jesus, knowing their evil intent, said, "You hypocrites, why are you trying to trap me? ¹⁹Show me the coin used for paying the tax." They brought him a denarius, ²⁰and he asked them, "Whose portrait is this? And whose inscription?"

²¹"Caesar's," they replied.

Then he said to them, "Give to Caesar what is Caesar's, and to God what is God's."

²²When they heard this, they were amazed. So they left him and went away.

Matthew now rejoins Mark (12:13–17) and Luke (20:20–26) in a series of confrontations, the third of which Luke omits. In each one Jesus is confronted in an attempt to show he is no better than any other rabbi, or even to ensnare him in serious difficulties. Not only does Jesus respond with superlative wisdom, but he ends the exchanges by challenging his opponents with a question of his own they cannot answer (vv. 41–46)—another bit of veiled self-disclosure. All this probably takes place in the temple courts on Tuesday of Passion Week.

15–16a "Then" (*tote*, v.15) may have purely temporal force (Mark and Luke have "and"), but there is probably a logical connection as well: "then"—after Jesus' further self-disclosure and ample warning to the Jewish leaders—the Pharisees went out from the temple courts where Jesus was preaching (21:23) and "laid plans to trap him in his words." Mark (12:13) says that "they" (presumably "the chief priests, the teachers of the law and the elders," 11:27) sent "some of the Pharisees and Herodians" to ensnare Jesus. Matthew says the Pharisees laid the plan and sent their disciples along with Herodians (v.16). Many think this difference reflects Matthew's "anti-Pharisaic bias." But several cautions must be sounded.

1. If Mark's "they" includes "the chief priests, the teachers of the law and the elders," we must remember that most of the latter two groups were Pharisees. Both Gospels therefore recognize the Pharisees' part in this confrontation.

2. Matthew's motive for making the Pharisees instigators need not be "anti-Pharisaic bias," any more than mention of the Sadducees in v.23 and synoptic parallels reflects "anti-Sadducean bias." It may owe something to literary balance—an explicit party in v.23, an explicit party in v.15. Or it may even reflect historical awareness since the Sadducees, most of whom got along with the Roman overlord better than the Pharisees, would be less likely to think up this first confrontation.

3. Both Matthew and Mark specify that Pharisees and Herodians approached Jesus, and the reason for this is obvious. Unlike most of the Jews, the Herodians openly supported the reigning family of Herod and its pro-Roman sympathies. Clearly both Pharisees and Herodians are more than mere envoys: they are active participants, seeking to put Jesus between a rock and a hard place.

A common enemy makes strange bedfellows; and common animus against Jesus erupts in plans to trip him up by fair means or foul. The verb *pagideuō* ("ensnare," "entrap," used only here [v.15] in the NT) reveals the motive: this is no dispassionate inquiry into a proper attitude to the Roman overlord. Paying the poll tax was the most obvious sign of submission to Rome. In A.D. 6 Judas of Galilee led a revolt against the first procurator because he took a census for tax purposes (Jos. Antiq. XVIII, 3[i.1]). Zealots claimed the poll tax was a God-dishonoring badge of slavery to the pagans. The trap, then, put Jesus into the position where he would either alienate a major part of the population or else lay himself open to a charge of treason.

16-17 The title "Teacher" and the long preamble (v.16) reflect flattery and pressure for Jesus to speak. If he does not reply after such an introduction, then he is not a man of integrity and is swayed by men. The question "Is it right?" is theological, as all legal questions inevitably were to a first-century Jew. The question raised here, and others like it, exercised the rabbis (e.g., b *Pesahim* 112b; b *Baba Kamma* 113a).

By NT times "Caesar," the family name of Julius Caesar, had become a title (cf. Luke 2:1, of Augustus; 3:1, of Tiberius; Acts 17:7, of Claudius; 25:8-12; Phil 4:22, of Nero). The reference here is to Tiberius. The wording of the question, with its deft "or not," demands a yes or a no.

18-20 But Jesus will not be forced into a reductionistic reply. He recognizes the duplicity of his opponents. "Trap" (v.18) is not *pagideuō* (as in v.15) but *peirazō* ("test" or "tempt," as in 4:1; 16:1). Jesus chooses to answer them on his own terms and asks for the coin (*nomisma*, a NT *hapax legomenon*) used for paying this tax (v.19). That he has to ask may reflect his own poverty or the fact that he and his disciples had a common purse. It was customary, though not absolutely essential, to pay the tax in Roman currency; and that such coins bore an image of the emperor's head along with an offensive inscription ("Tiberius Caesar, son of the divine Augustus" on one side and *"pontifex maximus"*—which Jesus would understand as "high priest"—on the other) would offend most Palestinian Jews. They hand Jesus a denarius (v.19); and, as in 21:23-27, he asks his questioners a question—this time one they have to answer (v.20).

21-22 Superficially Jesus' answer accords with Jewish teaching that men ought to pay taxes to their foreign overlords, since the great, even the pagan great, owe their position to God (cf. Prov 8:15; Dan 2:21, 37-38). But Jesus' answer (v.21) is more profound than that and can be fully understood only in the light of religion-state relations in first-century Rome. The Jews, with their theocratic heritage, were ill-equipped to formulate a theological rationale for paying tribute to foreign and pagan overlords, unless, like the Jews of the Exile, they interpreted their situation as one of divine judgment. But it was not only Jewish monotheism that linked religion and state. Paganism customarily insisted even more strongly on the unity of what we distinguish as civil and religious obligations. Indeed, some decades later Christians faced the wrath of Rome because they refused to participate in emperor worship—a refusal the state judged to be treason.

Seen in this light, Jesus' response is not some witty way of getting out of a predicament; rather, it shows his full awareness of a major development in redemption history. Jesus does *not* side with the Zealots or with any who expect his messiahship to bring instant political independence from Rome. The messianic community he determines to build (16:18) must render to whatever Caesar who is in power whatever belongs to that Caesar, while never turning from its obligations to

God. The lesson was learned by both Paul and Peter (Rom 13:1–7; 1 Peter 2:13–17). Of course, Jesus' reply is not a legal statute resolving every issue. Where Caesar claims what is God's, the claims of God have priority (Acts 4:19; 5:29; much of Rev). Nevertheless Jesus' pithy words not only answer his enemies but also lay down the basis for the proper relationship of his people to government. The profundity of his reply is amazing (v.22); but some of his enemies, no doubt disappointed at their failure to ensnare him, later on lie to pretend that their snare had worked (Luke 23:2).

Notes

16 The clause οὐ γὰρ βλέπεις εἰς πρόσωπον ἀνθρώπων (*ou gar blepeis eis prosōpon anthrōpon*, lit., "you do not look to the face of men") is idiomatically translated by NIV, "you pay no attention to who [men] are." The expression probably has the same force as לֹא חַכִּיר פָּנִים (*lō' takir pānîm*, "you shall not respect persons [NIV, 'show partiality'],", Deut 16:19; cf. Lev 19:15): cf. Sigal, "Halakah," pp. 74f.; contra Derrett, *Law*, pp. 313ff.

21 Some have interpreted ἀπόδοτε (*apodote*, "give") to mean "pay back": Give back to God what he has given you, and to Caesar what he has given you. Although the verb can have that force, it need only mean "give" or "pay"; but the former is more suitable in this context because in no real sense does Caesar "give back" his subjects' tax money. They pay what is his due, what properly belongs to him, not what he has given them.

6) *Marriage at the Resurrection*

22:23–33

> ²³That same day the Sadducees, who say there is no resurrection, came to him with a question. ²⁴"Teacher," they said, "Moses told us that if a man dies without having children, his brother must marry the widow and have children for him. ²⁵Now there were seven brothers among us. The first one married and died, and since he had no children, he left his wife to his brother. ²⁶The same thing happened to the second and third brother, right on down to the seventh. ²⁷Finally, the woman died. ²⁸Now then, at the resurrection, whose wife will she be of the seven, since all of them were married to her?"
>
> ²⁹Jesus replied, "You are in error because you do not know the Scriptures or the power of God. ³⁰At the resurrection people will neither marry nor be given in marriage; they will be like the angels in heaven. ³¹But about the resurrection of the dead—have you not read what God said to you, ³²'I am the God of Abraham, the God of Isaac, and the God of Jacob'? He is not the God of the dead but of the living."
>
> ³³When the crowds heard this, they were astonished at his teaching.

The questioners' intent is as malicious as in the last pericope. They hope to embroil Jesus in a theological debate where he must choose sides; but instead the exchange again demonstrates his wisdom and authority (cf. Mark 12:18–27; Luke 20:27–40).

23 "That same day" (lit., "in that hour") places this confrontation in the same situation as the former one. Pharisees believed in a resurrection from the dead, basing their belief in part on Isaiah 26:19 and Daniel 12:2. But Sadducees did not believe in a resurrection: both body and soul, they held, perish at death (cf. Acts 23:8; Jos. Antiq. XVIII, 12–17 [i.3–4]; Wars II, 162–66 [viii.14]). At Jesus' time Judaism as a whole held surprisingly diverse views of death and what lies beyond it (cf. G.W.E. Nickelsburg, *Resurrection, Immortality, and Eternal Life in Intertestamental Judaism* [Cambridge: Harvard University Press, 1972]). In support of his view that Matthew was written so late that it retains only vague and inaccurate impressions of Sadducees (who largely died out after A.D. 70), Hummel (pp. 18–20), followed by Bonnard, argues that this verse says that only *some* of the Sadducees say there is no resurrection; but the Greek text knows no such restriction, whatever variant is chosen (cf. Notes).

24–28 Like the Pharisees and Herodians, the Sadducees approach Jesus with insincere respect ("Teacher," v.24; cf. v.16). They begin by citing the Mosaic levirate law (Deut 25:5–6). The text form in Matthew is either a little closer to the Hebrew than in Mark and Luke, or else it assimilates more closely to Genesis 38:8 (LXX). According to biblical law, if a man dies without children (the pl. is generalizing: Zerwick, par. 7; and see on 2:20), his younger brother is to marry the widow and "have children for him," i.e., sire children who would legally be heirs of the deceased brother. Levirate marriage antedates Moses in the canon (Gen 38:8); i.e., Moses regulated the practice but did not initiate it. The OT gives us no case of it, though levirate law stands behind Ruth 1:11–13; 4:1–22. Probably in Jesus' day the law was little observed, the younger brother's right to decline taking precedence over his obligation.

Though the case brought by the Sadducees (vv.25–27) *could* have happened, it is probably hypothetical, fabricated to confound Pharisees and others who believed in resurrection. Their question presupposes that resurrection life is an exact counterpart to earthly life; and if so, the resurrected woman (v.28) must be guilty of incestuous marriages (see on 19:9) or arbitrarily designated the wife of one of the brothers. And if so, which one? Or—and this is the answer the Sadducees pressed for—the whole notion of resurrection is absurd.

29–30 In Jesus' mind the Sadducees were denying Scripture (v.29) because they approached its clear teaching on the subject (Isa 26:19; Dan 12:2; cf. Job 19:25–27), assuming that if God raises the dead he must bring them back to an existence just like this one. Jesus' response was acute. The Sadducees, Jesus insists, betray their ignorance of the Scriptures, which *do* teach resurrection, and of the power of God, who is capable of raising the dead to an existence quite unlike this present one. "For" (*gar*, untr. in NIV)—introducing an explanation as to how the power of God will manifest itself—"in" (*en*, not "at" [NIV], viewing the Resurrection, not as a single event, but as a state inaugurated by the event) "the resurrection" there will be a change in sexual relationships (v.30). In this way we shall be "like the angels in heaven," and marriage as we know it will be no more. In fact Jesus' use of angels contains a double thrust since the Sadducees denied their existence (cf. Acts 23:8).

Some have concluded from Jesus' answer that in heaven there will be no memory of earlier existence and its relationships, but this is a gratuitous assumption. The greatness of the changes at the Resurrection (cf. 1 Cor 15:44; Phil 3:21; 1 John 3:1–2) will doubtless make the wife of even seven brothers (vv.24–27) capable of loving all and the object of the love of all—as a good mother today loves all her children and is loved by them.

31–32 Jesus now turns from the power of God to the word of Scripture (cf. v.29). He may have drawn the passage to which he appeals (Exod 3:6) from the Pentateuch, because the Sadducees prized the Pentateuch more highly than the rest of Scripture. "Have you not read?" (v.31) is a rebuke (see on 21:42).

If God is the God of Abraham, Isaac, and Jacob even when addressing Moses, hundreds of years after the first three patriarchs died, then they must be alive to him (v.32), "for to him all are alive" (Luke 20:38). God is the eternal God of the covenant, a fact especially stressed wherever reference is made to the patriarchs (e.g., Gen 24:12, 27, 48; 26:24; 28:13; 32:9; 46:1, 3–4; 48:15–16; 49:25). He always loves and blesses his people; therefore it is inconceivable that his blessings cease when his people die (cf. Pss 16:10–11; 17:15; 49:14–15; 73:23–26). Yet at first glance the text Jesus cites is sufficient, along the lines of this argument, to prove immortality but not resurrection. Two observations largely alleviate the problem.

1. The Sadducees denied the existence of spirits as thoroughly as they denied the existence of angels (Acts 23:8). Their concern was therefore not to choose between immortality and resurrection but between death as finality and life beyond death, whatever its mode.

2. The mode that was the principal (though certainly not exclusive) option in Palestinian piety was a rather shadowy existence in Sheol followed by final resurrection.

Our problem is that we force on the text a neoplatonic dualism and demand a choice between immortality and resurrection (cf. Warfield, *Shorter Writings*, 1:339–47). The point is simply "that God will raise the dead because he cannot fail to keep his promises to them that he will be their God" (Marshall, *Luke*, p. 743), read against the background of biblical anthropology and eschatology (cf. also F. Dreyfus, "L'argument scripturaire de Jésus in faveur de la résurrection des morts [Mark, XII, 26–27]," RB 66 [1959]: 213–24—though he handles Luke 20:37–38 rather disappointingly).

33 Matthew does not tell us that the Sadducees are convinced but that the crowds are astonished at Jesus' teaching. The cause of the astonishment is probably Jesus' authority and incisive insight into biblical truth (cf. 7:28–29; 13:54; 22:22). Luke (20:39) remarks that some teachers of the law, almost certainly of Pharisaic persuasion, responded, "Well said, teacher!"

Notes

23 The two principal readings are "Sadducees saying" and "Sadducees, those who say" (for textual details, cf. Metzger, *Textual Criticism*, p. 58). The former is likely original, both on external evidence and because it almost suggests the Sadducees began the conversation with a denial, an unprecedented approach (though it is possible their "saying" is understood to be an aside, under their breath as it were). The second reading is then a partial assimilation to Mark 12:18; Luke 20:27. But even if the second reading is original, it is quite unnecessary to suppose "those who say" refers to some *part* of the Sadducees. The words most plausibly belong in apposition: "Sadducees, i.e., those who say." Matthew treats the verb ἔρχονται (*erchontai*, "come") in Mark 12:18 as a historical present; and if "saying" is a dependent participle, it takes on the same temporal force as Matthew's προσῆλθον (*proselthon*, "came").

31 This is the only place in the NT that speaks of resurrection τῶν νεκρῶν (*tōn nekrōn*, "of the dead"), though Rom 1:4 uses the anarthrous expression. More common is the insertion of the preposition ἐκ (*ek*, "from"). Despite various theories to explain these differences, the diverse forms are probably synonymous.

---

7) *The greatest commandments*

22:34–40

> [34] Hearing that Jesus had silenced the Sadducees, the Pharisees got together. [35] One of them, an expert in the law, tested him with this question: [36] "Teacher, which is the greatest commandment in the Law?"
>
> [37] Jesus replied: " 'Love the Lord your God with all your heart and with all your soul and with all your mind.' [38] This is the first and greatest commandment. [39] And the second is like it: 'Love your neighbor as yourself.' [40] All the Law and the Prophets hang on these two commandments."

The account as we have it is not in Luke (cf. Mark 12:28–34), though Luke 10:25–28 has something similar introducing the parable of the Good Samaritan. Because there are several verbal agreements between Matthew and Luke against Mark, it is usually held that the "double commandment" came down separately in Mark and Q (for recent discussion, cf. R.H. Fuller in Schottroff et al., pp. 41–56). This is quite possible; and the Lukan pericope (10:25–37) is so loosely connected to its setting that it could have come from almost any period in Jesus' ministry.

On the other hand, the rabbis of Jesus' day were much exercised to find summary statements of OT laws and establish their relative importance; and in all probability the question arose enough times in Jesus' ministry that he developed a fairly standard response to the question. In Luke, Jesus elicits the correct answer from the expert in the law, rather than providing it himself; but we have already seen this kind of diversity when the synoptists recount the same event (e.g., Mark 12:9 and Matt 21:40–41; cf. Mark 12:35–36 and Matt 22:42–44); so the distinction may not be significant. More telling is the fact that the pericope in Luke focuses primarily, not on the question of the greatest commandment, but on the question of how to inherit eternal life. While this is scarcely conclusive, it may suggest quite separate occasions (cf. E.E. Ellis, "New Directions," in Strecker, *Jesus Christus*, pp. 310–12).

34 Mark says that a teacher of the law—most of whom were Pharisees—posed the question (12:28) and gives a rather positive picture of the man. But Matthew maintains the polemical tone and portrays this confrontation as owing something to the machinations of the Pharisees, who saw how Jesus had silenced the Sadducees. Historically the Pharisees' leaders sent one of their "disciples" (cf. v.16)—himself a Pharisee—who turned out to be more sympathetic than his seniors. Mark focuses on the confrontation; Matthew looks at its core from the perspective of the Pharisees who plotted it. (For similar dissension among high Jewish authorities when assessing Jesus, see John 7:45–52; Acts 5:33–39.)

35–36 The *nomikos* ("expert in the law," assuming this is the correct reading and not an interpolation from Luke) is here a Pharisee, a "scribe" or "teacher of the law" considered particularly learned (v.35). The "law," of course, is Scripture, perhaps especially the Pentateuch. But because Scripture was applied to every area of life—including all civil matters—by means of certain interpretive rules and a vast complex of tradition, such an expert was, by modern standards, both a learned theologian and a legal expert. He "tested" Jesus, asking which is the greatest commandment (v.36; the positive is used for the superlative, a not uncommon way to speak of a group or class: Moulton, *Accidence*, p. 442; BDF, par. 245[2]; Zerwick, par. 146).

The Jews quite commonly drew distinctions among the laws of Scripture—great and small, light and heavy. Jesus does something similar in 23:23. Testament of Issachar 6 gives certain Scriptures as the epitome of the law; and Akiba's "negative golden rule" (see on 7:12) is proclaimed as "the whole law. The rest is commentary" (cf. b *Shabbath* 31a). Yet the Jewish evidence is not univocal. *Mekilta* Exodus 6 and *Sifre* Deuteronomy 12:8; 19:11 speak of the equal importance of all commandments (cf. futher SBK, 1:902ff.). We must allow not only for diversity of opinion among Jewish authorities but also for various opinions with different aims. Moreover, equality of various laws can refer to equality of reward for keeping them; Akiba's dictum was a response to a Gentile challenge to explain the whole law during the time he could stand on one leg.

Verse 36 shows that the question of the expert was probably a hotly debated one (cf. Urbach, 1:345–65). The scene is like an ordination council where the candidate is doing so well that some of the most learned ministers ask him questions they themselves have been unable to answer—in the hope of tripping him up or of finding answers.

37–39 Jesus first quotes Deuteronomy 6:5 (part of the Shema [Deut 6:4–9; 11:13–21; Num 15:38–41]) and then Leviticus 19:18. The first is from the MT; the second from the LXX (cf. Gundry, *Use of OT*, pp. 22–25). From the viewpoint of biblical anthropology, "heart," "soul," and "mind" (v.37) are not mutually exclusive but overlapping categories, together demanding our love for God to come from our whole person, our every faculty and capacity. "First and greatest" (v.38) refers to one, not two, qualities: the "and" is explicative, i.e., this command is primary because it is the greatest. The second (v.39) also concerns love, this time toward one's "neighbor," which in Leviticus 19:18 applies to a fellow Israelite or resident alien, but which Luke 10:29–37 expands to anyone who needs our help.

Bringing these two texts together does not originate with Jesus, as Luke's parallel suggests (confirmed also by T Issachar 5:2, 7:6; T Dan 5:3, if these texts are pre-Christian).

40 This verse is distinctive though enigmatic. "All the Law and the Prophets hang on [lit., 'are suspended from'] these two commandments." The following observations bring out the principal points of this summary.

1. The two commandments, Jesus says, stand together. The first without the second is intrinsically impossible (cf. 1 John 4:20), and the second cannot stand without the first—even theoretically—because disciplined altruism is not love. Love in the truest sense demands abandonment of self to God, and God alone is the adequate incentive for such abandonment.

2. But in what sense do the Law and the Prophets "hang" on these two commandments? It is unlikely that the verb implies "derivation"—that the Law and the Prophets can be deduced from these two commandments (so Berger, *Gesetzesauslegung*, pp. 227–32). Jesus has expanded the initial category ("the greatest commandment in the Law," v.36) to include all Scripture ("all the Law and the Prophets"). So even if "all the Law" could be derived from these two commandments, how could the same be said of "all the Prophets"?

3. It is equally unlikely that Jesus is appealing to these two commandments to abolish the necessity of formal adherence to all other law, thus entirely abandoning the rabbinical approach to the law and perhaps even making the love commandments a kind of hermeneutical canon for interpreting all OT law. This view, in one form or another, is very popular (Bornkamm, *Tradition*, pp. 76–78; id., "Das Doppelgebot der Liebe," *Geschichte*, pp. 37–45; Hummel, pp. 51ff.; and esp. B. Gerhardsson, "The Hermeneutic Program in Matthew 22:37–40," *Jesus, Greeks, and Christians*, edd. R. Hamerton-Kelly and R. Scroggs [Leiden: Brill, 1976], pp. 129–50). This radical interpretation of Jesus' answer is said to be necessary to make sense of the fact this confrontation is a test (Bornkamm, *Tradition*, p. 78). But the test can be understood in other ways (see on v.36); and the fact that Jesus' opponents are testing him does not require his answer to be radical, any more than in vv.23–33. There is no positive evidence in the text to support this view, if a better one can be found; and Moo ("Jesus") has rightly pointed out that in no case in the Gospels does love serve as grounds for abrogating any commandment (the Sabbath controversies are no exception, since there concern for fellow human beings is recognized as one important factor within the Sabbath law itself; see on 12:1–13). Indeed, G. Barth (Bornkamm, *Tradition*, p. 78) is reduced to pitting the love commands *against* the "jot and tittle" of 5:18, though both are taught by Jesus.

4. Kaiser rightly points out that this passage is in keeping with the prophetic tradition of the OT, which equally demands a heart relationship with God (Deut 10:12; 1 Sam 15:22; Isa 1:11–18; 43:22–24; Hos 6:6; Amos 5:21–24; Mic 6:6–8; cf. Prov. 15:8; 21:27; 28:9). Sterile religion, no matter how disciplined, was never regarded as adequate. Unfortunately Kaiser then arbitrarily links this pericope too closely with passages like 23:23–24 and argues that Jesus is saying that "the meticulous Scribes and punctilious Pharisees . . . must penetrate to the *more significant and abiding aspects of the law*" (p. 185; emphasis mine). But that is just what Jesus does *not* say at this point. The relative "greatness" of this command or some other one has no connection whatever in synoptic pericopes to continuity or discontinuity between the Testaments.

5. Nevertheless Kaiser's initial linking of 22:34–40 with the OT tradition demanding heart religion is valid. This matter is well treated by Moo ("Jesus"). There is no question here of the priority of love over law—i.e., one system over another—but of the priority of love within the law. These two commandments are the greatest because all Scripture "hangs" on them; i.e., nothing in Scripture can cohere or be truly obeyed unless these two are observed. The entire biblical revelation demands heart religion marked by total allegiance to God, loving him and loving one's neighbor. Without these two commandments the Bible is sterile. This pericope prepares the way for the denunciations of 23:1–36 and conforms fully to Jesus' teaching elsewhere. "Love is the greatest commandment, but it is not the *only* one; and the validity and applicability of other commandments cannot be decided by appeal to its paramount demand" (Moo, "Jesus," p. 12). The question of the continuity or discon-

tinuity of OT law within the teaching of Jesus is determined not with reference to the love commands but by a salvation-historical perspective focusing on prophecy and fulfillment (see on 5:17–48).

Notes

40 It is doubtful whether Paul (Rom 13:8–10) goes beyond the interpretation given above: see C.E.B. Cranfield, *The Epistle to the Romans*, 2 vols. (Edinburgh: T. & T. Clark, 1975, 1979), 2:673–79. This does not mean that Cranfield's entire view on the law in Paul is to be endorsed but that he rightly perceives the relation between love and law. For fairly detailed discussion of the place of law in the history of redemption, cf. Carson, *Sabbath*.

8) *The son of David*

22:41–46

> 41While the Pharisees were gathered together, Jesus asked them, 42"What do you think about the Christ? Whose son is he?"
> "The son of David," they replied
> 43He said to them, "How is it then that David, speaking by the Spirit, calls him 'Lord'? For he says,
>
> > 44" 'The Lord said to my Lord:
> > "Sit at my right hand
> > until I put your enemies
> > under your feet." '
>
> 45If then David calls him 'Lord,' how can he be his son?" 46No one could say a word in reply, and from that day on no one dared to ask him any more questions.

After silencing the Jewish leaders, Jesus in turn asks them a question. His purpose is not to win a debate but to elicit from them what the Scriptures themselves teach about the Messiah, thus helping people to recognize who he really is. The passage speaks to crucial christological and hermeneutical issues (see esp. on vv. 43–44).

The synoptic parallels (Mark 12:35–37; Luke 20:41–44) do not show that Jesus' questions were addressed to the Pharisees, or that they replied (see on 22:34–40). The historical setting is the temple courts, where crowds and leaders mingled together and alternately listened to the teacher from Nazareth and fired questions at him (21:23–23:36). Matthew's details probably stem from his memory of the events. That he mentions the Pharisees may reveal his desire to show his readers where the Pharisees were wrong. But one cannot be dogmatic about this, since Matthew omits Mark's gentle snub: "The large crowd listened to him with delight" (12:37), which shows that Mark, too, knows that Jesus aimed his exegesis of Psalm 110 against the biblical experts of his day.

41–42 Jesus' question (v. 41) focuses on the real issue—christology, not resurrection or taxes—that turned the authorities into his enemies. The Messiah's identity according to the Scriptures must be determined. One way to do that is to ask whose son he is (v.42). The Pharisees gave the accepted reply: "The son of David"—based on passages like 2 Samuel 7:13–14; Isaiah 11:1, 10; Jeremiah 23:5 (see on 1:1; 9:27–28; cf. Moore, *Judaism*, 2:328–29; Guthrie, *NT Theology*, pp. 253–56; Fitzmyer, *Semitic Background*, pp. 113–26; Longenecker, *Christology*, pp. 109–10).

43–45 But this view, though not wrong, is too simple because, as Jesus points out, David called the Messiah his Lord (v.43). How then could Messiah be David's son? The force of Jesus' argument depends on his use of Psalm 110, the most frequently quoted OT chapter in the NT. The Davidic authorship of the psalm, affirmed by the psalm's superscription, is not only assumed by Jesus but is essential to his argument. If the psalm was written by anyone else, then *David* did not call Messiah his Lord. The phrase "speaking by the Spirit" not only assumes that all Scripture is Spirit-inspired (cf. Acts 4:25; Heb 3:7; 9:8; 10:15; 2 Peter 1:21) but here reinforces the truth of what David said so it may be integrated into the beliefs of the hearers (cf. "and the Scripture cannot be broken," John 10:35). The text of Psalm 110:1 quoted by all three Synoptics is essentially Septuagintal (cf. Gundry, *Use of OT*, p. 25; on the variants, cf. Fee, pp. 163–64). The "right hand" (v.44) is the position of highest honor and authority (cf. Ps 45:9; Matt 19:28).

Many but not all Jews in Jesus' day regarded Psalm 110 as messianic (cf. SBK, 4:452–65; LTJM, app. 9; David M. Hay, *Glory at the Right Hand: Psalm 110 in Early Christianity* [Nashville: Abingdon, 1973], pp. 11–33). Most modern scholars say that Psalm 110 was not Davidic but was written *about* David or some other king, making "my Lord" a monarchical reference by an unknown psalmist. Because Psalm 110 is so frequently quoted in the NT, some scholars try to establish the "entry" of the psalm into Christian tradition, associating it with, say, "the pre-Pauline formula in Rom 1:3f." (D.C. Duling, "The Promises to David and Their Entrance into Christianity," NTS 20 [1974]: 55–77) or Pentecost (M. Gourgues, "Lecture christologique du Psaume cx et Fête de la Pentecôte," RB 83 [1976]: 1–24). A pattern is then plotted for the score of NT uses of Psalm 110, on which Matthew 22:41–46 plus parallels appear too late to be authentic words of Jesus.

Nevertheless there are many arguments for an interpretation more in conformity with the texts as we have them.

1. That Psalm 110 is about the king makes sense only if the superscription is ignored. If David is indeed the author, as both the psalm's superscription and Jesus insist, then either the psalm deals with some figure other than David or else David, caught up in high prophetic vision, is writing about himself in the third person.

2. The latter is by no means implausible. But we have already seen that much prophecy and fulfillment is in OT paradigms pointing forward, sometimes with the understanding of the OT writers, sometimes not (see on 2:15, 5:17; 8:16–17). David is regularly portrayed, even in the OT, as the model for the coming Anointed One; and David himself understood at least something of the messianic promise (2 Sam 7:13–14).

3. Psalm 110 uses language so reckless and extravagant ("forever," v.4; the mysterious Melchizedek reference, v.4; the scope of the king's victory, v.6) that one must either say the psalm is using hyperbole or that it points beyond David. That is exactly the sort of argument Peter uses in Acts 2:25–31 concerning another Davidic psalm (Ps 16).

4. Psalm 110 contains no allusion to the much later Maccabeans, who were priest-

kings, for they were priests who became "kings," whereas the figure in Psalm 110 is a king who becomes a priest.

5. As the text stands, this pericope has important christological implications. The widely held, if not dominant, view was that the coming Messiah would be the son of David (cf. Pss Sol 17). Jesus not only declares that view inadequate, but he insists that the OT itself tells us it is inadequate. If Messiah is not David's son, *whose son is he?* The solution is given by the prologue to Matthew (chs. 1–2) and by the voice of God himself (3:17; 17:5): Jesus is the Son of God. Even the title "Son of Man" (see on 8:20) offers a transcendent conception of messiahship.

6. However, in spite of Bultmann (*Synoptic Tradition*, pp. 136–37) and many others, this does not mean that Jesus or Matthew is *denying* that the Messiah is David's son, replacing this notion with a more transcendent perspective. This Gospel repeatedly recognizes that Jesus the Messiah is Son of David, not only by title (1:1; 9:27; 15:22; 20:30–31; 21:9, 15; cf. 12:23) and by the genealogy (1:2–16) but also by its portrayal of Jesus as King of the Jews (2:2; 21:5; 27:11, 29, 37, 42: cf. Hay, *Glory*, pp. 116–17). What Jesus does is synthesize the concept of a human Messiah in David's line with the concept of a divine Messiah who transcends human limitations (e.g., Ps 45:6–7; Isa 9:6; Jer 23:5–6; 33:15–16; Zech 12:10 [MT]; 13:7 [NASB]), even as Matthew elsewhere synthesizes kingship and the Suffering Servant. The OT itself looked forward to one who would be both the offshoot and the root of David (Isa 11:1, 10; cf. Rev 22:16).

7. Even the fact that Jesus' use of Psalm 110:1 was susceptible to an interpretation denying that the Messiah must be of Davidic descent argues strongly for the authenticity of this exegesis of the psalm, for it is unlikely that Christians would have placed this psalm on Jesus' lips when his Davidic sonship is taught throughout the NT (in addition to Matthew, cf. Mark 10:47–48; 11:10; Luke 1:32; 18:38–39; Rom 1:3; 2 Tim 2:8; Rev 3:7; 5:5; 22:16). Jesus' question (v.45) is not a denial of Messiah's Davidic sonship but a demand for recognizing how Scripture itself teaches that Messiah is more than David's son.

8. Against those who hold that this transcendent sonship could only have arisen as an issue after the Passion (e.g., Lindars, *Apologetic*, pp. 46f.), we must ask why Jesus himself could not have expressed the paradox of Messiah's dual paternity, since he certainly knew God as uniquely his "Father" (see esp. 11:27) and applies the transcendent title "Son of Man" to himself as well.

9. If this approach is substantially correct, then the entrance of Psalm 110 into Christian theology is traceable to Jesus himself. Moreover it can be credibly argued that *his* approach to the OT is adopted by the NT writers, even when they do not focus on the same OT texts to which he gave his primary attention.

10. Finally, the text has some eschatological implications, even though they are not of primary interest. Messiah is pictured at God's right hand of authority during a period of hostility from God's enemies, a hostility to be crushed at the end (cf. 28:18–20).

46 In Mark the opponents' silence (12:34) concludes the pericope of the greatest commandment. Matthew uses this comment to finish the entire section of confrontations (21:23–22:46). Many who were silenced were not saved; so Jesus' enemies went underground for a short time before the Crucifixion. Yet even their silence was a tribute. The teacher who never attended the right schools (John 7:15–18) confounds the greatest theologians in the land. And if his question (v.45) was unanswerable at this time, a young Pharisee, who may have been in Jerusalem at the time, was to answer it in due course (Rom 1:1–4; 9:5).

Notes

44 The variants "under your feet" or "your footstool" (cf. Nestle) were easily exchangeable in Greek because of (1) similarity in the Greek terms ὑποκάτω (hypokatō, "under") and ὑποπόδιον (hypopodion, "footstool"); (2) the demonstrable influence of Ps 8:6; and (3) the obvious relation between the two expressions (a footstool by definition is under one's feet). On the significance of the idea, cf. Josh 10:24; Ps 47:3.

e. *Seven woes on the teachers of the law and the Pharisees* (23:1–36)

1) *Warning the crowds and the disciples*

23:1–12

¹Then Jesus said to the crowds and to his disciples: ²"The teachers of the law and the Pharisees sit in Moses' seat. ³So you must obey them and do everything they tell you. But do not do what they do, for they do not practice what they preach. ⁴They tie up heavy loads and put them on men's shoulders, but they themselves are not willing to lift a finger to move them.

⁵"Everything they do is done for men to see: They make their phylacteries wide and the tassels on their garments long; ⁶they love the place of honor at banquets and the most important seats in the synagogues; ⁷they love to be greeted in the marketplaces and to have men call them 'Rabbi.'

⁸"But you are not to be called 'Rabbi,' for you have only one Master and you are all brothers. ⁹And do not call anyone on earth 'father,' for you have one Father, and he is in heaven. ¹⁰Nor are you to be called 'teacher,' for you have one Teacher, the Christ. ¹¹The greatest among you will be your servant. ¹²For whoever exalts himself will be humbled, and whoever humbles himself will be exalted.

Structurally, it is difficult to decide just where Matthew 23 belongs. Because it is essentially discourse, some have held that it either belongs to Matthew 24–25 or else is a separate discourse and must be treated as such. But the different audiences (23:1; 24:3) separate chapter 23 from chapters 24–25, as do their distinct, though related, themes. Nor is Matthew 23 a discourse on a par with the five major discourses of Matthew: it lacks the characteristic discourse ending (see on 7:28–29). Moreover, from a thematic viewpoint Matthew 23 is best perceived as the climax of the preceding confrontations.

Solutions to many of the important questions raised by Matthew 23 gradually emerge from exegesis of the whole; but several preliminary considerations will point the way ahead.

1. The literary origins of this chapter are disputed. Some see vv.1–12 as free expansion—by Matthew—of Mark 12:38–39, and vv.13–36 of Mark 12:40. Others hold that Mark has reduced material in Matthew because he is not interested in this debate; and still others that the two Gospels spring at this juncture from separate traditions. There is no way of proving the rightness of one of these options. Yet it must be said that Matthew's material is remarkably coherent and, when viewed dispassionately (see below), believably dominical. Even the changes of addressees

(23:1, 13, 37) admirably suit the larger context (21:23–22:46), with crowds and authorities milling around and coming and going, and the preacher addressing first this part of his audience, then that. The chapter *may* be a montage of sayings: there is ample evidence that Luke often compiled sayings in that way, without pretense of doing otherwise. On the other hand, there is no good reason for thinking 23:2–36 cannot be a report of what Jesus said on this occasion.

2. Attempts to define the situation in Matthew's church on the basis of this chapter are precarious. These turn on attitude toward the law (cf. vv.2–3 and v.23) or toward the Jewish religious leaders and lead to extended debate as to whether Matthew's church has broken from the synagogue and is therefore appealing to it, denouncing it from without, or still trying to win it over from within. Objections to the contrary, there is no real anachronism to warrant such discussion, which is scarcely more than fanciful though learned speculation. Obviously Matthew is telling us what Jesus says, not what the church says. Even if we assume that Matthew's choice of what he includes largely reflects the situation at the time he wrote, it is naive to think twentieth-century scholars can reconstruct the situation in detail (cf. Introduction, section 2). A certain amount of personal interest or a need to show his readers "how we got from there to here" may have led Matthew to many of his choices. The space he allots to it implies that he is interested in the continuity between the OT people of God and the church, the people of the Messiah, and how it happened that so many Jews, including the religious authorities, rejected Jesus. But Paul had similar aims in writing Romans, and no one thinks the church at Rome is theologically akin to Matthew's church in this respect.

3. The literary context of the chapter is extremely important. Not only does Matthew 23 climax a series of controversies with the Jewish religious authorities (21:23–22:46), but it immediately follows the christologically crucial confrontation of 22:41–46. The question "What do you think about Christ?" raised by Jesus (v.42) "was not simply a theological curiosity which could be thrashed out in the seminar room," as Garland (p. 24) puts it; it stands at the heart of the gospel. The failure of the Pharisees to recognize Jesus as the Messiah prophesied in Scripture is itself already an indictment, the more so since they "sit in Moses' seat" (see on v.2); and the woes that follow are therefore judicial and go some way toward explaining the prophesied destruction of Jerusalem in the Olivet Discourse (24:4–25:46).

4. Thus Jesus' strong language in this chapter ("fools," "hypocrites," "blind guides," "son of hell") is not the language of personal irritation at religious competition, nor the language of a suffering church tired of the restrictions and unbelief of the synagogue in the ninth decade A.D., but the language of divine warning (cf. vv.37–39) and condemnation. Those who see Matthew 23 as inconsistent with the Sermon on the Mount (esp. 5:43–48) neglect two things. First, they overlook the limitations inherent to the sermon itself: the love Jesus demands of his followers is more radical and more discriminating than modern liberal sentimentality usually allows. Second, the Sermon on the Mount, not less than Matthew 23, also presents Jesus as eschatological Judge who pronounces solemn malediction on those he does not recognize and who fail to do his word (7:21–23). To read Matthew 23 as little more than Matthew's pique about A.D. 85 is not only without adequate historical and literary justification but fails dismally to understand the historical Jesus, who not only taught his followers to love their enemies and gave his own life in supreme self-sacrifice, but proclaimed that he came not to bring peace but a sword (10:34) and presented himself as eschatological Judge (e.g., 7:21–23; 25:31–46).

1 Perhaps a year earlier Jesus had begun to denounce the Pharisees (15:7). Subsequently he warned his disciples of the teaching of the Pharisees and Sadducees (16:5–12). Now his warnings and denunciations are public. Current scholarship tends to see "crowds" and "his disciples" either as unhistorical, perhaps an invented transition (Walker, pp. 68–70), or else as an ambiguous pastiche of historical reminiscence and contemporizing, the "crowds" referring to Jews in Matthew's day and "disciples" to Christians in his day. All this is groundless. In the setting—the temple courts a few days before Passover (21:23)—"crowds" along with "disciples" and some religious authorities are to be expected. Matthew mentions both groups because he sees that the essential thrust of Jesus' warnings is to compel men to follow him, the Messiah as defined in 22:41–46, or the religious leaders. And those who do the latter will share their leaders' condemnation. The scene is therefore set for Jesus' lament over Jerusalem (vv.37–39) and the judgment that follows (chs. 24–25; cf. Garland, pp. 34–41).

2 Only here in Matthew do the Greek words behind "teachers of the law" and "Pharisees" take separate articles, implying two separate groups (cf. RHG, pp. 758f.). Therein lies a problem, for whereas "scribes" (NIV, "teachers of the law") had teaching authority, the Pharisees as such did not. Many were laymen without authority or responsibility to teach. Grundmann suggests that *kai* ("and") is epexegetical ("scribes, that is, the Pharisees"); Gaechter, that the phrase is a hendiadys ("scribes of the Pharisees"). But both views are unnatural and do not account for the use of "Pharisees" in ch. 23.

On the other hand, some hold that the "Pharisees" represent Matthew's opponents in A.D. 85 and are therefore anachronistically inserted into the Gospel (Kilpatrick, *Origins*, p. 113; Hummel, p. 31; Bonnard; and many others). Garland (p. 44, n. 32, and pp. 218–21), however, has pointed out that Luke attacks the Pharisees as vigorously as Matthew; yet no one holds that Pharisaic Judaism was a major concern for Luke's church. Walker (p. 20), van Tilborg (p. 106), and Garland (pp. 43–46) conclude that all categories of Jewish leaders (Pharisee, scribe, Sadducee, chief priest, etc.) in Matthew lose all historical distinction and become synonymous, ciphers for Jewish leadership in general that failed to recognize Jesus as Messiah. But some passages preserve fine historical distinctions (e.g., 21:23); and it is intrinsically unlikely that a writer as sensitive to Jewish background as Matthew would use words so clumsily. The problem is one of demanding too narrow definition of certain categories and, when they don't fit, charging the writer with anachronism.

A better approach is possible (cf. Carson, "Jewish Leaders"). The "teachers of the law," most of them Pharisees in Matthew's time, were primarily responsible for teaching. "Pharisee" defines a loose theological position, not a profession like "teacher." The two terms are distinct, even if there is much overlap on the personal level. An analogy might be the Puritan John Owen's denouncing "the prelates and Roman Catholics" and then continuing his discourse with epithets like "you prelates, you Catholics," "you prelates, Catholics." "Prelates" defines roles but does not mean that the only prelates are Catholics (some were Anglicans); the other— "Catholics"—defines theological position but does not require all Catholics to be prelates. This is how Jesus was attacking a theological position and those who promulgated it.

These leaders "sit in Moses' seat." E.L. Sukenik (*Ancient Synagogues in Palestine and Greece* [London: OUP, 1934], pp. 57–61) has shown that synagogues had a stone seat at the front where the authoritative teacher, usually a *grammateus* ("teacher of the law"), sat. Moreover, "to sit on X's seat" often means "to succeed X" (Exod 11:5; 12:29; 1 Kings 1:35, 46; 2:12; 16:11; 2 Kings 15:12; Ps 132:12; cf. Jos. Antiq. VII, 353[xiv.5]; XVIII, 2[i.1]. This would imply that the "teachers of the law" are Moses' legal successors, possessing all his authority—a view the scribes themselves held (M *Sanhedrin* 11:3; cf. Ecclus 45:15–17; M *Aboth* 1:1; M *Yebamoth* 2:4; 9:3).

3 The astounding authority conceded "the teachers of the law and the Pharisees" in v.2 becomes explicit in v.3. Even if the emphasis in v.3 falls at the end, where Jesus denounces the Jewish leaders' hypocrisy, the beginning of the verse gives them full authority in all they teach, even if they do not live up to it. *Panta hosa* ("everything") is a strong expression and cannot be limited to "that teaching of the law that is in Jesus' view a faithful interpretation of it"; they cover *everything* the leaders teach, including the oral tradition as well (Garland, pp. 48f.; contra Allen; Plummer; Schlatter; Stonehouse, *Witness of Matthew*, pp. 196f.; and others). Nor does the text say their authority rests in their roles but not in their doctrine: on the contrary, v.3 affirms their doctrine but condemns their practice. Meier (*Law*, pp. 106, 119, 156) argues that this pertains only to Jesus' earlier ministry but not to the church from the Resurrection on. But this settles nothing, because Jesus has during his ministry repeatedly criticized the scribes and Pharisees for their teaching, not least their oral tradition (5:21–48; 15:3–14; 16:12), will do so again (23:16–36), and has just finished exposing their ignorance of the Scriptures (22:41–46).

Many scholars hold that vv.2–3 reflect an earlier tradition, reflecting a time when Matthew's church was still part of and under the authority of the Jewish leaders and that somehow that early tradition was awkwardly preserved in a book that, on the whole, reflects later theological developments. But it is doubtful whether there ever was such a time (cf. Acts 3–4); and in any case the theory makes Matthew an extraordinarily incompetent editor.

The way around this thorny point, according to Hummel, van Tilborg, and Schweizer, is to recognize that Matthew preserves vv.2–3 because the rupture between synagogue and church has not yet taken place. So Matthew incorporates vv.2–3 to mollify and if possible win Jewish opponents, while at the same time giving a qualified interpretation of the statement in line with 5:17–20 (Schweizer). The remarkable thing, however, is that vv.2–3 are not in themselves qualified but are about as strong as can be imagined. If Matthew was interested in preventing a threatening rupture in the alleged union between synagogue and church, why does he not elsewhere mitigate his strong denunciation of the Jewish leaders' teaching and include the praise of the scribe (Mark 12:34)? First-century readers were no less alert than we. Could they not see that the Gospel repeatedly criticizes the Pharisees' doctrine, making the assurance of vv.2–3 empty and mocking?

Before proposing a solution, we must consider the force of v.4.

4 The Qumran covenanters called the Pharisees "the expounders of smooth things," because their casuistry made life easier than the covenanters themselves approved. To reconcile this DSS evidence with v.4, some have held that though the Pharisees made things easier for themselves, proving the covenanters right, they made it harder for everyone else; so v.4 is correct (cf. Hill, *Matthew*). The distinction is doubtful. Most Pharisees, including rabbis, worked in some full-time trade: they

were not secluded scholars but active members of society. It is hard therefore to see how their rulings could benefit only themselves. We must not forget that the DSS came out of a monastic community, which would negatively judge all rules less rigorous than their own. The real question about v.4 is whether (1) it contrasts in some way with vv.2–3 or (2) it merely illustrates v.3b. The latter will not stand close scrutiny (cf. Garland, pp. 50ff.).

Verse 4 speaks of the leaders' putting "heavy loads on men's shoulders—laying down irksome rules—and then refusing "to lift a finger" to help. This does not mean they were unwilling to obey burdensome rules themselves (contra Josef Schmid, in loc.; Bornkamm, *Tradition*, p. 24; Schweizer, *Matthew*; Sand, p. 89) but that they refused to help those who collapsed under their rules (Manson, *Sayings*, p. 101; McNeile; Filson; Garland, p. 51). This is the natural interpretation of *kinēsai* ("to move"; cf. BAGD, s.v.) and fits the allusion to 11:28–30. Thus the Pharisees are unlike Jesus, whose burden is light and who promises rest. But this means that v.4 does more than illustrate v.3b: it shows how the Pharisees are by their teaching doing more harm than good.

Thus vv.2–3 stand alone in their emphasis: their contexts flatly contradict them. It will not do to treat vv.2–3 as a concession to the leaders that Matthew then modifies, a "rhetorical preparation" drawn from conservative tradition that the evangelist proceeds to modify (Banks, *Jesus*, p. 176; Garland, pp. 54f.), for the tension is too sharp. The only way to make sense of the text is to follow Jeremias (*Theology*, p. 210) and see in vv.2–3 an instance of biting irony, bordering on sarcasm. This position is self-consistent and does not weaken the strong statements in vv.2–3. Moreover it is strengthened by the verb *ekathisan* ("sit") in v.2. The aorist is not normally translated as a present. In response many point out that the same aorist verb is used in Mark 16:19; Hebrews 1:3; 8:1; 10:12; Revelation 3:21—all of which refer to Jesus as still sitting. But that misses the point. The emphasis in each of these instances is not that Jesus is still sitting, though that is doubtless presupposed, but on the fact that as a result of his triumph he *sat down*. The aorist does not *require* that the action be at one point in time; it is the context that in each of these instances presupposes it. Moreover the gnomic aorist in the indicative mood (which is how NIV's "sit" takes the Greek in v.2) is so rare in the NT that it should not be our first option. But if vv.2–3a are ironic, then the aorist can have its natural force: the teachers of the law and the Pharisees *sat down* in Moses' seat (cf. NASB's "have seated themselves," which may be overtranslated but has the right idea). The Jewish religious leaders have "presumed" to sit in Moses' seat (so Adalbert Merx, *Das Evangelium Matthaeus* [Berlin: Georg Reimer, 1902]; Moulton, *Prolegomena*, p. 458; Zahn). It is, of course, of no help to say that such a translation must be followed in v.3a by "therefore, pay no attention to what they say" (contra Plummer; Banks, *Jesus*, p. 175; Garland, p. 48); for v.3a continues the irony. This generates a neat chiasm:

A:	v.2—the leaders have taken on Moses' teaching authority	}irony
	B: v.3a—do what they say	
	B¹: v.3b—do not what they do	}nonironical advice
A¹:	v.4—their teaching merely binds men	

Thus the first two elements are ironic, and the last two reveal in reverse order the painful futility of following the teachers of the law. Jesus warns the crowds and his disciples in the sharpest way possible. The reluctance of many scholars to admit that vv.2–3 are biting irony overlooks the tone of much of this chapter (e.g., vv.23–28) and superb parallels elsewhere in the NT (e.g., 1 Cor 4:8a, 10).

5–7 These verses illustrate some of the leaders' practices not to be copied (v.3b; cf. Mark 12:38–39; Luke 20:46). Jesus accuses them of being time-servers and applause-seekers (6:1–18). "Phylacteries" (v.5) were small leather or parchment boxes containing a piece of vellum inscribed with four texts from the law (Exod 13:2–10, 11–16; Deut 6:4–9; 11:13–21). They were worn on the arm or tied to the forehead according to Exodus 13:9, 16; Deuteronomy 6:8; 11:18 (though originally these passages were probably metaphorical). The peculiar term used here only in the NT has pagan associations ("amulet") and may insinuate that the *ṭôṭāpōṭ* ("frontlets," as they were called, though they are now referred to by Jews as *tᵉpillîn* [lit., "prayers"]) had become like pagan charms (cf. ZPEB, 4:786–87; SBK, 4:250–76; Urbach, 1:130, 366f.).

To show their piety to the world, these leaders made large, showy phylacteries. The same ostentation affected the length of tassels, worn by all Jews (including Jesus, 9:20; 14:36) on the corners of the outer garment, in obedience to Numbers 15:37–41; Deuteronomy 22:12. (The view that *ta kraspeda* ["tassels"] means "borders" [KJV] of garments is unlikely in this context: cf. BAGD, s.v.; on the details of Jewish ritualism, HJP, 2:479ff.)

Seeking a reputation for piety goes with seeking places of honor at great dinners or the most important seats—as close as possible to the law scrolls—in the synagogues (v.6). "Rabbi" (v.7), the transliteration of the Hebrew word meaning "my master" or "my teacher," was used in Hillel's time, a generation before Jesus; but it probably did not signify official ordination till after the Fall of Jerusalem. The title, originally merely a mark of respect, was applied to Jesus (26:25, 49; John 1:38; 3:26). But like other common terms, it became inflated. By Talmudic times a rabbi's status was immense: his disciple had to obey him without question, never walk beside or in front of him, never greet him first, and so forth (cf. Moses Aberbach, "The Relations Between Master and Disciple in the Talmudic Age," *Essays Presented to Chief Rabbi Brodie*, 2 vols., ed. H.J. Zimmels [London: Soncino, 1966–67]. 1:1–24; cf. Albright and Mann). The situation had not developed so far in Jesus' day; but if the process had begun, one can well imagine Jesus' exposing it (esp. in light of 18:1–5; 20:25–28; cf. also Introduction, section 11.f).

8–10 The "you" (v.8) is emphatic, but this does not mean that vv.8–10 are out of place in an address before a mixed audience. It is not implausible that out of the crowd Jesus is here speaking primarily to his disciples, just as he later addresses the Pharisees directly (vv.13–36). A good preacher knows that forthright words about what is required of believers can be at the same time a powerful incentive to decision on the part of the sympathetic but uncommitted. These verses could therefore serve as warning not to follow the "teachers of the law and the Pharisees" while laying down normative patterns for relationships among Jesus' disciples.

Unlike the religious authorities, Jesus says, his disciples are not to be called "Rabbi" (v.8), for they have but one *didaskalos* (better rendered "Teacher" than "Master"). The "one Teacher" is not God but Jesus himself (cf. v.10); but either way, in view of 22:41–46; 23:4, 13–36, this verse not only proscribes self-exaltation in teaching divine things but rejects the authority of the religious teachers of Jesus' day. Such authority has been taken from them (see on 21:43). Among those who follow Jesus, a brotherly relationship (see on 5:22–24, 47; 18:15, 21, 35; 25:40; 28:10) is required.

Verse 9 moves from "Rabbi" or "Teacher" to "Father." To the best of our knowledge, rabbis were not directly addressed as "Fathers." Some have therefore argued that the text is referring to the patriarchs ("fathers") and is saying, "Do not rely on your racial tie to Abraham, Isaac, and Jacob" (cf. 3:9; so J.T. Townsend, "Matthew xxiii.9," JTS 12 [1961]: 56–59; Schweizer *Matthew*; and others). Nothing in the context supports this, still less the suggestion that Greek Stoicism stands in the background (van Tilborg, p. 138). But K. Kohler ("Abba, Father: Title of Spiritual Leader and Saint," JQR 13 [1900–1901]: 567–80) showed long ago that "the fathers" became a very common way of referring to earlier teachers of the law, especially the great masters (cf. also Urbach, 1:186; 2:906, n. 38). The practice may have stretched back to the days of the prophets (cf. 2 Kings 2:12).

"On earth" does not mean the "fathers" were alive in Jesus' time but simply contrasts them with the Father in heaven: their domain is not exalted enough to warrant the latter title. This explains the change from the passive ("do not be called," vv.8, 10) to the active ("do not call [i.e., someone else," v.9): "do not be called" would be inappropriate since the title was not bestowed till after the teachers of law died and were memorialized. There may be an allusion to Malachi 2:7–10: like the priests of Malachi's day whose teaching caused many to stumble, so the revered Jewish fathers have so misinterpreted Scripture that they must not be called "fathers." There is but one Father, God.

But where, then, *is* the voice of authoritative teaching? Jesus returns to that theme in v.10, completing an A-B-A chiasm. Thus v.10 largely repeats v.8, using a different word for "Teacher" (cf. Notes); but it is not repetitious, still less anticlimactic, because it ends by identifying the sole Teacher as the Christ, the Messiah (Kingsbury, *Matthew*, p. 93). This not only picks up the theme of 1:1 and 16:16 but echoes the confrontation in 22:41–46 regarding Messiah. Jesus' enemies, the certified teachers of Israel, could not answer basic biblical questions about the Messiah. Now he, Jesus the Messiah, declares in the wake of that travesty that he himself is the only one qualified to sit in Moses' seat—to succeed him as authoritative Teacher of God's will and mind.

Two further observations need to be made. First, it is untrue to Jesus' teaching to deduce from this passage that no Jewish leader was sympathetic to his cause, nor that there is no place for distinctions in roles or respect for leaders in his church, any more than his prohibition of oaths (5:33–37) means it is unchristian to swear on oath in court. Certainly Jesus was not justifying that particularly perverse pride that cloaks itself in discourtesy. Yet once this has been noted, we must say that the risen Christ is as displeased with those in his church who demand unquestioning submission to themselves and their opinions and confuse a reputation for showy piety with godly surrender to his teaching as he ever was with any Pharisee.

Second, the continuing modern discussion as to what these verses show about the structure of Matthew's church finds no valid source here. For instance, Hummel (pp. 27f.) holds that vv.8–10 show that there must have been a sort of Christian rabbinate in Matthew's day, which Matthew was combatting or attempting to guide. That may be so, but the text does not say so. In any case other reasons for Matthew's including this material spring readily to mind. If Matthew *is* concerned to show Christian-Jewish readers of his own day "how we got from there to here," and if this material is basically authentic, no further reason is needed. The truth is that we know about Matthew's situation only from what he chose to write about Jesus, not a late first-century church.

11–12 The substance of v.11 is in 20:26: Matthew repeatedly emphasizes humility. For instances of exalting oneself, see on 20:20–28; of humbling oneself, on 18:4 (cf. Prov 15:33; 22:4; James 4:6; 1 Peter 5:5–6). "Will be your servant," "will be humbled," and "will be exalted" are pure futures without imperatival force (contra Zerwick, par. 280). The latter two could not be otherwise; so v.11 should be read the same way. The principle enunciated in these verses reflects not natural law but kingdom law: the eschatological reward will humble the self-exalted and exalt the self-humbled, after the pattern in Ezekiel 21:26. What is commended is humility, not humbug; service, not servility. The supreme example—the Messiah himself—makes this clear (20:26–28); for his astonishing humility and service to others was untainted by servility and was perfectly compatible with exercising the highest authority. Having done the greatest service, he has been most highly exalted.

Notes

4 For the variant "and hard to carry" (as in Luke 11:46), see Metzger, *Textual Commentary*, pp. 59–60.
8 For literature on the question of whether this use of "Rabbi" is anachronistic, see Garland, p. 58; Sigal, "Halakah."
9 The Greek word order suggests the rendering "for, for you there is only *one* Father—the heavenly Father" (Moule, *Idiom Book*, p. 166).
10 Καθηγητής (*kathēgetēs*, "teacher") is used only here in the NT. Many suggestions have been made as to why it should replace "rabbi" and διδάσκαλος (*didaskalos*, "teacher") in v.8. Some have assumed it to be Matthew's translation for Gentile readers (Grundmann; Strecker, *Weg*, p. 217) or an addition to dissociate Jesus from Hellenistic teachers as much as from "teachers of the law" (Frankmölle, pp. 99–100). C. Spicq ("Une Allusion au Docteur de Justice dans Matthieu, XXIII, 10?" RB 66 [1959]: esp. 393–96) suggests the word is the Greek equivalent of the Hebrew מוֹרֶה (*môreh*, "teacher"), used in the DSS for the "Teacher of Righteousness" at Qumran. Jesus is then seen as denouncing the sectarian religious authorities as well as the scribes. But the linguistic evidence is unconvincing, and it seems wiser to take *kathēgetēs* as a synonym for *didaskalos*, possibly prompted by homophony with ἐκάθισαν (*ekathisan*, "they sat down") and καθέδρα (*kathedra*, "seat") in v.2. "This would be further evidence that the authority of the scribes and Pharisees is null and void for Matthew" (Garland, p. 60, n. 100).

2) *The seven woes* (23:13–36)

Compare the six woes of Luke 11:37–54. The overlaps are considerable but the differences in order and wording no less remarkable. The three chief options are (1) Luke preserves the correct setting, and Matthew adds the woes to the end of vv.1–12; (2) Matthew preserves the correct setting, and Luke inserts some of the woes into his narrative; and (3) Jesus pronounced such woes on the Pharisees fairly frequently, perhaps following the pattern of the six woes of Isaiah 5:8–23 or the five woes of Habakkuk 2:6–20. (For discussion, cf. Marshall, *Luke*, pp. 491–93.)

The seven woes Matthew records fit into a neat chiastic pattern:

A: First woe (v.13)—failing to recognize Jesus as the Messiah
   B: Second woe (v.15)—superficially zealous, yet doing more harm than good
      C: Third woe (vv.16–22)—misguided use of the Scripture
         D: Fourth woe (vv.23–24)—fundamental failure to discern the thrust of Scripture
      C′: Fifth woe (vv.25–26)—misguided use of the Scripture
   B′: Sixth woe (vv.27–28)—superficially zealous, yet doing more harm than good
A′: Seventh woe (vv.29–32)—heirs of those who failed to recognize the prophets.

What stands out is the centrality of rightly understanding the Scriptures—a theme that is reflected in all the preceding controversies and is no less related to Jesus' rejection of the claims of the teachers of the law.

a) *First woe*

23:13[14]

> 13"Woe to you, teachers of the law and Pharisees, you hypocrites! You shut the kingdom of heaven in men's faces. You yourselves do not enter, nor will you let those enter who are trying to.

13[14] Verse 14 must be taken as an interpolation, derived from Mark 12:40; Luke 20:47. This is made clear, not only by its absence from the best and earliest Matthew MSS, but from the fact that the MSS that do include it divide on where to place it—before or after v.13. (For the meaning of v.14, cf. Derrett, *NT Studies*, 1:118–27.)

Verse 13 begins the first of seven "woes." A "woe" can be a compassionate "alas!" (24:19), a strong condemnation (11:21), or a combination of the two (18:17; 26:24). In Matthew 23 condemnation predominates; but it is neither vindictive nor spiteful so much as judicial. Jesus the Messiah pronounces judgment.

"Teachers of the Law" and "Pharisees" are anarthrous from here on throughout the chapter (see on 2:4; 3:7; 23:2; Introduction, section 11.f). (For "hypocrites," see on 1:2; for "kingdom of heaven," on 3:2.) The syntax of v.13 (cf. Notes) assumes that the messianic reign has begun. The teachers of the law and the Pharisees are "hypocrites" since they claim to teach God's way but refuse to enter the messianic kingdom and hinder those who try to do so. This does not refer to their casuistry that obscured fundamental questions of conduct and made it difficult for people to obey God's law fully, though this is the dominant interpretation (e.g., Hill, *Matthew*). Conduct is not mentioned here, only entrance into the kingdom. Though proper conduct is essential, it admits no one into the kingdom.

The last controversy (22:41–46) reveals the real failure—the teachers of the law and the Pharisees do not enter the kingdom because they refuse to recognize who

Jesus is. When the crowds begin to marvel at Jesus and suggest he may be the Messiah, the authorities do all they can to dissuade them (cf. 9:33–34; 11:19; 12:23–24; 21:15). The sheep of Israel are "lost" (10:6; 15:24) because the shepherds have led them astray. The "woe" pronounced on the authorities is therefore of a piece with 18:6–7.

Notes

13 The present substantival participle τοὺς εἰσερχομένους (tous eiserchomenous, "those entering") need not in itself have present force but can refer to sustained effort in the past (as in 2:20; for discussion, cf. BDF, par. 339[3]; RHG, pp. 858–64, 891–92; Zerwick, par. 274). However, in the context of the present finite verb οὐδὲ . . . ἀφίετε (oude . . . aphiete, "nor . . . do you permit"), there can be no doubt that the action envisaged by both participle and finite verb is portrayed as simultaneous with the speaker's words.

b) *Second woe*

23:15

> [15]"Woe to you, teachers of the law and Pharisees, you hypocrites! You travel over land and sea to win a single convert, and when he becomes one, you make him twice as much a son of hell as you are.

15 External sources for assessing the Pharisees' zeal to win converts are not easy to interpret, though a sizable body of scholarship convincingly argues that the first century A.D. till the Fall of Jerusalem marks the most remarkable period of Jewish missionary zeal and corresponding success (see esp. B.J. Bamberger, *Proselytism in the Talmudic Period* [Cincinnati: Hebrew Union, 1939]; W.G. Braude, *Jewish Proselytizing in the First Five Centuries of the Common Era* [Providence, R.I.: Brown University Press, 1940]; F.M. Derwacter, *Preparing the Way for Paul: The Proselyte Movement in Later Judaism* [New York: Macmillan, 1930]; D. Georgi, *Die Gegner des Paulus im 2. Korintherbrief* [Neukirchen-Vluyn: Neukirchener Verlag, 1964], pp. 83–187; Jeremias, *Promise*, pp. 11ff.; cf. Rom 2:24). Not the least important fact, as W. Paul Bowers observed ("Studies in Paul's Understanding of His Mission," Ph.D. dissertation, Cambridge, 1976), is that there is no evidence that Jews in any way opposed Paul's or anyone else's Christian Gentile mission: rather, what they disputed was the basis of admission to the people of God.

How much of the Pharisees' activity was aimed at converting to their views those who had already become loose adherents of Judaism (cf. Jos. Antiq. XX, 34–48[ii.3–4]), we cannot know for certain. But whether the scribes and Pharisees were winning raw pagans or sympathizers of Judaism, they were winning them to their own position. The converts in view, therefore, are not converts to Judaism but to Pharisaism. Pharisees and teachers of the law would travel extensively to make one "proselyte"—a word used in the NT only here and in Acts 2:11; 6.5; 13:43 and one that at this time probably refers to those who have been circumcised and have pledged to submit to the full rigors of Jewish law, including the oral tradition for which the Pharisees were so zealous.

Jesus did not criticize the *fact* of the Pharisees' extensive missionary effort but its *results:* the "converts" became twice as much a "son of hell" (gehenna; see on 5:32) as the scribes and Pharisees who won them. This means that the Pharisees' interpretations and the rules deduced from Scripture became so fully those of their converts that they "out-Phariseed" the Pharisees. Psychologically this is entirely possible, as every teacher of converts knows. As for the converts of whom Jesus was speaking, the Pharisees' teaching locked them into a theological frame that left no room for Jesus the Messiah and therefore no possibility of entering the messianic kingdom.

c) *Third woe*

23:16–22

> 16"Woe to you, blind guides! You say, 'If anyone swears by the temple, it means nothing; but if anyone swears by the gold of the temple, he is bound by his oath.' 17You blind fools! Which is greater: the gold, or the temple that makes the gold sacred? 18You also say, 'If anyone swears by the altar, it means nothing; but if anyone swears by the gift on it, he is bound by his oath.' 19You blind men! Which is greater: the gift, or the altar that makes the gift sacred? 20Therefore, he who swears by the altar swears by it and by everything on it. 21And he who swears by the temple swears by it and by the one who dwells in it. 22And he who swears by heaven swears by God's throne and by the one who sits on it.

16–22 See on 5:33–37 for the background and thrust of these verses. The striking designation "blind guides" (v.16) was introduced at 15:14. The "temple" here is *naos* (see on 4:5).

Because of the references to the temple—its gold, altar, and offerings—a surprising number of scholars focus on Matthew's attitude toward the cultic aspects of the temple (Hummel, pp. 78–82; van Tilborg, p. 105). This quite misses the point (Gaston, *No Stone*, p. 94). The pericope simply uses the language of the cultus in discussing the kinds of distinctions in oaths often favored in Jewish circles. Saul Lieberman (*Greek in Jewish Palestine* [New York: Jewish Theological Seminary, 1942], pp. 115–43), after studying the difficult and conflicting Jewish evidence, argues that the rabbis fought the abuses of oaths and vows among the unlearned masses. This is doubtless so. But the way they fought them was by differentiating between what was binding and what was not. In that sense, wittingly or unwittingly they encouraged evasive oaths and therefore lying. Jesus cut through these complexities by insisting that men must tell the truth.

Some writers have supposed that 5:33–37—which, formally at least, abolishes oaths—contradicts 23:20–22, which maintains that all oaths are binding but does not abolish them. In fact, however, vv.20–22 provide the rationale for 5:33–37. All oaths are in some way related to God. All are therefore binding, and thus evasive oaths are disallowed. On the other hand, the heart of the issue is telling the truth; and it is probably a new kind of casuistry that, failing to see this, insists that Jesus in 5:33–37 abolishes all oaths of every kind.

In the context of Matthew 23, Jesus charges the teachers of the law and the Pharisees with mishandling the Scriptures they claimed to defend and promulgate.

Notes

16–22 References to the temple and the cultus, which no longer existed after A.D. 70, do not prove that this Gospel was composed before that date, since Matthew, writing later, may be incorporating older material and describing what Jesus said at the time of his ministry. But the pericope is consistent with an early date; and, more importantly, if we think instead that Matthew writes about A.D. 85 but carefully preserves the right tense and distinctions appropriate to Jesus' ministry, why should we not expect him to be equally careful elsewhere?

---

d) *Fourth woe*

23:23–24

> ²³"Woe to you, teachers of the law and Pharisees, you hypocrites! You give a tenth of your spices—mint, dill and cummin. But you have neglected the more important matters of the law—justice, mercy and faithfulness. You should have practiced the latter, without neglecting the former. ²⁴You blind guides! You strain out a gnat but swallow a camel.

23–24 The OT law on tithing (Deut 14:22–29) specifies grain, wine, and oil, though Leviticus 27:30 is more comprehensive. Certainly in the first century there was debate about how far the law of tithing should extend. The consensus was to include greens and garden herbs (v.23; SBK, 1:932). Jesus does not condemn scrupulous observance in these things ("without neglecting the former"), but insists that to fuss over them while neglecting the "more important matters of the law" (cf. 22:34–40)— justice, mercy, and *pistis* (here rightly translated "faithfulness")—is to strain out a gnat but swallow a camel (v.24), both unclean creatures.

Several points deserve notice.

1. The "weightier" matters do not refer to the "more difficult" or "harder" but to the "more central," "most decisive" (Ridderbos, p. 302) or (as in NIV) "more important" versus "peripheral" or "trifling" ones (cf. TDNT, 1:554, 558; Kaiser, p. 184).

2. Yet it goes much too far to interpret vv.23–24 as expanding the love command into the central feature of the law (see on 22:34–40 and literature cited there; also Garland, p. 139).

3. In essence what Jesus accuses the teachers of the law and the Pharisees of is a massive distortion of God's will as revealed in Scripture. At a fundamental level, they fail to focus on the thrust of Scripture, a point made with equal force in the two references to Hosea 6:6 in this Gospel (see on 9:9–13; 12:1–14).

4. The chiastic structure of the "woes" centers on this fourth one, where the basic failure of the Pharisaic teachers is laid bare. Moving out from this center, it becomes clear that where Scripture is interpreted by the Pharisees, there is danger of misappropriation of truth (woes 3 and 5) and of corrupting other people (woes 2 and 6), coupled with blindness to true revelation when it comes supremely in the person of Jesus the Messiah (woes 1 and 7).

5. All this presupposes that Jesus holds readers of the OT responsible for discerning its purpose and recognizing its most important emphases (see on 22:40). Only

those who do this please God and recognize the Messiah (cf. Luke 24:44–46; John 5:39–40).

6. The current debate over the words "without neglecting the former"—viz., whether they show Jesus or Matthew as a very conservative interpreter of the law, or whether they can possibly come from the historical Jesus (cf. Garland, p. 140, n. 66; Westerholm, pp. 58f.)—badly misses the point. For neither Jesus nor Matthew do these verses focus on the problem of continuity–discontinuity between the OT and the reign of Jesus Messiah but on the relative importance of material within the OT. Jesus describes what the Pharisees should have done; he is not here questioning how the "former" will relate to the reign he now inaugurates (12:28) or the church he will build (16:19), any more than in vv. 16–22 he discusses what role the temple altar plays under the new covenant.

Notes

24 Black (*Aramaic Approach*, pp. 175f.) points out that in Aramaic this saying would be something of a pun, since "gnat" and "camel" sound much alike: קַמְלָא (*qamlā*) and גַּמְלָא (*gamlā'*) respectively.

e) *Fifth woe*

23:25–26

> 25"Woe to you, teachers of the law and Pharisees, you hypocrites! You clean the outside of the cup and dish, but inside they are full of greed and self-indulgence. 26Blind Pharisee! First clean the inside of the cup and dish, and then the outside also will be clean.

25–26 The most common interpretation of these verses is that Jesus begins with the metaphor of the cup and dish (v. 25a), reveals his nonmetaphorical concerns in the last words of v. 25, then returns to his metaphor in v. 26 now that its real purpose has been exposed. The Pharisees have been occupied with external religion instead of that of the inner person. Within themselves they remain "full of greed and self-indulgence [*akrasia*, found in the NT only here and in 1 Cor 7:5]." In the metaphor, cleaning the inside is basic and guarantees cleanliness of the outside.

Jacob Neusner (" 'First Cleanse the Inside,' " NTS 22 [1976]: 486–95) holds, largely on form-critical grounds, that pre–A.D. 70 Judaism was divided on the issue of clean vessels. The Hillelites thought that cleaning the inside of a vessel declared it "clean." The Shammaites, predominant before A.D. 70, held it was necessary to cleanse both inside and outside; the one did not affect the status of the other (cf. esp. M *Kelim* 2:1; 25:1, 7–9; j *Berakoth* 8:2). Consequently Jesus could not be refuting the Hillelites (who did not become predominant until after A.D. 70), telling them *first* to cleanse the inside, since they would have cleaned *only* the inside. Rather, the admonition was for the Shammaites.

From this debate about cleansing, it is argued, the saying was variously interpreted and applied (cf. Luke 11:41) in metaphorical ways. Garland (pp. 148–50) thinks the first part of v. 25 is literal but was taken over by Matthew to make his point. In his view the *ex* clause should not be rendered "full *of* greed and self-indulgence" but "full *because of* greed and self-indulgence" (Turner, *Syntax*, p. 260; Schweizer, McNeile, and others think this is possible). In other words Matthew turns the original saying into one that says the inside is most important but then draws "attention to the fact that the vessels were filled with food and drink which was [sic] obtained unjustly and consumed intemperately—a circumstance which cultic washing could not cleanse—and ultimately made the entire issue moot" (Garland, p. 149).

This interpretation will not do. The Pharisees were not as a class intemperate in food and drink but abstemious (cf. Luke 18:11–12). Moreover, if they were full *because* of greed and self-indulgence, the preceding "but" is nonsensical: the first clause should read "you empty the cup and dish," not "you clean the outside." Rather, the kind of historical background envisaged by Neusner is being used by Jesus to point away from the ceremonial question altogether. The Pharisees (here Shammaites) debate about what must be cleansed for a cup to be clean, without seeing that they themselves need to become inwardly clean. This approach is very close to the traditional interpretation of these verses (above; cf. Westerholm, pp. 85–90). Yet it also hints that Jesus holds that OT ceremonial distinctions have moral implications the avoiding of which betrays deep misunderstanding.

"Blind Pharisee!" (v.26, the singular has generic force), says the one who came to save his people from their sin (1:21), "first clean the inside . . . and then the outside also will be clean." "Inside" does not here encourage privatized pietism but total, moral renewal in terms of "justice, mercy, and faithfulness." The "outside," the bits of religious observance easily seen by men, will then take care of itself.

f) *Sixth woe*

23:27-28

> [27]"Woe to you, teachers of the law and Pharisees, you hypocrites! You are like whitewashed tombs, which look beautiful on the outside but on the inside are full of dead men's bones and everything unclean. [28]In the same way, on the outside you appear to people as righteous but on the inside you are full of hypocrisy and wickedness.

27–28 During the month of Adar, just before Passover, it was customary to whitewash with lime graves or grave-sites that might not be instantly identified as such (v.27), in order to warn pilgrims to steer clear of the area and avoid ritual uncleanness from contact with corpses (cf. M *Shekalim* 1:1; M *Kelim* 1:4; M *Moed Katan* 1:2; M *Masser Sheni* 5:1). Such uncleanness would prevent participation in the Passover (M *Kelim* 1:4; for similar concerns, cf. John 11:55; 18:28). But in that case whitewashed tombs would not have been objects of beauty ("which look beautiful on the outside") but of disgust: they were places to be shunned (cf. Luke 11:44, which mentions neither whitewash nor beauty).

Various solutions have been put forward (for a list, cf. S.T. Lachs, "On Matthew 23: 27–28," HTR 68 [1975]: 385–88). Perhaps the best proposal is Garland's (pp. 150–57), who suggests that the graves were beautiful because of their structure (cf. v.29), not their whitewash. Monuments were normally considered pure unless marked with whitewash; so if the memorial was built right over a grave, it would probably be whitewashed. Thus Jesus' mention of whitewashing has nothing to do with the beauty of sepulchers but is a further thrust at the Pharisees based on their distinctive preoccupation with avoiding defilement from corpses (cf. b *Baba Kamma* 57a; b *Baba Metzia* 85b). Jesus is saying that the scribes and Pharisees are sources of uncleanness just as much as the whitewashed graves are. There may also be an allusion to the white linen clothes that some men, impressed with their own eminence, used to wear (cf. b *Kiddushin* 72a; b *Shabbath* 25b; b *Nedarim* 20b; Jos. War II, 123 [viii.3]).

In the context of Matthew 23, the point Jesus is making is not that the scribes and Pharisees were deliberate and self-conscious hypocrites, but that in their scrupulous regulations they appeared magnificently virtuous but were actually contaminating the people. This woe parallels the second (v.15). The supreme irony is that their preoccupation with their law (*nomos*) left them steeped in *anomia*—a general term for "wickedness" (v.28; cf. 13:41; TDNT, 4:1085–86), but which may here suggest that their fundamental approach to the law was in fact, from the perspective of Jesus' hermeneutic, plain "lawlessness."

g) *Seventh woe*

23:29–32

> 29"Woe to you, teachers of the law and Pharisees, you hypocrites! You build tombs for the prophets and decorate the graves of the righteous. 30And you say, 'If we had lived in the days of our forefathers, we would not have taken part with them in shedding the blood of the prophets.' 31So you testify against yourselves that you are the descendants of those who murdered the prophets. 32Fill up, then, the measure of the sin of your forefathers!

29–30 Derrett (*NT Studies*, 2:68ff.) denies that Pharisees in Jesus' day would have been involved in building memorial tombs, but his evidence is late and may well represent reaction against earlier excesses (cf. Garland, p. 164). Herod led the way in tomb building (cf. Jos. Antiq. XVI, 179–82 [vii.1]; XVIII, 108 [iv.6]; XX, 95 [iv.3])—to atone for his attempts to plunder them! Jewish building was more likely to be commemorative; by erecting monuments the religious leaders thought themselves morally and spiritually above their forebears who had persecuted the prophets whose monuments they were building (v.29). They believed that they would not have joined their forebears in murdering the prophets (v.30)—just as many Christians today naively think they would have responded better to Jesus than the disciples or the crowds that cried, "Crucify him!"

31 But the distinction the Jews draw in v.30 Jesus now denies. Their own saying (not the tomb-building) testifies against them. They speak of their forefathers and so acknowledge themselves to be the sons (NIV, "descendants") of those who shed the blood of the prophets. But Jesus sees further irony here, based on the ambiguity of "fathers" and "sons" (see on 5:9). The Jews think in terms of their physical descent. Jesus responds by saying in effect that they are sons all right—more than they realize. They show their paternity by resembling their fathers. While piously claiming to be different, they are already plotting ways to put an end to Jesus (21:38–39, 46).

32 The conclusion is defiant and ironical. The idea behind "the measure of the sin" is that God can only tolerate so much sin; and then, when the measure is "full," he must respond in wrath (cf. Gen 15:16; 1 Thess 2:14–16). The idea is common in the intertestamental literature (e.g., Jub 14:16; 1 Enoch 50:2; 2 Esd 4:36–37; 4Q185 2: 9–10), but never before was the concept applied to Israel.

3) Conclusion

23:33–36

> [33]"You snakes! You brood of vipers! How will you escape being condemned to hell? [34]Therefore I am sending you prophets and wise men and teachers. Some of them you will kill and crucify; others you will flog in your synagogues and pursue from town to town. [35]And so upon you will come all the righteous blood that has been shed on earth, from the blood of righteous Abel to the blood of Zechariah son of Berekiah, whom you murdered between the temple and the altar. [36]I tell you the truth, all this will come upon this generation.

33 See on 3:7 and 12:34 for the epithets. The transition from the preceding verse is clear: if the teachers of the law and Pharisees are filling up the measure of the sin of their forefathers, how can they possibly escape the condemnation of hell (see on 5:22; 23:15)?

34 If this verse shares a common source (Q?) with Luke 11:49 (see above on 23:1–12), the differences between Matthew and Luke are noteworthy, though perhaps not quite so problematic as many think. The most noteworthy feature is the change from "the wisdom of God" (NIV, "God in his wisdom") as the sender of the emissaries to an emphatic "I." Not only is there little doubt that Christians identified Jesus with God's wisdom, but he who assigned to himself messianic titles and even OT texts referring exclusively to Yahweh would not have hesitated to make the same identification. Matthew's interpretation is therefore not necessarily wrong, even if a single saying stands behind both Luke and Matthew.

Hare (pp. 87–88) thinks the introductory *dia touto* ("Because of this," Luke 11:49; "Therefore," Matt 23:34) is drastically altered. In Luke it refers to 11:47–48—a tacit admission of blood-guiltiness for the prophets' death and for which reason "the wisdom of God" sends more prophets so that "this generation" (Luke 11:50) will be accountable. In Matthew, however, vv.32–33 separate the tacit admission from *dia touto* ("Therefore," v.34) so that the connective no longer explains God's wisdom in the past but an act Jesus performed in the present. But Hare's contrast is exaggerated. It is formally correct that *dia touto* in Luke 11:49 explains a statement made in the past by the wisdom of God. But that explains only that a statement was made, not the statement's content—which refers to an act done in the present, viz., Jesus' sending emissaries. Thus the two renderings of *dia touto* are very close and share the same function: they point out that because of the Jewish leaders' wicked reception of God's messengers, more messengers will "therefore" be sent; and they will be treated the same way. This will fill up the full measure of iniquity, and judgment will fall.

Luke (11:49) has "prophets and apostles," Matthew "prophets and wise men and teachers." The "wise man" and the "teacher" were "materially identical" (Garland, p. 175; TDNT, 8:505–7) at this time. Both Matthew and Luke here look forward to the sending out of Christian missionaries—disciples of Jesus (cf. 5:10–12; 9:37–38;

28:18–20). The terms used do not reflect post-A.D. 70 terminology (cf. van Tilborg, pp. 140f.).

Matthew adds "crucify." There is no evidence Jews used crucifixion as a mode of capital punishment after 63 B.C. "Crucify" may mean "cause to be crucified" (as in Acts 2:36; 4:10), surely a better possibility than Hare's suggestion (pp. 89–92) that the words "and crucify" are a gloss on what Matthew wrote. Garland (p. 177) holds that "and crucify" refers to Jesus' death. But this, too, requires a causative sense and seems strange when it is Jesus who is sending the emissaries to their deaths and Jesus who is (in this view) among those sent and killed. Perhaps v.34 echoes 10:24–25: the servant is not above his master. If Jesus is to be crucified, his servants may expect the same.

35 The very messengers who were beaten and killed for calling the people to repentance in the mystery of providence fill up the measure of the peoples' sin (v.32) —viz., shedding righteous blood of God's emissaries from Abel to Zechariah (cf. Notes). Verse 35 anticipates 27:24–25: Pilate tries to evade responsibility for crucifying Jesus, and the Jews clamor for that same dreadful responsibility because of their skepticism about who Jesus is. On the question of alleged anti-Semitism, see on 26:57–68.

36 All along in this chapter, the teachers of the law and the Pharisees have been Jesus' primary target. Now the reference is to "this generation," because the leaders represent the people (see on 21:43); and the people, despite Jesus' warnings, do not abandon their leaders for Jesus Messiah. This sets the stage for the concluding lament over Jerusalem (vv.37–39).

Notes

34 On flogging, see on 10:17; on persecution from city to city, cf. 10:23; Acts 9:2; 13:50–51; 14:4–7; 17:10–15. On indifference toward and harsh treatment of OT prophets, cf. 1 Kings 18:4, 13; 19:10, 14; 2 Kings 17:13–17; 1 Chron 16:22; 2 Chron 24:19; 36:14–16; Ps 105:15; Jer 7:25–26; 25:4; 26:5, 20–23; 29:19; 35:15; 44:4; Lam 2:20; 4:16.

35 Abel is the first victim of murder in the Scriptures (Gen 4:8); but the identity of this "Zechariah son of Berekiah" is problematic. Principal possibilities include:

1. It could refer to Zechariah the father of John the Baptist, but there is no evidence he was martyred.

2. It could be Zechariah son of Baris or Baruch or Bariscaeus (MSS vary), who was murdered by two Zealots in the temple (Jos. War IV, 334–44 [v.4]). But there is no evidence he was a prophet or a martyr; and, though he was killed ἐν μέσῳ (en mesō, "in the midst") of the temple precincts, it is unlikely he was killed between the actual sanctuary and the altar unless he was a priest; and there is no evidence for this.

3. It could be a reference to the OT prophet Zechariah son of Berekiah (Zech 1:1). But there is no account of his being killed.

4. It may be a Zechariah of whom we have no knowledge (Albright and Mann). This is possible but without proof.

5. Another possibility is Zechariah the son of Jehoiada (2 Chron 24:20–22). His murder took place in the courtyard of the temple and is related toward the end of what was probably the last book in the Hebrew canon. The sweep runs (to use Christian terms)

"from Genesis to Revelation." The problem is the patronymic. There is a possible solution. Just as Zechariah the prophet is alternately given his father's patronymic (Zech 1:1) or his grandfather's (Ezra 6:14), so it is possible Jehoiada was the grandfather (not father) of the Zechariah of 2 Chron 24—a suggestion that Jehoiada's living to be 130 years old (2 Chron 24:15) makes more plausible, since Zechariah's ministry immediately followed Jehoiada's death. An otherwise unknown Berekiah would therefore have had time to sire Zechariah, live to a good age, and die before the death of his own father gave him opportunity to serve as chief priest. That would allow time for a father named Berekiah. But we do not know. Substantive text-critical uncertainties in the relevant traditions (esp. LXX) complicate the problem. For literature and discussion, cf. Gundry, *Use of OT*, pp. 86–88; Garland, pp. 182–83.

---

f. Lament over Jerusalem

23:37–39

37"O Jerusalem, Jerusalem, you who kill the prophets and stone those sent to you, how often I have longed to gather your children together, as a hen gathers her chicks under her wings, but you were not willing. 38Look, your house is left to you desolate. 39For I tell you, you will not see me again until you say, 'Blessed is he who comes in the name of the Lord.' "

Almost exact verbal equivalence between these verses and Luke 13:34–35 makes it nearly certain that both Matthew and Luke are following the same written source (Q?) and therefore that at least one of the two evangelists displaced this prayer from its setting in the life of Jesus. Certainly the lament is more integral to the setting in Matthew than in Luke (cf. Suggs, pp. 64–66; Garland, pp. 187–97). Jesus undoubtedly lamented over the city on other occasions (Luke 19:41–44), and the broad compassion of his words is characteristic (Matt 9:35–38).

The effect of the lament is twofold. First, it tinges all the preceding woes with compassion (note the doubling of "Jerusalem" [cf. 2 Sam 18:33; 1 Kings 13:2; Jer 22:29; Luke 10:41; 22:31]). There is also a change of number from Jerusalem to people of Jerusalem: "you [sing.] who kill . . . sent to you [sing.] . . . your [sing.] children . . . your [pl.] house . . . you [pl.] will not see." The effect is to move from the abstraction of the city to the concrete reality of people. Jesus' woes in Matthew 23 therefore go far beyond personal frustrations: they are divine judgments that, though wrathful, never call in question the reality of divine love (see discussion on 5:44–45).

Second, the christological implications are unavoidable, for Jesus, whether identifying himself with God or with wisdom, claims to be the one who has longed to gather and protect this rebellious nation. Phrased in such terms, Jesus' longing can only belong to Israel's Savior, not to one of her prophets. The authenticity of the lament is frequently denied on the ground that the historical Jesus could not possibly have said it (e.g., Suggs, p. 66). But it is a strange criticism that a priori obliterates any possibility of listening to the text in such a way as to hear a historical Jesus who was not only conscious of his transcendent origins but who in many ways laid claims to his origins as part of his compassionate and redemptive self-disclosure.

37 Verses 37–39 preserve Jesus' last recorded public words to Israel. Jerusalem, the city of David, the city where God revealed himself in his temple, had become known as the city that killed the prophets and stoned those sent to her. Stoning to death, prescribed in the law of Moses for idolatry (Deut 17:5, 7), sorcery (Lev 20:27), and several other crimes, is also laid down in the Mishnah (M *Sanhedrin* 7:4) for false prophets. It could also be the outcome of mob violence (21:35; Acts 7:57–58) or conspiracy, which apparently is how Zechariah died (2 Chron 24:21). "How often" may look back over Israel's history—viz., Jesus' identifying himself with God's transcendent, historical perspective (John 8:58); but more probably "how often" refers to the duration of Jesus' ministry. During it he "often" longed to gather and shelter Jerusalem (by metonymy including all Jews) as a hen her chicks (cf. Deut 32:11; Pss 17:8; 36:7; 91:4; Jer 48:40); for despite the woes, Jesus, like the "Sovereign LORD" in Ezekiel 18:32, took "no pleasure in the death of anyone."

38 This verse may allude to both Jeremiah 12:7 and 22:5 (cf. Notes). "Your house" in this context could refer to Jerusalem, since the lament is first addressed to her (Klostermann; McNeile; Trilling [p. 86]), to Israel (Schniewind; Green; cf. Gal 4:25–26 for a similar use of "Jerusalem"), or to the temple in whose precincts Jesus was preaching (21:23; 24:1) and whose destruction was about to be predicted (24:2; cf. Manson [*Sayings*, p. 127]; Davies [*Setting*, p. 298]). There seems to be no need to choose only one of these options; all three are closely allied and rise and fall together. If "desolate" (*erēmos*) is not part of the text (cf. Notes), the verse means "your house is abandoned to the consequences of your misdeeds" (Plummer). More probably *erēmos* is original and makes the implied destruction explicit. Your "house" is left to you (i.e., abandoned), whether by God (as in Jer 12:7) or Jesus (cf. 24:1), who is "Immanuel," "God with us" (1:23; cf. Garland, pp. 202–3). The verb "left" (*aphietai*) can mean "abandoned to enemies," not just "abandoned." But since the ideas are related, a choice is unnecessary.

39 E. Haenchen ("Matthäus 23," *Zeitschrift für Katholische Theologie* 48 [1951]: 56) holds that in vv.33–36 "Wisdom" (cf. Luke 11:49) looks *forward* prophetically to sending the prophets but in vv.37–39 looks *back* on the sending of prophets. The latter passage must therefore be anachronistic. But the temporal relation between the two passages is not so sharp. If vv.33–36 look forward to the sending of the prophets, they also speak of judgment on "this generation." If vv.37–39 look backward on prophets already killed, the reference is to the way Jerusalem has acted in the *past* (v.37), a past that is even now bringing judgment (v.38), and that looks *forward* to future consummation (v.39).

The quotation is from Psalm 118:26 (also in 21:9; cf. 21:42 for another quotation from this psalm). The words may have been used by the priests in greeting the worshipers at the temple. Jesus, too, the true locus of Israel, must come, victorious and exalted, and receive greetings and homage from the religious authorities (cf. France, *Jesus*, pp. 58f.). Because of its location in Luke, "until" could refer to Palm Sunday, when people cried such words (Luke 19:38; cf. Matt 21:9); but as Marshall (*Luke*, pp. 576–77) points out, if Palm Sunday is in view in Luke, the cries of the people are but an ironic fulfillment that still looks forward to the consummation.

What Matthew refers to is perfectly clear. The Greek literally translated reads, "You will not see me from now [*ap'arti*] until you say"; and *ap'arti* is tied to the consummation (cf. 26:29, 64). Thus v.39 looks, not to Jesus' resurrection appearances, but to his parousia. When he returns, all will acknowledge him. The context strongly implies that the Parousia spells judgment (cf. 24:30–31; Phil 2:9–11; Rev 1:7); but the quotation of Psalm 118 keeps open the way Jesus will be received—as consuming Judge or welcomed King (cf. Benoit; Schlatter; Goulder, pp. 429–30; Bonnard; contra Garland, pp. 207–9 and the literature there cited). But whatever the outcome, the immediate prospect is disaster: "for I tell you, you will not see me, etc."; i.e., the proof that judgment is imminent is that Jesus turns away and will not be seen again till the End.

So Jesus leaves the temple and goes away (24:1); and his words, which have dealt with judgment on Israel and with the consummation, evoke his disciples' two-pronged question (24:3) and lead to the Olivet Discourse (chs. 24–25).

Notes

38 If ἔρημος (erēmos, "desolate") be omitted, as in B L [1184] it[ff2] et al., the allusion is to Jer 12:7 alone; if included, there may also be an allusion to Jer 22:5 (cf. Gundry, *Use of OT*, p. 88). WH, relying too heavily on B, omit it; but the external evidence is strong for inclusion in Matthew, even if omission in Luke—where the evidence is much weaker and principally Western—is more likely (cf. Garland, pp. 200–201, n. 120). The presence of the word makes the judgment theme slightly more emphatic.

B. *Fifth Discourse: The Olivet Discourse*

24:1–25:46

Few chapters of the Bible have called forth more disagreement among interpreters than Matthew 24 and its parallels in Mark 13 and Luke 21. The history of the interpretation of this chapter is immensely complex. G.R. Beasley-Murray's *Jesus and the Future* (London: Macmillan, 1954) is an admirable guide for works up to 1954; and David Wenham's "Recent Study of Mark 13" (*TSF Bulletin* 71 [Spring, 1975]: 6–15; 72 [Summer, 1975]: 1–9) succinctly summarizes and critiques several more recent works up to 1975, including A.L. Moore, *The Parousia in the New Testament* (Leiden: Brill, 1966); Lars Hartman, *Prophecy Interpreted: The Function of Some Jewish Apocalyptic Texts and of the Eschatological Discourse, Mark 13 Par.* (Lund: CWK Gleerup, 1966); J. Lambrecht, *Die Redaktion der Markus-Apokalypse: Literarische Analyse und Strukturuntersuchung* (Rome: PBI, 1967); R. Pesch, *Naherwartungen: Tradition und Redaktion in Markus 13* (Dusseldorf: Patmos, 1968); Gaston; and France (*Jesus*). In addition, there are major commentaries on each of the synoptic Gospels, as well as several important articles on these chapters, and some popular works on eschatology, not a few of them by conservatives (cf. the bibliography in Hoekema). Some of the difficulties and exegetical turning points must be cursorily introduced:

1. The literary nature of chapters 24–25 and of the parallels in Mark and Luke has occupied much scholarly attention. For a century or two before and after Jesus, writings now described as "apocalyptic literature" flourished in Jewish and Christian circles. At best the label is not precise, and the genre's various forms tend to fray around the edges. G.E. Ladd ("Why Not Prophetic-Apocalyptic?" JBL 76 [1957]:

192–200) has wisely suggested that the NT apocalypses, especially this chapter and most of Revelation, read like a merging of apocalyptic and prophetic literature. The symbolism is not so sharp as in works indisputably apocalyptic, and the "above–below" dualism typical of apocalyptic is here rather muted. Other features of this discourse are often noted, especially the frequent imperatives, whether in the second person ("Watch out that no one deceives you," v.4; "See to it that you are not alarmed," v.6) or the third person ("Let no one in the field go back," v.18).

2. As for the sources, first there is the question of whether the synoptists have simply put together a pastiche of Jesus' sayings (some of which may represent an "Olivet Discourse"), mingled with other traditions, or have selected and shaped material deriving from a single historical utterance. They undoubtedly give the latter impression. Matthew, with his framing formulas (see on 5:1–2; 7:28–29), is especially clear about this. Though this view is a minority one, nevertheless it can be strenuously argued that each evangelist felt his report of the discourse to be coherent. And if this is so, it seems too much to postulate, on the basis of disputable conceptual and grammatical discrepancies, unambiguous sources stemming from various traditions.

Second, the relation among the three synoptic accounts is still disputed. Some have argued that Luke 21 is sufficiently distinctive to spring from a separate tradition. Touching on both these questions, David Wenham, in some unpublished papers soon to appear in book form, argues for a source-critical solution, not only tying together all the synoptic Gospel records of this discourse, but also uniting them into a single comprehensive record. While Wenham's reconstruction is far from certain, the fact that he is able to develop his view so rigorously shows the dangers of the facile historical and literary disjunctions of which many critics are so fond.

Third, the Olivet Discourse is studded with OT quotations and allusions that add to the complexity.

Fourth, the discourse itself is undoubtedly a source for the Thessalonian Epistles (cf. G. Henry Waterman, "The Sources of Paul's Teaching on the 2nd Coming of Christ in 1 and 2 Thessalonians," JETS 18 [1975]: 105–13; David Wenham, "Paul and the Synoptic Apocalypse," France and Wenham, 2:345–75) and Revelation (cf. Gregory Kimball Beale, "The Use of Daniel in Jewish Apocalyptic Literature and in the Revelation of St. John [Ph.D. diss., Cambridge University, 1980], pp. 260–64, and the literature cited there). If so, then we may say that Jesus himself sets the pattern for the church's eschatology.

3. This last statement presupposes, of course, the authenticity of the discourse material in the Gospels. However, this is frequently denied on the grounds that the "prophecy" of the Fall of Jerusalem must in reality be *ex eventu*, based on the event itself. This will not do because, apart from antisupernatural presuppositions, Reicke ("Synoptic Prophecies") has shown the language in the Olivet Discourse prophesying the Fall of Jerusalem to be largely in OT categories. Not only is it general, it does not describe any detail peculiar to the known history of the Jewish War (A.D. 66–73). Reicke goes so far as to conclude that the Olivet Discourse as found in any of the Synoptics *could not* have been composed after A.D. 70, and that therefore the Synoptics themselves have earlier dates (cf. Introduction, section 6).

4. Numerous details in the text are much disputed and hard to understand: the meaning of "the abomination that causes desolation" (24:15), the significance of "let the reader understand" (v.15), whether the "coming of the Son of Man" (vv.27, 30) refers to his return at the consummation or to something else (the Resurrection,

Pentecost, the Fall of Jerusalem, and the growth of the church have all been suggested), the extent of "this generation" (v.34). The ideal solution is the one that treats all of these in the most natural way possible.

5. A disputed term, not in the text but in the forefront of interpretive theory, is "imminent," which has two related but distinct problems. One concerns the expectations of the historical Jesus and is linked to the way the various parts of the discourse relate to one another and to v.34: "I tell you the truth, this generation will certainly not pass away until all these things have happened." How "imminent" did Jesus think the coming of the Son of Man was? (See below, under 6.)

The other problem concerns the meaning of the word "imminent" itself as used in theological—especially evangelical—discussion. A dictionary defines it as "impending": as applied to Christ's return, an "imminent return of Christ" would then mean Christ's return was near, impending. Hardly anyone uses "imminent" that way but understands it in a specialized, theological sense to mean "at any time": "the imminent return of Christ" then means Christ may return at any time. But the evangelical writers who use the word divide on whether "imminent" in the sense of "at any time" should be pressed to mean "at any second" or something looser such as "at any period" or "in any generation."

Resolution turns on two issues. First, how are the various "signs" presaging Christ's return to be related to an "imminent" return? The classic dispensational response is to postulate two returns (or, as they hold, one return in two stages): one before any of the "signs" appear, a "Rapture" that removes the church alone and which could take place at any second; the other after the signs appear, a return that consummates history as we know it. Most will agree that no passage in the Bible unambiguously teaches a two-stage return. The theory is in the best sense a theological harmonization—certainly not a wrong approach in itself—of disparate texts.

Other theories clamor for attention, including that of J. Barton Payne (*The Imminent Appearing of Christ* [Grand Rapids: Eerdmans, 1962]), who proposes that, with the events of A.D. 70 now behind us, all the remaining "signs" are so general that they may be "fulfilled" in any generation. Distinctions regarding "imminency" therefore become moot. Other theories are not lacking. Unfortunately the meaning of "imminent" is so comprehensive a question that each theory is in fact an entire eschatological scheme, complete with detailed exegesis and sweeping synthesis. While the approach of this commentary is inductive and limited primarily to the text of Matthew, some implications for the debate will be spelled out in due course.

Second, on what is the "any second" view of imminency based and how well does it withstand close scrutiny? The truth is that the biblical evidence nowhere unambiguously endorses the "any second" view and frequently militates against it, as R.H. Gundry (*The Church and the Tribulation* [Grand Rapids: Zondervan, 1973], esp. pp. 29ff.) has demonstrated. Not only do all the relevant NT verbs for "looking forward to" or "expecting" or "waiting for" have a semantic range including necessary delay, but many NT passages also implicitly rule out an "any second" imminency (24:45–51 [see below]; 25:5, 19; Luke 19:11–27; John 21:18–19 [cf. 2 Peter 1:14]; Acts 9:15; 22:21; 23:11; 27:24). Yet the terms "imminent" and "imminency" retain theological usefulness if they focus attention on the eager expectancy of the Lord's return characteristic of many NT passages, a return that could take place soon, i.e., within a fairly brief period of time, without specifying that the period must be one second or less! This is not so rigid as the "any second" view, and it more fairly represents the exegetical evidence.

6. But the most difficult interpretive questions concern the structure of the discourse—how the parts relate to each other, to the initial questions of the disciples, and to the whole. On the face of it, the disciples' questions and the tenor of the discourse argue that Jesus is dealing with at least two issues—the Fall of Jerusalem and the return of the Son of Man. But these two issues appear to be so tightly intertwined that it is impossible to separate them, and therefore Jesus or Matthew wrongly (as it turned out) tied them together.

Many modern scholars adopt this view, and it has recently been given a new twist by Desmond Ford (*The Abomination of Desolation in Biblical Eschatology* [Washington, D.C.: University Press of America, 1979], p. 76). He argues that Jesus meant to say that the Parousia would immediately succeed the Fall of Jerusalem, all within the generation of his hearers, but that this was in reality a contingent promise, like Jonah's "Forty more days and Nineveh will be destroyed" (Jonah 3:4). Hence "it is possible that he [Jesus] believed that if the early church proved faithful to its missionary commission, and if the chastened Jewish nation repented, the end would transpire in the same Age."

But the parallel with Jonah is not very close, if only because the Parousia is invariably treated in the NT as qualitatively unlike all other divine visitations. It alone marks the end of history, the final outpouring of judgment and blessing, and thus is not an event that can be postponed. More important, v.22 seems to say that God will hasten the consummation, not postpone it; for the days of tribulation are shortened. And nowhere in the NT is there any clear suggestion that the delay of the Parousia was the result of the church's sin (2 Peter 3:12 is not a genuine exception). Yet Ford's view highlights the problem of the relation between the Fall of Jerusalem and the Parousia.

At the risk of oversimplification, we may lump together some other major interpretations of the Olivet Discourse according to their treatment of this problem.

a. In 1864, T. Colani published his "little apocalypse" theory. According to him the historical Jesus exhibited no interest in any future kingdom: as far as Jesus was concerned, the kingdom was exclusively present. The genesis of Mark 13 and parallels therefore must be accounted for as a tract by first-century Jewish Christians facing persecution just before A.D. 70. The answer of the historical Jesus to the disciples' questions was simply Mark 13:32 (Matt 24:36). Few follow Colani now, though some have tried to find in the Olivet Discourse not one "little apocalypse" but a number of different sources. Taken together, such theories follow a unifying method: the material in the discourse is assumed to be so disparate that it can only be accounted for by appealing to distinct sources not very well integrated by the evangelist-redactor. But too many details in the various theories seem unconvincing and fail to deal adequately with how each synoptist thought of the material he was editing. If he detected some unity, it must be found; and if found, then what methodological principle distinguishes between the unity imposed by a synoptist–redactor and a unity latent in a discourse delivered by Jesus? Indeed, one could make an a priori case for the apparent textual discrepancies based, not on the synoptist's failure to integrate separate sources, but on its condensed and selective reporting of much longer unified material in terms understandable to the first readers but more susceptible to misunderstanding today.

b. Among commentators who find comprehensive theological cohesion in the Olivet Discourse, the most common approach—and that of most evangelicals today —is exemplified by Broadus and Lane (*Mark*). Broadus holds that vv.15–21, 34 foretell the destruction of Jerusalem, and at least vv.29–31 foretell the Lord's return; but "every attempt to assign a definite point of division between the two topics has proved a failure." If Christ's return is placed between v.28 and v.29, then v.34 is difficult; if after v.34, v.36, or v.42, how are we to interpret vv.30–31, 36? The solution is that the two are purposely intertwined, perhaps under some kind of "prophetic foreshortening." The near event, the destruction of Jerusalem, serves as a symbol for the far event. (In addition to the commentaries, cf. also Hoekema; Ridderbos, *Kingdom*, pp. 477–510.) This approach is possible but has two weaknesses. It has to skate gingerly around the *time* references in the discourse (e.g., "immediately after those days," v.29; "this generation," v.34), and it leads some of its adherents to the view that on the *timing* of the Parousia Jesus was in error (e.g., Beasley-Murray). Verse 36 is scarcely sufficient to support all this, since it is one thing to admit ignorance and another to be quite mistaken.

c. A number of scholars have denied that any part of the Olivet Discourse deals with the Fall of Jerusalem: all of it concerns the Parousia. One form or another of this theory is held by Lagrange, Schlatter, Schniewind, and Zahn. Lagrange thinks the "abomination of desolation" deals with Jerusalem but not the "great distress" (v.21). Almost all who hold this view are forced to say that Luke 21:20–24, which is unavoidably historical, stems from another discourse or has been consciously modified by Luke. The latter suggestion seems a desperate expedient in support of a weak theory. It is very difficult to imagine that a Christian reader of any of the Synoptics at any period during the first one hundred years of the existence of these documents would fail to see a reference to the destruction of Jerusalem. Methodologically this approach belongs with those who flatten the discourse in other ways —e.g., by claiming that it represents a continuous account of Christian history.

d. An older view (e.g., Alexander), now again popular (Tasker; J.M. Kik, *Matthew Twenty-Four* [Swengel: Bible Truth Depot, 1948]) and newly given exegetical support (France, *Jesus*, pp. 231ff.), holds that the Fall of Jerusalem is in view in the discourse till the end of v.35. Only with the opening of v.36 does the second advent come into view. This interpretation has the advantage of being neat: there is a clear division between the two parts of the discourse and eliminates flipping back and forth or appealing to "prophetic foreshortening" or the like. Its proponents point out that this interpretation answers both questions put by the disciples. The first, concerning the destruction of Jerusalem and its temple, elicits the anticipation of an answer in v.15 ("When you see . . .") but finds an explicit answer only in vv.29–31. The verses before v.29 tell of great anguish *preceding* the events of A.D. 70. But unless vv.29–35 deal with the Fall of Jerusalem itself, it is held, the disciples' first question is never satisfactorily answered.

If someone objects that vv.29–35 more naturally read as a prophecy foretelling the Second Advent than the destruction of Jerusalem, this, we are told, would not be so obvious to the first readers. The celestial disturbances (v.29) are figurative, symbolic of political and national disasters (as in Isa 13:10; 34:4). The coming of the Son of Man in glory and power (v.30) is not Jesus' return to earth but, as in Daniel 7, a heavenly coming for vindication, a reference either to Jesus' vindication after the Resurrection or to the Fall of Jerusalem itself (26:64 is then commonly interpreted the same way). The sending of the "angels" is the commissioning of "messengers" or "missionaries" to gather the elect in the church (v.31); for despite the Lord's judgment on the Jews, the gathering in of the elect continues through the preaching of the gospel.

Casey (pp. 172ff.) has raised some criticisms, a few of them cogent. Detailed rebuttal is impossible, but the following difficulties in this interpretation must be faced.

1) Even if v.15 speaks only of the beginning of the Jerusalem distress (and this is debated), if France's view is right, it is hard to explain how vv.21–22 could describe the mere preliminaries to Jerusalem's fall. Verse 22 speaks of those days being cut short: surely this does not mean the preliminaries to the Fall of Jerusalem were cut short for the elect's sake, for that would entail the conclusion that the fall itself was a mercy on the elect.

2) Although vv.14–22 do not explicitly mention the Fall of Jerusalem, the same can be said with even greater vigor of vv.29–35. Similarly, if vv.29–35 do not mention the coming of the Son of Man *to the earth*, the same can be said of 1 Thessalonians 4:16, where in my opinion that is implied. In any case there may be other reasons for Jesus' not mentioning the Fall of Jerusalem explicitly in vv.15–22. The cryptic "let the reader understand" (v.15) may be thought hint enough of the true import of Jesus' reference to Daniel's "abomination that causes desolation"; or it may even be that the synoptists thought the Jerusalem reference obvious. Apparently Luke thought so (cf. Luke 21:20–24; and comments on v.15, below).

3) Although there can be no objection to coming-of-the-Son-of-Man language occasionally referring to something other than the Parousia (see on 10:23; 16:28), yet when that occurs the interpretive problems are invariably notoriously complex. This is because the *regular* way of taking this expression and related language is as a reference to the Parousia. Compare closely 13:40–41; 16:27; 25:31; 1 Corinthians 11:26; 15:52; 16:22; 1 Thessalonians 4:14–17; 2 Thessalonians 1:7; 2:1–8; 2 Peter 3:10–12; Revelation 1:7 (cf. *Didache* 16). Here are references to the Son of Man's coming, angels gathering the elect, trumpet call, clouds, glory, tribes of the earth mourning, celestial disturbances—all unambiguously related to the Second Advent. It seems very doubtful, to say the least, that the natural way to understand vv.29–35 is as a reference to the Fall of Jerusalem.

4) This approach to vv.29–35 is psychologically unconvincing for two reasons. First, it demands a close connection between the Fall of Jerusalem and the Gentile mission (v.31), when in fact the Gentile mission had been prospering, first informally and then formally, for several decades. The fall of the temple doubtless helped support Christian theology about Jesus as the true sacrifice, priest, and temple; but it did not clearly motivate Gentile mission per se. Why, then, should the link be tendered here, almost as the climax of the pericope? Second, even on the basis of the interpretation under review, Christians saw the destruction of Jerusalem as a terrible thing and the onslaught by the pagan Romans as an abomination. If they also saw it as Jesus' vindication and as judgment on the Jewish nation, that is comprehensible enough; but could they see it as fulfillment of Daniel 7? Daniel 7 portrays something glorious and wonderful, the end of the pagan emperor's reign; but A.D. 70 marks success by the pagan emperor. Even if one supposes that the Synoptics are operating under a reverse typology—the OT pagans being now equated with the Jews—is it psychologically convincing to hold that antipathy between Jews and Christians was running so high that the latter could be told the sack of Jerusalem was their "redemption" (Luke 21:28)?

5) The interpretation France (*Jesus*, pp. 236–38) offers of v.30, though plausible, is not convincing. He says that all the (Jewish) *tribes* of the land (*gē;* NIV, "earth"; see on 5:5) shall mourn. The word "tribe" (*phylē;* NIV, "nation"), used with cer-

tainty of Gentiles elsewhere in the NT only in Revelation, is not determinative (Rev 1:7; 5:9; 7:9; 11:9; 13:7; 14:6), though it must be admitted that all the other NT references either refer to a specific Jewish tribe or make a specifically Jewish connection unambiguous. More importantly, however, v.30 contains an allusion to Zechariah 12:10–12; and other similar NT use of this passage supports the view that the verse refers to the Parousia. This appears to be sufficient evidence to set against the ambiguous meaning of *phylē* proposed by France.

6) There are already hints, early in the discourse (esp. in Matt), that the reader is to bear in mind that there are at least two topics under discussion, not one: the Fall of Jerusalem and the Second Advent (cf. vv.3, 5, 14, 23–27). Thus, since the reader is already primed to expect mention of the Second Advent, it would be difficult for him to take vv.29–31 in any other way.

e. A strong minority of evangelicals adopts one form or another of the dispensationalist interpretation of the discourse (S.E. English; A.C. Gaebelein; Walvoord; cf. John F. Walvoord, "Christ's Olivet Discourse on the End of the Age," BS 128 [1971]: 109–16; 129 [1972]: 20–32, 99–105, 206–10, 307–15). Perhaps the most common view along these lines takes vv.36–40 to refer to a secret "Rapture" of the church, which could take place at any second, and vv.4–28 (or 15–28) to refer to the Great Tribulation, lasting seven years and culminating in the Second Advent (vv. 29–35). Walvoord adds refinements. He holds that v.2 refers to the destruction at A.D. 70. The disciples' question of v.3 is in *three* parts, the first of which, dealing with the Fall of Jerusalem, Jesus does not answer.

At this point there is a curious intersection of views with writers like Hare (pp. 177–79), who argues that Matthew, writing after the events of A.D. 70, eliminates all reference to the destruction of Jerusalem and "eschatologizes" even vv.15–28, and so does not answer the disciples' first question. Under Hare's view of Matthew's editorial activity, the strange thing is that Matthew retains that first question. The entire discourse, in Walvoord's view, deals with the general characteristics of the age (vv.4–14), the Great Tribulation (vv.15–25), and the Second Advent (vv.26–31), because the "Rapture" is not revealed till Paul. Thus "taken" in vv.40–41 means "taken in judgment." "This generation" (v.34) Walvoord takes to mean either "this race" or something like "the generation that is alive when the great tribulation starts."

This interpretation is difficult to discuss adequately without delving into dispensationalism, including its "parenthesis" view of the church, something beyond the range of this commentary. If dispensationalism were unambiguously defined elsewhere in Scripture, then the least to be said for its interpretation of chapter 24 is that it is self-consistent and makes sense of the time indicators (e.g., "Immediately after the distress of those days," v.29, etc.). Even then, however, this interpretation faces several difficulties, one or two of them well-nigh insuperable.

1) It is forced to adopt a possible but extraordinarily unlikely meaning for "this generation" (v.34; see below).

2) It rests heavily on Matthew's report of the Olivet Discourse and makes less sense of the parallels in Mark and Luke. One of many examples of problems it involves is Matthew's recording the disciples' question differently from Mark and Luke; and Walvoord's interpretation of the discourse depends almost entirely on Matthew. Even if through harmonizing Walvoord can show that v.3 best preserves the tripartite nature of the disciples' historical question, one must still ask why Mark and Luke have it as they do. If the discourse as they present it can only be ade-

quately explained by reference to the disciples' question as Matthew preserves it, then Mark and Luke cannot be intelligently read without referring to Matthew.

3) Much dispensationalism, especially the older kind, holds that the "Rapture" is not mentioned in this chapter and justifies this view on the ground that Jesus is not talking to the church but to Jews. Dispensationalists use this disjunction to justify a number of theological points, but they are insensitive to historical realities. Even after Pentecost the earliest church was entirely Jewish. Here, before the Passion, Jesus is not addressing the church, in its post-Pentecost sense; but he *is* addressing, not his Jewish opponents, but his Jewish disciples who will constitute the church. Rigid application of this doubtful disjunction between Jews and church likewise banishes the church from the Sermon on the Mount; but it fails to observe that 18:15–20, dealing with the church, is also addressed, before the Passion, to Jewish disciples.

4) Granted the dispensational interpretation, Jesus' answer must have not only been opaque to his auditors but almost deceptive. Their first question concerns Jerusalem's judgment. But since a substantial part of Jesus' answer is couched in terms dealing with Jerusalem's destruction, how could the disciples think Jesus was *not* answering their question but describing a *second* destruction of the city, unless Jesus explicitly disavowed their understanding? But he does nothing of the kind. So perhaps it is not surprising that the dispensational identification of vv.15–28 *exclusively* with the Great Tribulation after the Rapture of the church, whether revealed or unrevealed, finds no exponent till the nineteenth century. The dispensational approach to the Olivet Discourse must be judged historically implausible in reference to both the history of Jesus and the history of interpretation.

f. The view of Matthew 24 this commentary advocates finds clear breaks in the Olivet Discourse, thus differing from the second option, but deals with the location and significance of these breaks in a novel way. David Wenham and the writer, to our mutual surprise, came to independent but similar conclusions about the Olivet Discourse. Sustained discussion has benefited us both and enabled us to develop the original ideas with the result that I cannot say exactly what each of us contributed to the thinking of the other. Wenham will doubtless publish his own view of the discourse. But here I acknowledge indebtedness to him.

In my understanding of the Olivet Discourse, the *disciples* think of Jerusalem's destruction and the eschatological end as a single complex web of events. This accounts for the form of their questions. Jesus warns that there will be delay *before* the End—a delay characterized by persecution and tribulation for his followers (vv.4–28), but with one particularly violent display of judgment in the Fall of Jerusalem (vv.15–21; Mark 13:14–20; Luke 21:20–24). Immediately after the days of that sustained persecution characterizing the interadvent period comes the Second Advent (vv.29–31; cf. Guthrie, *NT Theology*, pp. 795–96). The warning in vv.32–35 describes the whole tribulation period, from the Ascension to the Second Advent. The tribulation period will certainly come, and the generation to which Jesus is speaking will experience all its features that point to the Lord's return. But the exact time of that return no one but the Father knows (vv.36–44). This structure works out in all three Synoptics (though with significant differences in emphasis), and the main themes developed have important ties with other NT books. The disciples' questions are answered, and the reader is exhorted to look forward to the Lord's return and meanwhile to live responsibly, faithfully, compassionately, and courageously while the Master is away (24:45–25:46).

1. *Setting*

24:1-3

> [1]Jesus left the temple and was walking away when his disciples came up to him to call his attention to its buildings. [2]"Do you see all these things?" he asked. "I tell you the truth, not one stone here will be left on another; every one will be thrown down."
>
> [3]As Jesus was sitting on the Mount of Olives, the disciples came to him privately. "Tell us," they said, "when will this happen, and what will be the sign of your coming and of the end of the age?"

Unlike Mark (12:41–44) and Luke (21:1–4), Matthew omits the story of the widow's offering, thus linking the Olivet Discourse more closely to the "woes" in chapter 23. This does not mean that chapters 24–25 continue a single discourse—the setting, audience, and principal themes all change. But Matthew does tie the prediction of desolation (23:37–39) to the destruction of the temple (24:1–2; for discussion, cf. Hummel, pp. 85–86; J. Lambrecht, "The Parousia Discourse," in Didier, pp. 314–18).

1 Jesus' departure from the *hieron* ("temple complex") may be symbolic (see on 23:39). It also gives the disciples a chance to call Jesus' attention to its various structures. In Mark and Luke the disciples call Jesus' attention to the beauty of the temple buildings and the great stones on which it rests (cf. Jos. Antiq. XV, 391–402 [xi.3]; Wars V, 184–226 [v.1–6]; Tacitus *Histories* 5.8.12). Whether or not the disciples thought they were speaking piously, they show that they have underestimated or even misunderstood the force of Jesus' denunciations in chapter 23 and Luke 11. They still focus on the temple, on which Jesus has pronounced doom, since the true center of the relation between God and man has shifted to himself. In chapter 23 Jesus has already insisted that what Israel does with him, not the temple, determines the fate of the temple and of Israel nationally.

2 Because *tauta panta* ("all these things") is neuter and "buildings" (v.1) feminine, some have suggested that Jesus' question refers, not to the buildings, but to the discourse in chapter 23, especially v.36, and should be rendered "You do understand [metaphorically 'see'] these things, don't you?"—the positive answer being suggested by the presence of the particle *ou* ("not," untr. in NIV). This may be oversubtle: the Greek demonstrative pronoun may have an irregular antecedent for various reasons (RHG, p. 704). Moreover, the particle *ou*, anticipating a positive response, detracts from this novel interpretation; for if Jesus thinks his disciples have understood, why then does he go on immediately to answer their question unequivocally? But if the sentence is taken in the usual way (NIV), then the expectation of a positive response is most natural: of course the disciples see the buildings! (Moule is nevertheless right in saying that English idiom prefers an open question here; cf. *Idiom Book*, p. 159.)

Jesus' forecast of the destruction of the temple complex is unambiguous, cast in OT language (cf. Jer 26:6, 18; Mic 3:12) and repeated variously elsewhere (23:38; 26:61; Luke 23:28–31).

3 The Mount of Olives (see on 21:1, 17) is an appropriate site for a discourse dealing with the Parousia (cf. Zech 14:4). Mark specifies that Peter, James, John, and Andrew (the first four in Matt 10:2) asked the question privately. Whether this means that they were the only disciples present or that they were the ones who raised the question is uncertain, since "privately" in both Matthew and Mark sets the disciples apart from the crowds, not some disciples from others. The form of the question varies from Gospel to Gospel, with Matthew showing the greatest independence. Yet if we make the reasonable assumption that in the disciples' mind their question as to the temple's destruction and the signs that will presage it are linked to the end of the age and Jesus' return (cf. 16:27–28; 23:39; Luke 19:11–27), there is little problem. Matthew makes explicit what was implicit and what Jesus recognized as implicit in their question.

"The end of the age" is used six times in the NT (13:39, 40, 49; 24:3; 28:20; Heb 9:26), five of which are in Matthew and look to final judgment and the consummation of all things. (Hebrews 9:26 sees the Cross as introducing the coming age and thereby marking out "the end of the ages" [NIV].) *Parousia* ("coming") is found twenty-four times in the NT, four of which are in Matthew 24 (3, 27, 37, 39). The term can refer to "presence," "arrival," or "coming"—the first stage of "presence"—and need not have eschatological overtones (2 Cor 7:6; 10:10). Yet *parousia* is closely tied with Jesus' glorious "appearing" or "coming" at the end of human history. (For views of its relation to NT eschatology, cf. Turner, *Christian Words*, pp. 404–8; DNTT, 2:898–935.)

2. The birth pains (24:4–28)

a. General description of the birth pains

24:4–14

> [4]Jesus answered: "Watch out that no one deceives you. [5]For many will come in my name, claiming, 'I am the Christ,' and will deceive many. [6]You will hear of wars and rumors of wars, but see to it that you are not alarmed. Such things must happen, but the end is still to come. [7]Nation will rise against nation, and kingdom against kingdom. There will be famines and earthquakes in various places. [8]All these are the beginning of birth pains.
>
> [9]"Then you will be handed over to be persecuted and put to death, and you will be hated by all nations because of me. [10]At that time many will turn away from the faith and will betray and hate each other, [11]and many false prophets will appear and deceive many people. [12]Because of the increase of wickedness, the love of most will grow cold, [13]but he who stands firm to the end will be saved. [14]And this gospel of the kingdom will be preached in the whole world as a testimony to all nations, and then the end will come.

Alexander goes too far in saying that Jesus' purpose in these verses "is not to tell what are but what are not the premonitions of the great catastrophe to which he refers." Instead, all things (vv.5–7) are signs that Jesus is coming back, and they all will be manifest before the generation Jesus was addressing had died. But though these things show that the End is near, none of them stipulates how near; and the tenor of the warning is that the delay will be substantial and that during this period Jesus' disciples must not be deceived by false messiahs.

4–5 One of the greatest temptations in times of difficulty is to follow blindly any self-proclaimed savior who promises help. It is the temptation to repose confidence (v.4) in false Christs. Those who "come in my name" (v.5) may refer to those who come as Jesus' representatives; but because of the words that follow, we must assume that their claim goes farther. They claim to be Messiah, Christ himself. They come "in his name," as if they were he. Would-be deliverers have appeared in every age, not least the first century (Acts 5:36; Jos. Antiq. XX, 97–99 [v.1], 160–72 [viii.5–6], 188 [viii.10]; Wars II, 259 [xiii.5], 433–56 [xvii.8–10]; VI, 285–87 [v.2]). That this governs vv.4–28 is made clear by the second half of the literary inclusion (vv.26–28) that brackets the section. (On Mark's parallel "I am he," see Lane, *Mark*, p. 457, n. 43.)

6–8 "Birth pains" (v.8) in this context (elsewhere in the NT in Acts 2:24 ["agony"]; 1 Thess 5:3) stems from such OT passages as Isaiah 13:8; 26:17; Jeremiah 4:31; 6:24; Micah 4:9–10. By this time it was almost a special term for "the birthpangs of the Messiah," the period of distress preceding the Messianic Age (cf. SBK, 1:905; 4:977 –78; TDNT, 9:667–74; cf. 2 Baruch 27:1–30:1; b *Shabbath* 118a; b *Sanhedrin* 98b). But the "wars and rumors of war, . . . famines and earthquakes" (vv.6–7, of which there were not a few in the first century; cf. Alford) do not so point to the End as to validate the false Christs' claims. Jesus' followers are not to be alarmed by these events. "Such things must happen"; yet the End is still to come (v.6). These are only "the beginning of [the] birth pains" that stretch over the period between the advents. Why "must [they] happen"? The reason may be hidden in God's providence, which can provide a haven for faith (cf. 26:54). But it may also be that during this time of inaugurated reign before the Messianic Age attains its splendor, conflict is inevitable, precisely because the kingdom is only inaugurated. The conflict extends not only to families (10:34–37), but to nations and even nature (cf. Rom 8:20–21; Col 1:16, 20).

The effect of these verses, then, is not to curb enthusiasm for the Lord's return but to warn against false claimants and an expectation of a premature return based on misconstrued signs.

9–13 *Tote* ("then," v.9) is an elusive word (see on 2:7). In this chapter alone it occurs in vv.9, 10, 14, 16, 21, 23, 30, 40. Translated "then" in v.9, it occurs as "At that time" in v.10. Certainly there is no suggestion of *sequence* between v.8 and v.9; it is *during* the "birth pains" that Jesus' disciples will be persecuted and killed. "You" quite clearly extends beyond the immediate disciples and includes all the followers Jesus will have. Persecution would break out early (cf. Acts 4:1–30; 7:59– 8:3; 12:1–5; Rev 2:10, 12) and keep on during the "birth pains," against a background of hatred by the whole world (cf. Acts 28:22).

Thlipsis ("persecution," "tribulation," "distress") occurs four times in Matthew, three in this chapter (13:21; 24:9, 21, 29), and relates significantly to the chapter's structure (see on vv.21, 29). Jesus establishes *thlipsis* as characteristic of this age (cf. 10:16–39)—a time when many will "turn away" (*skandalisthēsontas*) from the faith (for the verb, see on 5:29; 13:21, 57) and hate each other (v.10).

In this chapter there are several allusions to Daniel (cf. Dan 11:35; linguistically some LXX MSS of Dan 11:41; cf. D. Wenham, "A Note on Matthew 24:10–12," *Tyndale Bulletin* 31 [1980]: 155–62, and esp. Trotter) and a certain parallelism between v.10 and vv.11–12. Those who turn away from the faith are deceived by false prophets, and those who hate each other do so because wickedness abounds and the love of most grows cold (cf. Trotter). Professing believers are either included in this description or are the focus of interest; but only those who endure—in love (v.12) and despite persecution (vv.9–11); cf. Rev 2:10)—will be saved (v.13). They must "stand firm" [endure] to the *end*: individual responsibility persists to the end of life, but corporate responsibility to the final consummation. Part of the effect of this "tribulation," therefore, is to purify the body of professed disciples: those who endure are saved, as in Daniel 11:32, 34–35, and elsewhere in Matthew (see on 12:32; 13:21, 41; cf. 2 Tim 2:3, 10–13; 3:11; Heb 10:32; 11:27; 12:2–3; James 1:12; 5:11).

The reasons for falling away may differ. In 13:21 the cause is *thlipsis* ("persecution" or "tribulation"), and in 24:10–12 it is false prophets (see on 7:15–23). But even here the false prophecy finds some of its appeal in the matrix of trouble and persecution (vv.4–9) from which it emerges; and Matthew cares little whether faith is lost owing to fear of physical violence or to deception effected by false prophets. The result is the same and is to be expected throughout this age (cf. 7:15–23; 24:24; Acts 20:29–30; 2 Peter 2:1; 1 John 4:1).

14 But none of this means that the gospel of the kingdom (see on 4:23) is not preached or that its saving message does not spread throughout the world. Despite persecution—and often because of it (Acts 8:1, 4)—the Good News is "preached" (*kērychthēsetai*, see on 4:17) "as a testimony to all nations." The expression is itself neutral (see on 8:4), and the gospel will bring either salvation or a curse, depending on how it is received. Thus the theme of Gentile mission is again made explicit (see on 1:1; 2:1–12; 3:9; 4:15–16; 8:11–12; 21:43; 28:18–20).

Notes

10 The reciprocal pronoun ἀλλήλους (*allēlous*, "one another"), used twice in this verse, can scarcely be strictly reciprocal in either case.

b. *The sharp pain: the Fall of Jerusalem*

24:15–21

15"So when you see standing in the holy place 'the abomination that causes desolation,' spoken of through the prophet Daniel—let the reader understand— 16then let those who are in Judea flee to the mountains. 17Let no one on the roof of his house go down to take anything out of the house. 18Let no one in the field go back to get his cloak. 19How dreadful it will be in those days for pregnant women and nursing mothers! 20Pray that your flight will not take place in winter or on the Sabbath. 21For then there will be great distress, unequaled from the beginning of the world until now—and never to be equaled again.

Although many commentators hold that Matthew (but probably not Mark and certainly not Luke) here portrays not just the Fall of Jerusalem but also the Great tribulation before Antichrist comes (e.g., Hill, *Matthew*), the details in vv.16–21 are too limited geographically and culturally to justify that view. For other interpretations, see comments at the beginning of this chapter. For justification of a pericope termination at v.21 instead of the more common v.22, see below (on vv.21–22).

15 *Oun* ("so") can serve as either an inferential or merely a transitional conjunction (cf. BAGD, pp. 592–93; BDF, par. 451.1 plus app.; RHG, pp. 1191–92; Turner, *Syntax*, pp. 337–38), which can sometimes be left untranslated; it does not introduce something *temporally* new. If it retains any inferential force in this passage, it is very light—"accordingly, when you see . . . then flee." Having characterized the entire age during which the gospel of the kingdom is preached as a time of *thlipsis* ("distress"), Jesus goes on to talk about one part of it when there will be particularly "great distress."

To bdelygma tēs erēmōseōs means "the abomination characterized by desolation," leaving it unclear whether the abomination "causes" desolation (NIV; cf. McNeile, "the abominable thing that layeth waste"; RSV, "the desolating sacrilege") or is simply a token of it. The former is more likely. The expression occurs four times in Daniel (8:13; 9:27; 11:31; 12:11). Daniel 11:31 clearly refers to the desecration under Antiochus Epiphanes (168 B.C.; cf. 1 Macc 1:54–61), who erected an altar to Zeus over the altar of burned offering, sacrificed a swine on it, and made the practice of Judaism a capital offense. The other references in Daniel are more disputed. Matthew and Mark agree with the LXX of Daniel 12:11 only; and, "[despite] the primary importance of Dan 9:27 for the meaning of the expression, 12:11 is contextually the more suitable reference so far as the gospels are concerned, because allusions to Dan 11:40–12:13 surround this reference to the abomination of desolation" (Gundry, *Use of OT*, p. 48).

Jesus, then, is identifying Daniel 9:27 and 12:11 with certain events about to take place; and the parenthetical "let the reader understand" is designed to draw the attention of the *reader of Daniel* to the passages' true meaning. This parenthetical aside is not a Matthean addition (unless one holds to Matthew's priority), for it is already in Mark. Matthew clearly understood it, not as an aside by Mark to draw the attention of his readers to the importance of this Gospel text, but as an aside by Jesus to draw the attention of his hearers who read Daniel to the importance of Daniel's words; hence Jesus' mention of "the prophet Daniel." Whether the identification Jesus makes is a prediction fulfillment or a typological fulfillment largely depends on how one understands the various "abomination of desolation" passages in Daniel.

But to what event does Jesus make this text from Daniel refer? Some have suggested Caligula's plan to set up a pagan altar and standards in the temple precincts (A.D. 40), a plan never carried out; but the description in the following verses cannot apply to that. The obvious occasion, in general terms, is A.D. 70, though certain difficulties must be faced. Although *topos* ("place") can refer to the city of Jerusalem (cf. BAGD, p. 822), the normal meaning of *hagios topos* ("holy place") is the temple complex (cf. BAGD; Isa 60:13; 2 Macc 1:29; 2:18; Acts 6:13; 21:28). But by the time the Romans had actually desecrated the temple in A.D. 70, it was too late for anyone in the city to flee.

Mark's language is less explicit: "standing where it does not belong" (Mark 13:14), instead of "standing in the holy place." Luke resolves the matter: "When you see Jerusalem surrounded by armies, you will know that its desolation is near" (Luke 21:20)—but now there is no explicit mention of "the abomination of desolation." Possibly Jesus said something ambiguous, such as Mark reports. Luke, writing for a Gentile audience less concerned with Daniel, emphasizes the aspect of warning. Matthew, believing the allusions to Daniel important for his Jewish audience because Jesus drew attention to them, makes explicit reference to "the abomination of desolation" and to "the holy place," since the setting up of the abomination in the holy place is the inevitable result of the pagan attack.

By the time the Roman military standards (an eagle in silver or bronze over the imperial bust, to which soldiers paid homage not far removed from worship) surrounded Jerusalem, the city was defiled. Some have held that though Luke refers to the approaching armies, Matthew and Mark refer to the Zealot excesses that polluted the temple before A.D. 70 (including murder and the installation of a false high priest; cf. Jos. War IV, 147–57 [iii.6–8], 162–92 [iii.10], 334–44 [v.4]), when there was still time to flee (e.g., Lane, *Mark*, p. 469; Gaston, *No Stone*, pp. 458ff.). In any case, there is reasonably good tradition that Christians abandoned the city, perhaps in A.D. 68, about halfway through the siege.

16–19 The instructions Jesus gives his disciples about what to do in view of v.15 are so specific that they must be related to the Jewish War. The devastation would stretch far beyond the city; people throughout Judea should flee to the mountains, where the Maccabeans had hidden in caves. Most roofs were flat (cf. Deut 22:8; Mark 2:4; Acts 10:9)—pleasant places in the cool of the day. Verse 17 implies such haste that fugitives will not take time to run downstairs for anything to take with them but will run from roof to roof to evacuate the city as quickly as possible (cf. Jos. Antiq. XIII, 140 [v.3]). People in the fields will not have time to go home for their cloaks (see on 5:40). It will be especially dreadful (lit., "woe," here like a compassionate "alas!") for pregnant women and nursing mothers.

20 Flight is obviously harder in winter. As for fleeing on the Sabbath, travel would become more difficult because few would help, and many would try to prevent traveling farther than a Sabbath day's journey. Jesus clearly expects these events to take place while the strict Sabbath law is in effect.

21 "For" introduces the reason for flight in vv.17–20: *thlipsis* ("distress," "tribulation") and unprecedented suffering (cf. Dan 12:1; 1 Macc 9:27; Rev 7:14; Gundry, *Use of OT*, pp. 49f.). The savagery, slaughter, disease, and famine (mothers eating their own children) were monstrous (cf. Jos. War V, 424–38 [x.2–3]), "unequaled from the beginning of the world until now," and, according to Jesus, "never to be equaled again." There have been greater numbers of deaths—six million in the Nazi death camps, mostly Jews, and an estimated twenty million under Stalin—but never so high a percentage of a great city's population so thoroughly and painfully exterminated and enslaved as during the Fall of Jerusalem.

From this "great distress" Jesus' followers were to flee. Eusebius (*Ecclesiastical History* 3.5.2–3) says that during the siege under Titus (who did not replace his father Vespasian as commanding officer till A.D. 69, after the death of Galba), many were permitted to leave (cf. Jos. War V, 420–23 [x.1]). Others hold that the Christians left in 66 or 68.

That Jesus in v.21 promises that such "great distress" is never to be equaled implies that it cannot refer to the Tribulation at the end of the age; for if what happens next is the Millennium or the new heaven and the new earth, it seems inane to say that such "great distress" will not take place again. At the same time, by these remarks Jesus finishes his description of Jerusalem in Matthew and Mark (Luke goes to 21:24). (For the way Luke's version of the discourse fits this framework, see the forthcoming monograph by Wenham.)

Notes

---

18 Only here and in Luke 7:38 is ὀπίσω (*opisō*, "back") used as an adverb (cf. Moule, *Idiom Book,* p. 86).

---

c. *Warnings against false messiahs during the birth pains*

24:22–28

22If those days had not been cut short, no one would survive, but for the sake of the elect those days will be shortened. 23At that time if anyone says to you, 'Look, here is the Christ!' or, 'There he is!' do not believe it. 24For false Christs and false prophets will appear and perform great signs and miracles to deceive even the elect—if that were possible. 25See, I have told you ahead of time.

26"So if anyone tells you, 'There he is, out in the desert,' do not go out; or, 'Here he is, in the inner rooms,' do not believe it. 27For as the lightning that comes from the east is visible even in the west, so will be the coming of the Son of Man. 28Wherever there is a carcass, there the vultures will gather.

22 Many problems in interpreting the Olivet Discourse relate to the assumption that "those days" refers to the period described in vv.15–21 and also to v.29. But there are excellent reasons for concluding that vv.22–28 refer to the general period of distress introduced by vv.4–14 and that therefore "those days" refers to the entire period of which vv.15–21 are only one part—the "great distress" (v.21).

1. The term "elect" (in Matthew only at 22:14; 24:22, 24, 31; plus the variant at 20:16) most naturally refers to all true believers, chosen by God; so it is reasonable to assume that it does so here.

2. Similarly, *pasa sarx* (lit., "all flesh"; NIV, "no one"; cf. Notes) normally refers to all mankind and is more sweeping than "no one in Jerusalem."

3. The themes of the ensuing verses have already been taken up as characteristics of the entire age (vv.4–14), especially the warning against false Christs (cf. vv.4–5).

4. It has already been shown that v.21 makes a suitable ending to vv.15–21.

5. Wenham, in his forthcoming work (see at v.21), posits a neat presynoptic tradition that embraces the content of all three Gospels and suggests reasons for individual selection of materials. That tradition (slightly modified from Wenham) runs approximately as follows: Matthew 24:15–20 = Mark 13:14–18 = Luke 21:20–23a; Luke 21:23b–24; Matthew 24:20 = Mark 13:19; Matthew 24:22–28 = Mark 13:20–23; Matthew 24:29–42 = Mark 13:24–37 = Luke 21:25–36. Right or wrong as to source-critical details, this reconstruction at least makes sense of the relationship among the Synoptics at this point and supports a logical break between v.21 and v.22 of Matthew 24.

6. Further literary and structural arguments suggest that vv.4–28 must be taken as one time period, with vv.15–21 a critical part of it (see on v.29).

While none of these arguments is decisive, all are reasonable and help us understand the whole discourse. If they are correct, then v.22 tells us that this age of evangelism and distress—wars, famines, persecution, hatred, false prophets—will become so bad that, if not checked, no one would survive. In a century that has seen two world wars, now lives under the threat of extinction by nuclear holocaust, and has had more Christian martyrs than in all the previous nineteen centuries put together, Jesus' prediction does not seem farfetched. But the age will not run its course; it will be cut short. (For a somewhat similar idea, see the Jewish apocalypse 2 Baruch 20:1–2; 83:1.) This promise enables believers to look for God's sovereign, climactic intervention without predicting dates.

23–25 Empty-headed credulity is as great an enemy of true faith as chronic skepticism. Christian faith involves the sober responsibility of neither believing lies nor trusting imposters. As false Christs and false prophets proliferate (v.24), so will their heralds (v.23). Jesus' disciples are not to be deceived, even by spectacular signs and miracles (see on 7:21–23; 16:1; for the terms, 12:38; 18:12–13; cf. 24:4–5, 11). The imposter is perennial (Deut 13:1–4; Rev 13:13).

Ei dynaton ("if that were possible") no more calls in question the security of the elect (contra I.H. Marshall, *Kept by the Power of God*, rev. ed. [Minneapolis: Bethany, 1975], pp. 72–73) than it calls in question the inevitability of Jesus' cup (26:39). If "deceive" is telic (i.e., "in order to deceive"; cf. Notes), the "if possible" refers to the intent of the deceivers: they intend to deceive, if possible, even the elect—without any comment on how ultimately successful such attacks will be. "If that were possible" clearly suggests that "deceive" is not ecbatic (i.e., "with the result that"). That Jesus tells these things in advance (v.25) not only warns and strengthens his followers (cf. John 16:4) but also authenticates him (cf. Deut 13:1–4; John 14:29).

26–27 It is pointless to look for Messiah's return in the desert (v.26; cf. 4:1) or in inner rooms (cf. 6:6)—whether in some desert monastic community or in some hidden, unrecognized enclave for insiders (cf. Stendahl, Peake). Far from it! The coming of the Son of Man (see on 8:20; here his coming is clearly identified as "your [Jesus'] coming," v.3, and Messiah's coming, vv.23–24) will be public, unquestionable, and not confined to some little group of initiates. As the lightning (cf. Ps 97:4; Zech 9:14) comes out of the east but is everywhere visible, as far away as the west (Weiss, Broadus), so also the coming of the Son of Man will be visible to all people everywhere (TDNT, 8:433–34).

28 Here Jesus quotes a proverb (cf. Job 39:30; Luke 17:37). "Eagle" (KJV) is wrong: "vulture" (NIV) is correct. *Aetos* can mean "eagle," "kite," or "vulture"; but eagles are not normally carrion eaters. The proverb itself is a difficult one.

1. Calvin, following some of the Fathers, sees it portraying God's children, gathering to feed on Christ. But identifying carrion with Christ is strange indeed!

2. Others see an allusion to Roman military eagles, with the Roman forces swarming over corrupt Jerusalem. But eagles are not vultures; and the preceding verse relates to the Parousia, not the Fall of Jerusalem.

3. Hill and others think that the vultures' gathering indicates that the Parousia is near. But there must be carrion before the vultures gather; so the symbolism breaks down, because the "signs" attest the reality only after the fact.

4. Manson (*Sayings*, p. 147) emphasizes the swiftness of the coming of the Son of Man: the carrion is no sooner there than the vultures swoop down (Ezek 17:3, 7; Rev 4:7; 8:13; 12:4). But in passages where the *aetos* ("eagle" or "vulture") symbolizes speed, it is understood to mean an "eagle." Why then assign it to a setting where it must be taken as a vulture?

5. The proverb may be a colorful way of saying that things come to pass at just the right time (Broadus); so the proverb applies here and in Luke 17:37 to the Parousia of the Son of Man. Concluding this broader section (vv.4–28) is this thought: Do not be too eager for Christ's coming, or you will be deceived by false claimants (vv.23–26). When he comes, his coming will be unmistakable (v.27), in God's own time (v.28)—a time when the world will be ripe for judgment (Zahn; see on v.6).

6. Or this enigmatic proverb may simply mean that it will be as impossible for humanity not to see the coming of the Son of Man (cf. v.27) as it is for vultures to miss seeing carrion (Klostermann).

Notes

---

22 On the aorist verbs in this verse, see Zerwick, par. 317. The οὐ . . . πᾶς (ou . . . pas, lit., "not . . . all") construction is often said to represent the Hebrew כֹּל . . . לֹא (lōʾ . . . kōl), equivalent to Greek οὐδείς (oudeis, "no one"; e.g., Zerwick, par. 446; but the Semitizing stretches even farther to οὐ . . . πᾶσα σάρξ (ou . . . pasa sarx, lit., "not . . . all flesh," i.e., no person).

24 The construction ὥστε πλανῆσαι (hōste planēsai, "to deceive") would most naturally be expected to be consecutive, and so it may be (Moule, *Idiom Book*, p. 143); but the same construction can have final force (Zerwick, par. 352), as does the parallel expression in Mark 13:22.

---

3. The coming of the Son of Man

24:29–31

²⁹"Immediately after the distress of those days

" 'the sun will be darkened,
and the moon will not give its light;
the stars will fall from the sky,
and the heavenly bodies will be shaken.'

³⁰"At that time the sign of the Son of Man will appear in the sky, and all the nations of the earth will mourn. They will see the Son of Man coming on the clouds of the sky, with power and great glory. ³¹And he will send his angels with a loud trumpet call, and they will gather his elect from the four winds, from one end of the heavens to the other.

Matthew essentially follows Mark (13:24–27; cf. Luke 21:25–28) but adds the allusion to Zechariah about mourning (v.30) and the trumpet call (v.31).

29 For general arguments that vv.29–31 refer to the Parousia, not the coming of the Son of Man in the events of A.D. 70, see on vv.1–3. Mark brackets the last section (Mark 13:5–23 parallels Matt 24:4–28) with *blepete* ("watch out") in Mark 13:5, 23. Matthew has nothing similar, but the effect is the same because v.29 begins the new stage with "Immediately after the distress [*thlipsis*] of those days," a clear reference back to the *thlipsis* of vv.9, 22, not to the "great distress" of vv.15–21. Thus the celestial signs and the coming of the Son of Man do not immediately follow "the abomination that causes desolation" but "the distress of those days"—i.e., of the entire interadvent period of *thlipsis*.

The cosmic portents (cf. esp. Isa 13:9–10; 34:4; but also Ezek 32:7; Joel 2:31; 3:15; Amos 8:9; Rev 6:12) are probably meant to be taken literally, because of the climactic nature of the Son of Man's final self-disclosure. Yet this is not certain, since in some political contexts similar expressions are used metaphorically (see on 24:1–13).

30 "The sign of the Son of Man" has been interpreted in three principal ways.

1. Some of the Fathers after the Constantinian settlement thought it referred to Constantine's vision of a cross in the sky, with the words "In this sign, conquer"—an interpretation both anachronistic and fanciful.

2. More commonly "the sign" is assumed to be Jesus' coming, with "of the Son of Man . . . in the sky" being taken as standing in epexegetical relation to "the sign." The Jews had repeatedly asked for a sign (12:38; 16:1; cf. John 2:18), and the disciples had just asked for the sign of his coming (v.3). The supreme "sign" is his parousia at the end of the age. This interpretation is possible, though perhaps a bit forced. When the Jews asked for a sign, Jesus referred them to "the sign of Jonah" (12:39–41), not to his parousia. His disciples' more specific question (v.3) was partially answered by vv.4–28, with a fuller answer in vv.32–35.

3. T.F. Glasson ("The Ensign of the Son of Man (Matt. xxiv, 30)," JTS [1964]: 299f.) offers the best explanation. He points out that careful comparison of vv.30–31 with the synoptic parallels shows Matthew has added mention of both "sign" and "trumpet." But *sēmeion* ("sign") commonly meant "ensign" or "standard," both in pagan Greek literature and in the LXX; and "standard" and "trumpet" are both regularly associated with the eschatological gathering of the people of God (cf. v.31; Isa 11:12; 18:3; 27:13; 49:22; Jer 4:21; 6:1; 51:27; 1QM 3:1–4:2). Therefore *sēmeion* has two different meanings in this chapter (vv.3, 30)—a phenomenon common enough in the NT. Theologically this means that the kingdom is being consummated. The standard, the banner of the Son of Man, unfurls in the heavens, as he himself returns in splendor and power.

The event will prompt "all the nations of the earth" to mourn, an allusion to Zechariah 12:10–12, probably directly from the MT (cf. Gundry, *Use of OT*, p. 53; cf. John 19:37; Rev 1:7). In Zechariah the reference is to the tribes of Israel in the land, and the mourning is that of repentance. Those who follow Kik and France want to keep the first link with the OT (the tribes of Israel) but not the second (the mourning; see on 24:1–3). Most scholars see the mourning (v.30) as that of despair, not repentance (Rev 1:7; 6:15–17); and we have already argued for the translation "all the nations of the earth" (NIV) over "all the tribes of the land." So it seems that neither link with the OT is simple, and we must probe for a deeper link.

What we discover is an implicit a fortiori argument. In Zechariah 12, Yahweh enables the house of David and Judah to crush its enemies; and as a result the Jews weep, apparently in contrition for their past sins in light of Yahweh's merciful deliverance and salvation (cf. also Zech 13:1–2). But it is the Gentile enemies who are crushed. If, then, the Jews face judgment and mourning (vv.15–21), even though not only Jerusalem but also *all nations* (v.9) have hated Jesus' disciples, *how much more* will all the nations of the earth, to whom the gospel has been preached (v.14), also mourn at the Parousia, when the lost opportunities and the persecution of Jesus through persecuting his disciples are seen as they truly are?

The next allusion in v.30 is to Daniel 7:13–14. Some have objected that since in

Daniel's vision "one like a son of man" approaches the throne of "the Ancient of Days" and does not descend to earth, v.30 and parallels cannot be speaking about the Parousia, which requires the descent to earth. The objection misses the point. In Daniel "one like a son of man" approaches God to receive all authority, glory, sovereign power—"an everlasting dominion that will not pass away." In the framework of NT eschatology, we may imagine Jesus the Son of Man receiving the kingdom through his resurrection and ascension, his divine vindication, so that now all authority is his (28:18). Yet it is equally possible to think of him receiving the kingdom at the consummation, when his reign or kingdom becomes direct and immediate, uncontested and universal. Unless one thinks of the location of the Ancient of Days in some physical and spatial sense, it is hard to imagine why Christ's approaching God the Father to receive the kingdom might not be combined with his returning to earth to set up the consummated kingdom. This interpretation goes well with its vivid context.

The Son of Man, whose standard has been unfurled, comes "on [*epi*] the clouds of heaven" (cf. 26:64; Rev 14:14–16); it is doubtful whether sharp distinctions are to be drawn between this expression and "in [*en*] the clouds of heaven" (Mark 13:26; Luke 21:27) or "with [*meta*] the clouds of heaven" (Mark 14:62 [NIV, "on"]; Rev 1:7). The clouds symbolize God's presence (see on 17:5): Immanuel ("God with us") comes "with power and great glory." The latter phrase not only ensures that the coming is universally witnessed and unmistakably plain (cf. vv.26–28, 30) but may allude to Isaiah 11:10: the nations will rally to "the Root of Jesse," and his place of rest will be (lit.) "the Glory" (cf. M.G. Kline, "Primal Parousia," WTJ 40 [1977-78]: 274).

31 The sound of a loud trumpet (cf. Isa 27:13; 1 Cor 15:52; 1 Thess 4:16) is an eschatological figure (see on v.30). Only with considerable difficulty can v.31 be interpreted as referring to Christian missions: its natural linguistic relations are in 13:41. For comments on "his elect," see on 22:14; 24:22. The "four winds" represent the four points of the compass (Ezek 37:9; Dan 8:8; 11:4): the elect are gathered from all over (cf. 8:11), "from one end of the heavens to the other" (from every place under the sky), since that is how far the gospel of the kingdom will have been preached (v.14). Although all nations of the earth will mourn, nevertheless the elect are drawn from them.

4. The significance of the birth pains

24:32–35

> 32"Now learn this lesson from the fig tree: As soon as its twigs get tender and its leaves come out, you know that summer is near. 33Even so, when you see all these things, you know that it is near, right at the door. 34I tell you the truth, this generation will certainly not pass away until all these things have happened. 35Heaven and earth will pass away, but my words will never pass away.

32–33 This "lesson" (*parabolē*, lit., "parable"; see on 13:3a; 15:15) of the fig tree (cf. 21:18–22) is based on the common observation that the twigs get tender before summer and arouse expectations of summer (v.32). Although the Greek is ambiguous, NIV's "you know" is preferable to KJV's imperative ("know"). The "parable" points to the relation between "all these things" and "it is near" (v.33). It is uncertain whether the antecedent of "it" is the Parousia or Jesus, the Son of Man. Jesus sometimes spoke of himself in the third person (v.31) and may be doing so here. But whatever "it" refers to, it is certainly the nearness of the Second Advent that is in view.

"All these things" is more problematic. If the words include the celestial signs *and the Parousia itself* (vv.29–31), then vv.32–33 are illogical, because any distinction between "all these things" and "it is near" would be destroyed. Thus many have suggested that vv.32–33 constitute a displaced parable—once again making the synoptists out to be less intelligent than their critics two millennia later. The more natural way to take "all these things" is to see them as referring to the distress of vv.4–28, the tribulation that comes on believers throughout the period between Jesus' ascension and the Parousia.

Having warned his disciples of the course of this age (vv.4–28) and told them of its climax in the Parousia (vv.29–31), Jesus in these verses answers the part of his disciples' questions (v.3) dealing with timing. He makes two points. First, "all these things" (vv.4–28) must happen; and then the Parousia is "near, right at the door"—"imminent." In other words the Parousia is the next major step in God's redemptive purposes. Second, this does not mean that the period of distress pinpoints the Parousia, for "no one knows about that day or hour" (vv.36–42).

34 "I tell you the truth" emphasizes the importance of what it introduces. "This generation" (see on 11:16; 12:41–42; 23:36; cf. 10:23; 16:28) can only with the greatest difficulty be made to mean anything other than the generation living when Jesus spoke. Even if "generation" by itself can have a slightly larger semantic range, to make *"this* generation" refer to all believers in every age, or the generation of believers alive when eschatological events start to happen, is highly artificial. Yet it does not follow that Jesus mistakenly thought the Parousia would occur within his hearers' lifetime. If our interpretation of this chapter is right, all that v.34 demands is that the distress of vv.4–28, including Jerusalem's fall, happen within the lifetime of the generation then living. This does *not* mean that the distress must end within that time but only that "all these things" must happen within it. Therefore v.34 sets a *terminus a quo* for the Parousia: it cannot happen till the events in vv.4–28 take place, all within a generation of A.D. 30. But there is no *terminus ad quem* to this distress other than the Parousia itself, and "only the Father" knows when it will happen (v.36).

35 The authority and eternal validity of Jesus' words are nothing less than the authority and eternal validity of God's words (Ps 119: 89–90; Isa 40:6–8).

5. *The day and hour unknown: the need to be prepared* (24:36–42)

a. *The principle*

24:36

> 36"No one knows about that day or hour, not even the angels in heaven, nor the Son, but only the Father.

36 Many commentators read v.36 with the preceding paragraph; but it goes much better with the following verses, which constitute an exhortation to vigilance precisely because, the day and the hour being unknown to humanity, life goes on as it always has. The *gar* ("for") at the beginning of v.37 must not be overlooked, as in NIV.

The gist of v.36 is clear enough. Jesus' disciples are morally bound to repress all desires to know what no one knows but the Father—not even angels (cf. 18:10; 4 Ezra 4:52) or the Son (cf. Notes). If the Son himself does not know the time of the Parousia, "how cheerfully should we his followers rest in ignorance that cannot be removed, trusting in all things to our Heavenly Father's wisdom and goodness, striving to obey his clearly revealed will, and leaning on his goodness for support" (Broadus). Moreover it is ridiculous quibbling divorced from the context to say that though the day and hour remain unknown, we ascertain the year or month.

Jesus' self-confessed ignorance on this point has generated not a little debate. In fact, it is part of the NT pattern of his humiliation and incarnation (e.g., 20:23; Luke 2:52; Acts 1:7; Phil 2:7). John's Gospel, the one of the four Gospels most clearly insisting on Jesus' deity, also insists with equal vigor on Jesus' dependence on and obedience to his Father—a dependence reaching even to his knowledge of the divine. How NT insistence on Jesus' deity is to be combined with NT insistence on his ignorance and dependence is a matter of profound importance to the church; and attempts to jettison one truth for the sake of preserving the other must be avoided. (For an attempt to work some of these things out, cf. Carson, *Divine Sovereignty,* pp. 146–60.)

Notes

36 The words "nor the Son," while textually secure in Mark 13:32, are disputed here. The omission is supported by most late MSS and by אᵃ. Such omission may have been prompted by the doctrinal difficulty presented by the words; but it is mildly surprising that Mark 13:32 has not suffered similar distortion. One might in fact argue that the omission in Matthew is original and that the words were added by assimilation to Mark. The most convincing argument in favor of retaining the words in Matthew is grammatical (cf. Metzger, *Textual Commentary,* p. 62). The curious suggestion of Jeremias (*Prayers,* p. 37), that "nor the Son" is a late addition in both Matthew and Mark that makes explicit the implications of "but only the Father," is not only without textual warrant but also an intrinsically unlikely christological development.

b. Analogy of the days of Noah

24:37–39

> [37]As it was in the days of Noah, so it will be at the coming of the Son of Man. [38]For in the days before the flood, people were eating and drinking, marrying and giving in marriage, up to the day Noah entered the ark; [39]and they knew nothing about what would happen until the flood came and took them all away. That is how it will be at the coming of the Son of Man.

37–39 (See also Mark 13:33 and Luke 17:28–32, though the latter is in a different context and has quite different structure and wording.) The *gar* ("for") in the best

MSS further elucidates v.36: that the coming of the Son of Man takes place at an unknown time can only be true if in fact life seems to be going on pretty much as usual—just as in the days before the Flood (v.37). People follow their ordinary pursuits (v.38). Despite the distress, persecutions, and upheavals (vv.4–28), life goes on: people eat, drink, and marry. There is no overt typological usage of the Flood as judgment here, nor any mention of the sin of that generation. Yet Jesus' warning may well have given rise to 1 Peter 3:20–21. Jesus expects ceaseless vigilance of his followers, for the final climax of human history will suddenly come on ordinary life. In the human condition massive distress and normal life patterns coexist. For the believer the former point to the end; the latter warn of its unexpectedness.

c. *Two in the field; two with a mill*

24:40–41

40Two men will be in the field; one will be taken and the other left. 41Two women will be grinding with a hand mill; one will be taken and the other left.

40–41 These two vignettes do not "stress the sharp cleavage caused by the coming of the Son of Man, *rather than* the unexpectedness of the event" (Hill, *Matthew*, emphasis mine), but the unexpectedness of the event *by means of* the sudden cleavage. Two men are working in a field; one is taken, the other left (v.40). Two women work their hand mill (v.41)—one normally operated by two women squatting opposite each other with the mill between them, each woman in turn pulling the stone around 180 degrees. The two are apt to be sisters, mother and daughter, or two household slaves. Yet no matter how close their relationship, one is taken, the other left (cf. 10:35–36). It is neither clear nor particularly important whether "taken" means "taken in judgment" (cf. v.39, though the verb "took . . . away" differs from "taken" in vv.40–41) or "taken to be gathered with the elect" (v.31).

6. *Parabolic teaching: variations on watchfulness* (24:42–25:46)

a. *The homeowner and the thief*

24:42–44

42"Therefore keep watch, because you do not know on what day your Lord will come. 43But understand this: If the owner of the house had known at what time of night the thief was coming, he would have kept watch and would not have let his house be broken into. 44So you also must be ready, because the Son of Man will come at an hour when you do not expect him.

The exact relation between vv.42–51 and Mark 13:33–37 is obscure and has not been satisfactorily explained. On the nature of parables, see on 13:3a; on comparison with Luke 12:39–40, see discussion and chart at 19:1–2. Each of the five parables in 24:42–25:46 deal with some aspect of watchfulness. But watchfulness is not always passive: duties and responsibilities must be discharged (24:45–51), and foresight and wisdom are important (25:1–13). Responsible living under Jesus' directives is rewarded in the end (vv.14–46).

42–44 The first parable teaches both the unexpectedness of the return of "your Lord" (*kyrios*, v.42)—an expression that is not only identical to "the master" in the next parable (v.45), but lays the foundation for the church's cry, "Come, O Lord!" (1 Cor 16:22)—and her willingness to call Jesus *ho kyrios* ("the Lord"), a title hitherto reserved in its religious use by the Jews for God himself (1 Cor 12:3; Phil 4:5; 2 Thess 2:2; James 5:7; see on 8:2; 17:4, 14–16; 21:3; 22:41–46). It might be better to take *ginōskete* not as an imperative ("understand," NIV, v.43) but as an indicative ("you know"): the disciples know the owner of a house would watch if he knew when the thief was coming (on the tenses of the verb, cf. Zerwick, par. 317), so the thief could not break in (on the verb, see on 6:19). Since no one knows at what time, or during what "watch," the thief might strike, constant vigilance is required. "So you also must be ready" (v.44), because in this one respect—the unexpectedness of his coming—the Son of Man (see on vv.37, 39; 8:20) resembles a thief.

b. *The two servants*

24:45–51

> 45"Who then is the faithful and wise servant, whom the master has put in charge of the servants in his household to give them their food at the proper time? 46It will be good for that servant whose master finds him doing so when he returns. 47I tell you the truth, he will put him in charge of all his possessions. 48But suppose that servant is wicked and says to himself, 'My master is staying away a long time,' 49and he then begins to beat his fellow servants and to eat and drink with drunkards. 50The master of that servant will come on a day when he does not expect him and at an hour he is not aware of. 51He will cut him to pieces and assign him a place with the hypocrites, where there will be weeping and gnashing of teeth.

The good servant is prepared for his Lord at any time, is faithful throughout his delay, and in the end is highly rewarded. The wicked servant is faithless in his responsibilities, abusive to fellow servants, lax in waiting for his master's return, and ultimately earns the punishment that is his due (see chart and discussion at 19:1–2; cf. 21:34–36; cf. also Mark 13:34–37; Luke 12:35–38, 42–46).

45–47 The *doulos* ("servant") in this parable is the head over all the domestics (v.45). This, however, does not so much limit the application of the parable to leaders as establish that their responsibilities entail good personal relationships (v.49), requiring exemplary conduct and precluding harshness and lording it over others. The good servant is faithful and "wise" (i.e., prudent, judicious—cf. 7:24; 10:16), doing what is assigned him. When his master returns (v.46), he is *makarios* ("blessed"; NIV, "will be good"; see on 5:3) and promoted (v.47; cf. 25:21). In Mark 13:37 Jesus applies the necessity of watching to "everyone."

48–51 If the servant is wicked (v.48) and lacking faithfulness and wisdom (v.45), he may convince himself that the master "is staying away a long time"—perhaps a subtle hint that the Parousia could be considerably delayed (cf. 25:19). The wicked servant uses the delay to abuse his fellow servants and carouse (v.49). (For "begins to beat," cf. 11:7, 20.) But the wicked servant, surprised and unprepared for his master's return (v.50), is put with the "hypocrites" (v.51): his lot is with the punishment given those most constantly held up as vile in this Gospel (6:2, 5, 16; 16:3;

23:13–29). The master "will cut him to pieces" (cf. 1 Sam 15:33; Heb 11:37; Sus 55; on the punishments accorded Jewish slaves, cf. SBK, 4:698–744). *Dichotomeō* literally is "I cut in two" (found in the NT only here and Luke 12:46). Alleged parallels in 1QS 1:10–11; 2:16–17; 6:24–25; 7:1, 2, 16; 8:21–23 are unconvincing: the Hebrew "cut off from the midst of the sons of light" refers to excommunication. Here, however, the wicked servant is not cut off from anything; he is cut in pieces—a most severe and awful punishment—and joins the hypocrites in weeping and grinding of teeth (cf. 8:12).

Notes

---

50 This is one of only three places in Matthew where the relative pronoun is attracted to the case of its antecedent (see on 18:19; cf. 25:24).

---

c. *The ten virgins*

25:1–13

> [1]"At that time the kingdom of heaven will be like ten virgins who took their lamps and went out to meet the bridegroom. [2]Five of them were foolish and five were wise. [3]The foolish ones took their lamps but did not take any oil with them. [4]The wise, however, took oil in jars along with their lamps. [5]The bridegroom was a long time in coming, and they all became drowsy and fell asleep.
>
> [6]"At midnight the cry rang out: 'Here's the bridegroom! Come out to meet him!'
>
> [7]"Then all the virgins woke up and trimmed their lamps. [8]The foolish ones said to the wise, 'Give us some of your oil; our lamps are going out.'
>
> [9]"'No,' they replied, 'there may not be enough for both us and you. Instead, go to those who sell oil and buy some for yourselves.'
>
> [10]"But while they were on their way to buy the oil, the bridegroom arrived. The virgins who were ready went in with him to the wedding banquet. And the door was shut.
>
> [11]"Later the others also came. 'Sir! Sir!' they said. 'Open the door for us!'
>
> [12]"But he replied, 'I tell you the truth, I don't know you.'
>
> [13]"Therefore keep watch, because you do not know the day or the hour.

This parable has been widely discussed. Hill (*Matthew*), largely following Jeremias (*Parables*, pp. 51–53), notes the "allegorical" elements (bridegroom's coming = coming of the Son of Man; ten virgins = expectant Christian community; tarrying = delay of the Parousia; rejection of the foolish virgins = final judgment) and claims there is evidence for thinking these to be later additions by the church. This view is strengthened, it is claimed, by the fact that the equation Messiah = bridegroom is virtually unknown in late Judaism (cf. ibid., p. 52) and first appears in 2 Corinthians 11:2. The story Jesus actually told, stripped of its "allegorical accretions," involved wedding preparations and warned his hearers of the impending eschatological crisis. But this will not do. We have already seen that source criticism of Gospel parables based on theoretical distinctions between "parable" and "allegory" is ill-founded (see on 13:3a). The idea of Messiah as bridegroom springs from such OT passages as Isaiah 54:4–6; 62:4–5; Ezekiel 16:7–34; Hosea 2:19. There Yahweh is portrayed as the "husband" of his people. We have noted how readily Jesus in his parables places himself in Yahweh's place (see on 13:37–39). Moreover both John the Baptist (John 3:27–30) and Jesus himself (Matt 9:15; Mark 2:19–20) have already made the equation Jesus = Messiah = bridegroom, unless we deny the historicity of these passages. But the parable makes sense in its own setting and as it stands.

While dispensationalists divide on whether this parable relates to the "Rapture" of the church (A.C. Gaebelein) or the Second Advent, following the Tribulation (Walvoord), both views introduce eschatological structures that do not emerge naturally from the text (see above on 24:1–3). W. Schenk ("Auferweckung der Toten oder Gericht nach den Werken: Tradition und Redaktion in Matthäus xxv 1–3," NovTest 20 [1978]: 278–99) reconstructs a very simple "original" parable in which all the virgins have enough oil but only five of them sleep. When the bridegroom comes, they all enter and enjoy the feast. The point is that when the bridegroom comes, some are asleep and some are awake; but all enjoy the festivities (as in 1 Thess 4:15–17). But Matthew has allegorized this parable and required a store of good works (oil) as qualification for entry. It is hard to decide which of Schenk's options is more wrong—his reconstruction of the alleged original or his interpretation of the parable as it stands in Matthew.

Scarcely less idiosyncratic is J.M. Ford ("The Parable of the Foolish Scholars," NovTest 9 [1967]: 107–23), who, arguing largely from late rabbinic sources, claims the virgins represent Jewish scholars, the lamps Torah, and the oil good deeds. The foolish virgins are Jewish scholars who study Torah but who fail to practice good deeds. They are therefore excluded from the Chamber of Instruction.

Such ingenuity ignores both the narrative and the context, as J.M. Sherriff ("Matthew 25:1–13. A Summary of Matthean Eschatology?" in Livingstone, 2:301–5) has pointed out. The plot turns on the bridegroom's delay. The foolish virgins do not *forget* to bring oil; rather the delay of the bridegroom shows they did not bring enough. The oil cannot easily apply to "good works" or "Holy Spirit." It is merely an element in the narrative showing that the foolish virgins were unprepared for the delay and so shut out in the end. In a real sense it is the bridegroom's delay that distinguishes the wise from the foolish virgins. Any interpretation that ignores this central element in the story is bound to go astray (cf. also G. Bornkamm, "Die Verzögerung der Parusie," *Geschichte*, pp. 49f.). The context similarly shows that the overriding theme is preparedness for the coming of the Son of Man. Even when this involves certain forms of behavior (24:45–51; 25:14–30), that behavior is called forth by the unexpectedness of the master's return.

From this perspective vv. 1–13 fit well into this sequence of parables and agree with what we know Jesus taught. There is no good reason for doubting its authenticity or retreating to one of several reconstructed cores. The first parable (24:42–44) warns of the unexpectedness of Messiah's coming. The second (24:45–51) shows that more than passive watchfulness is required: there must be behavior acceptable to the master, the discharge of allotted responsibilities. This third parable (25:1–13) stresses the need for preparedness in the face of an unexpectedly long delay.

1 *Tote* ("At that time") is sufficiently vague in Matthew's usage (see on 2:7; 24:9) that not much can be built on it. The most natural way to take it here is as a reference to the coming of the Son of Man (cf. 24:29–31, 36–44). "At that time" the kingdom of heaven will become like the story of the ten virgins (so the Gr.; cf. Carson, "Word-Group")—i.e., the parable deals with the onset of the consummated kingdom.

The setting is fairly clear from what we know of the marriage customs of the day (cf. Broadus; Jeremias, *Parables*, pp. 173–74; TDNT, 4:1100; and esp. H. Granquist, *Marriage Conditions in a Palestinian Village*, 2 vols [Helsingfors: Centraltryckeriet, 1931, 1935]). Normally the bridegroom with some close friends left his home to go to the bride's home, where there were various ceremonies, followed by a procession through the streets—after nightfall—to his home. The ten virgins may be bridesmaids who have been assisting the bride; and they expect to meet the groom as he comes from the bride's house (cf. Kistemaker, p. 130), though this is uncertain. Everyone in the procession was expected to carry his or her own torch. Those without a torch would be assumed to be party crashers or even brigands. The festivities, which might last several days, would formally get under way at the groom's house.

That the bride is not mentioned in the best MSS (cf. Notes) has been variously interpreted. Some have thought this is the trip to the bride's house or that this is one of those rare occasions when all the festivities took place at her home, because the groom lived at a considerable distance. But then the bride's father, not the groom, would have refused entrance to the foolish virgins. To demand the presence of the bride is to demand that the parable walk on all fours: mention of her is not essential to the story.

For the meaning of *parthenos* ("virgin"), see on 1:23. The point is not these girls' virginity, which is assumed, but simply that they are ten (a favorite round number; e.g., Ruth 4:2; Luke 19:13; Jos. War VI, 423–24 [ix.3]) maidens invited to the wedding. The "lamps" (not the same word as in 5:15) are here either small oil-fed lamps or, more plausibly, torches whose rags would need periodic dowsing with oil to keep them burning. In either case the prudent would bring along a flask with an additional oil supply.

2–5 The "wise" (v.2) are called such because they are prepared (v.4) for the bridegroom's delayed coming. Both wise and foolish wait and doze (v.5); no praise or blame attaches to either group for this. There is no point in seeing hidden meanings in the oil or sleep. The sole distinction between the two groups is this: the wise bring not only oil in their lamps but an extra supply in separate jars, while the foolish bring no oil (either no extra oil or no oil at all [cf. Robertson, 1:196; Hendriksen; Lenski]: if the latter, then the lamps going out [v.8] is the sputtering of wicks or rags that burn brightly but don't last). The wise are prepared for delay; the foolish expect to meet the groom, but are either utterly unprepared or unprepared if he is delayed. And the bridegroom is a long time coming (24:48; 25:19).

6–9 At midnight (v.6), symbol of eschatological climax, "the cry rang out"—an admirable paraphrase of *krauge gegonen* (lit., "a cry has arisen": the perfect is unusual and probably dramatic; cf. Moule, *Idiom Book*, pp. 14, 202; BDF, par. 343[3]). All the virgins wake up and trim their lamps (v.7); but the lamps of the foolish virgins quickly go out (present tense, "are going out," contra KJV's "are gone out"). Apart from the identification of "oil" with "grace," Matthew Henry's observation is pertinent: "They will see their need of grace hereafter, when it should save them, who will not see their need of grace now, when it should sanctify and rule them." The wise virgins cannot help them. Whether the text reads "there may not be enough" or "there will certainly not be enough" (cf. Notes), the effect is the same: the foresight and preparedness of the wise virgins cannot benefit the foolish virgins when the eschatological crisis dawns (vv. 8–9). Preparedness can neither be transferred nor shared.

10–12 The bridegroom comes, the wise virgins enter, and the door is shut (v. 10; cf. 7:22–23; Luke 13:25). The intense cries of the ill-prepared and foolish latecomers— "Sir! Sir!" (on the doubling, cf. BDF, par. 493[1]; 7:21–23; 23:37)—are of no avail (v. 11). Because this parable concerns the consummation, the refusal to recognize or admit the foolish virgins (v. 12) must not be construed as calloused rejection of their lifelong desire to enter the kingdom. Far from it: it is the rejection of those who, despite appearances, never made preparation for the coming of the kingdom.

13 The theme is reiterated once more (cf. 24:36, 42, 44, 50). Jeremias (*Parables*, p. 52) and others suggest this verse is a late addition to the parable, since it is at variance with the fact that both the wise and the foolish virgins fell asleep. But this misses the purpose of v. 13. "Keep watch" does not mean "keep awake," as if an ability to fight off sleep were relevant to the story. Rather, in the light of the entire parable, the dominant exhortation of this discourse is repeated: Be prepared! Keep watching!

Notes

1 The words "and the bride," attested by D X* Θ f¹ et al., may have been added out of a sense of propriety, a desire for a well-rounded story in which the bride should be present. Alternatively one might argue that the words were original but omitted out of the widely held view that Christ would come and fetch his bride, the church. These and other internal considerations (how much did copyists know about marriage customs in Jesus' day?) are indecisive. On external evidence alone, omission is more likely original.

9 The two readings are (1) μήποτε οὐκ ἀρκέσῃ (*mēpote ouk arkesē*, "no, there may not be enough"), supported by ℵ A L Z (Θ) f¹³ et al.; and (2) μήποτε οὐ μὴ ἀρκέσῃ (*mēpote ou mē arkese*, perhaps "no, there will certainly not be enough"), attested by B C D K W Δ et al. The second option might be taken to introduce into the parable the notion of the absolute untransferability of the oil. But three things must be borne in mind: (1) though the grammatical points are much discussed, there is some ground for thinking that by NT times the second construction (*ou mē* plus the subjunctive) could itself be softened to the first meaning (cf. Zerwick, par. 444); (2) on internal grounds the first reading is considerably more likely, since copyists might well wish to change an *ouk* to an *ou mē* before the subjunctive; and (3) the effect on the story is the same—whether the wise virgins are certain they will not have enough oil to share or doubt that they will, the outcome is the same; and the reasons differ but little.

d. *The talents*

25:14–30

14"Again, it will be like a man going on a journey, who called his servants and entrusted his property to them. 15To one he gave five talents of money, to another two talents, and to another one talent, each according to his ability. Then he went on his journey. 16The man who had received the five talents went at once and put his money to work and gained five more. 17So also, the one with the two talents gained two more. ¹⁸But the man who had received the one talent went off, dug a hole in the ground and hid his master's money.

¹⁹"After a long time the master of those servants returned and settled accounts with them. ²⁰The man who had received the five talents brought the other five. 'Master,' he said, 'you entrusted me with five talents. See, I have gained five more.'

²¹"His master replied, 'Well done, good and faithful servant! You have been faithful with a few things; I will put you in charge of many things. Come and share your master's happiness!'

²²"The man with the two talents also came. 'Master,' he said, 'you entrusted me with two talents; see, I have gained two more.'

²³"His master replied, 'Well done, good and faithful servant! You have been faithful with a few things; I will put you in charge of many things. Come and share your master's happiness!'

²⁴"Then the man who had received the one talent came. 'Master,' he said, 'I knew that you are a hard man, harvesting where you have not sown and gathering where you have not scattered seed. ²⁵So I was afraid and went out and hid your talent in the ground. See, here is what belongs to you.'

²⁶"His master replied, 'You wicked, lazy servant! So you knew that I harvest where I have not sown and gather where I have not scattered seed? ²⁷Well then, you should have put my money on deposit with the bankers, so that when I returned I would have received it back with interest.

²⁸" 'Take the talent from him and give it to the one who has the ten talents. ²⁹For everyone who has will be given more, and he will have an abundance. Whoever does not have, even what he has will be taken from him. ³⁰And throw that worthless servant outside, into the darkness, where there will be weeping and gnashing of teeth.'

This parable goes beyond the first three (24:42–25:13) in that it expects the watchfulness of the servants to manifest itself during the master's absence, not only in preparedness and performance of duty, even if there is a long delay, but in an improvement of the allotted "talents" till the day of reckoning.

The parable is frequently compared with Luke 19:11–27, the parable of the ten minas. The majority opinion today is that there is only one original and that most likely Luke has borrowed from Matthew's version or from a precursor of it (cf. Marshall, *Luke*, pp. 700–703; chart and discussion at 19:1–2). Borrowing the other way is scarcely conceivable. Would Matthew, for instance, be likely to eliminate the "king" theme found in Luke? The language of the two pericopes is rather different, and most of the differing details cannot be reconciled on normal grounds. The few parallels are well within the bounds of the speech variation of any itinerant preacher. Moreover the emphasis in each of the two parables is somewhat different, and Luke's is tightly tied to the Zacchaeus episode. The somewhat similar parable in the later noncanonical Gospel of the Nazaraeans (Hennecke, 1:149) is undoubtedly secondary and dependent on Matthew. On the whole it seems best to side with certain older commentators (Plummer, Zahn) who discern two separate parables.

14 The introduction to this parable in the Greek is somewhat abrupt (lit., "for as," without mention of the kingdom, "it" [NIV]; or a verb [NIV, "will be"]: the closest parallel is Mark 13:34). Probably this parable is so tightly associated with the last one as to share its introduction (see on v.1).

Slaves in the ancient world could enjoy considerable responsibility and authority. The man going on a journey entrusts his cash assets to three of his slaves who are understood to be almost partners in his affairs and who may share some of his profits (cf. Derrett, *Laws*, p. 18). The departure and the property are integral parts of the story and should not be allegorized (to refer to the Ascension and the gifts of the Spirit), though doubtless some early readers after Pentecost read these into the text.

15 Modern English uses the word "talent" for skills and mental powers God has entrusted to men; but in NT times the *talanton* ("talent") was a unit of exchange. Estimates of its value vary enormously for four reasons.

1. A talent could be of gold, silver, or copper, each with its own value. *Argyrion* in v.18, a word that can mean either "money" or "silver," may hint at the second option.

2. The talent was first a measure according to weight, between fifty-eight and eighty pounds (twenty-six to thirty-six kg), and then a unit of coinage, one common value assigned it being six thousand denarii.

3. Although it is possible to calculate by weight or metallic value, another problem remains. For instance, eighty pounds of silver at fifteen dollars an ounce would mean that a talent was worth about nineteen thousand dollars. But modern inflation changes silver values so quickly that prices are soon obsolete. Yet such equivalences are passed on from generation to generation of reference texts (e.g., BAG [1957] and BAGD [1979] have the same figures!).

4. It may be more sensible to compare the talent with modern currency in terms of earning power. If a talent was worth six thousand denarii, then it would take a day laborer twenty years to earn so much—perhaps three hundred-thousand dollars. On any reckoning NIV's footnote ("more than a thousand dollars") is much too low.

So the sums are vast—much larger than in Luke 19:11–27, where a "mina" (one hundred drachmas) is very close to one hundred denarii, or one-third of a year's wages (perhaps five thousand dollars). Moreover in Matthew's parable the talents are distributed according to the master's evaluation of his servants' capacities, whereas in Luke each servant is given the same amount. In Matthew, therefore, the parable lays intrinsic emphasis on the principle "to whom much is given, from him also shall much be required."

Attempts to identify the talents with spiritual gifts, the law, natural endowments, the gospel, or whatever else, lead to a narrowing of the parable with which Jesus would have been uncomfortable. Perhaps he chose the talent or mina symbolism because of its capacity for varied application.

16–18 "At once" (v.16) relates to the servant's promptness to put the money to work (NIV), not with the owner's departure (KJV; cf. Metzger, *Textual Commentary*, p. 63). The point is that the good servants felt the responsibility of their assignment and went to work without delay. NIV's "put his money to work" does not mean the servant invested the money in some lending agency. Rather he set up some business and *worked* with the capital to make it grow. But one servant, unwilling to work or take risks, merely dug a hole and buried the money (v.18). This was safer than the deposit systems of the time. (In Luke's parable the money of the last servant is hidden in a piece of cloth.)

19–23 The accounting begins "after a long time" (v.19), the implication being that the consummation of the kingdom will be long delayed (24:48; 25:5). "Settled accounts" (*synairei logon*) is a standard commercial term (Deiss LAE, pp. 118–19). The first servant, who doubled his five talents (v.20), is praised, especially for his faithfulness, and given two things (vv.21, 23): increased responsibility and a share in his master's *chara* ("joy," as in John 15:11). But we should not conclude that the sole reward of fulfilled responsibility is increased responsibility. The eschatological setting, coupled with the promise of joy that bursts the natural limits of the story, guarantees that the consummated kingdom provides glorious new responsibilities and holy delight (cf. Rom 8:17).

The parallelism of vv.22–23 with vv.20–21 is not exact but close (cf. 7:26–27 with 7:24–25) and reflects a Semitic cast. The second servant has been faithful with what has been given him (v.22) and hears the same words as his more able fellow servant (v.23). Probably the "many things" assigned the two men are not exactly the same. The point is not egalitarianism, whether here (cf. 13:23) or in the consummated kingdom, but increased responsibility and a share in the master's joy to the limits of each faithful servant's capacity.

24–25 The third servant accuses his master of being a "hard" (*sklēros*) man (v.24). The word, both in Greek and English, can mean various things (elsewhere in the NT it is found only in John 6:60; Acts 26:14; James 3:4; Jude 15). The servant is saying that the master is grasping, exploiting the labor of others ("harvesting where you have not sown"), and putting the servant in an invidious position. Should he take the risk of trying to increase the one talent entrusted to him, he would see little of the profit. If he failed and lost everything, he would incur the master's wrath. Perhaps, too, he is piqued at having been given much less than the other two (cf. Derrett, *Law*, p. 26); so, in a rather spiteful act, he returns to his master what belongs to him, no more and no less (v.25).

What this servant overlooks is his responsibility to his master and his obligation to discharge his assigned duties. His failure betrays his lack of love for his master, which he masks by blaming his master and excusing himself. Only the wicked servant blames his master. "The foolish virgins failed from thinking their part too easy; the wicked servant fails from thinking his too hard" (Alf). Grace never condones irresponsibility; even those given less are obligated to use and develop what they have.

26–27 The master condemns the servant on the basis of the servant's own words, which prove his guilt (v.26). If the master was so hard and grasping, should not the servant have put the money where it would have been relatively safe, earn interest, and require no work (v.27)?

The OT forbade Israelites from charging interest against one another (Exod 22:25; Lev 25:35–37; Deut 23:19; cf. Ps 15:5; "usury" is from Lat. *usura*, "use," and came to refer to the interest charged for the use of money); but interest on money loaned to Gentiles was permitted (Deut 23:20). Doubtless the law was frequently broken (e.g., Neh 5:10–12). By NT times Jewish scholars already distinguished between "lending at interest" and "usury" (in the modern sense). According to Roman law the maximum rate of interest was 12 percent (cf. W.W. Buckland, *A Textbook of Roman Law*, 3d ed. [Cambridge: University Press, 1963], p. 465). It is wrong to assume that Jesus is here either supporting or setting aside the OT law. The question does not arise, for Jesus' parables are so flexible that he sometimes uses examples of evil to make a point about good (e.g., Luke 16:1–9; 18:1–8).

28–30 The talent entrusted to this wicked servant is taken from him (v.28); the relationship between master and servant is severed (cf. Derrett, *Law*, p. 28). It is given to the man who now has ten talents, following the kingdom rule (v.29) Jesus had already taught in 13:12. Moreover, there is OT warrant for this pattern: on this basis the kingdom of Israel was stripped from Saul and given to David (cf. also 21:43). The wicked servant is "worthless" (*achreios*, used only here [v.30] and in Luke 17:10), for to fail to do good and use what God has entrusted to us to use is grievous sin, which issues not only in the loss of neglected resources but in rejection by the master, banishment from his presence, and tears and gnashing of teeth.

The parable insists that the watchfulness that must mark all Jesus' disciples does not lead to passivity but to doing one's duty, to growing, to husbanding and developing the resources God entrusts to us, till "after a long time" (v.19) the master returns and settles accounts. The parable applies widely and cannot be restricted to Christian leaders or Jews who fail to recognize their Messiah.

e. The sheep and the goats

25:31–46

> 31"When the Son of Man comes in his glory, and all the angels with him, he will sit on his throne in heavenly glory. 32All the nations will be gathered before him, and he will separate the people one from another as a shepherd separates the sheep from the goats. 33He will put the sheep on his right and the goats on his left.
>
> 34"Then the King will say to those on his right, 'Come, you who are blessed by my Father; take your inheritance, the kingdom prepared for you since the creation of the world. 35For I was hungry and you gave me something to eat, I was thirsty and you gave me something to drink, I was a stranger and you invited me in, 36I needed clothes and you clothed me, I was sick and you looked after me, I was in prison and you came to visit me.'
>
> 37"Then the righteous will answer him, 'Lord, when did we see you hungry and feed you, or thirsty and give you something to drink? 38When did we see you a stranger and invite you in, or needing clothes and clothe you? 39When did we see you sick or in prison and go to visit you?'
>
> 40"The King will reply, 'I tell you the truth, whatever you did for one of the least of these brothers of mine, you did for me.'
>
> 41"Then he will say to those on his left, 'Depart from me, you who are cursed, into the eternal fire prepared for the devil and his angels. 42For I was hungry and you gave me nothing to eat, I was thirsty and you gave me nothing to drink, 43I was a stranger and you did not invite me in, I needed clothes and you did not clothe me, I was sick and in prison and you did not look after me.'
>
> 44"They also will answer, 'Lord, when did we see you hungry or thirsty or a stranger or needing clothes or sick or in prison, and did not help you?'
>
> 45"He will reply, 'I tell you the truth, whatever you did not do for one of the least of these, you did not do for me.'
>
> 46"Then they will go away to eternal punishment, but the righteous to eternal life."

Strictly speaking, this passage is not a parable. Its only parabolic elements are the shepherd, the sheep, the goats, and the actual separation. Moreover, because the pericope is unique to Matthew, criticism based on close parallels is impossible. It clearly functions in this discourse somewhat as 10:40–42 (with which it has some connections) does in the second discourse. Almost everyone praises the simplicity and power of the passage. Alford remarks, "It will heighten our estimation of the wonderful sublimity of this description, when we recollect that it was spoken by the Lord *only three days before His sufferings*" (emphasis his). But there is disagreement over the meaning and literary history of these eloquent words.

1. The great majority of scholars understand "the least of these brothers of mine" (vv. 40, 45) to refer to all who are hungry, distressed, needy. The basis of acceptance into the kingdom is thus established by deeds of mercy and compassion. This interpretation is often allied with a misunderstanding of 22:34–40 (see comments there). The overall interpretation can take on varying forms as it relies on source-critical conclusions or particular views of the "Son of Man" (U. Wilckens, "Gottes geringste Bruder—zu Mt 25, 31–46," in Ellis and Grässer, pp. 363–83; David R. Catchpole, "The Poor on Earth and the Son of Man in Heaven: A Re-appraisal of Matthew xxv. 31–46," BJRL 61 [1978–79]: 355–97).

Most authors stress the Jewish parallels relating to compassion and almsgiving. Bornkamm (*Tradition*, pp. 23–24) holds that the parable (as we shall call it) not only eliminates distinctions between Jews and Gentiles but also between Jesus' disciples and unbelievers. All will ultimately be judged by their response to human need, and on this basis some from each group will be numbered among the sheep (cf. P. Christian, *Jesus und seine geringsten Bruder* [Leipzig: St. Benno, 1975], who holds this is a sermon for the Christian church concerning the eschatological significance of human solidarity). J. Friedrich's tome (*Gott im Bruder?* [Stuttgart: Calwer, 1977]) includes much useful information about how this pericope has been interpreted; but its basic point—that Matthew narrowed down to Christians Jesus' teaching that the eschatological judgment would decide the fate of all men according to their response to all human need—is unconvincing because it rests on a redaction-critical methodology of dubious worth.

The weakness of this general position is the identification of the least of Jesus' brothers with the poor and needy without distinction. There is no parallel for this, but there are one or two excellent alternative interpretations with strong NT parallels.

2. If the first interpretation extends "one of the least of these brothers of mine" too far, the second does not go far enough. Several scholars (e.g., J.R. Michaels, "Apostolic Hardships and Righteous Gentiles," JBL 84 [1965]: 27–37; J. Mánek, "Mit wem identifiziert sich Jesus (Matt. 25:31–46)?" *Christ and Spirit in the New Testament*, edd. B. Lindars and S.S. Smalley [Cambridge: University Press, 1973], pp. 15–25) argue that Jesus' "least brothers" are apostles and other Christian missionaries, the treatment of whom determines the fate of all men. Those who receive them receive Christ; those who reject them reject Christ (cf. 10:40–42). This interpretation is much closer to the text than the first one. The only hesitation concerns the restriction to apostles and missionaries in any technical sense. Appeal to Matthew 10 cuts two ways: though that mission was first restricted to the Twelve, it is clear that Jesus was looking beyond the Twelve to all true disciples, who without exception must confess him before men (10:32–33). Proclaiming the gospel of the kingdom to all nations (24:14) takes place in obedience to a universal mandate (28:18–20); and the suffering that Jesus envisages for his disciples (24:9–13) is not restricted to missionaries, even if sometimes theirs is a special share of it. Without detracting from the Twelve, Matthew's report of Jesus' words makes it clear that all true disciples are his emissaries.

3. Another restrictive interpretation is that of George Gay ("The Judgment of the Gentiles in Matthew's Theology," *Scripture, Tradition, and Interpretation*, edd.

W.W. Gasque and W.S. LaSor [Grand Rapids: Eerdmans, 1978], pp. 199–215). Relying on Matthew 18, Gay holds that three mutually exclusive groups are involved: those outside the Christian community who think they are part of it, those inside the community but not the "little ones," and the "little ones" within the community. The basis for judgment is the attitude of professing believers to the "little ones," Jesus' favorites. The judgment is therefore not the judgment of the nations ("It would be unfair and illogical to judge the unrepentant who have never made any commitment to Jesus and know nothing of the demands of the Kingdom on the same basis" [ibid., p. 210]).

But Matthew 18 does not support Gay's tripartite distinction, and 12:46–50 makes it clear that Jesus' brothers are his disciples. Moreover the language of vv.31–32, 46, including a reference to "all the nations" gathered before the Son of Man "on his throne in heavenly glory," cannot easily be made to apply to anything as restricted as Gay suggests.

4. Dispensational writers see a reference to the Second Coming, after the church has been removed at the Rapture. Jesus' "brothers" are Jews who have been converted during the Tribulation; and the "nations" are converted Gentiles (the "sheep") because they side with the converted Jews during this period. But unconverted Gentiles (the "goats") continue to oppose Jesus' brothers (Jews converted during the Tribulation). The sheep enter the millennial kingdom with Jesus' "brothers." "All the nations" (v.32) therefore excludes Jews—though it is doubtful whether the same interpretation would be pressed in 28:18–20. Some older writers argue that the judgment determines what nations as opposed to individuals are admitted to the millennial kingdom, but see on 28:18–20. One or two nondispensationalist writers (e.g., Allen) think the "brothers" are Christian Jews.

This interpretation fails unless the dispensational interpretation of chapters 24–25 is sustained, something we have rejected on other grounds (see on 24:1–3). Moreover there is no such pinpointing in the passage itself. Jesus never speaks of Jews as his brothers, though he does speak of his disciples in that way (12:46–50).

5. By far the best interpretation is that Jesus' "brothers" are his disciples (12:48–49; 28:10; cf. 23:8). The fate of the nations will be determined by how they respond to Jesus' followers, who, "missionaries" or not, are charged with spreading the gospel and do so in the face of hunger, thirst, illness, and imprisonment. Good deeds done to Jesus' followers, even the least of them, are not only works of compassion and morality but reflect where people stand in relation to the kingdom and to Jesus himself. Jesus identifies himself with the fate of his followers and makes compassion for them equivalent to compassion for himself (cf. Kistemaker, pp. 146ff.; Manson, *Sayings*, p. 251; J.-C. Ingelaere, "La 'Parabole' du jugement dernier [Matthew 25/31–46]," *Revue de l'histoire et de philosophie religieuses* 50 [1970]: 23–60; G.E. Ladd, "The Parable of the Sheep and the Goats in Recent Interpretation," in Longenecker and Tenney, pp. 191–99; cf. Matt 10:40–42; Mark 13:13; John 15:5, 18, 20; 17:10, 23, 26; Acts 9:4; 22:7; 26:14; 1 Cor 12:27; Heb 2:17).

To the objection that this interpretation does not preserve an adequate distinction between the "sheep" and "the least of these brothers of mine," the answer is that (1) a similar ambiguity occurs in Matthew 18; (2) this interpretation emphasizes the kind of loving relationships that must exist within the Christian community, a constant theme in the NT; and (3) it prepares the way for the surprise shown by both sheep and goats (vv.37–39, 44) and for some important theological implications (see below).

31 Nowhere in this discourse does Jesus explicitly identify the "Son of Man" (see on 8:20) with himself (24:27, 30, 37, 39, 44). But since this epithet is used in answer to the question "What will be the sign of your coming?" (24:3), the inference is inescapable. There are clear allusions to Zechariah 14:5 (cf. also Dan 7; Joel 3:1–12); but the role of eschatological Judge is, like many other things (see on 13:37–39), transferred without hesitation from Yahweh to Jesus. The Son of Man will come "in his heavenly glory" (cf. 16:27; 24:30; 1 Thess 4:16; 2 Thess 1:8); for "nothing earthly could furnish the images for an adequate description" (Broadus). He sits on his throne, not only as Judge, but as King (see v.34); for all of divine authority is mediated through him (28:18; cf. 1 Cor 15:25; Heb 12:2). (On the role of the angels, see 13:41–42; 24:31; 2 Thess 1:7–8; Rev 14:17–20.)

32–33 Presupposed is the fulfillment of 24:14. "All the nations" (*panta ta ethnē*, v.32) means "all peoples" and clearly implies that "all the nations" includes more than Gentiles only (see on 28:18–20). As the gospel of the kingdom is preached to Gentiles as well as Jews (see on 1:1; 2:1–12; 3:15–16; 8:11), so also must all stand before the King.

In the countryside sheep and goats mingled during the day. At night they were often separated: sheep tolerate the cool air, but goats have to be herded together for warmth. In sparse grazing areas the animals might be separated during the day as well. But now these well-known, simple, pastoral details are freighted with symbolism. The right hand is the place of power and honor.

34–40 The change from "Son of Man" (see excursus on 8:20) to "King" (vv.31, 34) is not at all unnatural; for the Son of Man in Daniel 7:13–14 approaches the Ancient of Days to receive "a kingdom," and here that kingdom is consummated (see on 24:30). The kingship motif has long since been hinted at or, on occasion, made fairly explicit to certain persons (see on 3:2; 4:17; 5:35; 16:28; 19:28; 27:42). Yet Jesus still associates his work with his Father, something he loves to do (10:32–33; 11:25–27; 15:13; 16:17, 27; 18:10, 19; 20:23; 26:29, 53; and many references in John). He addresses the sheep, "Come, you who are blessed *by my Father*" (v.34). "Blessed" is not *makarioi* (as in 5:3) but *eulogēmenoi* (as in 21:9; 23:39). They are "blessed" inasmuch as they now take their inheritance (Rom 8:17; Rev 21:7), which presupposes a relationship with the Father. That inheritance is the kingdom (see on 3:2) prepared for them "since the creation of the world" (John 17:24; Eph 1:4; 1 Peter 1:20). This glorious inheritance, the consummated kingdom, was the Father's plan for them from the beginning.

The reason they are welcomed and invited to take their inheritance is that they have served the King's brothers (cf. Isa 58:7). The thought is antithetical to Paul only if we think this is all Matthew says and that all Paul says touches immediately on grace. Both assumptions are false: 2 Corinthians 5:10 is related to the thought of this parable, and Matthew has other things to say about the salvation of men and women (1:21; 11:25–30; 20:28). The reason for admission to the kingdom in this parable is more evidential than causative. This is suggested by the surprise of the righteous (vv.37–39; see further below). When he is questioned, the King replies that doing the deeds mentioned to the least of his brothers is equivalent to doing it to him (v.40), and by implication to refuse help to the King's brothers is sacrilege (Calvin).

There is no awkwardness in the scene that requires a disjunction between the sheep (the righteous) and "the least of these brothers of mine"; for in pronouncing sentence on each one, the King could point out surrounding brothers who had been compassionately treated.

41–45 The condemnation is even more awful than in 7:23. The "goats" are cursed: they are banished from the King's presence and sent to the eternal fire (v.41). Hell is here described in categories familiar to Jews (see on 3:12; 5:22; 18:8; cf. Jude 7; Rev 20:10–15). The kingdom was prepared for the righteous (v.34). Hell was prepared for the Devil (see on 4:1) and his angels (demons; see on 8:31; cf. Jude 6; Rev 12:7) but now also serves as the doom of those guilty of the sins of omission of which Jesus here speaks: they have refused to show compassion to King Messiah through helping the least of his brothers. There is no significance in the fact that the "goats" address Jesus as "Lord" (v.44); for at this point there is no exception whatever to confessing Jesus as Lord (cf. Phil 2:11).

More important is the surprise of the sheep (vv.37–39) and the goats (v.44), a major part of the parable, though rarely discussed. Three things can be said with confidence.

1. Contrary to what some have suggested (e.g., Gay, "Judgment of Gentiles"), neither the sheep nor the goats are surprised at the place the King assigns them but at the reason he gives for this—viz., that they are admitted or excluded on the basis of how they treated Jesus. Thus there is no need to say the goats expected to be welcomed or the sheep expected to be rejected.

2. Zumstein (p. 348) is right to point out that the surprise of the righteous makes it impossible to think that works of righteousness win salvation. How the sheep and the goats treated Jesus' brothers was not for the purpose of being accepted or rejected by the King. The sheep did not show love to gain an eschatological reward, nor did the goats fail to show it to flout eschatological retribution.

3. The parable therefore presents a test eliminating the possibility of hypocrisy. If the goats had thought that their treatment of Jesus' "brothers" would gain them eschatological felicity, they would doubtless have treated them compassionately. But Jesus is interested in a righteousness of the whole person, a righteousness from the heart (see on 5:20; 13:52). As people respond to his disciples, or "brothers," and align themselves with their distress and afflictions, they align themselves with the Messiah who identifies himself with them (v.45). True disciples will love one another and serve the least brother with compassion; in so doing they unconsciously serve Christ. Those who have little sympathy for the gospel of the kingdom will remain indifferent and, in so doing, reject King Messiah. So Paul learned at his conversion! Determined to persecute Christians, he heard the Voice from the heavenly glory declaring, "I am Jesus, whom you are persecuting" (Acts 9:5).

We must not think that the Bible is unconcerned for the poor and the oppressed (Deut 15:11; Matt 22:37–40; 26:11; Gal 2:10). But that is not the center of interest here.

46 The same word "eternal" (*aiōnion*) modifies "punishment" as modifies "life." *Aiōnion* can refer to life or punishment in the age to come, or it can be limited to the duration of the thing to which it refers (as in 21:19). But in apocalyptic and eschatological contexts, the word not only connotes "pertaining to the [messianic] age" but, because that age is always lived in God's presence, also "everlasting" (cf. BAGD, s.v.; and esp. DNTT, 3:826–33). (On penal notions in NT theology, cf. J.I.

Packer, "What Did the Cross Achieve? The Logic of Penal Substitution," *Tyndale Bulletin* 25 [1974]: 3–45.)

The final separation of "sheep" and "goats" is a recurring theme in the NT, including Matthew (e.g., 7:21–23; 13:40–43). Some have argued that this doctrine has turned many people into infidels; but so have other Christian doctrines. The question is not how men respond to a doctrine but what Jesus and the NT writers actually teach about it. Human response is a secondary consideration and may reveal as much about us as about the doctrine being rejected. Nevertheless two things should be kept in mind: (1) as there are degrees of felicity and responsibility in the consummated kingdom (e.g., 25:14–30; cf. 1 Cor 3:10–15), so also are there degrees of punishment (e.g., Matt 11:22; Luke 12:47–48); and (2) there is no shred of evidence in the NT that hell ever brings about genuine repentance. Sin continues as part of the punishment and the ground for it.

7. Transitional conclusion: fourth major passion prediction and the plot against Jesus

26:1–5

> [1]When Jesus had finished saying all these things, he said to his disciples, [2]"As you know, the Passover is two days away—and the Son of Man will be handed over to be crucified."
> [3]Then the chief priests and the elders of the people assembled in the palace of the high priest, whose name was Caiaphas, [4]and they plotted to arrest Jesus in some way and kill him. [5]"But not during the Feast," they said, "or there may be a riot among the people."

1–2 For the other major passion predictions, see on 16:21; 17:22–23; 20:18–19. One last time Matthew uses the formula by which he brings all his discourses to a close (v.1; see on 7:28–29). In the narrative line of Matthew, this pericope is a masterpiece of irony. The Judge of the universe, King Messiah, the glorious Son of Man, is about to be judged. After Jesus' warnings against hypocrisy (23:12–31) and his demand for righteousness that involves the whole person (25:31–46), the plot moves on by stealth and by a morally bankrupt expediency (26:4–5). The Passion begins.

The Passover began Thursday afternoon with the slaughter of the lamb. "Two days" (v.2) must be somewhat under forty-eight hours, or the "two days" would be "three days" (see on 12:40). According to the tentative chronology (see on 21:23–22:46; 23:1–36; 24:1–3), Jesus speaks these words on the Mount of Olives late Tuesday evening, which, by Jewish reckoning, would be the beginning of Wednesday.

The "Son of Man" (see on 8:20) is here both glorious and suffering: as often, the themes merge. The Passover is two days away; and it is during that festival, Jesus now reveals for the first time, that the Son of Man will be handed over (for reasons to take the Greek present as a future, cf. Moule, *Idiom Book*, p. 7) to be crucified. Thus Jesus provides a framework for his disciples to interpret his death correctly after it happens—a framework alluded to a little more clearly in the institution of the Lord's Supper (vv.17–29).

3–5 *Tote* ("then," v.3) is such a loose connective (see on 2:7) that it does not mean that the Jewish leaders only began to plot after Jesus had delivered his final passion prediction (vv.1–2). Certainly the opposition had been rising for some time (cf. 12:14; 21:45–46). On the other hand, by placing vv.3–5 immediately after vv.1–2,

Matthew gives the narrative the flavor of God's sovereign control. The leaders may plot; but if Jesus dies, he dies as a voluntary Passover sacrifice (vv.53–54; John 10:18).

Matthew mentions the chief priests and elders, probably meaning the clerical and lay members of the Sanhedrin (see on 21:23). The word *aulē* can mean "courtyard," "farm" or "farmyard," "temple court," or the "prince's court," hence, "palace" (NIV). Caiaphas is called the high priest in Matthew and John (11:49); Luke (3:2; Acts 4:6) specifies Annas. There is no real conflict. Annas was deposed by the secular authorities in A.D. 15 and replaced by Caiaphas, who lived and ruled till his death in A.D. 36. But since according to the OT the high priest was not to be replaced till after his death, the transfer of power was illegal. Doubtless some continued to call either man "high priest." Certainly Annas, Caiaphas's father-in-law (John 18:13), continued to exercise great authority behind the scenes. This joint high priesthood is presupposed by Luke 3:2 and probably by John 18, where the most natural reading of the passage names Caiaphas as high priest in v.13 but Annas as high priest in v.19 (cf. v.24).

The combination of *synagō* ("assembled") and *bouleuomai* ("plotted") in vv.3–4 strongly suggests an allusion to Psalm 31:13. Psalm 31 is the lament of a righteous sufferer and the source of Jesus' word from the cross in Luke 23:46 (cf. Moo, "Use of OT," pp. 234–35). Earlier that day the leaders had wanted to arrest Jesus but dared not do so for fear of the people (21:46; apparently earlier attempts had also failed, John 7:32, 45–52). Now they decide to do away with Jesus (v.4), recognizing that they must do this by *dolos* ("stealth," "cunning," "guile") so as not to excite the crowds and start a riot (v.5).

The leaders were right in fearing the people. Jerusalem's population swelled perhaps fivefold during the feast; and with religious fervor and national messianism at a high pitch, a spark might set off an explosion. They decided to suspend action; but Judas's offer to hand Jesus over at a time and place when the crowds were not present was too good an opportunity to pass up (vv.14–16). Thus in God's providence the connection between Passover and Jesus' death that he had just predicted (vv.1–2) came about.

VII. The Passion and Resurrection of Jesus (26:6–28:20)

A. *The Passion* (26:6–27:66)

1. *Anointed at Bethany*

26:6–13

> [6]While Jesus was in Bethany in the home of a man known as Simon the Leper, [7]a woman came to him with an alabaster jar of very expensive perfume, which she poured on his head as he was reclining at the table.
>
> [8]When the disciples saw this, they were indignant. "Why this waste?" they asked. [9]"This perfume could have been sold at a high price and the money given to the poor."
>
> [10]Aware of this, Jesus said to them, "Why are you bothering this woman? She has done a beautiful thing to me. [11]The poor you will always have with you, but you will not always have me. [12]When she poured this perfume on my body, she did it to prepare me for burial. [13]I tell you the truth, wherever this gospel is preached throughout the world, what she has done will also be told, in memory of her."

Because of the structure the five discourses impose on Matthew, some scholars (Bacon, *Studies in Matthew;* Stendahl, *School,* pp. 20ff.) have thought that the passion and resurrection narratives (26:6–28:20) stand outside the main framework, perhaps as a kind of epilogue to balance the "prologue" (Matt 1–2). But I have argued (see Introduction, section 14; and on 28:18–20) that the familiar pattern of narrative elements followed by discourse teaching continues here in a *sixth* section. In this case, however, the "teaching" part of the narrative-and-teaching structure is continued by the church after Jesus' ascension (28:18–20). From another viewpoint the Passion and Resurrection must, as in all the Gospels, be seen as the climax toward which a great deal of the earlier narrative has been moving.

As often noted, Matthew from now on follows Mark quite closely, though he omits Mark 14:51–52; 15:21b, adds certain bits (e.g., 27:3–10, 51–53), provides a completely independent ending, and offers a number of minor changes (e.g., some third-person reports in Mark are now given in direct speech). Many attempts have been made to identify what is exclusively Matthean in the passion narrative; but not a few such attempts suffer from reductionism. For instance, Dahl (*Jesus in Memory,* pp. 37–51) holds that Matthew's account is designed to highlight differences between church and synagogue. The former has accepted Jesus as Messiah; the latter has rejected and condemned him (cf. also Trilling, pp. 66–74). Others think Jesus' passion in Matthew has an ethical cast, designed to help young disciples learn obedience (e.g., Strecker, *Weg,* pp. 183–84). Many others see various christological elements in Matthew's account. Barth (Bornkamm, *Tradition*) claims that by his suffering and death, Jesus fulfills God's redemptive plan and establishes the kingdom; and Kingsbury (*Matthew*) stresses the confession of Jesus as "Son of God." (For an excellent survey, cf. D. Senior, "The Passion Narrative in the Gospel of Matthew," in Didier, pp. 343–57; A. Descamps, in Didier, pp. 359–415.)

Virtually every theme thought to be particularly strong in Matthew can be shown to be present in one or more of the other Gospels. For instance, that the events are all under God's control or that Jesus dies voluntarily is even more strongly attested in John than in Matthew. This is not to deny that Matthew has his own contribution to make. Instead it is to say that what Matthew offers is a great deal of commonly held theology, presented with a rich allusiveness and a complex intertwining of themes, subtly blended to lay stress on one part or another of the narrative, and capped with a few additions unknown in any other source. Thus it is best to examine Matthew's material inductively and trace its unfolding.

The first pericope (vv.6–13) is problematic because of its disputed relation to other Gospel accounts (Mark 14:3–9; John 12:2–8; cf. Luke 7:36–50). Some ancient commentators (e.g., Origen) thought there were three anointings: first, Luke 7:36–50, in Galilee; second, John 12:2–8, a few days earlier than the third, Mark 14:3–9 and Matthew 26:6–13. Most modern scholars believe that there was only one anointing and that variations in details arose during oral transmission and because of the hortatory use by each evangelist (see esp. R. Holst, "The One Anointing of Jesus: Another Application of the Form-Critical Method," JBL 95 [1976]: 435–46); but there is no consensus among these scholars as to the original setting or purpose of the story.

On the whole a third alternative seems preferable: there were two anointings, one in Galilee (recorded by Luke) and the other in Bethany (recorded by Matthew, Mark, and John; so Broadus; McNeile; A. Legault, "An Application of the Form-Critique Method to the Anointings in Galilee and Bethany," CBQ 16 [1954]: 131–

45). The only real similarities between the two incidents are the anointing by a woman and the name Simon. But "Simon," like "Judas," was a very common name; and the two incidents differ in many details. In Luke the woman is a "sinner"; in the other account there is no mention of this, and John says she is Mary of Bethany. In Luke the host is a Pharisee, in a Galilean home; here the host is "Simon the leper," at a home in Bethany. In Luke the host is critical of the woman's actions; here the disciples criticize her.

Small differences among Matthew, Mark, and John are fairly easily reconciled. John may place the incident where he does because he has just spoken of Bethany and will mention that town no more; but his links with the historical setting seem fairly strong and the most natural interpretation of his account is that the anointing took place before the Triumphal Entry (John 12:2, 12). Mark and Matthew, on the other hand, provide no chronological connection, only a thematic one. Out of Jesus' rebuke to the disciples, Judas Iscariot sets his course of betrayal (cf. John 12:4–6). To object to this two-incident theory on the grounds that the methodology and many of the presuppositions "are out of date due to the scholarly advances in the disciplines of form and redaction criticism. . . .[so that there is] no trajectory or *tendency* to explain the complexities of the final editions of the stories" (Holst, "The One Anointing," p. 435, emphasis his) is to make these tools intrinsically incapable of recognizing two superficially similar incidents.

6–7 For Bethany (v.6), see on 21:17. Contrary to common opinion, John does not say this took place at the home of Lazarus, Mary, and Martha; he may only mean that the well-known family was present. That Martha served is quite in keeping with village life at the time. Mark and Matthew set the scene in the home of "Simon the Leper," who was presumably cured—or else all there were violating Mosaic law. The action of the woman was not unprecedented: a distinguished rabbi might have been so honored. The evangelists stress the cost of the "perfume" (v.7, most likely a fairly viscous fluid, possibly from the nard plant native to India), which was extracted from the thin-necked alabaster flask by snapping off the neck. According to John 12:3, the nard was worth about three hundred denarii—approximately a year's salary for a working man.

8–9 Matthew mentions "the disciples" (v.8), Mark "some of those present," and John "Judas Iscariot." If the three accounts represent the same incident, it could be that, just as Peter voiced the sentiments of the group (v.35) and was answered directly by Jesus, so with Judas. Matthew shows the disciples' failure to understand what is taking place, not only in the anointing, but also in who Jesus truly is and in the rush of events toward the Cross (see on 16:21–28; 17:22–23; 20:18–19). Doubtless there were thousands of really poor people within a few miles of this anointing. Whatever Judas's motives (John 12:6), some people at least were motivated by righteous indignation (v.9); and thus in Jesus' view they revealed their distorted values and blindness as to the unique redemptive event about to take place.

10–11 The Greek *gnous de* ("aware of this") is also behind 16:8 ("Aware of their discussion"). It is possible that Jesus' knowledge is here supernatural; but perhaps the complaints were whispered and came to Jesus' attention because they troubled the woman. Jesus begins his rebuke by accusing the disciples of "bothering" her (v.10; the Greek idiom, found in the NT only here and in Luke 11:7; Gal 6:17, is a strong one). What they call waste, Jesus calls "a beautiful thing."

Hill's claim (*Matthew*) that Jesus' further statement (v.11) "distinguishes between a good work (i.e., almsgiving) and one done with reference to himself while he is present (with his disciples, and also as the 'living Christ' in the Matthean church)" entirely misses the point. Jesus distinguishes between giving to the poor and the extravagance lavished on himself *on the grounds that he will not always be there to receive it*. Far from referring to Jesus' spiritual presence in the church, Matthew *distinguishes* between Jesus' earthly presence and his postascension spiritual presence (28:20). His followers will always find poor people to help (cf. Deut 15:11); they will not always have the incarnate Jesus with them. Implicitly, the distinction Jesus makes is a high christological claim, for it not only shows that he foresees his impending departure but also that he himself, who is truly "gentle and humble in heart" (11:29), *deserves* this lavish outpouring of love and expense.

Lane (*Mark* pp. 493-94) follows F.W. Danker, ("The Literary Unity of Mark 14, 1-25," JBL 85 [1966]: 467-72) in suggesting that Psalm 41 may also be alluded to here—a psalm that speaks of the poor yet righteous sufferer who is betrayed by his closest friend, yet vindicated by God in the end. Jesus is the poor, righteous Sufferer par excellence; and the opportunity to help him in any way will soon be gone forever.

12 The anointing does not designate Jesus as Messiah but "prepares" him for his burial after dying the death of a criminal, for only in that circumstance would the customary anointing of the body be omitted (cf. D. Daube, "The Anointing at Bethany and Jesus' Burial," AThR 32 [1950]: 187-88). Jesus' defense of the woman does not necessarily mean that the woman understood what she was doing, though it allows this. Jesus may well be using the anointing to intimate again his impending crucifixion (cf. v.2).

13 Interpretations of this verse, with its solemn promise, differ. Jeremias (*Prayers*, pp. 112-24; *Promise*, p. 22) takes the saying as authentic but says that *hopou* here means not "wherever" (NIV) but "when"—i.e., when the triumphal news of this gospel is proclaimed by God's angel (cf. Rev 14:6-11) at the Parousia, before all the world, then her act will be remembered. Jeremias thus avoids any prediction by Jesus of a worldwide mission. But this uses "gospel" strangely and is too tightly linked with assumptions about what Jesus could or could not have said. Jesus did foresee Gentiles entering the kingdom (8:11), in response to his disciples' preaching, and that the word of God would be preached in the world (13:37; 24:14). Thus the groundwork has already been laid for this saying and also for the Great Commission (28:18-20).

The most natural interpretation of v.13 is that the woman and her deed would be remembered "wherever" the "gospel of the kingdom" would be preached (cf. Moore, pp. 203f.). Broadus remarks: "This very remarkable promise . . . was already in process of fulfillment when John wrote his Gospel, probably sixty years afterwards; for he distinguishes this Bethany from the one beyond Jordan (John 1:28) by calling it (John 11:1f.) the village of Mary (placed first) and Martha; and then makes all definite and clear by adding, 'It was that Mary who anointed the Lord with ointment', etc. He has not yet in his Gospel told the story of the anointing, but he assumes that it is familiar to all Christian readers."

2. Judas's betrayal agreement

26:14–16

> [14]Then one of the Twelve—the one called Judas Iscariot—went to the chief priests [15]and asked, "What are you willing to give me if I hand him over to you?" So they counted out for him thirty silver coins. [16]From then on Judas watched for an opportunity to hand him over.

All the Gospels speak of Judas's important role in Jesus' death (cf. Mark 14:10–11; Luke 22:3–6); but none explains what motives prompted his treachery. Like most human motives, his were mixed and doubtless included avarice and jealousy combined with profound disappointment that Jesus was not acting like the Messiah he had expected.

14–16 While *tote* ("then") is generally difficult to translate (see on 2:7), here (v.14) there is probably a logical connection with the preceding pericope. In Judas's view Jesus was acting less and less regal and more and more like a defeatist on his way to death. If Matthew's anointing (vv.6–13) is the same as the one in John 12:1–8, Judas may also have been smarting from Jesus' rebuke. Moreover, *if* his name ties him in with the Zealot movement (see on 10:4), then his disappointment is the more understandable, though not more excusable. He approaches the "chief priests" (see on 21:23). (One may ask in passing why Matthew makes no mention of the Pharisees if his antipathy toward them is as strong as some say.)

The chief priests "counted out for him thirty silver coins" (v.15); but Matthew's language (lit., "they weighed out to him"), unlike Mark's, is the distinctive language of the LXX and calls to mind Zechariah 11:12, to which Matthew will return in 27:3–10 (Moo, "Use of OT," pp. 187–89). In Zechariah 11, thirty pieces of silver is a paltry amount ("the handsome price at which they priced me" [v.13] is ironic)— the value of a slave accidentally gored to death by an ox (Exod 21:32). That Jesus is lightly esteemed is reflected not only in his betrayal but in the low sum agreed on by Judas and the chief priests.

Excursus

The traditional date of Jesus' death has been A.D. 30. But Hoehner (*Chronological Aspects*, pp. 65–93) has made a plausible case for A.D. 33, though the exact year has little effect on the exegesis. More important is the problem of the relationship between the synoptic Gospels and John. The Synoptics seem to indicate that Jesus and his disciples ate the Passover meal the evening before the Crucifixion (see esp. Mark 14:12–16; 15:1–25, and parallels), whereas John seems to suggest that the Passover lamb was slaughtered at the moment Jesus was being put to death, which would of course mean that he and his disciples did not eat the Passover at the Last Supper (cf. esp. John 18:28; 19:14).

The question is of more than chronological interest; for quite apart from harmonization of disparate historical records, the meaning of the Lord's Supper is affected by its connection with Passover. The literature about this question is immense. The aim of this excursus is to list some of the principal options and defend briefly the interpretation adopted here. Essential bibliography includes Hoehner, *Chronological Aspects*, pp. 81–90; Jeremias, *Eucharistic Words*, pp. 41ff.; SBK, 2:847–52; A. Jaubert, *The Date of the Last Supper* (Staten Island,

N.J.: Alba, 1965); E. Ruckstuhl, *Chronology of the Last Days of Jesus* (New York: Desclée, 1965); G. Ogg, "The Chronology of the Last Supper," *Historicity and Chronology in the New Testament*, ed. D.E. Nineham (London: SPCK, 1965), pp. 75–96; J.B. Segal, *The Hebrew Passover from the Earliest Times to A.D. 70* (London: OUP, 1963); S. Dockx, *Chronologies néotestamentaires et Vie de l'Eglise primitive* (Paris/Gembloux: Duculot, 1976), *passim*; Marshall, *Last Supper*, esp. pp. 57ff., and Table 4 (pp. 184–85); Moo, "Use of OT," pp. 318–23; and the major commentaries on the Gospels.

1. Many scholars maintain that the discrepancies are not historically reconcilable—that either the Synoptics are right or John is. There are many indications that the synoptists understand the Last Supper to be a Passover meal (see esp. Jeremias, *Eucharistic Words*, pp. 41–62; Marshall, *Last Supper*, pp. 59–62). Therefore attempts to turn the meal into something else—a *Kiddush* (prayer meal), though this was unknown till several centuries later, or an *Habburah* (fellowship meal) eaten just before Passover—are not convincing. That the meal was not Passover supper but that such elements were read back into it is a counsel of despair, especially in light of the Passover associations as early as 1 Corinthians 11.

Any theory of this kind depends on its explanation of why the discrepancy was introduced. If the Synoptics are historically correct (Jeremias), perhaps John changed the date to correspond with his Jesus–Passover-lamb typology; if John is historically correct (Ogg), perhaps the synoptists changed the date to make the Last Supper fit the Passover symbolism. Either way it is necessary to trace a theological development; but to date no such work has proved convincing. To argue that John has identified Jesus with the Passover lamb by so flimsy a device as changing two or three chronological references is not very credible in a book abounding with explanatory statements (1:42; 2:21–22; 12:38; 13:18 et al.). In fact, only the Synoptics mention the day the lambs were sacrificed (Mark 14:12; Luke 22:7). Finding theological motivation for a putative change in the Synoptics is even more problematic, because of the highly disputed question of which evangelist preserves the oldest form of the institution of the Lord's Supper (cf. Marshall, *Last Supper*, pp. 30ff.).

2. The second group of options brings together various theories of calendrical disputes in the first century. Jaubert argues that Jesus, as reported by the synoptists, was using a solar calendar known to us from Jubilees and apparently adopted at Qumran. Passover always occurred on *Tuesday* evening (14–15 Nisan); so Jesus and his men ate their Passover that night. But the "official" Pharisaic lunar calendar, followed by the fourth Gospel, places the Cross and the Sacrifice on the *lunar* 14–15 Nisan (Thursday–Friday, from nightfall to nightfall). In a somewhat different scheme some have argued that the Pharisees and Sadducees adopted different calendars (SBK), or that Jesus followed a Galilean (i.e., the Pharisees') calendar (Synoptics) and John reports on the basis of the Judean (Saducees') equivalent (so Hoehner).

At least all these theories based on diverse calendars join in affirming that Jesus and his disciples ate a Passover meal, whatever the date. But beyond that all these calendrical solutions have severe drawbacks. Part of Jaubert's view, for instance, turns on a third-century document (the *Didascalia*) concerned with justifying current fasting practices by appeal to Passion Week, rather than giving any useful historical information about that week. There is no evidence that Jesus followed a sectarian calendar; and quite certainly sacrifices were not offered in the temple on any day other than the "official" (lunar calendar) day. Moreover all four evangelists seem to agree that Jesus was arrested the evening before his crucifixion; and, despite objections, there was enough time between his arrest

Thursday night and his crucifixion Friday to allow for the various events discussed below. Some of the other theories are highly suspect because of poor attestation in primary sources and are little more than last resorts.

3. The third approach is to attempt historical harmonization between John and the Synoptics as they stand. Of these attempts, one, pursued at various times in church history, is reasonably successful.

Matthew 26:17 speaks of "the first day of the Feast of Unleavened Bread." According to Leviticus 23:6 and Numbers 28:17, Jews were forbidden to use yeast in their bread for seven days from 15 Nisan. However, Exodus 12:18 says that yeast should be removed from the house on 14 Nisan; and there is some evidence that Jews customarily removed it at noon on 14 Nisan so as to have everything ready in good time. Thus Josephus can in one place speak of the beginning of the feast as occurring on 15 Nisan (Antiq. III, 248–50 [x.5]) and in another as occurring on 14 Nisan (War V, 99 [iii.1]; cf. also Antiq. II, 315–16 [xv.1]). Matthew seems to presuppose Thursday, 14 Nisan. According to Exodus 12:6 and Numbers 9:3, the Jews were directed to kill the paschal lamb "at twilight" (NIV), i.e., "between the two evenings," which in Jesus' day meant middle to late afternoon till sundown (Deut 16:6). Hence Josephus (War VI, 423 [ix.3]) says the lambs were killed from the ninth to the eleventh hour (3:00 P.M. to 5:00 P.M.) and that on one occasion the number killed was 256,500—almost certainly an inflated figure.

It seems, then, that Jesus' disciples entered the city shortly after noon on Thursday, 14 Nisan, procured the room, took a lamb to the temple court and killed it, roasted it with bitter herbs (Exod 12:8–9), and made other arrangements for the meal, including the purchase of wine and unleavened bread. Matthew 26:19 explicitly says that they "prepared the Passover." After nightfall on Thursday evening, when it was 15 Nisan, Jesus joined his disciples and they ate the Passover. On these points the Synoptics agree; and this places Jesus' death on Friday, 15 Nisan, probably about 3:00 P.M.

The following passages in John are the most difficult to harmonize with this scheme.

John 13:1 "It was just before the Passover Feast" need not set the stage for the meal, which was about to be eaten, but for the footwashing. The footwashing took place before the "Passover Feast." John 13:2 in the best texts does not contradict this: we should not read "supper being ended" (KJV) but the "meal was being served" (NIV).

John 13:27 "What you are about to do, do quickly." John adds (13:29) that some of those present thought Jesus was telling Judas to buy what was necessary for the feast, or else give something to the poor. How could they think this, if they were just then *finishing* the feast? But one may also ask why, if the feast was still twenty-four hours away, anyone would think that there would be any rush to buy things. It is more reasonable to think that the disciples thought Judas needed to make some purchases for the *continuing* "Feast of Unleavened Bread"—e.g., some more unleavened bread. Since the next day, still Friday, 15 Nisan, was a high feast day and the day after a Sabbath, it was best to do things immediately. By Jewish reckoning the high feast day (15 Nisan) had begun that Thursday evening; but purchases were more than likely still possible, though inconvenient. After all one could buy necessities even on a Sabbath if it fell before a Passover, provided it was done by leaving something in trust rather than paying cash (M *Sanhedrin* 23:1). Moreover it was customary to give alms to the poor on Passover night. The temple gates were left open from midnight on, and beggars congregated there (cf. Jeremias, *Eucharistic Words*, p. 54; Ruckstuhl, *Last Days*, p. 132). On any other night it is difficult to imagine why the disciples would think Judas was being sent out for this purpose; the next day would have done as well.

John 18:28 Jesus stands before Pilate. "By now it was early morning, and to avoid ceremonial uncleanness the Jews did not enter the palace; they wanted to be able to eat the Passover." The precise nature of this "ceremonial uncleanness" is highly disputed. Certainly Jews had to purify themselves for Passover (cf. 2 Chron 30:18; Ezra 6:19–21; cf. John 11:55; 12:1), and Pilate respected the Jews' scruples (John 18:28–29). Contamination might come from the road dust brought in by foreign visitors (cf. M *Berakoth* 9:5), or from contact with Gentiles who had eaten or touched something unclean (e.g., a corpse or a menstruous woman). While there are numerous other possibilities, uncleanness from any of these sources could have been eliminated at the end of one day by a purifying wash at sundown (cf. Lev 15:5–11, 16–18; 22:5–7; cf. j *Peshahim* 36b, 92b); and then the Passover could be eaten. Thus close attention to John's text and the historical background makes it unlikely that John 18:28 can be used to defend the view that Jesus ate a meal the evening before Passover night. Instead, John 18:28 is more plausibly interpreted in one of two other ways.

1. It is possible that the priests had intended to eat the Passover that night; but, pressed by their temple duties and the thousands of sacrifices they had to perform, interrupted by Judas's unexpected offer of instant betrayal and delayed by the headlong pace of the ensuing judicial examinations, they still had not yet eaten their own Passover. This view is unlikely if Exodus 12:8–10, forbidding delay of the Passover dinner beyond midnight (M *Peshahim* 10:9; M *Zebahim* 5:8), was strictly interpreted. But these traditions may be late; and *Mekilta* on Exodus says that some rabbis interpreted Exodus 12:8–10 as being satisfied if the Passover were eaten by dawn. Even so, these Jewish leaders were being caught out by at least two or three hours.

2. More plausibly, "to eat the Passover" in John 18:28 may refer, not to the Passover meal itself, but to the continuing feast, and in particular to the *chagigah*, the feast-offering offered on the morning of the first full paschal day (cf. Num 28:18–19). This could explain the Jews' concern: ritual purification could be regained by nightfall, but not by the morning *chagigah*. Of course the *chagigah* could be eaten later in the week; but it is unlikely that the leaders, conscious of their public status, would be eager to delay it unless absolutely unavoidable. Deuteronomy 16:3 speaks of eating the Passover food of unleavened bread seven days. It may be, then, that the leaders wanted to avoid ritual uncleanness in order to continue full participation in the entire feast. Moreover this becomes the more plausible if our treatment of John 19:31 is correct. Morris's objection (*John*, pp. 778–79) that one may concede that "the Passover" can refer to Passover plus the Feast of Unleavened Bread but certainly not to the Feast of Unleavened Bread without the Passover meal may be setting up a straw man; for the interpretation being defended here does not claim that "the Passover" here refers to the Feast of Unleavened Bread *apart from* the Passover meal itself but to *the entire Passover festival*. Ritual uncleanness at this point in the festival would force temporary withdrawal from the festivities, from "eating the Passover."

John 19:14 Referring to the day of Jesus' crucifixion, the verse reads, "It was *paraskeuē tou pascha*" (lit., "the Preparation of the Passover"). There is strong evidence to suggest that *paraskeuē* ("Preparation [Day]") had already become a technical name for Friday, since Friday was normally the day on which one prepared for the Sabbath (Saturday); and we have no evidence that the term was used in the evangelist's time to refer to the eve of any festal day other than the Sabbath (cf. C.C. Torrey, "The Date of the Crucifixion according to the Fourth Gospel," JBL 50 [1931]: 241). In this context, then, *tou pascha* means "of Passover Week" or "of the Passover festival." Several diverse strands of evidence support this meaning of *pascha*. Josephus (Antiq. XIV, 21 [ii.1]; cf. XVII, 213 [ix.3]; War II, 10 [i.3]) uses "Passover" to refer to the entire Feast of Unleavened Bread, unless he is directly dependent on an OT passage, when he tends to keep the two distinct (Antiq. III, 248-51 [x.5]; cf. BAGD, s.v.). The same extended usage is found not only in M *Peshahim* 9:5 but in the NT (cf. Luke 22:1: "the Feast of Unleavened Bread, called the Passover," and probably also such passages as John 2:23; 6:4; 13:1; 19:31, 42). Thus John 19:14 most probably means "Friday in Passover Week" (hence NIV, "the day of Preparation of Passover Week"); and this understanding of *pascha* reinforces the comments on 18:28.

John 19:31 "And the next day was to be a special Sabbath." The most plausible view is that this does not refer to the day of the Passover meal but to Saturday, which would be considered a "high" or "special" Sabbath, not only because it fell during the Passover Feast, but because on the second paschal day, in this case a Sabbath (Saturday), the very important sheaf offering fell (cf. SBK, 2:582; Philo *De Specialibus Legibus* 2).

John 19:36 This verse refers to Exodus 12:46 to explain that Jesus, the Passover Lamb, did not have any of his bones broken; and some have thought this suggests that Jesus must have died while the lambs were being slaughtered. But this does not follow. John makes no such temporal connection; and the theological connection could spring either from the tradition regarding the witness of John the Baptist (John 1:29, 36) or from Jesus' words at the institution of the Lord's Supper, reported by the synoptists and Paul.

It seems, then, that the fourth Gospel can be fairly harmonized with the Synoptics as far as the chronology of the Last Supper and Jesus' death are concerned.

One final question remains. How could conscientious Jews be party to a trial and execution on a feast day, which, in terms of prohibitions and legal procedure, was to be regarded as a Sabbath (cf. Exod 12:16; Lev 23:7; Num 28:18; M *Betzah* 5:2)? But Mishnah (*Sanhedrin* 11:4) insists that the execution of a rebellious teacher *should* take place on one of the three principal feasts so that all the people would hear and fear (cf. also Deut 17:13; SBK, 2:826). Jeremias (*Eucharistic Words*, p. 79) examines other events reported in the Gospels (e.g., Jesus' burial) and alleged to be inconsistent with the sabbatical nature of Passover feast day and concludes that "the passion narratives portray no incident which could not have taken place on Nisan 15." There are numerous irregularities connected with the Sanhedrin trial; these, however, bear only marginally on the chronological problems and are treated in situ (see on 26:57–68).

Therefore we seem to be on safe ground in arguing that the Last Supper was a Passover meal and that some of its associations must be seen in that light.

3. *The Lord's Supper* (26:17–30)

a. *Preparations for the Passover*

26:17–19

> [17]On the first day of the Feast of Unleavened Bread, the disciples came to Jesus and asked, "Where do you want us to make preparations for you to eat the Passover?"
> [18]He replied, "Go into the city to a certain man and tell him, 'The Teacher says: My appointed time is near. I am going to celebrate the Passover with my disciples at your house.' " [19]So the disciples did as Jesus had directed them and prepared the Passover.

17 Problems of chronology and some of the steps needed to prepare for the Passover are discussed in the preceding excursus. A few more details shed light on the situation. Toward midafternoon of Thursday, 14 Nisan, the lambs (one per "household"—a convenient group of perhaps ten or twelve people) would be brought to the temple court where the priests sacrificed them. The priests took the blood and passed it in basins along a line till it was poured out at the foot of the altar. They also burned the lambs' fat on the altar of burnt offerings. The singing of the *Hallel* (Pss 113–18) accompanied these steps.

After sunset (i.e., now 15 Nisan), the "household" would gather in a home to eat the Passover lamb, which by this time would have been roasted with bitter herbs. The head of the household began the meal with the thanksgiving for that feast day (the Passover *Kiddush*) and for the wine, praying over the first of four cups. A preliminary course of greens and bitter herbs was, apparently, followed by the Passover *haggadah*—in which a boy would ask the meaning of all this, and the head of the household would explain the symbols in terms of the Exodus (cf. M *Pesahim* 10:4–5)—and the singing of the first part of the *Hallel* (Ps 113 or Pss 113–14). Though the precise order is disputed, apparently a second cup of wine introduced the main course, which was followed by a third cup, known as the "cup of blessing," accompanied by another prayer of thanksgiving. The participants then sang the rest of the *Hallel* (Pss 114–18 or 115–18) and probably drank a fourth cup of wine. Thus the preparations about which the disciples were asking were extensive.

18–19 Matthew's account is much simpler than Mark's. *Pros ton deina* ("to a certain man") refers to somebody one cannot or does not wish to name (v.18). A case can be made that the home belonged to the father of John Mark (Zahn), but this is far from certain. It is not clear whether Jesus had made previous arrangements or called on supernatural knowledge (cf. 21:1–3). Either way Jesus was carefully taking charge of this final Passover meal. Jesus' words "My appointed time is near" were probably purposely ambiguous. To the disciples and the owner of the house, they might have implied Jesus' timing for the Passover meal and prior arrangements for it. In the light of Easter, the words must refer to the now impending Crucifixion, the fulfillment of Jesus' mission.

The disciples do as Jesus has "directed" (v.19) or "instructed" them (*syntassō* is used in the NT only here and in 21:6; 27:10). *Syntassō* does not relate to discipleship, as many maintain, and still less to Jesus' authority in any abstract sense. Instead, it prepares the way for the Last Supper and Jesus' death and demonstrates that he is quietly and consciously taking the steps to complete his mission of tragedy and glory.

b. *Prediction of the betrayal*

26:20–25

> 20When evening came, Jesus was reclining at the table with the Twelve. 21And while they were eating, he said, "I tell you the truth, one of you will betray me."
> 22They were very sad and began to say to him one after the other, "Surely not I, Lord?"
> 23Jesus replied, "The one who has dipped his hand into the bowl with me will betray me. 24The Son of Man will go just as it is written about him. But woe to that man who betrays the Son of Man! It would be better for him if he had not been born."
> 25Then Judas, the one who would betray him, said, "Surely not I, Rabbi?"
> Jesus answered, "Yes, it is you."

Matthew agrees with Mark in placing this scene before the words of institution, whereas Luke's briefer account gives the impression that Judas did not leave till after those words. We cannot be certain which Gospel has preserved the chronological sequence; perhaps the Lukan account betrays greater marks of condensation and topical arrangement. Matthew omits the allusion to Psalm 41:9 preserved in Mark 14:18 but adds the brief exchange between Jesus and Judas in v.25 (cf. Mark 14:18–21; Luke 22:21–23; John 13:21–30).

20–22 The Passover meal could not be eaten till after sundown; and for those living within Palestine, it had to be eaten inside Jerusalem or not at all. That is why we find Jesus reclining at a table in a room in the city "when evening came" (v.20). Once the meal began—we do not know at what stage—Jesus solemnly says, "I tell you the truth, one of you will betray me" (v.21). The disciples respond uniformly: one after another, as the enormity of the charge sinks in, each man asks, "Surely not I, Lord?" (v.22).

23 NIV's "The one who has dipped his hand into the bowl" attempts to render an aorist participle (*ho embapsas*): contrast the present tense "one who dips" in Mark 14:20 (*ho embaptomenos*). Nevertheless NIV is misleading: it gives the impression that a particular "one" is in view, when in fact most if not all those present would have dipped into the same bowl as Jesus, given the eating styles of the day. Jesus' point is that the betrayer is a friend, someone close, someone sharing the common dish, thus heightening the enormity of the betrayal. The identification in John 13:22–30 probably took place just after this. If the main course, the roast lamb, was being eaten, the "bowl" would contain herbs and a fruit puree, which would be scooped out with bread.

24 For "woe," see on 23:13; for "Son of Man," see the excursus on 8:20. Here the Son of Man is simultaneously the glorious messianic figure who receives a kingdom and the Suffering Servant; indeed, the former highlights the evil of the person who hands him over to the latter role. No OT quotation explains "as it is written of him"; but one may think of OT passages such as Isaiah 53:7–9; Daniel 9:26, or else suppose that an entire prophetic typology (see on 2:15; 5:17–20) is in view, such as the Passover lamb, or some combination of the two.

The divine necessity for the sacrifice of the Son of Man, grounded in the Word of God, does not excuse or mitigate the crime of betrayal (cf. Acts 1:16–18; 4:27–28). Nor is this an instance of divine "overruling" after the fact. Instead divine sovereignty and human responsibility are both involved in Judas's treason, the one effecting salvation and bringing redemption history to its fulfillment, the other answering the promptings of an evil heart. The one results in salvation from sin for Messiah's people (1:21), the other in personal and eternal ruin (cf. Carson, *Divine Sovereignty*, pp. 130–32).

25 This exchange, preserved only in Matthew, magnifies Judas's effrontery and brackets the words of institution (vv.26–30) with the deceit of the betrayer (v.25) and the empty boast of the one who would disown Jesus with oaths (vv.31–35). Doubtless Judas felt he had to speak up; silence at this stage might have given him away to the others. Both here and in v.49, Judas uses "Rabbi" (see on 8:19; 23:7), which, in the pre-Easter setting, was probably more unambiguously honorific than the versatile *kyrios* ("Lord," v.22). As in v.22, the form of the question (using *mēti*) anticipates a negative answer; but the expected answer bears no necessary relation to the real answer (BDF, par. 427[2]). Jesus' response is identical in Greek to that in 26:64. It is affirmative but depends somewhat on spoken intonation for its full force. It could be taken to mean "You have said it, not I"; yet in fact it is enough of an affirmative to give Judas a jolt without removing all ambiguity from the ears of the other disciples. See further on v.64.

c. *The words of institution*

26:26–30

> 26While they were eating, Jesus took bread, gave thanks and broke it, and gave it to his disciples, saying, "Take and eat; this is my body."
> 27Then he took the cup, gave thanks and offered it to them, saying, "Drink from it, all of you. 28This is my blood of the covenant, which is poured out for many for the forgiveness of sins. 29I tell you, I will not drink of this fruit of the vine from now on until that day when I drink it anew with you in my Father's kingdom."
> 30When they had sung a hymn, they went out to the Mount of Olives.

John records nothing of the words of institution. Matthew and Mark are fairly close in their formulations, as are Luke and Paul; but Luke and Paul are sufficiently distinct to make it better to speak of three accounts instead of two (cf. Mark 14:23–26; Luke 22:19–20; 1 Cor 11:23–25). The numerous text-critical variations confirm the tendency toward assimilation, especially in material at the heart of Christian liturgy. The literature attempting to trace Jesus' exact words and to determine which of the synoptic forms is most primitive is immense (cf. Jeremias, *Eucharistic Words*, pp. 96–105; Marshall, *Last Supper*, pp. 30–56). Marshall's caution is sensible: "It must be emphasized that there is no good reason for supposing that any one of the three versions must necessarily be closer to the original form of the account than any of the others" (p. 38).

We may go farther and ask why we must limit ourselves to just one "original account." There were eleven or twelve witnesses. We have repeatedly referred to the evangelists' interest in reporting Jesus' *ipsissima vox*, not his *ipsissima verba* (see note on 3:17). The various criteria for getting behind this (number of Semitisms, redaction-critical distinctions) are inadequate. A good translation may reduce Semitisms but preserve authentic content; redaction criticism may determine that some statement is traditional but cannot prove authenticity or, conversely, that some formulation is redactional without disproving authenticity. We must be satisfied with the sources we have. (On the question of discerning by critical means Jesus' understanding of his own death, see esp. H. Schürmann, "Wie hat Jesus seinen Tod bestanden und verstanden? Eine methodenkritische Besinnung," in Hoffmann et al., *Orientierung*, pp. 325–63; and cf. Guthrie, *NT Theology*, pp. 436–48).

Close comparison of Mark and Matthew reveals few distinctive elements in Matthew. The first evangelist, unlike Mark, has "eat" in v.26 and replaces "they all drank from it" (Mark 14:23) with "Drink from it, all of you" (26:27). Matthew is usually judged more "liturgical" (Lohmeyer, Stendahl, Hill). This, though possible, is no more than a guess; we know almost nothing about first-century liturgy, and the variations are no more revealing in this regard than variations between Mark and Matthew in "nonliturgical" sections.

Appeal to liturgical influence is commonplace in current NT scholarship, and therefore the frequent assumption of such influence lends credibility to the claim; but it is in urgent need of reexamination. There may have been considerable diversity in the formulations used in church worship even *within each congregation*, as today in many nonliturgical denominations. Once again we must confess that our sources are inadequate for a confident conclusion. What is certain is that Jesus bids us commemorate, not his birth, nor his life, nor his miracles, but his death (cf. 20:28; 26:26–29).

26 This is the second thing Matthew records that takes place "while they were eating" (cf. v.21). Jesus takes *artos*, which can refer to "bread" generally (4:4; 6:11; 15:2, 26) but more commonly refers to a loaf or cake (4:3; 12:4; 14:17, 19; 15:33–34; 16:5–12). This loaf was unleavened (cf. Exod 12:15; 13:3, 7; Deut 16:3). He then gives thanks, probably with some such traditional formula as "Blessed art thou, O Lord our God, King of the universe, who bringest forth bread from the earth." He breaks it, distributes it (if the imperfect indicative variant is original, it may imply that he personally gave the bread to each of them), and says, "Take and eat; this is my body."

Few clauses of four words have evoked more debate than the last one. But three things must be said.

1. The words "this is my body" had no place in the Passover ritual; and as an innovation, they must have had stunning effect, an effect that would grow with the increased understanding gained after Easter.

2. Both the breaking and the distributing are probably significant: the bread (body) is broken, and all must partake of it. The sacrificial overtones are clearer in vv.27–28, but the unambiguous sacrificial language connected with Jesus' blood requires that v.26 be interpreted in a similar way.

3. Much of the debate on the force of "is" (In what sense *is* the bread Jesus' body?) is anachronistic. The verb itself has a wide semantic range and proves very little. "Take this, it means my body" (Mof) has its attractions, though it is scarcely less ambiguous. But what must be remembered is that this is a Passover meal. The new rite Jesus institutes has links with redemption history. As the bread has just been broken, so will Jesus' body be broken; and just as the people of Israel associated their deliverance from Egypt with eating the paschal meal prescribed as a divine ordinance, so also Messiah's people are to associate Jesus' redemptive death with eating this bread by Jesus' authority.

27 Assuming this is a Passover meal, this "cup" (with or without the article, by assimilation to Mark 14:23 or Luke 22:17 respectively) is probably the third, the "cup of blessing." Jesus again gives thanks, probably with some such prayer as "Blessed art thou, O Lord our God, King of the universe, Creator of the fruit of the vine." The wine was not grape juice, though it was customary to cut the wine with a double or triple quantity of water. Unlike Mark, Matthew records, not the performance, but the command: "Drink from it, all of you." As in Luke and Paul, this has the effect of describing exclusively what Jesus did, not what the disciples did. It should be noted that the participle *eucharistēsas* ("gave thanks"), cognate with *eucharistē* ("thanksgiving"), has given us the word "Eucharist." Some Protestants have avoided the term because of its associations with the traditional Roman Catholic mass, but the term itself is surely not objectionable.

28 This verse is rich in allusions; so attempts to narrow down its OT background to but one passage are reductionistic. "Blood" and "covenant" are found together in only two OT passages (Exod 24:8; Zech 9:11). Lindars (*Apologetic*, pp. 132–33) represents those who think the allusion must be to the latter, because allusion to the former would presuppose a typological exegesis not used so early in the tradition. But this fails to reckon with the extensive use of typology at Qumran; and the textual affinities are clearly in favor of Exodus 24:8 (see Gundry, *Use of OT*, pp. 57–58; Moo, "Use of OT," pp. 301ff.). The conclusion seems to be that, once again, we can penetrate near the heart of Jesus' own understanding of his relation to the OT (see on 5:17–20; 9:16–17; 11:9–13; 12:28; 13:52). And it is *his* understanding that sets a paradigm, not only for Matthew (see on 1:23; 2:15, 23; 8:16–17; 12:15–21; 13:35), but for other NT writers also (e.g., Heb 9:20). Equally without support are those theories that hold the covenant language to be original but not the blood–sacrifice language, making the primary allusion to Jeremiah 31:31–34; or that the sacrifice language is original but not the concept of covenant, making the primary allusion to the OT sacrificial system or to Isaiah 52:13–53:12. The primary reference is to Exodus 24:8, though other allusions are certainly present.

This means that Jesus understands the violent and sacrificial death he is about to undergo (i.e., his "blood"; cf. Morris, *Apostolic Preaching*, pp. 112–28; A.M. Stibbs, *The Meaning of the Word 'Blood' in Scripture* [London: Tyndale, 1954]) as the ratification of the covenant he is inaugurating with his people, even as Moses in Exodus 24:8 ratified the covenant of Sinai by the shedding of blood. "Covenant" is thus a crucial category (cf. DNTT, 1:365–72; Ridderbos, *Kingdom*, pp. 200–201; Morris, *Apostolic Preaching*, pp. 65–111; John J. Hughes, "Hebrews ix 15ff. and Galatians iii 15ff.; a Study in Covenant Practice and Procedure," NovTest 21 [1979]: 27–96; cf. Heb 8:1–13; 9:11–10:18, 29; 13:20). The event through which Messiah saves his people from their sins (1:21) is his sacrificial death; and the resulting relation between God and the messianic community is definable in terms of covenant, an agreement with stipulations—promises of blessing and sustenance and with threats of cursing all brought here into legal force by the shedding of blood.

Luke and Paul use the adjective "new" before covenant and thus allude to Jeremiah 31:31–34. Mark almost certainly omits the adjective; and the textual evidence for the word in Matthew is finely divided. But the passage from Jeremiah was almost certainly in Jesus' mind, as Matthew reports him, because "for the forgiveness of sins" reflects Jeremiah 31:34. Matthew has already shown his grasp of the significance of Jesus' allusion to covenant terminology in general and to the "new covenant" in particular; in 2:18 (see comments there) he cites Jeremiah 31 so as to show that he interprets the coming of Jesus as the real end of the Exile and the inauguration of the new covenant.

The words *to peri pollōn ekchynnomenon* ("which is poured out for many") could not fail to be understood as a reference to the Passover sacrifice in which so much blood had just been "poured out" (see on v.17). They also connote other sacrificial implications (e.g., Lev 1–7, 16), especially significant since at least *Jesus'* crucifixion did entail much bloodshed. The Mishnah (*Pesahim* 10:6), which in this instance may well preserve traditions alive in Jesus' day, uses Exodus 24:8 to interpret the Passover wine as a metaphor for blood that seals a covenant between God and his people. Jeremias (*Eucharistic Words*, pp. 222ff.) theorizes that the reason no mention is made of the Passover *lamb* in our accounts is that Jesus had already identified himself as the Lamb. This is possible because the failure to mention the lamb in any of the Synoptics is startling. But like most arguments from silence, it falls short of proof. Yet the allusions to the Passover—not least being the timing of the Last Supper—are cumulatively compelling.

It appears, then, that Jesus understands the covenant he is introducing to be the fulfillment of Jeremiah's prophecies and the antitype of the Sinai covenant. His sacrifice is thus foretold both in redemption history and in the prophetic word. The Exodus becomes a "type" of a new and greater deliverance; and as the people of God in the OT prospectively celebrated in the first Passover their escape from Egypt, anticipating their arrival in the Promised Land, so the people of God here prospectively celebrate their deliverance from sin and bondage, anticipating the coming kingdom (see on v.29).

Some take the preposition *peri* ("for [many]") to mean "on account of many" or "because of many" (BDF, par. 229[1]). But it is more likely equivalent in meaning to the *hyper* (NIV, "for [many]") of the parallel in Mark (Moule, *Idiom Book*, p. 63; Zerwick, par. 96) and possibly has the force of *anti* in 20:28 (cf. Morris, *Apostolic Preaching*, pp. 63, 172, 204, 206). As Karl Barth noted, the three prepositions point to Christ's "activity as our Representative and Substitute. . . . They cannot be understood if—quite apart from the particular view of the atonement made in Him which dominates these passages—we do not see that in general these prepositions speak of a place which ought to be ours, that we ought to have taken this place, that we have been taken from it, that it is occupied by another, that this other acts in this place as only He can, in our cause and interest" (cited in Morris, *Apostolic Preaching*, p. 63). For comments on "many," see on 20:28.

"For the forgiveness of sins" (cf. Heb 9:22) occurs in the words of institution only in Matthew and alludes to Jeremiah 31:31–34. Because the identical phrase is found in Mark 1:4 to describe the purpose of John's baptism but is omitted from the parallel in Matthew (3:1–2, 11), many suggest that Matthew purposely suppressed the phrase there because he wanted to attach it here and connect it exclusively to the work of Jesus Messiah. This is possible: NT writers understand that repentance and forgiveness of sin are tied together as tightly in the OT as in the period following Jesus' death, even though Jesus' death provides the real basis for forgiveness, a basis long promised by revelatory word, cultic act, and redemptive event. In one sense Mark might be willing to speak of John's baptism as a "baptism of repentance for the forgiveness of sins," while in another Matthew might be more interested in the ultimate ground of that "forgiveness of sin" and so reserve the phrase for Jesus. But several cautions should be kept in mind.

1. Matthew so regularly condenses Mark that it is usually risky to base too much on an omission.

2. Even in Matthew, John's baptism requires repentance (3:11) that demands confession of sin (3:6). It is hard to believe that Matthew thought that those who thus repented and confessed their sins were *not* forgiven!

3. Matthew may have slightly abbreviated the report of the Baptist's preaching (3:2) to maintain formal similarity to Jesus' early preaching (4:17).

4. In any case, a more important connection with v.28 is to be found in 1:21. It is by Jesus' death, by the pouring out of his blood, that he will save his people from their sins.

One more OT allusion is worth emphasizing. As in 20:28, it is very probable that Jesus is also portraying himself as Isaiah's Suffering Servant (cf. Moo, "Use of OT," pp. 127–32; France, "Servant of the Lord," pp. 37–39). This is based on three things: (1) "my blood of the covenant" calls to mind that the servant is twice presented as "a covenant for the people" (Isa 42:6; 49:8)—i.e., he will reestablish the covenant; (2) *ekchynnomenon* ("poured out") may well reflect Isaiah 53:12; and (3) "for many" again recalls the work of the Servant in Isaiah 52:13–53:12 (see on 20:28).

29 The "fruit of the vine" is a common Jewish way of referring in prayers to wine (cf. M *Berakoth* 6:1). Contrary to Jeremias (*Eucharistic Words*, pp. 207–18), Jesus' promise does not mean that he is abstaining from the cup of wine in this first "Lord's Supper" (cf. Hill, *Matthew*). Rather, just as the first Passover looks forward not only to deliverance but to settlement in the land, so also the Lord's Supper looks forward to deliverance and life in the consummated kingdom. The disciples will keep this celebration till Jesus comes (cf. 1 Cor 11:26); but Jesus will not participate in it with them till the consummation, when he will sit down with them at the messianic banquet (Isa 25:6; 1 Enoch 72:14; see on Matt 8:11; cf. Luke 22:29–30) in his Father's kingdom, which is equally Jesus' kingdom (cf. Luke 22:16, 18, 29–30; see on Matt 16:28; 25:31, 34). This point is greatly strengthened if we assume that Jesus speaks after drinking the *fourth* cup (see on v.17).

The four cups were meant to correspond to the fourfold promise of Exodus 6:6–7. The third cup, the "cup of blessing" used by Jesus in the words of institution, is thus associated with redemption (Exod 6:6); but the fourth cup corresponds to the promise "I will take you as my own people, and I will be your God" (Exod 6:7; cf. Daube, *New Testament*, pp. 330–31; Lane, *Mark*, pp. 508–9). Thus Jesus is simultaneously pledging that he will drink the "bitter cup" immediately ahead of him and vowing not to drink the cup of consummation, the cup that promises the divine presence, till the kingdom in all its fullness has been ushered in. Then he will drink the cup with his people. This is a veiled farewell and implies a sustained absence (see on 24:14; 25:5, 19). The Lord's Supper therefore points both to the past and to the future, both to Jesus' sacrifice at Calvary and to the messianic banquet.

30 The "hymn" normally sung was the last part of the *Hallel* (Pss 114–18 or 115–18). It was sung antiphonally: Jesus as the leader would sing the lines, and his followers would respond with "Hallelujah!" Parts of it must have been deeply moving to the disciples when after the Resurrection they remembered that Jesus sang words pledging that he would keep his vows (Ps 116:12–13), ultimately triumph despite rejection (Ps 118), and call all nations to praise Yahweh and his covenant love (Ps 117). It may be that Jewish exegesis had already interpreted Psalm 118:25–26 as a reference to Messiah's parousia (Jeremias, *Eucharistic Words*, pp. 255–62).

Notes

29 BDF, par. 12(3) points out that απαρτι (*aparti*) is ambiguous: it should most likely be taken as ἀπ᾿ ἄρτι (*ap' arti*, "from now on," NIV); but it could be construed as Ionic and Attic ἀπαρτί (*aparti*, "exactly," "certainly"), as, possibly, in Rev 14:13. But the customary rendering fits the context well and should be given the benefit of the doubt.

4. Prediction of abandonment and denial

26:31-35

31Then Jesus told them, "This very night you will all fall away on account of me, for it is written:

" 'I will strike the shepherd,
and the sheep of the flock will be scattered.'

32But after I have risen, I will go ahead of you into Galilee."
33Peter replied, "Even if all fall away on account of you, I never will."
34"I tell you the truth," Jesus answered, "this very night, before the rooster crows, you will disown me three times."
35But Peter declared, "Even if I have to die with you, I will never disown you." And all the other disciples said the same.

Mark (14:27-31) and Matthew place this pericope after Jesus and his disciples have left the Upper Room. Luke (21:31-38) implies that its contents occur before the departure for the Mount of Olives; John (13:36-38) clearly places it during the supper and before the farewell discourse. The abruptness with which Mark begins this pericope suggests that he displaced it, perhaps to keep intact the theological coherence of the preceding pericope. Matthew does the same thing and for the same reason: this use of *tote* ("then") is inconsequential (see on 2:7). It seems likely, therefore, that John gives us the historical sequence at this point, while Matthew and Mark place this pericope where it will emphasize the gravity of the disciples' defection and Peter's denial. Matthew adds some touches, such as the personal pronouns in v.31 (emphasis mine): "*You* will all fall away *on account of me*"—*you*, of all people, on account of *me*, your Messiah, by your own confession. Moreover, in laying out in advance much of the tragedy of the coming hours, the pericope shows that Jesus is not a blind victim of fate but a voluntary sacrifice; and simultaneously he is preparing his disciples for their dark night of doubt.

31 "This very night" makes clear how very soon the disciples' defection and Peter's denial will happen. The intimacy of the Last Supper is shortly to be replaced by disloyalty and cowardice. The disciples will all "fall away" on account of Jesus: they will find him an obstacle to devotion and will forsake him (for the verb, see on 5:29). As the quotation from Zechariah makes clear, their falling away is related to the "striking" of the Shepherd. Jesus has repeatedly predicted his death and resurrection, but his disciples are still unable to grasp how such things could happen to the Messiah to whom they have been looking (16:21-23; 17:22-23; see on v.33).

Yet Jesus' words "for it is written" show that the disciples' defection, though tragic and irresponsible, does not fall outside God's sovereign plan. The textual questions relating to Zechariah 13:7 are complex (Gundry, *Use of OT*, pp. 25-28; Moo, "Use of OT," pp. 182ff.; cf. John 16:32): apparently the quotation rests on a pre-Christian recension of the LXX or on the MT or on some combination of both. There is no reason to think that Zechariah's words have been altered to fit the events of Jesus' passion and thereby accord with Christian tradition to make the "prophecy" after the event seem to be scriptural (Jeremias, *NT Theology*, pp. 297f.). The change to the future *pataxō* ("I will strike") from the imperative *pataxon* ("Strike") is the only word that provides nominal support for this theory. However, the grammatical change was probably necessitated by the omission of a definite subject when the

Zechariah passage was condensed (France, *Jesus*, pp. 107–8), rather than by the pressure of an *ex eventu* "prophecy" or by a stress on the divine initiative for theological reasons—something already accomplished by "it is written." Even if it is the "sword" that does the striking in MT, it does so at Yahweh's command.

Matthew alone (cf. Mark) includes "of the flock" in the second line of the quotation (following LXX); but to what does "the flock" refer? In light of the context of Zechariah 13:1–6, many have suggested that a wicked prophet is in view there. But this is incompatible with "the man who is close to me [i.e., to Yahweh]" (13:7b). Instead, Yahweh pictures a day when, owing to the prevailing apostasy, the Shepherd who is close to him (as opposed to the false shepherd in Zech 11) is cut down and the sheep scattered. In 13:8–9 most of the sheep perish; but one-third are left, after being refined, to become "my people"—those who will say, "Yahweh is our God." If Jesus' quotation of Zechariah in the Gospels presupposes the full context of Zechariah 13:7, then the disciples themselves join Israel, the sheep of God, in being scattered as the result of the "striking" of the Shepherd. Their falling away "this very night" continues to the Cross and beyond and is emblematic of the coming dispersion of the whole nation. But a purified remnant, a "third," will survive the refining and make up the people of God, "my people." Thus at the very instant Jesus' disciples show by their scattering that they temporarily side with the unbelieving and apostate nation, God is taking action to make them his true people.

32 Lohmeyer (*Matthäus*) originated the notion that this verse refers to Jesus' future parousia, not his resurrection appearances. The Parousia is to take place, Lohmeyer thinks, in Galilee. But R.H. Stein ("A Short Note on Mark xiv.28 and xvi.7," NTS 20 [1974]: 445–52) has conclusively shown that v.32 must refer to a resurrection appearance. Others see in the verb *proagō* (which may mean either "will go ahead" [NIV] or "will lead" [as does a shepherd]) a continuation of the shepherd imagery. But the most natural way to take the verse, and one that vitiates the frequent insistence that it ill suits its context, is that of Stonehouse (*Witness*, pp. 170–73). The prediction that the shepherd will be stricken and the sheep scattered might suggest, apart from any further word, that the disciples would return disconsolate to their homes in Galilee, leaving Jesus behind in a grave in Judea. But this new word (v.32) promises that after Jesus has risen, he will arrive in Galilee before they get there: he will "go ahead of [them]."

33 Some have objected that Jesus' prediction of the scattering of *all* the disciples (v.31) conflicts with Peter's following Jesus into the high priest's courtyard (e.g., G. Klein, "Die Verleugnung des Petrus: Eine traditionsgeschichtliche Untersuchung," *Zeitschrift für Theologie und Kirche* 58 [1961]: 297; M. Wilcox, "The Denial-Sequence in Mark xiv.26–31, 66–72," NTS 17 [1970–71]: 426–36). But this overlooks the fact that all the disciples actually fled (v.56) and that Peter followed only "at a distance" (v.58) and then denied Jesus. At the end of the day, all the sheep were scattered; all had fallen away.

Peter does not respond directly to Jesus' quotation, nor to his promise to meet him in Galilee. But this does not mean that vv.31b–32 are misplaced redactional additions, for Peter's reply is psychologically convincing. On the one hand, he has learned more about Jesus than he knew at Caesarea Philippi (16:21–28); and as a result he is able to accept the idea of suffering for both Jesus and himself. On the other hand, his notion of suffering is bound up with the heroism of men like the

Maccabean martyrs, not with voluntary sacrifice—hence v.51 (cf. John 8:10). He is prepared for suffering but is not yet ready for what he thinks of as defeat. More important, he reacts on a primal level to Jesus' prediction in v.31a: "It would be natural for him to be too taken up with the implied slur on his loyalty to pay much attention to anything else" (Cranfield, *Mark*, p. 429).

34 Jesus' "I tell you the truth" (see on 5:18) introduces another warning about how near Peter's own defection is: "this very night," indeed, "before the rooster crows." If the idea of *two* cock crowings, preserved only in certain MSS of Mark 14:30, 68, 72, is original (and it may not be: cf. John W. Wenham, "How Many Cock-Crowings? The Problem of Harmonistic Text-Variants," NTS 25 [1978–79]: 523–25), then the "difference is the same as that between saying 'before the bell rings' and 'before the second bell rings' (for church or dinner)" (Alexander). Apparently it was usual for roosters in Palestine to crow about 12:30, 1:30, and 2:30 A.M. (Hans Kosmala, "The Time of the Cock-Crow," *Annual of Swedish Theological Institute* 2 [1963]: 118–20; 6 [1967–68]: 132–34); so the Romans gave the term "cock-crow" to the watch from 12:00 to 3:00 A.M. Despite Peter's claims of undeviating loyalty (v.33), Jesus says that Peter is within hours of disowning (same verb as in 16:24) him three times.

35 The language of Peter's protest (the rare subjunctive of *dei*) shows that he does not really think that Jesus' death was likely; he still has his visions of heroism. Nor is he alone in his brash protestations of loyalty—only quicker and more vehement than his peers.

5. Gethsemane

26:36–46

> 36Then Jesus went with his disciples to a place called Gethsemane, and he said to them, "Sit here while I go over there and pray." 37He took Peter and the two sons of Zebedee along with him, and he began to be sorrowful and troubled. 38Then he said to them, "My soul is overwhelmed with sorrow to the point of death. Stay here and keep watch with me."
>
> 39Going a little farther, he fell with his face to the ground and prayed, "My Father, if it is possible, may this cup be taken from me. Yet not as I will, but as you will."
>
> 40Then he returned to his disciples and found them sleeping. "Could you men not keep watch with me for one hour?" he asked Peter. 41"Watch and pray so that you will not fall into temptation. The spirit is willing, but the body is weak."
>
> 42He went away a second time and prayed, "My Father, if it is not possible for this cup to be taken away unless I drink it, may your will be done."
>
> 43When he came back, he again found them sleeping, because their eyes were heavy. 44So he left them and went away once more and prayed the third time, saying the same thing.
>
> 45Then he returned to the disciples and said to them, "Are you still sleeping and resting? Look, the hour is near, and the Son of Man is betrayed into the hands of sinners. 46Rise, let us go! Here comes my betrayer!"

Scholars usually see in this pericope an exhortation to foster vigilance and prayerfulness in the face of temptation (cf. Mark 14:32–42; Luke 22:40–46; also, John 12:28–33; 13:21; 16:32). Though this is doubtless present, far more central is the light the pericope sheds on Jesus' perception of what he is about to do. If the exegesis of v.39 is correct, we must ask why this Jesus who has for so long calmly faced the prospect of death (16:21; 17:22–23; 20:17–19; 26:1–2) should now seem to be less courageous than the Maccabean martyrs or the many thousands of his disciples who have faced martyrdom with great courage. The anguish in Gethsemane is not lightly to be passed over: three times Jesus prayed in deep emotional distress. The answer is found even in this first Gospel. The pericope must be interpreted in light of 1:21 and 20:28, on the one hand, and, on the other, in light of the reader's recognition that Jesus is the Messiah, the Son of God, "God with us," whose *sacrificial* death inaugurates the new covenant (vv.26–30) and redeems his people from their sins. Small wonder that NT writers make much of Jesus' unique and redemptive death (Rom 3:21–26; 4:25; 5:6, 9; 1 Cor 1:23; 2 Cor 5:21; Heb 2:18; 4:15; 5:7–9; 1 Peter 2:24).

Jesus did not suffer martyrdom. Can anyone imagine the words of 26:53 on the lips of a Maccabean martyr? Many of Jesus' followers throughout the centuries willingly suffer martyrdom because of the strength Jesus' death and resurrection give them. But Jesus went to his death knowing that it was his Father's will that he face death completely alone (27:46) as the sacrificial, wrath-averting Passover Lamb. As his death was unique, so also his anguish; and our best response to it is hushed worship (see K. Schilder, *Christ in His Suffering*, tr. H. Zylstra [Grand Rapids: Eerdmans, 1938], pp. 289–309).

36–38 "Gethsemane" (v.36) means "oil press," and here probably gave the name to the *chōrion* ("place"), usually a field or an *enclosed* piece of ground (cf. John 18:4, "went out") to which it was attached. Jesus and his disciples often frequented this spot (John 18:1–2) on the western slopes of Mount Olivet, separated from Jerusalem by the Kidron. Eight disciples remain at some distance, perhaps outside the enclosure, and the inner three join him (v.37). Jesus with stern self-control has so far masked his anguish; now he begins "to be sorrowful [*lypeisthai*, which connotes deep grief] and troubled" (*adēmonein*, found in the NT only here, in the parallel in Mark 14:33, and in Phil 2:26, and connoting deep distress).

Jesus' next words—"My soul is overwhelmed with sorrow" (v.38)—are almost a quotation from the refrain of Psalms 42–43 (LXX). The phrase *heōs thanatou* ("to the point of death") is so common in the LXX (e.g., Isa 38:1) that it should not be thought an allusion to Jonah 4:9 (contra Gundry, *Use of OT*, p. 59) but "merely a reflection of the OT-tinged language which Jesus used" (Moo, "Use of OT," p. 241). It suggests a sorrow so deep it almost kills (Taylor, *Mark*, p. 553; Hill, *Matthew*; and many others), not that Jesus is so sorrowful he would rather be dead (contra Bultmann, TDNT, 4:323, n. 2). Having revealed his deepest emotions and thus given his disciples the most compelling of reasons to do what he asks, he tells them to stay and "keep watch with me" while he goes a little farther on to pray alone. His words could be taken as no more than a request to protect him from intrusion in his deep anguish (so many older commentaries). But his words "with me" (only in Matthew) imply that he wanted them to keep awake and go on praying.

39 Jesus prays, prostrate in his intense anguish. He addresses God as "My Father" (see on 6:9); and Mark preserves the Aramaic *Abba*. The "cup" (*potērion*) refers not only to suffering and death but, as often in the OT (Pss 11:6 ["lot," NIV]; 75:7–8; Isa 51:19, 22; Jer 25:15–16, 27–29; 49:12; 51:57; Lam 4:21; Ezek 23:31–34; Hab 2:16; Zech 12:2; cf. Job 21:20; Ps 60:3; Isa 63:6; Obad 16), also to God's wrath (cf. C.E.B.

Cranfield, "The Cup Metaphor in Mark xiv.36 and Parallels," ExpT 59 [1947–48]: 137f.; Goppelt, TDNT, 6:153; Blaising, pp. 339–40). The frequent OT allusions in the passion narrative demand an OT meaning for *potērion* instead of "cup of death" in other Jewish literature. Thus the meaning here is fuller than in 20:22–23 and anticipates 27:46.

In one sense all things are possible with God (see on 19:26; Mark 14:36); in another some things are impossible. The two passages (Mark 14:36 and Matt 26:39) complement each other: all things are possible with God; and so, if it be morally consistent with the Father's redeeming purpose that this "cup" (Matthew) or "hour" (Mark) be taken from Jesus, that is what he deeply desires. But more deeply still, Jesus desires to do his Father's will. Though the precise wording of the synoptic accounts varies somewhat, if the prayer was of some duration ("one hour," v.40), and if Jesus after his resurrection told his disciples its contents, or if the disciples were within earshot, some variation in the tradition is not surprising. Jesus' deep commitment to his Father's will cannot be doubted. But in this crisis, the worst since 4:1–11, Jesus is tempted to seek an alternative to sin-bearing suffering as the route by which to fulfill his Father's redemptive purposes. As with his self-confessed ignorance in 24:36, Jesus may simply not have known whether any other way was possible. He prays in agony; and though he is supernaturally strengthened (Luke 22:43), he learns only that the Cross is unavoidable if he is to obey his Father's will.

Blaising has recently proposed an alternative exegesis. He observes that, what-ever the wording in the Synoptics, the conditional clause is grammatically "first class," a so-called real condition, which he interprets as follows: "This class of condi-tion assumes the condition to be a reality and the conclusion follows logically and naturally from that assumption" (p. 337; cf. RHG, p. 1007). From this Blaising concludes that what Jesus is asking for *is* possible with the Father and that Jesus knows it; so he cannot be asking that the cup (i.e., his passion) not come to him, an impossibility, for Jesus has repeatedly spoken of it, but that the cup not *remain* with him. In other words Jesus is tempted to fear that the "cup" of God's wrath will not pass away from him after he has drunk it but that it will consume him forever, and there would be no resurrection. He prays with faith, because he knows it is the Father's will: "Father, as you have promised in your Word, take the cup from me after I drink it; yet this is not my will alone, it is your will that this be done" (Blaising, p. 343).

This interpretation has certain attractions; yet along with several questionable details, it has two insuperable difficulties.

1. Despite Blaising's appeal to A.T. Robertson (i.e., RHG, p. 1007), a first-class condition in Greek does not necessarily assume the reality of the protasis but only that the protasis is as real as the apodosis. The speaker assumes the reality of the protasis for the sake of argument but does not thereby indicate that the condition described in the protasis is in fact real. Were Blaising to apply his understanding of first-class conditional clauses to Matthew 12:26–27; Mark 3:24–26, the result would be theologically incoherent, as Robertson himself recognizes (RHG, p. 1008; cf. Zerwick, pars. 303ff.).

2. Blaising introduces a novel interpretation, but only the traditional view contin-ues the line of temptation Jesus has earlier found most difficult to confront—viz., the temptation to avoid the Cross (see on 4:1–11; 16:21–23).

40–41 Jesus returns to his disciples—i.e., the inner three—and finds them sleeping (v.40; Luke 22:45 adds "exhausted from sorrow"). Jesus' question is addressed to

Peter but is in the plural and therefore includes them all (see on 16:16; 26:33–35). Though "one hour" need not be exact, it certainly indicates that Jesus has been praying for some time. "Watch and pray" could be a hendiadys (cf. Notes); alternatively it may suggest two components: spiritual alertness and intercession.

It is doubtful that "so that you will not fall into temptation" (v.41) means only "so that you will stay awake and not fall into the temptation to sleep." Indeed, Jesus' prediction of their spiritual defection that "very night" (v.31) should have served as an urgent call to prayer. So now he tells them that only urgent prayer will save them from falling into the coming "temptation" (see on 4:1; 6:13). Even in his own extremity, when he needs and seeks his Father's face, Jesus thinks of the impending but much lesser trial his followers will face. He speaks compassionately: "The spirit is willing, but the body [*sarx*, 'flesh'] is weak." This is not a reference to the Holy Spirit but makes a "distinction between man's physical weakness and the noble desires of his will" (Hill, *Matthew;* id., *Greek Words*, p. 242; Bonnard). But though compassionate, these words, which doubtless hark back to v.35, are not an excuse but a warning and incentive (Broadus). Spiritual eagerness is often accompanied by carnal weakness—a danger amply experienced by successive generations of Christians.

42–44 Some interpreters have seen a certain progression in Jesus' three prayers, but Matthew says that Jesus said "the same thing" (v.44). The variations between v.39 and v.42 must therefore be incidental. "May your will be done" mirrors one of the petitions of the prayer Jesus taught his disciples (6:10). As Jesus learned obedience (Heb 5:7–9), so he became the supreme model for his own teaching. In the first garden "Not your will but mine" changed Paradise to desert and brought man from Eden to Gethsemane. Now "Not my will but yours" brings anguish to the man who prays it but transforms the desert into the kingdom and brings man from Gethsemane to the gates of glory.

45–46 The word *loipon* as an adverb does not naturally mean "still" (NIV, v.45) or "meanwhile" but points to the future ("henceforth") or is inferential ("it follows that"). Therefore Jesus' words should not be taken as a question (NIV) but as a gently ironic command (cf. KJV, "Sleep on now, and take your rest"; cf. the irony in 23:2–3; cf. Moule, *Idiom Book*, p. 161). The hour of the Passion is near: it is too late to pray and gain strength for the temptations ahead. His disciples may as well sleep. The Son of Man (see on 8:20) is betrayed into the hands of sinners: he who is the resplendent, messianic King takes the path of suffering. Doubtless Jesus could see and hear the party approaching as it crossed the Kidron with torches and climbed up the path to Gethsemane. The sleepers for whom he would die have lost their opportunity to gain strength through prayer. By contrast Jesus has prayed in agony but now rises with poise and advances to meet his betrayer.

Notes

39 The distinctions Thrall (pp. 67–70) draws between Mark's (14:36) ἀλλά (*alla*, "but") and Matthew's πλήν (*plēn*, "but") are dubious, because the former adversative particle has so broad a semantic range.

41 If the ἵνα (*hina*, "that") clause is dependent only on the verb "pray," then it is probably nonfinal (as in 5:29) and gives the content of the prayer. If it depends on "watch and pray" together, it may have telic force.

43 The periphrastic pluperfect ἦσαν . . . βεβαρημένοι (*ēsan . . . bebarēmenoi*, lit., "were having been weighed down"; NIV, "were heavy") provides a good instance in which the perfect passive participle probably has no more than adjectival force (cf. Moule, *Idiom Book*, p. 19).

---

6. *The arrest*

26:47–56

> **47**While he was still speaking, Judas, one of the Twelve, arrived. With him was a large crowd armed with swords and clubs, sent from the chief priests and the elders of the people. **48**Now the betrayer had arranged a signal with them: "The one I kiss is the man; arrest him." **49**Going at once to Jesus, Judas said, "Greetings, Rabbi!" and kissed him.
> **50**Jesus replied, "Friend, do what you came for."
> Then the men stepped forward, seized Jesus and arrested him. **51**With that, one of Jesus' companions reached for his sword, drew it out and struck the servant of the high priest, cutting off his ear.
> **52**"Put your sword back in its place," Jesus said to him, "for all who draw the sword will die by the sword. **53**Do you think I cannot call on my Father, and he will at once put at my disposal more than twelve legions of angels? **54**But how then would the Scriptures be fulfilled that say it must happen in this way?"
> **55**At that time Jesus said to the crowd, "Am I leading a rebellion, that you have come out with swords and clubs to capture me? Every day I sat in the temple courts teaching, and you did not arrest me. **56**But this has all taken place that the writings of the prophets might be fulfilled." Then all the disciples deserted him and fled.

47 Judas Iscariot (see on 10:4; 26:14–16, 25; 27:3–10) arrived with armed men. What he received payment for was probably information as to where Jesus could be arrested in a quiet setting with little danger of mob violence. He may have first led the "large crowd" to the Upper Room and, finding it empty, surmised where Jesus and his disciples had gone (cf. John 18:1–3). The "large crowd" accompanying Judas had been sent "from the chief priests and the elders of the people"—the clergy and lay members of the Sanhedrin (see on 21:23). Luke 22:52 says some chief priests and elders accompanied the crowd. The military terms in John 18:3, 12 suggest that some Roman soldiers were among the number along with temple police and some others. Although many scholars have argued that no Romans were involved at this time, it is not unlikely that some were present. Especially during the feasts the Romans took extra pains to ensure public order; so a request for a small detachment from the cohort would not likely be turned down. Thus Pilate might have had some inkling of the plot from the beginning, and if he shared it with his wife, it might help explain her dream (27:19).

48–50 The need for pointing out the right man was especially acute, not only because it was dark, but because, in a time long before photography, the faces of even great celebrities would not be nearly so widely known as today. To identify Jesus, Judas chose the kiss (thereby turning it into a symbol of betrayal. "Greetings,

Rabbi!" (v.49; see on 8;19; 23:8), a tragic mockery, was for the crowd's ears, not Jesus'.

"Friend" (v.50) is an open-hearted but not intimate greeting. The next words, *eph ho parei* ("what you came for"), are notoriously ambiguous. If the relative pronoun *ho* functions as a direct interrogative pronoun, the expression means "Why [lit., 'for what'] have you come?" (NIV mg.; cf. Zerwick, par. 223; Turner, *Insights*, pp. 69–71; id., *Syntax*, pp. 49–50; BDF, pars. 495–96), and some verb like "do" must be supplied (NIV text; cf. BDF, par. 300[2]). If the clause is an imperatival statement, its force is like John 13:27 and reflects Jesus' newly regained poise and his sovereignty in these events. If it is a question, it elicits no information but administers a rebuke steeped in the irony of professed ignorance that knows very well why Judas has come.

51–54 "With that" (v.51) is NIV's acceptable effort to render *idou* in this context (cf. "Look," v.45; "Here," v.46; untr., v.47; see on 1:20). Many are skeptical of the authenticity of this passage, finding it out of keeping with the restrained spirit of the pericope as a whole and wondering why the offending disciple was not arrested. Moreover it is the latest Gospel that names Jesus' sword-wielding disciple (Peter) and his target (Malchus [John 18:10]). This might suggest that the story was growing and gaining accretions. Noteworthy are the following points.

1. The restraint belongs to Jesus, not the pericope. Moreover, we have already seen that earlier protestations of loyalty (vv.33–35) were probably grounded in some form of nationalistic messianism; so Peter's response is scarcely unexpected.

2. His response is psychologically convincing. After repeated warnings of defection, Peter may have felt that the crucial test of loyalty had arrived. He is magnificent and pathetic—magnificent because he rushes in to defend Jesus with characteristic courage and impetuousness, pathetic because his courage evaporates when Jesus undoes Peter's damage, forbids violence, and faces the Passion without resisting.

3. However one interprets the difficult verses in Luke 22:36–38, they show that the disciples had two swords with them; and if Peter actually wielded the sword, other disciples had the same idea (Luke 22:49).

4. There were probably many reasons why Peter was not arrested. Jesus not only quickly cooled the situation but healed the wound (omitted by Matthew). It was one thing to escort a nonresisting prisoner quietly back to the city; it was another to escort twelve men, eleven of them frightened and ready to fight. In any case before decisive action could be taken, the disciples fled in the darkness (v.56).

5. Over the centuries pious Christian imaginations have provided names for those not named in the NT (cf. B.M. Metzger, "Names for the Nameless in the New Testament: A Study in the Growth of Christian Tradition," *NT Studies*, pp. 23–43). Within the NT the evidence is mixed. Whatever order the Synoptics were written in, we must note that Matthew may preserve a name omitted by Mark (Matt 26:57; Mark 14:53) or drop a name preserved by Mark (Matt 9:18; Mark 5:22). Matthew and Luke both drop Mark's Bartimaeus (Mark 10:46) and Alexander and Rufus (Mark 15:21). Add to this the fact that many scholars now insist that John does not represent late tradition, and there remains little reason for skepticism concerning this sorry scene.

Some take Jesus' response—"for all who draw the sword will die by the sword" (v.52)—as a call to pacifism, whereas others observe that Jesus told Peter to put his sword "back in its place," not to throw it away. Both views ask the text to answer questions of no immediate relevance. The least we can say is that violence *in defense of Christ* is completely unjustified: certainly verse 52 separates Jesus from the Zealots. Moreover a simple request to his Father (the aorist infinitive is significant; cf. BDF, par. 471[2]) would bring twelve legions of angels (a full Roman legion was six thousand; cf. ZPEB, 3:907–8) to his assistance—perhaps one legion for Jesus and one for each of the Eleven (v.53). This is more than the eyes of faith seeing help as in 2 Kings 6:17 but the knowledge that help is available, while refusing to use it (cf. John 10:18). In addition, Jesus' stance regarding his own death is grounded on the fact the "Scriptures" (plural, v.54) must be fulfilled (see on vv.24, 31; cf. Luke 24:25–26). This divine "must" (*dei*) is not for Jesus sheer inevitability, since he still believes it possible to gain instant aid from his Father. Instead, it is the commingling of divine sovereignty and Jesus' unflagging determination to obey his Father's will.

Many commentators note that in 1QM 7:6 the angels are represented as joining forces with the righteous at the End. Jesus himself elsewhere pictures angelic participation at the consummation (e.g., 13:41; 24:30–31). But at this point in redemptive history, the angels are not called on. Jesus faces this battle alone, and the consummation of all things is not yet.

55–56 Every day for the preceding week, and presumably on earlier visits to the Holy City, Jesus had been teaching in the temple courts (v.55); yet the authorities had not arrested him. Why then do they seize him now as if he were a rebel (*lēstēs*, see on 27:16)? The implication is that there is no need to arrest him secretly and violently, except for reasons in their own minds that reveal more about them than about him. "At that time" (lit., "In that hour") seems a rather heavy-handed transition, but perhaps what follows it was a well-known saying of Jesus among Christians to whom Matthew was writing; and he is pointing out that this was the time when he spoke it.

After questioning the display of force by those who arrested him, Jesus said, "This has all taken place [see on 1:22; 21:4] that the writings [or 'Scriptures'] of the prophets might be fulfilled." Mark (14:49) simply has "But the Scriptures must be fulfilled." Matthew gives us more, doubtless because he is more interested in the prophetic nature of the Scriptures (see Introduction, section 11.b). "The writings of the prophets" therefore probably does not exclude the Law and the Writings, for elsewhere Moses and David are also considered "prophets." The reference is to the Scriptures (as in v.54), their human authors being considered primarily as prophets, not lawgivers, wise men, or psalmists.

All the disciples then fulfill one specific prophecy (see on v.31) and flee. Mark 14:51–52 adds the account of the young man who flees naked. Probably at this time Jesus is bound (John 18:12).

7. Jesus before the Sanhedrin

26:57–68

⁵⁷Those who had arrested Jesus took him to Caiaphas, the high priest, where the teachers of the law and the elders had assembled. ⁵⁸But Peter followed him at a distance, right up to the courtyard of the high priest. He entered and sat down with the guards to see the outcome.

⁵⁹The chief priests and the whole Sanhedrin were looking for false evidence

against Jesus so that they could put him to death. [60]But they did not find any, though many false witnesses came forward.

Finally two came forward [61]and declared, "This fellow said, 'I am able to destroy the temple of God and rebuild it in three days.'"

[62]Then the high priest stood up and said to Jesus, "Are you not going to answer? What is this testimony that these men are bringing against you?" [63]But Jesus remained silent.

The high priest said to him, "I charge you under oath by the living God: Tell us if you are the Christ, the Son of God."

[64]"Yes, it is as you say," Jesus replied. "But I say to all of you: In the future you will see the Son of Man sitting at the right hand of the Mighty One and coming on the clouds of heaven."

[65]Then the high priest tore his clothes and said, "He has spoken blasphemy! Why do we need any more witnesses? Look, now you have heard the blasphemy. [66]What do you think?"

"He is worthy of death," they answered.

[67]Then they spit in his face and struck him with their fists. Others slapped him [68]and said, "Prophesy to us, Christ. Who hit you?"

Few topics have caused more tension between Jews and Christians than the trial of Jesus. Those who have committed abominable atrocities against the Jews have often based their actions on the ground that Jews are the murderers of their Messiah, or God-killers, and have all too frequently turned to Matthew 27:25 for backing. As a reaction to this reprehensible attitude, more recent study (both Jewish and Christian) has argued that the Jews were very little involved and that most of the blame should be placed on the Romans. An excellent survey of Jewish and Christian exegesis of the trial narratives, from 1770 to the late 1960s, is given by Catchpole (*Trial of Jesus*); and representative modern treatments, in addition to commentaries and articles, are included in our bibliography under Bammel, Blinzler, Brandon, Cohn, Winter, Sherwin-White (ch. 2), and Benoit (*Jesus*, pp. 123–66).

Though there is no consensus, the dominant view in current scholarship runs something like this: The four Gospel accounts of the trial before the Sanhedrin cannot readily be reconciled. But the fourth Gospel, though making clear that both Jewish and Roman authorities were involved from the beginning (John 18:3, 12), stresses that the Sanhedrin did not have the power to inflict the death penalty (John 18:31) and places much more emphasis on the Roman trial. By contrast the Synoptics lay more blame on the Jews; and Matthew goes so far as to tell us that Pilate washed his hands of the whole affair, while the Jews called down curses on themselves (27:24–25). On the face of it, John's account is the more historically reliable, whereas the Synoptics are more seriously tainted by later church-synagogue tensions. In short, anti-Semitism has colored their narratives.

This is confirmed, it is alleged, when all the illegalities of the Jewish proceedings are noted. The Mishnah (*Sanhedrin*) makes it clear that legal procedure in capital cases forbade night trials, required at least two consecutive days, and provided for private interrogation of witnesses. The breaches in law are so numerous as to be unbelievable; and one Jewish writer (Cohn) has gone so far in reconstructing the evidence that he concludes the Sanhedrin actually tried to *save* Jesus from the Roman courts. Any trace of evidence that counters this thesis he ascribes to the polemic of later deteriorating church-synagogue relationships, compounded with the natural desire in Christian writers to avoid blaming the powerful Roman authorities.

Yet some things must not be overlooked.

1. The problem of illegalities in Jesus' trial is more complex than is customarily recognized. We have already shown (see excursus at v.17) that executions under certain circumstances could take place on a major feast day. Other irregularities include (1) the proceedings that apparently took place in Caiaphas's home, not the temple precincts; (2) Jesus' not being offered a defense attorney; (3) his being charged with blasphemy without actually blaspheming in the legally defined sense, which required that the accused actually pronounce the name of God; (4) the verdict's being rushed through at night without the minimum two days required in capital cases, which had the effect of banning the new opening of capital trials from the day before Sabbaths or festival days (M *Sanhedrin* 4:1). But quite apart from the difficult problem of dating Mishnaic traditions—for the sake of argument we may agree that they all date back to the beginning of the first century or earlier—five factors challenge the idea that legal considerations invalidate the authenticity of the Gospels on these points.

a. Some Mishnaic stipulations, not least in the tractate Sanhedrin, are almost certainly theoretical formulations only, which never had the force of obeyed law. Is there any independent historical evidence, for instance, that "burnings" of the sort described in *Sanhedrin* 7:2 ever took place?

b. Dalman (pp. 98–100) provides references to other occasions of flagrant breach of judicial regulations on the ground that "the hour demands it."

c. Similarly there is evidence that expediency partially motivated the religious authorities (cf. John 11:49–50). This could account for numerous irregularities. If the leaders feared mob violence, haste was required. Moreover it was legitimate to execute certain criminals on feast days, but not on the Sabbath. If Jesus was arrested Thursday night (Friday by Jewish reckoning), things had to move swiftly if he was to be buried by dusk on Friday, the onset of Sabbath. An all-night session of the Jewish authorities was demanded by the fact that Roman officials like Pilate worked very early in the morning and then refused to take on new cases for the rest of the day. If Jesus could not be presented to Pilate early Friday morning, the case would drag on till after Sabbath—along with mounting risks of mob violence.

d. The sources are sufficiently difficult that we do not know the precise relationship between the Pharisees of Jesus' day and the rabbis who compiled Mishnah. Even if Sigal (cf. Introduction, section 11.f) has exaggerated the distinctions, we may not always be wise in reading rabbinic regulations back into Jesus' day. For instance, the narrow and technical definitions of blasphemy in Mishnah may not have been popular with all Pharisees. After all, large parts of the population held to extraordinarily broad notions of blasphemy: Josephus (Antiq. XX, 108[v.2]) records that an angry crowd accused a Roman soldier of blasphemy because he had exposed his genitals to them. And we have *no* evidence for the way the Sadducees understood blasphemy.

e. We may go farther. A strong, if not entirely convincing, case can be made for distinguishing between *Sanhedrin* and *Beth Din*. The NT speaks of the former; the relevant Mishnaic tractate, though traditionally called *Sanhedrin*, in fact speaks almost thirty times of the latter and only three times of the former. From this some have deduced that what the Gospels describe is *not* the "Sanhedrin" in the religious, scholarly sense but the "Sanhedrin" that was essentially political and, to some extent, corrupt (most recently, cf. E. Rivkin, "Beth Din, Boule, Sanhedrin: A

Tragedy of Errors," HUCA 46 [1975]: 181–99). Even if this distinction does not prove valid, it must be admitted that "a way of removing an undesirable enemy is usually found when the will is there" (S. Rosenblatt, "The Crucifixion of Jesus from the Standpoint of Pharisaic Law," JBL 75 [1956]: 319 [though Rosenblatt does not accept the accounts as we have them in the Gospels]). Catchpole (*Trial of Jesus*, pp. 268f.) has convincingly shown that "the debate about illegalities should be regarded as a dead end, and at most able to make only a minor contribution."

2. More distinction is found between John and the Synoptics and between Matthew and Mark–Luke than is actually there. Although John places more emphasis on the Roman trial, only in John 19:12, and never in the Synoptics, do we find *the Jews* manipulating Pilate in order to secure a guilty verdict and a capital sentence. It is surely false to attribute the lesser prominence of Pilate in the Synoptics to Christian concern to get on with Rome; for long before the evangelists wrote, Pilate was deposed and banished by Rome. Moreover it is not at all clear that Matthew sees 27:24 as an effective absolution for Pilate; Matthew frequently records denunciations of hypocrisy and expects persecution from Gentile "governors and kings" (10:18–19). Equally it is not at all clear that 27:25 should be interpreted to mean that all Jews remain under a continuing curse. The first disciples were Jews to a man; and the fact that Matthew clearly insists the authorities were afraid of mob action (vv.3–4) shows he understands that many Jews were enthusiastically if superficially *for* Jesus, even if few of them were committed disciples.

3. But if such sharp distinctions between John's treatment of the trial and that of the Synoptics are scarcely supported by the text, even less defensible are sharp disjunctions. The attempt to blame the Romans and exonerate the Jews finds little support in the fourth Gospel; but even if it were an unquestionable theme there, responsible historiography attempts a synthesis of the sources, not a priori historical disjunctions—one of the classic "historians' fallacies" (cf. Fischer). And a believable synthesis is indeed possible (see below).

4. John 18:31, frequently cited to absolve the Sanhedrin, is not only historically credible (cf. Sherwin-White, pp. 35–43; Catchpole, *Trial of Jesus*, pp. 247–48) but also provides an important clue to the roles played by Jews and Romans. All the Gospels attest, repeatedly and in highly diverse ways, that many Jewish leaders wanted Jesus' removal because of his claims of messianic authority, coupled with his popularity among the populace at large and the unexpected kind of "messiah" he was proving to be—and especially his failure to show more respect to the religious authorities. When he finally came into their hands, political circumstances forced them to seek the death sentence from Pilate. For this purpose it was necessary for the Jewish leaders to tinge the charges against Jesus with political color. Thus he was made to seem less a Messiah than a competitor of Caesar. Only by a very selective handling of the evidence (e.g., S.G.F. Brandon, *The Trial of Jesus of Nazareth* [London: Batsford, 1968] can one conclude that the political charge came first, making Jesus some kind of Zealot rebel.

5. The Holocaust and other atrocities have blinded the eyes of both Jewish and Christian historians. Not a few modern Jews insist that the Holocaust is the result of centuries of bigoted Christian tradition, and that Christian solidarity entails corporate Christian guilt. Yet they would be loathe to assume that Jewish solidarity entails for the Jewish race a corporate Jewish guilt because of the contribution of a few Jews to the death of Jesus. Meanwhile Christian historians, alive to the legacy of

Western Christendom's persecution of the Jews, are embarrassed into making irresponsible judgments against the historical evidence, as a sort of atonement for past injustices. It is easier to blame the Romans, who are not present to defend themselves, than to face the survivors of the Holocaust with unpleasant historical realities. The wisest scholars of both sides have seen this. The Jewish scholar Samuel Sandmel writes: "Perhaps we might be willing to say to ourselves that it is not at all impossible that some Jews, even leading Jews, recommended the death of Jesus to Pilate. We are averse to saying this to ourselves, for so total has been the charge against us that we have been constrained to make a total denial" (*We Jews and Jesus* [London and New York: OUP, 1965], p. 141).

It is helpful to remember that, whatever Christendom has done, the NT writers, most if not all of whom were Jews, can scarcely or reasonably be labeled "anti-Semitic." Matthew and the other evangelists certainly blame some Jews for Jesus' death. They also blame some Romans. But the reasons for the blame are historical, theological, spiritual—not racial. The Twelve are Jews; and after the Crucifixion a Jew from Arimathea (27:57–60) shows great concern for Jesus' burial. The NT writers assess people by their response to Jesus, whom they have come to know as King Messiah and Son of God, not by their race.

6. From the viewpoint of NT theology, Christians must repeatedly remind themselves of two things. First, from a theological perspective every Christian is as guilty of putting Jesus on the cross as Caiaphas. Thoughtful believers will surely admit that their own guilt is the more basic of the two; for if we believe Matthew's witness, and Jesus could have escaped the clutches of Caiaphas (v.53), then what drove Jesus to the cross was his commitment to the Father's redemptive purposes. While this does not excuse Caiaphas and his peers, it keeps Christians from supercilious judgment of the Jews. Second, even if first-century Christians, whether Jews or Gentiles, rightly saw God's judgment in the destruction of Jerusalem and Judea (A.D. 66–73), that could not give them the right to put themselves in God's place and execute his judgment for him. Judgment belongs only to God. Any other view, including that which has often dominated Christendom, fails to recognize essential NT distinctions between the kingdom and the church (see on 13:37–39).

At this point we should consider one of several ways in which the complementary accounts of Jesus' passion in our Gospels can be reasonably harmonized so as to show how the proceedings against Jesus could have been completed within the few hours the chronology permits. There were two trials, one Jewish and the other Roman. The Jewish trial began with an informal examination by Annas (John 18:12–14, 19–23), perhaps while members of the Sanhedrin were being hurriedly gathered. A decision by a session of the Sanhedrin (vv.57–68; Mark 14:53–65) was followed by a formal decision at dawn and a dispatch to Pilate (27:1–2; Luke 22:66–71). The Roman trial began with a first examination before Pilate (vv.11–14; John 18:28–38a) and was quickly followed by Herod's interrogation (Luke 23:6–12) and the final appearance before Pilate (27:15–31; John 18:38b–19:16). This reconstruction is merely tentative; but it usefully coordinates the biblical data.

57 For the relationship between Annas and Caiaphas, see on v.3. If both men concurred in finding Jesus guilty and recommending the death penalty, the action would more likely win the acceptance of both the populace and the Romans than if only one agreed. Well-to-do homes were often built in a square shape with an open, central courtyard. If Annas lived in rooms on one wing of the court, then it is possible that he interviewed Jesus (John 18:14–16) in one wing while the Sanhedrin was assembling in another (NIV's "had assembled" is too strong: the Greek verb means no more than "assembled"). Not much time would be required.

Matthew mentions the teachers of the law and the elders; Mark 14:53 adds the chief priests, to whom Matthew refers in v.59. There is probably little significance to such variations, but they warn us against reading too much into particular details. No Pharisees are mentioned, though doubtless many teachers and lay elders belonged to that party. Their absence from Matthew's passion account is important for two reasons. First, it calls in question theories that pit the Matthean church against "Pharisees" of A.D. 85; for if Matthew sees the Pharisees as prime enemies of Jesus, why are they not mentioned in this final confrontation? Second, it accurately reflects the little we know of Jerusalem politics at the time. The Pharisees doubtless exercised throughout the land strong theological and social influence and through the synagogues in the towns and villages a great deal of moral persuasion and some political power. But for the Sanhedrin, where the final act of confrontation with Jewish leaders was played out, the shape of power was different. The high priest, almost certainly a Sadducee, presided; the priests, primarily if not exclusively Sadducees, enjoyed large and perhaps dominant influence; and the Pharisees exercised power only through the decision of the entire assembly.

58 Peter followed Jesus "at a distance," midway between courage (v.51) and cowardice (v.70) (Bengel). John 18:15–16 provides additional information on how Peter secured entrance to the high priest's courtyard. Peter joined the "servants" (the term is general but probably includes both household servants and temple police— hence NIV's "guards") around the courtyard fire, waiting to see the outcome.

59–63a If there was but one central Sanhedrin (see above), it was composed of three groups: leading priests (see on 21:23), teachers of the law, and elders. It had seventy members plus the high priest, but a mere twenty-three made a quorum. The "whole Sanhedrin" need not mean that everyone was present (cf. Luke 23:50–51) but only that the Sanhedrin as a body was involved. We do not know what proportion of the seventy came from constituent groups or whether the proportion had to be preserved in the quorum.

Many equate this meeting of the Sanhedrin with the one at daybreak described by Luke (22:66–71). But Matthew seems to make a distinction between the two (cf. 27:1–2). Perhaps the later meeting was in the temple precincts (the usual place) and was more fully attended; and if so, Luke may well be conflating the proceedings.

Matthew says the Sanhedrin was looking "for false evidence" (*pseudomartyria*, v.59) and obtained it from "false witnesses" (*pseudomartyres*, v.60). It is unlikely this means that the Sanhedrin sought liars only; if so, why not simply fabricate the evidence? Rather, the Sanhedrin, already convinced of Jesus' guilt, went through the motions of securing evidence against him. When people hate, they readily accept false witness; and the Sanhedrin eventually heard and believed just about what it wanted. Matthew knew that Jesus was not guilty and could not be; so he describes the evidence as "false."

The two men who came forward (v.60) may or may not have been suborned (cf. Acts 6:11). At least two witnesses were required in a capital case. In Greek *houtos* does not necessarily carry a sneering tone (NIV, "This fellow," v.61; similarly v.71) but may serve as an emphatic pronoun or equivalent to the British "this chap."

Their witness had some element of truth but was evilly motivated and disregarded what Jesus meant in John 2:19–21 (the reference is not to Matthew 24:2, where only disciples were present; see on 21:12–17). John did not interpret Jesus' saying allegorically (Hill, *Matthew*) but typologically. Though some will insist that even typological exegesis must be traced to the later church, we have already noted enough typological exegesis in Jesus' own teaching (see on v.28) to acknowledge that Jesus himself led the way in this regard. Interpreted with crass literalism, Jesus' words might be taken as a threat to desecrate the temple, one of the pillars of Judaism. Desecration of sacred places was almost universally regarded as a capital offense in the ancient world, and in this Jews were not different from the pagans (e.g., Jer 26:1–19; *Tosephta Sanhedrin* 13:5; b *Rosh ha-Shanah* 17a).

But what do Jesus' words in John 2:19–21 mean? If Jesus sees himself as the antitype of the Passover lamb, the true Suffering Servant, the revelation of the Father, and the fulfillment of OT Scriptures (e.g., vv.27–30; cf. 5:17–20; 11:25–30), it is not at all unlikely he would also see himself as the true temple, the ultimate point of meeting between God and man. In that case John's words accurately reflect Jesus' thought.

We have penetrated very close to the heart of the dispute between early Christianity and Judaism as attested elsewhere in the NT—a dispute that may be summarized by a series of questions: What is the nature of the continuity between the old covenant and the new? Must Gentiles become Jews before they can become Christians? In what sense and to what degree does the Mosaic law have binding force on Jesus' followers? The place of the temple is one element in that debate, raised in earliest Christianity (Acts 6:13–14), but traceable back to Jesus himself and a contributing factor to his own condemnation.

NIV and NASB are probably correct in translating v.62 as two questions from the high priest (cf. BDF, pars. 298[4]; 299[1]). He probably hoped Jesus would incriminate himself. But, true to Isaiah 53:7, Jesus kept silent (v.63a; cf. Moo, "Use of OT," pp. 148–51).

63b The high priest, frustrated by Jesus' silence, tried a bold stroke that cut to the central issue: Was Jesus the Messiah or was he not? The question has been raised before in one form or another (see on 12:38–42; 16:1–4; 21:1–11, 14–16, 23) and may have been prompted in the high priest's mind by Jesus' mention of the temple, since some branches of Judaism anticipated a renewal of the temple's glory when Messiah came (cf. Lane, *Mark*, p. 535). But whether or not this explains his motive, the high priest boldly charges Jesus to answer "under oath by the living God" (cf. McNeile; Benoit, *Jesus*, for justification of this rendering).

The form of the question in Mark 14:61 is slightly different: "Are you the Christ [see on 1:1; 2:4], the Son of the Blessed One?" Instead of the latter, Matthew uses his preferred title, "the Son of God." The two titles are formally equivalent and both may have been used at various points in the trial (cf. John 19:7). "Son of God" in Judaism can be equivalent to Messiah (see on 2:15; 3:17; 11:27; 16:13–20).

The outcome is now inevitable. If Jesus refuses to answer, he breaks a legally imposed oath. If he denies he is the Messiah, the crisis is over—but so is his influence. If he affirms it, then, given the commitments of the court, Jesus must be false. After all, how could the true Messiah allow himself to be imprisoned and put in jeopardy? The Gospels' evidence suggests that the Sanhedrin was prepared to see Jesus' unequivocal claim to messiahship as meriting the death penalty, and their unbelief precluded them from allowing any other possibility.

64 Perhaps this is what is meant by Jesus' "good confession" (1 Tim 6:13). There are four points of interest.

1. Unlike the unambiguous "I am" in Mark 14:62, Matthew uses an expression, found also in 26:25, that many have taken to be purposely ambiguous (e.g., Turner, *Insights*, pp. 72–75). But Catchpole has convincingly shown that the expression is "affirmative in content, and reluctant or circumlocutory in formulation" (David R. Catchpole, "The Answer of Jesus to Caiaphas (Matt.xxvi.64)," NTS 17 [1970–71]: 213–26). Certainly Caiaphas understood it as positive (v.65). The next clause, beginning with *plēn legō hymin* ("But I say to all of you"), found also in 11:22, 24, means something like "Indeed I tell you": there is likely no adversative force (Thrall, pp. 72–78). Instead it expresses "an expansion or a qualification" (Catchpole, "Answer of Jesus," p. 223) of the preceding statement. Jesus speaks in this way, not because Caiaphas has spoken the truth of himself without any revelation (Kingsbury, *Matthew*, p. 64), but because Caiaphas's understanding of "Messiah" and "Son of God" is fundamentally inadequate. Jesus is indeed the Messiah and so must answer affirmatively. But he is not quite the Messiah Caiaphas has in mind; so he must answer cautiously and with some explanation.

2. That explanation comes in allusions to two passages—Psalm 110:1 (see on 22: 41–46) and Daniel 7:13 (see on 8:20; 24:1–3, 30–31). Jesus is not to be primarily considered a political Messiah but as the one who, in receiving a kingdom, is exalted high above David and at the Mighty One's right hand, the hand of honor and power (cf. 16:27; 23:39; 24:30–31; 26:29). This is Jesus' climactic self-disclosure to the authorities and it combines revelation with threat.

3. Jesus uses "Son of Man" (see on 8:20) instead of "Christ" or "Son of God" (cf. v.63). Efforts to interpret "Son of Man" in terms of "Son of God" (Kingsbury, *Matthew*, pp. 113ff.) badly miss the point (cf. Hill, "Son and Servant"). The titles are parallel, and each is messianic. Certainly Caiaphas understands "Son of Man" that way. The most ambiguous title now reveals most about Jesus: it is his self-designation, associated with the glory of the Parousia, but uttered at the culmination of Jesus' ministry and in the face of suffering and death.

4. The Greek phrase *ap'arti* (lit., "from now; NIV, "in the future"; see on v.29) is difficult. Some have found it so difficult that they say v.64 must refer, not to the Parousia, but to the Resurrection (e.g., L. Hartman, "Scriptural Exegesis," in Didier, p. 145). But if "from now" or "from now on" ill suits the delay till the Parousia, it is equally unsuited to the delay till the Resurrection and the Ascension (see on 28:18–20). Moreover the records show that the high priest and other august leaders were not witnesses of the Resurrection; for according to the NT, no human being saw the actual event happen.

The best explanation of v.64 is that Jesus is telling the members of the Sanhedrin ("you" is pl.) that from then on they would not see him as he now stands before them but only in his capacity as undisputed King Messiah and sovereign Judge. "From now on" (i.e., "in the future," NIV) that is the way they will see him. Matthew does not include the word "only" or the like (e.g., "From now on you will only see the Son of Man sitting on the right hand. . . .") because it would imply a possibility they might not see him at all, which is not true. The phrase "from now on" makes this a forceful warning that at least some Sanhedrin members doubtless remembered after the Resurrection.

65–66 Rending garments (v.65) was prescribed for blasphemy (M *Sanhedrin* 7:5) but can also express indignation or grief (cf. 2 Kings 18:37; Jud 14:19; 1 Macc 11:71;

Acts 14:14). It appears that the definition of "blasphemy" varied over the years (see above, on vv.57-68; cf. John 5:18; 10:33). Whether the Sanhedrin thought Jesus was blaspheming because he claimed to be Messiah, because he put himself on the Mighty One's right hand, or because God had not especially attested who Jesus was (a requirement in certain rabbinic traditions) is uncertain. The decision of the assembled members of the Sanhedrin appears to have been by acclamation. "Worthy" (*enochos*, v.66) is the same word used in 5:21: Jesus is "liable" to the death penalty, mandated for blasphemy (Lev 24:16).

67-68 Although Luke portrays the examination and condemnation only at the trial that takes place after dawn (parallel to Matt 27:1-2), even he has this outrage first (Luke 22:63-65), which, in agreement with Matthew and Mark, suggests that some decisions had already been made. Though "they" (v.67) might well mean the members of the Sanhedrin, it might also refer to those under their control, their immediate servants (cf. Luke 22:63-65). In any case the messianic claims of the accused do not impress the Sanhedrin; and the indignities to which he is now subjected are probably meant to deride his false pretensions. The true Messiah would vanquish all foes and, according to some Jewish traditions, would be able to judge by smell without the need of sight (see Lane, *Mark*, pp. 539-40 and references there; cf. also Pss Sol 17:37ff.). But here is Jesus, spit on, punched, slapped (cf. Isa 50:6; the verb for "slapped" is also used in 5:39 and may mean "clubbed"), blindfolded (Mark 14:65; Matthew does not mention this detail), and taunted, without displaying any power.

"Prophesy" (v.68) does not here imply foretelling the future but revealing hidden knowledge (cf. 11:13): Messiah should be able to tell who hit him, even when blindfolded. The easiest way to explain Matthew's not mentioning blindfolding while including "Who hit you?" (not in Mark) is that Matthew and Mark have each kept one part of what Luke has kept intact (Notes). In any case Jesus remains silent, confirming their suspicions while fulfilling Isaiah 53:7.

Notes

61 The peculiar expression διὰ τριῶν ἡμερῶν (*dia triōn hēmerōn*, "in three days") uses the preposition in its primary sense of "between," which then extends to the notion of interval (contra B.F. Meyer; cf. Zerwick, par. 115; Moule, *Idiom Book*, p. 56).

63 Some MSS preserve only καί (*kai*, "and"), others καὶ ἀποκριθείς (*kai apokritheis*, "and he answered"), and a few ἀποκριθεὶς οὖν (*apokritheis oun*, "therefore he answered"). Although some have argued that the shortest reading came about because copyists felt "answered" was inappropriate immediately after a statement about Jesus' silence, Metzger (*Textual Commentary*, p. 65) says the majority of the UBS Committee preferred the shortest reading on the external evidence. But it is difficult to imagine why "answered" would have been introduced into the shortest reading, and easy to understand how the second reading could have generated the other two. If original, "answered" must be understood as in 11:25.

68 Although this is a remarkably clear "minor agreement" of Matthew and Luke (22:64) against Mark (14:65), it is scarcely adequate to overturn Mark's priority (cf. Introduction, section 3); but at very least it suggests that more independent accounts of the synoptic passion narratives were circulating (cf. Luke 1:1-4) than is commonly recognized. Some detect Luke's dependence on Matthew here. The literary relationships are too complex to sort out with certainty; but in view of the apparent independence of Luke's trial narrative as a whole, it seems wise to think that on this one point—the *combination* of the blindfolding and the question "Who hit you?"—Luke has preserved the *historical* connection, of which Matthew and Mark have each given one part (Tasker; for discussion and literature, cf. Moo, "Use of OT," p. 142, n. 2).

---

8. *Peter's denial of Jesus*

26:69-75

[69]Now Peter was sitting out in the courtyard, and a servant girl came to him. "You also were with Jesus of Galilee," she said.

[70]But he denied it before them all. "I don't know what you're talking about," he said.

[71]Then he went out to the gateway, where another girl saw him and said to the people there, "This fellow was with Jesus of Nazareth."

[72]He denied it again, with an oath: "I don't know the man!"

[73]After a little while, those standing there went up to Peter and said, "Surely you are one of them, for your accent gives you away."

[74]Then he began to call down curses on himself and he swore to them, "I don't know the man!"

Immediately a rooster crowed. [75]Then Peter remembered the word Jesus had spoken: "Before the rooster crows, you will disown me three times." And he went outside and wept bitterly.

The four Gospel accounts, though brief (cf. Mark 14:66-72; Luke 22:54-62; John 18:15-18, 25-27, and see above on v.34 for comments regarding two cock crowings [Mark]), contain substantial differences, and a variety of solutions have been proposed. Matthew and Mark are in close agreement and list three denials: (1) before a servant girl, in the courtyard; (2) before another girl, but out by the gateway; (3) before bystanders, apparently in the court. Luke also lists three: (1) before a servant girl, apparently near the fire; (2) before another person, place not specified; (3) before yet another person, still in the courtyard (22:60-61). The three denials recorded by John are (1) before a servant girl at the door; then, after a break in the narrative, (2) before some people—the verb is plural but may be a generalizing one—(3) before one of the high priest's servants, a relative of Malchus.

Several things may be said.

1. Some attempts to harmonize the texts have resulted in Jesus' predicting *three* denials at each of *two* different times, making *six* denials (most recently, cf. H. Lindsell, *The Battle for the Bible* [Grand Rapids: Zondervan, 1976], pp. 174-76). This is not only intrinsically unlikely but introduces major source-critical problems never addressed and handled.

2. It may help us to look at the location of the relevant pericopes in the four Gospels. If our treatment of the trial sequence is correct (see on vv.57-68), Matthew and Mark do not record the examination before Annas but simply say that Peter followed Jesus into the courtyard. Then they place Peter's three denials after the preliminary trial before the Sanhedrin. Luke records neither the examination before Annas nor the preliminary trial before the Sanhedrin and therefore places Peter's

three denials before recording the Sanhedrin trial at dawn. John has nothing about the Jewish trial (though it may be hinted at in 19:24) except Jesus' examination before Annas. If Peter's first denial took place about the time of that examination, it is understandable that John separates it from the other two, which he describes after Jesus has been led before Caiaphas.

3. The order of the first two denials may be reversed between John and the Synoptics (cf. the order of the temptations; see on 4:1-11), but which Gospel has the historical order cannot easily be determined. John has "the girl at the gate" asking the first question and implies, but does not state, that this occurs on Peter's way in. Matthew and Mark have Jesus move back out to the gate as the setting for their second denial. Several possibilities come to mind, but no adequate way of testing them.

4. Remaining differences are minor and are capable of many solutions. Problems arise from the brevity of the accounts. In a setting around a fire, two or three may speak up at once (see below on vv.69-70); or, more probably, the plural in the second denial (in John's order) is generalizing (as in Matt 2:20). The differences in the reports of the denial cannot adequately be accounted for on redactional grounds.

69-70 The article "a" in "a servant girl" masks an idiomatic use of "one" (*mia*, v.69; see on 8:19; 21:19; cf. Moule, *Idiom Book*, p. 125). Her remark to Peter reflects both an accusation and her curiosity; and "Jesus of Galilee" (Mark 14:67: "that Nazarene, Jesus") is the kind of derogatory remark one might expect from a Jerusalemite convinced of her geographical and cultural superiority. Peter denies her words "before them all" (v.70), implying that several people were listening and that some may have joined in the questioning. The form of Peter's denial is akin to a formal, legal oath (cf. M *Shebuoth* 8:3).

71-72 Peter "went out" (v.71) to the gateway, apparently retiring from the brighter light of the fire into the darkness of the forecourt. Again he denies the accusation, this time with an oath. "Oath" here (v.72) does not refer to "swearing" as we know it in profanity; rather, Peter invokes a solemn curse on himself if he is lying and professes his "truthfulness" by appealing to something sacred (see on 5:33-34; 23:16-22).

73-75 A little more time elapses (v.73). Luke says "about an hour later" (22:59). In any age accent in speaking varies with geography (e.g., Judg 12:5-6), and Peter's speech shows him to be a Galilean (cf. Hoehner, *Herod Antipas*, pp. 61-64). That one of those present at Peter's denial said that his accent proved him to be a disciple of Jesus shows how much Jesus' ministry had been in Galilee and how relatively few of his disciples were from Judea. Having lied twice Peter finds himself forced to lie again, this time with more oaths (v.74). Immediately the rooster crows, a bitter reminder (v.75) of Jesus' words (v.34). He who thought he could stand has fallen terribly (cf. 1 Cor 10:12). Luke tells us that Jesus looked at Peter—perhaps through a window or as he was being led across the courtyard. If we cannot credit the legend that after this Peter never heard a cock crow without weeping, we may justifiably assume that Peter's bitter tears led to his being "poorer in spirit" (5:3) the remainder of his days than he had ever been before.

Matthew does not mention Peter again.

9. Formal decision of the Sanhedrin

27:1–2

> [1]Early in the morning, all the chief priests and the elders of the people came to the decision to put Jesus to death. [2]They bound him, led him away and handed him over to Pilate, the governor.

Whether this formal decision was reached as a final stage of the first meeting or at a separate meeting held either in Caiaphas's house or the temple precincts, we cannot say with certainty (see on vv.57–68). But Luke 22:66 implies a meeting in the council chamber (Catchpole, *Trial of Jesus*, pp. 191f.).

1 *Symboulion elabon* ("came to the decision") is a Latinism for *consilium capere* (cf. RHG, p. 109; BDF, par. 5[3b]) and does not mean "hold a council" (Hill, *Matthew*). On the other hand, Catchpole (*Trial of Jesus*, p. 191) seems to go too far in denying that it refers to the same event as Luke 22:66–71. The term can refer to a plot (as in 12:14; 22:15) and also to an agreed decision (28:12) as here. *Hōste* plus the infinitive here clearly refers to intention (cf. Zerwick, par. 352; Moule, *Idiom Book*, p. 140). Probably, too, the religious authorities decided just how to present their case to Pilate. If their own concern was Jesus' "blasphemy" (26:65), they were nevertheless more likely to get Pilate to sentence him to death by stressing the royal side of messiahship rather than blasphemy, as to Pilate that would suggest treason (cf. Acts 17:5–9 for a similar reference to treason).

2 Jesus is led to Pontius Pilate, the "governor" (for the variant, cf. Metzger, *Textual Commentary*, p. 65). "Governor" is here a general title (cf. 10:18; 1 Peter 2:14); Pilate was in fact appointed prefect or procurator by Tiberius Caesar in A.D. 26 (cf. IBD, 3:1229–31; ZPEB, 4:790–93). Prefects governed small, troubled areas; and in judicial matters they possessed powers like those of the far more powerful proconsuls and imperial legates; in short, they held the power of life and death, apart from appeal to Caesar. Following the banishment of Archelaus in A.D. 6, Judea and Samaria were made into one Roman province governed by a prefect or procurator who normally lived at Caesarea but often came to Jerusalem during the feasts to be close to the potential trouble spot.

Extrabiblical sources portray Pilate as a cruel, imperious, and insensitive ruler who hated his Jewish subjects and took few pains to understand them (e.g., Jos. Antiq. XVIII, 35 [ii.2], 55–62 [iii.1–2], 177–78 [vi.5]; War II, 169–77 [ix.2–4]; Philo, *ad Gaium* 38; cf. Hoehner, *Herod Antipas*, pp. 172–83). He stole korban (see on 15:5) money to build an aqueduct; and when the population of Jerusalem rioted in protest, he sent in soldiers who killed many. He defiled Jerusalem more than once (cf. Luke 13:1). These known facts about Pilate are often thought to render the Gospel accounts incredible, for here Pilate is portrayed as weak, ineffectual, and cowardly, judicially fair enough to want to release Jesus but too cowardly to stand up to the Sanhedrin's brow-beating tactics. This transformation of Pilate's character, it is claimed, results from the evangelists' desire to exculpate the Romans and condemn the Jews.

Hoehner (*Chronological Aspects*, pp. 105–14) responds to these problems with his crucifixion date of A.D. 33, *after* Pilate had set up the embossed shields in Jerusalem that Tiberius Caesar directly ordered removed, and *after* the execution of Pilate's patron, the anti-Semite Sejanus (d. 19 Oct. A.D. 31), whose death endangered Pilate. At this time the Sanhedrin would have found it easier to make direct and telling application to the emperor. In Hoehner's view Pilate appears weak in the Gospels because he has just been severely rebuked by Caesar and fears that the Jews' threat (John 19:12) could lead to another rebuke. By A.D. 33 Pilate's administration had become so bad that in A.D. 36 he was recalled and finally banished.

Even without this chronology, far too wide a historical gap between the Pilate of the Gospels and the Pilate of extrabiblical sources is being assumed.

1. Modern psychology helps us understand that the weak, insecure, selfish man elevated to a position of authority may become despotic and insensitive. Thus the evidence about Pilate may be complementary rather than disjunctive.

2. Pilate hated the Jews and especially the Jewish leaders. In the crisis forced on him by the Sanhedrin, though he may have seemed to be *for* Jesus, in reality he was probably *against* the Sanhedrin. His final decision betrayed no trace of sympathy for the Sanhedrin; rather, the Jews' threat (John 19:12) could well have intimidated so corrupt a man at any point in his career.

3. Jesus was not the criminal or guerrilla fighter with which Pilate was familiar. Jesus' silence and poise, the wisdom of his brief answers, and the dreams of Pilate's wife (v.19) may have prompted less drastic action than Pilate usually took.

4. Arguably, v.24 does not exculpate Pilate or reserve exclusive blame for the Jews (see on vv.24–25). Instead, as in vv.3–5, Matthew uses irony to say that no one connected with this crisis could escape personal responsibility.

5. Both the Sanhedrin trial and the trial before Pilate were necessary for capital punishment. Without the Sanhedrin, Pilate would never have taken action against Jesus unless he had become convinced Jesus was a dangerous Zealot leader; without Pilate the Sanhedrin might whip up mob violence against Jesus, but not a legally binding death sentence (cf. John 18:31).

10. *The death of Judas*

27:3–10

> [3]When Judas, who had betrayed him, saw that Jesus was condemned, he was seized with remorse and returned the thirty silver coins to the chief priests and the elders. [4]"I have sinned," he said, "for I have betrayed innocent blood."
>
> "What is that to us?" they replied. "That's your responsibility."
>
> [5]So Judas threw the money into the temple and left. Then he went away and hanged himself.
>
> [6]The chief priests picked up the coins and said, "It is against the law to put this into the treasury, since it is blood money." [7]So they decided to use the money to buy the potter's field as a burial place for foreigners. [8]That is why it has been called the Field of Blood to this day. [9]Then what was spoken by Jeremiah the prophet was fulfilled: "They took the thirty silver coins, the price set on him by the people of Israel, [10]and they used them to buy the potter's field, as the Lord commanded me."

This account is peculiar to Matthew, though Acts 1:16–19 also records Judas's death. The differences between the two are considerable; and many scholars hold that Acts 1:16–19 or something like it circulated as a bit of independent tradition Matthew adapted to develop his "fulfillment" theme further. But Benoit (*Jesus,* pp. 189–207) finds greater historical accuracy in Matthew than in Acts. Many believe the only historically fixed points are Judas's sudden death and the purchase of a piece of land called "the Field of Blood" (cf. Stendahl, *School of Matthew*, pp. 120–27; Lindars, *Apologetic*, pp. 116–22). But if Matthew developed a fulfillment theme by adding to or changing an earlier tradition, numerous difficulties, including even misnaming the prophet (v.9), show that he botched the job.

Hill's suggestion that Matthew placed the story of Judas's suicide here to show that Judas's remorse depends on the Sanhedrin's decision, not Pilate's, is only a possibility. No matter where Matthew located the pericope, it would interrupt the narrative at this point; and other reasons may have led him to place it here. Matthew's prime interest in this pericope is to continue the fulfillment theme—that not only Jesus' death but the major events surrounding it were prophesied in Scripture. Verse 4 again stresses Jesus' innocence and sees the fulfillment of another of Jesus' predictions (26:24), which sets up an apologetic tool (cf. "to this day," v.8). In any case, neither Peter's tears nor Judas's remorse can remove their guilt.

3 On "the chief priests and elders," here governed by a single article suggesting a single entity (the Sanhedrin), see on 21:23. Verse 3 looks back to 10:4; 26:14–16, 20–25. Judas's "remorse" is not necessarily repentance, though the two Greek verbs *metamelomai* (here and in 21:29) and *metanoeō* can overlap.

4 Judas recognizes that he is not only guilty of betrayal but that Jesus whom he has betrayed is "innocent" (cf. Metzger, *Textual Commentary*, p. 66). The Jewish leaders' callous response "What is that to us?" is both a Semitic and classical idiom (cf. BDF, pars. 127[3], 299[3]). But their own words condemn them, for it *should* have been something to them. Judas has betrayed innocent blood; they have condemned innocent blood. "That's your responsibility" (lit., "you will see [to it]," as in v.24), they say—a remark correct in content but wrong in implying that they are absolved.

5–8 Exactly where Judas threw the money (v.5) is uncertain (cf. Notes). He then went out and hanged himself. *Apēnxato* ("hanged himself") occurs in 2 Samuel 17:23 LXX. On this basis some have made lengthy comparisons between Judas and Ahithophel—the one a treacherous friend of David, the other a treacherous friend of David's greater Son (e.g., B.F. Meyer, McNeile); but that Matthew intended such a comparison is doubtful (cf. Moo, "Use of OT," pp. 189–91).

The chief priests, in accord with Deuteronomy 23:18, refuse to allow the blood money to supplement the funds of the *korbanas* ("treasury," v.6; used only here in the NT—the place where a consecrated article is deposited and cognate with *korban*; see on 15:5; Jos. War II, 175 [ix.4]). Many scholars suggest that elements of the OT quotation (vv.9–10) have generated these "historical" details. They hold that the Hebrew *yôṣēr* ("potter") in Zechariah 11–13 was either confused with *'ôṣār* ("treasury") or that the latter was found in Matthew's copy of Zechariah (as in Peshitta). Alternatively *yôṣēr* can mean "smith," i.e., a worker in metals, and is so rendered by LXX. Does Zechariah therefore throw his money "to the potter" (NIV), to the treasury, or to the temple foundry, which made temple vessels and coins? The problem with this alternative to the MT is that if Matthew (or the tradition he used) understood the OT to refer to the treasury, then where did he find his reference to "potter" (vv.7, 10)? The OT text is indeed difficult, though a better analysis is possible (see below). What is clear is that Matthew is again pointing out the propensity of the Jewish leaders for ceremonial probity even in the face of gross injustice (cf. 12:9–14; 15:1–9; 23:23; 28:12–13; cf. John 18:28).

With this probity in view, the chief priests decide (same construction as in v. 1) to buy the potter's field to meet a public need (v. 7)—an accepted use of ill-gotten gains (cf. SBK, 1:37; Jeremias, *Jerusalem*, p. 140). The potter's field, used for the burial of foreigners, probably did not belong to "the potter" (surely there was more than one potter in Jerusalem) but was a well-known place, perhaps the place where potters had long obtained their clay. If depleted, it might have been offered for sale. There are no reliable early traditions of its location, though Matthew's "to this day" shows it was well known when he wrote. The best assumption is that it lay in the valley of Hinnom near the juncture with the Kidron.

There are three significant differences between these verses and Acts 1:18–19.

1. Matthew says that the chief priests bought the field; Acts, that Judas did. But if the priests bought it with Judas's money, it may well have been regarded as his. More important, the language in Acts is fine spun: "With the reward of unrighteousness, he acquired [*ktaomai*, not necessarily 'bought'] a field" (lit. tr.). "The money bought him a burial-place; that was to him the sole financial outcome of the iniquitous transaction" (Broadus).

2. Matthew says Judas hanged himself; Acts, that "he fell headlong, his body burst open and all his intestines spilled out." This does not imply a disease, or that Judas tripped, as some have held. If Judas hanged himself, no Jew would want to defile himself during the Feast of Unleavened Bread by burying the corpse; and a hot sun might have brought on rapid decomposition till the body fell to the ground and burst open. Alternatively, one long tradition in the church claims Judas hanged himself from a tree branch that leaned over a ravine (of which there are many in the area); and when the branch broke, whether before or after he died, Judas fell to a messy end. We are not so much beset by contradictory accounts as by paucity of information, making it difficult to decide which of several alternatives we should choose in working out the complementarity of the two accounts.

3. Matthew seems to ascribe the name "Field of Blood" to its being purchased with blood money; Acts, to the fact that Judas's blood was shed there. But again the paucity of information faces us with several possibilities. All the circumstances must have become public knowledge; and one reason, far from ruling out the other, actually complements it—provided that Judas died in the field purchased by the priests. Perhaps the priests bought the field (not necessarily the same day—Sunday would have been adequate); and Judas, informed as to what had been done with the blood money and driven to despair by futile remorse, decided to commit suicide in a field for the burial of aliens to Israel's covenants.

Moreover we must at least raise the question whether Acts 1:18–19 associates "Field of Blood" with Judas's blood. "Everyone in Jerusalem heard about this" (Acts 1:19); but does "this" refer to Judas's body splitting open, without mention of blood, or to securing the field with blood money, also without explicit mention of blood? This is not an attempt at forced harmonization. But if it is bad historiography to squeeze two diverse accounts of one incident into a contrived union, it is equally bad historiography to mistake an instance of too little information for contradiction.

9–10 Four aspects of this complex quotation need discussion.

1. *The ascription to Jeremiah.* On the face of it, the quotation is a rough rendering of Zechariah 11:12–13, with "I took" changed to "they took" and the price interpreted as referring to the sum paid for Jesus. The only obvious allusions ·to Jeremiah are 18:2–6; 32:6–15—Jeremiah did visit a potter and buy a field. But

though some of the language of those passages may have influenced Matthew 27:9–10, it is difficult to imagine why Matthew mentioned Jeremiah instead of Zechariah, even though Jeremiah is important in this Gospel (cf. 2:17; 16:14). Highly improbable "solutions" abound. Some have followed the minor textual variant "Zechariah" instead of "Jeremiah"; others have argued for an original text with no mention of the prophet's name, attributing "Jeremiah" to a copyist's error; many have assumed that Matthew made a minor error; others have appealed to a hypothetical writing of Jeremiah now lost; others have held that Jeremiah wrote Zechariah 9–11—though it is surely "a critical anachronism" (Morison) to see Matthew as anticipating modern source theories; and still others assume that Matthew is referring to the entire collection of prophetic books grouped under the name of the first book (though it is not at all certain that Jeremiah was first in Matthew's day).

The most believable solution comes from Hengstenberg (pp. 1095ff.) and is developed by Gundry (*Use of OT*, pp. 122–27), Senior (*Passion Narrative*, pp. 359ff.), and especially by Moo ("Use of OT," pp. 191–210). They note that no extant version of Zechariah 11 refers to a field; and Matthew's attributing the quotation to Jeremiah suggests we ought to look to that book. Jeremiah 19:1–13 (not Jer 18 or 32) is the obvious candidate. There Jeremiah is told to purchase a potter's jar and take some elders and priests to the Valley of Ben Hinnom, where he is to warn of the destruction of Jerusalem for her sin, illustrated by smashing the jar. A further linguistic link is "innocent blood" (Jer 19:4); and thematic links include renaming a locality associated with potters (19:1) with a name ("Valley of Slaughter") denoting violence (19:6). The place will henceforth be used as a burial ground (19:11), as a token of God's judgment. In the last clause in Matthew's quotation, "as the Lord commanded me" (v.19), Lindars (*Apologetic*, p. 121) sees an allusion to Exodus 9:12; but Moo ("Use of OT," pp. 196f.) has shown this is at best tenuous.

We have not yet tried to explain what Matthew understands by these OT texts, or what he means by "fulfillment." But it is fair to say that the quotation appears to refer to Jeremiah 19:1–13 along with phraseology drawn mostly from Zechariah 11:12–13 (MT in both cases), with the concluding clause a traditional "obedience formula" (cf. R. Pesch, "Eine alttestamentliche Ausführungsformel im Matthäus-Evangelium," *Biblische Zeitschrift* 10 [1966]: 220–45) used to paraphrase the opening words of Zechariah 11:13: "And the LORD said to me." Such fusing of sources under one "quotation" is not unknown elsewhere in Scripture (e.g., Mark 1:2–3); cf. 2 Chron 36:21, verbally drawn from Lev 26:34–35, yet ascribed to Jeremiah [25:12; 29:10; cf. Gundry, *Use of OT*, p. 125]; and see on Matt 3:17). Jeremiah alone is mentioned, perhaps because he is the more important of the two prophets, and perhaps also because, though Jeremiah 19 is the less obvious reference, it is the more important as to prophecy and fulfillment.

2. *Prophecy and history*. Many scholars hold that Matthew presents as history a number of "fulfillments" that did not happen. Rather he deduces that they must have happened because his chosen OT texts predict, as he understands them, that such events would take place. To this there are two objections. First, the more complex and composite a quotation (as here), the less likely is it that the "fulfillment" was invented. It is far easier to believe that certain historical events led Matthew to look for Scriptures relating to them. We may then ask how he has treated these Scriptures, but that is a separate problem. Second, when we examine Matthew's quotation clause by clause, we can see impressive reasons for holding that the narrative does not grow out of the prophecy (see esp. Moo, "Use of OT,"

pp. 198ff.). To give but one instance, the "thirty silver coins" (v.3) are mentioned in Zechariah 11:13; but Mark speaks of betrayal money without mentioning Zechariah. Even if Mark does not specify the amount, the *fact* that Judas had been paid became well known, independent of any Christian interpretation of Zechariah 11:12–13; and it is not unreasonable to suppose that the *amount* of money *also* became common knowledge.

3. *Meaning.* How did Matthew understand the OT texts he was quoting? The question is not easy, because the two OT passages themselves can be variously explained. It appears that in Zechariah 11 the "buyers" (v.5) and the three shepherds (vv.5, 8, 17) apparently represent Israel's leaders, who are slaughtering the sheep. God commands Zechariah to shepherd the "flock marked for slaughter" (v.7), and he tries to clean up the leadership by sacking the false shepherds. But he discovers that not only is the leadership corrupt, but the flock detests him (v.8). Thus Zechariah comes to understand the Lord's decision to have no more pity on the people of the land (v.6).

Zechariah decides to resign (11:9–10), exposing the flock to ravages. Because he has broken the contract, Zechariah cannot claim his pay (presumably from the "buyers"); but they pay him off with thirty pieces of silver (v.12). But now Yahweh tells Zechariah to throw this "handsome price at which they priced me" (probably ironical; cf. Notes) to the potter in the "house of the LORD," i.e., the temple (v.13). Temple ritual required a constant supply of new vessels (cf. Lev 6:28); so a guild of potters worked somewhere in the temple precincts. Certainly Jeremiah could point to a potter as he preached and could purchase pottery somewhere near the temple (Jer 18:6; 19:1).

The purpose of Zechariah's action is uncertain. Because a *yôṣēr* (lit., "shaper") was both a potter and a metal worker, it may be that the money in Zechariah 11:12–13 was thrown to the *yôṣēr* so that it would be melted down and turned into a figurine, a little "god." The people did not want the Lord's shepherd, and so they will be saddled with a silver figurine (cf. Ezek 16:17; Hos 2:8)—betrayal money, in effect, since it pays off the good shepherd who would have kept the people true to the Lord's covenant and who has been rejected by the people. The result can only be catastrophic judgment (11:14–17).

The parallel between Zechariah 11 and Matthew 26–27 is not exact. In Zechariah the money is paid to the good shepherd; in Matthew it is paid to Judas and returned to the Jewish leaders. In Zechariah the money goes directly to the "potter" in the temple; in Matthew, after being thrown into the temple, it purchases "the potter's field"—though at this point the influence of Jeremiah 19 has been introduced (see below). Nevertheless the central parallel is stunning: in both instances Yahweh's shepherd is rejected by the people of Israel and valued at the price of a slave. And in both instances the money is flung into the temple and ends up purchasing something that pollutes.

The reference to Jeremiah 19 (cf. above, under 1) provides equally telling parallels. The rulers have forsaken Yahweh and made Jerusalem a place of foreign gods (19:4); so the day is coming when this valley, where the prophecy is given and the potter's jar smashed, will be called the Valley of Slaughter, symbolic of the ruin of Judah and Jerusalem (19:6–7). Similarly in Matthew the rejection of Jesus (Yahweh; see on 2:6; 3:3; 13:37–39) leads to a polluted field, a symbol of death and the destruction of the nation about to be buried as "foreigners."

4. *Fulfillment.* In the light of these relationships between the events surrounding

Jesus' death and the two key OT passages that make up Matthew's quotation, what does the evangelist mean by saying that the prophecy "was fulfilled"? As in 2:17, the form of this introductory formula shrinks from making Judas's horrible crime the immediate result of the Lord's word, while nevertheless insisting that all has taken place in fulfillment of Scripture (cf. 1:22 with 2:17). Beyond that there is a tendency to apply standard Jewish categories to this use of the OT by Matthew. For instance, Doeve (pp. 185f.) characterizes Matthew 27:3–10 as "haggadah," a creative story the starting point of which was the link between "innocent blood" in v.4 and in Jeremiah 26:15, which led on by associations of word and theme to Jeremiah 19, 32 and Zechariah 11:13. But "innocent blood" is not an uncommon expression and is therefore an inadequate link between Matthew and Jeremiah. Lindars (*Apologetic*, pp. 116–22) detects an elaborate Midrashic development along somewhat different lines, and Stendahl (*School of Matthew*, pp. 120–26; 196–98) finds a parallel in Midrash Pesher at Qumran. Though these are invaluable studies, several cautions are needed.

France (*Jesus*, pp. 206–7) draws attention to two differences between Matthew's use of the OT in this passage and the Pesharim at Qumran, which claimed that various OT texts were in reality referring to certain recent historical events. First, Matthew changes the wording far more than was done at Qumran; second, he respects the central intentions of the OT authors far more than at Qumran. These two points are linked: Matthew does not need to devise farfetched explanations for each word and phrase, because in each case he has truly represented the central theme. The verbal differences he introduces in citing the OT are not an embarrassment to him, because he is not claiming that the OT text is a prophecy to be fulfilled by a simple one-on-one pattern. Pesher claims that what the OT text refers to *is* the specified historical event; and there are close parallels to this claim elsewhere in the NT (e.g., Acts 2:16). But what we find in Matthew, including vv.9–10, is not *identification* of the text *with* an event but *fulfillment* of the text *in* an event, based on a broad typology governing how both Jesus and Matthew read the OT (see on 2:15; 8:17; 13:35; 26:28, 54).

Because of this typological model, Matthew introduces the commonly noticed changes: the one on whom a price is set is no longer the prophet ("me," Zech 11:13) but Jesus ("him," Matt 27:9). Even Matthew's use of the concluding obedience formula—"as the Lord commanded me"—is best accounted for as a hint of the prophecy–fulfillment pattern. Here "me" can only refer to the prophet; yet Matthew keeps it even though he changes other parts of the quotation to "him," because he believes that in obeying the Lord, the prophet—whether Jeremiah or Zechariah—was setting forth typological paradigms that truly did point to Jesus and the greatest rejection of all.

"Midrash" and "haggadah" are deceptive categories. We have maintained that Matthew did not make up the events he relates to illustrate Scripture but that they stand as independent historical realities he now relates to Scripture. Normally, late Midrash (the only kind that is well defined: cf. Introduction, section 12.b) begins with the text as the point of departure, but in Matthew the narrative is the point of departure. The element of "fulfillment" is not present in Midrash in the way it is everywhere presupposed in the NT.

This is not a surreptitious plea to divorce Matthew from his Jewish roots. Doubtless it is correct to say that Matthew uses "midrashic techniques," at least on the level of what Moo calls "appropriation techniques"—i.e., devices by which an OT text is applied to or appropriated by events contemporary with the evangelist. But such procedures are so universally used that the expression "midrashic technique" conceals more than it reveals: it is a little like saying "interpretative techniques." What must not be overlooked is that, unlike any other broad, hermeneutical category used by the Jews, NT approaches to the OT are steeped in a salvation-historical perspective that finds in the sacred text entire patterns of prophetic anticipation (see esp. on 2:15; 5:17-20; 8:17; 11:11-13; 13:34-35). In this sense Matthew sees in Jeremiah 19 and Zechariah 11 not merely a number of verbal and thematic parallels to Jesus' betrayal but a pattern of apostasy and rejection that must find its ultimate fulfillment in the rejection of Jesus, who was cheaply valued, rejected by the Jews, and whose betrayal money was put to a purpose that pointed to the destruction of the nation (see on 15:7-9; 21:42).

Notes

---

5 The question of where Judas threw the money is beset by two problems.

1. O. Michel (TDNT, 4:882-85) and G. Schrenk (TDNT, 3:235) argue that there is no necessary difference between ναός (naos, "temple [sanctuary]") and ἱερόν (hieron, "temple [and its precincts]"). If so, then the use of the former in this verse means no more than that Judas threw the money somewhere in the temple area. But a fairly strong case can be made for maintaining a distinction between the words in Matthew's usage: naos is used only of the temple proper, the sanctuary, in 23:16-17, 21; 27:51, and, metaphorically, in 26:61; 27:40; whereas hieron is used of the temple and its precincts in 4:5; 21:12, 14-15, 23; 24:1; 26:55 (cf. Garland, p. 199, n. 117). It is possible that hieron is a trifle forced in 12:5; but since it is the encompassing term and not all the priests' functions took place in the temple proper, the use still admits the traditional distinction between the terms. That leaves only 27:5; but in the narrow sense of naos, Judas would normally not have been allowed to enter. That may be just the point: feeling damned already, he has nothing more to lose; and in desperation he runs into the temple proper and flings down his money before he can be stopped. Thus he deeply incriminates the priests, a further example of 23:35.

2. It is very difficult to decide between the variant εἰς τὸν ναόν (eis ton naon, "into the temple") and ἐν τῷ ναῷ (en tō naō, "in the temple") (cf. Metzger, Textual Commentary, p. 66).

8 The aorist passive ἐκλήθη (eklēthē, lit., "it was called") here takes on perfective force ("it has been called") because of the ἕως (heōs, "until") clause that follows (cf. Burton, Syntax, par. 18; Moule, Idiom Book, p. 14; somewhat similar, 28:15).

9 Although thirty shekels is the price of a slave (Exod 21:32), some argue (e.g., Joyce Baldwin, Haggai, Zechariah, Malachi, TOTC [London: Tyndale, 1972], pp. 183-86) that the amount is not paltry. The Code of Hammurabi distinguishes an ordinary citizen from a slave by saying that when either is gored to death by an ox, the payment in the former case is one-half mina, in the latter one-third mina, when a mina was probably worth about fifty shekels. Doubtless the biblical law puts more value on a human life, slave or not; but the fact remains that thirty shekels is a slave's price. If Baldwin is correct, then "the handsome price" of Zech 11:13 is not ironic but must be an indication of how willing the buyers were to get rid of this shepherd. This seems unlikely since Zechariah is going to leave anyway. If, however, "the handsome price" is meant sardonically, this makes good sense; for even if the amount represents a substantial sum, it is still the price of a slave and representative of how God's prophet is valued by an apostate people. The same kind of irony probably stands behind the paronomasia of Matt 27:9: τὴν τιμὴν τοῦ τετιμημένου ὃν ἐτιμήσαντο (tēn timēn tou tetimēmenou hon etimēsanto, lit., "the price of the one whose price had been priced [by the sons of Israel]").

10 The third person plural ἔδωκαν (edōkan, "they gave"; NIV, "they used") is to be preferred above the first person singular ἔδωκα (edōka, "I gave,") because the OT text and the "me" of the next clause would be strong inducement to change to the first person (cf. Senior, *Passion Narrative*, p. 356).

---

11. *Jesus before Pilate*

27:11–26

11Meanwhile Jesus stood before the governor, and the governor asked him, "Are you the king of the Jews?"

"Yes, it is as you say," Jesus replied.

12When he was accused by the chief priests and the elders, he gave no answer. 13Then Pilate asked him, "Don't you hear the testimony they are bringing against you?" 14But Jesus made no reply, not even to a single charge—to the great amazement of the governor.

15Now it was the governor's custom at the Feast to release a prisoner chosen by the crowd. 16At that time they had a notorious prisoner, called Barabbas. 17So when the crowd had gathered, Pilate asked them, "Which one do you want me to release to you: Barabbas, or Jesus who is called Christ?" 18For he knew it was out of envy that they had handed Jesus over to him.

19While Pilate was sitting on the judge's seat, his wife sent him this message: "Don't have anything to do with that innocent man, for I have suffered a great deal today in a dream because of him."

20But the chief priests and the elders persuaded the crowd to ask for Barabbas and to have Jesus executed.

21"Which of the two do you want me to release to you?" asked the governor.

"Barabbas," they answered.

22"What shall I do, then, with Jesus who is called Christ?" Pilate asked.

They all answered, "Crucify him!"

23"Why? What crime has he committed?" asked Pilate.

But they shouted all the louder, "Crucify him!"

24When Pilate saw that he was getting nowhere, but that instead an uproar was starting, he took water and washed his hands in front of the crowd. "I am innocent of this man's blood," he said. "It is your responsibility!"

25All the people answered, "Let his blood be on us and on our children!"

26Then he released Barabbas to them. But he had Jesus flogged, and handed him over to be crucified.

John gives most details of the trial before Pilate; Luke adds the account of the intervening trial before Herod; and Matthew follows Mark rather closely, but vv. 19, 24–25 have no parallel (cf. Mark 15:2–15; Luke 23:2–25; John 18:28–19:26).

The setting is uncertain. It might be the Tower of Antonia, on the northwest corner of the temple area; but more probably it is Herod's old palace on the west side of the city near the Jaffa gate (cf. Jos. Antiq. XX, 110; [v.3]; War II, 328 [xv.5]; Philo *ad Gaium* 38). The word "Praetorium" (v.27) can refer to a princely palace as readily as to a judicial or military seat. Probably Herod Antipas, tetrarch of Galilee, would also stay in his father's palace whenever he came to Jerusalem, which could explain the ease with which Jesus' brief interview with Herod (Luke 23:8–12) was arranged.

11 For comments regarding Pilate, see on vv. 1–2. Matthew's report, in which Pilate asks, "Are you the king of the Jews?" presupposes the background of Luke 23:2 and John 18:28–33. The Sanhedrin's concern with Jesus' "blasphemy" becomes his claim to kingship, a charge of treason with overtones of Zealot sedition, capped with a claim that Jesus refuses to pay taxes (see on 22:15–22). In Roman trials the magistrate normally heard the charges first, questioned the defendant and listened to his defense, sometimes permitted several such exchanges, and then retired with his advisors to decide on a verdict, which was then promptly carried out. The first step, the charge by the Jewish leaders, led to this particular formulation of Pilate's question to Jesus. Jesus answers, as in 26:25, 64, in an affirmative but qualified way. He is indeed the king of the Jews, but not exactly in the sense Pilate might think. The nature of Jesus' kingship is defined in the more detailed exchange John reports (18:34–37).

Verse 11 is important theologically as well as historically. It stands behind the inscription on the cross (v. 37) and prepares the way for Christianity, which rests on the conviction that Jesus of Nazareth, who rose from the dead, is indeed the promised Messiah, the King of the Jews—basic themes in Matthew even in the prologue. In other words, the vindicated Lord is the crucified Messiah (cf. N.A. Dahl, *The Crucified Messiah* [Minneapolis: Augsburg, 1974], pp. 10–36).

12–14 Persistent charges by "the chief priests and the elders" (v. 12) evoke only silence from Jesus. If Jesus had said nothing at all, Pilate would be bound to condemn him (Sherwin-White, pp. 25–26), since in the Roman system the defense depended heavily on the defendant's response. But Jesus *has* spoken (v. 11). Now, surrounded by unbelief and conscious that the hour has come, he makes no reply (v. 13). Thus he continues to fulfill Isaiah 53:7 (see on 26:63). Pilate's "great amazement" (v. 14) appears to be mingled with respect for Jesus and antipathy for the Jewish leaders, and so he takes tentative steps to release the prisoner. Meanwhile Jesus' silence testifies mutely to his willingness (cf. 26:53) to suffer as "a ransom for many" (20:28).

15 In Roman law an imperial magistrate could acquit a prisoner not yet condemned or pardon one already condemned; but the Gospel accounts makes this a regular custom, apparently associated with Judea alone (on the grammar, cf. Moule, *Idiom Book*, p. 59). Blinzler (pp. 218–21), followed by Lane (*Mark*, pp. 552f.), has shown that M *Pesahim* 8:6 ("they may slaughter [viz., a Passover lamb] for one . . . whom they have promised to bring out of prison") presupposes some kind of regular paschal amnesty; and the tractate in question is universally recognized as recording very old traditions.

16 "Barabbas" seems a strange name: "bar Abba" means "son of Abba," i.e., "son of the father." But there is evidence that the name or nickname was not unknown in rabbinic families (SBK, 1:1031). Perhaps Barabbas was the son of a famous rabbi (on such a use of "father," see on 23:9). Some MSS preserve his name as "Jesus Barabbas" (cf. Notes); but with what authority we cannot now be certain. Matthew says he was an *episēmos* ("notorious," NIV) prisoner. NIV's translation of the word implies Barabbas was universally reprobated, but the Greek is neutral ("notable," "conspicuous"); and in the only other NT occurrence of the word, NIV renders it "outstanding" (Rom 16:7). The point is not academic, for Barabbas was no ordinary villain but a *lēstēs* (cf. Mark 15:7; Luke 23:19; John 18:40). Although *lēstēs* can refer to a robber (as perhaps in John 10:1), it more probably refers to insurrectionists (cf. 26:55; John 18:40); and Josephus constantly uses it of the Zealots. Neither theft nor violent robbery was a capital offense, but insurrection was. Revolts and bloodshed fostered by guerrilla action were common (cf. Jos. Antiq. XVIII, 3–10 [i.1], 60–62 [iii.2]; Luke 13:1), and Barabbas had been caught. In the eyes of many of the people he would not be a "notorious" villain but a hero.

It may be that the two who were crucified with Jesus were co-rebels with Barabbas, for Matthew 27:38 calls them *lēstai* (better "rebels," "guerrillas," or "insurrectionists" than NIV's "robbers"), and their crucifixion indicates they were judged guilty of more than robbery. The fact that three crosses were prepared strongly suggests that Pilate had already ordered that preparations be made for the execution of the three rebels. If so, Jesus the Messiah actually took the place of the rebel [Jesus] Barabbas because the people preferred the political rebel and nationalist hero to the Son of God.

17–18 The "crowd" (v. 17) was not a crowd of Jesus' accusers but of those trying to influence the selection of the prisoner who would receive the paschal amnesty (cf. Mark 15:8). It is possible, though far from certain, that the crowd, knowing little as yet of the arrest and trial of Jesus Christ, was voicing its support for "Jesus" (i.e., Jesus Barabbas—if the variant is supported); and Pilate mistook their pleas as support for Jesus Christ (cf. Lane, *Mark*, p. 554, n. 29).

What is certain is that Pilate sized up the real motivation of the Jewish leaders (v. 18). They had no special loyalty to Rome; so if they were accusing Jesus of being a traitor to Rome, he must have been disturbing them for other reasons; and they were simply using Pilate to eliminate Jesus' challenge to them. Pilate, with his network of spies and informers, would be aware of how much popularity Jesus Christ enjoyed among the people at large. He could hardly have been unaware of the upsurge of acclaim the previous Sunday (21:1–16). He thought to administer a reversal to Sanhedrin policy by using the paschal amnesty to encourage the crowd to free Jesus; and therefore he offered them a choice: Barabbas or Jesus "who is called Christ." The last clause may be contemptuous.

19 In A.D. 21 it had been proposed in the Roman Senate that no provincial magistrate could be accompanied by his wife (cf. Tacitus *Annales* 3.33–35). The proposal was defeated; so Pilate's wife was on hand to speak of her dream. If Roman troops were involved in Jesus' arrest (see on 26:47–56), Pilate and perhaps his wife would have been informed. Her dream calls to mind the five dreams of Matthew 1–2; but it is quite unlike them and may not have been supernatural. God gave the earlier dreams for guidance to be obeyed, but this dream combines suffering with intimations of gloom. In any event the interruption of Pilate's wife while he was sitting "on the judge's seat" (cf. Jos. War II, 301[xiv.8]) further stresses Jesus' innocence (NIV rightly renders *dikaios* by "innocent") and gives the chief priests and elders a few moments to influence the crowd. On the idiom "Don't have anything to do with," see Turner (*Insights*, pp. 43–47).

20–23 Matthew and Mark both insist that the leaders ("chief priests," Mark; "chief priests and elders," Matthew) helped persuade the crowd (v. 20). But it is wrong to infer that either Matthew or Mark is whitewashing the crowd (contra Hill et al.), for then "all the people" (v.25) would make no sense. Historically the description of the crowd's response is comprehensible enough. They have come to demand Barabbas's release (see on v.17). When they are confronted with the choice of Barabbas or Jesus (v.21), both of whom were widely popular, their momentary faltering is resolved by their leaders. If the crowd must choose between Pilate's choice and the Sanhedrin's choice, especially if the Sanhedrin members are circulating stories of Jesus' "blasphemy," then there can be little doubt on which side of the issue they will come down. In Judea it was common to confront the Roman authorities with as noisy and large a delegation as possible (cf. Jos. Antiq. XVIII, 269–72[viii.3]). And now mob mentality begins to take over.

Tactically Pilate has blundered. Trying to save face he asks more questions. The first (v.22) offers the hope of milder sentence (high treason could be punished by crucifixion, facing wild animals in the arena, or banishment); and the second (v.23) attests Jesus' innocence (on NIV's sensitive rendering of *gar* [lit., "for"], cf. BDF, par. 423[1]). But mob psychology prevails (cf. Acts 19:34). The demand for crucifixion also assured that the executed person would be declared accursed (see on vv.32–44).

The people indicate their preference for a murderous, nationalistic guerrilla leader over their Messiah, who exhorted the people to love their enemies and said he would die as a ransom for many. As Luke points out, it would not be long before Peter would remind the people of Israel at large (not just the leaders): "You handed [Jesus] over to be killed, and you disowned him before Pilate, though he had decided to let him go. You disowned the Holy and Righteous One and asked that a murderer be released to you" (Acts 3:13b–14).

24 It is customary to interpret this verse as Matthew's fictitious attempt to show Pilate's positive response to his wife's advice (v.19) and place guilt on the Jews (cf. v.25). But this is not the most natural interpretation.

1. To the best of our knowledge, this hand washing was not a Roman custom. After living several years among the Jews he detested, Pilate picked up one of their own customs (Deut 21:6; cf. Ps 26:6) and contemptuously used it against them.

2. There is little reason to think the hand washing incompatible with the proceedings, because, whatever his motives, Pilate tried repeatedly to release Jesus. He sent him to Herod (Luke), suggested that the paschal amnesty be applied to him, proposed a compromise with a scourging (Luke), tried to turn the case back to Jewish authorities (John), remonstrated before pronouncing sentence (John), and here washes his hands. Matthew gives us only two of these steps; so it is difficult to see why he should be charged with exculpating the Romans simply because one of his two is the only one not mentioned by the other evangelists.

3. If Matthew were interested in exculpating Pilate, would he have included the soldiers' savage mockery of Jesus (vv.27–31)?

4. Pilate's claim to be "innocent of this man's blood" is no stronger than Luke 23:14. Why then should this verse in Matthew be thought to color the first gospel's passion narrative so uniquely?

5. We cannot be certain that Pilate actually thought his action would excuse him; it may have reflected his contempt for the Jews or have been a taunt. And even if he thought he had exculpated himself, he should have known better. Plumptre quotes Ovid's lines: "Too easy souls, who dream the crystal flood/Can wash away the fearful guilt of blood."

6. But regardless of what Pilate thought, Matthew does not think the hand washing exonerated Pilate. We have already seen how Matthew shows that all connected with Jesus' death are guilty (see on vv.2, 4–5). Now Matthew insists that Pilate's action was not prompted by desire for justice but by political and moral cowardice and fear of a mob. The Romans expected their magistrates to maintain peace. An uproar, especially one tinged with complaint to Caesar (John), would be enough to intimidate a corrupt governor whose past has caught up with him (see on 26:57–68). So when Pilate says, "It is your responsibility" (27:24), Matthew intends his readers to remember the same words spoken by the chief priests and elders to Judas (v.4).

7. Too much of the debate about v.24 implies that the text merely reflects church-synagogue relations at the end of the first century, with little connection with the trial of Jesus. This has led to so many historical disjunctions as to be no longer credible. Is it not remarkable that the fourth Gospel, which in recent literature is also regularly interpreted as a clash between church and synagogue, should contain much more about the Roman trial than the Synoptics?

25 To Pilate's words, "all the people" answer, "Let his blood be on us and on our children!" The idiom is familiar (2 Sam 1:16; 3:28; Acts 18:6; 20:26). In the narrative this is a swift retort to Pilate's taunt and mob pressure for him to pronounce the verdict. But it clearly is more than that. How much more? Many say that by "all the people" Matthew is saying that *the Jews as a whole* reject Jesus (Frankmölle, pp. 204–11) and therefore have incurred collective guilt. Thus v.25 becomes a prophecy of the destruction of Jerusalem and the nation; and a new people of God, the church, take over. There is some truth in this view, but it needs qualification.

1. Matthew probably means "all the people" to refer to the entire crowd that cries, "Let his blood be upon us," rather than limiting these words to the chief priests and elders (see on v.20).

2. Even if there is symbolism (as there appears to be) whereby the crowd's response reflects the response of the nation as a whole (cf. 23:37–39), Matthew certainly knows that *all* the first disciples were Jews. Thus the Gospel's denunciations of the Jews are not more severe than those of many OT prophets, and in both instances it is understood that a faithful remnant remains. So what Matthew actually says cannot be judged as anti-Semitic. It is only when Matthew's account is read as a description, not of Jesus' trial, but of later church-synagogue relations, that it begins to bear anti-Semitic nuances fostered, not by the trial itself, but by the expansion of the remnant to include Gentile believers. Thus the anachronism of the church-synagogue conflict, consciously adopted by more liberal critics and unconsciously presupposed by more conservative ones, injects into the passion narratives more "anti-Semitic" bias than was actually present in the events they describe. If v.25 joins Matthew 25 in anticipating the judgment of A.D. 70, it does so in a way akin to Jeremiah's prophecies of the Exile and not with the often cynical detachment of Gentile believers from the Fathers on.

26 Among the Jews scourging was limited to forty lashes (Deut 25:3; cf. 2 Cor 11:24), but the Romans were restricted by nothing but their strength and whim. The whip was the dreaded *flagellum*, made by plaiting pieces of bone or lead into leather thongs. The victim was stripped and tied to a post. Severe flogging not only reduced the flesh to bloody pulp but could open up the body until the bones were visible and the entrails exposed (cf. TDNT, 4:510–12; Jos. War II, 612[xxi.5]; VI,

304[v.3]). Flogging as an independent punishment not infrequently ended in death. It was also used to weaken the prisoner before crucifixion. Jesus' flogging took place before the verdict (cf. Luke 23:16, 22; John 19:1–5; cf. Blinzler, pp. 222ff.) and so was not repeated after the verdict. Repetition would doubtless have killed him. Pilate, after further entreaty (John 19:1–16), then "handed him over to be crucified" (v.16); the words recall the Suffering Servant (Isa 53:6, 12 LXX).

Notes

16–17 Only witnesses of the Caesarean text (e.g., Θ f^1 700* syr^s) preserve the name "Jesus" before "Barabbas"; but Origen knows the reading, as do several marginal glosses (in one uncial, S, and in about twenty miniscules); and it is probably presupposed in the ancestors of B 1010. The external evidence is not strong enough to be at all certain; but on the whole it is more likely that scribes deleted the name out of reverence for Jesus than added it in order to set a startling if grotesque choice before the Jews. The problem is compounded in v.17, where, in an uncial script, the abbreviated form of the accusative of "Jesus" could be easily lost by haplography (YMININ). See Metzger, *Textual Commentary*, pp. 67–68. UBS 3d edition and Nestle 26th edition include "Jesus" in brackets.

12. *The soldiers' treatment of Jesus*

27:27–31

> [27]Then the governor's soldiers took Jesus into the Praetorium and gathered the whole company of soldiers around him. [28]They stripped him and put a scarlet robe on him, [29]and then twisted together a crown of thorns and set it on his head. They put a staff in his right hand and knelt in front of him and mocked him. "Hail, king of the Jews!" they said. [30]They spit on him, and took the staff and struck him on the head again and again. [31]After they had mocked him, they took off the robe and put his own clothes on him. Then they led him away to crucify him.

Many think it unlikely that troops (auxiliary soldiers recruited from the non-Jewish population of Palestine and under Pilate's direct control) would mock a prisoner just scourged; but close parallels are not hard to find (Philo *In Flaccum* 6.36–39; Dio Cassius *History* 15.20–21; cf. Luther R. Delbrueck, "Antiquarisches zu den Verspottungen Jesu," ZNW 41 [1942]: 124–45). This pericope is meant to fulfill 17:22–23; 20:17–19 (cf. Mark 15:16–20; John 19:2–3).

27 That the governor's troops are the ones involved in these shameful actions belies any suggestion that Matthew exculpates Pilate (see on v.24). The "Praetorium" is probably the old palace of Herod (see on vv.11–26; cf. Benoit, *Jesus*, pp. 167–88); the soldiers take Jesus into the palace courtyard. The "whole company" would number six hundred if the cohort were at full strength and all were on duty, but more likely the expression simply refers to all the soldiers present.

28–31 Here we have humanity at its worst—a scene of vicious mockery. The Jews have mocked Jesus as Messiah (26:67–68); here the Roman soldiers ridicule him as king. Matthew's readers recognize that the soldiers speak more truly than they know, for Jesus is both King and Suffering Servant. The "robe" (*chlamys*, in the NT only here and in v.31) is probably the short red cloak worn by Roman military and civilian officials (v.28). Mark and John describe it as "purple," Matthew as "scarlet." Commentators have speculated that this redactional change serves to symbolize blood and its concomitant suffering. Such efforts are strained. The ancients did not discriminate among colors as closely as we do, and BAGD (p. 694) adduces a reference in which a Roman soldier's cloak is said to be "purple." The "purple" (Mark; John) calls to mind the robes worn by vassal kings (cf. 1 Macc 10:20, 62; 11:58; 14:43–44), and the "scarlet" (Matthew) shows what the garment probably was—a trooper's cloak.

For a crown (v.29) the soldiers plaited a wreath of thorns from palm spines or acanthus and crushed it down on Jesus' head in imitation of the circlet on the coins of Tiberius Caesar (cf. TDNT, 7:615–24, 632f.). The staff they put in his hand stood for a royal scepter; and the mocking "Hail, King of the Jews!" corresponded to the Roman acclamation "Ave, Caesar!" and capped the flamboyant kneeling. Not content with the ridicule and the torture of the thorns, they spat on him (v.30) and used the staff, the symbol of his kingly authority, to hit him on the head "again and again" (cf. the imperfect tense of the verb).

"After they had mocked him" (v.31, an aorist with pluperfect force; see on v.8; Moule, *Idiom Book*, p. 16), they dressed him again in his own clothes and led him off to be crucified. Normally a prisoner went naked to his place of execution and was scourged along the route. That this custom was not followed with Jesus may be because he had already been flogged and more flogging might have killed him. Or it may reflect an attempt not to offend too many Jewish sensibilities during a feast time. Jesus was led away by the execution squad of four soldiers, dragging the crosspiece to which his hands would be nailed (John 19:17, 23).

13. *The Crucifixion and mocking*

27:32–44

> [32]As they were going out, they met a man from Cyrene, named Simon, and they forced him to carry the cross. [33]They came to a place called Golgotha (which means The Place of the Skull). [34]There they offered Jesus wine to drink, mixed with gall; but after tasting it, he refused to drink it. [35]When they had crucified him, they divided up his clothes by casting lots. [36]And sitting down, they kept watch over him there. [37]Above his head they placed the written charge against him: THIS IS JESUS, THE KING OF THE JEWS. [38]Two robbers were crucified with him, one on his right and one on his left. [39]Those who passed by hurled insults at him, shaking their heads [40]and saying, "You who are going to destroy the temple and build it in three days, save yourself! Come down from the cross, if you are the Son of God!" [41]In the same way the chief priests, the teachers of the law and the elders mocked him. [42]"He saved others," they said, "but he can't save himself! He's the King of Israel! Let him come down now from the cross, and we will believe in him. [43]He trusts in God. Let God rescue him now if he wants him, for he said, 'I am the Son of God.'" [44]In the same way the robbers who were crucified with him also heaped insults on him.

Two thousand years of pious Christian tradition have largely domesticated the cross, making it hard for us to realize how it was viewed in Jesus' time. Two excellent recent studies discuss the relevant evidence (M. Hengel, *Crucifixion* [London:

SCM, 1977]; J.A. Fitzmyer, "Crucifixion in Ancient Palestine, Qumran Literature, and the New Testament," CBQ 40 [1978]: 493–513). Crucifixion was unspeakably painful and degrading. Whether tied or nailed to the cross, the victim endured countless paroxysms as he pulled with his arms and pushed with his legs to keep his chest cavity open for breathing and then collapsed in exhaustion until the demand for oxygen demanded renewed paroxysms. The scourging, the loss of blood, the shock from the pain, all produced agony that could go on for days, ending at last by suffocation, cardiac arrest, or loss of blood. When there was reason to hasten death, the execution squad would smash the victim's legs. Death followed almost immediately, either from shock or from collapse that cut off breathing.

Beyond the pain was the shame. The later rabbis excluded crucifixion as a form of capital punishment for just this reason, though there is some evidence that the Pharisees, their probable predecessors, did not oppose it in principle (cf. David T. Halperin, "Crucifixion, the Nahum Pesher, and the Rabbinic Penalty of Strangulation," *Journal of Jewish Studies* 32 [1981]: 32–46). In ancient sources crucifixion was universally viewed with horror. In Roman law it was reserved only for the worst criminals and lowest classes. No Roman citizen could be crucified without a direct edict from Caesar.

Among Jews the horror of the cross was greater still because of Deuteronomy 21:23: "Anyone who is hanged on a tree is under God's curse." In Israelite law this meant the corpse of a judicially executed criminal was hung up for public exposure that branded him as cursed by God. The words were also applied in Jesus' day to anyone crucified; and therefore the Jews' demand that Jesus be crucified rather than banished was aimed at arousing maximum public revulsion toward him. But in Christian perspective the curse on Jesus at the cross fulfills all OT sacrifices: it is a curse that removes the curse from believers—the fusion of divine, royal prerogative and Suffering Servant, the heart of the gospel, the inauguration of a new humanity, the supreme model for Christian ethics, the ratification of the new covenant, and the power of God (1 Cor 1:23–24; Gal 3:13; Rom 5:12–21; Col 2:14; Hebrews; 1 Peter 2:18–25, cf. Matt 3:17; 8:17; 16:21; 24–25; 20:25–28; 21:38–42; 26:26–29).

All four Gospels record the Crucifixion. No Gospel says much about the Crucifixion itself; the details were all too well known, and theological interest does not lie so much in crucifixion per se as in the attendant circumstances and their significance. Each evangelist gives his narrative an independent cast by what he includes or omits, though these differences are often exaggerated. Matthew largely follows Mark; but whereas Mark alludes to the OT, Matthew tends to be somewhat more explicit (v.34, Ps 69:21; v.35, Ps 22:18; v.39, Ps 22:7; v.43, Ps 22:8). The dominant note of the pericope is the continuing mockery (Bonnard); but the mockery by an awful irony reveals more than the mocker thinks, for Jesus is indeed King of the Jews (v.37), the new meeting place with God (v.40), the Savior of men (v.42), the King of Israel (v.42), and the Son of God (v.43).

The date is 15 Nisan A.D. 30 or 33, and the time fairly early in the morning, as the interchanges with Pilate and Herod and the scourging and the mocking need not have consumed more than two to three hours.

32 "As they were going out" presupposes "of the city," not "from the Praetorium," as Mark says that Simon was coming in "from the country." Executions normally took place outside the city walls (Lev 24:14; Num 15:35–36; 1 Kings 21:13; Acts 7:58), symbolizing still further rejection (cf. Heb 13:13). This suggests that Jesus, weak as he was, managed to carry the crossbeam as far as the city gates (cf. John 19:17). There the soldiers forced Simon to assume the load. His name suggests, but does not prove, that he was a Jew. He came from Cyrene, an old Greek settlement on the coast of North Africa (Acts 2:10; 6:9; 11:20; 13:1). Mark says that he was the father of Alexander and Rufus, who may be referred to in Acts 19:33 and Romans 16:13 and were obviously well-known to Mark's readers; but because the names were common, these passages may refer to other persons.

In 1941, N. Avigad ("A Depository of Inscribed Ossuaries in the Kidron Valley," IEJ 12 [1962]: 1–12) published an account of the discovery of a burial cave belonging to Cyrenian Jews, located on the southwest slope of the Kidron and dating from pre-A.D. 70. An ossuary from this find is twice inscribed in Greek: "Alexander son of Simon." But we cannot be certain the same family is in view.

The efforts of Christian piety to make Simon's act a deed of sympathetic magnanimity are invalid. Simon had no choice, and the text says nothing about his sympathy for Jesus.

33 The site of Golgotha (transliteration of Aram. *gālgāltā'*["skull"]) is uncertain. Gordon's Calvary is not an option (cf. Parrot, pp. 59–65). The most likely place is one near the Church of the Holy Sepulchre, in an area outside the northern wall, on a hill near the city wall (John 19:20), and not far from the road (Matt 27:39). Our English "Calvary" comes from the Latin *calva* ("a skull").

34 Mark says they offered Jesus wine mingled with myrrh, and he refused it; Matthew, that they offered him wine mingled with gall, and he tasted it and then refused it. A common explanation is that Mark describes a custom in which women of Jerusalem, responding to Proverbs 31:6–7 (the alleged custom is Jewish, not Roman), prepared a drink of wine and [frank]incense—Mark's mention of myrrh instead of frankincense is variously explained (e.g., Lane, *Mark*, p. 124)—as a narcotic to ease the pain of the sufferers (b *Sanhedrin* 43a). This Jesus refused so as to drink the full draught of suffering with all his senses intact. Matthew then changed "myrrh" (Mark) to "gall" in order to link the event to Psalm 69:21.

Though this interpretation remains popular, another one is more convincing (cf. Moo, "Use of OT," pp. 249–52). Neither Mark nor Matthew mentions women, and both imply that the soldiers administered the drink. Moreover that Matthew says Jesus tasted it before refusing it argues against the view that it was a customary narcotic to dull pain; for if customary, he would know what it contained: why should he have tasted it if he would in the end refuse it? It is much better to assume that the gesture in both Matthew and Mark was not one of compassion but of torment.

Myrrh may have been used with wine to strengthen the drink (TDNT, 7:458), but it has no effect on pain (cf. John Wilkinson, "The Seven Words from the Cross," SJT 17 [1964]: 77, n. 1). But myrrh tastes bitter; so a large dose of it mingled with wine would make the latter undrinkable. Whether customary or not, the drink was offered to Jesus; but it was so bitter he refused it, and, according to this view, the soldiers were amused. Mark keeps the word "myrrh" to describe the content, and Matthew uses "gall" to describe the taste and to provide a link with Psalm 69:21. In both Hebrew and Greek, the words for "gall" in Psalm 69:21 (*rō'š* and *cholē* respectively) refer to various bitter or poisonous substances. Like David his father, Jesus looked for sympathy but found none (Ps 69:20–21).

35 The victim was either tied or nailed to the crossbeam (in Jesus' case, the latter), which was then hoisted to its place on the upright. The feet were sometimes tied or, as in this instance, nailed to the upright. Crosses were made in various shapes—an X, a T, or the traditional †. The latter is in view here (v.37). How high the victim was from the ground varied from a few inches to several feet, in Jesus' case the latter (v.48; John 19:29). The Romans crucified their victims naked. Whether they permitted a loin cloth to avoid transgressing Jewish stipulations (M *Sanhedrin* 6:3) is unknown. The victim's clothes customarily became the perquisite of the executioners; here they divided them—probably an inner and outer garment, a belt, and a pair of sandals—among themselves by casting lots, oblivious to the OT lament in Psalm 22:18 that John 19:23–24 says was now fulfilled. (The variant reading in Matthew, preserved in NIV margin, is an assimilation to John.) Mark says this took place at the third hour, about 9.00 A.M.

36 This verse is peculiar to Matthew. The soldiers kept watch to prevent rescue (men were known to have lived after being taken down from a cross). Perhaps Matthew gives us this detail to eliminate any suggestion that Jesus was removed from the cross without dying.

37 The statement of the crime was often written on a white tablet in red or black letters and displayed on the cross. The charge against Jesus, written in Hebrew, Greek, and Latin (John 19:20), is highly ironic: Pilate, though desiring to offend the Jews (John 19:19–22), wrote more of the truth than he knew. Pilate rubs the noses of the Jews' in their vassal status. To a Jew, "king of the Jews" meant "Messiah"; so the charge on which Jesus was executed was, according to Pilate, that he was a messianic pretender. Matthew's Christian reader will remember the intertwining strands of royal Son and Suffering Servant and see their climax here.

38 On the two *lēstai* ("rebel guerrillas"; NIV, "robbers"), see on v.16. The King of the Jews is crucified along with rebels. Matthew may be thinking of Isaiah 53:12, but this is uncertain (cf. Moo, "Use of OT," pp. 154–55).

39–40 Crucifixion was always carried out publicly as a warning to others. With the day of the paschal meal behind them (see excursus at 26:17) and the restrictions of Sabbath not to begin till sundown, there was time and opportunity for people to walk by on the nearby road and "hurl insults" (*blasphēmeō*, v.39, as in 9:3; 12:31; 26:65) at Jesus. Shaking their heads, and so calling to mind the derision in Psalms 22:7; 109:25; Lamentations 2:15, the passers-by threw up the charge in Matthew 26:60–61. The Greek should probably be rendered "You who were trying to destroy the temple and rebuild it in three days" (v.40; cf. 2:20; cf. BDF, par. 339[3]; Turner, *Syntax*, pp. 80–81). The derision was palpable and identifies the mockers as those who had witnessed the proceedings of the Sanhedrin or had some report of them.

The second taunt, "If you are the Son of God," not only harks back to the trial (26:63), but for Matthew's readers recalls a dramatic parallel (4:3, 6). Through the passers-by Satan was still trying to get Jesus to evade the Father's will and avoid further suffering (Lohmeyer; cf. also 16:21–23).

41–43 The "chief priests, teachers of the law and the elders" (v.41) represent all the principal groups of the Sanhedrin (see on 21:23; 26:59). They do not address Jesus directly but speak of him in the third person, in a stage whisper meant for his ears. "He saved others" (v.42) is probably an oblique reference to Jesus' supernatural healing ministry. "But he can't save himself" is cutting because it questions that same supernatural power. But there is level on level of meaning. For the Christian reader "save" has full eschatological overtones. And though Jesus *could* have saved himself (26:53), he could *not* have saved himself if he was to save others.

The second of the three taunts, "He's the king of Israel," substitutes the covenant term Israel for "the Jews" in Pilate's words (v.11) and is in fact the normal Palestinian form of Jesus' claim (cf. TDNT, 3:359–62, 375f.). The words "Let him come down from the cross, and we will believe in him" have several levels of meaning. They constitute a malicious barb directed at Jesus' helplessness, while having the effrontery to suggest that the leaders' failure to believe was his fault. The taunt piously promises faith if Jesus will but step down from the cross; but the reader knows that, in the mystery of providence, if Jesus did step down, there would be no "blood of the covenant for the forgiveness of sins" (26:26–29), no ransom (20:28), no salvation from sin (1:21), no theological basis for healing (8:16–17), no gospel of the kingdom to be proclaimed to nations everywhere (28:18–20), no fulfillment of Scripture.

In an unconscious allusion to Psalm 22:8 (as Caiaphas uttered an unconscious prophecy in John 11:51–52), the religious leaders launch their third taunt: "He trusts in God" (v.43). They recognize that Jesus' claim to be the "Son of God" was at least a claim to messiahship and perhaps more. So assuming that God must crown every effort of Messiah with success, they conclude that Jesus' hopeless condition is proof enough of the vanity of his pretensions. Again their malice masks the ironic redemptive purposes of God. On the one hand, as Christian readers know, God will indeed vindicate his Son at the Resurrection: Matthew ends his Gospel, not at 27:56, but at 28:20 (cf. Acts 2:23–24; Rom 1:3–4). On the other hand, the leaders are right: Jesus is now facing his most severe test, the loss of his Father's presence, leading to the heart-rending cry of the following verses (esp. v.46).

44 The *lēstai* ("robbers"; see on v.16) crucified with him join in the abuse (cf. Luke 23:39–43; Zerwick, par. 7).

14. *The death of Jesus*

27:45–50

> [45]From the sixth hour until the ninth hour darkness came over all the land. [46]About the ninth hour Jesus cried out in a loud voice, "*Eloi, Eloi, lama sabachthani?*"—which means, "My God, my God, why have you forsaken me?"
> [47]When some of those standing there heard this, they said, "He's calling Elijah."
> [48]Immediately one of them ran and got a sponge. He filled it with wine vinegar, put it on a stick, and offered it to Jesus to drink. [49]The rest said, "Now leave him alone. Let's see if Elijah comes to save him."
> [50]And when Jesus had cried out again in a loud voice, he gave up his spirit.

45 The darkness that "came over all the land" from noon till 3:00 P.M. (that is what "sixth hour" and "ninth hour" refer to) was a sign of judgment and/or tragedy. The

Greek *gē* means "land" rather than "earth," since the darkness was meant to be a sign relating both to Jesus' death and to the Jewish people; and beyond the borders of Israel the darkness would lose this significance. SBK (1:1040–42) gives numerous rabbinic parallels, and Wettstein an array of Greek and Latin authors. But the most-telling background is Amos 8:9–10, and to a lesser extent Exodus 10:21–22. Both passages portray darkness as a sign of judgment; but Amos mentions noon, the turning of religious feasts into mourning, and says, "I will make that time like mourning for an only son" (Amos 8:10; see also on Matt 2:15). The judgment is therefore a judgment on the land and its people (cf. Best, pp. 98f.). But it is also a judgment on Jesus; for out of this darkness comes his cry of desolation (v.46). The cosmic blackness hints at the deep judgment that was taking place (20:28; 26:26–29; Gal 3:13).

It is futile to argue whether the darkness was caused by an eclipse of three hours(!) or by atmospheric conditions caused by a sirocco or something else, not because it did not happen, but because we do not know how it happened, anymore than we know how Jesus walked on the water or multiplied the loaves. The evangelists are chiefly interested in the theological implications that rise out of the historical phenomena.

46 The "cry of desolation" raises two important questions.

1. In what language did Jesus utter it? Almost all recognize that the words echo Psalm 22:1 (for a list of exceptions, cf. Moo, "Use of OT," pp. 264f.). But among the variant readings of a confused textual history (cf. Notes), Matthew keeps "*Eli, Eli*" (NIV, "*Eloi, Eloi*"), representing a Hebrew original, and Mark "*Eloi, Eloi*," representing an Aramaic original. The remaining words, "*lama sabachthani*," are Aramaic. Many suggest that Jesus quoted Psalm 22:1 in Hebrew, reverting to the ancient language of Scripture in his hour of utmost agony. Only this, it is argued, accounts for the confusion with "Elijah" in v.47 and provides a plausible explanation for the rendering "my power" (*hē dynamis mou*, presupposing Semitic *ḥêlî*) in the apocryphal Gospel of Peter. In this view Mark, or an early copyist of Mark, has turned Jesus' words into Aramaic, recognizing that Jesus more commonly spoke Aramaic than Hebrew.

However, though Jesus was probably at least trilingual (Hebrew, Aramaic, Greek —with perhaps some Latin), the overwhelming textual evidence for the rest of the cry supports an Aramaic original. Even Matthew's Hebraic-sounding "Eli" may in fact support an Aramaic original, because the Targum (written in Aramaic) to Psalm 22:1 has '*ēlî*. Apparently some Aramaic speakers preserved the Hebrew name for God in the same way some English speakers sometimes refer to him as Yahweh. The evidence of the Gospel of Peter is not decisive because "my power" may not rest on a Semitic original but may be an independent periphrasis for God, akin to 26:64. Moreover on the lips of a dying man crying out in agony, "*Eloi*" could as easily be mistaken for Elijah as "*Eli*" (cf. discussion by Broadus; Lagrange; Gundry, *Use of OT*, pp. 63–66; Moo, "Use of OT," pp. 264–75). Jesus' cry was most probably in Aramaic; and at least some of the variants stem from the difficulty of transliterating a Semitic language into Greek and others from the influence of the OT.

2. What does this psalm quotation signify? A large number of recent interpreters have interpreted the cry against the background of the *whole* of Psalm 22, which begins with this sense of desolation but ends with the triumphant vindication of the righteous sufferer. The chief difficulty with this is that though OT texts are frequent-

ly cited with their full contexts in mind, they are never cited in such a way that the OT context effectively annuls what the text itself affirms (Bonnard; Moo, "Use of OT," p. 272). If the context of Psalm 22 is carried along with the actual reference to Psalm 22:1, the reader of the Gospel is to understand that the vindication comes with the Resurrection in Matthew 28, not that Jesus' cry reflects full confidence instead of black despair.

Equally futile is the suggestion of Schweizer and others that these words constitute a more or less standard cry of a pious man dying with the words of a psalm on his lips. But why *this* psalm when others would be more suitable? Evidence for such a use of Psalm 22 is sparse and late. It is better to take the words at face value: Jesus is conscious of being abandoned by his Father. For one who knew the intimacy of Matthew 11:27, such abandonment must have been agony; and for the same reason it is inadequate to hypothesize that Jesus felt abandoned but was not truly abandoned (contra Bonnard; Green; McNeile; Senior, *Passion Narrative,* p. 298), because "it seems difficult to understand how Jesus, who had lived in the closest possible fellowship with the Father, could have been unaware whether he had, in fact, been abandoned" (Moo, "Use of OT," p. 274).

If we ask in what ontological sense the Father and the Son are here divided, the answer must be that we do not know because we are not told. If we ask for what purpose they are divided, the ultimate answer must be tied in with Gethsemane, the Last Supper, passion passages such as 1:21; 20:28 (see also 26:26–29, 39–44), and the theological interpretation articulated by Paul (e.g., Rom 3:21–26). In this cry of dereliction, the horror of the world's sin and the cost of our salvation are revealed. In the words of Elizabeth Browning:

Yea, once Immanuel's orphaned cry his universe hath shaken.
It went up single, echoless, "My God, I am forsaken!"
It went up from the Holy's lips amid his lost creation,
That, of the lost, no son should use those words of desolation.

47 According to 2 Kings 2:1–12, Elijah did not die but was taken alive to heaven in a whirlwind. Some Jewish tradition, perhaps as old as the first century, held that he would come and rescue the righteous in their distress (cf. Jeremias, TDNT, 2:930–31; SBK, 4:769–771).

48–49 See on v.34. The allusion is again to Psalm 69:21. What is not clear is whether the offer of a drink is meant as a gesture of mercy or as mockery (v.48). The Gospel parallels are somewhat ambiguous. The best explanation is that of mockery. *Oxos* (lit., "vinegar") probably refers to "wine vinegar" (NIV), sour wine diluted with vinegar drunk by foot soldiers; but this does not make the offer a compassionate act, since its purpose may have been to prolong life and agony, while with false piety the onlookers say they will wait for Elijah to rescue him (v.49). But if the Father has abandoned Jesus, will Elijah save him? The offer of a drink not only fulfills Scripture but makes the cry of dereliction (v.46) all the bleaker.

In this interpretation NIV's "But" (v.49) is too adversative a rendering of *de*, and "Leave him alone" should be taken to suggest (as in NIV on Mark 15:36) "Leave him alone now"—i.e., the proffered drink provides the context for more mocking. It is not clear whether Luke 23:36, where mockery is clearly intended, properly parallels Matthew 27:34 or 27:48–49. John's Gospel (19:28–29) is interested only in the fact of Scripture fulfillment, not the question of whether mockery is intended.

50 This loud cry reminds us once more of Jesus' hideous agony. Matthew's "he gave up his spirit" ("spirit" here is equivalent to "life") suggests Jesus' sovereignty over the exact time of his own death. It was at this moment, when he was experiencing the abyss of his alienation from the Father and was being cruelly mocked by those he came to serve, that he chose to yield up his life a "ransom for many" (see on 20:28).

Notes

46 Instead of ηλι or ηλει (ēli or ēlei,) from the Hebrew אֵלִי (ēlî, "my God"), some MSS agree with Mark 15:34: ελωι (elōi), from the Aramaic אֱלָהִי (ʾelāhî, "my God"), the long ō in Greek representing the Semitic ā by influence of Hebrew ʾelōhay. It is perhaps more probable that some MSS of Matthew have been assimilated to Mark than to MT. For other variants, see Metzger, *Textual Criticism*, pp. 70, 119.

49 The future participle σώσων (sōsōn, "to save") here functions as a supplement to the main verb. The construction is rare in the NT (cf. BDF, pars. 351 [1], 418 [4]; Zerwick, par. 282).

15. *Immediate impact of the death*

27:51–56

> ⁵¹At that moment the curtain of the temple was torn in two from top to bottom. The earth shook and the rocks split. ⁵²The tombs broke open and the bodies of many holy people who had died were raised to life. ⁵³They came out of the tombs, and after Jesus' resurrection they went into the holy city and appeared to many people.
>
> ⁵⁴When the centurion and those with him who were guarding Jesus saw the earthquake and all that had happened, they were terrified, and exclaimed, "Surely he was the Son of God!"
>
> ⁵⁵Many women were there, watching from a distance. They had followed Jesus from Galilee to care for his needs. ⁵⁶Among them were Mary Magdalene, Mary the mother of James and Joses, and the mother of Zebedee's sons.

51a There were two temple curtains, one dividing the Most Holy Place from the Holy Place and the other separating the Holy Place from the court. Tearing the latter would be more public, but tearing the inner veil could hardly be hushed up. Jewish parallels are interesting (b *Yoma* 39b reports the doors of the temple opened of their own accord during the forty years before the destruction of the temple) but difficult to interpret. The inner veil is presupposed in Hebrews 4:16; 6:19–20; 9:11–28; 10:19–22. Destruction of the outer veil would primarily symbolize the forthcoming destruction of the temple, while destruction of the inner veil would primarily symbolize open access to God (Best, *Temptation*, p. 99); but destruction of either veil could point in both directions.

There is more. If the death of Jesus opened up a fresh access to God that made the OT sacrificial system and the Levitical high priesthood obsolete, then an entire change in the Mosaic covenant must follow. It is impossible to grapple with Matthew's fulfillment themes (cf. esp. on 5:17–20; 11:11–13) and see how even the law points prophetically to Messiah and hear Jesus' promise of a new covenant grounded in his death (26:26–29) without seeing that the tearing of the veil signifies the obsolescence of the temple ritual and the law governing it. Jesus himself is the New Temple, the meeting place of God and man (see on 26:61); the old is obsolete. The rent veil does indeed serve as a sign of the temple's impending destruction—a destruction conceived not as a brute fact but as a theological necessity.

51b–53 On problems concerning the historicity of this narrative, see D. Wenham, "Resurrection" (esp. pp. 42–46). Only Matthew reports it, but it is of a piece with the tearing of the temple veil. Both are part of the initial impact of Jesus' death, along with the centurion's exclamation (v.54). Moreover, the earthquake apparently links them: it is possible that Matthew sees the earthquake (v.51b), itself a symbol of judgment and theophanic glory (cf. 1 Kings 19:11; Isa 29:6; Jer 10:10; Ezek 26:18; and esp. see the background materials gathered by R.J. Bauckham, "The Eschatological Earthquake in the Apocalypse of John," NovTest 19 [1977]: 224–33), as the means of tearing the veil as well as opening the tombs. The temple area lies on a geological fault; and the Muslim shrines on the site today have been damaged by tremors from time to time (cf. D. Baly, *The Geography of the Bible* [New York: Harper and Row, 1974], p. 25).

But the resurrection of the *hagioi* ("saints," i.e., "holy people," v.52) remains extraordinarily difficult for two reasons. First, its extreme brevity and lack of parallels raise many unanswered questions: What kind of bodies do these "holy people" have? Do they die again? How many people saw them? How public were these appearances? Second, a quick reading of the text gives the impression that though the holy people were raised when Jesus died, they did not leave the tombs and appear to the citizens of the "holy city" till after Jesus' resurrection (v.53). What were they doing in between?

The passage has elicited various explanations. Hutton thinks it a displaced resurrection account, originally connected with the earthquake of 28:2. Others have thought it a primitive Christian hymn. D. Senior ("The Death of Jesus and the Resurrection of the Holy Ones [Matthew 27:51–53]," CBQ 38 [1976]: 312–29), in addition to criticizing some other views, represents the approach currently most popular: these verses are a midrash, a symbolic representation of certain theological ideas about the triumph of Jesus and the dawning of the new age. But apart from questions of literary genre (cf. Introduction, section 12.b), one wonders why the evangelist, if he had nothing historical to go on, did not invent a midrash with fewer problems.

J.W. Wenham ("When Were the Saints Raised?" JTS 32 [1981]: 150–52) offers an alternative view. He has convincingly argued that a full stop should be placed, not after "split" (v.51), but after "broke open" (v.52). The tearing of the veil and the opening of the tombs together symbolize the first of twin foci in Jesus' death and resurrection. On the one hand, Jesus' sacrificial death blots out sin, defeats the powers of evil and death, and opens up access to God. On the other, Jesus' victorious resurrection and vindication promise the final resurrection of those who die in him.

The resurrection of "the holy people" begins a new sentence and is tied up only with Jesus' resurrection. So Matthew does not intend his readers to think that these "holy people" were resurrected when Jesus died and then waited in their tombs till

Easter Sunday before showing themselves. The idea is a trifle absurd anyway: there is no more reason to think they were impeded by material substance than was the resurrected Lord, the covering rock of whose grave was removed to let the witnesses in, not to let him out. The "holy people" were raised, came out of the tombs, and were seen by many after Jesus rose from the dead. There is no need to connect the earthquake and the breaking open of the tombs with the rising of "the holy people": the two foci must be differentiated.

On several details we are told little. For instance, it is unclear whether the resurrection of the "holy people" was to natural bodies (cf. Lazarus, John 11) or to supernatural bodies. The latter is perhaps more likely; and in that case they did not return to the tombs, and their rising testifies that the Last Day had dawned. Where they ultimately went Matthew does not say. Were they "translated"? Nor does he tell us who they were; but the language implies, though it does not prove, that they were certain well-known OT and intertestamental Jewish "saints," spiritual heroes and martyrs in Israel's history (cf. the terminology in Isa 4:3; Dan 7:18; Tobit 8:15; 1 Enoch 38:4–5; T Levi 18:10–11). If so, then Matthew is telling us, among other things, that the resurrection of people who lived before Jesus Messiah is as dependent on Jesus' triumph as the resurrection of those who come after him. The idea is not fanciful, given Matthew's grasp of prophecy and fulfillment (see on 5:17; Introduction, section 11.a).

One must still reflect on why the evangelist placed the account here instead of in chapter 28. He probably had at least three reasons.

1. The pericope would disrupt the narrative in Matthew 28.

2. The account is held together by two foci—Jesus' death and resurrection. Therefore Matthew's putting it with the resurrection pericopes would have possibly been even more awkward than putting it with the passion pericopes. Linking the Cross and the empty tomb in a unified theological application is not without its difficulties, regardless of whether the pericope in question is placed with the story of the Cross or with the account of the Resurrection.

3. More positively the placement of this pericope with other verses dealing with the immediate impact of Jesus' death may be peculiarly appropriate since they too point to the future. No Christian reader who saw in the torn veil a reference to judgment on the temple would fail to see the new means opening up for the meeting of God and man, a means dependent on Jesus' resurrection and continued ministry. Similarly the confession that Jesus was the Son of God (v.54) would appear to thoughtful readers as a deeper truth than the centurion and his men could have known, for Matthew 28 lies just ahead. Furthermore, if the text had ended at "broke open" (v.52) and resumed with v.54, the reader would have been given a wholly wrong impression. Jesus' work on the cross is tied to his impending resurrection; together they open up the new age and promise eschatological life.

54 Despite the fact that "Son of God" is one of several major christological titles in Matthew, it also appears in Mark as the climax of the Passion (Mark 15:38–39). What is not certain is exactly what the soldiers meant by "Son of God" (cf. Blair, pp. 60–68). They may have used the term in a Hellenistic sense, "a son of God" referring to a divine being in a pagan sense. But the governor's soldiers were probably non-Jewish natives of the land (see on 27:27). If so, or even if they were Romans who had been assigned to Palestine for some time, they may well have understood "Son of God" in a messianic sense (see on 26:63). Certainly the anarthrous noun

"Son" can mean *the* Son" instead of "*a* Son" in this construction (cf. Moule, *Idiom Book*, p. 116).

The darkness, the earthquake, and the cry of dereliction convinced the soldiers that this was no ordinary execution. The portents terrified them and probably led them to believe that these things testified to heaven's wrath at the perpetration of such a crime, in which the soldiers had participated. But this confession tells us something more: Jesus as the promised Messiah and unique Son of God is seen most clearly in his passion and death; but again the Jewish religious establishment, mistaking the nature of his messiahship, mocked him with the very title (vv.41–44) by which the pagans now confessed him (see also on 8:5–13; 15:21–28).

55–56 Along with the soldiers, certain women, generally not highly regarded in Jewish society, watched to the bitter end. They kept their distance (v.55), whether through timidity or modesty; and last at the cross, they were first at the tomb (28:1). Not only do they provide continuity to the narrative, but they prove that God has chosen the lowly and despised things of the world to shame the wise and strong (cf. 1 Cor 1:27–31). These women were Galileans who often traveled with the disciples to care for Jesus' needs out of their own resources (cf. Luke 8:2–3).

Comparison of the lists of names in Matthew, Mark, and John (19:25) produces these results:

Matthew	Mark	John
Mary Magdalene	Mary Magdalene	Jesus' mother
Mary the mother of James and Joses	Mary the mother of James the younger and Joses	Jesus' mother's sister
Mother of Zebedee's sons	Salome	Mary wife of Clopas
		Mary of Magdala

If we make two assumptions—(1) that John's second entry is distinguished from his third (i.e., they are not in apposition) and (2) that John's list of four includes the list of three in Matthew and Mark—then certain things become probable. First, the mother of Zebedee's sons was called Salome, unless a different woman is here introduced. Second, if Mary the mother of James and Joseph (or Joses) is Jesus' mother (cf. 13:55), then Jesus' mother and Mary Magdalene (of Magdala) appear on all three lists. That would make Salome Jesus' mother's sister—his aunt on his mother's side. Others suppose that Mary the wife of Clopas is the mother of James and Joses, who are not Jesus' half-brothers. Yet the result still equates Salome and Jesus' aunt on his mother's side. Although none of this is certain, it would help explain 20:20.

16. *The burial of Jesus*

27:57–61

> [57]As evening approached, there came a rich man from Arimathea, named Joseph, who had himself become a disciple of Jesus. [58]Going to Pilate, he asked for Jesus' body, and Pilate ordered that it be given to him. [59]Joseph took the body, wrapped it in a clean linen cloth, [60]and placed it in his own new tomb that he had cut out of the rock. He rolled a big stone in front of the entrance to the tomb and went away. [61]Mary Magdalene and the other Mary were sitting there opposite the tomb.

Because of Deuteronomy 21:22–23, Jesus' body, according to Jewish custom, could not remain on the cross overnight. The Roman custom was to let bodies of crucified criminals hang in full view till they rotted away. If they were buried at all, it was only by express permission of the imperial magistrate. Such permission was usually granted to friends and relatives of the deceased who made application, but never in the case of high treason.

57 The approaching evening—about 6:00 P.M. at that time of year—would mark the end of Friday and the beginning of Sabbath. Mark and Luke portray Joseph of Arimathea (the place is uncertain, but the best guess is Ramathaim, northwest of Lydda) as a prominent member of the Sanhedrin, and Luke says Joseph had not consented to the Sanhedrin's action. Only Matthew mentions he was rich. This may direct attention to Isaiah 53:9–12: though Jesus was numbered with the transgressors, yet in his death he was with the rich. To own a new tomb and use the quantity of spices reported by John, Joseph must have been well-to-do. Matthew tells us Joseph had become a disciple (on the verbal form, cf. BDF, par. 148[3]; Zerwick, par. 66; see on 13:52; 28:19); he learned from Jesus and to some extent was committed to following him, even if his discipleship was secret (John).

58–60 Matthew's account is more condensed than Mark's, who mentions Pilate's checking that Jesus was actually dead and describes Joseph's purchases. Joseph's initiative is remarkably courageous; and Pilate granted his request only because he was convinced that Jesus was not really guilty of high treason (v.58). Joseph could not have acted alone: removal of the body, washing, the weight of spices, and other preparations would be too much for one man with limited time. John mentions the assistance of Nicodemus; probably their servants also helped. Matthew does not mention the seventy-five pounds of spices (John) wrapped up with Jesus in the linen cloth.

The Church of the Holy Sepulchre is most probably the correct site of the tomb (cf. Parrot). Some centuries earlier the place had been a stone quarry, and the resulting rugged face became a place where tombs were cut from the rock. Joseph had prepared this tomb for his own use (v.60), but now he laid Jesus' body in it. Tombs were of various kinds. Many were sealed with some sort of boulder wedged into place to discourage wild animals and grave robbers. But an expensive tomb consisted of an antechamber hewn out of the rock face, with a low passage (cf. "bent over," John 20:5, 11) leading into the burial chamber that was sealed with a cut, disk-shaped stone that rolled in a slot cut into the rock. The slot was on an incline, making the grave easy to seal but difficult to open: several men might be needed to roll the stone back up the incline. This sort of tomb is presupposed in the Gospel records (cf. Parrot, pp. 43ff.).

61 No mourning was permitted for those executed under Roman law. The women followed with broken but silent grief and watched the burial. In addition to Joseph of Arimathea and Nicodemus, the women saw Jesus buried. This can only be factual, since the Jews placed little value on the testimony borne by women (M Rosh ha-Shanah 1:8). The witness of the women also prepares the way for 28:1. That Jesus was actually buried became an integral part of gospel proclamation (cf. 1 Cor 15:4).

17. *The guard at the tomb*

27:62–66

> [62]The next day, the one after Preparation Day, the chief priests and the Pharisees went to Pilate. [63]"Sir," they said, "we remember that while he was still alive that deceiver said, 'After three days I will rise again.' [64]So give the order for the tomb to be made secure until the third day. Otherwise, his disciples may come and steal the body and tell the people that he has been raised from the dead. This last deception will be worse than the first."
>
> [65]"Take a guard," Pilate answered. "Go, make the tomb as secure as you know how." [66]So they went and made the tomb secure by putting a seal on the stone and posting the guard.

This pericope is peculiar to Matthew; and it is often viewed as a piece of "creative writing" designed to provide "witnesses" to the Resurrection (Schniewind) or to provide "evidence" that Jesus' body had not been stolen. But there are several things in favor of the pericope's historicity.

1. It must be taken with 28:11–15. Thus the account of the guards at the tomb does less to assure us that the body was not stolen than to provide background for the report that it was.

2. This may be the reason why the other evangelists omit it. In the circles they were writing for, the report circulated by the Jews may not have been current; so no explanation was necessary. In Matthew's Jewish environment, he could not avoid dealing with the subject.

3. Matthew has regularly given information in the passion narrative that the other evangelists omit (e.g., 27:19, 34–35, 62–63); and it is methodologically wrong to doubt the historicity of all details that lack multiple attestation—not least because such "multiple attestation" may sometimes go back to one literary source.

4. If Matthew were trying to prove Jesus' body was not stolen, why does he not have the guards posted immediately, instead of waiting till the next day (v.62)?

5. On the other hand, the chief priests and the Pharisees would not necessarily be defiling themselves by approaching Pilate on the Sabbath, provided they did not travel more than a Sabbath day's journey to get there and did not enter his residence (cf. John 18:28). Their action is not implausible if they still saw some potential threat in the remains of the Jesus movement. A few more details are mentioned below. (See further D. Wenham, "Resurrection," esp. pp. 47–51.)

62 This strange way of referring to the Sabbath (for "Preparation Day," see excursus at 26:17) cannot reasonably be taken to spring from Matthew's desire to use the word he omitted at 27:57 (Mark 15:42; so Bonnard, Hill): Matthew is nowhere committed to using all of Mark's words. Rather, this may be a way to avoid using the word "Sabbath," which can be ambiguous during a feast, since it could refer to the last day of the week or to a feast-Sabbath.

63–64 "Sir" (*kyrie*, v.63) is merely a polite form of address. For comments on the phrase "after three days," see on 12:40. The objection that this scene is implausible because it shows the Jewish leaders believing something the disciples themselves cannot yet believe is insubstantial. They may have heard something of the content of 16:21; 17:9; 20:19 from Judas. Whatever the source of their information, they certainly do not *believe* Jesus' prediction, they are merely afraid of fraud—a fear fostered perhaps by the report that Jesus' body, against all judicial custom (see on vv.57–61), had been taken down from the cross and returned to Jesus' disciples by Joseph and Nicodemus. This could also account for the delay in the request to post a guard (v.64). The disciples disbelieved Jesus' words about rising again, not because they could not understand the plain words, but because they had no frame of reference capable of integrating a dying and rising Messiah into their own messianic expectations. Shattered by the demoralizing turn of events, they cowered in fear (John 20:19), unable and even unwilling to trust their judgment and understanding on anything, except for the terrible fact that their Messiah had been crucified.

The Jews could take no military action without Roman sanction; so they asked Pilate that a guard be posted against the possibility of the body being stolen (v.64). Jesus' "first deception" was his claim to messiahship; his "last deception" was his claim that he would rise from the dead. From their viewpoint, the Jewish leaders are protecting themselves and the people from deception; from Matthew's perspective they are deceiving themselves.

65–66 Greek *echete koustōdia* (v.65) could be imperative ("Take a guard," NIV), but it is more likely indicative ("You have a guard of soldiers," RSV; cf. KJV). Pilate refuses to use his troops but tells the Jewish authorities that they have the temple police at their disposal; and he grants the leaders permission to use them. This explains why, after the Resurrection, the guards reported to the chief priests, not to Pilate (28:11). Pilate's answer in v.65 must therefore be construed as cynical. He is saying, "You were afraid of this man when he was alive; now he is dead, and you are still afraid! By all means secure the tomb as tightly as possible, if you think that will help; but use your own police." So guards are posted and the stone sealed with cord and an official wax seal (v.66). But "death cannot keep his prey." With the dawn all the efforts to eliminate Jesus Messiah from the stage of redemptive history are held up for heavenly derision (Ps 2:4) in the irresistible triumph of the Resurrection.

B. *The Resurrection* (28:1–15)

1. *The empty tomb*

28:1–7

> ¹After the Sabbath, at dawn on the first day of the week, Mary Magdalene and the other Mary went to look at the tomb.
> ²There was a violent earthquake, for an angel of the Lord came down from heaven and, going to the tomb, rolled back the stone and sat on it. ³His appearance was like lightning, and his clothes were white as snow. ⁴The guards were so afraid of him that they shook and became like dead men.
> ⁵The angel said to the women, "Do not be afraid, for I know that you are looking for Jesus, who was crucified. ⁶He is not here; he has risen, just as he said. Come and see the place where he lay. ⁷Then go quickly and tell his disciples: 'He has risen from the dead and is going ahead of you into Galilee. There you will see him.' Now I have told you."

Because the Resurrection is central to Christian theology, few subjects have received more attention. Paul goes so far as to say that if Christ was not raised from the dead, Christian faith is vain; and we are still dead in our sins. Useful examples of modern redaction-critical approaches to the resurrection narratives are provided by N. Perrin, *The Resurrection Narratives* (London: SCM, 1977), and especially John E. Alsup, *The Post-Resurrection Appearance Stories of the Gospel-Tradition* (Stuttgart: Calwer, 1975). Older works like B.F. Westcott's *The Gospel of the Resurrection: Thoughts on Its Relation to Reason and History* (London and New York: Macmillan, 1906) are too readily passed over in the modern debate. Yet more recent treatments are also necessary to answer questions raised from new literary and philosophical angles. A useful place to begin is with G.E. Ladd, *I Believe in the Resurrection of Jesus* (London: Hodder and Stoughton; Grand Rapids; Eerdmans, 1975); Daniel P. Fuller, *Easter Faith and History* (Grand Rapids: Eerdmans, 1965); and two essays by W.L. Craig, "The Bodily Resurrection of Jesus" (in France and Wenham, 1:47–74) and "The Empty Tomb of Jesus" (France and Wenham, 2:173–200).

The textual problems at the end of Mark compound the difficulties in sorting out literary relationships. Most now hold that Mark intended to end his Gospel with 16:8, though some still cling to the authenticity of the "long ending" (Mark 16:9–20); others suggest some such ending as Matthew 28:9–10. What is certain is that, for those who wish to attempt it, the various resurrection appearances can be harmonized in at least three different ways (cf. Broadus; Ladd). But it is more important to come to grips with the distinctive emphasis of each NT writer.

The considerable number of "minor agreements" between Matthew and Luke over against Mark strongly suggests that Matthew and Luke, if they did not simply follow one account independent of Mark, either shared as one source a written account of some resurrection appearances, or one evangelist borrowed from the other. The theological implications of the Resurrection are not treated at length by the evangelists; but the theme constantly recurs in Paul (e.g., Rom 4:24–25; 6:4; 8:34; 10:9; 1 Cor 15; 2 Cor 5:1–10, 15; Phil 3:10–11; Col 2:12–13; 3:1–4; 1 Thess 4:14). Thought-provoking works in this area include W. Künneth, *The Theology of the Resurrection* (tr. J.W. Leitch [London: SCM, 1965]); T.F. Torrance, *Space, Time and Resurrection* (Edinburgh: Handsel, 1976).

1 The Greek *opse de sabbatōn* can be understood as meaning "late on the Sabbath"; then the next phrase would mean "as it began to dawn toward the first day of the week." Taken together these two temporal phrases must then mean one of two things: (1) unlike Mark 16:1, not to mention the consistent witness of the NT, the events described take place on *Saturday* evening, the end of the Sabbath; or (2) this is evidence for a scheme of counting days from sunrise to sunrise and takes place early Sunday morning.

Instead, it is far better to take *opse* as an irregular preposition, meaning "after" (as in NIV; cf. BDF, par. 164[4]; RHG, pp. 645f.; Moule, *Idiom Book*, p. 86). "After the Sabbath" is then a general time indicator; i.e., the women would not walk far *during* the Sabbath; so they waited till *after* the Sabbath. But by then Saturday night was drawing on; so early on the first day of the week (i.e., at dawn: cf. BAGD, p. 304), Mary Magdalene and "the other Mary"—the other one mentioned in 27:56 (still others are mentioned in Mark 16:1; Luke 24:10—"went to look at the tomb." Mark says they "bought spices so that they might go to anoint Jesus' body." It has been argued that Matthew must make the change to "late on the Sabbath" because he alone introduces the account of the posting of the guard (26:62–66), which would make admittance by the women impossible. The women would not have come once the guards were posted; so they must be presented as slipping in earlier. But if the women stayed home on the Sabbath and the guard was not posted till the Sabbath, would the women be likely to learn of it till they arrived on Sunday morning?

Matthew's brief "to look at the tomb" preserves the theme of witness (27:56, 61); but in addition it may reflect an ancient Jewish tradition that says Jews visited the tombs of the deceased till the third day to ensure that the party was truly dead (cf. Thomas R.W. Longstaff, "The Women at the Tomb: Matthew 28:1 Re-examined," NTS 27 [1981] 277–82).

2–4 The clause introduced by "for" (v.2) either suggests that the violent earthquake (see 27:51) came with the "angel of the Lord" (on angels, cf. 1:20–23; 18:10) or was the means the angel used to open the tomb. In Matthew and Luke the angel is more clearly portrayed as an angel than in Mark ("a young man dressed in a white robe"). But the distinction should not be pressed, as angelic beings often appear in human form in the OT; and Mark's "young man" is clearly an angel (cf. Lane, *Mark*, pp. 586–87; compare Jos. Antiq. V, 277 [viii.2]). The guards witnessed the earthquake, saw the angel, and "became like dead men" (v.4—i.e., "fainted in terror" or the like). There is no implication that the earthquake had anything to do with releasing Jesus: the stone was rolled back, the seal broken, and the soldiers made helpless, not to let the risen Messiah escape, but to let the first witnesses in.

Too much speculative "theologizing" has accompanied some modern treatments of these verses. In particular there is nothing to suggest that the soldiers were in any sense pagan witnesses of the Resurrection. They neither heard the angel's words nor saw the risen Jesus; and they would shortly lie about what really had happened (vv. 11–15). Furthermore it is doubtful whether Matthew intended to contrast the soldiers' terror, based on failure to understand, with the women's joy, who received the word of revelation. There is no evidence that the women witnessed the earthquake and the first descent of the angel; moreover their joy was mingled with fear (v.8), for the angel's "Do not be afraid" (v.5) is meaningless unless they were afraid. What is stunningly clear is the restrained sobriety of these accounts as compared with the later apocryphal Gospels (e.g., *Gospel of Peter*, 9:35–11:44).

5–7 The angel speaks (lit., "answered"; see on 11:25) words that allay the women's fears (cf. Mark 16:5–7; Luke 24:4–8). The empty tomb by itself is capable of several explanations (cf. John 20:10–15). This explanatory word of revelation narrows the potential interpretations down to one: Jesus has risen from the dead (v.6), a truth to be confirmed by personal appearances. In Matthew and Luke, but not in Mark, the fact of Jesus' resurrection, announced by the angel, is also tied into Jesus' promises —"as he said" (cf. 16:21; 17:23; 20:18–19). This is one of several significant "minor agreements" of Matthew and Luke against Mark in the resurrection narratives. The women are invited to see the place where Jesus lay and commanded to go "quickly" (v.7, a happy touch) to give his disciples the joyous message. Unlike Mark, Matthew does not explicitly mention Peter.

Jesus had promised to go ahead of his disciples into Galilee (see on 26:32); and the angel now reminds them of this (v.7). The present tense *proagei* ("is going ahead") cannot mean that Jesus is already on his way, because (1) v.10 places him still in Jerusalem; and (2) a verb like "go ahead," if pressed to mean Jesus was actually traveling, "would also seem to presuppose that the disciples also were on the way to Galilee" (Stonehouse, *Witness of Matthew*, p. 173). The verb is not a progressive present but a vivid future. As he promised, Jesus will arrive in Galilee before they do and meet them there, contrary to their expectation (see on 26:32; 28:10).

2. First encounter with the risen Christ

28:8–10

> 8So the women hurried away from the tomb, afraid yet filled with joy, and ran to tell his disciples. 9Suddenly Jesus met them. "Greetings," he said. They came to him, clasped his feet and worshiped him. 10Then Jesus said to them, "Do not be afraid. Go and tell my brothers to go to Galilee; there they will see me."

8–9 With mingled fear and joy, the women run to tell their news to the disciples (v.8), when "suddenly" (the probable force of *idou*, "behold," in this context) Jesus meets them (v.9). "Greetings" (*chairete*) is a normal Greek salutation (cf. 26:49). The women clasp his feet (possibly a generalizing plural: cf. Turner, *Insights*, p. 76; cf. John 20:11–14) and worship him. *Prosekynēsan* ("worshiped") can mean simply "knelt before" (see on 8:2). The same verb occurs in the only other resurrection appearance in Matthew (v.17) and encourages the view that the "kneeling" has instinctively become worship.

10 Like the angel (v.5), Jesus stills the women's fears and gives them a similar commission. Some have held that "my brothers" raises the status of Jesus' eleven surviving disciples. This ignores the use of the term in Matthew; for apart from the places where "brothers" denotes a natural relationship, the term is employed of spiritual relationships—even before the Passion—explicitly referring to the fellowship of those who acknowledge Jesus as Messiah (18:15; 23:8; cf. 5:22–24; 7:3–5; 18:21, 35). In the two other places where Jesus uses the full expression "my brothers" (12:49–50; 25:40), it refers to all Jesus' disciples and cannot possibly be limited to the apostles (cf. Stonehouse, *Witness of Matthew*, pp. 176–77).

Therefore the natural way to interpret "my brothers" in v.10 is not as a reference to the Eleven but to all those attached to his cause who were then in Jerusalem, most of whom had followed him from Galilee to Jerusalem as his "disciples" (see on 5:1–2, and esp. 26:32; 28:7). There were many others in addition to the Twelve who had followed Jesus (e.g., 20:17; 21:8–9, 15; 27:55; cf. 20:29; 21:46; 23:1). Apart from the Galileans, Joseph of Arimathea was certainly not Jesus' sole disciple from the Jerusalem region (19:13–15; 27:57–61).

If this interpretation of Jesus' words is reasonable, several interesting conclusions or possibilities are evident.

1. The view that interprets the "some" of v.17 as a reference to others than the apostles is supported, and the resurrection appearance of vv.16–20 may well be equivalent to the appearance before five hundred reported by Paul (1 Cor 15:6).

2. Obviously Matthew does not tell all he knows or recount every resurrection appearance of which he has information. Therefore it is tendentious to argue that 28:10, 16–20 means that Matthew thinks Jesus appeared to his disciples only in Galilee and denies any Jerusalem appearances.

3. The interpretation of v.10 offered here looks back to 26:32; 28:7: Jesus now confirms his earlier promise that, far from being left behind as a rotting corpse when his disciples return to Galilee, he will precede them there and meet them there. But now, after the resurrection, he makes the promise a command and includes all

his "brothers." Taken this way v.10 is far from eliminating other appearances to the believers (cf. John 20:3–10; Luke 24:13–49; John 20:11–29) before they return to Galilee. It is simply that Matthew, for his immediate purposes, is not interested in them.

4. But why not? Or why does Matthew record only the resurrection appearance to the women and the appearance in Galilee to his followers? Some have suggested that Galilee is introduced because it is the place of revelation and ministry, whereas Jerusalem is the place of rejection and judgment (see esp. E. Lohmeyer, *Galiläe und Jerusalem* [Göttingen: Vandenhoeck und Ruprecht, 1936], pp. 36ff.; R.H. Lightfoot, *Locality and Doctrine* [London: Hodder and Stoughton, 1938], pp. 66ff., 128ff.). But one must wonder whether enough weight has been assigned to various facts: viz., Jesus' ministry was not only to Galilee but to the whole of Israel (10:6, 23; 15:24); opposition was directed against Jesus in Galilee as well as in Jerusalem, where the plots to kill him were hatched; at Jerusalem Jesus revealed himself as King in fulfillment of Zechariah's prophecy (21:1–7); and Jerusalem, called the "holy city" (4:5; 27:53), peculiarly drew out Jesus' compassion (23:37–39), whereas cities in Galilee were excoriated (11:20–24).

Why, then, Matthew's record of a resurrection appearance in Galilee? The answer surely lies in the combination of two themes that have permeated the entire Gospel. First, the Messiah emerges from a despised area (see on 2:23) and first sheds his light on a despised people (see on 4:15–16); for the kingdom of heaven belongs to the poor in spirit (5:3). For this reason, too, the risen Jesus first appears to women whose value as witnesses among Jews is worthless (see on 27:55–56, 61; 28:1, 5–7). Second, "Galilee of the Gentiles" (4:15) is compatible with the growing theme of Gentile mission in this Gospel (see on 1:1; 2:1–12; 4:15–16; 8:5–13; 10:18; 12:21; 13:37; 15:21–28; 24:14 et al.) and prepares for the Great Commission (28:18–20).

3. *First fraudulent denials of Jesus' resurrection*

28:11–15

> [11]While the women were on their way, some of the guards went into the city and reported to the chief priests everything that had happened. [12]When the chief priests had met with the elders and devised a plan, they gave the soldiers a large sum of money, [13]telling them, "You are to say, 'His disciples came during the night and stole him away while we were asleep.' [14]If this report gets to the governor, we will satisfy him and keep you out of trouble." [15]So the soldiers took the money and did as they were instructed. And this story has been widely circulated among the Jews to this very day.

There is no sure way of dating the writing of this pericope by the closing words, "to this very day" (v.15). To conclude from *this* pericope that Matthew had in mind a period ten or fifteen years after the Fall of Jerusalem (so Bonnard) stretches the evidence too far. Matthew simply intends this paragraph to be an explanation of the stolen-corpse theory and an apologetic against it. He may also be drawing out a startling contrast: the chief priests use bribe money to commission the soldiers to spread lies, while the resurrected Jesus uses the promise of his presence to commission his followers to spread the gospel (vv.16–20).

11 Some of the guards (presumably the rest waited to be officially relieved) reported, not to Pilate, but to the chief priests; probably they were temple police (see on 27:65–66). When Matthew says the guards reported "everything that had happened," he is not suggesting that they actually witnessed the Resurrection but the earthquake, angel, and empty tomb (Bonnard).

12–14 It is very difficult to believe that the soldiers of Pilate would admit falling asleep (v.13): that would be tantamount to suicide. But the temple police could more easily be bribed, even though it took "a large sum of money" (v.12), and could more easily be protected from Pilate's anger. The plan devised (see on 12:14; 27:1) by the chief priests and elders (v.12; see on 21:23) proves to Matthew that their pious promises to believe if Jesus would only come down from the cross (27:42) were empty. Once again the instinctive concern of the Jewish leaders relates to expedience and the people's reaction, not to the truth. The story they concoct shows how desperate they are for an explanation, for if the guards were asleep, they could not know of the alleged theft; and if one of them awoke, why was not an alarm sounded and the disciples arrested? Molesting graves was a serious offense in the ancient world, subject at times to the death penalty. The famous "Nazareth Inscription," recording an ordinance of Caesar to this effect, confirms this, though the relation of this inscription to Jesus' death and burial is uncertain (cf. B.M. Metzger, "The Nazareth Inscription Once Again," in Ellis and Grässer, pp. 221–38).

It is equally improbable that the timid and fearful disciples could have mustered up the courage to open Jesus' tomb and run the risk of a capital indictment, or that the Jewish authorities would have failed to prosecute the disciples if they had possessed a scrap of evidence pointing to the disciples' guilt. Nor was the "large sum of money" an adequate measure of how far the Jewish leaders would go, for to "satisfy" the governor may well have involved further bribery (cf. parallels in Wettstein).

15 And this, Matthew explains, was the origin of the "widely circulated" Jewish explanation for the empty tomb, still common in the days of Justin Martyr (*Dialogue* 108).

C. *The Risen Messiah and His Disciples* (28:16–20)

1. *Jesus in Galilee*

28:16–17

> [16]Then the eleven disciples went to Galilee, to the mountain where Jesus had told them to go. [17]When they saw him, they worshiped him; but some doubted.

Partly because there is no close Gospel parallel to these verses, and partly because as the conclusion to Matthew's Gospel they have great significance, an enormous amount of study has centered on these verses. Much of it has gone into trying to distinguish between tradition and redaction or in establishing the *Gattung* or literary genre (e.g., B.J. Malina, "The Literary Structure and Form of Matthew 28:16–20," NTS 17 [1970–71]: 87–103; J. Lange, *Das Erscheinen des Auferstandenen im Evangelium nach Matthäus* [Würzburg: Echter, 1973]; B.J. Hubbard, *The Matthean Redaction of a Primitive Apostolic Commissioning: An Exegesis of Matthew 28:16–20* [SBLDS 19; Missoula: Scholars, 1974]). The most believable opinion is that of Hubbard, who avoids the classifications of his predecessors (enthronement hymn, official decree, covenant renewal manifesto) and opts for a commissioning narrative patterned after similar OT commissionings (e.g., Gen 12:1–4; Exod 3:1–10;

Josh 1:1–11; Isa 6; 49:1–6). After examining twenty-seven such narratives and finding a basic form consisting of seven elements, Hubbard finds five of them in Matthew 28:16–20: introduction (v.16), confrontation (vv.17–18a), reaction (v.17b), the commission (vv.19–20a), reassurance (v.20b). Missing are the protest before the reassurance and a conclusion stating the work is being carried out.

But several questions persist. Hubbard himself concedes that the form is not monolithic even in the OT; and absence of two of the seven common elements is disconcerting, the more so since Matthew's final clause is a perfectly suitable conclusion to his Gospel. More important, all the OT commissions Hubbard refers to are to individuals, whereas this one is to the disciples as a group. Some of the OT commissions are in reality the establishment of covenants; and if Frankmölle (pp. 42ff.) has somewhat exaggerated this theme in Matthew, it cannot be entirely ignored in a book that promises a new covenant (26:26–29) and seeks to demonstrate the continuity with and fulfillment of the OT covenant people in the messianic community being gathered around Jesus.

It seems best to conclude with John P. Meier ("Two Disputed Questions in Matt 28:16–20," JBL 96 [1977]: 407–24; cf. P.T. O'Brien, pp. 254–67) that this pericope does not easily fit any known literary form and must not be squeezed into a poorly fitting mold. Yet Meier's principal reason for this conclusion could be strengthened. He argues that these verses constitute a tradition so heavily redacted by the evangelist that conformity to a *Gattung* (or form) shaped primarily by oral transmission is in principal unlikely. That may be so, but this conclusion by no means makes impregnable judgments about the way the material came into Matthew's hands (cf. Introduction, section 2). Above all, the temptation to ascribe authenticity to "tradition" but not to "redaction" must be resisted (cf. Carson, "Redaction Criticism"; cf. G.R. Beasley-Murray, *Baptism in the New Testament* [London: Macmillan, 1962], pp. 77ff.).

Some have distinguished between "Christepiphanies" (appearances of the resurrected Christ on earth, as in 28:9) and "Christophanies" (appearances of the resurrected Christ from heaven, as at Paul's conversion, Acts 9; cf. Dunn, *Jesus*, pp. 116, 123). Those who make this helpful distinction are uncertain how to classify the resurrection appearance of vv.16–20. The dilemma is a false one. There has been no mention of the Ascension; and Paul seems to put his own experience of the risen Christ into a class of one (1 Cor 15:8), the sole "Christophany," which must also be distinguished from John's visionary experiences (e.g., Rev 1:12–16).

It is often pointed out that vv.16–20 recapitulate many of Matthew's themes. The point can be overstressed (e.g., Peter F. Ellis, *Matthew: His Mind and His Message* [Collegeville, Minn.: Liturgical, 1974]) but is an important insight that ties up several loose ends.

16 "Then" translates the mildly adversative *de* ("but"), not *tote* (see on 2:7). The fraudulent explanation of the empty tomb was purchased with a bribe and was widely circulated (vv.11–15), *but* the Eleven (designated as such in the NT only here and four times in Luke and Acts) do what Jesus says and go to Galilee. They go "to the mountain where Jesus had told them to go": the subordinate clause makes the expression *eis to oros* ("to the mountain") specific, though by itself it customarily means "into the hills." We do not know what mountain is meant, but the verse presupposes the arrangements implicit in 26:32; 28:7, 10. Associating the Great Commission (vv.18–20) with Galilee not only has nuances with Jesus' humble background and the theme of Gentile mission (see on v.10) but "ensures that the risen Christ and his teaching are not thought of as a substitute for, but as continuous with, Jesus' ministry and teaching in Galilee" (Hill, *Matthew*).

17 Doubt about Jesus' resurrection is expressed elsewhere (Luke 24:10–11; John 20:24–29), but only by those who have heard reports of Jesus' resurrection without actually seeing him. This verse is therefore unique. Two difficulties must be considered.

1. Does "some" refer to "some of the Eleven" or to "some others" in addition to the Eleven? The question is partly decided by one's interpretation of v.10, though more can be said. If *proskyneō* here means not merely "kneel" or "make obeisance to" but "worship" (see on v.9), then the "eleven disciples" and the "some" probably constitute two groups; for doubt about who Jesus is or about the reality of his resurrection does not seem appropriate for true worship. Especially if Matthew was an eyewitness, it is easy to believe that he describes a scene vivid in his own memory without taking all the precautions that would remove questions from the minds of readers who were not there. As a result, both here and in v.10 Matthew in an incidental fashion alludes to the larger crowd without providing useful specifics. Moreover *hoi de*, here as in 26:67, means "but some," in contrast with those already mentioned, rather than "but they" (cf. Gundry, *Matthew*). While this solution is not certain, the problem is not helped by suggesting that "some" refers to those in Matthew's community who have doubts (Hill, *Matthew*).

2. But why was there doubt at all? The verb used (*edistasan*, "[some] doubted") occurs in the NT only here and in 14:31 and does not denote disbelief but hesitation (cf. "though some hesitated," JB; cf. I.P. Ellis, " 'But some doubted,' " NTS 14 [1967–68]: 574–80). Even so, why did they hesitate, and why does Matthew include this information here? Even if others than the Eleven are the ones who hesitate, this does not solve the problem; it merely shifts it from the Eleven to other followers of Jesus.

Several solutions have been proposed, none of them convincing. There is no evidence of scribal emendation. It is barely possible that some doubted not the fact of the Resurrection but just who this person was (Hendriksen, Grosheide, Filson, Walvoord et al.). The pattern would then be somewhat akin to Luke 24:16; John 21:4–14, where the resurrected Jesus is not instantly recognized. But it must be admitted that this introduces a very subtle distinction into Matthew 28; and the parallels in Luke and John are not all that close, since Luke says the two on the Emmaus road "were kept from recognizing him," and John's narrative has other uncertainties—distance from shore and the aside in 21:12b. The most that can be said for this interpretation is that other passages show that Jesus in his postresurrection appearances was not always instantly recognized. Far less likely is the view of L.G. Parkhurst ("Matthew 28:16–20 Reconsidered," ExpT 90 [1978–79]: 179f.), who says that some doubted, not who Jesus was, nor the facticity of the Resurrection, but the propriety of worshiping the resurrected Jesus; and this hesitation Jesus dispels by the words of v.18: "All authority . . . has been given to me." Somewhat similar is the position of Gundry, who argues that vv.17–20 are Matthew's way of saying that only Jesus' *word* quiets doubt, and even the resurrection appearances will not do this. According to Gundry (*Matthew*), we "could hardly ask for better evidence of the authority of Jesus' teaching in Matthew's theology." But thematically v.18 is tightly related to v.19, not v.17. It is not at all clear that v.18 alleviates the doubt of v.17 (cf. Dunn, *Jesus*, p. 124; and to the contrary, Bornkamm, *Tradition*, p. 132). At very least we must admit that the text does not say that all doubts were removed, as is the case in Luke 24 and John 21. More important, Matthew's use of *proskyneō* ("worship") has been sufficiently ambiguous (see on 8:2; 28:9) that he would have needed to use a stronger verb such as *latreuō* ("worship," "serve [God]") if he were trying to make the various points Parkhurst and Gundry suggest.

We are left with some uncertainty about what Matthew means, owing primarily to the conciseness of his account. Perhaps it is best to conclude that, especially if the "some" refers not to the Eleven but to other followers, the move from unbelief and fear to faith and joy was for them a "hesitant" one. The Eleven, who according to the other Gospels had already seen the risen Jesus at least twice (Peter at least three times, Thomas at least once), respond instantly with worship on the occasion of this new epiphany, but some (others) hesitated—without further specification as to their subsequent belief or doubt. If this is what Matthew means, he may be using this historical reminiscence to stress the fact that Jesus' resurrection was not an anticipated episode that required only enthusiasm and gullibility to win adherents among Jesus' followers. Far from it, they still were hesitant; and their failure to understand his repeated predictions of his resurrection, compounded with their despair after his crucifixion, worked to maintain their hesitancy for some time before they came to full faith. Jesus' resurrection did not instantly transform men of little faith and faltering understanding into spiritual giants.

Another thing (not dealt with by Matthew) was necessary, viz., the enduement of the Spirit at Pentecost. Matthew's concise account presupposes this—for it is impossible that any evangelist could have been ignorant of that transforming event—but omits it in favor of pressing on to the Great Commission, which ties together some of his own thematic interests.

2. The Great Commission

28:18–20

> [18]Then Jesus came to them and said, "All authority in heaven and on earth has been given to me. [19]Therefore go and make disciples of all nations, baptizing them in the name of the Father and of the Son and of the Holy Spirit, [20]and teaching them to obey everything I have commanded you. And surely I am with you always, to the very end of the age."

18 "All" dominates vv.18–20 and ties these verses together: *all* authority, *all* nations, *all* things ("everything," NIV), *all* the days ("always," NIV). The authority of Jesus Messiah has already been heavily stressed in this Gospel (e.g., 7:29; 10:1, 7–8; 11:27; 22:43–44; 24:35; cf. John 17:2). Therefore it is incautious, if not altogether wrong, to claim that the Resurrection conferred on Jesus an authority incomparably greater than what he enjoyed before his crucifixion. The truth is more subtle. It is not that anything he teaches or does during the days of his flesh is *less* authoritative than what he now says and does: even during his ministry his words, like God's, cannot pass away (24:35); and he, like God, forgives sin (9:6). It is not Jesus' authority per se that becomes more absolute. Rather, the spheres in which he now exercises absolute authority are enlarged to include all heaven and earth, i.e., the universe. This authority has been "given" him by the Father; and so, of course, the Father is exempt from the Son's authority (cf. 1 Cor 15:27–28). The Son becomes the one through whom *all* God's authority is mediated. He is, as it were, the mediatorial King. This well-defined exercise of authority is given Jesus as the climactic vindication of his humiliation (cf. Phil 2:5–11); and it marks a turning point in redemptive history, for Messiah's "kingdom" (i.e., his "king-dominion," the exercise of his divine and saving authority; see on 3:2; 13:37–39) has dawned in new power. This is still clearer if we accept the view that there is a conscious allusion here to Daniel 7:13–14 (see esp. France, *Jesus*, pp. 142–43): the Son of Man, once humiliated and suffering, is given universal authority (same word in LXX).

Contrary to France, it does not follow from this that Matthew 26:64 and Mark 14:62 refer to this exaltation and not the Parousia. In the first place, the chief priests in no way witnessed this coming of the Son of Man; and, in the second place, we have repeatedly observed how the coming of the Son of Man to kingly authority cannot be reduced to a single moment in redemptive history.

19 "Therefore" is probably the correct reading; but even if the word is absent, the logical connection is presupposed by the flow of the commission. Two features tie the command to Jesus' universal authority.

1. Because he *now* has this authority, *therefore* his disciples are to go and make disciples—i.e., the dawning of the new age of messianic authority changes the circumstances and impels his disciples forward to a universal ministry he himself never engaged in during the days of his flesh, "except in reluctant anticipation" (Stendahl, Peake, 695k; Hill, *Matthew*). His promotion to universal authority serves as an eschatological marker inaugurating the beginning of his universal mission.

2. Because of that authority, his followers may go in confidence that their Lord is in sovereign control of "everything in heaven and on earth" (cf. Rom 8:28).

In the Greek, "go"—like "baptizing" and "teaching"—is a participle. Only the verb "make disciples" (see below) is imperative. Some have deduced from this that Jesus' commission is simply to make disciples "as we go" (i.e., wherever we are) and constitutes no basis for *going* somewhere special in order to serve as missionaries (e.g., Gaechter, *Matthäus*; R.D. Culver, "What Is the Church's Commission?" BS 125 [1968]: 243–53). There is something to this view, but it needs three careful qualifications.

1. When a participle functions as a circumstantial participle dependent on an imperative, it normally gains some imperatival force (cf. 2:8, 13; 9:13; 11:4; 17:27; cf. C. Rogers, "The Great Commission," BS 130 [1973]: 258–67).

2. While it remains true to say that the main imperatival force rests with "make disciples," not with "go," in a context that demands that this ministry extend to "all nations," it is difficult to believe that "go" has lost all imperatival force.

3. From the perspective of mission strategy, it is important to remember that the Great Commission is preserved in several complementary forms that, taken together, can only be circumvented by considerable exegetical ingenuity (e.g., Luke 24:45–49; John 20:21; Acts 1:8; cf. Matt 4:19; 10:16–20; 13:38; 24:14; see further below).

The main emphasis, then, is on the command to "make disciples," which in Greek is one word, *mathēteusate*, normally an intransitive verb, here used transitively (a not uncommon Hellenization; cf. BDF, par. 148[3]; Zerwick, par. 66; see on 13:52; 27:57). "To disciple a person to Christ is to bring him into the relation of pupil to teacher, 'taking his yoke' of authoritative instruction (11:29), accepting what he says as true because he says it, and submitting to his requirements as right because he makes them" (Broadus). Disciples are those who hear, understand, and obey Jesus' teaching (12:46–50). The injunction is given at least to the Eleven, but to the Eleven in their own role as disciples (v. 16). Therefore they are paradigms for all disciples. Plausibly the command is given to a larger gathering of disciples (see on vv. 10, 16–17). Either way it is binding on *all* Jesus' disciples to make others what they themselves are—disciples of Jesus Christ.

The words *panta ta ethnē* ("all nations") have been understood primarily in two ways.

1. They refer to all Gentiles—i.e., all nations except Israel. Israel has forfeited her place, and now the preaching of the Gospel must be kept from her (so Hare, *Jewish Persecutions*, pp. 147–48; Walker, pp. 111–13; D.R.A. Hare and D.J. Harrington, " 'Make Disciples of All the Gentiles' (Mt 28–19)," CBQ 37 [1975]: 359–69).

2. They refer to all people, including Israel (so Trilling, pp. 26–28; Hill, *Matthew;* Hubbard, *Matthean Reaction*, pp. 84–87; John P. Meier, "Nations or Gentiles in Matthew 28:19?" CBQ 39 [1977]: 94–102; O'Brien, pp. 262–63).

Now *ta ethnē* in its eight occurrences in Matthew (4:15; 6:32; 10:5, 18; 12:18, 21; 20:19, 25) normally denotes Gentiles, often pagans; but 21:43, where *ethnos* is used anarthrously, is an instance where "people" does not exclude Jews. Moreover, contrary to Hare and Harrington, a good case can be made for saying that the full expression, *panta ta ethnē*, used four times in Matthew (24:9, 14; 25:32; here), uses *ethnē* in its basic sense of "tribes," "nations," or "peoples" and means "all peoples [without distinction]" or "all nations [without distinction]," thereby including Jews. Could Matthew really be excluding Israel as one source of the hate his followers will have to endure (24:9)? Would he say that any Jewish Christians in any church known to him should not be baptized and taught?

More telling yet, Matthew's Gospel is now, in its final verses, returning to the theme introduced in the very first verse (see on 1:1)—that the blessings promised to Abraham and through him to all peoples on earth (Gen 12:3) are now to be fulfilled in Jesus the Messiah. And when that covenant promise is reiterated in Genesis 18:18; 22:18, the LXX uses the same words found here: *panta ta ethnē*. The expression is comprehensive; and, in line with all the anticipatory hints of Gentile witness in Matthew's Gospel (1:1; 2:1–12; 4:15–16; 8:5–13; 10:18; 13:38; 24:14 et al.), it would be as wrong to conclude that only Gentiles are in view as it would be to set up another restriction and see this commission as a command to evangelize only *Jewish* tribes.

Adherents of the "church growth movement" have attempted to justify their entire "people movement" principle on the basis of this phrase, used here and elsewhere, arguing that *ethnos* properly means "tribe" or "people" (most comprehensively, perhaps, by H.C. Goerner, *All Nations in God's Purpose* [Nashville: Broadman, 1979]). The latter point is readily conceded, but the conclusion is linguistically illegitimate. Plural collectives may have all-embracing force, whether in Greek or English. Doubtless God may convert people by using a "people movement"; but to deduce such a principle from this text requires a "city movement" principle based on Acts 8:40, where the same construction occurs with the noun "cities." In neither case may missiologists legitimately establish the normativeness of their theories.

The aim of Jesus' disciples, therefore, is to make disciples of all men everywhere, without distinction. Hill *(Matthew)* insists that such a command cannot possibly be authentic: "Had Christ given the command to 'make disciples of all nations,' the opposition in Paul's time to the admission of Gentiles to the Church would be inexplicable. It must be assumed that the Church, having learned and experienced the universality of the Christian message, assigned that knowledge to a direct command of the living Lord." But we have already seen how slow the disciples were to grasp what Jesus taught. More important, Acts and the Epistles betray no trace of opposition whatsoever to the *fact* of a Gentile mission. The debate between Paul and his Judaizing opponents was over *the conditions of entrance* into the Christian community (see on 23:15). The many hints throughout Jesus' ministry that show he anticipated a Gentile ministry after some delay (e.g., see on 10:16–20; 13:37–39; 24:14) would make it incongruous for him to have not given some commission about this.

The syntax of the Greek participles for "baptizing" and "teaching" forbids the conclusion that baptizing and teaching are to be construed solely as the *means* of making disciples (cf. also Allen, Klostermann, Lagrange, Schlatter); but their precise relationship to the main verb is not easy to delineate. Neither participle is bound to the other or to the main verb with the conjunction *kai* or a particle; and therefore "they must be viewed as dependent on one another or depending in differing ways on the chief verb" (Beasley-Murray, *Baptism*, p. 89; cf. BDF, par. 421). Most likely some imperative force is present, since the disciples are certainly to baptize and teach; but computer studies of the Greek NT have shown that although a participle dependent on an imperative normally gains imperatival force when it *precedes* the imperative, its chief force is not normally imperatival when it *follows* the imperative. Luke 6:35 has a close syntactic parallel: "And lend [*daneizete*] to them without expecting to get anything back [*apelpizontes*]." Not expecting anything in return is certainly not the *means* of the lending, but it is modal in that it characterizes the lending; and at the same time at least some imperatival force tinges the participle, even if the participle is primarily modal.

Similarly baptizing and teaching are not the *means* of making disciples, but they characterize it. Envisaged is that proclamation of the gospel that will result in repentance and faith, for *mathēteuō* ("I disciple") entails both preaching and response. The response of discipleship is baptism and instruction. Therefore baptism and teaching are not coordinate—either grammatically or conceptually—with the action of making disciples. The masculine pronouns *autous* ("them," vv.19–20) hint at the same thing, since *ethnē* ("nations") is neuter: the "them" who are baptized and taught are those who have been made disciples. But this is uncertain, because the case of "them" may be *ad sensum* (i.e., merely according to the general sense). In any case it would certainly misconstrue the text to absolutize the division between discipleship and baptism-instruction. The NT can scarcely conceive of a disciple who is not baptized or is not instructed. Indeed, the force of this command is to make Jesus' disciples responsible for making disciples of others, a task characterized by baptism and instruction.

Those who become disciples are to be baptized *eis* ("into," NIV mg.) the name of the Trinity. Matthew, unlike some NT writers, apparently avoids the confusion of *eis* (strictly "into") and *en* (strictly "in"; cf. Zerwick, par. 106) common in Hellenistic Greek; and if so, the preposition "into" strongly suggests a coming-into-relationship-with or a coming-under-the-Lordship-of (cf. Allen; Albright and Mann). For comments about baptism, see on 3:6, 11, 13–17. It is a sign both of entrance into Messiah's covenant community and of pledged submission to his lordship (cf. Beasley-Murray, *Baptism*, pp. 90–92).

The triple formula containing Father (or God), Son (or Christ), and Spirit occurs frequently in the NT (cf. 1 Cor 12:4–6; 2 Cor 13:14; Eph 4:4–6; 2 Thess 2:13–14; 1 Peter 1:2; Rev 1:4–6). Individually these texts do not prove there is any Trinitarian consciousness in the NT, since other threefold phrases occur (e.g., "God and Christ Jesus and the elect angels," 1 Tim 5:21). But contributing evidence makes it difficult to deny the presence of Trinitarian thought in the NT documents: (1) the frequency of the God–Christ–Spirit formulas; (2) their context and use: it is impossible, for instance, to imagine baptism into the name of God, Christ, and the elect angels; (3) the recognition by NT writers that the attributes of Yahweh may be comprehensively applied to Jesus and, so far as we have evidence, to the Spirit (cf. C.F.D. Moule, *The Holy Spirit* [London: Mowbrays, 1978], pp. 24–26; Carson, *Farewell Discourse*, esp. pp. 65–66).

Many deny the authenticity of this Trinitarian formula, however, not on the basis of doubtful reconstructions of the development of doctrine, but on the basis of the fact that the only evidence we have of actual Christian baptisms indicates a consistent monadic formula—baptism in Jesus' name (Acts 2:38; 8:16; 10:48; 19:5; similarly, passages such as Rom 6:3). If Jesus gave the Trinitarian formula, why was it shortened? Is it not easier to believe that the Trinitarian formula was a relatively late development? But certain reflections give us pause.

1. It is possible, though historically improbable, that the full Trinitarian formula was used for pagan converts, and "in the name of Jesus" for Jews and proselytes. But this is doubtful, not least because Paul, the Apostle to the Gentiles, never uses a Trinitarian formula for baptism.

2. Trinitarian ideas are found in the resurrection accounts of both Luke and John, even if these evangelists do not report the Trinitarian baptismal formula. The faith to be proclaimed was in some sense Trinitarian from the beginning. "This conclusion should not come as a great surprise: the Trinitarian tendencies of the early church are most easily explained if they go back to Jesus Himself; but the importance of the point for our study is that it means that Matthew's reference to the Trinity in chapter 28 is not a white elephant thoroughly out of context" (D. Wenham, "Resurrection," p. 53).

3. The term "formula" is tripping us up. There is no evidence we have Jesus' *ipsissima verba* here and still less that the church regarded Jesus' command as a baptismal *formula,* a liturgical form the ignoring of which was a breach of canon law. The problem has too often been cast in anachronistic terms. E. Riggenbach (*Der Trinitarische Taufbefehl Matt. 28:19* [Gütersloh: C. Bertelsmann, 1901]) points out that as late as the Didache, baptism in the name of Jesus and baptism in the name of the Trinity coexist side by side: the church was not bound by precise "formulas" and felt no embarrassment at a multiplicity of them, precisely because Jesus' instruction, which may not have been in these precise words, was not regarded as a binding formula.

20 Those who are discipled must not only be baptized but also taught. The content of this instruction (see on 3:1 for comments concerning *kerygma* ["preaching"] and *didache* ["teaching"]) is everything Jesus commanded the first disciples. Five things stand out.

1. The focus is on *Jesus'* commands, not OT law. Jesus' words, like the words of Scripture, are more enduring than heaven and earth (24:35); and the peculiar expression "everything I have commanded you" is, as Trilling (p. 37) has pointed

out, reminiscent of the authority of Yahweh (Exod 29:35; Deut 1:3, 41; 7:11; 12:11, 14). This confirms our exegesis of 5:17–20. The revelation of Jesus Messiah at this late stage in salvation history brings the fulfillment of everything to which the OT Scriptures pointed and constitutes their valid continuity; but this means that the focus is necessarily on Jesus.

2. Remarkably, Jesus does not foresee a time when any part of his teaching will be rightly judged needless, outmoded, superseded, or untrue: *everything* he has commanded must be passed on "to the very end of the age."

3. What the disciples teach is not mere dogma steeped in abstract theorizing but content to be *obeyed*.

4. It then follows that by carefully passing on everything Jesus taught, the first disciples—themselves eyewitnesses—call into being new generations of "earwitnesses" (O'Brien, pp. 264f.). These in turn pass on the truth they received. So a means is provided for successive generations to remain in contact with Jesus' teachings (cf. 2 Tim 2:2).

5. Christianity must spread by an internal necessity or it has already decayed; for one of Jesus' commands is to teach all he commands. Failure to disciple, baptize, and teach the peoples of the world is already itself one of the failures of our own discipleship.

But the Gospel ends, not with command, but with the promise of Jesus' comforting presence, which, if not made explicitly conditional on the disciples' obedience to the Great Commission, is at least closely tied to it. "Surely" captures the force of *idou* here (see on 1:20): he who is introduced to us in the prologue as Immanuel, "God with us" (1:23; cf. also 18:20), is still God with us, "to the very end of the age." The English adverb "always" renders an expression found in the NT only here— viz., *pasas tēs hēmeras*, strictly "the whole of every day" (Moule, *Idiom Book*, p. 34). Not just the horizon is in view, but each day as we live it. This continues to the end of the age (for this expression, see on 13:39–40, 49; 24:3; cf. Heb 9:26)—the end of history as we know it, when the kingdom will be consummated. Perhaps there is a small hint of judgment: the church dare not drift, because it, too, rushes to the consummation. The period between the commission and the consummation is of indefinite length; but whatever its duration, it is the time of the church's mission and of preliminary enjoyment of her Lord's presence.

Matthew's Gospel ends with the expectation of continued mission and teaching. The five preceding sections always conclude with a block of *Jesus'* teaching (3:1– 26:5); but the passion and resurrection of Jesus end with a commission *to his disciples* to carry on that same ministry (see Introduction, section 14), in the light of the Cross, the empty tomb, and the triumphant vindication and exaltation of the risen Lord. In this sense the Gospel of Matthew is not a closed book till the consummation. The final chapter is being written in the mission and teaching of Jesus' disciples.

MARK

Walter W. Wessel

MARK

Introduction

The Gospel of Mark is a succinct, unadorned yet vivid account of the ministry, suffering, death, and resurrection of Jesus. Mark presents the narrative in an appealing way, for he tells the Good News about Jesus Christ so simply that a child can understand it. Nevertheless his Gospel, as Peter said of Paul's letters, also contains "some things that are hard to understand" (2 Peter 3:16). Like a pool of pure water, it is far deeper than it looks. Therefore one ought to approach the study of this book humbly and with due recognition of the need for wisdom from almighty God and enlightenment from the Holy Spirit.

1. The Place of Mark's Gospel in Biblical Studies

Today the Gospel of Mark occupies a prominent place in biblical studies. It was not always so. Even though early tradition associated this Gospel with the apostle Peter, it soon was relegated to a position inferior to that of the other Gospels. In MSS of the Gospels, Mark never occupies the first position (with the one exception of Codex Bobiensis), and sometimes it occupies the last (e.g., codices Bezae and Washington). There are few quotations from Mark in the writings of either the apostolic fathers or the second-century Apologists. Augustine thought it was an abridgement of Matthew's Gospel, despite the fact that—though Matthew is longer —in almost every case where there are parallels, Mark's treatment is more extensive. The first commentary on Mark we have any record of is the one by Victor of Antioch in the fifth century. He sought in vain to find other commentaries on it and finally had to resort to gleaning incidental remarks on the text of Mark he found in commentaries on the other Gospels. From the time of Victor till the rise of modern biblical criticism, little attention was paid to Mark's Gospel. It is not difficult to explain this. Mark was not written by an apostle (as were Matthew and John); its language was rough and ungrammatical; and it was generally believed to be an abridgement of Matthew. So for centuries Mark remained in the shadows.

In the nineteenth century a dramatic change came. When as a result of modern biblical studies scholars concluded that Mark was the first Gospel to be written and that both Matthew and Luke used Mark in some form as a major source for writing their Gospels, interest in Mark's Gospel skyrocketed. The theory of "the priority of Mark" became one of the "sure results" of nineteenth-century biblical scholarship. This theory is usually credited to H.J. Holtzmann's *Die synoptischen Evangelien* (Leipzig: Wilhelm Engelmanns, 1863). Much work on the synoptic problem pointing in the direction of the priority of Mark had been done in Germany before Holtzmann's time, especially by Koppe, Lachman, Lessing, Reimarus, and Weisse; but it was Holtzmann who put it all together and popularized the theory.

The immediate response to Holtzmann's work brought Mark's Gospel to a place of prominence, especially in the Life-of-Jesus movement of the nineteenth century. Mark was seen as the original Gospel, containing the uninterpreted historical facts about Jesus of Nazareth. Whereas Matthew and Luke represented expansions and interpretations of the story of Jesus, Mark was considered to be pure gospel. And since this Gospel, with its emphasis on the humanity of Jesus lent itself in such a remarkable way to the preconceived christological notions of the nineteenth-century liberal theologians, they warmly embraced it. Martin (*Mark*, p. 37) observes that "with the Life-of-Jesus movement Mark's gospel came into its own, after centuries of neglect. Studies in literary criticism, gospel order and theological implicates all contrived to push this gospel into a prominent place."

The critical study of Mark's Gospel was in full swing. Martin Kähler (*The So-called Historical Jesus and the Historic, Biblical Christ* [Philadelphia: Fortress, 1964; German ed., 1896]) raised serious doubts about the Life-of-Jesus movement's understanding of Mark's Gospel by pointing out the kerygmatic nature of the Markan material (i.e., it contains essentially preaching rather than historical materials). Even more devastating was W. Wrede's *The Messianic Secret* (Greenwood, S.C.: Attic, 1971; German ed., 1901). Mark, Wrede argued, is far from being a simple, historical account of the life of Jesus. The truth is, the author had a theological axe to grind. Before the Resurrection, belief in Jesus as the Messiah never occurred to anyone. When, however, that belief did arise, there was an attempt to read it back into the accounts of Jesus. The messianic secret in Mark is such an attempt. Wrede's theory was so radical that it did not receive widespread acceptance. Nonetheless it succeeded in undermining further the assumption that Mark was a straightforward historical account of the life of Jesus.

The next stage in the history of Mark's Gospel in the church is form criticism—a school of Gospel criticism that dominated Markan studies from about 1919 to 1954. Its chief architects were the German scholars R. Bultmann, M. Dibelius, and K.L. Schmidt. The main assumption of form criticism is that the units of Gospel tradition circulated orally before they were written down and that in the oral period these units were shaped, even created, by the *Sitz im Leben* (life setting) of the early Christian community. This tradition, already formed and shaped, was collected and pieced together into our Gospels. Thus the Gospel writers were essentially scissors-and-paste men, collectors, vehicles of tradition, editors. The Gospels themselves are more the products of the community than of the individual authors they are ascribed to. Furthermore, they record the history of the church more than the history of Jesus.

This approach to the Gospels completely ruled out the possibility of an account of Jesus in any truly historical sense. Schmidt insisted that there were only separate units of tradition artificially put together, usually on a topical rather than a chronological basis; and since these units reflect more the life of the church than that of Jesus, they have little historical value.

Form criticism also undercut the tradition that Mark is based on the eyewitness reminiscences of Peter. It held that the Gospel is not to be regarded as a factual apostolic account of Jesus' life but is rather a community product, evoked and shaped by the vicissitudes of early Christianity.

With the emergence of redaction criticism, a more positive and constructive approach to the Gospels began. This new direction for Markan studies was initiated by Willi Marxsen. Form criticism, as we have seen, had not assigned any significant role to the Gospel writers. They were mere collectors, scissors-and-paste men. But with the coming of redaction criticism, attention turned to the editorial role of the Gospel writers. The chief concern was how these men handled the tradition, both oral and written, that came into their hands. Form criticism dealt with the individual units of tradition. Redaction criticism, however, focuses on each Gospel as a whole and on the distinctive manner in which each Evangelist wrote his Gospel. It is particularly interested in the Evangelists as theologians, i.e., as arrangers and shapers of the tradition in order to fulfill a particular theological purpose or set of purposes. Thus this approach recognizes a third life setting in the production of the Gospels. Not only is there (1) the life setting of Jesus and (2) that of the early church, but there is also (3) that of the Evangelist himself. Redaction criticism deals especially with investigating this third *Sitz im Leben*.

In Marxsen's hands redaction criticism does less than justice to the historicity of the Gospel of Mark. This, however, results more from his faulty presuppositions about the nature of the tradition than from his interpretive method. The insights of redaction criticism offer creative interpretive possibilities within a context of the historical reliability of Mark's Gospel. This hermeneutical approach is reflected in this commentary. (On redaction criticism, cf. also EBC 1:448–49.)

2. Authorship

a. Early Tradition

Although the Gospel of Mark is anonymous, there is a strong and clear early tradition that Mark was its author and that he was closely associated with the apostle Peter, from whom he obtained his information about Jesus. The earliest reference is found in the church historian Eusebius, who quoted from a lost work (*Exegesis of the Lord's Oracles*) written by Papias, bishop of Hierapolis, about A.D. 140. Papias, in turn, quotes the Elder, probably the elder John, referred to elsewhere by Eusebius. The quotation in Eusebius follows:

> The Elder said this also: Mark, who became Peter's interpreter, wrote accurately, though not in order, all that he remembered of the things said or done by the Lord. For he had neither heard the Lord nor been one of his followers, but afterwards, as I said, he had followed Peter, who used to compose his discourses with a view to the needs of his hearers, but not as though he were drawing up a connected account of the Lord's sayings. So Mark made no mistake in thus recording some things just as he remembered them. For he was careful of this one thing, to omit none of the things he had heard and to make no untrue statements therein. (*Ecclesiastical History* 3.39.15)

This tradition suggests several important points about Mark's Gospel: (1) behind Mark is the eyewitness account and apostolic authority of Peter; (2) Mark did not write his account about Jesus in chronological sequence; (3) nevertheless Mark was careful to record accurately what Peter said.

The Papias tradition, with its insistence on the apostolic, eyewitness source of Mark's Gospel, runs counter to the form-critical understanding of the tradition. Yet to accept Mark's dependence on Peter does not rule out Mark's role as the redactor of the received tradition. There may even be a hint of this possibility in Papias's reference to Mark's nonsequential arrangement of the tradition. If the tradition he received from Peter was in the form of disconnected homilies, Mark had much work to do in transforming Peter's preaching into a Gospel. This would allow him the freedom to impress on the received tradition his own theological concerns with a view to the special needs of the community he addressed his Gospel to. There do not seem to be any compelling reasons for rejecting the Papias tradition—even though, as Martin (*Mark*, pp. 80–83) has recently shown, Papias's immediate concern was to establish the apostolic authority of Mark in the face of Marcion's championing of the Gospel of Luke.

Another early tradition, the Anti-Marcionite Prologue to Mark (A.D. 160–80), mentions Mark as a Gospel writer and connects him with Peter. The passage, which is fragmentary, reads: ". . . Mark declared, who is called 'stump-fingered' because he had short fingers in comparison with the size of the rest of his body. He was Peter's interpreter. After the death of Peter himself he wrote down this same gospel in the regions of Italy." The two items of additional information found here are (1) Mark wrote his Gospel after the death of Peter and (2) he wrote it in Italy.

Irenaeus (c. A.D. 180) adds his testimony in agreement with the Anti-Marcionite Prologue: "And after their [Peter's and Paul's] death, Mark, the disciple and interpreter of Peter, himself also handed down to us in writing the things preached by Peter" (*Contra Haereses* 3.1.2).

The first line of the Muratorian Canon (c. A.D. 200) that has been preserved reads: "at which he was present so he wrote them down." The immediate context of the line makes it clear that "he" refers to Mark and "which" refers to the preaching of Peter.

The importance of the tradition cited above is increased by its geographical spread. At least three different church centers are represented: Hierapolis (Papias), Rome (Anti-Marcionite Prologue and the Muratorian Fragment), and Lyons (Irenaeus) (Lane, p. 10). The tradition is repeated later by Tertullian of North Africa and Clement of Alexandria.

b. John Mark in the Biblical Tradition

It is generally, though by no means unanimously, agreed that the Mark who is associated with Peter in the early tradition and identified as the author of the Gospel is also the John Mark of the NT. He is first mentioned in connection with his mother, who lived in the house in Jerusalem Peter went to on his release from prison (Acts 12:12). Mark accompanied Paul and Barnabas when they returned to Antioch from Jerusalem after the famine visit (Acts 12:25). Mark next appears as a "helper" (*hypēretēs*) to Paul and Barnabas on their first missionary journey (Acts 13:5). What Mark's function was is not clear; but whatever its nature, it brought him into close relationship with Paul and Barnabas.

Unfortunately Mark did not last long as a missionary helper. At Perga, in Pamphylia, he deserted to return to Jerusalem (Acts 13:13). Paul must have felt strongly about Mark's behavior on this occasion, because when Barnabas proposed taking Mark on the second journey, Paul flatly refused, a refusal that caused Barnabas to separate from Paul (Acts 15:36–39). Barnabas took Mark, who was his cousin, and sailed for Cyprus. No further mention is made of either of them in the Book of Acts.

In the Epistles Mark is seen with Paul at Rome at the time of the writing of Colossians. Paul sends Mark's greetings and adds: "You have received instructions about him; if he comes to you, welcome him" (Col 4:10; cf. Philem 24, written at the same time). Apparently Mark was at this point just beginning to win his way back into Paul's confidence. By the end of Paul's life, Mark was back in full favor. From Rome Paul wrote to Timothy: "Get Mark and bring him with you, because he is helpful to me in my ministry" (2 Tim 4:11). Peter also witnesses to Mark's presence in Rome about this time (1 Peter 5:13).

In summary we may say that though strictly speaking Mark's Gospel is anonymous, the early tradition of the church identifies the author with Mark, who was closely associated with the apostle Peter and from whom he received the tradition of the things said and done by our Lord. This tradition did not come to Mark as a finished, sequential account of the life of Jesus but in the form of the preaching of Peter, preaching that had been directed to the needs of the early Christian community. It is this material, arranged and shaped by Mark, that forms the nucleus of this Gospel.

The biblical material mentions a John Mark, cousin of Barnabas and associate of Paul, especially in the later stages of Paul's life. It is this Mark we identify as the author of the Gospel.

In addition to the early tradition, two other considerations point to the Markan authorship.

1. It seems unlikely that the church would have deliberately assigned the authorship of a Gospel to a person of secondary importance like Mark, who was neither an apostle nor otherwise prominent in the early church, unless there were strong historical reasons for doing this.

2. It may be, as Rawlinson (p. xxxi) points out, that "the interest in Mark displayed by Luke in the Acts . . . may be due not exclusively to the fact that he was the cause of the breach between Barnabas and Paul, but to the further fact also that Luke knew him to have been the author of a Gospel of which he had himself made use in the composition of his own."

The tradition of the Markan authorship, though called in question from time to time, remains secure.

3. Date

It is not possible to date Mark's Gospel with precision. The external evidence is divided. Both Irenaeus and the Anti-Marcionite Prologue say that Mark's Gospel was written after the death of Peter. (Irenaeus says that Paul also was dead at the time of its writing.) Against this is the claim of the Alexandrians that Mark was written while Peter was still alive. Irenaeus and the Anti-Marcionite Prologue are the more credible witnesses, though Irenaeus's testimony is not above question because of his erroneous statement that the Gospel of Matthew was written when Peter and Paul were still preaching.

The external evidence for the date of Mark suggests a *terminus a quo* of A.D. 64, the date of the martyrdom of Peter, or, if Irenaeus is right, A.D. 67, the most likely date of the martyrdom of Paul.

The internal evidence seems to support a date for the Gospel after Peter's death. Mark is very frank in pointing out the failures of Peter—a frankness more easily understood if Peter had already been martyred and had achieved a leading place in the affection of the early church. No recitation of his past failures could then threaten his high position. It could, however, be used to encourage and strengthen a suffering church, itself facing martyrdom.

The most likely *terminus ad quem* for the dating of Mark is the destruction of Jerusalem in A.D. 70, since the Gospel makes no reference to that catastrophe. In fact, Mark says nothing at all of the Jewish War (A.D. 66–70), which was climaxed by the destruction of the Holy City. This has led some scholars to suggest a *terminus ad quem* as early as 67, a date before the hostilities began in earnest. Also, the use of Mark by Matthew and Luke make a dating later than 70 unlikely.

The recent suggestion by the papyrologist Jose O'Callaghan that certain papyrus fragments found in Cave 7 at Qumran are bits of a copy of the Gospel of Mark and date from the first half of the first century A.D. has been largely rejected by NT scholars (cf. EBC 1:420–21, n. 1). The evidence O'Callaghan presents is far too fragmentary to be reliable.

Although we cannot be certain of it, the best estimate for dating the Gospel is the last half of the decade A.D. 60–70. This date embraces the period immediately following the great fire of A.D. 64, when intense persecution began to be directed against Christians in Rome. There are good reasons to believe that the Gospel of Mark was written to meet this crisis in the Roman church (see Section 5: Life Setting).

4. Origin and Destination

Although again certainty escapes us, we may arrive at reasonably reliable answers to the questions of the place of origin and the destination of the Gospel.

a. *Origin*

Early church tradition locates the writing of the Gospel either "in the regions of Italy" (Anti-Marcionite Prologue) or in Rome (Irenaeus, Clement of Alexandria). These church fathers also closely associate Mark's writing of the Gospel with the apostle Peter. The above evidence is consistent with (1) the historical likelihood that Peter was in Rome toward the end of his life and probably was martyred there and (2) the biblical evidence that Mark too was in Rome about the same time and was closely associated with Peter (cf. 2 Tim 4:11 and 1 Peter 5:13, where the word "Babylon" is probably a cryptogram for Rome). There is the further evidence that quotations from Mark's Gospel first appear in 1 Clement 15:2 and Hermas (*Similitudes* 5:2). Both these writings are associated with Rome.

The only contrary witness in the early tradition is Chrysostom, who locates Mark's writing in Egypt (*Homilies in Matt. i*); but he has probably misunderstood the statement of Eusebius (*Ecclesiastial History* 2.16.1): "They say that Mark set out for Egypt and was first to preach there the gospel which he composed" (cf. Johnson, p. 15).

Recent attempts to locate the writing of the Gospel in Antioch (Bartlett) or Galilee (Marxsen) have not met with much success. The arguments in favor of Rome are too strong.

b. Destination

Here too all indicators point to Roman or at least to Gentile readers. Mark explains Jewish customs that would be unfamiliar to Gentile readers (7:2–4; 15:42); he translates Aramaic words (3:17; 5:41; 7:11, 34; 15:22); he uses Latinisms and Latin loan words, a practice that in itself is no evidence of Gentile readership, but the large number of them (especially in comparison with Matthew and Luke) seems to suggest such readership; he reveals a special interest in persecution and martyrdom (8:34–38; 13:9–13), subjects particularly relevant to Roman Christians; and, finally, the immediate acceptance and widespread influence of his Gospel (Matthew and Luke built their Gospels on it) suggests a powerful church behind it. No church better fits the description than Rome.

5. Life Setting

Mark's Gospel is traditionally associated with Rome. It is in the Christian community there that we must look for its occasion and purpose. There are two suggestions as to the life setting of the Gospel.

a. In the persecutions of the Roman church A.D. 65–67

In A.D. 64 a devastating fire broke out in Rome. More than half the city was destroyed; and strong rumors persisted, despite all attempts to quash them, that the emperor Nero had himself deliberately set it. Tacitus, the Roman historian, describes the situation that followed:

> But neither human help, nor imperial munificence, nor all the modes of placating Heaven, could stifle scandal or dispel the belief that the fire had taken place by order. Therefore, to scotch the rumour, Nero substituted as culprits, and punished with the utmost refinements of cruelty, a class of men, loathed for their vices, whom the crowd styled Christians. Christus, the founder of the name, had undergone the death penalty in the reign of Tiberius, by sentence of the procurator Pontius Pilatus, and the pernicious superstition was checked for a moment, only to break out once more, not merely in Judaea, the home of the disease, but in the capital itself, where all things horrible or shameful in the world collect and find a vogue. First, then, the confessed members of the sect were arrested; next, on their disclosures, vast numbers were convicted, not so much on the count of arson as for hatred of the human race. And derision accompanied their end: they were covered with wild beasts' skins and torn to death by dogs; or they were fastened on crosses, and when daylight failed were burned to serve as lamps by night. Nero had offered his Gardens for the spectacle, and gave an exhibition in his Circus, mixing with the crowd in the habit of a charioteer, or mounted on his car. Hence, in spite of a guilt which had earned the most exemplary punishment,

there rose a sentiment of pity, due to the impression that they were being sacrificed not for the welfare of the state but to the ferocity of a single man. (*Annals* 15.44)

If the Gospel of Mark was written sometime during the period A.D. 65–67, this passage from Tacitus sheds much light on its life setting. The Roman church was experiencing the fires of persecution. Even martyrdom was not unknown among its members. Mark addresses himself to this situation. His purpose in writing was "not historical or biographical, but it was intensely practical. He was writing a book for the guidance and support of his fellow Christians in a situation of intense crisis. The martyrdoms had fallen off, but there was no assurance—with Nero on the throne—when they might begin again; the last days could not be far off (Ch 13), and every Christian's lamp must be trimmed, every Christian's loins girded for the struggle" (Grant, pp. 633–34).

The way Mark prepares his Christian readers for suffering is by placing before them the passion experience of Jesus. Jesus' way was a *via dolorosa*. The way of discipleship for Christians is the same way—the way of the Cross. About one-third of Mark's Gospel is devoted to the death of Jesus. And not only in the passion of Jesus is the theme of suffering found. Many explicit and veiled references occur elsewhere in the life of Jesus in Mark: in the temptation experience—he was in the wilderness with wild beasts (1:12–13); in the misunderstanding of his family (3:21, 31–35) and people generally (3:22, 30); in his statements about the cost of discipleship (8:34–38); and in his references to persecutions (10:30, 33–34, 45; 13:8, 11–13).

In addition, as Martin (following W. Popkes) has recently pointed out, it may be that *meta to paradothēnai ton Iōannēn* in 1:14 should be translated "after John was delivered over to death," rather than "after John was delivered over to prison." If this is true, then Mark's interest in John is more theological than historical. He wants to show that "the fate of John and the fate of Jesus run parallel; and both end by their being delivered up by God to death" (*Mark*, p. 67). On this understanding the implication for the Roman church is clear. Faithfulness and obedience as a follower of Jesus Christ will inevitably lead to suffering and perhaps even death.

b. *In the emergence of heretical theological teachings*

Most of the recent studies of Mark's Gospel have focused on its theology and particularly its christology (Luz, Schulz, Schweizer, Weeden). The most suggestive study to date is Martin's *Mark: Evangelist and Theologian*. The occasion for the writing of Mark's Gospel is traced to the "situation which arose after Paul's death or, at least, in areas where the influence of Paul's kerygmatic theology had sufficiently been diluted as to suggest a loss of grip on the historical events underlying his kerygma" (p. 161). Mark has caught the essence of Paul's thought and has stated it in language to which Paul had no access (the tradition about Jesus). Mark does this to compensate for a christology that exalted the divine-man status of Jesus at the expense of his true humanity. Thus in Mark we find the emphasis on Jesus' true humanity, underscored by his sufferings.

This setting for the Gospel has much to commend it. It recognizes the theological or, better, christological concerns of the author as well as his more directly pastoral concerns. Mark is no ivory-tower theologian. "The nature of the Christian life, as he understands it, carries the same pattern as his christology. The disciple is bidden to take up his cross and then follow the Lord who entered his glory by way of suffering and outward defeat" (ibid).

Perhaps the convergence of increased persecutions and false christological ideas in the Roman church constituted the life setting that gave rise to the writing of this first Gospel about Jesus Christ, the Son of God.

6. Literary Form

The nature of the literary form of Mark's writing has stimulated much discussion among NT scholars in recent years. Mark starts out with the statement "The beginning of the gospel about Jesus Christ." But what *is* a Gospel?

Perhaps it is best to state first what a Gospel is not. It is not a biography. A biography is an organized historical account of a person, usually beginning with a description of his background and family and continuing through each significant event or period of his life (birth, childhood, education, marriage, career, etc.). But Mark has no genealogy, no birth narrative, and says nothing of Jesus' boyhood or adolescence. Mark starts right out, after quoting from the OT, with Jesus as a full-grown man.

If the Gospel of Mark is not a biography of Jesus, what literary classification does it fall into? The word he uses is "gospel"—a word Mark himself seems to have created to describe the literary form of his work. The old Greek words used for biographies (*bioi* ["lives"], *praxeis* ["acts"], *apomnemoneumata* ["memoirs"]) would not do because Mark's work is not simply a historical account. It is rather "preaching materials, designed to tell the story of God's saving action in the life, ministry, death and resurrection of Jesus of Nazareth" (Martin, *Mark*, p. 21). Mark calls his work a Gospel because it contains the preached gospel.

This understanding of Mark's Gospel must not be taken as in any way depreciating the historical nature of the material it contains. The preaching that the Gospel enshrines arose out of the historical events of the career of Jesus. Without that history, the Good News that constitutes the gospel does not exist. Schweizer (p. 24), after stressing the kerygmatic nature of Mark's Gospel, remarks, "And yet it is really a history book, since Mark knows that these essentials [of the preached Good News] will not be found anywhere except in the record of the events of these years [of the ministry of Jesus]."

This means that though the material found in Mark's Gospel is rooted in what happened in Palestine during the first century of our era, it also bears the stamp of the man God chose to put it into its final form. Mark does not write as a disinterested historian. He writes as a preacher conveying God's good news of salvation by emphasizing Jesus' saving ministry (Mark devotes about one-third of his Gospel to Jesus' passion). Mark also writes as a theologian, arranging and interpreting the tradition to meet the needs of his hearers. (Mark has an intensely practical and theological purpose. See Section 5 of Introduction.)

7. Language and Style

The vocabulary of Mark's Gospel is rather limited. He uses 1,270 different words, of which 80 are peculiar to him among the NT writers. Luke's Gospel, by contrast, contains 250 words not found elsewhere in the NT.

Mark is fond of transliterating Latin words (at least ten of them) into Greek, and occasionally his Greek shows an underlying Latin construction or expression (cf. *symboulion edidoun* [3:6], *rhapismasin . . . elabon* [14:65], and *tini to hikanon poiē-sai* [15:15]).

A more important influence on Mark's language is Aramaic. Some of the more obvious evidences of this are the use of parataxis in preference to subordinating clauses, the use of *polla* ("many") as an adverb, the introduction of direct speech with the participle *legōn* ("saying"), the use of the *ērxato* ("began") as a redundant verb, and the use of the genitival pronoun. This strong Aramaic influence accounts in large measure for the rough, ungrammatical Greek often found in Mark's Gospel. Rawlinson (p. xxxi) likens Mark's Greek to that spoken by the lower classes at Rome, especially those who might have come from Palestine or Syria and who spoke Aramaic as their mother tongue.

Although Mark's facility with the Greek language is clearly inferior to that of Luke and other NT writers, he manages to achieve a remarkably forceful, fresh, and vigorous style. He uses the historical present (present tense used to describe a past event) over 150 times and the adverb *euthys* ("immediately") occurs 41 times. Thus he gives his readers the impression of listening to an on-the-spot report. Intimate details, such as one would expect from an eyewitness, abound: e.g., the reaction of the crowds (1:27; 2:12); the emotional responses of Jesus (1:41, 43; 3:5; 7:34); the reactions of the disciples (9:5-6, 10; 10:24, 32).

Another important feature of Mark's style is his vigorous interaction with his readers (cf. Lane, pp. 26ff.). He accomplishes this by (1) directly addressing them (cf. 2:10, where the words "But that you may know that the Son of Man has authority on earth to forgive sins" are probably a parenthetical statement by Mark addressed to his Roman readers—see commentary—and 7:19: "In saying this, Jesus declared all foods clean"); (2) addressing his readers through the words of Jesus (cf. 13:37: "What I say to you, I say to everyone: 'Watch!' "); (3) rhetorical questions addressed to them (cf. the question that occurs at the end of the story of the stilling of the waves, asked by the disciples but addressed to Mark's readers: "Who is his? Even the wind and the waves obey him" [4:41]). Mark wants his readers to be participants, not mere observers. He wants them to respond to what he tells them about Jesus by saying of him, "He is the Christ, the Son of God."

8. Bibliography

Books

Alexander, J.A. *The Gospel According to Mark*. New York: Scribner, 1858.

Anderson, Hugh. *The Gospel of Mark*. NCB. Greenwood, S.C.: Attic, 1976.

Beasley-Murray, G.R. *Jesus and the Future*. London: Macmillan, 1954.

————. *A Commentary on Mark Thirteen*. London: Macmillan, 1957.

Bratcher, R.G., and Nida, E.A. *Translator's Handbook on Mark*. Leiden: E.J. Brill, 1961.

Calvin, John. *Commentary on a Harmony of the Evangelists*. 3 vols. Grand Rapids: Baker, 1979.

Carrington, P. *The Primitive Christian Calendar*. Cambridge: Cambridge University Press, 1952.

Cole, A. *The Gospel According to Mark*. TNTC. Grand Rapids: Eerdmans, 1961.

Cranfield, C.E.B. *The Gospel According to Saint Mark*. Cambridge: Cambridge University Press, 1959.

Earle, Ralph. *The Gospel According to Mark*. The Evangelical Commentary on the Bible. Grand Rapids: Zondervan, 1957.

Farmer, W.R. *The Synoptic Problem*. New York: Macmillan, 1964.

_____. *The Last Twelve Verses of Mark*. Cambridge: Cambridge University Press, 1974.

Gould, E.P. *The Gospel According to Saint Mark*. ICC. Edinburgh: T. & T. Clark, 1932.

Grant, F.C. *The Gospel According to St. Mark*. Vol. 7. IB. New York: Abingdon, 1951.

Guy, Harold A. *The Origin of the Gospel of Mark*. London: Hodder & Stoughton, 1954.

Hunter, A.M. *The Gospel According to Saint Mark*. Torch Bible Commentary. London: SCM, 1967.

Johnson, S.E. *The Gospel According to St. Mark*. Harper's New Testament Commentary. New York: Harper and Brothers, 1960.

Klostermann, E. *Das Markusevangelium*. Handbuch zum Neuen Testament. Tübingen: Mohr, 1950.

Lagrange, M.J. *Évangile selon Saint Marc*. Études Bibliques. Paris: Librairie Le Coffre, 1947.

Lane, William L. *The Gospel According to Mark*. NIC. Grand Rapids: Eerdmans, 1974.

Lightfoot, R.H. *The Gospel Message of St. Mark*. Oxford: Clarendon, 1950.

Lohmeyer, E. *Das Evangelium des Markus*. Kritisch-Exegetischer Kommentar über das Neue Testament. Göttingen: Vandenhoeck und Ruprecht, 1967.

Martin, R.P. *Mark: Evangelist and Theologian*. Grand Rapids: Zondervan, 1972.

Marxsen, W. *Mark the Evangelist*. Nashville: Abingdon, 1969.

Mauser, Ulrich W. *Christ in the Wilderness*. London: SCM, 1963.

Moore, A.L. *The Parousia in the New Testament*. Leiden: Brill, 1966.

Morison, James. *A Practical Commentary on the Gospel According to St. Mark*. London: Hodder & Stoughton, 1889.

Moule, C.F.D. *The Gospel According to Mark*. The Cambridge Bible Commentary. Cambridge: Cambridge University Press, 1965.

Nineham, D.E. *Saint Mark*. Pelican Gospel Commentary. Baltimore: Penguin, 1963.

Plummer, A. *The Gospel According to St. Mark*. CGT. Cambridge: Cambridge University Press, 1914.

Rawlinson, A.E.J. *The Gospel According to St. Mark*. WC. London: Methuen, 1949.

Robinson, J.M. *The Problem of History in Mark*. London: SCM, 1957.

Ropes, J.H. *The Synoptic Gospels*. Harvard: Harvard University Press, 1934.

Schlatter, A. *Die Evangelien nach Markus und Lukas*. Stuttgart: Calwer Verlag, 1947.

Schweizer, Eduard. *The Good News According to Mark*. ET. London: SPCK, 1971.

Stonehouse, Ned B. *The Witness of Matthew and Mark to Christ*. Philadelphia: Presbyterian Guardian, 1944.

Swete, H.B. *The Gospel According to St. Mark*. Macmillan New Testament Commentaries. London: Macmillan, 1927.

Taylor, Vincent. *The Gospel According to St. Mark*. London: Macmillan, 1952.

Articles

Cranfield, C.E.B. "St. Mark 13." *Scottish Journal of Theology* 6 (1953): 189–96, 287–303; 7 (1954): 284–303.

_____. "Gospel of Mark." *The Interpreter's Dictionary of the Bible*. Vol. 3. Edited by George Buttrick. New York: Abingdon, 1962.

Dunn, J.D.G. "The Messianic Secret in Mark." *Tyndale Bulletin* 21 (1970): 92–117.

Grayston, K. "The Study of Mark XIII." *Bulletin of the John Rylands Library* 56 (1974): 371–87.

Longenecker, R.N. "The Messianic Secret in the Light of Recent Discoveries." *Evangelical Quarterly* 41 (1969): 207–15.

Marshall, I.H. "Son of God or Servant of Jahweh? A Reconsideration of Mark 1:11." NTS 15 (1965): 326–36.

Martin, R.P. "A Gospel in Search for a Life-Setting." *Expository Times* 80 (1969): 361–64.

Moule, C.F.D. "Mark 4:1–20 Yet Once More." *Neotestamentica et Semitica*. Studies in Honour of Matthew Black. Edited by E. Earle Ellis and Max Wilcox. Edinburgh: T. & T. Clark (1969), pp. 95–113.

Wenham, David. "Recent Study of Mark 13." *Theological Students' Fellowship Bulletin* 71 (1975): 6–15.

9. Outline

    I. Prologue (1:1–13)
       A. Preparing the Way (1:1–8)
       B. The Baptism of Jesus (1:9–11)
       C. The Temptation of Jesus (1:12–13)
   II. The Early Galilean Ministry (1:14–3:6)
       A. Calling the First Disciples (1:14–20)
       B. Driving Out an Evil Spirit (1:21–28)
       C. Healing Peter's Mother-in-law (1:29–31)
       D. Healing Many People (1:32–34)
       E. Leaving Capernaum (1:35–39)
       F. Healing a Leper (1:40–45)
       G. Conflict With the Religious Leaders (2:1–3:6)
          1. Healing a paralytic (2:1–12)
          2. Eating with sinners (2:13–17)
          3. A question about fasting (2:18–22)
          4. The Lord of the Sabbath (2:23–3:6)
             a. Picking grain on the Sabbath (2:23–28)
             b. Healing on the Sabbath (3:1–6)
 III. The Later Galilean Ministry (3:7–6:13)
       A. Withdrawal to the Lake (3:7–12)
       B. Selection of the Twelve (3:13–19)
       C. Jesus, His Family, and the Beelzebub Controversy (3:20–35)
          1. Charged with insanity (3:20–21)
          2. Charged with demon possession (3:22–30)
          3. Jesus' true family (3:31–35)
       D. Parables About the Kingdom of God (4:1–34)
          1. Parable of the sower (4:1–9)
          2. Secret of the kingdom of God (4:10–12)
          3. Interpretation of the parable of the sower (4:13–20)
          4. Parables of the lamp and the measure (4:21–25)
          5. Parable of the secretly growing seed (4:26–29)
          6. Parable of the mustard seed (4:30–32)
          7. Summary statement on parables (4:33–34)
       E. Triumph Over Hostile Powers (4:35–5:43)
          1. Calming the storm (4:35–41)
          2. Healing the demon-possessed man (5:1–20)
          3. Jairus's plea in behalf of his daughter (5:21–24)
          4. Healing a woman with a hemorrhage (5:25–34)
          5. Raising Jairus's daughter (5:35–43)
       F. Rejection at Nazareth (6:1–6a)
       G. Sending Out the Twelve (6:6b–13)
 IV. Withdrawal From Galilee (6:14–8:30)
       A. Popular Views of Jesus' Identity (6:14–16)
       B. Death of John the Baptist (6:17–29)
       C. Feeding the Five Thousand (6:30–44)
       D. Walking on the Water (6:45–52)

Text and Exposition

I. Prologue (1:1–13)

A. *Preparing the Way*

1:1–8

> ¹The beginning of the gospel about Jesus Christ, the Son of God. ²It is written in Isaiah the prophet:
>
>> "I will send my messenger ahead of you,
>> who will prepare your way"—
>> ³"a voice of one calling in the desert,
>> 'Prepare the way for the Lord,
>> make straight paths for him.' "
>
> ⁴And so John came, baptizing in the desert region and preaching a baptism of repentance for the forgiveness of sins. ⁵The whole Judean countryside and all the people of Jerusalem went out to him. Confessing their sins, they were baptized by him in the Jordan River. ⁶John wore clothing made of camel's hair, with a leather belt around his waist, and he ate locusts and wild honey. ⁷And this was his message: "After me will come one more powerful than I, the thongs of whose sandals I am not worthy to stoop down and untie. ⁸I baptize you with water, but he will baptize you with the Holy Spirit."

1 The first verse seems to be a title. Whether it is intended to refer to the entire Gospel or only to the ministry of John the Baptist is not clear. Since in Acts 1:22 the starting point of the Good News is stated to be "from John's baptism" (cf. also Acts 10:37; 13:24; Matt 11:12; Luke 16:16; John 1:6), Mark may have this in mind here. Another possibility, however, is that by the use of the word *archē* ("beginning") Mark is imitating the opening verse of the LXX (*en archē*, "in the beginning," Gen 1:1) and wants his readers to realize that his book is a new beginning in which God reveals the Good News of Jesus Christ. Taken in this way, the first verse is not only a title for the entire book but a claim to its divine origin.

The word "gospel" comes from the old English "god-spel" ("good news") and translates accurately the Greek *euangelion*. The Greek word originally meant the reward for bringing good news but later came to mean the Good News itself. In the NT the Good News is that God has provided salvation for all men through the life, death, and resurrection of Jesus Christ. For Mark to convey this Good News, he has created a new literary genre—"gospel." His use of this term strongly indicates the nature of the material as being kerygmatic. "Mark's book has come to be called *a* Gospel because it contains *the* Gospel—the announcement of the Christian good news" (Moule, *Gospel of Mark*, p. 8).

In the rendering "about Jesus Christ," the NIV translators have opted for the objective genitive. If a choice has to be made (and translators must make choices), this is probably to be preferred to the subjective genitive—"by Jesus Christ." Mark's intent seems to be to ·proclaim the gospel, already known and experienced by the Roman believers, by rooting it in the events of Jesus' life. There are indications that they had lost hold of these historical roots. Thus it is the gospel "about Jesus Christ."

"Jesus" is the Greek form of the Hebrew "Joshua," which means "Yahweh is salvation" or "salvation of Yahweh." It is the name revealed by the angel to Joseph before Jesus was born, and it was given as descriptive of our Lord's mission—"and you are to give him the name Jesus, because he will save his people from their sins" (Matt 1:21). "Christ" is the Greek word for "anointed," behind which is the Hebrew *māšîaḥ*, from which the English word "messiah" is derived (cf. 8:29 for a full discussion of the word).

Some MSS omit the last phrase of v.1, "the Son of God." There are good reasons, however, for including it: (1) the evidence from the MSS is very strong (see Notes at the end of this section); (2) it is easy to account for its omission by homoioteleuton (i.e., by the scribe accidentally omitting the two words *huiou theou*, "Son of God") because the two previous words (*Iēsou Christou*) have the same endings; (3) Son of God is an important theme in Mark's Gospel (cf. 1:11; 3:11; 5:7; 9:7; 12:6; 13:32; 14:36, 61; 15:39).

2–3 Mark cites the OT to show that any true understanding of the ministry of Jesus must be firmly grounded there. The verb translated "is written" (v.2) is in the perfect tense. It denotes completed action in the past with continuing results. "It was written and still is" is the sense. The frequency with which this tense of the verb is used by the writers of the NT to introduce OT quotations underscores their strong belief in the unchanging authority of the Scriptures.

In the KJV "in the prophets" is read for "in Isaiah the prophet." The attestation for KJV's reading is very weak. It doubtless arose because the quotations that follow are not only from Isaiah but include one from Malachi as well. The first part of the quotation in v.2 agrees verbatim with the LXX of Exodus 23:20a. The second part is from the Hebrew of Malachi 3:1 but differs from both the Hebrew and LXX in reading "your way" instead of "the way before me." By this change in persons, allowance was made for a messianic interpretation of this passage. These two texts were similarly combined by the rabbis (cf. Exodus R 23:20), who apparently identified Elijah (Mal 3:1) with the messenger of Exodus 23:20.

The quotation in v.3 is taken from the LXX text of Isaiah 40:3, the only difference being the substitution by Mark (or perhaps he found the text already altered) of "of him" for "of our God." This applies the statement to Jesus, since the antecedent is "Lord," a title the early church used for him.

Mark brings together these OT texts in a striking way. He probably found the Exodus text already combined with Malachi 3:1. It is God's promise of a messenger "to guard you on the way and to bring you to the place I have prepared" (Exod 23:20), i.e., through the wilderness to the Promised Land. Mark adds a third text to this matrix, Isaiah 40:3, which looks forward to the coming of another messenger "in the desert" who will go before the people of God in a second Exodus to prepare for the revelation of God's salvation in Christ.

4 Unlike Matthew and Luke, Mark has no nativity narrative. It is possible that the traditions concerning the birth and infancy of Jesus were unknown to him. More likely they were of no use for Mark's purpose. He has no interest in writing a biography, as such, of Jesus. His concerns are kerygmatic and theological, i.e., he wants to highlight the saving facts and their theological meaning for the Roman church. Thus he immediately begins with the ministry of John the Baptist as the forerunner of the Messiah. This is precisely where Peter begins in his proclamation of the gospel in Acts 10:37: "You know what has happened throughout Judea, beginning in Galilee after the baptism that John preached."

John appears suddenly, "baptizing in the desert region." Although the word *erēmos* ("desert," "wilderness") does not necessarily refer to dry, arid land but means essentially uninhabited territory—open, wild territory—in contrast to the cultivated and inhabited areas of the country, the specific reference here is to the arid regions west of the Dead Sea. (Matthew 3:1 locates John's ministry in the Judean desert.) This general area was the abode of the Qumran sect. It is likely that John came in contact with these people. He certainly must have known of them. What influences they exerted on him are not known. Perhaps his ascetic life and stern discipline were derived from them. However, neither his baptismal practices nor his great emphasis on ethical conduct and eschatological judgment seems to have come from them.

John was "preaching a baptism of repentance for the forgiveness of sins." "Of repentance" is a genitive of quality. It was a repentance-baptism John was preaching, i.e., the baptism indicated that repentance had already occurred or was being accompanied by it. *Metanoia* ("repentance") means etymologically "a change of mind"; but as Taylor (p. 154) says, "In the NT it is used in a deeper sense, indicating a deliberate turning." The end result (*eis*, "for") is the forgiveness of sins. God's direct response to true repentance is forgiveness.

5 John's preaching caused great excitement. Mark says, "The whole Judean countryside and all the people of Jerusalem went out to him." The verb "went out" (*exeporeueto*) is in the imperfect tense and suggests that they "kept going out" to him. Although there is an element of hyperbole in Mark's report, it nevertheless implies that John's preaching aroused much interest and created a great stir. Jerusalem is at least twenty miles from the Jordan River and about four thousand feet above it. It was hard going down the rugged Judean hills to the Jordan and even harder coming back up. No exclusively ethical preacher, as Josephus would have us believe John was (Antiq. XVIII, 117 [v.2]), could have attracted that kind of interest. John preached the coming of the Messiah. This raised popular excitement to a fever pitch. Although great numbers came seeking baptism, John baptized no one who did not make an open confession of sin.

6 John is described as a typical "holy man" of the Near East. His clothing was woven of camel's hair and held in place by "a leather belt around his waist" (cf. 2 Kings 1:8, where Elijah is similarly described). His food consisted of locusts (cf. Lev 11:21–22, where they are listed among clean foods) and wild honey. The wild honey is bees' honey and not, as has sometimes been suggested, carob pods or sap from various trees in the area.

7–8 In Mark's account John's message is very brief. Mark includes nothing of John's pointed ethical admonitions to the Pharisees and Sadducees (Matt 3:7–10), to the crowds (Luke 3:10–11), or to the tax collectors and soldiers (Luke 3:12–14). Instead he focuses on the coming of the Mighty One who will baptize with the Holy Spirit (v.7). So great is this Mighty One that John does not consider himself worthy even to untie his sandals for him.

John now contrasts his baptism with that of the Coming One (v.8). John's baptism is water baptism; that of the Coming One is Holy Spirit baptism. Again the emphasis is on the superiority (this time in terms of ministry) of the Coming One to John. Moule's comment is to the point: "The Baptist evidently meant that the great coming One would not merely cleanse with water but would bring to bear, like a deluge, the purging, purifying, judging presence of God himself" (*Gospel of Mark*, p. 10). This is what happened in a dramatic way at Pentecost (Acts 2) in fulfillment of Christ's promise (Acts 1:5).

Notes

1 For a complete discussion of the many interpretations of ἀρχή (*archē*, "beginning"), see Cranfield, *Gospel of Mark*, pp. 34–35.

The reading that includes υἱοῦ θεοῦ (*huiou theou*, "Son of God") is found in the great majority of MSS. It is however missing from Sinaiticus (א). What raises a question is the split between Vaticanus (B) and Sinaiticus. Otherwise there is little doubt that the phrase "Son of God" is original. Taylor (p. 120) remarks, "Beyond question this title represents the most fundamental element in Mark's Christology." It occurs at the beginning (1:1) and the end (15:39) in this Gospel.

3 The urgency of the action is stressed by the use of the aorist imperative ἑτοιμάσατε (*hetoimasate*, "Prepare now!"). In the OT passage cited (Isa 40:3), κύριος (*kyrios*, "Lord") refers, of course, to Yahweh. Here it refers to the Lord Jesus.

4 Grant (p. 649) thinks that βάπτισμα μετανοίας (*baptisma metanoias*) is "a Semitism, meaning 'a baptism which symbolized or expressed repentance.'"

B. The Baptism of Jesus

1:9–11

9At that time Jesus came from Nazareth in Galilee and was baptized by John in the Jordan. 10As Jesus was coming up out of the water, he saw heaven being torn open and the Spirit descending on him like a dove. 11And a voice came from heaven: "You are my Son, whom I love; with you I am well pleased."

Jesus probably began his public ministry about A.D. 27, when he was approximately thirty years old. His childhood and youth, about which we know almost nothing, were spent in the village of Nazareth in Galilee. Two events, however, immediately preceded the beginning of his ministry: his baptism by John and his temptation by the Devil.

9 "At that time" is a free translation of *en ekeinais tais hēmerais* ("in those days") and represents one of the frequent "seams" or connecting links in Mark's Gospel. These "seams" are Mark's way of putting together the stories about Jesus and often are helpful in probing into Mark's theological concerns.

The baptism of Jesus by John must have been a problem to the early church. Why did Jesus submit himself to a baptism of repentance for the forgiveness of sins? In Matthew's account John was reluctant to baptize Jesus: "I need to be baptized by you, and do you come to me?" (Matt 3:14). Jesus replied, "It is proper for us to do this to fulfill all righteousness" (v.15). "All righteousness" is a reference to God's plan and purpose for Jesus. Part of that plan was the complete identification of Jesus at the very outset of his ministry with man and his sin. This he did by submitting to baptism. He had no sins of his own to confess. Rather he was proclaiming his identity with human nature, weakness, and sin (cf. 2 Cor 5:21).

10 NIV does not translate the adverb *euthys* ("immediately") in this verse. The frequent use of this adverb is characteristic of Mark (it occurs forty-one times) and gives his Gospel a certain air of breathlessness.

Mark seems to suggest that only Jesus saw "heaven being torn open and the Spirit descending," though he may have been so focusing on Jesus' experience that he says nothing of John's. Mark's use of the verb *schizō* ("tear," "rend") to describe what happened to the heavens shows his graphic style of writing. Matthew and Luke use the ordinary word *anoigō* ("open"). The tearing open of the heavens is probably to be understood as signifying a cosmic event (cf. T Levi 18:5–12: "The heavens shall be opened . . . the Father's voice . . . sin shall come to an end . . . and Beliar shall be bound by him." The language echoes Isaiah 64:1: "Oh, that you would rend the heavens and come down, that the mountains would tremble before you"). Whatever else the descent of the Spirit on Jesus meant, it clearly indicated his anointing for ministry. Jesus himself claimed this anointing in the synagogue at Nazareth when he said, "The Spirit of the Lord is on me" (Luke 4:18).

11 The rabbis taught that when God speaks in heaven, "the daughter of his voice" (*baṯ qôl*, i.e., "an echo," is heard on earth. In what God says there is a fusing of the concept of the messianic King of the coronation Psalm (2:7) and that of the Lord's Servant of Isaiah (42:1). The main emphasis, however, is on the unique sonship of Jesus. Mark confesses Jesus as Son of God at the very outset of his Gospel (1:1). Here God confesses Jesus as his Son. "The Gospel is not a mystery story in which the identity of the main character has to be guessed; from the outset it is made clear who this is—the Son of God" (E. Best, *The Temptation and the Passion* [Cambridge: Cambridge University Press, 1965], p. 168).

The Father also witnesses to his approval of his Son. He knows the mission that has been given to the Son. At the very beginning of Jesus' fulfillment of that mission, God states his confidence in him. Lane (p. 58) points out that "the first clause of the declaration (with the verb in the present tense of the indicative mood) expresses an eternal and essential relationship. The second clause (the verb is in the aorist indicative) implies a past choice for the performance of a particular function in history."

Notes

11 "Whom I love" is a translation of ὁ ἀγαπητός (*ho agapētos*). Since seven out of fifteen times in the LXX *agapētos* translates יָחִיד (*yāḥîd*, "only one"), some commentators translate it "only" here (I.H. Marshall, "Son of God or Servant of Jahweh? A Reconsideration of Mark 1:11," NTS 15 [1965]: 326–36).

The verb εὐδόκησα (*eudokēsa*, "I am well pleased") may be taken as a timeless aorist or perhaps as representing the Hebrew stative perfect. The meaning then would be that God is always pleased with the Son.

C. The Temptation of Jesus

1:12–13

> ^{12}At once the Spirit sent him out into the desert, ^{13}and he was in the desert forty days, being tempted by Satan. He was with the wild animals, and angels attended him.

12 Mark emphasizes the close connection between the Baptism and the Temptation by the use of his characteristic word *euthys* ("at once"). The humbling of Jesus by his identification with man's failure and sin at the Baptism is continued by his subjection to the onslaughts of Satan. The same Holy Spirit who came on Jesus at the baptism drives him out into the desert.

13 Mark's account of the Temptation is very brief. He devotes only two verses to it whereas Matthew has eleven and Luke thirteen. No specific temptations are described and no victory over Satan is recorded. By this Mark wants to emphasize that Jesus' entire ministry was one continuous encounter with the Devil and not limited to a few temptations in the desert during a period of forty days. Indeed, in his Gospel he vividly describes this continuing conflict.

The forty days have symbolic significance and recall the experiences of Moses (Exod 24:18) and Elijah (1 Kings 19:8, 15) in the desert. Only Mark mentions the wild beasts—a touch that heightens the fierceness of Jesus' entire temptation experience.

Notes

12 The verb used to describe the Spirit's action is ἐκβάλλω (*ekballō*). Since Mark most often uses *ekballō* of the expulsion of demons (eleven times) and in this passage combines it with the vigorous word εὐθύς (*euthys*, "at once"), it ought to be translated by something stronger than NIV's "sent out"—e.g., "forced out" or "drove out." "Force is certainly involved. There is no need, however, of inferring resistance or unwillingness on the part of Jesus" (Bratcher and Nida, p. 32).

II. The Early Galilean Ministry (1:14–3:6)

A. Calling the First Disciples

1:14–20

> ^{14}After John was put in prison, Jesus went into Galilee, proclaiming the good news of God. ^{15}"The time has come," he said. "The kingdom of God is near. Repent and believe the good news!"
> ^{16}As Jesus walked beside the Sea of Galilee, he saw Simon and his brother Andrew casting a net into the lake, for they were fishermen. ^{17}"Come, follow me," Jesus said, "and I will make you fishers of men." ^{18}At once they left their nets and followed him.

¹⁹When he had gone a little farther, he saw James son of Zebedee and his brother John in a boat, preparing their nets. ²⁰Without delay he called them, and they left their father Zebedee in the boat with the hired men and followed him.

The purpose of this section (1:14–3:6) is to describe the opening stage of the Galilean ministry. The introductory statement (1:14–15) is followed by the account of the calling of the first disciples (vv.16–20), Jesus' ministry in and around Capernaum (vv.21–34), and a series of conflict stories (2:1–3:6) that reach their climax in a plot to put Jesus to death. The call of Levi the tax collector (2:13–14) introduces one of the conflict stories.

14–15 The opening of Jesus' public ministry is related to that of John the Baptist. Not until "after John was put in prison" (v.14) did Jesus begin his ministry. Mark apparently wants to show that John, the forerunner, completed his God-appointed task; and only after that had occurred did Jesus enter his ministry.

Although he gives neither the exact place nor the precise time of the beginning of Jesus' ministry (he shows little interest in such details), Mark says that the content of Jesus' preaching is "the good news of God." God is both its source (subjective genitive) and object (objective genitive); it is from God and about God. The gospel is good news, the very best news ever to come to the hearing of mankind, because it contains the message of forgiveness, restoration, and new life in Christ Jesus (cf. 2 Cor 5:17).

Jesus witnesses to God's action for man's salvation by saying, "The time has come" (v.15). Time here is not simply chronological time (*chronos*) but the decisive time (*kairos*) for God's action. With the coming of Jesus, God was doing something special. "He marks the fulfillment of the special salvation-time which is distinguished from all other time" (Schweizer, p. 45).

The concept of the kingdom of God is basic to the teaching of Jesus. Although the term "kingdom of God" does not occur in either the OT or the Apocrypha, the idea is abundantly present in both. The OT is full of such statements as "The LORD will reign for ever and ever" (Exod 15:18); "The LORD is enthroned as King forever" (Ps 29:10); "I am the LORD, your Holy One, Israel's Creator, your King" (Isa 43:15).

An examination of such passages reveals that the Lord's kingship is both a present reality (God is exercising his authority now) and a future hope (God will reign in the eschaton—the End—when he finally puts down all opposition to his reign).

The same tension between the kingdom of God as both present and future exists in the teaching of Jesus. At the outset of his Galilean ministry Jesus proclaimed, "The kingdom of God is near" (Mark 1:15). Later, after driving out the demons from a possessed man and being accused of being in league with Beelzebub, Jesus replied, "But if I drive out demons by the Spirit of God, then the kingdom of God has come upon you" (Matt 12:28; cf. Luke 11:20). In Jesus' actions God's rule has invaded this world. It is present with men. But in other sayings the kingdom is spoken of as still future; e.g., "I say to you that many will come from the east and the west, and will take their places at the feast with Abraham, Isaac and Jacob in the kingdom of heaven" (Matt 8:11; cf. Matt 20:21).

The solution to the dilemma of both a present and a future kingdom is not to be found in rejecting one or the other (e.g., realized eschatology rejects a future kingdom and consistent eschatology a present one). Bruce Metzger pointedly says: "The kingdom of God in its essence is the reign of God, the personal relationship between the sovereign God and the individual. Thus there is no point in asking whether the kingdom is present or future, just as there is no point in asking whether the fatherhood of God is present or future. It is both" (*The New Testament* [New York: Abingdon, 1965], p. 148).

In Mark 1:15 the approach of the kingdom is emphasized. It has drawn near *spatially* (in Jesus' person) and *temporally* (since it ushers in the events of the End). "In the person of Jesus men are confronted by the Kingdom of God in its nearness" (Lane, p. 65). The only appropriate response is repentance and faith. There is an urgency about the nearness of God's kingdom. Since it ushers in the End, it speaks of judgment. Jesus thus proclaims God's kingdom so that men will repent and believe.

16 Jesus has begun to preach his message. Now he must gather around him men whom he can teach so that they may become sharers in that message. He calls them in the midst of everyday life where they really live. God's reign does not operate in a void. It assumes a people—a people subject to that rule. It involves the formation of a community.

Jesus found Simon and his brother Andrew along the shore of the Sea of Galilee. This beautiful body of water, 682 feet below sea level, fourteen miles long and six miles wide, is an inland lake (Luke calls it the Lake of Gennesaret [5:1]; another designation was Sea of Tiberias). Much of Jesus' ministry took place near this lake. In NT times there were numerous towns along its shores, especially the northern and western ones. Since its waters abounded with fish, the local fishing industry flourished. Simon and Andrew were casting a net into the sea when Jesus called them.

17–18 Mark says nothing of a previous encounter of these two disciples with Jesus (cf. John 1:35–42). Even if he was aware of such a tradition, it is doubtful whether he would have used it. Mark wants to show the urgency of the situation, consistent with the eschatological significance of Jesus' mission. Jesus called Simon and Andrew to the urgent task of rescuing men from the impending judgment (v.17; cf. the use of fishing in the context of judgment in the OT: e.g., Jer 16:16; Ezek 29:4–5; 38:4; Amos 4:2) that the coming of the kingdom in the person and work of Jesus presages. The urgency demands an immediate response. "At once" the two fishermen left their nets and followed him (v.18).

19–20 The same call is now extended to James and John, sons of Zebedee (v.19). They too respond without any hesitation (v.20). In their case something of the price of discipleship is indicated by the breaking of family ties—the leaving of their father's business. The mention of the hired men may imply that Zebedee was a man of wealth. It may also be included to indicate that by leaving their father to follow Jesus, James and John were not leaving him entirely alone to run his fishing business. However, the main emphasis in this call, as in that of Simon and Andrew, is on the immediate response to it.

Notes

---

14 The words translated "was put in prison" represent the single Greek word παραδοθῆναι (*paradothēnai,* "to be delivered over"). NIV assumes the delivering over was to prison. It is possible, however, especially if Mark is more interested in theology than historical sequence (Mark reserves the details of John's death till ch. 6), that the delivering over is to death. By this means Marks wants to heighten the similarity between John's and Jesus' ministry. They both end in death. Thus the shadow of the Cross falls over the ministry of Jesus at its very outset.

15 The verb πιστεύετε (*pisteuete,* "believe") is followed by the preposition ἐν (*en,* "in")—the only occurrence in the NT. Scholars have debated whether it means "believe in [the sphere of] the gospel" (whatever that means!) or simply "believe the gospel" (the "in" being an example of "translation Greek," i.e., the Greek carries over the Hebrew idiom). Marxsen (p. 135) finds no problem with the translation "believe in" because to believe in the gospel is to believe in Jesus Christ who is present in the gospel.

18 Ἀκολουθεῖν (*akolouthein,* "to follow") is frequently used in the Gospels "to describe attachment to the person of Jesus, personal surrender to His summons, and acceptance of his leadership" (Taylor, p. 169). For an excellent statement of the concept of discipleship in Mark's Gospel, see Schweizer, p. 49.

B. *Driving Out an Evil Spirit*

1:21-28

> 21They went to Capernaum, and when the Sabbath came, Jesus went into the synagogue and began to teach. 22The people were amazed at his teaching, because he taught them as one who had authority, not as the teachers of the law. 23Just then a man in their synagogue who was possessed by an evil spirit cried out, 24"What do you want with us, Jesus of Nazareth? Have you come to destroy us? I know who you are—the Holy One of God!"
>
> 25"Be quiet!" said Jesus sternly. "Come out of him!" 26The evil spirit shook the man violently and came out of him with a shriek.
>
> 27The people were all so amazed that they asked each other, "What is this? A new teaching—and with authority! He even gives orders to evil spirits and they obey him." 28News about him spread quickly over the whole region of Galilee.

21 In vv.21-34 Mark records what seems to have occurred on one memorable Sabbath day. The first incident occurred in the synagogue in Capernaum. The word "synagogue" can refer either to the local congregation or to the building in which the congregation met. The synagogue originated in the Exile as the result of Jews meeting together for prayer and the study of the Torah. In NT times synagogues were found all over the Hellenistic world wherever there were sufficient numbers of Jews to maintain one. The synagogue became Judaism's most enduring institution.

Capernaum was the home of Peter and became a kind of base of operations for Jesus' Galilean ministry. Jesus, like Paul (cf. Acts 13:15), used the "freedom of the synagogue"—a Jewish custom that permitted recognized visiting teachers to preach (based on the reading from the Law or Prophets) in the synagogue by invitation of its leaders—to bring the Good News to his countrymen. Tell Hum, located on the northwest corner of the Sea of Galilee, almost certainly marks the site of Capernaum.

22 We are not told what Jesus said in the synagogue on this occasion, only what the reaction of the congregation was. They were "amazed." The verb used is *exeplēssonto* (cf. 6:2; 7:37; 10:26; 11:18), a compound from *plēssō* ("strike," "smite"); it has a very strong meaning. People were astonished at Jesus' teaching "because he taught them as one who had authority." Jesus did not have to quote the authorities ("Rabbi so-and-so says such-and-such"). His authority came straight from God.

NIV regularly translates *grammateis* as "teachers of the law." Most readers of the Bible know them as "scribes." They were the scholars of the day, professionally trained in the interpretation and application of the law. Jesus often came into direct conflict with them.

23 Suddenly the synagogue service was disrupted by the cry of a man "possessed by an evil spirit." Jesus thus early in his ministry came into conflict with Satan. This is significant, for Jesus came to destroy the power of the Devil (1 John 3:8). Although the belief that sickness or deviant behavior can be attributed to demon possession has usually been relegated by modern man to superstition or obscurantism, recent developments in the study of the occult and demonism have tended to leave the question open. (Popular books like C.S. Lewis's *Screwtape Letters* [1946; reprint ed., Old Tappan, N.J.: Revell, 1976] and films such as "The Exorcist" have contributed to this openness.) Reports of demon possession now come not only from distant and remote mission fields but from the most sophisticated of our urban centers. The NT accounts of demonism do not seem so bizarre after all.

24 Although v.23 states that the man cried out, it was really the demon who had the man under his control who shouted. (Notice that Jesus speaks to the demon in v.25.) The "us" in the question "What do you want with us?" shows that the demon in the man speaks for his fellow demons also. They clearly seem to recognize Jesus. This is evident not only because they call him "Jesus of Nazareth" but because they recognize his mission. The question "Have you come to destroy us?" could just as well be a statement of fact (punctuation marks were added later to the MSS): "You have come to destroy us." The demons recognize—far more clearly than the synagogue congregation—the role of judgment in the ministry of Jesus.

The utterance of the name of Jesus and his title "the Holy One of God" may have been an attempt by the demon to get control over Jesus, since "it was widely believed at that time that if you knew a person's true identity and could utter his name, you could gain a magic power over him" (Nineham, p. 75).

25–26 Jesus needed no magical formulas to exorcise the demon. After ordering him, "Be quiet!" (v.25), Jesus simply spoke his word of power and the evil spirit convulsed the man "and came out of him with a shriek" (v.26).

27–28 Mark again reports the reaction of the people (v.27). Their amazement, which also reveals some alarm, prompted them to ask one another, "What is this?" The answer stresses both the newness of Jesus' teaching and its authority. They had had no previous experience with this kind of teaching. Jesus' authority was inherent within himself and therefore did not have to appeal to spells or incantations to exorcise the demon. One command accomplished it. The inevitable result was that Jesus' fame was spread "over the whole region of Galilee" (v.28), which, in view of

Luke's "throughout the surrounding area" (Luke 4:37), means "all that part of Galilee that surrounds Capernaum."

C. *Healing Peter's Mother-in-law*

1:29–31

> ²⁹As soon as they left the synagogue, they went with James and John to the home of Simon and Andrew. ³⁰Simon's mother-in-law was in bed with a fever, and they told Jesus about her. ³¹So he went to her, took her hand and helped her up. The fever left her and she began to wait on them.

29–31 The eyewitness details of this story suggest its Petrine origin. After all, Peter had a special interest in what occurred. The incident took place after Jesus left the synagogue (v.29) and went to the house of Simon and Andrew (probably near by; only Mark's account mentions Andrew). We are not told what caused Peter's mother-in-law's fever (v.30). It had, however, put her in bed; and Jesus was told about her. The healing is described simply, yet with interesting detail: "He went to her, took her hand and helped her up" (v.31). The cure was instantaneous and complete, for she got out of bed and began to serve the needs of her guests, which probably means she prepared food for them.

D. *Healing Many People*

1:32–34

> ³²That evening after sunset the people brought to Jesus all the sick and demon-possessed. ³³The whole town gathered at the door, ³⁴and Jesus healed many who had various diseases. He also drove out many demons, but he would not let the demons speak because they knew who he was.

32–34 "That evening after sunset" (v.32) would be, according to Jewish reckoning, the following day, since the Sabbath ends at sundown. The Sabbath having ended, people could now bring, without breaking the law, their sick and demon-possessed to him. Apparently Mark wants to emphasize that the exorcism of v.26 and the healing of v.31 were not isolated cases. Jesus' healing power was extended to large numbers: "All the sick and demon-possessed" were brought, and "Jesus healed many" and "drove out many demons." Mark does not describe the healings and exorcisms individually but shows by the use of "all" and "many" the mighty power of Jesus.

Again Jesus muzzles the demons, "because they knew who he was" (v.34). Luke is more specific: "because they knew he was the Christ" (Luke 4:41). This reluctance by Jesus to have the demons reveal him as the Messiah is best explained by Jesus' desire to show by word and deed what kind of Messiah he was (viz., one quite different from the popular conception of the Messiah) before he declared himself.

E. *Leaving Capernaum*

1:35–39

> ³⁵Very early in the morning, while it was still dark, Jesus got up, left the house and went off to a solitary place, where he prayed. ³⁶Simon and his companions

went to look for him, ³⁷and when they found him, they exclaimed: "Everyone is looking for you!"

³⁸Jesus replied, "Let us go somewhere else—to the nearby villages—so I can preach there also. That is why I have come." ³⁹So he traveled throughout Galilee, preaching in their synagogues and driving out demons.

35 Although Mark makes no specific connection between v.35 and the preceding paragraph, he seems to be giving a sequence of events. Jesus, after a busy evening of healings and exorcisms, got up early the next morning and sought a quiet place to pray. In the other two places in Mark's Gospel where Jesus prays, he is faced with a crisis (6:46; 14:32–41). Here too there is a crisis, though not so definite a one as the other two. The crisis is the shallow and superficial response of the people to Jesus. They are only interested in what he can do to heal their physical afflictions. So Jesus seeks the strength that only communion and fellowship with the Father can provide.

36–37 The disciples (here [v.36] called "Simon and his companions"—not *mathētai*, perhaps because they are not acting like disciples) do not understand Jesus or his need for communion with the Father. So they go to look for him (Mark uses the verb *katadiōkein*, which literally means "to track down" or "hunt" and usually has a hostile sense). Apparently they think Jesus will be pleased to know that everyone was looking for him (v.37). They do not understand that this popular and shallow reception of him was the very reason he withdrew to pray.

38–39 Jesus' reply shows that he feared his healings and exorcisms were hindrances to understanding who he really was. The people of Capernaum were interested in him as a popular miracle-worker only. So Jesus suggests that they move on to other villages that he might "preach there also" (v.38). His coming into the world was more to proclaim God's Good News and all that was involved in discipleship and suffering than to be a popular miracle-worker. Healings and exorcisms had their place (v.39), but they were not to usurp the primary purpose for which Jesus had come. If Mark wrote his Gospel to refute a christological heresy that placed too much emphasis on Jesus as a miracle-worker, the relevance of these verses is clear.

F. *Healing a Leper*

1:40–45

⁴⁰A man with leprosy came to him and begged him on his knees, "If you are willing, you can make me clean."

⁴¹Filled with compassion, Jesus reached out his hand and touched the man. "I am willing," he said. "Be clean!" ⁴²Immediately the leprosy left him and he was cured.

⁴³Jesus sent him away at once with a strong warning: ⁴⁴"See that you don't tell this to anyone. But go, show yourself to the priest and offer the sacrifices that Moses commanded for your cleansing, as a testimony to them." ⁴⁵Instead he went out and began to talk freely, spreading the news. As a result, Jesus could no longer enter a town openly but stayed outside in lonely places. Yet the people still came to him from everywhere.

40 This pericope (vv.40–45) is connected with what precedes only by a *kai* ("and") and is followed by a story that is also introduced with a *kai*. The pericope apparently serves as a connecting link between 1:21–29 and 2:1–3:6—two clearly identifiable units in Mark's Gospel.

The word "leprosy" was used in biblical times to designate a wide variety of serious skin diseases. It was not limited to what we know as leprosy, or, to use the preferable medical term, Hansen's disease. Whatever variety of skin disorder the man had, it caused him much suffering. This suffering was social as well as physical. The law required that "the person with such an infectious disease must wear torn clothes, let his hair be unkempt, cover the lower part of his face and cry out, 'Unclean! Unclean!' As long as he has the infection he remains unclean. He must live alone; he must live outside the camp" (Lev 13:45–46). Instead of keeping his distance from Jesus, as the law demanded, the leper came directly to him and fell down on his knees to make his plea. He had no doubt that Jesus could heal him. He only wondered whether Jesus was willing. It is sometimes easier to believe in God's power than in his mercy.

41–42 On the assumption that the correct reading of v.41 is "being angered" and not "filled with compassion" (cf. Notes), the question arises why? Many answers have been suggested (cf. Cranfield, *Gospel of Mark*, p. 92). The best is that Jesus was angered in the presence of a foul disease that could only be the work of the Devil. Jesus' anger was focused neither on the man nor on the disease but on Satan whose work he came to destroy. Understood in this way, the incident becomes another example of the fierce conflict between Christ and Satan that plays such an important part in this Gospel.

Jesus also expressed compassion. He reached out and touched the unclean leper, an act that, according to the Mosaic Law, incurred defilement. Calvin (1:374) says: "By his word alone he might have healed the *leper*; but he applied, at the same time, the touch of his hand, to express the feeling of compassion. Nor ought this to excite our wonder, since he chose to take upon him our flesh, that he might cleanse us from our sins."

Jesus' touching of the leper not only resulted in his being cured (v.42) but also revealed Jesus' attitude toward the ceremonial law. He boldly placed love and compassion over ritual and regulation.

43 Both verbs in this verse seem to confirm the reading *orgistheis* ("being angry") in v.41. "Sent him away" is from *ekballō* (cf. note on 1:12), which often is used of driving out demons; and *embrimaomai* ("with a strong warning") is a word that originally meant "to snort like a horse." An element of anger or indignation is contained in Jesus' warning. Why? The best answer is that Jesus knew that the man would disobey him. The result was that Jesus could "no longer enter a town openly but stayed outside in lonely places" (v.45).

44 The reason Jesus didn't want the leper to tell anyone of his cure was that Jesus did not want to gain the reputation of being just another *theios anēr* ("a divine man," i.e., "a miracle-worker"). This would thwart the essential purpose of his ministry. Instead, he instructed the leper to go to those whose job it was to rule whether he was clean or not. Jesus also told the man to offer sacrifices that were required by the Mosaic Law. (These procedures are all given in detail in Lev 14:2–31). The last phrase of v.44—"as a testimony to them"—may be understood either as a testimony to the priest and the people of the reality of the cure or as a testimony against (cf. 13:9) the priests if they fail to accept the healing as having been done by Jesus. Although the latter is an attractive suggestion, it hardly seems consistent with Jesus' injunction to silence (presumably about his miraculous powers).

45 The leper acted consistent with human nature. The prohibition against telling what had happened to him made him all the more anxious to proclaim it everywhere. This resulted in curtailment of Jesus' public ministry. He avoided going into the towns and chose rather to stay in more isolated places. But even in his isolation, people managed to find him and "came to him from everywhere."

Notes

---

41 The translators of NIV may have been right in following the reading σπλαγχνισθείς (*splanchnistheis*, "filled with compassion") since the MS evidence strongly favors it. However, it is difficult to explain how the reading ὀργισθείς (*orgistheis*, "being angry") came into existence. It is much easier to explain the scribal origin of *splanchnistheis* as the result of embarrassment over the ascription of anger to our Lord. This solution is consistent with the use of ἐμβριμάομαι (*embrimaomai*, "speak harshly to") in v.43, which has an element of indignation or anger in it.

43 Some commentators argue that ἐμβριμάομαι (*embrimaomai*, "speak harshly to") simply expresses deep emotion and not anger. The use of the same verb, however, in Mark 14:5, in a context that clearly indicates anger, supports the element of anger here.

G. *Conflict With the Religious Leaders* (2:1–3:6)

Clearly 2:1–3:6 is a separate section in Mark's Gospel. In it Jesus comes into conflict with the Jewish religious leadership in a series of five separate incidents. It is highly unlikely that these incidents happened in chronological sequence or even come out of the same period in Jesus' ministry. Mark brought them together because they have a common theme: conflict with the religious authorities. There can be little doubt that such stories as we find here were used by the church in its ongoing struggle with Judaism.

1. *Healing a paralytic*

2:1–12

> [1]A few days later, when Jesus again entered Capernaum, the people heard that he had come home. [2]So many gathered that there was no room left, not even outside the door, and he preached the word to them. [3]Some men came, bringing to him a paralytic, carried by four of them. [4]Since they could not get him to Jesus because of the crowd, they made an opening in the roof above Jesus and, after digging through it, lowered the mat the paralyzed man was lying on. [5]When Jesus saw their faith, he said to the paralytic, "Son, your sins are forgiven."
> [6]Now some teachers of the law were sitting there, thinking to themselves, [7]"Why does this fellow talk like that? He's blaspheming! Who can forgive sins but God alone?"
> [8]Immediately Jesus knew in his spirit that this was what they were thinking in their hearts, and he said to them. "Why are you thinking these things? [9]Which is easier: to say to the paralytic, 'Your sins are forgiven,' or to say, 'Get up, take your mat and walk'? [10]But that you may know that the Son of Man has authority on

earth to forgive sins . . . ." He said to the paralytic, ¹¹"I tell you, get up, take your mat and go home." ¹²He got up, took his mat and walked out in full view of them all. This amazed everyone and they praised God, saying, "We have never seen anything like this!"

It has often been suggested (e.g., Bultmann, Schweizer, Taylor) that vv. 1–12 are the conflation of two stories. The first (vv. 1–5a, 10b–12) is a miracle story, and the other (vv. 5b–10a) is a separate story about the forgiveness of sins. But this dissection of the passage fails to recognize the close relationship between the healing of the body and the forgiveness of sins.

1 Jesus had been away from Capernaum and had been traveling throughout Galilee. He now returns to Capernaum, a kind of base of operations for him in the northern part of the country. His presence in town was soon discovered. "Home" was probably the house of Peter and Andrew referred to in 1:29.

2 Even the place Jesus called home afforded him no privacy. The house filled with people, and the overflow was so great that the space outside the door was blocked. They no doubt flocked to him because they wanted to see him perform more miracles (like the healing of the leper). But Jesus was not working miracles inside the house. He was preaching the gospel to the people.

3–4 In order to understand the action these verses describe, it is necessary to visualize the layout of a typical Palestinian peasant's house. It was usually a small, one-room structure with a flat roof. Access to the roof was by means of an outside stairway. The roof itself was usually made of wooden beams with thatch and compacted earth in order to shed the rain. Sometimes tiles were laid between the beams and the thatch and earth placed over them.

The four men brought the paralytic (v.3) to the house where Jesus was; but when they saw the size of the crowd, they realized it was impossible to enter by the door. So they carried the paralytic up the outside stairway to the roof (v.4). There they dug up the compacted thatch and earth (no doubt dirt showered down on those inside the house below), removed the tiles, and lowered the man through the now-exposed beams to the floor below.

5 Jesus recognized this ingenuity and persistence as faith. Mark says Jesus "saw their faith." It was evident in the actions of both the paralytic and his bearers. But instead of healing the man of his lameness, Jesus forgave his sins. This hardly seemed to be what the man needed—at least on the surface.

> It is not as if this sick man were unusually sinful, but his case makes the universal separation of man from God more conspicuous and illustrates the truth which is proclaimed over and over in the Old Testament, that all suffering is rooted in man's separation from God. For this reason, Jesus must call attention here to man's deepest need; otherwise the testimony of this healing would remain nothing more than the story of a remarkable miracle. (Schweizer, p. 61)

6 Mark has already mentioned the "teachers of the law" in 1:22 (q.v.), where their teaching is contrasted with Jesus' authoritative teaching. Here they become directly involved with Jesus. Luke (5:17) says that they had come from "every village of Galilee and from Judea and Jerusalem." Obviously they were there out of more than curiosity; they hoped to be able to ensnare him on some theological point. Jesus' statement about forgiveness gave them their opportunity.

7 For anyone but God to claim to forgive sin was blasphemy. Since for the teachers of the law Jesus was not God, therefore he blasphemed. If they were right about who Jesus was, their reasoning was flawless. In Jewish teaching even the Messiah could not forgive sins. That was the prerogative of God alone. Their fatal error was in not recognizing who Jesus really was—the Son of God who has authority to forgive sins.

8–9 The teachers of the law had not openly expressed their misgivings about Jesus' actions. They were "thinking in their hearts" (v.8). But Jesus knew their thoughts and challenged them with the question "Which is easier: to say to the paralytic, 'Your sins are forgiven,' or to say, 'Get up, take your mat and walk'?" (v.9). Of course, as he meant the words, neither of the two was easier. Both were alike impossible to men and equally easy for God. To the teachers of the law, it was easier to make the statement about forgiveness because who could verify its fulfillment? But to say, "Get up . . . and walk"—that could indeed be verified by an actual healing that could be seen.

10–11 The first half of v.10—"But that you may know that the Son of Man has authority on earth to forgive sins"—is usually understood to be addressed to the scribes. In that case the words "he said to the paralytic" constitute a parenthesis to explain that the following words are addressed not to the teachers of the law but to the paralytic. The change of addressee seems awkward; but, if this is the correct interpretation, presumably Jesus indicated his change by some sort of gesture. Another possibility is to take the entire verse as addressed to Mark's readers. This would not only solve the problem of awkwardness stated above but also the theological one of so early a public use of the title "Son of Man" (for a discussion of "Son of Man," cf. remarks at 8:31). In Mark's Gospel the use of this title seems to be reserved until after the crucial incident of 8:29 (cf. the remarks at 2:28 and also cf. Taylor, pp. 197–98).

The healing verified the claim to grant forgiveness. As sure as actual healing followed Jesus' statement "Get up" (v.11), so actual forgiveness resulted from his "your sins are forgiven." As Hunter (p. 38) says, "He did the miracle which they could see that they might know that he had done the other one that they could not see."

12 The man responded immediately (*euthys*) (not tr. in NIV). The cure was instantaneous. And "in full view of them all" (i.e., the entire crowd and especially the teachers of the law who had challenged Jesus' authority to forgive sins), the ex-paralytic walked out. Again the response of the crowd (the "all" includes the teachers of the law) was one of amazement, and there is the added response of giving praise to God for what had happened. Never before had they seen anything like this.

The significance of this story is not to be understood in terms of Jesus' pity on a helpless cripple that moves him to heal the man's paralyzed body. The emphasis is on the forgiveness of sins. This was at the root of the paralytic's problem, and it was to this that Jesus primarily addressed himself. In his act of forgiveness Jesus was also declaring the presence of God's kingdom among men.

Notes

2 "He preached the word to them" translates ἐλάλει αὐτοῖς τὸν λόγον (*elalei autois ton logon*, lit., "he was speaking to them the word"). *Logon* is here used of the "message of salvation," "the good news," "the gospel" (BAG, p. 479).

2. Eating with sinners

2:13–17

13Once again Jesus went out beside the lake. A large crowd came to him, and he began to teach them. 14As he walked along, he saw Levi son of Alphaeus sitting at the tax collector's booth. "Follow me," Jesus told him, and Levi got up and followed him.

15While Jesus was having dinner at Levi's house, many tax collectors and "sinners" were eating with him and his disciples, for there were many who followed him. 16When the teachers of the law who were Pharisees saw him eating with the "sinners" and tax collectors, they asked his disciples: "Why does he eat with tax collectors and 'sinners'?"

17On hearing this, Jesus said to them, "It is not the healthy who need a doctor, but the sick. I have not come to call the righteous, but sinners."

13 This is the second incident in the series of five in which Jesus comes into conflict with the religious leaders. The incident is introduced by the story of the calling of Levi, the tax collector. The only connecting word Mark uses is *palin* ("once again"), which makes it clear that this is a separate unit of tradition. The scene is the shore of the Sea of Galilee. Jesus' popularity with the crowds was still very evident—"a large crowd came to him, and he began to teach them."

14 Jesus may have done his teaching on this occasion as rabbis often did theirs—"as he walked along." If so, his teaching was interrupted by his encounter with Levi, at the tax collector's booth. This Levi is almost universally identified with Matthew (in the same incident in Matt 9:9, he is called Matthew). Levi was probably his given name and Matthew ("gift of God") his apostolic name. He was employed by Herod Antipas, the tetrarch of Galilee, as a tax collector. A traveler from either Herod Philip's territory or the Decapolis would naturally pass through Capernaum on entering Galilee. Tax collectors were despised by the Jews because they were considered traitors and because they often were, in fact, extortioners.

Jesus found Levi at the "tax collector's booth." This was probably the toll booth on the road that ran from Damascus through Capernaum to the Mediterranean coast. There was much at stake for Levi in accepting Jesus' challenge. Fishermen could easily go back to fishing (as some of the disciples did after Jesus' crucifixion), but for Levi there would be little possibility of his returning to his occupation. Tax collector jobs were greatly sought after as a sure way to get rich quickly.

15–16 The dinner held in Levi's house (v.15) was probably his farewell party since he was leaving to become one of Jesus' disciples, or perhaps he simply wanted to gather his friends together so that they too could have an opportunity to meet Jesus. "Eating with Jesus ['him' NIV]" (*synanekeinto tō Iēsou*) seems to suggest that the tax collectors and sinners were having dinner with Jesus; i.e., he was the host, not Levi! "When this is understood the interest of the entire pericope centers on the significance of Messiah eating with sinners. The specific reference in v.17 to Jesus' call of sinners to the Kingdom suggests that the basis of table-fellowship was *messianic forgiveness*, and the meal itself was an anticipation of the messianic banquet" (Lane, p. 106; emphasis his).

"Sinners" (v.16) denotes those people who refuse to follow the Mosaic Law as interpreted by the Pharisees. That Jesus would include in his most intimate circle a man associated with so disreputable a profession and would sit at table (in the ancient world a sign of intimacy) with tax collectors and "sinners" was too much for the "teachers of the law" to keep quiet about.

These particular teachers of the law were also Pharisees. Little is known of either the origin or the predecessors of this sect. The probability is that they were the successors of the Hasidim, the pious Jews who joined forces with Mattathias and his sons during the Maccabean period. After religious liberty was achieved, they largely deserted the Maccabees in their struggle for political independence. They first appear under the name "Pharisee" during the reign of the Hasmonean John Hyrcanus (135–104 B.C.) (cf. EBC, 1:192).

Josephus says, "The Pharisees [are] a body of Jews with the reputation of excelling the rest of their nation in the observances of religion, and as exact exponents of the laws" (War I, 110 [v.2]). Although many of them were doubtless pious and godly men, those Jesus came into conflict with represented some of the worst elements of traditional religion: jealousy, hypocrisy, and religious formalism. "Pharisaism is the final result of that conception of religion which makes religion consist in conformity to the Law, and promises God's grace only to the doers of the Law" (Metzger, *The New Testament*, p. 41). The consorting of Jesus with people who openly refused to keep the requirements of the law prompted the question "Why does he [supposedly a 'religious' or observant Jew] eat with tax collectors and 'sinners'?"

17 No statement of Jesus in this Gospel is more profound than this one. A doctor ministers not to healthy persons but to the sick. So Jesus came not to call the "righteous" (i.e., the self-righteous) but "sinners" (i.e., not merely people who refuse to carry out the details of the law but those who are alienated from the life of God). Jesus' call is to salvation; and, in order to share in it, there must be a recognition of need. A self-righteous man is incapable of recognizing that need, but a sinner can. "It would be true to say that this word of Jesus strikes the keynote of the Gospel. The new thing in Christianity is not the doctrine that God saves sinners. No Jew would have denied that. It is the assertion 'that God loves and saves them *as sinners*.' . . . This is the authentic and glorious doctrine of true Christianity in any age" (Hunter, pp. 40–41, emphasis his).

3. A question about fasting

2:18–22

> **18**Now John's disciples and the Pharisees were fasting. Some people came and asked Jesus, "How is it that John's disciples and the disciples of the Pharisees are fasting, but yours are not?"

¹⁹Jesus answered, "How can the guests of the bridegroom fast while he is with them? They cannot, so long as they have him with them. ²⁰But the time will come when the bridegroom will be taken from them, and on that day they will fast.

²¹"No one sews a patch of unshrunk cloth on an old garment. If he does, the new piece will pull away from the old, making the tear worse. ²²And no one pours new wine into old wineskins. If he does, the wine will burst the skins, and both the wine and the wineskins will be ruined. No, he pours new wine into new wineskins."

18 In the law only the fast of the Day of Atonement was required (Lev 16:29, 31; 23:27–32; Num 29:7), but after the Exile four other annual fasts were observed by Jews (Zech 7:5; 8:19). In NT times the stricter Pharisees fasted twice a week (Monday and Thursday; cf. Luke 18:12). The phrase "the disciples of the Pharisees" is unique in the NT. It presents some difficulty because the Pharisees as such were not teachers and thus did not have disciples. However, a small number of them were numbered among the scribes (NIV, "teachers of the law") and they did have disciples. Or perhaps the term is used in a nontechnical sense to refer to people who were influenced by the teachings and practice of the Pharisees. It is in this latter sense that the expression "John's disciples" (the Baptist) is also to be understood.

Why these two groups were fasting, Mark does not say. John's disciples may have been fasting because he was in prison at the time, or perhaps they were fasting in anticipation of the Messianic Age. The Pharisees' disciples were probably observing one of the biweekly fasts. In both instances fasting was a sign of true piety. This being the case, "some people" (Mark does not identify them specifically) were asking why Jesus' disciples were not evidencing true religious piety by fasting.

19–20 Jesus answers in a parable. Its great emphasis is on the joy the presence of Jesus makes possible. Therefore fasting—a sign of mourning—is not appropriate. A Jewish wedding feast was a particularly joyous occasion. The guests joined in the celebration that sometimes lasted a week. To fast during that time of great joy and festivity would be unthinkable. Jesus is the bridegroom (v.19) and his disciples the guests. While he remains with them they will rejoice, not fast. However, he will not always be with them. When he is taken away (v.20), fasting will be appropriate.

The mention of the removal of the bridegroom has often been explained as reading the death of Jesus back into the text on the ground that it was unlikely that he would so early have made mention of his death. On this two comments need to be made: (1) the reference to his death is veiled, and he only speaks of the bridegroom being "taken from them" and not specifically of death (though see note on this verse); and (2) we do not know when this incident took place, but it could conceivably have been late in Jesus' ministry.

21–22 These two parables, which occur side by side, were probably spoken on different occasions; but they belong together because they deal with a single theme. Obviously they bear on the question of fasting, but beyond that they also bear on the forms of Judaism generally. In ancient times wine was kept in goatskins. New skins were soft and pliable and would stretch when wine that had not yet completed fermentation was put in them. However, old wineskins that had been stretched would become brittle and, being no longer pliable, were thus unable to stretch. The gas from the fermenting wine burst them open, destroying both wine and wine-skins. Putting new wine into old wineskins (v.22) and patching an old garment with a new cloth (v.21) are just as inappropriate as fasting at a wedding feast. A wedding, new wine, and a new garment are all symbols of the New Age. The main teaching of the parable seems to be that the newness the coming of Jesus brings cannot be confined to the old forms.

Notes

20 'Απαρθῇ (*aparthē*, "will be taken away") is from ἀπαίρω (*apairō*) and occurs in the NT only here and in the parallels in Matthew and Luke. It means "take away," "remove." According to Bratcher and Nida (p. 92), "the verb as such does not state whether the removal is natural, or sudden and violent. The context of the whole saying, however, implies a violent removal which will provoke sorrow (cf. the use of the verb in the LXX Isa 53:8 [where, however, the simple form αἴρω is used])."

4. The Lord of the Sabbath (2:23–3:6)

a. Picking grain on the Sabbath

2:23–28

> 23One Sabbath Jesus was going through the grainfields, and as his disciples walked along, they began to pick some heads of grain. 24The Pharisees said to him, "Look, why are they doing what is unlawful on the Sabbath?"
> 25He answered, "Have you never read what David did when he and his companions were hungry and in need? 26In the days of Abiathar the high priest, he entered the house of God and ate the consecrated bread, which is lawful only for priests to eat. And he also gave some to his companions."
> 27Then he said to them, "The Sabbath was made for man, not man for the Sabbath. 28So the Son of Man is Lord even of the Sabbath."

The specific time or place of this incident is not given. Nor is it clear how it relates to what precedes or what follows except that it is a conflict story. The theme of the incident, not its chronological position in the life of Jesus, is what determined its inclusion at this point in Mark's Gospel. The conflict centers on the keeping of the Sabbath, something far more important in Judaism than the question of fasting.

23–24 The main point at issue was not the act of harvesting the heads of grain (v.23). Such activity as Jesus and his disciples were involved in was explicitly allowed in the law: "If you enter your neighbor's grain field, you may pick kernels with your hands, but you must not put a sickle to his standing grain" (Deut 23:25). What the Pharisees objected to (v.24) was doing this (regarded as reaping) on the Sabbath (cf. M *Shabbath* 7.2, where one of the thirty-nine acts forbidden on the Sabbath was reaping).

25–26 Jesus meets the accusation of the Pharisees with a counterquestion (v.25). The incident he refers to is recorded in 1 Samuel 21:1–6. David and his companions were hungry and ate the consecrated bread—the twelve loaves baked of fine flour, arranged in two rows or piles on the table in the Holy Place. Fresh loaves were brought into the sanctuary each Sabbath to replace the old ones that were then eaten by the priests (cf. Exod 25:30; 35:13; 39:36; Lev 24:5–9; cf. Jos. Antiq. III, 255–56, [x.7]). Although the action of David was contrary to the law, he was not condemned for it. Jesus does not claim that the Sabbath law has not been technically broken but that such violations under certain conditions are warranted. "Human need is a higher law than religious ritualism" (Earle, p. 49).

The problem associated with the phrase *epi Abiathar archiereōs* is well known (v.26). If it means "at the time when Abiathar was high priest," it is incorrect historically. At the time the incident occurred, Ahimelech, Abiathar's father, was high priest; and it was from him David received the consecrated bread. The difficulty is revealed by the fact that neither Matthew nor Luke records the phrase in the parallel passages, and it is not found in several MSS. In some MSS a definite article is inserted before "high priest." This would make possible the translation "in the time of Abiathar, the one who [later] became high priest." It is this reconstruction that NIV's "in the days of" reflects. Another possibility is to translate the preposition *epi* "in the account of," as is done in Mark 12:26 (*epi tou batou*, "in the account of the bush"). None of these solutions is entirely satisfactory. The OT itself seems to confuse Ahimelech and Abiathar (cf. 1 Sam 22:20 with 2 Sam 8:17; 1 Chron 18:16; 24:6).

27–28 The pronouncement is preceded by the phrase "Then he said to them" (v.27). Since this seems to be a literary device used by Mark (cf. 4:2b, 11, 21, 24, 26; 6:10; 7:9; 8:21; 9:1) to insert into the account an independent saying of Jesus that is relevant to the subject at hand, it seems best so to regard the pronouncement here. The larger context out of which this authentic saying of Jesus came is not given; but the crucial line is given, and that fact has special relevance to the controversy. To Jesus the Sabbath was not created for its own sake; it was a gift of God to man. Its purpose was not to put man in a kind of straight jacket. It was for his good—to provide rest from labor and opportunity for worship. Jesus' pronouncement was not as radical for his day as some would think. Rabbi Simeon ben Menasya (c. A.D. 180) said, "The Sabbath has been committed to you and not you to the Sabbath" (Melkilta *Shabbata* 1 to Exod 31:14).

The big question in v.28 is whether this is a statement of Mark about Jesus or of Jesus about himself. The question is not whether Jesus claims to be Son of Man in Mark's Gospel. That he does this is abundantly clear from such texts as 8:31, 38; 9:9, 12, 31; 10:33; 13:26; 14:21 (bis), 41, 62. But does he claim it here? If v.27 is a separate saying of Jesus inserted by Mark to climax the teaching of Jesus about the Sabbath, then it seems best to regard this verse as Mark's comment to the church, after the same pattern as 2:10. If taken as spoken by Mark of Jesus, the pronouncement is no less true. "Since the Sabbath was made for man, He who is man's Lord . . . has authority to determine its law and use" (Taylor, p. 219).

b. Healing on the Sabbath

3:1–6

¹Another time he went into the synagogue, and a man with a shriveled hand was there. ²Some of them were looking for a reason to accuse Jesus, so they

watched him closely to see if he would heal him on the Sabbath. ³Jesus said to the man with the shriveled hand, "Stand up in front of everyone."

⁴Then Jesus asked them, "Which is lawful on the Sabbath: to do good or to do evil, to save life or to kill?" But they remained silent.

⁵He looked around at them in anger and, deeply distressed at their stubborn hearts, said to the man, "Stretch out your hand." He stretched it out, and his hand was completely restored. ⁶Then the Pharisees went out and began to plot with the Herodians how they might kill Jesus.

1 This is the last in a series of five conflict stories. Again Mark gives no details of time or geographical location. It is simply another incident out of Jesus' life used to show what his attitude toward the Sabbath was. The story takes place in a synagogue where there is a man with a "shriveled hand." Apparently some sort of paralysis is meant.

2 Mark does not specifically identify the opposition here. Though he uses the indefinite "some," the identity is nonetheless clear (cf. v.6, where the Pharisees are mentioned; cf. also Luke 6:7, which says that they were the "Pharisees and the teachers of law"). Since Jesus had already raised suspicions in their mind because of his unorthodox actions, these men were present in the synagogue, not to worship God, but to spy on Jesus ("they watched him closely"). They "were looking for a reason to accuse Jesus." The statement "to see if he would heal him on the Sabbath" makes it clear that the Pharisees were convinced of Jesus' power to perform miracles. The issue was not "could he" but "would he?" Rabbinic law allowed healing on the Sabbath only in the event that life was actually in danger (cf. SBK, 1:623).

3–4 Jesus was fully aware of the designs of the opposition. Instead of acting carefully in the situation, he commanded the man to stand up and come to "center stage" so that all in the synagogue could see what he was going to do to him (v.3). There is no secrecy motif here!

No question had been asked Jesus by the religious leaders, but he knew what was racing through their minds. So he asked them, "Which is lawful on the Sabbath: to do good or to do evil, to save life or to kill?" (v.4). Several interpretations of Jesus' statement are possible.

1. Calvin (2:54) took it to mean that "there is little difference between manslaughter and the conduct of him who does not concern himself about relieving a person in distress."

2. The will of God is served better by saving (i.e., restoring to health) a life than by plotting to kill (as the Pharisees were doing; cf. v.6).

3. There may be a hint here of Jesus' mission to destroy the works of Satan. Disease and disfigurement are ultimately Satan's works. Jesus came to destroy these; and, since evil works seven days a week, "the warfare against Satan must go on on the Sabbath as well as on the other six days" (T.W. Manson, *The Sayings of Jesus* [Cambridge: Cambridge University Press, 1937], p. 190). The Pharisees were silent. They refused to debate the issue with Jesus.

5 Anger is rarely directly attributed to Jesus. The only other place in the Gospels he is said to be angry is in the reading rejected by the NIV in Mark 1:41. His anger was real, but it was never the expression of injured self-concern. It was more like "righteous indignation"—what a good man feels in the presence of stark evil. Such anger was particularly appropriate to this situation. But even such justifiable anger was couched in compassion. The tenses of the verbs are important here. The looking "around at them in anger" was momentary (aorist tense), but the being "deeply distressed" was continuous (present tense). Jesus' distress was caused by their "stubborn hearts," i.e., their consistent failure to recognize who he really was. "Their opposition rested on a fundamental misunderstanding—an inability, or refusal, to see that Jesus was God's eschatological agent and that his sovereign freedom with regard to law and custom sprang from that fact" (Nineham, p. 110).

When Jesus ordered the man to stretch out his hand, he obeyed; and it was instantly and completely restored.

6 "The consequence of the healing was neither surprise or acclamation, but increased enmity" (H. Van der Loos, *The Miracles of Jesus* [Leiden: Brill, 1965], p. 438). The Pharisees, joined now by the Herodians, began to plot Jesus' death. Although it is not clear who the Herodians were, it seems fairly certain that they were neither a religious sect nor a political party. The term probably refers to influential Jews who were friends and backers of the Herodian family. This meant, of course, that they were supporters of Rome, from which the Herods received their authority. They joined the Pharisees in opposition to Jesus because they feared he might be an unsettling political influence in Palestine.

Notes

5 "He looked around" translates περιβλεψάμενος (*periblepsamenos*) and is one of many eyewitness details in Mark's Gospel (cf. 3:34; 5:32; 9:8; 10:23; 11:11).

III. The Later Galilean Ministry (3:7–6:13)

A summary statement (3:7–12) begins this new section of Mark's Gospel, and it ends with the sending out of the Twelve (6:6b–13). In between are two obvious sections: parables about the kingdom (4:1–34) and miracles of Jesus' power over hostile powers (4:35–5:43). In addition there are several units that deal with hostility and rejection (3:20–30, 31–35; 6:1–6a), and there is a brief account of the selection of the Twelve (3:13–19). The fact that the renown of Jesus reaches the Jerusalem authorities, who send their representatives up to Galilee to observe what was going on, suggests an advanced stage in the ministry of Jesus, as does the sending out of the Twelve. Most of the action takes place in the vicinity of the Sea of Galilee.

A. Withdrawal to the Lake

3:7–12

> [7]Jesus withdrew with his disciples to the lake, and a large crowd from Galilee followed. [8]When they heard all he was doing, many people came to him from Judea, Jerusalem, Idumea, and the regions across the Jordan and around Tyre

and Sidon. [9]Because of the crowd he told his disciples to have a small boat ready for him, to keep the people from crowding him. [10]For he had healed many, so that those with diseases were pushing forward to touch him. [11]Whenever the evil spirits saw him, they fell down before him and cried out, "You are the Son of God." [12]But he gave them strict orders not to tell who he was.

7 Why did Jesus withdraw? Mark does not say, but Matthew's use of the participle *gnous* ("knowing," i.e., about the plot to kill him) in 12:15 makes it clear that Jesus left wherever he had been (Capernaum?) because he realized that the religious authorities were determined to get him. Since the time had not yet come for a serious confrontation, he withdrew to the Lake of Genessaret. This withdrawal, however, did not separate him from the crowds.

8 The crowds that came to Jesus were not only from the regions in the vicinity of Capernaum but also from the south (Jerusalem, Idumea), the east (across the Jordan), and the northwest (Tyre and Sidon). Mark includes the whole of Jewish Palestine. Schweizer (p. 79) points out that "to some extent, the locations named form an outline of the Gospel of Mark, since Jesus is active in Galilee (chs. 1–6); Tyre, Sidon and Decapolis (ch. 7); and finally beyond the Jordan and in Jerusalem (chs. 10ff.)." The only territory mentioned here in which Jesus was not active is Idumea, the area south of Hebron.

Some of the geographical terms in this verse require comment. Idumea was invaded and conquered, after the destruction of Jerusalem in 587 B.C., by the Edomites who came from the east and settled there. Judas Maccabeus had several successful campaigns against the Idumeans, and during the reign of John Hyrcanus they were forced to adopt Judaism. Herod the Great was an Idumean, and several of his sons played important roles in the political history of Palestine. "Tyre and Sidon" are terms used virtually interchangeably for the northwestern area of Palestine. The "regions across the Jordan" probably included Perea and the Decapolis, both of which were under the political control of Herod Antipas, as was Galilee.

9–10 Only Mark includes the detail about the boat (v.9). Its purpose was, of course, to provide escape for Jesus in case the crowd began to get unruly. The picture is that of great numbers of people pressing forward just to touch Jesus in the hope that by doing so they might be healed (v.10). The crowd seems to have had little interest in Jesus other than as a miracle-worker. Despite this, he graciously healed many of them.

11–12 Here again Jesus comes into conflict with the demonic (v.11). The evil spirits recognized who Jesus was—even if the crowds did not. Their crying out "You are the Son of God" is best understood as a "futile attempt to render him harmless. These cries of recognition were designed to control him and to strip him of his power, in accordance with the conception that knowledge of the precise name or quality of a person confers mastery over him" (Lane, p. 130). "Son of God" in this context is a true designation of who Jesus is, expressed by his bitter foes, the demons. Jesus silenced the outcries of the demons (v.12) because the time for the clear revelation of who he was had not yet come, and the demons were hardly appropriate heralds of him.

Notes

7 The word translated "withdrew" is ἀνεχώρησεν (*anechōrēsen*), used only here in Mark. It is not clear whether it contains the idea of forced withdrawal or not. MM (p. 40) give examples of it from the papyri meaning "take refuge."

B. *Selection of the Twelve*

3:13–19

[13]Jesus went up on a mountainside and called to him those he wanted, and they came to him. [14]He appointed twelve—designating them apostles—that they might be with him and that he might send them out to preach [15]and to have authority to drive out demons. [16]These are the twelve he appointed: Simon (to whom he gave the name Peter); [17]James son of Zebedee and his brother John (to them he gave the name Boanerges, which means Sons of Thunder); [18]Andrew, Philip, Bartholomew, Matthew, Thomas, James son of Alphaeus, Thaddaeus, Simon the Zealot [19]and Judas Iscariot, who betrayed him.

13 Lightfoot has a suggestive interpretation of the significance of the appointing of the Twelve. He understands the withdrawal of 3:7 as a withdrawal from the synagogue (the only other reference in Mark's Gospel to Jesus in the synagogue is in 6:2):

After withdrawing from the synagogue . . . he first meets a great multitude of enthusiastic followers on the shore of the lake, and proceeds to make a selection from them, with whom He withdraws to the high ground; and we then read of the appointment of the twelve, and a list is given of their names. We may see here, if we choose, the foundation of the new Israel, Israel after the flesh having proved itself unworthy." (p. 39)

Luke (6:12) says that Jesus spent a night in prayer before choosing the Twelve. Although literally *eis to oros* means "into the mountain," it is best to understand it to mean the hill country of Galilee near the lake. It was there that Jesus called "those he wanted," and they came to him. No delay in their response is indicated (cf. 1:18, 20; 2:14).

14–15 It may be (contra Lightfoot above) that the Twelve Jesus appointed (v.14) were the same he called in v.13. At any rate, from this point on there seem to be no persons designated "disciples" in Mark's Gospel other than the Twelve (cf. R.P. Meye, *Jesus and the Twelve* [Eerdmans: Grand Rapids, 1968], passim). The words "designating them apostles" entail textual problems and may not be original in Mark's Gospel. (UBS's apparatus assigns this a "C" rating, indicating considerable doubt as to its authenticity.) There can be little doubt that the number twelve has theological significance. The Twelve represent the new Israel in embryo.

The purpose for which the Twelve were appointed was twofold: (1) "that they might be with him"; (2) "that he might send them out to preach and to have authority to drive out demons." The Twelve were to be brought into the closest association possible with the life of the Son of God. They were to live with Jesus, travel with him, converse with him, and learn from him. Mark's Gospel indicates that much of Jesus' time was occupied with their training. The training was not an end in itself. They were to be sent out (in Mark's Gospel not until 6:7). And their ministry was to consist of preaching the Good News and driving out demons (v.15). The two are closely associated. The salvation Jesus brings involves the defeat of Satan and his demons.

16-19 There are three other lists of the apostles in the NT (Matt 10:2-4; Luke 6:14-16; Acts 1:13). The names of the Twelve as given in these lists naturally divide into four parts. Peter heads the three other names in the first section; Philip heads the second section; James the Son of Alphaeus (called "the Less" in Matthew) the third; the last section consists of the name of Judas (except in Acts since he had already committed suicide). Simon's nickname "the rock" (Peter) was given him by Jesus (v.16; cf. Matt 16:18). Why Jesus gave it to him is not clear since Peter is depicted in the Gospel narrative as anything but a rock. Perhaps Jesus saw in Peter, unreliable and fickle though he was, the potential for being firm and confident (cf. on Matt 16:18, this commentary).

James and John, the sons of Zebedee, were nicknamed "Sons of Thunder" (v.17). This was probably descriptive of their disposition; it had something of the thunderstorm in it. Since Bartholomew (v.18) is not a personal name but a patronymic, meaning "son of Talmai," he probably had another name (Nathaniel? cf. John 1:45). Matthew is doubtless to be identified with Levi (2:14), but Mark makes no point of it. Thaddaeus is probably the Judas son of James of Luke's lists (Luke 6:16; Acts 1:13). Simon is called "the Zealot." This may simply be a description of his religious zeal; but it is more likely a reference to his membership in the party of the Zealots, a Jewish sect bent on the overthrow at all costs of the Roman control of Palestine. Judas's surname is given as Iscariot (v.19), which probably means "the man from the place called Karioth." Karioth (Kerioth) is identified either with Kerioth Hezron (Josh 15:25), twelve miles south of Hebron, or with Kerioth in Moab (Jer 48:24). Judas is further identified as the man who betrayed Jesus.

It was a strange group of men our Lord chose to be his disciples. Four of them were fishermen, one a hated tax collector, another a member of a radical and violent political party. Of six of them we know practically nothing. All were laymen. There was not a preacher or an expert in the Scriptures in the lot. Yet it was with these men that Jesus established his church and disseminated his Good News to the end of the earth.

C. *Jesus, His Family, and the Beelzebub Controversy* (3:20-35)

The historicity of this incident can scarcely be denied. The church would not have invented a story that put the family of Jesus into such bad light. In the first verse of this section we are shown that

> ordinary, unprejudiced folk, recognizing (as we may assume) the goodness and God-given character of Jesus' power, flocked to avail themselves of it. In the rest of the section we are shown by contrast how those who might have been expected to share this attitude to the full, Jesus' own family and the religious leaders of the people, not only failed to recognize the true source and character of his actions, but insisted on attributing them to evil sources. (Nineham, p. 119)

Another feature of this section is the insertion of one incident (in this case the Beelzebub controversy) into another (the story of the relationship between Jesus and his family). This is a fairly frequent device in Mark's Gospel (cf. 5:21–43; 6:7–30; 11:12–25; 14:1–11). Mark may use this to heighten the suspense and allow for the passage of time. Lane suggests that in this incident Mark deliberately inserts the Beelzebub controversy between the earlier and later phases of the family narrative: "It suggests that those in Jesus' family who declare that he is mad (Ch. 3:21) are not unlike the scribes who attribute his extraordinary powers to an alliance with Beelzebul, the prince of the demons (Ch. 3:22)" (p. 137).

1. Charged with insanity

3:20–21

> [20]Then Jesus entered a house, and again a crowd gathered, so that he and his disciples were not even able to eat. [21]When his family heard about this, they went to take charge of him, for they said, "He is out of his mind."

20–21 Jesus again was being pressed by the crowds. The house (probably Peter and Andrew's; cf. 1:29) was so packed with people demanding his attention that both he and his disciples were prevented from eating (v.20). When Jesus' family heard that he was so engrossed by his work that he failed even to care for his physical needs, they decided to go to Jesus and "take charge of him" (v.21). This probably means that they wanted to take him back to Nazareth. This would remove him from the strain of having so many people constantly pressing on him to meet their physical and spiritual needs. The verb translated "take charge" is *kratēsai* and is used of arresting someone in 6:17; 12:12; 14:1, 44, 46, 49, and 51. The reason Jesus' family wanted to do this was because they feared that overwork had affected him mentally —he was "out of his mind." These are shocking words, but as C.L. Mitton says, "If they reveal his family's failure to understand him, they are also a measure of their concern for him" (*The Gospel According to Mark* [London: Epworth, 1957], p. 26).

2. Charged with demon possession

3:22–30

> [22]And the teachers of the law who came down from Jerusalem said, "He is possessed by Beelzebub! By the prince of demons he is driving out demons." [23]So Jesus called them and spoke to them in parables: "How can Satan drive out Satan? [24]If a kingdom is divided against itself, that kingdom cannot stand. [25]If a house is divided against itself, that house cannot stand. [26]And if Satan opposes himself and is divided, he cannot stand; his end has come. [27]In fact, no one can enter a strong man's house and carry off his possessions unless he first ties up the strong man. Then he can rob his house. [28]I tell you the truth, all the sins and blasphemies of men will be forgiven them. [29]But whoever blasphemes against the Holy Spirit will never be forgiven; he is guilty of an eternal sin." [30]He said this because they were saying, "He has an evil spirit."

Jesus' family was located in Nazareth. Jesus himself at this time was probably in Capernaum; so his family had to travel to Capernaum to get him and take him home. To allow for this time, Mark fills in the gap with the Beelzebub controversy.

22 The teachers of the law had come down from Jerusalem ("down" because Jerusalem was located at a higher elevation than Capernaum). This is a strong indication that the word about Jesus was spreading and was causing concern in high places. Their analysis of Jesus' condition was "he is possessed by Beelzebub!" (cf. John 10:20: "He is demon-possessed and raving mad"). Mark gives no account of the healing of the blind-and-dumb demoniac that prompted this statement (cf. Matt 12:22; Luke 11:14). Beelzebub is "the prince of demons," i.e., Satan. The further accusation is that Jesus and Satan are in collusion with each other.

23–27 Jesus replies to the charge "in parables" (v.23), which in this context means by making a comparison or by speaking proverbially. His argument is as follows: I have just cast out demons. Now if I am doing this by Satan's power, then Satan is actually working against himself. But that would be absurd. Just as a house (v.25) or a kingdom (v.24) cannot stand if it is divided against itself or opposes itself, so Satan will bring about his own destruction by working against himself (v.26). Furthermore, in order to enter the house of a strong man and plunder it, one must first tie up the strong man (v.27).

Two obvious conclusions may be drawn from the "parables": (1) Jesus cannot be in collusion with Satan; and (2) Jesus is actually destroying Satan's work, which means he is more powerful than Satan. The teachers of the law should have had the spiritual discernment to recognize something as obvious as this.

In v.27 it may be that *ta skeuē autou* ("his possessions") is a reference to people in bondage to Satan. Then the tying up of Satan is a reference to the coming of Jesus Christ into the world to deliver from bondage those under Satan's control. However, though "tied," Satan is on a long chain and will not be finally defeated till the End.

28–30 The pronouncement Jesus makes is meant to be a solemn one: "I tell you the truth" (v.28). Forgiveness is available for all the sins and blasphemies of men, except one. That exception is blasphemy against the Holy Spirit (v.29). What is that sin?

Verse 30—"because they were saying, 'He has an evil spirit'"—suggests an explanation for the unforgivable sin. Jesus had done what any unprejudiced person would have acknowledged as a good thing. He had freed an unfortunate man from the power and bondage of evil (cf. Matt 12:22; Luke 11:14). This he did through the power of the Holy Spirit, but the teachers of the law ascribed it to the power of Satan. Taylor (p. 244) says that the sin described here is "a perversion of spirit which, in defiance of moral values elects to call light darkness." Further, Mitton says, "To call what is good evil (Isa 5:20) when you know well that it is good, because prejudice and ill will hold you in bondage, that is the worst sin of all. The tragedy of the 'hardening of heart' (as in 3:5) is that it makes men capable of committing just this sin" (*Gospel of Mark*, p. 28).

The words of v.29—"will never be forgiven; he is guilty of an eternal sin"—have caused great anxiety and pain in the history of the church. Many have wondered whether they have committed the "unpardonable sin." Surely what Jesus is speaking of here is not an isolated act but a settled condition of the soul—the result of a long history of repeated and willful acts of sin. And if the person involved cannot be forgiven it is not so much that God refuses to forgive as it is the sinner refuses to allow him. Ryle's famous words are great reassurance to any who might be anxious about this sin: "There is such a thing as a sin which is never forgiven. But those who are troubled about it are most unlikely to have committed it" (J.C. Ryle, *Expository Thoughts on the Gospels* [New York: Revell], 2:59). On the other hand, those who actually do commit the sin are so dominated by evil that it is unlikely that they would be aware of it.

3. *Jesus' true family*

3:31–35

> [31]Then Jesus' mother and brothers arrived. Standing outside, they sent someone in to call him. [32]A crowd was sitting around him, and they told him, "Your mother and brothers are outside looking for you."
> [33]"Who are my mother and my brothers?" he asked.
> [34]Then he looked at those seated in a circle around him and said, "Here are my mother and my brothers! [35]Whoever does God's will is my brother and sister and mother."

31 Mark now turns back to the family of Jesus. By inserting the account of the Beelzebub controversy, he has both heightened the suspense and allowed for travel time from Nazareth to Capernaum. The family arrived where Jesus was, but they did not enter the place where he was. Instead they stood outside and sent someone in to call him. Specifically, only Jesus' mother (the only reference to her in Mark's Gospel) and his brothers are mentioned. Joseph is not mentioned. Presumably he was not living at this time.

32–34 When Jesus was told that his mother and his brothers were looking for him (v.32), he responded by asking the queston, "Who are my mother and my brothers?" (v.33). Then with a sweep of his eyes over those seated in a circle around him, he identified his true family: "Here are my mother and my brothers" (v.34). This statement probably included only the Twelve, who were seated nearest to Jesus. They had responded to his call to be with him. There were now spiritual ties between him and them that were far closer than blood ties.

35 Jesus' true family is not limited to the Twelve. It includes all who obey the will of God. It can easily be imagined what this statement meant to the original readers of Mark's Gospel. "In place of broken family relations, ostracism and persecution, was the close and intimate relation to the Son of God" (Grant, p. 694). In view of the Jewish attitude toward one's parents—an attitude adopted by the church—the authenticity of vv.31–35 is unimpeachable.

D. *Parables About the Kingdom of God* (4:1–34)

This is one of the few sections in Mark's Gospel devoted to teaching. Although Mark frequently shows us Jesus teaching (1:21; 2:13; 6:2, 6), only here and in 13: 2–37—and perhaps in 7:1–13—does he give any sustained account of the content of his teaching.

Chapter 4 contains four of Jesus' parables: the parable of the sower and its interpretation (vv.1–20), the parable of the lamp (vv.21–25), the parable of the secretly growing seed (vv.26–29), and the parable of the mustard seed (vv.30–32). Parables are the most striking feature in the teaching of Jesus. Although he did not invent this form of teaching (parables are found both in the OT and in the writings of the rabbis), he used it in a way and to a degree unmatched before his time or since.

The Sunday school definition of a parable—"an earthly story with a heavenly meaning"—is good as far as it goes. Many parables are stories taken out of ordinary life, used to drive home a spiritual or moral truth. But they are not always stories. Sometimes they are brief similes, comparisons, analogies, or even proverbial sayings. The Greek word *parabolē* (lit., "something placed along side") includes all these meanings. The word most often used in the OT is *māšal*. This can include anything from a simple metaphor to an elaborate story.

For centuries parables were interpreted allegorically; i.e., each element of the story was assigned a specific meaning. Thus Augustine found in the parable of the Good Samaritan references to Adam, Jerusalem, the Devil and his angels, the Law and the Prophets, and Christ and the church! Now we are more apt to look for the one main point a parable teaches. This is not to say that all Jesus' parables have only one point to make. Some clearly have more than one, but the principle is a generally valid one. We have also learned (from Dodd and Jeremias) that the teaching found in the parables is more than general religious truth. It is always related in a dynamic way to Jesus' message and mission, i.e., to the life situation of his ministry. This does not mean, of course, that the meaning of the parables are bound to the historical and theological situation of first-century Palestine. Like all Scripture, the parables contain truth relevant for God's people everywhere—those of the twentieth-century world as well as those of the first-century world.

1. Parable of the sower

4:1–9

¹Again Jesus began to teach by the lake. The crowd that gathered around him was so large that he got into a boat and sat in it out on the lake, while all the people were along the shore at the water's edge. ²He taught them many things by parables, and in his teaching said: ³"Listen! A farmer went out to sow his seed. ⁴As he was scattering the seed, some fell along the path, and the birds came and ate it up. ⁵Some fell on rocky places, where it did not have much soil. It sprang up quickly, because the soil was shallow. ⁶But when the sun came up, the plants were scorched, and they withered because they had no root. ⁷Other seed fell among thorns, which grew up and choked the plants, so that they did not bear grain. ⁸Still other seed fell on good soil. It came up, grew and produced a crop, multiplying thirty, sixty, or even a hundred times."

⁹Then Jesus said, "He who has ears to hear, let him hear."

1–2 Mark gives us no information as to when the situation in which Jesus spoke this parable took place but uses the indefinite "again" (v.1). The place was by the Lake of Galilee. The presence of the large crowd shows Jesus' popularity as a teacher. In fact, the crowd was so large that he found it convenient to use a small boat pushed out from the shore as his lectern (actually he sat while teaching). Whether the boat mentioned here is the same one "made ready" for him (3:9) is uncertain; if it is, the teaching reported in chapter 4 may have been given on that occasion and is only summarized in 3:9–11. What is contained in 4:1–34 is only part of Jesus' teaching in parables; for Mark says, "He taught them many things by parables" (v.2).

3–9 The parable of the "sower" (*ho speirōn;* NIV, "farmer") begins and ends with a call for careful attention. This suggests that its meaning may not be self-evident. Alert minds are needed to comprehend its truth. The background of the parable is rural life in Palestine. Seed was sown in broadcast fashion (v.3). The sower deliberately sowed it on the path (v.4), in rocky places (v.5), and among the thorns (v.7) because sowing preceded plowing. However, if plowing was delayed for any time at all, the consequences Jesus mentioned inevitably resulted.

The great emphasis in the parable is on the act of sowing the seed rather than on the soils into which it is sown. "The Kingdom of God breaks into the world even as seed which is sown on the ground. In the details about the soils there is reflection on the diversity of response to the proclamation of the Word of God, but this is not the primary consideration" (Lane, p. 154). Although difficulties face God's kingdom, it grows and ultimately produces an abundant harvest (v.8). This is no self-evident truth; so "he who has ears to hear, let him hear" (v.9), or as Moule paraphrases it: "Now think that one out for yourself, if you can!" (*Gospel of Mark*, p. 35).

2. Secret of the kingdom of God

4:10–12

> [10]When he was alone, the Twelve and the others around him asked him about the parables. [11]He told them, "The secret of the kingdom of God has been given to you. But to those on the outside everything is said in parables [12]so that,
>
> > " 'they may be ever seeing but never perceiving,
> > and ever hearing but never understanding;
> > otherwise they might turn and be forgiven!' "

10 The question about the parables must have been, in view of the answer given by Jesus, directed toward their purpose in his teaching. The plural "parables" is used because more is in view in Jesus' answer than the parable of the sower. Jesus had spoken other parables, and the disciples were inquiring into the purpose of parables generally. Mention is made of "others around him." These are followers of Jesus whom Mark distinguishes from the Twelve. This indicates that Jesus' teaching is not narrowly limited to the Twelve. He is no gnostic revealer whose esoteric teaching is only for the fortunate few. He came to reveal the truth to all who were open to receive it.

11–12 These verses are among the most difficult in the entire Gospel. It is important to look carefully at the terminology. The word translated "secret" (v.11) is *mystērion*. Although it occurs only here and in the parallels (Matt 13:11; Luke 8:10) in the Gospels, Paul uses it frequently in his epistles (twenty-one times); and it is found in the Book of Revelation four times (1:20; 10:7; 17:5, 7). In the NT it does not mean something only for the initiated few. The emphasis is on God's disclosure to man of what was previously unknown. It is proclaimed to all, but only those who have faith really understand. Here in Mark the mystery is the disclosure that the kingdom of God has drawn near in the person of Jesus Christ, or perhaps as G.E. Ladd suggests, the mystery "is that the Kingdom that is to come finally in apocalyptic power, as foreseen in Daniel, has in fact entered into the world in advance in a hidden form to work secretly within and among men" (*A Theology of the New Testament* [Grand Rapids: Eerdmans, 1974], p. 94).

The secret has been given to the disciples because they have responded in faith, but to "those on the outside" (i.e., men hardened by unbelief; cf. ch. 3), "all things," i.e., the entire significance of Jesus' person and mission, are "in parables." Here the word *parabolē* takes on the meaning of "riddle," a meaning well within the range of the word.

12 The introductory conjunction (*hina,* "so that") is Mark's. The quotation that follows is from Isa. 6:9–10, which in the MT is a command; this is not surprising, since in Semitic thought a command may be used to express a result.

Mark follows the LXX text. However, he omits the strong statements of the first part of v.10: "Make the heart of this people calloused, make their ears dull, and close their eyes," and changes the LXX's "and I heal them" (*kai iaomai autous*) to "and be forgiven" (*kai aphethē autois*). In doing this, Mark follows the Targum—an indication of the authenticity of the statement.

Taken at face value, the statement seems to be saying that the purpose of parables is that unbelievers ("those on the outside," v.11) may not receive the truth and be converted. That this statement was thought to be difficult theologically may be seen in Matthew's change of *hina* ("in order that") to *hoti* ("with the result that" NIV translates *hina* with the ambiguous, "so that"), and in Luke's dropping of the *mēpote* ("otherwise") clause.

Several recent attempts have been made to weaken the telic force of *hina:*

1. It is held that *hina* is used in the text to mean the same thing as *hoti.* Thus Jesus is not speaking of the purpose of parables but their result.

2. Mark has mistranslated the original Aramaic word *de.* It means "who," not "in order that." Thus the text should read, "The secret of the kingdom of God has been given to you. But to those on the outside *who* are ever seeing but never perceiving . . . everything is said in parables" (emphasis mine).

3. The purposive idea (expressed both by *hina* and *mēpote*) is not authentic with Jesus but represents Mark's theology.

4. *Hina* is an introductory formula to the free translation of Isa. 6:9–10. On this understanding *hina* would be almost equivalent to *hina plērōthē,* "in order that it might be fulfilled."

All of these attempts have their defects. Although 1 and 2 alleviate the problem of *hina,* they do not address that of *mēpote* ("otherwise"), which also suggests purpose (also cf. BAG, p. 378, which after discussing the possibility of *hina* meaning "with the result that," flatly rejects it for this passage). Solution 3 has no support at all, while 4, clearly the best choice of the four, founders on the fact that Mark elsewhere does not use *hina* to mean "in order that it might be fulfilled."

Perhaps the best way to understand v.12 is as an authentic saying that simply teaches that one reason Jesus taught in parables was to conceal the truth to "outsiders" (which I take to mean "persistent unbelievers"). Even a cursory reading of the Gospels reveals that Jesus' parables were not always clear. The disciples themselves had difficulty understanding (cf. Mark 7:17). So Jesus taught in parables (at least on some occasions) so that his enemies might not be able to comprehend the full significance of his words and bring false accusations or charges against him. He knew that in some cases understanding would result in more sin and not in accepting the truth. Furthermore, it is not foreign to the teaching of Scripture that God in his wisdom hardens some (again, I understand these to be "persistent unbelievers") in order to carry out his sovereign purposes (cf. Rom. 11:25–32). Marshall strikes a good balance when he says, "By this method of teaching in parables Jesus not only invited his audiences to penetrate below the surface and find the real meaning; at the same time he allowed them the opportunity—which many of them took—of turning a blind eye and a deaf ear to the real point at issue" (*Commentary on Luke*, p. 323). For an in-depth treatment of the purpose of parables in the teaching of Jesus, cf. R. Stein, *An Introduction to the Parables of Jesus* (Philadelphia: Westminster, 1981), pp. 25–35.

3. Interpretation of the parable of the sower

4:13–20

> [13]Then Jesus said to them, "Don't you understand this parable? How then will you understand any parable? [14]The farmer sows the word. [15]Some people are like seed along the path, where the word is sown. As soon as they hear it, Satan comes and takes away the word that was sown in them. [16]Others, like seed sown on rocky places, hear the word and at once receive it with joy. [17]But since they have no root, they last only a short time. When trouble or persecution comes because of the word, they quickly fall away. [18]Still others, like seed sown among thorns, hear the word; [19]but the worries of this life, the deceitfulness of wealth and the desires for other things come in and choke the word, making it unfruitful. [20]Others, like seed sown on good soil, hear the word, accept it, and produce a crop—thirty, sixty or even a hundred times what was sown.

Many modern scholars reject this passage as authentic because it allegorizes the parable. It is thought to be the work of the early church rather than the authentic teaching of Jesus. This is a good example of allowing unproved presuppositions to dominate exegesis: Jesus never used allegory; this is allegory; therefore it must not be from Jesus. The logic is sound, but the presupposition is faulty. Moule's word is to the point: "There is no evidence that Jesus never used allegory; and this is such a good and natural allegory, in which each point is itself a quite straightforward miniature parable, that Jesus may well have used it" (*Gospel of Mark*, p. 36). There is nothing in the interpretation of the parable that is contrary to the teachings of Jesus. Thus there is no reason to reject it as not having come from him.

13 There is a slight rebuke in Jesus' statement. The implication is that the meaning of the parable of the sower was clear and understandable. If the disciples could not understand this clear parable, how would they understand more obscure ones? Cranfield comments, "The blindness of men is so universal that even the disciples are not exempt from it" (*Gospel of Mark*, p. 97).

14–15 The "farmer" (v. 14), though not specifically identified here, is Christ himself; and the "word" is the word of the kingdom (cf. Matt 13:19), i.e., the coming of the reign of God in the person and work of Jesus. Whereas in the parable itself the emphasis is on the sowing of the word, in the interpretation it is on its reception. This must be understood in the historical setting of the parable in the ministry of Jesus. Jesus had already received negative responses to his proclamation (chs. 2–3). Mark clearly contrasts the belief of the disciples with "those on the outside" (4:11).

In the interpretation of the parable, Jesus describes in more detail the kind of reception the word of the kingdom receives. By some it receives a shallow reception. They are like seed sown on the hard-beaten path (v.15). Satan snatches the word from them before it has had an opportunity to take root.

16–17 Another hindrance to proper reception of the word is to be found in persecution and trials. This word of Jesus must have been particularly relevant to the Roman church and probably sounded a warning to any who, because of persecution and trials, may have been thinking of defecting from the faith. Those who do defect have no root in "themselves" (Gr.); they are "like seed sown on rocky places" (v.16). The word translated "fall away" (v.17) is *skandalizomai*. A *skandalon* was originally a stick placed in a trap or snare that, when touched by an animal, caused the trap to spring. In the NT it means "cause to stumble" or "fall away."

18–19 The third group of hearers are "like seed sown among thorns" (v.18). At first they seem to make good progress, but the word is choked out by "the worries of this life" (v.19)—a reference to whatever distracts people from the really important things—what Taylor (p. 260) calls "anxiety arising out of the times"; by "the deceitfulness of wealth"—deceitful because it gives to its possessor a false sense of security —a problem particularly evident in society today; and "the desires for other things" —an all-inclusive statement that includes everything that would choke out the sown word and prevent it from being productive.

20 Some seed does fall on good soil and is productive. The kind of person spoken of here is open and receptive to the word of the kingdom. He is neither hard, shallow, nor preoccupied. So the message gets through to him and issues forth in a productive life. In him truth becomes virtue. Moule sums up the meaning of the parable as follows:

> Words may be sound and lively enough, but it is up to each hearer to let them sink in and become fruitful. If he only hears without responding—without doing something about it and committing himself to their meaning—then the words are in danger of being lost, or of never coming to anything. The whole story thus becomes a parable about the learner's responsibility, and about the importance of learning with one's whole will and obedience, and not merely with one's head. (*Gospel of Mark*, p. 36)

Notes

19 Αἰών (aiōn) in αἱ μέριμναι τοῦ αἰῶνος (hai merimnai tou aiōnos, "the worries of this life") means "this age" and is often contrasted in the NT with the "age to come."
NIV translates ἀπάτη (apatē) as "deceitfulness." In Hellenistic Greek it can have the meaning "pleasure" or "delight" and may mean that here (cf. BAG, p. 81).

4. Parables of the lamp and the measure

4:21–25

21He said to them, "Do you bring in a lamp to put it under a bowl or a bed? Instead, don't you put it on its stand? 22For whatever is hidden is meant to be disclosed, and whatever is concealed is meant to be brought out into the open. [23]If anyone has ears to hear, let him hear."

[24]"Consider carefully what your hear," he continued. "With the measure you use, it will be measured to you—and even more. [25]Whoever has will be given more; whoever does not have, even what he has will be taken from him."

The sayings in vv.21–25 occur in different contexts in Matthew and Luke, but in each case they follow Mark's order. This group of sayings seems to be composite, being made up of two trilogies, both introduced by *kai elegen autois* ("and he said to them"). What the original contexts were, we do not know.

21–23 Only Mark has *erchetai* (lit., "does come") speaking of the "lamp" (*lychnos*); and he alone has the definite article (*ho*) before it (v.21). These may be keys for understanding the parable. The lamp represents Jesus who "comes," and the definite article "the" serves to identify him. As the purpose of the lamp is to be put on a lampstand and not under a bowl or a bed, so the present hiddenness of Jesus will not always be—hidden things are meant to be brought out into the open (v.22)—and God intends that one day Jesus will be manifested in all his glory, at the Parousia. But who Jesus really is, is now hidden. It is therefore of utmost importance for us to be careful hearers (v.23), i.e., to have spiritual perception.

24 The second trilogy of parables begins with an exhortation to spiritual perception. The proverb Jesus quotes occurs in other contexts (cf. Matt 7:2; Luke 6:38) with different applications. Here the meaning is that the more one listens to the word of Jesus with spiritual perception and appropriates it, the more the truth about Jesus will be revealed.

25 This proverb also occurs in other contexts (cf. Matt 13:12; 25:29; Luke 19:26). Here the meaning is that the more one appropriates the truth now, the more one will receive in the future (a reference to salvation in the End?); and whoever does not lay hold of the word now, even the little spiritual perception he has will be taken from him.

5. Parable of the secretly growing seed

4:26–29

[26]He also said, "This is what the kingdom of God is like. A man scatters seed on the ground. [27]Night and day, whether he sleeps or gets up, the seed sprouts and grows, though he does not know how. [28]All by itself the soil produces grain— first the stalk, then the head, then the full kernel in the head. [29]As soon as the grain is ripe, he puts the sickle to it, because the harvest has come."

26–29 Only Mark records this parable. Its emphasis is different from the parable of the sower. There the importance of proper soil for the growth of the seed and the success of the harvest is stressed. Here the mysterious power of the seed itself to produce a crop is emphasized.

The parable relates to the kingdom of God (v.26) and, more particularly, how that kingdom grows. All the farmer can do is plant the seed on suitable ground. He cannot make the seed grow. He does not even understand how it grows (v.27). But it does grow, and "all by itself the soil produces grain" (v.28). The point of the parable is as follows: "As seedtime is followed in due time by harvest, so will the present hiddenness and ambiguousness of the kingdom of God be succeeded by its glorious manifestation" (Cranfield, *Gospel of Mark*, p. 168).

A similar emphasis is suggested by J. Jeremias:

> The fruit is the *result* of the seed; the end is implicit in the beginning. The infinitely great is already active in the infinitely small. In the present, and indeed in secret, the event is already in motion. . . . Those to whom it has been given to understand the mystery of the Kingdom (Mark 4:11) see already in its hidden and insignificant beginnings the coming kingdom of God. (*The Parables of Jesus* [London: SCM, 1963], pp. 152–53; emphasis his).

The last part of the parable calls to mind Joel 3:13. The harvest spoken of (v.29) is the eschatological judgment.

6. *Parable of the mustard seed*

4:30–32

> [30]Again he said, "What shall we say the kingdom of God is like, or what parable shall we use to describe it? [31]It is like a mustard seed, which is the smallest seed you plant in the ground. [32]Yet when planted, it grows and becomes the largest of all garden plants, with such big branches that the birds of the air can perch in its shade."

30–32 This is the third and last of the parables about the seed sown. The mustard seed is "the smallest seed you plant in the ground" (v.31). NIV has interpreted the Greek, which really reads "which is smaller than any seed in the ground at its sowing" (NEB). The mustard seed was proverbial for its smallness (cf. SBK, 1:669), but it is not in fact the smallest known seed (e.g., the seed of the black orchid is smaller). Jesus obviously was not giving a lesson in botany. The mustard seed was the smallest seed his audience was familiar with. When grown, it becomes a huge treelike shrub (v.32). I myself have seen one about ten feet high, in front of the monastery on top of Mount Tabor, and another almost that size, near the Pool of Bethesda in Jerusalem.

The main point of the parable is that the kingdom of God (v.30) is like what happens to the mustard seed. It has insignificant and weak beginnings, but a day will come when it will be great and powerful. It is doubtful whether the detail in the parable about the birds taking shelter in the branches of the tree has any significance, though some interpreters see in it a mention of the inclusion of the Gentiles in the kingdom. Nineham (p. 144) makes a general practical application of the truth the parable teaches: "The example of the mustard seed should prevent us from judging the significance of results by the size of the beginnings."

7. *Summary statement on parables*

4:33–34

> [33]With many similar parables Jesus spoke the word to them, as much as they could understand. [34]He did not say anything to them without using a parable. But when he was alone with his own disciples, he explained everything.

33-34 Mark ends this section with its collection of parables with a statement about Jesus' use of them. Parables (here the word has its broad meaning to include similitudes, riddles, etc.) constituted one of Jesus' primary methods of speaking the word (i.e., the word of the kingdom—God's reign revealed in Jesus himself) to "them"— the crowd (v.33). He did this in order to help them understand by means of a veiled confrontation with the truth. It was his gracious means to stimulate their thinking and awaken their spiritual perception. The crowd was not ready for a direct revelation of the truth. In contrast, when Jesus was alone with his disciples (v.34), he could speak more directly with them; but even they needed his explanation to understand.

E. *Triumph Over Hostile Powers* (4:35–5:43)

1. *Calming the storm*

4:35-41

> [35]That day when evening came, he said to his disciples, "Let us go over to the other side." [36]Leaving the crowd behind, they took him along, just as he was, in the boat. There were also other boats with him. [37]A furious squall came up, and the waves broke over the boat, so that it was nearly swamped. [38]Jesus was in the stern, sleeping on a cushion. The disciples woke him and said to him, "Teacher, don't you care if we drown?"
>
> [39]He got up, rebuked the wind and said to the waves, "Quiet! Be still!" Then the wind died down and it was completely calm.
>
> [40]He said to his disciples, "Why are you so afraid? Do you still have no faith?"
>
> [41]They were terrified and asked each other, "Who is this? Even the wind and the waves obey him!"

The calming of the storm on the Lake of Galilee is a classic example of a nature miracle. Miracles of this kind seem to present the greatest problem to contemporary man. The NT, however, makes clear that Jesus Christ is not only Lord over his church but also Lord of all creation. "For by him all things were created: things in heaven and on earth, visible and invisible, whether thrones or powers or rulers or authorities; all things were created by him and for him"(Col 1:16). The Creator-Lord also controls what he has created. "He is before all things, and in him all things hold together" (Col 1:17). It is completely inadequate to explain this miracle of the sovereign Lord by coincidence or to relegate it to myth or imagination. One's conclusion about the historicity of this and similar stories in the Gospels will inevitably depend on one's christology. If Jesus was, as he claimed to be, the strong Son of God, a miracle of this kind is not inconsistent with that claim. If, on the other hand, he was less than God, there is a serious problem.

35-36 Note the details in the story: the mention of the time of day (v.35), the reference to Jesus "just as he was" (v.36), the statement about the "other boats," the position of Jesus in the boat (v.38), the mention of the cushion, the sharp rebuke made by the disciples, and their terror and bewilderment. Taken together these suggest the report of an eyewitness.

Jesus had been teaching the people from a boat pushed out from the shore a short distance (4:1). Evening had come; so Jesus decided to go over to the other side of the lake (v.35). Mark mentions no reason for this decision. Perhaps Jesus simply wanted to escape from the crowds for a little while and renew his strength. The disciples responded to Jesus' request by taking Jesus "just as he was, in the boat" (v.36). This presumably means "without going to shore." That is, Jesus wanted to go directly to the other side of the lake in the same boat he had been teaching the people from and without the delay his first going ashore might have caused.

The mention of "other boats with him" (v.36) seems to be a pointless detail and strongly suggests an eyewitness account. We are not told what happened to the other boats. Perhaps they were lost in the storm or driven back to the western shore of the lake.

37 The geographic location of the Sea of Galilee makes it particularly susceptible to sudden, violent storms. It is situated in a basin surrounded by mountains. Though at night and in the early morning the sea is usually calm, when storms come at those times, they are all the more treacherous. The storm is described as a "furious squall" (*lailaps megalē anemou*) that was driving the waves into the boat so that it was being swamped. Smith's description of the Sea of Galilee's susceptibility to storms is illuminating: "The atmosphere, for the most part, hangs still and heavy, but the cold currents, as they pass from the west, are sucked down in vortices of air, or by the narrow gorges that break upon the lake. Then arise those sudden storms for which the region is notorious" (G.A. Smith, *The Historical Geography of the Holy Land* [New York: Armstrong and Son, 1909], pp. 441–42).

38 Jesus, tired from a long day's teaching, was in the stern of the boat, asleep on a "cushion" (*proskephalaion*). Lagrange (p. 231) says that "in these boats, which will no doubt always have been the same, the place for any distinguished stranger is on the little seat placed at the stern, where a carpet or cushions are arranged." The cushion (the definite article is used) was apparently the only one on board, and Jesus used it as a pillow for his head. This is the only place in the Gospels where Jesus is said to have slept; but he did, of course, get tired and need sleep like any other man. He must have been very tired to have slept through such a violent storm.

The disciples' rebuke of Jesus—"Teacher, are we to drown for all you care?" (Mof)—indicates that they did not know who he really was. Such a rebuke of the Son of God was entirely inappropriate. Both Matthew and Luke eliminate the rebuke. "The rudeness of the Mk form, which is no doubt more original, is an eloquent pointer to the messianic veiledness—the Son of God subject to the rudeness of men" (Cranfield, *Gospel of Mark*, p. 174).

39–40 Jesus rebuked the wind and spoke to the waves. The result was that "the wind died down and it was completely calm" (v.39). The sovereign Lord spoke and his creation immediately responded. Mark alone records the words Jesus used.

Jesus also rebuked his disciples for their lack of faith (v.40). The preferred reading (*oupō*, "not yet"; NIV, "still") indicates that Jesus had expected them by this time to have demonstrated more mature faith. "Faith" here means faith in God's saving power as it is present and active in the person of Jesus. This is the first of several rebukes of the disciples by Jesus for their lack of understanding and faith (cf. 7:18; 8:17–18, 21, 32–33; 9:19).

41 "Were terrified" describes the feeling of awe that came over the disciples as the result of Jesus' mighty act. There was something about him revealed to them on this occasion that they had not experienced before. Thus they raised the rhetorical question "Who is this? Even the wind and the waves obey him!" The implied answer is "He is the strong Son of God."

It is not difficult to imagine what effect this story had on the members of the persecuted Roman church Mark wrote his Gospel for. It assured them that the strong Son of God would go with them into the storm of opposition and trial.

Notes

39 It has often been pointed out that the verbs ἐπιτιμᾶν (epitiman, "to rebuke") and φιμοῦν (phimoun, "to muzzle") are also found in the description of the exorcism of Mark 1:25. Lane (p. 177) sees in the use of these words evidence of "cosmic overtones in Mark's Gospel. The raging storm is an evil "force" threatening Jesus and his disciples. Jesus muzzled it by his sovereign word of authority.

2. Healing the demon-possessed man

5:1–20

¹They went across the lake to the region of the Gerasenes. ²When Jesus got out of the boat, a man with an evil spirit came from the tombs to meet him. ³This man lived in the tombs, and no one could bind him any more, not even with a chain. ⁴For he had often been chained hand and foot, but he tore the chains apart and broke the irons on his feet. No one was strong enough to subdue him. ⁵Night and day among the tombs and in the hills he would cry out and cut himself with stones.

⁶When he saw Jesus from a distance, he ran and fell on his knees in front of him. ⁷He shouted at the top of his voice, "What do you want with me, Jesus, Son of the Most High God? Swear to God that you won't torture me!" ⁸For Jesus had said to him, "Come out of this man, you evil spirit!"

⁹Then Jesus asked him, "What is your name?"

"My name is Legion," he replied, "for we are many." ¹⁰And he begged Jesus again and again not to send them out of the area.

¹¹A large herd of pigs was feeding on the nearby hillside. ¹²The demons begged Jesus, "Send us among the pigs; allow us to go into them." ¹³He gave them permission, and the evil spirits came out and went into the pigs. The herd, about two thousand in number, rushed down the steep bank into the lake and were drowned.

¹⁴Those tending the pigs ran off and reported this in the town and countryside, and the people went out to see what had happened. ¹⁵When they came to Jesus, they saw the man who had been possessed by the legion of demons, sitting there, dressed and in his right mind; and they were afraid. ¹⁶Those who had seen it told the people what had happened to the demon-possessed man—and told about the pigs as well. ¹⁷Then the people began to plead with Jesus to leave their region.

¹⁸As Jesus was getting into the boat, the man who had been demon-possessed begged to go with him. ¹⁹Jesus did not let him, but said, "Go home to your family and tell them how much the Lord has done for you, and how he has had mercy on you." ²⁰So the man went away and began to tell in the Decapolis how much Jesus had done for him. And all the people were amazed.

1 Jesus had demonstrated his power over the forces of nature by stilling the winds and the waves. Now he demonstrates his power over the forces of evil by casting out demons from a possessed man. The two stories go together. They reveal that Jesus is truly divine.

"Across the lake" means on the eastern side. That the population of this region was largely Gentile is shown by the name Decapolis (v.20) and the presence of a large herd of pigs, animals considered unclean by Jews and therefore unfit to eat (Lev 11:7-8).

The name of the place where the miracle was done is disputed. The correct reading in Mark is "the region of the Gerasenes" (so NIV). The textual variants (cf. Notes) arose because Gerasa, located about thirty miles southeast of the lake, seemed too far removed. However, Mark says the "region" of the Gerasenes, and this apparently included the entire district extending down from the city to the lake. Another possibility is that Gerasa is to be identified with the ruins of Kersa (Koursi), a village on the eastern shore. Not far from this site there is a cliff within forty meters of the shore and some old tombs.

2 From this verse it would appear that Jesus, on stepping out of the boat, was immediately confronted by the possessed man. Verse 6 clarifies the situation. The man actually saw Jesus from a distance and came running to him. Since it was already evening (cf. 4:35) when they started across the lake, by the time they reached the other side it was probably dark.

3-5 The possessed man lived in the tombs (v.3). Often in Palestine people were buried in natural caves or in tombs cut out of the limestone rock. These provided good shelter for anyone desiring to live in them. It was a natural place for a possessed man to dwell because of the popular belief that tombs were the favorite haunts of demons. This wretched man had probably been driven from ordinary society into the tombs. Efforts had been made to control him, but without success. Although bound "hand and foot," he had broken the chains; and no one was strong enough to subdue him (v.4). Verses 3-5 "give a vivid picture of the manic stage of a manic depressive psychosis" (Johnson, p. 101).

6 NIV correctly translates *prosekynēsen autō* as "fell on his knees in front of him" rather than "worshipped" (KJV). It was an act of homage rather than worship. The demon shows respect because he recognizes that he is confronted with one greatly superior to him.

7-8 The demon addresses Jesus (v.7) by shouting "at the top of his voice." His cry, "What do you want with me?" was a way of saying, "What have we in common?" The demon recognizes that he is in the presence of one who threatened his very existence. In addressing Jesus the demon uses his personal name. Had he heard it from the lips of the disciples? Or had Jesus' fame already spread into this territory? The demon also uses the title "Son of the Most High God," a title that implies that the demon recognized Jesus' deity. The demon, however, uses the title, not to express his belief in the dignity of Jesus, but in the hope of controlling him (cf. Mark 1:24). The demon fears that he will be exorcised; so he says to Jesus, "Swear to God that you won't torture me." The tormentor now changes his role; he pleads exemption from torment. This may be a reference to eschatological punishment (cf. 1:24: "Have you come to destroy us?").

Verse 8 seems to be an explanatory statement by Mark to make clear why the demon was acting so excitedly. Jesus had ordered him to come out of the man. Understood this way, there is no need to suggest that v.8 originally preceded v.7, perhaps in place of v.6, as does O. Bauernfeind (*Die Worte der Dämonen im Mark-usevangelium* [Stuttgart, 1927], pp. 48–49).

9 To Jesus' inquiry about his name, the demoniac replied, "Legion." The significance of his name is not clear. Perhaps he had had an unfortunate experience with a Roman legion and this had caused his madness. Or perhaps he felt as if he was possessed by thousands of demons (a legion consisted of over six thousand men). Perhaps the many demons in him combined to form one aggregate force, thus the name "Legion" (SBK, 2:9). Jesus may have asked him his name to help him establish an identity apart from the demons. So fully did they possess the man that he seemed to be unable to act apart from them.

10 Both the singular and the plural occur here: "He begged . . . not to send them." This is probably Mark's way of indicating that the demons are speaking through the lips of the demoniac. What they request is that they not be sent "out of the area." In Luke (8:31) the request is that they not be sent into the Abyss (Rev 20:1–3), the place of confinement before judgment.

11–13 The presence of a large herd of swine (v.11) in the Decapolis is not surprising. This region, on the eastern shore of the Sea of Galilee, was largely Gentile. Mark's account shows that what caused the stampede of the pigs (v.13b) was the entrance of the demons into them (vv.12–13a). The demons were bent on destroying. Not having been able to destroy the man, they destroyed the pigs. Demons are emissaries of Satan, the Destroyer. But why did Jesus, having exorcised the demons, allow them to enter the pigs, an act that ultimately resulted in the destruction of the entire herd? A tentative answer is that Jesus wanted to give tangible evidence to the man and to the people that the demons had actually left him and that their purpose had been to destroy him even as they destroyed the pigs.

14–15 The result of the stampede and destruction of the pigs was the flight of the herdsman to "the town" (probably the chief town of the district) and "countryside" to tell what had happened (v.14). This brought the people to the scene of the miracle. When they arrived, they could scarcely believe their eyes! The man who had been known as "crazy," who had been so violent that he could not even be controlled by chains, they saw now sitting quietly (v.15). Before he had roamed naked through the tombs (cf. Luke 8:27); now he was "dressed." Before he had been possessed by powerful evil forces; now he was in his "right mind." Calvin (2:436) makes a pointed application: "Though we are not tortured by the devil [I wonder?], yet he holds us as his slaves, till the Son of God delivers us from his tyranny. Naked, torn, and disfigured, we wander about, till he restores us to soundness of mind."

Instead of rejoicing because of the marvelous deliverance of the man from his pathetic state, the people "were afraid." Their fear was no doubt caused by the presence of one with power to perform such a miracle.

16–17 When those who had been eyewitnesses to the event reported what had happened (v.16), both to the man and to the pigs, the people decided it was time for Jesus to leave their region (v.17). In fact, they pleaded with him to leave. Why? They were afraid (v.15). They recognized that a mighty force was at work in Jesus that they could neither understand nor control. If it destroyed an entire herd of pigs, might not this power strike again with even more serious consequences? Fear, ignorance, and selfishness because of the material loss through the destruction of the pigs dominated their considerations rather than compassion for the former demoniac. So they asked Jesus to leave, and he did. He does not stay where he is not wanted.

18–19 Jesus had come to the east side of the lake by boat (5:2). Now he was about to return the same way. The man who had been possessed wanted to go with him (v.18)—a perfectly natural reaction. He was eager for Jesus' company, for no one had ever showed him such love and compassion. But our Lord did not allow it. Instead he gave him the much more difficult task of returning home to his family to bear testimony to what Jesus in his mercy had done for him (v.19). The command "Tell them how much the Lord has done for you" is in marked contrast to Jesus' instructions to the cleansed leper in 1:44—"See that you don't tell this to anyone." This is probably because in the case of the demoniac Jesus was in Gentile territory where there would be little danger that popular messianic ideas about him might be circulated. It was in Jewish territory that this possibility was always present. Or perhaps in the case of this man, Jesus realized that the true nature of his person and mission was perceived; therefore this man could be trusted to convey to others the truth about Jesus.

20 The man obeyed without argument and began to bear testimony of what "Jesus had done for him." The Decapolis was a league of ten originally free Greek cities located (except Scythopolis) on the east of the Sea of Galilee and the Jordan River. They had been organized on the Greek model during the Seleucid period, brought under Hasmonean control by John Hyrcanus, and liberated by the Roman general Pompey. These cities heard the testimony of the former demoniac and responded with amazement. Anderson (p. 150) says that Mark may have regarded this incident "as the inauguration of the mission to the Gentiles (whereas foreigners from beyond Jordan came to him (Mark 3:8), it is only now Jesus has moved out into their territory (cf. 5:1)."

Notes

1 There are three different readings of the place name: Γερασηνῶν (*Gerasēnōn,* "Gerasenes"), original in Mark; Γαδαρηνῶν (*Gadarēnōn,* "Gadarenes"), found in Matthew; Γεργεσηνῶν (*Gergesēnōn,* "Gergasenes"), a reading attributable to Origen. "The textual variations are due to the fact that Gerasa (30 miles to the S.E.) and Gadara (6 miles to the S.E.) are too far from the lake, and to the necessity of finding a site where the mountains run down steeply into the lake" (Taylor, p. 278).

3. Jairus's plea in behalf of his daughter

5:21–24

> 21When Jesus had again crossed over by boat to the other side of the lake, a large crowd gathered around him while he was by the lake. 22Then one of the synagogue rulers, named Jairus, came there. Seeing Jesus, he fell at his feet 23and pleaded earnestly with him, "My little daughter is dying. Please come and put your hands on her so that she will be healed and live." 24So Jesus went with him.
> A large crowd followed and pressed around him.

It is possible that Mark brought together the stories of the woman with the hemorrhage and the healing of Jairus's daughter with the story of the healing of the demoniac because they all have to do with ritual uncleanness. According to Jewish law contact with graves, blood, or death made one ceremonially unclean.

The account of the healing of the woman with a hemorrhage occurs within the story of the healing of Jarius's daughter. Both Cranfield (p. 182) and Taylor (p. 289) hold that the events actually occurred in the sequence in which Mark has them. But in view of the fact that Mark elsewhere uses the method of insertion (cf. 3:22–30; 6:14–29; 11:15–19) and that he frequently seems more interested in theology than in chronology, thematic interests here probably have determined the sequence of events (cf. Anderson, p. 151; Lane, p. 189). This seems to be a better solution than to understand the sandwiching of the two narratives as an artificial intercalation to allow for the passage of time or to heighten the suspense. Both incidents read like eyewitness accounts.

21 Again the scene shifts. Jesus has returned to the west side of the lake. On the east side he had been asked to leave. Here great crowds greeted him. The specific place where the incident occurred is not given, but most commentators conjecture that it was near Capernaum.

22–24 Jesus was probably busy teaching when he was interrupted by the plea of "one of the synagogue rulers" (v.22). This does not mean that Jairus was one of several rulers in a particular synagogue (though some synagogues did have more than one; cf. Acts 13:15), but that he belonged to that particular group called "synagogue rulers." These were laymen whose responsibilities were administrative, not priestly, and included such things as looking after the building and supervising the worship. Sometimes the title was honorary, given to prominent members of the congregation with no administrative duties attached. At Antioch Paul and Barnabas were invited by the synagogue rulers to participate in the service (Acts 13:15). Jairus's need was so urgent that he jettisoned all dignity and pride, fell at Jesus' feet, and begged for help (v.23). Jairus had apparently heard about Jesus and believed that he could heal his child. Mark records no oral reply by Jesus to Jairus's request. Here Jesus does not speak; he acts. He set out with Jairus to go to the child, and a large crowd—probably of curiosity seekers—followed along (v.24).

4. Healing a woman with a hemorrhage

5:25–34

> 25And a woman was there who had been subject to bleeding for twelve years. 26She had suffered a great deal under the care of many doctors and had spent all

she had, yet instead of getting better she grew worse. ²⁷When she heard about Jesus, she came up behind him in the crowd and touched his cloak, ²⁸because she thought, "If I just touch his clothes, I will be healed." ²⁹Immediately her bleeding stopped and she felt in her body that she was freed from her suffering.

³⁰At once Jesus realized that power had gone out from him. He turned around in the crowd and asked, "Who touched my clothes?"

³¹"You see the people crowding against you," his disciples answered, "and yet you can ask, 'Who touched me?'"

³²But Jesus kept looking around to see who had done it. ³³Then the woman, knowing what had happened to her, came and fell at his feet and, trembling with fear, told him the whole truth. ³⁴He said to her, "Daughter, your faith has healed you. Go in peace and be freed from your suffering."

25–26 The story of the healing of the woman with a hemorrhage is sandwiched between the report of Jairus's daughter's illness and Jesus' action in raising her to life. The precise nature of the woman's ailment is not stated. Probably some sort of uterine disease caused the bleeding that had persisted for twelve years (v.25). Luke (8:43) says of her condition that "no one could heal her." Mark includes vivid details: she had suffered much, had been treated by many doctors, had spent all she had; and, instead of getting better, her condition had gotten worse (v.26). Luke understandably tones down this verse.

27–29 The reports the woman had heard about Jesus' healings and her belief that he could help her led her to come to him. But her faith seemed to be mixed with a measure of superstition. She apparently shared the belief, common in her day, that the power of a person was transmitted to his clothing (v.27). So she went into the crowd and, because of her ceremonial uncleanness, approached Jesus surreptitiously from the rear. She thought, If I just touch his clothes, I will be healed (v.28). At once her faith, even though mixed with superstition, was rewarded. The bleeding was stopped, and she felt a soundness in her body that assured her that she had been healed (v.29).

30–32 Not only had something happened to the woman when she touched Jesus' clothes, he too was aware that something had happened to him (v.30). Healing energy had gone out of him for someone's benefit; and, insisting on knowing who it was, he asked, "Who touched my clothes?" To his disciples this seemed like a stupid question in view of the crush of the crowd all about him (v.31). Both Matthew and Luke soften the harshness of the disciples' response to Jesus—strong evidence of the historicity of Mark's account. The lack of understanding on the part of Christ's disciples and their harsh reply may have been caused by their concern to get Jesus to Jairus's daughter where a real emergency existed. The question raised by Jesus would only cause delay. But Jesus' spiritual sensitivity told him that someone had touched his clothes, and he "kept looking around" to find who it was (v.32). His purpose was not to rebuke her but to make personal contact with her. She needed to know that it was her faith, not her superstitious belief, that had caused God to heal her.

33–34 The woman responded to Jesus' searching eyes. She knew what had happened to her; and, though "trembling with fear," she came forward, prostrated herself before Jesus, and "told him the whole truth" (v.33). This must have taken great courage, especially since she was regarded as ceremonially unclean. Jesus addressed her as "daughter" (v.34)—the only occurrence in the Gospels of Jesus' addressing a woman by that word. He made clear to her that it was her faith (in Jesus, or God) that had healed her. The word translated "healed" is *sesōken* ("saved"). Here both physical healing and theological salvation are in mind. In Mark's Gospel the two go closely together (cf. 2:1–12).

The phrase "Go in peace" is a traditional Jewish formula of leave-taking (cf. *šālôm*, "shalom" [cf. Judg 18:6; 1 Sam 1:17]). The word *peace* here "means not just freedom from inward anxiety, but that *wholeness* or *completeness* of life that comes from being brought into a right relationship with God" (Anderson, p. 154, italics his; cf. also TDNT, II: 911).

By Jesus' last statement to the woman—"be freed from your suffering"—he actively participated in her healing and confirmed God's will to make her well.

5. *Raising Jairus's daughter*

5:35–43

[35]While Jesus was still speaking, some men came from the house of Jairus, the synagogue ruler. "Your daughter is dead," they said. "Why bother the teacher any more?"

[36]Ignoring what they said, Jesus told the synagogue ruler, "Don't be afraid; just believe."

[37]He did not let anyone follow him except Peter, James and John the brother of James. [38]When they came to the home of the synagogue ruler, Jesus saw a commotion, with people crying and wailing loudly. [39]He went in and said to them, "Why all this commotion and wailing? The child is not dead but asleep." [40]But they laughed at him.

After he put them all out, he took the child's father and mother and the disciples who were with him, and went in where the child was. [41]He took her by the hand and said to her, *"Talitha koum!"* (which means, "Little girl, I say to you, get up!"). [42]Immediately the girl stood up and walked around (she was twelve years old). At this they were completely astonished. [43]He gave strict orders not to let anyone know about this, and told them to give her something to eat.

35–37 While Jesus was still speaking to the woman, "some men" brought Jairus the news of the death of his daughter (v.35). Since death is final, they advised him not to bother Jesus any longer. But Jesus ignored what the messengers said (v.36). In an effort to encourage Jairus, Jesus turned to him and said, "Don't be afraid; just believe." This word of assurance must have been just what he needed. He in no way tried to dissuade Jesus from resuming his journey to the child's bedside. At this point Jesus decided to separate himself from the crowd following him (v.37). A momentous miracle was about to take place, and he would have only a chosen few witness it. Peter, James, and John had a particularly close relationship to Jesus. This, no doubt, is why he selected them to see this miracle.

38 When Jesus arrived at Jairus's house, a great commotion was taking place. Swete (p. 107) puts it succinctly: "The Lord has dismissed one crowd only to find the house occupied by another." As was the custom, professional mourners had been secured; and they were already at work. "The lamentations consisted of choral song or antiphony, accompanied by hand-clapping" (Van der Loos, *Miracles of Jesus*, p. 568; cf. SBK, 1:521ff.). Since Jairus occupied a prominent position in the Jewish community, the number of professional mourners was large. So along with members of his family, they were making a great uproar.

39–40 On entering the house, Jesus asked why they were making such a commotion since the child was not dead but only asleep (v.39). On the surface this statement is enigmatic. It could mean that she had slipped into a comatose state. From this he would awake her. Or it could be Jesus' way of indicating that he proposed to bring her back from the dead. Since her death was not final, he spoke of it as sleep. Luke's account clearly indicates that Jesus resurrected the girl from the dead: "Her spirit returned, and at once she stood up" (Luke 8:55). A careful reading of the text reveals that Mark too "intended his account to be understood in the same way" (Lane, p. 197; cf. Taylor, p. 295).

The mourners, however, misunderstood Jesus' reference to sleeping to mean that she was not really dead. So they laughed him to scorn (v.40). Tears were quickly changed to laughter—a clear indication of the superficiality of the grief of the professional mourners. Jesus did not want any noisy crowd present when he performed this stupendous miracle; so he put the mourners out. Their lack of sensitivity disqualified them from being present at such a beautiful event. Only Jesus' three most intimate disciples and the mother and father were allowed to enter the room where the dead child lay.

41 Jesus stood by the side of the child, took her hand, and spoke the Aramaic words *"Talitha koum,"* which Mark conveniently translates for his Gentile readers: "Little girl, I say to you, get up!" Mark is the only Evangelist who preserves the original Aramaic here. Aramaic was the language of Palestine in the first century A.D. and was probably the language Jesus and his disciples normally spoke. However, since they came from Galilee, which was surrounded by the Gentile Decapolis and by Syrian Phoenicia, it seems highly likely that they also knew Greek and on occasion spoke Greek. The suggestion that the original Aramaic words were preserved because Mark wanted to provide Christian healers with certain verbal prescriptions in the original language is farfetched and must be rejected. Mark usually uses foreign words in nonmiracle story contexts (cf. 3:17; 7:11; 11:9; 14:36; 15:22, 34). The only exceptions are this passage and 7:34 (the healing of the deaf mute).

42–43 The young girl (Mark tells us she was twelve years old) responded immediately to Jesus' words (v.42). She not only stood up, she began to walk around. "Strength returned as well as life" (Swete, p. 109). The reaction of the five witnesses to the miracle (Peter, James, John, and the parents) was one of complete amazement.

Jesus gave two orders to the witnesses (v.43). First, they were not to reveal the facts about the miracle. It has been suggested that since this was impossible (too many people had known of the death of the girl, and it was not likely that her parents could hide her), we have here an example of the artificiality of the Markan messianic-secret motif. Cranfield rightly replies that Jesus did not think that the miracle could be kept "absolutely private, but simply that he wanted it kept as private as possible—no one was to know about it who need not. There was at least a chance of avoiding unnecessary publicity" (*Gospel of Mark*, p. 191). Jesus' messianic dignity is revealed to some (the five witnesses to the miracle) who can be entrusted with it but veiled to those (like the raucous mourners) who cannot. Jesus' second order was that they should give the girl something to eat—beautiful evidence of his concern for man's ordinary needs.

Ellis sums up the theological meaning of this miracle: "Like its younger brother, sickness, death is an enemy. But it must yield to the powers of the messianic kingdom present in Jesus. In the presence of Christ, death becomes a 'sleeping.' . . . 'Finis' is transformed into prelude. Until the *parousia* its sting remains, but its ultimate threat is broken. If we 'believe,' we need not live in dread: 'fear not!' " (E. Earle Ellis, *The Gospel of Luke*, NCB [Greenwood, S.C.: Attic, 1966], p. 134).

Notes

39 The word καθεύδω (*katheudō*) has three meanings in the NT: "sleep" in the literal sense (cf. Matt 8:24; 13:25; 25:5; 26:40, 43, 45; Mark 4:27, 38; 13:36; 14:37, 40–41; Luke 22:46; 1 Thess 5:7); "sleep" in the figurative sense (1 Thess 5:6); and "sleep" in the sense of death (1 Thess 5:10). It is in the last sense that it is used here. Jesus says that she is not dead (in the sense that she will not be brought back to life), but she is asleep (dead, but only briefly, because she is soon to be raised to life).

F. *Rejection at Nazareth*

6:1–6a

[1]Jesus left there and went to his hometown, accompanied by his disciples. [2]When the Sabbath came, he began to teach in the synagogue, and many who heard him were amazed.

"Where did this man get these things?" they asked. "What's this wisdom that has been given him, that he even does miracles! [3]Isn't this the carpenter? Isn't this Mary's son and the brother of James, Joseph, Judas and Simon? Aren't his sisters here with us?" And they took offense at him.

[4]Jesus said to them, "Only in his hometown, among his relatives and in his own house is a prophet without honor." [5]He could not do any miracles there, except lay his hands on a few sick people and heal them. [6]And he was amazed at their lack of faith.

1 If Capernaum was the scene of the healing of Jairus's daughter, the movement of Jesus described here was to the southwest through the hill country of Galilee. Nazareth is not specifically mentioned here or in Matthew, but it is obviously meant. The Greek word *patris* usually means "home country" but may also be used of one's hometown. That Jesus was considered by the Galileans as a Nazarene is implied by Mark 1:9, 24; John 1:46. Even though he was born in Bethlehem, since his family lived in Nazareth and he had been brought up there, it was natural to regard it as his hometown. The incident Mark records here should not be thought of as a personal visit by Jesus to his family. Rather, he comes as a rabbi accompanied by his disciples, "a detail dropped in Mt., but important for Mark, because in this part of the gospel he is concerned with their training" (Cranfield, *Gospel of Mark*, p. 193).

2 On the Sabbath, Jesus went into the synagogue and began to teach. (On the custom that allowed visiting teachers to give the scriptural exposition in the synagogue, see comment at 1:21.) This probably was the first time his fellow townsmen had actually heard Jesus teach, and many of them were amazed. But with some of them, there was an undercurrent of doubt as their questions imply: "Where did this man get these things?" and "What's this wisdom that has been given him, that he even does miracles!" What was the source of his teaching and his miracles? They were either from God or from Satan. Which? Although we do not know of any miracles Jesus had done in Nazareth, his reputation as a miracle-worker had been spread abroad.

3 The hostility of Jesus' townspeople toward him comes out more clearly in the rhetorical questions in this verse. "Isn't this the carpenter?" i.e., Isn't he just a common ordinary fellow who makes his living with his hands like the rest of us? How is it that he's parading as a rabbi and miracle-worker? The second question, "Isn't this Mary's son?" seems also to be derogatory since it was not customary among Jews to describe a man as the son of his mother even when the father was not alive (cf. Taylor, pp. 299–300). Behind this question may be the rumor, circulated during Jesus' lifetime, that he was illegitimate (cf. John 4:41; 9:29; SBK, 1:39–43; Origen *Contra Celsum* 1. 28).

The brothers and sisters of Jesus mentioned here were not cousins (Jerome's view) or Joseph's children by a previous marriage (Epiphanius's view). Both Jerome and Epiphanius were greatly influenced by the Roman Catholic dogma of the perpetual virginity of Mary (Jerome's theory also made possible the virginity of Joseph!). But neither Epiphanius's nor Jerome's view finds support in Scripture. The children mentioned here were more probably children born to Mary and Joseph according to natural biological processes subsequent to the virgin birth of Jesus (Helvidius's view). James was probably the oldest and was certainly the best known of Jesus' brothers. He was closely identified with the church of Jerusalem (Acts 12:17; 15:13; 21:18; 1 Cor 15:7; Gal 1:19; 2:9, 12) and was probably the author of the Epistle of James (James 1:1). Both Josephus (Antiq. XX, 200 [ix. 1]) and Eusebius (*Ecclesiastical History* 2.33) preserve accounts of his violent death. Jude was probably the author of the Book of Jude. We know nothing of Joseph and Simon.

The word translated "they took offense" is from *skandalizomai*, from which the English word "scandal" is derived. The difficulty the word presents is reflected in the versions: "are repelled" (Mof); "fall away" (RSV); "stumble" (ASV); "fell foul of him" (NEB). "The idea conveyed by the Greek verb is that of being offended and repelled to the point of abandoning (whether temporarily or permanently, the word does not specify) belief in the Word (cf. Lk 8:13) or one's relation with Jesus (14:27, 29)" (Bratcher and Nida, pp. 139–40).

4 Jesus responded to the doubts raised about the legitimacy of his teaching and his miracles by a proverb that has parallels in both Jewish and Greek literature. One of these proverbs states the principle on which all of them are based: Familiarity breeds contempt. The basic difference between Jesus' proverb and the Jewish and Greek ones is his use of the word "prophet" (here it probably means "inspired teacher"). This word is not found in any of the Jewish or pagan proverbs. The people of Nazareth were incapable of appreciating who Jesus was because, like Jesus' own family, they identified him with themselves so closely.

5–6a Verse 5 opens with "one of the boldest statements in the Gospels, since it mentions something that Jesus could not do" (Taylor, p. 301). It was not, of course, that he did not have the power to do more miracles than he did at Nazareth. The inability was related to the moral situation. In the climate of unbelief he chose not to exercise his miraculous power. One of the great emphases of Mark's Gospel is that Jesus performs his miracles in response to faith.

Jesus expressed amazement at their lack of faith (v.6a). Apparently he did not expect such a response from his neighbors. It was their deep lack of faith that amazed him. It is significant that only here in Mark's Gospel is amazement ascribed to Jesus.

Notes

---

3 Matthew calls Jesus "the carpenter's son" (13:55), but only Mark says he was a "carpenter" (τέκτων, *tektōn*). The variant reading "son of a carpenter" is an obvious assimilation to Matthew. Origen (*Contra Celsum* 6.36) says that nowhere in the Gospels current in his day is Jesus called a carpenter. This statement apparently was due to either (1) a lapse of memory or (2) his acceptance of a Markan text assimilated to Matthew (probably because he preferred not to think of the Son of God as involved in so menial an occupation). The word *tektōn* can be used of masons or smiths but seems to have its usual meaning "carpenter" here.

G. Sending Out the Twelve

6:6b–13

> Then Jesus went around teaching from village to village. [7]Calling the Twelve to him, he sent them out two by two and gave them authority over evil spirits.
> [8]These were his instructions: "Take nothing for the journey except a staff—no bread, no bag, no money in your belts. [9]Wear sandals but not an extra tunic. [10]Whenever you enter a house, stay there until you leave that town. [11]And if any place will not welcome you or listen to you, shake the dust off your feet when you leave, as a testimony against them."
> [12]They went out and preached that people should repent. [13]They drove out many demons and anointed many sick people with oil and healed them.

6b There is some question whether 6b should go with vv.1–6 or vv.7–13. If with the former, it means that as a result of his rejection at Nazareth, Jesus decided to inaugurate a village ministry. If with the latter, it was as a result of the village ministry that he decided to send out the Twelve, presumably to increase his own ministry through them. NIV and NEB take v.6b with vv.7–13. RSV is noncommittal; it sets off the verse by itself.

7 Jesus had carefully prepared his disciples for this mission. He had called them with the promise "I will make you fishers of men" (1:17). He had withdrawn on several occasions to give them special attention (3:7, 13; 4:10). And, all the while they had been with him, they had witnessed his mighty acts and had listened to his wise words. Now it was time for them to be sent out (cf. 3:14–15: "that he might send them out to preach and to have authority to drive out demons").

The verb translated "sent" is *apostellein* and carries with it the idea of official representation. "Jesus authorized the disciples to be his delegates with respect to both word and power. Their message and deeds were to be an extension of his own" (Lane, p. 206). The Twelve were sent "two by two," apparently a Jewish custom (cf. Mark 11:1; 14:13; Acts 13:2, 4; 16:40). The purpose of their going in pairs was so that the truthfulness of their testimony about Jesus might be established "on the testimony of two or three witnesses" (Deut 17:6).

"Authority over evil spirits" was a part of the Twelve's commission. Mark especially highlights Jesus' power to exorcise demons. Here that power is given to the Twelve.

8–9 Inherent in the commission of the Twelve was absolute trust in God to supply all their needs. Here the physical needs are emphasized. They were to take only what they had on their backs. The only exception was a staff (v.8). (The account in Matthew does not even allow this.) No bread (i.e., food of any kind), no bag ("knapsack," "traveler's bag," or perhaps the passage has in mind the more specialized meaning of "beggar's bag" [BAG, p. 662]), and no money (the word is *chalkos*, a small copper coin, which BAG [p. 883] translates as "small change") were allowed.

Clothing, too, was to be minimal. Sandals were allowed and only one tunic (v.9). An extra tunic would come in handy at night because it could be used as a covering from the chilly night air. Jesus probably made this prohibition because he wanted the disciples to trust God for the provision of hospitality for each night. The total impression one receives from Jesus' instructions is that the mission he is about to send the Twelve on is extremely urgent.

The message Jesus gave them to preach was the same as the one he brought: "The kingdom of God is near. Repent and believe the good news!" (Mark 1:15). Cranfield rightly comments: "The particular instructions apply literally only to this brief mission during Jesus' lifetime; but in principle, with the necessary modifications according to climate and other circumstances, they still hold for the continuing ministry of the Church. The service of the Word of God is still a matter of extreme urgency, calling for absolute self-dedication" (*Gospel of Mark*, p. 200).

10–11 Jesus gave the instruction in this verse to protect the good reputation of the disciples. Whenever they accepted the hospitality of a home, they were to stay there until they left that town (v.10), even if more comfortable or attractive lodgings were offered them.

Jesus knew that the mission of the Twelve would not always be accepted. Had not he too been rejected by many? So he instructed them how to act in such circumstances. The shaking off the dust from their feet (v.11) may be understood in the light of the Jewish custom of removing carefully the dust from both clothes and feet before reentering Jewish territory (cf. SBK, 1:571). For the Jews heathen dust was defiling. The significance of the act here is to declare the place to be heathen and to make it clear that those who rejected the message must now answer for themselves. This seems to be the meaning of the phrase "as a testimony against them." The disciples' message, like that of Jesus, brings judgment as well as salvation. This always happens when the gospel is preached.

12–13 Mark now describes the actual mission of the Twelve. It was clearly patterned after Jesus' own ministry. Three activities are described: (1) preaching repentance (v. 12), (2) driving out demons (v. 13), and (3) healing the sick—all of them associated with Jesus' ministry. By these activities they were demonstrating that the kingdom of God had come with power. But the mission of the Twelve is a mere extension of the ministry of Jesus that completely overshadows it. Their independent mission waits till after Jesus' resurrection.

IV. Withdrawal From Galilee (6:14–8:30)

This fourth section of Mark's Gospel finds Jesus withdrawing from the territory of Galilee for the primary purpose of further instructing his disciples. Though one incident of public teaching occurs in the section 7:1–23, the focus of Jesus' teaching is now on the Twelve. The section begins with an account of the various views that people held as to Jesus' identity (6:14–16), including the view of Herod Antipas, followed parenthetically with the story of the death of John the Baptist (6:17–29). The section ends with the healing of a blind man at Bethsaida (8:22–26) and the disciples' recognition of Jesus as the Messiah (8:27–30). In between are several complexes of incidents including two stories of Jesus' feeding the multitudes: the five thousand (6:30–44) and then the four thousand (8:1–10). Jesus moves from Galilee into the territory of Tyre and Sidon and then back through Galilee to the Decapolis.

A. Popular Views of Jesus' Identity

6:14–16

14King Herod heard about this, for Jesus' name had become well-known. Some were saying, "John the Baptist has been raised from the dead, and that is why miraculous powers are at work in him."
15Others said, "He is Elijah."
And still others claimed, "He is a prophet, like one of the prophets of long ago."
16But when Herod heard this, he said, "John, the man I beheaded, has been raised from the dead!"

14 The Herod mentioned here is Antipas, son of Herod the Great and Malthace. When his father died, he became tetrarch ("ruler of the fourth part") of Galilee and Perea. He was not officially granted the title of "king." It was, in fact, his ambition to secure that title for himself that led to his downfall in A.D. 39 under Caligula. Mark may be using the title of "king" here ironically, or perhaps he is reflecting local custom (cf. Taylor, p. 308).

If the paragraph that begins with v. 14 goes with the one that precludes it, then the "this" refers to the mission of the Twelve. Herod heard about this. It is possible that the disciples of Jesus traveled as far as Tiberias on the southwestern shore of the Lake of Galilee, where Herod had built his capital and had named it after the ruling Caesar, Tiberias. On the other hand, the "this" of v. 14 may be a reference to the mighty works of Jesus. This latter view seems likely because the entire discussion focuses on the question of Jesus' identity.

Since NIV, correctly in my view, accepts the reading *elegon* ("some were saying") instead of *elegen* ("he [Herod] was saying"), what follows are popular views of who Jesus was. That some thought Jesus to be John the Baptist raised from the dead shows that they knew nothing of Jesus prior to his ministry in Galilee. John the Baptist did not perform miracles while he was alive, but apparently his resurrection status was thought to give him that power.

15 Another popular view identified Jesus with Elijah. John the Baptist had spoken of Jesus as "the Coming One"; and though he did not specifically identify who that was, to anyone who knew the OT it could be no one else but Elijah (cf. Mal 3:1; 4:5). Perhaps this popular view of Jesus owed its origin to John.

A third view was that "he is a prophet, like one of the prophets of long ago." This seems to be a lower estimate of Jesus than the previously mentioned one. He is just an ordinary prophet, not the Prophet foretold in Deuteronomy 18:15–19.

16 Herod's view—that Jesus was John the Baptist raised from the dead—arose not so much from what he had heard about Jesus as from the proddings of a guilty conscience, since Herod had been directly responsible for John's death. This view of Jesus suggests that Herod knew nothing about Jesus prior to the death of John. Otherwise he would hardly have viewed him as John redivivus. The mention of the death of John causes Mark to interrupt the account of the mission of the Twelve in order to tell the story of John's murder.

B. *Death of John the Baptist*

6:17–29

[17]For Herod himself had given orders to have John arrested, and he had him bound and put in prison. He did this because of Herodias, his brother Philip's wife, whom he had married. [18]For John had been saying to Herod, "It is not lawful for you to have your brother's wife." [19]So Herodias nursed a grudge against John and wanted to kill him. But she was not able to, [20]because Herod feared John and protected him, knowing him to be a righteous and holy man. When Herod heard John, he was greatly puzzled, yet he liked to listen to him.

[21]Finally the opportune time came. On his birthday Herod gave a banquet for his high officials and military commanders and the leading men of Galilee. [22]When the daughter of Herodias came in and danced, she pleased Herod and his dinner guests.

The king said to the girl, "Ask me for anything you want, and I'll give it to you." [23]And he promised her with an oath, "Whatever you ask I will give you, up to half my kingdom."

[24]She went out and said to her mother, "What shall I ask for?"

"The head of John the Baptist," she answered.

[25]At once the girl hurried in to the king with the request: "I want you to give me right now the head of John the Baptist on a platter."

[26]The king was greatly distressed, but because of his oaths and his dinner guests, he did not want to refuse her. [27]So he immediately sent an executioner with orders to bring John's head. The man went, beheaded John in the prison, [28]and brought back his head on a platter. He presented it to the girl, and she gave it to her mother. [29]On hearing of this, John's disciples came and took his body and laid it in a tomb.

17–18 Lane (p. 215) points out that in the scheme of Mark's Gospel there are two "passion narratives": the passion of John and the passion of Jesus. The passion of the Forerunner is a precursor to the passion of the Messiah. It is significant that Mark devotes fourteen verses to the death of John but only three to his ministry.

Numerous historical questions have been raised about Mark's account of John's death. Most of them arise out of his differences with Josephus. (For a complete discussion of these problems, see Cranfield, *Gospel of Mark*, pp. 208–9; Lane, pp. 215–16; and Taylor, pp. 310–11.)

John the Baptist had been arrested by Herod (v.17), who put him in prison because he had denounced Herod's adulterous union with Herodias, his brother Philip's wife (v.18). Josephus (Antiq. XVIII, 119 [v.2]) says that John was put in prison at Machaerus, the fortress situated in Perea, on the eastern side of the Dead Sea. Mark does not identify the place of John's imprisonment. Herodias was the daughter of Aristobolos, one of the sons of Herod the Great; so she was a niece of Herod Antipas. The Mosaic Law prohibited marriage to one's brother's wife while the brother was still alive (cf. Lev 18:16).

Josephus emphasizes the political motives behind the action of Herod against John. These were no doubt real. In order to marry Herodias, Herod had to rid himself of the daughter of King Aretas IV, whose kingdom lay just to the east of Perea. The situation there was already sensitive, and John's preaching had the potential to cause real trouble. Mark emphasizes the moral considerations. Calvin (2:222) comments: "We behold in John an illustrious example of that moral courage, which all pious teachers ought to possess, not to hesitate to incur the wrath of the great and powerful, as often as it may be found necessary: for he, with whom there is acceptance of persons, does not honestly serve God."

19–20 Herodias had not taken John's condemnation of her marriage lightly. In fact, she was infuriated by him and wanted to kill him (v.19). Herodias knew that "the only place where her marriage certificate could safely be written was on the back of the death warrant of John" (T.W. Manson, *The Servant Messiah* [London: Cambridge University Press, 1953], p. 40). She was thwarted in her design because Herod protected John (v.20). Motivated by fear and a recognition of John's righteous and holy character, Herod refused to allow him to be put to death. "Herod was awed by the purity of John's character, feared him as the bad fear the good" (Swete, p. 123). Yet "he liked to listen to him"; but he did not understand, being "greatly puzzled" by what he said.

21–23 Herodias finally got the opportunity she was waiting for (v.21). Herod celebrated his birthday with a banquet that he invited the military and political leaders of his tetrarchy to. At this festive occasion Herodias's daughter went before the guests to dance (v.22). A reading of the entire account suggests that Herodias sent her into the banquet hall to dance as part of her scheme to get rid of John the Baptist.

The dance was probably a lewd one. Objections to the historicity of the account have been raised on the basis of the unlikelihood of such a performance, but the low morals in Herod's court would not be inconsistent with it. Herod and his dinner guests were pleased with her performance—so much so that Herod offered her up to half his kingdom (v.23). The words "up to half my kingdom" may have been a kind of proverbial way of expressing openhanded generosity and were not to be taken literally.

24–25 The girl left the banquet hall to seek the advice of her mother (v.24). Herodias's quick reply betrayed the premeditated nature of her homicidal plan. Mark does not mention any surprise on the daughter's part when her mother made the request. In fact, when she went to convey the request for the head of John the Baptist, the daughter added two things: she wanted John's head "right now" and she wanted it "on a platter" (v.25).

26–28 Herod was in a quandary (v.26). Up to this point he had been able to protect John; but now, "because of his oaths and his dinner guests," he could hardly refuse the girl. Reluctantly (v.26 says he "was greatly distressed" about the whole thing) he ordered an executioner to be sent to the prison to decapitate John (v.27). John's head was brought to Herod (v.28), who presented it to Salome; and she gave it to her mother.

29 Mark ends the shocking story with John's disciples coming for the body to give it proper burial. Herod no doubt thought that he was now finished with the righteous prophet he both feared and respected. But this was not to be. The ministry of Jesus stirred up Herod's memories of John and his fears returned once more. Josephus says that when Herod's army was defeated by the Nabataeans in A.D. 30, the Jews thought it was a "punishment upon Herod and a mark of God's displeasure against him" (Antiq. XVIII, 119 [v.2]).

Notes

20 Some MSS read πολλὰ ἐποίει (*polla epoiei*, "he did many things"), but the reading adopted by NIV, πολλὰ ἠπόρει (*polla ēporei*, "he was greatly puzzled"), has the stronger MS support. It also seems consistent with what we know of Herod's character.

22 The external evidence supports the reading αὐτοῦ (*autou*, "his"). This identifies the girl as Herodias, the daughter of Herod. In v.24, however, she is identified as the daughter of Herodias; and we know from other sources that her name was Salome. The best solution seems to be to regard *autou* as an early scribal error and αὐτῆς (*autēs*, "her" as the original reading. In that case *autēs* would be used intensively to mean "herself" (cf. ASV: "When the daughter of Herodias herself came in").

26 The depth of the distress experienced by Herod at Salome's request for the head of John the Baptist is expressed graphically by the Greek word περίλυπος (*perilypos*, "greatly distressed"). This is the same word used to describe Jesus' agony in Gethsemane (Mark 14:34).

C. Feeding the Five Thousand

6:30–44

³⁰The apostles gathered around Jesus and reported to him all they had done and taught. ³¹Then, because so many people were coming and going that they did not even have a chance to eat, he said to them, "Come with me by yourselves to a quiet place and get some rest."

³²So they went away by themselves in a boat to a solitary place. ³³But many who saw them leaving recognized them and ran on foot from all the towns and got there ahead of them. ³⁴When Jesus landed and saw a large crowd, he had compassion on them, because they were like sheep without a shepherd. So he began teaching them many things.

35By this time it was late in the day, so his disciples came to him. "This is a remote place," they said, "and it's already very late. 36Send the people away so they can go to the surrounding countryside and villages and buy themselves something to eat."
37But he answered, "You give them something to eat."
They said to him, "That would take eight months of a man's wages! Are we to go and spend that much on bread and give it to them to eat?"
38"How many loaves do you have?" he asked. "Go and see."
When they found out, they said, "Five—and two fish."
39Then Jesus directed them to have all the people sit down in groups on the green grass. 40So they sat down in groups of hundreds and fifties. 41Taking the five loaves and the two fish and looking up to heaven, he gave thanks and broke the loaves. Then he gave them to his disciples to set before the people. He also divided the two fish among them all. 42They all ate and were satisfied, 43and the disciples picked up twelve basketfuls of broken pieces of bread and fish. 44The number of the men who had eaten was five thousand.

In Mark's Gospel the story of the feeding of the five thousand plays an important role. It begins with an elaborate introduction (6:35–38), is looked back to on two different occasions (6:52; 8:17–21), and has a sequel in the feeding of the four thousand (8:1–10). Its position immediately following the account of Herod's feast also serves a function. It contrasts the "sumptuous oriental aura of the Herodian court with the austere circumstances in which Jesus satisfied the multitude with the staples of a peasant's diet" (Lane, p. 227).

30 Mark now continues the account of the mission of the Twelve after having interrupted it by a flashback to the death of John the Baptist. The disciples returned to Jesus from their mission of preaching, casting out demons, and healing and reported to him "all they had done and taught." Only here does Mark use the word "apostles" for the disciples. (Its occurrence in 3:14 is highly doubtful textually.) The word is particularly appropriate because the Twelve were returning from doing their apostolic work (cf. Gould, p. 115).

31–32 The disciples had just returned from what was apparently an intensive mission. Their activities had created much interest. So many people were coming and going that the disciples had no time even to eat (v.31; cf. 3:20). Since the disciples were doubtless tired from their missionary activities and from the demands of the crowds, Jesus decided to seek rest for them. Where specifically they went we are not told. Mark merely says it was a "quiet" and "solitary place [*erēmos*, 'desert']" (v.32).
In addition to seeking rest, it is possible that there was another purpose in the withdrawal of Jesus to the wilderness. Mark seems to have in mind the "rest in the wilderness" theme in Scripture (for a full treatment of this theme in Mark, see Lane; Mauser, passim). It was in the wilderness that God gave rest to his ancient people in the Exodus from Egypt. In the preaching of the prophets Isaiah (63:14) and Jeremiah (31:2), this became a type of a second rest promised to the new people of God in a second exodus. Jesus and his disciples fulfill this promise. Jesus is God's presence (instead of the pillar and the cloud), and the Bread (instead of the manna) is God's provision of sustenance.
The best way for Jesus and his disciples to get away from the crowds was by boat. They probably went to the northeast side of the lake. Although the crowd that

followed by land would have had to cross the Jordan where it flows into the Lake of Galilee, this, according to Dalman, could have been possible: "On October 10, 1921, I saw that it was almost possible to cross over the Jordan dry-shod, just where it enters into the lake. An absolutely dry bar lay before the mouth" (G. Dalman, *Sacred Sites and Ways* [London: SPCK, 1935], p. 161). However, in the spring of the year, when this event apparently took place (cf. v.39: "green grass"), the Jordan had more water in it.

33-34 Perhaps the little boat faced a strong headwind, which slowed it down. At any rate the crowd was able to walk around the lake and arrive at the landing place ahead of the boat (v.33).

Jesus had every right to be annoyed with the crowd. They had prevented him and his disciples from having a much needed rest. But instead of being irritated, he responded compassionately and in love (v.34). He saw the multitude as "sheep without a shepherd" (cf. Num 27:17; Ezek 34:5). It is significant that in the context of these two OT passages the shepherd theme is associated with the wilderness. Mark seems to be working with these themes. Jesus, like Moses, leads his people into the wilderness; and, like David (cf. Ezek 34:23, 25), Jesus provides rest for them (cf. Lane, p. 226; Mauser, p. 135).

35-36 Jesus' disciples became concerned for the crowd (v.35). It was late in the day; and, since they were in a desolate place, there was little possibility of obtaining food. Their suggestion was that the crowd be dismissed so that they could get food for themselves in the neighboring towns and villages (v.36). This seemed to be a simple way for them to satisfy their hunger.

37 Jesus did not concur with the suggestion of his disciples that the food needed to feed the crowd was to be supplied from the resources of the neighboring towns and villages. The disciples themselves were to supply it! Jesus uses the emphatic personal pronoun to make the message plain: "*You* give them something to eat" (emphasis mine).

The reply of the disciples indicates how startled they were at Jesus' command. They could only think of the impossible amount of money it would take to feed a crowd like this one. Two hundred denarii represented the pay a common laborer earned in a period of about eight months (cf. Matt 20:2-15, where the usual pay for a day's wage is one denarius). Not even that amount of money would buy enough bread for all to eat (cf. John 6:7: "for each one to have a bite").

38 Jesus was not thinking of bread bought in the neighboring villages for two hundred denarii or whatever it might cost to supply the people. Before proceeding with his approach to the problem, he asked his disciples what the present status of the supply was. When they inquired, they found it to be meager: five loaves and two fish—a mere pittance in view of the number of people to be fed. The loaves, John tells us (6:9), were barley loaves. Unlike our modern loaves of bread, these were small and flat. One could easily eat several of them at a single meal.

39-40 At Jesus' direction (v.39), the disciples arranged the crowd into groups of hundreds and fifties (v.40). The words used to describe this arrangement mean literally "drinking parties by drinking parties" and "vegetable plots by vegetable plots" (cf. BAG, pp. 787, 705). Here they are used to describe the orderly arrangement of the crowd in order to facilitate the distribution of the food. Beyond that there may be a symbolic meaning. The arrangement may suggest the teacher-student relationship. The "rabbis compared their classes to vineyards because they were arranged in rows, 'shuroth shuroth'; and we may compare our own use of the word 'seminary,' which means a 'seed-plot'" (P. Carrington, *According to Mark* [Cambridge: Cambridge University Press, 1960], p. 136). Lane, in keeping with the wilderness motif, finds in this arrangement a recalling of the Mosaic camp in the wilderness. Thus the people taught by Jesus are shown to be the new people of God and Jesus is "the eschatological Saviour, the second Moses who transforms the leaderless flock into the people of God" (p. 230).

Mark notes that the grass was green (v.39). This shows that the incident took place in the late winter or early spring, when the grass in Galilee turns green after the rains.

41 Jesus did what any pious Jew would have done before eating—he prayed. The usual form of the prayer was a thanksgiving or eucharist: "Blessed art thou, O Lord our God, King of the Universe, who bringeth forth bread from the earth." As to how the miracle was performed, Mark does not give us so much as a hint. He simply says that Jesus broke the loaves, divided the fish, and gave them to the disciples to distribute among the people.

42–44 There can be no question but that Mark understood the actions of Jesus to have been miraculous. Temple correctly observes: "Every Evangelist supposed our Lord to have wrought a creative act; and for myself, I have no doubt that this is what occurred. This, however, is credible only if St. John is right in his doctrine of the Lord's Person. If the Lord was indeed God incarnate, the story presents no insuperable difficulties" (W. Temple, *Readings in St. John's Gospel* [London: Macmillan, 1940], p. 75). Not only were all the people fed and their hunger satisfied (v.42), but there was more left over at the end than there had been at the beginning—twelve basketfuls (v.43). These were the small wicker baskets (*kôphinōn*) every Jew took with him when away from home. In it he carried his lunch and some needed essentials so that he would not have to eat defiling Gentile food.

Mark says that the number of the men who had eaten was about five thousand (v.44)—a number that could easily have been calculated because of the division of the crowd into groups of hundreds and fifties.

Notes

40 The word πρασιαί (*prasiai*, "groups") is etymologically "leek beds." J.D.M. Derrett points out that leeks need a great deal of water and because of their need for irrigation must be planted in straight rows. Thus the explanation of arrangement of the crowd like leek beds was "to show that in the World to Come the righteous will be sated like the well-irrigated vegetables which the stupid and unbelieving Israelites lusted for in the desert" ("Leek Beds and Methodology," *Biblische Zeitschrift* 19, no. 1 [1975]: 102).

44 The word used for "men" here is not ἄνθρωποι (*anthrōpoi*), the generic sense, i.e., "human beings," but ἄνδρες (andres), "men" as opposed to women or children. Matthew makes this clear by adding "besides women and children" (14:21), though there probably were not many of them present. The number five thousand is very large when one realizes that the neighboring towns of Capernaum and Bethsaida had only two-to-three thousand people.

D. Walking on the Water

6:45–52

> ⁴⁵Immediately Jesus made his disciples get into the boat and go on ahead of him to Bethsaida, while he dismissed the crowd. ⁴⁶After leaving them, he went on a mountainside to pray.
> ⁴⁷When evening came, the boat was in the middle of the lake, and he was alone on land. ⁴⁸He saw the disciples straining at the oars, because the wind was against them. About the fourth watch of the night he went out to them, walking on the lake. He was about to pass by them, ⁴⁹but when they saw him walking on the lake, they thought he was a ghost. They cried out, ⁵⁰because they all saw him and were terrified.
> Immediately he spoke to them and said, "Take courage! It is I. Don't be afraid." ⁵¹Then he climbed into the boat with them, and the wind died down. They were completely amazed, ⁵²for they had not understood about the loaves; their hearts were hardened.

45 Mark records no reaction of the crowd to the multiplication of the loaves and fish, but there must have been one. The hurried departure of the disciples suggests that there was danger of a messianic uprising as a result of the miracle. (John's Gospel [6:15] refers specifically to this.) The suggestion that the crowd did not know a miracle had taken place and that Jesus wanted to get the disciples out of there before they divulged that one had happened seems farfetched. Bethsaida is on the northeast shore of the Lake of Galilee and could not have been far from the place where the miracle took place. Herod Philip elevated the village to the status of a city and named it after Julias, the daughter of the Roman emperor Augustus (cf. Jos. Antiq. XVIII, 28 [ii.1]). After sending his disciples away in the boat, Jesus stayed to dismiss the crowd. No doubt his purpose was to calm the people down.

46 Mark's mention of Jesus' praying is further evidence of the crisis nature of the situation. There are only three occasions in this Gospel in which Jesus withdraws to pray, and each time some sort of crisis is involved: after the excitement and activity of a busy Sabbath in Capernaum (1:35), after the multiplication of the loaves (6:46), and in Gethsemane after the Lord's Supper (14:32–36). Each incident involves the temptation not to carry out God's mission for him—a mission that would ultimately bring suffering, rejection, and death. These crises seem to represent an ascending scale and reach their climax in the agony of Gethsemane.

47–48 The time of this incident is "evening" (v.47). Since it was "already very late" (v.35) before the feeding of the five thousand, "evening" here must mean late at night. The Lake of Galilee is only about four miles wide. Thus a boat in the middle of the lake could easily be seen in the full moon of Passover time (assuming that the incident took place at that time) from the shore.

Apparently the wind was blowing from the north or northeast and had blown the disciples off their course. They were "straining at the oars" (v.48)—an indication of a stiff headwind. Jesus came to them "walking on the lake," about the fourth watch. According to Roman reckoning (and Mark follows this), the night was divided into four watches: 6–9 P.M., 9–12 P.M., 12–3 A.M., and 3–6 A.M. "He was about to pass by them" translates *kai ēthelen parelthein autous*, which literally means "and he was desirous to pass by them." NIV probably catches the correct meaning, showing that we have here not the intention of Jesus but the impression of an eyewitness as to what was happening.

49–50 To try to rationalize this incident by suggesting that what the disciples really saw was Jesus wading through the shallows at the edge of the shore is ridiculous. Although they did not recognize him at first—they thought they had seen some sort of water spirit (v.49)—Jesus calmed their fears with words of assurance: "Take courage! It is I. Don't be afraid" (v.50). It has sometimes been suggested that the statement "It is I" points to Mark's understanding this incident as a theophany (cf. the "I am who I am" of Exod 3:14). It is, however, simplest and best to regard the expression as a way by which Jesus was identifying himself ("It is I—Jesus").

51 Here another miracle is presupposed. When Jesus climbed into the boat, "the wind died down." Then Mark says, "They were completely amazed." There was unmistakenly some relationship between his getting into the boat and the calming of the wind. Only this explains the attitude of the disciples.

52 Mark relates his explanation of the disciples' panic at seeing Jesus walking on the water and their amazement at the calming of the wind to their failure to understand about the multiplication of the loaves. Had they understood about the loaves, i.e., that the sovereign Lord of the universe was in action there, they would have been prepared to understand walking on water and calming waves. Their problem was a christological one. Not unlike Jesus' opponents, "their hearts were hardened."

E. *Healings Near Gennesaret*

6:53–56

> 53When they had crossed over, they landed at Gennesaret and anchored there. 54As soon as they got out of the boat, people recognized Jesus. 55They ran throughout that whole region and carried the sick on mats to wherever they heard he was. 56And wherever he went—into villages, towns or countryside—they placed the sick in the marketplaces. They begged him to let them touch even the edge of his cloak, and all who touched him were healed.

53 Jesus stayed with the disciples in the boat and crossed over with them to Gennesaret, referring either to the plain north of Magdala on the western side of the lake or to a city in the plain (cf. Dalman, *Sacred Sites*, p. 128). The great fertility of the soil in the plain of Gennesaret enabled it to support a relatively large population. Josephus says of it, "One may call this place the ambition of nature, where it forces those plants that are naturally enemies to one another to agree together" (War III, 518 [x.8]).

54-56 This section serves as a summary of Jesus' work in Galilee before he withdrew to other regions. It resembles the summaries in 1:32-34 and 3:7-12, except that no mention is made of exorcising demons. In it we see the widespread fame of Jesus as a healer (vv.54-55). As a good Jew, he wore the fringes and tassels commanded by God in Numbers 15:37-39 and Deuteronomy 22:12. It was not the mere touch of the fringes of Jesus' garments that produced the healings (v.56). Though in some instances superstition was probably involved, it was the faith of those who came to touch Jesus' clothes that he responded to (cf. 5:25-34).

F. *Commands of God and Traditions of Men*

7:1-13

> [1] The Pharisees and some of the teachers of the law who had come from Jerusalem gathered around Jesus and [2] saw some of his disciples eating food with hands that were "unclean," that is, unwashed. [3] (The Pharisees and all the Jews do not eat unless they give their hands a ceremonial washing, holding to the tradition of the elders. [4] When they come from the marketplace they do not eat unless they wash. And they observe many other traditions, such as the washing of cups, pitchers and kettles.)
>
> [5] So the Pharisees and teachers of the law asked Jesus, "Why don't your disciples live according to the tradition of the elders instead of eating their food with 'unclean' hands?"
>
> [6] He replied, "Isaiah was right when he prophesied about you hypocrites; as it is written:
>
> > " 'These people honor me with their lips,
> > but their hearts are far from me.
> > [7] They worship me in vain;
> > their teachings are but rules taught by men.'
>
> [8] You have let go of the commands of God and are holding on to the traditions of men."
>
> [9] And he said to them: "You have a fine way of setting aside the commands of God in order to observe your own traditions! [10] For Moses said, 'Honor your father and your mother,' and 'Anyone who curses his father or mother must be put to death.' [11] But you say that if a man says to his father or mother: 'Whatever help you might otherwise have received from me is Corban' (that is, a gift devoted to God), [12] then you no longer let him do anything for his father or mother. [13] Thus you nullify the word of God by your tradition that you have handed down. And you do many things like that."

This incident appears to be linked with vv. 14-19 and vv. 20-23 by the common theme of "cleanness." It is similar to the conflict stories found in 2:1-3:6 but is placed here (along with vv.14-19 and vv.20-23) to function as an introduction to the extension of the ministry of Jesus to the Gentiles in vv.24-30 (the Syrophoenician woman), in vv.31-37 (the deaf-and-dumb man in the Decapolis) and, less obviously, in 8:1-10 (the feeding of the four thousand). No hint is given as to when or where the incident took place.

1-2 Another delegation of fact-finding theologians (Pharisees and teachers of the law) came down from Jerusalem (cf. 3:22) to investigate the Galilean activities of Jesus (v.1). What they discovered was that Jesus' disciples did not wash their hands before eating (v.2). Their complaint was not, of course, that the disciples by this failure were being unhygenic. The Pharisees had no concern with that. The question was one of ceremonial purity versus ceremonial defilement. We know that the Jews placed great importance on this as is shown by the fact that an entire division of the Mishnah (*Tohoroth*, "cleannesses") is devoted to this subject.

3–4 Verses 3–4 are a parenthesis (as in NIV). Mark felt it necessary to explain to his Gentile readers the Jewish custom of ceremonial handwashing, a custom based on the "tradition of the elders" (v.3). This consisted in a great mass of oral tradition that had arisen about the law. About A.D. 200 it was written down in the Mishnah, but in Jesus' day it was still in oral form. Its purpose was to regulate a man's life completely. If the law was silent or vague about a particular subject, one could be sure that the tradition would be vocal and explicit. The tradition, created and promulgated by the great rabbis, was passed on from one generation to the next and was considered binding.

Mark gives an example of the custom. Some versions translate v.4 as if what the Jews brought from the marketplace was washed before they ate it. But NIV is probably correct because the verb *baptisōntai* is middle voice ("wash themselves"). After being in the marketplace and coming into contact with Gentiles or even nonobservant Jews, the Pharisees would wash themselves to ensure their ritual cleanness. By way of further explanation, Mark adds that the Pharisees "observe many other traditions, such as the washing of cups, pitchers, and kettles."

5–7 To the question asked Jesus as to why his disciples acted as they did (v.5), he answered by quoting a passage from Isaiah, preceded by his own comment: "Isaiah was right when he prophesied about you hypocrites" (v.6). The word "hypocrite" (*hypokritēs*) means "play actor" and refers here to people whose worship is merely outward and not from the heart. In saying that Isaiah had prophesied about them, Jesus did not mean that Isaiah had in mind the Pharisees and the teachers of the law when he originally wrote these words but that his denunciation of the religious leaders of his day fitted those of Jesus' day. The quotation (Isa 29:13) is from the LXX, which, though differing somewhat from the MT, makes essentially the same point—viz., that in carrying out all their traditions and regulations, they were heartless hypocrites. Their outward appearance of piety was a lie, because it was not accompanied by a "total life commitment to the one who is the true object of religious devotion" (Anderson, p. 185). Jesus goes on (v.7) to equate neglect of true holiness to submission to man-made rabbinic tradition.

8–9 Here Jesus contrasts the "commands of God" with the "traditions of men" (v.8). It is clear that this great body of Jewish tradition had failed to get to the heart of God's commands. It was supposed to fence in the law so that the people would not infringe on it. Actually, however, the tradition distorted and ossified the law (v.9). In fact, it had even become a means of getting around God's law.

10–13 Jesus now cites a specific example of how the tradition was used to set aside God's commands. The first quotation is from the LXX of Exodus 20:12 and is a statement of the fifth commandment. The second quotation is from the LXX of Exodus 21:16 [17 MT]. In the latter the seriousness of failure to keep the fifth commandment is underscored—death is the penalty for anyone who curses his father or mother (v.10). But by means of the tradition, the responsibility of children to their parents could be easily circumvented (v.11). A son need only declare that what he had intended to give his father and mother be considered "Corban," i.e., a gift devoted to God, and it could no longer be designated for his parents. By devoting the gift to God, a son did not necessarily promise it to the temple nor did he prevent its use for himself. What he did do was to exclude legally his parents from benefiting from it (v. 12). So the very purpose for which the commandment was given was set aside by the tradition. This is what is meant by "nullifying" (akyrountes) the word of God (v. 13).

Notes

2 The word κοινός (koinos, "unclean") occurs again in v.5 and the verb form κοινόω (koinoō) in vv. 15, 18, 20, 23. It appears to be the theme word for the entire section (vv. 1–23). In classical Greek, koinos means "common" in contrast to ἴδιος (idios, "private"). It sometimes has the classical meaning in the LXX, but in 1 Macc 1:47, 62 it has the sense of "ritually unclean," which is its meaning here in Mark (cf. Acts 10:14, 28; 11:8; Rev 21:27).

3 NIV translates the Greek phrase ἐὰν μὴ πυγμῇ νίψωνται (ean mē pygmē nipsōntai) "unless they give their hands a ceremonial washing." Pygmē means literally "with a [the] fist." Taylor (p. 335) says that no satisfactory explanation of this difficult word can be given. The difficulty prompted some copyists to omit it (Δ syrˢ copˢᵃ Diatessaronᴾ) and others to substitute another word that to them made better sense, such as πυκνά (pykna, "often" or "thoroughly") (א W itᵇ·¹ vg al) or momento ("in a moment," itᵃ) or primo ("fist," itᵈ) (cf. Bruce Metzger, A Textual Commentary on the Greek New Testament, corrected ed. [New York: UBS, 1975], p. 93). The preferred reading (pygmē) has been taken to mean (1) with the clenched fist of one hand rubbing the palm of the other, (2) up to the wrist or elbow, or (3) with a handful of water (cupped hand). The RSV translation committee found the expression so difficult that they did not translate it at all.

6 Ὑποκρίτης (hypokritēs, "hypocrite")—"The thought here is probably not so much that the people concerned were consciously acting a part as that there was a radical inconsistency in their lives. . . . If they were themselves deceived as well as deceiving others, their situation was more, not less serious" (Cranfield, Gospel of Mark, p. 235).

G. True Defilement

7:14–23

¹⁴Again Jesus called the crowd to him and said, "Listen to me, everyone, and understand this. ¹⁵Nothing outside a man can make him 'unclean' by going into him. Rather, it is what comes out of a man that makes him 'unclean.' "

¹⁷After he had left the crowd and entered the house, his disciples asked him about this parable. ¹⁸"Are you so dull?" he asked. "Don't you see that nothing that enters a man from the outside can make him 'unclean'? ¹⁹For it doesn't go into his heart but into his stomach, and then out of his body." (In saying this, Jesus declared all foods "clean.")

²⁰He went on: "What comes out of a man is what makes him 'unclean.' ²¹For from within, out of men's hearts, come evil thoughts, sexual immorality, theft, murder, adultery, ²²greed, malice, deceit, lewdness, envy, slander, arrogance and folly. ²³All these evils come from inside and make a man 'unclean.' "

These verses form a part of the section vv. 1–23 and are not to be regarded as a separate, unconnected pericope. Their connection with what precedes is evident from Jesus' statement in v.15 that directly answers the question the Pharisees and teachers of the law raised (v.5).

14–15(16) Jesus has been speaking directly to the Pharisees and the teachers of the law. Now he calls the crowd around him (v.14) because he wants them to hear the crux of his teaching about what is clean. He prefaces his statement with a prophetic call to hear his words.

Jesus states clearly what does and does not make a person unclean (v.15). What is external cannot defile a person. Food, for example, cannot do this—not even if it is eaten with unwashed hands or declared unclean by kosher food laws. (This must have come as a startling statement to Jesus' hearers.) What really makes a person unclean comes from within, out of the heart and the will—what one thinks, says, desires, and does—these only can make a person unclean.

Verse 16 does not appear in NIV because, though it is present in the majority of the MSS, it does not occur in the important Alexandrian witnesses. "It appears to be a scribal gloss (derived perhaps from 4:9 or 4:23), introduced as an appropriate sequel to ver. 14" (Metzger, *Textual Commentary*, p. 95).

17–19 After leaving the crowd, Jesus entered a house (some have suggested it was Peter's house at Capernaum; but since the noun is without the definite article, no specific house is intended) and was teaching the disciples privately (v.17). Here, as in 9:28, 33 and 10:10, the place where Jesus reveals the true meaning of his teaching is in a "house." The explanation was prompted by the question of his disciples.

Although the disciples had already spent considerable time with Jesus and belonged to the inner circle of his concern, they were slow to grasp the meaning of his teaching. Jesus expressed surprise at this: "Are you so dull?" (v.18), i.e., "After all the time I have spent with you, do you still not comprehend spiritual truth?"

The reason nothing entering a person from the outside defiles him is because it enters into the stomach, not the heart (v.19). And it is in the heart that the true issues of life lie. In Semitic expression the heart is the center of human personality that determines man's actions and inaction (cf. Isa 29:13: "These people come near to me with their mouth and honor me with their lips, but their hearts are far from me").

In v.19b Mark explains for his readers the significance of Jesus' teaching about ceremonial purity.

> This statement clearly has its eye on a situation such as developed in the Pauline mission churches in which questions of clean and unclean foods (cf. Acts 10:9–16; 11:5–10 and see Rom 14:13ff.) and idol-meats became live issues (as we know from I Cor 8:10). This chapter in Mark 7 is perhaps the most obvious declaration of Mark's purpose as a Christian living in the Graeco-Roman world who wishes to publicize the charter of Gentile freedom by recording in the plainest terms Jesus' detachment from Jewish ceremonial and to spell out in clear tones the application of this to his readers. (Martin, *Mark*, p. 220). If Peter stands behind Mark's Gospel, these words are particularly apropos in the light of Acts 10:15.

20–23 Since v.20 is introduced by an indirect statement (*elegen de hoti*, "and he was saying that"; NIV, "he went on") and not a direct quotation, it is taken by some commentators to be Mark's further interpretation (cf. v.19b) or explanation of Jesus' teaching in vv.15–19a. The catechistical structure of section 19b–23 seems to lend support to this possibility. If it is Mark's interpretation, it is not inconsistent with Jesus' teaching in vv. 15–19a.

The main force of the passage is the same as in v.15b, which, in fact, is repeated in v.20. The source of uncleanness in anyone is the heart (v.21), for it is there that the true issues of life lie. The list that follows is "without parallel in the sayings of Jesus" (Taylor, p. 345), but it is typically Jewish (cf. Rom 1:29–31; Gal 5:19–23; 1 QS 4.9–11). The list is difficult to classify; it seems to move from overt sins to sinful attitudes or dispositions. "Evil thoughts" stand first, which suggests that what follows arises from these. *Porneia* ("sexual immorality") is a broader term than *moicheia* ("adultery") since it describes illegitimate sexual relations generally, while adultery is limited to illicit sex within marriage. *Aselgeia* ("lewdness") suggests open and shameless immorality. *Pleonexiai* ("greed," v.22) may have sexual overtones since it is frequently associated (as here) with words indicating sexual sins (e.g., Eph 4:19, 5:3; Col 3:5; 2 Peter 2:3). *Ophthalmos poneros* ("envy") is literally "evil eye," a Semitic term for "stinginess" (cf. Deut 15:9; Ecclus 14:10; 31:13) or perhaps better, "envious jealousy." *Blasphēmia* ("slander") includes speaking evil of either God or man, and *aphrosynē* describes "the stupidity of the man who lacks moral judgment" (Taylor, p. 346). The meanings of the rest of the words in the list are obvious.

Notes

15 Rawlinson (p. 96) tones down this statement of Jesus by arguing that since the Hebrew and Aramaic know no comparative degree, what Jesus is saying is that "pollutions from within are more serious than pollutions from without." But this fails to see the revolutionary nature of Jesus' teaching concerning the oral law.

H. *The Faith of the Syrophoenician Woman*

7:24–30

24Jesus left that place and went to the vicinity of Tyre. He entered a house and did not want anyone to know it; yet he could not keep his presence secret. 25In fact, as soon as she heard about him, a woman whose little daughter was possessed by an evil spirit came and fell at his feet. 26The woman was a Greek, born in Syrian Phoenicia. She begged Jesus to drive the demon out of her daughter.

27"First let the children eat all they want," he told her, "for it is not right to take the children's bread and toss it to their dogs."

28"Yes, Lord," she replied, "but even the dogs under the table eat the children's crumbs."

29Then he told her, "For such a reply, you may go; the demon has left your daughter."

30She went home and found her child lying on the bed, and the demon gone.

Why does Mark place this incident here? It seems to be a natural sequence to the preceding incidents in which Jesus breaks with the Jewish oral law and particularly the law of ceremonial cleanness. Jews normally had no relationship with Gentiles because associations with them made Jews ritually unclean. Jesus now shows by example that those oral laws are invalid and deliberately associates himself with a Gentile woman. Another purpose is to emphasize the mission to the Gentiles. The gospel of the kingdom is not limited to Israel, even though historically it came to her first (cf. v.27). Mark regards this story of the Syrophoenician woman as a natural consequence of Jesus' attitude toward the ceremonial law (vv.1–23); and by including it here, Mark wants to assure his Gentile readers that the "good news" is for them as it was for the Syrophoenician woman.

24 "Left that place" translates *ekeithen* (lit., "from here") and may refer to the house (7:17), to Gennesaret (6:53), or to some other place. The historical setting of the story is not known. Mark puts it here because of its theme ("the Gentiles hear the Good News") and not because it actually followed the preceding incident.

Phoenicia (now Lebanon), in which the city of Tyre was located, bordered on Galilee to the northwest. Why Jesus went there or how far he penetrated into this territory we are not told. Mark usually leaves such details up to the imagination of the reader. Apparently Jesus did not go there for public ministry. He went into a house "and did not want anyone to know it." This suggests that he went there to get out of the public eye, perhaps to rest and to prepare himself spiritually for what he knew lay ahead of him. But his hope of a time of quiet retirement was thwarted. His fame had apparently spread beyond the borders of Galilee into the territory of Phoenicia, and "he could not keep his presence secret."

25–26 One of the persons who sought out Jesus was a Gentile woman. No doubt she had heard about his healing powers and came to him because her daughter was possessed by an evil spirit (v.25). Mark says that the woman was "a Greek, born in Syrian Phoenicia" (v.26). Since she obviously was not a Greek by nationality, "Greek" is probably equivalent here to "Gentile" (in distinction from Jew) or to "Greek-speaking." By nationality the woman was a Syrophoenician. In those days Phoenicia belonged administratively to Syria. So Mark probably used Syrophoenician to distinguish this woman from the Libyo-Phoenicians of North Africa.

27–28 Jesus' conversation with this woman must have been in Greek, not Aramaic. There is no reason why Jesus, raised in Galilee, would not have known Greek. In the villages and towns of Palestine, he would ordinarily have used Aramaic. But in the coastal cities of the Gentiles, he spoke Greek.

Jesus' reply is in the form of a comparison between the children of the household and the little dogs (*kynarioi*, "puppies") that were kept as household pets (v.27). The contrast is between the privileged position of Israel ("children") and the less-privileged Gentiles ("little dogs"). First (*prōton*) the children are to be fed. Martin (*Mark*, p. 222) rightly attaches an eschatological sense to this verse, as in Mark 13:10, and treats the insertion of *prōton* "as a note required to indicate the passing of the exclusive privilege of Israel. The period immediately following the birth of the Jerusalem church saw the time of Israel's opportunity when the children 'first' would be fed; but this is no exclusive right belonging to the Jews. Later (ὕστερον) there would be provision made for Gentile dogs." So far as this woman was concerned, the "later" time had already come, because Jesus responded compassionately to her needs.

The reply of the woman (v.28) was remarkable. She admitted her status ("Yes, Lord"—the only time Jesus is called "Lord" in Mark) but refused to believe she was thereby excluded from any benefits. "Quite so, Lord; and in that case I may have a crumb" (Plummer, p. 189).

29–30 Jesus was pleased with the woman's reply (v.29). It revealed to him not only her wit but also her faith and humility, and he responded by declaring that her daughter had been healed ("the demon has left your daughter"). This is the only instance of healing at a distance found in Mark's Gospel. The woman returned home and discovered the truth of what Jesus had said (v.30). She found her daughter lying on the bed, perhaps as the result of the final convulsion of the demon as he came out of her (cf. Mark 9:26), and the demon gone.

I. Healing a Deaf and Mute Man

7:31–37

> [31]Then Jesus left the vicinity of Tyre and went through Sidon, down to the Sea of Galilee and into the region of the Decapolis. [32]There some people brought to him a man who was deaf and could hardly talk, and they begged him to place his hand on the man.
> [33]After he took him aside, away from the crowd, Jesus put his fingers into the man's ears. Then he spit and touched the man's tongue. [34]He looked up to heaven and with a deep sigh said to him, "*Ephphatha!*" (which means, "Be opened!"). [35]At this, the man's ears were opened, his tongue was loosened and he began to speak plainly.
> [36]Jesus commanded them not to tell anyone. But the more he did so, the more they kept talking about it. [37]People were overwhelmed with amazement. "He has done everything well," they said. "He even makes the deaf hear and the mute speak."

31 None of the other evangelists record this story. Mark includes it because it gives an account of another healing on Gentile territory, and this is its connection with the preceding story. The geographic references are difficult. Jesus journeys north from Tyre through Sidon and then apparently in a southeasterly direction through the territory of Herod Philip to the eastern side of the Sea of Galilee and into the territory of the Decapolis. The textual tradition indicates that the copyists had problems with this circuitous journey (cf. Notes). Yet the journey is not geographically impossible. Mark gives us no information as to what Jesus was doing during the journey. The Decapolis (the territory of the ten Greek cities) was largely Gentile, but there were also a significant number of Jews living there.

32 Mark says that the man brought to Jesus was "deaf and could hardly talk" (NEB has "had an impediment in his speech"). The adjective is *mogilalos* and is far from being a common word. This is its only occurrence in the entire NT; and it appears only once in the LXX, where its use is of great importance to the meaning of this story. Certainly Mark must have had Isaiah 35:6 in mind, which is a poetical description of the Messianic Age: "Then will the lame leap like a deer, and the tongue of the dumb [*mogilalos*] shout for joy." (For the rabbinic understanding of this text as fulfilled in the age of the Messiah, see R *Genesis* 95; Midrash *Tehillim* 146.8.)

The people brought the deaf mute to Jesus and begged him to lay his hands on him. Although they did not explicitly say so, they obviously wanted Jesus to heal the man. "They begged" (*parakalousin*) shows their concern for him, and Jesus responds to it. The deaf mute could make no intelligible request for himself.

33 In order to deal more personally with the mute, Jesus took him apart from the crowd. Mark emphasizes Jesus' desire to have personal contact with the people he heals. Here his actions seem to be done to help the man exercise faith—the fingers placed in his ears apparently indicate they were to be unblocked and the saliva on the tongue indicates it was going to be restored to normal use. Calvin (2:271–72) comments:

> The laying on of hands would of itself have been sufficiently efficacious, and even, without moving a finger, he might have accomplished it by a single act of his will; but it is evident that he made abundant use of outward signs, when they were found to be advantageous. Thus, by touching the tongue with spittle, he intended to point out that the faculty of speech was communicated by himself alone; and by putting his fingers into the ears, he showed that it belonged to his office to pierce the ears of the deaf.

(See also SBK, 2:17, where a similar understanding of the use of the fingers and spittle is offered.)

34–35 Jesus' looking up to heaven (v.34) is best understood as an attitude of prayer (cf. John 11:41; 17:1), and perhaps it was also a way of showing the man that God was the source of his power. The "deep sigh" should be interpreted together with the looking up into heaven. It was

> the "sighing" of the prayer, the sighing that accompanied the concealed communion of Jesus with the Father. If this looking up and sighing had been permanent technical aspects of the modus operandi of Jesus, we should definitely find references to them in early Christianity, but what we find there is that it is repeatedly stated that healing was simply performed only "in the name of Jesus"! (Van der Loos, *Miracles of Jesus*, p. 327)

Jesus' prayer consisted of only a single word—*Ephphatha*. According to his custom, Mark explains the meaning of this Aramaic word to his readers: "Be opened!" When Jesus spoke, as in this case, to the peasant people of Palestine, he used Aramaic (cf. Mark 5:41). To the Syrophoenician woman, he almost certainly spoke Greek.

The effect of the command was instantaneous (v.35). The man's ears were opened, his tongue loosed, and he spoke "plainly" (*orthōs*). He had not been completely mute; he had a speech impediment in his voice—"could hardly talk" (v.32).

36–37 Jesus again ordered the crowd not to divulge the miracle, but this had no effect at all (v.36). The more he insisted on their not talking about it, the more they blazed the miracle abroad. This is very much in contrast to the attitude of the crowd when, also in the Decapolis, he healed the Gadarene demoniac. Then the crowd was afraid and wanted to get rid of Jesus. His reason for enjoining silence here was probably the same as in 1:44. He did not want a false concept of him as only a miracle worker to spread lest it touch off a messianic insurrection and prevent him from accomplishing his God-appointed mission.

Another result of the healing was that the people were "overwhelmed" (*hyperperissōs*, a true *hapax legomenon*—i.e., a word occurring only once in Greek literature —that means "beyond measure," "in the extreme"). The statement "he has done everything well" reminds us of Genesis 1:31: "God saw all that he made, and it was very good." The reminder is not unsuitable, for in a profound sense Jesus' work is indeed "a new creation." And again we are reminded of the messianic significance of this miracle by words that reflect Isaiah 35:5–6 (already anticipated by the use of *mogilalon* ["hardly speak"] in v.32):

> Then will the eyes of the blind be opened and the ears of the deaf unstopped.
> Then will the lame leap like a deer, and the mute tongue shout for joy.

There can be no doubt that for Mark the significance of this miracle was the proclamation of the gospel in the territory of the Gentiles, a sign of the messianic activity of Jesus.

Notes

31 The best representatives of the Alexandrian and the Western texts, in addition to important Caesarean witnesses, support the reading ἦλθεν διὰ Σιδῶνος (*ēlthen dia Sidōnos*, "he went through Sidon"). This means that Jesus took a circuitous route, traveling from Tyre north through Sidon and thence southeast across the Leontes and south past Caesarea Philippi to the east of the Jordan and into the territory of the Decapolis on the east of the Lake of Galilee. The alternate reading καὶ Σιδῶνος ἦλθεν (*kai Sidōnos ēlthen*, "and he went to Sidon") arose because copyists either had difficulty with Mark's geography and deliberately changed the text or introduced it accidentally, being influenced by the well-known expression "Tyre and Sidon" (cf. Metzger, *Textual Commentary*, pp. 95–96).

J. *Feeding the Four Thousand*

8:1–10

¹During those days another large crowd gathered. Since they had nothing to eat, Jesus called his disciples to him and said, ²"I have compassion for these people; they have already been with me three days and have nothing to eat. ³If I send them home hungry, they will collapse on the way, because some of them have come a long distance."

⁴His disciples answered, "But where in this remote place can anyone get enough bread to feed them?"

⁵"How many loaves do you have?" Jesus asked.

"Seven," they replied.

⁶He told the crowd to sit down on the ground. When he had taken the seven loaves and given thanks, he broke them and gave them to his disciples to set before the people, and they did so. ⁷They had a few small fish as well; he gave thanks for them also and told the disciples to distribute them. ⁸The people ate and were satisfied. Afterward the disciples picked up seven basketfuls of broken pieces that were left over. ⁹About four thousand men were present. And having sent them away, ¹⁰he got into the boat with his disciples and went to the region of Dalmanutha.

Interest in Mark as an author in his own right, not merely a scissors-and-paste editor of the tradition, has focused attention lately on the structural arrangement of his Gospel. A study of the section 8:1–30 has revealed some important parallels with the section 6:31–7:37. Lane (p. 269) sets these out as follows:

6:31–44	Feeding the Multitude	8:1–9
6:45–56	Crossing the Sea and Landing	8:10
7:1–23	Conflict With the Pharisees	8:11–13
7:24–30	Conversation About Bread	8:13–21
7:31–36	Healing	8:22–26
7:37	Confession of Faith	8:27–30

The motif that seems to be behind this arrangement of the tradition is spiritual understanding—or lack of it. Jesus sounds a call to spiritual understanding in 7:14–18, but the disciples fail to understand after each feeding miracle (6:52; 8:14–21). The miracles of healing—the opening of the ears of the deaf man (7:31–36) and the eyes of the blind man (8:22–26)—are symbolic of and prepare the way for the opening of the spiritual understanding of the disciples. Mark's arrangement of the tradition to carry out his motif in no way decreases the historical reliability of the tradition.

The striking similarity between this story and the one in 6:34–44 raises the question whether there was one or two feedings of the multitude. The majority of scholars think there was only one and take 8:1–9 as a doublet of 6:34–44. Particularly important to this view is the disciples' apparent failure to remember the first feeding (cf. 8:4). Nonetheless there are strong reasons to support the view that 6:34–44 and 8:1–9 are indeed accounts of two separate events.

1. The language in the two accounts though similar also has significant differences (see commentary for details).

2. Jesus himself clearly refers to two feedings (8:18–21).

3. Verse 4 does not seem to be an insurmountable problem since it would be presumptuous to assume that the disciples always expected Jesus to meet a crisis situation by performing a miracle (cf. commentary for additional interpretations of 8:4).

The accounts certainly are similar. Yet their differences suggest that on two different occasions Jesus fed a multitude. There can be little doubt that Mark thought them to be two separate events.

1–3 "During those days" (v.1) probably connects this incident with the preceding one (7:31–37). Jesus remained in the Decapolis, on the east side of the Lake of Galilee. The presence of a large crowd is implied. They had been with Jesus for three days, probably receiving instruction from him. Taylor (p. 358) points out that "the reference to 'three days' is peculiar to the narrative, distinguishing it from 6:35–44, in which the crossing, the meal, and the recrossing all take place on the same day." Jesus, not the disciples (as in 6:35–36), recognized the physical needs of the crowds (v.2). He was moved with compassion for them because they had not had anything to eat for three days. Another difference in this amount is that Jesus immediately dismisses the idea that the crowd should be sent away for food ("If I send them home hungry, they will collapse on the way" [v.3]), whereas in 6:36 the disciples definitely ask him to send them away. The "long distance" that "some of them" had come may imply that the crowd was partly made up of local people.

4 The disciples' reply may indicate that they had completely forgotten the feeding of the five thousand. This is perhaps the strongest argument against the view that there were two separate feedings. But the argument is not so strong as it appears. Several things may be said in rebuttal (cf. Cranfield, *Gospel of Mark*, p. 205).

1. A considerable period of time may have elapsed between the two events.

2. Even mature Christians (which the disciples were not), having experienced God's power and provision, have subsequently acted in unbelief.

3. The reluctance of Jesus to perform miracles must have so impressed itself on the disciples that they did not expect to meet every crisis in that fashion.

4. Some allowance must be made for the assimilation of the language of the two accounts because of their repeated use in teaching and worship.

The disciples' answer here is in terms of the difficulty of finding enough food for such a huge crowd rather than sending them away to get their own as in 6:36.

5–7 Only seven loaves were available to feed the crowd (v.5). Again the details differ from the account in chapter 6. There is no ordering of the people into groups of hundreds and fifties. They are simply asked to sit down where they are on the ground (v.6). Jesus gives thanks separately for the bread and the fish—there were a few small ones, Mark tells us—and after each prayer the disciples distributed the food to the people. NIV does not distinguish between *eucharistein* ("to give thanks," v.6) and *eulogein* ("to bless," v.7), translating both as "give thanks." The difficulty copyists had with the idea of Jesus' "blessing" the fish is reflected by the variant *eucharistēsas* ("having given thanks") in v.7 and by the omission of *auta* ("them," referring to the fish) in the same verse. Mark's "having blessed them [in God's name]" is tantamount to giving thanks.

8 As always Jesus' provision was sufficient—"the people ate and were satisfied." But it was not merely sufficient. Seven (there were twelve in ch. 6) basketfuls of fragments were left over and collected by the disciples. The use of *spyris* for "basket" here instead of *kophinos* (6:43) is striking and suggests two different occasions. A *spyris* is a large basket—Paul was lowered from the wall of Damascus in one (Acts 9:25)—whereas a *kophinos* is a wicker basket in which Jews ordinarily carried their food when journeying.

9–10 Again the details are different. The crowd numbered "about four thousand" (v.9; five thousand in ch. 6). Jesus got into the boat with his disciples (v.10; in ch. 6 he had the disciples get into the boat and go to Bethsaida, while he stayed back to dismiss the crowd).

The identity of Dalmanutha is unknown. Matthew (15:39) says Jesus went to the vicinity of Magadan." Dalmanutha and Magadan (or Magdala), located on the western shore of the Lake of Galilee, may have been names for the same place or two places located near each other. This is the only reference anywhere to the name Dalmanutha.

K. Requesting a Sign From Heaven

8:11–13

> [11]The Pharisees came and began to question Jesus. To test him, they asked him for a sign from heaven. [12]He sighed deeply and said, "Why does this genera-

tion ask for a miraculous sign? I tell you the truth, no sign will be given to it."
13Then he left them, got back into the boat and crossed to the other side.

11 This paragraph seems quite separate from the one immediately preceding it. If it is to be understood as completing the pericope found in 3:22–30, a context would be provided that would be helpful for its interpretation. It seems best, however, to consider the paragraph as an isolated section Mark places here to form a parallel in this section (8:1–30) with 7:1–23 in the previous section (6:31–7:37). Both incidents relate to conflict with the Pharisees.

The request for a sign by the Pharisees was not sincere. It was "to test him." The word is *peirazō*, and in this context it probably should be translated "tempt" (cf. its use in 1:13 of Jesus' temptation). Jesus' temptation in the wilderness was not a once-for-all experience. The Devil came back again and again to tempt him. Here the temptation was for Jesus to produce a "sign from heaven." Two interpretations commend themselves. First, since the word *sēmeion* is used, a word by which the Synoptists denote an outward compelling proof of divine authority, what the Pharisees were asking was for more proof than Jesus' miracles (*dynameis*) afforded. Jesus resolutely refused the request for such a sign because it arose out of unbelief. Second, since the word *dynameis* ("mighty acts") is regularly used for Jesus' miracles in the Synoptics, and since the Pharisees ask for *semeia* ("signs"), what they are requesting is evidence of Jesus' trustworthiness, not of his supernatural power (Lane, p. 277). The former interpretation seems more likely and is in keeping with how NIV translates *sēmeion apo tou ouranou* ("a sign from heaven"). The mighty acts of Jesus are not clear enough for the Pharisees. Indeed, they had on one occasion ascribed them to Satan's power. They want a higher level of sign—from heaven, i.e., clearly from God.

12 Jesus responded to their request by sighing deeply. Here the word *anastenazō*, found only here in the NT, is used. It describes Jesus' grief and disappointment when faced with the unbelief of those who, because of their spiritual privileges, ought to have been more responsive to him. There is a note of impatience in Jesus' question "Why does this generation ask for a miraculous sign?" The designation "this generation" (*hē genea hautē*) is the equivalent of the rabbinic *ha-dôr ha-zeh* and includes more than the Pharisees. Jesus has in mind the entire people, i.e., the Jewish people. To them no sign will be given. This is a particularly strong statement by Jesus. It is introduced by the solemn asseveration "I tell you the truth," and the statement itself represents in Greek a shortened form of the Hebrew self-imprecation: "If I do such a thing may I die" (cf. Taylor, p. 136). Thus Jesus, with deep feeling and with an oath, flatly refuses to give any sign.

As to why Jesus refused to do this, Martin (*Mark*, p. 174) cogently says: "For Mark and Paul the answer to this wrongful instance is the same. There is no legitimating sign—save the ambiguity of the humiliated and crucified Lord; and to see in his cross the power and wisdom of God is to be shut up to the exercise of faith, which by definition can never rest in proofs or signs, or else its character would be lost." This teaching of Jesus was doubtless what the church in Rome needed to hear, especially if they had been too engrossed in an exalted-Lord christology.

13 Having so emphatically made his point, Jesus left the Pharisees, got into the boat, and, with his disciples (cf. v.14), crossed over to the east side of the lake.

L. *The Yeast of the Pharisees and Herod*

8:14–21

¹⁴The disciples had forgotten to bring bread, except for one loaf they had with them in the boat. ¹⁵"Be careful," Jesus warned them. "Watch out for the yeast of the Pharisees and that of Herod."

¹⁶They discussed this with one another and said, "It is because we have no bread."

¹⁷Aware of their discussion, Jesus asked them: "Why are you talking about having no bread? Do you still not see or understand? Are your hearts hardened? ¹⁸Do you have eyes but fail to see, and ears but fail to hear? And don't you remember? ¹⁹When I broke the five loaves for the five thousand, how many basketfuls of pieces did you pick up?"

"Twelve," they replied.

²⁰"And when I broke the seven loaves for the four thousand, how many basketfuls of pieces did you pick up?"

They answered, "Seven."

²¹He said to them, "Do you still not understand?"

14 For some reason the disciples (the Greek merely says "they," but NIV correctly assumes that the pronoun refers to the disciples) had forgotten to bring an adequate supply of bread with them for the trip across the lake. Had their quick departure from the Pharisees caused this? At any rate, their failure sets the stage for the teaching of our Lord in this pericope. Some commentators see in the "one loaf" a symbolic reference to Jesus. The disciples failed to see that the one loaf they had with them was none other than Jesus himself, and that was sufficient.

15 The connection of this verse with vv. 11–12 is clear, but its connection with the immediately preceding verses is obscure. Jesus warns his disciples about the yeast of the Pharisees and of Herod. Here, as generally in Scripture, yeast is a symbol of evil; and, as only a very small amount of it is necessary to leaven a loaf of bread, so evil has a permeating power. Here the yeast of the Pharisees clearly refers to their desire for a sign from God to validate the actions of Jesus. The yeast of Herod is mentioned because he too (cf. Luke 23:8) desired a sign. Jesus is warning his disciples not to make the same mistake the Pharisees and Herod did. He is appealing to them to understand that the authority he possesses cannot be proved by a sign. Only by faith can they recognize him as the bringer of God's salvation.

16 Since the meaning of v. 16 turns on which reading is adopted, that must be the first consideration in interpreting it. KJV, RSV, NEB, and NIV follow the majority of Greek MSS and read *echomen* ("we have"). However, *echousin* ("they have") has good attestation and is adopted as a "C" rated reading by the third edition of the UBS Greek text (a change of heart from the second edition). The rationale is that the reading *echomen* seems to be an accommodation to the following context and probably was also influenced by Matthew 16:7 (cf. Metzger, *Textual Commentary*, p. 98). If, following the reading *echousin, hoti* is taken as an indirect interrogative ("why"), the translation would be thus: "They discussed with one another why they had no bread." According to this reading, the disciples were so concerned to find out who was to blame for not bringing more bread that they completely ignored

Jesus' warning about the yeast of the Pharisees and of Herod. Such an understanding of this verse heightens Mark's depiction of the disciples' lack of understanding.

17–21 Jesus rebuked his disciples for their lack of understanding (v. 17). They were like those on the outside (cf. 4:11–12) who had eyes but did not see and ears but did not hear (v. 18). They should not have been so concerned over the bread. That concern had prevented them from profiting from the warning about the leaven of the Pharisees and of Herod. They should have remembered how abundantly Jesus had provided for them on two occasions—so much so that on both occasions they had leftover bread to collect (vv. 19–20). He, the Provider, was with them in the boat. What else could they want or need? Almost pleadingly Jesus asks, "Do you still not understand?" (v. 21).

Notes

11 The verb ζητεῖν (zētein, "ask") is used consistently in Mark in a negative sense (cf. 11:18; 12:12; 14:1). Here it is used in the same way. The asking was wrongheaded and misguided.

12 The introductory formula ἀμὴν λέγω ὑμῖν (amēn legō hymin, "I tell you the truth") is evidence that the form we have of the saying in Mark's Gospel, which allows for no exception in sign giving, "stands at the furthest recoverable point of the tradition. Indeed it may be claimed that we hear a true accent of *ipsissima vox Jesu*" (Martin, *Mark*, p. 165).

12 Εἰ δοθήσεται (ei dothēsetai, "will not be given") is a very strong negation, ei being equivalent to the Hebrew אִם (im), which introduces an oath (cf. Ps 7:4–5 LXX). Also, the fact that the verb is in the passive voice, thus indicating that Mark is using a circumlocution for the name of God, strengthens the statement even more. The meaning is "Surely God will not give a sign to this generation."

15 In the rabbinical writings, yeast is usually a symbol for "the evil influence" (יֵצֶר הָרַע yēṣer hara') or the wicked ways and dispositions of men (cf. SBK, 1:728). Paul also uses yeast in a negative sense (1 Cor 5:6–8).

19 As already noted in 8:8, two different words are used for basket in the two stories of the feeding of the multitude. Κόφινος (kophinos, "lunch basket") is used in all six references to the feeding of the five thousand (Matt 14:20; 16:9; Mark 6:43; 8:19; Luke 9:17; John 6:13), while σπυρίς (spyris, "hamper") is used in all four references to the feeding of the four thousand (Matt 15:37; 16:10; Mark 8:8, 20). This consistency argues powerfully in favor of two separate incidents.

M. *Healing a Blind Man at Bethsaida*

8:22–26

22They came to Bethsaida, and some people brought a blind man and begged Jesus to touch him. 23He took the blind man by the hand and led him outside the village. When he had spit on the man's eyes and put his hands on him, Jesus asked, "Do you see anything?"

24He looked up and said, "I see people; they look like trees walking around."

25Once more Jesus put his hands on the man's eyes. Then his eyes were opened, his sight was restored, and he saw everything clearly. 26Jesus sent him home, saying, "Don't go into the village."

22 This incident, which is recorded only in Mark, takes place at Bethsaida ("house of the fish") located on the east bank of the Jordan River, where it flows into the Sea of Galilee. At this place "some people" (Mark does not identify them) brought a blind man to Jesus for healing. The fact that the initiative seems to have come more from the people who brought him than from the man himself may account for the way Jesus dealt with him (cf. Mark 7:32ff.).

23–24 Why did Jesus lead the blind man out of the village (v.23)? Was it to avoid the clamor and excitement of the people or perhaps to make personal contact with the man apart from the distraction of the crowd? Most of the miracles in Mark were done in public. Only on three occasions did Jesus withdraw from the people to heal: viz., the raising of Jairus's daughter (5:35–43), where Jesus' motive is clearly to rid himself of the commotion caused by the professional mourners; the healing of the deaf mute (7:31–37), where Jesus wanted to establish a personal contact with the man to help his faith; and the present incident, where the motive seems to be the same as in the healing of the deaf mute.

Jesus performs a double action: he spits on the man's eyes and lays his hands on him. The only parallel anywhere near this double treatment occurs in the incident in John 9, where the blind man has his eyes anointed with clay and then washed in the Pool of Siloam. To Jesus' question "Do you see anything?" the answer of the blind man here in Mark is essentially "Yes, but not clearly" (v.24). Two things require comment: (1) the man had probably not been born blind or else he would not have been able to identify trees as trees and (2) the return of his sight was gradual. As to why Jesus abandoned his usual method of instantaneous healing, Calvin (2:285) said: "He did so most probably for the purpose of proving, in the case of this man, that he had full liberty as to his method of proceeding, and was not restricted to a fixed rule. . . . And so the grace of Christ, which had formerly been poured out suddenly on others, flowed by drops, as it were, on this man."

25–26 The second laying on of hands is unique in the healing ministry of Jesus (v.25). The result was a complete cure. Mark's account of it graphically records that fact: "his eyes were opened, his sight was restored, and he saw everything clearly." The word translated "clearly" (*tēlaugōs*) means "clearly at a distance" and indicates the completeness of the restoration of the man's sight. As for the reason why Jesus did this healing gradually, Mark gives us no hint. Jesus may have moved only as quickly as the man's faith would allow (in Mark's Gospel faith as a requisite for healing is emphasized). But Calvin's suggestion that Jesus was demonstrating his sovereign freedom seems more likely. One thing is certain. The early church did not make up this story!

In v.26 Jesus orders the man to go home directly without first going into the town of Bethsaida. The variant reading "Don't go and tell anybody in the city" is an attempt to clarify the reason why Jesus ordered the man not to go into the town. Doubtless it was influenced by other passages in Mark in which Jesus does enjoin silence.

The importance of this story for Mark is that it anticipates the opening of the eyes of understanding of the disciples. It is the second in a pair of incidents that only Mark records (the first one is 7:24–37) and that fulfill the OT messianic expectations of Isaiah 35:5–6. Mark uses both incidents to lead up to the revelation of the messianic dignity of Jesus to the disciples (8:27–30). Their eyes too are opened, not by

691

human perception, but by the miracle of God's gracious revelation, which was as much a miracle as the opening of the blind man's eyes.

N. *Recognizing Jesus as Messiah*

8:27–30

> 27Jesus and his disciples went on to the villages around Caesarea Philippi. On the way he asked them, "Who do people say I am?"
> 28They replied, "Some say John the Baptist; others say Elijah; and still others, one of the prophets."
> 29"But what about you?" he asked. "Who do you say I am?
> Peter answered, "You are the Christ."
> 30Jesus warned them not to tell anyone about him.

This incident is usually taken to mark the beginning of the second half of Mark's Gospel. While it is true that 8:27–30 has a close connection with 8:31–9:1, its relationship to 8:22–26 is even closer. This may be seen by the remarkable parallelism in the two stories—a parallelism that may be set out like this:

8:22	Circumstances	8:27
8:23–24	Partial Sight—Partial Understanding	8:28
8:25	Sight—Understanding	8:29
8:26	Injunction to Silence	8:30

Assuming that this arrangement is not by chance, Mark uses the account of the opening of the blind man's eyes to symbolize and anticipate the opening of the understanding of the disciples as to the true nature of the messiahship of Jesus. To be sure, their understanding was not complete, as 8:32 makes clear; yet the two accounts are generally parallel. Where the parallelism breaks down is at the point of partial understanding (8:28), for this is a partial understanding on the part of the people, not the disciples. Mark could have changed the story to force parallelism. That he did not do so supports the historicity of the account.

27 The first half of Mark's Gospel mounts to a climax with the story of the disciples' recognition of Jesus' messiahship. Caesarea Philippi was at the foot of Mount Hermon, on a shelf of land 1,150 feet above sea level and overlooking the north end of the Jordan River Valley. Originally the city was called Paneas (the name survives today as Banias) in honor of the Roman god Pan, whose shrine was located there. Herod Philip had rebuilt the ancient city and named it in honor of Tiberias Caesar and himself. Thus it was known as Caesarea Philippi and was distinguished from Caesarea, the Roman city on the Mediterranean coast. It was somewhere in the vicinity of Caesarea Philippi that Jesus put to his disciples the crucial question "Who do people say that I am?"

Cranfield is certainly right when he says:

> To argue that the content of the question and the fact that Jesus takes the initiative with it shows that the material is secondary, since according to Jewish custom it was the disciple, not the Rabbi, who asked the questions, and since Jesus would not have asked a question concerning something about which he must

have been as well informed as those whom he is supposed to question, is surely unimaginative. (*Gospel of Mark,* p. 268).

Jesus was no ordinary rabbi and did not ask the question simply to get information. He used it as preliminary to his second question (v.29).

28 The answers all reflect an inadequate view of Christ. John the Baptist had a preparatory role. He looked for another messenger far greater than himself (cf. Mark 1:7–8). A common Jewish concept of the day was that of "Elijah redivivus" (Elijah returned or revived), based on Malachi 3:1; 4:5; but he too was only a forerunner of the Messiah (cf. 6:14–15, where the same opinions are expressed about Jesus). "One of the prophets" reflects an even lower view of Jesus. He is merely one of many prophets who have come on the scene of Israel's history. It is surprising that the disciples do not report that anyone said that Jesus was the Messiah, especially since the demons recognized who he was and said so publicly (1:24; 3:11, 5:7). But his messiahship was veiled from the crowd.

29 Jesus now directs the question at the disciples. His use of *hymeis* ("you"), the emphatic pronoun, is particularly important. NIV catches this nuance by repeating the "you": "But what about you? . . . Who do you say I am?" In other words Jesus is asking, "Who do you, my most intimate and trusted friends—in contrast to the other people who neither know me nor understand me—think I am?"

Peter, true to form, had a ready answer: "You are the Christ." Peter speaks not only for himself. He is the spokesman for the Twelve, and in his confession one of the themes of this Gospel (cf. 1:1; "The beginning of the gospel about Jesus Christ") is stated.

The Greek word *Christos* ("Christ") translates the Hebrew *māšiaḥ* ("Messiah") and means the "Anointed One" of God. In the OT the word is used of anyone who was anointed with the holy oil, as, for example, the priests and kings of Israel (cf. Exod 29:7, 21; 1 Sam 10:1, 6; 16:13; 2 Sam 1:14, 16). The word carries with it the idea of chosenness by God, consecration to his service, and enduement with his power to accomplish the task assigned.

Toward the close of the OT period, the word "anointed" assumed a special meaning. It denoted the ideal king anointed and empowered by God to deliver his people and establish his righteous kingdom (Dan 9:25–26). Particularly important in the development of the concept was its use in the pseudepigraphal Psalms of Solomon (chs. 17–18). There the coming ruler is spoken of as restoring David's kingdom to its former prosperity and greatness. The ideas that clustered around the title "Messiah" tended to be political and national in nature. It is probably for that reason that Jesus seldom used the term. Of its seven occurrences in Mark, only three of them are in sayings of Jesus (9:41; 12:35; 13:21); and in none of these does he use the title of himself.

Because Jesus was reluctant to speak of himself as the Messiah does not mean that he did not believe himself to be the Messiah. In this passage (8:29) and in 14:6–62, he accepted it as used of him by others (cf. John 4:25–26).

And this is hardly surprising; for the title, in spite of all the false and narrow hopes which had become attached to it, was peculiarly fitted to express his true relation both to the OT and to the people of God. . . . the title, applied to Jesus,

693

designates him as the true meaning and fulfillment of the long succession of Israel's anointed kings and priests, the King and Priest . . . ; the Prophet anointed with the Spirit of God, who fulfills the long line of Israel's prophets; and the One in whom the life of the whole nation of Israel finds its fulfillment and meaning, in whom and for whose sake the people of Israel were, and the new Israel now is, the anointed people of God. (Cranfield, *Gospel of Mark*, pp. 270–71)

Peter's confession revealed real insight into the nature of Christ's person and mission, but his concept of Jesus' messiahship was far from being perfect. Peter still had much to learn of Messiah's suffering, rejection, and death, as the immediately following incident reveals.

30 Jesus' injunction of silence arose out of his knowledge of the disciples' defective view of his messiahship. They still needed instruction about it before they would be given permission to proclaim it without restraint.

V. The Journey to Jerusalem (8:31–10:52)

A new section in Mark's Gospel begins with 8:31. Its structure centers around three predictions Jesus makes of his passion (8:31; 9:31; 10:33–34). What had previously been veiled is now stated openly: the Son of Man must go up to Jerusalem, suffer and die, and on the third day be raised from the dead. This is the secret of Jesus' messiahship, and it is now revealed. Mark also stresses what this will mean for Jesus' followers. Throughout the section (cf. 8:34–38; 9:35; 10:29–30, 38–39) there are sayings about what true discipleship is, with the stress on suffering. Another purpose of this middle section of Mark's Gospel is to provide for Jesus' move from Galilee (where almost his entire ministry took place) to Jerusalem for the climactic events of his ministry. Mark does this by means of a travel narrative. Jesus progressively moves closer and closer to the Holy City. The final event, the healing of blind Bartimaeus (10:46–52), takes place when Jesus is coming out of Jericho with the crowds of people on the way to the Passover Feast in Jerusalem. Chapter 11 opens with the Triumphal Entry into the city.

This section with its emphasis on the suffering of the Messiah and of those that follow him must have had special meaning for the persecuted Christians in Rome. Mark is reminding them that to follow Jesus is to follow the path of suffering and even death.

A. *First Prediction of the Passion*

8:31–33

> [31]He then began to teach them that the Son of Man must suffer many things and be rejected by the elders, chief priests and teachers of the law, and that he must be killed and after three days rise again. [32]He spoke plainly about this, and Peter took him aside and began to rebuke him.
> [33]But when Jesus turned and looked at his disciples, he rebuked Peter. "Get behind me, Satan!" he said. "You do not have in mind the things of God, but the things of men."

31 Jesus now begins to teach his disciples what messiahship really meant. However he does not refer to himself as Messiah but as the Son of Man. Since this title is so important theologically, extended comment is in order.

"Son of Man" is by far the favorite expression Jesus uses in the Gospels to refer to himself. It occurs eighty-one times; and, with the possible exceptions of Mark 2:10 and 28—where the title "Son of Man" seems to be part of Mark's editorial comments—no one else, neither his friends nor his foes, refers to Jesus as the Son of Man.

"Son of Man" occurs in the OT. In the Psalms it means simply "man" (cf. Pss 8:4; 80:17); and in Ezekiel, where it occurs over ninety times, it is the particular name by which God addresses the prophet. These OT passages throw some light on the NT usage. The most helpful text, however, is Daniel 7:13–14:

> In my vision at night I looked, and there before me was one like a son of man, coming with the clouds of heaven. He approached the Ancient of Days and was led into his presence. He was given authority, glory and sovereign power; all peoples, nations and men of every language worshiped him. His dominion is an everlasting dominion that will not pass away, and his kingdom is one that will never be destroyed.

This passage, depicting the Son of Man as a heavenly figure who at the end time brings the kingdom to the oppressed on earth, is especially reflected in the sayings of Jesus in Mark's Gospel that speak of the coming of the Son of Man "in his Father's glory with the holy angels" (8:38; 13:26; 14:62). The title has, however, been infused with additional meaning, especially in those passages that associate the Son of Man with suffering and death (8:31; 9:9, 12, 31; 10:33, 45; 14:21, 41). The combining of the motif of eschatological glory with that of suffering and death is what characterizes the Son-of-Man idea in Mark's Gospel as elsewhere in the Synoptics. It is evident that Jesus considered "Son of Man" a messianic title because, immediately following Peter's confession of him as the Christ, he began to teach them that the Son of Man (equivalent to Christ in v.29) must suffer, etc. Son of Man was the title Jesus preferred in referring to himself because, unlike "Messiah," it was not freighted with connotations that might prove harmful to his God-appointed mission.

The Son of Man "must" (dei) suffer. Gould (p. 153) remarks: "The necessity arises, first, from the hostility of men; secondly, from the spiritual nature of his work, which made it impossible for him to oppose force to force; and thirdly from the providential purpose of God, who made the death of Jesus the central thing in redemption." If dei refers to God's will in Scripture, the most likely reference is to the Suffering Servant passage in Isaiah 52:13–53:12. The Targum to Isaiah shows how difficult it was for the Jews to associate suffering with the Messiah. There the sufferings are referred to the people and the other statements in the passage to the Messiah. However, the common view that Jesus was the first to associate sufferings with the Messiah is questionable. Cranfield (Gospel of Mark, p. 277) says that evidence for a suffering Messiah existed in Judaism before Jesus' day, and its rareness was due to Anti-Christian polemic.

Jesus predicted that the rejection of the Messiah would be by three groups: the elders, the chief priests, and the teachers of the law. The elders were the lay members of the Sanhedrin; the chief priests included not only Caiaphas, the high priest, and Annas, the emeritus high priest, but the members of the high priestly families; the teachers of the law were the professional scribes. These three groups made up the Sanhedrin, the Jewish high court.

The death of the Son of Man would be followed by his vindication: after three days he would be raised from the dead. "After three days" occurs also in Mark 9:31;

10:34. In Matthew 16:21; 17:23; 20:19; Luke 9:22; 18:33, "on the third day" is used. This change may indicate a difficulty with the Markan expression. Actually the two expressions are identical in meaning. Taylor (p. 378) points out that, contrary to English usage, in a Jewish context "after three days" can mean a period of less than seventy-two hours. Another possibility is that "after three days" is another way of saying "after a short period of time."

Verse 31 is particularly important because it is the only explanation in Mark's Gospel of "the messianic secret." Jesus did not want his messiahship to be disclosed because it involved suffering, rejection, and death. Popular expectations of messiahship would have hindered, if not prevented, the accomplishment of his divinely ordained (*dei*, "must") messianic mission.

32 Jesus now spoke plainly about his suffering role as Son of Man and Messiah. Before he had veiled it. The message got through to Peter, but he refused to accept it. Peter had the greatest difficulty in conceiving of messiahship in any other than the popular theological and political categories. A suffering Messiah! Unthinkable! The Messiah was a symbol of strength, not weakness. So Peter took Jesus aside and, amazingly, rebuked him. The word translated "rebuked" (*epitimaō*) is the same one used for the silencing of the demons (cf. 1:25; 3:12).

33 Jesus' words to Peter were not only very severe, they were deliberately spoken in the presence of the other disciples ("Jesus turned and looked at his disciples"). They probably shared Peter's views and needed the rebuke, too. The severity of the rebuke arises from Jesus' recognition in Peter's attempt to dissuade him from going to the Cross the same temptation he had experienced from Satan at the outset of his ministry. Satan offered him the option of using the world's means of accomplishing his mission (cf. Matt 4:8–10). On that occasion Jesus rebuked him, "Away from me, Satan! For it is written: 'Worship the Lord your God, and serve him only'" (Matt 4:10). Here, too, Jesus recognized the satanic opposition in Peter. "'Get behind me, Satan!' he said. 'You do not have in mind the things of God, but the things of men.'" Peter was opposing the divine will. He had in mind a popular messiahship. That was the way the world thought; it was not how God had planned Jesus' ministry and mission.

B. *Requirements of Discipleship*

8:34–9:1

> [34]Then he called the crowd to him along with his disciples and said: "If anyone would come after me, he must deny himself and take up his cross and follow me. [35]For whoever wants to save his life will lose it, but whoever loses his life for me and for the gospel will save it. [36]What good is it for a man to gain the whole world, yet forfeit his soul? [37]Or what can a man give in exchange for his soul? [38]If anyone is ashamed of me and my words in this adulterous and sinful generation, the Son of Man will be ashamed of him when he comes in his Father's glory with the holy angels."
>
> [9:1]And he said to them, "I tell you the truth, some who are standing here will not taste death before they see the kingdom of God come with power."

This section is composed of separate sayings already brought together in the tradition Mark received or, more probably, brought together by Mark himself. The purpose of the section is to encourage and strengthen the Roman Christians who are faced with persecution and trials. Mark is saying to them that such experiences are normal in the life of discipleship. "Jesus had called his own disciples to the realization that suffering is not only his destiny but theirs" (Lane, p. 306).

34 Now Jesus addresses the crowd as well as his disciples. The requirements for following him are not just for the Twelve but for all Christians. Two requirements of discipleship are (1) denial of self and (2) taking up one's cross and following Jesus. By denial of self, Jesus does not mean to deny oneself something. He means to renounce self—to cease to make self the object of one's life and actions. This involves a fundamental reorientation of the principle of life. God, not self, must be at the center of life.

Cross bearing does not refer to some irritation in life. Rather, it involves the way of the cross. The picture is of a man, already condemned, required to carry his cross on the way to the place of execution, as Jesus was required to do (cf. Luke 23:26). Although the cross was a Roman method of execution, it was well known to the Jews of Jesus' day. Certainly the Christians in Rome were acquainted with it. To bear the cross is to follow Jesus. This means suffering and death—a message especially relevant to the Roman Christians.

35 This statement relates to a situation in which Christians faced the alternatives of confessing Christ or denying him. Jesus warns that by denying him, one's physical life may be saved; but one's eschatological life—i.e., his eternal life, his salvation—will be lost. Conversely, to lose one's physical life by remaining true to Christ—i.e., by confessing him under duress—is to be assured of eternal life and salvation. This seems to be the meaning of the verse in this context in Mark. Thus it would have sounded a warning to any in Mark's church who might be thinking of defecting under trial. "For me" stresses the absoluteness of Jesus' claim for allegiance, and "for the gospel" is probably a reference to the preaching of the gospel for which men are to give their lives.

36–37 These two verses emphasize the incomparable worth of the *psychē* ("eschatological life," "soul"). Not even "the whole world" compares in value to it (v.36). And once a man has forfeited his share in eternal life (in this context, by a denial of Jesus), there is no way he can get it back (v.37). Even the whole world, if he had it, could not buy back eternal life for him—another stern warning against recanting the Christian faith.

38 Here is the climax of the warning. To be ashamed of Jesus and his words (the equivalent of saving one's life in v.35) has serious consequences. In the End, at the Judgment, the Son of Man will be ashamed of that person. The Hebrew parallelism in this verse clearly identifies the "of me" (Jesus) in the first part with the Son of Man in the second part. The mention of "his Father's glory with the holy angels" suggests the final judgment (cf. 2 Thess 1:7).

9:1 Since "and he said to them" is often used in Mark as an editorial link, the verse is probably an independent saying Mark has placed here. If this is true, then Mark's placement of this saying is for the purpose of making a transition between the

Transfiguration (9:2–8), a momentary manifestation of the power of the kingdom, and the Parousia (8:38), the full manifestation of it. On this understanding the Transfiguration anticipates and guarantees the Parousia.

Jesus prefaces his announcement with the solemn "I tell you the truth." The metaphor "taste death," is a reference to violent death for the sake of Jesus. Before that happens to some of them, they will see God's kingdom come in power. As the above interpretation suggests, it is not necessary to interpret this verse to mean that Jesus taught the Parousia would come in the lifetime of the disciples. Nowhere in the Gospels does Jesus say that.

C. The Transfiguration

9:2–8

> ²After six days Jesus took Peter, James and John with him and led them up a high mountain, where they were all alone. There he was transfigured before them. ³His clothes became dazzling white, whiter than anyone in the world could bleach them. ⁴And there appeared before them Elijah and Moses, who were talking with Jesus.
>
> ⁵Peter said to Jesus, "Rabbi, it is good for us to be here. Let us put up three shelters—one for you, one for Moses and one for Elijah." ⁶(He did not know what to say, they were so frightened.)
>
> ⁷Then a cloud appeared and enveloped them, and a voice came from the cloud: "This is my Son, whom I love. Listen to him!"
>
> ⁸Suddenly, when they looked around, they no longer saw anyone with them except Jesus.

The Transfiguration is a revelation of the glory of the Son of God, a glory now hidden but to be manifested completely and openly at the end of the age, when the Son of Man will come in the glory of his Father to render judgment on the world (cf. Mark 8:38).

The purpose of the Transfiguration is directed toward the disciples (observe the expressions "before them" [vv.2, 4] and "enveloped them" [v.7] and observe also that the Voice from the cloud speaks to them [v.7]). Mark places the Transfiguration here as a confirmation of the difficult teaching Jesus had given the disciples about his suffering and death (cf. 8:31–38). Six days had elapsed since that startling disclosure. So additional revelation of God's purpose in his Son was needed. To a select group of Jesus' disciples, this comes in the Transfiguration with God's voice booming out of the cloud: "This is my Son, whom I love. Listen to him!" (v.7). This was a direct order given to Peter, James, and John—and through them to the rest of the Twelve—to heed Jesus' disclosure at Caesarea Philippi.

2 "After six days" suggests that the Transfiguration is historical, connected with the previous event and not a throwback to a legendary postresurrection account of Jesus (Bultmann et al.). The revelation was given to Peter, James, and John, the inner circle of the disciples. The same three were present at the raising of Jairus's daughter and were with Jesus in Gethsemane. The high mountain is not identified. The traditional site is Mount Tabor, a loaf-shaped mountain in the middle of the Plain of Jezreel. But Tabor is not a "high mountain" (1,843 feet above sea level) and so is an unlikely site. Mount Hermon, which is over 9,000 feet high, is a more probable site. It is located near Caesarea Philippi, where the event Mark has just recorded took place. The word *metamorphoō* (on which see J. Behm, TDNT 4:755–59) means "to change into another form" and is used only here, in the parallel in Matthew 17:2, and in Romans 12:2 and 2 Corinthians 3:18, where it describes the believer's progressive change into the moral likeness of Christ.

3 It is difficult to know exactly what happened at the Transfiguration. Jesus' clothes became "dazzling white"—only Mark adds "whiter than anyone in the world could bleach them." If the event took place at night, its dazzling nature was enhanced. For a moment they saw the human appearance of Jesus "changed into that of a heavenly being in the transfigured world" (Behm, TDNT, 4:758).

4 Why the appearance of Elijah and Moses? (Matthew and Luke have Moses and Elijah, the more natural order.) If what the disciples saw was a glimpse of Jesus' final state of glory, then Moses and Elijah's function is to announce the End. In Jewish expectation, Elijah clearly played that role (cf. Mal 4:5; Mark 9:11–12). But what of Moses? The reappearance of Moses seems to have been a later Jewish idea (cf. Plummer, p. 214). Perhaps that is why he is mentioned second. Or Elijah and Moses may have been at the scene as representatives of the Law and the Prophets— i.e., the OT, which was being superseded, or at least fulfilled, by Jesus. Moses well represents the Law, but one would have expected one of the great writing prophets such as Isaiah or Jeremiah, instead of Elijah, to represent the Prophets. How Peter, James, and John recognized these men is not said. "The fact that both figures were, in the Old Testament, described as having ended their lives on earth in a mysterious way (Deut 34:6; II Kings 2:11) adds to the appropriateness of their mysterious reappearance in this preview of the glorious climax of Jesus' ministry" (Moule, *Gospel of Mark*, p. 70).

5 True to form, Peter responded impulsively. His words "Rabbi, it is good for us to be here" show that he was greatly moved by the experience yet did not understand it. He wanted to prolong it by erecting three shelters—"one for you [Jesus], one for Moses and one for Elijah." Lane (p. 319) says, "The desire to erect new tents of meeting where God can again communicate with men implies that Peter regards the time of the second exodus as fulfilled and the goal of the Sabbath rest achieved." But before that rest is achieved, the suffering and death of the Messiah must take place. Peter again stumbles at the necessity of a suffering Messiah.

6 This endeavor to excuse Peter's inept remark shows Mark's sensitive concern for Peter. He was frightened and at a loss as to what to say. So he impulsively spoke, and what he said was not worth saying.

7–8 The OT background of verse 7 lies in the passages where the cloud is "the vehicle of God's presence (Exod 16:10; 19:9; 24:15f.; 33:9; Lev 16:2; Num 11:25), the abode of His glory, from which He speaks" (Taylor, p. 391). The cloud "enveloped them"—viz., Elijah, Moses, and probably Jesus. At Jesus' baptism, the Voice had spoken to him (1:11); here the disciples are addressed. The Transfiguration experience was for their spiritual instruction. God's voice spoke authoritatively out of the cloud, and "this Voice assured the disciples that, although the Jews might reject Him and the Romans put Him to death (8:31), yet He was accepted and beloved by God" (Plummer, p. 215).

"Listen" must be given its full sense of obedience. The only true listening known in the Bible is obedient listening (cf. James 1:22–24). Calvin (2:314) rightly points out that when God "enjoins us to *hear him,* he appoints him to be the supreme and only teacher of his Church. It was his design to distinguish Christ from all the rest, as we truly and strictly infer from these words, that by nature he was God's *only Son*" (emphasis his). This uniqueness of Christ is highlighted by the fact that suddenly—as suddenly as they had appeared—Moses and Elijah were gone; and the three disciples "no longer saw anyone with them except Jesus" (v.8).

Notes

2 Another possible site for the Transfiguration has recently been suggested by W. Liefield, "The Transfiguration Narrative" (*New Dimensions in New Testament Study,* edd. R.N. Longenecker and M.C. Tenney [Grand Rapids: Zondervan, 1974], p. 167). His suggestion is Mount Meron, rising to the height of 3,926 feet, and located to the west of the Sea of Galilee. But Liefeld's evidence is not convincing. Since the name of the mountain on which the Transfiguration took place is not given in the Gospels, its clear identification is not possible.

D. *The Coming of Elijah*

9:9–13

9As they were coming down the mountain, Jesus gave them orders not to tell anyone what they had seen until the Son of Man had risen from the dead. 10They kept the matter to themselves, discussing what "rising from the dead" meant.
11And they asked him, "Why do the teachers of the law say that Elijah must come first?"
12Jesus replied, "To be sure, Elijah does come first, and restores all things. Why then is it written that the Son of Man must suffer much and be rejected? 13But I tell you, Elijah has come, and they have done to him everything they wished, just as it is written about him."

9 On the way down the mountain, Jesus gave the three disciples orders to keep their experience of the Transfiguration secret till after the resurrection of the Son of Man. The Transfiguration was a revelation of the glory of the Son of Man. To proclaim this before the Cross would have been too much in keeping with current popular ideas of messiahship. First must come suffering and death. Then after the Resurrection (in itself a manifestation of the glory of the Son of Man), divulging the Transfiguration experience would be appropriate. But until that time Jesus enjoined the disciples to keep what they had seen a secret.

In Mark's Gospel on numbers of occasions, especially after Jesus performs a miracle, he commands those involved to keep the matter quiet (cf. 1:34, 43–44; 3:11–12; 5:43, 7:36; 8:30). Based on these texts, William Wrede (*The Messianic Secret* (1901; reprint ed., Cambridge: James Clarke, 1971) developed his "messianic secret" theory. He held that the tradition about Jesus was nonmessianic; i.e., Jesus never actually claimed to be the Messiah. It was the post-Easter church that came to believe and teach that Jesus was the Messiah. In order to resolve this contradiction,

Mark, according to Wrede, created incidents in which Jesus commands that his messiahship be kept secret. This was Mark's way of accounting for the tradition being nonmessianic. The problem with Wrede's theory is that there is no evidence that a nonmessianic tradition about Jesus ever existed. Every stratum of Gospel material contains messianic implications. Thus there is no reason not to accept Mark's "messianic secret" as historical.

10 The disciples obeyed Jesus' injunction. But they were puzzled by his statement about the resurrection of the Son of Man. As Jews they were familiar with the idea of a general resurrection of the dead. But this special resurrection of the Son of Man baffled them, as their discussion of it showed.

11 Apparently the disciples did not feel free to ask Jesus what he meant by his "rising from the dead" (v.10). Instead they asked him about Elijah. No doubt the fact that three of them had seen Elijah at the Transfiguration reminded them of what the teachers of the law said about him—viz., he would come before the Messiah and restore all things (Mal 4:5–6). Restoring all things involved, among other things, leading the people to repentance. Now if Elijah comes first and does his preparatory work, how is it that when the Son of Man comes he finds people so unprepared for him that they completely reject him and, indeed, kill him? If this represents a correct reconstruction of the thinking of the disciples, behind their question lay the stumbling block of a suffering Messiah. They were still perplexed by this.

12 Jesus' answer is that the teachers of the law are right about Elijah. He will come first and restore all things. But whatever that involves it does not preclude the suffering of the Son of Man. The Scriptures, Jesus says, predict it: "It is written." This probably is a reference to the Suffering Servant passage in Isaiah 52:13–53:12.

13 Jesus' statement about Elijah goes beyond that of the teachers of the law: not only must Elijah come, he already has come in the person of John the Baptist. Though John is not named here, the reference to him is obvious. "They have done to him everything they wished" is a reference to his treatment by Herod, i.e., his imprisonment and death. "Just as it is written about him" refers to what the OT says about Elijah in his relationship to Ahab and Jezebel (cf. 1 Kings 19:1–2). Herod and Herodias were foreshadowed in Ahab and Jezebel. Although there is no prediction of suffering associated with Elijah's eschatological ministry, the main thrust of Jesus' reply in vv.12–13 makes clear to the disciples that the eschatological ministry of Elijah in no way does away with the necessity for the Son of Man to suffer and die.

E. *Healing a Boy With an Evil Spirit*

9:14–29

> [14]When they came to the other disciples, they saw a large crowd around them and the teachers of the law arguing with them. [15]As soon as all the people saw Jesus, they were overwhelmed with wonder and ran to greet him.
> [16]"What are you arguing with them about?" he asked.
> [17]A man in the crowd answered, "Teacher, I brought you my son, who is possessed by a spirit that has robbed him of speech. [18]Whenever it seizes him, it

throws him to the ground. He foams at the mouth, gnashes his teeth and becomes rigid. I asked your disciples to drive out the spirit, but they could not."

[19]"O unbelieving generation," Jesus replied, "how long shall I stay with you? How long shall I put up with you? Bring the boy to me."

[20]So they brought him. When the spirit saw Jesus, it immediately threw the boy into a convulsion. He fell to the ground and rolled around, foaming at the mouth.

[21]Jesus asked the boy's father, "How long has he been like this?"

"From childhood," he answered. [22]"It has often thrown him into fire or water to kill him. But if you can do anything, take pity on us and help us."

[23]" 'If you can'?" said Jesus. "Everything is possible for him who believes."

[24]Immediately the boy's father exclaimed, "I do believe; help me overcome my unbelief!"

[25]When Jesus saw that a crowd was running to the scene, he rebuked the evil spirit. "You deaf and mute spirit," he said, "I command you, come out of him and never enter him again."

[26]The spirit shrieked, convulsed him violently and came out. The boy looked so much like a corpse that many said, "He's dead." [27]But Jesus took him by the hand and lifted him to his feet, and he stood up.

[28]After Jesus had gone indoors, his disciples asked him privately, "Why couldn't we drive it out?"

[29]He replied, "This kind can come out only by prayer."

14 Mark has a more complete account of this story than either Matthew or Luke. This, the last exorcism story in Mark's Gospel, occurs when Jesus, Peter, James, and John rejoin the other disciples after the experience of the Transfiguration. The disciples were engaged in a debate with the teachers of the law while a large crowd looked on. If the Transfiguration took place on Mount Hermon, the presence of the teachers of the law so far north in Palestine indicates their concern in monitoring the teaching and preaching of Jesus.

15 Why were the people so amazed (Mark says that "they were overwhelmed with wonder") when they saw Jesus? Was this because the afterglow of the Transfiguration lingered on his face? This is unlikely, especially in view of his instruction for the disciples to keep the event a secret. It may have been because he arrived at an opportune time for meeting a critical need. Or perhaps it was simply because Jesus' very presence provoked wonder.

16-18 Jesus' inquiry as to what the other disciples and the crowd were arguing about (v. 16) brought a reply from a man who had brought his son for healing (v. 17). The description the father gives of his son's illness is graphic: he is possessed by a spirit, and this has caused a speech loss. He also has seizures accompanied by foaming at the mouth, grinding of the teeth, and bodily rigidity (v. 18). These symptoms suggest epilepsy (cf. SBK, 1:758), one of a group of diseases that have had particular attention because of their mysterious nature. In Jesus' absence the man had brought his possessed son to the disciples for healing. Doubtless the disciples had fully expected to be able to exorcise the demon. Had that not been a part of their commission (cf. 3:15), and had they not already been successful at it (cf. 6:13)?

19 It seems best to restrict the meaning of "unbelieving generation" to the disciples. Thus the cry of Jesus reveals his bitter disappointment with them. In the crucial moment they had failed because of their lack of faith. Van der Loos (*Miracles of Jesus*, p. 399) says, "It is not too bold to presume that during the absence of Jesus and His three intimates, a spirit of unbelief and laxity had overcome the disciples, perhaps partly as a result of conversations between them, leading to their impotence."

"How long shall I stay with you" suggests Jesus' longing, in the face of unbelief, for his heavenly Father. "How long shall I put up with you" suggests his weariness with the disciples' spiritual obtuseness. But in teaching his disciples, Jesus was never at the end of his patience. Mark seems particularly anxious to show him persisting in his instruction of them (9:30–31; 14:28; 16:7).

20–22 Here Mark describes the deadly conflict between Jesus and the demonic powers. Confronted by Jesus, the demon immediately threw the boy into a convulsion and made him fall on the ground and foam at the mouth (v.20). Mark alone tells us that Jesus asked how long the boy had had the disease (v.21)—a detail that shows Jesus' sympathetic concern. The boy had been sick since childhood and had experienced numerous attacks in which the demon had attempted to kill him by convulsing him and throwing him into fire and water (v.22). Mark uses the plural form of water (*hydata*), which in this context may mean pools or streams. Pathetically the father asked Jesus for help. When he left home to bring his son to Jesus' disciples, he apparently believed the boy would be healed. Now he is not sure and says, "If you can do anything."

23–24 Jesus immediately fixed on the father's "if" clause. The question was not whether Jesus had the power to heal the boy but whether the father had faith to believe Jesus could—"Everything is possible for him who believes." Or perhaps the reference is to the failure of the disciples. In that case the statement is not about belief as a condition necessary for receiving healing; it is about belief as an active force in the accomplishment of healing (cf. Van der Loos, *Miracles of Jesus*, p. 400). This would help explain Jesus' rebuke of his disciples in v.19. However, in view of Mark's emphasis in his Gospel of the importance of faith for healing, the first interpretation is to be preferred. Jesus' statement, which is really a promise, elicited faith from the father. "I do believe," he exclaimed; but he recognized that his faith was far from perfect (v.24). It was still mixed with unbelief. So in a beautiful display of honesty, he asked Jesus to help him overcome his unbelief. Calvin (2:325) comments: "He declares that he *believes* and yet acknowledges himself to have *unbelief*. These two statements may appear to contradict each other but there is none of us that does not experience both of them in himself" (emphasis his).

25 The mention of a crowd "running to the scene" seems strange in view of v.14, which states that a crowd was already there. No mention is made of the crowd withdrawing; so we conclude that the crowd of v.25 is in addition to the one already present. Jesus, wanting to avoid as much as possible further publicity, exorcised the demon before additional people arrived on the scene. "He did not want to perform miracles for gaping sightseers" (D.E. Hiebert, *The Gospel According to Mark* [Chicago: Moody, 1974], p. 223). The demon, referred to as "a deaf and mute spirit," i.e., one that causes deafness and muteness, was exorcised by Jesus' direct command. He was ordered to come out and stay out for good.

26–27 The demon's exorcism is accompanied by cries and convulsions (v.26). The effect on the boy was so severe that he seemed to the crowd to be dead. He was not in fact dead (*hōsei nekros*, "as one dead"), even though "many" declared him to be dead. Completely exhausted and looking like a corpse, the boy responded to the touch of Jesus (v.27). Lane (p. 334), though granting that the text does not say the boy was dead, remarks that "the accumulation of the vocabulary of death and resurrection in vv.26–27, and the parallelism with the narrative of the raising of Jairus' daughter, suggest that Mark wished to allude to a death and resurrection. The dethroning of Satan is always a reversal of death and an affirmation of life."

28–29 Why were the nine disciples powerless to act in behalf of this boy (v.28)? Here Mark gives us the answer. In private the disciples went to Jesus and asked him why they had failed. The question expressed their deep concern. They had been given authority over evil spirits (6:7) and had successfully cast out many demons before this incident (6:13). Why their failure now? Jesus answered, "This kind can come out only by prayer" (v.29). Apparently they had taken for granted the power given them or had come to believe that it was inherent in themselves. So they no longer depended prayerfully on God for it, and their failure showed their lack of prayer.

Notes

29 After ἐν προσευχῇ (*en proseuchē*, "by prayer") most MSS add καὶ νηστείᾳ (*kai nēsteia*, "and fasting"). But among the MSS that support the omission of "and fasting" are important representatives of the Alexandrian, Western, and Caesarean types of texts. In the light of the early church's increasing stress on fasting, the words *kai nēsteia* are probably an early scribal gloss.

F. *Second Prediction of the Passion*

9:30–32

> [30]They left that place and passed through Galilee. Jesus did not want anyone to know where they were, [31]because he was teaching his disciples. He said to them, "The Son of Man is going to be betrayed into the hands of men. They will kill him, and after three days he will rise." [32]But they did not understand what he meant and were afraid to ask him about it.

30–31 Jesus' return to Galilee (v.30) from the territory of Herod Philip was not for the purpose of pursuing another public Galilean ministry. His public ministry was finished in Galilee. Now he was on his way to Jerusalem to complete his redemptive mission. He was focusing his teaching ministry on the Twelve, and he sought seclusion to do this. The disciples needed to be away from the distractions of the crowds to concentrate on what Jesus was saying to them. Jesus continued to teach them about his passion (v.31) because they by no means had understood his first prediction of his passion. This second prediction of it included the new element of betrayal. The verb *paradidotai* ("is going to be betrayed") is a futuristic present. Although the betrayal is still in the future, it is as good as happening right now.

By translating *paradidotai* as "betrayed," NIV opts for Judas as the implied subject of the action. The word literally means "to be delivered up" or "to be handed over." As early as Origen, it was interpreted to mean "delivered up by God." Plummer (p. 222) points out that if this refers to Judas, "into the hands of men" is almost superfluous. It seems better to understand it as Origen did. God took the initiative in providing man's salvation. The delivering up of Jesus was part of God's plan for the world's redemption (cf. Rom 4:25; 8:32). If this is what the verb means, "the play on the words Son of man . . . men is no doubt deliberate; in a fallen world men had become so hostile to God that when, as the culmination of his plans for their salvation, he sent to them the Man, their Saviour and ultimate model, they regarded and treated him as their worst enemy. Men and the Son of Man stood on opposite sides in God's eschatological battle against the powers of evil" (Plummer, p. 222). (For a discusison of Son of Man, see commentary at 8:31.)

32 The disciples still did not understand. Mark does not soften this. But perhaps some light was getting through to them. Was their fear of asking Jesus about what he had said due to their fear of facing a full disclosure of the suffering that lay ahead? Or was it because before when they had asked about the coming of Elijah (9:1) they had not understood Jesus' answer? Or were they fearful of being rebuked as Peter had been (8:33)? Whatever their reasons, they were afraid to ask Jesus about it. Instead they chose to occupy themselves with arguing about who was the greatest among them (cf. vv. 33-34).

G. A Question About Greatness

9:33-37

> 33They came to Capernaum. When he was in the house, he asked them, "What were you arguing about on the road?" 34But they kept quiet because on the way they had argued about who was the greatest.
> 35Sitting down, Jesus called the Twelve and said, "If anyone wants to be first, he must be the very last, and the servant of all."
> 36He took a little child and had him stand among them. Taking him in his arms, he said to them, 37"Whoever welcomes one of these little children in my name welcomes me; and whoever welcomes me does not welcome me but the one who sent me."

Ropes (pp. 23-24) states clearly the purpose of this section in Mark's Gospel:

> The series of incidents and sayings in the last part of chapter nine . . . are not accidental in their place here, mere survivals of the crude context of an earlier source, nor are they due to a biographical motive. They are deliberately brought in by the evangelist as part of Jesus' instruction regarding the inseparable connection, both for Leader and for followers, of sufferings with the career and the cause of the Messiah. In this situation the dispute as to who is greatest (v.33ff.) betrays failure to understand; again, for them to reject any friends, however uninstructed and slight in their attachment (v.38ff.), is an arrogance that reveals their inadequate comprehension; what is requisite is sacrifice and self-denial, and persistence in it (vv.43-49), and that repression of jealousy and ill-feeling (v.50) which alone befits men who are entering on a march toward a cross.

33-34 Jesus returned to Capernaum (v.33) where his great Galilean ministry had begun (1:21) and where his headquarters in Galilee had been located. This time he did not linger there long, since his public ministry in the region had ended. He instructed his disciples "in the house," i.e., privately. The house is probably the one belonging to Peter and Andrew (cf. 1:29). The instruction runs from v.33 to v.50.

The disciples must have been embarrassed and ashamed of their arguing among themselves about who was greatest (v.34) because Jesus' question about it elicited only silence. And well might they have been ashamed. Instead of contemplating Jesus' passion and the suffering it would involve for both him and them, they had been occupied with senseless argument about greatness. Since questions of this sort were common among the Jews of the day, the disciples' dispute shows how much they were influenced by the culture of their time.

35 Jesus assumed the posture of a Jewish rabbi—he sat down (Matt 5:1; 13:1; Luke 5:3; John 8:2) and called the Twelve to him. True greatness comes through service of others. "The spirit of service is the passport to eminence in the Kingdom of God, for it is the spirit of the Master Who Himself became διάκονος πάντων ['servant of all']" (Swete, p. 205). This is a complete reversal of worldly values. How important this principle is can be seen by its repetition in the tradition (cf. Mark 10:31, 43–44; Matt 23:8–11; Luke 22:24–27). The very fact that the disciples were concerned about who was greatest underscores again their failure to understand Jesus' statements about his suffering and death. The kind of service Jesus was talking about involved sacrifice.

36–37 To illustrate the principle in v.35, Jesus took a child, perhaps one from the family in whose house he was teaching, and first stood him by his side (v.36). Then Jesus took him into his arms (cf. 10:16); and while all were watching, Jesus spoke. Black makes the suggestion that since the words "child" and "servant" represent one word in Aramaic, we have here a picture parable. The Twelve are to become like little children in their discipleship; and Jesus assures them that when they do this, they are his true representatives. Those who welcome them welcome Christ (v.37), and in welcoming Christ they welcome God himself (M. Black, "The Markan Parable of the Child in the Midst," ET 59 [1947–48]: 14–16). This is an attractive suggestion. It seems simpler and more natural, however, to take the saying as meaning that true greatness entails caring about people—insignificant people like children—because Jesus himself is concerned about them. When one cares about such people, one is really "receiving" Jesus and God himself. Moule (*Gospel of Mark*, p. 75) reminds us that "Jesus was one of the first ever to see how essentially precious any person is, particularly a young child. A concern for children was not invented by the welfare state: it goes back to the teaching of Jesus."

H. Driving Out Demons in Jesus' Name

9:38–42

38"Teacher," said John, "we saw a man driving out demons in your name and we told him to stop, because he was not one of us."

39"Do not stop him," Jesus said. "No one who does a miracle in my name can in the next moment say anything bad about me, 40for whoever is not against us is for us. 41I tell you the truth, anyone who gives you a cup of water in my name because you belong to Christ will certainly not lose his reward.

42"And if anyone causes one of these little ones who believe in me to sin, it would be better for him to be thrown into the sea with a large millstone tied around his neck.

38 John's use of "we" shows that he is speaking for all the disciples. This is the only time Mark mentions John alone. The exorcist had been driving out demons in Jesus' name, i.e., with his authority. What irked the disciples was that, though he was not one of them, he was being successful at it! What made things even worse was that they doubtless remembered their own failure to exorcise the demon from the epileptic (cf. 9:14-18). The strange exorcist must have been a believer. However, he was not one of the exclusive company of the Twelve, and this apparently was the sore point so far as they were concerned. So they took it on themselves to stop him.

39-40 Jesus' reply shows that he did not have as restrictive a view of who could legitimately participate in his mission as his disciples did (v.39). The casting out of demons was done by God's power, and his power was not limited to the Twelve. So Jesus tells his disciples not to stop the strange exorcist because he is not likely soon to speak badly of Jesus if he does a miracle in his name (cf. Num 11:26-29, where Joshua tried to get Moses to stop Eldad and Medad from prophesying in the camp of the Israelites). "The idea is, that if any man be conscious of exerting . . . a great and beneficent influence through the name of Jesus, *it will take a considerable time*, to say the least of it, before his mind can become so altered that he could either speak or think depreciatingly of the 'worthy name' in which he has found a source of power and blessing" (Morison, p. 261; emphasis his).

Casting out demons definitely demonstrated that the man was not against Jesus, and "whoever is not against us is for us" (v.40). Cranfield, p. 311, sees in this statement an indication of the messianic veiledness of Jesus. Jesus did not want to force men quickly into a decision about himself. He desired to give them plenty of time to decide, during which the principle in Mark 9:40 applies. But when the critical moment for decision arrives, then the principle laid down in Matthew 12:30 takes over: "He who is not with me is against me."

41 This verse seems to go best with v.37, before John's interruption. However, it could serve as a concrete example of the principle stated in v.40. Jesus introduced it with the solemn affirmation: "I tell you the truth." The giving of a cup of water is a very small act of hospitality. Yet if it is given to one who belongs to Christ, this act will be rewarded. Here again the Jewish idea that the representative of a man is as the man himself applies. To give a cup of water to one of Christ's followers is the same as giving it to Christ. The reward here is best understood as God's approval.

42 This verse is probably better taken with what precedes it than with what follows. On this understanding the warning it contains points back to the disciples' attempt to prevent the unknown exorcist from doing his work in Jesus' name (v.38) or to prevent anyone from giving a cup of water in his name. "Little ones" here does not refer to children as such but to followers of Jesus, and "to sin" (*skandalizein*) means to prevent them from acting in Jesus' name. The offense is so serious that it would have been better for one to be drowned than to commit it. The millstone referred to is the kind turned by donkey power rather than by hand—in other words, a big one!

Notes

41 The phrase ὅτι Χριστοῦ ἔστε (*hoti Christou este*, "because you belong to Christ") presents a problem since Jesus does not use the title "Christ" without the definite article in the synoptic Gospels. א * reads ἐμόν (*emon*, "me") instead of *Christou*. The suggestion that the original reading was ἐμοί (*emoi*, "mine") goes back to T.W. Manson in a verbal communication to Taylor. It is possible that Mark originally wrote *emoi* and that *emon* is a copyist's error. If this is true, then the meaning of the phrase would be "because you are mine" (Taylor, p. 408).

I. Demanding Requirements of Discipleship

9:43–50

⁴³If your hand causes you to sin, cut it off. It is better for you to enter life maimed than with two hands to go into hell, where the fire never goes out. ⁴⁵And if your foot causes you to sin, cut it off. It is better for you to enter life crippled than to have two feet and be thrown into hell. ⁴⁷And if your eye causes you to sin, pluck it out. It is better for you to enter the kingdom of God with one eye than to have two eyes and be thrown into hell, ⁴⁸where

" 'their worm does not die,
and the fire is not quenched.'

⁴⁹Everyone will be salted with fire.
⁵⁰"Salt is good, but if it loses its saltiness, how can you make it salty again? Have salt in yourselves, and be at peace with each other."

43–48 The main point of vv.43–50 is that it is so important to enter into life—i.e., eternal life, eschatological life—that radical means must be taken to remove what can prevent it, viz., sin. Here sin is connected with the physical self—the hand (v.43), foot (v.45), and eye (v.47). Jesus is not demanding the excision of our bodily members; he is demanding the cessation of the sinful activities of these members. Radical spiritual surgery is demanded. Nothing less is at stake than life, eternal life (cf. v.47, where "kingdom of God" stands in parallel to "life" in vv.43, 45).

The word translated "hell" is *gehenna*, a Greek form of the Hebrew words *gê hinnōm* ("Valley of Hinnom"). This was the valley along the south side of the city of Jerusalem, which was used in OT times for human sacrifices to the pagan god Molech (cf. Jer 7:31; 19:5–6; 32:35). King Josiah put a stop to this dreadful practice (2 Kings 23:10); and the Valley of Hinnom came to be used as a place where human excrement and rubbish, including animal carcasses, were disposed of and burned. The fire of *gehenna* never went out, and the worms never died. So it came to be used symbolically of the place of divine punishment. Isaiah 66:24 may reveal the beginning of this use, but it becomes much clearer during the intertestamental period, e.g., in the Book of Enoch: "This accursed valley is for those who are accursed forever; here will all those be gathered who utter unseemly words against God, and here is the place of their punishment" (27:2). "A like abyss was opened in the midst of the earth, full of fire, and they were all judged and found guilty and cast into that fiery abyss, and they burned" (90:26; cf. 48:9; 4 Ezra 7:36; M *Pirke Aboth* 1.5; 5.19–20).

Verses 44 and 46 (identical with v.48) are omitted in NIV. They are lacking in important early MSS but later on were added to round out the parallelism in vv. 47–48.

49 This is admittedly one of the most difficult verses in Mark. Over a dozen different interpretations are found in the commentaries. Of these, two commend themselves; and both take their clue from the insertion by a copyist (see Notes) of the words "and every sacrifice shall be salted with salt." This is a reference to Leviticus 2:13: "Season all your grain offerings with salt. Do not leave the salt of the covenant of your God out of your grain offerings; add salt to all your offerings."

One interpretation sees in the sacrificial salt a symbol of the covenant relationship the children of Israel had with God. For every disciple of Jesus, the salt of the covenant is the Divine Fire (cf. Matt 3:11), "which purifies, preserves and consummates sacrifice—the alternative to the Fire that consumes" (Swete, p. 213). The fire is the Holy Spirit.

Another interpretation sees in the fire the trials and persecutions of the disciples of Jesus. The previous verses relate to the dedication of the various members of the body (hand, foot, eye) to God. These must be sacrificed, if need be, to enter into the kingdom of God. Here in v.49 the total self is in mind. Every true disciple is to be a total sacrifice to God (cf. Rom 12:1); and as salt always accompanied the temple sacrifices, so fire—i.e., persecution, trials, and suffering—will accompany the true disciple's sacrifices (cf. 1 Peter 1:7; 4:12).

This saying, which is preserved only by Mark, must have had special meaning for the persecuted Roman church. It helped them understand that the purifying fires of persecution were not to be thought of as foreign to their vocation as Christians because "everyone will be salted with fire."

50 In this verse salt must be understood in a domestic setting and not in a religious or ritual one as in v.49. Salt played an important role in the ancient world. The rabbis considered it necessary to life. "The world cannot survive without salt" (*Sopherim* 15.8). It was also used as a preservative to keep food from spoiling. But salt could lose its saltiness. Jesus is warning his disciples not to lose that characteristic in them that brings life to the world and prevents its decay. But what is that characteristic that, if lost, will make the disciples of Jesus worthless? It is the disciples' spirit of devotion and self-sacrifice (cf. v.49) to Jesus Christ and his gospel. It will only be possible for disciples to be at peace with one another where that kind of devotion instead of self-interest prevails (cf. v.34).

Notes

49 The first words of this verse have come down to us in essentially three forms: (1) as translated in the NIV—"Everyone will be salted with fire." This reading has the best MS evidence; (2) "Every sacrifice will be salted with salt"; and (3) "Every one will be salted with fire and every sacrifice will be salted with salt." The history of these variants is probably as follows: The original reading was (1); a copyist finding Lev 2:13 a clue to the understanding of this difficult saying noted the OT passage in the margin; subsequently his marginal gloss was either substituted for (1) or added to it.

J. Teaching on Divorce

10:1–12

[1]Jesus then left that place and went into the region of Judea and across the Jordan. Again crowds of people came to him, and as was his custom, he taught them.

[2]Some Pharisees came and tested him by asking, "Is it lawful for a man to divorce his wife?"

[3]"What did Moses command you?" he replied.

[4]They said, "Moses permitted a man to write a certificate of divorce and send her away."

[5]"It was because your hearts were hard that Moses wrote you this law," Jesus replied. [6]"But at the beginning of creation God 'made them male and female.' [7]'For this reason a man will leave his father and mother and be united to his wife, [8]and the two will become one flesh.' So they are no longer two, but one. [9]Therefore what God has joined together, let man not separate."

[10]When they were in the house again, the disciples asked Jesus about this. [11]He answered, "Anyone who divorces his wife and marries another woman commits adultery against her. [12]And if she divorces her husband and marries another man, she commits adultery."

1 Jesus had completed his ministry in Galilee. He was moving closer and closer to the ancient city of Jerusalem where the final acts of the redemptive drama were to take place. He set his face to the accomplishment of his divine mission. Although the textual tradition (cf. Notes) reveals that the copyists had problems with the sequence of his journey ("into the region of Judea and across the Jordan"), there is no compelling reason why Jesus could not have traveled south from Capernaum, over the mountains of Samaria into Judea, and then eastward across the Jordan into Perea. Since 9:30 Jesus had been directing his teaching ministry toward his disciples, but now again he is among the crowds and teaching them.

2 The question posed by the Pharisees was not a sincere one, i.e., they were not honestly seeking information from Jesus about divorce. They were testing him, trying to catch him in some statement about a subject on which they themselves had no agreement, and then to use it against him. The fact that Jesus was in Perea, Herod Antipas's territory, may be significant. Antipas had put John the Baptist to death because John had denounced Antipas's marriage to Herodias. Perhaps the Pharisees hoped that Jesus, by his statements on marriage and divorce, would get himself into trouble with Antipas and would suffer the same cruel fate as John.

On the question of the lawfulness of divorce, there was general unanimity among the Jews: divorce was allowed. The real difference of opinion centered in the grounds for divorce. The crucial text was Deuteronomy 24:1: "If a man marries a woman who becomes displeasing to him because he finds something indecent about her, and he writes her a certificate of divorce . . ." The crucial words are "something indecent." What did that include? The school of Shammai, the stricter of the schools, understood these words to mean something morally indecent, in particular, adultery. The school of Hillel interpreted the words much more freely. Just about anything in a wife that a husband did not find to his liking was suitable grounds for divorce. Even if she burned his food! So where did Jesus stand in this? That was their question.

3 Jesus, as he often did when in controversy with the Jewish religious leaders, instead of answering the question directly, countered with a question of his own. Moses was their authority—what did *he* say? Jesus knew they would appeal to Moses; so he made them make the first commitment.

Johnson (pp. 169–70) writes:

> Jewish marriage was not a contract between equals; a woman did not marry, but was "given in marriage". It is only fair, however, to add that Pharisaic rules afforded a certain protection to the more helpless party. Her husband had to give her a writ of divorce that was valid in every respect, written on durable material and with ink that did not fade, and once he had delivered the writ he could not retract it; the woman was free. While a wife could not divorce her husband, she could go before the court and force him to divorce her if he engaged in disgusting occupations such as tanning, had certain diseases, took vows to her detriment, or forced her to take such vows. Furthermore, the rabbis bitterly condemned indiscriminate divorce even if it was legal.

4–5 Jesus did not question the law. But his answer reaches back to first principles. Moses' permission to divorce (v.4) was an accommodation to human weakness (v.5). It was an attempt to bring some sort of order in a society that disregarded God's standards. But that is not what God intended in marriage. His design in creating man and woman was that marriage should be an unbroken lifelong union. Cranfield (p. 319) points out that a distinction must be made between what is the absolute will of God and what the provisions are that take into account the sinfulness of man and are intended to limit and control its effects. Moses' bill of divorcement falls into the second category. The rabbis mistook God's gracious provision in allowing divorce as his approval of it.

6–8 Jesus refers back to the original creation (v.6), when God created them male and female.

> Marriage is grounded in this male and female constitution: as to its nature it implies that the man and the woman are united in one flesh; as to its sanction, it is divine; as to its continuance it is permanent. The import of all this is that marriage from its very nature and from the divine institution by which it is constituted is ideally indissoluble. It is not a contract of temporary convenience and not a union that may be dissolved at will. (J. Murray, *Divorce* [Philadelphia: Presbyterian and Reformed, 1974], p. 29)

Since marriage is a lifelong union between a man and a woman, its claims take precedence over ties to father and mother (v.7). "The forsaking of the house of one's father was far more meaningful at that time, since a man would forsake the solidarity and protection of his own clan" (Schweizer, p. 203). In the marriage relationship, husband and wife become one; "one flesh" is a Semitic expression that simply means "one" (v.8).

9 Behind the concept of the indissolubility of marriage is the authority of God himself. "Divorce is contrary to the divine institution, and contrary to the nature of marriage, contrary to the divine action by which the union is effected. It is precisely here that its wickedness becomes singularly apparent—it is the sundering by man of a union God has constituted. Divorce is the breaking of a seal which has been engraven by the hand of God" (Murray, *Divorce*, p. 33).

10–12 Mark records no response of the Pharisees to Jesus' teaching about divorce. Instead he moves directly to Jesus' private teaching of the Twelve. The disciples wanted a clarification of the teaching Jesus had just given (v.10). Jesus gave them a straightforward answer: divorce and remarriage by husband or wife is adultery (v.11). Jesus did what the rabbis refused to do: he recognized that a man could commit adultery against his wife. In rabbinic Judaism a woman by infidelity could commit adultery against her husband; and a man, by having sexual relations with another man's wife, could commit adultery against him. But a man could never commit adultery against his wife, no matter what he did. Jesus, by putting the husband under the same moral obligation as the wife, raised the status and dignity of women.

The phrase "and if she divorces her husband" (v.12) shows that Jesus recognized the right of a woman to divorce her husband, a right not recognized in Judaism. Matthew, writing for Jews, omits v.12; but Mark, writing for Romans, includes it.

Notes

1 The textual history of this verse reveals that the copyists had difficulty with Mark's geography. The most substantiated reading is that in NIV: "in the region of Judea and across the Jordan." KJV translates the reading of the TR: "into the coasts of Judaea by the farther side of Jordan." This is clearly an attempt by copyists to "correct" Mark's geography. A third reading omits the καὶ (*kai*, "and") before the word πέραν (*peran*, "across"). This probably represents an assimilation to the parallel in Matt 19:1.

9 Συνέζευξεν (*synezeuxen*) means literally "yoked together" (NIV, "joined together"). It graphically stresses the importance of husband and wife working together as a team of oxen yoked together. The word is often used in Greek literature of the marriage relationship.

12 Lane (p. 352) favors the reading, supported by the Western and Caesarean texts, that speaks of the woman "separating" (ἐξέλθῃ, *exelthē*) from her husband (without divorce) and marrying another man. His argument is that not only is the text tradition that supports this reading strong but it is particularly appropriate to the situation of Herodias and Herod Antipas. Taylor (pp. 420–21) also favors this reading. Cranfield (*Gospel of Mark*, p. 322), in support of the UBS text (followed by NIV), remarks: "The words in Mk may represent an adaptation of Jesus' teaching to the situation of a Gentile church (Jewish law did not allow a wife to divorce her husband), or it may be that Jesus himself was looking beyond the custom of his own people (he can hardly have been altogether unaware of Gentile practice)."

K. *Blessing the Children*

10:13–16

[13]People were bringing little children to Jesus to have him touch them, but the disciples rebuked them. [14]When Jesus saw this, he was indignant. He said to

them, "Let the little children come to me, and do not hinder them, for the kingdom of God belongs to such as these. ¹⁵I tell you the truth, anyone who will not receive the kingdom of God like a little child will never enter it." ¹⁶And he took the children in his arms, put his hands on them and blessed them.

13 Here we have a pronouncement story that has lost all details of time and place. Mark may have placed it at this point because a story about children is a fitting sequel to Jesus' teaching about marriage. Matthew also places it in this context but makes a closer connection with what precedes by the use of the word "then" (Mark uses the conjunction "and," untranslated in NIV).

Mark does not identify those who were bringing the children to Jesus. In the Greek the subject of the verb is indefinite—"they." NIV translates it "people were bringing." However, from the use of the masculine pronoun "them" (*autois*) in the last part of this verse, it may be assumed that, in addition to mothers, fathers and perhaps brothers and sisters also brought the children. Among Jews, as among other peoples, it was customary to bring children to great men to have them blessed (cf. Gen 48:13–20; SBK, 1:807–8). The word Mark uses for children (*paidia*) in this verse is the same one used of the twelve-year-old daughter of Jairus. Here, however, it denotes small children (Jesus took them into his arms). In the parallel passage in his Gospel, Luke uses the word *brephē*, which means "babies." Why the disciples wanted to prevent the children from coming to Jesus is not stated. Perhaps they wanted to protect his privacy and shield him from needless interruptions. Though their motives may have been commendable, they again show lack of spiritual sensitivity.

14 Only Mark records that Jesus was "indignant" when he realized what the disciples were doing. Mark never softens the human emotions of Jesus, nor is he less than candid about the failings of the disciples. Jesus was indignant that anyone should think children unimportant. The error of the disciples was in a smaller degree a repetition of the error of Peter (cf. 8:32). Peter wished to keep Jesus from future suffering and death; the disciples now wish to keep him from present trouble and fatigue. But Jesus wanted children to come to him and not to be hindered in their coming. His reason for this was that "the kingdom of God belongs to such as these"—i.e., children in their receptivity and dependence exemplify the characteristics of those who possess God's kingdom.

15 The solemn pronouncement "I tell you the truth" reiterates and expands the statement in v.14. The kingdom of God is to be received as a little child receives.

> The point of comparison is not so much the innocence and humility of children (for children are not invariably either innocent or humble): it is rather the fact that children are unselfconscious, receptive, and content to be dependent on others' care and bounty; it is in such a spirit that the kingdom must be "received" —it is a gift of God, and not an achievement on the part of man; it must be simply accepted, inasmuch as it can never be deserved. (Rawlinson, p. 137)

The kingdom is both a gift to be received and a realm to enter.

This saying is found in another context in Matthew 18:3. But it does not seem strange to the historical context of Mark and could be an independent saying placed here by him.

16 Jesus took the children in his arms (cf. 9:36)—a striking act showing his love for them. Apparently they were fairly small children. The verb *katalogein* means to "bless fervently," the prefix *kata* having an intensive force. This was the overflowing of Jesus' divine love for children. It was this experience that the disciples in their insensitivity were preventing the children from having and Jesus from giving! No wonder Jesus was indignant.

L. *Riches and the Kingdom of God*

10:17–31

> [17]As Jesus started on his way, a man ran up to him and fell on his knees before him. "Good teacher," he asked, "what must I do to inherit eternal life?"
> [18]"Why do you call me good?" Jesus answered. "No one is good—except God alone. [19]You know the commandments: 'Do not murder, do not commit adultery, do not steal, do not give false testimony, do not defraud, honor your father and mother.'"
> [20]"Teacher," he declared, "all these I have kept since I was a boy."
> [21]Jesus looked at him and loved him. "One thing you lack," he said. "Go, sell everything you have and give to the poor, and you will have treasure in heaven. Then come, follow me."
> [22]At this the man's face fell. He went away sad, because he had great wealth.
> [23]Jesus looked around and said to his disciples, "How hard it is for the rich to enter the kingdom of God!"
> [24]The disciples were amazed at his words. But Jesus said again, "Children, how hard it is to enter the kingdom of God! [25]It is easier for a camel to go through the eye of a needle than for a rich man to enter the kingdom of God."
> [26]The disciples were even more amazed, and said to each other, "Who then can be saved?"
> [27]Jesus looked at them and said, "With man this is impossible, but not with God; all things are possible with God.
> [28]Peter said to him, "We have left everything to follow you!"
> [29]"I tell you the truth," Jesus replied, "no one who has left home or brothers or sisters or mother or father or children or fields for me and the gospel [30]will fail to receive a hundred times as much in this present age (homes, brothers, sisters, mothers, children and fields—and with them, persecutions) and in the age to come, eternal life. [31]But many who are first will be last, and the last first."

This section is made up of three parts. The most satisfactory division is (1) vv. 17–22, which describe Jesus' encounter with a rich man; (2) vv. 23–27, a logion on the difficulty of a rich man's entering the kingdom of God; and (3) vv. 28–31, Peter's statement about leaving all to follow Jesus and Jesus' reply to it. It is possible that the three sections were historically connected. In view of the repetition of the amazement of the disciples (cf. vv. 24, 26) and Jesus' statement about the difficulty of a rich man's entering the kingdom (cf. vv. 23–24), it seems best to regard the three sections as separate sayings brought together by Mark because of their common theme.

The position of this section (vv. 17–31) in Mark's overall outline is significant. It follows Jesus' teaching about the importance of childlikeness—viz., a recognition of the necessity of weakness and dependence for entrance into the kingdom (vv. 13–16)

—and it precedes Jesus' third prediction of his passion. The impossibility of wealth as a means to gain the kingdom (v.27) looks back to the lesson from the children (v.15), and the call to commitment (vv.29–31) looks forward to the passion statement (vv.33–34).

17 This incident, unlike those in vv.2–12 and 13–17, is connected with the journey mentioned in 10:1 by the phrase "As Jesus started on his way." The man who ran up to Jesus is not identified by Mark (Luke calls him a ruler [18:18], meaning he was probably a member of some official council or court). Matthew says he was "young" (19:20). He fell on his knees before Jesus and addressed him by the revered title of "good teacher," thus expressing his high regard for Jesus. Nineham (p. 270) comments: "The stranger was altogether too obsequious and effusive in his approach." His question—"What must I do to inherit eternal life?"—indicates that he was thinking in terms of Jewish works of righteousness. He wanted to *do* something to merit eternal life, whereas Jesus taught that eternal life (the kingdom of God) is a gift to be received (cf. v.15).

18 Jesus' reply seems unnecessarily abrupt. But we must remember that he was calling attention to the man's unthinking use of language. "Jesus calls him to sober reflection. What does the epithet 'good' mean? It belongs to God who is good; and it should not be used unthinkingly or as a flippant gesture of praise" (Martin, *Mark*, p. 124). Or as Calvin (2:393) understands Jesus' reply, it is "as if he had said, 'Thou falsely calleth me a good Master, unless thou acknowledgest that I have come from God." In other words, Jesus is saying, "Before you address me with such a title, you had better think soberly about what the implications are, and especially what they are for you."

19–20 Jesus answered by giving the man a condensed summary of the second table of the law (v.19; cf. Exod 20:12–17). The prohibition of fraud is found only in Mark and seems to be a substitute for the commandment against coveting, fraud being a manifestation of coveting. It was a firm Jewish belief, based on OT teaching, that the man who kept the law would live (Deut 30:15–16). So Jesus began there.

The young man answered confidently. From boyhood he had kept all the commandments Jesus cited (v.20). This probably refers to the age of thirteen, when every Jewish boy became *bar miṣwāh* ("son of the commandment"; cf. Luke 2:42). At that point in a Jewish boy's life he became responsible to live by God's commands. The man spoke sincerely because to him keeping the law was a matter of external conformity. (Paul thought the same thing in his pre-Christian days [cf. Phil 3:6].) That the law required an inner obedience, which no man could comply with, apparently escaped him.

21 Recognizing the young man's sincerity, Jesus responded in love. Some commentators suggest that the words "loved him" mean that Jesus touched or hugged him. That may be, but nothing in the text indicates it.

The one thing that prevented this young man from having eternal life was the security of his wealth. Jesus put his finger on the sensitive place by commanding him to go, sell all he had, and give. These commands led up to the final and conclusive one: "Come, follow me." For this man there could be no following of

715

Jesus before he went, sold everything he had, and gave. His wealth and all it meant to him of position, status, comfort, and security prevented him from entering into eternal life. "The only way to 'life' is through the narrow gate of full surrender, and through that gate we may take, not what we want, but only what God allows. For this man his wealth was the hindrance" (Mitton, *Gospel of Mark*, p. 80). It must be emphasized, however, that there is no indication that in this incident Jesus' prescription for the young man was meant to be binding on all Christians. What Jesus does tell us is that we must not be attached to material things. Jesus' promise "you will have treasure in heaven" refers to eternal life; and since that is a gift of God and cannot be earned, no saving merit must be attached to the action of giving all to the poor.

22 Notice the intimate eyewitness details. When he heard the word of Jesus, the young man's "face fell." As Plummer (pp. 240–41) says, "He was gloomy and sullen with a double disappointment; no perilous exploit was required of him, but he was asked to part with what he valued most." To obey Jesus was too great a risk for him to take. So the security of wealth kept him out of the kingdom of God. He went away "with a heavy heart, for he was a man of great wealth" (NEB). Obedience to God brings joy; disobedience, sorrow.

23–26 The failure of the rich man to respond to the challenge led to one of Jesus' most striking pronouncements. He addressed it to the disciples, and it underscores the difficulty of a rich man's entering the kingdom of God (v.23).

The amazement of the disciples (v.24) at Jesus' words reflects their Jewish background, which placed great emphasis on the privileged position of the rich. To be wealthy was sure evidence of having the blessing of God. But with his penetrating spiritual insight, Jesus saw how wealth could hinder one from putting his trust and dependence in God.

The second half of v.24 may begin a new section, the last section ending with the amazement of the disciples. NIV considers it (along with vv.25–27) a part of the incident that begins with v.23. The fact that the disciples "were even more amazed" (v.26) looks back to their initial amazement in v.24 and supports the translators' decision.

Jesus supports his statement in v.23 by an amazing proverb. Moule paraphrases it thus: "It is easier to thread a needle with a great big camel than to get into the kingdom of God when you are bursting with riches" (*Gospel of Mark*, p. 80). Attempts have been made to play down the meaning of this proverb. A notable one identifies the "eye of the needle" with a gate leading into the city of Jerusalem before which camels had to kneel in order to get through. But the existence of any such gate is doubtful. As Rawlinson (p. 141) says, it has "no authority more trustworthy than the imaginative conjectures of modern guides to Jerusalem." Furthermore, this interpretation fails to recognize the picturesqueness of Jesus' speech or to grasp the full force of what he is saying—viz., that "for a rich man to enter the kingdom of God" is indeed "impossible." The proverb was not lost on the disciples. As their question "Who then can be saved?" shows, they completely understood it.

27 Now Jesus points to the solution. His answer makes clear that salvation is totally the work of God. Apart from the grace of God, it is impossible for any man—

especially a rich man—to enter God's kingdom. Humanly speaking, no one can be saved by his own efforts; but what we can never do for ourselves, God does for us. For he is the great Doer of the impossible. Was the rich man still within hearing and were these words meant for him, too? Mark does not say. Notice that "eternal life," "salvation," and "entrance into the kingdom" are all used synonymously here.

28 Mark makes no attempt to link vv.28–31 with vv.17–27. He does not even use a conjunction to connect the incidents. This seems to suggest that, though vv.17–22 and vv.23–27 go together historically, vv.28–31 are separate. Mark places them here because they fit the theme. Peter's response relates to what Mark had just reported: the failure of the rich man to give up what he had and to follow Jesus. By contrast they, i.e., the disciples, had given up everything to follow him. Matthew in the parallel passage reports Peter's additional words: "What then will there be for us?" (19:27). The disciples (Peter is their spokesman) were still thinking in terms of material rather than spiritual values.

29–30 Instead of rebuking Peter, Jesus makes a threefold promise introduced by the solemn "I tell you the truth" (v.29; cf. 10:15). No one who forsakes home, loved ones, or lands for Jesus' sake and the gospel's will fail (1) to receive back in his life a hundredfold what he has lost; (2) to suffer persecutions (only Mark includes this); and (3) to have eternal life in the age to come. The hundredfold return in this life (v.30) is to be understood in the context of the new community into which the believer in Jesus comes. There he finds a multiplication of relationships, often closer and more spiritually meaningful than blood ties. "God takes nothing away from a man without restoring it to him in a new and glorious form" (Lane, p. 372).

Jesus is also realistic about the Christian life. There will be persecutions. Again the relevance of this statement for the situation of the Roman church is obvious. It is through trials and persecutions that the new relationships as members of the Christian community develop and flourish. The promise is for a full, though admittedly difficult, life here and now, but not only here and now. Jesus promises eternal life in "the age to come." Everything that happens in the present is an earnest of that far richer and complete fulfillment in the future when there will no longer be any persecutions.

31 This saying of Jesus also appears in other contexts (cf. Matt 20:16; Luke 13:30). Jesus probably said it more than once; it lends itself to more than one application. Here it refers to the future when God will evaluate the lives of men and when human values will be reversed. At that time those who have rank and position now will not have them, and those who do not have them now will have them. This may be a kind of summary of Jesus' teaching in vv.17–31. In eternity the rich and the powerful will have the tables turned on them. Or perhaps it is a warning to the disciples in view of what they said, "we have left everything to follow you" (v.28). They must not conceive of their discipleship in terms of rewards. Discipleship entails suffering and service; it must be entered on in terms of love and commitment to Jesus, not because of what one hopes to get out of it either in this life or in the life to come. In his Gospel Matthew inserts the parable of the laborers in the vineyard here to illustrate the point (Matt 20:1–16).

717

Notes

---

19 "That man possesses the ability to fulfill the commandments of God perfectly was so firmly believed by the rabbis that they spoke in all seriousness of people who had kept the whole Law from A to Z" (SBK 1:814; quoted in Lane, p. 366).

24 The variant reading τοὺς πεποιθότας ἐπὶ [τοῖς] χρήμασιν (tous pepoithotas epi [tois] chrēmasin, "for those who trust in riches"), though found in the majority of Greek MSS, is probably a gloss intended to soften the force of the strong statement found in v.23.

M. *Third Prediction of the Passion*

10:32–34

> [32]They were on their way up to Jerusalem, with Jesus leading the way, and the disciples were astonished, while those who followed were afraid. Again he took the Twelve aside and told them what was going to happen to him. [33]"We are going up to Jerusalem," he said, "and the Son of Man will be betrayed to the chief priests and teachers of the law. They will condemn him to death and will hand him over to the Gentiles, [34]who will mock him and spit on him, flog him and kill him. Three days later he will rise."

32 The journey is resumed with Jesus taking the lead (cf. Luke 9:51). Jerusalem is mentioned for the first time as the destination of the journey southward. The astonishment of the disciples is not explained. Perhaps it was due to the determination with which Jesus proceeded to his goal (cf. Isa 50:7). He was already so preoccupied with what was to take place there that they were amazed. "Those who followed" were probably pilgrims on their way to the feast at Jerusalem. They were afraid because they sensed that something momentous was about to take place and they did not understand it. Jesus, as he so often does in Mark's Gospel, separated the Twelve from the crowd for renewed instruction about his coming passion.

33–34 This is the third major prediction of the Passion. The other two are in 8:31 and 9:31. In addition to these three, there is a brief reference to Jesus' death in the sequel to the Transfiguration narrative (cf. 9:9–12). Here the prediction is more detailed and precise than the others (for a helpful chart comparing these three predictions, see Taylor, p. 436). This prediction contains six details. Jesus is to be (1) betrayed (v.33); (2) sentenced to death; (3) handed over to the Gentiles; (4) mocked, spit on, and flogged (v.34); (5) executed; and (6) resurrected. This sounds like a brief summary of the passion narrative and so has led some scholars to consider vv.33–34 a prediction after the event—viz., that they represent postresurrection church tradition and not Jesus tradition. One's christology plays an important role in decisions like this. If Jesus was who he claimed to be—the unique Son of God—then it is not impossible that he predicted his passion in detail. If he is less than that, there are admittedly problems. That the events did not take place historically in the chronological sequence in which they are given in v.34 would tend to cast doubt on the prediction having been shaped by the passion narrative.

The word "crucify" does not occur in any of the passion predictions in Mark (cf. Matt 20:19, where it is used for the first time of Christ's death). But the statement that Jesus will be handed over to the Gentiles reveals in a veiled way his coming crucifixion. The climax of the passage is the prediction of the Resurrection. Mark does not record any response by the disciples to this startling statement. Luke (18:34), however, says, "The disciples did not understand any of this."

Notes

---

32 The phrase οἱ δὲ ἀκολουθοῦντες ἐφοβοῦντο (*hoi de akolouthountes ephobounto*, "while those who followed were afraid") created problems for the copyists because it suggests another group distinct from the disciples. The variants, none of which have strong MS support, try to eliminate this distinction. That Mark wanted to indicate two distinct groups is clearly shown by the definite article οἱ (*hoi*, "those") and the δὲ (*de*, "and," "but"; NIV, "while") used with it, which regularly indicates a change of subject. Two distinct groups are implicit in NIV's "the disciples were astonished, while those who followed were afraid."

N. *The Request of James and John*

10:35–45

> ³⁵Then James and John, the sons of Zebedee, came to him. "Teacher," they said, "we want you to do for us whatever we ask."
> ³⁶"What do you want me to do for you?" he asked.
> ³⁷They replied, "Let one of us sit at your right and the other at your left in your glory."
> ³⁸"You don't know what you are asking," Jesus said. "Can you drink the cup I drink or be baptized with the baptism I am baptized with?"
> ³⁹"We can," they answered.
> Jesus said to them, "You will drink the cup I drink and be baptized with the baptism I am baptized with, ⁴⁰but to sit at my right or left is not for me to grant. These places belong to those for whom they have been prepared."
> ⁴¹When the ten heard about this, they became indignant with James and John. ⁴²Jesus called them together and said, "You know that those who are regarded as rulers of the Gentiles lord it over them, and their high officials exercise authority over them. ⁴³Not so with you. Instead, whoever wants to become great among you must be your servant, ⁴⁴and whoever wants to be first must be slave of all. ⁴⁵For even the Son of Man did not come to be served, but to serve, and to give his life as a ransom for many."

Mark 10:35–45 parallels 9:30–37. Both contain discussions about true greatness and both follow a prediction of Jesus' passion. And in a woeful way both reveal how spiritually dense the disciples really were. It is not likely that the church created a story that cast such disrepute on the character of two of the best-known disciples.

35–37 The request made by James and John, sons of Zebedee, seems utterly preposterous (v.35). They wanted Jesus to do for them whatever they asked—a carte blanche request! When Jesus asked what that might be (v.36), their answer was that they might have the positions of highest honor in the messianic kingdom (v.37). The request reveals clearly that before the Crucifixion the disciples believed Jesus to be the Messiah; and since it was now clear that he was going up to Jerusalem, they expected his messianic glory to be revealed there. James and John wanted to be sure of a prominent place in this about-to-be-realized messianic kingdom. Calvin (2:417) comments: "This narrative contains a bright mirror of human vanity; for it shows that proper and holy zeal is often accompanied by ambition. . . . They who are not satisfied with himself alone, but seek this or the other thing apart from him and his promises, wander egregiously from the right path."

38 Jesus' answer is sharp and penetrating. The two disciples did not really know what they were asking. The way to privileged position in the messianic kingdom is not by grabbing for power but by relinquishing it through suffering and death. Jesus explains this to them by using the analogies of the cup and baptism. The cup, symbolizing trouble and suffering, is found in the OT. "In the hand of the LORD is a cup full of foaming wine mixed with spices; he pours it out, and all the wicked of the earth drink it down to its very dregs" (Ps 75:8). "Rise up, O Jerusalem, you have drunk from the hand of the LORD the cup of his wrath, you who have drained to its dregs the goblet that makes men stagger" (Isa 51:17; cf. also Mark 14:36; Jer 49:12; Ezek 23:31-34). Baptism is a symbol of a deluge of trouble (cf. Pss 18:16; 69:1-2 and the expression "baptism of fire").

39-40 With a confident "We can," the disciples answer Jesus' question about going through the suffering of his passion (v.39). How naive! James and John failed to understand what was involved in Jesus' sufferings; yet they would indeed participate in them. But to grant them privileged positions in his kingdom was not within his authority (v.40). Jesus refused to usurp the authority of his Father. God alone will grant the places at Jesus' right and left to "those for whom they have been prepared."

41-44 Although Jesus had previously rebuked the spirit of ambition and jealousy among his disciples (cf. 9:35), it was still very much alive in them. The other ten were indignant with James and John (v.41). None of the disciples had in the least comprehended what Jesus had meant when he spoke of his passion. So Jesus had to give them another lesson in what greatness is. The Gentile rulers "lord it over them," i.e., over their subjects (v.42). But this is not the way it is among true followers of Jesus (v.43). Among them greatness is not achieved by asserting rank but by humble service (v.44). "Here is the paradox of the Kingdom of God. Instead of being lords, its great ones become servants, and its chiefs the bond-servants of all" (Gould, p. 202).

45 The climax to this section (vv.35-45) comes in this verse. In the kingdom of God humble service is the rule, and even the Son of Man is not exempt from it. He is in fact par excellence the example of it, especially in his redemptive mission. Every part of this verse is important. "Son of Man" is the veiled messianic title Jesus often uses of himself (cf. comments at 8:31). "Did not come to be served, but to serve" describes his incarnate life. He did not come as a potentate whose every personal whim was to be catered to by groveling servants, but he came as a servant himself. And his coming issued in giving "his life as a ransom for many."

The word translated "ransom" is *lytron*, which also means "the price of release" (cf. BAG, pp. 483-84). In koine Greek it is often used of money paid for the release of slaves. In the NT, however, it no longer relates to a purchase price paid someone but simply means "redemption" or "release" as a theological concept based on the experience of Israel's release from the slavery of Egypt. *Lytron* may also contain an allusion to the Suffering Servant passage of Isaiah 53 and especially to v.6b: "And the LORD has laid on him the iniquity of us all."

The prepositional phrase "for many" translates *anti pollōn*. The ordinary meaning of the preposition *anti* is "in place of" or "instead of"—a clear indication of substitution. Although it can be used to mean "in behalf of," this is not the usual meaning of *anti*. Here its use with *lytron* seems to demand the meaning "instead of." The expression "the many" is not to be understood in the sense of "some but not all" but in the general sense of "many" as contrasted with the single life that is given for their ransom (cf. Bratcher and Nida, p. 337).

The entire phrase "to give his life a ransom for many" emphasizes the substitutionary element in Jesus' death. He takes the place of the many. What should have happened to them happened to him instead. The authenticity of this saying of Jesus has often been denied, usually on the basis that it represents a Markan insertion of Pauline thought into the teaching of Jesus. But surely Richardson is right in saying that "all such contentions reflect the theological outlook of their exponents rather than that of the NT. It would indeed be remarkable that St. Mark should have thus brilliantly summarized in a word the theology of St. Paul, in order to attribute it to Jesus, especially when we note that the word (λύτρον) is never used in the extant writings of the Apostle" (A. Richardson, *An Introduction to the Theology of the New Testament* [London: SCM, 1958], p. 220).

O. *Restoring Blind Bartimaeus's Sight*

10:46–52

> [46]Then they came to Jericho. As Jesus and his disciples, together with a large crowd, were leaving the city, a blind man, Bartimaeus (that is, the Son of Timaeus), was sitting by the roadside begging. [47]When he heard that it was Jesus of Nazareth, he began to shout, "Jesus, Son of David, have mercy on me!"
> [49]Jesus stopped and said, "Call him."
> So they called to the blind man, "Cheer up! On your feet! He's calling you."
> [50]Throwing his cloak aside, he jumped to his feet and came to Jesus.
> [51]"What do you want me to do for you?" Jesus asked him.
> The blind man said, "Rabbi, I want to see."
> [52]"Go," said Jesus, "your faith has healed you." Immediately he received his sight and followed Jesus along the road.

46 This last of the healing miracles in Mark's Gospel takes place near Jericho. Jericho is located five miles west of the Jordan and about fifteen miles southeast of Jerusalem. There was an old Jericho and a new Jericho. In Jesus' time the old Jericho was largely abandoned, but the new one extending to the south was an attractive city. It had been built by Herod the Great who had his winter palace there. Matthew, who speaks of two blind men, says the healing took place on the way into Jericho; Mark reports that it took place on the way out of the city. It is possible that the miracle was done somewhere between the old Israelite city and the new city of Herod. Mark is the only Evangelist who names the blind man. Bartimaeus probably means "son of Timai." In the Middle East, a blind man sitting along the road begging is a common sight.

47–48 Apparently Bartimaeus had heard of Jesus' reputation as a healer. When he discovered that Jesus was coming by, he seized the opportunity of approaching him (v.47). The title he used to address Jesus—"Son of David"—is messianic (cf. Isa 11:1, 10; Jer 23:5–6; Ezek 34:23–24). It was not an unambiguous title. In Mark's Gospel it is used only here (twice) of Jesus and in 12:35, where Jesus himself uses it in connection with the title "Christ." The crowd (they were pilgrims going up to Jerusalem for the Feast of Passover) did not appreciate Bartimaeus's loud shouting and tried to silence him, but he shouted all the more (v.49). Why they wanted him to keep quiet is not clear. Perhaps the title he gave Jesus offended them, or they did not want anyone to delay their journey to the feast.

Unlike the crowd, Jesus did not try to silence Bartimaeus. This implies that he did not reject the title "Son of David." Since Jesus was now close to the fulfillment of his messianic mission, it was no longer necessary to keep the secret. That Bartimaeus understood the significance of the title he used is doubtful. He was essentially appealing for mercy to be healed.

49–50 The loud cry stopped Jesus (v.49). Had the messianic title caught his attention? So he asked them to call the beggar to him. Only Mark gives us the graphic details of vv.49–50. The crowd's complete change of attitude toward the beggar is remarkable. Instead of trying to silence him, they encouraged him. The word translated "Cheer up!" is *tharsei*. It occurs only seven times in the NT (Matt 9:2, 22; 14:27; Mark 6:50; 10:49; John 16:33; Acts 23:11), and six of the seven are from the lips of Jesus. The exception is here. Bartimaeus's response was immediate (v.50). The cloak was his outer garment, which he had probably spread on the ground to receive the alms. The fact that he was able to get up and go to Jesus may imply that he was not completely blind.

51–52 Jesus did not immediately heal the blind beggar. Jesus first asked him a question to stimulate faith (v.51). Having done that, without any overt action or healing word on Jesus' part, he sent him away with the words "Go, . . . your faith has healed you" (v.52). The cure was immediate. Mark's statement that the blind man followed Jesus is best taken to mean, as NIV admirably brings out, that the man joined the crowd going up to the feast, not that he necessarily became a follower of Jesus in terms of discipleship.

The close of chapter 10 sets the stage for the climax of the story. The journey to Jerusalem is ended. Jesus is about to enter the Holy City where the last acts of the drama of redemption will take place. His opening the eyes of the blind man stands in sharp contrast to the blindness of the religious leaders he is about to encounter there.

VI. The Jerusalem Ministry (11:1–13:37)

At this point a new section in the Gospel of Mark begins. Jesus arrives in Jerusalem, and the rest of his ministry takes place within the confines of the city. Traditionally this period, beginning with the Triumphal Entry on Sunday and ending with the Crucifixion and Resurrection seven days later, has been designated the Passion Week. But if we had only Mark's Gospel, it would be possible to allow for a Jerusalem ministry longer than one week. Some scholars do in fact argue for an entrance into Jerusalem in the fall of the year at the time of the Feast of Tabernacles, extending Jesus' final ministry in the city to about six months. However, in view of John 12:1 and 12:12–15, which closely associate Jesus' final visit to Jerusalem with the Passover, a week-long ministry is more probable.

The section 11:1–13:37 is essentially made up of three parts: (1) the initial events of the entrance into the city and the cleansing of the temple (11:1–19); (2) instructions to his disciples (11:20–25; 12:35–44; 13:1–37); and (3) conflict with the religious leaders (11:27–33; 12:1–12, 13–17, 18–27, 28–34). The time sequence is difficult to sort out. In 11:1–25 three days are mentioned, but in 11:27–13:44 no time indicators are given. This gives rise to the possibility that some of the conflict stories could have been placed by Mark within the context of the final Jerusalem ministry of Jesus because they vividly reveal the opposition of the religious leaders that finally brought about his death. Whether or not this is true does not materially effect our understanding of the Jerusalem ministry.

A. *The Triumphal Entry*

11:1–11

> ¹As they approached Jerusalem and came to Bethphage and Bethany at the Mount of Olives, Jesus sent two of his disciples, ²saying to them, "Go to the village ahead of you, and just as you enter it, you will find a colt tied there, which no one has ever ridden. Untie it and bring it here. ³If anyone asks you, 'Why are you doing this?' tell him, 'The Lord needs it and will send it back here shortly.' "
>
> ⁴They went and found a colt outside in the street, tied at a doorway. As they untied it, ⁵some people standing there asked, "What are you doing, untying that colt?" ⁶They answered as Jesus had told them to, and the people let them go. ⁷When they brought the colt to Jesus and threw their cloaks over it, he sat on it. ⁸Many people spread their cloaks on the road, while others spread branches they had cut in the fields. ⁹Those who went ahead and those who followed shouted,
>
> > "Hosanna!"
> > "Blessed is he who comes in the name of the Lord!"
> > ¹⁰"Blessed is the coming kingdom of our father David!"
> > "Hosanna in the highest!"
>
> ¹¹Jesus entered Jerusalem and went to the temple. He looked around at everything, but since it was already late, he went out to Bethany with the Twelve.

1–2 The approach to Jerusalem was through Bethany and Bethphage (v.1). Bethphage ("house of figs") was a village close to Jerusalem. Its precise location is not known. Bethany, located on the eastern slope of the Mount of Olives, was about two miles from Jerusalem (cf. John 11:18). The Mount of Olives is directly east of the city, rising to an elevation of about twenty-six hundred feet. Its summit commands a magnificent view of Jerusalem and especially of the temple mount.

From the vicinity of Bethphage, Jesus sent two of his disciples (they are unnamed) "to the village ahead," presumably Bethphage, to get a colt (v.2). The word translated "colt" (*pōlos*) can mean the young of any animal; but here, as in the LXX and papyri, it means the colt of a donkey (cf. Matt 21:2; John 12:15). Because of the prophecy of Zechariah 9:9, the donkey was considered to be the beast of the Messiah. Jesus stipulated that the colt must be an unused one ("which no one has ever ridden"). Such animals were regarded as especially suitable for sacred purposes (cf.

Num 19:2; Deut 21:3; 1 Sam 6:7). Matthew says both the colt and his mother were brought (21:7).

3 Jesus anticipated that the actions of the disciples might be questioned; so he instructed them, when asked why they were taking the colt, to answer, "The Lord needs it." By capitalizing "Lord," NIV has interpreted the passage to mean that Jesus was referring to himself. But since neither Matthew nor Mark uses *ho kyrios* ("the Lord") as a title for Jesus, and since it occurs in Luke and John only after the Resurrection, some commentators regard *ho kyrios* as a reference to the owner of the colt. Perhaps the owner was with Jesus at the time. On this understanding of *ho kyrios*, the statement of the disciples ("the owner needs it") would have been more understandable, and the last phrase of v.3—"and will send it back here shortly"—is an assurance by the owner that the animal would be returned promptly after he was through with it. However, in view of Luke 19:33, which NIV translates, "As they were untying the colt, its owners [*hoi kyrioi autou*] asked them, 'Why are you untying the colt?'" it seems more likely that *ho kyrios* in Mark 11:3 refers to our Lord. Jesus probably was well known by this time in the area around Bethany, and his authority was recognized. The fact that the Gospel writers go into such detail to explain how the colt was obtained suggests that they attached some importance to it, "and this lay in its testimony to the authority and perhaps the prescience of Jesus" (I. H. Marshall, *Commentary on Luke* [Grand Rapids: Eerdmans, 1978], p. 714).

4-6 The disciples found it as Jesus had told them (v.4) and carried out his orders to the letter. No mention is made by Mark of the owners of the colt being present, but the phrase "some people standing there" (v.5) may be equivalent to Luke's "its owners" (Luke 19:33). The people (owners?) did not object to the disciples' taking the colt (v.6) because apparently they knew Jesus and recognized His authority.

7-8 The action of the crowd was completely spontaneous. The outer garments on the back of the donkey made a kind of saddle for Jesus to ride on (v.7). When he mounted the colt (Luke 19:15 says the people put Jesus on it), others in the crowd spread their garments on the road (an act of royal homage; cf. 2 Kings 9:13) and spread branches before him (v.8; cf. 1 Macc 13:51, a description of Simon Maccabaeus entering Jerusalem to the accompaniment of green branches and antiphonal singing). The word *stibadas* (translated in NIV as "branches") means "leaves," "leafy branches" (BAG, p. 776). These could easily have been cut from the fields located nearby. Only John mentions palm branches (12:13). These probably came from Jericho; they are not native to Jerusalem, though in protected places they are known to grow there.

9-10 The crowds surrounded Jesus. Some went ahead of him, some behind (v.9). All shouted, "Hosanna." Cranfield says:

> Perhaps the foliage that was being strewn to make a path of honour for Jesus reminded someone of the *lûlabim* (bundles of palm, myrtle and willow) which were carried at the Feast of Tabernacles and shaken at the occurrence in the liturgy of the word *hosiahnna* in Ps 118:25 . . . and so called to his mind and lips the passage of the psalm, which once repeated would quite naturally be taken up by the crowd of pilgrims. (*Gospel of Mark*, p. 351)

"Hosanna" literally means "save now," but it had become simply an exclamation of praise. "Blessed is he who comes in the name of the Lord" is an accurate quotation of Psalm 118:26, one of the Hallel Psalms (Pss 113–18), which were used liturgically at the feasts of Tabernacles and Passover. This quotation was a customary religious greeting or blessing pronounced on pilgrims who had come to Jerusalem for the feast, but as Lane (p. 397) suggests, that did not exhaust its meaning, since "the formulation is ambiguous and Mark may well have intended his readers to detect a deeper, messianic significance in the phrase 'he who comes in the name of the Lord' (cf. Gen 49:10)." Verse 10 seems to support that interpretation. The kingdom blessed is the "kingdom of our father David," clearly the messianic kingdom promised to David's son. Martin (*Mark*, p. 138) reminds us that not even this statement gives away the secret of Jesus' person, "since . . . the cry of Hosanna is related to the coming kingdom and does not directly designate Jesus as Davidic King." The crowd proclaims the kingdom and not the king.

11 On entering the city Jesus went to the temple. Mark uses the word *hieron*, which means "temple area," not building. Apparently the crowd had quickly dispersed and only the disciples remained with Jesus. "He looked around at everything," not as a tourist viewing the sacred precincts for the first time (Jesus had been to Jerusalem before), but as the sovereign Lord examining the institution to see whether it was fulfilling its divinely appointed mission. The examination was in preparation for the prophetic act of cleansing. But since the hour was late, Jesus delayed his action against the temple and instead withdrew with his disciples to Bethany for the night.

As for the significance of the Triumphal Entry, Rawlinson (p. 151) writes:

> On the whole, it seems to be the most probable conclusion that the entry in this peculiar fashion into Jerusalem was deliberate on the part of our Lord, and was meant to suggest that, though He was indeed the Messiah and "Son of David," yet the Messiahship which He claimed was to be understood in a spiritual and non-political sense, in terms of the prophecy of Zechariah, rather than in terms of the "Son of David" idea as interpreted by contemporary expectation (*e.g.*, in the Psalms of Solomon). The time had in fact come for our Lord to put forward His Messianic claims, and to make His appeal to Jerusalem in a deliberately Messianic capacity. He does so, however, in a manner which is suggestive rather than explicit, and which was so calculated as to afford the minimum of pretext for a charge of quasi-political agitation.

B. *The Unfruitful Fig Tree*

11:12–14

> [12]The next day as they were leaving Bethany, Jesus was hungry. [13]Seeing in the distance a fig tree in leaf, he went to find out if it had any fruit. When he reached it, he found nothing but leaves, because it was not the season for figs. [14]Then he said to the tree, "May no one ever eat fruit from you again." And his disciples heard him say it.

12–13 This is one of the most difficult stories in the Gospels. It is not found in Luke. (Did he too have problems with it and omit it, or was it unknown to him?) Many modern commentators would just as soon it were not here at all. Rawlinson

(p. 154) says that it "approximates more closely than any other episode in Mk to the type of 'unreasonable' miracle characteristic of the non-canonical Gospel literature." Hunter (p. 110) comments: "With our knowledge of Jesus from other sources, we find it frankly incredible that he could have used his power to wither a fig tree because it did not yield figs two or three months before its natural time of fruitage." While rejecting the historicity of this account, Hunter finds the kernel of history in this story in the parable of the barren fig tree found in Luke 13:6–9. What was originally a parable has been changed into a factual story. Though admittedly difficult, the incident is not impossible. An important consideration is the position it occupies. It is one of Mark's interrupted accounts, in the middle of which stands the record of the cleansing of the temple. This is the clue to its meaning. Like the cleansing of the temple, the story of the unfruitful fig tree has to do with judgment.

The incident occurred on the way to Jerusalem from Bethany (v. 12), where Jesus had spent the night. He was hungry; and, noticing a fig tree, he went to see whether it had any figs on it (v. 13). Fig trees around Jerusalem usually leaf out in March or April, but they do not produce figs till June. This tree was no exception. It was in full leaf; but, as Mark tells his readers, there were no figs on it "because it was not the season for figs." It is this phrase that makes the story such a problem. Grant (p. 828) says Mark's explanation "only increases the problem, as it reflects on the good sense of Jesus." An easy solution is to consider the phrase a scribal gloss. But that will not do, because there is no textual evidence to support it. Also there is the fact that explanatory notes are a feature of Mark's style (cf. 1:16; 5:42; 7:3–4, 19; 13:14). It seems best to consider the phrase Mark's own insertion to explain to people not familiar with the characteristics of a fig tree why one fully leafed out would not have fruit on it.

14 Jesus addressed the tree directly and by his words performed a miracle of destruction. It is the only miracle of destruction attributed to Jesus in the Gospels. Manson's verdict on the action here ascribed to Jesus is well known: "It is a tale of miraculous power wasted in the service of ill temper (for the supernatural energy employed to blast the unfortunate tree might have been more usefully expended in forcing a crop of figs out of season); and as it stands it is simply incredible" (T.W. Manson, "The Cleansing of the Temple," BJRL 33 [1951]: 259).

The best explanation is to see the miracle as an acted-out parable. Jesus' hunger provides the occasion for his use of this teaching device. The fig tree represents Israel (cf. Hos 9:10; Nah 3:12; Zech 10:2). The tree is fully leafed out, and in such a state one would normally expect to find fruit. This symbolizes the hypocrisy and sham of the nation of Israel, which made her ripe for the judgment of God. "A people which honoured God with their lips but whose heart was all the time far from him (7:6) was like a tree with abundance of leaves but no fruit. The best commentary on vv. 12–14 and 20f. is to be found in the narrative which these verses enframe" (Cranfield, *Gospel of Mark*, pp. 356–57).

C. *The Cleansing of the Temple*

11:15–19

15On reaching Jerusalem, Jesus entered the temple area and began driving out those who were buying and selling there. He overturned the tables of the money changers and the benches of those selling doves, 16and would not allow anyone to carry merchandise through the temple courts. [17]And as he taught them, he said, "Is it not written:

> " 'My house will be called
> a house of prayer for all nations'?

But you have made it 'a den of robbers.' "
[18]The chief priests and the teachers of the law heard this and began looking for a way to kill him, for they feared him, because the whole crowd was amazed at his teaching.
[19]When evening came, they went out of the city.

All three synoptic writers have the cleansing of the temple at the end of Jesus' ministry. Only John has it at the beginning. Most commentators prefer the synoptic placement and reject the possibility of the two cleansings. But why Jesus could not have cleansed the temple twice, once at the beginning and once at the end of his public ministry, is never adequately explained.

The temple cleansing is sandwiched between the two incidents of the fig tree, an arrangement meant to link the accounts. The judgment symbolized by the cursing of the fig tree is initiated by Jesus' cleansing of the temple, and the cleansing of the temple is prophetic of the destruction of Jerusalem and the eschatological judgment (cf. Mark 13).

15–16 The cleansing of the temple, in fulfillment of Malachi 3:1–3, was Jesus' second messianic act during the Passion Week, the first having been the Triumphal Entry.

When Jesus entered the temple area (v.15), the smell of the animals entered his nostrils; and the noise from the moneychangers' tables beat on his ears. For the convenience of pilgrims, the cattlemen and the moneychangers had set up businesses in the Court of the Gentiles. The animals were sold for sacrifices. It was far easier for a pilgrim in Jerusalem to purchase one that was guaranteed kosher than to have to bring an animal with him and have it inspected for meeting the kosher requirements. The Roman money the pilgrims brought to Jerusalem had to be changed into the Tyrian currency (the closest thing to the old Hebrew shekel), since the annual temple tax had to be paid in that currency. Exorbitant prices were often charged for changing the currency. By overturning the tables of the moneychangers and the benches of those selling doves, Jesus was directly challenging the authority of the high priest, because they were there by his authorization. In John's account Jesus drove them out with a whip made from pieces of rope. Mark does not mention a whip. Nevertheless the words "driving out" and "overturned the tables" suggest that Jesus used force.

The statement of v.16 occurs only in Mark. It has been suggested that it may be Peter's own recollection of the event. Jesus not only cleansed the temple of its profanation by the merchants, but he also put a stop to its casual use by those who used it as a shortcut between the city and the Mount of Olives. Such a use of the temple area is later prohibited in the Talmud (*Berakoth* 9.5).

17 The first passage quoted by Jesus is Isaiah 56:7, a prediction that non-Jews who worship God will be allowed to worship in the temple. By allowing the Court of the Gentiles, the only place in the temple area where Gentiles were allowed to worship God, to become a noisy, smelly public market, the Jewish religious leaders were preventing Gentiles from exercising the spiritual privilege promised them. How could a Gentile pray amid all that noise and stench? And God's house was supposed to be "a house of prayer for all nations." The second quotation—"But you have made it a 'den of robbers' "—is from Jeremiah 7:11 and emphasizes that instead of allowing the temple to be what it was meant to be, a place of prayer, they had allowed it to become a robber's den. This is to be understood not so much in terms of the Jews' dishonest dealing with the pilgrims as in terms of their robbing the Gentiles by merchandising activities of their rightful claim to the worship of Israel's God.

The significance of the cleansing of the temple is that with the coming of the Messiah, "[Jesus] seeks to make available to the Gentiles the privileges which belonged to the new age and thereby he proclaims that the time of universal worship, uninhibited by Jewish restrictions, has come" (Martin, *Mark*, p. 225). This would have been particularly meaningful for Mark's predominantly Gentile readers.

18–19 The Pharisees and Herodians in Galilee had decided that Jesus must be put out of the way (cf. 3:6). Now the chief priests and teachers of the law come to the same decision (v.18). This is the first time in Mark's Gospel that they reveal active hostility to Jesus. Jesus' action had challenged their authority and no doubt cost them a good deal of money. So they went into action against him, but not openly, because they feared what the response of the people might be. Jesus' teaching was getting through to them. If he could persuade the people to follow him, the power and authority of the chief priests and teachers of the law would be broken.

Again Jesus and his disciples withdrew from Jerusalem and spent the night in Bethany (v.19). Did they do this because Jerusalem was not a safe place for Jesus at night?

D. The Withered Fig Tree and Sayings on Faith and Prayer

11:20–25(26)

> [20]In the morning, as they went along, they saw the fig tree withered from the roots. [21]Peter remembered and said to Jesus, "Rabbi, look! The fig tree you cursed has withered!"
>
> [22]"Have faith in God," Jesus answered. [23]"I tell you the truth, if anyone says to this mountain, 'Go, throw yourself into the sea,' and does not doubt in his heart but believes that what he says will happen, it will be done for him. [24]Therefore I tell you, whatever you ask for in prayer, believe that you have received it, and it will be yours. [25]And when you stand praying, if you hold anything against anyone, forgive him, so that your Father in heaven may forgive you your sins."

The first three verses of this section form the second part of the story of the fig tree (11:12–14) that encloses the account of the cleansing of the temple. (For the theological significance of this, see the introductory paragraph to the exposition of 11:15–19.)

20–21 The next morning, on returning to Jerusalem from Bethany, Jesus and his disciples passed the fig tree again (v.20). It was totally destroyed ("withered from the roots"). Jesus had predicted that no one would ever eat fruit from it again (v.14); and Peter, remembering what Jesus had said, called his attention to the withered tree (v.21). Jesus does not in any way interpret the event. Yet the meaning is obvious: Jesus' predicted judgment on the temple will come to pass as surely as his prediction of the withering of the fig tree.

22 The sayings found in vv.22–25 occur elsewhere in the synoptic Gospels in various contexts (Matt 6:13–14; 7:7; 17:20; 18:19; Luke 11:9; 17:6). This suggests that here they have no historical connection with what precedes. It is, however, possible to see a connection. Jesus uses the incident of the fig tree to teach incidentally (for surely the main point of the incident is the sure judgment of God on the temple) some lessons on faith and prayer. The source of the power for performing the miracle is God. He must be the object of our faith.

23 This is another of Jesus' pronouncements preceded by the solemn introductory formula "I tell you the truth"—a way of implying its importance. Since Jesus was standing on the Mount of Olives, from which the Dead Sea can be seen on a clear day, he may have been referring specifically to the Mount. Of course Jesus is speaking figuratively. (For a mountain as a symbol of a great difficulty, cf. Zech 4:7 and references to SBK, 1:759.) Jesus is saying that the greatest possible difficulties can be removed when a person has faith (cf. James 1:6).

24 There is a close connection between the kind of faith Jesus speaks of here and prayer. Stauffer clearly brings this out: "What is it that distinguishes this faith from the self-intoxication that . . . is 'beyond one's powers' and makes a man and his work end up in a fiasco? The 'faith' of Mark 11:23f. is a faith that prays. . . . Prayer is the source of its power, and the means of its strength—God's omnipotence is its sole assurance, and God's sovereignty its only restriction (E. Stauffer, *New Testament Theology* [London: SCM, 1955], p. 169).

25 Admittedly the transition between v.24 and v.25 is abrupt (v.24 speaks of faith, v.25 of forgiveness). Still there is a connection. To be effective prayer must be offered in faith—faith in the all-powerful God who works miracles. But it must be offered in the spirit of forgiveness. Faith and the willingness to forgive—these are the two conditions of efficacious prayer.

26 This verse does not occur in NIV because it is not found in the best and most ancient MSS of the NT. It represents an insertion from Matthew 6:15.

Notes

22 The variant reading that inserts εἰ (*ie*, "if") before ἔχετε (*echete*, "you have") has rather strong MS support. But it is probably not original because (1) the solemn "I tell you the truth" is never preceded by a conditional clause, and (2) the introductory "if" probably arose by assimilation to the saying in Luke 17:6 (cf. Matt 21:21).
23 Verses 23–25 occur in the synoptic Gospels as follows: 11:23 = Matt 17:20; Luke 17:6; with 11:24, cf. Matt 7:7; 18:19; Luke 11:9; with 11:25, cf. Matt 6:14–15.

E. *The Question About Jesus' Authority*

11:27–33

> 27They arrived again in Jerusalem, and while Jesus was walking in the temple courts, the chief priests, the teachers of the law and the elders came to him. 28By what authority are you doing these things?" they asked. "And who gave you authority to do this?"
> 29Jesus replied, "I will ask you one question. Answer me, and I will tell you by what authority I am doing these things. 30John's baptism—was it from heaven, or from men? Tell me!"
> 31They discussed it among themselves and said, "If we say, 'From heaven,' he will ask, 'Then why didn't you believe him?' 32But if we say, 'From men'...." (They feared the people, for everyone held that John really was a prophet.)
> 33So they answered Jesus, "We don't know."
> Jesus said, "Neither will I tell you by what authority I am doing these things."

27–28 After the incident of the fig tree and the lesson on faith, prayer, and forgiveness, Jesus and his disciples came to Jerusalem and entered the temple area—the focal point of his ministry while in the city (v.27). On this occasion the opposition came from three elements of the Jewish religious establishment: chief priests, teachers of the law, and elders. These groups made up the Sanhedrin, the high court of the Jews. How drastic Jesus' action in cleansing the temple was is shown by their presence. They would have arrested Jesus on the spot, but his popularity among the people prevented that—at least for the time being. Instead they directed a question to him (v.28) about the source of his authority "for doing these things" (a reference to his cleansing the temple). Their hope was that by his answer Jesus would be brought into disrepute with the people and thereby clear the way for their arresting him.

29–30 Again Jesus answers a question by asking another one (v.29; cf. 10:2–3). Hunter (p. 113) paraphrases it thus: "Do you think God was behind John's mission or not?" The question was particularly appropriate for the situation. John had clearly testified to the divine source of Jesus' mission. If they recognized the divine authority of John's mission, they would be forced to recognize Jesus' also and his cleansing of the temple as the legitimate exercise of his authority. By "John's baptism" (v.30) Jesus meant John's ministry and teaching as evidenced by its outward expression. "From heaven" means "from God," since "heaven" was a common Jewish substitute for the divine name.

31–33 The question of Jesus proved too much for them. They clearly saw that either alternative—"from heaven" or "from men"—would place them in a difficult position (vv.31–32). An admission of John's divine authority would compel them to believe in Jesus; a denial would place them in an unfavorable position with the people who accepted John as a true prophet. So to save face they pleaded ignorance (v.33), which was tantamount to a refusal to answer Jesus' question. Jesus' reply was that he too would refuse to answer their question—at least directly. He had given them a veiled answer in his counterquestion (cf. v.30).

F. *The Parable of the Tenants*

12:1–12

> [1]He then began to speak to them in parables: "A man planted a vineyard. He put a wall around it, dug a pit for the winepress and built a watchtower. Then he rented the vineyard to some farmers and went away on a journey. [2]At harvest time he sent a servant to the tenants to collect from them some of the fruit of the vineyard. [3]But they seized him, beat him and sent him away empty-handed. [4]Then he sent another servant to them; they struck this man on the head and treated him shamefully. [5]He sent still another, and that one they killed. He sent many others; some of them they beat, others they killed.
>
> [6]"He had one left to send, a son, whom he loved. He sent him last of all, saying, 'They will respect my son.'
>
> [7]"But the tenants said to one another, 'This is the heir. Come, let's kill him, and the inheritance will be ours.' [8]So they took him and killed him, and threw him out of the vineyard.
>
> [9]"What then will the owner of the vineyard do? He will come and kill those tenants and give the vineyard to others. [10]Haven't you read this scripture:
>
> > " 'The stone the builders rejected
> >   has become the capstone;
> > [11]the Lord has done this,
> >   and it is marvelous in our eyes'?"
>
> [12]Then they looked for a way to arrest him because they knew he had spoken the parable against them. But they were afraid of the crowd; so they left him and went away.

Doubts have been raised about the authenticity of this parable because of its allegorical features. While it is true that most of Jesus' parables have but one point to make and the details have no separate significance, Jesus did use allegory on occasion (cf. Mark 4:13–20). There is no compelling reason to doubt the genuineness of this parable. Moule writes: "This story, so clearly directed against the irresponsible religious leaders of his own day, seems to furnish an example of a genuinely contemporary, unaltered piece of Jesus' teaching" (*Gospel of Mark*, p. 94).

Some scholars deny that the parable is an allegory. Its allegorical features, however, seem fairly obvious: the vineyard is Israel; the owner is God; the tenants are the Jewish leaders; the servants are the prophets; and the only son and heir is Jesus. Other details of the parable such as the wall, winepress, and tower have no separate significance.

1 Mark does not identify who Jesus' hearers were (he simply says "them"). Among "them" were included Jesus' opponents (the chief priests, teachers of the law, and elders; cf. 11:27), as the reaction recorded in v.12 makes clear. The description in v.1 reflects the language of Isaiah 5:1–2. The vineyard symbolizes Israel (cf. Ps 80:8–16; Isa 5:7; Jer 2:21). The details mentioned here—the wall (usually made of unmortared rocks); the pit (in which the juice of the grapes was collected); the press (usually made of solid limestone); the tower (for the protection of the vineyard and shelter for the farmer)—are all known to anyone who has traveled in Israel.

When the vineyard had been completely prepared, its owner rented it to tenants and went on a journey. This detail reflects a condition that actually prevailed in Galilee in Jesus' time, viz., much of the land was in the hands of absentee landowners who contracted with tenants on a crop-sharing basis.

2–5 When harvest time came (v.2), the absentee landlord sent one of his servants to collect what was due him from the tenants. The payment was to be made in produce of the land according to a previously agreed-on percentage. The landlord sent three servants in succession to collect the payment (vv.3–5), but the tenants repudiated the agreement. Instead they beat up the first two servants and killed the third. The detail of v.5b—"he sent many others"—Lane (p. 418) says, "was intended by Jesus to force his listeners beyond the framework of the parable to the history of Israel. In the OT the prophets are frequently designated 'the servants' of God (cf. Jer 7:25f; 25:4; Amos 3:7; Zech 1:6) and it is natural to find a reference to their rejection in the words 'beating some, and killing others.'"

6–8 The sending of the son underscores the serious view the owner of the vineyard took of the situation. He was an *agapētos* son (v.6). *Agapētos* probably means "only" here (as in the LXX of Gen 22:2, 12, 16; cf. Jer 6:26). The owner assumed that they would respect him. This statement is not to be taken as informing us as to God's expectation for the coming of Jesus into the world. He knew beforehand that Jesus would be rejected. It is simply a part of the story and should not be allegorized. The owner's expectations were thwarted. The tenants' greed led to outrageous action (v.7). They saw the coming of the son as a golden opportunity for seizing the property; they may have inferred from the son's coming that the owner had died. If they did away with his son (v.8), the property would be ownerless and therefore available to the first claimants (cf. M *Baba Bathra* 3.3 and b *Baba Bathra* 54a).

Jeremias points out that "there can be no doubt that in the sending of the son Jesus himself had his own sending in mind, but for the mass of his hearers the Messianic significance of the son could not be taken for granted, since no evidence is forthcoming for the application of the 'Son of God' to the Messiah in pre-Christian Palestinian Judaism" (*Parables of Jesus*, pp. 72–73). There was no question, however, in the minds of Jesus' hearers that he was the son in the parable; their reaction in v.12 makes this clear.

Throwing the son out of the vineyard is another detail of the story that should not be allegorized. Both Matthew and Luke have the killing of the son take place after (not before as in Mark) he is thrown out of the vineyard (v.8; cf. Matt 21:39; Luke 20:15).

9 Jesus draws out the meaning of the parable with a question and then proceeds to answer the question himself. (In Matt 21:41 the people answer the question.) Doubts have been cast on the authenticity of this verse because ordinarily Jesus does not answer his own questions (cf. Luke 17:9). But there is no inherent reason why he should not have done so in this situation. The answer underscores the seriousness of the action of the wicked tenants. Their punishment will be capital, and the vineyard will be let to other tenants who "will give him his share of the crop at the harvest time" (Matt 21:41). The allusion is to Isaiah 5:1–7. Cranfield points out that the warning "is directed specifically to the leaders of the people and not to the people at large," because "whereas in Isa 5 the vineyard was at fault, here it is only the husbandmen" (*Gospel of Mark*, pp. 367–68). The killing of the tenants may be a not-so-veiled prophecy of the destruction of Jerusalem, and the "others" to which the vineyard is given are the new Israel.

10–11 The quotation is from Psalm 118:22–23, the same psalm the joyful Hosanna cry came from (cf. 11:9). In the OT context the reference to "the stone" (v.10) is probably to the construction of Solomon's temple. One of the stones was rejected but became the *kephalē gōnias* ("capstone," NIV; "head of the corner," AV, RSV; "main cornerstone," NEB). Plummer (p.275) thinks the reference is to "a cornerstone uniting two walls; but whether at the base or at the top is not certain." Jeremias thinks it refers to a keystone that holds together and completes the building (TDNT, 1:792–93).

In the original context the rejected stone was Israel, despised by the pagan nations but, after her return from Exile, exalted to the status of nationhood. Here Jesus applies the psalm to himself. The "stoneship" of Jesus, based on this passage in Psalms, was a familiar theme in early Christianity, as shown by Acts 4:11 and 1 Peter 2:7. Although there is no specific reference to the Resurrection in the psalm, Jeremias remarks: "The early community found in Ps. 118:22 scriptural evidence for the death and resurrection of Jesus. The Crucified is the rejected stone which in the resurrection is made by God the chief corner-stone in the heavenly sanctuary (Ac. 4:11), to be manifested as such in the *parousia*" (TDNT, 1:793).

12 The application of the parable was obvious, but again the religious leaders did not dare harm Jesus because they feared the crowd (cf. 11:18, 32). It was getting close to the time of the feast, and more and more pilgrims from Galilee were arriving in Jerusalem. Many of these knew Jesus either by personal contact or by reputation. The religious leaders knew it would be unwise to make their move now; "so they left him and went away." The similarity of this verse with 11:18–19 may mark the end of Jesus' third day (Tuesday) in Jerusalem during the Passion Week.

G. The Question About Paying Taxes to Caesar

12:13–17

> [13]Later they sent some of the Pharisees and Herodians to Jesus to catch him in his words. [14]They came to him and said, "Teacher, we know you are a man of integrity. You aren't swayed by men, because you pay no attention to who they are; but you teach the way of God in accordance with the truth. Is it right to pay taxes to Caesar or not? [15]Should we pay or shouldn't we?"
>
> But Jesus knew their hypocrisy. "Why are you trying to trap me?" he asked. "Bring me a denarius and let me look at it." [16]They brought the coin, and he asked them, "Whose portrait is this? And whose inscription?"
>
> "Caesar's," they replied.
>
> [17]Then Jesus said to them, "Give to Caesar what is Caesar's and to God what is God's."
>
> And they were amazed at him.

13 Jesus again comes into conflict with the religious leaders. Mark does not say when or where this incident took place. It is generally agreed, however, that it was on the next day (Wednesday) and in one of the courts of the temple.

The Herodians were as obnoxious to the Pharisees on political grounds as the Sadducees were on theological grounds. Yet the two groups united in their opposition to Jesus. Collaboration in wickedness, as well as goodness, has great power. Their purpose was to trip Jesus up in his words so that he would lose the support of the people, leaving the way open for them to destroy him.

14–15a The question was prefaced with an obvious and, indeed, obnoxious piece of flattery (v.14). Moreover it was thoroughly insincere. The Pharisees and Herodians were intending "to impale [Jesus] on the horns of a dilemma" (Hunter, p. 116). Since the time of Archelaus's banishment in A.D. 6, Jews had been required by the Romans to pay tribute money into the *fiscus*, the emperor's treasury. Some Jews (e.g., the Zealots) flatly refused to pay it, because it was for them an admission of the Roman right to rule. The Pharisees disliked paying it but did not actively oppose it, whereas the Herodians had no objections to it. The intent of this question was to force Jesus to a direct answer (v.15a), identifying himself either with the Zealots or with the Herodians.

15b–16 Jesus was not about to fall into their trap. He recognized their question for the "hypocrisy" (*hypokrisin*) it was (v.15b). So he asked them for a Roman denarius. There is no indication that they had to send away for the coin; one was readily available. This implies that they had already answered their own question. It was Caesar's coinage they were using (v.16); and by using it they were tacitly acknowledging Caesar's authority and thus their obligation to pay the tax.

17 Jesus' answer avoided the trap. Caesar has a legitimate claim and so does God. Give to each his rightful claim. "So long as God's rights were safeguarded . . . there was no need to question the rights of Caesar. Civil obedience, attested by the payment of the tax, no more contradicted than it abolished the obedience due to God" (Hunter, p. 116). Jesus does not, however, say that the claims of God and those of Caesar are the same.

> Though the obligation to pay to Caesar some of his own coinage in return for the amenities his rule provided is affirmed, the idolatrous claims expressed on the coins are rejected. God's rights are to be honored. Here Jesus is not saying that there are two quite separate independent spheres, that of Caesar and that of God (for Caesar and all that is his belongs to God); but he is indicating that there are obligations to Caesar which do not infringe the rights of God but are indeed ordained by God. (Cranfield, *Gospel of Mark*, p. 372)

For a more complete doctrine of the Christian and his relationship to the state, this statement of Jesus must be taken with Romans 13:1–7; 1 Timothy 2:1–6; and 1 Peter 2:13–17.

The reply was not what they expected. It was simple yet profound, and "they were amazed at him." But because he did not give a direct yes-or-no answer, it was either misunderstood or deliberately distorted, as Luke 23:2 implies.

H. *The Question of Marriage at the Resurrection*

12:18–27

¹⁸Then the Sadducees, who say there is no resurrection, came to him with a question. ²⁹"Teacher," they said, "Moses wrote for us that if a man's brother dies and leaves a wife but no children, the man must marry the widow and have children for his brother. ²⁰Now there were seven brothers. The first one married and died without leaving any children. ²¹The second one married the widow, but he also died, leaving no child. It was the same with the third. ²²In fact, none of the seven left any children. Last of all, the woman died too. ²³At the resurrection whose wife will she be, since the seven were married to her?"

24Jesus replied, "Are you not in error because you do not know the Scriptures or the power of God? 25When the dead rise, they will neither marry nor be given in marriage; they will be like the angels in heaven. 26Now about the dead rising—have you not read in the book of Moses, in the account of the bush, how God said to him, 'I am the God of Abraham, the God of Isaac, and the God of Jacob'? 27He is not the God of the dead, but of the living. You are badly mistaken!"

18 Reliable information about the Sadducees (mentioned here for the first time by Mark) is difficult to obtain because no documents that are clearly Sadducean have been preserved. The word "Sadducee" probably comes from the name Zadok (*Saddouk* in Gr.) and is usually traced to the high priest of that name during the time of David. The Sadducees' relationship to the temple is not clear. Only one high priest, Hanan ben Hanan, during the 107-year period between Herod the Great's appointment to Ananel and the destruction of the temple in A.D. 70 is identified as a Sadducee by Josephus (Antiq. XX, 227 [ix.1]); and he only held the office for three months. Lane (p. 426) observes: "The disputes between Sadducean and Pharisaic scribes show a pronounced interest in the Temple but do not warrant the assertion that the Temple hierarchy was by conviction Sadducean or was inclined to follow the traditions of the Sadducees."

In the time of Jesus, the Sadducees were small numerically but exerted great influence politically and religiously. They were not, however, popular among the masses. Josephus says they were educated men and many of them held prominent positions (Antiq. XVIII, 17 [i.4]). The Sadducees represented the urban, wealthy, sophisticated class and were centered in Jerusalem. When Jerusalem was destroyed in A.D. 70, they disappeared from history.

In the NT the Sadducees are mentioned only fourteen times whereas the Pharisees are mentioned about one hundred times. Mark mentions them only in this verse and identifies them with the statement "who say there is no resurrection." The Sadducees held this position because they accepted only Scripture and rejected all beliefs and practices not found there. Since they claimed to be unable to find clear teaching about the Resurrection in the OT, they rejected the doctrine. This set them against the Pharisees, who considered the oral tradition as authoritative as the written Scriptures.

19–23 Although the Sadducees addressed Jesus with the honorific title "Teacher" (v.19), their purpose was not to learn from him. It was manifestly hostile: "the extreme case they offer for His opinion is clearly intended as a *reductio ad absurdum* of any view but their own" (Swete, p. 278). The case cited arose out of a provision in the Mosaic Law (Deut 25:5–6), which required that if a man died without children, his brother had to marry his widow. The purpose of the levirate law (from the Lat. *levir*, "brother-in-law"), as it was called, was to protect the widow and guarantee the continuance of the family line. With this law in mind, the Sadducees now presented a hypothetical case in which one woman married seven brothers in turn, all of whom died childless (vv.20–22). In the Resurrection whose wife of the seven would she be (v.23)? The case is so ludicrous it may have been a well-known Sadducean joke used for poking fun at the Pharisees' doctrine of the Resurrection.

24–25 In his answer Jesus accuses the Sadducees of ignorance of (1) the Scriptures and (2) the power of God (v.24). He then proceeds to take up the second accusation first. In the Resurrection there will be a new order of existence brought about by the power of God (v.25). "The questioners did not see that God could not only grant life in another world, but also make it very different from life in this world" (Plummer, p. 281). Marriage will not exist as it does now, but all life will be like that of the angels. This evidently means that the basic characteristics of resurrection life will be service for and fellowship with God. The mention of angels in this context is significant because it served as a correction of another theological error of the Sadducees (cf. Acts 23:8). Also, since in heaven there will be no more death, the need for marriage and the propagation of the race will not exist.

26–27 Jesus now turns to his first-mentioned cause of the Sadducees' erroneous thinking: ignorance of the teaching of the OT (cf. 2:25; 12:10). He directed them back to the story of Moses and the burning bush (v.26; Exod 3:6). His use of a text from the Pentateuch was significant because this part of the OT was considered particularly authoritative by the Sadducees. The quotation may be understood as follows: Abraham, Isaac, and Jacob had long since died when God made the statement to Moses. Nevertheless God said, "I am," not "I was," the God of Abraham, Isaac, and Jacob. Thus the patriarchs were still alive in Moses' time (v.27); and if they were alive then, we may be sure that in the Resurrection God will raise up their bodies to share in the blessedness of eternal life. The fact that the phrase "the God of Abraham, the God of Isaac, and the God of Jacob" carried with it the idea of the covenant God, the God whose promises can be relied on, underscores the basic thrust of Jesus' argument—viz., the faithfulness of God.

I. *The Question Concerning the Great Commandment*

12:28–34

> [28]One of the teachers of the law came and heard them debating. Noticing that Jesus had given them a good answer, he asked him, "Of all the commandments, which is the most important?"
>
> [29]"The most important one," answered Jesus, "is this: 'Hear, O Israel, the Lord our God, the Lord is one. [30]Love the Lord your God with all your heart and with all your soul and with all your mind and with all your strength.' [31]The second is this: 'Love your neighbor as yourself.' There is no commandment greater than these."
>
> [32]"Well said, teacher," the man replied. "You are right in saying that God is one and there is no other but him. [33]To love him with all your heart, with all your understanding and with all your strength, and to love your neighbor as yourself is more important than all burnt offerings and sacrifices."
>
> [34]When Jesus saw that he had answered wisely, he said to him, "You are not far from the kingdom of God." And from then on no one dared ask him any more questions.

28 Mark seems to suggest that the question asked by the teacher of the law, in contrast to many that had been asked by his colleagues, was a sincere one (but cf. Matt 22:34). He had been impressed by Jesus' answer to the previous question and so ventured one of his own. The rabbis counted 613 individual statutes in the law, 365 which were negative and 248 positive. Attempts were made to differentiate between the "heavy," or "great," and the "light," or "little," commandments. The rabbis also made attempts to formulate great principles from which the rest of the law could be deduced. The most famous example comes from Hillel, who when challenged by a Gentile, "Make me a proselyte on condition that you teach me the whole law while I stand on one foot," replied, "What you hate for yourself, do not do to your neighbor: this is the whole law, the rest is commentary; go and learn" (b *Shabbath* 31a). The question arose out of a works-righteousness understanding of the law and the keeping of its commandments.

29–30 In answer to the question, Jesus quoted two passages from the OT (Deut 6:4–5; Lev 19:18). Deuteronomy 6:4 is central to the Shema, named after the first word of the verse, which means "Hear" (v.29). In Hebrew liturgy Deuteronomy 6:4–9; 11:13–21; and Numbers 13:37–41 comprise the Shema. Deuteronomy 6:4–5 is a confession of faith that is recited by pious Jews every morning and evening. It basically affirms two things: (1) the unity of God ("the Lord is one") and (2) the covenant relationship of God to the Jewish people ("the Lord our God"). In telling this story only Mark included Deuteronomy 6:4 here. Its relationship to the words that follow is important. God is to be loved completely and totally (v.30) because he, and he alone, is God and because he has made a covenant of love with his people. In the covenant God gives himself totally in love to his people; therefore he expects his people to give themselves totally ("soul," "mind," and "strength") in love to him.

31 Jesus brought Leviticus 19:18 together with Deuteronomy 6:5 to show that love of neighbor is a natural and logical outgrowth of love of God. These two commandments belong together; they cannot be separated. Thus although the teacher of the law had asked for the one most important commandment, Jesus gave him two. In Leviticus 19:18 the neighbor is identified as "one of your people," i.e., fellow Israelites. The Jews of Jesus' day interpreted "fellow Israelites" even more narrowly than the OT passage; for there (cf. Lev 19:34) it included resident aliens, whereas for Jesus' contemporaries it included only Jews and full proselytes. Jesus redefined the term to mean "anyone with whom we have dealings at all" (cf. Luke 10:25–27). Mitton, in a most practical application of this verse, remarks that "neighbor" embraces

> all within our home, those we meet at work, in our church, and in recreations. And more than that: our employer is our neighbor too; so are our work people, all who serve us in shops, the men who empty our dust bins and those who try to keep streets and parks clean. So too are the people of Jamaica, of West Africa, of Kenya, of Germany and of Russia. If we love our neighbors as we love ourselves, we shall want for them the treatment we should want for ourselves, were we in their place. (*Gospel of Mark*, p. 99)

32–33 Only Mark records the favorable response of the teacher of the law and Jesus' statement that he was "not far from the kingdom of God" (v.34). In repeating the commandment he omitted the divine name "the Lord" in keeping with the practice of pious Jews of avoiding the pronunciation of God's name (v.32). The phrase "and there is no other but him" is an interpretive addition from Deuteronomy 4:35, which underscores the uniqueness of Israel's God. The statement by the teacher of the law that love of God and neighbor are "more important than all burnt offerings and sacrifices" (v.33) is in keeping with the teachings of the OT prophets (1 Sam 15:22; Hos 6:6); but it is an advance on the teaching of Judaism in his time. In

Judaism the law and sacrifices are set side by side with love (cf. M *Pirke Aboth* 1. 2), whereas the teacher of the law was declaring the superiority of love (cf. Taylor, p. 489). In his repetition of what Jesus said, the teacher of the law substitutes *synesis* ("understanding") for *dianoia* ("mind") and omits *psychē* ("soul"). There is, however, no appreciable difference in the meaning.

34 The reply of the teacher of the law shows that what Jesus said was getting through to him and elicits the statement by our Lord that he was close to the kingdom of God—a statement no doubt meant to stimulate and challenge him to further thoughtful reflection and decisive action. Whether or not he ever entered the kingdom is not stated.

Jesus had so forcefully demonstrated his ability to answer questions meant to trap him and to turn such questions back on his accusers that from this time on "no one dared ask him any more questions." Verse 34 points forward to the next incident recorded by Mark, where Jesus, not the religious leaders, asks the question about the "son of David."

J. The Question About David's Son

12:35-37

> 35While Jesus was teaching in the temple courts, he asked, "How is it that the teachers of the law say that the Christ is the son of David? 36David himself, speaking by the Holy Spirit, declared:
>
> > " 'The Lord said to my Lord:
> > "Sit at my right hand
> > until I put your enemies
> > under your feet." '
>
> 37David himself calls him 'Lord.' How then can he be his son?"
> The large crowd listened to him with delight.

35 Jesus was still in the temple courts. Up to this point he was being asked questions. Now he takes the initiative and asks a question himself. The Messiah (cf. commentary at 8:29), the Anointed One, the King appointed by God, was expected to be from the family of David (cf. Isa 9:2-7; 11:1-9; Jer 23:5-6; 30:9; 33:15, 17, 22; Ezek 34:23-24; 37:24; Hos 3:5; Amos 9:11). The Triumphal Entry clearly shows that the restored kingdom was a popular expectation ("Blessed is the coming kingdom of our father David," 11:10). Jesus' question is "In what sense [cf. NIV's 'How is it?'] is the Messiah the son of David?"

36-37 Jesus does not wait for an answer from his listeners. He provides it himself. The quotation is from Psalm 110:1. Both the Davidic authorship is assumed and his inspiration in writing it (v.36). "Speaking by the Holy Spirit" is a typical rabbinic formula to describe inspired utterance. A messianic interpretation of Psalm 110 is unknown before the third century A.D. It may be, however, that its messianic interpretation was dropped because of Christian usage and reintroduced at a later period. The main point of Jesus' reply presupposes the psalm's messianic usage.

David calls the Messiah "my Lord." How can he at the same time be David's son and David's Lord (v.37)? The answer Jesus intended to elicit was "The Messiah is indeed to be descended from David, but he has a more exalted role than that of a successor of David; he is the Son of God." Or as Moule puts the answer intended by Jesus: "Because, although he is his son by descent and therefore his junior in age, he is also in some mysterious way, superior to David and therefore his senior in rank" (*Gospel of Mark*, p. 99).

Mark says that the crowd was delighted to listen to Jesus. Apparently they enjoyed seeing the so-called experts stumped! The remark also serves to show that, though the religious leaders opposed Jesus, the common people were for him.

Notes

36 It was once held that Ps 110, stated by Jesus to have been written by David, was actually Maccabean in date (second century B.C.). This has now been disproved as the result of the discovery at Qumran of a complete Psalter that has been dated in the third century B.C.

K. *The Warning About the Teachers of the Law*

12:38–40

> [38]As he taught, Jesus said, "Watch out for the teachers of the law. They like to walk around in flowing robes and be greeted in the marketplaces, [39]and have the most important seats in the synagogues and the places of honor at banquets. [40]They devour widows' houses and for a show make lengthy prayers. Such men will be punished most severely."

38–39 This paragraph probably is a continuing account of Jesus' teaching in the temple courts (cf. 12:35), though it is possible that Mark placed it here because, like the previous paragraph, it concerns the teachers of the law (v.38). Moule rightly says: "There is no evidence that all the theologians of Jesus' day were frauds, using their position merely as a cloak for cruelty and greed. . . . But the most influential of them seemed to have conceived a bitter hatred of Jesus, and one can only guess that this was because they were indeed using their powers selfishly and irresponsibly and detested his exposure of their real motives" (*Gospel of Mark*, p. 100).

Here Jesus condemns "their love of religious uniform ('ecclesiastical millinery') and public deference ('the raised hats of the laity'); a failing not yet wholly extinct in the clerical class" (Hunter, p. 120). Teachers of the law wore long white linen robes that were fringed and reached almost to the ground. They also were shown special respect by the majority of the people, being addressed by the honorific titles "Rabbi," "Father," and "Master." In the synagogue they occupied the bench in front of the ark that contained the sacred scrolls of the Law and the Prophets (v.39). There the teachers could be seen by all the worshipers in the synagogue. They were often invited to banquets because of their prestige and were given special places of honor. What Jesus condemns is their seeking such honor for themselves instead of for God whom they professed to serve.

40 Since the teachers of the law were not allowed to be paid for their services, they were dependent on the gifts of patrons for their livelihood. Such a system was vulnerable to abuses. Wealthy widows especially were preyed on by the greedy and unscrupulous among these men. Jesus particularly condemns the hypocrisy of their long prayers that were used as a mask for their greed. "For a show" is a translation of the Greek work *prophasis*. It is difficult to know whether it should be taken with what precedes and be translated "and to cover it up" (i.e., to cover up their devouring of widow's houses) or with what follows (the long prayers) and translate it, as does NIV, "and for a show." In either case there is a connection between their long prayers and their greed. "To rob the poor and the bereaved under the guise of personal piety doubles the guilt" (Hiebert, *Gospel of Mark*, pp. 310–11). Jesus promises punishment to all such—a reference to God's judgment in the Last Day.

L. *The Widow's Offering*

12:41–44

> [41]Jesus sat down opposite the place where the offerings were put and watched the crowd putting their money into the temple treasury. Many rich people threw in large amounts. [42]But a poor widow came and put in two very small copper coins, worth only a fraction of a penny.
>
> [43]Calling his disciples to him, Jesus said, "I tell you the truth, this poor widow has put more into the treasury than all the others. [44]They all gave out of their wealth; but she, out of her poverty, put in everything—all she had to live on."

41–42 After this incident (the last in his public ministry), Jesus spends his time exclusively with the disciples. The placement of this story here may be to contrast the greed of the teachers of the law with the liberality of the widow. Or it may be that "with its teaching that the true gift is to give 'everything we have' (v.44) it sums up what has gone before in the Gospel and makes a superb transition to the story of how Jesus 'gave everything' for men" (Nineham, pp. 334–35). The setting is the court of the women, into which both men and women were allowed to come, and where the temple treasury was located. Jesus sat down on a bench where he could watch the people bring their offerings and put them in one of the thirteen trumpet-shaped boxes (*šôfār*) that were used for that purpose (v.41). It was not the rich with their large gifts who caught Jesus' attention but a poor widow (v.42). She placed in the box two copper coins (*lepta*), the smallest coins in circulation in Palestine (cf. Notes). Their value was, as NIV puts it, "only a fraction of a penny."

43–44 The disciples were not sitting with Jesus; so he called them to him (v.43). The lesson he wanted to teach them was important enough for them to be there to see it for themselves as well as to hear it. Again Jesus precedes his pronouncement with the solemn "I tell you the truth." The widow's offering was more (v.44) than all the others "in proportion, and also in the spirit in which she gave; it was in the latter that she was richer than all of them. . . . The means of the giver and the motive are the measure of true generosity" (Plummer, p. 290). Mark does not say how Jesus knew how much the widow gave or that what she gave constituted her entire livelihood.

Notes

42 A λέπτον (*lepton*, lit., "a tiny thing"; cf. the English word "mite"), the only Jewish coin mentioned in the NT, was worth one sixty-fourth of a denarius, the daily wage of a laborer (see IBD, II, 1022). Mark explains to his Roman readers, who would be unfamiliar with the value of the Palestinian coin, that a *lepton* was about equivalent to a *kodrantēs* (Gr. transliteration of the Lat. *quadrans*), which NIV translates in terms of its approximate value: "worth only a fraction of a penny." That Mark felt it necessary to explain the value of a *lepton* and that he does so by the use of a Latin coin (*quadrans*) only known in the west suggests strongly, in spite of contrary opinion, that he was writing to Romans.

M. *The Olivet Discourse* (13:1–37)

This is the longest connected discourse in Mark's Gospel. It is also the most difficult. The three major questions that present themselves in the study of Mark 13 are (1) What is the origin of the passage? (2) What is its purpose in Mark's Gospel? and (3) What is its meaning?

First, wide divergences of opinion exist as to the origin of this passage. Some scholars, concluding that Jesus teaches in Mark 13 that the end of the age will come within his own generation and being unwilling to ascribe such a serious mistake to him, have created the Little Apocalypse theory. By this means the apocalyptic element in chapter 13 is identified with a Jewish (or Jewish-Christian) apocalyptic tract that was written as a result of Pilate's placement of Roman ensigns in Jerusalem, or when Caligula, the Roman emperor, threatened to set up his image in the Jerusalem temple, or when the Roman armies surrounded the city of Jerusalem in A.D. 70. Since this apocalyptic tract was wrongly attributed to Jesus, none of the apocalyptic material in Mark 13 may be ascribed to him.

Although the Little Apocalypse theory has many adherents, it does not stand up under careful scrutiny. The chief problem with it is that the apocalyptic element in the discourse is too integrally bound up with the exhortative to posit an original apocalyptic tract. This is evident from the structure of the discourse. The apocalyptic statements are followed by exhortations that in turn are followed by clauses beginning with *gar* ("for") that state the reason for the exhortation (cf. vv.8, 11, 19, 22, 33, 35). Gaston accepts the readings that add *gar* to vv.6, 7b, and 9b and writes: "The importance of this word would have been noticed long ago were it not for the unfortunate fact that it is missing in several places from the Nestle text, even though it is required by a synoptic comparison and is well attested. . . . With the exception . . . of the longer sections 14–18 and 24–27, every apocalyptic element is attached to its context by a γάρ [*gar*]" (L. Gaston, *No Stone on Another* [Leiden: Brill, 1970], p. 52).

Other scholars opt for three kinds of material in Mark 13: (1) traditional sayings, (2) apocalyptic material, and (3) redactional comments. The difficulty of classifying the material in this way—evidenced by wide disagreement as to what falls into which category—creates skepticism as to the method. Beasley-Murray has shown that there are no compelling reasons for not accepting the discourse as substantially from Jesus. Whether he spoke its contents on a single occasion is another matter. Mark may have brought into the discourse material he felt was on the same theme (observe that Mark 13:9b–12 is not found in Matt 24 but in Matt 10:17–21 in the missionary discourse to the Twelve). Yet if Mark did this, he used the material within the bounds of its original intent and meaning in the teaching of Jesus. In summary, the discourse represents the teaching of Jesus but arranged and shaped by Mark to meet his theological purpose. This shaping and arranging was within the original intent and meaning of Jesus' words.

Second, why did Jesus speak these words and why were they included in Mark's Gospel? The discourse is patently apocalyptic in nature. This kind of literature was well known in the first century, especially to Jews. Daniel in the OT and the Revelation in the NT are examples of entire books that are apocalyptic in nature. These books, as well as the noncanonical apocalypses, are full of fantastic imagery and are highly symbolical. All of them purport to reveal information about the End. Mark's apocalypse is no exception. It has all the above characteristics, but in addition it has a distinctive exhortative character. The entire chapter is filled with exhortation and admonition. There are nineteen imperatives in vv.5–37. This makes it abundantly clear that the main purpose of the discourse is not to satisfy curiosity about the future but to give practical, ethical teaching. In this discourse Jesus combines eschatology with exhortation, with the emphasis on the latter. He is preparing his disciples—and beyond them the church—to live and to witness in a hostile world.

Mark's purpose is substantially the same. He desires "to present Jesus as Lord of history and as one in control of all events which may bring trouble to the church. Believers should in no way be startled or dispirited by what they see or have to endure. Their Lord has foretold these things. Better still, he will be with them in the Holy Spirit (v.11)" (Martin, *Mark*, p. 136).

Third, the problem of the meaning of the passage is closely tied in with the two major predictions in it: the destruction of the city of Jerusalem in A.D. 70 and the end of the age. The structure of the discourse is as follows: (1) Jesus' prophecy of the destruction of the temple and the questions of the disciples (vv.1–4—these verses form an introduction to the discourse); (2) warnings against deceivers and false signs of the End (vv.5–23); (3) the coming of the Son of Man (vv.24–27); (4) the lesson of the fig tree (vv.28–31); and (5) an exhortation to watchfulness (vv.32–37).

A simple solution to the problem of the relationship of the destruction of Jerusalem to the end of the age is to take vv.5–23 to refer to the destruction of the temple and the city, vv.24–27 to refer to the End, vv.28–31 back again to the same subject as vv.5–23, and vv.28–31 back again to the End (cf. vv.24–27). This arrangement takes the a—b a—b form. But the difficulty with this view is that the exegesis of the passage does not support it. The mention of the worldwide preaching of the gospel (v.10) and the unequaled days of distress (v.19) in vv.5–23 seem to point to something beyond A.D. 70, as does the appearance of "the abomination that causes desolation" (v.14; cf. commentary for details).

On the other hand, attempts to project the whole of vv.5–23 into the remote future with no reference to the destruction of Jerusalem are also unconvincing. The best solution is to see in vv.5–23 a shift back and forth between an immediate and a remote future. Some of the events even seem to have a dual fulfillment, one in the destruction of the city and the other in the end time. This shift from close to remote prediction may be due in part to Mark's arrangement of sayings of Jesus spoken on different occasions.

Problems of christology, i.e., whether Jesus mistakenly predicted the End within his own generation, are discussed in the commentary.

1. *Prophecy of the destruction of the temple*

13:1–2

> [1] As he was leaving the temple, one of his disciples said to him, "Look, Teacher! What massive stones! What magnificent buildings!"
> [2] "Do you see all these great buildings?" replied Jesus. "Not one stone here will be left on another; every one will be thrown down."

1 The last reference in Mark's Gospel to Jesus entering the temple area is in 11:27. In 13:1 he comes out of the temple. This does not necessarily mean that all the events recorded in Mark between 11:27 and 13:1 occurred within the temple area. This chapter may well refer to another occasion altogether.

What prompted Jesus' prophetic words was the exclamation of one of his disciples on looking at the temple in all its grandeur.

The temple area, including the temple building itself, had been rebuilt by Herod the Great. (The second temple, built by Zerubbabel, had fallen into bad disrepair.) The courtyard had been greatly enlarged (to about four hundred by five hundred yards) in order to accommodate the large throngs of Jews who came to Jerusalem for the festivals. To accomplish this a huge platform had to be erected to compensate for the sharp falling off of the land to the southeast. An enormous retaining wall was built to hold the platform in place. The massive stones used in the construction of this wall may still be seen today, since part of the wall escaped the destruction of A.D. 70. At the southeast corner the temple platform towered two hundred feet above the Kidron Valley.

In addition to the temple building itself, on the platform stood porticoes and cloistered courts flanked by beautiful colonnades. The temple area covered approximately one-sixth of the area of the city of Jerusalem. It was an architectural wonder and its size and location dominated the ancient city.

The disciples exclaimed over the beauty of the buildings and the massiveness of the stones. Josephus says the stones were twenty-five cubits long, eight cubits high, and twelve cubits wide (Antiq. XV, 392 [xi.3]).

2 Jesus' reply was startling. Great though the temple buildings were, they would be completely destroyed. This prophecy was fulfilled in A.D. 70, when Jerusalem and the temple were destroyed by the Roman general Titus. Jesus' prophecy is very specific: "Not one stone here will be left on another." Although some of the huge stones Herod's workmen used in the great walls supporting the temple platform were not battered down by Titus's soldiers, all the buildings on the temple platform, including the temple itself to which the prophecy refers, were utterly destroyed. So completely were they destroyed that no trace of them remains today. Even their exact location on the temple mount is disputed.

Notes

1 For a description of Herod's temple, see Josephus, War V, 184–226 (v. 1–6) and Antiq. XV, 380–425 (xi).

2 The word translated "do you see" ($\beta\lambda\acute{\epsilon}\pi\epsilon\iota\varsigma$, *blepeis*) may carry with it a slight rebuke: Are you allowing your attention to be taken up with these great and beautiful buildings when you shouldn't be? Swete (pp. 295–96) comments: "The disciples are warned that the pride which as Jews they naturally felt in this grand spectacle was doomed to complete humiliation."

2. The disciples' twofold question

13:3–4

> ³As Jesus was sitting on the Mount of Olives opposite the temple, Peter, James, John and Andrew asked him privately, ⁴"Tell us, when will these things happen? And what will be the sign that they are all about to be fulfilled?"

3–4 Between v.2 and v.3 the location shifts. Jesus is now on the Mount of Olives (v.3). With him are the four disciples who were the first to be called by him (cf. 1:16–20): Peter, James, John, and Andrew. From the top of the Mount they could clearly see the Kidron Valley running below the eastern wall of the city, and especially the temple mount. Its full grandeur was spread out below them.

The question the four disciples asked Jesus privately not only goes back to his statement made as they were leaving the temple area (cf. v.2) but actually expands it. "These things" (v.4) refers to the destruction of the temple. The disciples wanted to know when that would take place. They also wanted to know what the sign would be "that they are all about to be fulfilled?" Although from Mark's Gospel it would be possible to consider these two questions as essentially one (referring only to the destruction of the temple), Matthew's report of the questions makes this most unlikely: " 'Tell us,' they said, 'when will this happen, and what will be the sign of your coming and of the end of the age?' " (Matt 24:3). Ladd says, "There can be little doubt but that the disciples thought of the destruction of the temple as one of the events accompanying the end of the age and the coming of the eschatological Kingdom of God" (G.E. Ladd, *Theology of the New Testament* [Grand Rapids: Eerdmans, 1974], p. 196).

What the disciples wanted was a sign, some sure way by which they might know that the destruction of the temple was about to occur and that the end of the age was approaching. But Jesus refused to give them eschatological signs. Throughout the discourse he is more concerned to prepare them by exhortation and warning for the trials that lay ahead than to give them dates and signs.

3. Warnings against deceivers and false signs of the End

13:5–8

> ⁵Jesus said to them: "Watch out that no one deceives you. ⁶Many will come in my name, claiming, 'I am he,' and will deceive many. ⁷When you hear of wars and rumors of wars, do not be alarmed. Such things must happen, but the end is still to come. ⁸Nation will rise against nation, and kingdom against kingdom. There will be earthquakes in various places, and famines. These are the beginning of birth pains.

5–6 The first word of the discourse proper is *blepete* ("watch," v.5). This word reoccurs throughout the passage (cf. vv.9, 23, 33)—a clear indication that admonition is obviously one of Jesus' basic concerns. He is warning against false claimants to messiahship. This is apparently what "in my name" and "I am he" (i.e., the Messiah) refer to (v.6). That Jesus said there would be many such false messiahs suggests that his statement should be understood broadly. Speaking of the situation in Palestine before A.D. 70, Beasley-Murray writes: "Whereas the popular messianism hardly ever produced a claimant to the messianic office in the strictest sense, it both fostered and was nourished by men who asserted the possession of messianic authority or who regarded themselves as forerunners of the Kingdom" (*Mark Thirteen*, p. 31). The reference may not be limited to A.D. 70 but also look to the time preceding the End.

7–8 Wars and rumors of war are not to be a cause for alarm (v.7). These are within God's purposes. ("Such things must happen.") When they occur, they must not be mistaken as introducing the End. Jesus clearly says the "end is still to come." What "end" Jesus is talking about here is not clear. If the entire section (vv.5–23) deals only with the destruction of Jerusalem, then "the end" refers to the end of God's judgment on the Holy City. It is, however, more likely that it refers both to that event and the end of the age.

There will be other kinds of disturbances, too. In addition to international power struggles ("nation will rise against nation, and kingdom against kingdom"), there will be earthquakes and famine (v.8). These are indications of God's intervention in the historical process. Again, they are not to be taken as marking the End. They are rather the beginnings of "birth pains." The "birth pains" (*ōdin*) refer to the sufferings expected to occur in the period before the coming of the Messiah, and the word "beginning" suggests that there will be many more sufferings.

Ladd says that the last statement of v.8 is perhaps the most important of the discourse. He points out that

> the Old Testament speaks of the birth of a nation through a period of woes (Isa 66:8; Jer 22:23; Hos 13:13; Micah 4:9f.) and from these verses there arose in Judaism the idea that the messianic Kingdom must emerge from a period of suffering that was called the messianic woes or "the birth pangs of the Messiah." This does not mean the woes that the Messiah must suffer, but the woes out of which the messianic age is to be born. (*New Testament Theology*, pp. 201–2)

Notes

---

8 For the rabbinic expression "birth pangs of the Messiah," see SBK, 1:950. It probably was already in use in Jesus' day.

---

4. *Warnings of persecution and strife and a call to steadfastness*

13:9–13

9"You must be on your guard. You will be handed over to the local councils and flogged in the synagogues. On account of me you will stand before governors and kings as witnesses to them. 10And the gospel must first be preached to all nations. 11Whenever you are arrested and brought to trial, do not worry beforehand

about what to say. Just say whatever is given you at the time, for it is not you speaking, but the Holy Spirit.
12"Brother will betray brother to death, and a father his child. Children will rebel against their parents and have them put to death. 13All men will hate you because of me, but he who stands firms to the end will be saved.

9 Again Jesus warns his disciples to be on their guard, because persecutions of various kinds await them. The "local councils" to which they will be handed over are the religious courts. They were made up of the elders of the synagogues assembled for the purpose of exercising their disciplinary powers. From these courts, Jesus warns, they will be taken into the synagogues and publicly flogged. They will also be brought before secular authorities ("governors and kings"), most of whom were Gentiles. But persecution, whether by Jews or Gentiles, would be an opportunity for witness. This verse clearly anticipates fulfillment in the near future.

10 The Greek impersonal verb *dei* ("must") underscores the will of God. It has been decreed by him that the gospel be preached to all the nations (or Gentiles). This is Jesus' mandate to his disciples and through them to his church. "First" (*prōton*) may mean before the destruction of the city of Jerusalem. Those who hold this view see the promise fulfilled in the proclamation of the gospel throughout the Roman world by A.D. 60. It seems best, however, to understand "first" in terms of the End. Certainly Matthew understood it that way. He immediately follows the statement of the universal preaching of the gospel with "and then the end will come" (Matt 24:14). Jesus seems to be saying here, "Instead of looking for signs of the end, get busy and spread the 'good news'! All nations must hear before the End comes."

11 The disciples will be hauled into court and crossexamined by the authorities. Jesus promises them, in that situation, strength and resources beyond their own through the Holy Spirit. The Spirit will reveal to them on the spot the appropriate words to speak (cf. Jer 1:9; Acts 6:10; 7:55). To use this verse to justify lack of careful preparation for preaching is irresponsible exegesis.

12–13 The breaking of ties of natural affection will be another trial the disciples will have to face. In Luke 12:51–53 (cf. Mic 7:2–6) Jesus warns of families being split because of the gospel:

> Do you think I came to bring peace on earth? No, I tell you, but division. From now on there will be five in one family divided against each other, three against two and two against three. They will be divided, father against son and son against father, mother against daughter and daughter against mother, mother-in-law against daughter-in-law and daughter-in-law against mother-in-law.

Only a fanatical hatred of the gospel could bring about unnatural behavior such as these verses describe. Morison (p. 359) remarks: "As there is nothing that excites such love as the gospel, when intelligently received, so there is nothing that occasions such hate as this same gospel, when passionately rejected." Moreover the hatred will not be limited to relatives (v. 12), but "all men will hate you" (v. 13). Temple comments, "Not all that the world hates is good Christianity; but it does hate good Christianity and always will" (*Readings in John*, pp. 271–72).

Testing will be another feature of the last times. Not all will stand the test, but he who endures to the "end" (telos here is a reference to the end of a person's life, not, as in v.7, the end of the age) will be saved. Jesus is not here setting forth a doctrine of salvation by works. He is rather emphasizing that genuine faith will issue in Christian living that will endure trial and persecution. A good commentary on v.13b is 2 Timothy 2:12: "If we endure, we will also reign with him." This section (vv.9–13), with its warning and encouragements, must have had special relevance for the life situation of the Roman church.

The structure of vv.9–13 is especially interesting. The section includes three separate sayings of Jesus held together by the key word (paradidomi, translated in NIV as "handed over" (v.9), "arrested" (v.11), and "betray" (v.12). The first speaks of being handed over to religious courts and appearing before civil authorities; the second promises the presence of the Holy Spirit when they are arrested and brought to trial; and the last deals with the family hostility and hatred that loyalty to Jesus Christ will bring about. Verse 10, which is concerned with the worldwide preaching of the gospel, is sandwiched between the first and second sayings; and for this reason some scholars consider it a gloss. Verses 9–13 are not, with the exception of v.10, found in the parallel account in Matthew 24. They occur, with the exception of v.10, in Matthew 10:17–22 in the context of the mission charge to the Twelve. Luke has them in his parallel account (21:12–17), with the exception of v.10, and in another context (12:11–12) gives a variant of v.11 as a separate logion of Jesus. All this shows that the material in Mark 13:9, 11–13 was given by Jesus on more than one occasion or that Mark has collected sayings from other contexts and put them here because of their relevance.

Notes

9 Josephus in Antiq. IV, 214–18 (viii. 14) describes the συνέδρια (synedria, "local courts"). The phrase εἰς μαρτύριον αὐτοῖς (eis martyrion autois) may be translated "for evidence against them," i.e., the authorities. If this is the meaning, the assumption is that the witness of the disciples will be rejected by the authorities and on the day of judgment will be used against them (cf. TDNT, 4:502–3). In view of Luke 21:13, it seems best to follow the NIV rendering "as witnesses to them."

10 This verse interrupts the flow of thought of the passage. Because of this and other reasons, its authenticity has been questioned. A better solution is to regard it as an independent logion inserted here by Mark to stress the missionary enterprise of the church in spite of opposition and trial.

5. The abomination that causes desolation and the necessity of flight

13:14–23

14"When you see 'the abomination that causes desolation' standing where it does not belong—let the reader understand—then let those who are in Judea flee to the mountains. 15Let no one on the roof of his house go down or enter the house to take anything out. 16Let no one in the field go back to get his cloak.

> [17]How dreadful it will be in those days for pregnant women and nursing mothers! [18]Pray that this will not take place in winter, [19]because those will be days of distress unequaled from the beginning, when God created the world, until now—and never to be equaled again. [20]If the Lord had not cut short those days, no one would survive. But for the sake of the elect, whom he has chosen, he has shortened them. [21]At that time if anyone says to you, 'Look, here is the Christ!' or, 'Look, there he is!' do not believe it. [22]For false Christs and false prophets will appear and perform signs and miracles to deceive the elect—if that were possible. [23]So be on your guard; I have told you everything ahead of time.

14a This is one of the most difficult verses in Mark's Gospel if not in the entire NT. The key phrase is "abomination that causes desolation," an expression derived from the Book of Daniel (cf. Dan 9:27; 11:31; 12:11). In Matthew's Gospel (24:15) Jesus explicitly identifies it with that book. The first word of the phrase, *bdelygma* ("abomination"), suggests something repugnant to God, while the second, *erēmōsis* ("desolation"), suggests that because of the abomination the temple is left deserted, desolate. The holy and pious worshipers vacate it.

The fulfillment of Daniel's prophecy of the "abomination that causes desolation" is usually found in the profanation of the altar of burnt offering in the temple of Jerusalem by a representative of Antiochus IV, Epiphanes, in 167 B.C. (cf. 1 Macc 1:54–59; 6:7). The fact that Jesus uses the same expression here makes it clear that its fulfillment was not restricted to the events of the time of the Maccabees. What it does refer to has been hotly debated. Those who hold the view that all the events described in vv.5–23 have to do with the Fall of Jerusalem most often identify the "abomination" with either the Roman army (cf. Luke 21:20), and in particular the military standards that the Jews considered idolatrous and an abomination, or with the Zealots, or more specifically Phannias, whom they farcically made high priest (cf. Jos. War IV, 147–57 [iii.6–8]).

Others see this prophecy as being fulfilled in the end time by the Antichrist. Their evidence for this view is as follows:

1. The use of the masculine participal *hestēkota* ("standing") suggests a person (cf. NEB: "When you see the 'abomination of desolation' usurping a place that is not his").

2. Paul's statements in 2 Thessalonians 2:3–10 about the eschatological Antichrist seem to be derived from a similar tradition.

3. The person referred to must be associated with the End, because in Matthew's Gospel his appearance is immediately followed by the coming of the Son of Man (cf. 24:29–30).

A better solution, however, is to understand the abomination that causes desolation as having a multiple fulfillment in (1) the Maccabean period, (2) the events of A.D. 66–70, and (3) the end time.

The exhortation "let the reader understand" is probably Mark's editorial comment.

14b–18 It is difficult to consign the admonitions of these verses to the end time. No one will be able to flee from the judgment of God in that day. The warnings, however, make good sense in the context of the approach of the Roman army before the Fall of Jerusalem in A.D. 70. Two admonitions stress the urgency of the situation: (1) anyone on the roof of the house is not, on descending the outside staircase, to go inside to get any of his belongings (v.15); and (2) anyone in the field is not to return to the house even to get an outer garment (v.16).

The outer garment ("cloak") was used at night to keep one warm; in the daytime it was taken off to allow more freedom of movement in working. Though his cloak would be especially useful in case of the necessity of fleeing to the mountains (v.14b) where the night air is cold, the situation would be too urgent to allow one even to fetch it. A hurried flight to the mountains would be very hard for pregnant women and nursing mothers (v.17). And if the flight took place in winter (v.18), it would be all the more difficult, since both the cold and the rain-swollen wadis would present formidable hazards. These warnings and woes seem especially appropriate to what actually occurred at the time of the destruction of Jerusalem. The Christians in the city fled to the mountains—to Pella in Perea (Eusebius *Ecclesiastical History* 3.5.3).

19–20 The primary temporal reference now shifts back to the End. The language of v.19, though fulfilled partially in the great stress that occurred at the Fall of Jerusalem in A.D. 70, looks forward to the Great Tribulation that will precede the End. Mark uses language derived from Daniel's portrayal of the last days (Dan 12:1; cf. Jer 30:7). Nowhere else in Scripture is there a reference to the shortening of the time of tribulation (v.20), though the pseudepigraphical 3 Baruch contains the thought (ch. 9). In the context of A.D. 70, "the elect, for whose sake the siege was shortened, are probably the faithful members of the Church of Jerusalem . . . whose intercession or whose presence secured this privilege, though it did not avail to save the city" (Swete, p. 309). In the context of the End, the elect are the people of God generally.

21–23 The section (vv.5–23) ends as it began, with a warning against false Christs (v.21). A crisis like that of the fall of the city would be sure to produce many false pretenders. So would the crisis of the approaching End. They will wield supernatural power great enough to perform "signs and miracles" (v.22). Yet they will not be able to deceive God's people. This is the force of the phrase "if that were possible." But it is not possible; God will guard his elect. Beasley-Murray comments: "As in all the Scriptures, the assurance of God's care for his elect (implied in εἰ δύνατον [*ei dynaton*, 'if it were possible'], v.22), is not regarded as ground for presumption. 'Do on your part take care. If the temptations of false prophets are strong enough to endanger the chosen of God, you will not be exempt. I have told you all these things in order that you may be fully prepared. Remain on the alert' " (*Mark Thirteen*, p. 86). Again the hortatory purpose of the discourse is evident.

6. *The coming of the Son of Man*

13:24–27

24"But in those days, following that distress,

" 'the sun will be darkened,
and the moon will not give its light;
25the stars will fall from the sky,
and the heavenly bodies will be shaken.'

26"At that time men will see the Son of Man coming in clouds with great power and glory. 27And he will send his angels and gather his elect from the four winds, from the ends of the earth to the ends of the heavens.

24–25 Verses 24–27 form a unit and relate to the End. They are set off from the previous verses by the strong adversative *alla* ("but"). Whereas the preceding verses (5–23) point to both the destruction of Jerusalem and the end time, vv. 24–27 speak only of the end time. "In those days" (v. 24) is a common OT expression having eschatological associations (cf. Jer 3:16, 18; 31:29; 33:15–16; Joel 3:1; Zech 8:23). In Mark, Jesus speaks of a period "following that distress" (the NIV translators backed off from the word "tribulation" both here and in the Matthew parallel, but see RSV). In Matthew, however, the statement is more specific—"Immediately after the distress of those days" (24:29)—making it impossible to limit the "distress" of vv. 19–20 to the period preceding the destruction of the city of Jerusalem in A.D. 70, because the end time immediately follows.

The coming of the Son of Man will be associated with celestial phenomena. The imagery and language are derived from the OT descriptions of the Day of the Lord. The quotation is an echo of Isaiah 13:10, but other OT passages reveal similar language (cf. Isa 24:23; 34:4; Ezek 32:7–8; Joel 2:10, 30–31; 3:15; Amos 8:9). It is difficult to know whether the poetic language here is to be understood literally or figuratively. The repeated assertion in Scripture that the end times will be accompanied by cosmic disturbances seems to imply that there will be unprecedented celestial disturbances of some sort that are literal (cf. 2 Peter 3:10). This is not to deny that Mark may be using phenomenal language, but his language is nonetheless referring to objective events in the physical universe. These will occur when God brings history to an end by the coming of his Son. "This language does not mean necessarily the complete break-up of the universe; we know from similar language elsewhere that it designates the judgment of God upon a fallen world that has shared the fate of man's sin, that out of the ruins of judgment a new world may be born" (Ladd, *New Testament Theology*, p. 203).

26–27 The celestial drama reaches a climax when the Son of Man comes in the clouds with "great power and glory" (v. 26). Jesus describes his coming in these verses almost entirely in the words of Scripture. The reference here is to Daniel 7:13, the first time our Lord definitely connects the title "Son of Man" with the Daniel prophecy (cf. Mark 14:62). (For a discussion of the title "Son of Man," see commentary at 8:31.)

The great emphasis of these verses is on disclosure and triumph. Whereas the Son of Man has been hidden or at least veiled in his first coming, now he will be revealed. Men "will see" him and see him for who he really is. Whereas he has been the lowly Suffering Servant, despised and rejected by men, the Son of Man at his parousia will come in triumph—"with great power and glory." And his chief concern at his coming will be to bring together his people (v. 27) so that they may be with him. Therefore he sends forth his angels to gather the elect from all over the world. Calvin's comments (3:148) on v. 27 show its continuing relevance: "For, though the Church be now tormented by the malice of men, or even broken by the violence of the billows, and miserably torn in pieces, so as to have no stability in the world, yet we ought always to cherish confident hope, because it will not be by human means, but by heavenly power, which will be far superior to every obstacle, that the Lord will *gather* his Church" (emphasis his).

7. The lesson of the fig tree

13:28–31

28"Now learn this lesson from the fig tree: As soon as its twigs get tender and its leaves come out, you know that summer is near. 29Even so, when you see these things happening, you know that it is near, right at the door. 30I tell you the truth, this generation will certainly not pass away until all these things have happened. 31Heaven and earth will pass away, but my words will never pass away.

28 In Palestine most trees are evergreen, but the fig tree is an exception. In the fall it loses its leaves; and when in the spring the sap rises in its branches and the tree begins to leaf out, summer cannot be far off. The parable is essentially an antidote to despair. In contrast to the sufferings and persecutions promised in the previous verses, here the prospect of the coming of the Son of Man is offered.

29 The chief problem in this verse is the identification of "these things" (*tauta*). Do they refer to the events surrounding the fall of the city of Jerusalem or the events immediately preceding the end of the age? Ladd identifies them with the signs of the end outlined in vv.5–23. Also "*tauta* in verse 29 appears to be the antecedent of the *tauta panta* that are to take place in this generation [v.30]. What Jesus appears to be saying is that the signs that presage the end are not to be confined to a remote future; his hearers would themselves experience them" (Ladd, *New Testament Theology*, p. 209). Those signs were experienced in a special way at the fall of the city of Jerusalem.

The next phrase, *engys estin*, may be translated either "it is near" (NIV) or "he is near." Those who interpret this paragraph (vv.28–31) in its entirety to relate to the events surrounding the Fall of Jerusalem usually identify the "it" with the "abomination that causes desolation" (cf. v.14) or the fall of the city itself. If, on the other hand, vv.28–31 are descriptive of the End, then "he is near" would be a more fitting translation, though "it," referring to the Parousia, would also be suitable. Luke (21:31) has for "it" (or "he") the "kingdom of God."

30 Since Jesus' words are preceded by the solemn "I tell you the truth," they are not to be taken lightly. To suggest that Jesus was mistaken in the statement he made in this verse but that the mistake was in a matter of such small consequence that it makes no difference is to fail to take seriously the solemnity of the introductory words.

The interpretation hinges on the meaning of the expressions "this generation" (*he genea hautē*) and "all these things" (*tauta panta*). A multiplicity of interpretations have been given to "this generation"—mankind in general, the Jewish people, Christians, unbelievers. It seems best, however, to understand it to mean Jesus' own generation. Then *tauta panta* refers to the signs preceding the End found in vv.5–23. These are not confined to a remote future but "are to be experienced, though not necessarily exhausted, by the contemporary generation" (Moore, *The Parousia in the New Testament*, p. 133).

31 Jesus strongly emphasizes the certainty and reliability of his predictions in v.30. "Heaven and earth" is a reference to the whole of the universe, all creation. The certitude and absolute reliability of Jesus' words is far greater than the apparent continuance of the universe. It will some day cease to exist, but Jesus' words will always have validity (cf. Ps 102:25–27; Isa 40:6–8; 51:6).

Notes

30 The Greek word for "generation" is γενεά (*genea*). It "primarily denotes those descended from a single ancestor, a tribe, a race; then it comes to signify those born within the same period, a generation of contemporary men; finally a period of time occupied by a particular generation" (Beasley-Murray, *Mark Thirteen*, p. 99; cf. A-S, p. 89). Ellis, however, remarks that "in the Qumran writings the term, 'last generation' (1 Qp Hab 2.7; 7:2), apparently included several lifetimes. Their usage indicates that in the New Testament 'this (last) generation', like 'last hour' (I Jn 2.18) or 'today', means only the last phase in the history of redemption" (*Gospel of Luke*, p. 246). According to this interpretation "this generation" is the final period before the End, however long it may be.

An important problem raised by v.30, as interpreted in this commentary, is the NT insistence on the nearness of the End (cf. Rom 13:12; 1 Cor 7:29; Phil 4:5; Heb 10:25; James 5:8–9; 1 Peter 4:7; 1 John 2:18; Rev 22:20). Cranfield asks:

> Are we to say (with Dodd, Glasson, Taylor, *et al.*) that the primitive Church read into Jesus' ideas apocalyptic teachings that were alien to it? Or (with Schweitzer, Werner, T.W. Manson, Barrett, *et al.*) that Jesus was himself mistaken? Or is the solution to be found in a more theological understanding of what is meant by the nearness of the End? . . . If we realize that the Incarnation—Crucifixion—Resurrection—Ascension, on the one hand, and the Parousia, on the other, belong essentially together, and are in a real sense one Event, one divine Act, being held apart only by the Mercy of God who desires to give men opportunity for faith and repentance, then we can see that in a very real sense the latter is always imminent now that the former has happened. It was, and still is, true to say that the Parousia is at hand—and indeed this, so far from being an embarrassing mistake on the part either of Jesus or of the early Church, is an essential part of the Church's faith. Ever since the Incarnation men have been living in the last days. (*Gospel of Mark*, p. 408)

This type of thinking is difficult for contemporary man, but it seems consistent with the biblical material.

8. *The necessity of watchfulness*

13:32–37

³²"No one knows about that day or hour, not even the angels in heaven, nor the Son, but only the Father. ³³Be on guard! Be alert! You do not know when that time will come. ³⁴It's like a man going away: He leaves his house and puts his servants in charge, each with his assigned task, and tells the one at the door to keep watch.

³⁵"Therefore keep watch because you do not know when the owner of the house will come back—whether in the evening, or at midnight, or when the rooster crows, or at dawn. ³⁶If he comes suddenly, do not let him find you sleeping. ³⁷What I say to you, I say to everyone: 'Watch!' "

Jesus' call for vigilance pervades this paragraph—"Be on guard! Be alert!" (v.33); "Therefore keep watch" (v.35); "do not let him find you sleeping" (v.36); and "Watch!" (v.37).

32 Few would challenge the authenticity of this verse. The early church is unlikely to have created a logion that has resulted in such consternation and embarrassment as this one has. "That day" clearly refers to the Parousia. It is the great day, the eschatological day that will bring to an end "those days" (vv.17, 19, 24). Of "those days," i.e., the days that precede the time of the End, certain signs have been given; but of "that day" neither the angels of heaven nor Jesus himself knows the time. Only the Father knows that time. And Jesus, at his ascension, clearly says that it was not for the disciples "to know the times or dates the Father has set by his own authority" (Acts 1:7). A map of the future would be a hindrance, not a help, to faith. Their responsibility and ours is to get busy and do his work without being concerned about date setting. As Moule says:

> New Testament thought on the Last Things, at its deepest and best, always concentrates on what God has already done for men in Christ. It does not say, How long will it be before the last whistle blows full-time? Rather it says, Where ought I to be to receive the next pass? What really matters is that the kick-off has already taken place, the game is on and we have a captain to lead us on to victory. (C.F.D. Moule, *The Birth of the New Testament* [London: SCM, 1966], pp. 101–2)

Jesus' ignorance of the day or hour of his parousia must be understood in terms of the NT teaching concerning the Incarnation. A real Incarnation involved such lack of knowledge. Jesus purposely laid aside temporarily the exercise of his omniscience as part of what was involved in his becoming man.

33–36 Vigilance is the order of the day because the time of the Parousia is not known. *Blepete* ("be on guard") is the keynote of the entire discourse (v.33), and *gar* ("for"—not translated in NIV) states the reason watchfulness is necessary. "If the Master Himself does not know, the disciples must not only acquiesce in their ignorance, but regard it as a wholesome stimulus to exertion" (Swete, p. 317). The word for time here is *kairos*, meaning God's appointed time.

The parable has in it some of the features of that of the talents (Matt 25:14–30) and the pounds (Luke 19:12–27). There is a privilege (*exousia*, "charge") and a responsibility (*ergon*, "assigned task," v.34). The parable does not develop these elements but turns attention to the doorkeeper who has a special task. Then Jesus applies it to the disciples. Like a doorkeeper who must watch because he does not know when the owner will return, they too must be on guard (v.35). Evening, midnight, rooster crowing, and dawn are the names of the four watches of the night the Romans used. The Greek adverb *exaiphnēs* (NIV, "suddenly") emphasizes the suddenness of the Parousia (v.36). "The element of surprise is ineradicable from the parousia expectation. Signs, like the fig tree, are an indication of promise, not a clock" (Beasley-Murray, *Mark Thirteen*, p. 117).

37 The discourse that was addressed to four of the disciples (v.3) began with the imperative "Watch." This exhortation recurs during the discourse. Now at the end it is repeated once more, but this time it is no longer addressed only to the four disciples but to "everyone." In this way Jesus shows his concern not only for the disciples but for the whole community—all his followers for whom he was about to die—and his message is "Watch!" Beasley-Murray writes: "This word the first community took seriously. When their hour came they were ready. In crises since that day it has shone as a lamp in the gloom" (*Mark Thirteen*, p. 118).

VII. The Passion and Resurrection Narrative (14:1–16:8 [9–20])

The conflict of Jesus with the religious leaders, which in Mark's Gospel begins as early as 3:1, reaches its climax in the passion narrative and is followed by the triumph of the Resurrection on Easter morning. Since these events constitute the heart of the Christian gospel (cf. 1 Cor 15:1–4), they were the first part of the story of Jesus to be written down and circulated as a continuous whole. Mark had access to this narrative and seems to have incorporated it into his Gospel with little editorial revision. "He chose only to supplement it with parallel or complementary tradition and to orchestrate it for the development of certain themes" (Lane, p. 485).

The importance of the passion and resurrection of our Lord for the early church is evidenced by the relatively large amount of space the narrative takes in each of the Gospels and especially in Mark. Out of Mark's 661 verses, 128 are devoted to the passion and resurrection story, and a total of 242 are devoted to the last week (from the triumphal entry to the resurrection) of our Lord's life. The church obviously had more than a historical interest in Jesus' death and resurrection. These events formed the basis of the church's witness and worship—the lifeblood of early Christianity. The witnessing church proclaimed a crucified and living Savior, and the worshiping church reflected on the meaning of these events for its inner life.

This section in Mark's Gospel plays on two basic themes: suffering and triumph. The suffering of Jesus is highlighted by (1) his betrayal and denial (by Judas, Peter, and all the disciples); (2) his trial before the Sanhedrin and Pilate with its injustice and mockery; and (3) his crucifixion with its brutality and shame. The triumph of Jesus comes through his glorious resurrection on the third day after his crucifixion. This is the note on which Mark's Gospel, "the good news about Jesus Christ, the Son of God," comes to a close.

A. *The Plot to Arrest Jesus*

14:1–2

> [1]Now the Passover and the Feast of Unleavened Bread were only two days away, and the chief priests and the teachers of the law were looking for some sly way to arrest Jesus and kill him. [2]"But not during the Feast," they said, "or the people may riot."

1–2 These verses serve to introduce the passion and resurrection narrative. Passover (Heb. *pesaḥ*) is the Jewish festival commemorating the occasion when the angel of the Lord passed over (*pāsaḥ*) the homes of the Hebrews on the night he killed all the firstborn sons of the Egyptians (cf. Exod 12:13, 23, 27). The lambs used in the feast were slain on the fourteenth of Nisan (March/April), and the meal was eaten that evening between sundown and midnight. According to Jewish reckoning, that would be the fifteenth of Nisan, since the Jewish day began at sundown. The Feast of Unleavened Bread followed Passover and lasted seven days (15–21 Nisan; cf. Exod 12:15–20; 23:15; 34:18; Deut 16:1–8). Since the Last Supper was probably a

Passover meal and took place on Thursday night, the incident reported here must have taken place on Wednesday of Passion Week. This is calculated from the temporal· phrase *meta duo hēmeras*. If "after three days" means "on the third day" (cf. 8:31; 9:31; 10:34), then "after two days" would mean "on the second day," i.e., "tomorrow." NIV's "only two days away" (v.1) is ambiguous and must be understood in accordance with Jewish usage of the temporal phrase.

For a long time the religious authorities had been looking for a way to get rid of Jesus (cf. 3:6; 11:18; 12:12). Now they renewed and intensified their efforts. But it was necessary for them to proceed with the utmost caution. Since Passover (like Tabernacles and Pentecost) was one of the pilgrim feasts, great throngs of people invaded the Holy City to celebrate it. It is said that the population doubled (from twenty-five thousand to fifty thousand) during the week. The chief priests and teachers of the law (the two main bodies that made up the Sanhedrin, the Jewish high court) realized that it would be too risky to move in on Jesus with such a highly excitable crowd present. The possibility of a riot was too great (v.2). It would be wiser to wait for a more propitious moment—perhaps after the pilgrims had left the city to go home. God's purposes were otherwise, and this part of their plan miscarried. Perhaps the unexpected help from one of Jesus' disciples (14:10–11) changed their minds, and they decided to go through with their wicked scheme despite the presence of the Passover pilgrims.

B. *The Anointing at Bethany*

14:3–9

> [3]While he was in Bethany, reclining at the table in the home of a man known as Simon the Leper, a woman came with an alabaster jar of very expensive perfume, made of pure nard. She broke the jar and poured the perfume on his head.
> [4]Some of those present were saying indignantly to one another, "Why this waste of perfume? [5]It could have been sold for more than a year's wages and the money given to the poor." And they rebuked her harshly.
> [6]"Leave her alone," said Jesus. "Why are you bothering her? She has done a beautiful thing to me. [7]The poor you will always have with you, and you can help them any time you want. But you will not always have me. [8]She did what she could. She poured perfume on my body beforehand to prepare for my burial. [9]I tell you the truth, wherever the gospel is preached throughout the world, what she has done will also be told, in memory of her."

3 The placing of this incident in the narrative is different in John's Gospel. There it occurs before the Passion Week begins (cf. John 12:1: "six days before the Passover"). Theological emphasis is more important than chronology to Mark—at least here. His placing contrasts the hatred of the religious leaders (immediately preceding [vv.1–2]) and the betrayal of Judas (immediately following [vv.10–11]) with the love and devotion of Mary demonstrated by her anointing of Jesus with expensive perfume. Although Luke 7:36–50 is similar to John 12:1–8 and Mark 14:3–9, the differences are significant and thus it no doubt records a different incident (see Notes).

The incident takes place in the home of Simon the Leper at Bethany. The occasion for the dinner is not specified. Simon was probably a leper who had been healed. The retention of the name "the Leper" would suggest this—indeed he may have been healed by Jesus. Was the dinner an expression of gratitude for this? Mark does not identify the woman who anointed Jesus, but we know from John's Gospel (12:3) that she was Mary, the sister of Martha and Lazarus. The "alabaster jar" that contained the perfume was a "vessel w. a rather long neck which was broken off when the contents were used" (BAG, p. 33). The "nard" (perfume) was made from the root of a plant found chiefly in India and was very expensive. Mary took the bottle and broke the neck so that she could pour the ointment profusely over Jesus' head.

4–5 Mark does not name those who reacted so indignantly at the "waste" of the costly perfume (v.4). Matthew, however, says it was the disciples (26:8), while John says it was Judas Iscariot (12:4–5). Judas probably expressed the most vigorous dissent because he was the treasurer of the Twelve. The chief concern of the objectors was mercenary (v.5). The perfume had a value of more than three hundred denarii (a denarius was what a man received for a day's work—thus NIV's "more than a year's wage"). The mention of the poor is natural because it was the custom for the Jews to give gifts to the poor on the evening of the Passover. The insensitivity of Jesus' disciples to this beautiful expression of love and devotion is amazing. Mark uses the word *embrimaomai* ("to be angry," "to express violent displeasure") to describe the feeling of the disciples toward Mary. This is all the more surprising since they had often enjoyed the generous hospitality of Mary, her sister, Martha, and her brother, Lazarus, while in Bethany.

6–8 Jesus rushed to Mary's defense (v.6). Instead of condemning her, they should have commended her. Her action of anointing Jesus with a bottle of expensive perfume was a beautiful expression of her love and devotion to him, and she should not be berated. In addition he would not be with them very long (v.7). Before Jesus lay Gethsemane, the trial, Golgotha, the Resurrection, and the return to glory. Time for such expression of devotion and love while he was still here was running out. In contrast, opportunities for helping the poor would continue. There is no evidence in Jesus' statement of a lack of concern for the poor. On the contrary, there is ample evidence elsewhere that their interests and needs lay close to his heart (cf. Matt 5:3; 6:2–4; 19:21; Luke 6:20, 36–38; 21:1–4; John 13:29).

In addition to being an expression of devotion, Mary's act was interpreted by Jesus as an anointing of his body beforehand in preparation for his burial (v.8). Was Mary aware of this aspect of what she was doing? Perhaps not, but it is possible that she had a greater sensitivity to what was about to happen to Jesus than the Twelve did. In Luke's Gospel she is depicted as a good listener (10:39); and perhaps by this means she wanted to do for Jesus what she knew would ordinarily not be done for one who would die the death of a criminal. Jesus' statement serves as yet another prediction of his passion.

9 This pronouncement is preceded by the solemn "I tell you the truth." In an indirect way Jesus is here predicting his resurrection, because the preaching of the gospel presupposes the Resurrection. The central message of the Good News is Jesus' defeat of sin, death, and hell by his resurrection. And anywhere in the world that Good News is preached, Mary's act of love and devotion will be remembered. Thus Jesus—in marked contrast to the disciples—assesses the significance of her act.

Notes

3 The incident in vv.3–9 should not be confused with that in Luke 7:36–50. The details, except the name Simon, are very different. "The Leper" may be added to Simon's name to differentiate him from the Simon in Luke 7:36–50, since Simon was a very common name. Plummer (p. 312) rightly comments: "The difficulty of believing in two anointings is infinitesimal. . . . Whereas the difficulty of believing that Mary of Bethany had ever been 'a sinner' is enormous. There is no evidence of a previous evil life, and what we know of her renders a previous evil life almost incredible."

C. The Betrayal by Judas

14:10–11

> ¹⁰Then Judas Iscariot, one of the Twelve, went to the chief priests to betray Jesus to them. ¹¹They were delighted to hear this and promised to give him money. So he watched for an opportunity to hand him over.

10–11 These verses are connected with vv.1–2. The chief priests and teachers of the law were looking for "some sly way to arrest Jesus" (v.1), and Judas "watched for an opportunity to hand him over" (v.11). Judas is identified specifically as "one of the Twelve" (v.10). He had all the advantages of being in the inner circle yet betrayed Jesus. Spiritual privilege in itself is not enough. There must be the response of faith and love.

Judas's offer to betray Jesus was readily accepted by the chief priests and teachers of the law because, being on the inside, he could choose the most opportune time to hand Jesus over to them. In that way they could avoid what they feared most, a riot of the people. It was undoubtedly the offer of Judas—he, not the religious leaders, took the initiative—that changed their minds about not arresting Jesus during the feast. It was a golden opportunity, and they were not about to lose it! Money was involved in the deal, though from Matthew's Gospel (26:15) we learn that Judas received for his treacherous act the pitiful sum of thirty silver coins.

What motivated Judas? Many guesses have been made—jealousy, greed, disappointment with Jesus' mission, to name a few. None of the Evangelists answer the question. There can be little doubt, however, that Judas was the betrayer. It is not likely that the church would have invented this story.

D. The Lord's Supper (14:12–26)

1. Preparation of the meal

14:12–16

> ¹²On the first day of the Feast of Unleavened Bread, when it was customary to sacrifice the Passover lamb, Jesus' disciples asked him, "Where do you want us to go and make preparations for you to eat the Passover?"
> ¹³So he sent two of his disciples, telling them, "Go into the city, and a man carrying a jar of water will meet you. Follow him. ¹⁴Say to the owner of the house he enters, 'The Teacher asks: Where is my guest room, where I may eat the Passover with my disciples?' ¹⁵He will show you a large upper room, furnished and ready. Make preparations for us there."

¹⁶The disciples left, went into the city and found things just as Jesus had told them. So they prepared the Passover.

12 Ordinarily "the first day of the Feast of Unleavened Bread" would mean 15 Nisan, the day following Passover. But the added description of the day—"when it was customary to sacrifice the Passover lamb"—makes it clear that 14 Nisan is meant, because Passover lambs were killed on 14 Nisan. The entire eight-day celebration, including Passover, was sometimes referred to as the Feast of Unleavened Bread (cf. Jos. Antiq. II, 315–17 [xv.1]); and there is some evidence that 14 Nisan was loosely referred to as the "first day of Unleavened Bread" (cf. SBK, 2:813–15).

The day of the week was Thursday. Jesus and his disciples were probably in Bethany. It is clear from v.13 that they were outside the city of Jerusalem. Since the Passover had to be eaten within the walls of the city (cf. M. *Pesachim* 7.9), the disciples asked Jesus where in Jerusalem they were to go to make preparation. There was no time to lose because the Passover meal had to be eaten between sundown and midnight, the first hours of 15 Nisan.

13–16 Jesus gave explicit instructions to two of his disciples (v.13). We know from Luke that the two were Peter and John (Luke 22:8). The "man carrying a jar of water" would easily be identified because customarily women, not men, carried water jars. He was to lead them to the house where the owner had a guest room (v.14). Jewish custom required that if a person had a room available, he must give it to any pilgrim who asked to stay in it, in order that he might have a place to celebrate the Passover (cf. SBK, 1:989). Mark seems to indicate that Jesus had made previous arrangements with the owner of the house. The upstairs room is described as "furnished and ready" (v.15), i.e., with what was necessary for the celebration: table, couches, cushions, etc. The disciples would have to get the food and prepare it. This would include the unleavened bread, wine, bitter herbs, sauce (*hărôset*), and the lamb. The two disciples went into the city as instructed by Jesus, found everything as he had said, and made the necessary preparations (v.16).

Notes

12 Πάσχα (*pascha*) here means "the Passover lamb" as translated in NIV. In 14:1 it means the feast day and in 14:12b, 14, and 16 it means the Passover meal.

2. Announcement of the betrayal

14:17–21

¹⁷When evening came, Jesus arrived with the Twelve. ¹⁸While they were reclining at the table eating, he said, "I tell you the truth, one of you will betray me—one who is eating with me."

¹⁹They were saddened, and one by one they said to him, "Surely not I?"

²⁰"It is one of the Twelve," he replied, "one who dips bread into the bowl with me. ²¹The Son of Man will go just as it is written about him. But woe to that man who betrays the Son of Man! It would be better for him if he had not been born."

17 Jesus and his disciples had probably spent the day in Bethany. In the evening they returned to the city. Mark says Jesus "arrived with the Twelve." This suggests that Peter and John, after making preparations, returned to Bethany, a distance of only a couple of miles, and then accompanied Jesus when he went into the city in the evening. The other possibility is that "the Twelve" was a designation of the close followers of Jesus whether all twelve were present or not. Jesus and his disciples went to the room prepared by Peter and John to celebrate the Passover. Since the Jewish day began at sundown, it was now Thursday night, 15 Nisan.

18 The Passover meal was originally eaten standing: "This is how you are to eat it: with your cloak tucked into your belt, your sandals on your feet and your staff in your hand. Eat it in haste; it is the Lord's Passover" (Exod 12:11). But in Jesus' time it had become customary to eat it in a reclining position. Jesus uses the solemn formula "I tell you the truth" to disclose the fact that one of them would betray him.

"'One of you!' It came as a bolt from the blue. It was a stunning blow. What! Did the Master actually mean to say that one of their own number was going *to hand him over to the authorities,* for them to deal with as they pleased? Why, it was almost unbelievable—Yet, the One who never told an untruth and whose very name was 'the Truth' (John 8:46; 14:6) was saying this; so it must be true" (W. Hendriksen, *The Gospel of Matthew* [Grand Rapids: Baker, 1973], p. 905; emphasis his).

Jesus further identified the betrayer as "one who is eating with me." To betray a friend after eating a meal with him was, and still is, regarded as the worst kind of treachery in the Middle East. Jesus may have had in mind Psalm 41:9: "Even my close friend, whom I trusted, he who shared my bread, has lifted his heel against me."

19 The response of the disciples to Jesus' startling disclosure was one of sadness and self-distrust. One by one they asked Jesus, "Surely not I?" In Matthew's Gospel even Judas asks the question (Matt 26:25). It was an honest question coming from the rest of the disciples and was prompted by fear and lack of confidence in their own spiritual and moral strength. With Judas it was hypocritical and an attempt to cover his intent; for him not to have asked the question with the other disciples would have made him liable to suspicion.

20 Jesus had already given two clues as to the identity of the betrayer: he was one of the Twelve; he was eating with them at that moment. Now Jesus gives a third clue: the betrayer is the "one who dips bread in the bowl with me." The reference is to dipping a piece of unleavened bread in the sauce (*ḥārôseṭ*) that was part of the Passover meal. This clue does not specifically reveal the betrayer but emphasizes again that it is one who enjoys the closest relationship with Jesus—he even dips his bread into the same bowl with him!

21 Behind Judas's action a divine purpose is being carried out. What happens to the Son of Man does not just happen. In all this the Scriptures are being fulfilled. As Hunter (p. 130) comments: "Beyond reasonable doubt Jesus is referring to Isa. 53. His words mean: 'The Son of Man travels the road marked out for the suffering Servant of the Lord, but alas for that man through whose agency he is being delivered up!' The 'delivering-up' is that predicted of the Servant: 'And he bore the sins of many and was delivered up because of their iniquities' (Isa. 53:12, LXX)."

The woe pronounced on the betrayer emphasizes the personal responsibility of Judas in his wicked deed. "The fact that God turns the wrath of man to his praise does not excuse the wrath of man" (Cranfield, *Gospel of Mark*, p. 424).

3. Institution of the Lord's Supper

14:22–26

22While they were eating, Jesus took bread, gave thanks and broke it, and gave it to his disciples, saying, "Take it; this is my body."
23Then he took the cup, gave thanks and offered it to them, and they all drank from it.
24"This is my blood of the covenant, which is poured out for many," he said to them. 25"I tell you the truth, I will not drink again of the fruit of the vine until that day when I drink it anew in the kingdom of God."
26When they had sung a hymn, they went out to the Mount of Olives.

The NT records four accounts of the Lord's Supper (Matt 26:26–30; Mark 14:22–26; Luke 22:19–20; 1 Cor 11:23–25). Matthew's account closely follows Mark's, while those of Luke and Paul have certain agreements. All four include the taking of the bread, the thanksgiving or blessing, the breaking of the bread, the saying "This is my body," and the taking of the cup. Only Paul (and Luke if the longer reading [22:19b–20] is adopted) records Jesus' command to continue to celebrate the Supper. Mark may not have included it because it was well known in the church he was writing to.

22 The bread Jesus took was the unleavened bread of the Passover meal. He first gave thanks. Two different Greek verbs are translated "give thanks" in vv.22–23. Both are equivalent to the Hebrew verb *bārak*, to "bless" or "praise" God. At Passover the blessing for the bread that immediately preceded the meal itself went thus: "Praised be Thou, O Lord, Sovereign of the World, who causes bread to come forth from the earth." After the blessing Jesus divided the bread and gave it to his disciples with the words "This is my body." Since this saying of Jesus was separated from the cup-saying by the eating of the main part of the meal, it is best to understand it as separate from that saying. The significant action of Jesus was the distribution of the bread, not its breaking. The bread represented his body, i.e., his abiding presence, promised to the disciples on the eve of his crucifixion; and the words become a pledge of the real presence of Jesus wherever and whenever his followers celebrate the Supper. Sacrificial ideas, though crucially important in the cup-saying, are not of primary importance here.

That Jesus did not mean that the bread became his body is clear. There is no indication that the bread was changed—it remained ordinary bread. Furthermore, Jesus often used symbolic language to speak of himself. He spoke of himself as the true vine, the way, the door, etc., by which he meant that certain aspects of his person or work were symbolized by these objects. In the same way the bread symbolized his body, i.e., his abiding presence; and the wine symbolized his blood about to be shed. Our Lord desired

that by means of the supper here instituted, the church should remember his sacrifice and *love* him, should *reflect* on that sacrifice and embrace him by *faith*, and should look forward in living *hope* to his glorious return. Surely, the proper celebration of communion is a loving remembrance. It is, however, more than that. Jesus Christ is most certainly, and through his Spirit most actively, present at this genuine feast! Cf. Matt. 18:20. His followers "take" and "eat." They appropriate Christ by means of living faith, and are strengthened in this faith. (Hendricksen, *Matthew*, p. 910; emphasis his)

23–24 The cup Jesus referred to (v.23) is the third cup of the Passover meal, which was drunk after the meal was eaten. Again Jesus gave thanks. The verb is *eucharisteō*, from which "Eucharist" is derived. The meaning of the cup, unlike that of the bread, is clearly placed in a sacrificial context. The phrase "my blood of the covenant" (v.24) echoes Exodus 24:8 LXX: "Behold the blood of the covenant that the Lord has made with you." The word *diathēkē* means "testament" or "will" in classical Greek, but here it translates the Hebrew *berît* ("covenant"). It is "that relationship of lordship and obedience which God establishes between Himself and men, and the 'blood of the covenant' is the sign of its existence and the means by which it is effected" (Taylor, p. 546). Although the reading "new" found in some MSS before the word "covenant" may be an assimilation to 1 Corinthians 11:25, it expresses an important truth. Jesus' death inaugurated a new era. Jeremiah had prophesied of just such a new day (Jer 31:31–33). The blood that establishes the covenant will be "poured out" (a clear reference to Christ's death) "for many." "Many" here means "all," as Calvin (3:214) clearly recognized: "By the word *many* he means not a part of the world only, but the whole human race" (emphasis his). The language seems to echo Isaiah 53:12.

25–26 Solemnly Jesus declared that this would be his last festal meal with them till the dawn of the messianic kingdom (v.25). "The fruit of the vine" is a liturgical formula for wine used at the feast. The drinking of the cup at the Supper anticipates the perfected fellowship of the Messianic Age. (For the idea of the messianic banquet, cf. Isa 25:6; 1 Enoch 72:14; Matt 8:11; Luke 22:29–30.) The vow of Jesus consecrated him for his sacrificial death, but it also held out the promise of victory and salvation. He will drink the festal cup anew, i.e., with a new redeemed community, in the kingdom of God (cf. Luke 14:15; Rev 3:20–21; 19:6–9).

Assuming the meal to have been a Passover meal, it ended with the singing (v.26) of the second part of the Hallel (Pss 115–118). It is significant that Jesus went to Gethsemane and its agony with such promises as follows:

> The LORD is my strength and my song;
> he has become my salvation.
>
> Shouts of joy and victory
> resound in the tents of the righteous:
> "The LORD's right hand has done mighty things!
> The LORD's right hand is lifted high;
> the LORD's right hand has done mighty things!"
>
> I will not die but live,
> and will proclaim what the LORD has done.
> (Ps 118:14–17)

E. *The Prediction of Peter's Denial*

14:27–31

27"You will all fall away," Jesus told them, "for it is written:

" 'I will strike the shepherd,
and the sheep will be scattered.'

28But after I have risen, I will go ahead of you into Galilee."
29Peter declared, "Even if all fall away, I will not."
30"I tell you the truth, Jesus answered, "today—yes, tonight—before the rooster'
crows twice you yourself will disown me three times."
31But Peter insisted emphatically, "Even if I have to die with you, I will never
disown you." And all the others said the same.

27–28 The predictions recorded here were probably spoken by Jesus as he walked with his disciples from the Upper Room to the Mount of Olives. The verb *skandalizō* ("fall away," NIV) is difficult (v.27). (Notice the many variant renderings in the versions.) Here it seems to be defined by the words from Zechariah that immediately follow. Thus it means, not that the disciples will lose their faith in Jesus, but that their courage will fail and they will forsake him. When the Shepherd (Jesus) is struck, the sheep (the disciples) will be scattered. The quotation is from Zechariah 13:7 and clearly indicates that the death of Jesus is the result of the action of God and that it results in the scattering of the sheep. The prediction was fulfilled. The disciples were fearful to be identified with Jesus in his trial and death, and that caused them to forsake him. This was especially true of Peter, whose actions are often representative of the rest of the disciples.

After the death of the Shepherd, however, there will be a glorious resurrection and a reunion of Shepherd and sheep in Galilee (v.28). Marxsen (pp. 86–87) sees in this verse and in the statement in Mark 16:7 a reference to the Parousia. But the obvious reference is to a postresurrection appearance.

29–31 Jesus' prediction of failure on the part of the disciples was too much for Peter to accept (v.29). For the other disciples it may come true, but certainly not for himself. But Jesus' reply emphasizes the absolute certainty of Peter's denial (v.30). Not only does Jesus use the *amēn* ("I tell you the truth") formula, but he also uses the emphatic "today—yes, tonight." The denial is not only certain, it is imminent. It was also to be a repeated denial (three times), and that in spite of warning (twice repeated) of the crowing of the rooster. The second crowing is found only in Mark and may have come from Peter himself. Cranfield rightly points out that the prediction cannot be a *vaticinium ex eventu* (postevent "prophecy"): "The early Church would hardly have created a prediction which aggravated the baseness of Peter's denial, even for the sake of showing that Jesus was not surprised" (*Gospel of Mark*, p. 429).

Jesus' explicit description of Peter's forthcoming denial was not convincing to him. He insisted on his willingness even to die with Jesus rather than deny him (v.31). But Peter did not know how weak he really was—nor did the rest of the disciples know their weakness, for they quickly chimed in with him to declare their allegiance (cf. 14:50, 71–72).

F. *The Agony of Gethsemane*

14:32–42

> [32]They went to a place called Gethsemane, and Jesus said to his disciples, "Sit here while I pray." [33]He took Peter, James and John along with him, and he began to be deeply distressed and troubled. [34]"My soul is overwhelmed with sorrow to the point of death," he said to them. "Stay here and keep watch."
>
> [35]Going a little farther, he fell to the ground and prayed that if possible the hour might pass from him. [36]"*Abba*, Father," he said, "everything is possible for you. Take this cup from me. Yet not what I will, but what you will."
>
> [37]Then he returned to his disciples and found them sleeping. "Simon," he said to Peter, "are you asleep? Could you not keep watch for one hour? [38]Watch and pray so that you will not fall into temptation. The spirit is willing, but the body is weak."
>
> [39]Once more he went away and prayed the same thing. [40]When he came back, he again found them sleeping, because their eyes were heavy. They did not know what to say to him.
>
> [41]Returning the third time, he said to them, "Are you still sleeping and resting? Enough! The hour has come. Look, the Son of Man is betrayed into the hands of sinners. [42]Rise! Let us go! Here comes my betrayer!"

Gethsemane reveals the humanity of Jesus with astonishing fidelity. He is shown to be "anything but above temptation. So far from sailing serenely through his trials like some superior being unconcerned with this world, he is almost dead with distress" (Moule, *Gospel of Mark*, p. 117). It is inconceivable that the early church could or would have created a story like this one about Jesus.

32–34 The name "Gethsemane" (v.32) is probably from the Hebrew *gat šᵉmānî* ("press of oils"). It was a garden located somewhere on the lower slopes of the Mount of Olives, in which there were olive trees and olive presses. It was one of Jesus' favorite spots (cf. Luke 22:39; John 18:2), no doubt often used by him and his disciples as a place to be alone. Here he faced one of his most crucial tests.

Leaving the rest of the disciples behind, Jesus took with him the three of the inner circle—Peter, James, and John (v.33). He must have felt his need for their presence in this time of crisis. The two verbs translated "deeply distressed and troubled" together "describe an extremely acute emotion, a compound of bewilderment, fear, uncertainty and anxiety, nowhere else portrayed in such vivid terms as here" (Bratcher and Nida, p. 446). This deep agony Jesus shared with his disciples (v.34). Why? Probably because he wanted them to know something of the depths of suffering he was about to experience for the redemption of the world. Then Jesus, having shared his feelings with Peter, James, and John, withdrew to be alone with his Father. Jesus' command to them to keep watch meant either that they were to stay awake and so share in his agony or that they were to be on the lookout for those Jesus knew were on their way to arrest him. John 18:2 says that Judas knew the place where Jesus was accustomed to pray.

35–36 Jesus did not die serenely as both Christian and Jewish martyrs have. He was no mere martyr; he was the Lamb of God bearing the penalty of the sins of all mankind. The wrath of God was turned loose on him. Only this can adequately explain what happened in Gethsemane. The burden and agony were so great he could not stand up (v.35). His prayer, uttered in a prone position, was addressed to "*Abba*, Father" (v.36). The word "*Abba*" is the Aramaic intimate form for father ("Daddy")—a word the Jews did not use to address God because they thought it disrespectful. Since Jesus was the unique Son of God and on the most intimate terms with him, it was natural for him to use it. Jesus believed that with God anything was possible and therefore prayed for the cup to be removed from him. This cup is the same one Jesus referred to in 10:38–39—the cup of the wrath of God. In the OT it is regularly used as a metaphor of punishment and judgment. Here it obviously refers to Jesus' death. Jesus' desire was for the removal of the cup. But he willingly placed his will in submission to his Father's will.

37–38 Returning to his disciples, Jesus found them sleeping. They were doubtless very tired; the hour was late, probably past midnight, and they had experienced some exciting events during the long day. Nevertheless it was a critical time, and they were expected to be awake. Jesus' rebuke in v.37 is addressed to Peter whereas in v.38 it is addressed to all three disciples. Peter is probably singled out because he was the one who had boasted of his fidelity to Jesus. He who had said he was willing to die, if need be, with Christ (v.31) could not watch for one hour.

The verbs "watch" (*grēgoreite*) and "pray" (*proseuchesthe*) are both imperatives and are addressed to all three disciples, not just Peter. The conquest of temptation (to "enter into temptation" means to yield to it) can only come through these two actions. The spirit (a reference to the human spirit) might be willing to do what is right, but the human body (*sarx*) is weak. Some commentators take *sarx* to mean our poor unaided human nature. Here, however, it seems to mean the physical body and refers to the inability of the disciples to stay awake.

39–40 Again, after having left his disciples to pray (v.39), Jesus returned to find them sleeping (v.40). Because of sheer fatigue, they were unable to stay awake. When confronted by Jesus, they "did not know what to say to him"—probably because they were so embarrassed and ashamed. Even Peter had nothing to say on this occasion (cf. 9:6).

41 A third time Jesus left them to pray (cf. Matt 26:44) and on returning again found the disciples asleep. The next words may be either ironic—"Sleep then, since that's what you want; rest if you are able"—or a question—"Are you still sleeping and resting?" (NIV). The latter seems better in view of the situation. The rendering of the next word (*apechei*) is difficult, as the many translations of it indicate. NIV renders it "Enough!" apparently meaning "enough of sleep," i.e., it is time for the disciples to wake up. Some other explanations for *apechei* are (1) "he has received it," meaning that Judas has received the money for the betrayal; (2) "the account is closed," i.e., the end has come; and (3) "it is settled," i.e., it is now clear to Jesus that it is God's will for him to go to the cross; the cup will not be taken from him. It is hard to choose between (2) and (3) since both are supported by Jesus' next statement: "The hour has come," i.e., the time of his betrayal and death. The "sinners" into whose hands the Son of Man is to be betrayed are the satanic agents who bring about his death.

42 The disciples apparently were still lying on the ground; so when Jesus heard the approach of the arresting party, he told the disciples to get on their feet. "The call to 'go' ends the scene in Gethsemane, but cannot be intended to suggest flight, for the Lord had always reserved Himself for this 'hour,' and had now finally embraced the Divine Will concerning it" (Swete, p. 349). Jesus did not go to flee from Judas but to meet him.

Rawlinson (p. 211) explains the significance of the experience of the disciples in Gethsemane for the Christians at Rome to whom Mark is writing as follows:

> For the Church of Mk's day the example of Jesus in the Garden, as contrasted with the behaviour of the three disciples, must have had special value as setting forth the spirit in which the vocation of martyrdom should be approached. The Christian witness must not presume upon the fact that his spirit is willing: he must ever be mindful also of the weakness of the flesh. It is essential therefore that he should *watch and pray,* that when the hour of trial comes he may not break down (emphasis his).

Notes

33 Ἐκθαμβεῖσθαι (*ekthambeisthai*) is peculiar to Mark (1:27; 9:15; 16:5–6). It is a difficult word to translate. Swete has "terrified surprise"; Rawlinson, "shuddering awe"; Taylor, "amazement amounting to consternation."

Ἀδημονεῖν (*adēmonein*) is translated in NIV "troubled." Swete (in loc.) says it describes the "distress that follows a great shock"; NEB has "My heart is ready to break with grief"; Martin (in loc.) says "The impact of the two words is incalculable and carries its own power to stab the reader wide awake."

41 For the many interpretations of ἀπέχει (*apechei*), see Cranfield, *Gospel of Mark*, pp. 435–36, and Lane, p. 514.

42 Ἄγωμεν (*agōmen*) may be translated "Let us advance to meet them."

G. *The Betrayal and Arrest*

14:43–52

⁴³Just as he was speaking, Judas, one of the Twelve, appeared. With him was a crowd armed with swords and clubs, sent from the chief priests, the teachers of the law, and the elders.

⁴⁴Now the betrayer had arranged a signal with them: "The one I kiss is the man; arrest him and lead him away under guard." ⁴⁵Going at once to Jesus, Judas said, "Rabbi!" and kissed him. ⁴⁶The men seized Jesus and arrested him.

⁴⁷Then one of those standing near drew his sword and struck the servant of the high priest, cutting off his ear.

⁴⁸"Am I leading a rebellion," said Jesus, "that you have come out with swords and clubs to capture me? ⁴⁹Every day I was with you, teaching in the temple courts, and you did not arrest me. But the Scriptures must be fulfilled." ⁵⁰Then everyone deserted him and fled.

⁵¹A young man, wearing nothing but a linen garment, was following Jesus. When they seized him, ⁵²he fled naked, leaving his garment behind.

43 The fact that Judas is described as "one of the Twelve," as if it were the first mention of him in the narrative, strongly suggests that at this point Mark is inserting into his account the primitive passion narrative that had no prior mention of Judas

in it. Another possibility is that "one of the Twelve" is repeated "to keep this tragic element of the situation before us" (Gould, p. 273). Judas was accompanied by a crowd sent from the three constituent groups of the Sanhedrin: chief priests, teachers of the law, and elders. This was not a motley crowd; as John's Gospel tells us, it consisted of a detachment of soldiers and some official attendants of the Sanhedrin (18:3). They came armed with swords and clubs. Apparently they thought they would meet with resistance.

44–46 The prearranged "signal" (*syssēmon*) or means of identifying Jesus was for Judas to kiss him (v.44). This suggests that the members of the arresting party did not know Jesus, or perhaps since it was dark they wanted to be sure not to arrest the wrong person (v.46). Rabbis customarily were greeted by their disciples with a kiss. Thus Judas's act would not be suspected for what it really was. Judas's instructions to the crowd were designed to assure the successful accomplishment of the arrest. They were to lead Jesus away securely—with no chance of escape. Once having become involved in the wicked affair, Judas did not want to make a fiasco of it.

47 Mark does not say who wielded the sword. But we know from John that it was Peter and that the ear belonged to Malchus, a servant of the high priest (John 18:10). Apparently Peter aimed at his head; but Malchus sidestepped, and Peter only caught his ear. Jesus' rebuke to Peter (Matt 26:52) and the restoration of the ear (Luke 22:51) are not recorded by Mark. He uses the diminutive *ōtarion* for "ear." Perhaps only the lobe was cut off. This would explain Luke's statement that Jesus healed the ear instead of replacing it (Luke 22:51).

48–50 Jesus protested against the manner of his arrest (v.48). The crowd sent from the Sanhedrin had come after him with swords and clubs, as if he were a dangerous criminal or insurrectionist of some kind. He had been teaching every day in the temple courts (v.49). They could have arrested him there. Why then had they come at night? and why had they chosen to arrest him outside the city? The obvious answer is that they feared the people's reaction to Jesus' arrest. So they carefully chose both the time and the place. Jesus' statement about his teaching daily in the temple courts may point to a period longer than two or three days and thus imply that Jesus had spent a longer period in Jerusalem before his arrest than is ordinarily supposed.

The circumstances of Jesus' arrest were a fulfillment of Scripture. Mark does not say what Scripture specifically Jesus had in mind. It may have been Isaiah 53:12: "And [he] was numbered with the transgressors." But in view of v.50—"Then everyone deserted him and fled"—he may have had Zechariah 13:7 in mind, which Jesus quoted in 14:27 and which is fulfilled here. The words of v.50 "drive home, as it were with hammer-blows, the failure of the disciples without exception . . . and the complete forsakenness of Jesus" (Cranfield, *Gospel of Mark*, p. 438).

51–52 Only Mark records this mysterious episode. The "young man" (v.51) is not identified, but the consensus is that he is Mark. Why else would he insert such a trivial detail in so solemn a story? Was this Mark's way of saying, "I was there"? Why he was there is not explained.

Ordinarily men wore an undergarment called a *chitōn*. This young man had only a *sindōn*, an outer garment. Usually this garment was made of wool. His, however, was linen, an expensive material worn only by the rich. Since he had no *chitōn*, when he fled without his *sindōn*, he was actually naked (v.51). Perhaps the main point of the story—and the reason Mark included it—was to show that the forsakenness of Jesus was total. Even this youth forsook him.

Notes

45 The verb καταφιλέω (*kataphileō*), a compounded form of φιλέω (*phileō*, "to kiss"), usually means "to kiss fervently" and here probably indicates a lingering kiss to ensure the identification of Jesus.

H. *Jesus Before the Sanhedrin*

14:53–65

53They took Jesus to the high priest, and all the chief priests, elders and teachers of the law came together. 54Peter followed him at a distance, right into the courtyard of the high priest. There he sat with the guards and warmed himself at the fire.
55The chief priests and the whole Sanhedrin were looking for evidence against Jesus so that they could put him to death, but they did not find any. 56Many testified falsely against him, but their statements did not agree.
57Then some stood up and gave this false testimony against him: 58"We heard him say, 'I will destroy this man-made temple and in three days will build another, not made by man.'" 59Yet even then their testimony did not agree.
60Then the high priest stood up before them and asked Jesus, "Are you not going to answer? What is this testimony that these men are bringing against you?" 61But Jesus remained silent and gave no answer.
Again the high priest asked him, "Are you the Christ, the Son of the Blessed One?"
62"I am," said Jesus. "And you will see the Son of Man sitting at the right hand of the Mighty One and coming on the clouds of heaven."
63The high priest tore his clothes. "Why do we need any more witnesses?" he asked. 64"You have heard the blasphemy. What do you think?"
They all condemned him as worthy of death. 65Then some began to spit at him; they blindfolded him, struck him with their fists, and said, "Prophesy!" And the guards took him and beat him.

The trial of Jesus took place in two stages: a religious trial followed by a civil one. Each had three episodes. The religious trial included (1) the preliminary hearing before Annas (reported only in John 18:12–14, 19–23); (2) the trial before Caiaphas and the Sanhedrin (Mark 14:53–65); and (3) the trial before the same group just after daybreak (Mark 15:1). The three episodes of the civil trial were (1) the trial before Pilate; (2) the trial before Herod Antipas (recorded only in Luke 23:6–12); and (3) the trial before Pilate continued and concluded. In Mark, since there is no account of Jesus being sent to Herod Antipas, the trial before Pilate is a continuous and unbroken narrative (15:2–15).

53 Mark makes no mention of the preliminary hearing before Annas (cf. John 18:12–14, 19–23). Annas had been high priest from A.D. 7–14 but had been deposed by

Valerius Gratus, Pilate's predecessor. Caiaphas, Annas's son-in-law, held the office; but some of the Jews probably regarded Annas as the true high priest. Caiaphas probably lived in the same palace. Jesus, according to Mark, was taken directly to Caiaphas (Mark never mentions his name), with the entire Sanhedrin present. The meeting took place in the palace of Caiaphas in an upstairs room (cf. v.66). This must have been a large room to accommodate the Sanhedrin. If all the members were present, there would have been seventy of them, though Mark's use of "all" does not necessarily mean all seventy were present. Certainly there were enough of them there to constitute a quorum, and that may be what Mark's "all" means. Since the Sanhedrin usually met in one of the market halls, the use of Caiaphas's house may have been to ensure secrecy.

54 This verse seems to interrupt the flow of the narrative. It is inserted here to prepare for the full account of Peter's denial (vv.66–72) and to indicate that the trial and the denial were concurrent. "When the first panic was over Peter's affection re-asserted itself" (Plummer, p. 335). He followed at a distance because he was afraid, but he *did* follow. Apparently he could not bring himself to desert Jesus completely. Eventually he arrived at the high priest's palace. John's Gospel informs us that there was "another disciple" with Peter; and, since this unnamed disciple knew the high priest, he spoke to the girl on duty at the gate, and Peter was let in. The palace was built around an open courtyard (*aulē*) that was entered through an archway (cf. v.68). Spring nights are cool in Jerusalem (which is at an elevation of about twenty-five hundred feet); so Peter sat with the guards and warmed himself before a charcoal fire (cf. John 18:18). From where he was sitting, he could see the upstairs room where the Sanhedrin was meeting to decide Jesus' fate.

55–56 Just how rigged the trial of Jesus was is made clear by these verses. Though it was late at night (in fact, it probably was very early Friday morning), false witnesses were available (v.56). But a problem developed—the witnesses could not agree with one another! According to the law (Num 35:30; Deut 17:6; 19:15), it was necessary in cases that required the death penalty to have two witnesses. These witnesses must, however, give consistent evidence. The smallest inconsistency was sufficient to discredit them. As is always true when witnesses testify falsely, there was no consistency in their testimony. Many came to witness against Jesus (the Sanhedrin had made careful preparation for the trial [v.55]), but the contradictory nature of the evidence frustrated the court's wicked intent.

57–59 The lack of consistent evidence did not thwart Caiaphas and the Sanhedrin for long. Although the first round of testimony proved to be of no value, soon a definite charge was made. Jesus had said he would destroy this "man-made temple" and rebuild another "not made by man" in three days (v.58). There is no statement just like this in the Gospels. The allusion is probably to Jesus' statement in John 2:19, made two years previously; but on that occasion he did not predict that he would do the destroying, and the reference is not to the Jerusalem temple but to his body. It may have been that Jesus' statement in Mark 13:2, where he predicts the destruction of the temple, was combined with John 2:19; and out of the two the charge was formulated. The charge, however, proved invalid because again the testimony of the witnesses was inconsistent (vv.57, 59).

60–61 The situation had become extremely tense. There were plenty of witnesses, but they could not pass the test of Deuteronomy 17:6. Finally in exasperation the high priest stood up in the Sanhedrin to interrogate Jesus himself (v.60). Caiaphas apparently wanted Jesus to respond to the charges made againt him in the hope of provoking an incriminating answer. But Jesus refused to give him that opportunity (v.61). "In majestic silence, Jesus refused to dignify the self-refuting testimony by any explanation of His own" (Hiebert, *Gospel of Mark*, p. 371).

The silence of Jesus to the first questions prompted the high priest to ask him another. The question "Are you the Christ, the son of the Blessed One?" indicates that by this time the religious authorities either knew or suspected that Jesus regarded himself as the Messiah. "The Blessed" is a reverential circumlocution to avoid the pronunciation of the name of God and stands in apposition to the title "Christ" or "Messiah." "Son of God" was understood by the Jews of Jesus' time solely in a messianic sense; and since the Messiah in Jewish expectations was to be a man, the question of the high priest was about Jesus' claim to messiahship and had nothing to do with deity (cf. Lane, p. 535). The question proved to be a stroke of genius. Blasphemy was a capital crime. If the religious authorities could not effect an accusation by the testimony of others, Jesus' own testimony about himself would do. Had Jesus refused to answer this question, the Sanhedrin would have had to devise some other plan.

62 Jesus' reply is a straightforward "I am." This is in sharp contrast to his deliberate avoidance of calling himself the Messiah or having others proclaim his messiahship up to this point in his ministry. It clearly was not because he had no consciousness of being the Messiah. His avoidance of the messianic claim was because of the false concepts of messiahship that were popular in his day and with which he did not want to be identified. Also, there was always the danger that an open claim to messiahship would bring about a premature crisis and abort his ministry. Now, however, the time of veiledness had passed. He was ready to unequivocally state his messiahship.

Jesus' affirmation of messiahship is followed by a Son-of-Man saying that brings together Daniel 7:13 and Psalm 110:1. The two main ideas are the enthronement of the Son of Man and his eschatological coming. Jesus is looking to the future, beyond the Crucifixion and Resurrection, to the Ascension, when he will take his place at the right hand of God—the place of authority—and to his parousia, when he will come in judgment. Now Caiaphas and the Sanhedrin are sitting in judgment on him. In that day Jesus will pass final and irrevocable judgment on them. The author of Revelation points to that day: "Look, he is coming with the clouds,/ and every eye will see him,/ even those who pierced him" (1:7). Jesus' words are a solemn warning.

63–64 The tearing of one's clothes was originally a sign of great grief (cf. Gen 37:29; 2 Kings 18:37; Jud 14:19; Ep Jer 31; 2 Macc 4:38). In the case of the high priest (v.63), it became "a formal judicial act minutely regulated by the Talmud" (Taylor, p. 569). The action of the high priest showed that he had just heard a blasphemous statement (v.64; cf. M. *Sanhedrin* 7.5). During this period the Jews defined blasphemy fairly loosely. They identified it not only with overt and definite reviling of the name of God (cf. Lev 24:10–23) but also with any affront to the majesty and authority of God (cf. Mark 2:7; 3:28–29; John 5:18; 10:33; see also SBK 1:1007ff.). Jesus' claim to be the Messiah was understood by Caiaphas in the latter sense and was therefore considered to be blasphemy. All the members of the Sanhedrin concurred with Caiaphas's judgment and condemned Jesus "as worthy of death." The death sentence had been handed down as Jesus had predicted in Mark 10:33. Leviticus 24:14 prescribes stoning as the manner of death for the sin of blasphemy.

65 The decision that Jesus deserved the death penalty was the signal for the Sanhedrin to release their pent-up hostilities against him. Although Rawlinson's suggestion (p. 223) that Mark's grammar is careless ("we are to understand a change of subject at the beginning of the verse") absolves the Sanhedrin of this barbarous display, it is almost certainly wrong. "Some" at the beginning of v.65 is in contrast to "all" in v.64, and both refer to members of the Sanhedrin. This interpretation is supported by the mention of the guards as a second and distinct group of participants in the barbarous acts.

Spitting and hitting were traditional means of expressing rejection and repudiation (cf. Num 12:14; Deut 25:9; Job 30:10; Isa 50:6). Light is shed on the significance of the covering of the face followed by blows and the demand to prophesy by the additional words in Matthew 26:88 and Luke 22:64: "Who hit you?" This was their way of trying to make a mockery of Jesus' messianic claims because a rabbinic interpretation of Isaiah 11:2–4 stated that the Messiah could judge by smell and did not need sight (cf. Lane, p. 540; b *Sanhedrin* 93b). Jesus refused to respond to their vicious jests. When the Sanhedrin had its fill of brutality and mockery, they turned Jesus over to the guards who continued the beatings.

Notes

62 The variant reading σὺ εἶπας ὅτι ἐγώ εἰμι (*sy eipas hoti egō eimi*, "You say that I am") has the support of the Caesarean text (Θ Φ pc arm geo Origen). Taylor thinks this is the original text because it is more in keeping with Jesus' reluctance in Mark's Gospel in revealing straight-out his messiahship and because it would account for Matt 26:64 and Luke 22:67–68. If this is the correct reading, Jesus' reply is affirmative, "but it registers a difference of interpretation: 'The word is yours, Yes, if you like'; as if to indicate that the Speaker has His own ideas about Messiahship" (Taylor, p. 568). Against this is the MS evidence that overwhelmingly supports the shorter reading. Also at this point Jesus was ready to reveal clearly his identity as the Messiah.

I. *Peter's Denial of Jesus*

14:66–72

66While Peter was below in the courtyard, one of the servant girls of the high priest came by. 67When she saw Peter warming himself, she looked closely at him.

"You also were with that Nazarene, Jesus," she said.

68But he denied it. "I don't know or understand what you're talking about," he said, and went out into the entryway.

69When the servant girl saw him there, she said again to those standing around, "This fellow is one of them." 70Again he denied it.

> After a little while, those standing near said to Peter, "Surely you are one of them, for you are a Galilean."
>
> [71]He began to call down curses on himself, and he swore to them, "I don't know this man you're talking about."
>
> [72]Immediately the rooster crowed the second time. Then Peter remembered the word Jesus had spoken to him: "Before the rooster crows twice you will disown me three times." And he broke down and wept.

66–68 The incident begun in v.54 is now developed. When Jesus was being mocked, spit upon, and beaten in the upstairs room of the high priest's palace, Peter was below in the courtyard (v.66). He was waiting to see what would happen to Jesus. The fact that Peter was there at all indicates that he loved Jesus and was concerned about him, but his love did not stand the test of fear. The servant girl (probably the "girl at the door," John 18:17) recognized Peter as he stood in the light of the fire, warming himself (v.67). Perhaps she had seen Peter with Jesus in the temple during the days immediately preceding or remembered that she had admitted him at the request of John, another one of Jesus' disciples. Her contempt for Jesus is revealed in the order of the words she used to speak about him—"that Nazarene, Jesus." Peter denied her charge (v.68) by "using the form common in rabbinical law for a formal, legal denial (e.g., M. *Shebuoth* VIII. 3: 'Where is my ox?' He said to him, 'I do not know what you are saying'" Lane, p. 542). Fearful of being identified and apprehended, Peter retreated into the archway that led into the street. He was anxious for his own safety. Yet he still could not bring himself to abandon Jesus completely. So he slunk into the darkness and safety of the archway.

69–72 Peter's retreat to safety was short-lived. The servant girl saw him slip into the entryway and reiterated her contention—this time to "those standing around," presumably the guards and others in the pay of the high priest (v.69). Her words—"This fellow is one of them"—seem to show that she recognized Peter as part of a group or movement whose leader was Jesus. Peter's second denial (v.70) was not convincing. So the next time, not the servant girl, but the others, apparently having their suspicions aroused by her and detecting Peter's Galilean accent (Jesus was known to have come from Galilee), accused him. Peter was now like a cornered animal. He called down curses on himself if he was lying and swore that he didn't know "this man you're talking about" (v.71). The first two times Peter had denied being identified with Jesus. The last time he denied Jesus himself. Hendriksen comments: "How deceitful is man's heart! It is 'exceedingly corrupt. Who can know it?' (Jer. 17:9). . . . Think of it: 'Thou art the Christ, the Son of the living God.'—'I don't even know the man'" (*Matthew*, p. 937).

The third denial was followed by the second crowing of the rooster (v.72). Luke (22:61) tells us that at that very moment the Lord "turned and looked straight at Peter." The first time the rooster crowed, Peter's conscience was not awakened. This time he remembered what Jesus had said about his denial of him. The look of Jesus and the reminder of the crowing rooster proved too much for Peter. "He broke down and wept."

The importance and relevance of Peter's denial for the church to which Mark writes is obvious. To a church under severe pressure of persecution it provided a warning. If denial of Jesus Christ was possible for an apostle, and one of the leaders of the apostles at that, then they must be constantly on guard lest they too deny

Jesus. The story also provided assurance that if anyone did fail Jesus under the duress of persecution, there was always a way open for repentance, forgiveness, and restoration (cf. 16:7).

Notes

68 NIV omits the reading καὶ ἀλέκτωρ ἐφώνησεν (*kai alektōr ephōnēsen*, "and the rooster crowed") at the end of this verse. It is included in the UBS Greek NT but is put in brackets and given a "D" rating (very high degree of doubt). Reasons for excluding it are (1) if Peter heard the crowing of the rooster, why didn't he repent? and (2) the MS evidence favors excluding it (this was presumably the primary reason for excluding it from NIV). Reasons for including it are (1) it was omitted by copyists to make Peter's denial seem a little less shameful; (2) why do not the majority of the MSS that omit it not omit ἐκ δευτέρου (*ek deuterou*, "twice") in v.72? and (3) exclusion represents an assimilation to Matthew and Luke where only one rooster crowing is mentioned. The decision is a very difficult one. I agree with NIV.

72 The last words of this verse, καὶ ἐπιβαλὼν ἔκλαιεν (*kai epibalōn eklaien*), are very difficult to translate. Some of the renderings are as follows: "he began to cry"; "he set to and wept"; "he burst into tears"; "he thought on it and wept"; "he covered his head and wept"; "he threw himself on the ground"; "he dashed out." Plummer (p. 342) is probably right when he says that "we must be content to share the ignorance of all the ages" as to its meaning.

J. The Trial Before Pilate

15:1–15

¹Very early in the morning, the chief priests, with the elders, the teachers of the law and the whole Sanhedrin, reached a decision. They bound Jesus, led him away and handed him over to Pilate.

²"Are you the king of the Jews?" asked Pilate.

"Yes, it is as you say," Jesus replied.

³The chief priests accused him of many things. ⁴So again Pilate asked him, "Aren't you going to answer? See how many things they are accusing you of."

⁵But Jesus still made no reply, and Pilate was amazed.

⁶Now it was the custom at the Feast to release a prisoner whom the people requested. ⁷A man called Barabbas was in prison with the insurrectionists who had committed murder in the uprising. ⁸The crowd came up and asked Pilate to do for them what he usually did.

⁹"Do you want me to release to you the king of the Jews?" asked Pilate, ¹⁰knowing it was out of envy that the chief priests had handed Jesus over to him. ¹¹But the chief priests stirred up the crowd to have Pilate release Barabbas instead.

¹²"What shall I do, then, with the one you call the king of the Jews?" Pilate asked them.

¹³"Crucify him!" they shouted.

¹⁴"Why? What crime has he committed?" asked Pilate.

But they shouted all the louder, "Crucify him!"

¹⁵Wanting to satisfy the crowd, Pilate released Barabbas to them. He had Jesus flogged, and handed him over to be crucified.

1 What seems to be spoken of here is not another gathering of the Sanhedrin but the final stages of the meeting that had begun late the night before. The phrase *symboulion poiēsantes* is difficult. The best translation seems to be "reached a decision" (NIV) or "made a resolution" (cf. its use in Mark 3:6; Matt 12:14; 22:15; 27:7; 28:12). Apparently the resolution or decision made by the Sanhedrin in the final stages of its meeting was to accuse Jesus before the civil authority, not of blasphemy, but of high treason. The Roman government would not have considered blasphemy a punishable crime. It had to do with Jewish religion, and this was of little or no concern to the Roman authorities. But high treason was a crime they could not overlook. Moule points out the overpowering irony of the situation: "Jesus, who is, indeed, king of the Jews in a deeply spiritual sense, has refused to lead a political uprising. Yet now, condemned for blasphemy by the Jews because of his spiritual claims, he is accused by them also before Pilate by being precisely what he had disappointed the crowds for failing to be—a political insurgent" (*Gospel of Mark*, p. 124).

Having made their decision, the members of the Sanhedrin led Jesus away and handed him over to Pilate. Mark does not mention who Pilate is or why he was in Jerusalem at that time. Apparently he presupposes this knowledge on the part of his readers.

The official residence of the Roman governors of Judea was at Caesarea on the Mediterranean coast. Whenever they came to Jerusalem, they occupied the palace of Herod. This palatial residence, constructed by Herod the Great, was located in the northwestern section of the city. It was here that the trial of Jesus before Pilate took place. Mark uses the word "Praetorium" to indicate Herod's palace in v. 16. Early in the morning Jesus was led from the palace of the high priest, located in the southwestern part of the city, through the streets of Jerusalem to Herod's palace. He was taken "early in the morning" because that is when Pilate held trials. This explains why the Sanhedrin held their session late at night and very early in the morning.

2 Pilate's first question to Jesus—"Are you the king of the Jews?"—shows that the charges against Jesus, though Mark does not mention this, had already been made known to Pilate. Mark gives us only a summary of the trial. According to Luke, the Sanhedrin brought before Pilate three charges against Jesus: (1) he is "subverting our nation"; (2) he "opposes payment of taxes to Caesar"; and (3) he "claims to be Christ, a king" (Luke 23:2). Pilate was primarily interested in the third accusation. This is clear from his question: "Are you the king of the Jews?" Jesus' answer to Pilate's question was affirmative yet somewhat qualified: "Yes, it is as you say." He seems to be saying, "Yes, I am the king of the Jews; but your concept of what that means and mine are poles apart."

3–5 The chief priests were now taking the lead in the attack against Jesus (v.3). Luke specifically mentions three accusations against Jesus (see commentary at v.2 above. But the "many" of this verse suggests there were more. Jesus, however, in his majestic serenity, refused to defend himself (v.4). His composure in the face of vicious accusations completely amazed Pilate (v.5).

6 The custom referred to here of releasing a prisoner at the Passover Feast is unknown outside the Gospels (cf. Matt 27:15; John 18:39. Luke 23:17—not included in NIV—reads: "Now he was obliged to release one man to them at the Feast"). It was, however, a Roman custom and could well have been a custom in Palestine. An example of a Roman official releasing a prisoner on the demands of the people occurs in the Papyrus Florentinus 61.59ff. There the Roman governor of Egypt, G. Septimus Vegetus, says to Phibion, the accused: "Thou hast been worthy of scourging, but I will give thee to the people" (cited in Taylor, p. 580).

7–8 According to Luke 23:19, there had been an uprising in the city, and one of the insurrectionists was a man named Barabbas (v.7). He and his fellow insurrectionists had been thrown in prison for revolution and murder. Mark speaks of the revolt as if it were well known, but there is no record of it in any of our sources. This is not surprising because the period was one of frequent insurrections. Barabbas was probably a member of the sect of the Zealots, who deeply resented the Roman occupation of Palestine.

The crowd seems to have come to Pilate's tribunal for the primary purpose of asking for Barabbas's release since it was customary for a prisoner to be released at the Passover Feast (v.8). It was Pilate who deliberately faced them with the choice between Jesus and Barabbas.

9–10 This statement (v.9) implies that the crowd had asked for the release of Jesus. If Barabbas also had the name "Jesus" (see note on v.7), it is possible that Pilate may have mistaken the crowd's request for releasing Jesus Barabbas as a request for releasing Jesus of Nazareth. Pilate, of course, used the title "king of the Jews" contemptuously, as in 15:2. He was too shrewd a politician to believe that the chief priests had handed Jesus over to him out of loyalty to Caesar! He reasoned, and rightly so, that they envied Jesus' popularity and influence with the people (v.10). Swete (p. 371) comments: "The pretense of loyalty to the Emperor was too flimsy to deceive a man of the world, and he detected under this disguise the vulgar vice of envy."

11 The original purpose of the crowd was to gain the release of the insurrectionist Barabbas. Pilate had attempted to deflect that purpose and substitute the release of Jesus instead. This was a serious threat to the murderous purposes of the chief priests. They had already condemned Jesus to death in their secret councils; now they were not about to allow Jesus to slip through their fingers through some Passover Feast clemency custom. No other alternative was open to them but to urge the crowd to force Pilate to carry out their request—the release of Jesus Barabbas, not Jesus of Nazareth. How the chief priests stirred up the crowd is not told us by Mark.

12–14 Pilate's question is surprising (v.12). Apparently he held out other options than crucifixion for Jesus. In Matthew's account Pilate had just before this received his wife's warning not to have anything to do with "that innocent man" (27:19). Perhaps his question reflects this warning. If Barabbas was to be released, what would Pilate do with Jesus? Was Pilate suggesting the possibility of releasing Jesus too? Whatever was going through his mind, it is clear that he was reluctant to carry out the murderous intent of the chief priests. His attempt to change the mind of the crowd, if it actually was that, failed. There was no dissuading them. The chief priests had stirred them up to a frenzy. "Crucify him!" they shouted (v.13). And when Pilate, in a final attempt to save Jesus, asked, "Why? What crime has he committed?" the crowd, now a mob, ignored his question (v.14). They had reached a stage where they were beyond reason. No death for Jesus but crucifixion would satisfy them. They wanted him to suffer the full ignominy of the cross. So they shouted all the louder, "Crucify him!"

15 Pilate saw that he could not change the mind of the mob. He would have to go through with Jesus' crucifixion. His previous handling of matters relating to the Jews' religion had not endeared him to the people. To risk alienating them in this crisis would be too dangerous for him politically. His wife's message had made him think more deeply about Jesus than he might otherwise had done (cf. v.12). Yet he was a Roman career politician, and a great deal was at stake for him. An official complaint to Rome by the Jewish authorities might well result in his recall. So to protect his own interests and placate the priests and the people, he released the insurrectionist and murderer Barabbas and ordered Jesus flogged.

Since flogging did not necessarily precede crucifixion, Pilate was still hoping he could dissuade the crowd from their demand for Jesus' crucifixion (cf. John 19:1–7, where after the flogging Pilate tried to persuade them against crucifixion) by administering a severe flogging instead. In any case, flogging was no light punishment. The Romans first stripped the victim and tied his hands to a post above his head. The whip (flagellum) was made of several pieces of leather with pieces of bone and lead embedded near the ends. Two men, one on each side of the victim, usually did the flogging. The Jews mercifully limited flogging to a maximum of forty stripes; the Romans had no such limitation. The following is a medical doctor's description of the physical effects of flogging.

> The heavy whip is brought down with full force again and again across Jesus' shoulders, back and legs. At first the heavy thongs cut through the skin only. Then, as the blows continue, they cut deeper into the subcutaneous tissues, producing first an oozing of blood from the capillaries and veins of the skin, and finally spurting arterial bleeding from vessels in the underlying muscles. . . . Finally the skin of the back is hanging in long ribbons and the entire area is an unrecognizable mass of torn, bleeding tissue. (C. Truman Davis, "The Crucifixion of Jesus. The Passion of Christ from a Medical Point of View," *Arizona Medicine* 22, no. 3 [March 1965]: 185)

It is not surprising that victims of Roman floggings seldom survived.

After going through this terrible ordeal, Jesus was handed over by Pilate to be crucified. The use of the phrase "handed over" may be a deliberate attempt to identify Jesus with the Suffering Servant of Isaiah 53:6, 12, since these words are used there (LXX) of the Servant.

Notes

1 The traditional site of Jesus' trial shown to most visitors to Jerusalem—the ancient pavement of the Fortress of Antonia—is almost certainly erroneous. The Antonia, located adjacent to the temple area on the northwest, served primarily as a barracks for soldiers on duty in Jerusalem. It is highly doubtful whether the Roman governors visiting Jerusalem

would prefer the spartan accommodations of the Antonia to the luxurious facilities of Herod's palace. We know from Josephus that Gessius Florus, one of the Roman procurators, resided in Herod's palace and had his tribunal set up in the square in front of it (Jos. War II, 301 [xiv.8]).

In 1961 at Caesarea on the Mediterranean coast, Italian archaeologists discovered a two-by-three foot stone that has on it the following inscription in three-inch lettering:

CAESARIENS TIBERIEVM
PONTIVS PILATVS
PRAEFECTVS IVDAEAE
DEDIT

"Pontius Pilatus, Prefect of Judea, has presented the Tiberieum to the Caesareans." What the Tiberieum was is not clear (perhaps a building or monument). What is important is that this discovery marked the first archaeological evidence for the existence of Pontius Pilate (cf. J. Vardaman, "A New Inscription which Mentions Pilate as 'Prefect,'" JBL 81 [1962]: 70–71).

2 Jesus' answer was σὺ λέγεις (*sy legeis*, "you say"). This appears to be intentionally qualified. Had he wanted to declare his kingship openly, he would have answered ναί (*nai*, "Yes!"). Martin suggests the paraphrase "You do well to ask"—"a reply which deflects the thrust of Pilate's interrogation and makes possible a continuation of the dialogue in the Trial scenario" (*Mark*, p. 178).

3 The variant reading at the end of v.3 that is included in KJV, αὐτὸς δὲ οὐδὲν ἀπεκρίνατο (*autos de ouden apekrinato*, "but he answered nothing"), is supported by predominantly Caesarean witnesses. Taylor thinks the reading may be original because the following verse (4) seems to require some such statement. The external evidence is, however, so weak that the UBS Greek text does not even list it as a variant.

6 In addition to the example of clemency cited in the commentary, there is in the Mishnah a rule that a paschal lamb may be slaughtered for one who has been promised release from prison (M *Pesachim* 8.6a). It is notoriously difficult to date passages in the Mishnah, but this one probably originated early enough to represent what may have been a custom as early as the first century A.D.

7 According to a variant reading of Matt 27:16–17, the full name of Barabbas is "Jesus Barabbas." This reading was known to Origen but rejected for theological reasons. Cranfield (*Gospel of Mark*, in loc.) thinks it may be original in Matt 27:16–17 and, since Matthew is dependent on Mark, was originally present here. Its omission is explained by the reluctance of copyists to give to Barabbas the revered name Jesus. But Jesus was actually a common name among Jews.

K. *The Mocking of Jesus*

15:16–20

> ¹⁶The soldiers led Jesus away into the palace (that is, the Praetorium) and called together the whole company of soldiers. ¹⁷They put a purple robe on him, then twisted together a crown of thorns and set it on him. ¹⁸And they began to call out to him, "Hail, king of the Jews!" ¹⁹Again and again they struck him on the head with a staff and spit on him. Falling on their knees, they paid homage to him. ²⁰And when they had mocked him, they took off the purple robe and put his own clothes on him. Then they led him out to crucify him.

16 The scourging of Jesus took place out in front of the palace of Herod and in the presence of all the people. Afterward Jesus was taken by the soldiers into the *aulē* ("palace," ordinarily "court," "courtyard"). NIV translates it "palace" because of Mark's explanatory clause—"that is, the Praetorium." It is used in 1 Maccabees 11:46 in this sense. Another possibility is that the courtyard (aulē), being the most public part of the Praetorium, "may well have been known by the Latin name of the whole" (Swete, p. 374). "Praetorium" is a Latin loan word in Greek. Used originally of a general's tent or the headquarters in a camp, here it designates the Roman governor's official residence. (For the identification of the Praetorium with Herod's palace, see commentary at 15:1.) The soldiers who led Jesus into the palace and then mocked and manhandled him were a part of the auxiliary troops Pilate had brought up to Jerusalem from Caesarea. They were non-Jews recruited from Palestine and other parts of the empire. Mark says the whole company (speira) took part in their perverted humor. Since a speira (the tenth part of a legion) consisted of two hundred to six hundred men, the word is probably used loosely here by Mark to include only the soldiers immediately at hand.

17–18 The soldiers thought it was a great joke that this gentle Jew claimed to be a king. So they took a purple robe and threw it across his shredded and bleeding back (v.17). It was probably a scarlet military cloak (cf. Matt 27:28), "a cast-off and faded rag, but with color enough left in it to suggest the royal purple" (Swete, p. 375). The crown was made of some kind of prickly plant such as abounds in Palestine. This they pressed into his scalp. Again there must have been copious bleeding because the scalp is one of the most vascular areas of the body. The royal purple and the crown were symbols of royalty. The soldiers decked him out with these for the purpose of making sport of him. "Hail, king of the Jews!" (v.18) is a parody of "Hail, Emperor Caesar!"

19 The mocking was followed by further physical violence. The blows hitting his head from the staff drove the thorns more deeply into Jesus' scalp and caused even more profuse bleeding. Matthew (27:29) says that they first forced Jesus to hold the staff as a mock scepter. They also kept spitting (Gr. imperfect tense) on him, and the climax came when they mockingly fell on their knees and paid homage to him. It is difficult to imagine a greater demonstration of insensitivity and cruelty than the soldiers' treatment of Jesus.

20 At last, tiring of their sadism, the soldiers tore the robe from Jesus' back. The fabric had probably stuck to the clots of blood and serum in the wounds. Thus when it was callously ripped off him, it caused excruciating pain, just as when a bandage is carelessly removed. Jesus' own clothes were now put back on him. The custom was for men condemned to death by crucifixion to be led naked to the place of execution and to be flogged on the way (Jos. Antiq. XIX, 269 [iv.5]). Jesus, however, had already been scourged and was too weak to have survived an additional brutal beating.

In John's account Pilate makes one final appeal to the crowd (19:4–16). He brings Jesus, badly beaten and with blood streaming down his face, before them and says, "Here is the man!" (v.5). Perhaps he wanted to appeal to their sympathy. But Satan had possessed them. The scourging was not enough. "Crucify him!" they shouted. John says that Pilate wanted to set Jesus free, but the Jews' warning that if he let Jesus go he was no friend of Caesar forced his hand. His political future was at stake. So Pilate acquiesced to their bloodthirsty cries.

L. *The Crucifixion*

15:21-32

21A certain man from Cyrene, Simon, the father of Alexander and Rufus, was passing by on his way in from the country, and they forced him to carry the cross. 22They brought Jesus to the place called Golgotha (which means The Place of the Skull). 23Then they offered him wine mixed with myrrh, but he did not take it. 24And they crucified him. Dividing up his clothes, they cast lots to see what each would get.

25It was the third hour when they crucified him. 26The written notice of the charge against him read: THE KING OF THE JEWS. 27They crucified two robbers with him, one on his right and one on his left. 29Those who passed by hurled insults at him, shaking their heads and saying, "So! You who are going to destroy the temple and build it in three days, 30come down from the cross and save yourself!"

31In the same way the chief priests and the teachers of the law mocked him among themselves. "He saved others," they said, "but he can't save himself! 32Let this Christ, this King of Israel, come down now from the cross, that we may see and believe." Those crucified with him also heaped insults on him.

21 Men condemned to die by crucifixion were customarily required to carry the heavy wooden crosspiece (*patibulum*), on which they were to be nailed, to the place of execution. Jesus started out carrying his cross (John 19:17), but it proved too much for him. The *patibulum* usually weighed thirty or forty pounds and was usually strapped across the shoulders. One can hardly imagine the pain caused by the rough heavy beam pressing into the lacerated skin and muscles of Jesus' shoulders. The scourging and loss of blood had so weakened him that he could not go on carrying the heavy crossbeam. So apparently at random they apprehended one Simon of Cyrene and forced him into service. Since Cyrene (in North Africa) had a large Jewish population, Simon was no doubt a Jew (not an African black as some have suggested) and was on his way to the city of Jerusalem for the Passover celebration. Mark probably mentions Simon's two sons Alexander and Rufus because they were known to the Roman church (cf. Rom 16:13).

22 Both Roman and Jewish executions were customarily performed outside the city. John (19:20) says that the place where Jesus was crucified was near the city, but it was outside the city wall. In the first century A.D., as closely as it can now be determined, the northern wall of the city ran northward from Herod's palace, turned sharply to the east past Golgotha, which was just west of it, and then went on to the Fortress of Antonia.

"Golgotha" is a slightly modified transliteration of the Aramaic word for skull, whereas the name "Calvary" is derived from the Vulgate translation "*Calvariae locus*," *calva* being the Latin word for skull. How this site was named Golgotha is not known. The common conjecture is that the place looked like a skull. The traditional site is located inside the famous Church of the Holy Sepulchre, which is within the present walls of the city.

Recent archaeological excavations tend to support the historicity of the traditional site. For example, Kathleen Kenyon's excavations in 1967 discovered a rock quarry on the south side of the church. Rock quarries were seldom found inside the walls of cities simply because the crowded conditions made it impossible to work them. Also, just west of the Church of the Holy Sepulchre, tombs have been discovered. Since burials were not allowed within the city walls, this also supports the Church of the Holy Sepulchre site. Gordon's Calvary, located on a skull-shaped knoll outside the present northern wall of the city and between the Damascus and Herod gates, though a major tourist attraction, has no historical support as the site of the crucifixion of Jesus.

23 Jesus was offered wine mixed with myrrh when he arrived at the place of execution. Mark does not identify who it was that offered Jesus the drink. Lane (p. 564) thinks it may have been the women of Jerusalem who provided a narcotic drink to condemned criminals in order to deaden the pain (cf. b *Sanhedrin* 43a). Michaelis (*TDNT*, 7:457–59) thinks Jesus, because he was weak and exhausted, was offered soldier's wine by the executioner. In any case it must have been meant to deaden the pain. Jesus refused the drink, choosing rather to experience the terrible sufferings of the Crucifixion with his senses intact.

24 Mark simply says, "And they crucified him." What incredible restraint! Especially when one considers that crucifixion was, as Cicero said, "the cruelest and most hideous punishment possible" (*In Verrem* 5.64.165). What took place physically is vividly described by Davis ("Crucifixion of Jesus," pp. 186–87).

> Simon is ordered to place the patibulum on the ground and Jesus is quickly thrown backwards with His shoulders against the wood. The legionnaire feels for the depression at the front of the wrist. He drives a heavy, square, wrought-iron nail through the wrist and deep into the wood. Quickly, he moves to the other side and repeats the action, being careful not to pull the arms too tightly, but to allow some flexion and movement. The patibulum is then lifted in place at the top of the stipes [the vertical beam]. . . .
>
> The left foot is pressed backward against the right foot, and with both feet extended, toes down, a nail is driven through the arch of each, leaving the knees moderately flexed. The Victim is now crucified. As He slowly sags down with more weight on the nails in the wrists, excruciating, fiery pain shoots along the fingers and up the arms to explode in the brain—the nails in the wrists are putting pressure on the median nerves. As He pushes Himself upward to avoid this stretching torment, He places His full weight on the nail through His feet. Again there is the searing agony of the nail tearing through the nerves between the metatarsal bones of the feet.
>
> At this point, another phenomenon occurs. As the arms fatigue, great waves of cramps sweep over the muscles, knotting them in deep, relentless, throbbing pain. With these cramps comes the inability to push Himself upward. . . . Air can be drawn into the lungs, but cannot be exhaled. Jesus fights to raise Himself in order to get even one small breath. Finally carbon dioxide builds up in the lungs and in the blood stream and the cramps partially subside. Spasmodically He is able to push Himself upward to exhale and bring in the life-giving oxygen. . . .
>
> Hours of this limitless pain, cycles of twisting, joint-rending cramps, intermittent partial asphyxiation, searing pain as tissue is torn from His lacerated back as He moves up and down against the rough timber: Then another agony begins. A deep crushing pain deep in the chest as the pericardium slowly fills with serum and begins to compress the heart. . . .
>
> It is now almost over—the loss of tissue fluids has reached a critical level—the compressed heart is struggling to pump heavy, thick, sluggish blood into the tissues—the tortured lungs are making a frantic effort to gasp in small gulps of air. . . .

> The body of Jesus is now in extremis, and He can feel the chill of death creeping through His tissues. . . .
>
> His mission of atonement has been completed. Finally he can allow His body to die.

All this Mark describes with the words "And they crucified him"!

Death by crucifixion could come very slowly, especially if the victim was tied (as sometimes happened) instead of nailed to the cross. Nailing caused loss of blood and this hastened death. The physical condition of the victim and the severity of the scourging also affected the length of survival. If the victim was slow in dying, his legs would be broken by a club. Jesus had been so brutally beaten that when the soldiers came to him to see whether they would have to break his legs, he was dead already (cf. John 19:31–33).

Jesus' clothes had been removed when he was nailed to the cross. They were now in the hands of the soldiers who proceeded to while away their time by casting lots for them (cf. Ps 22:18).

25 Mark says that Jesus was crucified the third hour, i.e., 9:00 A.M. This conflicts with John's account, which says that the trial before Pilate was not quite over by the sixth hour, i.e., 12:00 noon, therefore implying that the Crucifixion took place later still. Several solutions to this difficult problem have been suggested.

1. John was using Roman time. Thus the sixth hour was 6:00 A.M., not 12:00 noon; and the three-hour interval was taken up with the scourging, mocking, and preparations for the Crucifixion.

2. An early copyist has confused a Greek Γ—the letter that stands for three—with a ϝ—the letter that stands for six.

3. Verse 25 is a gloss; i.e., it was added by an early copyist. Of these the first seems to be a desperate attempt at harmonization since there is no evidence whatever for it; the third is a possibility since both Matthew and Luke do not include this verse, and they ordinarily follow Mark's indications of time in the passion narrative; the second seems most likely since such a copyist error could very easily have occurred.

26 A wooden board stating the specific charge against the condemned man was commonly fastened on the cross above his head. Over Jesus' head was placed the inscription "THE KING OF THE JEWS." None of the Gospels agree on the precise wording of the inscription, but they all assert that Jesus was crucified on the charge of claiming to be the King of the Jews. For the Romans, this was high treason.

27 The two criminals crucified on either side of Jesus are called *lēstas*, a word normally meaning "robbers." Here, however, it means "insurrectionists" (cf. 14:48, where the NIV has "Am I leading a rebellion"). They had probably been a part of the same insurrection Barabbas was involved in (cf. 15:7) and had been sentenced at the same time as Jesus. They seemed to know that the charges against him were false (cf. Luke 23:41). His placement in the middle, between the two criminals, was probably to mock him as the insurrectionist par excellence. Rengstorf points out that the crucifixion of Jesus by the Jews was a decision "against His Messianism and in favour of that of the Zealots, and which thus elected war against Rome and its own crucifixion instead of the peace which the Messiah of God brings. . . . How far this decision affected the judgment of Judaism on Him is nowhere more clearly seen than when Celsus calls Jesus a λῃστής [lēstēs, 'insurrectionist'] and thus seeks to dismiss Him as a false Messiah" (TDNT, 4:262).

28 This verse (NIV mg.) does not appear in the most ancient MSS of the NT. Most textual critics consider it an interpolation from Luke 22:37 (quoting Isa 53:12), where it is authentic. Mark does not usually point out OT fulfillment.

29–30 It is evident from these verses that the Crucifixion took place in a public area, perhaps beside a thoroughfare where people were coming and going. As they passed by, they took the opportunity to vent their hostility on Jesus (v.29). Their words echo the OT (cf. Lam 2:15 and esp. Ps 22:7). They particularly remembered the charge made against him of destroying and rebuilding the temple (cf. 14:58), and they throw that into his teeth. Surely if he could destroy and rebuild the temple, he could save himself now (v.30)! Swete (p. 383) comments: "The jest was the harder to endure since it appealed to a consciousness of power held back only by the self-restraint of a sacrificed will." Here, obviously, "save" means physical deliverance.

31–32 The chief priests and teachers of the law were also there to add their mockery to that of the passersby (v.31). This must have been especially difficult for Jesus to bear. As the spiritual leaders of the people, they should have championed Jesus' cause; instead, they had condemned him and demanded his crucifixion. One would have thought that would have satisfied them. But their shriveled souls demanded more: they "mocked him among themselves," no doubt within the hearing of Jesus. Yet as they did, they unconsciously bore witness to his miraculous powers: "He saved others"—a reference to his healing miracles and perhaps the raising of Lazarus. Their statement "he can't save himself" is both false and true. In the sense they meant it—he does not have the power—it is false. But in a profound sense, if Jesus was to fulfill his messianic mission, he could not save himself. His death was necessary for man's redemption.

The epithet "This Christ, this King of Israel" is full of derision (v.32). Pilate had placed over Jesus the title "King of the Jews." But the religious leaders referred to him as "King of Israel," mocking his claim to be the King of the people of God. And they tauntingly demanded a demonstration of his power—"come down from the cross, that we may see and believe." Gould (p. 293) paraphrases as follows: "A crucified Messiah, forsooth! Let us hear no more of it. If he is really the Messianic King, let him use his Messianic power, and deliver himself from his ridiculous position by coming down from the cross. He wants us to believe in him and here is an easy way to bring that about."

Jesus also had to bear the insults of the criminals who were crucified on either side of him.

M. *The Death of Jesus*

15:33–41

> ³³At the sixth hour darkness came over the whole land until the ninth hour. ³⁴And at the ninth hour Jesus cried out in a loud voice, *"Eloi, Eloi, lama sabachthani?"*—which means, "My God, my God, why have you forsaken me?"
> ³⁵When some of those standing near heard this, they said, "Listen, he's calling Elijah."

³⁶One man ran, filled a sponge with wine vinegar, put it on a stick, and offered it to Jesus to drink. "Now leave him alone. Let's see if Elijah comes to take him down," he said.

³⁷With a loud cry, Jesus breathed his last.

³⁸The curtain of the temple was torn in two from top to bottom. ³⁹And when the centurion, who stood there in front of Jesus, heard his cry and saw how he died, he said, "Surely this man was the Son of God!"

⁴⁰Some women were watching from a distance. Among them were Mary Magdalene, Mary the mother of James the younger and of Joses, and Salome. ⁴¹In Galilee these women had followed him and cared for his needs. Many other women who had come up with him to Jerusalem were also there.

33 All three synoptic Gospels report the darkness; none say what caused it. It hardly could have been an eclipse of the sun at the time of the Passover full moon. Perhaps it was dark clouds obscuring the sun or a black sirocco—a wind that comes in from the desert, not uncommon in Jerusalem in the month of April. Whatever its cause, it lasted for three hours (12:00 M. to 3:00 P.M.) and was "over the whole land," i.e. Judah, not the whole earth. There can be little doubt that Mark understood the darkness as God's supernatural act and associated it with his judgment.

34 This is the only one of Jesus' seven words from the cross Mark records. The meaning of the cry of agony "My God, my God, why have you forsaken me?" lies beyond human comprehension. Taylor (p. 549) remarks: "The depths of the saying are too deep to be plumbed, but the least inadequate interpretations are those which find in it a sense of desolation in which Jesus felt the horror of sin so deeply that for a time the closeness of His communion with the Father was obscured."

Some have felt that Jesus' cry of dereliction shows his utter agony in tasting for us the very essence of hell, which is separation from God. Elizabeth Barrett Browning in her poem "Cowper's Grave" has powerfully expressed the meaning of that cry:

> Deserted! God could separate from his own essence rather;
> And Adam's sins have swept between the righteous Son and Father.
> Yea, once, Immanuel's orphan'd cry his universe hath shaken—
> It went up single, echoless, "My God, I am forsaken!"

"The orphan'd cry" of Jesus reflects something of the depth of meaning of Paul's statement in 2 Corinthians 5:21: "God made him who had no sin to be sin for us."

Interpretations that suggest that Jesus began to recite Psalm 22 with the intent of reciting the entire psalm, which ends on a note of triumph, but died before getting past v.1 are desperate attempts to dodge the reality of Jesus' forsakenness.

Matthew's version of Jesus' cry is a mixture of Hebrew and Greek with the important words in Hebrew. Jesus probably spoke the words in Hebrew, and they were in Hebrew in the earlier stage of the tradition; but, according to Nineham (p. 429), this was "changed by someone who knew that Aramaic was the language normally spoken in Jesus' time."

35 The ignorant and heartless bystanders mistook the first words of Jesus' cry *"Eloi, Eloi"* ("My God, my God") to be a cry for Elijah. (Or, instead of mistaking *"Eloi"* for "Elijah," were they indulging in a cruel joke?) Elijah was regarded as the forerunner and helper of the Messiah and was also regarded as a deliverer of those in trouble. So tauntingly they said, "Listen, he's calling Elijah."

36 Mark does not identify the person who went to get the wine vinegar. If the drink referred to is the *posca*, the sour wine drunk by laborers and soldiers, then it was probably one of the soldiers who got it. A sponge was filled with this wine vinegar and placed around the tip of a stick (*hyssōp* [John 19:29]) and held up to Jesus' lips so that he could suck the liquid from it. NIV translates *aphete* "Now leave him alone." But the equally valid rendering "Let me alone" seems more in keeping with the context. Apparently some of the bystanders wanted to prevent the soldier from giving the wine vinegar to Jesus. He insisted on doing it, however, and then added his own taunt: "Let's see if Elijah comes to take him down." Gould's paraphrase (p. 295) of the last part of this verse catches its meaning: "Let me give him this, and so prolong his life, and then we shall get an opportunity to see whether Elijah comes to help him or not."

37 After six hours of torture, Jesus cried out and died. Usually those who were crucified took long to die (cf. 15:44, where Pilate expresses surprise on hearing that Jesus had already died). The loud cry of Jesus is unusual because victims of crucifixion usually had no strength left, especially when near death. But Jesus' death was no ordinary one, nor was his shout the last gasp of a dying man. It was a shout of victory that anticipated the triumph of the Resurrection.

38 All the synoptic writers record this event. The curtain referred to was the one that separated the Holy Place from the Most Holy Place in the temple. It was torn from the top to the bottom. Mark must have regarded this as a supernatural act. Although he does not assign theological significance to it, later Christian writers so interpreted it (cf. Heb 9:1–14; 10:19–22). This information was known originally only to the priests who alone were permitted entrance into the Holy Place, but it probably became part of the tradition through the report of priests who were subsequently converted to Christianity (cf. Acts 6:7). Perhaps the experience of witnessing the tearing of the curtain in the temple prepared their hearts for receiving Jesus Christ as their Savior.

39 The Roman centurion in command of the detachment of soldiers at the cross had witnessed the scourging, mocking, spitting, crucifixion, wagging of heads, and now heard Jesus' last cry and watched him die. The soldier was deeply impressed. He had never seen anything like this before! Although it is unlikely that his statement "Surely this man was the Son of God" is to be taken in its full theological sense, yet it is the word of a man deeply moved and drawn to the person of the Righteous Sufferer on the cross (cf. Luke 23:47, where the centurion says, "Surely this was a righteous man"). In view of Mark's opening words—"The beginning of the gospel about Jesus Christ, the Son of God" (1:1)—the confession of the centurion at the climax of Jesus' passion takes on added significance. Whether or not the centurion realized the full import of his words, they were for Mark a profoundly true statement of the identity of the Man on the cross.

40–41 Women too were present at the Crucifixion, but they kept their distance (v.40). Out of the many who had come up to Jerusalem with Jesus from Galilee, Mark identifies three of the group of women who were "watching from a distance"— Mary Magdalene; Mary the mother of James the younger and Joses; and Salome, the wife of Zebedee and mother of James and John. Mary Magdalene (i.e., Mary of

Magdala, a fishing village on the west shore of the Sea of Galilee), is mentioned only here in Mark. From Luke 8:2, however, we learn that Jesus had cast seven demons out of her. The second Mary is designated as the "mother of James the younger and Joses." Although little is known about her, her sons were apparently well known in the early church. She is referred to as the "mother of Joses" in 15:47 and the "mother of James" in 16:1. In the NIV James is described as "the younger." The Greek adjective *mikros* can also mean "the less," i.e., "the smaller," "less important," or "less known." It is difficult to decide which meaning applies here. The third woman Mark mentions here is Salome, Zebedee's wife and the mother of James and John (cf. Matt 27:56). These three women had been with Jesus in Galilee (v.41) and had served him there. They had come up to Jerusalem, along with many other women also, especially to be with him and to serve him.

Notes

39 Although there is no definite article ὁ (*ho*, "the") before υἱὸς (*huios*, "son") in the centurion's confession, NIV translates it "Surely this man was *the* Son of God" (emphasis mine) because a definite predicate noun that precedes the verb usually does not have the article (cf. John 1:1).

N. *The Burial of Jesus*

15:42–47

⁴²It was Preparation Day (that is, the day before the Sabbath). So as evening approached, ⁴³Joseph of Arimathea, a prominent member of the Council, who was himself waiting for the kingdom of God, went boldly to Pilate and asked for Jesus' body. ⁴⁴Pilate was surprised to hear that he was already dead. Summoning the centurion, he asked him if Jesus had already died. ⁴⁵When he learned from the centurion that it was so, he gave the body to Joseph. ⁴⁶So Joseph bought some linen cloth, took down the body, wrapped it in the linen, and placed it in a tomb cut out of rock. Then he rolled a stone against the entrance of the tomb. ⁴⁷Mary Magdalene and Mary the mother of Joses saw where he was laid.

42–43 Preparation Day was the name given to the day before a festival or a Sabbath (v.42). Here it refers to the day before the Sabbath, as Mark explains for the benefit of his Gentile readers. Since the Jewish Sabbath began at sundown, and it was now late in the afternoon (probably around 4:00 P.M.), there was not much time to take Jesus' body down from the cross. This is apparently what spurred Joseph of Arimathea into action. (Arimathea is probably to be identified with Ramathaim-Zophim, a village in the hill country of Ephraim about twenty miles north of Jerusalem. It was the birthplace of Samuel [1 Sam 1:1].)

Joseph's request for the body of Jesus (v.43) is described by Mark as a bold act, as indeed it was, because it would inevitably have identified him with Jesus and his followers. For a man in Joseph's position ("a prominent member of the Council," i.e., Sanhedrin), such an act could have serious consequences. But he was a pious man who, according to Luke, had not consented in the decision and action of the council (Luke 23:51); and he "was himself waiting for the kingdom of God."

Ordinarily a relative or close friend would have requested the body, but apparently the mother of Jesus was so distraught that she was incapacitated; and all of Jesus' disciples but John had fled. There is no evidence that Jesus' brothers and sisters were in Jerusalem at the time of the Crucifixion.

44–45 Pilate was surprised to hear that Jesus had already died (v.44) because death usually came much more slowly to crucified victims than it had to Jesus. Only after he received confirmation of Jesus' death from the centurion was Pilate willing to turn Jesus' body over to Joseph (v.45). Had it not been for this loving act of Joseph, Jesus' body would have been buried in a common criminal's grave. For Pilate to release the body of a condemned criminal—especially one condemned of high treason—to someone other than a relative was highly unusual. It suggests that Pilate did not take seriously the charge of high treason against Jesus and had only pronounced sentence against him because of political expediency. This action of Pilate is consistent with Mark's account (15:1–15) of Jesus' trial before Pilate.

46 Mark does not mention anyone assisting Joseph in the actions described here. He must, however, have had help in removing the body from the cross, preparing it for burial, and carrying it to the place of burial. Matthew 27:57 describes Joseph as being rich (cf. Isa 53:9); so he doubtless had servants to help him. Moreover John says that Nicodemus, who had previously come to Jesus at night, helped Joseph and supplied some of the spices used in the preparation of the body for burial (John 19:39). Although no specific mention is made of washing the blood-soaked body, this important Jewish rite must have been performed before the body was wrapped for burial in the linen cloths. After being properly prepared for burial (cf. John 19:40), it was placed in "a tomb cut out of rock." Matthew tells us that the tomb belonged to Joseph and that it was new; i.e., it had not been used before (Matt 27:60; cf. John 19:41).

The location of the tomb was in a garden very near the site of the Crucifixion (John 19:41). Archaeological excavation has shown that the traditional site of the burial of Jesus (Church of the Holy Sepulchre in Jerusalem) was a cemetery during the first century A.D. Tombs cut out of the rock were closed by rolling a stone against the entrance. This could be either a flat stone disc that rolled in a sloped channel or simply a large rock that could be rolled in front of the opening. (For an interesting discussion of what kind of stone is meant, see Dalman, *Sacred Sites*, pp. 374ff.)

47 The two Marys mentioned in 15:40 as being witnesses of the Crucifixion were also present at Jesus' burial. Mark mentions this in anticipation of 16:1 and particularly 16:5. The two women could identify the tomb on Sunday morning because they had been present at the burial.

O. The Resurrection

16:1–8

> ¹When the Sabbath was over, Mary Magdalene, Mary the mother of James, and Salome bought spices so that they might go to anoint Jesus' body. ²Very

early on the first day of the week, just after sunrise, they were on their way to the tomb ³and they asked each other, "Who will roll the stone away from the entrance of the tomb?"

⁴But when they looked up, they saw that the stone, which was very large, had been rolled away. ⁵As they entered the tomb, they saw a young man dressed in a white robe sitting on the right side, and they were alarmed.

⁶"Don't be alarmed," he said. "You are looking for Jesus the Nazarene, who was crucified. He has risen! He is not here. See the place where they laid him. ⁷But go, tell his disciples and Peter, 'He is going ahead of you into Galilee. There you will see him, just as he told you.' "

⁸Trembling and bewildered, the women went out and fled from the tomb. They said nothing to anyone, because they were afraid.

The climax to Mark's Gospel is the Resurrection. Without it the life and death of Jesus, though noble and admirable, are nonetheless overwhelmingly tragic events. With it Jesus is declared to be the Son of God with power (Rom 1:4), and the disciples are transformed from lethargic and defeated followers into the flaming witnesses of the Book of Acts. The Good News about Jesus Christ is that God, by the resurrection of Jesus, defeated sin, death, and hell. It was this message that lay at the heart of the apostolic preaching.

All four Gospels tell the story of the Resurrection and do so with the same dignity and restraint they use in telling the story of the Crucifixion. As the Crucifixion was a historical event—viz., something that actually happened at a specific time and place—so the tomb in which Jesus had been placed on Friday afternoon was actually found to be empty on the following Sunday morning. To this fact all four Evangelists bear witness. The explanation of the historical event, unavailable to men apart from divine revelation, is given by the young man (his white robe identifies him as an angelic being): "He has risen!" This word of revelation, the truth of the resurrection of Jesus, is the focal point in all four gospel accounts. Any claim that the Resurrection was a fabrication (cf. Matt 27:62–65) or a delusion is implicitly denied.

1 When the Sabbath was over (about 6:00 P.M. Saturday evening), the three women mentioned at the Crucifixion (15:40), two of whom were also present at Jesus' burial (15:47), bought aromatic oils to anoint the body of Jesus. These were apparently in addition to the spices and perfumes that were prepared before the Sabbath began (cf. Luke 23:56). The anointing was not for the purpose of preserving the body (embalming was not practiced by the Jews) but was a single act of love and devotion probably meant to reduce the stench of the decomposing body. Palestine's hot climate causes corpses to decay rapidly. Thus the action of the women seems strange. Perhaps they thought that the coolness of the tomb would prevent the decomposition process from taking place as rapidly as it otherwise would. In any case, as Cranfield (*Gospel of Mark*, p. 464) says, their action "is not incredible, since love often prompts people to do what from a practical point of view is useless."

2 Since it would have been too dark Saturday night after the end of the Sabbath to go to the tomb, the women waited till Sunday morning. The expressions *lian prōi* ("very early") and *anateilantos tou hēliou* ("just after sunrise") present a problem, evidenced by the variation of readings that appear in the MS tradition. Ordinarily, "very early" would refer to the period before 6:00 A.M., when it would still be dark

(cf. John 20:1); but used here with the expression "just after sunrise," it must mean the period of time immediately after the sun rose on Sunday morning.

3 As the women walked to the tomb, their chief concern was with the heavy stone they knew had been rolled in front of the opening of the tomb (cf. 15:46–47). Of the sealing of the tomb or the posting of the Roman guard, they knew nothing (cf. Matt 27:62–66). Their concern with moving the stone was a real one because, no matter what kind of stone it was, it would have been difficult to move. A circular stone, though relatively easy to put in place since usually it was set in a sloped track, once established in place was very difficult to remove. It would either have to be rolled back up the incline or lifted out of the groove and then removed. Any other kind of stone placed in front of the tomb's entrance would be as difficult or even more difficult to remove.

4–5 Mark makes no attempt to explain how the stone was removed. He does, however, say that it was very large and leaves the matter there (v.4). Once inside the tomb, the women saw a young man (*neaniskos*) dressed in a white robe (v.5). His dress suggests an angel, and though Mark does not explicitly identify him as such, Matthew 28:2 does. Cranfield's note on angels is worth repeating:

> A protest must be made against the widespread tendency to dismiss the angels as mere pious fancy. . . . It may be suggested that the purpose of the angel's presence at the tomb was to be the link between the actual event of the Resurrection and the women. Human eyes were not permitted to see the event of the Resurrection itself. But the angels as the constant witnesses of God's action saw it. So the angel's word to the women, "He is risen", is, as it were, the mirror in which men were allowed to see the reflection of this eschatological event. (*Gospel of Mark*, pp. 465–66)

The reaction of the women to the angel was what one would expect: "They were dumbfounded" (NEB)—*exethambēthēsan*, a strong verb used only by Mark in the NT.

6 The women's fright was calmed by words of reassurance: "Don't be alarmed." The angel knew whom they were seeking. These were Galilean women, and the mention of Jesus of Nazareth struck a familiar note in their memories. The angel then spoke the revelatory word "He has risen!" and invited them to see the evidence of the empty tomb. An empty tomb, however, only invites the question What happened to the body of Jesus? There needed to be a word from God to interpret the meaning of the empty tomb, and the angel was God's gracious provision. The explanation is Resurrection! Across the centuries many other explanations have been proposed: the body of Jesus was stolen; the women came to the wrong tomb; Jesus did not actually die on the cross but walked out of the tomb; etc. Some of them have had success with skeptics. But the only adequate explanation is still what the angel said to the women who were at the tomb on the first Easter morning: "He has risen!"

7 "Go, tell his disciples and Peter" reveals how gracious was the provision God made for Peter's special need through the word of the angel. Peter is singled out because he had denied Jesus (14:66–72) and now needed reassurance that he was not excluded from the company of the disciples. Jesus had forgiven and restored him. Not only had Jesus predicted the scattering of the sheep (14:27) but also their regathering in Galilee (14:28). What was the purpose of the meeting in Galilee? Jesus had done a large part of his work in Galilee. Perhaps he wanted to meet not only with the disciples but with the community of believers there to give them his last instructions before his ascension.

Galilee was a fitting place for the launching of a Gentile mission. The contention of some scholars (e.g., Lohmeyer, Marxsen) that the reference to Galilee in 14:28 and here is to the Parousia (the Second Coming) and not to a postresurrection appearance of Jesus has little to support it and has been largely rejected. Meye (*Jesus and the Twelve*, pp. 80–87) suggests that the purpose of the reunion in Galilee was to fulfill Jesus' promise in 1:17 to make the disciples fishers of men.

8 The confrontation with the angel proved to be too much for the women. They fled "trembling and bewildered." It was a natural and to-be-expected reaction. Only Mark tells us, "They said nothing to anyone," which probably means that they were so frightened and confused that they were at first silent. After they had collected their wits, they did a lot of talking (cf. Matt 28:8; Luke 24:9).

If the Gospel of Mark ends with 16:8, as some believe, Mark intentionally emphasizes the mystery and awesomeness of the Resurrection. The women were afraid because God's eschatological action in the resurrection of his Son had been revealed to them, an event Mark understood to be the climax of all God's saving acts and the inauguration of the time of the End.

Notes

2 In D ἀνατέλλοντος (*anatellontos*, "while [the sun] was rising") in place of ἀνατείλαντος (*anateilantos*, "after [the sun] rose") solves the temporal problem but is obviously a copyist's emendation.

3 k (Codex Bobiensis) has a gloss to this verse that is an attempt to describe how the Resurrection actually took place: "Suddenly at the third hour of the day there was darkness over the whole earth, and angels descended from heaven, and rising in the splendor of the living God they ascended together with him, and immediately it was light." Another early attempt to describe the Resurrection is found in the pseudepigraphical Gospel of Peter (35–44).

P. *The Longer Ending—The Appearances and Ascension of Jesus*

16:9–20

> [9]When Jesus rose early on the first day of the week, he appeared first to Mary Magdalene, out of whom he had driven seven demons. [10]She went and told those who had been with him and who were mourning and weeping. [11]When they heard that Jesus was alive and that she had seen him, they did not believe it.
>
> [12]Afterward Jesus appeared in a different form to two of them while they were walking in the country. [13]These returned and reported it to the rest; but they did not believe them either.

> ¹⁴Later Jesus appeared to the Eleven as they were eating; he rebuked them for their lack of faith and their stubborn refusal to believe those who had seen him after he had risen.
> ¹⁵He said to them, "Go into all the world and preach the good news to all creation. ¹⁶Whoever believes and is baptized will be saved, but whoever does not believe will be condemned. ¹⁷And these signs will accompany those who believe: In my name they will drive out demons; they will speak in new tongues; ¹⁸they will pick up snakes with their hands; and when they drink deadly poison, it will not hurt them at all; they will place their hands on sick people, and they will get well."
> ¹⁹After the Lord Jesus had spoken to them, he was taken up into heaven and he sat at the right hand of God. ²⁰Then the disciples went out and preached everywhere, and the Lord worked with them and confirmed his word by the signs that accompanied it.

There are four sections of the Longer Ending: (1) the appearance to Mary Magdalene (vv.9–11); (2) the appearance to the two men (vv.12–13); (3) the appearance to the Eleven and the Great Commission (vv.14–18); and (4) the Ascension, session, and the disciples' response (vv.19–20). A discussion of the problem of the authenticity of this ending follows the commentary on vv.9–20.

9 The break in the continuity of the narrative seems to indicate that vv.9–20 were not originally a part of Mark's Gospel but are rather a summary of postresurrection appearances of Jesus composed independently. The Greek text of this verse has no subject (it is supplied for clarification by NIV), as if Jesus, not Mary, had just been mentioned. Also, Mary Magdalene is mentioned for the fourth time (cf. 15:40, 47; 16:1). It is strange, assuming 16:9 to be part of Mark's original Gospel, that the detail "out of whom he had driven seven demons" is for the first time mentioned here.

10–11 Mary carried out the command of the angel given in 16:7. She found the disciples in a state of mourning (v.10). While the people of Jerusalem were celebrating the Passover and the Feast of Unleavened Bread, the disciples were weeping, but not for long. Her witness to them was that Jesus was alive, and she knew it to be so because she had seen him. The reluctance of the disciples to believe her is certainly understandable (v.11; cf. Matt 28:17; Luke 24:11). A resurrection is no ordinary event!

12–13 These verses are obviously a shortened account of the story of the two men on the way to Emmaus (cf. Luke 24:13–35). It adds nothing to Luke's account except the statement "but they did not believe them either" (v.13). The element of unbelief on the part of the disciples on hearing the report of the two men may represent a different tradition. It certainly is not dependent on Luke. Plummer (p. 372) comments: "The Apostles may have been allowed to hear of the Resurrection before seeing the risen Christ in order that they might know from personal experience what it was to have to depend upon the testimony of others, as would be the case with their converts."

14 Again the account in Luke (24:36–44) is briefly summarized. The rebuke Jesus gave his disciples is particularly severe—more severe, in fact, than any other rebuke he gives them elsewhere in the Gospels. Neither of the words used here, *apistia* ("without faith") and *sklērokardia* ("stubborn refusal to believe," "obtuseness") is ever used by Jesus of his disciples. Taylor (pp. 611–12) concludes that the rebuke "can be understood only by the supreme importance attached to the Resurrection by the writer, who has in mind the conditions of his day."

At this point in W (the Gr. MS Washingtonianus, also called Freer), the following interpolation occurs:

> And they excused themselves, saying, "This age of lawlessness and unbelief is under Satan, who does not allow the truth and power of God to prevail over the unclean things of the spirits. Therefore, reveal thy righteousness now"—thus they spoke to Christ. And Christ replied to them, "The term of years of Satan's power has been fulfilled, but other terrible things draw near. And for those who have sinned I was delivered over to death, that they may return to the truth and sin no more, in order that they may inherit the spiritual and incorruptible glory of righteousness which is in heaven."

This, of course, is clearly not a part of Mark's Gospel but was probably inserted at this point to tone down the severe condemnation of the disciples in v.14 and to provide a smoother transition to v.15.

15–16 The Great Commission given here seems to be an independent version of Matthew 28:18–20. The unusual scope of the preaching of the gospel is not new to Mark's Gospel. It is clearly anticipated in 14:9. Belief and baptism are so closely associated that they are conceived of as virtually a single act. The inward reception (belief) is immediately followed by the external act or witness to that faith (baptism). The result is salvation. Here the word has its eschatological sense. Refusal to believe results in judgment. One of the primary themes of this entire section (vv.9–20) is the importance of belief and the sinfulness of unbelief.

17–18 The promise of signs (v.17) is not limited to the apostles. They will accompany "those who believe." These include the converts of the apostles. The apostles had already been given power to exorcise demons; now this power was to be shared by other believers. Speaking in tongues is not mentioned elsewhere in the Gospels and seems to reflect a post-Pentecost situation. Luke 10:19 speaks of trampling on snakes but not of picking them up with one's hands (v.18; cf. Acts 28:3–6). The drinking of poison without harm is unknown in the NT. Anointing the sick with oil is mentioned in 6:13, but no laying on of hands by the apostles occurs in the Gospels. Paul, however, lays hands on Publius's sick father (cf. Acts 28:8). Superstitious use of this verse has given rise to the snake-handling and poison-drinking sects of Appalachia.

19–20 "After the Lord Jesus had spoken to them" (v.19) may refer to vv.15–18 or to some other occasion. Mark gives us no geographical or time references. The ascension and session of Jesus are stated in the simplest terms: "he was taken up into heaven and he sat at the right hand of God." The Ascension was predicted by Jesus (cf. 14:7) and witnessed by the apostles (cf. Acts 1:9); the session was a matter of faith but firmly believed and preached in the early church (cf. Acts 2:33–35; 7:56).

There is nothing like v.20 in any of the Gospels. It sounds more like a summary statement from the Book of Acts of the activities of the apostles.

Notes

9 In addition to the Longer Ending (vv. 9–20), a Shorter Ending has come down to us in the MS tradition. It reads as follows: "But they reported briefly to Peter and those with him all that they had been told. And after this Jesus himself sent out by means of them, from east to west, the sacred and imperishable proclamation of eternal salvation." The witnesses to this ending are four uncial MSS of the seventh, eighth, and ninth centuries (L Ψ 099 0112), Old Latin k, the margin of the Harclean Syriac, several Sahidic and Bohairic MSS, and a good number of Ethiopic MSS. All of them, except k, continue with vv. 9–20. Both the external and internal evidence are clearly against the authenticity of this ending.

The Ending of the Gospel of Mark

The Gospel of Mark has four different endings in the MS tradition. The Freer or Washingtonianus addition, which occurs after v. 14 in the Longer Ending, is clearly an interpolation intended to soften the severe condemnation of the disciples in v. 14. It has extremely limited external attestation (only one MS—W). The Shorter Ending, cited above in the note to v. 9, also has weak external evidence and seems to be either an attempt to provide an ending in itself (in only one MS, however, does it appear without vv. 9–20 following it) or to provide a smoother transition between v. 8 and v. 9. This leaves only two endings that have any significant claim to authenticity: (1) the ending that concludes the gospel with v. 8 and (2) the so-called Longer Ending (vv. 9–20).

1. *External Evidence*

(The material cited here is mainly from Metzger, *Textual Commentary*, pp. 122–26). Evidence for (1) above (i.e., the absence of vv. 9–20) is as follows: ℵ and B (the two oldest Gr. uncial MSS of the NT), the Old Latin codex Bobiensis, the Sinaitic Syriac MS, about one hundred Armenian MSS, and the two oldest Georgian MSS (A.D. 897 and A.D. 913). Neither Clement of Alexandria nor Origen show any knowledge of the existence of vv. 9–20. Almost all the Greek copies of Mark known to Eusebius and Jerome did not contain these verses. The original form of the Eusebian sections makes no provision for numbering sections beyond 16:8. Some MSS that include the verses have scribal notes stating that they are absent in older Greek copies, and in other Greek MSS the verses are marked with obeli or asterisks to indicate they are spurious.

In addition there is the evidence provided by those MSS and versions in which the Shorter Ending (followed by the Longer Ending) is found. Warfield rightly says: "The existence of the shorter conclusion . . . is *a fortiori* evidence against the longer one. For no one doubts that this shorter conclusion is a spurious invention of the scribes; but it would not have been invented, save to fill the blank." (B.B. Warfield, *An Introduction to the Textual Criticism of the New Testament* [New York: Whittaker, 1890], p. 200).

The Longer Ending is contained in the great majority of the MSS. This includes A C D K X W Δ Θ Π Ψ 099 0112 f¹³ 28 33 et al. Irenaeus and Tatian's Diatessaron are the earliest patristic witnesses for the inclusion. Justin Martyr is uncertain. The external evidence seems to indicate that the Longer Ending was in circulation by the middle of the second century and was probably composed in the first half of the same century.

2. Internal Evidence

(The evidence cited here is from Bratcher and Nida, pp. 519ff.)

a. *Vocabulary*. In the Nestle Greek text there are 101 different words in vv.9–16 (167 words totally). After disregarding unimportant words such as the definite article, connectives, proper names, etc., there remain 75 different significant words. Of these, 15 do not appear in Mark and 11 others are used in a sense different from Markan usage. This means that slightly over one-third of the words are "non-Markan." After due allowance is made for different subject matter requiring different vocabulary, it would seem that the marked difference in vocabulary between 16:9–20 and the rest of Mark's Gospel makes it difficult to believe that they both came from the same author.

b. *Style*. Here the argument against Markan authorship of vv.9–20 is even stronger. The connection between v.8 and and vv.9–20 is abrupt and awkward. Verse 9 begins with the masculine nominative participle *anastas,* which demands for its antecedent "he," i.e., Jesus; but the subject of the last sentence of v.8 is the women, not Jesus. Mary Magdalene is referred to as if she had never been mentioned before; yet she appears three times in the crucifixion, burial, and resurrection narratives that immediately precede. Also, the women who were commissioned in v.7 to go tell Peter and the disciples of Jesus' resurrection are not mentioned at all (except Mary Magdalene, and she in another capacity) in the Longer Ending. The angel at the tomb spoke of a postresurrection appearance in Galilee to the disciples, but Jesus' appearances are confined to Jerusalem and its immediate vicinity. All these factors weigh heavily against the Longer Ending. To this evidence should be added the words of Bratcher and Nida (p. 520): "The narrative is concise and barren, lacking the vivid and lifelike details so characteristic of Markan historical narrative."

3. Content

It is in the area of content that the most serious objections are found. The first has to do with the severe rebuke by Jesus of his disciples. Nothing like this is found in the rest of Mark's Gospel (see commentary at v.14). The second relates to the "signs" of vv.17–18.

> The bizarre promise of immunity from snakes and poisonous drinks is completely out of character with the person of Christ as revealed in the Gospel of Mark, the other Gospels and in the whole of the New Testament. Nowhere did Jesus exempt himself or his followers from the natural laws which govern this life, nor did he ever intimate that such exemptions would be given those who believe in him. That such miracles have in fact occasionally taken place is a matter of record; what is to be doubted is that the Lord should have promised them indiscriminately to all believers as part of the blessings which would have been bestowed upon them. (Bratcher and Nida, pp. 520–21)

External and especially internal evidence make it difficult to escape the conclusion that vv.9–20 were originally not a part of the Gospel of Mark.

One further question arises: Did Mark actually intend to end his Gospel at 16:8? If he did not, then either (1) the Gospel was never completed, or (2) the last page was lost before it was multiplied by copyists.

Although there are staunch supporters of the view that it was Mark's intention to end his Gospel with 16:8, this view does not adequately explain (1) why the early church felt so strongly its lack of completion, witnessed by the insertion of both the Shorter and Longer endings; (2) why a book that purports to be the "good news about Jesus Christ" should end with the women being afraid (even allowing for Mark's emphasis on the awesomeness and mystery of Christ's person); and (3) why there is no recorded fulfillment of Jesus' promised postresurrection appearance in Galilee to Peter and the other disciples (cf. 16:7).

Thus the best solution seems to be that Mark did write an ending to his Gospel but that it was lost in the early transmission of the text. The endings we now possess represent attempts by the church to supply what was obviously lacking.

LUKE

Walter L. Liefeld

LUKE

Introduction

Had modern methods of book publishing been available in the first century, the books of Luke and Acts might have been found standing side by side in paperback editions on a bookseller's shelf. Possibly they would have been bound together in one hardback volume. Though Acts has some characteristics of the ancient novel, this need not be understood as impugning its historical value. One can picture a Gentile reader going from adventure to adventure, delighting in the story of Paul's shipwreck and learning something of the gospel through reading the various speeches. Likewise the Gospel of Luke contains narratives and sayings of Jesus cast in a variety of literary forms. No doubt among its readers would have been the "God-fearers," those Gentiles who had already been convinced of Jewish monotheism and of Jewish ethical standards.[1] They, in turn, would have interested their friends in reading Luke-Acts.

1. Literary Genre

It is difficult for us today to know with what literary genre, if any, the first-century reader would have identified the Gospels. There has been much discussion of this in recent years. R.H. Gundry has evaluated the literature up to the early 1970s in "Recent Investigations into the Literary Genre 'Gospel.'"[2] More recently David E. Aune has provided an excellent discussion of some of the alleged first-century parallels to the Gospels, as well as a critical evaluation of twentieth-century

---

[1]See, however, Max Wilcox, "The God-Fearers in Acts-A Reconsideration," *Journal for the Study of the New Testament* 13 (1981): 102–22.

[2]In *New Dimensions in New Testament Study*, pp. 97–114. See also Frank E. Gaebelein, "The Bible as Literature," ZPEB, 3:944.

approaches, in his article "The Problem of Genre of the Gospels: A Critique of C.H. Talbert's *What Is a Gospel?* "[3]

2. Distinctive Features

Before proceeding further it will be helpful at least to recognize some of the distinctive features of Luke's Gospel, especially in comparison with other Gospels. Among these are Jesus' concern for all people, especially those who were social outcasts—the poor, women, and those who were known as "sinners"; Luke's universal scope; his alteration of some of the terminology of Mark to facilitate the understanding of Luke's readers—e.g., the Greek term for "lawyer" (*nomikos*) instead of the Hebrew term "scribe" (*grammateus*); an emphasis on Jesus' practical teaching (e.g., chs. 12 and 16 deal with finances); Luke's sense of purpose, fulfillment, and accomplishment; his sense of joy and praise to God for his saving and healing work; Jesus' strong call to discipleship; Jesus' dependence on the Holy Spirit and prayer; and many examples of the power of God.

In the first century, when pagans had not only long since turned from the traditional gods but had also wrestled unsuccessfully with issues of luck and fate and had turned to the false hopes of the so-called Eastern or mystery religions, such a narrative as Luke's doubtless had a genuine appeal. Here was a "Savior" who actually lived and cared about people. He was here among people; he was crucified and actually raised from the dead. And Luke tells all this with a conviction and verisimilitude that brought assurance to Theophilus and continues to bring assurance down to our day.

3. Authorship

The unique relation of Luke to Acts sets the authorship of Luke apart from the problem of the authorship of the other Gospels. The following facts are important: (1) both Luke and Acts are addressed to an individual named Theophilus (Luke 1:3; Acts 1:1); (2) Acts refers to a previous work (1:1), presumably Luke; (3) certain stylistic and structural characteristics, such as the use of chiasm and the device of focusing on particular individuals, are common to both books and point to a single author; and (4) not only do the two volumes have a number of themes in common, but some of these receive a distinctive emphasis in this third Gospel that are not found elsewhere in the NT. These things point to a common author.

The author of the Gospel indicated that he was a second-generation Christian who was in a position to investigate the traditions about Jesus. As for the Book of Acts, the author associated himself with Paul in the well-known "we passages" (Acts 16:10–17; 20:5–15; 21:1–18; 27:1–28:16). The use of the first person plural in the "we passages" certainly does not prove that Luke was the author of Acts, but it does accord with other data pointing in this direction.[4] Paul mentioned Luke as a

---

[3]In R.T. France and D. Wenham, edd., *Gospel Perspectives*, 2:9–60.

[4]See V.K. Robbins, "The We–Passages in Acts and Ancient Sea Voyages," *Biblical Research* 20 (1975): 5–18, for a negative assessment; R.N. Longenecker, "Acts," EBC, 9:235–38 in support of Lukan authorship.

companion in Colossians 4:14, Philemon 24, and 2 Timothy 4:11 (assuming a genuine tradition of Paul here).

The tradition of the early church is consistent in attributing the third Gospel to Luke. Thus the Muratorian Canon (c. A.D. 180) says, "The third book of the Gospel, according to Luke, Luke that physician, who after the ascension of Christ, when Paul had taken him with him as companion of his journey, composed in his own name on the basis of report." But even before this, the heretic Marcion (c. A.D. 135) acknowledged Luke as the author of the third Gospel. This tradition of authorship was continued by Irenaeus and successive writers.

As seen in the above quotation from the Muratorian Canon, tradition also held that Luke was a physician (cf. 4:14). In 1882 Hobart attempted to prove that Luke and Acts "were written by the same person, and that the writer was a medical man" (p. xxix). His study of the alleged medical language is informed, rich, and still useful; but it does not necessarily prove his point. Cadbury argued that though the terminology cited by Hobart was used by medical writers in the ancient world, others who were by no means physicians also used it.[5] Cadbury's work does not, of course, disprove that Luke was a physician, much less that he wrote Luke and Acts; but it does weaken the linguistic evidence for the former assumption.

Irenaeus not only attested to Luke's authorship of the Gospel but also said that Luke was Paul's "inseparable" companion (*Adversus Haereses* 3.14.1). While there were periods of time when Luke was not with Paul, their relationship was deep and lasting. Taking 2 Timothy 4:11 as a genuine comment of Paul's, only Luke was with him during his final imprisonment. Paul's comment in Colossians 4 leads us to assume Luke was a Gentile, because in vv.10–11 Paul listed several friends and said, "These are the only Jews among my fellow workers for the kingdom of God." Then he mentioned Luke (v.14). This, however, falls short of a direct statement that Luke was a Gentile. Some have held that he was a Jewish Christian, even (according to an early church tradition) one of the seventy-two disciples in Luke 10:1. The Semitic elements of style in Luke, especially in chapters 1–2 and in the Jerusalem narrative in Acts (chs. 1–15), might also suggest that he was a Jewish Christian. But as we shall note below, there are other possible reasons for these stylistic traits. There is a church tradition that Luke came from Antioch in Syria. It is generally accepted, not on its own authority, but because of Luke's involvement with the church in Antioch. This would mean, of course, that Luke was not (as some think) the "man of Macedonia" Paul saw in his vision at Troas (Acts 16:8–9).[6]

4. Purpose

Can we discern a single purpose for the Gospel of Luke? The answer must be based on a consideration of the prologue to the Gospel (1:1–4),[7] of the apparent purposes of Acts (cf. Longenecker, "Acts," EBC, 9:216–21), of the major themes and

---

[5]Henry J. Cadbury, *The Style and Literary Method of Luke*, pp. 39–72.

[6]For more detail and a citation of scholars on each side of this question, see Joseph A. Fitzmyer, *The Gospel According to Luke I–IX* (Garden City: Doubleday, 1981), pp. 35–53, 59–61.

[7]Schuyler Brown, "The Role of the Prologue in Determining the Purpose of Luke-Acts," in Talbert, *Perspectives*, pp. 99–111.

theology of the book, and of its life situation. The following proposals are worth weighing.

a. Evangelism

The centrality of the theme and theology of salvation and the frequent proclamation of Good News, both in Luke and in Acts, make the evangelization of non-Christians a possible purpose for Luke-Acts.

b. Confirmation of the factual basis for faith

This is supported by the prologue (Luke 1:1–4), the historical references throughout the two books, the references to eyewitnesses (e.g., Luke 1:2; Acts 10:39), and the apologetic value of proof from prophecy (e.g., Acts 10:43).

c. Personal assurance

Confirmation of the factual basis for faith is not sufficient unless it brings a corresponding conviction and assurance within the reader. Luke 1:4 says that Luke wrote so that Theophilus might "know the certainty of the things" he had "been taught."

d. Narration of history

Did Luke write simply because he sensed the need of preserving the record of the origin and growth of the early church? Few, if any, ancient writers wrote history simply to preserve a chronicle of events. Also, it would be difficult to explain the disproportionate space given to early events and figures in the life of the church if Luke were merely doing a historical chronicle. Fitzmyer (*Gospel of Luke*, p. 9) sees value in Nils Dahl's proposal that this is a "continuation of biblical history" in that it shows the validity of apostolic tradition as part of that continuity and locus of salvation truth. But see further at "f" below.

e. An apologetic

One version of this purpose, which was occasionally proposed in an earlier generation, was that Luke wrote Acts as a brief for Paul's trial at Rome. The contents are too broad for that purpose, and it does not explain the Gospel of Luke. A more likely proposal is that the Gospel is an apologetic for Christianity as a religious sect. Jews had certain rights under the Roman Empire, and Luke may have written to demonstrate that Christianity should also have such rights as a *religio licita* ("legitimate religion") along with Pharisaism and the other sects of Judaism. At his trials Paul tried to identify himself with Judaism, especially Pharisaism. He himself called Christianity a "sect" in Acts 24:14, a term used in the accusation against him in v.5.

f. Solution of a theological problem

It has been common in recent years to assume that Luke was writing to explain the delay of the Parousia. According to this theory, proposed by Conzelmann and others, the early Christians were troubled because Christ did not return immediately as they had expected; and they therefore needed both assurance and some explanation for this delay. This is questionable and will be dealt with below (cf. 11.k). Another possible problem relates to the identity of the Christian church with

Israel. Is the church a new entity? Are all Christians to be considered part of Israel spiritually, or is there some other way to view this new group (cf. below at 11.j)?

g. *Conciliation*

The well-known contention of F.C. Baur and the so-called Tübingen School was that the Book of Acts was an example of the Hegelian principle of thesis, antithesis, and synthesis. Baur and his group saw Peter and Paul as representing opposing parties, with Luke trying to bring the antithetical viewpoints together in a synthesis of organized, normative Christianity. That there were differences is obvious, and Luke may well have written in part to show that these differences were not unresolvable. But the process as described by Tübingen scholars does not fit the facts and requires too long a period of time.

h. *Defense against heresy*

During the period when Gnosticism was being proposed as a problem dealt with by several NT books, C.H. Talbert proposed a short-lived hypothesis that Luke was written against this heresy. Not only is there insufficient evidence in Luke's writings to support this, but it also leaves unanswered the question as to why so much else is included in these books that is not relevant to the Gnostic issue.

i. *Instruction*

This is a very general proposal, which covers a great deal of what we have in these writings. As a generality the proposal is valid but lacks focus.

j. *Dealing with social problems*

Recent works have made a good deal of the prominence of the theme of poverty and wealth in both Luke and Acts (cf. n.34). This concern was hardly large enough in comparison to other more major matters to be considered a major purpose for Luke's writing, but it does call for a response from the reader.

k. *Multiple purposes*

If none of the above qualifies as *the* purpose for the writing of Luke-Acts, is it then wrong to seek a single overarching purpose in Luke? Should we think instead of primary and secondary purposes? If we take this approach, almost everything mentioned above has value. In this case we may take the prologue to the Gospel as articulating the primary purpose of not only the Gospel but, at least to an extent, of Acts as well, providing enough information about Jesus to supplement the instruction Theophilus had already received, to confirm him in his faith. By extrapolation we may assume that Luke wrote to bring the gospel, and the assurance of salvation that follows its acceptance, to a larger audience than Theophilus. This certainly does not exclude subsidiary purposes, especially in the second volume (Acts). Since Luke clearly distinguishes the second volume from the first, there is no reason why he could not have accomplished his purpose mainly in the first volume and then continued the story of "all that Jesus began to do and teach" in the second one to accomplish yet further objectives.

If in addition to winning and establishing individual converts, Luke is concerned with forwarding the Christian movement, such subsidiary aims as establishing the legitimacy of that movement as a true sect of Judaism, demonstrating the innocence of Jesus and Paul at their trials, clarifying the relationship of Jewish and Gentile believers to Israel, and rooting the Gospel record in Jewish and secular history all have their place. It was important for Luke to deal with specific problems, whether eschatological or social, if such problems threatened to hinder the forward movement of the church. Far from producing a simplistic or a fragmented work, the author (Luke) brings together all the data and addresses all the issues he feels it necessary to deal with in order to advance Christ's cause throughout the world.

5. Intended Readership

Any conclusions as to the readership of the Gospel must be drawn primarily from the prologue (1:1–4) and secondarily from conclusions about the purpose of the Gospel. As to the first, see the commentary on 1:1–4 for remarks about Theophilus. From our brief survey of theories about Luke's purpose, it would appear that while Luke-Acts had an appeal to the non-Christian, Luke expected and desired it to be read by Christians, especially new converts. Some of the characteristics of the Gospel, such as its orientation to the secular world, its references to Judaism, its Septuagintisms, along with the prominence of God-fearers in both books, make it plausible that Luke had those God-fearers in mind. They were Gentiles (though see n.1), at home in secular society but monotheistic by conviction; and they were accustomed to hearing the Jewish Scriptures read in the synagogue, though not familiar with Palestinian geography and society. Like the God-fearers reached through Paul's mission (cf. the Acts narrative), they formed an ideal bridge from the synagogue to the Gentile world. It is possible, though unprovable, that Luke himself had been a God-fearer. While it is impossible to restrict Luke's readership to the God-fearers, it is difficult to imagine him writing without at least having them in mind.[8]

6. Literary Characteristics

Moulton called Luke "the only *littérateur* among the authors of NT books."[9] He said this mainly because of Luke's rare use of the optative. To Moulton, Luke was a Greek who had the "native instinct" not only to write well but to vary his style scene by scene. While there is no uniform agreement today regarding Luke's background or the reasons for his distinctive style, nevertheless his writings are generally held to be superb in style and in structure.[10]

---

[8]Maddox (p. 187) says, "[Luke] writes to reassure the Christians of his day that their faith in Jesus is no aberration, but the authentic goal towards which God's ancient dealings with Israel were driving."

[9]James Hope Moulton, *A Grammar of New Testament Greek*, vol. 2, *Accidence and Word-Formation*, ed. W.F. Howard (Edinburgh: T. & T. Clark, 1929), p. 7.

[10]Cf. Cadbury, *Style and Method of Luke*, who demonstrates the excellence of Luke's style. Among Luke's distinctive words are many with a literary flavor, medical terms (see earlier on Hobart's theory and Cadbury's response), and distinctive theological terms. The following are the major sources for word statistics: Gaston, *Horae Synopticae Electronicae*; Hawkins, *Horae Synopticae*; R. Morgenthaler, *Statistik des neutestamentlichen Wortschatzes*.

As to the linguistic and syntactical idioms of Luke's Gospel, we find a mystifying combination of literary Greek and Semitic style. The latter includes expressions characteristic of Hebrew, Aramaic, or both, and Septuagintisms. This "translation Greek" betrays its Hebrew or Aramaic original. Some of these characteristics can be easily seen in familiar KJV expressions such as "he answering said" (where the participle "answering" is redundant, e.g., 1:19; 4:12; 5:5, 22, 31), "before the face of" (e.g., 2:31), the use of the verb *egeneto* with a finite verb (familiar from the KJV "it came to pass that . . ."), and the intensive "with desire I have desired" (22:15), to name a few. (NIV's idiomatic renderings generally eliminate these awkward expressions.)

These characteristics occur more often in Luke 1 and 2 and in Acts 1–15 than in the rest of the books. There are fewer such in the "we passages," which leads Turner to suggest that these are from a diary Luke wrote earlier than he did the rest of the work, before he was exposed to Septuagintal idioms through Paul.[11]

Among the theories advanced to explain this occurrence of Hebrew and Aramaic "interference" in Luke's fine Greek style and the traces of Septuagintal influence are (1) Luke was actually Jewish; (2) he was a Gentile but had a long exposure to Semitic idioms; (3) he was a Greek who perhaps unconsciously adopted a Septuagintal style, possibly through association with Paul; (4) he artificially affected a Semitic style to give a ring of genuineness to certain sections of his works; and (5) at times he was using a source with a tradition that went back to a Semitic original. Though these idioms occur in some places more heavily than in others, they are found scattered throughout Luke's works. Of the theories mentioned above, the most likely are (2), supported by Fitzmyer, or (3), supported by Turner, with (5) applying in certain parts. The idea of a Semitic source behind Luke 1–2 has received recent cautious support from S.C. Farris's "On Discerning Semitic Sources in Luke 1–2,"[12] based on the research of R.A. Martin.

As to structure, Luke also shows literary skill. Talbert (*Literary Patterns*) has demonstrated Luke's ability to use the device of chiasm (a sequence of topics repeated in reverse order) as a major structural means of presenting his message. Talbert notes other examples of this in some of the finest Greek writings. It is widely acknowledged that the two books attributed to Luke exhibit a unit of structure (which, as noted above, is significant with regard to the issue of authorship). Cadbury has observed two striking pairs of stylistic characteristics.[13] The first is "repetition and variation," i.e., Luke at times has obvious repetitions—e.g., "the growth of a child in Luke 1:80; 2:40; 2:52" (to which we could add the growth of the church under the favor of God and of people, Acts 2:47). The second pair of characteristics is "distribution and concentration." By this he means the tendency to use a term frequently in a passage or in a sequence of passages, only to use it rarely or never elsewhere. All in all it is evident that Luke's writings are rich in linguistic, stylistic, and structural creativity.

---

[11]James Hope Moulton, *A Greek Grammar of the New Testament*, vol. 4, *Style*, Nigel Turner (Edinburgh: T. & T. Clark, 1976), p. 55, cf. p. 61. The most useful survey of data is by Fitzmyer, *Gospel of Luke*, pp. 107–25. For a useful survey of scholarship on this matter, see Fred Horton, "Reflections on the Semitisms of Luke-Acts," in Talbert, *Perspectives*, pp. 1–23.

[12]In France and Wenham, *Gospel Perspectives*, vol. 2. The Semitic character of Luke 1–2 also forms a significant step in establishing the historicity of the Virgin Birth in Machen, pp. 62–101.

[13]Henry J. Cadbury, "Four Features of Lucan Style," in Keck and Martyn, pp. 87–102.

7. Method of Composition

Since the synoptic problem and the proposed frameworks for its solution involve some of the same data for Matthew as for Luke, the reader should consult the introduction to Donald A. Carson's commentary on Matthew in this volume (see also "The Synoptic Gospels" by J. Julius Scott, Jr., EBC, 1:501–14).

The first written Gospel in the NT form was probably Mark. Matthew apparently had access to Mark, as well as other traditions that contained sayings of Jesus. These other traditions are referred to by scholars as "Q," but whether or not that was a written collection is now impossible to determine. Scholars have been increasingly reluctant to accept the hypothesis of the relation of Matthew and Luke to the two sources of Mark and "Q"; but it still seems to be, with modifications, the most satisfactory hypothesis at this time. In the reconstruction of synoptic traditions by Streeter,[14] he called the other material known to Luke beside Mark and "Q" by the letter "L." Although this terminology is less used today, it is customary to assume that, in addition to other materials, Luke had one main special source. The parts of the Gospel unique to Luke include 1:5–2:52 (birth and childhood narratives); 3:10–14 (John the Baptist's ethical teaching); 7:12–17 (the raising of the widow of Nain's son); a good deal of the material in 9:51–19:44; and a number of incidents in the passion narrative, along with other small sections.[15] Whether, as Streeter and others have supposed, Luke wrote an earlier Gospel (which Streeter called "Proto-Luke") before he became acquainted with Mark or with the content of his first two chapters is extremely doubtful.

Since publication of Conzelmann's work *Die Mitte der Zeit* in 1953 (English tr., *The Theology of St. Luke*), major attention has been given to the redaction criticism of Luke. The term comes from the German *Redaktionsgeschichte* and has to do with the analysis of the editorial work of an author as he shaped the written or oral materials that came to his hand. To some this implies creativity to the extent of changing or slanting the materials received for the purpose of imposing the editor's theological viewpoint on that material. Such a radical handling of sources is, however, not a necessary presupposition to a redactional study of the synoptic Gospels. There is no question but that each of the Gospels contributes a distinctive perspective on the life and teachings of the Lord Jesus. It is to the enrichment of our total understanding of the person and work of Christ that we thoroughly investigate these distinct contributions. But extreme caution is needed lest we superimpose on the Gospel the supposed conditions of the church communities at the time Luke wrote and to do this so as to alter what Jesus actually taught. The same caution applies to superimposing our own schemes of theology on the Gospel.[16]

In 1971 Schramm[17] showed that much of the distinctive material in Luke was due not so much to his redactional activity as to his use of sources different from those available to Matthew and Mark. Also it has long been assumed that many of the differences in Luke are due to his stylistic improvements of Mark. Various scholars have analyzed individual pericopes (sections) of Luke to determine the extent of his

---

[14]B.H. Streeter, *The Four Gospels* (New York: Macmillan), 1930.

[15]For a fuller list, a useful discussion of the entire matter of Luke's sources, and a full bibliography, see Fitzmyer, *Gospel of Luke*, pp. 63–106.

[16]See also section 11 below on "Themes and Theology."

[17]T. Schramm, *Der Markus-Stoff bei Lukas*.

redaction. A recent example is Bruce Chilton's "Announcement in Nazara: An Analysis of Luke 4:16–21."[18] The most detailed study of the passion narrative was done in a series of studies originally published as separate monographs by H. Schürmann.[19] There are, in summary, three main reasons why a passage in Luke may be different from parallel passages in Matthew or Mark: theology, literary style, and source material.

Those who have engaged in redaction criticism of Luke have not necessarily followed the radical conclusions of Conzelmann. One of the first full-scale responses was that of Helmut Flender. His work included a fascinating study of the dialectical structure of Luke-Acts, which has not received complete acceptance. Robinson employed a redactional approach but criticized Conzelmann and proposed a geographical scheme for Luke's theology.[20] Another major study that counters some of Conzelmann's ideas is Schuyler Brown's *Apostasy and Perseverance*. Brown debates Conzelmann's theory that between the temptation of Jesus and the betrayal of Judas, Satan was not actively opposing the ministry of Jesus. Brown answers this by reexamining the meaning of *peirasmos* ("temptation" or "trial") in Luke.

The negative assessment Conzelmann made of Luke's knowledge of Palestinian geography and of historical matters has also been challenged by a number of writers. The finest assessment of Luke as both a theologian and a historian is Marshall's *Luke: Historian and Theologian*. Nevertheless a good deal of skepticism about Luke's accuracy persists, and unfortunately redaction criticism is often carried on under such negative assumptions.

One of the more recent approaches to the material in the Gospels is that of structuralism. This does not pertain uniquely to Luke; and it is a large, complex, and much-debated approach. Structuralism seeks to understand reality—relating to sociology and a number of other disciplines as well as to linguistics and literature—in what might be called universal terms. Scholars using it construct theoretical structural models to explain particular linguistic and literary elements, such as the roles and actions within a narrative or parable.[21]

A final comment on Luke's method of composition relates to the central section of the Gospel (9:51–19:44). This part has no parallel in the other Gospels, though some of the stories and parables within it do. It has long been a matter of debate whether Luke is merely following some literary or historical procedure in the composition of this section, or whether he has some theological purpose in mind. The most persistent supposition is that he is consciously constructing a parallel to Deuteronomy.

---

[18]In France and Wenham, *Gospel Perspectives*, 2:147–72.

[19]*Der Paschamahlbericht, Der Einsetzungsbericht* (Münster: Aschendorffsche Verlag, 1955), and *Jesu Abschiedsrede*.

[20]W.C. Robinson, Jr., *Der Weg des Herrn*.

[21]The following works are useful for understanding structuralism: R. Barthes et al., *Structural Analysis and Biblical Exegesis: Interpretational Essays*, tr. A.M. Johnson, Jr., Pittsburgh Theological Monograph Series Number 3 (Pittsburgh: Pickwick, 1974); Daniel Patte, *What is Structural Exegesis?* New Testament Guides to Biblical Scholarship Series (Philadelphia: Fortress, 1976); Daniel and Aline Patte, *Structural Exegesis: From Theory to Practice* (Philadelphia: Fortress, 1978); R.M. Polzin, *Biblical Structuralism: Method and Subjectivity in the Ancient Texts* (Philadelphia: Fortress, 1977); V.S. Poythress, "Structuralism and Biblical Studies," JETS 21 (1978); Robert W. Funk, ed., "A Structuralist Approach to the Parables," *Semeia* 1 (1978); A.C. Thiselton, "Keeping Up With Recent Studies: II. Structuralism and Biblical Studies: Method or Ideology?" ExpT 89 (1977–78): 329–35. On the state of parable research in particular, see Carson's introduction to Matthew in this volume.

(For further remarks and a bibliography on this subject, see the introduction to that section in the commentary.)

8. Text

There are some textual problems in Luke that demand the attention of the exegete, though not so many as in Acts. In general the so-called Alexandrian tradition of the text has proved reliable, especially since the discovery in 1961 of the papyrus P[75]. In some cases (e.g., Luke 22:19b–20; 24:3, 6, 12, 36, 40, 51–52) the omission of words from the so-called Western text, which tends to add rather than omit words, was so unusual that these omissions were considered significant. Recent studies have challenged that assessment,[22] and it is fairly certain that the inclusion of the wording in question in the Alexandrian text tradition is correct. See remarks on the verses in question in the Notes portions of the commentary.[23]

9. History and Geography

Discussion of the historical value of Luke usually proceeds along one or more of the following lines: (1) Luke's careful observation of the historical setting of his narratives; (2) the question as to whether a work so tendential, so committed to establishing certain theological conclusions, can possibly be historically objective; (3) the authenticity and accuracy of Luke's sources; (4) his own claim to historical accuracy in his introduction; (5) problems caused by apparent errors (e.g., his reference to the census under Quirinius in 2:1–2; see commentary in loc.); and (6) apparent discrepancies between Luke and the other Gospels.

The first of these has to do with the kind of data collected by W.M. Ramsay in his well-known works[24] and by A.N. Sherwin-White.[25] Cassidy (p. 13) calls these data "empire history," that is, things "within the broad category of political affairs . . . [such as] the description of rulers and officials . . . the dating of specific events in relation to other events more widely known throughout the empire" and so on. It is important to recognize that where Luke can be checked historically (except for the few problem texts under 8 above), his accuracy has been validated. We should, however, acknowledge that this does not in itself guarantee Luke's accuracy in everything he relates.

Second, as indicated earlier, Luke's theological intentions should not be taken as invalidating his historical accuracy. Even so careful a scholar as Fitzmyer assumes that Luke's theological concern sets him apart from both ancient and modern historians, noting that his introduction "reveals his historical concern as subordinate to a theological one" (*Gospel of Luke*, p. 16). But it does not logically follow that

---

[22]So K. Snodgrass, "Western Non-Interpolations."

[23]See also Gordon D. Fee, "The Textual Criticism of the New Testament," EBC, 1:419–33, and Fitzmyer, *Gospel of Luke*, pp. 128–33.

[24]E.g., *St. Paul the Traveller and the Roman Citizen* (New York: Putnam, 1898); *Was Christ Born in Bethlehem?; The Bearing of Recent Discovery on the Trustworthiness of the New Testament* (1915, reprint, Grand Rapids: Baker, 1953).

[25]*Roman Society and Roman Law*.

because historical concern is subordinate, error must result.[26] Likewise we must remember that other ancient historians were seeking to establish certain viewpoints as they wrote their histories.

Third, the matter of sources was briefly discussed under Method of Composition above. So was the question of whether Luke's use of Semitic constructions indicates Semitic source material (cf. Literary Characteristics). If it does, the presence of such sources (with the tradition handed down either in the original Semitic idiom or in Septuagintal Greek) points to an early Palestinian origin of the book. Though this does not guarantee authenticity or accuracy, it certainly increases their probability. It appears that in some instances Luke follows an even earlier tradition than Matthew or Mark does. An example is the tradition of the institution of the Lord's Supper, where the wording in Luke is close to that found in 1 Corinthians 11, which had probably been committed to writing earlier than Matthew or Mark. Apparently both Luke and Paul had access to a very early tradition.

Fourth, the terminology of Luke's prologue (1:1–4) certainly implies careful historical research. Such a claim to historical accuracy does not in itself prove accuracy. But the honesty of the writer in distinguishing himself from the eyewitnesses and the care he took to provide an orderly, accurate account cannot be overlooked. Historians in the ancient world were, contrary to what many have thought, interested in accurate reporting.[27]

Fifth, there are indeed several serious historical problems in Luke's writings, such as the reference to Quirinius (Luke 2:2) and the reference to Theudas (Acts 5:36–37). A few others are more easily handled. Nevertheless, as the commentary shows, there are possible solutions that obviate extreme skepticism as to Luke's historical accuracy.

Sixth, the issues involved in the apparent discrepancies between the Gospels are so complex as to preclude brief discussion of them here. However, it must at least be said that, unfortunately, attempts at reasonable reconciliation are often summarily dismissed as "harmonization," as though any attempt to give the benefit of the doubt to one of two parallel ancient documents was somehow unworthy. To think that one can either "prove" or "disprove" the historical value of an ancient historical work on the basis of the slight amount of information we have about the remote events it deals with is presumptuous.

10. Date

The dating of Luke depends largely on four factors: (1) the date of Mark and Luke's relationship to it, (2) the date of Acts, (3) the reference to the destruction of Jerusalem in chapter 21, and (4) the theological and ecclesiastical tone of Luke-Acts.

First, the date of Mark is, of course, relevant only if Luke used Mark as one of his sources. That probability is strong enough to assume here. With rare exceptions, scholars today hold that Mark was written about A.D. 70, probably just a few years before that date, which was marked by the destruction of Jerusalem. Yet there is no compelling reason why it could not have been written a few years earlier, toward

---

[26]See the strong comments on this topic by Martin Hengel in *Acts and the History of Earliest Christianity*, tr. J. Bowden (Philadelphia: Fortress, 1979), pp. 59–68.

[27]See A.W. Mosley, "Historical Reporting in the Ancient World," NTS 12 (1965–66): 10–26.

A.D. 60. At this time it is not possible to be certain about this (cf. Introduction to Mark in this volume).

Second, the issues surrounding the date of Acts are more complex (cf. Longenecker, "Acts," EBC, 9:235–38). Presumably Luke completed his Gospel before writing Acts, though this has been debated. Apart from its connection with the writing of the Gospel and the implications of the theological climate of the two books, which will be discussed below, the main considerations in the dating of Acts relate to the time of Paul's imprisonment and the date of the Neronian persecution. Acts 28:30 takes leave of Paul with a reference to his two-year imprisonment at Rome. This is generally agreed to have taken place around A.D. 60 to 62. This provides a *terminus a quo* for the date of Acts. The fact that there is no record in Acts of the subsequent persecution under Nero in A.D. 65 and of Paul's death at about that time suggests that Luke wrote Acts before these events. There is no hint of further hostilities between the Jews and the Romans or of the climax in A.D. 70. One might have expected Luke to cite the destruction of Jerusalem in his attempt to show the innocence of Christianity and the culpability of the Jewish rulers. On the ground of these historical matters alone, Acts can be dated anywhere between A.D. 61 and 65, probably around A.D. 63 or 64.

Third, Luke's reference to the destruction of Jerusalem in his version of the Olivet Discourse (21:8–36) complicates the problem of dating the Gospel. Most scholars see it as a *vaticinium ex eventu*, a "prophecy" given after the event. In that case Luke would have added sufficient detail to the discourse in Mark 13, once the event had occurred, to show his readers what he thought Jesus must have intended. An obvious response to this, though not in itself conclusive, is that one cannot assume that Jesus did not, or could not, actually have included Jerusalem in his prediction. Also, if Luke had adapted the prediction to the event, it is strange that he did not also modify the prediction of the accompanying apocalyptic events, including the coming of the Son of Man. These did not happen in A.D. 70, at least in the literal sense in which Luke probably would have understood them (cf. Morris, *Luke*, p. 23). But the conventional apocalyptic terminology does stand in Luke 21, and the passage has very little additional detail about the destruction of Jerusalem, as might be expected were it written after the event. Furthermore, if Jesus had, either explicitly or implicitly, referred in the Olivet Discourse to the destruction of Jerusalem, why was Luke the only one of the synoptic writers to include that specific reference, unless he were indeed writing after the event? The answer would seem to be that it is only Luke who throughout his Gospel stresses Jerusalem as the city of destiny. His Gospel opens with a scene in the temple in Jerusalem; Jesus is constantly pressing toward Jerusalem (see commentary passim); and Luke includes a lament of Jesus over the city (19:41–44). It is natural that he would pick up any tradition of Jesus' words about the fate of that city, even before the event occurred. The question of whether Jesus specifically predicted the Fall of Jerusalem and whether Luke wrote chapter 21 before or after the event should, therefore, not be decided subjectively.

Fourth, another reason why many date Acts and also Luke later (even as late as the early second century) is that they believe Acts reflects a theological climate and ecclesiastical situation nonexistent in the 60s or 70s. They base their view largely on the assumption that the author of Acts shows little knowledge of the apostle Paul as the early epistles portray him and also that the author reflects a view of the church more in common with the later Pastoral Epistles and "early Catholicism." On this complex matter, see I. Howard Marshall's " 'Early Catholicism' in the New Testament," in Longenecker and Tenney (*New Dimensions*, pp. 217–31), and Longenecker's Introduction to Acts (EBC, 9:235–38). Longenecker offers several internal evidences for an early date for Acts. See also the discussion in Ellis, *Gospel of Luke* (pp. 44–51), and his treatment of the date of Luke (pp. 55–60). Among other points, Ellis sees evidences in Luke of a troublesome time such as that begun by the Neronian persecution. He prefers a date around A.D. 70 for Luke. In my judgment the only compelling reason for assigning a date much earlier than this would be the lack of allusions in Acts to the death of Paul and to the Neronian persecution. Even this conclusion is based on the assumption that Luke would have alluded to such events had he written later—though he might not have done so if he had intended to write a third volume covering that period. All things considered, then, it seems preferable to date the completion of Luke's two works somewhere in the decade of A.D. 60–70.

11. Themes and Theology

A word of caution is necessary on beginning this section. Fitzmyer (*Gospel of Luke*, pp. 6ff.) has warned against superimposing a "thesis" about Lukan theology on the data of Luke and Acts themselves. Though his warning is directed largely against Conzelmann's *Theology of Luke* and J.C. O'Neill's *The Theology of Acts in Its Historical Setting*, rev. ed. (London: SPCK, 1970), it applies to other works as well and serves as a warning to all expositors. It is constantly necessary to check one's understanding of an author against the actual data in his work. But what constitutes evidence for biblical theology? It is one thing to exegete the propositions in the logical argument of an epistle (and even here there is much room for disagreement); it is another thing to reconstruct the theology of a narrator such as Luke. The evidence ranges from overall patterns of structure (cf. Talbert's *Literary Patterns*) to the possible significance of (e.g., the use or nonuse of) an article before the word "mountain" in Matthew or Luke. Word frequency is certainly one valuable clue. Yet it is not enough to make a simple word count and draw conclusions from it. As Gaston has shown in *Horae Synopticae Electronicae*, it is necessary to use modern statistical methodology, such as standard deviation, to assess the significance of word counts. We also need to bear in mind the source of the material under consideration. If a word appears frequently in one of Luke's special sources (assuming that we know when he is using such a source), should we use that as evidence for Luke's own theological viewpoint? Does the very fact that he selected that source indicate that he wanted to express its theology? One would assume this to be the case and that Luke was being divinely led in weaving together his materials into a cohesive theology.

Moreover, those passages in the Gospel that are of most theological weight must be taken into account, namely, not only passages that contain specific teachings, but also those that contain a confluence of significant Lukan terminology. For example, Jesus' conversation with Zacchaeus in 19:1–10 includes the word "today" (bis), "salvation," "save," and the name "Abraham." Such terminology is relatively frequent in Luke. Also, Zacchaeus, who was a tax collector and so was called a "sinner" by the people, exemplifies the kind of people Luke uses to show God's grace. This incident is of high significance (see commentary).

Jesus' preaching at Nazareth (4:16–21) exemplifies the kerygmatic (proclamation) theme in Luke and provides a programmatic statement regarding Jesus' ministry (see commentary).

While the proper use of redaction criticism in discerning the theology of a Gospel author must depend on careful comparison with parallel passages in the other Gospels, the coherence of themes *within* a Gospel is as important as a comparison of themes *between* the Gospels. For example, the messiahship of Jesus and the kingdom of God must be recognized as important themes in Luke's theology whether or not they appear with unusual frequency as compared with Matthew and Mark.

History and geography play an important part in Luke's theology (we object to the criticism that this implies that Luke is less reliable in these areas). Luke's "empire history" (to use Cassidy's term) as well as the local context of events in his Gospel demonstrate the reality and importance of salvation-history in time and space. The providence of God in history has an important relation to the sequence of events in Luke-Acts.

In Luke's central section (9:51–18:14), we can discern a theological motif in the way Jesus orients his thinking and his ministry toward Jerusalem, the city of destiny, which would be the scene of the passion and ascension of Christ (9:51). That Luke, in contrast to the other Gospels, does not describe the actual entrance of Jesus into Jerusalem itself is significant. (See comments on 19:28–44. Other historical and geographical matters of theological importance will be treated in loc. See also remarks on Luke's scheme of history as understood by Conzelmann, under "Eschatology" below [k].)

The following are some of the more significant topics in Luke.

a. Christology

The Gospel opens with a series of birth narratives alternating between Jesus and John the Baptist. Among other purposes, these narratives effect a contrast between the two figures, both of whom are identified in Luke as prophets.[28] From the beginning it is apparent that Jesus is also the Son of God, born of a virgin (1:26–33). The atmosphere of chapters 1–2 is that of the OT. In them Jesus is presented in terms of messiahship (cf. 1:32b–33, 68–75). Simeon and Anna give testimony to the baby Jesus in the temple and announce that God's day of redemption has dawned, since the coming of the Savior means light to the Gentiles and glory to Israel (2:25–38). At the age of twelve, Jesus expresses his filial consciousness—his unique awareness that God is his Father (2:49).

There are hints throughout the Gospel that Jesus came as a "prophet" (e.g., 4:24; 13:33; 24:19). Luke effectively focuses on the messiahship of Jesus (unlike Mark) by taking the reader directly from the question of Herod—"Who, then, is this I hear such things about?" (9:9)—to the messianic act of feeding the five thousand (9:10–17) and then immediately to Peter's affirmation that Jesus is "the Christ of God" (9:20).

Unlike the other Gospels, Luke's narrative concludes with the ascension of Jesus. This marks both the conclusion of the Gospel and the beginning of Acts and is thus also pivotal in the two-volume work. Moreover, Luke makes mention of the Ascension in 9:51, at the beginning of the central section of his Gospel.

---

[28]Minear, *Heal and Reveal*, pp. 95–96; cf. Marshall, *Luke: Historian and Theologian*, pp. 125–28.

b. Doxology

The prominence of the Ascension in Luke contributes to his "theology of glory." It has often been observed that Luke has emphasized the resurrection, ascension, and vindication of Christ (taking into account also the early chapters of Acts). The descriptive term "glory" (*doxa*) is also appropriate because there is a sense of doxology—i.e., of ascribing glory to God—throughout Luke's work. Those who observe or benefit from the healing power of Christ are filled with wonder and bring glory to God (e.g., Luke 5:25–26; Acts 3:8–10). Other examples of praising and blessing God in Luke are 1:46–55, 68–79; 2:13–14, 20, 28–32; 7:16; 10:21; 18:43; 19:37–38; 24:53.

c. Soteriology

If Luke has a theology of glory, this does not mean he lacks a theology of the Cross. It is true that the gospel as proclaimed in the first chapters of Acts does not feature the doctrine of the atonement as we have come to understand it from Paul. Nevertheless the Cross is central. Even before the first passion prediction of Luke 9:22, there are foreshadowings of Jesus' sufferings (2:35; 5:35). Jesus is clearly moving toward the Cross in 13:33. His words instituting the Last Supper must not be overlooked as evidence of his understanding of the Cross (22:19–20).

d. Salvation

"The central theme in the writings of Luke is that Jesus offers salvation to men." This is the thesis of Marshall in *Luke: Historian and Theologian* (p. 116). This offer of salvation is not to be dissociated from the concept of salvation-history that, properly understood, has a significant place in Luke and elsewhere in Scripture. It does, however, focus on the person and the saving work of the Lord Jesus Christ, rather than a scheme of history (as in Conzelmann). *Sōzō* ("save") occurs in Luke 6:9; 7:50; 8:12, 36, 48, 50; 9:24, 56 mg.; 13:23; 17:19; 18:26, 42; 19:10; 23:35, 37, 39; *sōtēr* ("Savior") in 1:47; 2:11; *sōtēria* ("salvation") in 1:69, 71, 77; 19:9; and *sōtērion* in 2:30; 3:6.

We observed above that one of the key passages in Luke is 19:1–10, which concludes with the statement that the Son of Man "came to seek and to save what was lost." The entire Gospel of Luke pictures Jesus as reaching out to the lost in forgiveness. We see this exemplified in the beautiful story of the sinful woman (7:36–50). In the well-known parables in Luke 15, Jesus, in contrast with the attitude of the Pharisees, identifies himself with the heavenly Father in rejoicing over the return of those who are lost. See Marshall's *Luke: Historian and Theologian* (pp. 116–44) for a fine discussion of Jesus' ministry of salvation. Also, see further under "Sense of Destiny" below (h).

e. The Holy Spirit

The prominence of the Holy Spirit in Luke-Acts has received considerable attention. It is through the overshadowing spirit and power of God that Mary conceives the one who will be called the Son of God (1:35). The same Spirit would fill John the Baptist (1:15) and his mother, Elizabeth (1:41). The Spirit was on Simeon, and through the Spirit he gave testimony to the Messiah (2:25–35). Jesus was full of the Spirit and was led by the Spirit at the time of his temptation (4:1). The great passage from Isaiah that Jesus quoted in the synagogue at Nazareth begins: "The Spirit of the Lord is on me" (4:18). Furthermore, Jesus promised the Holy Spirit both as an answer to prayer (11:13) and in anticipation of Pentecost (24:49; Acts 1:4). The Holy Spirit, of course, has a major place throughout Acts.

f. Prayer

Not only was prayer significant throughout Jesus' life and in the early church, but it seems to have been especially important in times of transition and crisis. Only Luke records that Jesus was praying at his baptism when the Holy Spirit descended on him (3:21). He prayed before choosing the twelve apostles (6:12). Again only Luke records that Jesus was praying on the Mount of Transfiguration (9:29). Luke 11:1–13 and 18:1–8 contain his special teaching and parables on prayer. Other instances of Jesus praying in Luke are 5:16; 9:18; 11:1.

g. Miracles

All four Gospels record miracles of Christ. In Luke, as noted above, the performance of miracles often results in expressions of praise to God. The word *dynamos* ("power") occurs frequently in Luke, though not significantly more than in Matthew or Mark. It also occurs a number of times in Acts.

h. Sense of destiny

The word *dei* ("it is necessary") is prominent in Luke and in Acts. Jesus "had to" be in his Father's house (2:49); he "must preach the good news of the kingdom of God," because that "is why I was sent" (4:43); he "must suffer" (9:22; cf. Matt 16:21; Mark 8:31); he must finish the way appointed to him, the way that culminated in the Cross (13:33); and it was necessary for the Son of Man to be betrayed and crucified, suffering first before entering his glory (24:7, 26, 44–47). In this way Jesus occupies the central place in salvation history, fulfilling the plan of God.

i. Prophecy and fulfillment

God's plan in Christ was in accordance with OT prophecy. Although Luke does not use the fulfillment formulas of Matthew, the idea is in his Gospel. This is especially notable in the programmatic statement in 4:16–21. The quotation of Isaiah 61:1–2, which Jesus concluded with the words "the year of the Lord's favor," became contemporary as Jesus said, "Today this scripture is fulfilled in your hearing" (4:21).[29] The theme of fulfillment also has apologetic value in Luke. "Proof from prophecy" is significant, especially in Luke 24 and in the early chapters of Acts.[30]

j. Israel and the people of God

The term *laos* ("people") is to be distinguished, as Minear ("Jesus' Audiences," pp. 81–109) points out, from the more general *ochlos* ("crowd"). In his Gospel, Luke uses it to describe believers and sympathetic Jews. In Acts it seems at one or two

---

[29]For the significance of this in connection with the OT Year of Jubilee, see Robert B. Sloan, Jr., *The Favorable Year of the Lord* (Austin: Schola, 1977).

[30]Cf. Nils A. Dahl, "The Story of Abraham in Luke-Acts," in Keck and Martyn; cf. also Tiede.

points to include potential believers among Gentiles. Whereas the crowds are sometimes hostile to Jesus, the "people" are responsive. But what happens to the Jewish people who become believers in Christ? Once they are part of the Christian church, are they separated from Israel? Or, at the other extreme, is the entire church to be considered "Israel"? Richardson has shown that the term "Israel of God" (Gal 6:16) does not refer to the church itself but rather to "those within Israel to whom God will show mercy."[31] Jervell (pp. 41–74) likewise refrains from applying the term "Israel" to the church as a whole. There is a group of repentant Jews who have accepted the gospel. The Gentile mission grows out of the fulfillment of the biblical promises to Israel. Jervell's view is consistent with the emphasis in Acts on the conversion of great numbers of Jews, even Jewish priests. See especially the summary in Acts 21:20: "many thousands of Jews have believed."

k. *Eschatology*

The continuity of the true people of God and the mission to the Gentiles are part of the plan of God that, as many have seen, is a major theme in Luke. The opening chapters of Luke emphasize the messianic promises, especially through the songs of Mary (1:46–55) and Zechariah (1:68–79). The ultimate fulfillment of these still lies in the future. Luke, in common with the other synoptic Gospels, contains teachings of Jesus about his return and about the glorification of the Son of Man.[32] It has been common to picture Luke, however, as writing at a time when Christians were despairing over the return of Christ, which they had expected immediately. This "delay of the Parousia" was of such major concern to Luke that he devised a scheme that divided history into three phases. The first of these was the OT period, the second the life of Jesus, and the third the period of the church. This idea is set forth in Conzelmann's *Theology of Luke*, the German title of which—*Die Mitte Der Zeit* (i.e., the central point in time)—reflects his theory. But one of the problems with Conzelmann's idea is that it makes Luke distort the traditions of Jesus' sayings regarding his return by superimposing on them a concept of an extended period of the church in which life is to go on without the return of Christ.

A number of studies have addressed this issue, maintaining the importance of those eschatological teachings that Luke does incorporate and that were not reinterpreted as radically as Conzelmann had thought.[33] It is possible to see stages in the fulfillment of predictions made both in the OT and by Jesus, with a partial fulfillment now and a consummation later. The problem, says Ellis (*Eschatology in Luke*, p. 19), is "not the delay of the parousia . . . but false apocalyptic speculation that has misapplied the teachings of Jesus and threatens to pervert the church's mission." Thus Luke contains vivid warnings against coming judgment, an encouragement to watchfulness (e.g., 12:40), and the description of the coming of the Son of Man (17:22–37), but warns against misguided speculation (17:20–21). Faithfulness is needed during the time the Master is away (12:42–48; 19:11–27). In another response to Conzelmann, which seeks to maintain the eschatological

---

[31]Peter Richardson, *Israel in the Apostolic Church* (Cambridge: Cambridge University Press, 1969), p. 82.

[32]See the excursus on "Son of Man" in Carson's commentary in this volume at Matt 8:17.

[33]E.g., I.H. Marshall, *Eschatology and the Parables;* cf. Ellis, *Eschatology in Luke;* and Mattill, *Luke and the Last Things*.

element in Luke, Franklin sees the ascension and proclamation of Jesus as Lord as an eschatological climax.

There are other subjects related to eschatology that cannot be discussed here. The concept of present and future stages in the fulfillment of prophecy naturally includes the idea of the kingdom of God with its present or "inaugurated" aspects and its later consummation. Likewise, we see Luke's emphasis on the present reality of God's work in the use of the word "today" (sēmeron), alluded to earlier. The following passages are significant: 2:11; 4:21; 5:26; 12:28; 13:32–33; 19:5–9; 22:34, 61; 23:43. "Today" also occurs nine times in Acts.

I. *Discipleship and the Christian in the world*

This topic covers a multitude of subjects that cannot be discussed in this brief introduction but which have occasioned much attention in recent years. Only Luke contains the narrative of 9:57–62 on would-be disciples and the teaching of Jesus on the cost of discipleship in 14:25–35.

A major question in Luke is whether Jesus requires the sacrifice of material possessions for salvation or for discipleship, or whether he just presents it as an ideal for those who are especially devoted. The first idea is not taught in Luke. The case of the rich ruler (18:18–30) is unique (see commentary). Likewise those who want to be disciples should *yield* up all their possessions but not necessarily *disperse* them (see commentary on 14:33). But if this is an ideal, it is an ideal strongly taught. Luke includes Jesus' woes as well as blessings (6:24–26), which speak strongly against the wealthy. He also addresses the matter of possessions in chapter 12 and in chapter 16. In addition Acts not only mentions but emphasizes the sacrificial giving of the early church (2:45; 3:6; 4:32–37; 5:1–11).[34]

Recent attention to the social and political teachings of Jesus has focused on their implications for possible political revolution.[35] Cassidy, dealing particularly with the Gospel of Luke in *Jesus, Politics and Society*, concludes that Luke gives an accurate description of Jesus' social and political stance, and that, though he rejected the use of violence, Jesus challenged the social status quo under the Roman Empire. Cassidy holds that the teachings of Jesus as found in the Gospel of Luke would, if carried out widely, have seriously challenged the principles of the -Roman government. He bases his conclusions on Jesus' social teachings in general and on specific texts such as Luke 20:23–25, the familiar "give to Caesar what is Caesar's, and to God what is God's."

---

[34]A number of recent works have addressed the theme of poverty and wealth in the NT. See especially Martin Hengel, *Property and Riches in the Early Church* (Philadelphia: Fortress, 1974); Luke T. Johnson, *The Literary Function of Possessions in Luke-Acts*; R.J. Karris, "Poor and Rich: The Lukan *Sitz im Leben*," in Talbert, *Perspectives on Luke-Acts*; G.W.E. Nickelsburg, "Riches, the Rich and God's Judgment in 1 Enoch 92–105 and the Gospel According to Luke"; Walter E. Pilgrim, *Good News to the Poor*. Regarding the understanding of the early church on biblical teachings, see L. Wm. Countryman, *The Rich Christian in the Church of the Early Empire* (New York and Toronto: Edwin Mellon, 1980).

[35]Oscar Cullmann, *The State in the New Testament* (New York: Scribner's, 1956); id., *Jesus and the Revolutionaries* (New York: Harper and Row, 1970); Martin Hengel, *Was Jesus a Revolutionist?* tr. W. Klassen (Philadelphia: Fortress, 1971). For a different position, see S.G.F. Brandon, *Jesus and the Zealots* (Manchester: Manchester University Press, 1967). See the critical review of Brandon's book by Martin Hengel in JSS 14 (1969): 231–40. See also Harold J. Yoder, *The Politics of Jesus* (Grand Rapids: Eerdmans, 1972).

m. *The word of God*

This is a more important theme in Luke than is generally realized. The first appearance of *logos* is in 1:2: "servants of the word." Luke emphasizes the graciousness and effectiveness of Jesus' word in 4:22, 32, 36. The term is prominent in the parable of the sower (8:4–15). It is those who "hear the word, retain it, and by persevering produce a crop" who are truly related to Jesus. We also learn from Luke that, not only is the word of God in the OT fulfilled in the life of Jesus, but also that Jesus' own words are fulfilled (e.g., 19:32: "just as he had told them"). Thus we have the prophetic word, the authoritative word of Jesus, and the inspired word that is the Gospel of Luke itself.[36]

12. Bibliography

Books

Arndt, William F. *The Gospel According to St. Luke*. St. Louis: Concordia, 1956.
Bailey, Kenneth. *Poet and Peasant: A Literary-Cultural Approach to the Parables in Luke*. Grand Rapids: Eerdmans, 1977.
_____. *Through Peasant Eyes*. Grand Rapids: Eerdmans, 1980.
Barrett, C.K. *Luke, the Historian in Recent Study*. Facet Books, Biblical Series 24. Philadelphia: Fortress, 1970.
Black, Matthew. *An Aramaic Approach to the Gospels and Acts*. 3rd ed. Oxford: Clarendon, 1967.
Bode, E.G. *The First Easter Morning*. Rome: Biblical Institute Press, 1970.
Brown, R.E. *The Birth of the Messiah: A Commentary on the Infancy Narratives in Matthew and Luke*. Garden City: Doubleday, 1977.
Brown, Schuyler. *Apostasy and Perseverance in the Theology of Luke*. Rome: Pontifical Biblical Institute, 1969.
Cadbury, Henry J. *The Making of Luke-Acts*. New York: Macmillan, 1927.
_____. *The Style and Literary Method of Luke*. Cambridge: Harvard, 1920.
Cassidy, Richard J. *Jesus, Politics, and Society. A Study of Luke's Gospel*. Maryknoll, N.Y.: Orbis, 1978.
Conzelmann, Hans. *The Theology of St. Luke*. Translated by Geofrey Buswell. New York: Harper and Row, 1960.
Creed, J.M. *The Gospel According to St. Luke. A Commentary on the Third Gospel*. London: Macmillan, 1930.
Danker, F.W. *Jesus and the New Age According to St. Luke. A Commentary on the Third Gospel*. St. Louis: Clayton, 1972.
_____. *Luke*. Proclamation Commentaries. Philadelphia: Fortress, 1976.
Dillon, R.J. *From Eyewitnesses to Ministers of the Word*. Rome: Biblical Institute Press, 1978.

---

[36]Since the writing of this Introduction, two significant works have appeared. Charles H. Talbert's *Reading Luke* has important insights and information on fulfillment of prophecy and miracles. But his concept of martyr theology (pp. 221–25) has been heavily critiqued by Robert J. Karris in a paper, unpublished at this date, delivered at the Chicago Society for Biblical Research, on 16 April, 1983. Eduard Schweizer, *Luke*, says that Luke's christology is "far from being clear" (p. 43) and that his usage of "Son of God" is "chaotic" (p. 44). Schweizer's insistence that one's approach to theology should be molded by the approach of a biblical author (e.,g., Luke) shows the importance of rightly understanding Luke.

Drury, John. *Tradition and Design in Luke's Gospel*. London: Daston, Longman and Todd, 1976.

Edwards, O.C., Jr. *Luke's Story of Jesus*. Philadelphia: Fortress, 1981.

Ellis, E.E. *The Gospel of Luke*. NCB. New York: Nelson, 1966.

———. *Eschatology in Luke*. Facet Books. Biblical Series 30. Philadelphia: Fortress, 1972.

Fitzmyer, Joseph A. *Essays on the Semitic Background of the New Testament*. Missoula, Mont.: Scholars, 1974.

Flender, Helmut. *St. Luke: Theologian of Redemptive History*. Translated by R.H. and I. Fuller. Philadelphia: Fortress, 1967.

France, R.T., and Wenham, D., edd. *Gospel Perspectives*, 2 vols. Sheffield: J.S.O.T., 1981.

Franklin, Eric. *Christ the Lord: A Study in the Purpose and Theology of Luke-Acts*. Philadelphia: Westminster, 1975.

Gaston, Lloyd. *Horae Synopticae Electronicae; Word Statistics of the Synoptic Gospels*. Missoula, Mont.: Society of Biblical Literature, 1973.

Geldenhuys, Johannes Norval. *Commentary on the Gospel of Luke*. NIC. Grand Rapids: Eerdmans, 1951.

Godet, Frederic. *A Commentary on the Gospel of St. Luke*. Translated by E.W. Shalders and M.D. Cusin. Edinburgh: T. & T. Clark, 1893.

Grundmann, Walter. *Das Evangelium nach Lukas*. Berlin: Evangelische Verlagsanstalt, 1974.

Hawkins, John Caesas. *Horae Synopticae; Contributions to the Study of the Synoptic Problem*. 1909. Reprint. Grand Rapids: Baker, 1968.

Hendriksen, William. *Exposition of the Gospel According to Luke*. Grand Rapids: Baker, 1978.

Hobart, William K. *The Medical Language of St. Luke*. Reprint. Grand Rapids: Baker, 1954.

Hoehner, H.W. *Chronological Aspects of the Life of Christ*. Grand Rapids: Zondervan, 1977.

Jeremias, Joachim. *The Parables of Jesus*. Rev. ed. Translated by S.H. Hooke. New York: Scribner, 1963.

Jervell, J. *Luke and the People of God. A New Look at Luke-Acts*. Minneapolis: Augsburg, 1972.

Johnson, L.T. *The Literary Function of Possessions in Luke-Acts*. Society of Biblical Literature Dissertation Series no. 39. Missoula, Mont.: Scholars, 1977.

Keck, Leander, and Martyn, J. Louis, edd. *Studies in Luke-Acts*. New York: Abingdon, 1966.

Leaney, A.R.C. *A Commentary on the Gospel According to St. Luke*. Harper's New Testament Commentaries. New York: Harper and Brothers, 1958.

Longenecker, R.N., and Tenney, M.C., edd. *New Dimensions in New Testament Study*. Grand Rapids: Zondervan, 1974.

Machen, J. Gresham. *The Virgin Birth of Christ*. Reprint. Grand Rapids: Baker, 1965.

Maddox, Robert. *The Purpose of Luke-Acts*. Göttingen: Vandenhoeck und Ruprecht, 1982.

Manson, T.W. *The Sayings of Jesus*. London: SCM, 1949.

Marshall, I. Howard. *Eschatology and the Parables*. London: Tyndale, 1963.

———. *Luke: Historian and Theologian*. Grand Rapids: Zondervan, 1971.

———. *The Gospel of Luke: A Commentary on the Greek Text*. Grand Rapids: Eerdmans, 1978.

Mattill, A.J., Jr. *Luke and the Last Things*. Dillsboro, N.C.: Western North Carolina, 1979.

Minear, Paul S. *To Heal and to Reveal*. New York: Seabury, 1976.

Morganthaler, R., *Die lukanische Geschichtsschreibung als Zeugnis. Gestalt und Gehalt des Kunst des Lukas*. 2 vols. Abhandlung zur Theologie des Alten und Neuen Testaments, 14–15. Zürich: Zwingli, 1949.

———. *Statistik des neutestanmentlichen Wortschatzes*. Zürich: Gotthelf, 1973.

Morris, Leon. *The Gospel According to St. Luke*. TNTC. Grand Rapids: Eerdmans, 1974.

Navone, J. *Themes of St. Luke*. Rome: Gregorian University, 1970.

Nineham, D.E., ed. *Studies in the Gospels*. Naperville, Ill.; Allenson, 1955.

Pilgrim, W.E. *Good News to the Poor*. Minneapolis: Augsburg, 1981.

Plummer, Alfred. *A Critical and Exegetical Commentary on the Gospel According to St. Luke*. ICC. 5th ed. Edinburgh: T. & T. Clark, 1922.

Ramsay, W.M. *Was Christ Born in Bethlehem? A Study on the Credibility of St. Luke*. New York: Putnam, 1898.

Robinson, W.C. *Der Weg des Herrn: Studien zur Geschichte und Eschatologie im Lukas-Evangelium: Ein Gespräch mit Hans Conzelmann*. Theologische Forschung, 36. Hamburg-Bergstedt: H. Reich, 1964.

Schramm, T. *Der Markus-Stoff bei Lukas. Eine literarkritische und redaktionsgeschlichtliche Untersuchung*. Society for New Testament Studies Monograph Series 15. New York and Cambridge: Cambridge University Press, 1971.

Schürmann, H. *Das Lukasevangelium. Erster Teil: Kommentar zu kap. 1.1—9.50*. Herders Theologischer Kommentar zum Neuen Testament. Band III. Freiburg-Vienna: Herder, 1969.

_____. *Der Paschamahlbericht*. Münster: Aschendorffsche Verlag. 1953.

_____. *Jesu Abschiedsrede*. Münster: Aschendorffsche Verlag, 1957.

Schweizer, E. *Luke: A Challenge to Present Theology*. Atlanta: John Knox, 1982.

Sherwin-White, A.N. *Roman Society and Roman Law in the New Testament*. Oxford: Clarendon, 1963.

Sloan, R.B. *The Favorable Year of the Lord*. Austin: Schola, 1977.

Stanton, G.H. *Jesus of Nazareth in New Testament Preaching*. SNTS Monograph Series 27. London: Cambridge University Press, 1974.

Stonehouse, Ned B. *The Witness of Luke to Christ*. Grand Rapids: Eerdmans, 1951.

Summers, R. *Commentary on Luke*. Waco: Word, 1972.

Talbert, Charles H. *Luke and the Gnostics*. New York: Abingdon, 1966.

_____. *Literary Patterns, Theological Themes and the Genre of Luke-Acts*. Society of Biblical Literature Monograph Series 20. Missoula, Mont.: Scholars, 1974.

_____, ed. *Perspectives on Luke-Acts*. Edinburgh: T. & T. Clark, 1978.

_____. *Reading Luke: A Literary and Theological Commentary on the Third Gospel*. New York: Crossroad, 1982.

Thompson, G.H.P. *The Gospel According to Luke*. Oxford: Clarendon, 1972.

Tiede, David L. *Prophecy and History in Luke-Acts*. Philadelphia: Fortress, 1980.

Wilcock, Michael. *Savior of the World. The Message of Luke's Gospel*. Downers Grove, Ill.: Inter-Varsity, 1979.

Articles

Only articles that bear significantly on more than one part of the Gospel of Luke are listed here. Others will be found at the appropriate passages.

Minear, Paul S. "Jesus' Audiences, According to Luke." Nov Test 16 (1974): 81–109.

Nickelsburg, G.W.E. "Riches, the Rich and God's Judgment in 1 Enoch 92–105 and the Gospel According to Luke." NTS 25 (1979): 324–44.

Snodgrass, K. "Western Non-Interpolations." JBL 91 (1972): 369–79.

Talbert, Charles H. "Shifting Sands: the recent study of the Gospel of Luke." Int 30, 4 (October 1976): 381–95.

13. Outline

    I. Introduction (1:1–4)

    II. Birth and Childhood Narratives (1:5–2:52)
       A. Anticipation of Two Births (1:5–56)
          1. The birth of John the Baptist foretold (1:5–25)
          2. The birth of Jesus foretold (1:26–38)
          3. Mary's visit to Elizabeth (1:39–45)
          4. Mary's song: The Magnificat (1:46–56)
       B. Birth Narratives (1:57–2:20)
          1. The birth of John the Baptist (1:57–66)
          2. Zechariah's song: The Benedictus (1:67–80)
          3. The birth of Jesus (2:1–7)
          4. The announcement to the shepherds (2:8–20)
       C. Jesus' Early Years (2:21–52)
          1. Presentation of Jesus in the temple (2:21–40)
          2. The boy Jesus at the temple (2:41–52)

    III. Preparation for Jesus' Ministry (3:1–4:13)
       A. The Ministry of John the Baptist (3:1–20)
       B. The Baptism of Jesus (3:21–22)
       C. Jesus' Genealogy (3:23–38)
       D. The Temptation of Jesus (4:1–13)

    IV. The Galilean Ministry (4:14–9:50)
       A. Initial Phase (4:14–6:16)
          1. First approach and rejection at Nazareth (4:14–30)
          2. Driving out an evil spirit (4:31–37)
          3. Healing many (4:38–44)
          4. Calling the first disciples (5:1–11)
          5. The man with leprosy (5:12–16)
          6. Healing a paralytic (5:17–26)
          7. Calling Levi (5:27–32)
          8. The question about fasting (5:33–39)
          9. Sabbath controversies (6:1–11)
         10. Choosing the twelve apostles (6:12–16)
       B. Jesus' Great Sermon (6:17–49)
          1. Blessings and woes (6:17–26)
          2. Love for enemies (6:27–36)
          3. Judging others (6:37–42)
          4. A tree and its fruit (6:43–45)
          5. The wise and foolish builders (6:46–49)
       C. Ministry to Various Human Needs (7:1–9:17)
          1. The faith of the centurion (7:1–10)
          2. Raising a widow's son (7:11–17)
          3. Jesus and John the Baptist (7:18–35)
          4. Anointed by a sinful woman (7:36–50)
          5. Parable of the sower (8:1–15)
          6. Parable of the lamp (8:16–18)
          7. Jesus' true family (8:19–21)
          8. Calming the storm (8:22–25)

Text and Exposition

I. Introduction

1:1-4

¹Many have undertaken to draw up an account of the things that have been
fulfilled among us, ²just as they were handed down to us by those who from the
first were eyewitnesses and servants of the word. ³Therefore, since I myself have
carefully investigated everything from the beginning, it seemed good also to me to
write an orderly account for you, most excellent Theophilus, ⁴so that you may
know the certainty of the things you have been taught.

The introduction to Luke is a long, carefully constructed sentence in the tradition
of the finest historical works in Greek literature. It stands in contrast to the genealogical table of Matthew, the concise opening sentence of Mark, and the theological
prologue of John. It was customary among the great Greek and Hellenistic historians, including the first-century Jewish writer Josephus, to explain and justify their
work in a preface. Their object was to assure the reader of their capability, thorough
research, and reliability. While such a weighty introduction does not in itself guarantee the honesty of the writer, neither should its conventional form be dismissed as
a merely formal pretension.

The classical literary style of the preface contrasts with the remainder of the
Gospel, in which Semitisms abound (cf. comment in Introduction in loc.; cf. also
introductory comments on vv.5-25).

1 The preface opens with the Greek word *epeidēper* (KJV, "forasmuch as"; RSV,
"inasmuch as"), a classical word used only here in the NT but found in such major
authors as Thucydides, Philo, and Josephus. It stands in stylistic contrast to the
colloquial *egeneto* ("there was"), which in v.5 opens the narrative. NIV omits *epeidēper* for the sake of concise English style, adding "therefore" in v.3. This clarifies
the meaning—that Luke's account was written after those of many others.

"Many have undertaken" implies that by the time Luke wrote there was considerable interest in data about Jesus and his ministry. Luke does not say he himself
actually reproduced material from any of the existing accounts, though that could be
assumed from this and subsequent evidence. The choice of the word "undertaken"
(*epecheirēsan*) need not mean that earlier attempts to write gospel narratives had
failed (cf. MM, pp. 250-51). Obviously Luke would not be writing if there were no
need for something further, but this does not necessarily reflect adversely on his
predecessors. "To draw up an account" (*anataxasthai diēgēsin*) means to write a
report or narrative, relating events in an orderly way (cf. MM, p. 38). The verbal
form of *diēgēsis* ("accounts") occurs in Luke 8:39; 9:10; Acts 9:27; 12:17.

"Fulfilled" is a better translation of *peplērophorēmenōn* than "most surely believed" (KJV) in this context. The word and its cognate *plērophoria* can be translated "full assurance" or "assurance," when their basic reference is to the confident
attitude of a person (cf. Rom 4:21; 14:5; Col 2:2; Heb 6:11; 10:22). Otherwise, and
especially with reference to things rather than people, the idea of accomplishment
or completion is foremost. (See "discharge all the duties" and "fully proclaimed" in
2 Tim 4:5, 17.) Further, if the accomplishment of the purposes of God in the life and

ministry of Jesus is one of Luke's themes, it is appropriate for the preface to reflect this.

2 "Just as they were handed down" stresses the validity of the tradition of Jesus' words and deeds. The same emphasis occurs in Paul, who was careful to pass on to others what had been "handed down" to him (1 Cor 11:23; 15:3; cf. also O. Cullmann, *The Early Church: Studies in Early Christian History and Theology* [Philadelphia: Westminster, 1956], pp. 59–75).

Although the "eyewitnesses and servants" may have included some of the "many" (v.1), they are mostly to be distinguished from them because they were prior to them. Luke is establishing the validity of the information both he and his predecessors included in their narratives. Witnesses are important to Luke. While the concept of "witness" is not as prominent in Luke as in John (see esp. John 5:31–47), it is integral to Luke's historical and theological purposes.

The words "from the first" (probably meaning from the early days of Jesus' ministry) are tied to the word "eyewitnesses" as closely as grammar permits—viz., "the from-the-first witnesses" (*hoi ap' archēs autoptai*). These were not passive observers but "servants of the word." Luke is probably referring primarily to the apostles, whose authority he upholds throughout Luke-Acts. In Acts 10:39–42, Peter speaks as one of those who were both witnesses and preachers.

"Word" (*logos*) here means the message of the Gospel, especially as embodied in the words and deeds of Jesus. Ancient Greek writers often stressed the importance of matching one's words with appropriate deeds. In Acts 1:1, Luke combines the words "do" and "teach" when he describes Jesus' ministry. This is essential to the fulfillment mentioned in v.1. While all four Gospels use the term *logos* (with particular significance in John 1:1, 14), Luke uses it surprisingly often. This is especially true in passages unique to Luke (see Gaston, pp. 64, 76; Hawkins, pp. 20, 43). In summary, v.2 makes a serious claim regarding careful historical research that has weighty implications for our estimate of the entire Gospel.

3 The opening words in the Greek order are "it seemed good also to me" (*edoxe kamoi*). This establishes a balance and pattern of comparison between vv.1–2 and 3–4: "Many have undertaken" and "it seemed good also to me"; "to draw up an account" and "to write an orderly account"; "handed down to us" and "so that you may know."

Luke now describes his own work of investigation and writing. The word "everything" may partially explain how his work differed from that of the "many" (v.1) and also from that of Mark—namely, in its greater comprehensiveness. "From the beginning" translates *anōthen*, which can mean, according to the context, either "above" or "again." Here in its relation to historical research, it has a temporal sense. Luke did his research "carefully" (*akribōs*, lit., "accurately") and wrote an "orderly" (*kathexēs*) account. We cannot determine from this preface alone whether Luke is referring to a chronological or to a thematic order. He does not specifically claim to have aimed at chronological sequence. Perhaps he may have followed an order found in his sources. If so, this could explain his occasional differences from Matthew and Mark. Or he may have rearranged his sources according to another pattern. Taken alone the prologue is not conclusive as to these possibilities. In any event Luke intended his claim of working in an orderly way to inspire confidence in his readers.

The identity of Theophilus is unknown. The name ("friend of God") might be either a symbol or a substitute for the true name of Luke's addressee. Theophilus was, however, a proper name, and "most excellent" naturally suggests an actual person of some distinction. He may have been Luke's literary patron or publisher, after the custom of the times (cf. E.J. Goodspeed, "Some Greek Notes: I. Was Theophilus Luke's Publisher?" JBL 73 [1954]: 84).

4 Though it is not clear whether Theophilus was a believer, he had doubtless received some instructions in the faith. The genitive plural (*logōn*) of *logos* ("word") is here translated by NIV as "things," a legitimate extended use. Theophilus has learned of both the words and the deeds of Jesus. "Taught" (*katēchēthēs*) may refer to formal church teaching (Gal 6:6), but not necessarily. For some reason Theophilus needed assurance, or "certainty" (*asphaleian*), as to the truth of the things taught him. Possibly he was troubled by denials of the Resurrection and other historical foundations of the faith that Gnostic speculation was challenging. Such are not to be countered by mere speculation but by the factual narrative Luke is about to write. His book will set forth evidences and purposes ancillary to the one he has stated in this preface.

According to the prologue, Luke's purpose in writing was to assure Theophilus of the "certainty" of the Gospel tradition. His Gospel can still fulfill that purpose. This does not exclude other purposes for Luke-Acts (cf. Introduction: Purpose).

Notes

1–4 Among the many useful articles on the Lukan prologue and the method of his historical investigation, see Stonehouse, *The Witness to Christ*, pp. 24–25, in which he especially surveys the contributions of H.J. Cadbury. Supplementary to this is Stonehouse's *Origins of the Synoptic Gospels* (Grand Rapids: Eerdmans, 1963), pp. 113–31. For more recent perspectives, see D.J. Sneen, "An Exegesis of Luke 1:1–4 with Special Regard to Luke's Purpose as a Historian," ExpT 83 (1971–72): 40–43, and I.I. du Plessis, "Once More: The Purpose of Luke's Prologue," NovTest 16 (1974): 259–71 (contains useful comparisons with other ancient historical introductions, and S. Brown, "The Role of the Prologues in Determining the Purpose of Luke–Acts," in C.H. Talbert, ed., *Perspectives on Luke–Acts*). A most important recent work on the purpose of Luke is Maddox's *Purpose of Luke-Acts*.

II. Birth and Childhood Narratives (1:5–2:52)

A. *Anticipation of Two Births* (1:5–56)

1. *The birth of John the Baptist foretold* (1:5–25)

⁵In the time of Herod king of Judea there was a priest named Zechariah, who belonged to the priestly division of Abijah; his wife Elizabeth was also a descendant of Aaron. ⁶Both of them were upright in the sight of God, observing all the Lord's commandments and regulations blamelessly. ⁷But they had no children, because Elizabeth was barren; and they were both well along in years.

⁸Once when Zechariah's division was on duty and he was serving as priest

before God, [9]he was chosen by lot, according to the custom of the priesthood, to go into the temple of the Lord and burn incense. [10]And when the time for the burning of incense came, all the assembled worshipers were praying outside.

[11]Then an angel of the Lord appeared to him, standing at the right side of the altar of incense. [12]When Zechariah saw him, he was startled and was gripped with fear. [13]But the angel said to him: "Do not be afraid, Zechariah; your prayer has been heard. Your wife Elizabeth will bear you a son, and you are to give him the name John. [14]He will be a joy and delight to you, and many will rejoice because of his birth, [15]for he will be great in the sight of the Lord. He is never to take wine or other fermented drink, and he will be filled with the Holy Spirit even from birth. [16]Many of the people of Israel will he bring back to the Lord their God. [17]And he will go before the Lord, in the spirit and power of Elijah, to turn the hearts of the fathers to their children and the disobedient to the wisdom of the righteous—to make ready a people prepared for the Lord."

[18]Zechariah asked the angel, "How can I be sure of this? I am an old man and my wife is well along in years."

[19]The angel answered, "I am Gabriel. I stand in the presence of God, and I have been sent to speak to you and to tell you this good news. [20]And now you will be silent and not able to speak until the day this happens, because you did not believe my words, which will come true at their proper time."

[21]Meanwhile, the people were waiting for Zechariah and wondering why he stayed so long in the temple. [22]When he came out, he could not speak to them. They realized he had seen a vision in the temple, for he kept making signs to them but remained unable to speak.

[23]When his time of service was completed, he returned home. [24]After this his wife Elizabeth became pregnant and for five months remained in seclusion. [25]"The Lord has done this for me," she said. "In these days he has shown his favor and taken away my disgrace among the people."

This narrative introduces a section in Luke unparalleled in the other Gospels (cf. Introduction for critical and stylistic issues). Its distinctive characteristics include (1) an atmosphere reminiscent of the OT, with a grammatical and stylistic Semitic cast; (2) an alternation of focus on John the Baptist and on Jesus; (3) the awesomeness of heavenly beings appearing to humans; and (4) a note of joy, especially as heard in four songs: Mary's (1:46–55), Zechariah's (1:68–79), the angels' (2:14), and Simeon's (2:29–32).

1. The Semitic style fits the religious and historical connection Luke is establishing between the OT and NT periods. Luke does not use the fulfillment formulas Matthew used but shows that OT predictions stand behind the events he describes. This he does by giving his style and vocabulary a flavor of the LXX. He also takes pains to ground the Christian message in Jerusalem and in its temple. Machen (pp. 62–101) uses the Semitic style in his arguments for the Virgin Birth.

2. To make this connection with the OT, Luke also uses a pattern of alternation, in which attention shifts back and forth between John the Baptist and Jesus. Far from being a confusion of sources, as is sometimes supposed, this alternation is a literary device to focus attention successively on each person (cf. G.N. Stanton, *Jesus of Nazareth in New Testament Preaching*, SNTS Monograph Series 27 [London: Cambridge University Press, 1974], pp. 55–56). Luke clearly identifies John as a successor to the OT prophets. Through his alternating presentations, Luke links John and Jesus, whom Luke apparently also identifies as a prophet (Minear, *Heal and Reveal*, pp. 95–96). Since he also sees in Jesus far more than a prophet, Luke's device of alternation goes beyond comparison to contrast, with Jesus presented as "Son of the Most High" and messianic Deliverer (1:32–33, 69, 76; 2:11, 30). The

structure of the section then is (1) the announcement of John's coming birth, (2) the announcement of Jesus' coming birth, (3) Elizabeth's blessing of Mary, (4) Mary's praise to God, (5) John's birth, and (6) Jesus' birth, which is acclaimed by angels in heaven and by saintly Jews in the temple.

3. The appearance of angels is likewise appropriate for an account that teaches that God has acted decisively in the history of his people to accomplish our salvation. Some reject this supernatural activity, attempting to explain the narratives as an accretion of legends. To do so deprives the event of an effective cause. Actually the appearance of an angel is no more remarkable than the Incarnation itself.

4. The theme of joy finds expression not only in the songs but in the tone of the whole passage. The gospel is always "good news of great joy" (2:10). Moreover, the passage realistically includes a reminder both of the pain of sin and of the cost of our deliverance, as Simeon's allusion to the ultimate death of Mary's son (2:35) shows.

Another pattern of themes may be seen in the repetition of the phrase "Most High": (1) Jesus is the "Son of the Most High" (1:32); (2) Mary's conception by the Holy Spirit is said to be by the "power of the Most High" (1:35); and (3) John is called a "prophet of the Most High" (1:76) (H.H. Oliver, "The Lucan Birth Stories and the Purpose of Luke-Acts," NTS 10 [1963–64]: 215–26).

While the phrases just outlined do not occur in close sequence, they should probably be taken together as relating to three major themes in Luke's Gospel: (1) John is the final prophet of the OT period, the forerunner of the Messiah, and the first proclaimer of the kingdom; (2) Jesus is the unique Son of God, the true eschatological prophet and Messiah; and (3) the Holy Spirit's ministry both validates and empowers the ministry of Jesus. (The Holy Spirit is mentioned frequently in this section; viz., 1:15, 35, 41, 67, 80; 2:25–27.) Other themes prominent in Luke occur in these opening narratives and will be pointed out in the exposition.

5 As has already been said, the style of this section is different from the classical style of vv.1–4. Likewise, the method of dating differs from that used later in 3:1, where Luke is interested in establishing a more precise point of historical reference. In this verse his only concern is to locate the events in the reign of Herod (king of Judea 37–4 B.C.).

Luke emphasizes the Jewish roots of Christianity by mentioning that, not only was Zechariah (whose name means "God remembers") a priest, but that his wife had also been born into the priestly line. (See comment on v.8 for the functioning of this "priestly division.")

6 This is a description of a truly pious couple wholly devoted to God. The language of the verse "implies a religious rather than a purely ethical character" (Marshall, *Gospel of Luke*, p. 53). Marshall remarks that v.6 shows that their childlessness did not imply any sin. The OT would use the Hebrew *tām* or *tāmîm* to describe such a couple (tr. "blameless" in Gen 6:9; Job 1:8).

7 To be childless brought sorrow and often shame. At her advanced age, Elizabeth could no longer entertain the hope of each Jewish woman to be the mother of the Messiah. While her situation and the subsequent intervention of God had its precedents in the OT (cf. Sarah, Gen 17:16–17; Hannah, 1 Sam 1:5–11), no other woman had such a total reversal in fortune as to bear the forerunner of the Messiah.

8–9 The "division" (v.8; cf. v.5) was one of twenty-four groups of priests divided by families and structured after the pattern of 1 Chronicles 23 and 24 (note Abijah, Zechariah's ancestor [1 Chron 24:10]). The Exile had interrupted the original lines of descent; so the divisions were regrouped, most of them corresponding to the original in name only. Each of the twenty-four divisions served in the temple for one week, twice a year, as well as at the major festivals (J. Jeremias, *Jerusalem in the Time of Jesus* [London: SCM, 1969], pp. 198–207). An individual priest, however, could offer the incense at the daily sacrifice (cf. Notes) only once in his lifetime (v.9), since there were so many priests. Therefore this was the climactic moment of Zechariah's priestly career, perhaps the most dramatic moment possible for the event described to have occurred. God was breaking into the ancient routine of Jewish ritual with the word of his decisive saving act. Considering his interest in the Jewish origin of Christianity, Luke probably viewed this dramatic moment not so much as a judgment against Judaism as an appropriate and significant context for the new revelation.

10 Mention of the worshipers outside not only heightens the suspense but prepares the reader for vv.21–22. They were probably pious Jews who loved to be near the temple when sacrifices were offered. NIV's "assembled worshipers" obscures the important word *laos* ("people"; cf. comments on v.27).

11–12 The suddenness of the appearance of the angel (v.11) accords with other supernatural events in Luke and elsewhere in Scripture (cf. 2:9, 13). Luke does not describe the angel, but the fact that he tells exactly where the angel appeared shows the reality of the vision. Only a heavenly being had the right to appear in the Holy Place with the priest. "Startled" (v.12) represents a word of deep emotion (from *tarassō*) and is coupled with the descriptive phrase "gripped with fear." This is not only a natural reaction to such an appearance but is also consistent with what the Gospels say about the response of the disciples and others to the presence of the supernatural (e.g., 5:8–10). Sometimes this betrayed unbelief. But this was certainly not true of Mary (v.38). Rather her attitude (v.29) showed her genuine awe and quite natural trepidation at being confronted by the heavenly visitor.

13 This is the first indication of prayer on the part of Zechariah. The word Luke used (*deēsis*) indicates a specific petition. If this was for a child (probably a son), the aorist tense in the phrase "has been heard" refers to Zechariah's lifelong prayer. Otherwise, his just-offered prayer in the temple was probably for the messianic redemption of Israel. Actually, the birth of his child was bound up with redemption in a way far beyond anything Zechariah expected. That the prayer included a petition for a son is substantiated by the further description of the child, beginning with his name. "John" (*Iōannēs*) combines in its Hebrew form the name of God with the word *ḥānan* ("to show favor" or "be gracious"). God did indeed answer Zechariah's prayer. That the child was named before his birth stresses God's sovereignty in choosing him to be his servant.

14–15 The description of the child's mission has a counterpart in Gabriel's words to Mary (vv.32–33). This is part of the literary device that connects and compares the roles of Jesus and John.

The "joy" (v.14) so characteristic of the day of God's salvation and so prominent in

Luke came first to the parents of the forerunner, then spread to "many people [lit., 'sons'] of Israel" (v. 16). Also "joy and gladness" stand in contrast to Zechariah's fear (v. 12). The child will be "great" (*megas*) as the prophetic forerunner of the Messiah (v. 15). "Great" also describes Jesus in v. 32, though in the latter case it is absolute greatness without the qualifying "in the sight of the Lord." Later there would be those who found it hard to relinquish their devotion to John to follow Jesus. They would need to realize that while both were great, Jesus was the greater (3:16). Also John's greatness related to the pre-Messianic Age (7:28). "In the sight of the Lord" indicates divine choice and approval. This expression, or its equivalent, is used frequently in Luke and Acts (cf. Notes).

It is difficult to identify John with a particular religious group simply by this description or that in Mark 1:6. Abstinence from wine suggests the Nazirite vow (Num 6:1–12), but no mention is made of John's hair. Nazirites were to let their hair grow (Num 6:5). Danker (*Jesus*, p. 8) refers to the priests' abstinence from strong drink prior to entering the tabernacle and sees John as a priestly figure calling the people to repentance. On the other hand, the radical elements in John's appearance and behavior may exemplify his radical message of repentance. The Spirit's control is contrasted with the control wine can have over a person (cf. Eph 5:18). In the life of Jesus, the Spirit's ministry will be even more prominent than in John's life.

16–17 The OT prophets were repeatedly concerned with turning the erring people back to God, i.e., to repentance (v. 16). In this work none was more prominent than Elijah on Mount Carmel (1 Kings 18:20–40). Luke does not here identify John as a reincarnated Elijah but qualifies his statement with the words "in the spirit and power of Elijah" (v. 17). Moreover Luke uses the language of Malachi 4:5–6 (cf. Mal 3:1) to compare John's ministry with that of Elijah. (See comments on 9:30 for further discussion of Elijah.)

"To turn the hearts of the fathers to their children" must be interpreted with reference to both the expanded form in Malachi 4:6 and the next phrase in this context (v. 17). If the words are parallel to the phrase "wisdom of the righteous," then "the fathers," previously disobedient, may be following the example of their children who are presumably listening to the message of John—"the wisdom of the righteous." Grammatically less likely but more probable, it might mean that when those who disobey heed wisdom, their Jewish ancestors would, if they knew of it, be pleased with them (Godet, pp. 79–80). In their OT context, the words "turn the hearts," etc., relate to averting divine wrath, a concept certainly basic in the ministry of John.

"People" (*laos*) is a significant word in Luke. Thirty-five of its forty-nine occurrences in the synoptic Gospels are in Luke (Gaston, p. 76; cf. Hawkins, pp. 20–21, 45). Minear ("Jesus' Audiences," pp. 81–109) holds that the term *laos* as used by Luke, in contrast to *ochlos* ("crowd"), "normally refers to Israel as the elect nation which forever retains the specific identity given to it by God." This suggestion accords with Luke's interest in Jewish origins of Christianity, though it may be too comprehensive. Minear (ibid.) also comments that "it is this specific entity ['people'] which Luke sees as the initial and ultimate audience for all God's messengers, whether John the Baptist (Acts 13:24) or the apostles ([Acts] 3:12f.)." The "people prepared for the Lord" ultimately includes not only these initial Jewish hearers but those who formerly were "not a people" (1 Peter 2:10), the Gentiles (see also Jervell).

18–20 Zechariah's question (v.18) seems innocent, but v.20 reveals that it was asked in doubt. In contrast Mary's question—"How can this be?" (v.34)—arises from faith (v.45). Mary simply inquired as to the way God would work; Zechariah questioned the truth of the revelation. "How can I be sure of this?" apparently was a request for a sign. Though we are told that Zechariah was devout (v.6), his quest for confirmation was perilously close to the attitude described in Luke 11:29. Since the gospel requires a response of faith, and since Zechariah, of all people, should have believed without question, the angel's reply (v.20) is not overly severe. The narrative gains solemnity by mentioning that Gabriel stood "in the presence of [*enōpion*] God" (v.19; cf. "in the sight of" [v.15] and "before"[v.17]). The "good news" will come to fulfillment in spite of human unbelief, but Zechariah must nevertheless bear the sign of his doubt. "Will come true" (*plērōthēsontai*) means "will be fulfilled" and forms part of Luke's presentation of the fulfilled word of God.

21–22 The element of suspense during the unusually long prayer-time contributes to the vividness of Luke's narrative (v.21; cf. v.10). The worshipers who had been praying outside now understood without anyone telling them that Zechariah had seen a vision. Verse 22 reinforces the extraordinary nature of his experience and his loss of speech.

23–25 As with the announcement to Mary, the word concerning Zechariah and Elizabeth's promised son was given before his conception (v.24; cf. Joseph's experience [Matt 1:18–25]). It is characteristic of Luke to mention Elizabeth's grateful acknowledgment of the Lord's grace in removing the stigma of her childlessness (v.25).

Notes

5–25 The literature on Luke 1 and 2 is extensive. The following are especially useful for the birth narratives: R.E. Brown, *Birth of the Messiah*, pp. 233–533; Marshall, *Luke: Historian and Theologian*, pp. 96–102; Paul S. Minear, "Luke's Use of the Birth Stories," in Keck and Martyn, pp. 111–30; and Oliver, "Lucan Birth Stories," pp. 202–26.

6 Ἄμεμπτοι (*amemptoi*, "blamelessly") does not imply sinlessness. Abraham was told to be "blameless" before the Lord (Gen 17:1 [LXX, *amemptoi*]). Paul, who affirms universal sinfulness (Rom 3:23), says he had been "faultless" (*amemptoi*) as regards "legalistic righteousness" (Phil 3:6).

8 Ἐγένετο δὲ (*egeneto de*, "once") reflects the Hebrew idiom וַיְהִי (*wayᵉhî*, "and it came to pass") in the narrative construction. This is a common expression in Luke, used in various combinations. In this form and in others, the verb γίνομαι (*ginomai*, "be") is used frequently in Luke, more than in Matthew and Mark together. Of the 107 occurrences, 31 in Luke are apparently editorial additions to his sources (Gastron, p. 70).

9 "According to the custom of the priesthood" could go with v.8, but NIV is probably right in taking it with "he was chosen by lot."

"Incense" was offered in connection with the morning and evening sacrifice (M *Tamid* 2.5; 5.2; 6.3). Marshall (*Luke: Historian and Theologian*, p. 54) connects the offering of incense, which symbolizes prayer in Scripture (Ps 141:2; Rev 5:8; 8:3–4), with Luke's particular interest in prayer.

13 "Prayer" here means, as noted above, a specific request. The more general word is προσευχή (*proseuchē*, cf. 6:12; 19:46; 22:45).

15 Luke is the only synoptic writer to use ἐνώπιον (*enōpion*, "in the sight of"). He does so twenty-two times.

19 Gabriel (cf. Dan 8:16; 9:21) is one of two angels named in Scripture, the other being Michael (Dan 10:13; 21; 21:1; Jude 9; Rev 12:7).

Εὐαγγελίζομαι (*euangelizomai*, "to tell . . . good news") has a special significance in Luke. Of its eleven occurrences in the Synoptics, ten are in Luke (cf. 2:10; 3:18; 4:8, 43; 7:22; 8:1; 9:6; 16:16; 20:1). The noun εὐαγγέλιον (*euangelion*, "good news," "gospel") occurs in Mark but not in Luke. The words do not always denote news that is good (TDNT, 2:707–37; cf. Marshall, *Luke: Historian and Theologian*, pp. 123–24).

---

2. The birth of Jesus foretold

1:26–38

> [26]In the sixth month, God sent the angel Gabriel to Nazareth, a town in Galilee, [27]to a virgin pledged to be married to a man named Joseph, a descendant of David. The virgin's name was Mary. [28]The angel went to her and said, "Greetings, you who are highly favored! The Lord is with you."
>
> [29]Mary was greatly troubled at his words and wondered what kind of greeting this might be. [30]But the angel said to her, "Do not be afraid, Mary, you have found favor with God. [31]You will be with child and give birth to a son, and you are to give him the name Jesus. [32]He will be great and will be called the Son of the Most High. The Lord God will give him the throne of his father David, [33]and he will reign over the house of Jacob forever; his kingdom will never end."
>
> [34]"How will this be," Mary asked the angel, "since I am a virgin?"
>
> [35]The angel answered, "The Holy Spirit will come upon you, and the power of the Most High will overshadow you. So the holy one to be born, will be called the Son of God. [36]Even Elizabeth your relative is going to have a child in her old age, and she who was said to be barren is in her sixth month. [37]For nothing is impossible with God."
>
> [38]"I am the Lord's servant," Mary answered. "May it be to me as you have said." Then the angel left her.

Continuing in the same style in which he has described Zechariah's encounter with the angel of the Lord, Luke now weaves deep theological meaning into his simple and delicate narrative. This section is the highest of several summits of revelation in chapters 1 and 2. The account of Jesus' nativity, beautiful and essential as it is, rests theologically on the angel Gabriel's announcement to Mary. Luke presents the theology of the Incarnation in a way so holy and congruent with OT sacred history that any comparisons with pagan mythology seem utterly incongruous. Instead of the carnal union of a pagan god with a woman, producing some kind of semidivine offspring, Luke speaks of a spiritual overshadowing by God himself that will produce the "holy one" within Mary.

Several themes are intertwined in this passage: (1) the divine sonship of Jesus (vv.32, 35); (2) his messianic role and reign over the kingdom (vv.32–33); (3) God as the "Most High" (vv.32, 35; cf. v.76); (4) the power of the Holy Spirit (v.35); and (5) the grace of God (vv.29–30, 34–35, 38).

26 The mention of Elizabeth's "sixth month" (cf. v.24) points to the pattern of alternation and establishes a link with the prophet John the Baptist (cf. comments on vv.5–25). The same chronological device points in v.36 to God's power over human reproduction. This theme of the direct action of God is one of the basic ones in Luke-Acts. (See v.19 in reference to the angel Gabriel.) Luke calls Nazareth a *polis*, which can often be translated "city," but here describes a "town" (NIV) or "village." It was off, though not totally inaccessible from, the main trade routes. Its relatively insignificant size contrasts with Jerusalem, where Gabriel's previous appearance had taken place. John 1:46 records the contemporary Judean opinion of Nazareth.

Likewise, the region of Galilee contrasts with Judea. Surrounded as they were by Gentiles, the Galileans were not necessarily irreligious. They were, however, somewhat lax respecting such things as keeping a kosher kitchen (cf. Sean Freyne, *Galilee from Alexander the Great to Hadrian 323 B.C.E. to 135 C.E.* [Wilmington, Del.: Michael Glazier and Notre Dame: University of Notre Dame Press, 1980], pp. 259–97). Though the Galileans had a reputation for pugnacity, Galilee was not a hotbed of revolutionary activity, as some have thought (ibid., pp. 208–55).

27 The young virgin Mary contrasts with the old priest Zechariah, who was past the time for having children. The word "virgin" refers here to one who had not yet had sexual relations (cf. Notes). Mary's question in v.34 and the reference in v.27 to her being "pledged to be married" make this clear. Since betrothal often took place soon after puberty, Mary may have just entered her teens. This relationship was legally binding, but intercourse was not permitted until marriage. Only divorce or death could sever betrothal; and in the latter event the girl, though unmarried, would be considered a widow.

In v.27 Luke calls Joseph "a descendant of David." Even though the genealogy in 3:23–37 is often taken as showing Mary's line, this is never stated. Neither does Luke nor any other NT writer say that Mary was descended from David. Since Joseph is named here and in 3:23 and is explicitly linked with the royal line, we should probably assume that Luke considers Jesus a legitimate member of the royal line by what we today might call the right of adoption. This has an important bearing on the promise in v.32b.

28 Here Luke establishes another contrast with the preceding narrative—this time by relating Gabriel's greeting (vv.30–32) to Mary. But Zechariah had received no such greeting.

"Highly favored" renders *kecharitōmenē*, which has the same root as the words for "Greetings" (*chaire*), and "favor" (*charin*, v.30). Mary is "highly favored" because she is the recipient of God's grace. A similar combination of words occurs in Ephesians 1:6—"his glorious grace . . . which he has freely given [same Gr. word as for 'highly favored'] us." Some suggest that Luke implies that a certain grace has been found in Mary's character. While this could be so, the parallel in Ephesians (the only other occurrence of the verb in the NT) shows that the grace in view here is that which is given all believers apart from any merit of theirs. Mary has "found favor with God" (v.30); she is a recipient of his grace (v.28), and she can therefore say, "My spirit rejoices in God my Savior" (v.47).

"The Lord is with you" recalls the way the angel of the Lord addressed Gideon to assure him of God's help in the assignment he was to about to receive (Judg 6:12).

29–30 Zechariah had been "gripped with fear" (v.12) at the very appearance of the angel, but it was the angel's words—viz., his greeting (v.28)—that "greatly troubled" Mary (v.29). He responded first by assuring her that she had indeed "found favor" with God (v.30; cf. Gen 6:8, where Noah is spoken of as having found favor with God). God's grace, like his love, banishes fear of judgment (1 John 4:17–18).

31 Gabriel now explains why his preliminary assurance of Mary's having found grace with God is so significant for her. The wording here is virtually identical to the "virgin" passage in Isaiah 7:14 (LXX) and to the assurance the angel of the Lord gave the fugitive Hagar (Gen 16:11 LXX). The word "virgin" is not, however, mentioned in the allusion to Isaiah, though Mary's question (v.34) shows she was a virgin, a fact Luke has mentioned in v.27.

The name Jesus (Joshua) had been common in OT times and continued to be a popular name through the first century A.D. (TDNT, 3:284–93). Matthew 1:21 provides an explanation for giving the child a name that contains, in its Hebrew form, the word "saves" (*yāšaʿ*): "because he will save his people from their sins."

32–33 Some scholars consider it significant that whereas in v.15 Gabriel had qualified his prophecy of the greatness of John ("he will be great in the sight of the Lord"), here his statement of the greatness of Mary's Son has no qualification whatever. The striking term "Son of the Most High" (v.33; cf. vv.35, 76) leads to a clear messianic affirmation—the reference to the "throne of his father David." Jesus' divine sonship is thus linked to his messiahship in accord with 2 Samuel 7:12–14 and Psalm 2:7–9 (cf. Ps 89:26–29). The description of Jesus' messianic destiny follows the statement of his sonship, and that sonship is related in v.35 to his divine origin. Clearly Luke sees the messianic vocation as a function of God's Son, rather than seeing sonship as just an aspect of messiahship.

The OT concepts of "throne," Davidic line, "reign" (v.33), and "kingdom" are spoken of as eternal—i.e., "will never end." Though this idea is found in Micah 4:7, it is not common in Jewish thought.

34 Unlike Zechariah, Mary does not ask for a confirmatory sign (cf. comments on v.18) but only for light on how God will accomplish this wonder. As Luke has it, the question does not relate to the remarkable person and work of her promised Son but arises from the fact that she "does not know [*ou ginōskō*, i.e., has not had sexual relations with] a man" (NIV, "I am a virgin"). "While the tense is present, it describes a state resultant from a past pattern of behavior—Mary has not known *any* man and so is a virgin" (R.E. Brown, *Birth of the Messiah*, p. 289; emphasis his).

Because she was betrothed, we may assume that Mary fully expected to have normal marital relations later. It is difficult, therefore, to know why she saw a problem in Gabriel's prediction. The text does not say that Mary had Isaiah 7:14 in mind and wondered how she, still a virgin, could conceive. Perhaps Luke's condensed account is intended to suggest (1) that Mary assumed an immediate fulfillment before marriage and (2) that the informed reader should understand the issue in terms of Isaiah 7:14, already hinted at in v.31. Marshall (*Luke: Historian and Theologian*, pp. 69–70) lists several alternative explanations, none of which is satisfactory by itself (cf. also R.E. Brown, *Birth of the Messiah*, pp. 303–9).

35 Once again (cf. v.15) Luke mentions the Holy Spirit, as he does six more times in his first two chapters (1:41, 67, 80; 2:25, 26, 27). The word for "overshadow" (*episkiazō*) carries the sense of the holy, powerful presence of God, as in the description of the cloud that "covered" (Heb. šākan; NIV, "settled upon") the tabernacle when the tent was filled with the glory of God (Exod 40:35; cf. Ps 91:4). The word is used in all three accounts of the Transfiguration to describe the overshadowing of the cloud (Matt 17:5; Mark 9:7; Luke 9:34). Likewise, in each account the voice comes out of the cloud identifying Jesus as God's Son, a striking reminder of Luke 1:35 where the life that results from the enveloping cloud is identified as the Son of God.

The child whose life is thus engendered by the power of God, which power is identified as the Holy Spirit, is himself called by Gabriel "the holy one." Because of this connection with the Holy Spirit, and because of the ethical meaning of "holy" in v.49, that word probably relates here to the purity of Jesus instead of relating to separation for a divine vocation.

36-37 The angel cites the pregnancy of Elizabeth (v.36) as further evidence of God's marvelous power and concludes with the grand affirmation of v.37—surely one of the most reassuring statements in all Scripture.

38 Mary's exemplary attitude of servanthood recalls that of Hannah, when she was praying for a son (1 Sam 1:11, where the LXX also has *doulē*, "servant"). Nothing is said about the relation of Mary's submission to her consciousness of the shame a premarital pregnancy could bring her. Her servanthood is not a cringing slavery but a submission to God that in OT times characterized genuine believers and that should characterize believers today (cf. v.48). Understandably Mary doubtless felt an empathy with Hannah's sense of being at the Lord's disposal in part of life a woman before modern times had little or no control over. Mary's trusting submission at this point in her life may be compared with her attitude toward her Son later on (cf. John 2:5).

Notes

---

27 The meaning of παρθένος (*parthenos*) is not in doubt here since it is amplified in v.34 (where NIV introduces the term "virgin" to explain the text). Therefore, while it is alleged on the basis of some other literature that *parthenos* occasionally had a broader meaning under special circumstances (J. Massingbyrde Ford, "The Meaning of 'Virgin,'" NTS 12 [3, 1966]: 293-99), the meaning here is not affected. See commentary on 3:23. In addition to the works cited in the Bibliography, especially Machen, literature on the Virgin Birth includes James Orr, *The Virgin Birth of Christ* (New York: Scribner's, 1907); Thomas Boslooper, *The Virgin Birth* (Philadelphia: Westminster, 1962); R.E. Brown, *The Virginal Conception and Bodily Resurrection of Jesus* (New York: Paulist, 1973); Robert Gromacki, *The Virgin Birth: Doctrine of Deity* (Nashville: Nelson, 1974).

28 The meaning of "Greetings" (KJV, "Hail") for Χαῖρε (*chaire*) is debated. It is the simple Greek word for a greeting. In the LXX of Zeph 3:14, it means "Rejoice" (cf. Zech 9:9). Some have seen a connection—significant for Roman Catholic interpreters—between Mary and the "Daughter of Zion" addressed in Zephaniah. Although an allusion to Zeph 3:14 is dubious, the parallel between "mighty to save" in Zeph 3:17 and Mary's reference to God as "Savior" and "Mighty One" in Luke 1:47, 49 may make it a remote possibility. The Latin form of the greeting is preserved in the familiar words "Ave Maria."

Ὁ κύριος μετὰ σοῦ (ho kyrios meta sou, "the Lord is with you") is followed, in many MSS, by the words εὐλογημένη σὺ ἐν γυναιξίν (eulogēmenē su en gynaixin, "blessed are you among women"). This clause, familiar from the Roman Catholic "Hail Mary," is in the later MSS represented in the KJV and is probably copied from v.42 (B. Metzger, *A Textual Commentary on the Greek New Testament* [New York: United Bible Societies, 1971], p. 129). Since it is hard to explain why Sinaiticus (ℵ) and Vaticanus (B) omitted it if it were authentic, and since its presence in other MSS can be explained as a transfer from v.42, it is best left out. It was included in the KJV and Douay Version.

28, 30 For studies on χάρις (charis, "grace," "favor"), see H. Conzelmann, TDNT, 9:372–402, and H.H. Esser, DNTT, 2:115–24.

32, 35 Ὁ ὕψιστος (ho hypsistos, "Most High") is found seven times in Luke, twice in Acts, and only four times elsewhere in the NT. It is frequent in the LXX. See Marshall, *Luke: Historian and Theologian*, p. 67, for a defense of the Semitic rather than Hellenistic character of the term as used here. The issue affects the question of the Palestinian origin and, therefore, of the authenticity of the narrative.

35 Observe that the title υἱὸς θεοῦ (huios theou, "Son of God") occurs in a Jewish Palestinian setting here. Formerly its use in the NT was commonly attributed to Hellenistic influence. Recent scholarship has corrected this error. The literature on this subject is vast. For a summary of the data, see E. Schweizer, TDNT, 8:334–92, esp. pp. 376–82; cf. Martin Hengel, *The Son of God: The Origin of Christology and the History of the Jewish-Hellenistic Religion* (Philadelphia: Fortress, 1976). R.E. Brown, *Birth of the Messiah*, pp. 311–16, surveys the relevant data in this passage.

The syntax of τὸ γεννώμενον ἅγιον κληθήσεται υἱὸς θεοῦ (to gennōmenon hagion klēthēsetai huios theou, "the holy one to be born will be called the Son of God") is difficult. The alternate possibilities can be visualized as follows:

NIV: The holy one to be born
RSV: The   child to be born
NIV: . . . will be called   the Son of God
RSV: . . . will be called holy, the Son of God

The second possibility takes "holy" as a predicate adjective, rather than as a modifier of the subject. In supporting the second rendering, R.E. Brown (*Birth of the Messiah*, p. 291) cites Isa 4:3 and Luke 2:23 as parallels. (The parallel in Luke 2:23 is not clear in NIV, which substitutes "consecrated" for "called holy.") In both parallels, the verb καλέω (kaleō) follows the predicate, which is the normal order (Marshall, *Luke: Historian and Theologian*, p. 71). If v.35 follows this pattern, "holy," not "Son of God," is in the predicate position, with "Son of God" in apposition to "holy," as in RSV and RV. In either case, "will be called" is "tantamount to saying 'he will be'" (R.E. Brown, *Birth of the Messiah*, p. 291); so the virginal conception brings into human existence one who is the Son of God.

---

3. Mary's visit to Elizabeth

1:39–45

[39]At that time Mary got ready and hurried to a town in the hill country of Judea, [40]where she entered Zechariah's home and greeted Elizabeth. [41]When Elizabeth heard Mary's greeting, the baby leaped in her womb, and Elizabeth was filled with the Holy Spirit. [42]In a loud voice she exclaimed: "Blessed are you among women, and blessed is the child you will bear! [43]But why am I so favored, that the mother of my Lord should come to me? [44]As soon as the sound of your greeting reached my ears, the baby in my womb leaped for joy. [45]Blessed is she who has believed that what the Lord has said to her will be accomplished!"

At this point Luke deftly combines the two strands about Elizabeth and Mary. So far the narrative has not stressed Jesus' superiority to John. But now attention centers on Jesus and his mother (v.43). Even so, the pattern of alternation continues, giving John his own important place as the prophet who goes before the Lord.

39–40 Mary apparently started on her journey as soon as possible (v.39). Luke does not specify the town she went to, but we can assume that it was fifty to seventy miles from Nazareth to Zechariah's home (v.40), a major trip for Mary.

41–42 To speculate about how Mary's greeting caused the child to leap in Elizabeth's womb (v.41) would be to miss the unaffected beauty of this narrative in which the stirring of the unborn child becomes a joyful prelude to Elizabeth's being filled by the Holy Spirit, who enlightened her about the identity of the child Mary was carrying (v.42).

43 Nowhere in the NT is Mary called "Mother of God." Deity is not confined to the person of Jesus (we may say, "Jesus is God," but not [all of] "God is Jesus"). She was, however, the mother of Jesus the Messiah and Lord. In Luke "Lord" is a frequently used title (95 out of 166 occurrences in the Synoptics; so Gaston, p. 76). Jesus is called "Lord" two other times in the Lukan birth narratives (1:76; 2:11).

44–45 "Blessed" (v.45) describes the happy situation of those God favors. Elizabeth gave the blessing Zechariah's muteness prevented him from giving. See vv.68–79 for the blessing he later gave the infant Jesus. Luke uses the blessing Elizabeth gave Mary to call attention to Mary's faith.

4. Mary's song: The Magnificat

1:46–56

46And Mary said:

> "My soul glorifies the Lord
> 47 and my spirit rejoices in God my Savior,
> 48for he has been mindful
>   of the humble state of his servant.
> From now on all generations will call me blessed,
> 49 for the Mighty One has done great things for me—
>   holy is his name.
> 50His mercy extends to those who fear him,
>   from generation to generation.
> 51He has performed mighty deeds with his arm;
>   he has scattered those who are proud in their
>   inmost thoughts.
> 52He has brought down rulers from their thrones
>   but has lifted up the humble.
> 53He has filled the hungry with good things
>   but has sent the rich away empty.
> 54He has helped his servant Israel,
>   remembering to be merciful
> 55to Abraham and his descendants forever,
>   even as he said to our fathers."

56Mary stayed with Elizabeth for about three months and then returned home.

This song, commonly known as the Magnificat, has several striking features. First, it is saturated with OT concepts and phrases. Plummer (pp. 30–31) cites twelve different OT passages it reflects line by line, in addition to Hannah's prayer in 1 Samuel 2:1–10, on which the song seems to have been modeled.

Second, assuming that the song is correctly attributed to Mary (see below), it shows her deep piety and knowledge of Scripture. Such familiarity with the OT was not at that time so unusual for a pious Jewess like Mary as to bar her from consideration as its author. Moreover, it reflects qualities suitable to the mother of the Lord.

Third, though it reveals a God who vindicates the downtrodden and ministers to the hungry (cf. 1 Sam 2:1–10), it also strikes a revolutionary note. If Hannah spoke of the poor being raised to sit with nobles (1 Sam 2:8), Mary sees the nobles toppled from their places of power (Luke 1:52). Yet Hannah's song is not without its elements of judgment in which the hungry and those who arrogantly oppose God are routed (1 Sam 2:3, 5, 10; cf. Luke 1:51, 53). Luke conveys a strong social message to us, one that is rooted in the OT and that, with cultural adaptations, is of continued meaning.

Fourth, Mary's Magnificat markedly transcends Hannah's song. It does this through its messianic element and implies Mary's consciousness of her own exalted role as the kingdom dawns (v.48).

This song can be divided into four strophes: (1) vv.46–48 praise God for what he has done for Mary, a theme that continues into the first part of the next strophe; (2) vv.49–50 mention certain attributes of God—power, holiness, and mercy; (3) vv.51–53 show God's sovereign action in reversing certain social conditions; and (4), finally, vv.54–55 recall God's mercy to Israel.

How much of the Magnificat was originally spoken by Mary rather than composed by Luke? Apart from basic matters of inspiration and literary or critical factors, several considerations ought to be kept in mind. One is the creative potential of even a poorly educated girl from a rural area. Another is the ability of people in ancient times to absorb and remember the spoken word, especially the biblical word. This applies both to Mary's knowledge of OT phraseology and to her repetition of these phrases.

Further, we are not told that Mary composed the song on the spot. Even a few days of meditation during her journey would have been sufficient time for her to produce the composition, especially since she was a girl who reflected deeply (cf. 2:51).

Finally, the song may be taken as prophecy in the broad biblical sense, in which case the Holy Spirit who instructed Elizabeth (v.41) may well have led both Mary and Luke in the composition and transmission of the song.

46–47 The excitement of Elizabeth, who actually shouted her benediction (v.42), gives way to a restraint that is no less joyful. A synonymous parallelism like that in the Psalms characterizes vv.46b–47.

This first major song in Luke derives its name Magnificat from the first word of the Latin version of the song, which translates *megalynei*. NEB's translation "Tell out . . . the greatness of the Lord" is a beautifully phrased expression of Mary's intent. The word *megalynei* literally means "enlarge." In this context it connotes the ascription of greatness to God.

Mary's song begins on the note of salvation, as she acknowledges her dependence on God (v.47). Her words are comparable to those of Habakkuk, who came through his trials rejoicing in God his Savior (Hab 3:18). Note that in beginning the Magnificat by praising "God my Savior," Mary answered the Roman Catholic dogma of the immaculate conception, which holds that from the moment of her conception Mary was by God's grace "kept free from all taint of Original Sin." Only sinners need a Savior.

48 Mary's "humble state" probably refers to her lowly social position. The word does not usually convey the idea of "humiliated." For the meaning of "servant," see comments on v.38; for that of "blessed," see v.45 and 6:20.

49 Mary is in awe of the "Mighty One," whose great power has been exercised in her life. The word "great" (*megala*) recalls "praises" (*megalynei*) in v.46. God's "name" is, according to the common ancient meaning, his whole reputation or character.

50 "Mercy" expresses an aspect of God's character sometimes overlooked when his power and holiness are stressed. A false dichotomy between holiness and mercy characterized some of the Pharisees (Matt 23:23). "Fear" means here, as often in Scripture, a pious reverence.

51–55 The main verbs in the next two strophes are in the past or aorist tense. The use of the aorist tense could be gnomic (somewhat like a proverb, e.g., v.53: "God always fills the hungry"). If not gnomic, the aorists could recall the specific times in the OT when God acted (vv.51–52). We must not, however, overlook the fact that Mary's references to the acts of God relate to the coming of the Messiah and indicate, as mentioned above, radical social reversals. Also, use of the past tenses here could actually be predictive (as in Isa 53:1–9), though general in content.

Mary recalls God's covenant (vv.54–55). The words translated "forever" (*eis ton aiōna*) occur emphatically as the final words in the original text of the song. To avoid the impression that "to Abraham and his descendants" are indirect objects of "as he said" (as though parallel with "to our fathers"), NIV reverses v.55a and 55b (cf. Notes).

56 Luke leaves us perplexed as to whether Mary's stay of "about three months" ended before or continued after the birth of John (cf. vv.26, 36, 39). His reticence should preclude rather than stimulate needless speculation.

Notes

46 There are several reasons—textual and contextual—for questioning the word "Mary" here. Some theorize that Elizabeth, not Mary, composed the Magnificat. Among the contextual reasons is the fact that the earlier social shame of Elizabeth's childless condition corresponds both to the situation of Hannah, whose prayer in 1 Samuel 2 is similar to this, and, possibly, to the description of the author of the Magnificat in v.48. The former parallel is significant, but the meaning of v.48 is equally or more appropriate to Mary. Of the contextual reasons, the strongest is the wording of v.56, which is, literally, "Mary stayed with her" (i.e., with Elizabeth; so NIV). If Mary had just sung the Magnificat, one might expect the verse to say, "She stayed with Elizabeth." Yet this is hardly conclusive.

Textually, there is only scant testimony to the reading "Elizabeth" in v.46 (Metzger, *Textual Commentary*, pp. 130–31). The editors of the UBS considered alternate possibilities but found the evidence for the originality of "Mary" in the text "overwhelming." (For a presentation of the argument that Elizabeth was the author of the Magnificat, see Creed, pp. 22–23.)

47 'Ηγαλλίασεν (*ēgalliasen*, "rejoices"), unlike μεγαλύνει (*megalynei*, "praises") in v.46, is in the aorist (past) tense. It may be a Semitism (*waw* conversive) or just an example of an aorist used with a perfective sense, i.e., describing a present state that is the continuation of a past event (cf. James Hope Moulton, *A Grammar of New Testament Greek*, vol. 3, *Syntax*, Nigel Turner [Edinburgh: T. & T. Clark, 1963], pp. 68–81).

49–55 A certain militant tone in the song calls to mind some extrabiblical phraseology as well as some of the ideals of the Zealots. For a significant, even if not entirely convincing, discussion of this, see J. Massingbyrde Ford, "Zealotism and the Lukan Infancy Narratives," NovTest 18 (1976): 281–92, especially pp. 284ff.

49 Ὁ δυνατός (*ho dynatos*, "the Mighty One") is a phrase that has no exact OT parallel, though God was often lauded for his power. Psalm 24 (23 LXX):8 does have the word *dynatos* ("mighty") twice, but the closest expression is in Zeph 3:17: "The LORD your God is in your midst, A victorious warrior" (lit. LXX; "mighty to save," NIV).

55 The words "to our fathers" clearly go with the verb "said." The second half of the verse, beginning with "to Abraham," probably completes "remembering to be merciful" in v.54.

B. *Birth Narratives* (1:57–2:20)

1. *The birth of John the Baptist*

1:57–66

> [57]When it was time for Elizabeth to have her baby, she gave birth to a son. [58]Her neighbors and relatives heard that the Lord had shown her great mercy, and they shared her joy.
>
> [59]On the eighth day they came to circumcise the child, and they were going to name him after his father Zechariah, [60]but his mother spoke up and said, "No! He is to be called John."
>
> [61]They said to her, "There is no one among your relatives who has that name."
>
> [62]Then they made signs to his father, to find out what he would like to name the child. [63]He asked for a writing tablet, and to everyone's astonishment he wrote, "His name is John." [64]Immediately his mouth was opened and his tongue was loosed, and he began to speak, praising God. [65]The neighbors were all filled with awe, and throughout the hill country of Judea people were talking about all these things. [66]Everyone who heard this wondered about it, asking, "What then is this child going to be?" For the Lord's hand was with him.

This is a brief sequel to vv.5–25 and serves to introduce the Benedictus (vv.67–79). It pictures a rural, close-knit society where personal experiences are shared by the community.

57–61 These verses give the impression that no one in the neighborhood knew of Elizabeth's pregnancy (v.57). Perhaps a seclusion that would have prompted suspicion in the case of a younger woman seemed normal for an older one. On one level, the "joy" (v.58) is over Elizabeth's emergence from the shadow of childlessness; on another it accords with the messianic joy of vv.44, 46.

Circumcision on the eighth day (v.59) was in accord with Genesis 17:9–14. Luke offers no explanation as to why the child had not been publicly named at birth. Possibly the narrative reflects the Hellenistic custom of waiting a week or so to name a newborn child. In any event there was obviously a considerable audience for the naming at the circumcision. To choose a name after a baby's grandfather or father, especially if one of them was highly esteemed, was natural (v.61). The objection from Elizabeth (v.60) was against custom and was apparently discounted, probably because she was only a woman.

62–63 Zechariah may have been deaf as well as mute, though this has not been indicated. Luke says he was "unable to speak" (1:22), but the word used (*kōphos*) can also mean "deaf" (as in 7:22). In any case the relatives and neighbors made signs (v.62), to which he responded on a waxed writing tablet (v.63). The present tense in the statement "his name is John" has the ring of deliberate emphasis.

64–66 When the time of his disability (v.20) was over, Zechariah's first words were words of praise (v.64; cf. Acts 2:4, 11—"declaring the wonders of God"). Luke stresses the widespread response (v.65) to the events surrounding the birth of John, just as he later stresses the fame of Jesus (e.g., 2:52). A child whose birth was attended by such marvelous circumstances would surely have an unusual destiny (v.66).

Notes

58 The word "great" is actually a verb, ἐμεγάλυνεν (*emegalynen*), the same used in v.46, meaning to "magnify" or "make great." The idea of greatness is also repeated in v.49. For "mercy," see vv.50, 54.

59 The imperfect ἐκάλουν (*ekaloun*) could mean that they were already naming him John, or, as in NIV, that they were trying or "were going to name him."

66 The verb ἦν (*ēn*, "was") in the clause "for the Lord's hand was with him" probably indicates that the comment was not made by the people at the time but that it is Luke's own later reflection. A few Western texts omit the verb. The omission probably was a deliberate change to make the comment fit in as part of the dialogue (Metzger, *Textual Commentary*, p. 131).

2. *Zechariah's song: The Benedictus*

1:67–80

[67]His father Zechariah was filled with the Holy Spirit and prophesied:

> [68]"Praise be to the Lord, the God of Israel,
>   because he has come and has redeemed his people.
> [69]He has raised up a horn of salvation for us
>   in the house of his servant David
> [70](as he said through his holy prophets of long ago),
> [71]salvation from our enemies
>   and from the hand of all who hate us—
> [72]to show mercy to our fathers
>   and to remember his holy covenant,
> [73] the oath he swore to our father Abraham:

74to rescue us from the hand of our enemies,
and to enable us to serve him without fear
75 in holiness and righteousness before him all our days.
76And you, my child, will be called a prophet of the
Most High;
for you will go on before the Lord to prepare the way
for him,
77to give his people the knowledge of salvation
through the forgiveness of their sins,
78because of the tender mercy of our God,
by which the rising sun will come to us from heaven
79to shine on those living in darkness
and in the shadow of death,
to guide our feet into the path of peace."

80And the child grew and became strong in spirit; and he lived in the desert until he appeared publicly to Israel.

This second major song in Luke is called the Benedictus, the first word in the Latin version, which is a translation of the Greek *eulogētos* ("blessed"). The song has two main parts: (1) praise to God for messianic deliverance (vv.68–75), and (2) celebration of the significant role John the Baptist will have in this work of deliverance. In both sections there is a strong emphasis on salvation, national and personal, and on the covenant and preparation that are about to be realized in their fulfillment. There is striking use of chiasmus (a rhetorical device that entails inversion in parallel literary structures) in the first part of Zechariah's song. From the ends to the center, the following terms recur, usually in reverse order: "come" or "visit" (vv.68, 78 [some versions have "dawn" in v.78]); "his people" (vv.68, 77); "salvation" (vv.69, 77); prophet(s) (vv.70, 76); "hand of our enemies" (vv.71, 74); father(s) (vv.72–73); "covenant" and "oath" (vv.72–73). With the words "covenant" and "oath" in juxtaposition at the center, i.e., at the end of the first and the beginning of the second sequence of the chiasm (vv.72–73), God's faithfulness to his covenant occupies a central position theologically in the Benedictus. Once again Luke makes the connection between the Christian gospel and its OT roots. Plummer (p. 39) notes sixteen OT parallels in the Benedictus.

67 Zechariah the priest now prophesies. As the Holy Spirit had filled Elizabeth (v.41), he now fills Zechariah. Observe that Zechariah's previous doubt and his discipline through loss of speech did not mean the end of his spiritual ministry. So when a believer today has submitted to God's discipline, he may go on in Christ's service.

68 The NIV uses "praise" to translate both *eulogētos* in this verse and *megalynei* in v.46. The word *eulogētos* can refer both to a human being on whom God has showered his goodness (i.e., "blessed," as in vv.42, 45) and to God, to whom we return thanks for that goodness (i.e., "praise"). A form of the same word occurs in v.64. It is as though vv.68–79 provide the content of the blessing expressed in the earlier verse. "Israel" is paralleled by "his people" in vv.68, 77, carrying along the promise of v.17 (cf. comments there).

The action is centered in two verbs: "has come" and "has redeemed." The first, "has come," is from the verb *episkeptomai*. In secular Greek it means simply "to look at," "reflect on," or "visit" (often in a charitable way, such as a doctor visiting the sick; cf. Matt 25:36, 43; James 1:27). The element of special concern is deepened to the spiritual level in the LXX use of the word. A particular example is that of God "visiting" people in grace or in judgment (Exod 4:31; Zech 10:3; cf. TDNT, 2:599–605). The idea of God graciously "visiting" or "coming" to his people in the sense of vv.68, 78 appears also in 7:16. In these three verses, as well as in Acts 15:14, where *episkeptomai* is translated "showed his concern," the word "people" also occurs. Tragically, Jerusalem did not recognize the day of her "visitation" (19:44; NIV, "the time of God's coming").

The second verb, "redeemed," represents two Greek words: *epoiēsen lytrōsin* ("accomplished redemption"). The idea of redemption runs through Scripture, with the Exodus being the great OT example of rescue from enemies and captivity. Luke 24:21 shows the expectation Jesus' followers had that he would do a similar work of freeing God's people. Luke, though committed to the universal application of the gospel, includes these words of redemption that apply especially to Israel (see esp. v.69). Not only does this reflect his emphasis on the Jewish roots of Christianity, it also underlines the political aspects of redemption foremost in the minds of Zechariah's contemporaries.

69–70 "Horn" (v.69) is a common OT metaphor for power because of the great strength of the horned animals of the Near East. The word "salvation" describes the kind of strength Zechariah had in mind. The power of salvation resides in the Savior. Again, the messianic theme occurs—this time in an allusion to Psalm 132 (131 LXX): 17, where, in fulfilling the Davidic covenant, God "will make a horn grow for David." The verb "raised up" (*ēgeiren*) in v.69 is not used in the LXX of Psalm 132. Here it is appropriate for stressing God's sovereignty. Later in Luke's writing this verb will assume great importance in relation to the resurrection of Christ (24:6, 34; Acts 3:7, 15; 4:10).

The messianic motif is further emphasized by a reference to the "house of . . . David." The mention of the "holy prophets of long ago" (v.70), while placed in parenthesis in NIV for clarity, is not theologically parenthetical. Like a similar reference in Hebrews 1:1, it serves to confirm the OT origin of and support for the messianic role of Jesus.

71–73 Placing v.70 in a parenthesis clarifies the relationship of vv.71–75 to v.69. "Salvation" (v.71) is the link. It is the first of three aspects of God's redeeming work, the others being "mercy" (v.72) and the remembrance of God's "covenant." The salvation Zechariah is speaking of is at this stage clearly political. Mercy to the "fathers" seems to mean that God has not thwarted their hopes. This mercy may be related to v.17 and Malachi 4:6. The "oath" (v.73) to Abraham in view here is recorded in Genesis 22:16–18, where the Lord promised Abraham not only that his descendants' enemies would be subdued but also that universal blessing would result from his obedience. Therefore, the salvation in view here involves both political deliverance and spiritual blessing (cf. the next verses).

As noted earlier, the words "covenant" and "oath" form the central point of the chiasm (inverse repetition of terms). This has the effect of emphasizing the importance of God's covenant and his faithfulness to it. Not only does this serve an important theme in Luke, but it gives encouragement to us to trust the promises of God.

74–75 The fulfillment of God's promise does not mean passivity for Israel but a new opportunity for service—negatively, service "without fear" (v.74) and, positively, "in holiness and righteousness" (v.75; cf. Mal 3:3).

76–77 The second part of Zechariah's hymn begins with a direct word to his son (v.76). The role of John, like that of Paul and the Lord's servants throughout history, derives its significance and greatness from God's purpose and, even more, from the greatness of the Person served. Before addressing the theme of salvation, Zechariah speaks of the "Most High" and "the Lord" John represents.

The description of John in v.76, when compared with Isaiah 40:3; Malachi 3:1; 4:5, clearly links him with Elijah, dispelling any doubts about the recognition of this link in Luke. Such doubts have arisen largely from Luke's omission of the conversation (cf. Matt 17:10–13; Mark 9:11–13) about Elijah following the Transfiguration. There Jesus says that Elijah has "already come," i.e., the predictions about Elijah were fulfilled in John the Baptist. Also Luke's parallel to Matthew 11:12 (Luke 16:16) has seemed to some to detach John from the age of Jesus and the church. Thus some have considered it unlikely that Luke thought of John as the Elijah figure whose coming was to usher in the last days. We must keep in mind that as a physician Luke was strongly aware of corporeality. More than the other Gospel writers, he stressed the physical resurrection of Jesus ("they did not find the body of the Lord Jesus" [24:3]), the reality of Jesus' ascension, and the Spirit's descent in "bodily form" like a dove (3:22) at Jesus' baptism. It would, therefore, be understandable for Luke to hold that John had indeed come "in the spirit and power of Elijah" (1:17), yet for him to avoid saying anything that might imply the reincarnation of Elijah as John. If Elijah could still appear in recognizable form, as he did at the Transfiguration, Luke may have hesitated to include in his Gospel anything about his apparent identification with John. Verse 76, though consistent with the idea that John came in the "spirit and power of Elijah," avoids the kind of terminology Luke may still have had some hesitation about. See also Walter Wink, *John the Baptist in the Gospel Tradition* (London: Cambridge University Press, 1968), pp. 42–45.

The theme of "salvation" (v.77) for God's "people," expressed in political terms in v.71, now finds its spiritual identity through forgiveness. John will go on to preach "a baptism of repentance for the forgiveness of sins" (3:3).

78–79 NIV's "rising sun" (v.78; cf. Notes) has a dynamic quality that suits the word "come" or "visit" (cf. v.68). Verse 79 uses a beautiful quotation from Isaiah 60:1–3 to carry forward the imagery of light (the sun) and to offer hope of peace to those who were then outside the faithful remnant of Judaism (cf. Eph 2:12).

80 This brief description of John's boyhood reflects Luke's interest in human beings. Later he will comment more fully on Jesus' personal developments (2:40, 52). Since the discovery of the DSS near Qumran, there has been speculation about the possibility of contact between John and the Qumran community. If his elderly parents had been unable to care for him, or if they had died in his youth, it is conceivable that John might even have lived for a time at Qumran. Taking in young men was the only way the celibate community could reproduce itself. Nevertheless, such a connection lacks supporting evidence.

Notes

67 Both the unity and the literary history of the Benedictus are disputed. But its theology arises from the OT, the themes of the two parts (vv.68–75 and vv.76–79) are intertwined, and the concepts in each part are appropriate to Jesus and John respectively. For a discussion of the issues, see Marshall, *Luke: Historian and Theologian*, p. 87.

68–79 This passage is so thoroughly Jewish in its orientation and theology that it would be difficult to imagine that it originated in the Hellenistic church and was adapted back into this context. The distinction between "we" and "they" is ingrained throughout—e.g., "us" in vv.69, 74, which is parallel to "his people," over against the "enemies . . . all who hate us." Only at the end does a salvation seem to extend beyond Israel, and that promise is rooted in Isa 60.

68 The noun λύτρωσις (*lytrōsis*, "redemption") is found only twice in Luke—here (where the NIV renders the noun as a verb for smoother English) and in Anna's prophecy about the infant Jesus (2:38). The verbal form occurs in 24:21. Luke is the only Gospel to use the longer form ἀπολύτρωσις (*apolytrōsis*), which is of major importance in the Epistles. For a discussion of redemption in the NT, see Leon Morris, *The Apostolic Preaching of the Cross* (Grand Rapids: Eerdmans, 1955), pp. 9–59; cf. also David Hill, *Greek Words and Hebrew Meanings: Studies in the Semantics of Soteriological Terms*, SNTS 5 (London: Cambridge University Press, 1967). Significantly, despite Luke's stress on the concept of redemption, when λύτρον (*lytron*) occurs in Matt 20:28 and Mark 10:45, Luke omits it in his parallel of these verses. This may be because the concept is already inherent in the narrative of the Last Supper that, in the Lukan order, just precedes it. Luke 22:24–27 may not, however, be a true parallel.

69 Σωτηρία (*sōtēria* "salvation") is also mentioned in vv.71, 77; 2:30; 3:6, σωτήρ (*sōtēr*, "Savior" in 1:47; 2:11, and numerous occasions of σώζω (*sōzō*, "save"). See Marshall, *Luke: Historian and Theologian*, pp. 92–102.

71 The use of the accusative σωτηρίαν (*sōtērian*, "salvation") here is debatable. It seems to function as the object of ἐλάλησεν (*elalēsen*, "said") in v.70. Or it could stand in apposition to κέρας (*keras*, "horn"), which is already identified in v.69 with salvation.

78 Ἀνατολή (*anatolē*) is interestingly rendered "dayspring" in KJV, "day" in RSV, "sunrise" in NASB, and "rising sun" in NIV. These represent attempts to translate a word with a basically simple meaning, the rising of the sun or stars, yet one that the LXX used in translating the distinctive messianic term צֶמַח (*ṣemaḥ*, "sprout," "branch") in Jer 23:5; Zech 3:8; 6:12. However *anatolē* is translated, it is important to keep this messianic aspect in mind (see TDNT, 1:352–53).

80 Ἐκραταιοῦτο πνεύματι (*ekrataiouto pneumati*) probably means "became strong in spirit" in the sense of development of moral character, though somewhat similar wording in Eph 3:16 describes a strengthening by God's Spirit.

The plural form ἐν ταῖς ἐρήμοις (*en tais erēmois*, "in the desert") is idiomatic. John ministered near the Jordan River, but it is not certain that he grew up in the same area. While the desert had various popular connotations (e.g., the home of demons), here it simply implies relative isolation.

Ἀναδείξεως (*anadeixeōs*, "until he appeared publicly") is literally "until the day of his appearance" or "commissioning" (so BAG, s.v.).

3. The birth of Jesus

2:1–7

> [1]In those days Caesar Augustus issued a decree that a census should be taken of the entire Roman world. [2](This was the first census that took place while Quirinius was governor of Syria.) [3]And everyone went to his own town to register.

⁴So Joseph also went up from the town of Nazareth in Galilee to Judea, to Bethlehem the town of David, because he belonged to the house and line of David. ⁵He went there to register with Mary, who was pledged to be married to him and was expecting a child. ⁶While they were there, the time came for the baby to be born, ⁷and she gave birth to her firstborn, a son. She wrapped him in cloths and placed him in a manger, because there was no room for them in the inn.

In comparison with the complex narrative in chapter 1, the actual birth narrative of Jesus is brief. In it Luke stresses three things: (1) the political situation (to explain why Jesus' birth took place in Bethlehem); (2) that Bethlehem was the town of David (to stress Jesus' messianic claim); (3) the humble circumstances of Jesus' birth.

The mention of Caesar Augustus may not only be for historical background but also to contrast the human with the divine decrees. A mere Galilean peasant travels to Bethlehem ostensibly at the decree of the Roman emperor. Actually, it is in fulfillment of the divine King's plan, which, as noted passim, is reflected in Luke's frequent reference to what "must" (*dei*) be done.

1–3 Luke clearly intends to secure the historical and chronological moorings of Jesus' birth. Ironically, it is precisely this that has led some to question Luke's accuracy.

The first census (i.e., enrollment prior to taxation) known to have occurred under the governorship of Quirinius took place later (i.e., A.D. 6) than usually reckoned as the time of Jesus' birth. Reference to this census is found in both Acts 5:37 and Josephus (Antiq. XVIII, 26 [ii.1]). Many have supposed that Luke confused this census of A.D. 6 with one he thinks was taken earlier, but which lacks historical support. The most satisfactory solutions that have been proposed follow.

1. Quirinius had a government assignment in Syria at this time and conducted a census in his official capacity. Details of this census may have been common knowledge in Luke's time but are now lost to us (cf. E.M. Blaiklock, "Quirinius," ZPEB, 5:5–6). An incomplete MS describes the career of an officer whose name is not preserved but whose actions sound as if he might have been Quirinius. He became imperial "legate of Syria" for the "second time." While this is ambiguous, it may be a clue that Quirinius served both at the time of Jesus' birth and a few years later (cf. F.F. Bruce, "Quirinius," NBD, p. 1069).

2. The word *prōtē* can be construed to mean not "first," as usually translated, but "former" or "prior." The meaning of v.2 is then "This census was *before* that made when Quirinius was governor" (N. Turner, *Grammatical Insights into the New Testament* [Edinburgh: T. & T. Clark, 1966], pp. 23–24; idem, *Syntax*, p. 32).

It was customary to return to one's original home for such a census. Also, powerful as he was, Herod was only a client king under Rome and, like others, was subject to orders for a census. Furthermore, it is scarcely conceivable that Luke, careful researcher that he was (1:1–4), would have stressed the census unless he had reasonable historical grounds for doing so. (See further F.F. Bruce, *Jesus and Christian Origins Outside the New Testament* [Grand Rapids: Eerdmans, 1974], pp. 192–94; Marshall, *Luke: Historian and Theologian*, pp. 98–104.)

Notes

1–3 For a negative judgment on the historicity of Luke's account of the census, see HJP, 1:399–427.

4–7 Luke does not say how long in advance of Jesus' birth Joseph left for Bethlehem (v.4) nor why he took Mary with him. It is possible that he used the emperor's order as a means of removing Mary from possible gossip and emotional stress in her own village. He had already accepted her as his wife (Matt 1:24), but apparently they continued in betrothal (v.5: "pledged to be married") till after the birth. The text neither affirms nor denies the popular image of the couple arriving in Bethlehem just as the baby was about to be born. Luke simply states that the birth took place "while they were there" (v.6). Since she had stayed three months with Elizabeth, Mary was at least three months pregnant. It is possible that they went down during her last trimester of pregnancy, when the social relationships in Nazareth would have grown more difficult. They may have stayed in a crowded room in the home of some poor relative till the birth of the baby necessitated their vacating it for privacy and more space. Any such reconstruction is, however, merely speculative.

The word *katalyma*, usually translated "inn" (v.7), may mean a room (e.g., the "guest room" used for the Last Supper [22:11], referred to as an "upper room" in 22:12), a billet for soldiers, or any place for lodging, which would include inns. It is not, however, the usual Greek word for an inn—*pandocheion*, to which the Good Samaritan took the robbery victim (10:34). As the etymology of the word—*pan* ("all") and *dechomai* ("receive")—suggests, inns accepted all kinds of people, often the worst. Stories were told of discomfort and even of robberies at inns.

Luke could have painted a sordid picture, had he so desired. Instead he uses the general word for a lodging place and states the simple fact that when Mary's time came, the only available place for the little family was one usually occupied by animals. It may have been a cave, as tradition suggests, or some part of a house or inn. Even today in many places around the world farm animals and their fodder are often kept in the same building as the family quarters. The eating trough, or "manger," was ideal for use as a crib. Luke does not seem to be portraying a dismal situation with an unfeeling innkeeper as villain. Rather, he is establishing a contrast between the proper rights of the Messiah in his own "town of David" and the very ordinary and humble circumstances of his birth. Whatever the reason, even in his birth Jesus was excluded from the normal shelter others enjoyed (cf. 9:58). This is consistent with Luke's realistic presentation of Jesus' humanity and servanthood. As to the "cloths," see comment on v.12.

4. The announcement to the shepherds

2:8–20

8And there were shepherds living out in the fields nearby, keeping watch over their flocks at night. 9An angel of the Lord appeared to them, and the glory of the Lord shone around them, and they were terrified. 10But the angel said to them, "Do not be afraid. I bring you good news of great joy that will be for all the people. 11Today in the town of David a Savior has been born to you; he is Christ the Lord.

¹²This will be a sign to you: You will find a baby wrapped in cloths and lying in a manger."

¹³Suddenly a great company of the heavenly host appeared with the angel, praising God and saying,

¹⁴"Glory to God in the highest,
and on earth peace to men on whom his favor rests."

¹⁵When the angels had left them and gone into heaven, the shepherds said to one another, "Let's go to Bethlehem and see this thing that has happened, which the Lord has told us about."

¹⁶So they hurried off and found Mary and Joseph, and the baby, who was lying in the manger. ¹⁷When they had seen him, they spread the word concerning what had been told them about this child, ¹⁸and all who heard it were amazed at what the shepherds said to them. ¹⁹But Mary treasured up all these things and pondered them in her heart. ²⁰The shepherds returned, glorifying and praising God for all the things they had heard and seen, which were just as they had been told.

The pastoral scene described in this section actually conveys more theological significance than is sometimes realized. Both the words of the angel and the symbolism of what happened have theological implications.

8 There may be several reasons for the special role of the shepherds in the events of this unique night. Among the occupations, shepherding had a lowly place (SBK, 2:114). Shepherds were considered untrustworthy and their work made them ceremonially unclean. Thus the most obvious implication is that the gospel first came to the social outcasts of Jesus' day. This would accord with a recurring emphasis in Luke. Moreover, it may be significant that in the Lord's instructions to Nathan about giving David the covenant the Lord reminds David, who was to become Messiah's ancestor, that he was called from the shepherd's life (2 Sam 7:8). Finally, in both testaments shepherds symbolize those who care for God's people, including the Lord himself (Ps 23:1; Isa 40:11; Jer 23:1–4; Heb 13:20; 1 Peter 2:25; 5:2). The shepherds of Luke 2 may, therefore, symbolize all the ordinary people who have joyfully received the gospel and have become in various ways pastors to others.

That the shepherds were out in the fields at night does not preclude a December date, as the winter in Judea was mild. But, of course, the text says nothing about the time of year. The traditional date for the Nativity was set, long after the event, to coincide with a pagan festival, thus demonstrating that the "Sol Invictus," the "Unconquerable Sun," had indeed been conquered. December 25 was widely celebrated as the date of Jesus' birth by the end of the fourth century. January 6 was also an important date in the early church, held by many as the occasion of the arrival of the wise men and known as Epiphany. (See Frank E. Gaebelein, "The Most Beautiful Story Ever Told," CT 23 [1979]: 1612–14 [18–20].) Morris (*Luke*, p. 84) suggests that, if the birth did take place in winter, the shepherds may have been raising sheep for sacrifice at Passover a few months later.

9 First a single angel (cf. 1:11, 26) appears; the multitude of angels does not appear till v.13. The shepherds' terror recalls that of Zechariah (1:12). It was not just the angel that terrified them but the visible manifestation of the glory of God—something neither Zechariah nor Mary had seen. Again, as in 1:13 and 1:30, the angel speaks reassuringly.

10–11 The angel's announcement (v.10) includes several of the most frequently used words in Luke's Gospel (cf. Notes)—a fact that shows the tremendous importance of the angelic pronouncement. It is a bold proclamation of the gospel at the very hour of Jesus' birth (v.11).

Thus in this whole section Luke shares his perception of major themes that support the declaration: the time has come ("today") for the fulfillment of the prophetic expectation of Messiah's coming.

12 The "cloths" (KJV, "swaddling clothes," from the verb *spargano*, "to swathe") would constitute a "sign." Babies were snugly wrapped in long strips of cloth, giving them warmth, protection of extremities, and a sense of security in their newborn existence. The combination of a newborn baby's wrappings and the use of the manger for a crib would be a distinctive "sign." Perhaps they also imply that in spite of seeming rejection, symbolized by the manger, the baby was the special object of his mother's care. In Ezekiel 16:1–5, Jerusalem is symbolically described as a heathen child who was neglected from birth till God rescued and cared for her. She had not been given the usual postnatal care and so was not wrapped with strips of cloth (Ezek 16:4). But Jesus was not so neglected. On the other hand, the "sign" might be only the strange circumstance of the newborn child being in the manger at all.

13 "Suddenly" (*exaiphnes*), along with cognate words, often describes the unexpected nature of God's acts, especially the eschatological events. Malachi had predicted the sudden coming of the Lord to his temple (Mal 3:1). Now the angels suddenly announce his arrival at Bethlehem. The Spirit's coming at Pentecost was sudden (Acts 2:2), as was the appearance of the Lord to Saul on the road to Damascus (Acts 9:3). Mark 13:36 and 1 Thessalonians 5:3 describe the suddenness of future events.

The "heavenly host," which often meant heavenly bodies in the OT, refers here to an army or band of angels (cf. 1 Kings 22:19).

14 The doxology "Glory to God in the highest" is the climax of the story. Its two parts relate to heaven and to earth respectively. In Luke's account of the Triumphal Entry, the crowds say, "Peace in heaven and glory in the highest" (19:38). In Ephesians 3:21, Paul ascribes glory to God, not now in the heavens, but "in the church and in Christ Jesus." Verse 14b is best translated as in NIV: "and on earth peace to men on whom his favor rests." For reasons discussed in the Notes, "good will to men" (KJV) is inaccurate. Luke emphasizes the work of Christ on earth. (See also Jesus' own declaration that "the Son of Man has authority on earth to forgive sins"— Luke 5:24; Matt 9:6; Mark 2:10.)

The "peace" here is that which the Messiah brings (cf. 1:79). Those whom Jesus healed or forgave on the basis of their faith could "go in peace" (7:50; 8:48). Those on whom God's "favor" (*eudokia*) rests are the "little children" (10:21) to whom God graciously reveals truth according to his "good pleasure" (the only other use of *eudokia* in the Gospels, except for the parallel in Matt 11:26).

15–16 Luke does not say that the angels disappeared but that they went "into heaven" (v.15), an expression typical of his attention to spatial relationships (cf. comments on the Ascension at 24:51, where the same words appear in what is probably the original text; cf. Acts 1:11). The realization of God's promise ("this thing [*rhema*] . . . which the Lord has told us") is expressed also in v.29: "as you have promised" (*kata to rhēma sou,* lit., "according to your word"). Luke combines the phenomena of ancient (v.15) and recent (v.29) prophetic words, thus emphasizing the connection between the old and new ages, the Jewish orientation of the gospel and the reality of the heavenly in the earthly.

Both the idiomatic particle *dē,* which conveys a note of urgency (BAG, s.v.), expressed in NIV's "Let's go" (v.15), and the words "hurried off" (*ēlthon speusantes,* v.16) heighten the sense of excitement and determination that propelled the shepherds to the baby's side.

17–18 Then they "spread the word" (v.17) and became the first evangelists of the Christian Era. Luke's observation (v.18) that those who heard them "were amazed" (*ethaumasan*) is the first of his many comments on the enthusiastic response to the messianic proclamation. The next occurrence is when Mary and Joseph "marvel" at what Simeon says about their child (v.33). In v.47 everyone is "amazed" (*existanto*) at Jesus' answers in the temple discussion. The initial reaction of the audience of Jesus' opening declaration in the synagogue of Nazareth that the prophecy of Isaiah 61 was at that moment fulfilled was amazement (4:22; cf. 8:25; 9:43; 11:14, 38; 20:26; 24:12, 41). There are also passages that use other words to describe a similar response (e.g., 4:15, 36; 5:26).

19–20 In contrast to the overreaction of the people, Mary (*hē de Mariam,* "Mary on the other hand") meditates on the meaning of it all (v.19; cf. v.51; cf. also Gen 37:11). Just as the seventy-two disciples returned (*hypestrepsan*) with joy after their preaching mission (10:17), so the shepherds returned (*hypestrepsan*) "glorifying and praising God" (v.20). It is clear that in Luke this spirit of doxology is the proper response to the mighty works of God (cf. 5:25–26; 7:16; 13:13; 17:15; 18:43; 23:47, along with similar occurrences in Acts).

Notes

9–11 The significant terms characteristic of Luke that occur in these verses include εὐαγγελίζομαι (*euangelizomai,* "bring good news" [always in the verbal form in Luke], v.10); χαρά (*chara,* "joy"), which occurs more often in Luke than in Matthew and Mark combined; λαός (*laos,* "people"), used 35 times in Luke against 14 in Matthew and none in Mark (with Luke using it some 47 additional times in Acts); σήμερον (*sēmeron,* "today"), which occurs more in Luke than in Matthew and Mark together (see comment on 4:21 for its significance in Luke); σωτήρ (*sōtēr,* "Savior," v.11), used only by Luke among the Synoptics; and κύριος (*kyrios,* "Lord"), which occurs 95 times in Luke out of 166 in the Synoptics. The word δόξα (*doxa,* "glory"), which occurs in v.9 and reappears in v.14, is also distinctively Lukan. Along with the verb δοξάζω (*doxazō,* "glorify"), Luke uses it more than the two other Synoptics combined.

14 In KJV "good will" is the subject of the clause because KJV followed the TR, which has the nominative εὐδοκία (*eudokia*). However, the oldest MSS have an added sigma (ς), indicator of the genitive case (εὐδοκίας, *eudokias*). The inadvertent *omission* of the small elevated half-circle that was customarily used to indicate the genitive sigma is more likely than the *addition* of a sigma. On the principle that the harder reading is more likely the original one, the genitive should be assumed, since a nominative would read more smoothly. And since similar phrases, describing people "of [God's] good pleasure" are now known from hymns in the DSS (1QH 4.32–33; 8.6; 9.9), there is no difficulty in accepting this reading. More recently an Aramaic text from Cave 4 with a syntactical structure even closer to Luke's has confirmed the matter (Fitzmyer, *Semitic Background*, pp. 101–4). It is also more in accordance with the doctrine of grace than is the idea that those of "good will" are rewarded with peace (cf. also Metzger, *Textual Commentary*, p. 133).

C. *Jesus' Early Years* (2:21–52)

1. *Presentation of Jesus in the temple*

2:21–40

21On the eighth day, when it was time to circumcise him, he was named Jesus, the name the angel had given him before he had been conceived.

22When the time of their purification according to the Law of Moses had been completed, Joseph and Mary took him to Jerusalem to present him to the Lord 23(as it is written in the Law of the Lord, "Every firstborn male is to be consecrated to the Lord"), 24and to offer a sacrifice in keeping with what is said in the Law of the Lord: "a pair of doves or two young pigeons."

25Now there was a man in Jerusalem called Simeon, who was righteous and devout. He was waiting for the consolation of Israel, and the Holy Spirit was upon him. 26It had been revealed to him by the Holy Spirit that he would not die before he had seen the Lord's Christ. 27Moved by the Spirit, he went into the temple courts. When the parents brought in the child Jesus to do for him what the custom of the Law required, 28Simeon took him in his arms and praised God, saying:

29"Sovereign Lord, as you have promised,
 you now dismiss your servant in peace.
30For my eyes have seen your salvation,
31 which you have prepared in the sight of all people,
32a light for revelation to the Gentiles
 and for glory to your people Israel."

33The child's father and mother marveled at what was said about him. 34Then Simeon blessed them and said to Mary, his mother: "This child is destined to cause the falling and rising of many in Israel, and to be a sign that will be spoken against, 35so that the thoughts of many hearts will be revealed. And a sword will pierce your own soul too."

36There was also a prophetess, Anna, the daughter of Phanuel, of the tribe of Asher. She was very old; she had lived with her husband seven years after her marriage, 37and then was a widow until she was eighty-four. She never left the temple but worshiped night and day, fasting and praying. 38Coming up to them at that very moment, she gave thanks to God and spoke about the child to all who were looking forward to the redemption of Jerusalem.

39When Joseph and Mary had done everything required by the Law of the Lord, they returned to Galilee to their own town of Nazareth. 40And the child grew and became strong; he was filled with wisdom, and the grace of God was upon him.

21–24 It is important to understand the sequence and background of these events. According to Jewish law a woman became ceremonially unclean on the birth of a child. On the eighth day the child was circumcised (cf. 1:59; Gen 17:12), after which the mother was unclean an additional thirty-three days—sixty-six if the child was female (Lev 12:1–5). At the conclusion of this period, the mother offered a sacrifice, either a lamb or, if she was poor, two doves or two young pigeons (Lev 12:6–8). In addition, the first son was to be presented to the Lord and then, so to speak, bought back with an offering (Num 18:15; cf. 1 Sam 1:24-28, where Hannah actually gives up Samuel to the Lord).

Luke, conflating the performance of these OT obligations into this single narrative, shows how Jesus was reared in conformity with them. His parents obeyed the Lord (1:31) in naming him. The offering of birds instead of a lamb shows that he was born into a poor family. Perhaps this helped him identify with the poor of the land (cf. 6:20).

25 In vv.25-38 Luke presents two pious figures who, under divine inspiration, testify to the significance of Jesus. Once again Luke assures us of the credentials of Jesus as Messiah, taking care to show that each witness is an authentic representative of Judaism.

"Now" represents the attention-getting word *idou* ("behold"). Luke neither associates Simeon with a leading sect or party nor calls him a priest. The important thing is that he is "righteous and devout" (cf. Zechariah and Elizabeth, 1:6). He could be described as one of the believing remnant of Judaism, looking forward to the Messianic Age in its spiritual aspect. It is appropriate that the Spirit who is the Consoler (cf. Notes) was upon one who awaited the consolation.

26-28 The same Spirit had revealed to Simeon (v.26) that the Messiah ("the Lord's Christ") would come before Simeon died. This may, but need not necessarily, imply that he was an old man.

Mary and Joseph are referred to as Jesus' "parents" (v.27) and as "the child's father and mother" (v.33). Jesus would have been considered Joseph's own son; so Luke's terminology is not inconsistent. In the genealogy, however, the particulars of the relationship had to be made more explicit (3:23). Here, as in v.38, Luke notes the providential timing, as the Spirit brings Simeon to the temple courts to be ready for the family's arrival. In this touching scene, Luke again shows the presence of Jesus, now in Simeon's arms (v.28), as an occasion of praise (*eulogeō*) to God. Actually, the word is "blessed," the same as in v.34.

29-32 Simeon's psalm begins with the word *nun* ("now"), emphasizing the fact that the Messiah has indeed come (hence the Latin title Nunc Dimittis ["Now Dismiss"]). "Dismiss" (*apolyō*) here means "allow to die" (BAG, s.v.; cf. Num 20:29 LXX). NIV loses the emphasis of the Greek word order because it reverses the phrases. Nevertheless it does retain the words "in peace" in their place of final emphasis (cf. 1:79; 2:14). On "as you promised," see comment on v.15. Note the contrast between "Sovereign Lord" and "servant." God's servant is now ready for his final order—to depart in death (cf. Gen 15:15 LXX; Num 20:29)—because he has indeed seen the "Lord's Christ" (v.26).

Simeon does not say, however, that he has seen the Messiah but rather that his eyes have seen God's salvation (v.30). To see Jesus is to see salvation embodied in him, a theme already noted as prominent in Luke (cf. 1:69, 71, 77; 19:9, and comments). Luke's concern for the universal application of the gospel finds support in the words "in the sight of all people" (v.31). Verse 31 echoes Isaiah 52:10 and Psalm 98:3. The parallel structure in v.32 may involve a detailed contrast as well as a larger one. That is, not only are Gentiles and Jews put in contrast, but the same light (Isa 49:6) that brings "revelation" to pagans (cf. 1:78-79) brings "glory" to Israel (cf. 1:77). Note also "all people" (v.31) and "your people" (v.32; cf. comments on 1:77).

33–35 In spite of what they already know, Joseph and Mary are amazed (v.33; cf. comment on v.17) at Simeon's song. Moreover, in it a somber note is sounded. In vivid language Simeon predicts that because of the child "many in Israel" (v.34) would be brought to moral decision, some to a point of collapse (*ptōsis;* NIV, "falling") and others to what can well be called a resurrection (*anastasis;* NIV, "rising"). Some think there is but one group that falls and then rises (Marshall, *Luke, Historian and Theologian,* p. 122). But there will be a cost to Jesus. As the one who himself is the ultimate "sign," the visible affirmation of God's declared intentions, he will be vulnerable to the hostility of unbelievers. A negative attitude toward him, however, serves to brand the unbeliever as one who has rejected not only him but the whole of God's revelation (v.35; cf. John 5:45–47). This clash will inevitably wound Jesus' mother.

36–38 Luke's attention to the renewal of prophecy at the coming of the Messianic Age continues with the introduction of Anna as a "prophetess" (v.36). Zechariah had been "filled with the Holy Spirit and prophesied" (1:67). Simeon, though not called a prophet, was filled with the Spirit and also prophesied. Prophetesses functioned in both OT and NT times (Exod 15:20; Judg 4:4; 2 Kings 22:14; Neh 6:14; Isa 8:3; Acts 2:17; 21:9; 1 Cor 11:5). Apparently Anna could trace her genealogy; and, though the tribe of Asher was not outstanding (Gen 30:12–13; 35:26), Luke considered it important to show her true Jewishness. She was a familiar figure at the temple. Possibly she lived in one of the rooms surrounding the temple precinct; or she may have, like the disciples in 24:53, centered her life there. She was the ideal widow (v.37) described in 1 Timothy 5:5. Once more Luke points out the providential timing (v.38; cf. v.27). He may be underlining the desire for the messianic deliverance of Jerusalem (cf. Isa 52:9) by describing Anna's thanksgiving with a rare verb (*anthōmologeomai*), which ocurs in a psalm lamenting the defilement of the Jerusalem temple (Ps 79 [78 LXX]:13). Later Luke will mention another pious Jew who had been expecting the messianic kingdom, Joseph of Arimathea (23:51).

39–40 Luke takes another opportunity to mention the fidelity of Jesus' parents to the Jewish law as he continues the narrative (v.39). He omits mention of the flight to Egypt. It is important to Matthew, providing another example of fulfilled prophecy (Matt 2:13–15); but this is not so significant at this point in Luke. What is significant is that Jesus' parents were faithful to the Jewish law and that the child grew normally, the object of God's grace (v.40; cf. v.52).

Notes

25 The "consolation [παράκλησις, *paraklēsis*] of Israel" refers to the time when, according to Isa 40:1–2, God would end Israel's time of alienation and suffering through the advent of the Messiah (cf. Isa 49:13; 57:18; 61:2; and contrast the promise of 5:4 with Luke 6:24). Notice also the theme of encouragement in Acts 4:36; 9:31; 13:15; 15:31. The time of the "consolation" would also be the age of the promised Holy Spirit, who himself is the one who consoles and encourages—παράκλητος (*paraklētos,* "Counselor," John 14:16; 15:26; 16:7).

33 Understandably, the designation ὁ πατὴρ αὐτοῦ καὶ μήτηρ (ho patēr autou kai mētēr, "his father and mother") for Joseph and Mary raises questions in the minds of believers in the Virgin Birth. Some early scribes doubtless felt the need for making it clear that Joseph was not Jesus' biological father. As a result there are far too many readings and sources to cite here (see UBS apparatus in loc. and Metzger, *Textual Commentary*, p. 134). NIV's rendering has strong MS support and is the natural way the family would be described.

37 "Until she was eighty-four" is the most natural way to understand ἕως ἐτῶν ὀγδοήκοντα τεσσάρων (heōs etōn ogdoēkonta tessarōn). Goodspeed's conclusion is that if Luke meant "for eighty-four years" (which would make her 105 years old), he would have omitted heōs ("until") and used the accusative instead of the genitive, or used heōs with an ordinal, rather than cardinal, numeral in the genitive (E.J. Goodspeed, *Problems of New Testament Translation* [Chicago: University of Chicago Press, 1945], pp. 79–81). If Anna were 105 years old, she would have been the same age as Judith in the Apocrypha (Jud 16:23).

---

2. The boy Jesus at the temple

2:41–52

41Every year his parents went to Jerusalem for the Feast of the Passover. 42When he was twelve years old, they went up to the Feast, according to the custom. 43After the Feast was over, while his parents were returning home, the boy Jesus stayed behind in Jerusalem, but they were unaware of it. 44Thinking he was in their company, they traveled on for a day. Then they began looking for him among their relatives and friends. 45When they did not find him, they went back to Jerusalem to look for him. 46After three days they found him in the temple courts, sitting among the teachers, listening to them and asking them questions. 47Everyone who heard him was amazed at his understanding and his answers. 48When his parents saw him, they were astonished. His mother said to him, "Son, why have you treated us like this? Your father and I have been anxiously searching for you."

49"Why were you searching for me?" he asked. "Didn't you know I had to be in my Father's house?" 50But they did not understand what he was saying to them.

51Then he went down to Nazareth with them and was obedient to them. But his mother treasured all these things in her heart. 52And Jesus grew in wisdom and stature, and in favor with God and men.

This section provides the only account of Jesus' boyhood we possess apart from apocryphal legends. The focal point is not his precocious wisdom, noteworthy as that was. Rather, Luke leads us to the real climax, Jesus' reference to God as "my Father" (v.49). This is the first instance of Jesus' "filial consciousness," his awareness that in a unique way he was the Son of God.

41–42 Luke takes yet another opportunity to emphasize the fidelity of Jesus' family to Judaism. Adults were supposed to attend the three major feasts in Jerusalem annually—Passover, Pentecost, and Tabernacles. For many this was impossible, but an effort was made to go at least to Passover. With puberty, a boy became a "son of the covenant," a custom continued in the present bar-mitzvah ceremony. It was considered helpful for a boy to attend the Jerusalem festivals for a year or two before becoming a son of the covenant so that he would realize what his new relationship involved. Luke calls Jesus a "boy" (*pais*, a term also used for servanthood, v.43) in contrast to "child" (*paidion*, v.40).

43–47 At this intermediate age, Jesus might have been either with the women and children or with the men and older boys, if the families were grouped this way in the caravan. Each parent might have supposed he was with the other (v.43). We need not assume that his parents neglected him. It was after a day of travel that they missed Jesus (v.44); another day would have been required for the trip back (v.45), and on the next day ("after three days," v.46) the successful search was made.

The questions Jesus put to the teachers (v.46) were probably not merely boyish inquiries but the kind of probing questions used in ancient academies and similar discussions. He also gave answers (v.47). J.W. Doeve suggests that Jesus engaged in a midrashic discussion of biblical texts: "Their amazement must relate to his deducing things from Scripture which they had never found before" (*Jewish Hermeneutics in the Synoptic Gospels and Acts* [Assen: Van Gorcum, 1954], p. 105).

48 Luke vividly describes the parents' emotions. The first is astonishment (cf. v.33). There is no inconsistency or lapse in Luke's attributing surprise to those who should have known best the uniqueness of Jesus' person and mission. It is one of the characteristics of Luke to observe the various responses of awe at the words and deeds of Jesus, which is also consistent with ancient narratives touching on the observation of wonders. His mother's natural concern then issues very humanly in a hint of scolding. Next she uses the word "anxiously" (the participle *odynōmenoi*) to describe her and Joseph's feelings as they hunted for him. The word is unusually strong, often indicating pain or suffering (16:24–25; Acts 20:38; cf. TDNT, 5:115).

49–50 Jesus' answer, "Why were you searching for me?" (v.49), pointedly prepares the hearer for a significant statement that is then understood as being theologically inevitable. The same pattern occurs in 24:5: "Why do you look for the living among the dead?" followed by "He is not here; he has risen!" (24:6). In the present instance, the second part of the statement is of extraordinary significance. The importance of Jesus' use of the phrase "my Father," with its implied designation of himself as the unique Son of the Father, is heightened not only by the preceding question but by the subsequent statement of v.50. By saying that Mary and Joseph did not understand, Luke underlines the awesome mystery of Jesus' statement of filial consciousness. There may also be, though it is doubtful, a subtle contrast between the words "your father" (v.48) and "my Father" (v.49).

51 Immediately following this intimation of Jesus' divinity, Luke assures us also of his perfect humanity by noting his obedience to his parents. Once more Mary reflects inwardly on the significance of it all (cf. Gen 37:11). Like the boy Samuel (1 Sam 2:26) and the responsible son in Proverbs 3:4, Jesus matures into a person both God and men approve.

52 Jesus' growth was normal. Unlike some stories in the apocryphal gospels, Luke does not try to portray Jesus as exhibiting unusual powers. To say Jesus "grew in wisdom" does not detract from his deity. Even if wisdom means innate knowledge, Philippians 2:7 suggests that as a servant Jesus was willing to forgo the full use of his divine powers; so a normal development of knowledge is not ruled out. "Stature" (*hēlikia*) is ambiguous, referring either to physical growth or, more likely, personal development, i.e., maturity. The good reputation Jesus enjoyed "with men" was continued in the church (Acts 2:47).

Notes

---

49 The tendency in recent versions has been to understand the Greek idiom ἐν τοῖς τοῦ πατρός μου (*en tois tou patros mou*, "in the [noun omitted] of my Father") to refer to the temple rather than to affairs or "business" of God. The latter is not impossible (cf. 1 Cor 7:33; 1 Tim 4:15), but the former is more appropriate to the context (cf. Gen 41:51 LXX; cf. also Creed, p. 46).

III. Preparation for Jesus' Ministry (3:1–4:13)

A. *The Ministry of John the Baptist*

3:1–20

[1]In the fifteenth year of the reign of Tiberius Caesar—when Pontius Pilate was governor of Judea, Herod tetrarch of Galilee, his brother Philip tetrarch of Iturea and Traconitis, and Lysanias tetrarch of Abilene—[2]during the high priesthood of Annas and Caiaphas, the word of God came to John son of Zechariah in the desert. [3]He went into all the country around the Jordan, preaching a baptism of repentance for the forgiveness of sins. [4]As is written in the book of the words of Isaiah the prophet:

> "A voice of one calling in the desert,
> 'Prepare the way for the Lord,
>   make straight paths for him.
> [5]Every valley shall be filled in,
>   every mountain and hill made low.
> The crooked roads shall become straight,
>   the rough ways smooth.
> [6]And all mankind will see God's salvation.' "

[7]John said to the crowds coming out to be baptized by him, "You brood of vipers! Who warned you to flee from the coming wrath? [8]Produce fruit in keeping with repentance. And do not begin to say to yourselves, 'We have Abraham as our father.' For I tell you that out of these stones God can raise up children for Abraham. [9]The ax is already at the root of the trees, and every tree that does not produce good fruit will be cut down and thrown into the fire."

[10]"What should we do then?" the crowd asked.

[11]John answered, "The man with two tunics should share with him who has none, and the one who has food should do the same."

[12]Tax collectors also came to be baptized. "Teacher," they asked, "what should we do?"

[13]"Don't collect any more than you are required to," he told them.

[14]Then some soldiers asked him, "And what should we do?"

He replied, "Don't extort money and don't accuse people falsely—be content with your pay."

[15]The people were waiting expectantly and were all wondering in their hearts if John might possibly be the Christ. [16]John answered them all, "I baptize you with water. But one more powerful than I will come, the thongs of whose sandals I am not worthy to untie. He will baptize you with the Holy Spirit and with fire. [17]His winnowing fork is in his hand to clear his threshing floor and to gather the wheat into his barn, but he will burn up the chaff with unquenchable fire." [18]And with many other words John exhorted the people and preached the good news to them.

19But when John rebuked Herod the tetrarch because of Herodias, his brother's wife, and all the other evil things he had done, 20Herod added this to them all: He locked John up in prison.

This narrative, like the foregoing, bears Palestinian Jewish characteristics in its language, themes, and setting. An example of this is vv.1–2. Here Luke not only shows classical historical precision in the dates he provides but also reflects the opening words of the OT prophets (e.g., Isa 1:1; Jer 1:1–3; Hos 1:1; Amos 1:1). God's word is not simply the vehicle for timeless truth; it is a word in and to specific human circumstances. At this point in history, after a long silence, the prophetic word was again being heard.

1 The dating provided in this verse was more immediately useful to Luke's first-century readers than to the average reader today who does not know the period when Luke was writing. If the reign of Tiberius was dated from the occasion of his predecessor's death (Augustus died on 19 August A.D. 14), his "fifteenth year" would be from August, A.D. 28, to August, A.D. 29, according to the normal Roman method of reckoning. If Luke was following the Syrian method as a native of Antioch, Tiberius's "fifteenth year" would have been from the fall of A.D. 27 to the fall of A.D. 28 (cf. discussion in Notes). For Luke to use the Roman method would have been in keeping with his cultural environment and appropriate for his readers.

"Herod" is Herod Antipas, son of Herod the Great who ruled Galilee and Perea 4 B.C.–A.D. 39 (cf. Luke 3:19–20; 13:31; 23:7). Philip, like Herod Antipas, was a son of Herod the Great. He ruled a group of territories to the northeast of Palestine, Iturea and Traconitis (4 B.C.–A.D. 33/34). Lysanias, unlike an earlier ruler of the same name, is unknown except through inscriptions (see Creed, pp. 307–9). Pontius Pilate was governor (Luke uses the general term *hegemoneuontos*, not the disputed "procurator") from A.D. 26–36 (cf. F.F. Bruce, "Procurator," NBD, 2d ed., pp. 973–74).

2 The official high priesthood of Annas had ended in A.D. 15, but his influence was so great, especially during the high priesthood of his son-in-law Caiaphas (A.D. 18–36) (cf. John 18:13), that his name is naturally mentioned along with that of Caiaphas. With the reference to the high priests, we move from the secular world to the religious and are ready for the introduction of the prophet John. He is in the desert, where he had gone (1:80). The desert held memories for the Jews as the locale of the post-Exodus wanderings of Israel. It also had eschatological associations (cf. not only Isa 40:3 but also Hos 2:14). Some thought demons inhabited the desert, and it was later alleged that John had a demon (Matt 11:18). Luke's interest is not only in the coming of John (Matt 3:1; Mark 1:4: "John came") but in the message "the word of God came" (cf. Notes).

3 The impression Luke, more than the other Gospels, gives is that John had an itinerant ministry. Apparently he not only preached in the wilderness but followed the Dead Sea coast to the Jordan River and then away a distance from there. The "desert" is a barren rocky area that covers a large territory. Naturally he went where there was enough water to perform baptisms (see John 3:23).

John's baptism was "of repentance" (*metanoias*), that is, its chief characteristic was that it indicated sorrow for sin and a moral change on the part of those he baptized (vv.8–14). The noun *metanoia* ("repentance") appears also in 3:8; 5:32; 15:7; and 24:47. The verb *metanoeō* ("repent") occurs in Luke 10:13; 11:32; 13:3, 5; 15:7, 10; 16:30; and 17:3–4. The basic idea comes from the Hebrew *šûḇ* ("turn," i.e., from sin to God; cf. TDNT, 4:975–1008). Repentance is an ancient prophetic theme (e.g., Ezek 18:21, 30). "For [*eis*, or 'with a view to'] forgiveness of sins" expresses the result of the repentance shown in baptism.

4–6 Isaiah 40:3 was used by the community at Qumran as a rationale for leading a separated life in the desert, where they believed they were preparing the way of the Lord by means of a constant reading of the Law (1QS 8.12–16; 9.19–20). For Luke, as for Matthew and Mark, the Isaiah passage was a clear prophecy of the ministry of John the Baptist. Luke includes more of the quotation than Matthew and Mark do. First he cites the extraordinary way in which, on the analogy of preparations made for a royal visitor, even the seemingly immovable must be removed to make way for the Lord (vv.4–5). What needs removal is the sin of the people.

Luke concludes the Isaiah quotation with words that aptly describe his own evangelistic and theological conviction: "And all mankind will see God's salvation" (v.6). Luke finds here, following the LXX, a biblical basis for his own universal concern and his central theme of salvation (Morris, *Luke*, p. 95). The words concerning the appearance of God's glory (Isa 40:5) are omitted. Luke does stress the glory of God often elsewhere, beginning with 2:14; but for some reason he apparently does not think it appropriate to stress it here.

7 The word "crowds" represents *ochlos*, an assorted group of people, rather than *laos* (cf. v.18). Luke does not specify who was in this group (Matt 3:7 says that they were Pharisees and Sadduccees; cf. John 1:19, 24). Perhaps Luke wants to leave the first narration of a specific confrontation with the Pharisees till they have one with Jesus himself (5:17). Similarly, no mention is made of people coming from Jerusalem (cf. Mark 1:5).

John's language is strong, as was that of OT prophets who preceded him. His words (vv.7–9) are virtually identical with those in Matthew 3:7–10. Luke has, however, omitted one element and added another. Matthew's reference to John's words "Repent, for the kingdom is near" (Matt 3:2) is not found anywhere in Luke's account. Although Luke does emphasize the kingdom, he reserves its introduction for Jesus (4:43). What he adds here is a list of specific instances in which his audience ought to exhibit behavioral changes consistent with repentance.

Later on Jesus himself used the epithet "brood of vipers" against the Pharisees (Matt 23:33). Here John uses it as a prophet of judgment under the direction of God's Spirit. OT prophets had spoken strongly also and made similar allusions to reptiles (Isa 59:5). The question "Who warned you to flee from the coming wrath?" suggests that while their "coming out to be baptized by him" was the proper thing to do, their motives were in question.

8–9 The language is picturesque. Two images are presented. First, a tree that does not produce fruit should be chopped down and removed to make way for one that will. Jesus speaks later about appropriate fruit (6:43–45) and also tells a parable about cutting down a barren fruit tree (13:6–9). The imagery may be intended to call to mind the figure of Israel as a fig tree or vine (cf. Isa 5:1–7). Black, p. 145, suggests a possible word-play in the original Aramaic that would have included *raq* and *qar* (twice) in the words for "flee," "root," and "cut down." The second image, the axe "at the root," symbolizes an impending radical action, the destruction of the whole tree. The theme of Abraham's children (v.8) is found in John 8:31–41, Romans 4:12–17, and Galatians 3:6–9.

Mere physical descent from Abraham is not important; God can create his own children out of stones just as he can cause inanimate stones to praise his Son, if humans remain silent (19:40). The threat of judgment is heightened through the imagery of fire, a theme reintroduced in the reference to Jesus' ministry (vv.16–17).

10–11 This prophetic word of judgment elicits a response, first from the crowd in general (v.10), then from the unpopular and greedy tax collectors (v.12), and finally from the soldiers (v.14). The conversations, which are unique to Luke, provide opportunity for some clear statements about social justice and responsibility.

The crowd, which is mixed, in contrast to the groups of tax collectors and soldiers (vv.12, 14), is told to share clothing and food with the needy (v.11). John is not requiring a strict communal life like that at Qumran but "fruit in keeping with repentance" (v.8; cf. Gal 5:22–23). The "tunic" was the short garment (*chitōn*) worn under the longer robe (*himation*). One might have an extra tunic, for warmth or a change of clothes (cf. 9:3: "Take . . . no extra tunic"). Those who had broken the biblical law of love needed to demonstrate their repentance in this kind of sharing.

12–13 The "tax collectors" (v.12) were part of a despised system (cf. 5:27; 15:1). Of the three groups, they would have been considered most in need of repentance. The chief tax collectors (*architelōnēs*), such as Zacchaeus (19:2), bid money for their position. Their profit came from collecting more than they paid the Romans. The chief tax collectors hired other tax collectors to work for them. Because their work and associations rendered them ritually unclean and because they regularly extorted money, they were alienated from Jewish society and linked with "sinners." While John shows social concern, he does not advocate overthrow of the system but rather advocates a reform of the abuses. Since these abuses arose out of individual greed, a radical change in the practice of the collectors themselves was required (v.13).

14 The "soldiers" (*strateuomenoi*) were probably not Roman but Jewish, assigned to internal affairs (cf. comment on "officers" at 22:4). The very nature of their work gave them opportunity to commit the sins specified. Soldiers could use threats of reprisal to extort money from the people. The soldiers' question suggests the seriousness of their moral need, by means of the added words *kai hemeis* ("even we")— "What about us?" as JB puts it. Here again the need of others is set over against personal greed. The second great commandment (cf. 10:27b) needs to be applied.

15–17 The question naturally came to the minds of "the people" (v.15; cf. v.18) whether such a radical prophet as John might be the Messiah. In John 1:19–25 popular opinion about him is reported in greater detail. Here John answers the unexpressed question in several ways. The Messiah is "more powerful" than he is (v.16). The Messiah is worthy of such reverence that even the task of tying his sandals is more than John feels worthy of (cf. John 3:30).

The Messiah will baptize, not with water in a preparatory way, as John had done, but actually "with the Holy Spirit and with fire" (v.16). These are not two separate categories of baptism. The single word "with" (*en*) combines the two (cf. Matt 3:11; Mark 1:8). The coming of the Spirit is to have the effect of fire. John uses an agricultural image to explain this. The grain is tossed in the air with a "winnowing fork" (v.17). The lighter and heavier elements are thus separated, the heavier grain falling on the "threshing floor." The "chaff," which is not the true grain, is burned up and the wheat stored in the barn.

Interpreters have discussed whether the fiery work of the Spirit is judgment or purification also. Modern readers find it difficult to understand how the concepts of the Spirit, baptism (usually associated with water), and fire relate to one another. The biblical background (e.g., Isa 44:3; Ezek 36:25–27; Joel 2:28–29) and also 1QS 4.20–21 show that the concept of washing and refreshing was associated with the Spirit. Fire is an ancient symbol of judgment, refinement, and purification (cf. Notes). We may conclude that John and his contemporaries were already acquainted with all these nuances. The Holy Spirit was understood as being active in saving, purifying, and judging. The Spirit had definitely, but not frequently, been associated with the Messiah (Isa 11:1–2), whose coming would mean also the availability of the Spirit's ministry.

18 That John not only "exhorted" the people but "preached the good news" shows that grace accompanies the warning to flee from judgment. It is noteworthy that here and in v.21 Luke uses the word *laos* ("people"; cf. v.21)—the term he specifically employs to describe not just a "crowd" (*ochlos;* v.7) but a potentially responsive group (see comments on 1:68, 77). It is this "people," who apparently stayed on to hear more of John's message, who heard the further proclamation of "good news."

19–20 "Herod" (v.19) is Herod Antipas, mentioned in v.1. His brother is Philip, whose wife, Herodias, left him for Herod. His marriage to her was one of many sins, and the climactic sin "added" (v.20) to this sordid series was his imprisonment of John. For John's death, see 9:7–9 and the fuller account in Mark 6:17–29. By his brief anticipation here of John's imprisonment, Luke underscores both the boldness of John and the sickness of the society he called to account. Verse 20 also indicates that John's ministry was completed before that of Jesus began. The same point is made in Peter's sermon to Cornelius (Acts 10:37–38). (C. Talbert, "The Lukan Presentation of Jesus' Ministry in Galilee," *Review and Expositor* 64 [1967]: 490, presents this relationship between John's and Jesus' ministry as part of a comprehensive theological scheme in Luke.)

Notes

1 Several alternate methods of chronological reckoning have been applied to the data in this verse. Some have proposed that Luke followed a chronology used at that time in the Near East by which the reign would have been counted, not from the actual date, but by a regnal year scheme. According to the Julian calendar, 19 August to 31 December A.D. 14 would have been the accession year, with the first full year beginning 1 January A.D. 15. The fifteenth year would have been 1 January to 31 December A.D. 29. This calculation and that cited in the commentary above allow for an A.D. 33 crucifixion date, which many now think likely.

It is also possible that a Syrian system was used, by which Tiberius's fifteenth year was 21 September A.D. 27 to 8 October A.D. 28. Still other possibilities exist (see Harold W.

Hoehner, *Chronological Aspects of the Life of Christ*, pp. 29–37; cf. G. Ogg, "Chronology of the New Testament," NBD, pp. 222–25). These dates must be correlated with those of Luke 3:23; John 2:20; 8:57, and other passages relating to the Crucifixion, as well as those pertaining to Jesus' birth. For further information about Herod Antipas, see Harold W. Hoehner, *Herod Antipas* (Grand Rapids: Zondervan, 1972).

2 Ῥῆμα (*rhēma*, "word") emphasizes the actual words spoken, whereas λόγος (*logos*, "word") looks more at the expression of thought (cf. A–B, s.v.). Seventeen of *rhēma*'s twenty-three occurrences in the Synoptics are in Luke.

3 Dipping and washing ritually in water was becoming increasingly common in the first century A.D. (cf. J. Thomas, *Le mouvement baptiste en Paletine et Syrie* [Gembloux: J. Duculot, 1935]). Such lustrations were used at Qumran, both as one confessed his sins and entered the community (1QS 5.7–20) and on subsequent occasions (1QS 2.25ff.; 3.4–5). John's probable knowledge of the Qumran community, which was in the Judean desert, has led some to see a connection between his baptism and theirs. His baptism was not, however, intended for frequent repetition, nor did it link the participants with a community like theirs. Probably as early as John's day, baptism along with circumcision (for males) and the offering of a sacrifice marked the full conversion of a proselyte to Judaism. The striking difference between Jewish proselyte baptism and that which John practiced is that John's subjects were already Jews. For them to be baptized carried negative implications as to the sufficiency of Judaism. Josephus (Antiq. XVIII, 117 [v.2]) has a different understanding of John's baptism, perhaps seeing it only as a lustration such as he knew was practiced at Qumran. In Josephus's view, John wanted people to do righteous deeds and then be baptized. But Luke shows John baptizing repentant sinners, who then go on to live righteous lives.

4 Αὐτοῦ (*autou*, "for him") is parallel with κυρίου (*kyriou*, "for the Lord") and has the pronoun *autou* whereas Isa 40:3 LXX has τοῦ θεοῦ ἡμῶν (*tou theou hēmōn*, "our God"). In this way, Luke makes it easier to understand that the words "the Lord" here refer to Christ (cf. Matt 3:3; Mark 1:3).

7 On ἀπὸ τῆς μελλούσης ὀργῆς (*apo tēs mellousēs orgēs*, "from the coming wrath"), see also Rom 2:5; 1 Thess 1:10; Rev 6:15–17. John will allude to this in Luke 3:9 (cf. TDNT, 5:422–47).

16 In the clause "with the Holy Spirit and with fire," the second "with" (ἐν, *en*) was omitted in the 1973 edition of NIV. That was technically correct, as the Greek does not repeat the word. The 1978 edition added the second "with" possibly for stylistic reasons.

17 Among the relevant passages in OT, intertestamental, and NT literature on the Spirit, water, fire, purification, and judgment are Gen 19:24 (cf. Luke 17:29); Amos 7:4; Mal 3:2; Enoch 90:24–27; Pss Sol 15:6; 1QS 2.8; 1QpHab 2.11ff.; Matt 5:22; 13:40; 25:41; 1 Peter 1:7; Rev 20:14. For the association of fire with fluidity, see Dan 7:9–10 and 1QH 3.29–32. See also J.D.G. Dunn, *Baptism in the Holy Spirit*, Studies in Biblical Theology, 2d series, 15 (Naperville, Ill.: A.R. Allenson, 1970), pp. 8–22.

B. *The Baptism of Jesus*

3:21–22

> [21]When all the people were being baptized, Jesus was baptized too. And as he was praying, heaven was opened [22]and the Holy Spirit descended on him in bodily form like a dove. And a voice came from heaven: "You are my Son, whom I love; with you I am well pleased."

21 For a comprehensive study of the events contained in vv.21–22, the parallels in Matthew 3:13–17; Mark 1:9–11; and John 1:32–34 should be consulted. As in the birth narratives, there is at Jesus' baptism a supernatural attestation. Many see in the event his "call" to his mission. His baptism comes as the climax of the baptism of "all the people" (cf. Notes).

Jesus was baptized, not because he was a sinner in need of repentance, but as a way of identifying himself with those he came to save. His reasons are expressed in Matthew 3:15. This is the first of several important events in Luke that took place when Jesus prayed (cf. esp. 6:12; 9:18, 29; 22:41). Though Luke's description of the opening of the heavens is not so dramatic as Mark's (1:10), it does make clear that Jesus had a true vision of the Deity (cf. Ezekiel's vision, Ezek 1:1; Stephen's, Acts 7:56; and Peter's, Acts 10:11). In contrast, the disciples on the Mount of Transfiguration were enveloped by a cloud. Although they heard God speaking, their vision was of Christ and the heavenly visitors rather than of God in heaven.

22 God had appeared in OT times through theophanies. Now the Spirit appears as a dove. Only Luke has the expression "in bodily form," giving more substance to the experience of the Spirit's presence. Luke does not say that anyone other than Jesus was aware of the Holy Spirit. Perhaps others present saw only a dove without realizing its significance. The descent of the Spirit is reminiscent of Genesis 1:2, but no specific parallel is drawn (cf. Notes).

"You are my Son, whom I love" designates Jesus as the unique Son of God. The words, like those heard at the Transfiguration (9:35; cf. Matt 17:5; Mark 9:7), effect a blend of OT christological passages: Psalm 2:7 and Isaiah 42:1. Present scholarly opinion holds that the concept of divine sonship in Jewish thought was not only applicable to angels (Job 1:6; 2:1) and to the nation of Israel and her kings (Exod 4:22; 2 Sam 7:14; Hos 11:1) but was coming into use, at least at Qumran, as a designation for the Messiah (4QFlor 10-14). At the Annunciation Jesus was designated the "Son of the Most High" (1:32). On his sonship and OT passages, see the comments on the Transfiguration (9:35) for a full discussion of the wording common to both passages. Here we may simply observe that the words "love" and "well pleased" convey the idea of choice and special relationship. Jesus has now received his commission. He is ready (following the Temptation, 4:1-12) to begin his ministry.

Notes

---

21 The infinitive phrase βαπτισθῆναι (*baptisthēnai*, "were baptized"; NIV, "were being baptized") could, because the verb is an aorist, imply antecedent action. In this case it would indicate that the baptism of the people had ended, thus distinguishing Jesus' baptism from theirs. The construction does not necessarily imply this, however.

Luke also uses an aorist, this time in participial form, βαπτισθέντος (*baptisthentos*, "was baptized") to describe Jesus' own baptism, perhaps in contrast to the durative idea of the present participle προσευχομένου (*proseuchomenou*, "was praying"). Jesus' baptism, like that of the people, was a single event in time; but his praying continued for his lifetime. The most striking aspect of Luke's use of grammar in vv:21-22 is his use of dependent clauses leading up to the affirmation "You are my Son. . . ."

22 The significance of the dove's descent has been much discussed (cf. L.E. Keck, "The Spirit and the Dove," NTS 17 [1970-71]: 41-67; Marshall, *Luke: Historian and Theolo-*

gian, pp. 151–52. While it may be impossible to determine the symbolism with certainty, its basic significance relates to God's presence, call, and approval.

Scholars have debated the relationship of the "voice . . . from heaven" to the בַּת קוֹל (*bat qôl*, lit., "daughter of a voice," i.e., the voice of God heard not directly but as an echo). The rabbis thought that God, having ceased speaking through prophets as in the OT, now spoke indirectly. O. Betz (TDNT, 9:288–90, esp. 298) shows that the voice was still considered a shared communication from God. The heavenly voice to Jesus was not identical to the *bat qôl*, being directed to one person and involving a first-person address: "*You* are *my* Son, whom *I* love" (emphasis mine).

Against the view that the word υἱός (*huios*, "son") is a later substitute for an original παῖς (*pais*, "servant") under Hellenistic influence, see I.H. Marshall, "Son of God or Servant of Jehovah?—A Reconsideration of Mark I.11," NTS 15 (1968–69): 326–36.

An early variant in the Western text, "This day I have begotten you," echoing Ps 2:7 and the synoptic parallels, is not supported by the best MSS (Metzger, *Textual Commentary*, p. 136).

C. *Jesus' Genealogy*

3:23–38

23Now Jesus himself was about thirty years old when he began his ministry. He was the son, so it was thought, of Joseph,

the son of Heli, 24the son of Matthat,
the son of Levi, the son of Melki,
the son of Jannai, the son of Joseph,
25the son of Mattathias, the son of Amos,
the son of Nahum, the son of Esli,
the son of Naggai, 26the son of Maath,
the son of Mattathias, the son of Semein,
the son of Josech, the son of Joda,
27the son of Joanan, the son of Rhesa,
the son of Zerubbabel, the son of Shealtiel,
the son of Neri, 28the son of Melki,
the son of Addi, the son of Cosam,
the son of Elmadam, the son of Er,
29the son of Joshua, the son of Eliezer,
the son of Jorim, the son of Matthat,
the son of Levi, 30the son of Simeon,
the son of Judah, the son of Joseph,
the son of Jonam, the son of Eliakim,
31the son of Melea, the son of Menna,
the son of Mattatha, the son of Nathan,
the son of David, 32the son of Jesse,
the son of Obed, the son of Boaz,
the son of Salmon, the son of Nahshon,
33the son of Amminadab, the son of Ram,
the son of Hezron, the son of Perez,
the son of Judah, 34the son of Jacob,
the son of Isaac, the son of Abraham,
the son of Terah, the son of Nahor,
35the son of Serug, the son of Reu,
the son of Peleg, the son of Eber,
the son of Shelah, 36the son of Cainan,
the son of Arphaxad, the son of Shem,
the son of Noah, the son of Lamech,
37the son of Methuselah, the son of Enoch,

the son of Jared, the son of Mahalalel,
the son of Kenan. 38the son of Enosh,
the son of Seth, the son of Adam,
the son of God.

23–38 The age of Jesus is given in very approximate terms. He might have been in his mid-thirties. "Thirty" is a round number and might also indicate that, like the priests who began their service at that age, he was ready to devote himself to God's work. Compare the extreme comment recorded in John 8:57. Both Matthew and Luke recognize the importance of establishing a genealogy for Jesus, in accordance with the care given such matters in ancient Israel.

In their handling of Jesus' genealogy, Matthew and Luke differ in several ways.

1. Matthew begins his Gospel with the genealogy, thereby establishing an immediate connection with the OT and with Israel. Luke waits till the significant part of the ministry of John the Baptist is completed and Jesus stands alone as the designated Son of God.

2. Matthew begins with Abraham, stressing Jesus' Jewish ancestry; Luke, in reverse order, goes back to Adam, probably with the intention of stressing the identification of Jesus with the entire human race.

3. Matthew groups his names symmetrically; Luke simply lists them.

4. Both trace the lineage back through ancestral lines that diverge for a number of generations from Luke's, though both meet at the generation of David.

5. Matthew includes the names of several women (a feature one might have expected in Luke because of his understanding and respect for women).

The significance of the genealogy in Luke probably lies in the emphasis on Jesus as a member of the human race, a son of Adam; in the contrast of Jesus, the obedient Second Adam (a theme implicit but not explicit in Luke), with the disobedient first Adam; and in Jesus as the true Son of God (cf. "Adam," v.38).

The differences outlined above, as well as some problems of detail, have been explained in part by one or more of the following assumptions: (1) Joseph's lineage is given in Matthew, Mary's in Luke; (2) the legal line is traced in Matthew, the actual line of descent in Luke; and (3) there was a levirate marriage at one or more points in the line.

The first assumption is without solid foundation and does not seem to accord with the emphasis on Joseph in 1:27. Nevertheless, Luke's narrative seems to be from Mary's point of view, whereas Matthew's is from that of Joseph (cf. Machen, pp. 202–9; 229–32). The second assumption is possible; it allows for breaks in Matthew's line, with heirship still retained. The levirate marriage assumption has been a popular option since ancient times (proposed by Africanus, third century, as cited in Eusebius, *Ecclesiastical History* 1.7). The widow of a childless man could marry his brother so that a child of the second marriage could legally be considered as the son of the deceased man in order to perpetuate his name. In a genealogy the child could be listed under his natural or his legal father.

Joseph is listed as the son of Heli in Luke but as the son of Jacob in Matthew. On the levirate marriage theory, Heli and Jacob may have been half-brothers, with the same mother but fathers of different names. Perhaps Heli died and Jacob married his widow.

To all this it must be added that we possess not a poverty but a plethora of possibilities. Therefore the lack of certainty due to incomplete information need not imply error in either genealogy. Morris (*Luke*, p. 100) observes that it is not possible to know how Luke would have handled a genealogy involving a virgin birth and so "the case is unique."

Recent studies include M.D. Johnson, *The Purpose of the Biblical Genealogies* (Cambridge: University Press, 1969); E.L. Abel, "The Genealogies of Jesus HO CHRISTOS," NTS 20 (1974): 203–10; and H.C. Waetjen, JBL 95 (1976): 205–30. M.D. Johnson summarizes the data (and his viewpoint that the genealogies are "probably examples of the tendency to historicize traditional motifs in the Gospel material") in his article "Genealogy," ISBE (rev. ed.), 2:424–31. For a conservative approach to this complex subject, see the concise summary in Marshall, *Luke: Historian and Theologian*, pp. 157–66.

D. *The Temptation of Jesus*

4:1–13

> [1]Jesus, full of the Holy Spirit, returned from the Jordan and was led by the Spirit in the desert, [2]where for forty days he was tempted by the devil. He ate nothing during those days, and at the end of them he was hungry.
> [3]The devil said to him, "If you are the Son of God, tell this stone to become bread."
> [4]Jesus answered, "It is written: 'Man does not live on bread alone.' "
> [5]The devil led him up to a high place and showed him in an instant all the kingdoms of the world. [6]And he said to him, "I will give you all their authority and splendor, for it has been given to me, and I can give it to anyone I want to. [7]So if you worship me, it will all be yours."
> [8]Jesus answered, "It is written: 'Worship the Lord your God and serve him only.' "
> [9]The devil led him to Jerusalem and had him stand on the highest point of the temple. "If you are the Son of God," he said, "throw yourself down from here. [10]For it is written:
>
> > " 'He will command his angels concerning you
> > to guard you carefully;
> > [11]they will lift you up in their hands,
> > so that you will not strike your foot against a stone.' "
>
> [12]Jesus answered, "It says: 'Do not put the Lord your God to the test.' "
> [13]When the devil had finished all this tempting, he left him until an opportune time.

This vivid narrative (vv.1–13) contains an important blend of theological themes— the divine sonship and messiahship of Jesus, the warfare between Christ and Satan, OT theology, and principles of obedience to the divine Word.

1–2 These two verses shed light on the significance of the episode. Jesus is in the "desert" (v.1) for a period of "forty days" (v.2). This probably relates to Israel's experience in the desert after the Exodus. It may also allude to Moses' forty days without food on the mountain (Deut 9:9). The parallel with Israel becomes stronger if it is meant as a comparison between Israel as God's "son" (Exod 4:22–23; Hos 11:1) who failed when tested and Jesus as his unique Son who conquered temptation. God led Israel into the desert; likewise the Spirit led Jesus. In the former case, God tested his people. Now God allows the devil to tempt his Son.

It is important here to distinguish between three kinds of tempting (*peirasmos*, "testing").

1. Satan tempts people, i.e., lures them to do evil. God never does this nor can he himself be tempted in this way (James 1:13). Further, not all temptation comes directly from Satan; often it comes from our own lower nature (James 1:14–15).

2. People may tempt (test) God in the sense of provoking him through unreasonable demands contrary to faith. This is what Israel did in the desert and what is probably referred to in Jesus' quotation of Deuteronomy 6:16 (cf. v.12).

3. God tests (but does not tempt) his people, as he did in the desert (Deut 8:2). All three kinds of testing are involved in the parallels between the desert experiences of Israel and Jesus. (On this theme, see B. Gerhardsson, *The Testing of God's Son*, Coniectanea Biblica NT Series 2:1 [Lund: C.W.K. Gleerup, 1966].)

Although God already knows all about us, he reveals the thoughts and intents of our hearts through our response to him in times of trial. Thus he tested Israel in the desert to "see" whether the people would obey (Exod 16:4).

In this temptation by the devil, the Lord Jesus shows the validity of what God had just said of him: "With you I am well pleased" (3:22).

In this section we see several contrasts. One—between Israel and Jesus—has just been discussed. Another is the absolute contrast between Jesus, who is both filled and led by the Spirit (note Luke's emphasis on the Spirit), and the devil, who opposes both Christ and the Spirit. (The unpardonable sin is called blasphemy against the Spirit [12:10; cf. Matt 12:31–32].) Another contrast is the one implied between Jesus as "hungry," i.e., physically empty, and yet as "full of the Spirit." Our own experience is usually the reverse.

3–4 The "devil" (*diabolos*, v.3) has several names in biblical and other Jewish literature, notably the OT name "Satan," which is used often in the NT (*Satanas*; cf., e.g., 4:8; 10:18; 11:18). He opposes God and God's servants (1 Chron 21:1; Job 1:6–12; 2:1–7; Zech 3:1–2). He may seem to be ubiquitous but is not omnipresent. Sometimes he works indirectly through the evil spirits who form his domain (cf. 11:14–20). Here the devil's statement "If you are the Son of God" picks up the declaration of Jesus' sonship in 3:22. The conditional construction does not imply doubt but is a logical assumption in the dialogue.

The reference to bread is conceivably an allusion to God's provision of manna for Israel during the Exodus. Apparently some of Jesus' contemporaries expected that the coming Messiah would perform some such miracle of provision for them (cf. John 6:30). Consequently this temptation may have been an appeal for Jesus to do a work of messianic significance. Alternately, and more probably, his temptation may have been to satisfy his own need and gratify himself. Bread, however, is necessary, not evil, and hardly an object of "the cravings of sinful man" (1 John 2:16). Further, Jesus' temptation is not the same as the self-engendered lusting described in James 1:14–15—a fact to keep in mind when we question how Jesus could have been perfect and yet truly tempted. The issue, therefore, is not one of allurement to perverted self-gratification but a challenge to act apart from faithful dependence on God.

Jesus' reply is brief, a partial quotation of Deuteronomy 8:3 (found more fully in Matt 4:4). In Deuteronomy Moses was reminding Israel that during the forty years in the desert God had led them "to humble you [i.e., Israel] and to test you in order to know what was in your heart, whether or not you would keep his commandments" (Deut 8:2). The next verse (Deut 8:3) specifically refers to hunger and the provision of manna, which the Lord gave Israel so that the people might know that man needs not merely bread but the sustaining word of God.

Thus while he is being "tempted" by the devil, Jesus is also proving faithful to God in contrast to Israel's response when "tested" by him. Jesus proves by his response that his heart is not divided but that he is dependent on God and obedient to his word (v.4). So he becomes our example in temptation (Heb 4:14–16; 5:8).

5–8 The second temptation, though of a different nature, involves similar issues. The devil takes Jesus to a "high place" (v.5; cf. "mountain" in Matt 4:8, where a parallel with Moses on Mount Nebo may be implied [Deut 32:49; 34:1–3]). "In an instant" probably shows that this part of the Temptation involved a vision. It was not necessary for Jesus to see every part of the world physically for this to be an actual temptation. Once again, what the devil offered was legitimate in itself. The Messiah would one day rule all the world, possessing all "authority and splendor" (v.6). In this temptation the devil claims to possess the world. Jesus does not challenge the claim (cf. John 12:31); neither does he acknowledge it. To worship the devil in order to recapture the world, even for its good, would have meant "casting out devils by Beelzebub" (Morris, *Luke*, p. 103).

Had Jesus accepted the devil's offer, our salvation would have been impossible. First, Jesus would have sinned by giving worship to the devil and thus could not have offered himself a perfect sacrifice for our sins. (The same thing applies to all three temptations.) Second, Scripture teaches that the Messiah should first suffer and only then "enter his glory" (24:26). Third, since the devil tried to prevent Christ's voluntary death for our sins, the implication of this second temptation was that accepting an immediate kingdom would avoid the Cross.

The temptations deal with both the divine sonship and messiahship of Jesus—related concepts in biblical thought. But the temptations also tested his perfect manhood. This aspect of them especially interested Luke. Moreover, they show us Jesus as our example. By quoting Deuteronomy 6:16, he responded as the perfect man—the obedient last Adam (Rom 5:19)—should respond, worshiping and serving his only God (v.8). Both the OT texts Jesus quoted so far (vv.4, 8) are more than weapons against the devil; they apply to Jesus himself.

9–12 Luke records this temptation in the last rather than second place (cf. Matt 4:5–7). It may be that Matthew preferred to conclude with a kingdom reference. Possibly Luke wants to center on the city of Jerusalem (v.9), which Matthew does not mention by name, because of his theme of the progression of the gospel from Jerusalem to the Gentile nations. The essence of this temptation is that of presuming on God (v.12) and displaying before others one's special favor with him. In this instance the devil quotes a passage of Scripture (Ps 91:11–12) out of context—notice that the mere use of Bible words does not necessarily convey the will of God (v.10). Further, Satan omits the words "in all your ways" (Ps 91:11), possibly to facilitate application to an act inconsistent with the normal "ways" of the godly person. Gerhardsson ("Testing God's Son," pp. 54ff.) sees here a theme of protection (cf. Deut 1:31 with the context of Ps 91, from which the devil quotes). He sees the temple as a place of protection and finds a play on words between "wings" (Ps 91 [90 LXX]:4, *pterygas*) and "highest point" or "pinnacle" (*pterygion*). But it is doubtful whether Luke intended this parallel. The rabbinic tradition that the Messiah would appear on top of the temple (SBK, 1:151) may provide a background that accounts for the form of this temptation, even though the idea of jumping down is absent.

Again Jesus responds with Scripture (v.12), this time by quoting Deuteronomy 6:16. This quotation could be understood as applying to the devil, who "tempted" Jesus in the first sense of the word (cf. comments on temptation, v.2). More probably it is applied to Jesus, who thus refuses to "tempt" God in the second sense of the word. That is, he will not repeat the sin that Israel committed in the desert by putting God to the test. To do that would be to provoke God by making inappropriate demands for a divine sign to be used for display. This request for a sign would actually be an act of unbelief, masquerading as extraordinary faith.

13 This verse may be considered the conclusion of this section rather than the beginning of the next (so NIV 1978 ed.). The devil leaves only temporarily—"until an opportune time."

Notes

9 Τὸ πτερύγιον (to pterygion, "the highest point") may be the corner of the walls that encompassed the temple area. The southeastern corner was directly above a cliff, making a terrifying drop down to the Kidron Valley possible.

13 Conzelmann's view (*Theology of Luke*, p. 38) that Luke thought Satan was inactive during Jesus' ministry imposes an artificial scheme on this Gospel. Conzelmann reads too much into the first half of this verse and holds that the "opportune time" does not come till Luke 22:3. Schuyler Brown (*Apostasy and Perseverance*, in loc.) counters this concept. He maintains that Satan is active throughout Luke's Gospel, a conclusion based on a view of the nature of temptation in Luke that differs from Conzelmann's.

IV. The Galilean Ministry (4:14–9:50)

A. *Initial Phase* (4:14–6:16)

1. *First approach and rejection at Nazareth*

4:14–30

¹⁴Jesus returned to Galilee in the power of the Spirit, and news about him spread through the whole countryside. ¹⁵He taught in their synagogues and everyone praised him.

¹⁶He went to Nazareth, where he had been brought up, and on the Sabbath day he went into the synagogue, as was his custom. And he stood up to read. ¹⁷The scroll of the prophet Isaiah was handed to him. Unrolling it, he found the place where it is written:

> ¹⁸"The Spirit of the Lord is on me,
>   because he has anointed me
>   to preach good news to the poor.
> He has sent me to proclaim freedom for the prisoners
>   and recovery of sight for the blind,
> to release the oppressed,
> ¹⁹ to proclaim the year of the Lord's favor."

²⁰Then he rolled up the scroll, gave it back to the attendant and sat down. The eyes of everyone in the synagogue were fastened on him, ²¹and he began by saying to them, "Today this scripture is fulfilled in your hearing."

²²All spoke well of him and were amazed at the gracious words that came from his lips. "Isn't this Joseph's son?" they asked.

²³Jesus said to them, "Surely you will quote this proverb to me: 'Physician, heal yourself! Do here in your hometown what we have heard that you did in Capernaum.'"

²⁴"I tell you the truth," he continued, "no prophet is accepted in his hometown. ²⁵I assure you that there were many widows in Israel in Elijah's time, when the sky was shut for three and a half years and there was a severe famine throughout the land. ²⁶Yet Elijah was not sent to any of them, but to a widow in Zarephath in the region of Sidon. ²⁷And there were many in Israel with leprosy in the time of Elisha the prophet, yet not one of them was cleansed—only Naaman the Syrian."

²⁸All the people in the synagogue were furious when they heard this. ²⁹They got up, drove him out of the town, and took him to the brow of the hill on which the town was built, in order to throw him down the cliff. ³⁰But he walked right through the crowd and went on his way.

14–15 Once again, as Jesus enters a new phase of his experience, Luke mentions the special activity of the Holy Spirit (v.14; cf. 4:1). Shortly Jesus will make a significant declaration about the meaning of the Spirit's ministry in his life (v.18). So far we have seen the Spirit's activity at Jesus' conception (1:35), baptism (3:22), and temptation (4:1). The "news" that spread about Jesus and the fact that "everyone praised him" (v.15) are the first of several observations Luke makes about public response to Jesus' ministry (cf. vv.22, 28, 32, 36–37).

This passage (vv.16–30) has an important place in the Lukan presentation. It not only marks the beginning of Jesus' ministry; it is also the first major narrative about his ministry that is not largely paralleled in Matthew or Mark. The setting is Nazareth, the place of Jesus' childhood. A lengthy quotation from Isaiah (vv.18–19) issues in a proclamation of immediate fulfillment. Jesus also implies, at the very outset of his ministry, the selection of Gentiles for divine favor (vv.24–27). Observe that this event occurs in Luke much earlier than what appears to be the same occurrence later in presentations of Matthew and Mark. Whatever the literary and historical relationship may be between this passage and Mark 6:1–6, its placement here shows that Luke considers it of prime importance and a bold introductory statement as Jesus begins his ministry in Galilee. Also a pattern appears here that is unveiled more clearly later on in Luke-Acts: (1) the presentation of the gospel to Jews in their synagogues, (2) rejection, and (3) turning to the wider Gentile world (cf. Acts 13:46; cf. also commentary on Acts, R.L. Longenecker, EBC, vol. 9).

16–17 Luke emphasizes that Jesus was in his hometown by the words "where he had been brought up." Luke stresses Jesus' Jewish piety with a reference to his custom of synagogue attendance. This strengthens the contrast with his rejection. Luke does not say whether Jesus had publicly read from the Scriptures before; nor does Luke say whether Jesus chose Isaiah 61 himself (v.17), or whether the passage was assigned for that Sabbath (cf. Notes). The passage was Isaiah 61:1–2, with the words "to release the oppressed" taken from Isaiah 58:6. The variation from the usual wording may simply reflect the interpretive translation in use at that time.

18–19 The quotation has significance both as our Lord's statement of his call to his saving ministry and as Luke's affirmation of this ministry as thematic in his Gospel. In saying "Today this scripture is fulfilled in your hearing" (v.21), Jesus identifies himself as the subject of Isaiah's prophetic word. As such he is (1) the bearer of the Spirit (v.18); (2) the eschatological prophet, proclaimer of the "good news"; and (3) the one who brings release to the oppressed (a messianic function). His role as Suffering Servant is not specified here, but an association may be assumed on the basis of the place of Isaiah 61 among the Servant passages.

1. We have already observed Luke's frequent mention of the Holy Spirit in Jesus' life (cf. comment on 4:14). Now we see that Jesus' ministry will be uniquely marked by the presence of the Spirit as prophetically foretold.

2. His role as eschatological prophet is intertwined with that of John the Baptist as prophetic forerunner. For the sense in which John was a prophet and was characterized by the spirit of Elijah, see comments on 1:17 and 7:24–28. However Jesus, not John, was *the* prophet predicted in Deuteronomy 18:18 (cf. John 1:19–24, esp. v.21). Luke gives special attention to Jesus as a prophet in a number of ways. Among them are sayings of Jesus not found in other Gospels (v.24 in this chapter; 13:33) and comments by others (7:16, 39; 24:19, only in Luke, and 9:8, 19; see also Acts 3:22; 7:37, 52). In the present passage, the prophetic mission described by Isaiah, a mission of proclamation, is accepted by Jesus.

3. The prophetic role of Jesus overlaps his role as Messiah (cf. discussion in Marshall, *Luke: Historian and Theologian*, pp. 124–28). His ministry of deliverance is messianic in character. This assumption probably lay behind the doubts in John's mind when release from prison was not forthcoming (7:18–19).

The "good news" (v.18) Jesus was to proclaim recalls both the joyful announcement in 1:19 and the frequent use of the term elsewhere in Luke. It also builds on Isaiah 40:9; 41:27; and especially 52:7. The "poor," like the "prisoners," the "blind," and the "oppressed," are not only the unfortunate of this world but those who have special need of dependence on God (cf. comment on 1:53; 6:20). The words "to release the oppressed" fill out the meaning of the previous words. Luke 7:22 cites some ways Jesus fulfilled this mission.

The "year of the Lord's favor" (v.19) is reminiscent of the Jubilee (one year in every fifty) when debts were forgiven and slaves set free (Lev 25:8–17). It means not so much a time that is "acceptable" to people but the time in history when God in sovereign grace brings freedom from the guilt and effects of sin. The inclusion of this quotation is consistent with Luke's stress on the dawning of the new age of salvation.

The omission of the next phrase in Isaiah 61:2—"the day of vengeance of our God"—is also significant. Jesus' audience would suppose that the day of their own salvation would be the day of judgment on their pagan enemies. But the delay of judgment means that this time of the Lord's favor benefits the Gentiles also. Jesus affirms (vv.24–27) that Gentiles are also recipients of God's grace, even when Jews were not so blessed. It has been suggested that the omission of the vengeance phrase is the cause of the hostility in v.28. But while the two may be related, Luke does not say so.

In summary, Luke presents the quotation and Jesus' ensuing comments as a programmatic statement of Jesus' ministry. As prophet and Messiah, he will minister to the social outcasts and needy, including Gentiles, in the power of the Spirit.

20 We now have a description of the synagogue procedure. Jesus hands back the scroll to the "attendant." In addition to other services rendered to the synagogue (including at times the teaching of children), the attendant had the sacred duty of handling the revered scroll. After this was replaced in its cabinet or ark, the reader took the customary sitting position for instructive comments on the passage. Luke now makes the first of several comments on the response of the congregation, which is at first intense attention and ultimately hostility.

21 Jesus' comment is short but of the highest importance. We do not know whether he said more than Luke recorded. But that is not important, for the single sentence recorded is of profound significance. It announces the fulfillment of the reading from Isaiah concerning the subject of the prophecy (Jesus) and the time of God's gracious work ("today"). Since the Isaiah quotation lacks the phrase about the day of God's wrath, it must be understood that "today" refers only to the part about God's grace.

The term "fulfilled" (*peplērōtai*) is not as prominent in Luke as in Matthew. Usually it occurs with a unique Lukan meaning (cf. comment on 7:1). Only here and in the Emmaus conversation (24:44) does Luke use the word in relation to the fulfillment of OT prophecy, and in both cases the Matthean formula "to fulfill what was spoken" is lacking. These two lone references to fulfillment stand out then at the beginning and end of Jesus' public appearances, emphasizing the fulfillment of God's eternal purpose in the ministry of Christ.

22 The response of the audience to Jesus' comment on Isaiah's words has been variously interpreted. Most expositors take the words "bore him witness" (*emartyroun autō*) as implying a positive attitude toward what he had said; hence NIV translates them "spoke well of him." The same verb is used in Acts 22:12 of Ananias, where NIV translates it "was . . . highly respected." But J. Jeremias (*Jesus' Promise to the Nations. Studies in Biblical Theology* [London: SCM, 1958], pp. 44–45) takes it in a negative sense, as he does the statement in v.20b, assuming that hostility against Jesus began when he did not refer to the day of God's judgment. The ambiguous nature of the passage continues with *ethaumazon* ("were amazed"), which does not indicate clearly either favor or disfavor. The cause of their amazement was Jesus' "gracious words" (*hoi logoi tēs charitos*)—i.e., the kind and wise manner of his speech or of what he said about the grace of God. A near parallel in Acts 14:3 suggests the latter, but there it is "word" (*ho logos*, singular, i.e., "message") of grace, which is closer to the phrase "the gospel of God's grace" in Acts 20:24.

Certainly Luke appreciates and conveys the gracious nature of Jesus' ministry. But at some point, here or shortly after, the hostility of the audience begins. Does the question "Isn't this Joseph's son?" indicate hostility? The question does seem to express perplexity and irritation at this man who grew up in the home of a fellow Nazarene and is now making such impressive claims. The question could be colloquially rendered "He's Joseph's son, this one, isn't he?"

23 Jesus' response is not intended to reassure his audience but rather to draw out their subconscious attitudes. The future tense in "you will quote" (*ereite*) might refer to another occasion, especially if we assume that Jesus has not yet preached in Capernaum. Yet this incident might be the same as that recorded in Matthew 13: 53–58 and Mark 6:1–6. Both Gospels have made prior references to Jesus' preaching in Capernaum. Matthew 4:13 says Jesus lived there and Mark 1:21–28 tells of his teaching and his popularity there. It is not necessary, however, to go to the other Gospels for support; Luke himself records an apparently extensive and popular ministry in Galilee prior to this time (4:14–15). It would be strange if this had not included Capernaum. It is, therefore, more likely that Jesus is expressing the reply he would expect the people to make in response to his message in the synagogue—namely, that they would challenge him to fulfill Isaiah's prophecy by doing miracles in the presence of those who heard him. Throughout his ministry Jesus would be challenged to do miraculous signs (e.g., 11:16, 29) to prove his claims.

24 "I tell you the truth" (*amēn legō hymin*) is used six times in Luke to introduce a solemn assertion. This expression shows the authority with which Jesus spoke and is clearly an authentic word of Jesus. This introductory formula with the Greek word for "amen" appears often in Mark and even more frequently in Matthew, especially in the material unique to that Gospel. Luke includes a few other quotations in which he changes the "amen" to its equivalent in idiomatic Greek, most notably in 9:27: *legō de hymin alēthōs* ("I tell you the truth").

Here the statement so solemnly introduced anticipates Jesus' rejection. It sees him as a prophet and may be a variation of the saying found in Matthew 13:57 and Mark 6:4. The difference is in the sentence structure and in Luke's use of the word "accepted," the same adjective (*dektos*) used in v.19 to describe the year of the Lord. The double use of this word in this context may be intended to show that, though God desires to accept the people, they do not respond by accepting the prophet who tells them of God's grace. The "proverb" (*parabolē*, v.23) itself is apparently a version of a common adage making the point that whoever achieves greatness is never fully trusted back home. But here its meaning is the deeper one that Jesus stands in the line of the prophets who were rejected by their own people.

25–27 These verses are introduced by Jesus saying, "I assure you" (v.25), a phrase very like the "amen" formula in v.24. Observe that Jesus does not state here that the prophets Elijah (v.26) and Elisha (v.27) went to Gentiles because they were rejected by the Jews; rather, they went because they were sent there by God. Jesus' audience is becoming more and more enraged as they realize that they will receive no special favors from him and that he considers himself above home ties and traditions.

28–30 Nazareth lay among the ridges of the southern slopes of the Galilean hills. Jesus allowed the crowds to drive him (v.29) out of the town (as he later did on going to the place of crucifixion). But it was not yet his time to die, and by some unexplained means he made his way out (v.30).

Notes

16–30 The location of this narrative in Luke has been a major problem of critical scholarship. If the similar incident recorded in Matthew 13:53–58 and Mark 6:1–6 is actually a different and later occurrence, several questions arise. Did the same sort of event take place twice? In that case it would seem strange that Jesus would return a second time and meet a similar incredulous response, as though no such incident had occurred before. Yet even though this may seem improbable, it is not for us to judge it impossible. Also the wording in Matthew and Mark, including most of the dialogue portion, is almost totally different from that in Luke. (Note another variation in John 6:42.)

Nevertheless, a case may be made for the same incidents being described in all three Synoptics. If so, Luke has simply placed it earlier in his narrative. It may be, as often suggested, that he had theological reasons for placing it early, in order to show the progression of the gospel from Jewish environs to the Gentile world and Rome (at the end of Acts). Luke emphasizes this progression by featuring here the statements about the extent of God's grace to the Gentiles. On the other hand, the order may reflect Luke's care in following a source or combination of sources in which this incident did in fact stand at the beginning of Jesus' ministry. This explanation is congruous with the remarkable fact that not only Mark but even Matthew, who is so interested in the fulfillment theme, does not include the quotation from Isaiah. If Luke has used a different source than those known to Matthew, the whole matter is clarified and Luke has written an "orderly account" (1:3).

At any event, this is a crucial passage in Luke. Recent significant studies include H. Anderson, "Broadening Horizons: The Rejection at Nazareth Pericope of Lk 4, 16–30 in Light of Recent Critical Trends," Int 18 (1964): 259–75; D. Hill, "The Rejection of Jesus at Nazareth," NovTest 13 (1971): 161–80; Robert Sloan, *Favorable Year* (cf. n. 29); and the discussion in Marshall, *Gospel of Luke*, pp. 175–90; cf. the treatment of the text by J. Jeremias, *Jesus' Promise to the Nations*, pp. 44–46. On the Isaiah quotation itself and its use by Jesus, see J.A. Sanders, "From Isaiah 61 to Luke 4," in *Christianity, Judaism and other Graeco-Roman Cults: Studies for Morton Smith at Sixty*, Part One (Leiden: E.J. Brill, 1975), pp. 75–106.

16 Ἀνέστη ἀναγνῶναι (anestē anagnōnai, "he stood up to read") shows the synagogue custom of standing to read Scripture and sitting to preach. The first reading, following the shema—"Hear, O Israel . . ." (Deut 6:4)—and prayers, was of the passage for the day from the lectionary (selected verses of Bible readings) of the Pentateuch. The second reading was from the Prophets. The choice of the passage may have still been up to the reader in Jesus' day.

18 Ἔχρισεν (echrisen, "anointed") designates appointment to the messianic mission, possibly referring to Jesus' baptism (3:22–23). Εὐαγγελίσασθαι (euangelisasthai, "to preach") is a significant word in Luke, already found in 1:19; 2:10; 3:18. Ἀπέσταλκεν (apestalken, "sent") is from ἀποστέλλω (apostellō), commonly used in relation to sending someone on a mission. It could refer, as in John 3:17 and elsewhere in John, to the Father's sending Jesus into the world.

19 Ἐνιαυτὸν κυρίου δεκτόν (eniauton kyriou dekton) is literally the "acceptable" (RSV) or "favorable" (NASB) "year of the Lord." NIV both expresses the meaning here and follows the Hebrew text (cf. Isa 61:2 NIV). Luke's text follows the LXX.

20 The verb ἀτενίζω (atenizō, "to fasten on"), in the phrase οἱ ὀφθαλμοὶ ἦσαν ἀτενίζοντες αὐτῷ (hoi ophthalmoi ēsan atenizontes autō, "the eyes . . . were fastened on him"), is used once more in Luke (22:56) and ten times in Acts. It is usually found in situations of extreme emotion, e.g., of those watching the ascension of Christ (Acts 1:10), and of Stephen looking into heaven just before his martyrdom (Acts 7:55). It can connote hostility (Acts 13:9). In a somewhat parallel situation, the Sanhedrin "looked intently" at Stephen at the beginning of his trial, "and they saw that his face was like the face of an angel." Here (v.20), since no hostility to Jesus has yet been expressed, we cannot take atenizontes as meaning more than intense anticipation of how Jesus will interpret the Isaiah passage.

21 Ἤρξατο λέγειν (ērxato legein, "began to say") is omitted by NIV. It may be "simply a case of redundant usage," but more likely "what follows is the arresting opening of a sermon, so that the use of the verb is justified" (Marshall, *Gospel of Luke*, pp. 184–85).

Σήμερον (sēmeron, "today") occurs relatively often in Luke (2:11; 5:26; 12:28; 13:32–33;

19:5, 9; 22:34, 61; 23:43) and nine times in Acts. Its use is consistent with Luke's interest in the presence of the kingdom and of the time of salvation.

2. Driving out an evil spirit

4:31–37

³¹Then he went down to Capernaum, a town in Galilee, and on the Sabbath began to teach the people. ³²They were amazed at his teaching, because his message had authority.

³³In the synagogue there was a man possessed by a demon, an evil spirit. He cried out at the top of his voice, ³⁴"Ha! What do you want with us, Jesus of Nazareth? Have you come to destroy us? I know who you are—the Holy One of God!"

³⁵"Be quiet!" Jesus said sternly. "Come out of him!" Then the demon threw the man down before them all and came out without injuring him.

³⁶All the people were amazed and said to each other, "What is this teaching? With authority and power he gives orders to evil spirits and they come out!" ³⁷And the news about him spread throughout the surrounding area.

31–32 Luke has already mentioned Capernaum (v.23) as a center of miraculous activity in the ministry of Jesus. Capernaum was on the northwest shore of the Sea of Galilee. Luke adds a geographical note for Gentile readers. The ruins of a later (probably third-century) synagogue may be seen today in that vicinity. The expression "went down" reflects the descent necessary from the elevated situation of Nazareth to the coastal plain.

The implication of the imperfect periphrastic *ēn didaskōn* ("was teaching") may be that it was Jesus' custom to attend the synagogue (v.33) and to teach there. Though the plural *tois sabbasin* can have a singular meaning (NIV, "on the Sabbath") as it does in the Markan parallel (Mark 1:21), if it has a plural meaning here in Luke, it would support the possibility that the imperfect implies repeated action. This would be true to the pattern Jesus had established. It is more likely, however, that the imperfect means he was "just in the process of teaching" (NIV, "began to teach") when the demon-possessed man interrupted him.

The incident Luke next gives is perhaps more striking than the parallel in Mark (1:21–34) because it exemplifies the liberating work described in the preceding Isaiah quotation (vv.18–19). The reaction of the people, though comparable to that in the preceding incident (vv.20–22), differs from it in one important aspect. Now they are astonished that this teacher, who in their eyes was not even a rabbi, taught with authority (v.32). The contrast is sharpened in Mark 1:22 by the additional words "not as the teachers of the law." The majority of rabbis would base their teaching on the chain of tradition, citing the opinions of their predecessors. By omitting this specific comparison, Luke may simply be deferring to his Gentile readership, who would perhaps not be as aware as Jewish readers of rabbinical custom. But it may also be that Luke is emphasizing the absolute authority of Jesus. In support of this is Luke's use of the word "message" (*logos*, lit., "word"). For the importance of the "word" in Luke, see comment on 1:1–4. Keeping in mind that the parallel passage in Mark does not use "word" but says "he taught them," Luke would seem to be emphasizing the "authority" of Jesus' "word" (cf. v.36).

33–35 Demon possession is too frequent and integral to the Gospel narratives to minimize or, worse, to discard it as Hellenistic superstition. This is only the first mention of it in Luke, the climax of such incidents coming in 11:14–22. Significantly, Jesus is confronted by demonic activity during his first public ministry Luke describes following the introductory sermon at Nazareth. The "good news of the kingdom of God" (v.43) Jesus was proclaiming signaled an attack on the forces of evil. Luke wants us to understand the centrality of the kingdom in Jesus' ministry and in that of his disciples. (See his unique use of the expression "kingdom of God" in such passages as 9:27, 60, 62.) A holy war is being launched and, as v.34 suggests, the demons know it. This war will be carried on by Jesus' disciples (9:1–2; 10:8–9, 17).

The man is possessed by a spirit (v.33) that is "evil" (*akathartou*, "unclean," so NIV mg.). Though some would see in the terms "evil" and "unclean" evidence for different kinds of demons, there is little biblical support for this. In 8:2 "evil" spirits are mentioned; several verses later we read simply of a "demon" (8:27), which is said to be "unclean" (8:29, NIV mg.). There seems to be no difference and NIV uses the same term "evil" in both cases. An evil spirit is unclean in contrast to the holiness of God and may well cause both moral and physical filth in a possessed human (cf. R.K. Harrison, "Demon, Demoniac, Demonology," ZPEB, 2:92–101).

The possessed man shrieks and utters an expression of "indignant surprise" (Creed, p. 70). The word "Ha" (v.34) is followed by an idiomatic rhetorical question (*ti hēmin kai soi*, "What do you want with us?") that may be rendered "What do we have to do with each other?" or, loosely, "Why this interference?" (Danker, *Jesus*, p. 61). The demon, perhaps exemplifying James's comment that "the demons believe and shudder" (James 2:19), senses the purpose of Jesus' presence. In keeping with the pattern in the Gospels, testimony to the truth about Christ comes from a number of different and unexpected sources. The term "the Holy One of God" (*ho hagios tou theou*) contrasts strongly with the remark that this was an unclean demon.

Jesus responded sternly (cf. Notes) with a command to be silent (v.35). In Jesus' action we may see the beginning of a pattern of prohibiting the premature proclamation of his identity. Throughout the Gospels Jesus guards the fact of his messiahship, probably (1) to prevent a misinterpretation that would draw to him revolutionary minded dissidents seeking a leader against Rome; (2) to allow his messianic works themselves to establish his authority among true believers (cf. 7:18–23); and (3) to avoid an inappropriate self-proclamation as Messiah, especially if there was, as it now appears (cf. R.N. Longenecker, *The Christology of Early Jewish Christianity*, Studies in Biblical Theology, Second Series 17 [London: SCM, 1970], pp. 71–74), an understanding that the true Messiah would allow others to proclaim him as such, rather than doing so himself. If none of these is the reason here, Jesus is at least maintaining his authority by silencing the enemy.

What follows is not technically an exorcism, because Jesus does not use an incantation or invoke the authority of another. Instead he speaks a simple word of command on his own authority. Luke, always interested in the physical condition of people, observes that the demon came out violently but without hurting the man.

36–37 Once again Luke notes the amazement of the people (v.36). The astonishment this time is not only at his teaching and authority (*logos*, cf. above on v.32) but at his power. Luke's theme of the spread of the gospel finds expression in the conclusion of the narrative (v.37).

Notes

35 Ἐπετίμησεν (*epetimēsen*, "said sternly") is a strong word of rebuke or warning (cf. v.39; 8:24; 9:42, and note on v.39).

3. Healing many

4:38–44

> ³⁸Jesus left the synagogue and went to the home of Simon. Now Simon's mother-in-law was suffering from a high fever, and they asked Jesus to help her. ³⁹So he bent over her and rebuked the fever, and it left her. She got up at once and began to wait on them.
> ⁴⁰When the sun was setting, the people brought to Jesus all who had various kinds of sickness, and laying his hands on each one, he healed them. ⁴¹Moreover, demons came out of many people, shouting, "You are the Son of God!" But he rebuked them and would not allow them to speak, because they knew he was the Christ.
> ⁴²At daybreak Jesus went out to a solitary place. The people were looking for him and when they came to where he was, they tried to keep from leaving them. ⁴³But he said, "I must preach the good news of the kingdom of God to the other towns also, because that is why I was sent." ⁴⁴And he kept on preaching in the synagogues of Judea.

38–39 Jesus' healing ministry continues in a more private setting (v.38). This account lacks the vivid detail of Mark's, but Luke stresses the miraculous by adding the word "immediately" (*parachrēma*, v.39; NIV, "at once"). Luke mentions Simon Peter here without special introduction, though he has not yet described Peter's call. Probably Peter was so well known by Luke's readership that this did not seem abrupt, and the call does follow immediately. Both this passage and 1 Corinthians 9:5 inform us that Peter was married. A crisis of serious illness in the family gives occasion for Jesus to help. The fact that Jesus "rebukes" (cf. Notes) an impersonal fever, as he had earlier rebuked the demon, has led some to assume that a personal evil force had caused the fever. If so, one might also suspect this in 8:24. Otherwise either the fever is simply personified in effect, through the use of a vivid verb, or Luke is emphasizing the active force of Jesus' word. The vividness of the scene continues as Jesus bends over the woman; she immediately rises; and, doubtless in keeping with her character, she begins to serve the group.

40 One of the most beautiful scenes in Scripture now follows. The crowds have apparently waited till evening, after the Sabbath was over. In the remaining hours of diminishing light, they perform the labor of love they could not do on the Sabbath, carrying the sick to Jesus. It is noteworthy that Jesus himself has not yet ventured out on the Sabbath to perform healings publicly. This bold action will take

place later (6:1–11). Luke carefully distinguishes between those who were just sick (v.40) and those who were demon-possessed (v.41). This warns us not to assume that the Gospel writers thought all disease was caused by demons. Luke mentions that Jesus laid his hands on the people who came to him, a detail not found in the parallel accounts (Matt 8:16; Mark 1:34). Though laying on hands was a common practice in ancient religious acts, here it shows that Jesus is the source of the healing power and that he had a personal concern.

41 Luke is also the only synoptic writer who says at this point that the demons called Jesus the Son of God. As already mentioned (cf. comment on v.34), the Gospel writers show various people testifying to the identity of Christ, including even unbelievers and demons. This provides a broad base for the case the Gospels are establishing. The injunction to silence (v.35) is here amplified. This knowledge of the demons is in ironic contrast to the unbelief of the crowds.

42–44 Shifting quickly from dusk to dawn, Luke portrays Jesus in a sharply contrasted setting. He is alone (v.42). Surprisingly, in view of his special attention to prayer (cf. 5:16), Luke does not tell us, as Mark does (1:35), that Jesus is praying. Luke, however, does express with greater force than Mark the reason for Jesus' refusal to linger at Capernaum. The difference gives us a clue to one of the dominant themes in Luke. The words "must," "kingdom of God," and "sent" (v.43) are unique to Luke's narrative at this point (cf. Notes). Along with "preach," these words constitute a programmatic statement of Jesus' mission and also of Luke's understanding of it. Verse 44 emphasizes the continuation of the misson, as Jesus preaches in the synagogues throughout the "land of the Jews" (NIV mg.; cf. Notes).

Here, then, Luke has provided representative incidents from the ministry of Jesus. It is the kind of activity summarized in Acts 10:38 as "doing good and healing all who were under the power of the devil."

Notes

---

38 Mark (1:29) connects this incident more closely with the synagogue incident than Luke by using the word εὐθύς (*euthys*, "immediately"; NIV, "as soon as"), but the implication in Luke is also that it occurs on the same Sabbath day.

Luke's use of πυρετῷ μεγάλῳ (*pyretō megalō*, "high fever") shows that he follows the ancient medical custom in distinguishing levels of fever.

39 "In NT ἐπιτιμάω [*epitimaō*] has no other meaning than 'rebuke'" (Plummer, p. 134; cf. note on v.35 above). It is a "prerogative of Jesus in the Gospels. . . . which declares His position as the Lord. . . . He is also Lord over the demons and bends them to do His will" (E. Stauffer, TDNT, 2:625–26). This being the case, some think that here and in Luke 8:24 (cf. Matt 8:26; Mark 4:39) there must be demonic influence behind fever and storm. However, this is not the case in God's shaking of the heavens or the Red Sea (Job 26:11; Ps 106 [105 LXX]:9) and need not be assumed here.

Παραχρῆμα (*parachrēma*, "at once") is one of Luke's favorite words, though he does not use it as frequently as Mark does εὐθύς (*euthys*, "at once," "without delay"; cf. note above on v.38). *Parachrēma* contributes to the sense of urgency in Luke (see below).

43 Δεῖ (*dei*, "must") conveys a strong sense of urgency. Two thirds of its occurrences in the Synoptics are in Luke, most of these in the material unique to this Gospel and the others added by Luke as he edited his work. While the number of occurrences is not great, the proportion is statistically significant and the particular applications striking. Among the significant examples of its use are 2:49; 13:33; 22:37; 24:7, 26, 44.

Luke's distinctive stress on the sovereign purpose of God and the relationship of that to Jesus' mission appears also in Luke's use of the word ἀποστέλλω (apostellō, "send"). Luke uses it only slightly more times than Mark, but it has greater significance in Luke because of the way he introduces it into the narratives. The present passage is an example of this, because where Mark 1:38 has ἐξῆλθον (exēlthon, "have come"), Luke has the stronger ἀπεστάλην (apestalēn, "was sent").

Τὴν βασιλείαν τοῦ θεοῦ (tēn basileian tou theou, "the kingdom of God") is a major topic in Jesus' teaching and in Luke's presentation of that teaching. Several passages that summarize Jesus' ministry and that of his disciples specify that the kingdom is the core of Jesus' message (e.g., 8:1; 9:2; cf. 9:62; 10:9; 16:16). The occurrences of the term in Matthew and the proportion of occurrences in Matthew's work are even greater than in Luke. For a full study of the kingdom in Jesus' teaching, see G.E. Ladd, *The Presence of the Future* (Grand Rapids: Eerdmans, 1974).

44 Τῆς Ἰουδαίας (tēs Ioudaias, "of Judea") is a difficult reading since Luke is clearly describing Jesus' Galilean ministry. For that very reason early copyists of the NT seem to have welcomed alternative possibilities: τῆς Γαλιλαίας (tēs Galilaias, "of Galilee"), in conformity with Mark 1:39 and Matt 4:23, and τῶν Ἰουδαίων (tōn Ioudaiōn, "of the Jews"). By using a slight paraphrase, "the land of the Jews," the NIV margin has conveyed what is probably Luke's intention. The word "land" is the traditional word for all of Palestine, the home of the Jews. In Luke's mind Judea may have had the same significance. Marshall notes that it is not correct to draw a sharp distinction between "the two parts of Jesus' ministry" (i.e., Galilee and Judea), for "v.43 indicates that Jesus' ministry is directed to the Jews as a whole; the point is theological rather than geographical" (*Gospel of Luke*, p. 199).

---

4. Calling the first disciples

5:1–11

¹One day as Jesus was standing by the Lake of Gennesaret, with the people crowding around him and listening to the word of God, ²he saw at the water's edge two boats, left there by the fishermen, who were washing their nets. ³He got into one of the boats, the one belonging to Simon, and asked him to put out a little from shore. Then he sat down and taught the people from the boat.

⁴When he had finished speaking, he said to Simon, "Put out into deep water, and let down the nets for a catch."

⁵Simon answered, "Master, we've worked hard all night and haven't caught anything. But because you say so, I will let down the nets."

⁶When they had done so, they caught such a large number of fish that their nets began to break. ⁷So they signaled their partners in the other boat to come and help them, and they came and filled both boats so full that they began to sink.

⁸When Simon Peter saw this, he fell at Jesus' knees and said, "Go away from me, Lord; I am a sinful man!" ⁹For he and all his companions were astonished at the catch of fish they had taken, ¹⁰and so were James and John, the sons of Zebedee, Simon's partners.

Then Jesus said to Simon, "Don't be afraid; from now on you will catch men."

¹¹So they pulled their boats up on shore, left everything and followed him.

This narrative (vv.1–11) is similar in certain details to Matthew 4:18–22 and Mark 1:16–20. Luke's account is much fuller, containing the unique encounter between

Jesus and Peter. The climax of each account is a call to "catch men" and the obedience of the disciples. Luke lacks the specific command "Follow me." The sequence in which this account occurs in Luke is different from that in Mark, who records the call in 1:16–20, before the Capernaum incidents (1:21–28), which Luke put just prior to the present narrative (4:31–41). Naturally these similarities and differences have led scholars to different conclusions about the relationship of the two accounts and the history of the tradition behind them. In the light of Luke's method of focusing on individuals as a means of them drawing attention to Jesus, we can understand the placement and character of the narrative (cf. G.N. Stanton, *Jesus of Nazareth in NT Preaching*, pp. 20, 59). Although Jesus might have called the disciples several times (one such calling has already taken place according to John 1:35–51), to attempt a harmonization by defining the Lukan narrative and that in Matthew and Mark as separate incidents is unnecessary. Luke focuses on Peter, shows the sovereignty and holiness of Jesus in a way Matthew and Mark do not, and alone mentions the total abandonment of the disciples' possessions as an act of discipleship (cf. 14:33).

The difference in placement is likewise understandable. None of the Synoptics ties the incident into a strict chronological sequence; so the placement is flexible. Luke first establishes the program of Jesus' ministry (4:16–30, 43). Now he is ready to establish the sovereign lordship of Christ in his relationship first with Peter as representative of the disciples and then with the social outcasts and "sinners" whom he has come to save (5:32; 19:10), such as the man with leprosy (5:12–15) and Levi also (5:27–32).

Elements of this narrative also resemble the postresurrection story in John 21:1–14. Scholars are not agreed as to the relation between the traditions represented in the two passages (see discussions in Creed, pp. 73–74; Marshall, *Gospel of Luke*, pp. 199–200; R.E. Brown, *The Gospel According to John*, II, AB [Garden City: Doubleday, 1970], pp. 1089–92). The Johannine issues aside, the Lukan narrative is coherent and natural in its context. Arguments for an original postresurrection setting for Luke's tradition are unconvincing.

1–3 "One day" (v.1) represents the simple *egeneto* ("it happened [that]"; KJV, "it came to pass"). It does not indicate a specific chronological sequence. The geographical description is more precise: "lake" is used instead of the more general word "sea." Luke mentions the pressure of the crowds, as he occasionally does elsewhere (8:42, 45; 19:3). Their attention is on the "word of God," another instance of Luke's focus on the "word" (cf. 4:32, 36). The shore of the lake provided an excellent, acoustically serviceable amphitheater. Luke, being observant of detail, draws our attention to two boats (v.2). Next he singles out Simon as the owner of one of them (v.3). The description in v.2 along with the comment in v.5 serve to emphasize the futility of the night's work. Luke is careful to mention that Jesus again teaches—now from the boat, from which his voice would carry across the water to the crowd. Not even the next event, miraculous as it is, may, in Luke's narrative, be allowed to direct attention away from Jesus' teaching ministry.

4–5 The sharp contrast between the expert but unsuccessful fisherman and Jesus needs no comment. Jesus' command (v.4) must have seemed unreasonable to them after their failure during the night (v.5). Peter, here called by his old name, Simon, demurs; but he does what Jesus says.

6–10a Luke now moves quickly to three focal points in his narrative. First, he describes the gathering of the fish (v.6). This extraordinary happening is similar to that in John 21 (cf. also Jesus' uncanny ability to direct Peter to a fish with a coin in its mouth [Matt 17:24–27]). The details of the breaking nets and loaded boats (v.7) help give the narrative the ring of truth. Second, the miracle moves Peter (Luke now uses his full name, Simon Peter), who is overcome by awe (v.9), to abase himself before Jesus (v.8). He now calls Jesus "Lord" (*kyrios*), with a greater depth of meaning than the common "Sir." Peter is gripped not merely by a sense of his inferiority but of his own sinfulness. The experience of Isaiah 6:5 comes to mind, but Peter needs no such vision; he is face to face with Jesus. Luke's reason for including this incident may be not only to portray the confrontation of human sinfulness with Jesus but also to show that to receive the saving grace of Christ a "sinful" (*hamartōlos*, cf. Notes) man must repent. Long before Luke speaks of the Gentiles with their gross sins and their being included in saving grace, we are faced with the realization that even Peter, who in Luke's time was known for his obedience to the Jewish laws, must take his place as a sinner (Danker, *Jesus*, p. 65). Luke (v.10a) mentions James and John, but only in passing; the central figures are Jesus and Peter.

10b–11 The third focal point in the narrative following Peter's obedience to Jesus in letting down the net is Jesus' declaration that he will "catch men" from then on (v.10b). Here interpretations vary. But in view of Luke's emphasis on the kindness of God reaching out to embrace all mankind, it is more likely to signify a beneficent rather than judgmental ingathering. It presages the widening horizons of both Luke and Acts, culminating, in a sense, in Peter's vision symbolizing the reception of Gentiles into the church and his subsequent witness to the Gentile Cornelius (Acts 10:9–48, esp. vv.34–35).

After the declaration about catching men, the disciples followed Jesus (v.11). Luke's observation that they left everything, which is not stated in Matthew and Mark, underscores the condition of discipleship Jesus taught later on (14:33). Compare also his words to the rich ruler (18:22).

Notes

5 All seven synoptic occurrences of ἐπιστάτα (*epistata*, "Master") are in Luke. In all but one of these (17:13), it is the disciples who use the title. It is used instead of διδάσκαλος (*didaskalos*, "teacher") in 8:24 (cf. Mark 4:38), 9:49 (cf. Mark 9:38), and instead of "rabbi" in 9:33 (cf. Mark 9:5). It was a term Luke's readers understood, and it often referred to officers.

8 Ἁμαρτωλός (*hamartōlos*, "sinner") is one of Luke's characteristic words. Of twenty-two occurrences in the Synoptics, fifteen are in Luke, mainly in material unique to his Gospel and usually assigned to the "L" source. Luke does not use the term pejoratively but compassionately, as a common term applied to those who were isolated from Jewish religious circles because of their open sin, their unacceptable occupation or lifestyle, or their paganism. Luke shows that these sinners are the objects of God's grace through the ministry of Jesus.

10 Ἀπὸ τοῦ νῦν (*apo tou nyn*, "from now on") is an important indicator of transition in Luke (cf. 22:18, 69; Acts 18:6). Ἔση ζωγρῶν (*esē zōgrōn*, "you will catch") is a future periphrastic suggesting continuity of action.

5. The man with leprosy

5:12–16

¹²While Jesus was in one of the towns, a man came along who was covered with leprosy. When he saw Jesus, he fell with his face to the ground and begged him, "Lord, if you are willing, you can make me clean."
¹³Jesus reached out his hand and touched the man. "I am willing," he said. "Be clean!" And immediately the leprosy left him.
¹⁴Then Jesus ordered him, "Don't tell anyone, but go, show yourself to the priest and offer the sacrifices that Moses commanded for your cleansing, as a testimony to them."
¹⁵Yet the news about him spread all the more, so that crowds of people came to hear him and to be healed of their sicknesses. ¹⁶But Jesus often withdrew to lonely places and prayed.

Luke not only presents the gospel of salvation but supports it with signs and witnesses (though not as prominently as John does). In this section Jesus performs a miracle that is to be a "testimony" (v.14).

12 Leprosy is a general term in Scripture for certain skin diseases. They were not necessarily equivalent to what we know as Hansen's disease. While their interpretation as a type of sin may have been overdrawn by some commentators, such an application is consistent with the nature of such diseases. They were repulsive and resulted in physical, social, and psychological isolation of their victims (cf. Lev 13, esp. v.45). Luke is once again careful to note the nature and extent of a disease ("covered with leprosy"). The assumption is that the man has some knowledge of Jesus' prior miracles. Just as Peter fell at Jesus' feet for shame at his sinfulness, this man falls face downward for shame at his uncleanness. The disease was of such nature as to give the impression of filth, and the appeal for cleansing was appropriate to the condition. The appellation "Lord" doubtless has less meaning than on Peter's lips (v.8), meaning here no more than "Sir." The condition "if you are willing" may express a sense of unworthiness rather than doubt as to Jesus' ability or kindness.

13 The very act of touching is significant, especially since lepers were always kept at a distance. Later, Jesus touched a coffin (7:14), an act ritually prohibited. Perhaps our contemporary society, having rediscovered the significance of touching as a means of communicating concern, can identify to an extent with Jesus' kindness in touching the leper. Such contact also symbolized the transfer of healing power (cf. being touched by a suppliant, 8:44). Jesus' "I am willing" meets the man's need of reassurance, just as his "Don't be afraid" reassured Peter (v.10). Luke notes that the healing was accomplished "immediately" (*eutheōs*, more common in Mark).

14 The command to silence follows the pattern noted above in 4:41. Jesus wanted first to do the works of the Messiah and to fulfill his basic mission of sacrificial suffering before being publicly proclaimed as Messiah. The healing of lepers is one of the messianic signs that John the Baptist in prison was reminded of (7:22). Also, as has often been observed, the crowds could all too easily apply to Jesus their commonly held view of the Messiah as a military or political liberator.

For the cleansed leper to show himself to the priest was essential. One reason often suggested for this is that Jesus wanted to observe the ritual prescribed in Leviticus 14. (In 17:14 he gives the same command.) Here, however, something further is involved: the messianic act of healing was to be "as a testimony to them" (see comments on 7:21–23).

15–16 If the command to silence is part of a pattern in the Gospels, so is the failure to obey it. The immediate effect of the healing is Jesus' increased popularity. Though this popularity leads others to come and be healed (v.15), Jesus is forced to withdraw in order to seek quiet (v.16). Once again Luke speaks of Jesus' habit of prayer (cf. note on 3:21). In contrast to his earlier freedom to minister in "the towns" (v.12), Jesus must now make a practice of finding solitude in deserted areas.

Notes

12 Ἀνήρ (anēr, "man") occurs far more often in Luke than in all the other synoptic Gospels. On leprosy, see R.H. Pousma, "Diseases of the Bible," ZPEB, 2:138.

16 "Often" represents an imperfect periphrastic, ἦν ὑποχωρῶν (ēn hypochōrōn, lit., "was withdrawing"), suggesting repeated action.

6. Healing a paralytic

5:17–26

> [17]One day as he was teaching, Pharisees and teachers of the law, who had come from every village of Galilee and from Judea and Jerusalem, were sitting there. And the power of the Lord was present for him to heal the sick. [18]Some men came carrying a paralytic on a mat and tried to take him into the house to lay him before Jesus. [19]When they could not find a way to do this because of the crowd, they went up on the roof and lowered him on his mat through the tiles into the middle of the crowd, right in front of Jesus.
> [20]When Jesus saw their faith, he said, "Friend, your sins are forgiven."
> [21]The Pharisees and the teachers of the law began thinking to themselves, "Who is this fellow who speaks blasphemy? Who can forgive sins but God alone?"
> [22]Jesus knew what they were thinking and asked, "Why are you thinking these things in your hearts? [23]Which is easier: to say, 'Your sins are forgiven,' or to say, 'Get up and walk'? [24]But that you may know that the Son of Man has authority on earth to forgive sins...." He said to the paralyzed man, "I tell you, get up, take your mat and go home." [25]Immediately he stood up in front of them, took what he had been lying on and went home praising God. [26]Everyone was amazed and gave praise to God. They were filled with awe and said, "We have seen remarkable things today."

Jesus' activities inevitably brought him into confrontation with the religious authorities. Far from minimizing this, the Gospels actually focus on several such occasions. (See, for example, the Sabbath controversies in ch. 6 and the encounters in ch. 20.) Luke is especially concerned in his Gospel and in Acts to clarify the original relationship beween Christianity and Judaism and to show the reasons why the gospel had to break out of the confines of Judaism. Here he stresses the authority of

Jesus once more. In 4:32 Jesus' teaching was authoritative; 4:36 shows his authority over demons; 5:24 shows his authority to forgive sins.

17 The opening words, "one day," loosely connect this narrative with the preceding ones. The implication is that Jesus was teaching over a period of some time. Luke mentions, as often, the teaching ministry of Jesus. The word "teach" does not occur in this context in Matthew or Mark. While this is not specifically stated, it seems that Jesus' reputation had aroused the attention of the Jewish religious authorities, who considered it important to hear what he was teaching. Whereas Mark (2:6) introduces the scribes (NIV, "teachers of the law," *grammateis*) almost casually later in the narrative, Luke centers attention on them immediately, even specifying that they had come from as far away as Jerusalem. By doing this he lays stress on the crucial nature of the religious issues to be raised. This is also Luke's first introduction of the Pharisees and "teachers of the law."

The Pharisees had, earlier in their history, helped the Jews maintain the purity of their religion by teaching how the Mosaic Law and the traditions that grew up along side it ought to be applied in daily life. Many of them became rigid, imbalanced, and hypocritical (cf. comments on 11:37–54). Here Luke introduces them without any comment.

The "teachers of the law" were not a religious party, like the Pharisees, though most of them were also Pharisees. They were respected as having expert knowledge of the details of the Jewish legal tradition and so would be expected to form an opinion about the correctness of Jesus' teaching.

Luke now turns from Jesus' teaching ministry to that of healing, a subject of great interest to him. These two elements, doctrine and healing power, climax this narrative. The presence of the Lord's power to heal means that God himself was there.

18–19 Attention now focuses on a different group motivated by earnestness and faith (v. 18). The typical flat roof could be reached by an outside stairway (v. 19). Roofing materials, whether tiles (as in Luke) or mud thatch (as implied, though not stated, in Mark 2:4; cf. Notes) were separable without being damaged.

20 Two declarations form the focal point of this narrative, which, because it appears in the Gospel in order to provide a context for a pronouncement, may be called a "pronouncement story" (without prejudice to its historicity). The first is a declaration of forgiveness, the second an affirmation of Jesus' authority to make that declaration (v. 24). The plural reference in the term "their faith" is to the four who brought the man, though we may assume from his subsequent forgiveness that he also believed. Jesus' attention to the faith of the man's helpers demonstrates the important fact that God responds to the intercession of others regarding a person in need. This does not imply, of course, that faith that trusts Jesus for salvation can ever be by proxy. Those who brought the paralytic to Jesus believed that Jesus would save him. But the paralytic's salvation was an intensely personal matter between him and Jesus. Indeed, we are not even told that he had faith. Jesus chose to heal him; and, out of the totality of his need, the paralytic looked in faith to Jesus. Perhaps when he did what Jesus asked him to do, *that* was his declaration of faith in Jesus.

Jesus' declaration of the forgiveness of the paralytic's sin does not imply that sin was the immediate cause of his disease. To be sure, this was commonly assumed, even by Jesus' own disciples (John 9:2). Although correct theology sees sickness and death as part of the deterioration mankind has suffered because of universal sin, and though some specific ills may be connected with a particular sin (1 Cor 11:29-30), no such connection appears in this context.

21 In Jewish law conviction of blasphemy, which was a capital crime penalized by stoning, had to be based on unmistakable and overt defilement of the divine name. Luke shows that with his divine insight, Jesus probed the unvoiced thoughts of the Pharisees and teachers of the law, who were convinced that he had arrogated to himself the divine prerogative.

22-23 Without making a point of it, Luke indicates that Jesus exercises extraordinary knowledge (v.22). In a typical dialogue form of question and counterquestion, the challengers are impaled on the horns of a hypothetical dilemma (v.23; cf. 6:9; 20:3-4, 44). Obviously while the two sentences are in one sense equally easy to say (and equally impossible to do), in another sense it is easier to say that which cannot be disproved: "Your sins are forgiven."

24 The structure of this sentence is broken by the redirecting of Jesus' comments from the leaders to the man. This presents no problem. The form of the sentence is virtually identical in all three Synoptics, which deliberately retain its irregular structure. Thus a focus is maintained both on Jesus' running controversy with the religious leaders and on his ministry to the paralytic.

Here (v.24) is the first appearance of the term "Son of Man" in Luke (cf. Notes). It occurs earlier in the Gospel than we might have expected, certainly before the issues of Jesus' identity and titles have been spelled out. Further, it occurs in connection with the right to pronounce forgiveness rather than with the themes of suffering and glory that characterize its specific use in the other passages where it is used.

25-26 The healing validates the declaration of forgiveness. The command to the paralyzed man is impossible of fulfillment—except for the power of God. To respond took an act of obedience based on faith. He stood up "immediately" (*parachrēma*, which appears ten times in Luke out of twelve in the Synoptics). The result is the glorification of God (v.25), both by the man and by the crowd (v.26). As we have already observed (cf. comment on 2:20), to glorify God is one of Luke's important objectives. This praise is offered by the one who is the object of God's power and by the witnesses of that power. The onlookers were "amazed" (v.26); Luke uses the same word to describe the response of the crowds to the events at Pentecost, when by God's power the disciples told of his great works (Acts 2:11-12). In this case the people say that what they have observed is contrary to expectation (*paradoxa*, from which our word "paradox" is derived; NIV, "remarkable"). The final word in both the Greek and the NIV is "today." Its use in this particular position, at the very end of the passage, strikingly recalls its occurrence as the first word said by Jesus after reading the Isaiah passage in Nazareth (4:21). The other Gospels do not have the word in this final sentence. By including it here Luke assures the reader that this indeed is the awaited eschatological "today."

Notes

17 Literature on the Pharisees is vast. Among recent significant studies are W.D. Davies, *Introduction to Pharisaism* (Philadelphia: Fortress, 1954, 1967); A. Finkel, *The Pharisees and the Teacher of Nazareth* (Leiden: Brill, 1964). See also J. Jeremias, *Time of Jesus*, and the summary article "Pharisees" by D.A. Hagner, ZPEB, 4:745–52.

Luke thoughtfully avoids the Jewish word γραμματεύς (*grammateus*, "scribes"), using instead νομοδιδάσκαλοι (*nomodidaskaloi*, "legal experts"; NIV, "teachers of the law") for the benefit of his largely Gentile readership (see J. Jeremias, TDNT, 1:740–42; and K. Rengstorf, TDNT, 2:159).

19 Much discussion has centered around what is alleged to be a contradiction between Mark, who describes an action suitable to a roof made of thatch held together with mud, and Luke, who uses the word κέραμος (*keramos*, cf. "ceramic"). But it is wrong to call it a contradiction, for at most Luke is adapting the terminology in order to communicate the scene vividly to those used to tile roofs. Even so, tile was not unknown in Palestine; and Luke's terminology may be even more suitable to the specific nature of the roof than we realize.

20 "Friend" translates Ἄνθρωπε (*Anthrōpe*, "[O] Man"), a surprising use by Luke of a less tender term than that used by Matthew and Mark: τέκνον (*teknon*, "son," Matt 9:2; Mark 2:5). For the sake of theological precision, it should be noted that Jesus does not say here that *he* forgives sins but that they *are forgiven*. The passive ἀφέωνται (*apheōntai*, "are forgiven") probably suggests that God is the source of forgiveness (cf. 7:48, where, in the only other similar pronouncement, the passive is also used). The premise was correct: only God can forgive sins, but the leaders failed to recognize who stood before them.

24 Ὁ υἱὸς τοῦ ἀνθρώπου (*ho huios tou anthrōpou*, "the Son of Man") is common in the Synoptics and was certainly used often by Jesus. However, many think that its inclusion in this narrative is redactional or due to the influence of the early church during the history of its tradition. This conclusion is partly based on the assumption that Jesus did not attach to the OT figure of the Son of Man (e.g., Dan 7:13), or to himself, the authority to forgive sins. The immense concentration of study on the development of concepts about the Son of Man still leaves enough questions to prevent dogmatizing here. But to forgive sins is certainly a legitimate function of an eschatological figure who is concerned with righteous judgment.

There is no textual evidence against the genuineness of this saying, nor does the literary structure of the passage in Luke or Mark require a negative judgment against its appropriation in the passage. Nor does Son of Man here mean man in general. It is inconsistent with the rest of the Gospels and NT literature to allow mankind the authority implied in this statement. For a survey that incorporates much of the extensive discussion and conclusions of work during the 1960s, see C. Colpe, TDNT, 8:400–477; for conservative approaches, see I.H. Marshall, "The Synoptic Son of Man Sayings in Recent Discussion, NTS 12 (1965–66):327–51. Two more recent and very fine surveys of the topic, including citation of the significant literature, will be found in D. Guthrie, *New Testament Theology* (Downers Grove, Ill.: Inter-Varsity, 1981), pp. 270–91; G.E. Ladd, *A Theology of the New Testament* (Grand Rapids: Eerdmans, 1974), pp. 145–58. Another significant work is A.J.B. Higgins, *The Son of Man in the Teaching of Jesus*. SNTS Monograph Series, 39 (New York: Cambridge, 1980). On the passage in question, see Marshall, *Gospel of Luke*, pp. 214–16.

7. Calling Levi

5:27–32

> 27After this, Jesus went out and saw a tax collector by the name of Levi sitting at his tax booth. "Follow me," Jesus said to him, 28and Levi got up, left everything and followed him.
>
> 29Then Levi held a great banquet for Jesus at his house, and a large crowd of tax collectors and others were eating with them. 30But the Pharisees and the teachers of the law who belonged to their sect complained to his disciples, "Why do you eat and drink with tax collectors and 'sinners'?"
>
> 31Jesus answered them, "It is not the healthy who need a doctor, but the sick. 32I have not come to call the righteous, but sinners to repentance."

The succession of people on whom the Lord bestows his favor continues. We have seen his grace to a demoniac, a leper, and a paralytic; and now we see it given to a tax collector. So Jesus liberates those suffering from malign spirits, physical handicap, and social disfavor. The antagonists, Pharisees and teachers of the law, who were merely named in the preceding narrative, are again on the scene. D. Daube has discerned a pattern here (cf. 4:15–30; 5:17–26; 6:1–11; 11:14–54; 13:10–17; 20:1–8): "(1) Jesus and his disciples perform a revolutionary action, (2) the Pharisees remonstrate with him—or, on occasion, merely 'marvel'—and (3) he makes a pronouncement by which they are silenced" (*The New Testament and Rabbinic Judaism* [New York: Arno, 1973], p. 170).

27–28 Levi (v.27) is identified as Matthew in Matthew 9:9. He was a tax collector (cf. Notes); as such he had incurred the dislike of those who looked on such officials as crooked and serving an unpopular government (see comments on 15:1; 19:2). Levi himself was not a "chief" tax collector, as Zacchaeus was (cf. Notes; cf. also comments on 3:12); nor is it said that he, like Zacchaeus, was wealthy, but he obviously was treated by the Pharisees as a religious outcast.

The direct command of Jesus to follow him results in Levi's immediate and total obedience, a paradigm of the kind of discipleship Jesus will later specify in detail. Luke notes both the negative aspect (leaving everyting) and the positive one (following Jesus) of what Levi did (v.28; cf. also 9:23–25).

29–30 A banquet (v.29) in the NT symbolizes joy and often hints at the eschatological banquet, the future celebration of God's people with the patriarchs in the presence of God. Jesus is the guest of honor; but Levi does not, as might be expected, limit the guest list to his new Christian friends, the disciples of Jesus. Instead of immediately cutting off his old associates, Levi invites them into his home, probably to bring them also into contact with Jesus. Luke mentions "others," who turn out (v.30) to be "sinners," as far as the Pharisees are concerned. The joy of the participants is now opposed by the dour criticism of the religious leaders, a contrast we can see running throughout the Gospels.

The complaint of the Pharisees, and particularly of those among them who were also scribes, is more than a superficial attempt to find fault. To join in table fellowship with irreligious "sinners" is to cast doubt on one of the essential assumptions of Pharisaic teaching. This sect was dedicated to upholding the purity of Jewish faith and life. Implicit in their teachings was strict adherence to both law and tradition, including necessary rites of purification and separation from all whose moral or ritual purity might be in question. The Galilean people had a reputation (not always deserved) for disdaining such scruples and disregarding the traditions.

The Pharisees' complaint is specifically directed to the act of eating and drinking because in their society table fellowship implied mutual acceptance. No act, apart from participation in the actual sinful deeds of the guests, could have broken the wall of separation more dramatically. Yet the Pharisees are not yet ready to argue with Jesus himself. In the previous incident they did not even express their thoughts openly (v.21). They direct their question to Jesus' disciples and also (in Luke only) charge the disciples themselves, not just Jesus, with this unacceptable conduct.

31–32 It is important to recognize that Jesus not only originated proverbs and parables but also made wise use of current ones. So, citing a self-evident proverb of his day (v.31), he described his mission in terms that he would go on to amplify in the parables in chapter 15. Since none are truly "righteous" (v.32; cf. 18:19; Rom 3:23), Jesus used the word here either in a relative sense or with a touch of sarcasm. The Prodigal Son's older brother, for example, could rightly claim that he had not deserted his father as the Prodigal had. If, therefore, Jesus meant by "righteous" those who are generally loyal or devout, v.32 means that he gave more help to those in greater need. But if, as is more likely, Jesus implied that the Pharisees only *thought* that they were righteous, the point is that one must first acknowledge himself to be a sinner before he can truly respond to the call to repentance. Luke allows the proverb Jesus quoted to come full circle theologically by including the word "repentance," omitted in Matthew 9:13 and Mark 2:17. With this word, Luke introduces a topic of major importance. While the gospel of grace and forgiveness is for everyone (2:10), repentance is a prerequisite to its reception. The tax collector in 18:13–14 met this prerequisite, but not the Pharisee (18:11–12). The Lukan theme of joy is linked with that of repentance in 15:7, 10, 22–27, 32. Repentance was previously mentioned in Luke 3:3, 8, but only in the context of John the Baptist's ministry.

Notes

27 "Tax collector" is the proper translation for τελώνης (*telōnēs*), not "publican" (KJV). The latter comes from the Latin *publicanus*, which was normally applied to chief tax collectors (Gr. ἀρχιτελώνης, *architelōnēs*), like Zacchaeus (19:2). Levi is not further mentioned by that name in Luke but is called "Matthew" in 6:15.
30 On the connotation of the word ἀμαρτωλόι (*hamartōloi*, "sinners") in Jesus' day, see Rengstorf, TDNT, 1:327–33.

8. The question about fasting

5:33–39

33They said to him, "John's disciples often fast and pray, and so do the disciples of the Pharisees, but yours go on eating and drinking."
34Jesus answered, "Can you make the guests of the bridegroom fast while he

is with them? 35But the time will come when the bridegroom will be taken from them; in those days they will fast."

36He told them this parable: "No one tears a patch from a new garment and sews it on an old one. If he does, he will have torn the new garment, and the patch from the new will not match the old. 37And no one pours new wine into old wineskins. If he does, the new wine will burst the skins, the wine will run out and the wineskins will be ruined. 38No, new wine must be poured into new wineskins. 39And no one after drinking old wine wants the new, for he says, 'The old is better.' "

In all three Synoptics the issues related to Levi's banquet lead to further questions about religious practices. From Jesus' mention of fasting and prayer along with almsgiving as "acts of righteousness" in the Sermon on the Mount (Matt 6:1–18), we know that these practices were considered significant indications of religious devotion. In contrast to the two previous incidents (vv.21, 30), this time the leaders challenge Jesus directly.

33 The question, which is stated as a fact, not a query, is cleverly expressed. First, the Pharisees and the disciples of John the Baptist, who were assumed to be particularly sympathetic to Jesus, are lined up against Jesus' disciples, who are thus made to appear out of step. Second, there is a hint that Jesus' disciples were neglecting the important duty of prayer. Again Jesus himself is not criticized directly but through his disciples. Fasting was actually only prescribed for one day in the year (cf. Notes) but was practiced as a religious exercise more often—viz., twice a week by the Pharisees (cf. 18:12). The disciples are now criticized, not only for eating with sinners, but for having a lifestyle that seems to be in contrast to proper religious decorum.

34–35 Jesus' answer is so remarkable that many have assumed that the saying in v.35 must not be an authentic prophecy but is a reflection of the church after Jesus' death. The first part of the saying is clear (v.34). Jesus compares the situation to a wedding, which naturally calls for joy. (The image of the bridegroom is most fully treated in Eph 5:25–33; Rev 19:6–9.) But to think at a wedding of the possibility of the groom's death is highly unusual. The allusion is so abrupt that we cannot ignore it. Neither can we ignore the fact that Jesus anticipated his rejection and his death at the hands of his enemies.

36 The context provides opportunity for Jesus to state a basic principle in a series of parabolic figures. His mission involved a radical break with common religious practices. Jesus neither affirms nor denies the value of fasting, and he does not mention prayer here at all. He teaches rather that he has not come merely to add devotional routines to those already practiced, for what he brings is not a patch but a whole new garment. Merely to "patch things up"—i.e., to have a dinner celebration in place of fasting—would fail for two reasons. First, it would ruin the rest of the new garment from which it is taken. Second, just one new patch will not help preserve the old garment but will in fact be conspicuously incongruous. The form of the saying in Luke carries the image beyond the way Matthew and Mark state it.

37–38 The second illustration has a slightly different connotation—viz., Jesus' teaching is like fermenting wine that seems to almost have inherent vigor and cannot be contained within an old rigid system. Later on Jesus will speak of a new covenant (22:20), which is indeed new and not merely an improved extension of the old.

39 Jesus is not reversing himself and saying that his new teaching is not as good as the old it replaces. The point emphasized is that people tend to want the old and reject the new, assuming (wrongly in this case) that the old is better.

9. Sabbath controversies

6:1–11

> ¹One Sabbath Jesus was going through the grainfields, and his disciples began to pick some heads of grain, rub them in their hands and eat the kernels. ²Some of the Pharisees asked, "Why are you doing what is unlawful on the Sabbath?"
> ³Jesus answered them, "Have you never read what David did when he and his companions were hungry? ⁴He entered the house of God, and taking the consecrated bread, he ate what is lawful only for priests to eat. And he also gave some to his companions." ⁵Then Jesus said to them, "The Son of Man is Lord of the Sabbath."
> ⁶On another Sabbath he went into the synagogue and was teaching, and a man was there whose right hand was shriveled. ⁷The Pharisees and the teachers of the law were looking for a reason to accuse Jesus, so they watched him closely to see if he would heal on the Sabbath. ⁸But Jesus knew what they were thinking and said to the man with the shriveled hand, "Get up and stand in front of everyone." So he got up and stood there.
> ⁹Then Jesus said to them, "I ask you, which is lawful on the Sabbath: to do good or to do evil, to save life or to destroy it?"
> ¹⁰He looked around at them all, and then said to the man, "Stretch out your hand." He did so, and his hand was completely restored. ¹¹But they were furious and began to discuss with one another what they might do to Jesus.

The uneasy tension between Jesus and the Pharisees described in chapter 5 hardens into controversy over one of the main institutions of Judaism, the Sabbath. The Gospels list three Sabbath controversies. Two occur in the Synoptics and one in John 5. In each instance Jesus allows or even stimulates the controversy, providing several types of response: (1) the Sabbath is for man's benefit (Mark 2:27); (2) the Son of Man is "Lord of the Sabbath" (v.5); (3) the Sabbath is for helpful deeds, the omission of which would be evil (v.9); and (4) the Father works even on the Sabbath and so may the Son (John 5:17).

Keeping the Sabbath provided an appropriate issue for debate because it (1) had roots both in the creation account and in the Ten Commandments, (2) involved every seventh day and consequently called for many decisions about what was permitted or forbidden on that day, (3) consequently became the subject of two tractates in the Mishna (*Shabbath* and *Erubin*), and (4) afforded a public disclosure of one's observance or nonobservance of the day.

1–2 Luke centers attention on the disciples (v.1), though in accordance with custom their teacher was held responsible. To glean by hand (not using a sickle) in someone's field was permitted by law (Deut 23:25). But to do this and to rub the heads of grain (a detail Luke alone has) was considered to be threshing. The Mishnah forbids threshing (v.2) on the Sabbath (*Shabbath* 7.2).

3–4 Jesus' response (v.3) centers in an analogy from Scripture (1 Sam 21:1–6). He is not providing a specific teaching, such as would be necessary to establish a rabbinical rule (W. Lane, *The Gospel According to Mark* [Grand Rapids: Eerdmans, 1974], p. 117). Instead he simply calls to mind an instance in which the infringement of a rule to meet human need received no condemnation (v.4). His illustration is apt because the general principle then and in his time continues to be the same and because a leader (David and David's messianic descendant) is involved along with his companions. The point is that ceremonial rites (being only means to an end) must give way to a higher moral law.

5 Following this analogy, on which the Pharisees offer no comment, Jesus makes a statement in which for the second time in Luke he uses the phrase "Son of Man" (cf. 5:24). While some have argued that "Son of Man" simply means "man" here (cf. Creed, pp. 84–85), Morris (*Luke*, p. 122) objects that "Jesus never taught that man is Lord over a divine institution." Therefore what Jesus says at this point is a claim to unique authority and takes the argument of vv.3–4 a step further.

6–8 The second Sabbath controversy involves basically the same issue as the first— human need versus ceremonial law. Luke presents some specific details, lacking in the parallels in the other Synoptics, that show this event occurred on a different Sabbath, and that it was the man's right hand Jesus healed (v.6). As in 4:15–16, 31–33, Jesus is teaching in the synagogue. Luke does not say that the man actually asked for healing; Jesus simply took the initiative. The hand was "shriveled," i.e., atrophied and useless. As in 5:17, the "Pharisees and teachers of the law" (v.7) are present, scrutinizing Jesus' every action to find fault. Now, after the first Sabbath controversy, they think they have a case against him. Man's reasonings tend to be evil (Gen 6:5; 8:21; Eph 5:17–18); Jesus is aware of their thoughts (v.8) and in the light of that knowledge performs the healing. He has the man stand in front of the people so that all will see what follows.

9 Jesus' question goes beyond the fact that the healing could have been postponed a day. After all, it was not a critical illness that might take a turn for the worse if not treated immediately. Were that the case, rabbinical law would have permitted healing on a Sabbath. But Jesus implies in his double question that if any illness is left unattended when healing can be provided, evil is done by default. Jesus is not breaking the Sabbath; he is using it to do good to a human being in need.

10 Here Jesus commanded the impossible. Presumably the man exercised obedience born of faith, though Luke has not said that the man had faith or asked to be healed. Jesus healed the withered hand completely.

11 The response is violent; the opposition to Jesus mounts in a crescendo of fury more intense than that after the previous miracle. So now, near the very start of Jesus' ministry, a plot against him was beginning to form.

Notes

1 Σαββάτῳ δευτεροπώτῳ (*sabbatō deuteropōtō*, "second-first Sabbath"), an alternative reading to σαββάτῳ (*sabbatō*, "a Sabbath"), has puzzled textual critics. First, the meaning of the variant is uncertain. There is an attractive speculation that Luke keeps a careful chronological record and that this is the second Sabbath after Jesus' major sermon (4:16, followed by 4:31 and 6:1). Marshall (*Gospel of Luke*, p. 230) calls this "a solution born of despair." This reading could refer to a sequence of Sabbaths beginning with the one occurring after Passover, during the week-long Feast of Unleavened Bread. The Sabbath in 6:1 would be the first after that feast, the second after Passover. But this also seems a strained solution, except that Lev 23:15–16 shows that this period, leading up to Pentecost, is carefully numbered by weeks (cf. TDNT, 7:23, n. 183). Also Luke seems to be interested in the Sabbath along with the Jubilee (cf. comments on 4:19) as symbols of God's work of salvation and freedom. However, this variant reading seems to have little support (cf. UBS apparatus). While it is the more difficult reading, and on that ground more likely to be the original, it may not be original. Instead, it may have arisen if the word πρώτῳ (*prōtō*, "first") had been (1) written in, (2) crossed out, with δευτέρῳ (*deuterō*, "second") substituted, and then (3) through scribal confusion reinstated along with *deuterō* (Metzger, *Textual Commentary*, p. 139). This, too, seems strained; but at least it might balance the claim that as the more difficult reading it should be accepted, by showing how it might have arisen. The MS evidence is the least problematic factor in the decision and should probably lead to a rejection of the extra word.

---

10. *Choosing the twelve apostles*

6:12–16

> [12]One of those days Jesus went out to a mountainside to pray, and spent the night praying to God. [13]When morning came, he called his disciples to him and chose twelve of them, whom he also designated apostles: [14]Simon (whom he named Peter), his brother Andrew, James, John, Philip, Bartholomew, [15]Matthew, Thomas, James son of Alphaeus, Simon who was called the Zealot, [16]Judas son of James, and Judas Iscariot, who became a traitor.

At this point in the narrative sequence, Mark (3:7–12) summarizes Jesus' ministry of healing. Luke postpones that summary to 6:17–19 as his introduction to the Sermon on the Plain. He puts the call of the disciples first, though not necessarily "in order to gain an audience for the sermon" (Marshall, *Gospel of Luke*, p. 237), since a statement about a crowd of disciples and others already stood available in the Markan summary (Mark 3:7).

12 Jesus spent an entire night in prayer, a sure indication that the circumstances were pressing: the preceding controversy, the resultant threatening atmosphere, and the selection to be made of the twelve apostles. The second clause indicates that the first was not a routine devotional exercise.

How many of us Christians today have ever spent a whole night in prayer? In his prayer life, as in all else, the Lord Jesus stands far above even the best of us whose words about prayer need to be matched by the consistent practice of it.

13–16 The "disciples" (v.13) up to this time were a group of followers interested in attaching themselves to Jesus the teacher. (See further on discipleship in the comments on 9:23–27; 14:25–33.) From among these followers, Jesus chose the Twelve. Luke alone tells us that Jesus gave them the designation "apostles" (cf. Notes). That Luke does this accords with his regard for apostolic authority.

Most interpreters assume that Jesus intended the number of apostles to correspond with the number of the tribes of Israel, thereby indicating that a new people of God was coming into existence. The apostles' names appear several other times in the Gospels and Acts (Matt 10:2–4; Mark 3:16–19; Acts 1:13), with the same grouping, differing only in the form of a few names.

"Judas son of James" (v.16) apparently had, like many people, two names and is to be identified with Thaddaeus in Mark and Matthew. One of the two Simons was a "Zealot," i.e., one who had advocated revolutionary opposition to Rome. The other Simon, Peter, is at the head of every list. Judas Iscariot (cf. Notes) is always last. From a promising beginning he "became a traitor." The group is not distinguished by particular abilities or position in life (cf. the principle in 1 Cor 1:26–29).

Notes

12 Conzelmann (*Theology of Luke*, p. 44) thinks that Luke has enlarged Mark's concept of the mountain as "the place of revelation," and that "there is no question of locating 'the' mountain." It is a mythical place, to which the people "cannot come." Mountains did provide an environment that seemed very near to heaven, but it is unnecessary to assume that Luke uses mountains (NIV, "hills") or any other topographical or geographical site merely as a symbol (cf. comment and Note on 9:28).

13 From later Jewish literature we learn that an "apostle" was a messenger who, during his particular mission, acted with the full authority of the one who sent him (jHag. 1.8). It may be anachronistic to see that particular meaning here, but there is no reason why the basic concept cannot be attributed to Jesus' situation (cf. TDNT, 1:398–447).

16 Ellis (*Gospel of Luke*, p. 110) and Marshall (*Gospel of Luke*, p. 240) support the option that the name Ἰσκαριώθ (*Iskariōth*, "Iscariot") means the "false one," a derivation from the Aramaic שְׁקַר (*šeqar*, "falsehood"). Other suggestions are an unlikely derivation from *sicarius* (lit., "dagger man" or "assassin") and the traditional "man of Kerioth" (cf. Josh 15:25), which still remains a possibility.

B. *Jesus' Great Sermon* (6:17–49)

1. *Blessings and woes*

6:17–26

[17]He went down with them and stood on a level place. A large crowd of his disciples was there and a great number of people from all over Judea, from Jerusalem, and from the coast of Tyre and Sidon, [18]who had come to hear him and to be healed of their diseases. Those troubled by evil spirits were cured, [19]and the people all tried to touch him, because power was coming from him and healing them all.

[20]Looking at his disciples, he said:

> "Blessed are you who are poor,
> for yours is the kingdom of God.

²¹Blessed are you who hunger now,
    for you will be satisfied.
Blessed are you who weep now,
    for you will laugh.
²²Blessed are you when men hate you,
    when they exclude you and insult you
and reject your name as evil,
    because of the Son of Man.

²³"Rejoice in that day and leap for joy, because great is your reward in heaven.
For that is how their fathers treated the prophets.

²⁴"But woe to you who are rich,
    for you have already received your comfort.
²⁵Woe to you who are well fed now,
    for you will go hungry.
Woe to you who laugh now,
    for you will mourn and weep.
²⁶Woe to you when all men speak well of you,
    for that is how their fathers treated the false prophets.

The settings of this passage and of the Sermon on the Mount in Matthew 5–7 are not indisputably the same, and there is considerable difference in content. Therefore many scholars call the Lukan material the "Sermon on the Plain," with the implication that it is, in Luke's opinion, an entirely different sermon. The probability is that there was one sermon among many that Jesus preached on similar themes that was something like a "keynote" address. This was a basic affirmation of the kingdom message, beginning with beatitudes and ending with a parable about builders. Within this framework Matthew and Luke present samples or selections of Jesus' teachings that differ at points; Luke (Matthew also to a lesser extent) distributes some of the sermon's teachings, which Jesus probably repeated frequently, in other contexts in the Gospel narrative. One clear example is the Lord's Prayer in Luke 11:2–4 (cf. Matt 6:9–13).

The sermon as presented in this chapter includes the "Blessings and Woes" (vv. 20–26), "Love for Enemies" (vv.27–36), "Judging Others" (vv.37–42), and a final section on the test of genuineness in two parts: "A Tree and its Fruit" and "The Wise and Foolish Builders" (following the divisions in the NIV text). However, vv.39–49 may be viewed as a unified section from a literary perspective, as this part is marked by a parabolic style.

17–19 The "level place" (*epi topou pedinou*, v.17) is apparently an area on the "mountainside" mentioned in Matthew 5:1. If it were a plain, such as Jesus often used for his teaching near the sea, just the words *epi pedinou* would probably have been used (Godet, p. 295). Luke mentions a "large crowd" of Jesus' disciples plus "a great number of people" (cf. 4:14–15 and Luke's stress on Jesus' popularity). Matthew mentions disciples in 5:1, speaking of "crowds" only at the end of the sermon (7:28).

Although Jesus directs his comments to the disciples (v.20), he is surely conscious of his larger audience. His teachings in the sermon, especially those in Matthew 5:17–20, keep a balance between two extreme viewpoints that would have been familiar to any crowd. One is the strong legalistic "righteousness" often characteristic of the Pharisees; the other is the attitude attributed to many of the "people of the land," who knew little of the rabbinic tradition and were thought to disregard many religious practices. The emphasis in vv.18–19 on "power" and "healing" is characteristic of Luke. (For another instance of Jesus' power being drawn on by a "touch," see 8:43–46.) Luke clearly distinguishes here between those affected by demons and those whose illness was basically physical.

20–23 Luke's version of the blessings (or "Beatitudes") is shorter than Matthew's and is different in some particulars. Also the Beatitudes appear in negative form in the woes. Both blessings and woes are familiar forms in the OT (e.g., Ps 1, which also carries an implication of woes; Isa 5:8–23). The entire theme of reversal of fortune has already been encountered in the Magnificat (1:51–55). It is also implicit in the attention Luke gives to social and religious outcasts throughout his Gospel.

"Blessed" (vv.20–22), as elsewhere in the NT, "refers to the distinctive religious joy which accrues to man from his share in the salvation of the Kingdom of God" (Hauck, TDNT, 4:367). "Poor" (*ptōchoi*) in Luke implies those who are utterly dependent on God (v.20). They are the special recipients of the "good news" Jesus came to preach (4:18). Often the economically destitute sense their need of God more than others. Whether voluntary poverty such as that practiced at Qumran is in view is not clear (cf. Ellis, *Gospel of Luke*, p. 113). Marshall (*Gospel of Luke*, p. 249) shows that nonviolence is implied. Matthew 5:3 specifies the spiritual poverty —i.e., recognition of one's spiritual need. To inherit the kingdom of God is the antithesis of poverty. Note the emphatic sense of assurance the present tense gives: "yours *is*" (emphasis mine). There may also be an element of "inaugurated eschatology" in the present tense—i.e., the presence of some aspects of the coming kingdom of God. In this case, the poor can rejoice even in the midst of their destitution because they are already able to partake of some of the kingdom blessings.

"Hunger" (*peinōntes*) is presented in its reality without spiritualization (v.21). It may well carry the connotation of hungering for righteousness (Matt 5:6). Those who "weep" (*klaiontes*) may be those who carry the burden not only of personal grief but of a hurting society. (The passage Jesus quoted in his synagogue sermon [4:18–19] goes on to speak of mourning giving way to gladness [Isa 61:2b–3a].) Both parts of v.21 stress the contrast between the situation "now" and the future blessing. Notice the difference in tone between Luke's "laugh" (*gelasete*) and Matthew's "be comforted" (*paraklēthēsontai*, 5:4).

The idea of laughter is vividly carried forward in the next section on persecution (vv.23–26). Persecution is described in some detail and the contrasting "rejoice" (*charēte*) and "leap for joy" (*skirtēsate*) stand out all the more (v.23). Note the progression from hate (v.22) to exclusion (which later took the form of being banned from the synagogue) to insult (cf. 1 Peter 4:14) to defamation of their name (cf. Matt 5:11). Those who share the rejection of the "Son of Man" relive the experience of the prophets (cf. comments on 20:9–12).

The promise of "reward in heaven" (v.23) does not suggest that the disciples are to work for some future gain but that there will be personal vindication and appropriate recognition and blessing from the Lord. Luke emphasizes the vindication of God's people who patiently wait for him (cf. 18:1–8 and comments). He also presents Jesus' teaching on reward for faithful servants (12:37, 42–44).

24–26 The woes in both structure and content form a direct contrast to the blessings. This again is after the Magnificat. "He has filled the hungry with good things but has sent the rich away empty" (1:53).

Woe comes to the "rich" (*tois plousiois*), not simply because they are wealthy, but (1) because the implication is that they have chosen present gratification over future blessing (v.24); (2) because rich people criticized in Luke disregard spiritual realities (e.g., 12:15–21); and (3) perhaps because, as was generally assumed, the wealthy became so at the expense of others (cf. James 2:6–7). The same thought runs through v.25—"well fed"—and probably v.26—where those who "laugh now" presumably do so at the expense of others.

The word "all" in the clause "when all men speak well of you" (v.26) should be carefully noted, lest we distort the basic concepts of honor and praise. False prophets plagued God's people in OT times; they were a threat in Jesus' day (Matt 7:15–23), in Paul's day (Acts 13:6; cf. 20:29–30), and on into the church age (cf. *Didache* 11:5–6; 12:5).

Notes

22 In its parallel to ἕνεκα τοῦ υἱοῦ τοῦ ἀνθρώπου (*heneka tou huiou tou anthrōpou*, "because of the Son of Man"), Matt 5:11 lacks *tou huiou tou anthrōpou* ("Son of Man"), having only ἕνεκεν ἐμοῦ (*heneken emou*, "because of me"). Since Luke does not add the title "Son of Man" where it does not appear in the tradition as he received it, its appearance here is authentic, contrary to some critical opinion (cf. Marshall, *Gospel of Luke*, p. 253).

24 Ἀπέχετε (*apechete*) means "you have received your full payment," hence NIV's "you have already received." This is in contrast to the blessed ones whose full reward lies ahead (v.23).

2. *Love for enemies*

6:27–36

27"But I tell you who hear me: Love your enemies, do good to those who hate you, 28bless those who curse you, pray for those who mistreat you. 29If someone strikes you on one cheek, turn to him the other also. If someone takes your cloak, do not stop him from taking your tunic. 30Give to everyone who asks you, and if anyone takes what belongs to you, do not demand it back. 31Do to others as you would have them do to you.

32"If you love those who love you, what credit is that to you? Even 'sinners' love those who love them. 33And if you do good to those who are good to you, what credit is that to you? Even 'sinners' do that. 34And if you lend to those from whom you expect repayment, what credit is that to you? Even 'sinners' lend to 'sinners,' expecting to be repaid in full. 35But love your enemies, do good to them, and lend to them without expecting to get anything back. Then your reward will be great, and you will be sons of the Most High, because he is kind to the ungrateful and wicked. 36Be merciful, just as your Father is merciful.

In place of the five antitheses of Matthew 5:21–48, Luke selects one theme (contained in two of the antitheses, Matt 5:38–42, 43–48) and enlarges on it. As might be expected from his basic concern for people, he chooses the theme of love. He does not present the teaching of Jesus over against the prevalent distortion of the OT (cf. Matt 5:43–44). Instead he conveys only the positive command. The Golden Rule, which Matthew apparently postpones to use as a summary statement later in the sermon (7:12), occurs in Luke in what seems to be a natural context. Also, the conclusion in v.36 is significantly different from Matthew 5:48, each expression being eminently appropriate to its context (see below).

27–31 "You who hear me" (v.27) are probably those who are taking in what Jesus is saying, not casual listeners. The word "love" (*agapē* in the noun form) must be understood in its classic Christian sense of having a genuine concern for someone irrespective of his or her attractiveness or of the likelihood of any reciprocation in kind. The spirit of Jesus' words finds expression in Romans 12:14–21. Here in Luke the specifics are spelled out. In the first instance (v.28), apparently no physical harm has been done; so the response also is not physical but to "bless" (*eulogeite*) and to "pray" (*proseuchesthe*). The next situations involve action that must be met by some physical response. Opinions differ as to whether when "someone strikes you on the cheek" (v.29), it is (1) a mere insult (in Matt 5:39 it is the right cheek, indicating a backhanded slap, (2) the "ritual slap on the cheek given a Christian 'heretic' in the synagogue" (Ellis, *Gospel of Luke*, p. 115), or (3) "a punch to the side of the jaw," on the basis that *siagōn* means jaw, not cheek (Morris, *Luke*, p. 129, but cf. Notes). In any case, the injunction is directed to individuals (the form of the Greek imperatives and pronouns here is singular, not plural) who desire to live as "sons of the Most High" (v.35). Jesus is not advocating the suspension of normal civil judicial procedures. If pagan governments abandoned the protection of civil rights, the result would be an unbiblical anarchy (Rom 13:4).

"If someone takes your cloak" (v.29) may refer to a street robbery (since the clothing seized is the immediately accessible outer robe [*himation*]). In Matthew (5:40) the short tunic (*chitōn*), which is worn underneath, is taken first, possibly in court action. Nevertheless the implication seems to be that the person has a need or thinks he does. The teaching of the passage as a whole relates not so much to passivity in the face of evil as to concern for the other person. Inevitably, as ancient Greek philosophers recognized, to refrain from doing evil often means suffering evil. This was the path of the Lord Jesus (cf. 1 Peter 2:20–24), who prayed for his enemies (Luke 23:34) and died for them (Rom 5:10).

The same spirit is expressed in v.30, where the practical application of this hyperbolic command would be to refuse to demand that which would genuinely be to the good of the other person, even at our expense. The Golden Rule is now cited (v.31), not with theological comment, as in Matthew 7:12, but as a practical governing principle (cf. Notes).

32–36 At this point we have a remarkable series of comparisons between the courtesies of believers and those of worldly people. Even "sinners" act decently to others when kindnesses are reciprocated. In the sermon in Matthew, three basic comparisons are made with unbelievers regarding the quality of their relationship (1) to God (Matt 6:7–8), (2) to people (Matt 5:46–47; cf. the present passage), and (3) to material possessions (Matt 6:32; cf. Luke 12:30).

Loving (v.32) is augmented by doing good (v.33), which, in turn, is expressed in lending (v.34). Marshall (*Gospel of Luke*, p. 263) argues that *hina apolabōsin ta isa* ("expecting to be repaid in full," v.34) means "the reception of loans in return." One hardly makes a loan "expecting to" receive back the principal; that is assumed. Nor would a good Jew normally charge interest. Therefore some kind of equal treatment in return seems to be implied. One should benefit the helpless as well as one's friends.

Believers are to be like what they really are, "sons of the Most High" (v.35), and as such will have recognition. Jesus is not teaching that one earns sonship (cf. John 1:12–13). Rather, the day will come when the world will recognize God's children (Rom 8:19, 23).

"Be merciful" (*ginesthe oiktirmones*, v.36) singles out that area of life in which, given the preceding examples, one is very likely to come short. The Pharisees tithed spices but neglected "justice, mercy and faithfulness" (Matt 23:23). The believer's righteousness must exceed theirs (Matt 5:20). It should be measured against the perfection of God himself (Matt 5:48). Since Luke omits a discussion of law and Pharisees that would not be appropriate for his readership, he omits the imperative about being perfect and replaces it with one about being merciful. This accords with his emphasis on kindness to others in need (cf. 10:25–37).

Notes

29 Although σιαγών (*siagōn*) meant "jaw" in earlier classical literature, it came to mean "cheek" (so NIV) in the Hellenistic period. With the omission of Matthew's δεξιὰν (*dexian*, "right") (5:39), any allusion to a ritual slap is gone (it would have been meaningless to his Gentile audience anyway); so the idea of outright violence is stressed here in Luke. This is heightened by his statement about yielding the cloak, which he presents as a robbery rather than a court action.

31 No claim to originality is inherent in Jesus' use of the Golden Rule. It existed in a negative form, attributed to Rabbi Hillel, to the effect that one should not do to others what he does not want to happen to himself (*Shabbath* 31a; Tobit 4:15). Jesus uses and strengthens the "rule." There is a change from the singular verb form in the preceding injunctions to the plural in this general command καθὼς θέλετε . . . ποιεῖτε (*kathōs thelete . . . poieite*, "As you desire . . . do").

32–34 Χάρις (*charis*) here means "favor" or "credit" (cf. μισθὸς [*misthos*, "reward"] in v.35 and Matt 5:46). God will not overlook what is done for him at personal sacrifice.

35 On υἱοὶ ὑψίστου (*huioi hypsistou*, "sons of the Most High"), cf. 1:32 and comments.

3. *Judging others*

6:37–42

> 37"Do not judge, and you will not be judged. Do not condemn, and you will not be condemned. Forgive, and you will be forgiven. 38Give, and it will be given to you. A good measure, pressed down, shaken together and running over, will be poured into your lap. For with the measure you use, it will be measured to you."
>
> 39He also told them this parable: "Can a blind man lead a blind man? Will they not both fall into a pit? 40A student is not above his teacher, but everyone who is fully trained will be like his teacher.
>
> 41"Why do you look at the speck of sawdust in your brother's eye and pay no

attention to the plank in your own eye? ⁴²How can you say to your brother,
'Brother, let me take the speck out of your eye,' when you yourself fail to see the
plank in your own eye? You hypocrite, first take the plank out of your eye, and
then you will see clearly to remove the speck from your brother's eye.

37–38 These verses deal with the kind of mercy expected of the Lord's disciples. If
the preceding imperative about being merciful refers indirectly to the lack of mercy
among the Pharisees, then this one may refer to the kind of judgmental attitude
religious people like the Pharisees often have. Since "do not judge" (v.37) could be
misunderstood as ruling out any ethical evaluation at all, it is important to note the
further definition provided by the parallel "Do not condemn" (*mē katadikazete*). In
Matthew (7:6) the injunction not to "give dogs what is sacred," which obviously
requires some discernment, provides the balance. Just as God will give a suitable
reward to the merciful (vv.32–36), so v.37 implies that he will bring appropriate
judgment on the unmerciful. The idea of suitable reward carries over in the next
illustration of an overflowing measuring cup (v.38). Those who are generous (both
materially [vv.27–36] and in their estimation of others [v.37]) will be abundantly
repaid.

39–40 Some have found vv.39–40 difficult to relate to the context. If Jesus still has
the Pharisees in mind (cf. Schürmann, *Das Lukasevangelium*, 1:365–79), it is not
necessary to assume that he is directly accusing them. Rather his thought in addressing the disciples runs like this: The disciple of a rabbi dedicates himself to his
master's teachings and way of life. Thus he cannot be expected to be different from,
or better than, his master (v.40). If the rabbi lacks a proper view of life, his student
will be also misled (v.39). The criticism and hostility already apparent in the Pharisees may unfortunately crop up in their disciples, but it must never find a place
among Jesus' disciples.

This interpretation assumes that v.40 carries on the thought of v.39, in which both
teacher and follower are blind—not a description of Jesus and his disciples. If,
however, v.40 introduces a new comparison, it might mean that Jesus' disciples
ought not to go beyond what they have learned from him—viz., a merciful uncen-
sorious spirit. In that instance v.39 could refer to the Pharisees or others.

41–42 The humorous illustration (v.41) of the "speck" (*karphos*) and the "plank"
(*dokon*) hits the mark with force when the person who casually calls the person he
is criticizing "brother" (v.42) suddenly hears himself called "hypocrite" by the Lord.
Danker (*Jesus*, p. 89) observes, "What is criticized by Jesus is the moralist's patron-
izing attitude." He cites Democritus (fifth century B.C.): "Better it is to correct one's
own faults than those of others." Jesus' humor makes the point vividly.

Notes

38 Εἰς τὸν κόλπον ὑμῶν (*eis ton kolpon hymōn*, "into your lap") refers to the fold of one's
robe used as a pocket.

4. A tree and its fruit

6:43–45

43"No good tree bears bad fruit, nor does a bad tree bear good fruit. 44Each tree is recognized by its own fruit. People do not pick figs from thornbushes, or grapes from briers. 45The good man brings good things out of the good stored up in his heart, and the evil man brings evil things out of the evil stored up in his heart. For out of the overflow of his heart his mouth speaks.

43–45 The thought of v.40 continues—like teacher, like student; like tree, like fruit. The parallel passage in Matthew 7:15–20 refers to false prophets—a fact that supports a link between this verse (43) and v.39 about a blind leader. Throughout the preceding section and this one, the idea is that of consistency between source and product (cf. the teaching of John the Baptist [3:7–9 and comments]).

Notes

45 Ἐκ τοῦ ἀγαθοῦ θησαυροῦ τῆς καρδίας (ek tou agathou thēsaurou tēs kardias) is literally "out of the good treasure of the heart." The heart is a treasury in which good or evil is "stored up" (NIV). See also Matt 15:19 and Mark 7:21, both of which are in contexts criticizing the Pharisees.

46 "Already . . . during his [Jesus'] ministry, the address of Κύριε [kyrie, 'Lord'] was taking on a deeper significance than a mere honorific 'Sir' " (Marshall, *Gospel of Luke*, p. 274).

5. The wise and foolish builders

6:46–49

46"Why do you call me, 'Lord, Lord,' and do not do what I say? 47I will show you what he is like who comes to me and hears my words and puts them into practice. 48He is like a man building a house, who dug down deep and laid the foundation on rock. When a flood came, the torrent struck that house but could not shake it, because it was well built. 49But the one who hears my words and does not put them into practice is like a man who built a house on the ground without a foundation. The moment the torrent struck that house, it collapsed and its destruction was complete."

46–49 If Jesus' audience was relaxing in the assumption that the preceding teachings were directed only at the Pharisees and their followers, they could not dodge the direct force of this challenge. It is specifically directed to those who profess to follow Jesus (v.46). In Matthew the statement is amplified with a description of self deception, probably at first deliberate and then habitual. Here only the basic point is made: It is not mere words, nor even generally ethical behavior or religious practice, that mark true believers but whether they "do" (*poieite*) what Jesus says (cf. James 1:22–25). The thrust of the parable is clear. Luke includes reference to the foundation (v.48), but he omits some of the graphic detail found in Matthew 7:24–27. Luke also omits the response of the people (cf. Matt 7:28–29).

C. Ministry to Various Human Needs (7:1–9:17)

1. The faith of the centurion

7:1–10

> ¹When Jesus had finished saying all this in the hearing of the people, he entered Capernaum. ²There a centurion's servant, whom his master valued highly, was sick and about to die. ³The centurion heard of Jesus and sent some elders of the Jews to him, asking him to come and heal his servant. ⁴When they came to Jesus, they pleaded earnestly with him, "This man deserves to have you do this, ⁵because he loves our nation and has built our synagogue." ⁶So Jesus went with them.
>
> He was not far from the house when the centurion sent friends to say to him: "Lord, don't trouble yourself, for I do not deserve to have you come under my roof. ⁷That is why I did not even consider myself worthy to come to you. But say the word, and my servant will be healed. ⁸For I myself am a man under authority, with soldiers under me. I tell this one, 'Go,' and he goes; and that one, 'Come,' and he comes. I say to my servant, 'Do this,' and he does it."
>
> ⁹When Jesus heard this, he was amazed at him, and turning to the crowd following him, he said, "I tell you, I have not found such great faith even in Israel." ¹⁰Then the men who had been sent returned to the house and found the servant well.

This incident has an important place in Luke's narrative. First, it marks a pivotal point in the progress of the word of the Lord from its original Jewish context to the Gentile world. The Jews' appreciation of a pious Gentile (the centurion) is an important theme in Luke, which was written partly to show the compatibility of early Christianity with Judaism. At the same time, Jesus compares the Gentile's faith more than favorably with that of the Jews, which serves Luke's desire to justify the prominence of Gentiles in the church.

Second, the incident is paralleled by the conversion of Cornelius (Acts 10), which itself marks a historic transition from a purely Jewish church to one including Gentiles. Luke is careful to speak well of each centurion and his religious concern. Third, Luke has been careful to note those who had "faith" (*pistis*), beginning with Mary (1:45) and then the four men who brought the paralyzed man to Jesus (5:20). Further, the authority of Jesus is stressed, and his "word" (v.7) is believed to have power (cf. 4:32, 36).

1–5 The introductory words "When Jesus had finished saying all this" (v.1) provide more than just a transition from the preceding sermon. They suggest another step in the mission Jesus came to fulfill (1:1) because the word "finished" translates *eplērōsen* ("fulfilled"). Matthew's formula following a collection of sayings uses *etelesen* ("finished," e.g., 7:28). "In the hearing of the people" (*eis tas akoas tou laou*) echoes "you who hear me" (6:27) and establishes the reliability of the witnesses from Galilee who would later bear testimony to the truth about Jesus' words and deeds.

On behalf of his seriously ill "servant" (*doulos*, v.2; cf. below on v.7), the centurion "sent some elders [*presbyterous*] of the Jews" (i.e., the leaders of the community) to Jesus (v.3). At this point a comparison with Matthew 8:5–13 shows a significant difference of detail. Luke, with his great interest in the character and importance of the centurion, gives us a fuller narrative than Matthew. Two groups come from the centurion to talk with Jesus on his behalf. Matthew provides a more condensed version, as is his custom, relating the words of the centurion to Jesus as though he had been there in person.

In v.4 we learn why the village elders were willing to intercede for the centurion. They were genuinely indebted to him for his generosity (v.5).

6–8 It seems strange that at this point, having invited Jesus to come, the centurion now sends another group of "friends" (*philous*) to stop him short of entering (v.6). They express the centurion's sense of unworthiness (v.7). Indeed, one wonders why at this point the centurion did not simply come out and speak for himself. Luke, however, apparently wishes to stress the humility of the man and possibly also his concern, on second thought, that Jesus might be criticized for entering a Gentile's house.

The focal point of the section is the centurion's concept of Jesus' authority (v.8). The wording is significant: "For I myself am a man under authority" (*gar egō anthrōpos eimi hypo exousian tassomenos*). He compares Jesus' relationship to God with his own to his superiors. The position of responsibility implies "authority" (*exousia*) to command others. Therefore he has faith that Jesus' authoritative "word" (*logos*) will accomplish the healing.

9–10 Jesus is not criticizing the faith he has found among Jews but rather says that "not even" (*oude*) in Israel has he found such faith (v.9). The Jews would be expected to have faith, considering their possession of God's revelation in their Scriptures (cf. Rom 3:1–2). "But not all the Israelites accepted the good news" (Rom 10:16), missing the element of personal faith (Rom 10:6–13). This failure to respond to their privileges was ending in Jesus' day, and the response of the centurion stood out in welcome contrast.

Notes

2, 6 'Ο ἑκατοντάρχης (*ho hekatontarchēs*, "the centurion") is presumably a Roman, though stationed not over Roman but Jewish soldiers, hired by the Herodian rulers to maintain their position. A centurion was comparable to an army lieutenant, though a noncommissioned officer, and was responsible for about a hundred men.

2. Raising a widow's son

7:11–17

[11]Soon afterward, Jesus went to a town called Nain, and his disciples and a large crowd went along with him. [12]As he approached the town gate, a dead person was being carried out—the only son of his mother, and she was a widow. And a large crowd from the town was with her. [13]When the Lord saw her, his heart went out to her and he said, "Don't cry."

[14]Then he went up and touched the coffin, and those carrying it stood still. He said, "Young man, I say to you, get up!" [15]The dead man sat up and began to talk, and Jesus gave him back to his mother.

[16]They were all filled with awe and praised God. "A great prophet has appeared among us," they said. "God has come to help his people." [17]This news about Jesus spread throughout Judea and the surrounding country.

Jesus is now about to perform the ultimate kind of miracle that will certify him as the Messiah and will be reported to John the Baptist ("the dead are raised," v.22). Luke also wants his readers to understand that while John the Baptist came in the spirit and power of Elijah, it is Jesus himself who is the great prophet of the end time. This miracle bears significant resemblance, as we shall note, to one performed by Elijah. Luke has already included a reference to the widow Elijah ministered to (4:25–26).

11 The time reference is vague. The trip to Nain would not have taken more than a day; it lay a few miles to the southeast of Jesus' hometown, Nazareth. Nain lay on the other side of the Hill of Moreh from Shunem, where Elisha raised the son of the Shunammite woman. Perhaps the local people recalled this. Luke typically notes the "large crowd" (e.g., 5:15, 29; 6:17, 8:4).

12–13 The cortege has already gone through the town and is on the way to the place of burial, which was customarily outside the town (v.12). The deceased was the "only son" (*monogenēs*) of his mother (cf. Notes). The compassion of the Lord Jesus, and of Luke as well, goes out to the woman. She is a widow (*chēra*) who, without a man in her family, would probably become destitute, unable in that society to earn a living. Our Lord's words are deeply human: "Don't cry" (*mē klaie*, v.13), but only he could say that and at the same time remove the cause of the tears. Otherwise such words would be hollow, though well meant.

14–15 Jesus risked ritual defilement by touching the "coffin" (*sorou*, a litter on which the shrouded body was laid, v.14). One can only imagine the thoughts of the pallbearers as they stopped. Jesus did what would seem useless—he spoke to a dead person. On the young man's return to life, Jesus "gave him back to his mother" (v.15), words similar to those in 1 Kings 17:23 regarding Elijah and the widow.

16–17 Once more Luke records the response of the people, noting that they "praised" (*edoksazon*, lit., "glorified") God (v.16; cf. 5:26; 18:43; 23:47). The similarities we have noted with Elijah and Elisha would naturally cause the people to use the word "prophet" to describe Jesus. They also echo an OT expression: "God has come to help his people" (e.g., Ruth 1:6). For the significance of "come" (*epeskepsato*), see comment on Luke 1:68. Once again Luke emphasizes the spread of the "news" (*logos*) about Jesus (v.17).

Notes

12 Whenever μονογενὴς υἱός (*monogenēs huios*, "the only son") is used in Scripture, it is of an only son who is either in mortal danger or already dead (cf. 8:42; 9:38; cf. also Judg 11:34–35, Zech 12:10; John 3:16; Th.C. de Kruif, "The Glory of the Only Son, John 1:14," *Studies in John*, Presented to J.N. Sevenster [Leiden: Brill, 1970], pp. 111–23). Luke shows his compassion and the beauty of God's saving grace by showing that these were precious only children even where Matthew and Mark do not have the term.

3. *Jesus and John the Baptist*

7:18–35

¹⁸John's disciples told him about all these things. Calling two of them, ¹⁹he sent them to the Lord to ask, "Are you the one who was to come, or should we expect someone else?"

²⁰When the men came to Jesus, they said, "John the Baptist sent us to you to ask, 'Are you the one who was to come, or should we expect someone else?' "

²¹At that very time Jesus cured many who had diseases, sicknesses and evil spirits, and gave sight to many who were blind. ²²So he replied to the messengers, "Go back and report to John what you have seen and heard: The blind receive sight, the lame walk, those who have leprosy are cured, the deaf hear, the dead are raised, and the good news is preached to the poor. ²³Blessed is the man who does not fall away on account of me."

²⁴After John's messengers left, Jesus began to speak to the crowd about John: "What did you go out into the desert to see? A reed swayed by the wind? ²⁵If not, what did you go out to see? A man dressed in fine clothes? No, those who wear expensive clothes and indulge in luxury are in palaces. ²⁶But what did you go out to see? A prophet? Yes, I tell you, and more than a prophet. ²⁷This is the one about whom it is written:

" 'I will send my messenger ahead of you,
who will prepare your way before you.'

²⁸I tell you, among those born of women there is no one greater than John; yet the one who is least in the kingdom of God is greater than he."

²⁹(All the people, even the tax collectors, when they heard Jesus' words, acknowledged that God's way was right, because they had been baptized by John. ³⁰But the Pharisees and experts in the law rejected God's purpose for themselves, because they had not been baptized by John.)

³¹"To what, then, can I compare the people of this generation? What are they like? ³²They are like children sitting in the marketplace and calling out to each other:

" 'We played the flute for you,
and you did not dance;
we sang a dirge,
and you did not cry.'

³³For John the Baptist came neither eating bread nor drinking wine, and you say, 'He has a demon.' ³⁴The Son of Man came eating and drinking, and you say, 'Here is a glutton and a drunkard, a friend of tax collectors and "sinners." ' ³⁵But wisdom is proved right by all her children."

In Luke 3:16–17, John had described the one who would come baptizing with the Holy Spirit and with fire. Then Jesus was baptized, receiving divine approval and anointing for his work. In 4:16–21 Jesus assumed the task prophesied in Isaiah 61:1–2. Now, after a cycle of teachings and healings, the validity of his messianic calling is once more under consideration; and John the Baptist is the other central figure.

18–20 "These things" (v.18), i.e., the healings and presumably also the raising of the widow's son, apparently have not sufficed to convince John of Jesus' messiahship. This reluctance seems strange, considering John's role in announcing the Coming One and in baptizing Jesus. There are several reasons why John needed further confirmation (v.19). He was in prison (Matt 11:2). This could lead to depression and, in turn, doubt. Further, he might wonder why, if the Messiah was to release prisoners (Isa 61:1), and if Jesus was the object of that prediction (Luke 4:18), he had not freed John. Also, though he had received reports of Jesus' ministry, John himself had apparently not witnessed spectacular messianic miracles such as he might have expected; nor had he heard Jesus claim outright that he was the Messiah. The fact that John still had "disciples" (vv.18, 20) does not necessarily mean he had been continuing a separate movement because of uncertainty about the Messiah. A number continued with John even after he had pointed them to Jesus.

21–23 Jesus responds by listing the messianic works (some of them just described in Luke) that he has accomplished (v.21). It was understood in those days that the true Messiah would not proclaim himself such but would first do appropriate messianic works that would lead to public acknowledgment of his identity (R. Longenecker, *The Christology of Early Jewish Christianity*, Studies in Biblical Theology, Second Series 17 [London: SCM, 1970], pp. 71–74). The works of Jesus echo not only Isaiah 61, quoted at Nazareth, but other passages from Isaiah (e.g., 42:7). Isaiah 35:5–6 declares that in the Messianic Age those who could not see, hear, walk, or speak would be healed. Jesus pronounces a blessing (v.23) on the person who accepts his credentials rather than being trapped (*skandalisthē*, NIV, "fall away") because of a false evaluation of Jesus.

24–28 The topic now changes from the role of Jesus to that of John (v.24). Jesus asks a couple of gently ironic questions that, through obviously negative answers, stress the inflexibility and austerity of John. Jesus uses the term "prophet" (v.26) and adds the role of "messenger" (v.27) from Malachi 3:1. If John is the messenger, obviously this forcefully implies the significance of Jesus' own role.

Jesus now puts John into historical perspective. John came in advance of the kingdom, which has now become a reality (16:16). Great as John was (v.28), it is greater to participate in the kingdom than to announce it. We are not to conclude from this, however, that John himself is excluded. Luke 13:28 says that all the prophets will be in the kingdom.

29–35 Attention now turns to the response of the people and of their leaders to John and Jesus also. Observe the contrast between the "people" (*laos*, v.29; see comment on 1:17) and the hostile religious leaders. In v.24 the neutral word "crowd" is used. The "tax collectors" (*telōnai*) are mentioned along with the "people" as those who stood ready to believe Jesus and thereby to "acknowledge that God's way was right." Notice that the issue is not only the role of Jesus and John but the entire counsel of God, whose "purpose [*boulēn*] for themselves" (v.30) was rejected by the "Pharisees and experts in the law [*nomikou*]." John's baptism was a symbol they chose to reject. The obdurate opposition to each of God's messengers is described as childish fickleness (v.32; cf. their earlier attempt to play John against Jesus, 5:33). The children's words are those of annoyed leaders who want their friends to play "grownup" and, when the leaders play cheerful or sad music, pretend that they are at a celebration, like a wedding, or at a funeral. They become petulant when their friends refuse to play. Jesus and John, when in confrontation with the Jewish leaders, refused to "play their game" and so are the object of their taunts. The people not only criticize but exaggerate the habits both of John (v.33), calling his asceticism demonic (demons were said to inhabit the desert where John was), and Jesus (v.34), calling his normal habits of food and drink gluttony and drunkenness. The concluding saying (v.35) probably means that those who respond to wisdom prove its rightness (cf. Notes).

Notes

19 Κύριον (*kyrion*, "Lord") does not have convincing MS support, but UBS chose it because "it is not likely that copyists would have deleted the name Ἰησοῦν [*Iēsoun*, 'Jesus'], and since κύριος is in accord with Lukan style" (Metzger, *Textual Commentary*, p. 143).

Ὁ ἐρχόμενος (*ho erchomenos*, "he who is coming"; NIV, "the one who was to come") alludes to the coming Messiah or prophet (John 6:14; 11:27; cf. Dan 7:13; Hab 2:3 and Heb 10:37; Mal 3:1).

27 Danker (*Jesus*, p. 97) sees a reminder here to the angel who went before the people of Israel in the desert (Exod 23:20).

30 Οἱ νομικοί (*hoi nomikoi*, "experts in the law") is a term used almost exclusively by Luke. It was more readily understood by his Gentile readers than γραμματεύς (*grammateus*, "scribe"; cf. Note on 5:17).

---

4. *Anointed by a sinful woman*

7:36–50

36Now one of the Pharisees invited Jesus to have dinner with him, so he went to the Pharisee's house and reclined at the table. 37When a woman who had lived a sinful life in that town learned that Jesus was eating at the Pharisee's house, she brought an alabaster jar of perfume, 38and as she stood behind him at his feet weeping, she began to wet his feet with her tears. Then she wiped them with her hair, kissed them and poured perfume on them.

39When the Pharisee who had invited him saw this, he said to himself, "If this man were a prophet, he would know who is touching him and what kind of woman she is—that she is a sinner."

40Jesus answered him, "Simon, I have something to tell you."

"Tell me, teacher," he said.

41"Two men owed money to a certain moneylender. One owed him five hundred denarii, and the other fifty. 42Neither of them had the money to pay him back, so he canceled the debts of both. Now which of them will love him more?"

43Simon replied, "I suppose the one who had the bigger debt canceled."

"You have judged correctly," Jesus said.

44Then he turned toward the woman and said to Simon, "Do you see this woman? I came into your house. You did not give me any water for my feet, but she wet my feet with her tears and wiped them with her hair. 45You did not give me a kiss, but this woman, from the time I entered, has not stopped kissing my feet. 46You did not put oil on my head, but she has poured perfume on my feet. 47Therefore, I tell you, her many sins have been forgiven—for she loved much. But he who has been forgiven little loves little."

48Then Jesus said to her, "Your sins are forgiven."

49The other guests began to say among themselves, "Who is this who even forgives sins?"

50Jesus said to the woman, "Your faith has saved you; go in peace."

The criticism Jesus has received (v.34) does not preclude Luke from setting down another example of Jesus' concern for sinners. The story contrasts a sinner and a

Pharisee. It is similar to another incident (cf. Matt 26:6–13; Mark 14:3–9; John 12:1–8). A woman brings perfume to Jesus while he is at a banquet hosted by a Pharisee named Simon (anonymous in John). There are several differences: the other incident occurs immediately before Jesus' crucifixion, the host is a leper (Matt and Mark), the woman pours the perfume on Jesus' head (Matt and Mark), and the controversy centers in the cost of the perfume, not the character of the woman.

The differences are sufficient to require two traditions. Some of the similarities may be coincidental (e.g., Simon was a common name); others may be due to cross influence.

36–38 Since he accepted an invitation from a Pharisee (v.36), Jesus cannot be accused of spurning the Pharisees socially. The woman (v.37) took advantage of the social customs that permitted needy people to visit such a banquet to receive some of the leftovers. She came specifically to see Jesus, bringing a jar or little bottle of perfume. Since Jesus was reclining (*kateklithē*) at the table according to custom (v.36), she prepared to pour the perfume on his feet (v.38), a humble act (cf. 3:16). A flow of tears preceded the outpouring of the perfume; so she wiped his feet lovingly with her hair and, perhaps impulsively, kissed them before using the perfume.

39–43 In this masterly narrative, Luke now directs attention to the Pharisee (v.39). He mulls over the matter and reaches three conclusions: (1) if Jesus were a prophet, he would know what kind of woman was anointing his feet; (2) if he knew what kind of a woman she was, he would not let her do it; and (3) since he does let her anoint his feet, he is no prophet and should not be acknowledged as such. But Jesus does let her expend the perfume on him and does not shun her. He shows that he does have unique insight into the human heart, for he knows what the Pharisee is thinking. When Jesus tells Simon his host that he has something to say to him (v.40), Simon, perhaps expecting some stock word of wisdom from his teacher-guest, replies perfunctorily, "Tell me, teacher."

The point of the incident (vv.41–42) is clear, and Simon is made to give the conclusion that will condemn him. His "I suppose" (v.43) probably implies an uneasy reluctance.

44–50 Again the woman is the focal point of the narrative. Surprisingly, Jesus first contrasts her acts of devotion with a lack of special attention on Simon's part as host (vv.44–46; cf. Notes). The main point is reached swiftly. Jesus can declare that her sins (which he does not hesitate to say were "many") have been forgiven (v.47). He can affirm this (v.48) because her act of love shows her realization of forgiveness. Her love is not the basis of forgiveness; her faith is (v.50). As in the event itself, the forgiveness was unearned; and it is this fact that elicits her love (cf. note on v.47).

As the episode ends, attention rapidly shifts from one person to the other. Simon obviously knows little of either forgiveness or love (v.47). Jesus pronounces the woman forgiven. Then he becomes the object of another discussion because he presumes to absolve her from her sins (v.49; cf. 5:21). The woman receives his pronouncement of salvation—"saved" (*sesōken*) is in the perfect tense, expressing an accomplished fact—and his benediction "go in peace" (v.50), traditional and common words that have true meaning only for those who have been saved by faith

(8:48; 17:19; 18:42; cf. Judg 18:6; 1 Sam 1:17; 2 Sam 15:9; 1 Kings 22:17; Acts 16:36; James 2:16).

Notes

37 Ἀμαρτωλός (*hamartōlos*, "sinner"; NIV, "who lived a sinful life") is the word Luke often uses to identify a person who has a reputation for gross immorality. The woman's unbound hair (v.38) might indicate that she was a prostitute.

41 A δηνάριον (*dēnarion*, "denarius") was the approximate daily wage of a laborer.

44–46 Schürmann (*Das Lukasevangelium*, 1:435–36), followed by Marshall (*Gospel of Luke*, pp. 312–13), holds that Simon was not actually at fault as a host, because the amenities mentioned, while customs of the day, were not necessary acts of hospitality. Bailey (*Peasant Eyes*, p. 5), on the other hand, says, "The formal greetings were clearly of crucial significance in first-century times." The contrast remains strong in either case because of the extraordinary nature of what the woman did.

47 NIV (so UBS) has a comma before and after "I tell you," making the phrase οὗ χάριν λέγω σοι (*hou charin legō soi*, "Therefore, I tell you") parenthetical, which links "therefore" with "her many sins have been forgiven." While this is grammatically possible, KJV, RSV, NASB, and JB are probably correct in linking the deeds of the woman (described in vv.44–46) with Jesus' response rather than with her forgiveness (e.g., JB: "For this reason I tell you"). The use of ὅτι (*hoti*, "for") here is not to show causality but evidence (see discussions in C.F.D. Moule, *An Idiom-Book of New Testament Greek*, 2d ed. [Cambridge: University Press, 1959], p. 147; M. Zerwick, *Biblical Greek* [Rome: Pontifical Biblical Institute, 1963], par. 422). TEV has "the great love she has shown proves that her many sins have been forgiven."

---

5. Parable of the sower

8:1–15

[1]After this, Jesus traveled about from one town and village to another, proclaiming the good news of the kingdom of God. The Twelve were with him, [2]and also some women who had been cured of evil spirits and diseases: Mary (called Magdalene) from whom seven demons had come out; [3]Joanna the wife of Cuza, the manager of Herod's household; Susanna; and many others. These women were helping to support them out of their own means.

[4]While a large crowd was gathering and people were coming to Jesus from town after town, he told this parable: [5]"A farmer went out to sow his seed. As he was scattering the seed, some fell along the path; it was trampled on, and the birds of the air ate it up. [6]Some fell on rock, and when it came up, the plants withered because they had no moisture. [7]Other seed fell among thorns, which grew up with it and choked the plants. [8]Still other seed fell on good soil. It came up and yielded a crop, a hundred times more than was sown."

When he said this, he called out, "He who has ears to hear, let him hear."

[9]His disciples asked him what this parable meant. [10]He said, "The knowledge of the secrets of the kingdom of God has been given to you, but to others I speak in parables, so that,

" 'though seeing, they may not see;
though hearing, they may not understand.'

[11]"This is the meaning of the parable: The seed is the word of God. [12]Those along the path are the ones who hear, and then the devil comes and takes away

the word from their hearts, so that they may not believe and be saved. [13]Those on the rock are the ones who receive the word with joy when they hear it, but they have no root. They believe for a while, but in the time of testing they fall away. [14]The seed that fell among thorns stands for those who hear, but as they go on their way they are choked by life's worries, riches and pleasures, and they do not mature. [15]But the seed on good soil stands for those with a noble and good heart, who hear the word, retain it, and by persevering produce a crop.

1–3 The opening verses provide a summary of yet another preaching tour (cf. the previous circuit described in 4:44). Luke states Jesus' mission both in that passage and here as announcing the "good news of the kingdom of God." During this time, Jesus has chosen the "Twelve." Luke is careful to mention them here, as they will serve as witnesses and authorities in the days following Jesus' ascension.

What is new is the mention of several women who not only accompany Jesus but share in his support (vv.2–3). It was not uncommon for ancient itinerant cult leaders, fortune tellers, and their kind to solicit the financial support of wealthy women (Lucian, *Alexander the False Prophet* 6; cf. 2 Tim 3:6–7). In this case, however, it is in a Jewish, not a pagan, culture; and the relationship is morally pure. Some of these women, at least, had a great debt of love to Jesus, as did the woman in the preceding incident (7:36–50). Luke does not say that Mary Magdalene, as often thought, had been a prostitute; she is not identified with the woman of 7:36–50. He does refer to her as an object of the grace and power of God in being released from seven demons. "Joanna the wife of Chuza" is otherwise unknown, but her presence at the Crucifixion (in contrast to the flight of most of the disciples) shows her faithfulness. She is the first person connected with the Herodian household to be mentioned in this Gospel. Later on, the gospel often reached into distinguished and royal homes through the witness of Christian servants. It is noteworthy that these women were industrious, in their time truly "liberated," and helped in the support not only of Jesus but of the Twelve, to whom the word "them" (*autois*) in v.3 refers.

As in Matthew 13:1–23 and Mark 4:1–20, the sequence in vv.4–15, is (1) the parable of the sower, (2) Jesus' reason for using parables, and (3) the interpretation of the parable of the sower. Each part deals with the mixed response Jesus was receiving from his audiences, a response also basic in the next two pericopes (vv.16–18; 19–21). Jesus' realism regarding the failure of people to believe his message also appears elsewhere in Luke, notably in the saying about the persistent widow and others who cry for vindication. They will receive justice quickly, but "when the Son of Man comes, will he find faith on the earth?" (18:8). Jesus explains the present parable and his reasons for using the parabolic form—both to warn those who neglect the word they hear and to encourage his disciples when that word is not fully accepted.

4 Luke begins with an observation on the size of the crowds (so also Matt 13:2; Mark 4:1). But whereas Matthew and Mark specify a location by the lake, Luke omits this. Instead, he adds to the comment on the crowd by speaking of those who were coming to Jesus from "town after town." The effect is to help the reader visualize a large mixed group of people who represent the various types of "soil" in the parable.

5–8 This particular parable reflects a situation well known to the audience, and the details of the parable would have immediately been grasped by the hearers. The very fact that circumstances so familiar need still further comment before the spiritual meaning is clear underlines the paradox presented in v.10—namely, that those who see and hear do not understand.

The focal point of the parable has been variously interpreted. In none of the Gospels is the sower (v.5; NIV, "farmer") the center of attention (not even in Mark, though some have taken Mark 4:14 as directing attention to the sower). Nor is particular stress laid on the seed—certainly not as in the parable of the secretly growing seed (Mark 4:26–29). This is not to say that the seed is unimportant. On the contrary, it represents the word of God (v.11); and the whole act of sowing the seed is proclaiming the gospel of the kingdom (cf. Mark 4:14).

What does catch attention is the variety of soils. Contrary to what a modern Western perspective might lead us to expect, the sower is not immediately concerned about the kind of soil. Since plowing followed sowing in Jesus' culture, the trampled ground where people crossed the field might later be plowed under with seed; so it is not excluded from the sowing. The same could be true of young thorn bushes (v.7). Furthermore, the rocky subsoil (v.6) might not be visible at the time of sowing. The low yield from the poor soil is overshadowed by the very large yield from the good soil (v.8)—an encouragement for Jesus' disciples to realize that the ultimate greatness of the kingdom will make all their efforts worthwhile.

9–10 Here in Luke the disciples' question (v.9) refers only to this parable, not to Jesus' larger ministry as in Matthew 13:10 and Mark 4:10. The reference to the "secrets" (*mystēria*, v.10) occurs in this context in all three Synoptics. Mark 4:11 uses the singular form *mystērion;* and Matthew (13:11), like Luke, includes the word "knowledge" (*gnōnai*, lit., "to know"). Only in this situation does *mystērion* occur in the teachings of Jesus. A word of immense significance in biblical literature, *mystērion* is found also in extrabiblical Jewish literature. Biblical scholars, now freed from the earlier idea that NT references to a "mystery" derived from the Hellenistic mystery religions, have been finding a rich meaning in the word. While it occurs in the LXX only in Daniel 2, where God is praised as the one who reveals secrets (Dan 2:20–23, 28–30), it appears in varied frames of reference in the NT. The basic concept of *mystērion* is that of the purpose and plan of God, which he works out phase by phase in human history and through the church. The issues of the problem of evil, suffering, and the delay of vindication will be resolved when God finally reveals his "secret," which is "accomplished" (*etelesthē*) after the "delay" (*chronos*) has ended in Revelation 10:6–7. The "mystery" or "secret" is only revealed by God's sovereign grace to his people. As Luke says here, "The knowledge of the secrets of the kingdom of God has been given to you."

"To others" (*tois loipois*, lit., "to the rest") is not as specific as Mark's "those on the outside" (*tois exō*, 4:11). The quotation from Isaiah 6:9 in v.10—"though seeing . . . not understand"—shows that Jesus' teaching is in accord with the consistent principle in Scripture that those who fail to respond to a saving word from God will find that they are not only under judgment for rejecting what they have heard but that they are unable to understand further truth (cf. John 3:17–19 with John 9:39–41, which contains words similar to Isa 6:9; Exod 8:32, regarding Pharaoh, with Exod 9:12 and Rom 9:17–18; and see Acts 28:26–27, another quotation from the Isaiah passage; Matt 7:6; Luke 20:1–8; Rev 22:11). For such, the very parable that reveals truth to some hides it from them. Given this sober reality, it is all the more important that the interpretation of the present passage be in full accord both with the Greek syntax of this sentence and with the whole biblical revelation of God's character and the way he deals with unbelief (see also B. Lindars, *New Testament Apologetic* [Philadelphia: Westminster, 1961], pp. 159–67).

While "so that" (*hina*, v.10) may be understood as indicating result, it more normally indicates purpose. The thought may be that the principle of Isaiah 6:9 may be fulfilled. Luke does not include the additional difficult words from Isaiah that are found in Mark 4:12—"otherwise they might turn and be forgiven" (see commentary on this verse in this vol.)—but instead hastens on to the interpretation of the parable in question.

11–12 Having shown the danger of unbelief in v.10, Jesus now returns to the parable, explaining why the proclaimed "word of God" (v.11) fails to bring a uniform response of faith. Luke's inclusion of the clause "so that they may not believe and be saved" (v.12; lacking in Matthew and Mark) reflects his intense concern regarding salvation. The clause is introduced by *hina* ("so that"); and here, unlike its use in v.10, there is no doubt that it expresses deliberate purpose. Note the contrast between the devil's purpose and God's purpose (2 Peter 3:9).

13–14 In the next two instances (seed fallen on the rock, v.13; seed fallen among thorns, v.14), there is an initial response. The superficial reception given the word may be compared to those who "believed" Jesus (John 8:31), only to be called children of the devil (John 8:44). Obviously they did not go on to true liberating faith (vv.31–32). Luke alone among the synoptic writers says these people actually "believe for a time" (*pros kairon pisteuousin*, v.13; cf. Matt 13:21 and Mark 4:17—"last only a short time"). It is "in the time of testing" (*en kairō peirasmou*; cf. *thlipseōs ē diōgmou* ["trouble or persecution"], Matt 13:21; Mark 4:17) that they "fall away" (*aphistantai*; cf. the use of *skandalizo* ["stumble"], Matt 13:21; Mark 4:17). In all three Synoptics the response is superficial and cannot endure adversity. Schuyler Brown (*Apostasy and Perseverance*, p. 14) would see this as characteristic of Luke's concern for apostasy under external testing.

The third example (v.14) has to do, not with adversity, but with distractions, like those Jesus warned against in Matthew 6:19–34; Luke 11:34–36; 12:22–32; 16:13. The comment that the hearers in this example "do not mature" (*ou telesphorousin*, often used of fruit; cf. *akarpos* ["unfruitful"], Matt 13:22; Mark 4:19) is comparable to the statements in James 2:14–26 on a "dead" (*nekra*, v.17) and "useless" (*argē*, v.20) faith and in 2 Peter 1:8 on those who are "ineffective" (*argous*) and "unfruitful" (*akarpous*; NIV, "unproductive"). That this matter of being fruitful is not simply a matter of the quality of one's Christian life but of whether one has life at all is suggested by Jesus' parallel teaching on wealth in Matthew 6:19–34. There the "single ['good'] eye" (see on Luke 11:34) is opposed to the total darkness that envelops a divided heart (Matt 6:22–24; cf. Hos 10:1–2: "Israel was a spreading vine . . . their heart is deceitful"). The unresponsive people described here (v.14) apparently lack the following essentials to true saving faith: understanding (Matt 13:23; cf. v.19), accepting the word (Mark 4:20), and retaining it (Luke 8:15).

15 Luke's stress on the character of the individual is in contrast to Matthew's reference (13:23) to "understanding" (*synieis*) the word. This is in accord with Matthew's interest in comprehending the secrets of the kingdom (cf. Matt 13:11, 14–15, 19, 25). The description "noble and good" (*kalē kai agathē*) is a Christian adaptation of an ancient Greek phrase. The word "heart" (*kardia*) means the spiritual, intellectual, volitional center of a person's being, i.e., the whole person. This person is marked by singleness of purpose, unlike those of divided heart mentioned in Hosea 10:1–2 (cf. Ps 101[100 LXX]:2—*en akakia kardias mou* ["with blameless heart"] and 1 Chron 29:17–19). Jesus' emphasis here is not so much on whether a person perseveres but on the kind of person who does persevere. RSV's "bring forth fruit with patience" (*en hypomonē*) is more literal and perhaps more accurate than NIV's "by persevering produce a crop."

Notes

4 Teaching in παραβολαί (*parabolai*, "parables," i.e., placing things alongside of others for comparison) was common among the rabbis of Jesus' day.

The ancient Greeks used the literary form of parable. In the Hebrew tradition, there were a variety of figures of speech all subsumed under the word מָשָׁל (*māšāl*), usually translated *parabolē* in the LXX. Contemporary NT scholars generally recognize that while the parable is distinct from allegory, in that the various features in the parable do not each convey a particular meaning, neither does the parable convey a simplistic ethical truth. Rather the parable is an art form offering various possibilities of expression to the speaker or writer. In the NT it usually conveys a message about the kingdom of God, which, in its very telling by Jesus, involved the hearer in a crisis of personal response. Among the useful works on parables are K.E. Bailey, *Poet and Peasant;* id., *Peasant Eyes;* A.M. Hunter, *The Parables Then and Now* (Philadelphia: Westminster, 1971); J. Jeremias, *Parables of Jesus;* R.H. Stein, *An Introduction to the Parables of Jesus* (Philadelphia: Westminster, 1981). Recent critical and literary studies include John Dominic Crossan, *In Parables* (New York: Harper and Row, 1975); Geraint Vaughn Jones, *The Art and Truth of the Parables* (London: SPCK, 1964); Eta Linneman, *Parables of Jesus* (London: SPCK, 1966); R.W. Funk, ed., "A Structuralist Approach to the Parables," *Semeia* 1; Mary Ann Tolbert, *Perspectives on the Parables* (Philadelphia: Fortress, 1979); Dan O. Via, *The Parables: Their Literary and Existential Dimension* (Philadelphia: Fortress, 1967). On the parables and Luke 8:4–15, see P.B. Payne, "Metaphor as a Model for Interpretation of the Parables of Jesus with Special Reference to the Parable of the Sower" (Ph.D. dissertation, Cambridge University, 1975).

5 Τὸν σπόρον αὐτοῦ (*ton sporon autou*, "his seed") is found only in Luke and is probably merely a stylistic addition, not a theological emphasis on "seed."

6–8 Φυὲν (*phuen*, "when it came up") occurs only in Luke; so also συμφυεῖσαι (*symphueisai*, "grew up with") in v.7. *Phuen* again occurs in v.8.

6 Διὰ τὸ μὴ ἔχειν ἰκμάδα (*dia to mē echein ikmada*, "because they had no moisture") replaces διὰ τὸ μὴ ἔχειν ῥίζαν (*dia to mē echein rhizan*, "because they had no root") in Mark 4:6. The statement is less vivid than in Mark and Matthew because Luke does not refer to the scorching heat of the sun.

8 Ἐφώνει (*ephōnei*, "called out") is unique to Luke here and perhaps emphasizes the opportunity of the crowds, to whom Jesus has given special attention (v.4), to receive the teaching. The call to "hear" (ἀκουέτω, *akouetō*) prepares for the saying in v.10 (cf. a similar exhortation in 14:35; Matt 11:15; Rev 2:7 [and in each letter to the seven churches]; 13:9).

10 Ἵνα (*hina*, "so that") can be causal, but grammarians are reluctant to acknowledge it as such in this passage or Mark 4:12 (cf. Zerwick, *Biblical Greek*, p. 413; BDF, par. 369 [2]). Moule (*Idiom Book*, pp. 142–43) notes this reluctance but hesitates to see this as a final (purpose) clause because of the apparent incongruity of a purpose sense here with the rest of NT thought. Zerwick notes that after the parallel verse in Mark 4:12, Mark (4:33) says that Jesus spoke in parables "according as they were able to hear."

11–15 The interpretation of the parable often has been attributed to the early church rather than to Jesus. Jeremias acceded to this view on the basis of the vocabulary and theology, which he thought were more characteristic of the primitive church than of Jesus (*Parables of Jesus*, pp. 77–79; 149–50). Gerhardsson concluded that it is not possible to identify here a later hortatory application by the early church distinct from the original eschatological teaching given by Jesus (B. Gerhardsson, "The Parable of the Sower and its Interpretation," NTS 14 [1968]: 165–93). The supposition that Jesus could not have employed a multiple form of interpretation such as we have in this passage can no longer be sustained in view of the allegorical methods used by rabbis in the first century. Luke's own modifications of the tradition expand but do not alter the theological teaching in Mark (cf. I.H. Marshall, "Tradition and Theology in Luke. Luke 8:5–15," *Tyndale Bulletin* 20 [1969]: 56–75). We can conclude that the interpretation in vv.11–15 belongs to Jesus' authentic teaching.

13 Ἀφίστανται (*aphistantai*, "fall away") is related to ἀποστασία (*apostasia*), from which our word "apostasy" is derived (cf. 1 Tim 4:1 and Heb 3:12, where the verbal form clearly means to depart from a biblical faith in God).

---

6. *Parable of the lamp*

8:16–18

> [16]"No one lights a lamp and hides it in a jar or puts it under a bed. Instead, he puts it on a stand, so that those who come in can see the light. [17]For there is nothing hidden that will not be disclosed, and nothing concealed that will not be known or brought out into the open. [18]Therefore consider carefully how you listen. Whoever has will be given more; whoever does not have, even what he thinks he has will be taken from him."

This section contains three distinct sayings. The order of the sayings is the same in Mark and Luke, but Matthew places the first two in entirely different contexts. The considerable dissimilarities in wording between the Gospels suggest that the sayings were repeated on many occasions and written down separately.

16–17 Here the theme is the same as that of vv.11–15—viz., that what is genuine can and will be tested for its authenticity. If what is "hidden" (v.17) is evil, this saying affirms that God's judgment on those referred to in v.10 and in vv.12–15 will be just. If what is "hidden" is good, the saying may refer to the truth of Jesus' private teachings to his disciples, which they are exhorted to proclaim publicly. More likely it indicates that God's truth, now partially hidden from those who reject it, will one day be publicly vindicated. The absurdity of lighting a lamp (v.16) only to hide it reinforces the point.

18 In Matthew 13:11 this saying relates to personal response to the proclamation of the kingdom of heaven. There the meaning is that those who accept the message of the kingdom will also be given the knowledge of the "secret," but those who reject it will lose even the opportunity of hearing more teaching. Here Luke has the verse in a different setting, though its meaning may well be the same as in Matthew. Notice the additional word "think" in Luke: "even what he thinks he has."

7. Jesus' true family

8:19–21

19Now Jesus' mother and brothers came to see him, but they were not able to get near him because of the crowd. 20Someone told him, "Your mother and brothers are standing outside, wanting to see you."

21He replied, "My mother and brothers are those who hear God's word and put it into practice."

19–21 Matthew and Mark continue with parabolic teaching at this point, but Luke turns to an incident Matthew and Mark locate at the conclusion of the Beelzebub controversy. When he comes to this controversy (11:14–28), Luke inserts something different, though on the same theme of obedience to God's word. Here the theme of obedience appropriately continues vv.5–15.

Jesus is not, of course, dishonoring his family (vv.19–20) but honoring those who obey God (v.21). The incident Luke now gives us teaches a profound lesson about how believers may be near to the Lord Jesus. Most Christians would probably say that we come closest to him through prayer and reading the Bible. But with searching practicality Jesus says that the way to be close to him—even as close as his own family—is through being receptive to ("hearing") God's word and then doing it. Hours of praying and reading the Bible will not bring disobedient Christians as close to the Lord as doing his truth brings even the simplest believer. Elsewhere Luke shows the place family must take in the life of one who desires to be Jesus' disciple (14:25–26).

Notes

20 Οἱ αδελφοί (hoi adelphoi) is most naturally translated "brothers." To render it "cousins" or "step-brothers" on the theory that Mary remained a virgin is to strain the meaning.

21 Τὸν λόγον τοῦ θεοῦ (ton logon tou theou, "God's word") may be an alternate term Luke uses to express the idea behind "the will of God" in the parallels (Matt 12:50; Mark 3:35) in order to stress again God's "word" (cf. v.11), which is the expression of his will.

8. Calming the storm

8:22–25

22One day Jesus said to his disciples, "Let's go over to the other side of the lake." So they got into a boat and set out. 23As they sailed, he fell asleep. A squall came down on the lake, so that the boat was being swamped, and they were in great danger.

24The disciples went and woke him, saying, "Master, Master, we're going to drown!"

He got up and rebuked the wind and the raging waters; the storm subsided, and all was calm. 25"Where is your faith?" he asked his disciples.

In fear and amazement they asked one another, "Who is this? He commands even the winds and the water, and they obey him."

Luke resumes the sequence of narratives illustrating the powerful, authoritative word of Jesus (notice esp. 8:25, 29, 32, 54; cf. 4:36). Jesus exercises his power against natural forces, demons, illness, and death. Then he delegates this power to his disciples (9:1–2). Shürmann (*Das Lukasevangelium,* 1:472–73) groups the incidents in 8:22–56 as a trilogy of "*Grosswunder*" ("great miracles") that are "*fast johanneische* σημεῖα ("almost Johannine signs").

The story itself is noteworthy for its vividness and for its portrayal of the Lord Jesus in complete control of himself and his environment. The climax comes not with the miracle itself but with the question of the disciples (v.25) concerning the identity of the Master. It is a nature miracle, marking the first time in Luke that Jesus applied his power to a nonliving object rather than to a person. Jesus is affirming sovereignty over storm and sea as God did in the Exodus.

22–23 Luke omits some of the detail found in Mark, including a specific reference to the time of day. His words "Let us go over to the other side of the lake" (v.22) should have assured the disciples that they would indeed complete their trip across the water (as the Jews did in the Exodus). Luke uses vivid language, as Mark does, to describe the fury of the storm. Luke mentions the wind three times (vv.23, 24, 25). This was an intense squall (*lailaps anemou,* lit., "windstorm of wind"), such as characteristically swept down on the Sea of Galilee, which lies in a shallow basin rimmed by hills. Luke mentions earlier in the narrative than do Matthew and Mark that Jesus was asleep. This placement heightens the contrast between the turmoil of the storm and Jesus' peaceful rest.

24–25 The fear and unbelief of the disciples is in contrast not only to the calm of their Master but also to the endurance they themselves should have had in "the time of testing" (cf. v.13). Even so, in Luke's account Jesus does not say, "Do you still have no faith?" as in Mark 4:40, but only, "Where is your faith?" (v.25). The double "Master, Master" (v.24) expresses both respect and terror (contrast the less respectful question in Mark 4:38). The fear of being lost at sea is a common human fear and typical of helplessness in the immensity of life (cf. Ps 107:23–31). Also the Christian church has thought of herself as a boat navigating treacherous waters. Jesus' miracle would have had special meaning during the unsettling and threatening conditions the church encountered through persecutions during its early period.

The question of the disciples, "Who is this?" serves to show not only their amazement but also the slowness of their apprehension of the "Master's" true identity. This question not only marks the climax of this story but is a key question in Luke. In fact, because Luke omits a large amount of material found in Mark (6:45–8:26, which otherwise would come between v.17 and v.18 of Luke 9), he can move quickly from the next occurrence of this question (9:9) to the question at Caesarea Philippi: "Who do you say I am?" (9:20).

Notes

24 Ἐπετίμησεν (*epetimēsen,* "rebuked") suggests to some interpreters that there is a demonic presence behind the storm (cf. comments on 4:39). On the other hand, the word may simply reflect the tendency of Semitic and other peoples to personify natural forces. In the LXX the word ἐπιτιμάω (*epitimaō*, "to blame, reprove") often expresses the "creative or destructive" work of God (TDNT, 2:624). It would be natural for the disciples to say that these forces "obey" (ὑπακούω *hypakouō*, lit., "hearken to") him (v.25).

---

9. Healing a demon-possessed man

8:26–39

> ²⁶They sailed to the region of the Gerasenes, which is across the lake from Galilee. ²⁷When Jesus stepped ashore, he was met by a demon-possessed man from the town. For a long time this man had not worn clothes or lived in a house, but had lived in the tombs. ²⁸When he saw Jesus, he cried out and fell at his feet, shouting at the top of his voice, "What do you want with me, Jesus, Son of the Most High God? I beg you, don't torture me!" ²⁹For Jesus had commanded the evil spirit to come out of the man. Many times it had seized him, and though he was chained hand and foot and kept under guard, he had broken his chains and had been driven by the demon into solitary places.
>
> ³⁰Jesus asked him, "What is your name?"
>
> "Legion," he replied, because many demons had gone into him. ³¹And they begged him repeatedly not to order them to go into the Abyss.
>
> ³²A large herd of pigs was feeding there on the hillside. The demons begged Jesus to let them go into them, and he gave them permission. ³³When the demons came out of the man, they went into the pigs, and the herd rushed down the steep bank into the lake and was drowned.
>
> ³⁴When those tending the pigs saw what had happened, they ran off and reported this in the town and countryside, ³⁵and the people went out to see what had happened. When they came to Jesus, they found the man from whom the demons had gone out, sitting at Jesus' feet, dressed and in his right mind; and they were afraid. ³⁶Those who had seen it told the people how the demon-possessed man had been cured. ³⁷Then all the people of the region of the Gerasenes asked Jesus to leave them, because they were overcome with fear. So he got into the boat and left.
>
> ³⁸The man from whom the demons had gone out begged to go with him, but Jesus sent him away, saying, ³⁹"Return home and tell how much God has done for you." So the man went away and told all over town how much Jesus had done for him.

This narrative provides the strongest expression yet of the power of Jesus against the forces of evil. (A previous instance of Jesus' casting out demons [4:33–35] offered little descriptive comment.) Luke gives us far more detail than Matthew, though not quite as much as Mark, and provides a lively, forceful picture of the destructive effects of demon possession. If a raging sea is a threat, demonic force is much worse. Not only the power of the kingdom (11:20), but also the power of the Messiah to release the captives of the kingdom of darkness move against this demonic force. The very narrative that describes this power of Jesus grips the reader. First, there are several progressive levels of action (in both Luke and Mark) involving the demoniac, the demons, the swine, the townspeople, and finally the demoniac after his healing. Second, Luke by his literary skill has inserted part of the description of the demoniac's past life in between the lines of dialogue to heighten the readers' awareness of the man's helplessness under demonic control.

26–29 "They sailed" (v.26) connects this episode with the previous one, suggesting the accomplishment of the goal stated in v.22. If the purpose of the trip across the lake was to liberate the demoniac (no other activity is recorded in the region of the Gerasenes), we are probably to understand the storm at sea as the deliberate attempt of evil forces to prevent Jesus' arrival, though biblical teaching is not clear on this point. Also, the connection between the calming of the sea and the healing of the demoniac is more likely to underscore the sequence of Jesus' mighty works rather than suggest a continuum of demonic activity (cf. v.40).

The NIV has adopted the reading "Gerasenes" (cf. Notes). Luke may have added the clause at the end of v.26 simply as a geographical explanation. Yet the fact that the locale was in Gentile territory is especially important to Luke as validating the Christian mission to Gentiles. Verse 27 implies that the man was right by the shore when Jesus arrived.

In vv.27 and 29 we have a classic description of demon possession. The symptoms of such possession are like those of certain psychic illnesses known today, but Luke does not confuse illness with demon possession (cf. 4:40–41), though he does link the two when appropriate. Certain effects of demon possession cited in this passage are (1) disregard for personal dignity (nakedness), (2) social isolation, (3) retreat to the simplest kind of shelter (caves, often containing tombs, were also used for shelter by the very poor), (4) demons' recognition of Jesus' deity, (5) demonic control of speech, (6) shouting, and (7) extraordinary strength. The basic tragedy of the demoniac lay not in mental or physical symptoms; in his case a human being was controlled by powers totally antithetical to God, his kingdom, and the kingdom blessings of "righteousness, peace and joy in the Holy Spirit" (Rom 14:17).

The term "Most High God" (v.28) appears in the NT in an orthodox sense, as in the OT (Gen 14:18–22; Num 24:16; Isa 14:14; Dan 3:26; 4:2), and also as a general term for deity apart from worship (contrast Luke 1:32, 35, 76, with Acts 16:17). Here it is used in the latter sense. The words "fell at his feet" do not indicate worship: the plea "I beg you, don't torture me!" (v.28) along with the dialogue in vv.30–31 make it clear that the man's words and actions are not his own. The "torture" (from *basanizō*, which can indicate either physical or mental torture) is presumably that of being cast into the "Abyss" (cf. v.31), or else the advance threat of that fate. Matthew 8:29 adds "before the appointed time," i.e., the eventual judgment of Satan and his followers after his incarceration in the Abyss (Rev 20:1–3, 10; cf. the intertestamental literature: 1 Enoch 15–16; Jub 10:8–9; T Levi 18:12).

30–31 Jesus was not actually an exorcist, because he did not need formulas nor invoke the authority of another in driving out demons. Therefore his asking the demoniac's name (v.30) should not be interpreted as an attempt to control the demons through knowing their host's name. That was pagan magical procedure. Moreover, it is not clear whether Jesus asked the name of the man or of the demons, though the response comes from the latter. "Legion" was not normally used as a proper name. It refers to a Roman military unit consisting of thousands of soldiers (the precise number varied). Thus "Legion" implies that there were many demons. As for "Abyss" (*abyssos*, v.31), the word has a long history and varied meanings ranging from the idea of primeval chaos to the abode and prison of evil beings (cf. Notes).

32–39 When the demons entered them, the swine were carried into the lake (v.33). In ancient thought, waters of the sea or a large lake was one form of the Abyss. The cosmology behind this, however, is not clear; nor is it clear that the demons, intent on carrying out their destructive work even on animals, met the fate they wanted to avoid.

The episode of the pigs, often considered a legendary accretion, is integral to the present narrative in two ways. Theologically, it completes the cycle just described. Psychologically, it is essential for understanding the complex response of the towns-people. The report of what happened to the swine (vv.34, 36) first triggered the people's fear, which merged into overwhelming awe on seeing the former demoniac "dressed and in his right mind" (vv.35, 37).

But what about the ethical aspect of the pigs' destruction? Obviously the good of the man was more important than that of the pigs. Moreover, the demons them-selves insisted on entering the pigs; Jesus permitted them to do this but did not actively send them there. Inevitably the discussion moves from exegesis to theology and the problem of evil—why it exists and why God in his wisdom, power, and love permits evil in this world.

The narrative does not say that the demons were destroyed so that they could never again be at large. The biblical references to the Abyss connote that God may allow evil beings to go abroad from there, just as Satan, though defeated, still roams the earth (1 Peter 5:8). In any event, once the demons are off the scene, attention centers on the man and Jesus (vv.38–39). Now healed and a new man (observe the contrast between vv.27–29 and 35), the former demoniac is commissioned by Jesus, not to go with him as a disciple, but to be a witness where he lived. Jesus has different ways for different believers to serve him (cf. John 21:21–22).

Notes

26 Γερασηνῶν (Gerasēnōn, "of the Gerasenes") is the preferred reading (UBS, 3d ed.) over Γεργεσηνῶν (Gergesēnōn, "of the Gergesenes") and Γαδαρηνῶν (Gadarēnōn, "of the Gadarenes"). The appearance of several names at this point in the various MSS results not only from possible phonetic confusion but also from the existence of several towns with similar names east and south of the Sea of Galilee. "Gerasenes" seems original in Luke, as in Mark, having good MS support (see Metzger, *Textual Commentary*, p. 145). Perhaps Mark had reasons unknown to us for assuming that the territory of Gerasa extended some thirty miles from the town of that name (southeast of the sea) to the place on the shore of Galilee, which, with its steep slopes and modern city of Kursi (or Kersa) may have been the scene of the incident (cf. V. Taylor, *The Gospel According to St. Mark* [London: MacMillan, 1963], p. 278).

Another suggestion is that there may have been another town with the name Gerasa, or a phonetically similar name, on the sea coast near modern Kursi (Kersa) and near the steep slopes (C.E.B. Cranfield, *The Gospel According to St. Mark, An Introduction and Commentary* [Cambridge: University Press, 1960], p. 176; Marshall, *Gospel of Luke*, p. 337). But it is also possible that Kursi marks the site of Gergesa rather than a second Gerasa. Origen, writing on John 6, suggested that the town was Gergesa, a suggestion reflected in some MSS.

The claim of Gadara (the modern Umm Qeis) to be the site of the miracle lies in the importance of that name in MSS of Matthew, in its location six miles from the shore of the lake, and from the possibility that the territory named after the town might have extended to the shore of Galilee. It is possible that people in the area were identified by the name of the more important city of Gerasa rather than by that of the smaller Gadara (cf.

E. Smick, *Archaeology of the Jordan Valley* [Grand Rapids: Baker, 1973], pp. 135–37). However, Smick did not deal with M. Avi-Yonah's evidence against Gadara (*The Holy Land* [Grand Rapids: Baker, 1966], p. 174). Without more certain knowledge, the textual reading *Gerasēnōn* should tentatively be considered correct. Also we must keep in mind that all three Synoptics use a general expression, εἰς τὴν χώραν (*eis tēn chōran*, "into the region"), leaving the precise location unspecified.

29 παρήγγειλεν (*parēngeilen*, "had commanded") is aorist. The twenty-fifth edition of the Nestle text had the imperfect παρήγγελλεν (*parēngellen*, "was commanding"), a reading assumed by Turner (*Syntax*, p. 65) and by Marshall (*Gospel of Luke*, p. 338). However, the UBS text has the aorist, following B and P[75], among other MSS, but with no footnote, and consequently no comment in Metzger, *Textual Commentary*.

31 Ἄβυσσος (*abyssos*, "abyss") is used only here in Luke (cf. Rom 10:7; Rev 9:1–3; 11:7; 17:8; 20:1–3; cf. ZPEB, 1:30–31).

---

10. *Jesus' power to heal and restore life*

8:40–56

[40]Now when Jesus returned, a crowd welcomed him, for they were all expecting him. [41]Then a man named Jairus, a ruler of the synagogue, came and fell at Jesus' feet, pleading with him to come to his house [42]because his only daughter, a girl of about twelve, was dying.

As Jesus was on his way, the crowds almost crushed him. [43]And a woman was there who had been subject to bleeding for twelve years, but no one could heal her. [44]She came up behind him and touched the edge of his cloak, and immediately her bleeding stopped.

[45]"Who touched me?" Jesus asked.

When they all denied it, Peter said, "Master, the people are crowding and pressing against you."

[46]But Jesus said, "Someone touched me; I know that power has gone out from me."

[47]Then the woman, seeing that she could not go unnoticed, came trembling and fell at his feet. In the presence of all the people, she told why she had touched him and how she had been instantly healed. [48]Then he said to her, "Daughter, your faith has healed you. Go in peace."

[49]While Jesus was still speaking, someone came from the house of Jairus, the synagogue ruler. "Your daughter is dead," he said. "Don't bother the teacher any more."

[50]Hearing this, Jesus said to Jairus, "Don't be afraid; just believe, and she will be healed."

[51]When he arrived at the house of Jairus, he did not let anyone go in with him except Peter, John and James, and the child's father and mother. [52]Meanwhile, all the people were wailing and mourning for her. "Stop wailing," Jesus said. "She is not dead but asleep."

[53]They laughed at him, knowing that she was dead. [54]But he took her by the hand and said, "My child, get up!" [55]Her spirit returned, and at once she stood up. Then Jesus told them to give her something to eat. [56]Her parents were astonished, but he ordered them not to tell anyone what had happened.

The third part of the section on Jesus' power is composed of two intertwined stories—a pattern of alternation common to all the synoptic accounts and apparently one that goes back to the tradition (see Introduction: Method of Composition). We must ask why the two events are so closely connected. In both, the power and compassion of Jesus are notably displayed. Also, in both we see the importance of faith. Another point of comparison may be that Jairus's daughter was about twelve years old, while the woman (vv.43–48) had suffered a hemorrhage the same period of time. Perhaps we ought also to reflect on the tension created for Jesus and his disciples by the two pressing needs: prevention of impending death, and helping a pathetic woman whose illness had isolated her from normal life and relationships.

40–42a The words "Now when Jesus returned" (v.40) establish a continuity with the preceding episodes and alert the reader to this sequence of Jesus' mighty works. Once again Luke shows us the popularity of Jesus. The only recent event to have caused such expectation was the episode in Gerasene territory, word of which must have spread immediately. The present section now before us ends, by contrast, with Jesus' command not to speak of the girl's healing (v.56). As a leader of the synagogue, Jairus was locally prominent (v.41; cf. Notes). In the extremity of his need, he humbled himself as a suppliant. Luke describes the girl as Jairus's "only" (*monogenēs*) daughter (v.42a). The term "only" (or "one and only," as in John 3:16 NIV) adds to the pathos, as it is used in Scripture to designate an only child who has died or is in mortal danger (cf. note on 7:12). The further detail "about twelve" points out that in Jewish society she was about to become a young lady of marriageable age. This intensifies the poignancy.

42b–46 The "crowds" (*ochloi*), now an integral part of the narrative, cover the woman's furtive approach to Jesus (42b). The verbs "almost crushed" (*synepnigon*), "crowding" (*synechousin*, v.45), and "pressing against" (*apothlibousin*) bring the scene to life. Luke does not specify the nature of the "bleeding" (v.43), which is usually taken to have been a gynecological problem. The restrictions imposed by Leviticus 15:25–33 and by Jewish custom (codified in M *Zabim*) would have radically affected the woman's life. But her primary problem was the discomfort and embarrassment of her prolonged malady. If Luke did not mention the failure of the physicians to help the woman (v.43; cf. Mark 5:26) because he was one himself, that would be understandable. Yet the omission may be of no more significance than others (as in v.42; cf. Mark 5:23).

More serious questions are raised by (1) the woman's touching his cloak (v.44), as though magical power could be transferred, and (2) by Jesus' awareness of the transfer of power apparently without knowledge of who had done this (vv.45–46). As to the first, the intrusion of Hellenistic ideas and superstitions may indeed have influenced her action; but Jesus did not quench the "smoldering wick" (Matt 12:20) of her faith; instead, he fanned it into flame (v.48). Elsewhere it is implied that God honored even stranger expressions of faith, presumably because imperfect knowledge did not hinder confidence in the Lord himself (cf. Acts 5:14; 19:11–12).

Regarding Jesus' awareness of the transfer of some of his power, his question (v.45) need not imply ignorance of the woman's identity but only his intention of singling her out. The dialogue (vv.45b–46) suggests that he knew only the fact that power had been transferred. (Just as Jesus was the bearer of the Spirit [see comment on 3:22], so he was the bearer of the power of God.) While at times he chose to heal people who had not expressed any faith, the reverse seems to be true here—viz., that someone with faith in him drew on his power without his conscious selection of that person. Since he bore the very power of God, and since God the Father had not assumed the voluntary human limitations the incarnate Son had, God could have extended his healing power through his Son even though Jesus may not yet have been aware of the woman's identity. "Power has gone out from me" (v.46) does not mean that Jesus' power was thereby diminished, as though it were a consumable commodity.

47–48 The woman had desired to go unnoticed (v.47), possibly because of the embarrassment of her illness or because of her audacity in breaking her ritual isolation to touch Jesus' cloak. Her public confession of faith may constitute the purpose for which Jesus asked, "Who touched me?" (v.45). Jesus prefaced his traditional words of benediction (v.48) by words of grace (see comment on 7:50).

49–50 The episode of the sick woman delayed Jesus until word of the death of Jairus's daughter reached him (v.49). Yet the woman's healing also paved the way for Jesus' words in v.50.

51–56 It was only on particular occasions that Jesus selected Peter, James, and John alone (v.51) to be with him—e.g., at the Transfiguration (Matt 17:1; Mark 9:2; Luke 9:28) and in Gethsemane (Matt 26:37; Mark 14:33). The secrecy involved and the command to silence (v.56) may seem incomprehensible to some apart from the awkward theory of the "messianic secret" (see comments on 7:20–23; 9:21 and on Mark 9:9 in this volume). In actuality Jesus often tried to avoid publicity to prevent premature or misguided declarations of his messiahship from being made. Of course, it would be hard to keep silent about the girl's restoration to active life; but the use of the word "asleep" (v.52) might have diverted the attention of the mourners and others from Jesus to the girl. While Jesus' statement "she is . . . asleep" (*katheudei*) meant that her death was not forever but only till the Resurrection (cf. John 11:11; 1 Thess 4:13–14), the others probably assumed that she had, after all, only been in a coma. If they thought she was only revived, not raised from death, Jesus could thus reserve the public acknowledgment of his messiahship till the proper time. But the words "her spirit returned" (v.55) plainly imply that the child actually was dead. Because of these words, Marshall (*Gospel of Luke*, p. 348) suggests that the miracle is not to be described as a resuscitation of a body but as the calling back of the girl's spirit. The secrecy of this miracle is in contrast with the public nature of the raising of the young man from Nain (7:16–17).

11. Sending out the Twelve

9:1–6

> ¹When Jesus had called the Twelve together, he gave them power and authority to drive out all demons and to cure diseases, ²and he sent them out to preach the kingdom of God and to heal the sick. ³He told them: "Take nothing for the journey—no staff, no bag, no bread, no money, no extra tunic. ⁴Whatever house you enter, stay there until you leave that town. ⁵If people do not welcome you, shake the dust off your feet when you leave their town, as a testimony against them." ⁶So they set out and went from village to village, preaching the gospel and healing people everywhere.

Luke describes the mission of the Twelve in less detail than does Matthew, who presents it as one of his five major discourses. Some of the instructions that appear in Matthew 10:1–10 (as well as the saying about the harvest in Matt 9:37–38) are not found here in Luke 9 but rather among the instructions to the group of seventy-two Jesus sent out (Luke 10:1–12). There are a large number of verbal similarities between the accounts in Matthew 10, Mark 6, Luke 9, and Luke 10, along with some apparent discrepancies (see comments on each passage in this volume of EBC). The usual approach to these textual phenomena is to postulate an intertwining of traditions. There is also the possibility that Jesus gave approximately similar instructions on different occasions, and that parts of these instructions were also repeated in the early church as normative guidelines. (For example, the teaching in Matt 10:10 about the worker being worth his keep is repeated in Luke 10:7; 1 Cor 9:14; 1 Tim 5:18; and in *Didache* 13:1.) What is described in these "sending" passages in the Gospels is not appointment to a permanent office but commissioning for an immediate task. The practice of sending a man on a mission empowered to act with full authority on behalf of the sender is known from the Talmud (j Hagigah 1.8). Such an appointment could therefore be repeated using words essentially similar though varying in detail. The common theme that is found in the biblical passages cited above, and in others such as 3 John 5–7, is that the servants of Christ should go forth, not seeking support from unbelievers, but trusting God completely to supply their needs through his people.

1–2 The "Twelve" (*dōdeka*) receive both the "power" (*dynamis*) and the "authority" (*exousia*) to do works of the sort Jesus has performed in the episodes Luke has thus far reported. Luke includes the word *dynamis*, which does not occur in either Matthew 10 or Mark 6. While the word *dynamis* itself is not usually prominent in Luke's vocabulary (it is absent in 9:27, but the parallel in Mark 9:1 has it), nevertheless signs and wonders are important in his books, especially in Acts. This is because Luke stresses the validation of the Gospel by, among other means, the apostles' miraculous power as God's messengers. Others were claiming supernatural powers (cf. the Jewish sorcerer Bar-Jesus, or Elymas, and the itinerant Jewish exorcists, Acts 13:6–10; 19:13); so it was necessary for Jesus' disciples to have both "authority" (*exousia*) and "power" (*dynamis*). This principle appears in a different context in Luke 5:24. The connection between casting out demons and the coming of the kingdom is not as clear there as in 11:20; but the double mention of the ministry of healing here in 9:1–2 suggests that relationship. The authority of the Twelve extends over "all" (*panta*) demons. None is too powerful for them.

3 The instructions indicate the urgency of the task. The severely limited provisions Jesus allows the Twelve to take with them may be intended to express their dependence on God alone. Without bread or money they would need to be given daily food. The forbidden "bag" (*pēra*) may be the kind frequently used by itinerant philosophers and religious mendicants for begging (cf. Notes). The disciples are learning to trust God for food, protection, and shelter. (See comment on the apparent reverse of these instructions in Luke 22:3.)

4 The disciples should receive hospitality graciously. Hospitality was important as well as necessary in days of difficult travel conditions and poor accommodations at inns. The disciples are not to move about from house to house, a practice that might gain them more support but would insult their hosts.

In "The Passing of Peregrinus," the satirist Lucian described a Cynic preacher, Peregrinus, who for a time pretended to be a Christian and lived off the generosity of Christian hosts. The *Didache* (chs. 11–12) also warns of wandering false prophets and contains careful instructions about receiving prophets.

5 The disciples will also encounter those who refuse them a welcome. As a solemn symbol of judgment, the disciples are to shake the dust of an unresponsive town off their feet, just as Jewish travelers might do on returning from pagan territory (SBK, 1:571). This action expressed symbolically what Jesus would say about Korazin and Bethsaida in 10:13–15. Jesus himself later wept over Jerusalem's unresponsiveness (19:41).

Elsewhere, Jesus specifies the kind of person who is to have the privilege of supporting the disciples. He must be a "worthy [*axios*] person" (Matt 10:11), a "man of peace" (*huios eirēnēs*, lit., "son of peace," Luke 10:16). Such a person is clearly in sympathy with the message brought by Jesus' disciples.

6 Luke concludes this section with a summary of the mission of the Twelve, including another reference to preaching and healing. Their instructions had not included any limitation of scope such as in Matthew 10:5. "Everywhere" (*pantachou*) may even indicate the opposite.

Notes

1, 2, 6 Luke uses two words for healing without a difference in meaning: θεραπεύω (*therapeuō*) and ἰάομαι (*iaomai*). See DNTT, 2:164–69.

3 The problem of Luke's "no staff" (μήτε ῥάβδον, *mēte rhabdon*, lit., "neither a staff"; cf. Matt 10:10—μηδὲ ῥάβδον [*mēde rhabdon*, "nor a staff"]) over against the apparently contradictory words in Mark 6:8—μηδὲν . . . εἰ μή ῥάβδον μόνον (*mēden . . . ei mē rhabdon monon*, "nothing . . . except a staff") has several possible explanations.

1. Luke follows Q, which contains the original wording; he is not intentionally changing Mark (Marshall, *Luke: Historian and Theologian*, p. 352). This may well be so, but the difference remains.

2. The authors had different types of staves in mind, one for walking and the other, a club, for protection (E. Power, "The Staff of the Apostles, a Problem in Gospel Harmony," *Biblica* 4 [1923]: 241–66). But only one Greek word is used for "staff."

3. Mark adapts his wording so as to parallel the instructions to Israel (Exod 12:11). But the difference remains.

4. Two similar sounding Aramaic words are used, meaning "except" and "and not" respectively (M. Black, *An Aramaic Approach to the Gospels and Acts*, 3d ed. [Oxford: Clarendon, 1967], pp. 216ff.). This is attractive but improbable; it does not solve the problem for those who hold to the inerrancy of the canonical Greek text.

5. Jesus taught that the disciples were not to procure a staff if they lacked one. But this fits Matt 10:10 better than Luke, for Matt 10:9 uses κτάομαι (*ktaomai*, "acquire"), whereas Luke uses αἴρω (*airō*, "take").

6. Jesus meant that they were not to take an *extra* staff. This would fit the wording of each Gospel, but it leaves the question of whether anyone would normally carry two staffs.

The answer probably lies near the approaches of 1, 5, and 6. Whether or not one chooses some such explanation or does not attempt a harmonization of detail, the intent in all three Synoptics is the same: travel light, trust God, accept the gracious help of pious people, and do not let a mere staff interfere with these principles.

Πήρα (*pēra*, "bag") was commonly used to designate both a leather pouch in which provisions could be carried and a wallet for collecting alms (cf. LSJ, s.v.; BAG, s.v.; Deiss LAE, pp. 108–10). The latter use was so well known and such a symbol of itinerant, begging preachers that it probably has that sense here.

12. Herod's perplexity

9:7–9

> [7]Now, Herod the tetrarch heard about all that was going on. And he was perplexed, because some were saying that John had been raised from the dead, [8]others that Elijah had appeared, and still others that one of the prophets of long ago had come back to life. [9]But Herod said, "I beheaded John. Who, then, is this I hear such things about?" And he tried to see him.

Jesus has come to the end of his great Galilean ministry. The subsequent events take place to the north and east of Galilee and culminate in the confession of Jesus' messiahship, followed by the first passion prediction (vv. 19–27). These events are related more fully in Mark 6:30–8:26 along with other episodes Luke chose not to include, perhaps (1) because of their similarity with the other examples of Jesus' ministry he includes elsewhere, (2) because of the limitations of space, and (3) in order to move quickly to Peter's confession in 9:18–21. It is also possible that Luke used an earlier draft of Mark that lacked these parts, but this cannot be proved. Luke does include the event that is most important for his purpose, the feeding of the five thousand (9:10–17). And here, prior to that narrative, he states that Herod "was perplexed" (*diēporei*) about Jesus. This is of great importance in the sequence of Luke's Gospel because it introduces the question "Who then is this . . .?" (v.9; cf. Mark 6:16, where Herod answers his own question). This all-important question is picked up again in vv. 18–20.

7–9 "All that was going on" (*ta ginomena panta*, v.7) probably refers to the activities of both Jesus (cf. Matt 14:1) and the disciples on their mission. In Matthew 14:2 and Mark 6:14, Herod is interested in the "powers" (*dynameis*) Jesus was reputed to have. (On the identity of Herod the tetrarch, see comments on 3:1. Luke uses the proper official title.) The questions of Jesus' identity and also of the reappearance of a dead prophet (v.8) are reintroduced in vv. 18–19 and parallels (cf. John 1:19–22). John the Baptist is naturally on Herod's mind (and doubtless also on his conscience). Luke makes only a brief reference to John's execution (cf. 3:19–20, described more fully in Matt 14:3–12; Mark 6:17–29). Herod was not able to see Jesus (v.9) but had his curiosity satisfied when Pilate sent Jesus to him (23:8–11).

13. Feeding the five thousand

9:10–17

> [10]When the apostles returned, they reported to Jesus what they had done. Then he took them with him and they withdrew by themselves to a town called Bethsaida, [11]but the crowds learned about it and followed him. He welcomed them and spoke to them about the kingdom of God, and healed those who needed healing.
> [12]Late in the afternoon the Twelve came to him and said, "Send the crowd

away so they can go to the surrounding villages and countryside and find food and lodging, because we are in a remote place here."
[13]He replied, "You give them something to eat."
They answered, "We have only five loaves of bread and two fish—unless we go and buy food for all this crowd." [14](About five thousand men were there.)
But he said to his disciples, "Have them sit down in groups of about fifty each." [15]The disciples did so, and everybody sat down. [16]Taking the five loaves and the two fish and looking up to heaven, he gave thanks and broke them. Then he gave them to the disciples to set before the people. [17]They all ate and were satisfied, and the disciples picked up twelve basketfuls of broken pieces that were left over.

The fact that this miracle is in all four Gospels indicates its importance. Luke's account is sparse and straightforward, a little shorter than Mark's, though including some additional words (e.g., on the kingdom, v.11).

10 The return of the disciples is the occasion for Jesus' withdrawal to Bethsaida (for the purpose of resting, according to Mark 6:31). This town was on the northeast side of the lake outside Herod's territory. Only Luke mentions its name.

11 The image of the shepherd in the parallels (Mark 6:34; cf. Matt 14:14) is here replaced by that of the Savior who "welcomed" (*apodexamenos*) all who came and told them about the kingdom. Thus even a time set aside for rest becomes an opportunity to fulfill the purpose expressed in Luke 4:43. As in Matthew 14:14, Luke mentions healings. He presents Jesus as having ministered to the total needs of people as he taught, healed, and fed those who came to him.

12–13 Each of the Synoptics records the disciples' unimaginative suggestion that the crowds be sent away to find their own food (v.12; Matt 14:15; Mark 6:36) and Jesus' response, "You give them something to eat" (v.13; Matt 14:16; Mark 6:37), putting the responsibility back on the disciples. The loaves (*artoi*) were a basic food, often eaten stuffed with fish (*ichthys*) from the Sea of Galilee.

14–17 The crowd was much greater than five thousand, since there were that many men (*andres*, v.14), plus women and children (Matt 14:21). Luke briefly summarizes the miracle, showing the orderliness of the distribution, Jesus' thanks (v.16, providing a lasting example for Christian table fellowship in the presence of God), and the adequacy of the food (v.17). Luke's description of the miracle does not direct attention to the Lord's Supper, though there are some common factors.

Notes

16 Εὐλόγησεν αὐτούς (*eulogēsen autous*) could mean "he blessed them," i.e., the fish, as an act of consecration (KJV, NASB), or "he gave thanks for them," which is the sense of NIV. The latter meaning is supported by Marshall, who takes *autous* to be an accusative of respect rather than a direct object; so "Jesus' prayer of thanks will here be one of thanks for what God is able to do to the bread" (*Gospel of Luke*, p. 362).

D. *Climax of Jesus' Galilean Ministry (9:18–50)*

1. *Peter's confession of Christ*

9:18–21

> [18]Once when Jesus was praying in private and his disciples were with him, he asked them, "Who do the crowds say I am?"
> [19]They replied, "Some say John the Baptist; others say Elijah; and still others, that one of the prophets of long ago has come back to life."
> [20]"But what about you?" he asked. "Who do you say I am?"
> Peter answered, "The Christ of God."
> [21]Jesus strictly warned them not to tell this to anyone.

Luke moves directly from the miracle of multiplying the loaves and fishes, which pointed to Jesus' messiahship, to Peter's confession of that messiahship. To do this, Luke omits, or includes elsewhere, the material in Mark 6:45–8:26 (cf. comments on 9:7–9).

If the priority of Mark (or Matthew) is assumed, questions regarding the genuineness and literary history of this narrative properly belong to the study of those Gospels (cf. comments on Matt 16:13–20; Mark 8:27–30 in this volume.) However, it is important to recognize the contextual integrity of its position at this point in Luke, following Herod's question about Jesus' identity (v.9) and the feeding of the five thousand, with its messianic implications. It leads directly to the transfiguration narrative through the natural transition of v.28.

Theologically, this is the most important statement thus far in Luke. It is the first time a disciple refers to Jesus as Messiah (cf. 2:11, 26; 3:15; 4:41). Observe that immediately after Peter's great declaration, Jesus predicts his rejection, death, and resurrection (v.22), thus shedding light on the implications of his messiahship.

18–19 Luke's introduction to the dialogue between Jesus and his disciples is unique in two respects: he omits reference to Caesarea Philippi and inserts a reference to Jesus at prayer (v.18; cf. Matt 17:13; Mark 8:27). The omission is surprising because one might have expected Luke, with his interest in the Gentile world, to show Jesus' penetration of the area of Caesarea, where extant inscriptions still show the influence of Hellenistic religion. On the contrary, Luke apparently disconnects Peter's confession from time and space in order to emphasize the link between the miraculous feeding and also Jesus' intimate fellowship with God, as exemplified in his praying. This is one of the insights Luke gives us into Jesus' prayer life (cf. 3:21; 6:12; 11:1). Jesus asks for the opinion of the "crowds" (*ochloi*, in place of *anthrōpoi* ["men"], Matt 16:13; Mark 8:27), a word Luke frequently uses to draw attention to the uncommitted masses of people who heard Jesus. The responses (v.19) echo the rumors expressed in vv.7–8.

20 "Christ" (*Christos*) represents the Hebrew word for "anointed" and was first an adjective before it came to be used as a proper name. Its OT occurrences with the idea of a coming anointed King include Psalm 2:2 and Daniel 9:26. The idea, without the title, appears in such passages as Isaiah 9:6–7; 11:1–16. The additional words "of God" in Luke do not explicitly express sonship as does the longer phrase in the parallel in Matthew 16:17, but they do emphasize Jesus' divine commission.

21 The command not to tell others (cf. comments on 8:51–56) probably stems from two circumstances: (1) the Jewish people, chafing under the domination of Rome, were all too ready to join a messianic revolutionary; and (2) there was apparently an understanding that one should not claim messiahship for himself but should first do the works of the Messiah and then be acclaimed as such by others (see Longenecker, *Early Jewish Christianity*, pp. 71ff.). The idea that Mark had imposed a motif of secrecy (the so-called messianic secret) on the tradition of Jesus' teachings is neither a necessary nor a provable hypothesis for explaining Jesus' commands to silence in Mark and the other Gospels (cf. comments on 7:20–23; 8:56).

2. The suffering and glory of the Son of Man

9:22–27

> [22]And he said, "The Son of Man must suffer many things and be rejected by the elders, chief priests and teachers of the law, and he must be killed and on the third day be raised to life."
>
> [23]Then he said to them all: "If anyone would come after me, he must deny himself and take up his cross daily and follow me. [24]For whoever wants to save his life will lose it, but whoever loses his life for me will save it. [25]What good is it for a man to gain the whole world, and yet lose or forfeit his very self? [26]If anyone is ashamed of me and my words, the Son of Man will be ashamed of him when he comes in his glory and in the glory of the Father and of the holy angels. [27]I tell you the truth, some who are standing here will not taste death before they see the kingdom of God."

22 This statement is known as the first passion prediction. Although there had been foreshadowings of a dark fate for Jesus—Simeon's prediction (2:35) and Jesus' statement about the bridegroom (5:35)—here in Jesus' words is the first explicit recitation in Luke of the sequence of events at the close of his life. Some scholars find it difficult to accept the authenticity of such a prediction. Arguments pro and con tend to revolve around subjective judgments as to what Jesus might or might not have foreseen at this point in his ministry and what may or may not have been added editorially. The entire following teaching on discipleship requires some basic understanding of the Passion and, indeed, of the Crucifixion, since Jesus mentions the Cross (v.23). The use of the term "Son of Man" in vv.22, 26 is understandable, assuming that (1) Jesus used it frequently, (2) that he used it especially in connection with his passion, and (3) that the occurrence of the term in Matthew 16:14 is not editorial but reflects Jesus' actual use of it in his initial question to the disciples.

23 The person who wants to be Jesus' disciple—viz., "come after me" (*opisō mou erchesthai*)—can only truly be said to "follow" (*akoloutheitō*) him when he has made and implemented a radical decision to "deny" (*arnēsasthō*) himself. This verb functions as a polar opposite to the verb "confess" (*homologeō*), which has the sense of acknowledging a thing or a person. We should therefore on the one hand "confess" Christ, i.e., acknowledge him and identify ourselves with him, but on the other hand "deny" ourselves. This means that as Christians we will not set our desires and our will against the right Christ has to our lives. It does not mean cultivating a weak, nonassertive personality or merely denying ourselves certain pleasures. Furthermore, we are to recognize that we now live for the sake of Christ, not for our own sake. The next words about the daily cross explain and intensify this principle. A condemned criminal was forced to carry one bar of his cross to the place of execution. He was "on a one-way journey. He'd not be back" (Morris, *Luke*, p. 170). To take up the cross daily is to live each day, not for self, but for Christ.

24–26 These two statements (vv.24–25) show the futility of clinging to one's "life" (*psyche*), because that, paradoxically, would result in losing the very self one wants to preserve. In contrast, the person who invests his life for God finds that, like the kernel of wheat planted in the ground (John 12:24), the "buried" life is not lost after all. Jesus next uses a "magnificent hyperbole" (Morris, *Luke*, p. 170) to emphasize his point. The world the disciple is willing to forfeit rather than lose his "very self" is, after all, to be succeeded by the new order when the Son of Man comes in glory (v.26). If one seeks gain by letting the world's view of Christ make him ashamed of the Lord, he rightly draws a corresponding response from the glorified Son of Man. Mention of the fact that the glory is Christ's own, along with that of the Father and of the angels, heightens the contrast with the shame Christ experienced in the world.

27 This is a perplexing verse. "Some who are standing here" (*tines tōn autou hestekotōn*) may refer to the disciples as a group as opposed to the crowd, or to some of the disciples as opposed to the rest of the disciples. Marshall (*Gospel of Luke*, in loc.) argues well for the former. But both are possible. Even if the larger group from whom the "some" are selected is broader than the Twelve, that does not mean that the select group includes all or even most of the Twelve.

There have been a number of different proposals as to what specific experience Jesus had in mind when he said these words. If he meant the future consummation of a literal kingdom, he would have been mistaken, as that has not yet occurred. He may have meant Pentecost, for the coming of the Spirit brought the dynamic of the kingdom (Mark 9:1 has the word "power" [*dynamis*]), but the imagery is not obvious. The resurrection of Christ declared him "with power to be the Son of God" (Rom 1:4), but that event does not seem to be understood in Scripture as an expression of the kingdom as such. It is true that Pentecost and the Resurrection are expressions of the same power, by which the kingdom of God proved itself over the kingdom of Satan and his demons in Jesus' casting out of demons.

There is, however, another event, the Transfiguration (vv.28–36), which Luke is about to describe, that may suit the saying better. It focuses even more sharply on the kingdom. The Transfiguration is, among other things, a preview of the Parousia, which event is clearly connected with the reign of Christ (see comment below on vv.28–36). Moreover, the specific reference to the brief interval of time between this saying and the Transfiguration, which is made even more specific by Luke— "about eight days after Jesus said this" (v.28)—tightens the connection between the saying and that event. In 2 Peter 1:16–18, Peter mentions in connection with the Transfiguration the elements of power and the coming of Jesus that are associated with the kingdom. If Jesus was referring to the Transfiguration in this saying, then the "some" who would not die before seeing the kingdom were Peter, James, and John, who saw Jesus transfigured. Why Jesus said they would "not taste death" before participating in an event only days away is perplexing. But he may have chosen those words because most people despaired of seeing the glory of the kingdom in their lifetime.

3. The Transfiguration

9:28–36

[28]About eight days after Jesus said this, he took Peter, John and James with him and went up onto a mountain to pray. [29]As he was praying, the appearance of his face changed, and his clothes became as bright as a flash of lightning. [30]Two men, Moses and Elijah, [31]appeared in glorious splendor, talking with Jesus. They spoke about his departure, which he was about to bring to fulfillment at Jerusalem. [32]Peter and his companions were very sleepy, but when they became fully awake, they saw his glory and the two men standing with him. [33]As the men were leaving Jesus, Peter said to him, "Master, it is good for us to be here. Let us put up three shelters—one for you, one for Moses and one for Elijah." (He did not know what he was saying.)
[34]While he was speaking, a cloud appeared and enveloped them, and they were afraid as they entered the cloud. [35]A voice came from the cloud, saying, "This is my Son, whom I have chosen; listen to him." [36]When the voice had spoken, they found that Jesus was alone. The disciples kept this to themselves, and told no one at that time what they had seen.

This glorious transformation of the appearance of Christ is the most significant event between his birth and passion. In each of the synoptic Gospels, it stands as a magnificent christological statement. Both the transformation itself and the divine commentary expressed in the Voice from heaven declare Jesus Christ to be the beloved Son of God. Luke emphasizes a further dimension of the event—the suffering that lay ahead of God's chosen Servant. Luke does this both through the conversation of Moses and Elijah (vv.30–31) and through a slightly different wording of the message of the Voice. In addition to the main elements of the Transfiguration itself and the words from heaven, the narrative contains several motifs of deep significance: the eight day interlude (v.28), the mountain, Moses and Elijah (v.30), Jesus' impending "departure" (*exodos*, v.31), the shelters (v.33), and the cloud (v.34).

Two frames of reference will help us understand these motifs. One is the Exodus of the people of Israel from Egypt with the events at Mount Sinai, especially Moses' experience on the mount (Exod 24). The other is the second coming of Christ, the "Parousia" (cf. reference in v.26). These two frames of reference—one past, the other future—will help us understand the biblical imagery the events of the transfiguration episode would have brought to the minds of the disciples and all later readers familiar with Scripture.

There seems to be a pattern involving the two adjoining sections—vv.18–27 and vv.28–36. Three themes are stated and then repeated in reverse (chiastic) order. The first theme is the affirmation of Jesus' identity as the Messiah (v.20); the second is the prediction of his passion (v.22); and the third is the promise of his glory (v.26). In the transfiguration narratives the order is reversed (not only in Luke, but also, except for the words about his "departure," in Matthew and Mark), and the three themes are portrayed dramatically. The third theme, that of Jesus' glory, is first portrayed (v.29). The prediction of his passion is confirmed by the conversation between Moses and Elijah (v.30). The identity of Jesus is the subject of the heavenly proclamation (v.35).

28 Luke's note on the passage of time—"about eight days after Jesus said this" (*meta tous logous toutous hōsei hēmerai oktō*, lit., "after these words about eight days")—is less precise than "after six days" in Matthew and Luke. It is obviously an alternative way of indicating the passage of approximately one week. However, commentators have not agreed as to any specific reason for the different wording. Luke is, as pointed out above, more precise than the other Synoptics in linking the Transfiguration with Jesus' preceding sayings by a specific reference to Jesus' "words." There may be an allusion here to the time Moses waited on Mount Sinai for the revelation of God (Exod 24:15-16). This is even more likely in Matthew and Mark, where the phrase "after six days" corresponds directly to the period Moses waited.

Peter, James, and John had been taken into Jesus' confidence elsewhere, e.g., at 8:51 and in the Garden of Gethsemane (Mark 14:33). Luke uses the definite article *to* ("the") with "mountain," from which we may infer that the original readers knew what location he had in mind. On the other hand, the construction might indicate that Luke uses "mountain" symbolically. Symbolism is not infrequent in references to mountains, in Matthew especially; but this does not rule out a specific geographical location. The locale of the Transfiguration could have been any high mountain (Mark 9:2; cf. Notes). The article with *oros* ("mountain") is normal in similar grammatical constructions in the Gospels (except for Matt 5:14). If we think of the Exodus as a frame of reference, then Sinai is symbolically in mind; if the Parousia, then the Mount of Olives may be symbolized (Zech 14:4; Acts 1:10-12).

Once again Luke mentions that Jesus is at prayer, an observation repeated in v.29 but absent from the account in Matthew 17:1-2; Mark 9:2.

29 Luke omits the actual word "transfigured" (*metemorphōthē*, used in Matt 17:2, Mark 9:2), possibly to avoid a term that might have suggested Hellenistic ideas of an epiphany, the appearance of a god. Instead he describes the remarkable alteration of Jesus' face and the dazzling whiteness of his clothing, "bright as a flash of lightning" (*exastraptōn*).

30-31 Moses and Elijah also appear in this scene of supernatural glory (NIV, "glorious splendor," *en doxē*, lit., "in glory," only in Luke). Nevertheless, Luke still describes them in ordinary human terminology (*andres*, "men"; cf. 24:4 and comments). Scholars debate the significance of Moses' and Elijah's presence. The old view that they represent the Law and the Prophets respectively does not do justice to the rich associations each name has in Jewish thought. Moses had a mountaintop experience at Sinai; his face shone (Exod 34:30; 2 Cor 3:7); he was not only a lawgiver but also a prophet—indeed the prototype of Jesus (Deut 18:18). Elijah was not only a prophet but was also related to the law of Moses as symbolizing the one who would one day turn people's hearts back to the covenant (Mal 4:4-6). In Jewish thought, Elijah was an eschatological figure, that is, one associated with the end times. So one may say that in the transfiguration scene Moses is a typological figure who reminds us of the past (the Exodus), Moses being a predecessor of the Messiah, while Elijah is an eschatological figure pointing to the future as a precursor of the Messiah. Each man was among the most highly respected OT figures; both had one distinctive thing in common—their strange departure from this world. Elijah was taken up to heaven in a whirlwind (2 Kings 2:11), and Moses was buried by the Lord (Deut 34:6). (The disposition of Moses' body was a matter of speculation in ancient Judaism, cf. Jude 9.) In summary, it seems that the presence of Moses and Elijah on the Mount of Transfiguration draws attention, first, to the place of Jesus in continuing the redemptive work of God from the Exodus to the future eschatological consummation; second, to the appropriateness of Jesus' association with heavenly figures; and, third, to the superiority of Jesus over even these great and divinely favored heroes of Israel's past.

The conversation (v.31) is about Jesus' "departure" (*exodos*, lit., his "exodus"). In 2 Peter 1:15 the term means death. But here in Luke it also recalls the redemptive work of God in the Exodus from Egypt. Jesus' coming death was one that he would deliberately accomplish (*hēn ēmellen plēroun*, "which he was about to bring to fulfillment"). Luke portrays Jesus as moving unhurriedly toward the accomplishment of his goals (e.g., 4:43; see comments there). He specifies Jerusalem as the city of destiny for Jesus (v.31; see esp. comments on 13:31–35; cf. 9:51; 18:31). Thus Luke, having knowledge of this saying, which perhaps Matthew and Mark did not, included it to reinforce Jesus' passion prediction in v.22.

32 The writers of the Gospels use fear and sleepiness to indicate the slowness of the disciples to understand and believe. On this point see the explanation of Peter's words in v.33 in Mark 9:6 and the way Mark and Luke handle the sleepiness of the disciples at Gethsemane in different ways [Mark 14:40; Luke 22:45].) It is not clear from the Greek whether they were only drowsy but managed to keep awake or whether they actually fell asleep and woke up. At the least they were far from alert during the conversation about Jesus' approaching passion; and the spectacular scene aroused them thoroughly.

33 Only Luke mentions that it was as Moses and Elijah "were leaving" (*diachōrizesthai*, present tense) that Peter made the suggestion to make three shelters. This may imply that Peter did this to keep them from going. Both Luke's parenthesis here and Mark's in 9:6 show that Peter's suggestion was highly inappropriate. His use of "Master" (*epistata*, cf. 5:5) is itself appropriate (cf. "Lord" in Matt 17:4; "Rabbi" in Mark 9:5). His comment "It is good," though banal given the grandeur of the occasion, is not entirely out of order. The idea of three shelters is the main problem. These would have been temporary shelters, such as were used at Sukkoth, the Feast of Tabernacles. Peter's proposal of three, presumably equal, shelters may have implied a leveling perspective, putting Jesus on a par with the others. More than that, it connotes an intention to perpetuate the situation as though there were no "departure" (v.31) for Jesus to accomplish. Whether the shelters symbolize a future or present rest is not completely clear (cf. TDNT, 7:380; Marshall, *Gospel of Luke*, pp. 386–87; W. Liefeld, "Theological Motifs in the Transfiguration Narrative," in Longenecker and Tenney, *New Dimensions*, pp. 174–75). What does seem clear is that Peter wanted to prolong the stay of the heavenly visitors because he still failed to grasp the significance of the passion prediction of v.22 and its confirmation in v.31.

34 The cloud, like other elements in this narrative, can symbolize more than one thing, among them the cloud in the wilderness after the Exodus (Exod 13:21–22; 16:10; 24:16; 40:34–38). But clouds are also associated with the future coming of the Son of Man (Dan 7:13; cf. Mark 14:62), of the Messiah in intertestamental literature (2 Baruch 53:1–12; 4 Ezra 13:3), and with the two prophets in Revelation 11:12.

G.H. Boobyer (*St. Mark and the Transfiguration Story* [Edinburgh: T. & T. Clark, 1942]) sees in this symbolism a possible reference to the Parousia. H. Riesenfeld (*Jésus transfiguré. L'arrière-plan du récit évangélique de la Transfiguration de Notre-Seigneur*. Acta Seminarii Neotestamentici Upsaliensis 16 [Copenhagen: Ejnar Munksgaard, 1947], p.296) thinks it relates to Jewish concepts of eschatology, especially a future enthronement of the Messiah. Isaiah 4:5 describes a cloud, reminiscent of that which showed God's "shekinah" glory in the wilderness, which will appear during a future time of rest under the Messiah. The word "shekinah" is from the Hebrew *šākan*, which is translated by the Greek *episkiazō* ("overshadow") in Exodus 40:35 LXX. The same Greek verb is used here in v.34 ("enveloped"). But above all the cloud symbolizes the glorious presence of God (cf. Exod 19:16). This is notably true in the passage so clearly recalled by the Transfiguration (Exod 24:15–18). Matthew's use (17:5) of *phōteinē* ("bright") also suggests the shekinah glory. Though the disciples enter the cloud (v.34), a sense of the transcendence of God is retained as the Voice comes "from" (*ek*) the cloud (v.35).

35 The Voice speaking from the cloud is that of God the Father himself. No indirect or mediated message, no mere echo or "daughter of a voice," as Jewish writings put it, was sufficient to unmistakably identify Jesus. The awesome voice of God himself must be heard. The message expressed by the Voice is so clear that any uncertainty about the meaning of some of the other aspects of this great scene become comparatively unimportant. Whether seen in relation to the Exodus or to the second coming of the Son of Man, the focus throughout the Transfiguration is on the supreme person and glory of the Lord Jesus Christ. And now he is expressly declared to be God's Son—a declaration similar to that spoken by the Voice at Jesus' baptism (cf. 3:22; cf. also Matt 3:17; Mark 1:11). In Mark the Voice addresses Jesus directly; here it addresses the three disciples. In John 12:28–30, just preceding Jesus' passion, the Voice from heaven speaks for the "benefit" (v.30) of a whole crowd. In each case the Voice from heaven affirms that Jesus is the one who is sent by God and who has God's authority. These words spoken by the Voice on these three occasions affirm that Jesus is the Son of God, is obedient to him, and possesses divine authority for his mission. The words "this is my Son" (*houtos estin ho huios mou*), also in Matthew and Mark, recall Psalm 2:7. "Chosen" (*eklelegmenos*) for "whom I love" (Matt 17:5; Mark 9:7; KJV, "beloved") points us to Isaiah 42:1 ("my servant . . . my chosen one") and the concept of the Suffering Servant found in the broader context of Isaiah, especially 52:13–53:12.

"Listen to him" is not only a command; it is a correction of the human tendency to substitute human opinion for divine revelation (e.g., Peter after his confession in Matt 16:22, also implied here in the Transfiguration [v.33]). The words also fulfill Deuteronomy 18:15, which predicts the coming of the prophet God would raise up and commands, "You must listen to him." Jesus alone is the True Prophet, the Chosen Servant, and the Son of God.

36 All three synoptic Gospels note that at the end of the Transfiguration only Jesus was there with the disciples. So the scene ends with Jesus as the center of their attention. Luke's statement is concise and ends emphatically with the word "alone" (*monos*). Luke's comment on the silence of the disciples is shorter than Mark's very significant treatment of this (cf. Wessel's commentary on Mark, this vol., at Mark 9:9–10).

Notes

28 Τὸ ὄρος (*to oros*, "the mountain") has usually been identified as either Tabor, in Galilee, or Hermon, north of Caesarea Philippi. The former is doubtful, not only because of its distance from Caesarea Philippi, where Jesus had been about a week earlier, but because shortly after that time Josephus mentions that a Roman fortress was there (War II, 572–73 [xx.6]; IV, 54–61 [i.8]). Furthermore, though Tabor does stand out as the only mountain in its immediate area, it is not really "high" (Mark 9:2) but only 1,929 feet. Hermon, on the other hand, is high—9,232 feet. If Jesus went all the way to the summit, that would have required an exhausting climb of about six hours. Also, considering Hermon's remoteness, it is difficult to imagine such a large crowd (v.37), including scribes (cf. Mark 9:14), at its base. Moreover, the return trip from Hermon would not have been in the main "through Galilee" (Mark 9:30). A more likely place, not mentioned in tradition, is Meron, the highest mountain within Israel itself, 3,926 feet. It is just to the northwest of the Sea of Galilee. The distance from Caesarea Philippi is moderate; privacy would have been possible in the higher levels above the city of Safed (which, at 2,790 feet, is possibly the "city on a hill" of Matt 5:14); crowds, including scribes, would be normal on the lower slopes of the mountainside; and the subsequent short trip to Capernaum would have literally been "through Galilee" (Mark 9:30).

Literature on the Transfiguration includes H. Baltensweiler, *Die Verklärung Jesu* (Zurich: Zwingli-Verlag, 1959); Boobyer, *St. Mark and the Transfiguration;* H.C. Kee, "The Transfiguration in Mark: Epiphany or Apocalyptic Vision?" *Understanding the Sacred Text: Essays in Honor of Morton S. Enslin*, ed. J. Reumann (Valley Forge, Pa.: Judson, 1972); W. Liefeld, "Theological Motifs in the Transfiguration Narrative," Longenecker and Tenney, *New Dimensions*, pp. 162–79; H.-P. Müller, "Die Verklärung Jesu," ZNW 51 (1960): 56–64; A.M. Ramsay, *The Glory of God and the Transfiguration of Christ* (London: Darton, Longman and Todd, 1967); Riesenfeld, *Jésus transfiguré;* M. Thrall, "Elijah and Moses in Mark's Account of the Transfiguration," NTS 16 (1970): 305–17.

4. Healing a boy with an evil spirit

9:37–45

> [37]The next day, when they came down from the mountain, a large crowd met him. [38]A man in the crowd called out, "Teacher, I beg you to look at my son, for he is my only child. [39]A spirit seizes him and he suddenly screams; it throws him into convulsions so that he foams at the mouth. It scarcely ever leaves him and is destroying him. [40]I begged your disciples to drive it out, but they could not."
>
> [41]"O unbelieving and perverse generation," Jesus replied, "how long shall I stay with you and put up with you? Bring your son here."
>
> [42]Even while the boy was coming, the demon threw him to the ground in a convulsion. But Jesus rebuked the evil spirit, healed the boy and gave him back to his father. [43]And they were all amazed at the greatness of God.
>
> While everyone was marveling at all that Jesus did, he said to his disciples, [44]"Listen carefully to what I am about to tell you: The Son of Man is going to be betrayed into the hands of men." [45]But they did not understand what this meant. It was hidden from them, so that they did not grasp it, and they were afraid to ask him about it.

This healing is another significant example of the power of God over demons. It also implies Jesus' strong censure of the disciples for not performing the exorcism. But it is much shorter than the account in Mark and lacks the specific comment on prayer that concludes Mark's account. Moreover, Luke omits the intervening discussion on the coming of Elijah (Matt 17:10–13; Mark 9:11–13).

37–42 "The next day" (*tē hexēs hēmera*, v.37) may imply that the Transfiguration happened at night. If so, then that great event would have been even more striking, were that possible. The descent of Jesus and the disciples "from the mountain" meant a descent into the earthly world of illness, evil, and unbelief. The "large crowd" would be surprising if the location of the Transfiguration were Mount Hermon (cf. note on v.28). Since Luke was a physician, it is interesting that he does not identify the boy's condition as epilepsy, as Matthew 17:15 does. Clearly Luke is more concerned with the demonic aspect of the boy's affliction (v.42). The physical manifestations were similar to those of epilepsy—a fact that has contributed to the unfortunate misunderstanding of epilepsy down through the ages. Luke alone notes the continual debilitating oppression the boy endured (v.39). While three of the disciples were witnessing the Transfiguration, the others were helpless in the face of demonic power (v.40).

43a Instead of centering attention on the efficacy of prayer in exorcism, as Matthew and Mark do, Luke concludes his account of the boy's healing by speaking of the greatness of God. We might have expected Luke to dwell on the role of prayer, given his interest in it. He does have a saying similar to the one Matthew includes in his parallel to this narrative (Matt 17:21 mg.), but that is in another context (Luke 17:6). Actually the climax in the present story is typical of Luke, for it records the reaction of those who observe a healing by Jesus. They were "amazed" (*exeplēsonto*; cf. 4:32) at the "greatness" of God. Elsewhere Luke speaks similarly of people giving God glory (5:25; 7:16).

43b–45 This repetition of the prediction of Jesus' passion (cf. 9:22 and comments) might be considered as a separate section, had not Luke connected it closely with the preceding incident. This is not the case in Matthew 17:22 or Mark 9:30. Luke uses another word, *thaumazontōn* ("marveling," v.43b; cf. 43a), to describe the amazed reaction of the people to the healing. The passion prediction (v.44) serves to emphasize that Jesus' ultimate purpose went beyond such miracles. This time Jesus includes a reference to his betrayal. The failure of the people to understand (v.45), even at the very time they are marveling at the greatness of God's work through Jesus, is comparable to Peter's resistance to the first passion prediction immediately after his great confession (Matt 16:22). The people were not granted understanding of the meaning of Jesus' words. See the comparable situation in Luke 8:10 and its parallels (cf. commentary there). Here, however, the implication is that had they asked Jesus for help in understanding his words, they might have been given it.

5. Two cases of rivalry

9:46–50

> [46]An argument started among the disciples as to which of them would be the greatest. [47]Jesus, knowing their thoughts, took a little child and had him stand beside him. [48]Then he said to them, "Whoever welcomes this little child in my name welcomes me; and whoever welcomes me welcomes the one who sent me. For he who is least among you all—he is the greatest.

⁴⁹"Master," said John, "we saw a man driving out demons in your name and
we tried to stop him, because he is not one of us."
⁵⁰"Do not stop him," Jesus said, "for whoever is not against you is for you."

46–48 This passage naturally follows the preceding two verses. The disciples did not
understand Jesus' role as the Suffering Servant and so could not grasp its implications for them as his disciples. They were still thinking of the Messiah only in terms
of triumph, assuming, quite naturally, that their position was important. The issue
was not whether there would be rank in the kingdom but the nature and qualifications of such rank (v.46) The point of Jesus' reference to the "little child" (*paidion*,
v.47) does not illustrate simple faith (as in Matt 18:2–4). Nor does it refer to receiving a disciple who comes in the name of Jesus, as in Matthew 10:40–42. Rather, it
refers to receiving for the sake of Christ a person who has no status (v.48; cf. Matt
18:5). This is consistent with Jesus' (and Luke's) concern for neglected people. The
meaning, then, is that instead of seeking status for ourselves (out of pride as an
associate of the Messiah) we Christians should, as Jesus did, identify ourselves with
those who have no status at all, welcoming them to join us in the kingdom. To put
it another way, in Matthew 10 one receives a Christian apostle as consciously receiving Christ himself, whereas here in Luke 9 by ministering to a child one ministers,
without realizing it, to Christ himself.

49 The next episode reveals the apostles' attitude of rivalry. The issue is not orthodoxy but association. Far from merely invoking the name of Jesus in a formula
and without genuine faith (as did the seven sons of the Jewish priest Sceva, to whose
formula the demon refused to respond, Acts 19:13–16), the man referred to here
had actually been "driving out demons" through Jesus' name.

50 This verse is proverbial in form. The man was not against Jesus. Apparently he
had not yet joined the group of Jesus' disciples. Perhaps he represents those who
are "on the way" to joining the body of believers and who should be welcomed
rather than repulsed. In a different situation (Matt 12:30), Jesus used a reverse form
of this proverb and did so without contradicting the truth set forth here in Luke.

V. Teaching and Travels Toward Jerusalem (9:51–19:44)

This extensive section has no counterpart in Matthew or Mark, though much of its
material is found in other contexts in those Gospels. Luke 9:51 implies that Jesus
was setting out on a journey one would expect to be described in the succeeding
chapters. Yet these chapters say comparatively little about Jesus' traveling from one
place to another.

To be sure, we do find some clues showing that Jesus is moving toward Jerusalem:
e.g., 9:52—approaching Samaria; 10:38—"on their way . . . to a village where . . .
Martha opened her home" (presumably Bethany, near Jerusalem); 13:22—"Jesus
went through towns and villages . . . as he made his way to Jerusalem"; 13:32–33—
"I will reach my goal. . . . no prophet can die outside Jerusalem"; 17:11—"Now on
his way to Jerusalem, Jesus traveled along the border between Samaria and Galilee."

Following this section, Luke further notes Jesus' words "We are going up to Jerusalem" (18:31). Then he mentions Jesus' approach to Jericho (18:35; 19:1) and finally his arrival near Jerusalem (19:28–29). It is clear from all this that Jesus is now heading toward Jerusalem, not Galilee. However, he did not make one continuous journey from Galilee to Jerusalem. (See 10:38 and the subsequent note on 17:11, which poses a notorious problem [see comments, in loc.].)

To assume that Luke intends to describe a single continuous journey involves difficult problems, including the question of Luke's knowledge of geography raised by Conzelmann (*Theology of Luke*, pp. 60–73). To see the travel motif in this section as a mere literary or theological device entails some wrong preconceptions about what certainly appears to be a straightforward narrative. It is more reasonable and more consistent with the data to understand this section as showing that Jesus' ministry has entered a new phase and has taken on some new characteristics. Jesus follows routes that bring him away from Galilee and nearer to Jerusalem than his former itineraries did (except for visits for the feasts, as in John 2:13; 5:1 et al.). During this period Jesus is no longer committed to the locale of his former ministry but is looking toward Jerusalem and the Cross. Much of his teaching at this time is directed to the disciples. Warnings to the rich and complacent are prominent, as well as words aimed at the Pharisees. On several occasions he actually visits Jerusalem, where he proclaims the truth about himself and enters into controversy with those who oppose his claims.

If there is a travel motif in this section, it is not an artificial scheme but one that is (1) consistent with the nature of Jesus' ministry, which has been itinerant all along; (2) consistent with the emphasis on travel in both Luke and Acts, possibly to maintain the reader's interest; and (3) consistent with the fact that, while Jesus did not go directly from Galilee to Jerusalem, his mind was definitely set on the impending events he faced in that city. Even at times when he may have traveled north again, his ultimate goal was Jerusalem. This also accords with the prominence of Jerusalem in the Gospel of Luke (see comments especially on 13:33–34; 19:28, 41). (For bibliography on the characteristics of Luke 9:51–19:44, cf. Notes.)

Notes

9:51–19:44 There are many approaches to the characteristics of this large section of Luke. Some, such as the search for chiasms by Bailey and by Talbert and the comparison with Deuteronomy most recently by Drury, are suggestive and useful, even if overdone. The following is a partial bibliography of significant contributions to the subject: Bailey, *Poet and Peasant*, pp. 79–85; Drury, *Tradition and Design in Luke's Gospel*, pp. 138–64; C.F. Evans, "The Central Section of St. Luke's Gospel," in D.E. Nineham, ed., *Studies in the Gospels*, 1955), pp. 37–53; C.C. McCown, "The Geography of Luke's Central Section," JBL 57 (1938): 51–66; G. Ogg, "The Central Section of the Gospel According to St. Luke," NTS 18 (1971–72): 39–53; W.C. Robinson, Jr., "The Theological Context for Interpreting Luke's Travel Narrative (9:51ff.)," JBL 79 (1960): 20–31; Talbert, *Literary Patterns*, pp. 51–56.

A. *The New Direction of Jesus' Ministry* (9:51–10:24)

1. *Travel south through Samaria*

9:51–56

> [51]As the time approached for him to be taken up to heaven, Jesus resolutely set out for Jerusalem. [52]And he sent messengers on ahead, who went into a Samaritan village to get things ready for him, [53]but the people there did not welcome him, because he was heading for Jerusalem. [54]When the disciples James and John saw this, they asked, "Lord, do you want us to call fire down from heaven to destroy them?" [55]But Jesus turned and rebuked them, [56]and they went to another village.

51 Luke uses the transitional *egeneto de* (the Semitic "and it came to pass"), omitted by NIV for stylistic reasons. As observed above, there is now a major change in Jesus' orientation. At this significant turning point, Luke once again uses a word expressing fulfillment, *sympleroō*, translated "approached" in NIV (cf. Notes). God's plan is another step nearer fulfillment. The approaching goal is not only the death and resurrection but especially the ascension of Christ (cf. note on *analēmpsis*). In the account of the Transfiguration, Luke has a reference to Jesus' "exodus" (v.31; cf. v.22). But now that Jesus faces the Cross, Luke mentions the exaltation that would follow his "exodus." He "resolutely set out" (NIV's contemporary idiom for the Semitic is "set his face towards") for Jerusalem, the designated place of his passion. We shall be reminded again of this destination as Jesus draws nearer Jerusalem (19:28, 41).

52 Jesus "sent messengers on ahead." This custom is described further in the particular mission of the seventy-two disciples (10:1–16). In this instance they were not told to preach but simply to "get things ready for him," a fact that makes the attitude of James and John (v.54) even less appropriate.

53–54 The residents of the Samaritan village (v.52) reciprocated the hostile attitude of the Jews (v.53; cf. John 4:9). They were especially negative because Jesus was going to Jerusalem, which they refused to acknowledge as a valid center of worship (cf. John 4:20).

The history of the Samaritans is uncertain. Many hold that they were a mixed race since the fall of the northern kingdom of Israel. The king of Assyria deported the leaders of Israel, among them the religious teachers, replacing them with foreigners (2 Kings 17:6; 24–26). From that time on, the northern kingdom inhabitants received no further prophetic instruction and refused to acknowledge the continuing revelation received by the Jews in the southern kingdom. Some think that the Samaritans known in the NT arose in the early Hellenistic period (cf. H.G.M. Williamson, "Samaritans," NBD, rev. ed., 1062–63). Being semipagan, the Samaritans were a fringe segment of the Jewish world for which Jesus, and Luke following him, had a concern. They are not mentioned unfavorably elsewhere in Luke; on the contrary, he mentions them favorably in 10:30–37 and 17:11–19. James and John may have thought that Jesus would respond as Elijah had (v.54; 2 Kings 1:9–12).

55 Jesus' strong disapproval of James and John's suggestion is seen in his use of the word "rebuked" (*epetimēsen;* cf. 4:35, 41; 8:24). If the Samaritans were consciously rejecting Christ by rejecting his disciples, one would have expected that v.5 would apply—a mild reaction compared to that of James and John. But Jesus' messengers were rejected merely because they were Jews going to Jerusalem, as v.53 indicates.

Notes

51 Ἐν τῷ συμπληροῦσθαι τὰς ἡμέρας (en tō symplērousthai tas hēmeras) literally means "as the days were [or 'time was'] being fulfilled" rather than "as the time approached" (NIV; cf. RSV, NASB). It is true that συμπληρόω (symplēroō) can mean "approach," and the NIV translation does convey a sense of destiny. But in view of Luke's significant use of words of fulfillment and accomplishment (e.g., in 1:1; 4:21; 9:31; 22:16; 24:44), symplēroō probably continues that theme here. It would be awkward, in an English translation, to describe days as being "fulfilled"; but from the perspective of God's plan, that is the meaning (cf. TDNT, 6: 308-9). See also Jer 25:12, where the LXX ἐν τῷ πληρωθῆναι τὰ ἑβδομήκοντα ἔτη (en tō plērōthēnai ta hebdomēkonta etē) is translated "when the seventy years are fulfilled" (NIV).

Ἀναλήμψεως (analēmpseōs, "of his ascension"; NIV, "for him to be taken up to heaven") can refer to Jesus' death, since the word can be so used (BAG, s.v.). However, not only is there evidence in extracanonical literature for its use with reference to ascension, but also that is clearly the meaning of the verb form (ἀναλαμβάνω, analambanō) Luke used to describe the ascension of Jesus in Acts 1:2, 11.

54 The parallel between the disciples' suggestion and Elijah's action probably gave rise to the gloss "even as Elijah did" (see NIV mg.). The words were included in KJV but are absent from such important early texts as P 45,75 א B.

55 Some ancient texts add "And he said, 'You do not know what kind of spirit you are of, for the Son of Man did not come to destroy men's lives but to save them.' " The first part of the sentence, up to "you are of," is in the Western text D and a couple of versions. The rest is, with varying details, found in a number of texts generally lacking the stature of those MSS that omit them. Those that lack the questionable reading are P45,75 א A B C L W, among many others. The longer reading is in KJV, is bracketed in NASB, and is placed in a footnote in RSV and NIV. Marshall, after weighing arguments pro and con, including (pro) the appropriateness of the saying in the context and (con) the weak MS evidence and likelihood that a scribe would add words that seemed appropriate, concludes that in view of the "considerable doubt" the words should be either omitted or bracketed (*Gospel of Luke*, p. 408). Metzger (*Textual Commentary*, p. 148) also considers the claim to genuineness weak.

2. The cost of following Jesus

9:57-62

⁵⁷As they were walking along the road, a man said to him, "I will follow you wherever you go."

⁵⁸Jesus replied,"Foxes have holes and birds of the air have nests, but the Son of Man has no place to lay his head."

⁵⁹He said to another man, "Follow me."

But the man replied, "Lord, first let me go and bury my father."

⁶⁰Jesus said to him, "Let the dead bury their own dead, but you go and proclaim the kingdom of God."

⁶¹Still another said, "I will follow you, Lord; but first let me go back and say good-by to my family."

62Jesus replied, "No one who puts his hand to the plow and looks back is fit for service in the kingdom of God."

This is the second major treatment of discipleship in Luke (cf. v.23). The first two conversations (vv.57–60 through the words "bury their own dead") are found in Matthew 8:18–22. It is difficult to tell whether Matthew has omitted part of the material they had in common or whether Luke has used a combination of sources. There are some differences. The order of the dialogue in v.59 is the reverse of that in Matthew 8:21–22. Also, while a saying about the kingdom would have been equally at home in Matthew or Luke, the words "you go and proclaim the kingdom of God" are lacking in Matthew but made the central statement in Luke's section. The "man" of v.57 is a "teacher of the law" in Matthew 8:19.

The structure of this passage is noteworthy. The familiar "rule of three" is employed by Luke in recording three conversations. There is an interchange of order: in the first conversation the inquirer initiates the conversation and Jesus states the objection; in the second this is reversed; in the third the man both initiates the dialogue and raises the objection, with Jesus adding a comment. (On this structure, see Johannes P. Louw, "Discourse Analysis and the Greek New Testament," *Bible Translator* 24 [1973]: 104–8.) Each dialogue contains some theological language: "Son of man" (v.58), "proclaim the kingdom of God" (v.60), "service in the kingdom of God" (v.62). This shows that discipleship is not simply following Jesus in one's lifestyle but is involvement in the important work of the kingdom.

57–58 The man uses the terminology of discipleship, "follow" (v.57), and amplifies it with a sweeping promise. Jesus' reply is in accord with his prior definition of discipleship in v.23 and constitutes a comment on the man's "wherever you go." Since most men do have homes, "Son of Man" (v.58) must refer specifically to Jesus. The idea of the rejection—if not his actual suffering—of the Son of Man is implied in Jesus' words.

59–60 Since it was a religious, social, and family obligation to provide a suitable funeral for one's father, Jesus' refusal to permit this is a striking example of the radical transfer of loyalty he demanded in 14:25–27. To conjecture that the length of time required for mourning was the reason Jesus did not accept the excuse of the second man he asked to follow him, or that the man's father was not yet dead, misses the point. "The dead" who are to perform the burial are usually thought to be the spiritually dead who do not follow Jesus but remain at home. Manson's understanding (*Sayings of Jesus*, p. 73) of this as a paradoxical saying, meaning, "That business must look after itself," is appealing; but it loses the sharp thrust of the saying.

61–62 Although to "say good-by" (*apotaxesthai*, v.61) is not at all the emotional equivalent of a funeral (cf. vv.59–60), it still represents family duty that must be forsaken for service to Jesus. Danker (*Jesus*, p. 125) sees here (v.62) an allusion to the call of Elisha while plowing and his request to say good-by to his family (1 Kings 19:19–21; cf. Marshall, *Gospel of Luke*, p. 412). A further illustration of discipleship is keeping the hand on the plow. Jeremias (*Parables of Jesus*, p. 195, drawing on E.E. Bishop, *Jesus of Palestine* [London: Lutterworth, 1955], pp. 93–94) describes the plowman concentrating on the furrow before him, guiding the light plow with his left hand while goading the oxen with the right. Looking away would result in a crooked furrow.

Notes

62 The word "service" is not in the Greek text but is implied by the word εὔθετος (*euthetos*, "fit") and by the context.

3. Sending out the seventy-two

10:1–24

¹After this the Lord appointed seventy-two others and sent them two by two ahead of him to every town and place where he was about to go. ²He told them, "The harvest is plentiful, but the workers are few. Ask the Lord of the harvest, therefore, to send out workers into his harvest field. ³Go! I am sending you out like lambs among wolves. ⁴Do not take a purse or bag or sandals; and do not greet anyone on the road.

⁵"When you enter a house, first say, 'Peace to this house.' ⁶If a man of peace is there, your peace will rest on him; if not, it will return to you. ⁷Stay in that house, eating and drinking whatever they give you, for the worker deserves his wages. Do not move around from house to house.

⁸"When you enter a town and are welcomed, eat what is set before you. ⁹Heal the sick who are there and tell them, 'The kingdom of God is near you.' ¹⁰But when you enter a town and are not welcomed, go into its streets and say, ¹¹'Even the dust of your town that sticks to our feet we wipe off against you. Yet be sure of this: The kingdom of God is near.' ¹²I tell you, it will be more bearable on that day for Sodom than for that town.

¹³"Woe to you, Korazin! Woe to you, Bethsaida! For if the miracles that were performed in you had been performed in Tyre and Sidon, they would have repented long ago, sitting in sackcloth and ashes. ¹⁴But it will be more bearable for Tyre and Sidon at the judgment than for you. ¹⁵And you, Capernaum, will you be lifted up to the skies? No, you will go down to the depths.

¹⁶"He who listens to you listens to me; he who rejects you rejects me; but he who rejects me rejects him who sent me."

¹⁷The seventy-two returned with joy and said, "Lord, even the demons submit to us in your name."

¹⁸He replied, "I saw Satan fall like lightning from heaven. ¹⁹I have given you authority to trample on snakes and scorpions, and to overcome all the power of the enemy; nothing will harm you. ²⁰However, do not rejoice that the spirits submit to you; but rejoice that your names are written in heaven."

²¹At that time Jesus, full of joy through the Holy Spirit, said, "I praise you, Father, Lord of heaven and earth, because you have hidden these things from the wise and learned, and revealed them to little children. Yes, Father, for this was your good pleasure.

²²"All things have been committed to me by my Father. No one knows who the Son is except the Father, and no one knows who the Father is except the Son and those to whom the Son chooses to reveal him."

²³Then he turned to his disciples and said privately, "Blessed are the eyes that see what you see. ²⁴For I tell you that many prophets and kings wanted to see what you see but did not see it, and to hear what you hear but did not hear it."

Luke's account of Jesus' commissioning of the seventy-two, while in some points similar to that of the Twelve (9:1–6) but differing from it, fits well its immediate context; and in several respects it resembles Matthew's account of the commissioning of the Twelve. It continues the procedure of sending messengers ahead during Jesus' journey (9:52). At the same time, the obedient response of the seventy-two provides a contrast to the three men (9:57–62) whose excuse disqualified them from discipleship. The mere repetition of some travel instructions given the Twelve does not constitute a doublet. While the question of sources is complex (see comments at introduction to 9:1–6), the material here seems to be drawn from Q (cf. Matt 9:37–38; 10:7–16) and is properly included in this place. As noted in the introduction to 9:1–6, the instructions prescribed by Jesus were undoubtedly repeated frequently by Jesus and in the early church.

1 "After this" (*meta de tauta*) establishes the connection we have just observed with the context. The title "Lord" (*ho kyrios*) occurs only here among the various accounts of commissioning, possibly to emphasize the serious dominical aspect of the instructions—namely, that they came from the Lord Jesus himself. Not only does the commissioning of the seventy-two lack any restriction to Jewish hearers (Matt 10:5–6), but the number of missionaries sent out (cf. Notes) parallels the number of nations thought to exist in the world and so suggests the deliberate inclusion of Gentiles.

Sending messengers "two by two" (*ana duo*) was common not only among the early Christians (Mark 6:7; Luke 7:18–19; Acts 13:2; 15:27, 39–40; 17:14; 19:22) but also among the Jews. It provided companionship, protection, and the double witness prescribed in Deuteronomy 17:6; 19:15 (cf. Joachim Jeremias, *New Testament Theology. The Proclamation of Jesus* [New York: Scribners, 1971], p. 235). The seventy-two were to go everywhere Jesus was going. The extent of this mission underscores that of the church: to reach the "plentiful harvest." It may also look toward the conclusion of the church's mission at Jesus' return (cf. Matt 10:23).

2 Although the harvest imagery in Scripture usually refers to God's intervention in history through gathering his people together (cf. Matt 13:37–43), here it applies to the urgent missionary task of the present age (cf. Matt 9:37–38; John 4:35).

3 The imperative "go" (*hypagete*) and the untranslated exclamation *idou* ("behold") anticipate the difficulties of the journey. Wolves are natural enemies of sheep. No specific enemies are pointed out; the warning is a general one. The disciples are like "lambs" (*arnas*)—defenseless and dependent on God alone.

4 The limitations on what the seventy-two may take with them increases their vulnerability (see comment and note on 9:3). They must also be single-minded even to the extent of not becoming involved in time-consuming greetings (cf. 2 Kings 4:29).

5–6 Greetings (cf. v.4), which go beyond mere formality, are to be reserved for the hosts of the seventy-two. "Peace" (*eirēnē*), so familiar in Jewish salutations, has a rich connotation here (v.5). If the host has a proper attitude toward God (v.6), he will receive the blessing of the kingdom (v.9). "Man of peace" is literally "son of peace" (*huios eirēnēs*)—an idiomatic way of expressing not only a person's character but also the destiny he is worthy of. Such a person would be open to the kingdom message.

7 Like the Twelve (9:4), the seventy-two are to remain with their original hosts. As the Lord's servants, they are deserving of support by the Lord's people (cf. 1 Tim 5:18). For the definitive discussion of this principle of support for Christian workers, see 1 Corinthians 9:3–18, where Paul speaks (v.14) of what the Lord "commanded." Likewise John says that Christians are obligated to support the Lord's messengers who, unlike the other itinerant preachers of the first century, sought no help from unbelievers but trusted in God alone (3 John 5–8).

8 It is not clear whether the messengers feared being offered food prohibited to Jews. This would have been less likely in Samaria and central Judea than elsewhere. The words may have been preserved because of their appropriateness to later situations (cf. Acts 10:9–16; 1 Cor 10:27).

9 Healing and the proclamation of the kingdom are linked together. This accords both with the mission of the Twelve and with the ministry of Jesus (Luke 9:1–2, 11).

10–11 These verses introduce a transition to the consequences of rejecting the kingdom message. In 4:18–19, Jesus' quotation of Isaiah 61:1–2 stopped short of the words "and the day of vengeance of our God." Nevertheless that day is coming, and Luke includes such warnings of it as 6:24–26; 12:46–48; 16:23–24; 21:22.

12 Sodom, destroyed along with Gomorrah (Gen 19:24–29), represents the consequences of ignoring God's warning to repent (cf. Matt 10:15; 11:20–24 [almost verbally identical with the present text]; Rom 9:29 [quoting Isa 1:9]; 2 Peter 2:6; Jude 7). "More bearable" (*anektoteron*) probably relates not so much to the degree of punishment as to the degree of culpability. If Sodom cannot escape judgment, what hope does a city that rejects the Lord Jesus have?

13–14 The probable site of Korazin along with that of Bethsaida is near Capernaum, at the north end of the Sea of Galilee, where Jesus concentrated his ministry. The comparison with the pagan Phoenician towns of Tyre and Sidon suggests utter rebellion against the Lord. Those ancient towns suffered drastic judgment for their proud opposition to God and his people (Isa 23:1–18; Jer 25:22; 47:4; Ezek 26:1–28:23; Joel 3:4–8; Amos 1:9–10).

"Sackcloth" was a coarse, black material worn as a sign of mourning or repentance (cf. 1 Kings 21:27 for an example). "Ashes" could also symbolize repentance or contrition (e.g., Job 42:6). "Sitting" (or lying) on these was one custom; another was wearing the sackcloth and putting ashes on the head (cf. Esth 4:2–3, where both customs are followed).

15 Capernaum had the high privilege of hearing Jesus preach there frequently, but this privilege guaranteed neither its fame nor its survival. On the contrary, in language like that of Isaiah 14:12–15, Jesus graphically portrays Capernaum's fall to the "depths" (*heōs tou hadou*, lit., "to Hades"; cf. the fall of Satan in v.18; cf. also Rev 12:10).

16 Reception or rejection of Christ's messengers shows one's attitude to the Lord himself (cf. Christ's identification of himself with the "least" of his "brothers" in Matt 25:31–46). In the parable of the vineyard, both son and servants were rejected (Luke 20:9–17). Moreover, whoever rejects Christ also rejects Moses (John 5: 45–47).

17 Whatever their experiences may have been, the messengers returned to Jesus filled with joy. The power of the kingdom was effective against demons just as it was in the ministry of Christ (11:20). Exorcism must be done in the name of Christ; it is not an incantation but signifies his authority (contrast Acts 19:13–16).

18 The taunt-song describing the fall of the king of Babylon (Isa 14:4–11) and the fall of the "morning star" ("Lucifer," KJV, vv.12–21), to which Luke 10:15 alludes, also relates to Revelation 12:9. When the disciples exorcise demons, the forces of evil are shaken, symbolizing the defeat of Satan himself.

19 To have authority "to trample on snakes and scorpions" relates to the victorious work of Christ, who, according to the first promise of the gospel in Genesis 3:15, was to bruise (NIV, "crush") the head of the Serpent, the devil. The ultimate implication of overcoming "all the power of the enemy" is to be victorious over the chief enemy, i.e., through whose temptation Adam and Eve fell and sin entered into humanity. Therefore, Jesus' saying is far from an invitation to snake handling (cf. the instructions and context in vv.17–18 of the questionable ending of Mark 16).

20 This verse with its call to rejoicing in the supreme blessing of assurance of heaven is one of Jesus' great sayings. "Do not rejoice" does not exclude the disciples' taking joy in spiritual victories but rather introduces a strong and typically Semitic comparison. The idea of the names of God's faithful people being written down in heaven is common in biblical and extrabiblical Jewish writings. In those days it was natural to refer to this through the metaphor of a book or scroll (e.g., Exod 32:32–33; Ps 69:28; Dan 12:1; Mal 3:16; Rev 20:12–15).

21–22 The emphasis on joy combines with another subject of Luke's special interest —the Holy Spirit in the life of Christ. The apparent parallel to this passage (Matt 11:25–27) lacks the reference to joy and the Holy Spirit. Correspondingly, Luke omits the words that follow in Matthew—the invitation to those who are weary and burdened. With their allusion to the "yoke" (Matt 11:29–30) of the Jewish law, these words are not as appropriate for Luke's audience as for Matthew's.

Verses 21–22 are of great doctrinal importance because they show (1) God's sovereignty in imparting revelation, (2) the relationship between the Father and the Son, and (3) the privilege the disciples had of participating in this instance of messianic revelation and salvation.

Jesus' words relate to the time (*hōra*, lit., "hour"; cf. *kairos*, "time" or "season," in Matt 11:25) in which the power of the kingdom is revealed. Jesus himself participates in the joy that characterizes the day of God's salvation, a theme established at the beginning of Luke's Gospel (e.g., 1:44). Like Mary (in the Magnificat, 1:46–47), he combines joy with thanksgiving on the occasion of God's mighty saving work. Jesus had already spoken about God's sovereignty in hiding and revealing divine mysteries in explaining his use of parables (8:10 and synoptic parallels; cf. 1 Cor

1:18–25). A remarkable thing—and one that Jesus' thanksgiving stresses—is not that the wise do not understand but that the simple do. This has to do with revelation and does not negate what Scripture teaches (e.g., in Proverbs) about the importance of study and pious wisdom. The "children" (*nēpiois*) are those whose open, trusting attitude makes them receptive to God's word. The theme of revelation appears in both v.21 and here, in v.22, first the revelation of "things" and now of God himself. The knowledge God gives is "committed" (*paredothē*, lit., "delivered," "handed over") directly to the Son. This explains why Jesus spoke with authority (4:32) in contrast to the scribes (Matt 7:29, Mark 1:22, cf. Matt 28:18), who received their ideas through tradition, passed on from rabbi to rabbi. Jesus' sayings confirm other teachings in the Synoptics and in John about the fatherhood of God and the unique sonship of Christ. While some aspects of his sonship relate to his role as the Messiah, who was designated God's Son, the relationship expressed here is clearly personal rather than functional. The same truth is one of the major themes in John's Gospel (see also Matt 24:36; Mark 13:32).

23–24 Here Jesus congratulates the disciples privately on participating in this revelation (v.23). The woes (vv.13–15) on those whose pride will be broken are balanced by the blessings of those granted salvation. This pattern has already appeared in the Magnificat (1:52–55) and in Jesus' beatitudes and woes (6:20–26). See also 1 Corinthians 2:9–10.

Notes

1 Ἑβδομήκοντα [δύο] (*hebdomēkonta [duo]*, "seventy [-two]") has strong MS support, including P75 B D, but the number "seventy" has a stronger precedence in the OT. There were seventy descendants of Jacob according to the MT of Exod 1:5, seventy elders in the Sanhedrin (Sanh 1.6), seventy nations in the world and so on (cf. TDNT, 2:634). There are fewer significant instances of the number seventy-two, if one is looking for possible precedents, though S. Jellicoe ("St. Luke and the Seventy-two," NTS 6 [1960]: 319–21) suggests that the seventy-two translators of the LXX, mentioned in L Aristeas, may have relevance. Marshall (*Gospel of Luke*, p. 415) suspects that Luke wrote that number thinking of the table of nations in the LXX of Gen 10, which lists seventy-two rather than seventy nations. Copyists, who were more familiar with the number seventy, may have changed the text in that direction. This is a reasonable proposal, which fits both the MS evidence and the background situation.

2 Τοῦ κυρίου τοῦ θερισμοῦ (*tou kyriou tou therismou*, "the Lord of the harvest") is presumably God the Father. Although Jesus is called "Lord" in v.1, his reference to the Lord of the harvest as the hearer of prayer is clearly in the third person in meaning as well as form.

4 Ὑποδήματα (*hypodēmata*, "sandals") are not mentioned in 9:3. The summary in 22:35 mentions them among prohibited equipment. See note on 9:3 regarding the differences between the Synoptics as to what was or was not allowed.

6 Ἐπαναπαήσεται ἐπ᾽ αὐτὸν ἡ εἰρήνη ὑμῶν (*epanapaēsetai ep' auton hē eirēnē hymōn*, "your peace will rest on him") portrays peace almost as an objective, personal power. God's spoken word had this characteristic in Semitic thought. It was to leave the host if he was not the kind of person who would be receptive to the kingdom message.

9 Ἔγγικεν ἐφ᾽ ὑμᾶς ἡ βασιλεία τοῦ θεοῦ (*engiken eph' hymas hē basileia tou theou*, "the kingdom of God is near you") is one of many statements of Jesus that teach the nearness

of the kingdom. It is not so clear in this passage that the kingdom has actually arrived as it is in 11:20, where the verb ἔφθασεν (ephthasen) means "has come." In the latter case, Jesus' casting out demons was an act of kingdom power. Here (v.9) it is not clear whether the disciples actually embodied or brought the kingdom, or whether they just announced it. The prepositional phrase eph hymas occurs both here and in 11:20, giving rise to the question of whether a common Aramaic saying underlies both, even though the Greek verbs are difficult. While this is improbable (Marshall, Gospel of Luke, p. 422), the potential of ἐγγίζω (engizō, "draw near," "approach") to indicate actual arrival plus the idea of proximity in the prepositional phrase are sufficient to establish the point: the hearers had adequate assurance of the coming of the kingdom to them in time and space through the arrival and ministry of Jesus' representatives.

11 On καὶ τὸν κονιορτὸν (kai ton koniorton, "even the dust"), cf. comment on, 9:5.

21 Ἠγαλλιάσατο [ἐν] τῷ πνεύματι τῷ ἁγίῳ (ēgalliasato [en] tō pneumati tō hagiō) presents a textual and a theological problem. In turn (as often) the theological problem may have produced the textual. The wording here (UBS text) may be translated "rejoiced [or 'exulted'] in the Holy Spirit." Metzger (Textual Commentary, p. 152) says, "The strangeness of the expression . . . (for which there is no parallel in the Scriptures) may have led to the omission of τῷ ἁγίῳ [tō hagiō, "the holy"] from P⁴⁵ A W Δ Ψ f¹³ itq goth Clement al." The more important MSS have hagiō; and it is most likely that it is in the Spirit of God, not his own human spirit, that Jesus exulted. The use of square brackets around en in the UBS text acknowledges that some significant MSS omit that word. NIV interprets the word en as instrumental and has "full of joy through the Holy Spirit." In the theology of Luke this clause is especially significant because of his stress both on Jesus and the Holy Spirit and on joy.

B. Teachings (10:25–11:13)

1. Parable of the Good Samaritan

10:25–37

²⁵On one occasion an expert in the law stood up to test Jesus. "Teacher," he asked, "what must I do to inherit eternal life?"

²⁶"What is written in the Law?" he replied. "How do you read it?"

²⁷He answered: "'Love the Lord your God with all your heart and with all your soul and with all your strength and with all your mind'; and, 'Love your neighbor as yourself.'"

²⁸"You have answered correctly," Jesus replied. "Do this and you will live."

²⁹But he wanted to justify himself, so he asked Jesus, "And who is my neighbor?"

³⁰In reply Jesus said: "A man was going down from Jerusalem to Jericho, when he fell into the hands of robbers. They stripped him of his clothes, beat him and went away, leaving him half dead. ³¹A priest happened to be going down the same road, and when he saw the man, he passed by on the other side. ³²So too, a Levite, when he came to the place and saw him, passed by on the other side. ³³But a Samaritan, as he traveled, came where the man was; and when he saw him, he took pity on him. ³⁴He went to him and bandaged his wounds, pouring on oil and wine. Then he put the man on his own donkey, took him to an inn and took care of him. ³⁵The next day he took out two silver coins and gave them to the innkeeper. 'Look after him,' he said, 'and when I return, I will reimburse you for any extra expense you may have.'

³⁶"Which of these three do you think was a neighbor to the man who fell into the hands of robbers?"

³⁷The expert in the law replied, "The one who had mercy on him."

Jesus told him, "Go and do likewise."

This parable, unique to Luke, requires the utmost care in its interpretation. It must neither be overallegorized, as it was by the early church fathers, nor reduced to a simplistic meaning hardly worthy of Jesus' teaching. Above all, it must be understood in its context, with attention to the questions of v.25 and v.29 and to Jesus' application in vv.36–37.

The dialogue that precedes the parable in Luke is similar to the one Matthew and Mark locate in Jerusalem (Matt 22:34–40; Mark 12:28–34). It is possible that Luke incorporates the same conversation in this section of Jesus' sayings; but it is equally possible, if not more likely, that the somewhat different wording indicates a different conversation. Questions about achieving eternal life and about the essence of the law were common in Judaism. Totally different conversations follow the recitation of the two commandments in Mark and in Luke.

25 The man's expertise lay in details of the Jewish religion. The fact that he wanted to "test" (*ekpeirazōn*) Jesus may, but does not necessarily, indicate hostility. He addressed Jesus as "teacher" (*didaskalē*). Note his assumption of human responsibility in the attainment of eternal life, and see the similar assumption on the part of the rich ruler in 18:18. "Eternal life" (*zoēn aiōnion*) here means the life of the kingdom (18:18, 24–25, 29; cf. John 3:3, 5, 15–16, 36). This concern regarding life is seen in two stories found in later Jewish tradition in which a rabbi and a merchant respectively ask who desires life. They then quote Psalm 34:12–14 as the means of achieving it (*Abodah Zara* 19b; R Lev 16).

26 Jesus' counterquestion does not constitute an affirmation of the assumption behind the question but directs the questioner back to the law, the commandments of the OT, which are not only his special field but also the ultimate source of religious knowledge. "How do you read it?" invites the expert's personal interpretation.

27 In Luke it is the interlocutor, not Jesus, who quotes the commandment (cf. Matt 22:37–40; Mark 12:29–31). The answer is satisfactory so far as it goes. It is based on the OT (Deut 6:5; Lev 19:18; cf. Rom 13:9). The words "as yourself" will provide the crucial means of evaluating one's love of neighbor. The ultimate evaluation will have to be based on deeds, not words, as the parable shows. It is noteworthy that the command to love one's neighbor is not subordinated to the first commandment as strongly in Luke (where it is joined by the coordinate conjunction "and," *kai*) as it is in Matthew 22:39 and Mark 12:31, where the word "second" (*deutera*) is used. (On the command itself, see V.P. Furnish, *The Love Command in the New Testament* [Nashville and New York: Abingdon, 1972].)

28 Jesus affirms that the man has answered correctly (*orthōs*, "right," "properly," from which our word "orthodox" is derived). This does not mean that the inquirer has grasped the full meaning of the law, nor does it support the idea held by many Pharisees that by keeping the law, as some kind of contract with God, a person can earn eternal life.

29 The only way he (or any person) can "justify himself" is to limit the extent of the law's demand and consequently limit his own responsibility. This maneuver not only fails but has an opposite effect. Jesus will change the man's very words "who is my neighbor?" from a passive to an active sense (v.36).

942

30 The overallegorization of the parable (vv. 30–35) that saw the Samaritan as Christ, the inn as the church, etc., must be rejected. The characters of the story must have the same significance they had to the original hearers. The religious persons act contrary to love, though not contrary to expectation. It is made clear that the priest, at least, is pursuing his religious duty, going "down," i.e., back from Jerusalem (v. 31). To an extent, the "Law" (vv. 26–27) was being observed, but studious readers will recognize the neglect of mercy (cf. Matt 23:23 and especially the occurrence of "merciful" in Luke 6:36 in place of "perfect" in Matt 5:48). The "rule of three" is fulfilled by the appearance of a third character, but unexpectedly he is not just a layman (in contrast to the clerical characters) but a Samaritan (in contrast to the Jewish victim).

The distance from Jerusalem to Jericho is about seventeen miles, descending sharply toward the Jordan River just north of the Dead Sea. The old road, even more than the present one, curved through rugged, bleak, rocky terrain where robbers could easily hide. It was considered especially dangerous, even in a day when travel was normally full of hazards.

31–32 Priests served in the temple; their highest duty was to offer sacrifices. Levites assisted in the maintenance of the temple services and order. It has been suggested that the priest (v. 31) and the Levite (v. 32) refrained from helping the man because he appeared to be dead and they feared ritual defilement. Jeremias rejects this explanation on the grounds that (1) ritual purity was only significant when carrying out cultic activities; (2) the priest was going "down" (v. 31), i.e., away from Jerusalem, presumably having finished with those duties; (3) the Levite by implication (v. 32) was probably also going away from Jerusalem; and (4) when priests and Levites were on their way to serve in the temple, they traveled in groups; but these two were alone and therefore not on their way to Jerusalem (*Parables of Jesus*, pp. 203–4). Also, the point of the story seems to require that the priest and the Levite be without excuse.

33–36 "Took pity" (*esplanchnisthē*) implies a deep feeling of sympathy (v. 33), a striking response that stands in contrast, not only to the attitude of the priest and the Levite, but also to the usual feelings of hostility between Jew and Samaritan. This pity is translated into sacrificial action. The Samaritan probably used pieces of his own clothing to make the bandages (v. 34); he used his own wine as a disinfectant and his own oil as a soothing lotion (Jeremias, *Parables of Jesus*, p. 204). He put the man on "his own donkey" and paid the innkeeper out of his own pocket (v. 35), with a promise to pay more if needed.

The NT parables aim to lead one to a decision; Jesus' second counterquestion (v. 36) forces the "expert in the law" to voice his decision. In his question, Jesus does not focus on the object of neighborly love, the Jewish victim, but on the subject, the Samaritan who made himself a neighbor. This reversal of the "expert's" question (v. 29) provides in itself the key to the meaning of the parable and to Jesus' teaching on love. Love should not be limited by its object; its extent and quality are in the control of its subject. Furthermore, love is demonstrated in action, in this case in an act of mercy. It may be costly: cloth, wine, oil, transportation, money, and sacrifice of time. There is a striking reversal of roles here. The Jewish "expert" would have thought of the Jewish victim as a good person and the Samaritan as an evil one. To a Jew there was no such person as a "good" Samaritan. Jesus could have told the story with a Samaritan victim and a Jewish helper, but the role reversal drives the story home by shaking the hearer loose from his preconceptions.

37 The "expert" cannot avoid the thrust of the parable, though he apparently finds it impossible to say the word "Samaritan" in his reply. Jesus now refers back to the original question, "What must I do?" by saying, "Go and do likewise." Both this man and the rich ruler of 18:18–25 needed to learn that God does not bestow the life of the kingdom on those who reject the command to love. Such rejection shows that they have not truly recognized how much they need the love of God themselves. In this respect they are identified with Simon the Pharisee rather than with the woman who was forgiven much and therefore loved much (7:36–50).

Notes

30–37 The literature on this parable is extensive. For a summary of various recent works to 1965, see R.W. Funk, "The Old Testament in Parable. A Study of Luke 10:25–37," *Encounter* 26 (1965): 251–67. Since that article was written, much further work has been done, especially using the methodology of structuralism. See, for example, John Dominic Crossan, ed., *Semeia* 2 (1974), which is entirely devoted to this parable.

2. The home of Martha and Mary

10:38–42

> [38]As Jesus and his disciples were on their way, he came to a village where a woman named Martha opened her home to him. [39]She had a sister called Mary, who sat at the Lord's feet listening to what he said. [40]But Martha was distracted by all the preparations that had to be made. She came to him and asked, "Lord, don't you care that my sister has left me to do the work by myself? Tell her to help me!"
>
> [41]"Martha, Martha," the Lord answered, "you are worried and upset about many things, [42]but only one thing is needed. Mary has chosen what is better, and it will not be taken away from her."

In 8:1–3 Luke mentioned several women who traveled with Jesus and the disciples and contributed to their support. Now he tells about a woman who entered into discipleship. Once again Luke portrays the way Jesus transcended the prejudices of his day.

38–40 The travel theme appears in v.38 ("on their way"), but Luke refrains from mentioning that the "village" was Bethany (John 11:1). Possibly he wants to reserve mention of Jesus' ministry in Jerusalem and its environs till later (cf. 13:32–33; 17:11; 19:28; cf. comments on 9:51). The way Martha is mentioned seems to give her the role of hostess (cf. John 12:1–2). It is Mary, however, who takes the place of a disciple by sitting at the feet of the teacher (v.39; cf. Acts 22:3—"under Gamaliel," lit., "at his feet"). It is unusual for a woman in first-century Judaism to be accepted by a teacher as a disciple. Notice that Jesus is called "Lord" (*kyrie*) throughout this passage. Martha was "distracted" (v.40), the verb *periespato* implying that her attention was drawn away by the burden of her duties. One can only speculate about the actual feelings she had toward her sister beyond what she said and about the personal differences between Martha and Mary. Martha's concern seems to have been that she had to work alone rather than that she could not sit at Jesus' feet.

41–42 The Lord shows concern for Martha's anxiety (v.41), but the precise meaning of his saying (v.42) is partly obscured because of a textual problem (cf. Notes). There is no explanation of "what is better" (*tēn agathēn merida*, lit., "the good part"). Some have understood this to be the contemplative life, or placing worship over service. Manson (*Sayings of Jesus*, pp. 264–65) thought it was seeking the kingdom first. This interpretation has the merit of explaining Mary's seeming neglect of household duties, which in comparison with the kingdom would have a radically diminishing demand on her. The word of the Lord has first claim. For the disciple an attitude of learning and obedience takes first place. The preceding narrative and parable establish the importance of priorities in the Christian life—i.e., heeding the commands to love God and neighbor. Martha must now learn to give the Lord and his word priority even over loving service. There are important human needs, whether of the victim in vv.30–35 or of Jesus himself. But what is most "needed" goes beyond even these. The thoughtful reader will recognize, however, that this spiritual priority is not the same as the sterile religion of the priest and Levite in vv.31–32.

Notes

42 As the NIV footnote indicates, there is a textual problem here. Of the several variant readings, none has a clear claim to originality. Among these, the most probable choices resolve into (1) "few things are needed," (2) "one thing is needed," and (3) "few things are needed—or only one." NIV has chosen (2) for its text; the UBS text gives it a "C" rating. The NIV footnote has (3). Reading (1) has slim support from the MSS, but Marshall (*Gospel of Luke*, p. 453) thinks it is worth considering because "it is indirectly attested in the good MSS which have the conflate reading" (i.e., the one reflected in the NIV footnote). Also, if "few" means "few dishes of food," Marshall says, "the change from 'few' to 'one' is comprehensible; scribes were perhaps more likely to think that Jesus would give teaching not about practical hospitality but about the one spiritual goal." In any case the basic meaning is clear—Martha's and Mary's priorities are contrasted.

3. *Teaching on prayer*

11:1–13

¹One day Jesus was praying in a certain place. When he finished, one of his disciples said to him, "Lord, teach us to pray, just as John taught his disciples."
²He said to them, "When you pray, say:

" 'Father,
hallowed be your name,
your kingdom come.
³Give us each day our daily bread.

4Forgive us our sins,
   for we also forgive everyone who sins against us.
   And lead us not into temptation.' "

5Then he said to them, "Suppose one of you has a friend, and he goes to him at midnight and says, 'Friend, lend me three loaves of bread, 6because a friend of mine on a journey has come to me, and I have nothing to set before him.'

7"Then the one inside answers, 'Don't bother me. The door is already locked, and my children are with me in bed. I can't get up and give you anything.' 8I tell you, though he will not get up and give him the bread because he is his friend, yet because of the man's boldness he will get up and give him as much as he needs.

9"So I say to you: Ask and it will be given to you; seek and you will find; knock and the door will be opened to you. 10For everyone who asks receives; he who seeks finds; and to him who knocks, the door will be opened.

11"Which of you fathers, if your son asks for a fish, will give him a snake instead? 12Or if he asks for an egg, will give him a scorpion? 13If you then, though you are evil, know how to give good gifts to your children, how much more will your Father in heaven give the Holy Spirit to those who ask him!"

The Lord's Prayer in Luke appears in connection with Jesus' own practice and teaching on prayer. Matthew presents the prayer in somewhat different form as part of the Sermon on the Mount (Matt 6:9–13). The prayer fits each context, and the differences indicate separate traditions. It would be difficult to prove that either Matthew or Luke had significantly changed the prayer from the form in which he knew it. The Matthean form is undoubtedly more "liturgical" in that the successive petitions are parallel, are balanced, and in Aramaic may even have rhymed at points. In Matthew 6 the prayer has petitions that may supplement or substitute for some feature of the Jewish prayers of that day. Luke offers a basic prayer to say what is characteristic of Jesus' teaching.

1–4 Once more Luke speaks of Jesus at prayer (cf. 3:21; 6:12; 9:28). His exemplary practice introduces the exemplary prayer. Since prayer inevitably expresses one's theology, the prayers of the Jewish sects in the first century were distinctive. This was true of John the Baptist (v.1). Jesus responds to the request of "one of the disciples" with a model that, while not to be thoughtlessly repeated (Matt 6:7), provides words disciples can use with the confidence that they express Jesus' own teachings. The words "when [or 'whenever,' *hotan*] you pray" (v.2) imply frequent repetition of the actual prayer.

The word "Father" (*patēr*) expresses the essence of Jesus' message and the effect of his atoning work on our relationship with God. Through the use of this intimate but respectful term of address, the Son of God expressed his own unique relationship to God. It is very probable (so TDNT, 1:6) that in every prayer he spoke to God, Jesus used the Aramaic word *Abba* ("dear Father"), which would naturally be translated *pater* in the Greek text. The notable exception is the prayer of dereliction from the cross (Mark 15:34). Through his atoning death on the cross, the Savior brought about reconciliation with God, making it possible for us to become his spiritual children through the new birth. While we cannot use the term *Abba* on an equal basis with the Son of God, there is a sense in which both he and we may address God as "dear Father" (John 20:17; Rom 8:14–17). (For the originality of the simple term *Abba* as a form of direct address to God by Jesus, see Joachim Jeremias, *The Lord's Prayer* [Philadelphia: Fortress, 1964], pp. 17–21.)

The petitions that follow are two kinds—the first two petitions relate to God, the last three to us. "Hallowed be your name" is an ascription of worship basic to all prayer and is found in various forms in the OT (e.g., Ps 111:9) and in ancient Jewish prayers (the *Kaddish* and the Eighteen Benedictions; see also SBK, 1:406–8). "Hallowed" (*hagiastheto*) means "let [your name] be regarded as holy." It is not so much a petition as an act of worship; the speaker, by his words, exalts the holiness of God. God's people were told in the OT to keep his name holy (Lev 22:32; cf. Ps. 79:9; Isa 29:33). God told Israel that because they failed to honor his name, he would do it himself so the nations would know that he was LORD (Ezek 36:22–23). The aorist tense here suggests that a specific time of fulfillment is in mind. This may be the coming of the kingdom. The next clause, which is about the kingdom, also contains a verb in the aorist tense.

In the *Kaddish* the petition for the exaltation and hallowing of God's name was immediately followed by a request that we might know the rule of God in our lives now. These requests, that the glory and reign of God may be realized soon, are suitable for the Lord's Prayer because Jesus came to announce and bring the kingdom. Though its consummation is still future, in his ministry the kingdom was inaugurated in power. The form of the prayer in Luke lacks these words in Matthew —"your will be done on earth as it is in heaven" (Matt 6:10).

Thus far, apart from the address "Abba" (see above), the wording has been close to what any Jew expecting the kingdom might pray. The three petitions that follow are closely connected with the "Abba" and give a more distinctive character to the prayer as a whole.

The first of the three petitions relating to us is for "bread" (*artos*), representing food in general (v.3). The meaning of *epiousion* (tr. "daily" in NIV) is obscure (cf. Notes), and so the context of the word becomes crucial. If we transliterate it instead of translating it, the petition can be paraphrased in the Greek word order as follows: "Our bread, the daily, keep giving to us each day" (the verb is in the present tense, indicating continuing, daily provision). This contrasts with Matthew 6:11—"Our bread, the daily, give to us today" (the verb is in the aorist tense, indicating a simple act). "Today" in Matthew and "each day" in Luke are in an emphatic position at the end of the clause. Rather than meaning "daily," *epiousion* may mean "for tomorrow." "Tomorrow" may be literally the next day. This would be appropriate if it were an evening prayer. It could also signify the eschatological bread, that is, God's abundant provision at the consummation of the kingdom. Thus the Matthean form is a request for that kind of bread to be given in advance—on this very day. In Luke, however, any gap between present and future (assuming the future meaning of *epiousion*) is bridged by the substitution of the present imperative "keep giving us" and by the words "each day." Thus the petition, as Luke has it, would then be for the provision of this aspect of the future feast in our own lives now.

The word *epiousion* can also have a more general meaning—"sufficient" or "necessary" (cf. E.M. Yamauchi, "The Daily Bread Motif in Antiquity," WTJ 28 [1965–66]: 147–56). This would make a smoother reading than having two terms that mean "daily" ("each day" . . . "daily"). It would also fit Luke's stress on present needs better than "for tomorow" (if that means the eschaton). To trust God for sufficient food day by day was important to people in Jesus' time who were hired only a day at a time (cf. Matt 20:1–5). When the people of Israel were in the wilderness, they learned to trust God for manna day by day (Exod 16:4; Deut 8:6).

"Forgive us our sins" (*aphes hemin tas hamartias hemon*) uses the aorist tense (v.4), which may refer to a single declaration of forgiveness, when all accounts are settled. More probably, however, it simply describes a petition repeated as needed. The word "sins" is the familiar *hamartia* rather than the Jewish idiom "debts" (*opheilēmata*) in Matthew 6:12. Since the petitioner has called God "Father," he is a believer, already justified and without guilt through the death of Christ. Therefore the forgiveness he must extend to others is not the basis of his salvation but a prerequisite for daily fellowship with the Father in the sense of 1 John 1:5–10. Conversely, one who does not forgive others may actually be revealing that he has not really known God's forgiveness (cf. Luke 7:47).

"Lead us not into temptation [*eis peirasmon*]" does not imply that God might otherwise entice us to do evil. James 1:1–15 rules this out. God does, however, allow his people to be tested as to their faithfulness (see comments on 4:1–12 and the references there to Deut 6–8). The word *peirasmos* here probably means "testing" rather than "temptation" (i.e., to sin), though severe testing may be the occasion for one to sin. Further, there is a coming *peirasmos* that will severely try all those who undergo it, and this petition may have reference to that. In any case, the request is clearly for the Father to keep his children from falling away in the hour of trial, with a possible allusion to the temptation and fidelity of Christ. With this petition the Lord's Prayer comes to a close, lacking, except in a variant (cf. Notes), the additional words in Matthew.

5–6 Jesus' teaching on prayer continues (vv.5–13) with a parable unique to Luke, the meaning of which has been variously assessed.

The scene is that of a Palestinian home in which the family are all asleep in one room—perhaps the only room in the house—and probably all on one mat. The father could not get over to the door and slide back the heavy bolt that bars it without waking up his family. In such a situation no one would be happy to respond, especially in the middle of the night. Nevertheless the man does respond to his friend at the door (v.5), for a reason to be discussed below.

The midnight arrival of the hungry friend (v.6) has usually been thought normal because "journeys were often undertaken by night to avoid the heat of the day" (Marshall, *Gospel of Luke*, p. 464). Bailey (*Poet and Peasant*, p. 121) maintains that, on the contrary, while this is true in desert areas, the elevation of central Palestine and Lebanon and the sea breeze along the coast made travel during the day customary. The night arrival would therefore be unusual. In either case, a host in that first-century society would be expected to provide a welcome. Rather than insult his guest with too little bread (or with a broken loaf, if it was of the large variety of that area), the host would seek out a person with a good supply, knowing who in his small town had recently done baking. The visitor would have been the guest, not only of the individual and his family, but of the whole community. This placed a great responsibility both on the traveler's host and on the friend he approached at midnight (see Bailey on these customs, *Poet and Peasant*, pp. 121ff.).

7–8 The point of the parable depends partly on the context and partly on the meaning of the word *anaideia* (v.8), translated "persistence" (NIV, NASB) or "importunity" (RSV, KJV). If *anaideia* does mean persistence, the parable would seem to teach that if we persist long enough, God will finally answer our prayers. But since the larger context, especially vv.10, 13, as well as the rest of Scripture, teaches God's eagerness to hear and grant our requests, the meaning persistence has little in its favor. Reference is sometimes made to 18:1–8 in support of the persistence theory.

(But see the comment on that passage.) On the other hand, this parable with its reluctant host and persistent visitor may present not a comparison but a contrast to the way God answers prayer. In that case the point would be that if in human circumstances one will respond to a request, even though reluctantly, if pressed hard enough, surely God will answer and do so far more graciously.

Yet another interpretation has been proposed. The word *anaideia* can mean "avoidance of shame" (Bailey, *Poet and Peasant*, pp. 125–33). While it did come to have the meaning of "persistence," the concept of shame was linked with it in the first century. The parable would thus mean that just as the man in bed would respond so as not to incur shame (for having refused the needs of a visitor to his community), so God will always do what is honorable and consistent with his character.

9–10 In threefold poetic form, Jesus teaches that "everyone who asks" (*pas ho aitōn*, v.10)—not only the persistent—will receive from God. This saying of great assurance is preserved here in Luke and also in Matthew 7:7–8.

11–13 The bizarre examples in vv.11–12 reinforce the point that God will respond to our petitions only in kindness. There are two steps in the argument: (1) God is our heavenly Father (v.13) and will do no less for his children than would an earthly father; (2) God is perfect and will do "much more" than sinful man would. The parallel passage in Matthew 7:11 has the general term "good gifts." Luke specifically mentions the Holy Spirit, who was "promised" (Acts 2:33; cf. Luke 24:49; Acts 1:4).

Notes

2–4 Helpful works on the Lord's Prayer include J. Carmignac, *Recherches sur le "Notre Père"* (Paris: Letouzey & Ané, 1969), R.A. Guelich, *The Sermon on the Mount* (Waco: Word, 1982), pp. 283–97, 307–20; A. Hamman, *Prayer in the N.T.* (Chicago: Franciscan Herald Press, 1971), pp. 103–45; J. Jeremias, "The Lord's Prayer in Modern Research," *Exp. T.* 71 (1960), 141–46; J. Jeremias, *The Prayers of Jesus* (Philadelphia: Fortress, 1978); W.L. Liefeld, "The Lord's Prayer," in ISBE (rev. ed., forthcoming); T.W. Manson, "The Lord's Prayer," *Bull. John Rylands Lib.* 38 (1955–56), 99–113; C.F.D. Moule, "An Unresolved Problem in the Temptation-Clause in the Lord's Prayer," *Ref. Theol. Rev.* 33 (1974), 65–75; J.J. Petuchowski and M. Brocke, *The Lord's Prayer and Jewish Liturgy* (New York: Seabury, 1978); E.M. Yamauchi, "The Daily Bread Motif in Antiquity," WTJ 28 (1965–66), 145–56.

3 Ἐπιούσιον (*epiousion*, "daily") may be derived from a combination of ἐπί (*epi*) used as a preposition or as a prefix with εἰμι (*eimi*, "to be," "to exist") or with εἰμι (*eimi*, with a circumflex accent, "to come," "to go"). Thus it could refer to present or to future time (the latter usage being common in Jesus' time), including the presence of something needed at the moment.

5–6 Jeremias thinks that as Jesus originally told it, the parable was addressed not to the visitor but to the man in bed. The words translated "suppose one of you" (τίς ἐξ ὑμῶν, *tis ex hymōn*, lit., "who [or 'which'] of you?") imply "surely none of you would do what I am going to describe" (cf. Jeremias, *Parables of Jesus*, pp. 157ff.). But though the immediate transition to the third person "he" in v.5 makes for some ambiguity, the hearer of the parable is not to imagine himself as the man in bed but as the visitor.

Bailey (*Poet and Peasant*, pp. 124–25) cites as a close parallel Luke 17:7, which he thinks helpful in determining the understood subject of the verb πορεύσεται (*poreusetai*, "goes") here in v.5. If the parallel holds, the hypothetical person ("one of you") is the one who "goes" rather than the friend going to him. Thus the hearer identifies himself with the visitor, who, according to Bailey's interpretation, receives the bread not because of his own persistence but because the man in bed does not want to incur shame.

C. *Growing Opposition* (11:14–54)

1. *Jesus and Beelzebub*

11:14–28

¹⁴Jesus was driving out a demon that was mute. When the demon left, the man who had been mute spoke, and the crowd was amazed. ¹⁵But some of them said, "By Beelzebub, the prince of demons, he is driving out demons." ¹⁶Others tested him by asking for a sign from heaven.

¹⁷Jesus knew their thoughts and said to them: "Any kingdom divided against itself will be ruined, and a house divided against itself will fall. ¹⁸If Satan is divided against himself, how can his kingdom stand? I say this because you claim that I drive out demons by Beelzebub. ¹⁹Now if I drive out demons by Beelzebub, by whom do your followers drive them out? So then, they will be your judges. ²⁰But if I drive out demons by the finger of God, then the kingdom of God has come to you.

²¹"When a strong man, fully armed, guards his own house, his possessions are safe. ²²But when someone stronger attacks and overpowers him, he takes away the armor in which the man trusted and divides up the spoils.

²³"He who is not with me is against me, and he who does not gather with me, scatters.

²⁴"When an evil spirit comes out of a man, it goes through arid places seeking rest and does not find it. Then it says, 'I will return to the house I left.' ²⁵When it arrives, it finds the house swept clean and put in order. ²⁶Then it goes and takes seven other spirits more wicked than itself, and they go in and live there. And the final condition of that man is worse than the first."

²⁷As Jesus was saying these things, a woman in the crowd called out, "Blessed is the mother who gave you birth and nursed you."

²⁸He replied, "Blessed rather are those who hear the word of God and obey it."

This event shows the real nature of the increasing opposition Jesus faced. Mark and Matthew also include it, but in different contexts. Mark follows it with the parable of the sower, which illustrates the varying responses to Jesus' teaching (Mark 3:20–4:20). Matthew (like Luke) follows it with Jesus' comments on the sign of Jonah but then (unlike Luke) has the parable of the sower, followed by the so-called parables of the kingdom, which also show the contrast between good and evil (Matt 12:22–13:52). In Luke the Beelzebub controversy leads to the sign of Jonah (as in Matthew) and then on to the woes against the unbelieving religious leaders. Each of the other Synoptics also includes a comment regarding Jesus' mother together with a statement that obedience to God's word is more important than even the closest human ties to Jesus.

Whether the arrangement is due to each evangelist's plan or to the order of events in his source, every occurrence of the Beelzebub incident in the Synoptics comes at a crucial point in the narrative. The incident shows that Jesus' hearers must choose between good (Jesus, the Spirit, and God's kingdom) and evil (Satan and his demons).

The issue is nothing less than the source of Jesus' authority and power. This is especially important for Luke, who is deeply aware of the importance of the supernatural as a testimony that Jesus is the promised Messiah (cf. the apostolic testimony he records in Acts 2:22, 43; 4:30; 5:12; 10:38, as well as the miracles in the Gospel itself). The climax of the passage comes in v.20, which, as we shall see, links the display of God's power in the Exodus and the same potential power in the kingdom of God with Jesus' successful attack on the kingdom of Satan. Although Luke continues this theme in vv.21–26, he postpones the issue of blasphemy against the Holy Spirit (located at this point in Matthew and Mark) until 12:19. This may have been the order in his source for this passage.

14–16 The setting of this account of the Beelzebub controversy is the healing (v.14) of a deaf mute (*kōphos*). Such a healing was among the signs of his messiahship that Jesus reminded John the Baptist of (7:22). Once more, as in 4:36 and elsewhere, the crowds are amazed at Jesus' power over demons. The crowd is divided, however, between those who either opposed him outrightly by attributing his power to the head demon, "Beelzebub" (v.15; cf. Notes), or taunted him to give them an even more dramatic sign, which constitutes a "testing" or provocation (v.16).

17–20 Jesus "knew their thoughts" (v.17; cf. 5:22; 7:39–47). The identification of Beelzebub with Satan (v.18) is the basis of vv.17–19. The head of any army would hardly work with the enemy against his own troops. Moreover, if demons are exorcised by the power of their own leader, how do the Jews explain the power their own exorcists (v.19; cf. Acts 19:13–14) are supposed to have? Jesus' illustration shows the drastic antithesis between the powers of evil, darkness, and Satan on the one hand and the power of God the Holy Spirit and the kingdom of light (cf. Col 1:12–13) on the other hand. When the magicians in Egypt were unable to duplicate all the miracles Moses did before the Exodus, they said to Pharaoh, "This is the finger of God" (Exod 8:19). So here Jesus is affirming that the source of his power is "the finger of God" (v.20), i.e., God himself, a statement Matthew specifically identifies with the Holy Spirit (Matt 12:28). If this is true, then Jesus' driving out demons is a messianic sign and "the kingdom of God has come" (cf. Notes).

21–23 Here the imagery is more vivid than in Matthew and Mark, for the strong man (v.21) guards his own house. Jesus' victory against Satan during his temptation may be alluded to here (v.22). In any event, we have in these verses a principal reference to Jesus' tactics in his war against Satan. The ultimate and actual means of Jesus' victory is the Cross. The critical place in Jesus' ministry of his victory over Satan means that we also must take a stand for or against Jesus as the one who brings the kingdom (v.23). Whoever does not "gather" (*synagōn*) the sheep "scatters" (*skorpizei*) them by default and thus works counter to Jesus (so Marshall, *Gospel of Luke*, p. 478). In John 10:11–13, the hired hand neglects his duty and the wolf "scatters" (*skorpizei*) the flock.

24–26 "Evil spirit" (*akatharton pneuma*) is a Jewish term for a demon (v.24). Luke does not say that the demon has been exorcized. When it is, the Holy Spirit in the power of the kingdom will accomplish that work and will indwell the person who has been possessed. In vv.24–26 a spiritual renewal has taken place, but without the indwelling Spirit. Marshall (*Gospel of Luke*, p. 479) suggests that this refers to the work of the Jewish exorcists mentioned in v.19. The evil spirit wanders through the "arid places" (v.24), a description in accord with the popular idea that demons inhabited the desert (cf. the accusation that John the Baptist, who lived in the desert, had a demon [7:33]). Some see Isaiah 13:21; 34:14 as a source for this idea. The demon seeks a human body and, in order to repossess its previous abode, enlists the aid of seven demons even worse than itself (v.26). This combination of seven plus one is reminiscent of the same grouping of spirits in the *Testament of Reuben*, 2 and 3. Contrast the "seven spirits" before the throne (Rev 1:4). The demons "live" (*katoikei*, lit., "settle down") there. The same verb is used in Ephesians 3:17 of Christ's full indwelling. The parallel in Matthew 12:43–45 applies the demons' settling down directly to "this wicked generation" and thus suggests that those who repented on hearing the initial proclamation of the kingdom through John the Baptist but failed to allow Jesus to bring the power of the kingdom into their lives were the ones who were worse off than formerly.

27–28 This saying (v.27) is unique to Luke and provides another instance of his identification of Jesus' sayings (v.28) as the "word of God." It must not be taken as reflecting unfavorably on Mary.

Notes

15 "Beelzebub" is a difficult name to analyze. It has been compared to a similar sounding word meaning "Lord of the Flies." There are several variants of the name. "Beelzebub" (NIV) has come down through the Latin MS tradition. The form "Beelzeboul" (NIV mg.) is the most common one in the Greek MSS—Βεελζεβούλ (*Beelzeboul*). Among the various etymologies suggested is that which incorporated a Hebrew word for a dwelling, זְבֻל (*zᵉbul*), which was used in Jesus' day to refer to the temple (L. Gaston, "Beelzebul," *Theologische Zeitschrift* [1962]: 247–55). This would have been a parody of the one who was truly "head of the house" (Matt 10:25).

Whatever its etymology, the significance of the name is clear. The wording in v.18 suggests that Beelzeboul was another name for Satan. That Beelzeboul was more than an ephithet formed for the occasion is not certain. But Jesus' response points to a known and sinister figure. It is possible, though unlikely, that this "prince of demons" (v.15) is to be understood as an inferior being representing Satan's cause (cf. ZPEB, 1:505).

20 In ἔφθασεν ἐφ' ὑμᾶς (*ephthasen eph' hymas*, "has come to you"), we have what is perhaps the strongest single affirmation in the Gospels of the presence of the kingdom. While ἐγγίζω (*engizō*, "approach," "draw near") implies imminent arrival (e.g., in Mark 1:15), the verb here, from φθάνω (*phthanō*), can mean not only to "arrive" but even, in the proper context, to "precede," as in 1 Thess 4:15. The prepositional phrase *eph' hymas* secures the meaning that the kingdom was actually there. See G.E. Ladd, *Theology of the New Testament*, pp. 65–68, for a discussion of the presence of the kingdom, centering on the parallel passage in Matt 12:28.

2. The sign of Jonah

11:29–32

²⁹As the crowds increased, Jesus said, "This is a wicked generation. It asks for a miraculous sign, but none will be given it except the sign of Jonah. ³⁰For as Jonah was a sign to the Ninevites, so also will the Son of Man be to this generation. ³¹The Queen of the South will rise at the judgment with the men of this generation and condemn them; for she came from the ends of the earth to listen to Solomon's wisdom, and now one greater than Solomon is here. ³²The men of Nineveh will stand up at the judgment with this generation and condemn it; for they repented at the preaching of Jonah, and now one greater than Jonah is here.

This passage gives us Jesus' response to those who were prodding him for a "sign [*sēmeion*] from heaven" (v.16). The Gospel of John builds on the premise that Jesus performed miracles as signs (*sēmeia*). The present passage does not stand in opposition to the meaningful use of signs but rather to the unbelief that resists the testimony already obvious in the messianic works (cf. v.14 above). The Synoptics oppose an inordinate demand for extraordinary miracles beyond those needed for a witness to Jesus' authority. An even stronger statement, though not incompatible with this, occurs in Mark 8:12.

29–30 The transitional phrase "as the crowds increased" (v.29) encourages the reader to understand this comment on "sign" in terms of the previous passage, especially v.16. Only Luke has the phrase, just as only Luke has the reference to a sign in v.16. The "sign" of Jonah is Jonah himself, whose presence and brief message (cf. v.32, *kērygma*, NIV, "preaching"), though far minimal compared with the preaching of Jesus, triggered immediate and widespread repentance. Matthew 12:40 adds a reference to Jonah's experience in the huge fish as pointing to the duration of Jesus' entombment. This is not mentioned in Luke, and Marshall's attempt (*Gospel of Luke*, p. 483) to introduce it here may be unnecessary. For Luke the preaching of Jesus—viz., his "word"—carried its authority, especially when affirmed by the power of God in miracles (e.g., 4:32, 36). This does not mean that Jesus' resurrection as a parallel to Jonah's delivery from the fish was not the ultimate sign—only that Luke did not have that part of the tradition.

31–32 The inclusion of the "Queen of the South" (the queen of Sheba) fortifies the judgment on Jesus' generation, because she traveled a great distance to hear the wisdom of Solomon (v.31). A double contrast is implied in these two examples: (1) the response of the audience, (2) the greatness of the preacher. The "one greater" (v.32) than Solomon and Jonah is, of course, Jesus, unless one interprets the neuter form of the word "greater" (*pleion*) to cover the whole mission of Jesus or perhaps the kingdom (though the latter would call for the feminine form).

Notes

29 On the meaning of σημεῖον (*sēmeion*, "sign") in Scripture, see Rengstorf, TDNT, 7:200–261 (esp. pp. 233–34 on Jonah); Hofius and Brown, DNTT, 2:626–33 (p. 630 on Jonah).

Hofius takes the sign of Jonah to be the Parousia of the Son of Man; cf. Colpe, TDNT, 8:449–50. Colpe holds that while this would be significant with respect to judgment, it comes too late to validate Jesus' ministry. But in Luke, where the emphasis on judgment is without explicit reference to Jesus' resurrection (cf. Matt 12:40), this would not be as much of a problem and does not require, as clearly as Matthew does, a sign that was observable during Jesus' ministry apart from the very preaching of the word itself. On the tradition-history of the Jonah and sign passages, R.A. Edwards has a major work, *The Sign of Jonah in the Theology of the Evangelists and Q*, SBT, 2d series 18 (Naperville, Ill.: Allenson, 1971). Edwards attributes not only the form of the saying but also its christology to the early church rather than to Jesus.

---

3. *The lamp of the body*

11:33–36

> [33]"No one lights a lamp and puts it in a place where it will be hidden, or under a bowl. Instead he puts it on its stand, so that those who come in may see the light. [34]Your eye is the lamp of your body. When your eyes are good, your whole body also is full of light. But when they are bad, your body also is full of darkness. [35]See to it, then, that the light within you is not darkness. [36]Therefore, if your whole body is full of light, and no part of it dark, it will be completely lighted, as when the light of a lamp shines on you."

33 Hearing Jesus' message lays a responsibility on the hearer. The metaphors of light, signs, and judgment (cf. vv.29–32) are akin to what we have in John (e.g., 3:19–21; 9:39–41) and elsewhere in the NT (e.g., Acts 26:18; 2 Cor 6:14–15; Eph 5:5–14). Much of this passage is paralleled in Matthew 6:22–23. There the Jewish concept of the bad eye symbolizing covetousness provides a link with the preceding saying about treasures. In the Lukan context there is no reference to possessions.

34–35 "Good eyes" (cf. Notes) admit light (v.34); bad ones do not. The implication is that the individual is responsible for receiving light. The eye is thus a "lamp" (*lychnos*), not in the sense that it emits light, but that through it (subject to the individual's will) the body receives light. The real source of light is outside the body; if we think we can generate our own light, we must beware lest that inner "light" prove to be darkness (v.35).

36 This seemingly repetitive verse resembles in its repetitiveness and its subject Ephesians 5:13–14a. Its meaning becomes clear in the light of vv.34–35. The body is only completely lighted when a lamp shines on it from the outside. The repetition of two Greek words is chiastic (in reverse order): *holon phōteinon* ("whole body is full of light") and *phōteinon holon* ("completely lighted"). The concluding *holon* is emphatic. The words are repeated to introduce an analogy that describes how the body is fully lighted: "As when [*hōs hotan*] the light of a lamp shines on you." Taking vv.34–36 together, we learn that full illumination only comes when one is willing to receive light from the lamp of God's truth.

Notes

34 The word ἁπλοῦς (*haplous*, "healthy," "sound") can have the idea of "sincere" or "generous" (e.g., in Matt 6:22, where, as noted above, the matter of possessions has been discussed). Here it means eyes that see clearly and do not deliberately obscure reality, so NIV's "are good."

4. Six woes

11:37–54

³⁷When Jesus had finished speaking, a Pharisee invited him to eat with him; so he went in and reclined at the table. ³⁸But the Pharisee, noticing that Jesus did not first wash before the meal, was surprised.

³⁹Then the Lord said to him, "Now then, you Pharisees clean the outside of the cup and dish, but inside you are full of greed and wickedness. ⁴⁰You foolish people! Did not the one who made the outside make the inside also? ⁴¹But give what is inside ˌthe dishˌ to the poor, and everything will be clean for you.

⁴²"Woe to you Pharisees, because you give God a tenth of your mint, rue and all other kinds of garden herbs, but you neglect justice and the love of God. You should have practiced the latter without leaving the former undone.

⁴³"Woe to you Pharisees, because you love the most important seats in the synagogues and greetings in the marketplaces.

⁴⁴"Woe to you, because you are like unmarked graves, which men walk over without knowing it."

⁴⁵One of the experts in the law answered him, "Teacher, when you say these things, you insult us also."

⁴⁶Jesus replied, "And you experts in the law, woe to you, because you load people down with burdens they can hardly carry, and you yourselves will not lift one finger to help them.

⁴⁷"Woe to you, because you build tombs for the prophets, and it was your forefathers who killed them. ⁴⁸So you testify that you approve of what your forefathers did; they killed the prophets, and you build their tombs. ⁴⁹Because of this, God in his wisdom said, 'I will send them prophets and apostles, some of whom they will kill and others they will persecute.' ⁵⁰Therefore this generation will be held responsible for the blood of all the prophets that has been shed since the beginning of the world, ⁵¹from the blood of Abel to the blood of Zechariah, who was killed between the altar and the sanctuary. Yes, I tell you, this generation will be held responsible for it all.

⁵²"Woe to you experts in the law, because you have taken away the key to knowledge. You yourselves have not entered, and you have hindered those who were entering."

⁵³When Jesus left there, the Pharisees and the teachers of the law began to oppose him fiercely and to besiege him with questions, ⁵⁴waiting to catch him in something he might say.

37–38 In a way typical of his use of material, Luke puts the major discourse in the setting of a dinner (v.37; cf. 14:1–24) Jesus himself attended (cf. the similar discourses in Matt 15:1–20; 23:1–36; Mark 7:1–22). Having accepted table fellowship with a Pharisee, Jesus offended his host, a proponent of ritual separation, by omitting the customary ritual washing prior to eating (v.38). Luke's introduction lacks the details about Jewish customs found in Mark 7:1–4. The reference to Isaiah 29:13 in Mark and in the similar passage in Matthew 15:1–9 is also lacking; and the comments in vv.39–54 have their parallel, not in Mark 7 and Matthew 15, but in Matthew 23:1–36, where the order is different and the comments on each indictment fuller. Luke gives us a concise selection of indictments. These point up some of the most common of the sins that characterize strict religious persons ("churchmen," as Ellis, *Gospel of Luke*, pp. 168f., calls them). These include hypocrisy (vv.39–41), imbalance (v.42), ostentation (v.43), impossible demands (v.46), intolerance (vv.47–51), and exclusiveness (v.52).

39–44 The "Pharisees" (v.39), originally a group of laymen who sought to be separate from impure things and people and attempted to apply Mosaic law to all parts of life, had, for the most part, by the time of Jesus lost the heart of their religion. In vv.41–42b Jesus offered a positive corrective that clearly shows he did not oppose strict attention to religious duties but rather the neglect of caring about people that strict religionists often fall into. This is consistent with his teaching in 6:27–36 and 10:25–37. Seen merely from the religious point of view, to wash externally was in reality only a halfway measure. Moreover, vv.39–41 imply that in their "greed and wickedness" (v.39) the Pharisees had deprived the poor of the very food and drink that were "inside" (v.40) their own carefully washed dishes. Alternatively, "inside" also refers to their inner moral life ("you are full," v.39). Likewise (v.42) they apparently were tithing possessions that they should have shared with (or that rightfully belonged to) the needy. Marshall (*Gospel of Luke*, p. 498) remarks that though it might seem inconsistent that Jesus, while not practicing ritual washing, commended meticulous tithing, tithing was an OT principle. The vivid simile in v.44 is an example of Jesus' use of irony. Though the Pharisees avoided touching a grave for fear of ritual defilement, they themselves, through their own unrecognized corruption, were defiling those who came into contact with them. In Matthew 23:27 the figure is that of whitewashed tombs.

45–46 These verses are directed against the "experts in the law" (v.45). Many of them were Pharisees, and they were often mentioned together. Yet they were distinct groups, and Jesus addressed them separately. Their religious legalism explains v.46. They could interpret the OT and the traditions built on it in such a way as to leave little room for personal moral decisions. As "experts," they could, of course, find ways of circumventing the rules themselves.

47–48 Some lavish tombs were built for royalty and others before and during the time of Christ. It was all very well for the experts in the law to build new tombs for prophets long since martyred by the experts' forefathers (v.47). Yet this very act ironically symbolized approval of their forefathers' crimes against God's messengers (v.48; cf. the longer version of this saying in Matt 23:29–32).

J.D.M. Derrett (" 'You Build the Tombs of the Prophets' [Luke 11:47–51, Matt 23:29–31]," *Studia Evangelica* 4 [1968]:187–93) suggests that the building of tombs was a way of acknowledging guilt analogous to the offering of blood money to a victim's survivors by a relative of one guilty of murder.

49–51 These verses relate the grim truth behind the parable of the tenants (20:9–19). (See Notes on "wisdom" [v.49] and on "Zechariah" [v.51].)

52–54 Jesus directed his final woe against the experts in the law at their sin of taking away not just physical but eternal life. Those who should have opened the meaning of the OT with their "key" not only declined to use it themselves but prevented others from "entering" (v.52). (The present participle *eiserchomenous* may be conative: "trying to enter.") The implied subject of "knowledge" is probably the kingdom of God, which people were seeking to "enter." The connection of "keys" with the "kingdom" in Matthew 16:19 comes to mind here. Jesus charged the experts in the law with dereliction of their most important duty. His series of woes made the violent hostility against him described in vv.53–54 inevitable. His opponents followed him out of the house and fired at him a barrage of difficult questions (v.53), such as those later used to embarrass rabbinic scholars. He had challenged those who professed to be the expert biblical teachers. They were out to defend their reputation by discrediting his (v.54).

Notes

---

42 In its wild state, πήγανον (*pēganon*, "rue") was exempt from tithing. But Luke is referring to kitchen herbs among which cultivated rue was subject to tithing (D. Correns, "Die Verzehntung der Raute. Lk xi, 42 and M Schebi ix," 1 NovTest 6 [1963]: 110–12).

49 NIV translates ἡ σοφία τοῦ θεοῦ εἶπεν (*hē sophia tou theou eipen*, lit., "the wisdom of God said") as "God in his wisdom said." This interpretation is one way to understand this unusual introduction to a quotation that has no known source in the OT. Some think it is from an apocryphal source. Ellis (*Gospel of Luke*, pp. 170–73) takes it as referring to NT prophets bringing new revelations from the risen Christ. It may embody the essence of several OT passages. Many of the prophets God sent were opposed and even persecuted (e.g., 1 Kings 19:10, 14; Jer 7:25–26; Mal 3:10). The apostles were likewise "sent" on a mission that may be described as prophetic (Luke 6:22–23). Thus the saying applies all that God said "in his wisdom" in the OT to the NT apostles and prophets. Each of the above attempts to understand this difficult saying is plausible, and others could be cited. It is not clear whether there is an allusion to wisdom in its technical sense in Proverbs and other Jewish writings known as wisdom literature. There is no apparent reason for such an allusion, but it is otherwise difficult to explain why wisdom is introduced at all here, since nothing in the saying has a unique "wisdom" characteristic. It may simply refer to the sovereign wisdom of God in allowing evil men to continue and the good (here the prophets) to suffer.

51 Bloodguiltiness is emphasized here by the specific mention of Abel (Gen 4:8–10) and of a "Zechariah" (Matt 23:35—"Zechariah the son of Berakiah"), whose identity is much disputed. Some consider him to be a man, whose father's name was similar to that in Matthew, who was killed in the temple precincts in A.D. 67–68. This assumes that the saying either did not originate in the time of Jesus' earthly ministry or was expanded later. Marshall (*Gospel of Luke*, p. 506) argues that without any reference to Jesus as a martyr-prophet, or to the apostles, the saying cannot be classified as a Christian addition.

It is more common to identify "Zechariah" with the person mentioned in 2 Chron 24:20–25. Not only was that Zechariah murdered in the temple precincts, but the account follows a description similar to those mentioned above, of the prophets whom God "sent" who were resisted (2 Chron 24:19). J. Barton Payne ("Zechariah Who Perished," *Grace Journal* 8 [1967]: 33–35) points out, however, that the murder must have been done in the inner court (1 Kings 6:36; 2 Chron 4:9), in contrast to the location mentioned in 2 Chron 24:20–25; that Jesus is speaking of prophets, a term recalling the minor prophet Zechariah rather than the son of Jehoida the priest; that Jewish tradition favors the prophet; and that taking Josephus's order of the canon, Jesus' placing of Zechariah as last in a series could well refer to the canonical order rather than a chronological order. Further, Matthew adds the detail that the victim was the son of Berakiah, which accords with Zech 1:1. The problem is more vexing for interpreters of Matthew; Luke's version lacks the reference to Berakiah; so neither of the two biblical Zechariahs mentioned above is excluded.

52 Τὴν κλεῖδα τῆς γνώσεως (tēn kleida tēs gnōseōs, "the key to knowledge") could also be understood as an appositive: "the key that is knowledge." The parallel (Matt 23:13) has "you shut [or 'lock up' (κλείετε, kleiete)] the kingdom of heaven." The construction τὰς κλεῖδας τῆς βασιλείας (tas kleidas tēs basileias, "the keys of the kingdom") in Matt 16:19 is grammatically close enough to suggest that NIV's "key to knowledge" is preferable here in Luke 11:52.

53–54 "To besiege him with questions" is perhaps the best translation of ἀποστοματίζειν (apostomatizein), but its meaning is hard to determine. It seems to have connoted "mouthing" something one was supposed to learn and repeat. Here it could have the sense of pressing a series of questions to which certain "correct" answers must be given or the subject is considered heretical. Questions were sometimes used in rabbinic circles of the first centuries of our era to demonstrate one's own superiority over another (a possible clue to the meaning of 1 Cor 14:34–35). But the meaning is not at all certain. BAG (s.v.) says, "Ancient commentators interpreted it (prob. correctly) as *catch* (him) *in someth.* he says = vs. 54; then approx. *watch his utterances closely*" (*emphasis theirs*). The uncertainty led to changes in the Western text. Our problem probably comes from not knowing the development of an idiomatic use that may have had a brief lifespan.

D. *Teachings on Times of Crisis and Judgment* (12:1–13:35)

1. *Warnings and encouragements*

    12:1–12

    ¹Meanwhile, when a crowd of many thousands had gathered, so that they were trampling on one another, Jesus began to speak first to his disciples, saying: "Be on your guard against the yeast of the Pharisees, which is hypocrisy. ²There is nothing concealed that will not be disclosed, or hidden that will not be made known. ³What you have said in the dark will be heard in the daylight, and what you have whispered in the ear in the inner rooms will be proclaimed from the roofs.

    ⁴"I tell you, my friends, do not be afraid of those who kill the body and after that can do no more. ⁵But I will show you whom you should fear: Fear him who, after the killing of the body, has power to throw you into hell. Yes, I tell you, fear him. ⁶Are not five sparrows sold for two pennies? Yet not one of them is forgotten by God. ⁷Indeed, the very hairs of your head are all numbered. Don't be afraid; you are worth more than many sparrows.

    ⁸"I tell you, whoever acknowledges me before men, the Son of Man will also acknowledge him before the angels of God. ⁹But he who disowns me before men will be disowned before the angels of God. ¹⁰And everyone who speaks a word against the Son of Man will be forgiven, but anyone who blasphemes against the Holy Spirit will not be forgiven.

    ¹¹"When you are brought before synagogues, rulers and authorities, do not worry about how you will defend yourselves or what you will say, ¹²for the Holy Spirit will teach you at that time what you should say."

The crisis in Jesus' relationship with the teachers of the law at the end of chapter 11 gives rise to a series of strong statements about the eternal issues involved. Jesus' audience must choose sides. He gives promises and warnings, appropriate to each hearer's circumstance. Much of these exhortations is also found in Matthew's account of Jesus' instructions to the Twelve (Matt 10:19–20, 26–33). Similar ideas occur in the Olivet Discourse (Luke 21:12–19 and parallels). These other passages suggest an application not only to Jesus' immediate audience but also to the future church with its martyr missionaries.

1–3 "Meanwhile" (*en hois*, v.1) specifically connects this section with the preceding one. Again Luke notes the crowds, emphasizing the size of this one by the word "thousands" (*myriadōn*, lit., "of tens of thousands"—viz., an extremely large crowd). The same word in Acts 21:20 designates the great number of Jewish people who were believers, presumably far more than the few thousand mentioned at the beginning of Acts (e.g., 2:41, 47). Jesus addresses the disciples "first" (*prōton*, in an emphatic position). The crowds received his words later (vv.54–59). The key word "hypocrisy" (*hypokrisis*) was triggered by the charges in chapter 11. Jesus compares the insidious way this attitude can influence others to the action of "yeast" (*zymēs*). His next words about concealment and disclosure seem at first to be a warning that what hypocrites try to cover up will be revealed (v.2). But vv.3–4 have a positive thrust. Verse 3 is much like Matthew 10:26–27, where the disciples are encouraged not to be afraid but to declare publicly what they have heard privately from Jesus. This sense also fits the similar saying in the context of the parables of the kingdom (Mark 4:22; Luke 8:17). The idea of disclosure is linked to that of acknowledgment in v.8.

4–7 "Friends" (*philois*) is an expression of confidence (John 15:14–15) and is antithetical to the hostility of the Pharisees (v.4). Jesus does not guarantee protection from death but affirms that (1) God alone controls the final destiny of men, and people should "fear" (*phobēthēte*) him rather than those who can merely inflict physical death (v.5); and (2) God is intimately aware of all that befalls us. "Hell" (*geenna*) is mentioned only here in Luke but several times in Matthew and Mark, where it is clearly a place of torment ("the fire of," Matt 5:22; cf. Matt 18:8–9; Mark 9:43–48).

Geenna is a Greek transliteration of the Hebrew words for "Valley of Hinnom" (*ge hinnōm*), a ravine to the south and southwest of Jerusalem. Because it had been used for infant sacrifices (2 Chron 28:3; 33:6), it was repulsive to the Jews. Josiah attempted to prevent its use in this way (2 Kings 23:10), but apparently its reputation continued. Jeremiah labels it as a place of future judgment (Jer 7:32; 19:6). The idea of a place, of which this valley was an analogy, for punishment after death was developed in the intertestamental period. Jesus taught the reality of hell unambiguously.

Sparrows (v.6) and hairs (v.7) are so insignificant that this kind of argument (from lesser to greater) has a great effect in pointing up the supreme worth of the disciples in God's eyes.

8–9 Jesus underscores the seriousness of the issues by referring to the ultimate issue—whether or not one sides with him (v.8). Although he has already given the substance of this warning in his first passion prediction (9:26 and parallels), the cruciality of the present situation called for its restatement. The reference to "the Son of Man" in the third person has led some to think that Jesus is referring to a coming figure other than himself. But this would make Jesus a personage inferior to him. In point of fact, however, the third-person usage is consistent with Jesus' guarded use of titles. Not until his trial does he publicly combine the terms "Son of Man," "Son of God," and "Messiah" in an eschatological context. "Acknowledge" (*homolgēsei*) and "disown" (*arnēsetai*) are semantic polar opposites (KJV and NASB: "confess" and "deny"). The reference is apparently to a future scene when the Lord Jesus, having achieved victory and honor, acknowledges those who supported him and disowns (v.9) those who repudiated him during the present age. He does this publicly before God the Father (Matt 10:32–33) and the assembled angels.

10 The final one of this progression of warnings relates to the "unpardonable sin." The context of this saying in Luke differs from that of Matthew and Mark and the saying itself is separate from the Beelzebub controversy. This separation not only raises questions of tradition history beyond the scope of this commentary but also makes exegesis of the passage difficult. The separation does allow for the continued buildup of hostility between Jesus and the teachers of the law and for the sequence of warnings in 12:1–9, so that it occupies a climactic place. Nevertheless, it is difficult to determine its meaning without the contextual explanations in Matthew and Mark.

Matthew 12:33–36 and Mark 3:30 make it clear that the blasphemy against the Holy Spirit is the attribution of the works of Jesus to the very prince of demons. Moreover, this oral blasphemy involves not merely careless words but the expression of an incorrigibly evil heart. This background must be kept in mind as an aid to the theological application of Luke's reference to the unpardonable sin. If dishonoring the Son of Man is such a serious matter as vv.8–9 indicate, then total rejection of God by insinuating that his "Holy" Spirit is "evil" is so much the worse. One may reject Christ and later, by God's grace, accept him; but there is no remedy for absolute and complete denial of the one holy God—Father, Son, and Holy Spirit. This is what the "blasphemy" seems to be here. Some would relate this to Hebrews 6:4–6; 10:26–31 and to apostasy, but the Scriptures lack a sufficient interconnection to make this clear. The same caution should be applied to any attempt to connect this sin with the "sin that leads to death" (1 John 5:16–17).

11–12 The foregoing series of warnings and encouragements conclude with this striking contrast to the blasphemy against the Holy Spirit. Far from committing that sin of speaking against him, the believers find that the Spirit speaks through them. Observe the comparison with the mission of the Twelve and with the Olivet Discourse, especially in Matthew 10:19–20 and Luke 21:14–15. The circumstance of the Spirit's speaking through believers is not preaching but persecution, in which preparation of an adequate defense is hardly possible.

2. Parable of the rich fool

12:13–21

> ¹³Someone in the crowd said to him, "Teacher, tell my brother to divide the inheritance with me."
>
> ¹⁴Jesus replied, "Man, who appointed me a judge or an arbiter between you?"
> ¹⁵Then he said to them, "Watch out! Be on your guard against all kinds of greed; a man's life does not consist in the abundance of his possessions."
> ¹⁶And he told them this parable: "The ground of a certain rich man produced a

good crop. ¹⁷He thought to himself, 'What shall I do? I have no place to store my crops.'

¹⁸"Then he said, 'This is what I'll do. I will tear down my barns and build bigger ones, and there I will store all my grain and my goods. ¹⁹And I'll say to myself, "You have plenty of good things laid up for many years. Take life easy; eat, drink and be merry."'

²⁰"But God said to him, 'You fool! This very night your life will be demanded from you. Then who will get what you have prepared for yourself?'

²¹"This is how it will be with anyone who stores up things for himself but is not rich toward God."

Although the narrative flows smoothly, with the word "crowd" (v.13) making the transition from vv.1–12, the change in topic seems abrupt. A comparison with chapter 16 shows a similar placement of controversy with Pharisees alongside teaching about worldly wealth. There the words "the Pharisees, who loved money" (v.14) serve to link the two subjects. Chapters 12 and 16 have much in common. If Talbert (*Literary Patterns*, pp. 51–63) is right, they may be part of an overall pattern in which the two chapters are in a chiastic relationship. In any event, the topic of wealth is prominent in Luke's writing. In this instance, Jesus turns a question into an opportunity for ministry to an individual's underlying need.

13–14 A person who recognized Jesus as a "teacher" (v.13) would naturally expect him to have the ability to render a judgment in ethical matters (v.14). Rabbis were often thus consulted, and in later years some traveled from place to place to render legal decisions. Jesus' refusal to answer is not a denial of his right or ability to answer, nor of his concern for social and ethical matters. Rather he turns directly to an area in which others have no right to judge (cf. Matt 7:1)—viz., the question of motivation. We are not told whether the inquirer had legal ground for his request—a point that is unimportant here.

15 The audience (*autous*, "them") is probably now the whole crowd, not just the two brothers. The issue revolves around the very nature of "life" (*zōē*). Greed seeks possessions, which are not to be equated with true "living." In fact, they become a substitute for the proper object of man's search and worship—God. Therefore, "greed . . . is idolatry" (Col 3:5).

16–21 Since this is a parable (v.16), not an actual incident, Jesus can heighten certain elements that illustrate his point, even to the point of having God speak directly to the rich man. The man expresses in his words (vv.17–19) the attitude Jesus discerns not only in the inquirer but in others (cf. "anyone" in v.21). The word "fool" (*aphrōn*, v.20) is not used lightly but in the OT sense of one who rejects the knowledge and precepts of God as a basis for life. God addresses the man on his own pragmatic terms, dealing not with matters of the kingdom or of life beyond death but with the question of the disposition of the man's possessions. This underscores the fact that he will have to "leave it all." If we read the question "Who will get?" with Ecclesiastes 2:18–19 in mind, there is also the irony that after years of careful management the man's possessions might be frittered away by an incompetent heir.

Verse 21, which uses the contrasting words "for himself" (*heautō*) and "toward God" (*eis theon*), ends powerfully with the participle "rich" (*ploutōn*) as the final word. "Stores up things for himself" resembles Matthew 6:19: "Do not store up for yourselves treasures on earth." Both passages introduce similar encouragements about God's care (cf. vv.21–22 here with Matt 6:19, 25).

Notes

13 Διδάσκαλε (*didaskale*, "teacher") has the same sense as "rabbi," which Luke does not use in his Gospel. Formerly some thought that the term "rabbi" was anachronistic in the Gospels, as it was only later that ordination was practiced in Judaism. But now it is clear that both terms were used in an honorific sense in Jesus' day (see H. Shanks, "Is the Title 'Rabbi' Anachronistic in the Gospels?" JQR 53 [1963]: 343–44). Jesus' contemporaries recognized that, while he was not rabbinically trained, he was a competent teacher (John 7:15). Luke has already stressed the crowds' assessment of Jesus' teaching authority (4:31–32).

19–20 NIV translates ψυχή (*psychē*) in three ways—"myself," "you," and "life"—thereby showing the broad sense of the word customarily translated "soul."

3. Anxiety over possessions

12:22–34

22Then Jesus said to his disciples: "Therefore I tell you, do not worry about your life, what you will eat; or about your body, what you will wear. 23Life is more than food, and the body more than clothes. 24Consider the ravens: They do not sow or reap, they have no storeroom or barn; yet God feeds them. And how much more valuable you are than birds! 25Who of you by worrying can add a single hour to his life? 26Since you cannot do this very little thing, why do you worry about the rest?

27"Consider how the lilies grow. They do not labor or spin. Yet I tell you, not even Solomon in all his splendor was dressed like one of these. 28If that is how God clothes the grass of the field, which is here today, and tomorrow is thrown into the fire, how much more will he clothe you, O you of little faith! 29And do not set your heart on what you will eat or drink; do not worry about it. 30For the pagan world runs after all such things, and your Father knows that you need them. 31But seek his kingdom, and these things will be given to you as well.

32"Do not be afraid, little flock, for your Father has been pleased to give you the kingdom. 33Sell your possessions and give to the poor. Provide purses for yourselves that will not wear out, a treasure in heaven that will not be exhausted, where no thief comes near and no moth destroys. 34For where your treasure is, there your heart will be also.

This section (vv.22–34), except for vv.32–34, is virtually identical to Matthew 6:25–33 in the Sermon on the Mount. As noted in the comment above on v.21, which forms a transition to this section, both passages are connected with sayings against "storing up" things for oneself. The passage ends (v.34) with a saying about one's "treasure" (cf. Matt 6:21). The Greek word for "treasure" (*thēsauros*) is related to that for "store up" (*theaurizō*). The passage then both introduced and concluded with a saying about "treasuring" is thereby given its theme. What was implied in the warning parable of vv.16–20 is explicitly commanded here (note the *dia touto*, "therefore," of v.22). Believers should not act like the "pagan world" (*ta ethnē tou kosmou*, v.30), represented by the rich fool of the parable.

22-23 Having addressed the crowds in vv.1–21, Jesus turns to his disciples. The word for "life" in vv.22–23 (and cf. v.20) is *psychē*, which often means "soul." Here the translation "life" is appropriate. Observe the parallelism between v.22 and v.23. A comment on food comes first in each verse, followed by one on clothing. Verse 23 provides the support for the exhortation in v.22: there is more to life than these. The exhortation "do not worry" (*mē merimnate*) stands alongside the implied "do not covet" in this passage and the preceding one (cf. v.15). Actually one can both worry and be covetous whether he is poor or rich. "Do not worry" is the first of a series of four prohibitions. The others are "Do not set your heart on" (v.29), "Do not worry" (again v.29), and "Do not be afraid" (v.32).

24-26 The thrust of the comparison "how much more valuable?" is similar to the argument from the lesser to the greater in vv.6–7. There the sparrows represent birds of little value. Here the ravens (v.24) may represent birds that were considered unclean (Lev 11:13–20, esp. v.15) and therefore unworthy of God's care. Jesus assures us that the God who cares for such birds surely will care for us. Verses 25–26 constitute still another argument from the lesser (adding inches of height or minutes of life [cf. Notes]) to the greater (totality of life and its needs). The point here is that if it is futile to worry about small matters we cannot control, it is even more futile to worry about the larger matters that lie even farther beyond our control.

27-28 Jesus gives a final example of the lesser to greater argument in contrasting the grandeur of Solomon, who could afford the finest clothing, to common flowers, which can do nothing toward making clothes (v.27). His second contrast is between the limited lifespan of flowers and the (implied) eternal life that lay before the disciples (v.28). God's meticulous and lavish care for mere perishing flowers assures us of his unfailing care for his own people. In view of this, the disciples' "little faith" is all the more shameful.

29 "Do not worry" is the third of four prohibitions (cf. comment on v.22). The word for "worry" here (*meteōrizesthe*) differs from that in v.22 (*merimnate*). *Meteōrizesthe* meant in classical Greek "be raised up" or "suspended." While it came metaphorically to mean "worry," the literal meaning might be expressed by "be in suspense" or "be up in the air."

30-31 "The pagan world" (*ta ethnē*, lit., "the nations," i.e., the Gentiles) contrasts with believers. In Matthew's report of the Sermon on the Mount, believers are cautioned three times not to behave as the pagans do: (1) in their relation to people (Matt 5:47), (2) in their relation to God in prayer (Matt 6:7), and (3) in their relation to material possessions (Matt 6:32)—the application it has here in Luke. In Matthew the contrast to Gentiles is especially significant in view of the Jewish slant of that Gospel. Luke 6:32, the equivalent of Matthew 5:47, has "sinners" (*hamartōloi*), a Lukan term. Pagans do not have the same relation believers have with a loving, caring, providing heavenly Father. To know that he knows their needs is sufficient assurance for all believers. Secure in that knowledge, his disciples can turn all their attention to the kingdom they are commanded to seek (v.31).

32 "Do not be afraid" (*mē phobou*) introduces another contrast. The "little flock" (*to* *mikron poimnion*), which now needs to be fed and defended, will one day inherit the kingdom, possessing its benefits and authority. The fatherhood of God and its connection with the giving of the kingdom are themes not only characteristic of Matthew but also foundational in the Sermon on the Mount, of which this passage may have been originally a part. The encouragement not to fear is appropriate in view of the hostility of the "experts in the law" who, instead of opening the way to the kingdom and its truth (11:52), stand in the way of those who seek it.

33 With the injunction to "sell your possessions" (*pōlēsate ta hyparchonta hymōn*), we come to the concluding exhortations on the "treasure" theme. It is difficult to know whether the reason for this exhortation is to benefit the poor or to rid the disciples of encumbering possessions. While the poor are mentioned, the point of the passage as a whole seems to be the total dependence of disciples on God. The second reason, therefore, is probably primary and the first secondary in *this* context but still important in itself and in Luke's thought throughout his Gospel.

The word "all" is neither present nor implied before the word "possessions." As we have seen, the point of Jesus' teaching on treasures is that they are not to be hoarded for one's own selfish pleasure (cf. v.21 and Matt 6:19). Nevertheless the interpreter must be careful neither to blunt Jesus' strong teaching as expressed in Luke regarding a life of abandonment and giving (cf. 6:27–36; 14:26, 33) nor to introduce teachings given to one audience into a discussion with another group. One should live on such a modest level of subsistence that the only "purses" needed (see the metaphor in v.33) are those one needs for heavenly "treasure." By their nature, such purses are never motheaten or stolen.

34 This verse shows the essential thrust of Jesus' teaching. It is not the *extent* but the *place* of one's possessions that is emphasized, because it is the direction of one's "heart," heavenward or earthward, that is all important.

Notes

---

25 NIV's translation "add a single hour to his life" of ἐπὶ τὴν ἡλικίαν αὐτοῦ προσθεῖναι πῆχυν (*epi tēn hēlikian autou prostheinai pēchyn*) is debatable (cf. NIV mg). *Hēlikia* can mean "age" or "bodily stature" (cf. BAG, s.v.). *Pēchys* means "cubit," a unit of measure the length of one's forearm, roughly eighteen inches. It could be used to describe the extent of the *hēlikia* in either of its senses. NIV takes *hēlikia* in the sense of "age," which fits well with the parable about the rich fool (vv.16–21) who could not add to his life. Yet the words "how the lilies grow" (v.27) suggest the idea of height. A person of normal stature would scarcely want to add another foot and a half to his height; so that meaning may be unlikely. The meaning could, however, be that one normally grows inch by inch without giving it any thought. Even if one thought about it, he could not suddenly gain eighteen inches and be full-grown. While to live on some "borrowed time" may seem important and to grow a foot-and-a-half taller is to gain about an additional fourth of one's stature, these are both insignificant in comparison with the entire scope of one's life, especially considered in its spiritual dimension. At any rate, neither is possible; so why worry at all?

27 Τὰ κρίνα (*ta krina*, "the lilies") may be some specific flower of Jesus' land, but more probably Jesus was "thinking of all the wonderful blooms that adorn the fields of Galilee" (BAG, s.v.; see also Morris, *Luke*, p. 214).

Οὐ κοπιᾷ οὐδὲ νήθει (*ou kopia oude nēthei*, "they do not labor or spin") receives a cautious "D" rating by UBS. The Western text has οὔτε νήθει οὔτε ὑφαίνει (*oute nēthei oute hyphainei*, "they neither spin nor weave"). Metzger (*Textual Commentary*, p. 161) says the Western reading was rejected "after much hesitation . . . as a stylistic refinement." Marshall (*Gospel of Luke*, p. 528) considers this to be "over-subtle for a scribe" but still finds support by only one Greek MS (D) weak. It is probably best to keep the UBS reading as does NIV.

---

4. Readiness for the coming of the Son of Man

12:35–48

35"Be dressed ready for service and keep your lamps burning, 36like men waiting for their master to return from a wedding banquet, so that when he comes and knocks they can immediately open the door for him. 37It will be good for those servants whose master finds them watching when he comes. I tell you the truth, he will dress himself to serve, will have them recline at the table and will come and wait on them. 38It will be good for those servants whose master finds them ready, even if he comes in the second or third watch of the night. 39But understand this: If the owner of the house had known at what hour the thief was coming, he would not have let his house be broken into. 40You also must be ready, because the Son of Man will come at an hour when you do not expect him."

41Peter asked, "Lord, are you telling this parable to us, or to everyone?"

42The Lord answered, "Who then is the faithful and wise manager, whom the master puts in charge of his servants to give them their food allowance at the proper time? 43It will be good for that servant whom the master finds doing so when he returns. 44I tell you the truth, he will put him in charge of all his possessions. 45But suppose the servant says to himself, 'My master is taking a long time in coming,' and he then begins to beat the menservants and maidservants and to eat and drink and get drunk. 46The master of that servant will come on a day when he does not expect him and at an hour he is not aware of. He will cut him to pieces and assign him a place with the unbelievers.

47"That servant who knows his master's will and does not get ready or does not do what his master wants will be beaten with many blows. 48But the one who does not know and does things deserving punishment will be beaten with few blows. From everyone who has been given much, much will be demanded; and from the one who has been entrusted with much, much more will be asked.

The emphatic use of the personal pronoun "you" (*hymeis*) twice in the Greek text of vv.35–36 sets the attitude of the alert Christian in contrast to that of the pagans (v.30) who seek only the things of this present world. The word "watching" (*grēgorountas*, v.37) expresses the theme of this passage. Luke introduces it earlier in his Gospel than do Matthew and Mark, who use it only in the Olivet Discourse (and in the parables following in Matthew and in the Lord's words to the disciples at Gethsemane (cf. Matt 24:42–43; 25:13; 26:38, 40–41). Luke does not use the actual verb "to watch" in either of the parallel contexts (17:26–30, 34–36; 22:45–46). Here he seems to be impressed by the connection in our Lord's teaching between warnings about future judgment. The verses following the figure about "watching" (vv.39–40) and the next section also (vv.41–46) are parallel to part of Matthew's version of the Olivet Discourse (Matt 24:43–51). They are usually considered to be from Q and interwoven with other material. The scene in vv.36–37 and the parable in v.39 point clearly to the necessity of being ready for the Son of Man (v.40).

35–38 In Jesus' time, a person "dressed ready for service" (v.35) tucked his flowing outer robe under his belt or sash. This was done to prepare for travel, fighting (Eph 6:14), or work (cf. the metaphorical use in 1 Peter 1:13).

Matthew 25:1–13 also describes a time of waiting with burning lamps for the return of a bridegroom for his wedding. In Matthew the lamps are *lampades;* here they are *lychnoi.* There virgins wait for the bridegroom; here servants wait for their masters (v.36). The strong affirmation "I tell you the truth" (*amēn*, v.37) appears for the first time in Luke since 4:24. There is a striking reversal of roles as the master dresses himself to serve (cf. v.35) and waits on the servants. This contrasts with Luke 17:7–10, where a different point is being made. If the return is very late in the night or toward morning, in the "second or third watch" (the middle and last division of the night hours according to Jewish reckoning), the alertness of the servants is even more commendable (v.38).

39–40 The image now changes to one of burglary (v.39). The absence of figurative or parabolic terminology (cf. "like" in v.36) may indicate that this is not a story but a recent incident known to Jesus' audience. Moreover, Jeremias (*Parables of Jesus,* pp. 48–49) notes that the use of the aorist tense in the story gives the impression of a straightforward narrative. It is unusual, but not impossible, for an evil character, such as a thief, to represent a good person (see the unjust judge [18:1–8], who stands in contrast to God). Actually, it is the story as a whole, not the individual characters in it, that provides the comparison here. The concluding exhortation (v.40) to "be ready," because the time of the Son of Man's coming is unknown, is similar to Matthew 24:42–44, in the Olivet Discourse, where the burglary figure is also used (cf. Matt 25:13; Mark 13:33–37). Luke's version of the Olivet Discourse lacks this saying, as well as the saying about ignorance of the day and hour, which is recorded in Matt 24:36 and Mark 13:32. Here Luke is clearly concentrating much of the Lord's teaching on the implications of his sudden return.

41–44 Peter responds, in his accustomed role as spokesman for the apostles, with a question about the extent of their responsibility (v.41). Jesus answers, as often, with a counterquestion (v.42). Although he says elsewhere that exhortations to "watch" apply to everyone (Mark 13:37), in this case the parable that follows (vv.42–46) shows that the apostles have a special responsibility. In the illustration the "manager" (or "steward," *oikonomos*) in charge of the "servants" is a "servant" (or "slave," *doulos*) himself (v.43). This was a common situation in that first-century society. The passage teaches the importance of faithfulness in doing the will of the master. Verses 42–46 emphasize responsibility one has for those who have been placed under his leadership. Conversely, the following paragraph (vv.47–48) focuses on response to the master's command.

45–46 As in 18:7 and 19:12, the clear implication is that Jesus himself would not return immediately but that there would be an interval of waiting and serving (cf. Notes). The attitude of the manager in v.45 is contrary to that commanded in v.40. The word "begins" (*arxētai*, v.45) suggests that the action is interrupted by the master's unexpected return. The severe treatment of the servants may be hyperbolic, but Acts 20:29–30 warns against false leaders who ravage the congregation (cf. the warning in Matt 7:15–23). Likewise the vivid description of the manager's punishment, "cut to pieces" (*dichotomēsei*), stresses the seriousness of his default of responsibility (v.46, cf. Notes). "A place with the unbelievers" applies to the false religious leaders alluded to rather than merely to the secular characters in the story.

47–48 If this punishment seems too severe, the explanation of God's principle of judgment now clarifies matters. The servant in v.47 may represent those who sin "with a high hand," committing "presumptuous sins" (Num 15:30–31; Ps 19:13, RSV). If so, the servant who "does not know" (v.48) sins "unwittingly" and has "hidden faults" (Num 15:27–29; Ps 19:12, RSV). In either case there is some definite personal responsibility and therefore judgment, because the servant should have made it his business to know his master's will. All have some knowledge of God (Rom 1:20), and God judges according to individual levels of responsibility (Rom 2:12–13). The closing statement (v.48) would apply especially to the apostles and church leaders throughout the successive centuries.

Notes

35–48 This passage is important in determining Luke's view of the Parousia. Many scholars have assumed that Luke modified the tradition of Jesus' teaching about his return, reducing the element of imminency to accommodate the fact that Jesus was obviously not returning as soon as expected. A more realistic view, however, is that Jesus not only taught the certainty of his return at an unexpected moment but also implied, through various instructions for his disciples, that the community of believers would continue for an unspecified time serving their Lord till his return in the indefinite future (see comments at 19:11–27; cf. Ellis, *Eschatology in Luke,* and Marshall, *Eschatology and the Parables*). There is neither any necessary nor substantial ground for postulating that in the transmission of Jesus' teaching about the Parousia the audience has been changed from the crowds to the disciples so as to make the teaching apply to the church in view of a delayed Parousia rather than to those who need to repent in view of impending judgment (cf. Jeremias, *Parables of Jesus,* p. 48).

46 Διχοτομήσει αὐτὸν (*dichotomēsei auton,* "he will cut him to pieces") seems to be such an extreme punishment to modern readers that various attempts have been made to explain it. Marshall (*Gospel of Luke,* p. 543) surveys some of these explanations, favoring that of O. Betz ("The Dichotomized Servant and the End of Judas Iscariot," *Revue de Qumran* 5 [1964]: 43–58). According to Betz, the original Aramaic statement was "he was cut off," i.e., from the "sons of light" as in the theology of Qumran (cf. 1QS 2.16). The words in v.46 would then express this same idea in different terms.

5. *Division over Jesus*

12:49–53

49"I have come to bring fire on the earth, and how I wish it were already kindled! 50But I have a baptism to undergo, and how distressed I am until it is completed! 51Do you think I came to bring peace on earth? No, I tell you, but division. 52From now on there will be five in one family divided against each other, three against two and two against three. 53They will be divided, father against son and son against father, mother against daughter and daughter against mother, mother-in-law against daughter-in-law and daughter-in-law against mother-in-law."

49–50 The Lord's teaching about preparation for his return and impending judgment (vv.35–48) leads to this paragraph about the personal crises Christ precipitates. It is difficult to determine the precise meaning of "fire" (v.49) because the word can signify either judgment or purification, to say nothing of other less probable meanings. The verses that follow v.49 may, consistently with the preceding paragraphs, connote judgment. While Jesus came to bring salvation rather than judgment (Luke 4:19; John 3:17), his coming also meant judgment (John 9:39). A comparison with earlier teaching in Luke, however, suggests that "fire" means purification as well as judgment. The ministry of John the Baptist included not only judgment (3:9, 17) but also the promise that Jesus would "baptize . . . with the Holy Spirit and fire" (see commentary and OT references at 3:16). Luke 9:51–56 shows that Jesus did not intend to bring an immediate fire of judgment on those who rejected him. Since 3:16 links fire with the Holy Spirit, it is possible that this fire was to be "kindled" by the baptism of the Spirit (Acts 2:1–4). This could only occur after Jesus' own "baptism" of death, to which he referred here (v.50). Mark 10:38 mentions baptism as a symbol of Jesus' death, along with the "cup" Jesus spoke of at Gethsemane (Luke 22:42). He felt "distressed" (*synechomai*) in anticipation of that. "The prospect of his sufferings was a perpetual Gethsemane" (Plummer, p. 334).

51–53 Although the Messiah was to bring peace (v.51), this was not his only mission, nor, in the political sense, his immediate one. Isaiah 11:1–9 shows that even in the final period of peace, the Messiah, enabled by the Spirit, will exercise judgment. Already in his earthly ministry ("from now on," v.52), there is division. The parallel to v.51 in Matthew 10:34 has "sword" (*machaira*) instead of "division" (*diamerismon*). In 22:36 Luke reports Jesus' speaking of a "sword" (*machaira*) when the crisis deepens. The expression "from now on" (*apo tou nyn*) is, apart from 2 Corinthians 5:16, unique to Luke in the NT. It is an important part of Luke's vocabulary of time (cf. esp. 5:10; 22:69; also the use of "today" in 4:21; 13:32; 19:5, 9). Luke is stressing the element of crisis, both immediately and at the Lord's return. During this time his disciples must be prepared for a break in their family relationships if others do not concur with their decision to follow Christ (vv.52–53; cf. 14:26). The wording of v.53 is probably from Micah 7:6.

The mention of six people in v.53 does not contradict the number five in v.52, since one person can have two relationships, e.g., a woman can be both a mother and a mother-in-law.

Notes

51 Ἐν τῇ γῇ (*en tē gē*, "on earth") may possibly refer to the "land" of Israel. This meaning of *gē* is possible (TDNT, 1:677–78). "Peace on earth" in 2:14 has ἐπί (*epi*, "on"; so 12:49), not *en* as here. If this was the case, Jesus' words would be referring even more clearly to the Jewish messianic expectations current in his day.

Οὐχὶ λέγω ὑμῖν (*ouchi, legō hymin*, "No, I tell you") is emphatic.

6. Interpreting the times

12:54–59

54He said to the crowd: "When you see a cloud rising in the west, immediately you say, 'It's going to rain,' and it does. 55And when the south wind blows, you say, 'It's going to be hot,' and it is. 56Hypocrites! You know how to interpret the appearance of the earth and the sky. How is it that you don't know how to interpret this present time?

57"Why don't you judge for yourselves what is right? 58As you are going with your adversary to the magistrate, try hard to be reconciled to him on the way, or he may drag you off to the judge, and the judge turn you over to the officer, and the officer throw you into prison. 59I tell you, you will not get out until you have paid the last penny."

54–56 Though the text does not link this section with the preceding one, there is a common element of crisis. The words "interpret this present time [*kairon*, or 'season']" (v.56) imply this by comparing the observation of changing weather (vv.54–55) with God's "time" of opportunity and responsibility. This emphasis on the opportune time recurs more emphatically in 19:41–44 (cf. "on this day . . . but now . . . you did not recognize the time"). Here the word "hypocrites" (v.56) shows that the people Jesus was speaking to were not sincere in their professed inability to "interpret this present time."

57–59 Here Jesus' appeal to human judgment regarding a time of personal decision (v.57) is similar to, though not verbally identical with, Matthew 5:25–26. In human affairs one resolves a crisis situation wisely to avoid penalty (v.58). This is a secular illustration, and v.59 should not be applied spiritually in point-for-point detail aside from its basic application of reconciliation with God before the day of judgment.

Notes

54–55 Δυσμῶν (*dysmōn*, "west") is the direction of the Mediterranean, and the νότον (*noton*, "south wind") comes from the desert.

7. A call to repentance

13:1–9

1Now there were some present at that time who told Jesus about the Galileans whose blood Pilate had mixed with their sacrifices. 2Jesus answered, "Do you think that these Galileans were worse sinners than all the other Galileans because they suffered this way? 3I tell you, no! But unless you repent, you too will all perish. 4Or those eighteen who died when the tower in Siloam fell on them—do you think they were more guilty than all the others living in Jerusalem? 5I tell you, no! But unless you repent, you too will all perish."

6Then he told this parable: "A man had a fig tree, planted in his vineyard, and he went to look for fruit on it, but did not find any. 7So he said to the man who took care of the vineyard, 'For three years now I've been coming to look for fruit on this fig tree and haven't found any. Cut it down! Why should it use up the soil?'

⁸" 'Sir,' the man replied, 'leave it alone for one more year, and I'll dig around it and fertilize it. ⁹If it bears fruit next year, fine! If not, then cut it down.' "

At this point, dialogue about the problem of human suffering and evil introduces a parable that, like Jesus' teaching in chapter 12, deals with crisis and judgment.

1–5 We cannot be certain as to the exact incident v.1 refers to. The social tension made revolutionary activity in those days possible at any time. Pilate's position as governor of a troubled province far distant from Rome was precarious. Josephus (Life, 92 [17]) says that Galileans were especially susceptible to revolt, though see comment at 1:26. Any attack against Jews who had come to offer sacrifices was horrendous whatever its reason. The fact that the people "told Jesus" about the event implies that he was not at Jerusalem when it happened. Jesus (v.4) refuses to attribute tragedy (v.2) or accident (v.3) directly to one's sin as the Jews did (cf. John 9:1–3). On the contrary, he affirms the sinfulness of all people (v.5). "Too" (*hōsautōs*) means "similarly" or even "in the same way," showing that one who flouts God cannot count on immunity from sudden adversity. Whereas the two victims of the calamities referred to in vv.1–5 perished physically, "all" (*pantes*) who do not repent face spiritual death.

6–9 Once more Jesus alludes to Micah 7 (cf. comments on 12:53), this time to Micah 7:1, with its lament over unproductive fig trees. The symbolism, like that of the vine in Isaiah 5:1–7, applies to Israel. Jesus' mention (v.6) of both a fig tree and a vineyard makes the figure doubly clear. Luke includes this parable instead of the cursing of the fig tree (found only in Matt 21:18–22; Mark 11:12–14, 20–25). Here the tree is not immediately destroyed, as it was in the cursing incident, but is given an extra year of grace (v.8), even beyond the three years its owner had already waited (v.7). Israel failed to recognize her season of opportunity (cf. 12:56; 19:41–44).

Notes

3, 5 Οὐχί (*ouchi*, "No!") is the first word in each sentence for emphasis.
4 The tower of Siloam was probably near the Pool of Siloam in the southeastern corner of Jerusalem.

8. Healing a woman on the Sabbath

13:10–17

¹⁰On a Sabbath Jesus was teaching in one of the synagogues, ¹¹and a woman was there who had been crippled by a spirit for eighteen years. She was bent over and could not straighten up at all. ¹²When Jesus saw her, he called her forward and said to her, "Woman, you are set free from your infirmity." ¹³Then he put his hands on her, and immediately she straightened up and praised God.
¹⁴Indignant because Jesus had healed on the Sabbath, the synagogue ruler said to the people, "There are six days for work. So come and be healed on those days, not on the Sabbath."

15The Lord answered him, "You hypocrites! Doesn't each of you on the Sabbath untie his ox or donkey from the stall and lead it out to give it water? 16Then should not this woman, a daughter of Abraham, whom Satan has kept bound for eighteen long years, be set free on the Sabbath day from what bound her?"

17When he said this, all his opponents were humiliated, but the people were delighted with all the wonderful things he was doing.

The Sabbath issue, a major cause of dissension earlier (6:1–11), now reappears. As in 6:6, and for the last time in Luke's narrative sequence, Jesus is teaching in a synagogue. This incident, like the others in this chapter, shows that in spite of the failure of the religious leaders to acknowledge the time of God's working, the kingdom is still being manifested.

10–13 "Was teaching" (*ēn didaskōn*) suggests that as Jesus was speaking (v.10), he suddenly became aware of the woman (*kai idou,* "and look!" untranslated in NIV [v.11], with perhaps some loss of effect). As often in healing narratives, Luke mentions the seriousness and duration of the disease to highlight the greatness of the cure.

The "spirit" (v.11) presumably was a demon, though Luke does not specifically say the woman was demon possessed. Any activity by a demon is ultimately Satan's responsibility (v.16; cf. comments on 11:14–20). The fact that Jesus touched her (v.13) has led some to conclude that she was not demon possessed, on the ground that nowhere else in the Gospels are we told that Jesus touched a demon-possessed person. But the Gospel narratives by no means record every detail of Jesus' actions. Far more important, and emphasized by Luke, is the woman's instant healing and its direct attribution to God. This, of course, shows that Jesus was truly acting with God's authority. "Praised [*edoxazen*] God" reflects Luke's special interest in the glory of God (cf. 5:26). And Luke may have used *endoxois* (v.17), which sounds similar and means "wonderful things," to remind his readers of this theme of praise.

14–17 The controversy over Jesus' Sabbath activities now comes to the fore (v.14), as the synagogue ruler speaks to the people on the ground of Exodus 20:9–10. Notice that he avoids addressing Jesus directly. There was ample evidence of rabbinic precedent for helping animals in emergencies on the Sabbath. So Jesus uses a lesser-to-greater argument to move from helping animals (v.15) to helping human beings (v.16; cf. 12:24). "A daughter of Abraham" means a Jewess. In keeping with Luke's purpose, this designation highlights the priority of the Jews in the program of the Gospel. It also shows that she deserved immediate healing. As he often does, Luke gives us the crowd's reaction (v.17; cf. 4:15, 22, 32, 36–37; 5:26).

9. Parables of the mustard seed and the yeast

13:18–21

18Then Jesus asked, "What is the kingdom of God like? What shall I compare it to? 19It is like a mustard seed, which a man took and planted in his garden. It grew and became a tree, and the birds of the air perched in its branches."

20Again he asked, "What shall I compare the kingdom of God to? 21It is like yeast that a woman took and mixed into a large amount of flour until it worked all through the dough."

971

18–21 In Luke's narrative, his presentation of these two kingdom parables comes later than in Matthew and Mark. Isolated from other parables, they receive the added support of the account of the miraculous healing Luke has just described. In Jesus' teaching the "mustard seed" (v.19) represents that which is tiny but effective (cf. 17:6). The full-grown mustard tree may reach ten feet or so in height (see ZPEB, 4:324–25) and thus be quite large enough for birds to settle in its branches. It is not certain whether birds are mentioned as vivid detail in accord with the occasional OT use of birds to symbolize the Gentiles (cf. Notes). The point of the parable is not the growth of the tree, nor a comparison between the seed and the tree, but the power inherent in the seed. This power is implicit in the kingdom (v.18), as Jesus' healing of the woman has just demonstrated. Likewise the point of Jesus' simile of the yeast and the kingdom is not that yeast penetrates the dough but the inherent power— i.e., of the kingdom—that enables it to do this. This interpretation fits Mark's parable of the growing seed (Mark 4:26–29).

Notes

19 Πετεινά (*peteina*, "birds") are specifically mentioned in each version of the parable (Matt 13:32; Mark 4:32) and may therefore be significant in symbolizing Gentile nations. Plummer (p. 345) cites Ezek 17:23; 31:6; Dan 4:9, 18[12, 21 MT] as OT evidence for this.

21 Ζύμη (*zymē*, "leaven") when used metaphorically usually symbolizes evil. This is true in both biblical and secular literature. See reference notes on Matt 13:33 in J.J. Wettstein's edition (1751–52) of the Greek NT for examples. But it is difficult without reading extraneous ideas into the text to find anything other than a positive straightforward description of the kingdom here.

10. *Entering the kingdom*

13:22–30

> [22] Then Jesus went through the towns and villages, teaching as he made his way to Jerusalem. [23] Someone asked him, "Lord, are only a few people going to be saved?"
> He said to them, [24] "Make every effort to enter through the narrow door, because many, I tell you, will try to enter and will not be able to. [25] Once the owner of the house gets up and closes the door, you will stand outside knocking and pleading, 'Sir, open the door for us.'
> "But he will answer, 'I don't know you or where you come from.'
> [26] "Then you will say, 'We ate and drank with you, and you taught in our streets.'
> [27] "But he will reply, 'I don't know you or where you come from. Away from me, all you evildoers!'
> [28] "There will be weeping there, and gnashing of teeth, when you see Abraham, Isaac and Jacob and all the prophets in the kingdom of God, but you yourselves thrown out. [29] People will come from east and west and north and south, and will take their places at the feast in the kingdom of God. [30] Indeed there are those who are last who will be first, and first who will be last."

Jesus' teaching now turns to personal responsibility. Several themes appear in this section that occur in other NT settings in Matthew and Mark (cf., in sequence, Matt 7:13–14; 25:10–12; 7:22–23; 8:11–12; 19:30; 20:16, along with Mark 10:31).

22–23 Here we have one of the few specific travel references in what is sometimes called Luke's "travel section" (9:51–19:44). Nevertheless, the travel theme appears repeatedly in connection with the verb *poreuomai* and its cognates (cf. *dieporeueto*, "went," v.22; see comment on v.33). The words "made his way to Jerusalem" are especially significant because the important element is not merely travel but Jesus' orientation toward that city (cf. 9:51; 13:33–34; 17:11; 19:28, 41 and comment on 19:28). Like the question on divorce (Matt 19:3), this one about whether few or many people will be saved (v.23) was the occasion of differing opinions among the rabbis.

24–27 Jesus' reply (v.24) emphasizes not "how many?" but "who?" The saved are those who seize their opportunity now (in the "year of the Lord's favor," 4:19). Once the time for decision has passed (v.25), attempts to enter into salvation afterward (note the future "will try . . . will not be able," v.24) will be futile. Likewise Esau "afterward" sought his inheritance in vain (Heb 12:17). Does the "narrow door" limit the number of people who are admitted or the opportunities a person has to enter? Verse 24 by itself suggests the former; v.25 with its reference to the closing door suggests the latter. In John 10:9, entrance to salvation is only through Christ, who himself is the gate. The use of the third person in "But he will reply" (v.27) does not refer to anyone other than Jesus as the Son of Man (cf. Matt 7:23: "I will tell them") and simply follows the pattern of v.25. The repetition of "I don't know you or where you come from" (v.27; cf. v.25) heightens the sense of utter rejection (cf. Matt 7:23: "I never knew you"). Familiarity with Jesus (v.26) will be of no benefit then (cf. the even stronger plea in Matt 7:22).

28–30 The contrast is heightened between those inside—note the reference to the patriarchs of Israel—and those outside the door, i.e., outside the kingdom (v.28). Every Jew expected to sit with the patriarchs at the messianic banquet or "feast in the kingdom of God" (v.29). The concept of such a feast in heaven as a celebration with the Messiah is alluded to throughout the OT and other Jewish literature over a long period of time (cf. 14:5). The tragedy would not only be that of looking at the patriarchs from the outside but also that of seeing Gentiles inside with them. Verse 30 describes a total reversal of positions. Here it clearly means the exclusion from future blessings of those who thought they were first in line for them. Its thrust is stronger here than its use in different contexts in Matthew 19:30; 20:16; and Mark 10:31. Exclusion from the kingdom will lead to "weeping and grinding of teeth"—an expression found only here in v.27 but used several times in Matthew (8:12; 22:13; 24:51; 25:30) to express the horror of future doom.

Notes

24 "Make every effort" is ἀγωνίζεσθε (*agōnizesthe*), a word often used in an athletic or a military context. It does not imply working for salvation but rather earnestness in seeking it (cf. its use regarding prayer in Col 4:12).

11. *Concern over Jerusalem*

13:31–35

[31]At that time some Pharisees came to Jesus and said to him, "Leave this place and go somewhere else. Herod wants to kill you."
[32]He replied, "Go tell that fox, 'I will drive out demons and heal people today and tomorrow, and on the third day I will reach my goal.' [33]In any case, I must keep going today and tomorrow and the next day—for surely no prophet can die outside Jerusalem!
[34]"O Jerusalem, Jerusalem, you who kill the prophets and stone those sent to you, how often I have longed to gather your children together, as a hen gathers her chicks under her wings, but you were not willing! [35]Look, your house is left to you desolate. I tell you, you will not see me again until you say, 'Blessed is he who comes in the name of the Lord.' "

This is the main passage in Luke in which Jesus expresses a strong sense of destiny in his final journey to Jerusalem. Note the sense of divine purpose expressed by such characteristic Lukan words as "today" (*sēmeron*) and "must" (*dei*). The passage is peculiar to Luke and shows Luke's editorial care in making a significant transition at this point. It marks a stage in Jesus' progress to Jerusalem and prepares the reader for chapter 14 (note v.1).

31 Now the Pharisees warn Jesus of Herod's designs on his life. Later in his Gospel, Luke will speak out in blaming the Jewish leaders for their drastic actions against Jesus but will minimize the role of the people in opposing him (e.g., 19:47). At this point, however, he attributes no evil motive to those who warn Jesus. Apparently these Pharisees have Jesus' safety at heart. "At that time" (*en autē tē hōra*) makes a strong transition from the warning in vv.28–30, which would have caused strong reactions among the Jewish leaders. We do not know where Jesus was at that time; if he was in Herod's territory, he was obviously not near Jerusalem.

32–33 In Luke's last mention of him, Herod was troubled at the reports of Jesus' miracles. By having John the Baptist beheaded, Herod thought he had done away with prophetic opposition. But Jesus, far from being threatened by Herod, called him "that fox" (v.32). Today foxes connote cleverness; in Jesus' day they also connoted insignificance (cf. Neh 4:3; S of Sol 2:15). Either or both connotations may apply here. Jesus' intent was to continue his ministry and manifest the power of the kingdom—"drive out demons and heal people"—but not to do this indefinitely. "Today and tomorrow" (*sēmeron kai aurion*) signifies the time of present opportunity in Jesus' ministry. That time, however, was short. Since "today and tomorrow" are not literal days, so with the "third day," which must have reminded Luke's readers of the day of Jesus' resurrection. Perhaps it was intended to do so. Verses 32 and 33 are parallel, with the idea of "three days" implicit in each. In v.32 "the third day" is followed by "I will reach my goal" (*teleioumai*, "be completed," "be perfected"). In v.33 it is followed by a reference to Jesus' death. Clearly the expressions are equivalent, and there may well be an anticipation of the profound phrase in Hebrews 2:9: "perfect through suffering." In one sense v.33 marks the completion of Jesus' mission, especially in Luke's theology (cf. 9:31). Ellis (*Gospel of Luke*, p. 190) suggests that it refers to consecration to the high priestly work, since the Greek word for "perfected" is used in the LXX of Exodus 29 and Leviticus 8.

The programmatic statement of Jesus' purpose and progress continues in v.33 with two additions: the specific reference to suffering ("die") and the word "must" (*dei*). Luke conveys Jesus' sense of purpose and necessity more strongly than the other Synoptics do. Well over two-thirds of the synoptic uses of *dei* are in Luke (cf. comment on 4:43). Another key word that reappears here is the verb *poreuomai* ("keep going"; cf. comment on "went" at v.22). Luke emphasizes the "way" of Jesus, which led to the cross and on to glory (cf. John 7:35; 14:12, 28; 16:7, 28). Jesus expected to suffer as a "prophet." Jeremias (TDNT, 5:714) says that to a great extent "martyrdom was considered an integral part of the prophetic office" in those days (cf. TDNT, 6:834–35). Stephen's speech (Acts 7:52) accords with this.

34–35 The word "Jerusalem" appears three times in a row: once at the end of v.33 and twice at the beginning of the lament (v.34). The effect is to draw the reader's attention to that city of destiny, both as the place of our Lord's passion and as the pathetic, unwilling object of his love. The "house," perhaps specifically the temple, which had been visited by Jesus as a boy (2:41–50), will now lose him till Psalm 118:26, quoted here ("Blessed . . . Lord"), is fulfilled. The lament and the quotation do not appear in Matthew till after the Triumphal Entry (23:37–39), where Jesus includes the word "again" (*ap' arti*, v.39), apparently to make it clear that there was to be a future fulfillment of the word quoted from Psalm 118:26. The substance of the quotation is recorded by all four Gospels in their account of the Triumphal Entry; but the words are said, not by the Jerusalemites, but by Jesus' supporters. Luke specifies that they were Jesus' disciples (19:37–38).

E. *Further Teaching on Urgent Issues* (14:1–18:30)

1. *Jesus at a Pharisee's house*

14:1–14

> [1]One Sabbath, when Jesus went to eat in the house of a prominent Pharisee, he was being carefully watched. [2]There in front of him was a man suffering from dropsy. [3]Jesus asked the Pharisees and experts in the law, "Is it lawful to heal on the Sabbath or not?" [4]But they remained silent. So taking hold of the man, he healed him and sent him away.
>
> [5]Then he asked them, "If one of you has a son or an ox that falls into a well on the Sabbath day, will you not immediately pull him out?" [6]And they had nothing to say.
>
> [7]When he noticed how the guests picked the places of honor at the table, he told them this parable: [8]"When someone invites you to a wedding feast, do not take the place of honor, for a person more distinguished than you may have been invited. [9]If so, the host who invited both of you will come and say to you, 'Give this man your seat.' Then, humiliated, you will have to take the least important place. [10]But when you are invited, take the lowest place, so that when your host comes, he will say to you, 'Friend, move up to a better place.' Then you will be honored in the presence of all your fellow guests. [11]For everyone who exalts himself will be humbled, and he who humbles himself will be exalted."
>
> [12]Then Jesus said to his host, "When you give a luncheon or dinner, do not invite your friends, your brothers or relatives, or your rich neighbors; if you do, they may invite you back and so you will be repaid. [13]But when you give a banquet, invite the poor, the crippled, the lame, the blind, [14]and you will be blessed. Although they cannot repay you, you will be repaid at the resurrection of the righteous."

This passage and the following one incorporate several elements—healing, conversations, and a parable—all tied together in dinner-table conversation—a familiar device in ancient literature. The conversation, except for its opening, revolves around the response and behavior of dinner guests. This leads into the response of would-be followers of Jesus and the cost of discipleship.

1–4 Since this is the fourth time Luke records a controversy over the Sabbath (v.1), it is obvious that this was a major issue between Jesus and the religious leaders (cf. 6:1–5, 6:11; 13:10–17). The host was "prominent"—literally, one of the "ruling" (*archontōn*) Pharisees, possibly a member of the Sanhedrin. The NIV rendering "he was being carefully watched" brings out the durative aspect of the imperfect periphrastic tense, which Luke uses effectively (cf. "was teaching" and "were sitting," 5:17). Luke pictures the Pharisees as watchdogs of the faith as they waited for some theological flaw to appear in Jesus' teaching (vv.1–3; cf. 5:17; 6:7). "There [*kai idou*, lit., 'and behold'] in front of him" (v.2; cf. 13:11) draws attention to a man who some commentators think was "planted" there to test Jesus. That would not be improbable, but the text does not affirm it. "Dropsy," an "abnormal accumulation of serous fluid in the tissues of the body" (R.H. Pousma, "Diseases of the Bible," ZPEB, 2:134), may have popularly been considered a curse for sin (Num 5:11–27). As in 6:9, Jesus took the initiative with a question designed to shift the burden of proof to the opposition (v.3). "Is it lawful" may have been intentionally ambiguous, a leading question that could be answered in terms of either OT or rabbinical "law." During the silence of the "Pharisees and experts in the law," Jesus met the man's need (v.4). His condition could have waited another day, but Jesus was concerned to establish a principle. This may be why he dismissed the man without including him further in the conversation and then turned to the Pharisees.

5–6 The phrase "If one of you" (v.5) draws Jesus' listeners into the illustration (cf. 11:5, 11; 12:25; 14:28). "Immediately" (*eutheōs*) stresses the urgency of meeting the need, a pointed reference back to the man with dropsy. The principle exampled in the case of a beast is in accord not only with the OT but with rabbinic law (cf. SBK, 1:629; *Shabbath* 128b, though cf. the forbidding of helping such an animal in the Qumran sect, CD 11:13–17). In the face of this, the silence of Jesus' opponents was no longer by choice (e.g., v.4) but of necessity; they "had nothing to say" (*ouk ischysan antapokrithēnai*, lit., "could not respond," v.6). A dilemma also silences a group of Jewish leaders in 20:3–7 (cf. also 20:26).

7–11 Jesus continued to take the initiative (v.7). In his time the guests at a formal dinner reclined on couches, several on each one, leaning on their left elbows. The seating was according to status. The "head of the table" was the couch at one end, with other couches extending from it and facing each other like the arms of a "U." The important places, the places of "honor" (v.8), were those nearest the head couch position. If an important guest came late, someone might have to be displaced to make room for him (v.9). Jesus' practical advice (cf. Prov 25:6–7) illustrates the spiritual principle he stated in v.11. The significance of this principle—and indeed of vv.7–11—is clarified by Luke's use in the parable of the Pharisee and the tax collector (18:14). The ultimate reference of the principle (v.11) is to God's final judgment. Luke follows the custom of using passive verbs ("will be humbled . . . will be exalted") to avoid direct reference to God, the real subject of this profound sentence. The same may hold for 16:9 (cf. Ellis, *Gospel of Luke*, on both passages; cf. also comment on 15:7 for another way Luke reverently avoids the use of God's name). This practice seems strange to us, but we need to realize that in the culture of that day a name both designated and represented a person. Therefore it was safe to refer to God obliquely by a descriptive title, "Lord"; a phrase, "the Holy One," "Blessed be he"; a circumlocution, "He who sits in heaven"; or a term such as "the heavens," whereas to say the divine Name itself without proper reverence could be blasphemy.

12–14 Having addressed the Pharisee's guests, Jesus turns to his host (v.12). What he says resembles his words in 6:32–36 (see comments)—viz., in view of ultimate reward from God, doing good to those who cannot repay it. Also, v.13 recalls Luke's report of Jesus' concern for the poor and oppressed (cf. 4:18; 6:20–21). As Jesus said (6:35), believers are to do good, not with the expectation of a future reward, but unselfishly. Then God will remember and reward them (v.14). (Scripture distinguishes between the resurrection of the righteous and that of the wicked [Dan 12:2; Acts 24:15; Rev 20:4–5].)

Notes

5 The reason some MSS read ὄνος (*onos*, "donkey," NIV mg.) instead of υἱός (*huios*, "son") is probably because the combination of two animals, donkey and ox, seems more likely than that of a son and an ox. Vaticanus (B) and Alexandrinus (A), significant papyri, and other early MS witnesses have *huios*.

2. Parable of the great banquet

14:15–24

[15]When one of those at the table with him heard this, he said to Jesus, "Blessed is the man who will eat at the feast in the kingdom of God."
[16]Jesus replied: "A certain man was preparing a great banquet and invited many guests. [17]At the time of the banquet he sent his servant to tell those who had been invited, 'Come, for everything is now ready.'
[18]"But they all alike began to make excuses. The first said, 'I have just bought a field, and I must go and see it. Please excuse me.'
[19]"Another said, 'I have just bought five yoke of oxen, and I'm on my way to try them out. Please excuse me.'
[20]"Still another said, 'I just got married, so I can't come.'
[21]"The servant came back and reported this to his master. Then the owner of the house became angry and ordered his servant, 'Go out quickly into the streets and alleys of the town and bring in the poor, the crippled, the blind and the lame.'
[22]" 'Sir,' the servant said, 'what you ordered has been done, but there is still room.'
[23]"Then the master told his servant, 'Go out to the roads and country lanes and make them come in, so that my house will be full. [24]I tell you, not one of those men who were invited will get a taste of my banquet.' "

Jesus continues the figure of the banquet with a striking parable about the "feast in the kingdom of God" (v.15)—the so-called eschatological banquet. Luke 13:28–30 had shown that some who expect to be present will be excluded; this passage teaches that those excluded have only themselves to blame.

15 The exuberant remark seems like a boorish counterpart to Peter's "It is good for us to be here" (9:33); Manson (*Sayings of Jesus*, p. 129) calls it "a characteristic piece of apocalyptic piety." The concept of future celebration in the kingdom is certainly biblical. Jesus does not repudiate it but rather addresses the presumption by some present, perhaps including the speaker in v.1, that they would inevitably participate.

16–17 It is not certain whether the invited guests (v.16) were waiting for the second invitation customary in fashionable circles or whether this was simply to remind those who had already accepted the invitation that it was time to come (v.17). "People had no watches . . . and . . . a banquet took a long time to prepare" (Morris, *Luke*, p. 233.)

18–20 The striking thing is that "all" of them declined (v.18). "Alike" (*apo mias*, a unique expression in Greek) does not mean "in the same way" but probably "with one accord" or "all at once" (Jeremias, *Parables of Jesus*, p. 176).

The excuses are weak. One man "must" go to see a purchased field he probably had seen before he bought it (v.18). Contrast his urgent attention to material things with Jesus' healing a man on the Sabbath (vv.2–4). The second excuse (v.19) is as worthless as the first; would anyone have bought oxen without examining them? Going "to try them out" sounds like preoccupation with a new possession rather than urgent business. In both instances materialism got in the way of honoring an invitation already extended.

The third excuse (v.20) has more validity in the light of Deuteronomy 24:5. Also, only men were invited to banquets (Jeremias, *Parables of Jesus*, p. 177). Yet marriage was not, especially in that society, an abrupt decision and could hardly have been an unexpected factor intervening between the first (v.16) and second (v.17) invitations. With his superb narrative art, Jesus uses these three excuses to show that just as a host may be snubbed, so God's gracious invitation may be flouted.

21–24 The host "became angry" (v.21) because the rejections were a personal insult. A "street" (*plateia*) was broader and traveled by a greater variety of people than a neighborhood road. In contrast an "alley" (*rhymē*) was a small lane or side path, likely to harbor the loitering outcasts of society. Those brought from these places were precisely the same unfortunates Jesus had told his host to invite in v.13 (see comment). With room still available (v.22), the servant is to go outside the town and search even the "country lanes" (v.23). To "make them come in" is not compulsion but "an insistent hospitality" (Manson, *Sayings of Jesus*, p. 130).

Although Jesus does not interpret the parable, it is reasonable to link it with 13:28–30 and find in it an allusion of the extension of the gospel to the Gentiles. Those who had the benefit of the original invitation are perhaps best described by Paul in Romans 9:4–5—Jews with all their heritage and spiritual advantages. "Not one" (v.24) refers to the parable and should not be taken literally but understood as stressing the seriousness of the consequences of rejecting God's invitation.

Notes

16–23 As to the similarity of this parable to the one in Matt 22:1–10, there can be only two explanations. Either there was one original parable handed down in different forms and edited by Matthew and Luke and placed in different settings, or Jesus told similar parables on two different occasions with appropriate variations. Ellis (*Gospel of Luke*, p. 194) observes that the "use of the same parabolic theme to teach different truths is frequent in rabbinical writings." Comparing Luke 15:3–7 with Matt 18:12–14 will show this. The second alternative is reasonable and does not preclude legitimate editing. The same basic story is found in the Gospel of Thomas (Logion 64). For a critical analysis, see Jeremias, *Parables of Jesus*, pp. 63–69. Bailey, *Peasant Eyes*, pp. 88–113, has a number of keen insights into the significance of this parable.

3. The cost of being a disciple

14:25–35

25Large crowds were traveling with Jesus, and turning to them he said: 26"If anyone comes to me and does not hate his father and mother, his wife and children, his brothers and sisters—yes, even his own life—he cannot be my disciple. 27And anyone who does not carry his cross and follow me cannot be my disciple.

28"Suppose one of you wants to build a tower. Will he not first sit down and estimate the cost to see if he has enough money to complete it? 29For if he lays the foundation and is not able to finish it, everyone who sees it will ridicule him, 30saying, 'This fellow began to build and was not able to finish.'

31"Or suppose a king is about to go to war against another king. Will he not first sit down and consider whether he is able with ten thousand men to oppose the one coming against him with twenty thousand? 32If he is not able, he will send a delegation while the other is still a long way off and will ask for terms of peace. 33In the same way, any of you who does not give up everything he has cannot be my disciple.

34"Salt is good, but if it loses its saltiness, how can it be made salty again? 35It is fit neither for the soil nor for the manure pile; it is thrown out.

"He who has ears to hear, let him hear."

The serious tone of the preceding parable continues as attention now turns to those who profess allegiance to Jesus.

25–27 With the words "large crowds" (v.25), Luke again draws attention to Jesus' popularity (see comment on 4:15). These crowds formed an entourage along with Jesus' own group (cf. 8:1–3). They were "traveling," an indication of further progress toward Jerusalem (see comment on 13:22). "Hate" (v.26) is not an absolute but a relative term. To neglect social customs pertaining to family loyalties would probably have been interpreted as hate. Jesus is not contravening the commandment to honor one's father and mother. Moreover, he says a disciple should hate "even his own life," whereas he speaks elsewhere of loving ourselves (10:27; cf. Matt 22:39; Mark 12:31). It is important to understand the ancient Near Eastern expression without blunting its force. (For the meaning of v.27, see comment on 9:23.)

28–32 Jesus uses two different circumstances to illustrate his basic point: discipleship requires a conscious advance commitment, made with a realistic estimate of the ultimate personal cost. The practical nature of the circumstances Jesus so vividly pictures underlines the fact that Christian discipleship is not some theoretical abstract ideal but hard reality.

33 This is clearly a crucial verse. But does it mean that it is impossible to retain any possessions at all if one wants to be a true disciple? The key word is *apotassetai* ("give up"). When used of persons, the verb means to take leave of or say good-by to someone. When used of things, it means to give up or renounce (BAG, s.v.). Here, in contrast to the cares of the rich young ruler (18:22), Jesus does not say a disciple should sell all his possessions and give everything away. His thought probably is that of abandonment of things, yielding up the right of ownership, rather than outright disposal of them. The disciple of Jesus may be given the use of things in trust, as a stewardship, but they are no longer his own. The present tense implies that what Jesus requires in relation to possessions is a continual attitude of abandonment.

In his recent work (cf. n. 34), Pilgrim (*Good News*, pp. 101f.) sides cautiously with those who take the view that abandonment was total only for Jesus' disciples in his lifetime. Pilgrim nevertheless sees this radical abandonment as speaking to the rich of Luke's day, urging them to share their goods with their needy brethren. But the principle of stewardship makes a spirit of abandonment—i.e., the willingness to part with our goods (which are not ultimately ours anyway)—necessary today. This is consistent with the command to *use* our possessions wisely (cf. 16:1–12).

34–35 This saying (v.34) poses two questions: Why does it occur here? and How does salt lose its saltiness? Its place here is due to the common element it shares with the preceding illustrations—the consistent quality of life Jesus expects of his disciples. We do not know with certainty what he had in mind in speaking of salt losing its saltiness. The reference may be to adulteration either by impurities in the beds by the Dead Sea from which salt slabs were taken or by inert fillers introduced by unscrupulous dealers. The point is that tasteless salt is useless. The one who "has ears" is expected to apply the lesson to himself (v.35).

Notes

34 On the Aramaic background of μωρανθῇ (*mōranthē*, "loses its saltiness"), see Jeremias, *Parables of Jesus*, p. 168, and Black, *Aramaic Approach*, pp. 166–67.

4. *Parables of joy* (15:1–32)

a. *The lost sheep*

15:1–7

> ¹Now the tax collectors and "sinners" were all gathering around to hear him. ²But the Pharisees and the teachers of the law muttered, "This man welcomes sinners and eats with them."

3Then Jesus told them this parable: 4"Suppose one of you has a hundred sheep and loses one of them. Does he not leave the ninety-nine in the open country and go after the lost sheep until he finds it? 5And when he finds it, he joyfully puts it on his shoulders 6and goes home. Then he calls his friends and neighbors together and says, 'Rejoice with me; I have found my lost sheep.' 7I tell you that in the same way there will be more rejoicing in heaven over one sinner who repents than over ninety-nine righteous persons who do not need to repent.

This section begins what Manson (*Sayings of Jesus*, p. 282) has called the "Gospel of the Outcast." The large body of material in chapters 15–19 is unique to Luke and dramatically shows Jesus' concern for the social outcasts of his day (N.B. 15:1; 16:19–25; 17:11–19; 18:1–8; 9–14; 19:1–10). The twin parables (vv.3–7, 8–10) along with the longer one about the lost son (vv.11–32) depend for their interpretation on vv.1–2.

1 "Tax collectors" were among those who were ostracized because their work was considered dishonest or immoral (Jeremias, *Parables of Jesus*, p. 132). NIV appropriately puts "sinners" in quotation marks to show that this was not Luke's designation but the way others, i.e., the Pharisees, thought of them. For an explanation of the attitude of Pharisees to such "sinners," see comments on 5:29–30. "All" signifies either all such persons (wherever Jesus was at the time) or, generally speaking, the large proportion of them among the crowds who usually came to hear him. The imperfect periphrastic "were gathering" (cf. comment on 14:1) could indicate either the process of gathering at the time of the story or the habitual coming of "sinners" throughout Jesus' ministry.

2 In OT times it was taken for granted that God's people did not consort with sinners (cf. Ps 1), but the Pharisees extended this beyond the biblical intent. To go so far as to "welcome" them and especially to "eat" with them, implying table fellowship, was unthinkable to the Pharisees. The parables that follow show that the return of "sinners" to God should be a cause for joy to the religious leaders, as it was to God. Furthermore, "Jesus makes the claim for himself that he is acting in God's stead, that he is God's representative" (Jeremias, *Parables of Jesus*, p. 132.)

3–7 For the phrase "suppose one of you" (v.4), see comment on 14:5. There is a parallel between the expression *tis anthrōpos ex hymōn* (lit., "what man of you") and *tis gynē* ("what woman," v.8, where the lack of the additional words "of you" may indicate that no women were present). The situation described was a common one. One hundred sheep was a normal-sized flock. A count was taken nightly. The "open country" was a safe place to leave the sheep ("wilderness" [KJV, RSV] is misleading), though they would have to be left in someone's care. The frightened, confused, and perhaps injured sheep would have to be carried (v.5).

Two things are striking. First, in the obvious analogy to the search for the sheep, Jesus takes the initiative in seeking out lost people—a major theme in Luke (cf. 19:10). In contrast were some rabbis in the early centuries who hesitated to seek Gentile converts. But that does not invalidate Jesus' comment in Matthew 23:15 about Pharisees who were proselytizing aggressively. They were apparently trying to gain adherents to their sect, rather than compassionately seeking the lost. Second, the climax of the story is not only the return of the sheep but the triumphant rejoicing in its rescue (v.6). Jesus is stressing, both by parable and direct statement (v.7), that his seeking and receiving sinners pleases God.

"In heaven" (v.7) is a customary way of referring reverently to God without saying his name (cf. v.10 and comment on 14:11). The NIV rendering "there will be . . . rejoicing" brings out the future (*estai*, "will be"), which may include the day yet future of gathering and feasting (cf. 13:29). There are none who are truly "righteous" (cf. Rom 3:10); the "righteous persons" referred to in v.7 are devout people (cf. 1:6), or those who seem so (Matt 6:1), who have no gross, open sins to repent of.

b. *The lost coin*

15:8–10

> 8"Or suppose a woman has ten silver coins and loses one. Does she not light a lamp, sweep the house and search carefully until she finds it? 9And when she finds it, she calls her friends and neighbors together and says, 'Rejoice with me; I have found my lost coin.' 10In the same way, I tell you, there is rejoicing in the presence of the angels of God over one sinner who repents."

8–10 This parable is clearly linked to the preceding one, and the opening words are comparable (see comment on "suppose" at v.4). The "coins" (v.8) are *drachmas* (see NIV mg. on their value). They may have formed part of the woman's headdress, which, being part of her dowry, she constantly wore (Jeremias, *Parables of Jesus*, p. 134; cf. Marshall, *Gospel of Luke*, p. 603). Whether or not that is the case here, the mention of ten coins implies that they were all she had. "A lamp" was needed because the house would have had at best a few small windows or only a low doorway. She would "sweep" the hard earthen floor to find the coin by the sound of its clinking. As in v.6, the extent of joy expressed is striking (v.9). Considering the neighborly feelings in a small village, this is understandable, especially if the coin represented a tenth of the woman's savings. Moreover, Jesus' final comment (v.10) reinforces the point. "In the presence of the angels of God" is, like "in heaven" (v.7), a reverential reference to God. This parable, like that of the lost sheep, justifies Jesus' welcome of sinners (v.2).

c. *The lost son*

15:11–32

> 11Jesus continued: "There was a man who had two sons. 12The younger one said to his father, 'Father, give me my share of the estate.' So he divided his property between them.
>
> 13"Not long after that, the younger son got together all he had, set off for a distant country and there squandered his wealth in wild living. 14After he had spent everything, there was a severe famine in that whole country, and he began to be in need. 15So he went and hired himself out to a citizen of that country, who sent him to his fields to feed pigs. 16He longed to fill his stomach with the pods that the pigs were eating, but no one gave him anything.
>
> 17"When he came to his senses, he said, 'How many of my father's hired men have food to spare, and here I am starving to death! 18I will set out and go back to my father and say to him: Father, I have sinned against heaven and against you. 19I am no longer worthy to be called your son; make me like one of your hired men.' 20So he got up and went to his father.
>
> "But while he was still a long way off, his father saw him and was filled with compassion for him; he ran to his son, threw his arms around him and kissed him.

²¹"The son said to him, 'Father, I have sinned against heaven and against you. I am no longer worthy to be called your son.'

²²"But the father said to his servants, 'Quick! Bring the best robe and put it on him. Put a ring on his finger and sandals on his feet. ²³Bring the fattened calf and kill it. Let's have a feast and celebrate. ²⁴For this son of mine was dead and is alive again; he was lost and is found.' So they began to celebrate.

²⁵"Meanwhile, the older son was in the field. When he came near the house, he heard music and dancing. ²⁶So he called one of the servants and asked him what was going on. ²⁷'Your brother has come,' he replied, 'and your father has killed the fattened calf because he has him back safe and sound.'

²⁸"The older brother became angry and refused to go in. So his father went out and pleaded with him. ²⁹But he answered his father, 'Look! All these years I've been slaving for you and never disobeyed your orders. Yet you never gave me even a young goat so I could celebrate with my friends. ³⁰But when this son of yours who has squandered your property with prostitutes comes home, you kill the fattened calf for him!'

³¹" 'My son,' the father said, 'you are always with me, and everything I have is yours. ³²But we had to celebrate and be glad, because this brother of yours was dead and is alive again; he was lost and is found.' "

The great parable of the lost son speaks even more eloquently than its predecessors to the situation set forth in vv.1–2. The first part (vv.11–24) conveys the same sense of joy on the lost being found the other two parables have; in contrast, the second part deals with the sour attitude of the elder brother. Like the Pharisees, he could not comprehend the meaning of forgiveness. The positions of the two sons would, in a structural analysis, be considered binary opposites, the lost son rises and the elder brother falls in moral state. The central figure, the father, remains constant in his love for both. As in v.2 (cf. comment), by telling the story Jesus identifies himself with God in his loving attitude to the lost. He represents God in his mission, the accomplishment of which should elicit joy from those who share the Father's compassion. The parable is one of the world's supreme masterpieces of storytelling. Its details are vivid; they reflect actual customs and legal procedures and build up the story's emotional and spiritual impact. But the expositor must resist the tendency to allegorize the wealth of detail that gives the story its remarkable verisimilitude. The main point of the parable—that God glady receives repentant sinners—must not be obscured.

11–12 The "share of the estate" (v.12) that a younger son would receive on the death of the father would be one-third, because the older (or oldest) son received two-thirds, a "double portion"—i.e., twice as much as all other sons (Deut 21:17). If the property were given, as in this case, while the father lived, the heirs would have use of it (cf. v.31); but if they sold it, they could not normally transfer it as long as the father lived. The father also would receive any accrued interest (see Jeremias, *Parables of Jesus*, pp. 128–29). The son may have been asking (v.12) for immediate total ownership, but the parable does not specify the exact terms of the settlement. The property was "divided"; so the elder son was made aware of his share (cf. v.31).

13–16 NIV captures the vivid wording of the account, including "squandered his wealth" and "wild living" (v.13). The famine made employment and food even harder than usual to get. The "distant country" was apparently outside strictly Jewish territory, and the wayward son found himself with the demeaning job of feeding pigs (v.15), unclean animals for the Jews. He would even have eaten "pods" (v.16), which were seeds of the carob tree, common around the Mediterranean and used for pigs' food. He had fallen so low and had become so insignificant that "no one gave him anything"—an indication of total neglect.

17–20 "Came to his senses" (*eis eauton elthōn;* lit., "came to himself," v.17) was a common idiom, which in this Jewish story may carry the Semitic idea of repentance (Jeremias, *Parables of Jesus,* p. 130; cf. Bailey, *Poet and Peasant,* pp. 171–73). Certainly repentance lies at the heart of the words the son prepared to tell his father. The motivation for his return was hunger, but it was specifically to his "father" (v.18) that he wanted to return. The words "against heaven" (*eis ton ouranon*) can mean "to heaven," meaning that his sins were so many as to reach to heaven; more probably the meaning is that his sins were ultimately against God—veiled in the word "heaven" (cf. Ps 51:4). Assuming this latter meaning, we see that the parable is far more than an allegory, with the father representing God, for the father and God have distinct roles. The father in the story does, of course, portray the characteristics and attitudes of a loving heavenly Father. This does not mean that God is heavenly Father to everyone (note John 1:12; 8:42–44). Yet the Jews knew God's loving care was like that of a father (Ps 103:13). The son knew he had no right to return as a son (v.19), having taken and squandered his inheritance. He therefore planned to earn his room and board.

The description of his return and welcome is as vivid as that of his departure, with several beautiful touches. Because his father saw him "while he was still a long way off" (v.20) has led many to assume that the father was waiting for him, perhaps daily searching the distant road hoping for his appearance. This prompted the title of H. Thielicke's book of Jesus' parables, *The Waiting Father* (New York: Harper, 1959). The father's "compassion" assumes some knowledge of the son's pitiable condition, perhaps from reports. Some have pointed out that a father in that culture would not normally run as he did, which, along with his warm embrace and kissing, adds to the impact of the story. Clearly Jesus used every literary means to heighten the contrast between the father's attitude and that of the elder brother (and of the Pharisees, cf. vv.1–2).

21–24 The son's speech was never completed (v.21). Instead the father more than reversed the unspoken part about becoming a "hired man" (v.19). The robe, ring, and sandals (v.22) signified more than sonship (Jeremias, *Parables of Jesus,* p. 130); the robe was a ceremonial one such as a guest of honor would be given, the ring signified authority, and the sandals were those only a free man would wear. Marshall (*Gospel of Luke,* p. 610) doubts Manson's assertion that the robe was "a symbol of the New Age." The calf was apparently being "fattened" for some special occasion (v.23); people in first-century Palestine did not regularly eat meat. Note the parallel between "dead" and "alive" and "lost" and "found" (v.24)—terms that also apply to one's state before and after conversion to Christ (Eph 2:1–5). As in the parables of the lost sheep and the lost coin, it was time to "celebrate."

25–32 It seems strange that the older son was not there when the celebration began (v.25). Jesus' parables, however, are a fictional way of teaching enduring truth; and we may imagine that the celebration began so quickly that the older son was not aware of it (vv.26–27). Or, more likely in view of the dialogue in vv.26–31, his absence showed his distant relationship with his family. Verse 28 contrasts the older son with the father. The son became angry; but the father "went out," as he had for the younger brother, and "pleaded" rather than scolded. The older son's abrupt beginning—"Look!" (v.29)—betrays a disrespectful attitude toward his father. Likewise, "slaving" is hardly descriptive of a warm family relationship. "You never gave me," whether true or not, shows a long smoldering discontent. "This son of yours" (*ho huios sou houtos,* v.30) avoids acknowledging that the prodigal is his own brother, a disclaimer the father corrects by the words "this brother of yours" (v.32). The older brother's charges include sharp criticism of both father and brother. The story has made no mention of hiring prostitutes (v.30).

The father's response is nevertheless tender: "My son" (or "child," *teknon*) is followed by words of affirmation, not weakness (v.31). "We had to celebrate" (*euphranthenai . . . edei*) is literally "It was necessary to celebrate"; no personal subject is mentioned. This allows the implication that the elder brother should have joined in the celebration. The words "had to" (*edei*) introduce once more the necessity and urgency so prominent in Luke (see comment on 4:43).

Notes

11–32 Two issues, one literary and one theological, are often raised concerning this parable. Because the first part of the parable revolves around the younger brother and the latter around the older (and also for other reasons), some have found the parable's literary structure complex—i.e., originally consisting of two independent stories. If so, the resultant unit is well edited; for the older son appears from the very beginning, the two parts complement each other, and the latter part fits as well as the former into the context of vv.1–2. But this view cannot be sustained (cf. Marshall, *Gospel of Luke,* p. 605).

The theological issue centers in the absence of any hint of anything more than repentance and returning to God as Father being involved in salvation. (God's fatherhood is discussed in the comment on v.18.) It must, however, be kept in mind that this is a parable and thus is intended to portray only one aspect of the gospel—God's willingness to receive "sinners" and his joy over their return. Elsewhere in Luke's presentation of Christ as Savior, the Cross has its place (see Manson, *Sayings of Jesus,* p. 286; cf. Marshall, *Luke: Historian and Theologian,* pp. 170–75).

16 Χορτασθῆναι (*chortasthēnai,* "to feed on") has more MS support than γεμίσαι τὴν κοιλίαν (*gemisai tēn koilian,* "to fill the stomach"). NIV appears to have followed the latter but may simply be using a contemporary idiom to express the general idea of both verbs.

5. Parable of the shrewd manager

16:1–18

¹Jesus told his disciples: "There was a rich man whose manager was accused of wasting his possessions. ²So he called him in and asked him, 'What is this I hear about you? Give an account of your management, because you cannot be manager any longer.'

³"The manager said to himself, 'What shall I do now? My master is taking away my job. I'm not strong enough to dig, and I'm ashamed to beg—⁴I know what I'll do so that, when I lose my job here, people will welcome me into their houses.'

⁵"So he called in each one of his master's debtors. He asked the first, 'How much do you owe my master?'

⁶" 'Eight hundred gallons of olive oil,' he replied.

"The manager told him, 'Take your bill, sit down quickly, and make it four hundred.'

⁷"Then he asked the second, 'And how much do you owe?'

" 'A thousand bushels of wheat,' he replied.

"He told him, 'Take your bill and make it eight hundred.'

⁸"The master commended the dishonest manager because he had acted shrewdly. For the people of this world are more shrewd in dealing with their own kind than are the people of the light. ⁹I tell you, use worldly wealth to gain friends for yourselves, so that when it is gone, you will be welcomed into eternal dwellings.

¹⁰"Whoever can be trusted with very little can also be trusted with much, and whoever is dishonest with very little will also be dishonest with much. ¹¹So if you have not been trustworthy in handling worldly wealth, who will trust you with true riches? ¹²And if you have not been trustworthy with someone else's property, who will give you property of your own?

¹³"No servant can serve two masters. Either he will hate the one and love the other, or he will be devoted to the one and despise the other. You cannot serve both God and Money."

¹⁴The Pharisees, who loved money, heard all this and were sneering at Jesus. ¹⁵He said to them, "You are the ones who justify yourselves in the eyes of men, but God knows your hearts. What is highly valued among men is detestable in God's sight.

¹⁶"The Law and the Prophets were proclaimed until John. Since that time, the good news of the kingdom of God is being preached, and everyone is forcing his way into it. ¹⁷It is easier for heaven and earth to disappear than for the least stroke of a pen to drop out of the Law.

¹⁸"Anyone who divorces his wife and marries another woman commits adultery, and the man who marries a divorced woman commits adultery.

Chapter 16 follows the pattern characteristic of this part of Luke—viz., a combination of parables and sayings pointing again and again to the need for decision. Here (ch. 16), in spite of obvious diversity, one theme occurs several times. It is that of Jesus' teaching about material possessions—first in the parable of the shrewd manager, then in the comment about the Pharisees "who loved money" (v.14), and finally in the parable of the rich man and Lazarus.

The interpretation of this parable is notoriously difficult. Prior to any overall interpretation and application of it is a series of decisions regarding vv.8–13. Several interdependent questions face the expositor.

1. Is the "master" (*kyrios*) in v.8 the "master" in the parable (vv.3, 5) or the Lord Jesus?

2. Why did the "master" commend a dishonest manager?—a question that becomes more acute if the "master" is the Lord Jesus.

3. Where does the parable end, before v.8 (in which case the "master" is the Lord), in the middle of v.8 (in which case the sentence beginning "For the people" begins the comment on the parable), or at the end of v.8 (with the words "I tell you" [v.9] initiating the comment)?

4. Finally, are vv.10–12 and 13 part of the same unit or do they represent a separate tradition?

Discussion of these issues will help us interpret the parable. First, the "master" may refer to the Lord Jesus (1) because Luke normally uses *kyrios* to refer to Jesus and God, (2) because the latter part of v.8 (taking it as a unity) refers to believers and unbelievers rather than to characters in the story, and (3) because in 18:6 *kyrios* is used to refer to Jesus when he begins the explanation of a parable (see Ellis,

Gospel of Luke, p. 199). On the other hand, it more likely refers to the rich "master" in the story, as (1) this would not be an unusual secular use of the word *kyrios;* (2) the religious terminology of v.8 (e.g., "people of the light") seems to refer to real people (in contrast to the characters of the secular illustration) and therefore sounds like the beginning of Jesus' explanation; (3) the real parallel to 18:6 ("the Lord said") may not be in this verse ("The master commended") but in v.9 ("I tell you"); and (4) v.8a seems to form a better conclusion to the parable than v.7 (so Fitzmyer, "The Story of the Dishonest Manager," *Semitic Background*, pp. 161–84, originally published in *Theological Studies* 25 [1964]: 23–42).

Second, even if the "master" of v.8 is the one in the story, the Lord Jesus seems to agree with the commendation; so we are left with the second question in either case: Why was a dishonest manager commended? The answer on the surface is "because he had acted shrewdly" (v.8). But was his shrewd act not dishonest? The text does not say that the manager's action in writing off the debts was dishonest. Rather the word "dishonest" may be used here because it serves a double purpose. First, it refers back to his initial act of mishandling the master's funds. Yet even one who had thus acted could do something commendable. Second, it introduces a chain of words using the same root. "Dishonest" (*adikos*) is recalled by "worldly" (*tēs adikias*) in v.9 and reappears twice in v.10 and once in v.11. Ellis suggests that *adikia* is a "technical theological expression," equivalent to a term used at Qumran describing the character of that age. When *adikia* is applied to people, it is because "they belong to this age and live according to its principles" (Ellis, *Gospel of Luke*, p. 199).

The reason the manager was now commended, though he had previously acted dishonestly, may be that he had at last learned how one's worldly wealth can be wisely given away to do good. This assumption is reasonable if Fitzmyer's suggestion (*Semitic Background*, pp. 175–76) is correct that the amount taken off the bills in vv.5–7 was not part of the debt owed the master but rather represented the interest the manager himself was charging. Though this would have been contrary to Jewish law (Exod 22:25; Lev 25:36–37; Deut 15:7–8; 23:19–20), charging a poor Jew such interest (actually usury) was often rationalized. The bill would be written in terms of the commodity rather than in monetary figures, with the interest hidden in the total. By law a master could not be held accountable for illegal acts of an employee. So the master in the parable was in a position to view the manager's activities objectively. If this explanation is correct, the manager's transaction was not illegal. In any event, the master would lose no money if the amount forfeited was simply the interest the manager would have gained. Furthermore, such a forgiveness of debts would hardly have hurt but would probably have helped the master's own reputation. Therefore, the master admires the manager's shrewdness. The manager knew his job and reputation were gone because of his previous mishandling of funds. He needed friends; and, by foregoing the customary interest, he won friends among the creditors. Jesus then uses this story to show that the "people of the light" could also accomplish much by wisely giving up some of their "worldly wealth."

This explanation follows in the main that of Fitzmyer, who draws on and expands J.D.M. Derrett, "Fresh Light on St. Luke xvi. I. The Parable of the Unjust Steward," NTS 7 (1960–61): 198–219. Even if some details of this view turn out to be unsatisfactory, the basic interpretation remains valid, that Jesus uses the story of the manager's actions not to commend graft but to encourage the "prudent use of material wealth" (Fitzmyer, *Semitic Background*, p. 177). The repetition of the idea of the cessation of the present scheme of things, first in v.4 ("when I lose my job here") and then in v.9 ("when it is gone"), emphasizes the need for prudent preparation for the inevitable.

Some commentators see this parable as an exhortation to act decisively in time of eschatological crisis, just as the manager acted in his personal crisis. This interpretation, while possible, ignores the fact that, though the theme of decision is important in Luke, here, as well as in other passages (e.g., 6:17–36; 13:13–34), the prudent use of material wealth predominates.

Third, the answer to the question of where the parable ends depends partly, as has been said, on who is designated "master" in v.8. It also depends on whether the reference to "people" in v.8b is to those in the world of the story or in the religious world of Jesus' time. In the former case, the reference is part of the story; in the latter, it is part of the commentary on it. If it is commentary, is it by Jesus or by Luke? If by Luke, the opening words of v.9, "I tell you," seem an abrupt reintroduction of Jesus' words. Since v.8b seems inappropriate as part of the story, it is best to assume that the parable ends with v.7 or, more likely, with the "master's" (rich man's) commendation of the manager.

Fourth, whether or not vv.10–13 were part of the original discourse (cf. Notes), as they stand in the text, they provide an integrated sequence of teachings structured around the ideas of dishonesty (see second discussion above) and responsibility ("trusted," *pistos*, "trusted" or "trustworthy," four times, and *pisteusei*, "will trust," once in vv.10–12).

1–4 "Manager" (*oikonomos*, v.1, often tr. "steward") is a broad term for an employee or agent who was entrusted with the management of funds or property. Mismanagement was possible, as in this parable, because strict accounts were not always kept. When word came from others—"What is this I hear about you?" (v.2) —he had to "give an account" (*apodos*, cf. Matt 12:36; Heb 13:17; 1 Peter 4:5). The manager's plight (v.3) was that he had a respectable "desk job" but could do little else. His decision, therefore, is made with a view to his personal security after his dismissal. The word "welcome" (*dexōntai*, v.4) will be dealt with in the comment at v.9.

5–8a As already noted, the bills may have been written in terms of commodities rather than cash, perhaps in order to hide the actual amount of interest. The amounts owed were large; the wheat is said to be equal to the yield of about one hundred acres (Jeremias, *Parables of Jesus*, p. 181). The difference in the percentage of reduction may be due to the difference in the relative value of the two commodities. The actual value of the reduction in each case has been computed to equal about five hundred denarii, roughly eighty dollars, or sixteen months' wages for a day laborer. The meaning of v.8a, as noted above, is not that a manager is commended for an act of dishonesty but that a dishonest manager is commended for an act of prudence.

8b–9 The contrast between those who belong to (lit., "are sons of") this age and those who belong to the light (v.8b) is familiar from Qumran (1QS 1:9; 2:16; 3:13; cf. Eph 5:8). Christians do not belong to this evil age, but they can nevertheless make responsible use of "worldly wealth" (v.9, cf. Notes). The "friends" may not refer to any particular people but simply be part of the parable's imagery (Danker, *Jesus*, p.

174). Usually they have been understood as being poor people, for whom Jesus (and Luke also) had a deep concern, and to whom we are here urged to give alms (cf. 12:33). "Worldly wealth" should not be stored up for oneself (cf. 12:21), since one day it will be "gone." "You will be welcomed" echoes v.4. The future passive of NIV is a good way of representing *dexōntai hymas* ("they will receive you"), which has no expressed subject. Although, if we follow the context closely, the subject may be the "friends," the use of the plural may reflect the Jewish custom of referring to God obliquely.

10–13 The theme of stewardship is now discussed in terms of trustworthiness as over against dishonesty (v.10). "Worldly wealth" (v.11) appears for the second time (cf. v.9). The property here is "someone else's" (v.12), presumably God's, in contrast to the parable's imagery in which, at least in Fitzmyer's view, the amount forgiven was the manager's own commission. Except for the word "servant," v.13 appears in precisely the same form in Matthew 6:24. The verse is equally appropriate in each context; here, however, it is connected to the context, not only topically, but verbally, through the use, for the third time, of *mamōnas* (cf. "worldly wealth," vv.9, 11), this time translated "money" in NIV. The addition of "servant" stresses the point that though one may *have* both God and money, we cannot *serve* them both.

14–15 Money (v.14) links this section (vv.14–18) with the preceding one. The charge that the Pharisees do not have a proper sense of values (v.15) leads to the saying about the value of the kingdom and the law (vv.16–17). In turn, reference to the permanence of the law becomes the context for a specific example of a contested moral standard, divorce and remarriage (v.18). Jesus' charge of greed is not leveled at the Pharisees elsewhere in the Gospels, nor is it intended to be an absolute generalization. Jewish teachers who had been influenced by Hellenistic culture were aware that philosophers often taught for fees. Rabbis in the first centuries of our era often had secular jobs. The Pharisees would not have been immune to desires for remuneration commensurate with their own sense of importance. Later on, Paul was to work at a trade so he could say that he did not "put on a mask to cover up greed" (1 Thess 2:5; cf. 1 Cor 9:12). Self-justification (v.15) is a temptation for religious people (cf. Matt 5:20; 6:1).

16–17 The Pharisees had the truth of the "Law" of Moses (Genesis to Deuteronomy) and the "Prophets" (v.16, here representing the rest of the OT). They failed to respond not only to the Good News of the kingdom but even to their own Scriptures (cf. Mark 7:8–9), whose authority continued into the present age (v.17). Verse 29 also alludes to their failure to heed the Law and the Prophets (see comments). For the relationship of John the Baptist to the kingdom (v.16a), see 7:28 and comment on that verse. Verse 16 appears in slightly different form—and with the sentences reversed—in Matthew's passage about John the Baptist (Matt 11:12–13). The wording in Matthew is notoriously difficult to interpret, but the substitution in Luke (v.16b) of "being preached" (*euangelizetai*) for "forcefully advancing" (*biazetai*, possibly, "suffered violence," see comments on Matt 11:13) limits the meaning here. *Biazetai*, which occurs in Matthew 11:13 though not in Luke 16:16b, does occur in v.16c—"is forcing his way," a translation that takes the verb, probably correctly, to be in the middle voice. Matthew has "forceful men lay hold of it" (*biastai* *harpazousin autēn*), conveying a sense of violence not necessarily implied in Luke's "everyone is forcing his way into it" (*pas eis autēn biazetai*). This could be understood as expressing violence if one interprets it in accord with what Matthew has; otherwise it could simply express the enthusiastic drive of those determined to enter the kingdom (cf. Luke 13:24). However one interprets this difficult verse, it is clear that the Pharisees had missed what was really of value (v.15), while all around them were people whose values were in order and who were energetically seeking the kingdom (cf. Matt 13:44–46). The truth of v.17 is also expressed in the Sermon on the Mount (Matt 5:17–20).

18 This brief excerpt from Jesus' teaching on divorce and remarriage is included as an example of one aspect of the law the Pharisees tended to minimize. The teaching is essentially the same as in Matthew 5:32, except that Luke (1) omits the phrase "except for marital unfaithfulness," (2) says that the remarried man commits adultery rather than that he causes his first wife to do so, and (3) includes a comment about a man who marries a divorced woman. See comments on Matthew 5:32 for the basic teaching.

Notes

4 The use of the aorist ἔγνων (*egnōn*, "I know") rather than the present tense γινώσκω (*ginōskō*) has often been commented on. Exegetes have tended to read too much into the simple aorist and to stress too much its punctiliar aspect. Here it could imply a flash of inspiration, "I've got it!" or, more likely as the culmination of his deliberations, "I've decided."

9 Μαμωνᾶς τῆς ἀδικίας (*mamōnas tēs adikias*, "worldly wealth," lit., "the mammon of injustice" or "of unrighteousness") is probably a Semitic expression used idiomatically to signify money. *Adikias* probably carries the thought, found in the Qumran writings, of that which characterizes the godless world (Ellis, *Gospel of Luke*, p. 199).

10–13 These verses appear to have been independent sayings brought together here by Luke because they share certain catchwords with the preceding verses. This is not impossible; there are no transitional words that indicate that the sayings were given on the same occasion in Jesus' ministry as the preceding. Verses 10–12 are unique to Luke and presumably come from his special source. Verse 13 is found, without the word "servant," in Matt 6:24 and is usually ascribed to Q.

6. *The rich man and Lazarus*

16:19–31

19"There was a rich man who was dressed in purple and fine linen and lived in luxury every day. 20At his gate was laid a beggar named Lazarus, covered with sores 21and longing to eat what fell from the rich man's table. Even the dogs came and licked his sores.

22"The time came when the beggar died and the angels carried him to Abraham's side. The rich man also died and was buried. 23In hell, where he was in torment, he looked up and saw Abraham far away, with Lazarus by his side. 24So he called to him, 'Father Abraham, have pity on me and send Lazarus to dip the tip of his finger in water and cool my tongue, because I am in agony in this fire.'

25"But Abraham replied, 'Son, remember that in your lifetime you received your good things, while Lazarus received bad things, but now he is comforted here and you are in agony. 26And besides all this, between us and you a great chasm has been fixed, so that those who want to go from here to you cannot, nor can anyone cross over from there to us.'

27"He answered, 'Then I beg you, father, send Lazarus to my father's house, 28for I have five brothers. Let him warn them, so that they will not also come to this place of torment.'

29"Abraham replied, 'They have Moses and the Prophets; let them listen to them.'

30" 'No, father Abraham,' he said, 'but if someone from the dead goes to them, they will repent.'

31"He said to him, 'If they do not listen to Moses and the Prophets, they will not be convinced even if someone rises from the dead.' "

The expositor's basic concern is not the nature and history of this story (cf. Notes) but its primary significance in its Lukan context. It is set in a series of encounters with the Pharisees (cf. 15:1–2; 16:14). Its meaning must be understood in that context. The Pharisees did not follow their own Scriptures, the "Law and the Prophets" (v.16); so they were no better than the rich man's brothers who "have Moses and the Prophets" (v.29). The Pharisees professed belief in a future life and in future judgment. However, they did not live in conformity with that belief but rather in the pursuit of wealth (v.14), just like the rich man of the parable. Even Jesus' resurrection (possibly alluded to in v.31) would not convince them. It is implicit in the account that one's attitude to God and his word is confirmed in this life and that it cannot be altered in the next one.

While the parable does contain a few doctrinal implications, the expositor must keep in mind that one cannot build an eschatology on it. To do that will result in an anachronism; for though Revelation 20:14 places the throwing of death and Hades into the lake of fire at the end of history (the "second death"), in this story the rich man is already in a torment of fire, in his body, while his brothers are still living. It should be understood as a story containing some limited eschatological ideas familiar to Jesus' audience. Thus understood, the story makes a powerful case for (1) the future reversal of the human condition (cf. 6:20–26), (2) the reality of future judgment based on one's decisions in this life, and (3) the futility of even a resurrection to persuade those who persist in rejecting God's revealed word.

19–20 This paragraph vividly pictures the earthly state of the two men and prepares the hearer and reader for the reversal in vv.22–24. The latter is both striking and consistent with Luke's presentation of Jesus' teaching, but it is not in itself the main feature of the story. The fact that Jesus named the "beggar" (v.20) while not naming the "rich man" (v.19) may imply that one was ultimately more important. The naming of a character in the story need not lead to the conclusion some have drawn that Lazarus was a real person, though parables usually do not have named characters. Nor is there convincing evidence that this Lazarus is the same one Jesus raised from the dead (John 11). Admittedly, the similarity is remarkable, since both stories deal with death and resurrection (cf. v.30), and since in both instances resurrection does not convince unbelievers (see Marshall, *Gospel of Luke*, p. 635). Nevertheless, Lazarus was a common name, the Greek form (*Lazaros*) of the Hebrew Eleazar (*'el'āzār*, "[whom] God has helped"). It is probably used symbolically. Tradition has given the name of "Dives," meaning "rich," to the anonymous rich man (cf. Notes).

"Purple" (v.19) was a dyed cloth worn by the wealthy. The Roman soldiers mocked Jesus by putting a purple robe on him in the Praetorium before the Crucifixion (Mark 15:17, 20). In a vivid contrast to the rich man, Jesus depicts Lazarus as neglected and subjected to insult even by "the dogs" (v.20).

21–24 After his death, Lazarus is escorted by "the angels," in contrast to the rich man who was merely "buried" (v.22). Angelic activity is not foreign to the biblical scene (Heb 1:14), but here Jesus' reference to the angels is probably simply an artistic touch.

"Abraham's side" may picture reclining at a banquet, like the "feast in the kingdom of God" at which Abraham will be present (13:28–29). If so, it may contrast with vv.20–21, where the rich man sits at the table while Lazarus longs for the scraps. Otherwise it might be a symbol of reunion with Abraham and the other patriarchs at death. "Hell" (v.23) is "Hades" (NIV mg.). In early classical literature Hades was a term for the place of departed spirits. In the LXX it represents the Hebrew Sheol, the realm of the dead. It occurs ten times in the NT, two of them in Luke (cf. 10:15). In the NT Hades is never used of the destiny of the believer. Neither is it identified with Gehenna (*geenna*), which is usually connected with fiery judgment, as in Matthew 5:22, 29–30 (Luke only in 12:5, q.v.). Here (v.23) Hades stands in contrast to the place and state of Lazarus's blessing. The division between the two is absolute and final (v.26). "Father Abraham" (v.24) expresses the normal attitude a Jew, conscious of his heritage, would have (John 8:39).

25–26 Abraham's response, "Son" (*teknon*, v.25), like the identical term on the lips of the Prodigal Son's father (15:31), conveys something of the compassion God himself shows even to those who spurn him. The possessive pronoun in "your good things" is similar in its force to the words "for himself" in 12:21. In a masterly summary Jesus contrasts the previous states of the rich man and Lazarus with the "now" and "here" of their situations after death. Verse 26 shows the utter and unchangeable finality of their decision.

27–31 This unchangeability comes from a hardness not only toward Christ but toward "Moses and the Prophets" (v.29; cf. John 5:46). Not even a spectacular "sign," like one returning from the dead (vv.27, 30), can change those whose hearts are set against God's word, as the response of many to the resurrection of Jesus was to show.

Notes

19–31 Over the years some commentators have held that this is not a parable but a story about two men, possibly known to Jesus' audience. (For a recent example of this view, see Summers, *Luke*, p. 195.) The usual reasons for supporting this interpretation are (1) the story lacks an introduction similar to the introductions to most of Jesus' parables and (2) at least one of the characters is named. At the other extreme is the view that follows a study by Gressmann (see Creed, pp. 209–10) and assumes that the story originated in Egyptian folklore. A more recent structural approach is more concerned with the structure and contemporary symbolism of the story itself than with any extended history of tradition.

As indicated in the introductory comments to this section, to interpret the story literally introduces a difficult anachronism, that the man is already being tormented by fire, though the event of Rev 20:14 has not yet taken place. The story can be understood as a parable that realistically portrays the fate of those who have rejected the Lord. If Luke had clearly indicated that Jesus was referring to an actual event, we would have to attempt to resolve the anachronism. But since Luke has not done so, and since the story is powerfully didactic, it seems best to interpret it as a parable. However, it is no mere story chosen for its usefulness as an illustration but a rather sober portrayal of yet unseen realities.

The expositor will do best by expounding this passage in its Lukan context, stressing those elements that are clearly affirmed in biblical teaching elsewhere. Issues of source or of background are not as important in this instance as are its immediate purpose and message.

19 The vagueness of ἄνθρωπος . . . τις (anthrōpos . . . tis, "a certain man") was intolerable for early readers, and some early "improvements" were made, such as the insertion of the name Νευης (Neuēs) in P⁷⁵ (see Creed, p. 211, and Marshall, *Gospel of Luke*, pp. 634–35).

---

7. Sin, faith, duty

17:1–10

> ¹Jesus said to his disciples: "Things that cause people to sin are bound to come, but woe to that person through whom they come. ²It would be better for him to be thrown into the sea with a millstone tied around his neck than for him to cause one of these little ones to sin. ³So watch yourselves.
>
> "If your brother sins, rebuke him, and if he repents, forgive him. ⁴If he sins against you seven times a day, and seven times comes back to you and says, 'I repent,' forgive him."
>
> ⁵The apostles said to the Lord, "Increase our faith!"
>
> ⁶He replied, "If you have faith as small as a mustard seed, you can say to this mulberry tree, 'Be uprooted and planted in the sea,' and it will obey you.
>
> ⁷"Suppose one of you had a servant plowing or looking after the sheep. Would he say to the servant when he comes in from the field, 'Come along now and sit down to eat'? ⁸Would he not rather say, 'Prepare my supper, get yourself ready and wait on me while I eat and drink; after that you may eat and drink'? ⁹Would he thank the servant because he did what he was told to do? ¹⁰So you also, when you have done everything you were told to do, should say, 'We are unworthy servants; we have only done our duty.'"

As the heading indicates, this unit contains various brief teachings. As with some other parts in this special section of Luke, it is difficult to understand why these teachings are brought together. The introductory words "Jesus said to his disciples" are similar to those in other places where there apparently is no attempt to establish a chronological sequence (e.g., 12:22, 54; 13:6; 16:1). This does not rule out the possibility that the parables in these instances were originally given sequentially, but they could be understood as merely marking a break from the preceding section. Yet it is also possible to see a logical connection between the end of chapter 16 and the beginning of chapter 17, if we understand "the things that cause people to sin" (v.1) to be the sins of the Pharisees, such as those mentioned in 16:14.

Some may feel that logical connections within this passage are difficult to discern, e.g., between v.4 and v.5. However, there is a common unifying theme of attitudes in the Christian community. The connections are no weaker than those that join similar teachings in Matthew 18 about care for the little ones, the problem of sin in the community, and prayer. Actually, though we expect to find material in topical rather than chronological order in Matthew (in contrast to most of Luke), in Matthew 18 the pericopes are joined by chronological indicators, while those in Luke are not. The contexts of the two passages are totally different, and here in Luke the teachings on prayer are not parallel to those on prayer in Matthew 18 but rather to those in Matthew 17:19–20 and 21:21–22. Here, as throughout the Synoptics, each Gospel must be studied and interpreted in its own context.

1–3a Jesus has been addressing the Pharisees since 16:14. Now he resumes his conversation with the disciples. The "things that cause people to sin" (v.1) are the familiar *skandala* (lit., "traps," but symbolically whatever causes people to fall into sin). "Woe" recalls 6:24–26. A "millstone" (v.2) was a stone of sufficient weight to crush grain as it was being rotated in a mill. The "little ones" would seem to be either young or new believers or people the world takes little notice of. There is no mention here of children as in Matthew 18:1–6. There is no antecedent for "these." So if the conversation stands alone, it must be taken to refer to those who were actually standing there with Jesus. In the NIV paragraph structure, v.3a—"So watch yourselves"—is joined with the preceding saying rather than with the following (as in RSV, NASB). Either way makes sense.

3b–4 The two members of v.3b must be given equal weight. Rebuke of the sinner and forgiveness of the penitent are both Christian duties. Verse 4 does not, of course, establish a specific number of times for forgiveness but rather shows the principle of being generous in forgiving others (cf. Matt 6:12). This is the only right response for those who have themselves been forgiven.

5–6 The apostles may have felt that this kind of forgiveness would demand more faith than they had (v.5). The "mulberry tree" (v.6) in Luke corresponds to the mountain in Matthew 17:20; 21:21; and Mark 11:23. In each instance the object is to be disposed of in the "sea" (probably Galilee). The black mulberry tree (KJV "sycamine," not to be confused with "sycamore") grew quite large, to a height of some thirty-five feet, and would be difficult to uproot. The mustard seed is proverbially small, a suitable metaphor for the amount of faith needed to do the seemingly impossible. Jesus' answer to the request for additional faith seems to be that they should use the faith they had to petition God.

7–10 This is one of the passages in which Luke presents Jesus' teaching about the ideal of servanthood. The world's idea of success is to lord it over others; Jesus' way is the reverse—namely, servanthood—which is actually the way to true greatness. Two earlier parables on this theme occur in 12:35–37; 42–48. The circumstances Jesus describes here were normal in that society and the point obvious. In contrast, in the parable in 12:35–37, Jesus presented a reversal of the normal procedure, with the master doing just what 17:7 rules out. The master's extraordinary act depicted in 12:35–37 symbolizes God's grace, while the normal expectation of the master here in Luke 17 symbolizes the proper servant attitude. Jesus did not intend to demean servants but to make their duty clear. In this respect the NIV translation "unworthy" for *achreioi* (v.10) is an improvement over KJV's "unprofitable."

8. Ten healed of leprosy

17:11–19

> ¹¹Now on his way to Jerusalem, Jesus traveled along the border between Samaria and Galilee. ¹²As he was going into a village, ten men who had leprosy met him. They stood at a distance ¹³and called out in a loud voice, "Jesus, Master, have pity on us!"
>
> ¹⁴When he saw them, he said, "Go, show yourselves to the priests." And as they went, they were cleansed.
>
> ¹⁵One of them, when he saw he was healed, came back, praising God in a loud voice. ¹⁶He threw himself at Jesus' feet and thanked him—and he was a Samaritan.
>
> ¹⁷Jesus asked, "Were not all ten cleansed? Where are the other nine? ¹⁸Was no one found to return and give praise to God except this foreigner?" ¹⁹Then he said to him, "Rise and go; your faith has made you well."

Not only is this narrative peculiar to Luke, but it also stresses several characteristically Lukan themes. Jerusalem is the goal of Jesus' journey (cf. 9:51; 13:33); Jesus has mercy on social outcasts; he conforms to Jewish norms by requiring that the lepers go for the required priestly declaration of health (cf. Lev 14); faith and healing should bring praise to God (cf. 18:43; Acts 3:8–9); and the grace of God extends beyond Judaism, with Samaritans receiving special attention (cf. 10:25–37).

11–13 That Luke does not mention the particular place where the healing was done implies that he did not consider the exact locale important historically or theologically. What is important is the reminder (possibly to indicate a new phase of his ministry) of Jesus' progress toward Jerusalem (v.11). The "village" (v.12) lies somewhere in the border territory between Galilee and Samaria (cf. Notes); so Jewish and Samaritan lepers share their common misery at its edge. The lepers maintain their proper distance, call Jesus by a term found only in Luke—"Master" (*epistata*, v.13; cf. 5:5)—and ask only for pity without specifying their request.

14–19 Jesus' command (v.14) required obedience based on some faith in the reliability of the speaker (cf. Matt 12:13; Mark 3:5; Luke 6:10). On their way to the priests, the lepers are "cleansed" (*ekatharisthēsan*). Jesus, however, uses the more comprehensive word "made well" (*sesōken*, v.19) on speaking to the Samaritan who returned to give thanks. Though Luke does not say whether the others had faith, it need not be denied them. The stress is on the openly expressed gratitude of the Samaritan, who alone brought praise to God (vv.15–16).

Notes

11 Διὰ μέσον (*dia meson*, "along the border between") is a troublesome phrase. This accusative is well attested, but the Byzantine tradition has the genitive μέσου (*mesou*, KJV, "through the midst"). Conzelmann (*Theology of Luke*, pp. 68–72) considered this a theological use of geography, with Luke trying to establish a travel theme based on an allegedly distorted view of the geographical relationship of Samaria to Galilee. On Conzelmann's assumption, Luke thought that Judea was directly south of Galilee, with Samaria alongside both. On this view, Jesus was going south along this supposed north-south border. Actually, Luke does not state that Jesus made just one journey from north to south but rather suggests that he crisscrossed the area, making perhaps several trips to Jerusalem before his final stay there. In this case he might have been on his way east to Perea, to turn south on the highway along the east side of the Jordan River.

---

9. The coming of the kingdom of God

17:20–37

20Once, having been asked by the Pharisees when the kingdom of God would come, Jesus replied, "The kingdom of God does not come with your careful observation, 21nor will people say, 'Here it is,' or 'There it is,' because the kingdom of God is within you."

22Then he said to his disciples, "The time is coming when you will long to see one of the days of the Son of Man, but you will not see it. 23Men will tell you, 'There he is!' or 'Here he is!' Do not go running off after them. 24For the Son of Man in his day will be like the lightning, which flashes and lights up the sky from one end to the other. 25But first he must suffer many things and be rejected by this generation.

26"Just as it was in the days of Noah, so also will it be in the days of the Son of Man. 27People were eating, drinking, marrying and being given in marriage up to the day Noah entered the ark. Then the flood came and destroyed them all.

28"It was the same in the days of Lot. People were eating and drinking, buying and selling, planting and building. 29But the day Lot left Sodom, fire and sulfur rained down from heaven and destroyed them all.

30"It will be just like this on the day the Son of Man is revealed. 31On that day no one who is on the roof of his house, with his goods inside, should go down to get them. Likewise, no one in the field should go back for anything. 32Remember Lot's wife! 33Whoever tries to keep his life will lose it, and whoever loses his life will preserve it. 34I tell you, on that night two people will be in one bed; one will be taken and the other left. 35Two women will be grinding grain together; one will be taken and the other left."

37"Where, Lord?" they asked.

He replied, "Where there is a dead body, there the vultures will gather."

Luke contains two major discourses about the future, the present passage and 21:5–33. Both have close parallels in Matthew 24 and Mark 13. (See comments on 21:5–33 for a discussion of interpretive and critical issues a comparison with these parallels involves.) Luke 17 is more uniformly apocalyptic than Luke 21—i.e., no human agency appears here (in contrast to the besieging armies of 21:20); God acts directly from heaven. Also the prohibition against lingering is stronger here than in chapter 21. People on the rooftop when the Son of Man is revealed dare not take a moment to go inside their houses. But those addressed in chapter 21 are threatened by a military siege and should avoid getting caught in the city. The urgency in chapter 17 is greater with less time to spare than in chapter 21.

20–21 The Pharisees' question about the kingdom initiates this new cycle of Jesus' teachings. This includes (1) a saying about the coming of the kingdom that is unique to Luke's Gospel (vv.20–21), (2) the discourse on the coming of the Son of Man (vv.22–37), and (3) a parable of encouragement for those who wait for vindication when the Son of Man comes (18:1–8).

The time of the coming of the kingdom was important to both Pharisees and Christians, though for different reasons. By the time Luke was written, rumors were abroad that the day of the Lord had already come (2 Thess 2:1–2). Later, others would question whether the Lord would return at all (2 Peter 3:3–4). Before this point in Luke, Jesus had made it clear that the kingdom had already come, insofar as God's power was unleashed against demons (11:20). Jesus will shortly indicate by a parable that the full expression of the kingdom does not take place in the immediate future (19:11–27). The present passage is therefore important as a further definition of the nature of the kingdom.

To the question "When?" (v.20; cf. v.37, "Where?"), Jesus says that the kingdom will not come *meta paratēreseōs* (lit., "with observation"). This may have one of three meanings, none of them excluding the others: (1) it cannot be foreseen from signs; (2) it is not an observable process; and (3) it does not come with or through observing rites. The second meaning accords most naturally with the most common usage of *paratērēsis* and with the context, which emphasizes suddenness, though the first meaning may fit the Pharisees' frame of reference better. The NIV "within you" (for *entos hymōn*, v.21) is a questionable translation. Jesus would hardly tell Pharisees, most of whom (especially those who interrogated him) were unbelievers, that the kingdom was within them (cf. Marshall, *Gospel of Luke*, p. 655, who considers the word "you" to be indefinite, though he also rejects the translation "within"). The NIV margin ("among you") is surely right.

Luke's presentation of the kingdom in Jesus' teaching is dynamic rather than psychological, as seen in 11:20: "But if I drive out demons by the finger of God, then the kingdom of God has come to you." The idea behind " 'Here it is' or 'There it is' " is that of the kingdom's authoritative presence. Jesus is thus saying that people are the subjects, not the timekeepers, of God's kingdom. Whether he means here that the kingdom is already present (which was true, in the sense of 11:20), or whether he used the present "is" in a vivid futuristic sense, he is emphasizing its suddenness.

22–25 In this paragraph, which begins with a saying not found in Matthew or Mark, Jesus continues the emphasis on the suddenness of the kingdom's coming. Does "one of the days" (v.22) refer back to the time of his earthly ministry or forward to his return? Does "one" mean any "one" or "the first" of a series as in Matthew 28:1 and parallels? Since Jesus now addresses his disciples, who will have reason to long for his return, and since what follows deals with that return, "one of the days" probably refers to the initiation of the reign of the coming Son of Man (cf. Notes). "You will not see it" implies "not yet" rather than "never." His coming will be obvious, "like the lightning" (v.24); so rumors of seeing him in various places ("here," "there," vv.21, 23) cannot be true. (For Jesus' use of the plural "days" [v.22] and of the third person referring to the Son of Man [e.g., "in his day"] and the combination of these with the passion prediction in v.25, see Notes.)

The inclusion of the passion prediction (v.25) is natural in Luke, who stresses the order of suffering before glory (cf. 24:26, 46; Acts 17:3). "This generation" may obliquely refer back to the Pharisees. Broadly it refers to Jesus' contemporaries, elsewhere called by him "unbelieving and perverse" (9:41) and "wicked" (11:29; cf. 11:31–32, 50–51).

26–29 Jesus' references to Noah (vv.26–27) and Lot (v.28) serve to illustrate the suddenness of the revelation of the Son of Man. The words "eating, drinking," etc. (vv.27–28) describe the usual round of life's activities. NIV accurately represents the Greek use of asyndeton (i.e., a sequence of words without connectives such as "and"). This effectively gives the impression of continually repeated activities. Unexpected destruction came as a judgment on people in the times of Noah and of Lot. God's sudden interruption of human affairs is part of the apocalyptic perspective on the divine ordering of history. The term "apocalyptic" (from the Gr. *apokalypto*, "reveal") occurs in v.30: "the Son of Man is revealed" (*apokalyptetai*). The consummation of history, indeed, of the kingdom of God itself, is realized in the revelation of the Son of Man.

30–36 As already noted, unlike the siege of Jerusalem described in chapter 21, the sudden coming of the Son of Man (v.30) leaves no time even for a quick gathering of possessions from one's home (v.31). This theme of imminency blends into a call for decision between eternal values and present possessions reminiscent of chapter 12. The reason for returning to house or field is to salvage possessions. Lot's wife (v.32), reluctant to leave her old life, looked back to Sodom (Gen 19:26). This leads to the saying in v.33 (used elsewhere in an ethical sense) regarding discipleship (Matt 10:39) but employed here with a very concrete application.

The solemn words, "I tell you" (v.34) introduce a warning that the apocalyptic moment reveals ultimate destinies. Even those closely associated (in bed and at work) are separated. "Will be taken" (*paralēmphthēsetai*, vv.34–35) probably has its normal sense of being taken into fellowship (in Noah's case into safety), rather than being taken into judgment, for which there seems to be no precedent (cf. TDNT, 4:11–14). The one "left" (*aphethēsetai*) is thereby abandoned to judgment. The alternate interpretation, however, is possible in this context. The two illustrations reflect either simultaneous activities early in the morning (Danker, *Jesus*, p. 183) or, more likely, activities selected to show that the Son of Man could come at any time, day or night.

37 The Pharisees had asked "When?" (v.20); the disciples asked "Where?" For us Jesus' reply is somewhat obscure. The hovering "vultures" (*aetoi*, usually tr. "eagles," but here probably meaning scavengers such as vultures [BAG, s.f.]) may symbolize judgment on the spiritually dead. Also they may merely represent the place of carnage.

Notes

21 The phrase ἐντὸς ὑμῶν (*entos hymōn*, "within you") can also mean "in your control," according to an exegetical note by C.H. Roberts (" Ἐντος Ὑμῶν," HTR 41 [1948]: 1–8) and one by J.G. Griffiths ("The Kingdom of Heaven [Lk XVII.21]," ExpT 63 [1951–52]: 30–31 [reprinted in the *Bible Translator* 4 (1953): 7–8]). This would not mean that the Pharisees controlled the kingdom but that response to it was under their control. C.F.D. Moule provides evidence against this view in his *Idiom Book of New Testament Greek* (Cambridge: Cambridge University Press, 1959), pp. 83–84.
22 Μίαν τῶν ἡμερῶν (*mian tōn hēmerōn*, "one of the days") seems to combine both the singular "day" (vv.24, 30) and the plural "days" (vv.26, 28). It seems to be an echo of the Day of the Lord, a term denoting the occasion on which God acts mightily in history, especially the inception of the Messianic Age. A parallel in which both singular and plural are used with the same point of reference is Amos 8:11, 13.

24 Ἐν τῇ ἡμέρα αὐτοῦ (*en tē hēmera autou,* "in his day") sharpens, by its use of the third instead of the first person, the issue as to whether Jesus spoke of himself in such sayings. A common conclusion of recent studies on the "Son of Man" is that the sayings using this designation may be grouped into those that use the phrase as a neutral (or covert) reference to the speaker, those that refer to the expected suffering of Jesus, and those that refer to the future glory of the Son of Man. Some claim that the future (apocalyptic) sayings of Jesus refer to someone else, not him. Jeremias (*New Testament Theology,* p. 276), however, correctly observes that "quite apart from the absence of evidence in the sources, it is impossible that in the 'Son of Man' Jesus should have seen a future saving figure who was to be distinguished from himself. In that case, one would have to suppose that Jesus had seen himself as a forerunner, as the prophet of the Son of Man." Jesus undoubtedly saw himself, not some other, as the one who fulfilled the OT prophecies. The use of the third person is common in all three types of Son-of-Man sayings. (For a fuller bibliography, see note on 5:24). Both the suffering and the apocalyptic type sayings are found in this passage (vv.24–25).

Regarding the textual evidence for "in his day," a variety of significant MSS omit it (e.g., P75 B D). The omission could have been accidental, if a copyist's eyes mistakenly jumped from the ending of "man" (-πον, *pou*) to the ending of "his" (-του, *tou*), the last word of the Greek phrase in question. However, the MSS cited are probably correct.

---

10. *Parable of the persistent widow*

18:1–8

> [1]Then Jesus told his disciples a parable to show them that they should always pray and not give up. [2]He said: "In a certain town there was a judge who neither feared God nor cared about men. [3]And there was a widow in that town who kept coming to him with the plea, 'Grant me justice against my adversary.'
>
> [4]"For some time he refused. But finally he said to himself, 'Even though I don't fear God or care about men, [5]yet because this widow keeps bothering me, I will see that she gets justice, so that she won't eventually wear me out with her coming!' "
>
> [6]And the Lord said, "Listen to what the unjust judge says. [7]And will not God bring about justice for his chosen ones, who cry out to him day and night? Will he keep putting them off? [8]I tell you, he will see that they get justice, and quickly. However, when the Son of Man comes, will he find faith on the earth?"

1 This parable must be interpreted with reference to the eschatological theme in chapter 17, as v.8b makes clear. The story is not intended to apply to prayer in general, as though one needed to pester God for every need until he reluctantly responds. The theme is that of the vindication of God's misunderstood and suffering people, as v.7 states. God's people in OT days needed to "wait" on God as he worked out justice with apparent slowness. "Do not . . . let my enemies triumph over me. No one whose hope is in you will ever be put to shame" (Ps 25:2–3). In the final days the martyrs wait for vindication (Rev 6:9–11). Ultimately delay is ended and the "mystery" of God completed (Rev 10:6–7). Meanwhile we wrestle with the problem of evil and with issues of theodicy. Under these circumstances we should "always pray and not give up."

2–3 The designation "unjust judge" (*ho kritēs tēs adikias,* v.6) is similar to the idiom in 16:8, "the dishonest manager" (*ton oikonomon tēs adikias*). *Adikia* ("injustice" or "dishonesty") also appears in connection with wealth in the Greek of 16:9, where it has the connotation of "worldly" (cf. 16:11). Therefore we should probably understand the judge (v.2) to be a "man of the world," who, though crooked, prided himself on shrewd judicial decisions. The judge is typical of a local Gentile judge known throughout the Hellenistic world (cf. *Livy* 22. 3 and comments in Danker, *Jesus*, p. 184). J.D.M. Derrett ("Law in the NT: The Unjust Judge," NTS 18 [1971–72]: 178–91) suggests that as a local secular administrative officer he would be approached by those who could not bring their cases to the high religious court. Being easily accessible and having the authority to make quick decisions, he would naturally be besieged by people such as the widow of the story (v.3).

4–6 The words "wear me out" (*hypōpiazē me*, v.5) are difficult to translate, for they literally mean "strike under the eye, give a black eye to" (BAG, s.v.). Commentators usually give them a figurative meaning. Derrett ("Unjust Judge," p. 191) shows that they are common idiom in eastern countries, where to have one's face blackened means to suffer shame. Probably we can also compare our American idiom "to give a black eye to," meaning "to damage one's reputation." If this is so, the story may be compared to that of the friend at midnight, where, if Bailey (*Poet and Peasant*, pp. 125–33) is correct, the friend responds to his friend's request for fear of public shame (see comment on 11:5–13). In each parable the reputation on the one being petitioned is at stake. Therefore, though God is not compared to a crooked judge, there *is* a partial basis of comparison in that God will also guard his reputation and vindicate himself.

7 "Chosen ones" (*eklektōn*) is a term used throughout Scripture that is especially significant in describing those who, at the end of history, are marked out as on the victorious side (Matt 24:31; Mark 13:27; Rev 17:14). "Will he keep putting them off?" (*kai makrothymei ep' autois*) is one of several possible translations of these words (cf. Notes). The point of the verse is that God patiently listens to his elect as they pray in their continuing distress, waiting for the proper time to act on their behalf.

8 Help is on the way, and the delay will prove shorter than it seems from our perspective (cf. Notes). The noun "faith" (*tēn pistin*) is probably to be understood here in relation to its content or quality. True believers who still wait with patient trust will seem few when the Son of Man comes (cf. vv.24–25). This may reflect the theme of perseverance that Schuyler Brown sees as characteristic of Luke (*Apostasy and Perseverance*, pp. 45–46).

Notes

1–8 For a representative of the older interpretation of the parable that both minimizes the eschatological reference and assumes a strong contrast between God and the judge, see Benjamin B. Warfield, "The Importunate Widow and the Alleged Failure of Faith," ExpT 25 (1913–14): 69–72, 137–39.

7 Καὶ μακροθυμεῖ ἐπ' αὐτοῖς (*kai makrothymei ep' autois*, "Will he keep putting them off?") is very difficult to exegete. The difficulty is both lexical and syntactical. Does the verb mean to "delay," "put off," or "be patient"? What is the relationship of *ep' autois* to the

verb? Does the question anticipate a positive answer or, like the preceding question, a negative one? If the verb means "be patient," if *ep' autois* is taken with it to mean "with them" (as in Matt 18:29; James 5:7), and if it calls for a positive response, the meaning is "He will also be patient with them, won't he?" For a thorough discussion of a number of possibilities, see Marshall, *Gospel of Luke*, pp. 674–75.

8 "Speedily" is a translation of ἐν τάχει (*en tachei*, NIV, "quickly"), which assumes v.7 means that God will not delay his act of vindication. Others think "suddenly" is the meaning here, since a period of time has intervened (recognized especially in Luke). A similar expression, ταχύ (*tachy*), occurs in Rev 22:20. The prophetic scroll is not to be sealed (cf. Dan 12:4, 9), for the time of fulfillment is near (Rev 22:10).

---

11. *Parable of the Pharisee and the tax collector*

18:9–14

> [9]To some who were confident of their own righteousness and looked down on everybody else, Jesus told this parable: [10]"Two men went up to the temple to pray, one a Pharisee and the other a tax collector. [11]The Pharisee stood up and prayed about himself; 'God, I thank you that I am not like other men—robbers, evildoers, adulterers—or even like this tax collector. [12]I fast twice a week and give a tenth of all I get.'
>
> [13]"But the tax collector stood at a distance. He would not even look up to heaven, but beat his breast and said, 'God, have mercy on me, a sinner.'
>
> [14]"I tell you that this man, rather than the other, went home justified before God. For everyone who exalts himself will be humbled, and he who humbles himself will be exalted."

Danker (*Jesus*, p. 185) observes that whereas Paul "discusses the *process* of justification . . . Luke describes the nature of the *recipients* of God's verdict of approval" (emphasis his). This is true throughout Luke's Gospel, but it is in this story of "The Churchman and the Politician" (Ellis, *Gospel of Luke*, p. 214) that we see the characteristics of recipients and rejectors most sharply defined. The Pharisee shows the attitude of pride and self-vindication alluded to in Matthew 23:5–7; Mark 7:6; Philippians 3:4–6. The implication of his words is a contractual relationship with God whereby he would accept the Pharisee's merit in exchange for justification. Actually not only this parable but the two following stories (vv.15–17, 18–30) deal with conditions for entering the kingdom. Each stresses human inability.

9–12 Elements of this parable need little interpretation, only careful observation. Luke does not say whom the parable was directed at (v.9) but rather describes the two men (v.10) so that the parable can be understood by his readers. The characters represent extremes, but the sketches are true to life. The Pharisee follows custom in praying in the temple and in standing while praying (v.11). His prayer expresses the essence of Pharisaism—separation from others. This in itself was not reprehensible, because at the inception of Pharisaism there was a need for a distinctive group who would maintain a piety that stood in contrast to the encroaching pagan Hellenism. This initial good hardened into obnoxious self-righteousness on the part of many (not all) Pharisees, as seen not only in Matthew 23 and Mark 7, but in Jewish literature as well. Luke has observed the Pharisees' hostility thus far (cf. 5:17; 6:2, 7; 7:39; 11:37–54; 15:2; 16:14). Pharisees did tithe (v.12), even their herbs (11:42). They did fast, though twice in the week was more than necessary and was only practiced by the most pious. The problem was that this Pharisee's prayer was a farce, being created only in himself (notice the sarcastic phrase "about himself" [v.11] and the mention of God only at the beginning of his prayer).

13–14 The description speaks for itself. The tax collector (v.13), generally thought of as a greedy politician whose very business depended on knuckling under to the despised Roman government, was one of the social outcasts so prominent in Luke as recipients of God's grace (e.g., 5:12, 27; 7:34, 37; 15:1–2; 16:20). His justification was immediate (v.14), granted by God in contrast to the fantasy of self-justification the Pharisee was futilely caught up in. Verse 14b states the principle that is further illustrated in vv.15–17.

The modern reader will probably not feel the impact of this story to the extent a first-century reader would. We already think of the Pharisees as hypocrites and the tax collectors as those who received the grace of God. Jesus' original hearers would have thought, on the contrary, that it was the pious Pharisee who deserved acceptance by God.

12. *The little children and Jesus*

18:15–17

> [15]People were also bringing babies to Jesus to have him touch them. When the disciples saw this, they rebuked them. [16]But Jesus called the children to him and said, "Let the little children come to me, and do not hinder them, for the kingdom of God belongs to such as these. [17]I tell you the truth, anyone who will not receive the kingdom of God like a little child will never enter it."

15–17 Luke's special section has now reached its conclusion. With v.15 the narrative rejoins that of Matthew (19:13) and Mark (10:13). Jesus' words about little children provide Luke's second example of the attitude essential for receiving God's grace. It is not age per se that is in view but childlike qualities such as trust, openness, and the absence of holier-than-thou attitudes. Therefore, this passage does not directly bear on the question of infant baptism. Nevertheless v.15 shows through the use of *brephē* ("babies") that Jesus had compassion even on infants too young to understand the difference between right and wrong. The ones he invites in v.16 (*paidia*, "children") include a broader age spread. Only in recent years have we begun to understand the importance of communication through touching, though the instinct has always been present in those who care about other human beings.

13. *The rich ruler*

18:18–30

> [18]A certain ruler asked him, "Good teacher, what must I do to inherit eternal life?"
> [19]"Why do you call me good?" Jesus answered. "No one is good—except God alone. [20]You know the commandments: 'Do not commit adultery, do not murder, do not steal, do not give false testimony, honor your father and mother.' "
> [21]"All these I have kept since I was a boy," he said.
> [22]When Jesus heard this, he said to him, "You still lack one thing. Sell everything you have and give to the poor, and you will have treasure in heaven. Then come, follow me."

²³When he heard this, he became very sad, because he was a man of great wealth. ²⁴Jesus looked at him and said, "How hard it is for the rich to enter the kingdom of God! ²⁵Indeed, it is easier for a camel to go through the eye of a needle than for a rich man to enter the kingdom of God."

²⁶Those who heard this asked, "Who then can be saved?"

²⁷Jesus replied, "What is impossible with men is possible with God."

²⁸Peter said to him, "We have left all we had to follow you!"

²⁹"I tell you the truth," Jesus said to them, "no one who has left home or wife or brothers or parents or children for the sake of the kingdom of God ³⁰will fail to receive many times as much in this age and, in the age to come, eternal life."

After the parable of the Pharisee and the tax collector and the incident of the little children, the story of the rich ruler illustrates once more the need for receptiveness if one is to experience God's grace. Then, lest it be thought that this response lies within human power, Jesus makes the point that it is only by the power of God that anyone is saved (vv.25–27). The story thus emphasizes both the responsibility and the helplessness of human kind.

18 "Ruler" (only in Luke) is too broad a term to permit precise identification of the man's background. Only Matthew says that he was young (Matt 19:20). The appellation "Good teacher" is not a common one and called for comment by Jesus. "What must I do?" indicates a desire to discover if any deed has been overlooked in qualifying for eternal life. John 3:3–15 shows that eternal life is life in the kingdom and that it is received only through the new birth.

19 Jesus replies by asking the ruler a question that has puzzled many. Whatever its ultimate meaning, the question does not constitute a denial that he himself is good. Some commentators hold that he is subtly urging the ruler to see that if Jesus is good, and if only God is good, then there is a clear conclusion to be drawn as to his true identity. Whether or not that is Jesus' purpose (the logic is certainly true), his more obvious purpose in this question is to establish a standard of goodness infinitely higher than the ruler supposes it to be. In other words, he brings us close to the principle in Matthew 5:20, 48.

20–21 Jesus now addresses this standard of righteousness. The first step is a summary of several of the Ten Commandments (v.20), omitting the first few that relate to God and the final one about covetousness. The man, like Paul (Phil 3:6), has kept the letter of the law (v.21).

22 Jesus now moves to the heart of the tenth commandment by leading the ruler to face his attitude toward his possessions. Paul recognized his sinfulness when he became aware of the thrust of the command against covetousness (Rom 7:7–8). In Colossians 3:5 he said that greed is idolatry. The ruler had broken the first commandment by breaking the last. Actually, by the act of giving away his goods, he would have shown himself rid of that sin; and by following Jesus, he would have indicated his allegiance to God. Luke's report of this part of the conversation—"You still lack one thing"—corresponds to Matthew's—"If you want to be perfect" (19:21) —in the same way that Luke 6:36—"Be merciful"—corresponds to Matthew 5:48— "Be perfect." In each case the record in Matthew speaks generally of righteousness, whereas that in Luke (and also Mark) concentrates on that which is yet needed in order to produce righteous perfection.

The command to sell everything and give to the poor is difficult to interpret as well as to apply. It goes a step further than 14:33, where Jesus says that whoever does not "give up" (*apotassetai*) everything he has cannot be his disciple (see comments there). Here the ruler must not only surrender all rights to his possessions but must also actually dispose of them. This does not seem to be a universal requirement; it seems rather to be designed particularly for this man to shatter his covetousness. According to Jesus' teaching in 6:30–31, such an act would also benefit others; so his wealth should be dispensed among poor people. Even this is insufficient, however, unless the ruler truly follows Jesus. The command "Come, follow me" (*deuro, akolouthei moi*) means to become a disciple.

23–25 The ruler's sorrow (*perilypos*, only here in Luke; NIV, "very sad") over the decision about his wealth (v.12) recalls the far deeper sorrow rich people who have incurred Jesus' "woe" will experience (6:24). Only Luke mentions that Jesus looked at the man as he spoke to him about the problem of wealth (v.24). This keeps the focus on the ruler even during the transition to the next dialogue. It also limits the application of v.24 to the kind of attitude the ruler had. The vivid hyperbole about the camel (v.25) makes the point unforgettable (cf. Notes).

26–30 If wealth is such a hindrance in respect to salvation, the situation for the rich is hopeless, as the disciples realize (v.26). Jesus' reply about God's power (v.27) provides the assurance the audience needed and evokes an enthusiastic outburst from Peter (v.28), who feels that the disciples have done what the ruler did not do. Jesus acknowledges this with assuring his disciples who have "left all to follow [him]" of abundant recompense, not only in the future age, but also in the present (v.30). In v.29 Luke has "for the sake of the kingdom of God" instead of "for my [name's] sake" (Matt 19:29; Mark 10:29). This again identifies Jesus with the cause of God's kingdom and ties in with v.25. (In Matthew this is accomplished by an added saying [19:28].) Luke lacks the saying about the first and the last (Matt 19:30; Mark 10:31).

Notes

18–29 Luke is following both the Markan sequence of events and, during the first part of this pericope, the Markan wording fairly closely. (See the comments on Matt 19:16–30 for the significant divergences from Mark 10:17–31 in that account.)

24 It is possible, though doubtful, that the original Greek text of v.24 had the words περίλυπον γενομένον (*perilypon genomenon*, "being sorrowful," referring to the ruler). Some Western and other texts have it; UBS puts it in square brackets, showing its uncertainty. See Metzger, *Textual Commentary*, pp. 168–69. The nearly similar words in v.23, however, are original.

F. Final Approach to Jerusalem (18:31–19:44)

1. A further prediction of Jesus' passion

18:31–34

³¹Jesus took the Twelve aside and told them, "We are going up to Jerusalem, and everything that is written by the prophets about the Son of Man will be fulfilled. ³²He will be handed over to the Gentiles. They will mock him, insult him, spit on him, flog him and kill him. ³³On the third day he will rise again."
³⁴The disciples did not understand any of this. Its meaning was hidden from them, and they did not know what he was talking about.

This is generally referred to as the third passion prediction because it is basically similar to those in 9:22 and 9:44 (found in fuller form in Matt 17:22–23; Mark 9:31). Luke, however, has preserved other sayings that predict or foreshadow Jesus' death, including, up to this point, 5:35; 12:50; 13:32; and 17:25. Also, he does not follow this saying with the dialogue in Mark 10:35–45 with its further allusions to Jesus' passion. Since Luke normally stresses the role of Jerusalem, it is surprising that he omits the reference to it preserved in Matthew 20:17 and Mark 10:32. This may be because Jerusalem appears in v.31 or because Jesus had already emphasized Jerusalem as the place of his destiny (13:32–33), thereby accomplishing what Matthew and Mark do in this context.

31 Once again Luke, by stressing these words of Jesus, stresses the fulfillment of prophecy (cf. the first two chapters, esp. 2:25–38; 22:37). The parallels in Matthew 20:18 and Mark 10:33 omit any reference to prophecy here.

32–34 In this prediction, Jesus for the first time mentions the Gentiles as his executors (v.32). Luke attributes the ignorance of the disciples (a theme much emphasized by Mark) to what is apparently a supernatural withholding of understanding (v.34; cf. the experience of the two on the road to Emmaus, 24:16).

2. Healing a blind beggar

18:35–43

³⁵As Jesus approached Jericho, a blind man was sitting by the roadside begging. ³⁶When he heard the crowd going by, he asked what was happening. ³⁷They told him, "Jesus of Nazareth is passing by."
³⁸He called out, "Jesus, Son of David, have mercy on me!"
³⁹Those who led the way rebuked him and told him to be quiet, but he shouted all the more, "Son of David, have mercy on me!"
⁴⁰Jesus stopped and ordered the man to be brought to him. When he came near, Jesus asked him, ⁴¹"What do you want me to do for you?"
"Lord, I want to see," he replied.
⁴²Jesus said to him, "Receive your sight; your faith has healed you." ⁴³Immediately he received his sight and followed Jesus, praising God. When all the people saw it, they also praised God.

This incident shows that Jesus, who was on his way to the royal city of Jerusalem, was actually the "Son of David" (vv.38–39), i.e., the Messiah. It also allows Luke to point again to Jesus' concern for the needy and especially to show his healing of the blind as a messianic work (cf. 4:18). In addition, this miracle emphasizes the importance of faith (v.42) and (in Luke only) the glory that God receives through the ministry of Jesus (v.42).

35–36 Jesus' final approach to Jerusalem is under way. Luke is establishing a very important sequence: the healing of the blind man just outside Jericho (v.35), the call of Zacchaeus in Jericho (19:1–10), and then Jesus' triumphal entry to Jerusalem, his city of destiny (19:11, 28; N.B. the comment on 19:28). Luke apparently makes reference to the crowds here (v.36) to explain how the blind beggar knew that something special was happening (v.37).

38–43 The description of the man's insistent calling (vv.38–39) draws attention to his faith, which was based on the messiahship of Jesus, the "Son of David." So does Jesus' question in v.41, which allows the man to voice his request. Only Luke speaks of the praise both the man who had been blind and the people gave to God after the miracle (v.43). This is a unique Lukan feature (5:26; 17:18; Acts 2:47; 3:9).

Notes

18–43 It is well known that in Matt 20:29 and Mark 10:46, Jesus is leaving, not approaching, Jericho at this point. In Luke's concern to maintain the important thematic order described above (healing, call of Zacchaeus, approach to Jerusalem), might he have described the healing before the Jericho incident in order to prevent confusion within his own narrative? This would have been acceptable to his contemporaries, though it is troublesome to us.

If this were the case, the problem would be cleared up. Luke, contrary to his custom, does not draw attention to the crowds that followed Jesus out of Jericho but only mentions them in passing (v.36). There must be some reason for the unusual omission here, especially when the crowds are stressed in the parallel passages (Matt 20:29; Mark 10:46). If Luke were following a thematic order, rather than a geographical one, so that Jesus is just entering Jericho after the healing, there would be no opportunity for the crowds to follow him out of the city, as in Matthew and Mark. If this suggestion is inadequate, we can turn to one of the various harmonizing suggestions that have been made. The most plausible probably is that Jesus was between the remains of OT Jericho and the new city, with its large Herodian palace to the south of the old city. Thus he could be "leaving" OT Jericho (Matthew and Mark) and "approaching" the NT city (Luke) at the same time.

3. Zacchaeus the tax collector

19:1–10

¹Jesus entered Jericho and was passing through. ²A man was there by the name of Zacchaeus; he was a chief tax collector and was wealthy. ³He wanted to see who Jesus was, but being a short man he could not, because of the crowd. ⁴So he ran ahead and climbed a sycamore-fig tree to see him, since Jesus was coming that way.

⁵When Jesus reached the spot, he looked up and said to him, "Zacchaeus, come down immediately. I must stay at your house today." ⁶So he came down at once and welcomed him gladly.

7All the people saw this and began to mutter, "He has gone to be the guest of a 'sinner.' "

8But Zacchaeus stood up and said to the Lord, "Look, Lord! Here and now I give half of my possessions to the poor, and if I have cheated anybody out of anything, I will pay back four times the amount."

9Jesus said to him, "Today salvation has come to this house, because this man, too, is a son of Abraham. 10For the Son of Man came to seek and to save what was lost."

This narrative contains what may well be considered the "key verse" of Luke—viz., 19:10. The incident contains several primary Lukan features: the universal appeal of the gospel (vv.2–4); the ethical problem of wealth (v.2); the call of a "sinner" who was in social disfavor (v.7); the sense of God's present work (vv.5, 9); the feeling of urgency ("immediately," *speusas*, v.5), of necessity ("must," v.5), and of joy (v.6); restitution, with goods distributed to the poor (v.8); and, above all, salvation (vv.9–10).

1–4 Zacchaeus was a "chief tax collector" (*architelōnēs*, v.2), holding a higher office in the Roman tax system than Levi did (5:27–30). This system, under which an officer gained his income by extorting more money from the people than he had contracted to pay the Roman government, had evidently worked well for Zacchaeus. His location in the major customs center of Jericho was ideal. Being both a member of a generally despised group and wealthy, he is a notable subject for the saving grace of God. Observe the proximity of this story to that of the rich ruler, whose attitude toward wealth kept him from the Lord (18:27). Zacchaeus's desire to see Jesus, though commendable, was surpassed by the fact that Jesus wanted to see *him*.

5–6 Not only did he want to see Zacchaeus, Jesus had to stay with him—"I must stay at your house today" (v.5). This divine necessity is stressed in Luke (see comment on 4:43). Luke also has the word "today," with its special meaning (see comment on 4:21). The reciprocity of the divine, sovereign call and the human response is striking (v.6; cf. v.10).

7 In chapter 15 Luke gave us three parables Jesus told to answer the "Pharisees and teachers of the law" who opposed his eating with tax collectors and "sinners" (15:1–2). Now "all the people" complain that Jesus was consorting with a sinner. Similar criticism was made of Jesus' visit with Levi the tax collector (5:29–30). In each case table fellowship was involved—something that had a far deeper significance than our dinner parties. (See comments on 5:29–30; 15:1 for the significance of the word "sinner" from the Pharisees' point of view.)

8 Zacchaeus's announcement sounds abrupt and is probably intended to seem so. After all, for Luke (following Jesus) the use of possessions is a major indicator of one's spiritual condition (cf. 14:33; 18:22, and comments). There is no doubt that Zacchaeus had really "cheated" people. "Four times the amount" was far more than what the OT specified for restitution (Lev 5:16; Num 5:7). Whether or not Zacchaeus knew of these laws, his offer was unusually generous and was the sort of "fruit in keeping with repentance" earlier sought by John the Baptist (3:8).

9–10 Salvation did not "come to this house" because Zacchaeus finally did a good deed but because he was "a son of Abraham" (v.9), which may mean because he was a believer and thus a spiritual descendant of Abraham (Ellis, *Gospel of Luke*, p. 220). On the other hand, it may mean that "a Jew, even though he has become one of the 'lost sheep of the house of Israel', is still a part of Israel; the good Shepherd must seek for such" (Marshall, *Gospel of Luke*, p. 698).

Verse 10 could well be considered the "key verse" of Luke. As noted in the introductory comments to this section, the context is rich with Lukan themes, an appropriate setting for a significant verse. The verse itself expresses the heart of Jesus' ministry as presented by Luke, both his work of salvation and his quest for the lost. Luke has portrayed the "lost" throughout his gospel, from Jesus' own statements (e.g., the programmatic statement in 4:18–19) to the disdainful comments of the self-righteous (e.g., the Pharisee in 18:11 and here in v.7). Jesus has sought and found another of the "lost" in Jericho. He uses the occasion and the criticism of the people in v.7 as an opportunity to restate his mission.

This whole incident is the epitome of the messianic mission described in Luke 4.

4. Parable of the ten minas

19:11–27

> ¹¹While they were listening to this, he went on to tell them a parable, because he was near Jerusalem and the people thought that the kingdom of God was going to appear at once. ¹²He said: "A man of noble birth went to a distant country to have himself appointed king and then to return. ¹³So he called ten of his servants and gave them ten minas. 'Put this money to work,' he said, 'until I come back.'
>
> ¹⁴"But his subjects hated him and sent a delegation after him to say, 'We don't want this man to be our king.'
>
> ¹⁵"He was made king, however, and returned home. Then he sent for the servants to whom he had given the money, in order to find out what they had gained with it.
>
> ¹⁶"The first one came and said, 'Sir, your mina has earned ten more.'
>
> ¹⁷" 'Well done, my good servant!' his master replied. 'Because you have been trustworthy in a very small matter, take charge of ten cities.'
>
> ¹⁸"The second came and said, 'Sir, your mina has earned five more.'
>
> ¹⁹"His master answered, 'You take charge of five cities.'
>
> ²⁰"Then another servant came and said, 'Sir, here is your mina; I have kept it laid away in a piece of cloth. ²¹I was afraid of you, because you are a hard man. You take out what you did not put in and reap what you did not sow.'
>
> ²²"His master replied, 'I will judge you by your own words, you wicked servant! You knew, did you, that I am a hard man, taking out what I did not put in, and reaping what I did not sow? ²³Why then didn't you put my money on deposit, so that when I came back, I could have collected it with interest?'
>
> ²⁴"Then he said to those standing by, 'Take his mina away from him and give it to the one who has ten minas.'
>
> ²⁵" 'Sir,' they said, 'he already has ten!'
>
> ²⁶"He replied, 'I tell you that to everyone who has, more will be given, but as for the one who has nothing, even what he has will be taken away. ²⁷But those enemies of mine who did not want me to be king over them—bring them here and kill them in front of me.' "

This parable fulfills four important functions: (1) it clarifies the time of the appearance of the kingdom of God; (2) it realistically portrays the coming rejection and future return of the Lord; (3) it delineates the role of a disciple in the time between the Lord's departure and his return; and (4), while it is similar to the parable in

Matthew 25:14–30 (cf. Notes), it makes a unique contribution at this point in Luke's narrative.

11 The parable of the ten minas is connected with the pericope about Zacchaeus by the clause "While they were listening to this." The transition can be viewed in two complementary ways. First, Marshall, referring back to Jesus' words in v.9, notes that "although salvation has come *today* . . . the End, and the coming of the Son of Man to judgment, still lie in the future" (*Gospel of Luke*, p. 703, emphasis his). Second, "Son of Man" in v.10 of the Zacchaeus incident and "kingdom of God" at the beginning of this parable are conceptually related (cf. Doeve, *Jewish Hermeneutics*, pp. 128, 130, 142f). The one who has the right to reign is precisely the same Son of Man who came to seek lost sheep (v.10).

In addition to its connection with the Zacchaeus pericope, this parable is appropriate to Luke, which, in passage after passage, deals with Jesus' teaching about the future in general, the present and future aspects of the kingdom, and the consummation of God's purposes in history. (On Luke's eschatology, see Introduction: Themes and Theology). Obviously this parable teaches that Jesus predicted an interval of time between his ascension and return. For the time when the kingdom will be restored to Israel, see the beginning of Luke's second volume (Acts 1:6–7).

12–14 The historical background for the parable was the visit of Archelaus, son of Herod the Great, to Rome to secure permission to reign as a so-called client king, i.e., over a territory actually subject to Rome. This petition was opposed by a delegation of Archelaus's own subjects (Jos. Antiq. XVII, 213–49 [ix.3–7], 299–320 [xi.1–4]; War II, 14–22 [ii.1–3]). Similarly, Jesus has gone to the heavenly seat of authority till the time for his return. In the meantime, though his qualifications for kingship are impeccable, he has been rejected by those who should serve him as his subjects (v.14).

The money each servant received was worth about three months' wages (NIV mg.) or perhaps a little more (v.13). Their responsibility was to "put this money to work" in business, trading, or by investment.

15–19 Jesus singles out three of the ten servants as examples. The first two did well (vv.16, 18), one so well as to receive a special commendation for being "trustworthy" (v.17). The test was "small" (i.e., on a small scale), not because the amount itself was so small, but because of its relative insignificance in comparison to the cities awarded the trustworthy servants (vv.17, 19). We need not seek any particular symbolism in the cities other than the contrast between the extraordinary responsibility of ruling them and the responsibility of simply investing the sums of money (minas).

20–23 What some have called the "rule of end stress" leads the reader to concentrate on the last of the three examples. This servant allowed his fear (justified on the basis of experience) of the nobleman's anger (v.21) to prevent him from fulfilling his responsibility of putting the money given him to work (v.20). To be sure, its investment was risky. But he was specifically charged to take the risk of investing the money (vv.22–23). In his case conservatism was born of fear and was wrong (cf. Thielicke, *The Waiting Father*, pp. 143–45).

24–27 The principle of taking from one who has little and giving to one who has much (v.24) strikes us today as strange and unfair (v.25). In the original setting, as similarly in the kingdom parables (Matt 13:12), whether a person has little or much depends on his use of opportunities to increase what he already has.

The nobleman's anger (vv.26–27) is not intended to attribute such behavior to Jesus himself. Rather it does picture the kind of response one might have expected in Jesus' day, especially from the Herodians. It also reveals the seriousness of flouting the orders of the King whom God has appointed Judge (John 5:22; Acts 17:31; cf. 1 Peter 1:17).

Notes

11–27 In structure this parable is very similar to the parable of the talents in Matt 25:14–30. It has been argued, on the one hand, that both go back in tradition history to one story, and, on the other hand, that there were two stories told on two different occasions in Jesus' ministry. The structural similarities seem in regard to the meaning of the story more significant than the differences in detail. Yet while some of the differences—e.g., the number of servants mentioned, the amounts entrusted, and the conclusion (ten cities being mentioned only in Luke)—are relatively minor, the description of the main figure is not. The figure of a king who is rejected is distinctive to Luke and belongs to a deep stratum of his narrative and theology.

5. *The Triumphal Entry*

19:28–44

²⁸After Jesus had said this, he went on ahead, going up to Jerusalem. ²⁹As he approached Bethphage and Bethany at the hill called the Mount of Olives, he sent two of his disciples, saying to them, ³⁰"Go to the village ahead of you, and as you enter it, you will find a colt tied there, which no one has ever ridden. Untie it and bring it here. ³¹If anyone asks you, 'Why are you untying it?' tell him, 'The Lord needs it.'"

³²Those who were sent went and found it just as he had told them. ³³As they were untying the colt, its owners asked them, "Why are you untying the colt?"

³⁴They replied, "The Lord needs it."

³⁵They brought it to Jesus, threw their cloaks on the colt and put Jesus on it. ³⁶As he went along, people spread their cloaks on the road.

³⁷When he came near the place where the road goes down the Mount of Olives, the whole crowd of disciples began joyfully to praise God in loud voices for all the miracles they had seen:

³⁸"Blessed is the king who comes in the name of the Lord!"
"Peace in heaven and glory in the highest!"

³⁹Some of the Pharisees in the crowd said to Jesus, "Teacher, rebuke your disciples!"

⁴⁰"I tell you," he replied, "if they keep quiet, the stones will cry out."

⁴¹As he approached Jerusalem and saw the city, he wept over it ⁴²and said, "If you, even you, had only known on this day what would bring you peace—but now it is hidden from your eyes. ⁴³The days will come upon you when your enemies will build an embankment against you and encircle you and hem you in on every side. ⁴⁴They will dash you to the ground, you and the children within your walls.

They will not leave one stone on another, because you did not recognize the time of God's coming to you."

Luke does not mention Jesus' actual entry into Jerusalem—the Triumphal Entry. Instead, he shows us Jesus only as approaching Jerusalem (v.11), and after the crowd's welcome he is still "approaching" Jerusalem (v.41).

The story comes to its climax, not in Jesus' entering Jerusalem, but in his lamenting over the city (vv.41–44). Therefore, while Jesus deserves a triumphal entry as "king" (v.38), Luke emphasizes that he is moving instead to the place of his rejection. This continues the movement Jesus spoke of in 13:33. It does not contradict Matthew or Mark, for v.45 shows that Jesus did eventually enter the city. Luke simply omits the statement that he entered (cf. Matt 21:10; Mark 11:11) to make his theological point.

28–34 The transition "After Jesus said this" (v.28) links his approach to the city with the parable of the ten minas that denies an immediate appearance of the kingdom and portrays the rejection of its ruler. Luke's mention of Bethphage and Bethany (v.29) locates where Jesus went. Bethany was, of course, important as the home of Mary, Martha, and Lazarus. The Mount of Olives had a significant place in prophecy as the place of the coming Messiah's appearance (Zechariah 14:4). The incident of securing the colt (vv.30–31) "just as he told them" (v.32) reminds us, as did 2:15, 20, 29, of the dependability of the prophetic word. The "owners" are called *kyrioi* by Luke (v.33), which may (as Danker, *Jesus*, suggests) contrast with the one who is supreme Lord (*kyrios*) and rightful owner of all we possess (v.34).

35–38 As does Matthew, Luke shows us the humble king as he portrays Jesus riding on the colt (v.35). (For the custom of spreading cloaks along the path [v.36], see 2 Kings 9:13.) Only Luke mentions the descent from the Mount of Olives (cf. comment above), showing that Jesus was still outside Jerusalem (v.37). The reference to praising God for Jesus' miracles is unique to Luke (cf. comment on 18:43). Luke omits from v.38 the word "Hosanna," which might have been strange to his Gentile readers. He also omits the messianic quotation from Zechariah 9:9 given in Matthew 21:5 but instead stresses the messianic theme with the word "king" (v.38). The word "comes" is reminiscent of the designation "the coming one" for the Messiah. Luke has already quoted v.26 of the festival Psalm 118 in Jesus' previous lament over Jerusalem (13:35). In addition to using the specific word "king," Luke gives us the words about peace, reminiscent of the angels' proclamation at the Nativity (2:14), including the identical words "glory in the highest" (*doxa en hypsistois*). Once again he omits a "Hosanna."

39–40 Here (v.40) is another saying of Jesus found only in Luke. It is a fitting prelude to vv.41–45. Ellis (*Gospel of Luke*, p. 226) suggests that the words about the stones, similar to Habakkuk 2:11, may be a link to the idea of the capitulation of Jerusalem found in the Qumran Habakkuk commentary (1QpHab 9:6ff.).

41–44 Jesus is still outside Jerusalem (v.41) as he utters this lament, which only Luke records. Once more Luke focuses on Jesus' concern for the city and adds his prediction of its destruction, which is not given in 13:34. "This day" (v.42; cf. 4:21, "today," and comment) of peace has arrived; and the city ("even you," *kai su*), whose very name means "peace," has failed to recognize it. For the meaning of "hidden," see comment on 18:34. For a further description of Jerusalem's fate, see 21:20–24. God's "coming" (*episkopē*, v.44) has here the sense of a "visitation" that brings good or ill—in this case, either salvation or judgment.

VI. Concluding Events (19:45–24:53)

A. *Teaching in the Temple Area* (19:45–21:38)

1. *Jesus at the temple*

19:45–48

> ⁴⁵Then he entered the temple area and began driving out those who were selling. ⁴⁶"It is written," he said to them, " 'My house will be a house of prayer'; but you have made it a 'den of robbers.' "
> ⁴⁷Every day he was teaching at the temple. But the chief priests, the teachers of the law and the leaders among the people were trying to kill him. ⁴⁸Yet they could not find any way to do it, because all the people hung on his words.

45–48 Luke states—still without specifically saying that Jesus had entered Jerusalem (cf. comments on the previous section)—that Jesus is now in the temple area (v.45). Luke has omitted the episode of the fig tree (Matt 21:18–22; Mark 11:12–14, 20–26). At first thought this is surprising, since through the strange episode Jesus taught the efficacy of the prayer of faith, a matter of particular interest to Luke. However, Luke may have felt that the drastic overtones of the cursing of the fig tree with its relation to the fruitlessness of Israel (symbolized by the fig tree) would be inappropriate here, perhaps because of Jesus' strong words recorded in vv.41–44. The cleansing of the temple lacks the vivid detail in Matthew 21:12–13 and Mark 11:15–17. Luke mentions the importance of the temple as a house of prayer (v.46), though he omits the reference to the nations (cf. Mark 11:17). Verses 47–48 are not in Matthew and are different in form from Mark 11:18–19. Whereas Mark mentions Jesus' "teaching" (noun form of *didachē*) at the end of his brief paragraph (11:18), Luke uses the verbal form of the same word (in a vivid periphrastic construction: *ēn didaskōn*, "was teaching"), evidently to emphasize Jesus' teaching ministry (cf. comment on 20:1). This is appropriate because Luke has consistently portrayed Jesus as a teacher, especially since the beginning of the central section of the Gospel (9:51–19:44). He adds "the leaders among the people" (*hoi prōtoi tou laou*) to those Mark says are trying to kill Jesus, but by careful omission Luke indicates that the people (*laos*) themselves are not hostile to him. On the contrary, they "hung on his words" (v.48). This fits in with Luke's attempt to distinguish between the "people," who were responsive to Jesus, and their leaders and the "crowds" (*ochloi*), who were not. This, in turn, forms part of Luke's attempt to show that Christianity is properly seen as a continuation of true Judaism (cf. 1:68, 77; 2:10, 31–32, and comments).

2. *Jesus' authority questioned*

20:1–8

> ¹One day as he was teaching the people in the temple courts and preaching the gospel, the chief priests and the teachers of the law, together with the elders,

came up to him. ²"Tell us by what authority you are doing these things," they said. "Who gave you this authority?"

³He replied, "I will also ask you a question. Tell me, ⁴John's baptism—was it from heaven, or from men?"

⁵They discussed it among themselves and said, "If we say, 'From heaven' he will ask, 'Why didn't you believe him?' ⁶But if we say, 'From men,' all the people will stone us, because they are persuaded that John was a prophet."

⁷So they answered, "We don't know where it was from."

⁸Jesus said, "Neither will I tell you by what authority I am doing these things."

With this controversy Luke initiates a series of dialogues, most of which are common to all three Synoptics. They include the familiar form in which a question is answered by another question designed to catch the interrogator in his own inconsistency. The controversies are typical examples of the kind of challenges thrown at Jesus by the various sects and parties: "the chief priests and the teachers of the law" (v.1; cf. vv.19, 39), the Pharisees and Herodians (cf. Mark 12:13; Luke alone has "spies," v.20), and the Sadducees (v.27). Jesus also addresses the "rich" in 21:1. These dialogues sharpen the issues so that the reader sees the hostility and the theological errors of the leaders of the people.

Jesus' authority is of paramount importance, and his work as teacher and prophet (especially strong in Luke) requires validation. It is therefore appropriate that each synoptic Gospel begins the controversy section with this question: "By what authority are you doing these things?" (Matt 21:23; Mark 11:28; cf. Luke 20:2).

1–2 "One day" is indefinite in contrast to Mark 11:27, which, unlike Luke (cf. comment on his omission of the actual entry to Jerusalem in 19:28–38) speaks of Jesus' return to Jerusalem. As in 19:47, Luke emphasizes Jesus' role as a teacher. He also mentions the "people" (*laos*), who (in Luke) are always receptive to his teaching (cf. comment on 19:45–48). Luke further adds "preaching the gospel" (*euangelizomenou*), lacking in the other Synoptics. This is consistent with Luke's significant use of that verb (though not the noun *euangelion*).

3–8 The implication of Jesus' question is clear (vv.3–4). Jesus refused to give more light to those who refused to accept the light they had (v.8) and make a decision concerning it (vv.5–7). They refused to live according to what Minear (*Heal and Reveal*, pp. 3–30, 37–38) calls "Consciousness B"—an awareness of the heavenly dimension of life (v.7), choosing to stay on a worldly level, Minear's "Consciousness A." The word "heaven" is a surrogate for God in vv.3, 5.

3. Parable of the tenants

20:9–19

⁹He went on to tell the people this parable: "A man planted a vineyard, rented it to some farmers and went away for a long time. ¹⁰At harvest time he sent a servant to the tenants so they would give him some of the fruit of the vineyard. But the tenants beat him and sent him away empty-handed. ¹¹He sent another servant, but that one also they beat and treated shamefully and sent away empty-handed. ¹²He sent still a third, and they wounded him and threw him out.

¹³"Then the owner of the vineyard said, 'What shall I do? I will send my son, whom I love; perhaps they will respect him.'

¹⁴"But when the tenants saw him, they talked the matter over. 'This is the heir,'

they said. 'Let's kill him, and the inheritance will be ours.' ¹⁵So they threw him out of the vineyard and killed him.

"What then will the owner of the vineyard do to them? ¹⁶He will come and kill those tenants and give the vineyard to others."

When the people heard this, they said, "May this never be!"

¹⁷Jesus looked directly at them and asked, "Then what is the meaning of that which is written:

> " 'The stone the builders rejected
> has become the capstone'?

¹⁸Everyone who falls on that stone will be broken to pieces, but he on whom it falls will be crushed."

¹⁹The teachers of the law and the chief priests looked for a way to arrest him immediately, because they knew he had spoken this parable against them. But they were afraid of the people.

The refusal of the leaders to accept Jesus' authority (vv.1–8) leads to this parable that not only clearly affirms that authority but also alludes to Jesus' death and his subsequent vindication. The parable draws its imagery from the Song of the Vineyard (Isa 5:1–7), though Luke's account omits the quotation of Isaiah 5:2 found in Matthew 21:33 and Mark 12:1. The details of the story vary between the Synoptics. In Matthew and Mark, one of the servants is killed; in Luke only the son is killed. The story tends more toward allegory than Jesus' parables usually do. The vineyard may be compared to Israel on the basis of Isaiah 5. The owner represents God; the son, Jesus; the tenants, the religious leaders charged with cultivating the religious life of Israel (as they acknowledge in v.19); and the servants correspond to the prophets.

9–12 The circumstances were not such as to provoke a violent reaction (v.9). Nothing but a sample of the fruit was requested (v.10). In the early years of a vineyard's existence, the tenants would own little if anything (J.D.M. Derrett, *Law in the New Testament* [London: Longman & Todd, 1970], pp. 296ff.).

13 The expression "whom I love" (*agapēton*, "beloved") must be understood with respect to its meaning in ancient Near Eastern family relationships. In the LXX *agapētos* was at times virtually used as a synonym for *monogenēs*, "one and only" (cf. de Kruif, "Only Son" pp. 112ff.) The latter term did not necessarily refer to origin, as the KJV translation "only begotten" in John 3:16 implies, but rather to the unique status of the person as a beloved only child. See Luke 7:12, where the statement that the deceased son was her "only" (*monogenēs*) son shows the widow's desolate situation. The most relevant use in the LXX of *agapētos* is Genesis 22:2: "Take your beloved son, whom you love" (LXX *Labe ton huion sou ton agapēton, hon ēgapēsas*). This is reflected in the Transfiguration account in Matthew 17:15: "This is my Son, whom I love" (*ho huios mou ho agapētos*, cf. Mark 9:7). God spoke similar words at Jesus' baptism (Matt 3:17; Luke 3:22). Luke did not include *agapētos* in his account of the Transfiguration but does include it here in 20:13 (cf. Mark 12:6[Gr.], but cf. Matt 21:38). "What shall I do?" introduces a soliloquy similar to those in 16:3–4 and 18:4–5. Luke's amplification here (cf. Mark 12:6) adds to the pathos.

14–16 Jesus' audience was in a better position than we are to surmise what would have motivated these tenants to kill the son (v.14). But we are in a better position than they to understand the meaning of the story. Certainly the vivid description of the son's murder (v.15) and the father's vengeance (v.16; cf. 19:43–44) evoked from the people who heard the parable a strong "May this never be!" (*mē genoito;* cf. the Pauline use, Rom 3:4, 6, 31 et al.). They sensed the horror of the story and its drastic application, however imperfectly they understood its details.

17–19 The quotation (v.17) is from Psalm 118:22. (In 19:38 the same psalm was quoted.) Luke shows the point of this quotation by referring to the reaction of the people in v.16 (cf. Matt and Mark). Not only will God vindicate his Son, who is the "stone" (v.17, an important NT theme), but those who oppose him will meet destruction (v.18). The point is tacitly acknowledged in the reaction of the leaders (v.19). This carries forward the hostile scheming against Jesus referred to in 19:47.

4. Paying taxes to Caesar

20:20–26

> ²⁰Keeping a close watch on him, they sent spies, who pretended to be honest. They hoped to catch Jesus in something he said so that they might hand him over to the power and authority of the governor. ²¹So the spies questioned him: "Teacher, we know that you speak and teach what is right, and that you do not show partiality but teach the way of God in accordance with the truth. ²²Is it right for us to pay taxes to Caesar or not?"
>
> ²³He saw through their duplicity and said to them, ²⁴"Show me a denarius. Whose portrait and inscription are on it?"
>
> ²⁵"Caesar's," they replied.
>
> He said to them, "Then give to Caesar what is Caesar's, and to God what is God's."
>
> ²⁶They were unable to trap him in what he had said there in public. And astonished by his answer, they became silent.

Luke is blunt about the motives of the visitors, calling them "spies" (*egkathetoi,* people hired to lie in wait) and speaking of their insincerity ("pretended" is *hypokrinomenous,* related to *hypokritēs* "hypocrite"). They try to catch Jesus between two positions they considered mutually exclusive and irreconcilable.

20–22 Luke, writing for an audience to whom the distinctions between Jewish parties might be unfamiliar, does not mention the Pharisees and Herodians as Matthew and Mark do. His readers would, however, certainly know about the various forms of the heavy Roman taxation (v.22). These totaled over one-third of a person's income and included a poll tax, customs, and various indirect taxes.

23–26 The portrait on the coin (vv.24–25) represented submission to Rome. Jesus' statement may seem ordinary to us, as we have become so used to the saying. But it was an unexpected and telling response to the question. Jesus' questioners were sure his answer would alienate either the government officials or the pious people and zealots who opposed foreign domination. Actually Jesus appealed neither to those who preached revolution nor to the political compromisers. He stated a principle, not an accommodation or a compromise. This principle appears in the classic passage on Christian social ethics (Rom 13:1–7). To give what the government requires is not only not antithetical to religious duty but part of it. This even goes beyond the idea of dual citizenship. In spite of Jesus' balanced position, he was later accused at his trial of promoting an insurrection against Rome.

5. The Resurrection and marriage

20:27–40

> 27Some of the Sadducees, who say there is no resurrection, came to Jesus with a question. 28"Teacher," they said, "Moses wrote for us that if a man's brother dies and leaves a wife but no children, the man must marry the widow and have children for his brother. 29Now there were seven brothers. The first one married a woman and died childless. 30The second 31and then the third married her, and in the same way the seven died, leaving no children. 32Finally, the woman died too. 33Now then, at the resurrection whose wife will she be, since the seven were married to her?"
>
> 34Jesus replied, "The people of this age marry and are given in marriage. 35But those who are considered worthy of taking part in that age and in the resurrection from the dead will neither marry nor be given in marriage, 36and they can no longer die; for they are like the angels. They are God's children, since they are children of the resurrection. 37But in the account of the bush, even Moses showed that the dead rise, for he calls the Lord 'the God of Abraham, and the God of Isaac, and the God of Jacob.' 38He is not the God of the dead, but of the living, for to him all are alive."
>
> 39Some of the teachers of the law responded, "Well said, teacher!" 40And no one dared to ask him any more questions.

27 This controversy section continues with still another group challenging Jesus. The Sadducees, who tended to be more conservative than the Pharisees, did not accept what they considered theological accretions to their beliefs. The OT has little specific to say about the future state of the individual after death. Greek thought sharply divided between the soul and the body, the soul's temporary prison, and saw immortality as a quality of the soul. The Pharisees leaned toward a belief in resurrection that owed more to Greek ideas than to the OT. However, the Sadducees refused to even face the clear implications of OT teaching about the future state and were skeptical of the nature of personal future existence related to rewards or punishment.

28–33 This hypothetical case of a woman who had successively had seven husbands rests on the Jewish custom of "levirate marriage" (from the Lat. *levir*, "husband's brother," "brother-in-law"). It provided for the remarriage of a widow to the brother of a husband who died childless, the purpose of the remarriage being to provide descendants to carry on the deceased husband's name (Deut 25:5–6; cf. Gen 38:8). The Sadducees made this custom the basis for an argument ad absurdum that assumed that the idea of resurrection involves sexual reunion with one's earthly partner(s).

34–40 Jesus responded along these lines: It is not legitimate to project earthly conditions into the future state (vv.34–35). Eternal life is actually the life of the age to come (v.36). The believer already participates in that life (vv.37–38); but its full expression, involving the resurrection of the body, must wait till the new age has fully come. (Note the link in v.36 between "that age" and the "resurrection.") "Worthy" probably has somewhat the same meaning as in Matthew 10:11, 13, where it apparently refers to a person or home honoring God and blessed by him.

Though in the new age believers do not become angels (or gods), they do share certain characteristics of angels. This may refer to the absence of the sexual aspect of marriage without denying the continuation of mutual recognition and love. The Greek syntax, however, places the comment about angels nearer to "no longer die" than to "neither marry." This moves the emphasis from the issue of marriage to that of the nature of the Resurrection. God's children are also "children of " (i.e., are characterized by) the Resurrection. Note the repetition of the word "resurrection" and the absence of any reference to the Greek concept of "immortality." It is not persistence of life but that "the dead rise" (v.37) that Jesus is teaching. Invoking, so to speak, the authority of Moses, whom the Sadducees revered (rejecting later oral tradition), Jesus shows that Abraham, Isaac, and Jacob are also going to "rise." Therefore their existence does not lie only in the past but in the future; and God is called, in contemporary terms, their God.

Jesus' answer is approved by some of the teachers of the law (v.39), who are happy to see the Sadducees lose their argument. Jesus' wisdom has silenced all his questioners (v.40).

6. The sonship of Christ

20:41–47

> [41]Then Jesus said to them, "How is it that they say the Christ is the Son of David? [42]David himself declares in the Book of Psalms:
>
> > " 'The Lord said to my Lord:
> > "Sit at my right hand
> > [43]until I make your enemies
> > a footstool for your feet." '
>
> [44]David calls him 'Lord.' How then can he be his son?"
>
> [45]While all the people were listening, Jesus said to his disciples, [46]"Beware of the teachers of the law. They like to walk around in flowing robes and love to be greeted in the marketplaces and have the most important seats in the synagogues and the places of honor at banquets. [47]They devour widows' houses and for a show make lengthy prayers. Such men will be punished most severely."

The opponents silenced, the controversy section concludes with a rhetorical question Jesus puts to his questioners—one that is designed to clarify from Scripture who the Christ is. The interpretation of these three verses has been complicated by three factors: (1) the paradox inherent in Psalm 110; (2) Jesus' not answering his own question, thus leaving its significance to be implied; and (3) the reluctance of some to accept the christological understanding the interpretation of these verses demands.

41–43 The term "Christ" (v.41) is, of course, used here, not as a proper name, but as a title, "the Messiah." The Messiah was understood by the Jewish people to be a Son (descendant or "sprout," as in 4QFlor 11). If this is so, the question is Why does David, in Psalm 110:1, call his descendant his "Lord" (v.42)? In that passage "The Lord" is the translation of the LXX *ho kyrios*, which in turn represents the Hebrew

Yahweh, the sacred name of God. "To my Lord" represents the same word in the LXX but *'aḏōnay* in the Hebrew. This word conveyed a sense of dignity and was often used as a substitute for the name of God. Although the rabbis of the first Christian centuries did not interpret *'aḏōnay* as referring to the Messiah, that is the only meaning that makes sense here.

44 Jesus' question is not intended to suggest that there could not be a descendant of David who was also "Lord" but that the seemingly irreconcilable has meaning only if he is more than just a human descendant. Paul expressed the complete answer to the question in Romans 1:3–4, which says that Jesus was a descendant of David as to his human nature but declared Son of God by his resurrection.

45–47 Having responded with such authority to his opponents' controversial questions, Jesus now comments on those who sought to disprove his authority. His incisive portrayal of them here is shorter than in 11:37–52. Here he stresses their pride and ostentation, as well as accusing them of taking advantage of widows. Apparently they misused their responsibility as legal arbiters (cf. 12:13 and comment) and betrayed the financial trust innocent widows placed in them (cf. J.D.M. Derrett, " 'Eating up the Houses of Widows: Jesus' Comment on Lawyers?" Nov-Test 14 [1972]).

Notes

41–47 This section has occasioned much debate. Among the many alternatives to the interpretation offered above, the most common element is the idea that Jesus was not affirming but specifically denying the apparent teaching of Psalm 110:1 on the identity of character of the Messiah.

For a discussion of these issues, see Marshall, *Gospel of Luke,* pp. 744–47; for an extended critical treatment of the place of Psalm 110 in early Christian interpretation, see D.M. Hay, *Glory at the Right Hand: Psalm 110 in Early Christianity* (Nashville: Abingdon, 1973).

7. The widow's offering

21:1–4

> [1]As he looked up, Jesus saw the rich putting their gifts into the temple treasury. [2]He also saw a poor widow put in two very small copper coins. [3]"I tell you the truth," he said, "this poor widow has put in more than all the others. [4]All these people gave their gifts out of their wealth; but she out of her poverty put in all she had to live on."

The connection between this passage and the preceding one is that both refer to widows: one, how teachers of the law victimized them (20:47); the other, how a poor widow set an example of acceptable giving.

1–4 The "temple treasury" (*to gazophylakion,* v.1) was either a room in the temple or a "contribution box" (BAG, s.v.). Marshall (*Gospel of Luke,* p. 751) argues for the former (following SBK, 2:37–45) and suggests that Jesus would have heard an announcement as to how much was being donated. The widow's "two very small copper coins" (lepta, v.2, the familiar "mites") were each worth only a small fraction of a day's wage. Proportionate to her total financial worth, however, the woman's gift was far more valuable than the gifts of the wealthy (vv.3–4).

8. *Signs of the end of the age*

21:5–38

⁵Some of his disciples were remarking about how the temple was adorned with beautiful stones and with gifts dedicated to God. But Jesus said, ⁶"As for what you see here, the time will come when not one stone will be left on another; every one of them will be thrown down."

⁷"Teacher," they asked, "when will these things happen? And what will be the sign that they are about to take place?"

⁸He replied: "Watch out that you are not deceived. For many will come in my name, claiming, 'I am he,' and, 'The time is near.' Do not follow them. ⁹When you hear of wars and revolutions, do not be frightened. These things must happen first, but the end will not come right away."

¹⁰Then he said to them: "Nation will rise against nation, and kingdom against kingdom. ¹¹There will be great earthquakes, famines and pestilences in various places, and fearful events and great signs from heaven.

¹²"But before all this, they will lay hands on you and persecute you. They will deliver you to synagogues and prisons, and you will be brought before kings and governors, and all on account of my name. ¹³This will result in your being witnesses to them. ¹⁴But make up your mind not to worry beforehand how you will defend yourselves. ¹⁵For I will give you words and wisdom that none of your adversaries will be able to resist or contradict. ¹⁶You will be betrayed even by parents, brothers, relatives and friends, and they will put some of you to death. ¹⁷All men will hate you because of me. ¹⁸But not a hair of your head will perish. ¹⁹By standing firm you will gain life.

²⁰"When you see Jerusalem being surrounded by armies, you will know that its desolation is near. ²¹Then let those who are in Judea flee to the mountains, let those in the city get out, and let those in the country not enter the city. ²²For this is the time of punishment in fulfillment of all that has been written. ²³How dreadful it will be in those days for pregnant women and nursing mothers! There will be great distress in the land and wrath against this people. ²⁴They will fall by the sword and will be taken as prisoners to all the nations. Jerusalem will be trampled on by the Gentiles until the times of the Gentiles are fulfilled.

²⁵"There will be signs in the sun, moon and stars. On the earth, nations will be in anguish and perplexity at the roaring and tossing of the sea. ²⁶Men will faint from terror, apprehensive of what is coming on the world, for the heavenly bodies will be shaken. ²⁷At that time they will see the Son of Man coming in a cloud with power and great glory. ²⁸When these things begin to take place, stand up and lift up your heads, because your redemption is drawing near."

²⁹He told them this parable: "Look at the fig tree and all the trees. ³⁰When they sprout leaves, you can see for yourselves and know that summer is near. ³¹Even so, when you see these things happening, you know that the kingdom of God is near.

³²"I tell you the truth, this generation will certainly not pass away until all these things have happened. ³³Heaven and earth will pass away, but my words will never pass away.

³⁴"Be careful, or your hearts will be weighed down with dissipation, drunkenness and the anxieties of life, and that day will close on you unexpectedly like a trap. ³⁵For it will come upon all those who live on the face of the whole earth. ³⁶Be always on the watch, and pray that you may be able to escape all that is about to happen, and that you may be able to stand before the Son of Man."

³⁷Each day Jesus was teaching at the temple, and each evening he went out to spend the night on the hill called the Mount of Olives, ³⁸and all the people came early in the morning to hear him at the temple.

Jesus concludes his teaching ministry (apart from the Upper Room Discourse in John 14–16) with this discourse on the end times. It is immediately followed in Luke by the conspiracy by Judas. The corresponding passages in Matthew 24 and Mark 13 are called the Olivet Discourse because, unlike Luke, they tell us that Jesus was on the Mount of Olives when he spoke.

Jesus' teachings in this discourse provide both a realistic warning about future events and a strong encouragement to persevere. They entail some notable difficulties of interpretation and literary analysis. But if the expositor concentrates on the series of exhortations in the discourse, then the supporting teachings along with the problems of interpretation will come into focus. These exhortations are ninefold.

1. Do not follow false leaders (v.8).

2. Do not be frightened by the awesome events associated with the end times in apocalyptic literature (vv.9–11).

3. Do not worry about your legal defense when you are persecuted and face legal charges because of your Christian witness (vv.12–16).

4. When all turn against you, persevere and take a firm stand (vv.17–19).

5. Flee Jerusalem when it is besieged (vv.20–24).

6. When the final apocalyptic events (the portents in heaven and on earth) do take place, take heart at your coming redemption when the Son of Man returns (vv.25–28).

7. Recognize also that these things point to the approach of the kingdom of God (vv.29–31).

8. Be assured that throughout the apocalyptic period the Lord's words endure (vv.32–33).

9. Be watchful and pray so that you will come through all these things in a way the Son of Man will approve of (vv.34–36).

Of these exhortations, only numbers 5–7 are affected by serious interpretive problems. These include the relationship of the destruction of Jerusalem to other future events and the literary problem of the tradition history of this pericope, specifically its relationship to Matthew 24 and Mark 13. (For comment on the latter, see Notes as well as commentary in loc.)

The exhortations can be grouped under five major topics in the discourse: (1) warnings against deception (vv.5–11); (2) encouragement during persecution (vv.12–19); (3) the destruction of Jerusalem (vv.20–24); (4) future events (vv.25–28); and (5) assurances concerning these events (vv.29–36).

5–11 The opening of the discourse resembles, with several exceptions, that in Matthew 24 and Mark 13. Luke does not mention that Jesus himself was at the temple (though the mention of architectural details and the "gifts" shows that Jesus and his disciples were on the premises, v.5). As observed above, Luke does not mention the Mount of Olives. The Matthean part of the question—"and of the end of the age" (Matt 24:3)—is missing. For the temple to be totally destroyed was unthinkable (v.6). Its sanctuary and surrounding structure were huge, solid, and glistening, a symbol of Jewish religion and Herodian splendor. The disciples do not ask for a "sign" (v.7) because they are doubting but because they need a clue as to when the end will come.

The word "deceived" (*planēthēte*, v.8) was frequently used in the early Christian centuries to describe the activities of heretics and false prophets (e.g., 2 John 7; cf. Rev 2:20). Even as late as the time of Origen (died c. 254), pretenders were making such claims as v.8 describes (Origen, *Contra Celsum* 7.9). Certain frightening events (vv.9–11) are typically linked in apocalyptic literature with the end times (e.g., Isa 13:10, 13; 34:4; Ezek 14:21; 32:7–8; Amos 8:9; Hag 2:6; 4 Ezra 13:30 ff.; 1QH 3:29–39). Jesus is teaching that, while such things are indeed to take place as history moves toward its climax, Christians should not be terrified by them (Luke alone has *mē ptoēthēte*, "do not be frightened," v.9). The reason is that wars, revolutions, natural calamities are not a signal that the end of history is to come immediately (*eutheōs*), as is commonly supposed even today. The sample summary of apocalyptic events in v.11 includes the familiar "famines and pestilences" (*limoi kai loimoi*, a literary device called paronomasia, words with similar sound).

12–19 In its content this section resembles Mark 13:9–13 and also the account of the sending out of the Twelve (Matt 10:17–22). Yet the actual similarities are minimal—only thirteen words or syllables (Gr.) in vv.12–16 and all of v.17. It is not certain whether Luke edited Mark or drew on a different source, or whether Jesus repeated this teaching on different occasions. Among the differences between vv.12–19 and the passages in Matthew and Mark are (1) Luke's omission of the preaching of the gospel to the Gentiles (Matt 10:18) and around the world (Mark 13:10, possibly because he has in mind only the period just before the destruction of the temple in A.D. 70 (see Marshall, *Gospel of Luke*, p. 768); (2) a promise of wisdom in time of persecution (v.15) in place of a reference to the Holy Spirit (cf. Matt 10:20; Mark 13:11), an unusual omission for Luke with his strong interest in the Holy Spirit; (3) the addition of the saying "not a hair of your head" (v.18), the idea of which had already appeared in 12:7; and (4) a change in the wording of v.19. Whereas Matthew 10:22 (cf. 24:13) and Mark 13:13 have "He who stands firm to the end will be saved" (which encourages those who are standing firm, because God will bring rescue, cf. Luke 18:7–8), the Lukan expression is stronger: literally, "you will gain your lives" (*ktēsasthe tas psychas hymōn*). Luke uses a different Greek word—*sōthēsetai;* ("shall be saved"). The meaning is close to that of Matthew 16:25; Mark 8:35; Luke 9:24; Matthew 10:39; Luke 17:33, which state, with some verbal differences, that whoever loses his life for the sake of Christ will preserve it, the implication being spiritual survival. If perseverance is indeed a major concern of Luke (cf. S. Brown, *Apostasy and Perseverance*, in loc.), then the particular wording of 21:19 in comparison to its parallels is significant.

20–24 The reference to Jerusalem (v.20) need not be construed as a *vaticinium ex eventu* (a prophecy after the event). It is often pointed out that, were this so, Luke could have included more precise details. Furthermore, the vocabulary was already at hand and well known (cf. 2 Chron 15:6; Isa 3:25–26; 8:21–22; 13:13; 29:3; Jer 20:4–5; 34:17; 52:4; Ezek 4:1–4; Dan 9:26–27; Hos 9:7; 14:1; Zeph 1:14–15).

The description of the siege of Jerusalem, a protracted event, contrasts with the sudden events in Luke's earlier apocalyptic passage (17:22–37). There the one on the roof will not even have time to reenter his house. But here those out in the country are warned not to try to get back into the city during the siege (v.21). *Kykloumenēn* ("surrounded," v.20) refers to the siege itself, not its completion; so reentry was still possible (Morris, *Luke*, p. 298). The vivid description is painful to read. It is certainly possible to assume that Jesus' predictions incorporated two phases: (1) the events of A.D. 70 involving the temple and (2) those in the distant future, described in more apocalyptic terms. The latter takes us back to 17:20–37, where Jesus' words about the end time naturally fit in with the Pharisees' question (17:20). Thus what Luke has there can now be omitted from chapter 21. In its place, using much of the same vocabulary, Luke now substitutes a prophetic oracle on Jerusalem. Among the words common to Mark 13 and Luke 21 are different forms of *erēmōsis* ("desolation")—a fact that suggests that Luke edited this section from Mark. Yet the word "desolation" is a natural one for this passage even if it were not in the source.

Luke's preservation of the saying in v.24, where *plērōthōsin*, another word for fulfillment, occurs, shows his interest in the Gentiles. Verse 24 implies that an extended period of time is needed for this fulfillment—an idea consistent with Luke's twofold emphasis on a period of waiting along with an expectation of Christ's imminent return. It also implies an end to the period when Gentiles are prominent in God's plan (cf. Rom 11:11–27, esp. v.25, "until the full number of the Gentiles has come in").

25–28 The words in Matthew 24 and Mark 13 about false Christs are omitted; Luke has placed them in 17:23. Now he again takes up material from the Olivet Discourse in v.25, where Jesus speaks of apocalyptic signs of the end time. The "roaring . . . of the sea" is reminiscent of Isaiah 17:12; in biblical prophecy the sea often symbolizes chaos or stands for a source of fear. Daniel 7:13 is the main OT source for v.27 and the NT concept of the glorified "Son of Man." "Power," "coming," and "glory" are terms appropriate to Christ as Son of Man and King (cf. Matt 16:27–28; Mark 9:1; Luke 9:26–27; 2 Peter 1:16–17). Luke omits the saying about the gathering of the elect (cf. Matt 24:31; Mark 13:27), which might have followed v.27. Instead he has Jesus' words of encouragement in expectation of redemption (v.28).

29–38 The illustration of the fig tree, found in the parallel passages in Matthew and Mark, is clear. Luke, perhaps to avoid any thought of exclusiveness based on the fig tree's symbolizing Israel, adds the words "and all the trees" (v.29). "Generation" (*genea*, v. 32) could refer here to a span of time or to a class or race of people. In the former sense it could mean the decades following Jesus' lifetime. (Ellis, *Gospel of Luke*, p. 246, notes that in 1QpHab 2:7; 7:2, it includes several lifetimes.) If this whole passage thus referred to the destruction of Jerusalem, the heavenly portents would have to be understood figuratively (so J. Marcellus Kik, *Matthew Twenty-Four* [Swengal, Penn.: Bible Truth Depot, 1948]). If *genea*, still in the sense of a span of time, referred to the period of time following the initial events of the end time, it could indicate that once the sequence began, it would be brought through to conclusion without delay. This does not necessarily demand a predictable time framework beginning with some identifiable event such as would permit setting dates for the Lord's return. The references cited above in the Habakkuk commentary preclude this. The span of time would be too great to calculate precisely.

The other major alternative, "generation" as a class or race of people, would make most sense if understood as meaning the Jewish people. The point then would be that the Jewish people would be preserved throughout the ages till the consummation of history by Christ's return. The usage of *genea* in the Gospels is inconclusive. It frequently refers to Jesus' contemporaries, classing them as evil and unbelieving (e.g., 9:41); but that is hardly the meaning in this discourse. *Genea* here probably means the people living in the end time, who "will be sure that the last events have begun and will be brought to a consummation" (Marshall, *Gospel of Luke*, p. 780). The next most reasonable interpretation would be that it means the Jewish race, but that is hardly the emphasis here. (For a different approach, see comments on Matt 24:34, this volume.)

The conclusion of the discourse again emphasizes faithfulness, with warnings not only against carousing but against the "anxieties of life" (v.34; cf. 8:14; 12:22–26). Only Luke discloses that Jesus taught in the temple by day but spent each night outside Jerusalem on the Mount of Olives (v.37). It is difficult to know whether Luke mentions this to show the danger awaiting Jesus in the city or to show that Jesus dissociated himself from it (see comments at introduction to 19:28–44), or whether it is simply a matter-of-fact statement. He is careful to tell us, just as he did in his earlier narratives of Jesus' ministry (4:14–15, 22, 32, 37, 42; 5:19, 26, 29), how popular Jesus was. Here it is the "people" (*laos*), the responsive group as distinguished from the mere "crowds" (*ochloi*) and from the leaders, who come to hear his teaching "early in the morning" (v.38).

Notes

The problem of the tradition history of this pericope and the issues surrounding Luke's possible editing of Mark 13 is a complex one. A concise summary with careful judgments will be found in Marshall (*Gospel of Luke*, at several points within pp. 752–84, esp. pp. 754–58). An overlooked treatment of the relationship between Luke 17 and Luke 21 is in J. Oliver Buswell, Jr., *A Systematic Theology of the Christian Religion*, 2 vols. (Grand Rapids: Zondervan, 1962–63), 2:368–71. Written before the widespread use of redaction criticism, it contains some original and useful suggestions. Among the major contributions to the problem are V. Taylor, *Behind the Third Gospel* (Oxford: Clarendon, 1926), pp. 101–25, on the possibility of a source other than Mark, and T. Schramm, *Der Markus-Stoff* (cf. n. 17), pp. 171–82, on the same issue. A useful survey is found in D. Wenham, "Recent Study of Mark 13," *Theological Students Fellowship Bulletin* 71 (1975): 6–15; 72 (1975): 1–9. See also Colin Brown, "The Parousia and Eschatology in the NT," DNTT, 2:901–31. An extensive bibliography follows on pp. 931–35.

B. *The Passion of Our Lord* (22:1–23:56)

1. *The agreement to betray Jesus*

22:1–6

¹Now the Feast of Unleavened Bread, called the Passover, was approaching, ²and the chief priests and the teachers of the law were looking for some way to get rid of Jesus, for they were afraid of the people. ³Then Satan entered Judas, called Iscariot, one of the Twelve. ⁴And Judas went to the chief priests and the officers of the temple guard and discussed with them how he might betray Jesus. ⁵They were delighted and agreed to give him money. ⁶He consented, and watched for an opportunity to hand Jesus over to them when no crowd was present.

Luke's passion narrative begins ominously with a description of Judas's plot. Only Luke says that "Satan entered Judas" (v.3). Although Conzelmann's theory that the period between Jesus' temptation and this event is free from satanic activity is wrong (cf. Notes), there is certainly a focus on these two times of heightened satanic opposition. Ellis (*Gospel of Luke*, p. 248) observes, "In the temptation Satan entices; in the passion he threatens."

1–2 The "Feast of Unleavened Bread" (v.1) lasted seven days (Exod 12:15–20). The Jewish dates for Passover were Nisan 14–15 (early spring). The Feast of Unleavened Bread followed it immediately and also came to be included under the Passover.

Earlier the Pharisees were prominent in opposing Jesus (cf. comment on 5:17). Now the "chief priests and teachers of the law" were taking the initiative against him (v.2). In that society the priests were not only religious leaders, but they also wielded great political power. The scribes (teachers of the law) were involved doubtless because their legal expertise would be useful in building a case against Jesus. Matthew, Mark, and Luke all take pains to show that "the people" (*ton laon*) were a deterrent to the schemes of the leaders.

3–6 Among the Synoptics only Luke exposes Judas's plot as the work of Satan (v.3; but cf. John 13:2, 27). Moreover Luke alone mentions the presence of the "officers of the temple guard" (v.4). It was probably their soldiers who captured Jesus (John 18:3). Municipalities had their own officers and so did the Jerusalem religious establishment. Luke alone mentions that, in betraying Jesus, Judas sought to avoid the crowds (vv.4–6).

Notes

1–6 The theory by Conzelmann (*Theology of Luke*, in loc.), alluded to above, about a period in Jesus' ministry that was free from satanic activity, is ably refuted by S. Brown, *Apostasy and Perseverance*, pp. 6–12.

4 Στρατηγοῖς (*stratēgois*, "officers of the temple guard") is literally "soldiers." On soldiers in the ancient world and in Luke's writings, see TDNT, 7:704, 709–10.

6 Ἐξωμολόγησεν (*exōmologēsen*, "consented," "promised") is, contrary to customary usage, in the active, thereby apparently giving emphasis to Judas's eagerness (Marshall, *Gospel of Luke*, p. 789).

2. *The Last Supper*

22:7–38

7Then came the day of Unleavened Bread on which the Passover lamb had to be sacrificed. 8Jesus sent Peter and John, saying, "Go and make preparations for us to eat the Passover."

9"Where do you want us to prepare for it?" they asked.

10He replied, "As you enter the city, a man carrying a jar of water will meet you. Follow him to the house that he enters, 11and say to the owner of the house, 'The Teacher asks: Where is the guest room, where I may eat the Passover with my disciples?' 12He will show you a large upper room, all furnished. Make preparations there."

¹³They left and found things just as Jesus had told them. So they prepared the Passover.

¹⁴When the hour came, Jesus and his apostles reclined at the table. ¹⁵And he said to them, "I have eagerly desired to eat this Passover with you before I suffer. ¹⁶For I tell you, I will not eat it again until it finds fulfillment in the kingdom of God."

¹⁷After taking the cup, he gave thanks and said, "Take this and divide it among you. ¹⁸For I tell you I will not drink again of the fruit of the vine until the kingdom of God comes."

¹⁹And he took bread, gave thanks and broke it, and gave it to them, saying, "This is my body given for you; do this in remembrance of me."

²⁰In the same way, after the supper he took the cup, saying, "This cup is the new covenant in my blood, which is poured out for you. ²¹But the hand of him who is going to betray me is with mine on the table. ²²The Son of Man will go as it has been decreed, but woe to that man who betrays him." ²³They began to question among themselves which of them it might be who would do this.

²⁴Also a dispute arose among them as to which of them was considered to be greatest. ²⁵Jesus said to them, "The kings of the Gentiles lord it over them; and those who exercise authority over them call themselves Benefactors. ²⁶But you are not to be like that. Instead, the greatest among you should be like the youngest, and the one who rules like the one who serves. ²⁷For who is greater, the one who is at the table or the one who serves? Is it not the one who is at the table? But I am among you as one who serves. ²⁸You are those who have stood by me in my trials. ²⁹And I confer on you a kingdom, just as my Father conferred one on me, ³⁰so that you may eat and drink at my table in my kingdom and sit on thrones, judging the twelve tribes of Israel.

³¹"Simon, Simon, Satan has asked to sift you as wheat. ³²But I have prayed for you, Simon, that your faith may not fail. And when you have turned back, strengthen your brothers."

³³But he replied, "Lord, I am ready to go with you to prison and to death."

³⁴Jesus answered, "I tell you, Peter, before the rooster crows today, you will deny three times that you know me."

³⁵Then Jesus asked them, "When I sent you without purse, bag or sandals, did you lack anything?"

"Nothing," they answered.

³⁶He said to them, "But now if you have a purse, take it, and also a bag; and if you don't have a sword, sell your cloak and buy one. ³⁷It is written: 'And he was numbered with the transgressors'; and I tell you that this must be fulfilled in me. Yes, what is written about me is reaching its fulfillment."

³⁸The disciples said, "See, Lord, here are two swords."

"That is enough," he replied.

7–13 Luke now sharpens his chronology (in v.1 he only mentioned that the Passover was "approaching"). NIV adds the word "lamb" (v.7) as an implication of the text. A kid could also be used. Luke clearly states that it was the day of sacrifice—normally Nisan 14. The actual Passover meal was celebrated after sundown, when, according to Jewish reckoning, the next day, Nisan 15, had begun.

Luke shows that Jesus initiated plans for the Passover arrangements (v.8; Matt 26:17 and Mark 14:12 mention only the disciples' question, v.9). Jesus' instructions guaranteed privacy, indeed, secrecy, perhaps to avoid his premature arrest. Verses 10–12 show his supernatural knowledge. The right person Jesus asked his disciples to follow would be a man carrying a water jar (v.10). Ordinarily only women carried jars; men used leather skins for water.

The "large upper room" (v.12) was on the second story under a flat roof, accessible by an outside stairway. It was "furnished" with the couches for reclining at a Passover meal and with necessary utensils. Things were "just as Jesus told them" (v.13), showing that he was far more than a "teacher" (v.11), though that term was customary.

14–18 Sometimes, as has often been observed, Luke does not use the terminology of vicarious atonement when we might expect him to. Thus in vv.24–27, the passage describing the rivalry between the disciples and the contrasting servant role Jesus adopted, Luke does not include the "ransom saying" in Mark 10:45. Nevertheless, the strong link Luke forges with the Passover underscores the redemptive motif. In the Transfiguration narrative (9:31), he has already used the Greek word *exodos* (NIV, "departure"), with its redemptive connotations, to describe Jesus' approaching death. This passage also exhibits the strong orientation to the future that characterizes Luke's Gospel.

Both of Jesus' opening statements are strongly worded. "I have eagerly desired" (v.15) represents a strong double construction with a Semitic cast—*epithymia epethymēsa* (lit., "with desire I have desired"). The second statement begins with an emphatic future negative: "I will not eat" (*ou me phagō*, v.16). A similar construction occurs in v.18. Together the sentences convey the depth of Jesus' feelings at this time and the immense significance of what is taking place. Grammatically the statements may imply that, though he had greatly desired to do so, Jesus would not partake of the Passover (so J. Jeremias, *The Eucharistic Words of Jesus*, 2d ed. [London: SCM, 1966], pp. 207–18). Luke's placement of the saying may also imply this, as he puts it before the actual meal, in contrast to Mark and Matthew, who place it after the meal (Matt 26:29; Mark 14:25). It is still likely, however, that Jesus actually did partake when, as the host at the meal, he "took" the cup and the bread (vv.17, 19, 20). The word "again" (*apo tou nyn*, lit., "from now on") in v.16 accords with this likelihood. But insofar as it represents the word *ouketi*, it might be better omitted, for the text is uncertain and probably not original here (cf. Notes). In any case, what Jesus would not eat till the coming of the kingdom is described simply as "it" (*auto*, v.16) and probably means the lamb rather than the meal as a whole (Marshall, *Gospel of Luke*, p. 796).

Unlike the other accounts of the Last Supper, Luke mentions a cup before (v.17), as well as after (v.20), the bread. That vv.19–20 are missing from some Western texts complicates this difference. If the words were not in Luke's original account, there would be a difficult problem—the mention of a cup before but not after the bread (v.17). In spite of some arguments to the contrary, it seems reasonable to hold the authenticity of vv.19b–20. Luke has apparently combined his data from various sources to describe both the Passover setting of the supper (vv.7–18) and the institution of the Lord's Supper (vv.19–20) instead of following Mark (cf. Notes). If so, the seeming disjunction and the problem of the two cups are understandable. The cup of v.17 may be the first of the traditional four cups taken during the Passover meal. In this case, Jesus' comments come at the beginning of that meal. This cup was followed by part of the Passover meal and the singing of Psalms 113 and 114. Alternately, the cup of v.17 may be the third cup, mentioned both here in connection with the Passover setting and again in connection with its place in the Eucharist, on which Luke focuses (v.20).

The uncertainties of the passage should not detract from the high significance of the saying itself. The meal is a turning point. Jesus anticipated it; and he likewise anticipates the next genuine meal of its kind that he will eat sometime in the future, when the longed-for kingdom finally comes, or, in Luke's characteristic vocabulary, "finds fulfillment" (*plērōthē*, v.16; the saying in v.18 has a near parallel in Matt 26:29; Mark 14:25). The believer in the present age observes the Lord's Supper "until he comes" (1 Cor 11:26).

19–20 As stated above, the words of institution in these verses may come from a non-Markan source. Similar wording in 1 Corinthians 11:24–25, written before A.D. 60, shows that it was probably an early source, used by both Luke and Paul. This supports the reliability of Luke's research (1:1–4). The suffering motif is consistent with Jesus' understanding of his mission as the Suffering Servant.

The "bread" (*arton*, v.19) was the thin, unleavened bread used in the Passover. "Gave thanks" translates the verb *eucharisteō*, the source of the beautiful word Eucharist, often used to signify the Lord's Supper. Luke alone has "given for you" (*hyper hymōn didomenon*) in the saying over the bread, as well as "poured out for you" (*to hyper hymōn ekchynnomenon*) in the cup saying (v.20).

"In remembrance of me" (v.19) directs our attention primarily to the person of Christ and not merely to the benefits we receive (of whatever nature we may understand them to be) from taking the bread and cup. The final cup, following the sequence of several refillings during the Passover, signifies the "new covenant" (v.20) in Jesus' blood. The disciples would have been reminded of the "blood of the covenant" (Exod 24:8), i.e., the blood used ceremonially to confirm the covenant. The new covenant (cf. Jer 31:31–34) carried with it assurance of forgiveness through Jesus' blood shed on the cross and the inner work of the Holy Spirit in motivating us and enabling us to fulfill our covenantal responsibility.

21–23 Because this saying follows the Last Supper, one might assume that Judas was present at the institution of the Lord's Supper. Matthew 26:21–25 and Mark 14:18–21, along with John 13:21–27, indicate that Judas was there at least for the Passover, for he had dipped the bread in the dish. John 13:30 says that Judas went out immediately after that; so apparently he was not there for the supper itself. But since John does not actually relate the events of the supper, this is only an implication. By mentioning the "hand" of Judas (v.21), Luke draws attention to his participation in the Passover (or supper), thus heightening the tragedy. In each of the Synoptics, this saying about the Son of Man (v.22) includes reference to the "man" who will betray him. The Greek word *anthrōpos* thus appears twice, making a sober play on the word "man."

The use of "decreed" (*hōrismenon*, v.22) emphasizes divine sovereignty, a theme dominant in Luke, though this particular word occurs rarely in the NT (cf. Acts 2:23; 10:42; 17:31; cf. also Rom 1:4). Instead of "decreed," Matthew (26:24) and Mark (14:21) have "it is written" (*gegraptai*). Divine sovereignty is balanced by human responsibility; so Jesus pronounces a "woe" on the betrayer. The same balance occurs in Acts 2:23. Luke alone among the Gospels has v.23, which shows not only the disciples' concern but also the secrecy that still surrounded Judas's treachery.

24–27 Their questions about this treachery leads immediately, in Luke's order of events, to the disciples' argument—shocking on this solemn occasion—about precedence. See also the similar grasping after status that follows the passion prediction in Matthew 20:17–28 and Mark 10:32–45. The differences between the Gospels warrant our treating Luke's account of this argument as distinct from its near parallels. The word "considered" (*dokei*, "seems," "is regarded") in v.24 is well chosen since status has to do with self-perception and with how one desires to be perceived by others. Jesus replies by reminding the disciples of two objectionable character-istics of secular rulers. First, they "lord it over" (*kyrieuousin*) others (v.25). First Peter 5:3 warns elders in the church against this attitude. Second, they are given the title "Benefactor" (*euergetēs*, v.25), which was actually a title, not merely a description (cf. TDNT, 2:654–55). The form of the verb "call" (*kalountai*) may be middle or passive. If the former, it may imply that these Gentile rulers were not passively waiting to be called Benefactor but sought the title for themselves. In Matthew 23:7, Jesus disapproved of a similar kind of status seeking. Actually he himself is the true "Benefactor." In Acts 10:38 Peter uses a verbal form of the word, describing Jesus as going about "doing good" (*euergetōn*).

In v.26 "but you" is emphatic, with the word "you" standing at the very beginning of the clause (*hymeis de*). Jesus makes two points about true greatness. First, one should not seek the veneration given aged people in ancient Near Eastern society but be content with the lower place younger people had. This allusion to youthful-ness does not appear in Mark 10:43 and is one of the variations that point to a different setting for Luke's record of the conversation. In v.27 Luke includes an-other fresh illustration from social custom. The person sitting at a dinner table had a higher social position than the waiter, who was often a slave. This illustration recalls the example of the Lord Jesus, who washed his disciples' feet as they re-clined at the table of the Last Supper (John 13:12–17).

28–30 Verse 28 is not in Matthew or Mark; it shows that Jesus' trials kept on be-tween his temptation by Satan (ch. 4) and the passion events. It also recognizes the faithfulness of the disciples during this time. The fidelity of one of them is about to be tested severely (v.31). This theme of testing and faithfulness is prominent in Luke (S. Brown, *Apostasy and Perseverance*). The comparison "just as" (*kathōs*, v.29) is like that Jesus gave his disciples in the commission in John 20:21, which was comparable to the one he received from his Father. Here in Luke the picture is not just that of a commission but of a conferral similar to a testament. There may also be a suggestion of the new covenant referred to in v.20. The verb *diatithemai* ("confer") here (v.29) is cognate to *diathēkē* ("covenant") there. (For a similar promise in noncovenantal language, see 12:32.) The idea of a messianic banquet is reflected in v.30 (cf. 13:28–30 and comments). Matthew's parallel to this verse is preceded by a reference to the "renewal of all things" (*palingenesia*) instead of to the kingdom (Matt 19:28). The parallel in Matthew speaks of twelve thrones, but Luke omits the number, possibly to avoid the problem of Judas's occupying one of them. Since Luke does specify that there are twelve tribes, the omission is not important. (On the role of the Son of Man and the saints in judgment, see Dan 7:9–18.) Specific designation of the number of tribes of Israel with respect to their future role does not appear again in the NT till Revelation 7:1–8.

31–34 Only Luke records these words to Peter, at the same time omitting Jesus' prediction of the disciples' failure and their being scattered (Matt 26:30–32; Mark 14:26–28). He also omits any reference to Jesus' postresurrection appearance in Galilee, likewise omitted in his Resurrection narrative (cf. comment on 24:6). While Luke has stressed the faithfulness of the disciples and might not wish to mention their defection, he does refer forthrightly to Peter's coming defection (v.31), where he attributes it to the direct activity of Satan. In Matthew and Mark there is a transition from the scene of the Last Supper to the Mount of Olives before the prediction of the disciples' defection is given. In Luke, Jesus' warning to Peter comes immediately after Jesus' commendation for the disciples' faithfulness and his promise concerning the kingdom. This makes a strong contrast. The repetition of Simon's name adds weight to the warning. The metaphor of sifting implies separating what is desirable from what is undesirable. Here the thought is that Satan wants to prove that at least some of the disciples will fail under severe testing. The first occurrence of "you" in v.31 is in the plural (*hymas*). This refers to all the disciples in contrast to Peter, who is addressed (v.32) by the singular "you" (*sou*). Notice the use of the name "Simon" for Peter, apparently characteristic of Luke or of his special source.

Jesus' prayer that Simon's faith would not fail (v.32) has occasioned discussion over whether it was or was not answered. The verbal phrase "may not fail" (*mē eklipē*) probably means "may not give out" or "may not disappear completely" (as the sun in a total eclipse). If this is correct, then Jesus' prayer was certainly answered. Peter's denial, though serious and symptomatic of a low level of faith, did not mean that he had ceased, within himself, to believe in the Lord. Nevertheless his denial was so contrary to his former spiritual state that he would need to "return" (*epistrephō*) to Christ. The whole experience, far from disqualifying Peter from Christian service, would actually issue in a responsibility for him to strengthen his brothers. Peter's overconfident reply (v.33) includes a reference to death found among the four Gospels only here and in John 13:37. The prediction of his denial (v.34) is substantially the same in all four Gospels, despite some differences in detail. Luke alone specifies that in the denial Peter will say he does not even know Jesus.

35–38 This short passage is difficult to interpret. The difficulties lie in (1) the syntax of v.36 (cf. Notes); (2) the problem of Jesus' apparent support for using weapons, which is hard to reconcile with his word to Peter when the latter used the sword (Matt 26:52); and (3) the seeming reversal of the instructions Jesus gave the Twelve and the seventy-two on their missions (9:1–3; 10:1–3). Thus there is a question as to which principle regarding the use of force is normative for the church.

It is common to solve difficulties (2) and (3) by taking Jesus' words as ironical. But if that were so, v.38b—"That is enough"—would be hard to understand; for it would seem to continue the irony when one would have expected a correction of the disciples' misunderstanding of it. Any approach to a solution must take into account the fact that later, when the disciples were armed with these swords, Jesus opposed their use (vv.49–51). Moreover, the tone of v.52 is nonmilitant. Verse 36 clearly refers back to 10:4, the sending of the seventy-two; both passages mention the "purse" (*ballantion*) and the "bag" (*pēra*). (See also the sending of the Twelve in 9:1–6, where the bag is mentioned, but not the purse.) Here in v.35 there seems to be an affirmation of those principles in the question "Did you lack anything?" Yet a contrast is also clearly intended. That contrast may imply that Jesus' earlier instructions were a radical statement applicable only to discipleship during his lifetime. On the other hand, however, it more likely indicates, not a reversal of normal rules for the church's mission, but an exception in a time of crisis (cf. "but now," *alla nyn*). Jesus is not being ironic but thoroughly serious. Since he told them not to buy more swords than they had (v.38), and since two were hardly enough to defend the group, the swords may simply be a vivid symbol of impending crisis, not intended for actual use.

Verse 37a is one of several clear quotations of Isaiah 53 in the NT. (The UBS Index of Quotations cites John 12:38; Rom 10:16; Matt 8:17; Acts 8:32–33; 1 Peter 2:22.)

Notes

7–23 The composition of this passage is complex. Verses 7–13 seem to be dependent on Mark 14:12–16. Verse 14 differs from Matthew and Mark and may be from a special source. Verses 15–17 are unique to Luke, with v.18 showing some similarity to Mark 14:25. Except for the first and last phrases, vv.19–20 appear to be from a non-Markan source, possibly one also used by Paul for 1 Cor 11:23–26, modified in the process. If this is so, it reflects a very early form of the tradition that contains the words of institution of the Eucharist. Taken together, the verses constitute an original narrative edited by Luke from different sources.

7 Ἦλθεν δὲ ἡ ἡμέρα τῶν ἀζύμων (ēlthen de hē hēmera tōn azymōn, "then came the day of Unleavened Bread"). It is not certain on what day of the week Jesus celebrated the Passover. Few scholars question that Jesus was crucified on a Friday. There is considerable doubt, however, as to the chronological relationship between the Passover, the Last Supper, and the Crucifixion. Some infer from John 13:1; 18:28; 19:14, 31, 42, that the Passover did not occur till after Jesus was crucified. In that case the Paschal lambs would have been killed in preparation for the Passover at the very time Jesus was on the cross, which would have had strong symbolic significance. But if that inference is correct, then, assuming the chronological reliability of all four Gospels on this point, the Synoptics could not be describing a Passover meal as the setting for the Last Supper, in spite of all appearances that it was. Another approach interprets the Johannine texts above as being consistent with a pre-crucifixion Passover. N. Geldenhuys has a clear discussion of this possibility in *The Gospel of Luke*, NIC (Grand Rapids: Eerdmans, 1951), pp. 649–70.

Most scholars now look elsewhere for a solution. A. Jaubert (*The Date of the Last Supper* [New York: Alba House], 1965) proposed that the Last Supper was held on an earlier evening in the week when sectarians such as those at Qumran (site of the DSS) celebrated the Passover. This would allow more time for the trial of Jesus, as well as solving the Passover chronology. But the theory conflicts with other data. H. Hoehner (*Chronological Aspects of the Life of Christ* [Grand Rapids: Zondervan], 1977, pp. 65–93) suggests that the differences between the Synoptics and John arise from differences caused by different methods of reckoning dates by Jewish groups. If some calculated the date from evening to evening and others from dawn to dawn, both groups could celebrate the Passover on the same *date* but on different *days*. The Judeans (and John) might have followed one method and the Galileans (and the Synoptics) the other. Whether or not any of the schemes mentioned here is correct, at least we have several plausible solutions to this chronological problem.

16 Οὐκέτι (ouketi, "never again," "no longer") is not in some of the most reliable MSS (e.g., B or, apparently, P75). It may have been added by a copyist who thought it made better sense (cf. Metzger, *Textual Commentary*, p. 173).

19–20 The words τὸ ὑπὲρ ὑμῶν . . . ἐκχυννόμενον (to hyper hymōn . . . ekchynnomenon, "given for you . . . poured out [for you]") are found in every Greek uncial MS except D. They are lacking in the Western text and some other sources. Those who have followed the assumption that because the Western text tends to include rather than omit questionable readings and that on those few occasions when it does omit readings it should be given special weight apply that principle here. Also, since copyists have a tendency to include anything they believe may be genuine, any shorter reading is given strong consideration. Furthermore, the wording is similar to 1 Cor 11:24–25, including words unusual in Luke; so there is a suspicion that this was copied from another source, perhaps combining elements from Paul and Mark.

Arguments for the longer text include the judgment that the Western text is not to be given preference (cf. K. Snodgrass, "Western Non-Interpolations," JBL 91 [1972]: 369–79), the weight of all the MSS that include it, the probability that the source of the words is a very old tradition that Paul also followed, and the likelihood that the sequence of cup-bread-cup in the longer reading was perplexing to later copyists, who preferred readings that simplified the narrative. The following are among the more significant discussions: preferring the shorter text: A. Vööbus, "A New Approach to the Problem of the Shorter and Longer Text in Luke," NTS 15 (1968–69): 457–63; preferring the longer text: H. Schürmann, *Traditionsgeschichtliche Untersuchungen* (Düsseldorf, 1968), pp. 159–92; cf. Ellis, *Gospel of Luke*, pp. 254–56; Marshall, *Gospel of Luke*, pp. 799–801.

36 Ὁ μὴ ἔχων (*ho mē echōn*, lit., "the [person] not having"; NIV, "if you don't have") lacks a direct object. It is not clear whether we should (1) supply the same object as in the first clause, "purse," meaning that if they lacked money they should sell their cloaks to get money for swords, or (2) supply the word "sword" from the end of the clause, where it serves as the object of the verb ἀγορασάτω (*agorasatō*, "buy"), since a sword is the needed item. The first is more balanced grammatically, but the final command to buy a sword is the same either way.

---

3. Prayer on the Mount of Olives

22:39–46

> [39]Jesus went out as usual to the Mount of Olives, and his disciples followed him. [40]On reaching the place, he said to them, "Pray that you will not fall into temptation." [41]He withdrew about a stone's throw beyond them, knelt down and prayed, [42]"Father, if you are willing, take this cup from me; yet not my will, but yours be done." [43]An angel from heaven appeared to him and strengthened him. [44]And being in anguish, he prayed more earnestly, and his sweat was like drops of blood falling to the ground.
>
> [45]When he rose from prayer and went back to the disciples, he found them asleep, exhausted from sorrow. [46]"Why are you sleeping?" he asked them. "Get up and pray so that you will not fall into temptation."

Luke's account of this prayer differs in several respects from Mark's and Matthew's: (1) Luke does not specify the location as being Gethsemane; (2) he alone includes at the beginning an exhortation to the disciples to ward off temptation by means of prayer; and (3) his account omits much of the narrative included in Mark and Matthew. Such differences raise perplexing questions about Luke's sources—questions that lie beyond the scope of this commentary, though they may bear on Luke's theology. Also there is considerable doubt as to the genuineness of vv.43–44 (cf. Notes). Theologically, there has been much discussion over the purpose of Jesus' prayer. Some have proposed a meaning for the "cup" of v.42 that would avoid any inference that Jesus had difficulty facing death.

39–42 Luke singles out Jesus in v.39 by using a verbal ending in the third person singular (Mark 14:32 uses a plural ending). NIV inserts the name "Jesus" for clarity.

This reminds us of the way Luke focused attention on Jesus' initiative (cf. comments on 19:38). Jesus went to the Mount of Olives "as usual" (*kata to ethos*, cf. the virtually identical *kata to eiōthos*, 4:16), as mentioned in 21:37. He did not change his habits to elude Judas. Luke may have omitted the name "Gethsemane" to direct the reader's attention to the Mount of Olives. But since he did not mention the Mount of Olives as the scene of the eschatological discourse but introduced it only after the conclusion of the discourse (21:37), it may be that in both places he is simply following his practice of omitting names and other words not familiar to his wide readership. That Luke uses geographical features mainly as symbols is doubtful (see comment on 9:23).

While it is natural to think that the "temptation" (or "trial," *peirasmon*, v.40) has something to do with that of the end time, in view of vv.16, 18 (so Danker, *Jesus*, p. 225), Marshall is probably correct that without the definite article the word does not refer to that specific time. The themes of prayer and temptation are common in Luke. So it is not surprising that only he has the saying in v.40. It is repeated in v.46, to which Matthew 26:41 and Mark 14:38 are parallel. Marshall (*Gospel of Luke*, p. 830) interprets it in terms of vv.28–38. Kneeling in prayer (v.41) was not customary in Jesus' time (standing was the normal posture). But this scene is one of intense emotional strain (cf. Eph 3:14). Matthew and Mark say that Jesus fell to the ground (Matt 26:39; Mark 14:35). It is fitting that Luke, who throughout his Gospel stresses Jesus' conscious fulfillment of the purposes of God, should now emphasize Jesus' concern for the will of God. "If you are willing" (*ei boulei*, v.42) is absent from Matthew and Mark at this point, though they do have the rest of v.42.

As in Matthew 20:22 and Mark 10:38, Jesus uses the cup as a metaphor of his imminent passion. Some, however, have imagined that this metaphor implies that Jesus faced death with less bravery than others have faced it. (But to shrink from a painful death is not necessarily cowardice; the highest bravery may consist in being fully cognizant of impending and agonizing death and yet to embrace it voluntarily.) At any rate, it has been suggested that the cup Jesus feared was that he might die from the strain he was under before he could willingly offer himself on the cross. But this view fails to recognize that Jesus would not have been as concerned with the physical pain of his death as with the spiritual desolation of bearing our sin and its judgment on the cross (2 Cor 5:21; 1 Peter 2:24). Moreover, in the OT the wrath of God expressed against sin was sometimes referred to by the metaphor of a cup (e.g., Ps 11:6, where NIV translates *kôs* as "lot" rather than "cup"; cf. Ps 75:8; Isa 51:17; Jer 25:15–17).

43–44 These verses have some formidable textual difficulties (cf. Notes). Since they have a claim to genuineness and are included in most texts of the Greek testament, they require comment. Luke has already mentioned angels (v.43) many times—in the Nativity narrative and elsewhere, e.g., 9:26; 12:8–9; 15:10; 16:22. So the appearance of an angel here in Gethsemane is not strange.

Luke describes Jesus' agony in physical terms, as we might expect a physician to do. The sweating was apparently so profuse that it looked like blood dripping from a wound (v.44).

45–46 Luke does not dwell on the weakness of the disciples, nor does he describe in further detail Jesus' agony. Matthew and Mark refer to another prayer of Jesus and mention two more instances of the disciples' falling asleep. For Luke a single reference to each suffices, with the addition of an explanation for the disciples' sleep: exhaustion from sorrow (v.45). Luke does repeat the injunction for the disciples to pray lest they fall into temptation (v.46).

Notes

43–44 These verses are textually uncertain. Their mention of angels and their description of Jesus' physical agony are not incompatible with Luke's perspective. Also it is unlikely that copyists would have omitted the verses because of their supernatural element, even if they seemed an intrusion into this report of Jesus' intensely human suffering. Yet the MS support is weak. UBS cites "ancient and diversified witnesses," among them P⁷⁵ ℵ A B, that omit the verses. Their inclusion in square brackets in the UBS text does not indicate that the UBS committee thought them genuine but rather its respect for the antiquity of the verses. Even if vv.43–44 did not appear in the canonical Luke in early stages of the tradition, they may be authentic in their substance and message and may have conceivably been composed by Luke himself at some point.

4. Jesus' Arrest

22:47–53

⁴⁷While he was still speaking a crowd came up, and the man who was called Judas, one of the Twelve, was leading them. He approached Jesus to kiss him, ⁴⁸but Jesus asked him, "Judas, are you betraying the Son of Man with a kiss?"

⁴⁹When Jesus' followers saw what was going to happen, they said, "Lord, should we strike with our swords?" ⁵⁰And one of them struck the servant of the high priest, cutting off his right ear.

⁵¹But Jesus answered, "No more of this!" And he touched the man's ear and healed him.

⁵²Then Jesus said to the chief priests, the officers of the temple guard, and the elders, who had come for him, "Am I leading a rebellion, that you have come with swords and clubs? ⁵³Every day I was with you in the temple courts, and you did not lay a hand on me. But this is your hour—when darkness reigns."

47–48 Luke drops the introductory "and" (*kai*). Thus this pericope "is joined as closely as possible to the preceding one" (Marshall, *Gospel of Luke*, p. 835). All the Synoptics make the point that Jesus was still speaking to his disciples when Judas and the crowd arrived (v.47). This emphasizes the sudden intrusion of Judas and the crowd into the somber scene in Gethsemane. In making the transition to Judas, Luke first refers to the crowd (not mentioned by Matthew or Mark). In Luke "the crowd" (*ochlos*), in contrast to the "people" (*laos*), is sometimes presented as being unfeeling, perhaps even hostile. From the crowd attention moves to "the man who was called Judas" (*ho legomenos Ioudas*, "one called Judas"). The designation occurs only in Luke and seems to be a dramatic way of isolating Judas—holding him off at a distance for a derogatory look and comment, viz., "this Judas person." Each of the synoptic writers feels compelled to say that Judas was "one of the Twelve." The betrayal was accomplished with a kiss. In Judas's scheme of betrayal, the kiss was the way he identified Jesus in the darkness of the night (Mark 14:44). But in the high drama of the actual situation, it was cruelly hypocritical. In the Greek word order, following Judas's name, three elements come together in stark succession—"with a kiss/the Son of Man/are you betraying?" (v.48).

49–51 (See comments on vv.33–38 for the background to this incident.) John 18:10 (but none of the Synoptics) tells us that it was Peter who drew the sword. Luke alone tells us in words a physician might use about Jesus' healing of the ear of the high priest's servant (v.51).

52–53 In v.52 the details regarding the makeup of the crowd—religious, political, and military leaders—are peculiar to Luke. These details may be part of his design to show that it was not the believing Jews who brought about Jesus' crucifixion but their arrogant leaders. Matthew and Mark do not bring this out till later (e.g., Matt 27:20; Mark 15:11, the substance of which is not in Luke). Jesus' comment shows the underhanded nature of their act. "This is your hour [*hōra*]" (v.53) sounds Johannine (e.g., John 17:1 and passim), especially since it refers to the Passion. But Luke also uses the word "hour" frequently, as well as other words designating a time of opportunity or destiny. The verb "reigns" represents the noun *exousia* ("power," "authority"). Satan had previously offered Jesus *exousia* in the Temptation (4:6); but Jesus, who after obediently going to the cross would receive "all authority" from the Father (Matt 28:18), was willing to have Satan exercise his authority for a time under the divine plan of salvation.

Notes

51 Ἐᾶτε ἕως τούτου (*Eate heōs toutou*, "No more of this") means literally "Permit, or let go, up to this [point]." It is usually taken to mean "Stop what you are doing." Marshall (*Gospel of Luke*, p. 837) prefers understanding *autous* ("them") after *eate*, with the meaning "Let them [i.e., the police] have their way," as in NEB.

5. Peter's denial

22:54–62

[54]Then seizing him, they led him away and took him into the house of the high priest. Peter followed at a distance. [55]But when they had kindled a fire in the middle of the courtyard and had sat down together, Peter sat down with them. [56]A servant girl saw him seated there in the firelight. She looked closely at him and said, "This man was with him."

[57]But he denied it. "Woman, I don't know him," he said.

[58]A little later someone else saw him and said, "You also are one of them."

"Man, I am not!" Peter replied.

[59]About an hour later another asserted, "Certainly this fellow was with him, for he is a Galilean."

[60]Peter replied, "Man, I don't know what you're talking about!" Just as he was speaking, the rooster crowed. [61]The Lord turned and looked straight at Peter. Then Peter remembered the word the Lord had spoken to him: "Before the rooster crows today, you will disown me three times." [62]And he went outside and wept bitterly.

Throughout this and the succeeding sections, dramatic tension mounts. A contributing feature is the simultaneous action taking place in the house of the high priest with Jesus (v.54) and in the courtyard with Peter (v.55). Luke separates the two sequences of events instead of intertwining them as Matthew and Mark do. While this literary device differs from his alternation of stories about the births of Jesus and of John the Baptist (ch. 1), it does enable the reader to follow Peter's experience and then Jesus' trial separately. Luke does not tell us anything about a night session of the trial but allows for it in v.54 (cf. vv.63–65; cf Notes). The story of Peter's denial could not have been invented. It presents a sober and utterly real picture of the prominent apostle; and, along with vv.31–32, it offers a deep spiritual lesson about humility and the spiritual conflict.

54–57 A number of problems surround the account of the meeting in the high priest's house (v.54)—possibly the house of Annas, father-in-law of the high priest Caiaphas (cf. John 18:13). But this meeting seems also to have been a trial before the entire Sanhedrin (cf. Matt 26:59; Mark 14:55; cf. the other commentaries in this volume on the verses just cited from Matt and Mark).

Though he followed Jesus at a distance, Peter is the only disciple who, so far as we know, followed him at all. The fire in the courtyard (v.55) was needed because the evenings were—and still are—cool in springtime in Jerusalem. The denial had three phases. All four Gospels identify the first speaker as a servant girl (v.56). As many have observed, the girl and what she said were relatively harmless and did not deserve such a drastic response. Peter, however, realized that many ears were listening. Peter's response is called a denial. The word "deny" (*arneomai*, v.57) is used in the NT as the polar opposite of the word "confess" (*homologeō*). We are to confess (i.e., acknowledge) Christ but deny ourselves (i.e., disown our private interests for the sake of Christ; cf. comment on 9:23). Peter here does the reverse. He denies Christ in order to serve his own interests. While Peter's language may recall the language of the rabbinic ban (SBK, 1:469; cf. "I never knew you," Matt 7:23, and, more distantly, Luke 13:25, 27), this is unlikely to have been in Peter's mind.

58 After a brief time, someone else, not described by Luke, made another charge. Notice that in none of these dialogues as reported by Luke does Jesus' name actually appear. The assumption is that the recent events in Jesus' life were already known to the group in the courtyard. Luke's description of the speakers is also limited. It is only from Peter's response that we know that the second speaker was a man.

59–60 Verse 59 is typical of Luke's way of indicating the passage of time. The third speaker then makes a definite assertion; the verb translated "asserted" (*diischyrizeto*) means to "insist, maintain firmly" (BAG, s.v.). Peter's response is stated more mildly in Luke than in Matthew and Mark, where he accompanies his statement with an oath. Also here (v.60) Peter does not directly deny Jesus but professes ignorance of him, though this amounts to the same thing. Luke emphasizes the fulfillment of Jesus' words about the cock crowing by indicating that the third denial was just being uttered (*parachrēma eti lalountos*, lit., "immediately while he was still speaking") when the cock crowed.

61–62 In telling how the Lord looked at Peter (v.61), Luke uses the word John used (John 1:42) to describe the way Jesus looked at Peter when they first met—*emblepō*.

It "usually signifies a look of interest, love or concern" (DNTT, 3:519; cf. Mark 10:21). Peter's feelings (v.62) need no further comment.

Notes

54–62 Immediately after his description of how Peter and the others made a fire in the courtyard and sat around it, Luke tells us about Peter's denial. Then, without a break, Luke goes on to describe how the soldiers mocked Jesus, after which he gives us his account of Jesus' trial. Matthew and Mark alternate episodes from the denial and the trial. It may be that Luke (1) followed a different source or (2) arranged his material for dramatic effect in bringing Peter's denial closer to Jesus' prediction of it. While there are difficulties in reconciling the accounts of the denial in the four Gospels, Luke's narrative with its designation of the three questioners as "a servant girl," "someone else," and "another" is consistent with the other narratives. Though John 18:25 has a plural verb for the second question, this does not pose a serious problem because it does not exclude the possibility of one man in a group being spokesman.

6. The mocking of Jesus

22:63–65

⁶³The men who were guarding Jesus began mocking and beating him. ⁶⁴They blindfolded him and demanded, "Prophesy! Who hit you?" ⁶⁵And they said many other insulting things to him.

63–65 Marshall (*Gospel of Luke*, p. 845) says that the beginning of this section is "badly linked" to the incident just preceding. Though the accusative *auton* ("him") in the Greek text of v.63 clearly refers to Jesus (NIV substitutes "Jesus" for *auton*), grammatically it should refer to the subject of v.62—Peter. Again we probably have a matter of sources. Be that as it may, the incident itself is put in a position of sharp contrast between Jesus' sufferings and Peter's attempt to avoid any identification with Jesus. Also, the soldiers' taunting Jesus about prophesying who hit him while he was blindfolded (v.64) contrasts with Luke's clear portrayal in his Gospel of Jesus as a prophet.

7. Trial before the Jewish leaders

22:66–71

⁶⁶At daybreak the council of the elders of the people, both the chief priests and teachers of the law, met together, and Jesus was led before them. ⁶⁷"If you are the Christ," they said, "tell us."
Jesus answered, "If I tell you, you will not believe me, ⁶⁸and if I asked you, you would not answer. ⁶⁹But from now on, the Son of Man will be seated at the right hand of the mighty God."
⁷⁰They all asked, "Are you then the Son of God?"
He replied, "You are right in saying I am."
⁷¹Then they said, "Why do we need any more testimony? We have heard it from his own lips."

This section presents special difficulties of a literary and historical nature. Jesus' trial had several phases. Between them there is some overlapping of persons and charges. There were some irregularities in the proceedings, especially in the light of later evidence from Jewish jurisprudence. Moreover, the Synoptics are not uniform in covering all aspects of the trial; each writer makes his own choice as to what to include or omit in order to fulfill his distinctive editorial purpose. While the Notes will present some details about these things, most of them do not affect the exposition itself.

66–69 Luke has already indicated that Jesus was arrested during the night (see comment on v.47) and has implied that he was confronted by the authorities while in the house of the high priest (v.64). All three Synoptics mention the early morning trial, though the substance of vv.66–71 has already been given in the account of the night trial in Matthew 26:63–65 and Mark 14:61–64. Luke summarizes the crucial exchange between Jesus and the leaders and adds a time note that it was becoming day (v.66). Matthew and Mark refer to the same time of day, when the religious authorities reached a decision, as "very early in the morning [*prōi*]" (Mark 15:1). Luke's way of reporting the questioning separates the questions regarding messiahship and regarding the Son of God (cf. the Matthew and Mark passages just cited).

The word "Christ" (v.67) at this time had not yet become a proper name; so the question is whether Jesus was claiming to be the Messiah (NIV mg.). Jesus' answer, a simple affirmation as in Mark 14:62, is twofold. First, he says that they would not believe him even if he answered them. D. Catchpole (*The Trial of Jesus* [Leiden: E.J. Brill, 1971], p. 195) notes the similarity of this to Jesus' answer to a similar question in John 10:24–25. Jesus also says that were he to question them they would not answer (v.68). The truth of this had already been demonstrated in 20:1–8.

The second part of Jesus' answer (v.69) concerns the exaltation of the Son of Man (who must be identified with Jesus here or the saying is irrelevant) and vindicates Jesus and proves who he is. Luke's report of this differs considerably from its form in Matthew 26:64 and Mark 14:62. Significant among these differences is the phrase "from now on" (*apo tou nyn*), which Mark does not have, though he has "you will see" (*opsesthe*) where Luke has "will be" (*estai*). Thus Mark stresses the future revelation of the Son of Man, whereas Luke stresses the fact that from that very time in his appearance before the council he was to be exalted. This fits in with Luke's emphasis on the present reality of events that may appear, in Matthew and Mark, to have their main significance in the future. Here Luke is concerned with the present vindication of Jesus. Matthew combines both ideas (a fact that complicates the question of sources), though his *ap' arti* is understood by NIV to mean "in the future," or, better, "hereafter" (RSV, NASB).

70–71 Only Luke has this question (v.70). Standing independent of and subsequent to the question about messiahship, it serves to emphasize that Jesus is himself the Son of God and is not merely called such as an honorific title because of his role as Messiah. Jesus' reply—lit., "You say that I am" (*hymeis legete hoti egō eimi*)—while not a direct affirmation, was taken as such, as v.71 shows. The nature of this reply is understandable in view of Jesus' remarks in vv.67b–68.

Notes

66–71 The probable order of Jesus' trial appearances in the four Gospels is (1) before Annas (John), (2) before Caiaphas and the Sanhedrin (Synoptics), (3) before Pilate (Synoptics, John), (4) before Herod Antipas (Luke), and (5) before Pilate (Luke). The charges before Caiaphas and the Sanhedrin were (1) threatening to destroy the temple and (2) blasphemy. The charges before Pilate were (1) subverting the Jewish nation, (2) opposing the payment of taxes to Caesar, (3) claiming to be king, and (4) sedition ("stirs up the people," 23:5).

The procedures at the Jewish trial have been frequently questioned. A brief summary, drawn from Lohse (TDNT, 7:868), of the alleged illegalities in this capital case includes the following: night session, trial on a holy day, failure to wait for a second session on the following day, definition of blasphemy, and holding the trial away from the official chambers. These issues are more complex than appear from this summary. Yet it would appear that the items cited stand in contradiction to the legal procedures in the Jewish Talmud. Out of much recent discussion, the following are some solutions that have been proposed.

1. The Sanhedrin did act illegally. Few, however, would still hold that the situation was clear-cut.

2. The Gospels are in error. Recently, however, scholars have been treating the Gospels with more confidence as to their accuracy in recording these emotionally charged events.

3. The legal procedures described in the Talmud were not all in effect at the time of Jesus' trial. This is probably true to some degree and may help considerably in reconciling the Jewish and Christian positions.

4. There were two Sanhedrins; different rules might have applied to a smaller group meeting first and the whole group meeting later. This is at best uncertain.

5. The trial lasted longer than it appears; so the first three illegalities listed above did not actually occur. The trial may have lasted longer if the Last Supper were earlier, as proposed by Jaubert and others (see Notes on vv.7–23 above). We are not yet certain enough of the facts to accept this proposal without question.

6. Numbers 1, 4, and 5 of the alleged illegalities listed above do not apply to Luke. The Lukan account should be given priority, though its final editing was later than the other Gospels. Not only is it true that the sources Luke followed were early and accurate, it is also true that Luke's account presents fewer problems than the others. But this still leaves questions regarding the other Gospels, as it assumes that they are in error. All things considered, there are enough variables in the different accounts to preclude any blanket accusation against the historical reliability of Luke's account.

The following works represent recent approaches to the problems relating to Jesus' trials: E. Bammel, ed., *The Trial of Jesus* (Naperville, Ill.: A.R. Allenson, 1970); J. Blinzler, *Der Prozess Jesu*, 4th ed. (Regensburg: F. Pustet, 1969); Catchpole, *Trial of Jesus;* A.N. Sherwin-White, *Roman Society and Roman Law in the New Testament* (Oxford: Clarendon, 1963), pp. 24–47; and P. Winter, *On the Trial of Jesus*, 2d ed. (Berlin: De Gruyter, 1974). Of these, Blinzler, Catchpole, and Sherwin-White take the historicity of the Lukan narrative most seriously.

---

8. *Trial before Pilate and Herod*

23:1–25

¹Then the whole assembly rose and led him off to Pilate. ²And they began to accuse him, saying, "We have found this man subverting our nation. He opposes payment of taxes to Caesar and claims to be Christ, a king."

³So Pilate asked Jesus, "Are you the king of the Jews?"

"Yes, it is as you say," Jesus replied.

⁴Then Pilate announced to the chief priests and the crowd, "I find no basis for a charge against this man."

⁵But they insisted, "He stirs up the people all over Judea by his teaching. He started in Galilee and has come all the way here."

⁶On hearing this, Pilate asked if the man was Galilean. ⁷When he learned that Jesus was under Herod's jurisdiction, he sent him to Herod, who was also in Jerusalem at that time.

⁸When Herod saw Jesus, he was greatly pleased, because for a long time he had been wanting to see him. From what he had heard about him, he hoped to see him perform some miracle. ⁹He plied him with many questions, but Jesus gave him no answer. ¹⁰The chief priests and the teachers of the law were standing there, vehemently accusing him. ¹¹Then Herod and his soldiers ridiculed and mocked him. Dressing him in an elegant robe, they sent him back to Pilate. ¹²That day Herod and Pilate became friends—before this they had been enemies.

¹³Pilate called together the chief priests, the rulers and the people, ¹⁴and said to them, "You brought me this man as one who was inciting the people to rebellion. I have examined him in your presence and have found no basis for your charges against him. ¹⁵Neither has Herod, for he sent him back to us; as you can see, he has done nothing to deserve death. ¹⁶Therefore, I will punish him and then release him."

¹⁸With one voice they cried out, "Away with this man! Release Barabbas to us!" ¹⁹(Barabbas had been thrown into prison for an insurrection in the city, and for murder.)

²⁰Wanting to release Jesus, Pilate appealed to them again. ²¹But they kept shouting, "Crucify him! Crucify him!"

²²For the third time he spoke to them: "Why? What crime has this man committed? I have found in him no grounds for the death penalty. Therefore I will have him punished and then release him."

²³But with loud shouts they insistently demanded that he be crucified, and their shouts prevailed. ²⁴So Pilate decided to grant their demand. ²⁵He released the man who had been thrown into prison for insurrection and murder, the one they asked for, and surrendered Jesus to their will.

The trial now moves into its Roman phase. While there had doubtless been more interrogation than the Synoptics report before Pilate declared he found no basis for a charge against Jesus (v.4), it obviously did not take Pilate long to determine Jesus' innocence. The larger part of this section deals, not with the trial as such, but with the difficulty the authorities had in trying to convict an innocent man.

1–5 Verse 1 links the Jewish and Roman trials. The "whole assembly" is the Sanhedrin. Pilate was Roman governor (procurator) of the province of Judah. His name appears in an inscription found in 1961 at Caesarea, his official residence. Caesarea was a large, magnificent city boasting Roman culture, where Pilate would no doubt have preferred to be at the time of Jesus' trial, were it not the Passover season, when special precautions were needed in Jerusalem against civil disturbances.

The Sanhedrin's accusation contains three distinct charges. The first (subverting the Jewish nation) would have been of concern to Pilate, who wanted no internal strife among the Jewish people. But it was not a matter for Roman jurisprudence. The second (opposing payment of taxes to Caesar) and third (claiming to be king) were more to the point. Luke has already shown (20:20–26) that the second charge was untrue. The third one became the key issue. Jesus' responses to the questions asked him (22:66–71) were understood as being clearly affirmative. It is also clear that the word Christ, or Messiah (v.2), was deliberately used to imply to Pilate that

Jesus was a political activist. The word "king," put in apposition to Messiah, implies a threat to Roman sovereignty to the point where Pilate would have to take action. (In v.5 the Sanhedrin summarized all this by insisting that Jesus was guilty of sedition.)

In Pilate's question (v.3), the word "you" (*su*) comes first in the Greek sentence for emphasis. Jesus' answer, like those in the Jewish trial, implies a positive answer and at the same time returns the issue to Pilate. The answer (*su legeis*, "you say") is the same in all three Synoptics and is virtually similar to Matthew's report of Jesus' answer in the Jewish trial (Matt 26:64, using the synonym *su eipas*, "you say"), which interprets the "I am" of Mark 14:62.

Luke's account lacks the further dialogue in Mark 15:3–5. But Luke is the only Gospel that has Pilate's declaration of Jesus' innocence (v.4). Presumably the source containing that statement was not available to Mark or Matthew, for they would certainly have wanted to make that point. Yet the point is especially important for Luke, who seeks throughout his Gospel and Acts to vindicate Christianity through the vindicating of both Jesus and Paul in their appearances in court. The response from the Sanhedrin is clever. It implies seditious actions by saying that the people are being stirred up by Jesus' (unspecified) teaching.

6–12 Only Luke has this incident. It is appropriate for his narrative; he had more interest in politics than Matthew or Mark and has already mentioned Herod Antipas whereas they have not (3:1; 9:7–9; 13:31). Herod had a more protracted and more intimate experience with Jewish politics and religion than Pilate had. For a long time he had desired to learn more about Jesus (v.8; cf. 9:7–9). Like Pilate, Herod was probably in Jerusalem because of the Passover. For Jesus' attitude toward him, see 13:31–33. Herod's territory, as a local king under the authority of Rome, was Galilee (vv.6–7) and Perea. Verse 11 probably reflects a certain frustration on his part. He apparently had no legal accusation to make; so he vented his anger by echoing the hostility of the priests and teachers (vv.9–11). Mockery (v.11) was an unworthy aspect of the whole trial scene, repeated later on (Mark 15:17–20 and parallel passages). The robe was "elegant" (*lampros*, "bright," "gleaming"—a word used in both biblical and secular literature to describe clothes and other adornments like those of the rich man in James 2:2). This impetuous use of someone's fine clothes contrasts with the later scene (Mark 15:17–20) where the soldiers used a purple robe and other symbols to mock Jesus' claim to kingship.

13–16(17) This section, also unique to Luke, like v.4, demonstrates Jesus' innocence (vv.13–14). As Marshall (*Gospel of Luke*, in loc.) observes, the presence of the people here is "strange," because elsewhere in Luke they are either friendly or neutral. Actually Luke seems to be making a significant point by mentioning their presence. The "people" (v.13) are the *laos*, as distinguished from the crowd (*ochlos*). Throughout his Gospel, Luke has been careful to distinguish these two groups. He has also been careful to show that it is not the people but their leaders who oppose Jesus. Even here the people do not take an active stand against Jesus. Summoned by Pilate, they, like the crowds in v.4, hear a declaration of Jesus' innocence (vv.14–15). The "people" appear again in v.27, following Jesus to the place of crucifixion, and then in v.35, watching Jesus die. Once more (24:19) Luke mentions them as witnesses of Jesus' mighty works. At their first mention in Acts, Luke refers to the "people" as approving the young Jerusalem church (2:47).

English translations usually imply that Pilate punished Jesus (v.16) because he was innocent (e.g., NIV, "Therefore, I will punish him and then release him"). In the Greek structure, the word for "punish" may be a participal (*paideusas*) for stylistic reasons; but it also throws the emphasis on the main verb "release" (*apolysō*). The thought probably is "Because he is innocent, I will let him go with a light scourging [*paideusas*]." In this way Luke shows that Pilate, a Roman official, wanted to treat Jesus as fairly as possible. This would fit in with one of Luke's apparent goals in writing the Gospel and Acts—viz., to show that Christianity deserved to be favorably treated by Rome. The word "scourged" (*paideusas*) is different from the one used by Matthew and Mark to describe the flogging that preceded the Crucifixion (*phragellōsas*, Matt 27:26; Mark 15:15).

18–22 Luke provides only a brief statement about Barabbas compared with Mark 15:6–11 and has nothing about the message from Pilate's wife mentioned in Matthew 27:19. Again the writers are apparently following different sources. While Luke does mention Barabbas's crimes, he does not explain the custom Mark refers to (15:6). Barabbas has been romanticized, but since he was probably only an unimportant leader of a small riot, history has no record of him apart from the Gospels. We see Luke's concern to vindicate Jesus (and Christianity) to his readers again in v.22. He emphasizes Jesus' innocence by noting that this is the "third time" that Pilate spoke on Jesus' behalf, probably counting the appeals after Jesus' return from Herod (vv.15, 20, 22). On the "punishment," see v.16 and comment.

23–25 In vivid Greek (v.23), Luke brings the crowd's action to a climax. Although he does not refer to Pilate as washing his hands of responsibility for Jesus (cf. Matt 27:24), or to the Jews' acceptance of responsibility for Jesus' death (cf. Matt 27:25), or to Pilate's wishing to "satisfy" the people (cf. Mark 15:15), he effectively shifts attention from Pilate to the people by ending the Greek sentence, not with the verb (as in the English rendering), but with a final reference to the crowds, in the words *hai phōnai autōn* ("their voices"; NIV, "their shouts").

Luke omits the incident (Mark 15:17–20) of the soldiers' mockery (cf. v.11 and comment above) and proceeds directly to Pilate's action. He makes it clear in both v.24 and v.25 that Pilate acted in accord with the crowd's wishes. Having emphasized God's plan and will throughout his Gospel, Luke now notes the human factor: Jesus is delivered to the "demand" (v.24) of the crowd. Acts 2:23 shows how God's purpose was fulfilled even in their decision.

9. The Crucifixion

23:26–43

26As they led him away, they seized Simon from Cyrene, who was on his way in from the country, and put the cross on him and made him carry it behind Jesus. 27A large number of people followed him, including women who mourned and wailed for him. 28Jesus turned and said to them, "Daughters of Jerusalem, do not weep for me; weep for yourselves and for your children. 29For the time will come when you will say, 'Blessed are the barren women, the wombs that never bore and the breasts that never nursed!' 30Then

> " 'they will say to the mountains, "Fall on us!"
> and to the hills, "Cover us!" ' "

³¹For if men do these things when the tree is green, what will happen when it is dry?"

³²Two other men, both criminals, were also led out with him to be executed. ³³When they came to the place called the Skull, there they crucified him, along with the criminals—one on his right, the other on his left. ³⁴Jesus said, "Father, forgive them, for they do not know what they are doing." And they divided up his clothes by casting lots.

³⁵The people stood watching, and the rulers even sneered at him. They said, "he saved others; let him save himself if he is the Christ of God, the Chosen One."

³⁶The soldiers also came up and mocked him. They offered him wine vinegar ³⁷and said, "If you are the king of the Jews save yourself."

³⁸There was a written notice above him, which read: THIS IS THE KING OF THE JEWS.

³⁹One of the criminals who hung there hurled insults at him: "Aren't you the Christ? Save yourself and us!"

⁴⁰But the other criminal rebuked him. "Don't you fear God," he said, "since you are under the same sentence? ⁴¹We are punished justly, for we are getting what our deeds deserve. But this man has done nothing wrong."

⁴²Then he said, "Jesus, remember me when you come into your kingdom."

⁴³Jesus answered him, "I tell you the truth, today you will be with me in paradise."

In their accounts of Jesus' crucifixion, the four Gospels relate essentially the same series of events, but with varied selection of details and of Jesus' words. None of them portrays the physical agony of crucifixion in the shocking details that might have been given. The stark facts are there but are presented with sober restraint. What was most important for the four evangelists was the inner reality of Jesus' atoning death and his spiritual anguish in being identified with the sins of the world. As Cecil Alexander put it in the great hymn "Green Hill": "We may not know, we cannot tell, What pains he had to bear; But we believe it was for us He hung and suffered there."

26 Jesus was required, like others condemned to crucifixion, to carry the cross-bar. The wood was heavy, and Jesus was weakened by the maltreatment. The soldiers could press civilians such as Simon into service. Mark 15:21 has the word *angareuō* ("forces"), the same word Jesus used in the famous saying about going the second mile (Matt 5:41). Cyrene is a port in North Africa.

27-31 Once more Luke gives us an incident that is neither in Matthew nor Mark. For Luke it is important because it again expresses his concern for the fate of Jerusalem (cf. 19:41-44). The terrible destruction Jesus was speaking of also reflects his prediction in 21:20-24. Jewish women (v.27) had always considered barrenness a misfortune and children a blessing (v.28). In the day of Jerusalem's destruction, however, women would have the horror of seeing their children suffer and would wish they could have been spared that agony (v.29). A person standing out in the open in Jerusalem, or in the Judean hills, would probably not think of mountains (v.30) as a means of destruction as much as a means of protection. Therefore, Marshall (*Gospel of Luke*, p. 864) is probably right in suggesting that the words from Hosea 10:8 are a plea for protection rather than for quick death. Fire spreads much more rapidly through a dry forest than through a wet one; so Jesus' words in v.31 warn of a situation in the future even worse than the events surrounding his crucifixion.

32–34 It is not certain why, in contrast to Matthew and Mark, Luke mentions the two criminals (v.32) in advance of Jesus' conversation with them. The effect is to emphasize the humiliation of his execution and perhaps also (cf. Hendriksen, p. 1027) his identification with sinners in his death as well as in his life. Luke omits the name Golgotha, either because it would not be significant to his readers or because it was not in his source. His omission of the drink offered to Jesus may be for the latter reason. Luke's narrative is concise (v.33) and effective in presenting the brutal facts. Nor is it surprising that he, who constantly portrayed Jesus as offering God's grace and forgiveness to sinners (e.g., 7:40–43), is the only one who records his prayer for the forgiveness of his executors (v.34; cf. Notes on the textual problem here). Stephen followed his Lord's example and prayed for those who stoned him (Acts 7:60).

35 It is difficult to know whether the connective "and . . . even" (*de kai*, possibly "but even" or "but also") identifies the "people" (*laos*) with the sneering of the rulers or whether Luke intends the reader to understand the role of the "people" still to be passive rather than hostile, while everyone else, "even" the rulers, sneered. NIV takes it in the latter sense, which is probably correct. The word "saved" (*esōsen*) does not mean that the rulers believed in the claim of Jesus to forgive people but alludes to his reputation for restoring the sick and disturbed. Instead of the words "king of Israel" (Matt 27:42; Mark 15:32), Luke has "Christ of God, the Chosen One," which is consistent with his frequent presentation of Jesus as a prophet chosen by God (cf. the words "whom I have chosen," which occur only in Luke's version of the Transfiguration, in 9:35; cf. Isa 42:1).

36–37 The taunts continue. Luke places this incident earlier in his narrative than Matthew and Mark do in theirs, possibly to bring together in one place the people, rulers, and soldiers (Hendriksen, p. 1030). Although in the other Gospels the offering of wine vinegar (v.36) seems to be an act of kindness, the drink being a thirst quencher carried by soldiers, Luke connects it with their mockery of Christ (v.37). It may have been a compassionate act done in the midst of taunts.

38 All four Gospels contain the superscription, with John offering an explanation of the circumstances (19:19–22). The full text of the superscription may be seen by comparing all the Gospels. Luke's record shows the issue as Pilate, Jesus' Roman judge, saw it. Luke reserves the word "this" (*houtos*) for the end of the sentence, conveying the emphatic idea "The King of the Jews, this one!"

39–43 This conversation, unique to Luke's account, reinforces two characteristics of his Gospel. One (v.41) is the innocence of Jesus (cf. v.22 and comment). The other (v.43) is the immediate ("today") realization of God's saving grace through Christ (cf. 4:21 and comments).

As elsewhere (e.g., with Peter in 5:1–11), Luke focuses on one person in a group. In Matthew 27:44 and Mark 15:32 both criminals insult Jesus; here this attitude is attributed to one in particular (v.39). "Hurled insults" does not express the more serious aspect of the verb *eblasphēmei*. Marshall, following Beyer (TDNT, 1:623), observes, "To mock Jesus by refusing to take his powers seriously is to blaspheme against him; the use of the verb represents a Christian verdict in the light of who Jesus really is" (*Gospel of Luke*, p. 871). The criminal's taunt, "Aren't you the Christ?" is "bitterly sarcastic" (Morris, *Luke*, p. 328).

The other criminal (v.40) recognizes that Jesus is no mere pretender and that he will reign as king (v.42). Jesus' response (v.43) assures this criminal that he need not wait for any future event but that he would have an immediate joyful experience of fellowship with Jesus "in paradise" (*en tō paradeisō*). This Persian word, which had been taken over into Greek, symbolizes a place of beauty and delight. It means "park" or "garden" and refers to the Garden of Eden in Genesis 2:8 (LXX) and to the future bliss the garden symbolizes (Isa 51:3; cf. Rev 2:7). Paul said he was caught up into paradise (2 Cor 12:4), which may preclude the idea that Jesus descended into hell after his death.

Notes

34 The familiar words "Father, forgive them . . . doing" may not have been in the original text. While it is (with some variations) in ℵ A C f¹ 13 33, among other MSS, the following are among the significant and diverse MSS that omit it: P⁷⁵ B D W Θ and some versions. Reasons for and against its genuineness are not easy to weigh. Did the idea come from Stephen's prayer in Acts 7:60; or, more probably, was his prayer inspired by Jesus' prayer? Do we take it as a genuine saying of Jesus that was omitted only because later events—viz., the destruction of the temple and other misfortunes of the Jews—seemed to show that they were not forgiven? (The latter view applies the saying to the Jews rather than to the Roman soldiers.) Or did some anti-Semitic feeling cause it to be dropped? Does the fact that it so beautifully reflects what we know both of Jesus' attitude and of Luke's theology and style lead us to conclude that it must be original? Or should we think that it was skillfully woven into the narrative later, since it is hard to suppose that anything so appropriate to the context would have been dropped? Ellis (*Gospel of Luke*, pp. 267f.) and Marshall (*Gospel of Luke*, pp. 867f.) have especially fine treatments of the issue. Ellis argues well that the "ignorance motif" ("they do not know") is "part of Luke's theological emphasis," deriving from the OT. Deliberate and persistent ignorance, far from being excusable, is sinful. Considerations such as this and others mentioned above speak strongly for the genuineness of the saying in its context. The UBS editors concluded that even though they thought it was not originally part of this context, it "bears self-evident tokens of its dominical origin" (Metzger, *Textual Commentary*, p. 180). They therefore included it, but in double square brackets.

42 Εἰς τὴν βασιλείαν σου (*eis tēn basileian sou*, "into your kingdom") presents a double problem, textual and interpretive. While that reading is supported by P⁷⁵ B L, ἐν τῇ βασιλείᾳ σου (*en tē basileia sou*, "in your kingdom") occurs in other significant MSS (e.g., ℵ A C K W X Δ Θ) and a number of minuscules. Also, there is uncertainty as to what either of these readings means when viewed against Luke's other passages on the kingdom. While it is questionable whether a spatial concept of the kingdom is intended by *eis* ("into") and the accusative, the phrase would seem, from the perspective of Luke's eschatology, to indicate that the thief expected that Jesus would in some way assume his reign immediately. See the wording of 22:69 in contrast to the parallels (see comments above). *En* plus the dative would seem to refer to the return of Jesus. Put another way, does the thief speak of Jesus leaving this world for his kingdom? The latter would accord, in Marshall's view, with a Semitism meaning "as king" (*Gospel of Luke*, p. 872). With such a division of MSS and with such uncertainties, not only regarding what Luke might have written, but as to what a thief barely acquainted with Jesus' teaching might be expected to have meant, a firm conclusion is not possible. The balance textually seems to be on the side of *eis* with the accusative.

10. *Jesus' death*

23:44–49

⁴⁴It was now about the sixth hour, and darkness came over the whole land until the ninth hour, ⁴⁵for the sun stopped shining. And the curtain of the temple was torn in two. ⁴⁶Jesus called out with a loud voice, "Father, into your hands I commit my spirit." When he had said this, he breathed his last.

⁴⁷The centurion, seeing what had happened, praised God and said, "Surely this was a righteous man." ⁴⁸When all the people who had gathered to witness this sight saw what took place, they beat their breasts and went away. ⁴⁹But all those who knew him, including the women who had followed him from Galilee, stood at a distance, watching these things.

44–46 Luke refrains from giving a precise time ("about the sixth hour," v.44; cf. "about eight days," 9:28) but does imply by the word *ēdē* ("already"; NIV, "now") that the preceding events had filled the morning. Time was less precisely noted in those days, which may help explain some apparent differences between the Gospels. Matthew, Mark, and Luke agree that there was darkness from about the sixth hour to the ninth, i.e., from noon to three o'clock. The whole "land" (*gē*) could refer to all the "land" of Israel or, possibly, to the local area only. Luke does not say what caused the sun's light to fail (v.45; cf. Notes); nor does he say what significance should be given this fact, recorded in all three Synoptics. Certainly it emphasized the somberness of the event; some think it was to symbolize, or possibly to veil, the judgment endured on our behalf by Christ. Hendriksen (p. 1035) lists a number of Scriptures that link darkness with God's judgment.

Like Matthew and Mark, Luke states that the temple curtain was torn apart. This curtain was doubtless the one separating the Holy Place from the inner Most Holy Place (Exod 26:31–33). It might be argued that the word refers to the curtain at the entrance to the Holy Place (Exod 26:36–37), which would have been visible to passersby. The LXX uses the same word Luke does (*katapetasma*) for the curtain in each location. But in this extraordinary circumstance, which would have been accompanied by the sound of the tearing, the priests would have been aware of what had happened even if it had occurred inside the Holy Place. Such questions cannot be settled by typology. Neither can we ignore the allusion to this in Hebrews 10:19–22, where the veil can only be the one hiding the Holy of Holies. Access to the most holy God is now open through the death of Christ.

Normally a person in the last stages of crucifixion would not have the strength to speak beyond a weak groan, but each synoptic Gospel says that Jesus spoke with a "loud voice" (v.46). Jesus' words are from Psalm 31:5 (LXX 30:6), which was used by the Jews as an evening prayer. To the Christian reader who knows that Jesus' death was a voluntary act, they are beautifully appropriate. All four Gospels describe Jesus' moment of death in terse, restrained words.

47–49 All three Synoptics call on the centurion (v.47) as a witness to Jesus' uniqueness. To the modern reader, Luke's words "a righteous man" (*anthrōpos . . . dikaios*) may seem less significant than "Son of God" in Matthew 27:54 and Mark 15:39. The emphasis in Luke is on Jesus' innocence (cf. v.22 and comment); so this form of the saying is appropriate. Also the term "Son of God" might have been misunderstood by Luke's largely Gentile readership, as it was not unusual for pagans to use such terminology with a different meaning. The "people" referred to in v.48 are not the *laos*, who are so significant in Luke, but the *ochloi* ("crowds"), a mixed group. They were deeply affected, as were Jesus' own followers, who endured their inexpressible grief standing at a distance. Luke's Gospel does not name the women (v.49), as do all the other Gospels at this point, probably because he had named some of them in 8:3. All the Synoptics say that the women stood at a distance (cf. Ps 38:11).

Notes

45 Τοῦ ἡλίου ἐκλιπόντος (*tou hēliou eklipontos*, "the sun stopped shining") need not mean that the sun went through an eclipse. While the verb (our English word "eclipse" comes from it) can mean that, it can also mean any darkening or fading of the light. It is the same word Jesus used in his prayer for Peter's faith not to disappear (22:32). It may be that copyists used the variant ἐσκοτίσθη (*eskotisthē*, "was darkened") to avoid the idea of an eclipse. P[75] ℵ B retain a form of ἐκλείπω (*ekleipō*), while A and others have *eskotisthē*.

11. *Jesus' burial*

23:50–56

> [50]Now there was a man named Joseph, a member of the Council, a good and upright man, [51]who had not consented to their decision and action. He came from the Judean town of Arimathea and he was waiting for the kingdom of God. [52]Going to Pilate, he asked for Jesus' body. [53]Then he took it down, wrapped it in linen cloth and placed it in a tomb cut in the rock, one in which no one had yet been laid. [54]It was Preparation Day, and the Sabbath was about to begin.
> [55]The women who had come with Jesus from Galilee followed Joseph and saw the tomb and how his body was laid in it. [56]Then they went home and prepared spices and perfumes. But they rested on the Sabbath in obedience to the commandment.

50–54 Luke is careful to assure his readers of the credentials of the man who offered to bury Jesus. Here again Luke presents someone qualified to affirm by word or action that Jesus was a just and innocent man and that by inference the claims of Christianity are valid. He describes Joseph as *agathos kai dikaios* ("good and upright," v.50). He is also a good Jew, "waiting for the kingdom of God" (v.51), and so joins others in Luke whose piety and expectation of the Messiah validates their testimony (e.g., Simeon and Anna, 2:25–38). He was a member of the Council (the Sanhedrin) but had disagreed with their decision against Jesus.

Joseph laid the body in a tomb "cut in the rock" (v.53). We can still see such tombs today in rocky hillsides in Palestine; in fact, one was recently excavated at Tel Midras. They often have more than one chamber, with a special place for initial care of the body. Luke's description of the shroud does not provide enough detail to allow a comparison with the "shroud of Turin." We learn in v.54 that it was Friday (the probable meaning here of the word *paraskeuē*), and the Sabbath was about to begin at sundown.

55–56 Although Matthew and Mark mention the presence of the women at this point (v.55), they do not speak of the women's preparation of the spices in advance of Easter morning, as Luke does (v.56). He carefully notes that the women did not do this on the Sabbath, even though Jewish tradition apparently would have allowed care for the dead on a Sabbath (SBK, 2:52–53). In this way Luke stresses one more time the fidelity of Jesus and his followers to the Jewish laws.

C. *The Resurrection and Ascension* (24:1–53)

1. *The Resurrection*

24:1–12

> ¹On the first day of the week, very early in the morning, the women took the spices they had prepared and went to the tomb. ²They found the stone rolled away from the tomb, ³but when they entered, they did not find the body of the Lord Jesus. ⁴While they were wondering about this, suddenly two men in clothes that gleamed like lightning stood beside them. ⁵In their fright the women bowed down with their faces to the ground, but the men said to them, "Why do you look for the living among the dead? ⁶He is not here; he has risen! Remember how he told you, while he was still with you in Galilee: ⁷'The Son of Man must be delivered into the hands of sinful men, be crucified and on the third day be raised again.' " ⁸Then they remembered his words.
>
> ⁹When they came back from the tomb, they told all these things to the Eleven and to all the others. ¹⁰It was Mary Magdalene, Joanna, Mary the mother of James, and the others with them who told this to the apostles. ¹¹But they did not believe the women, because their words seemed to them like nonsense. ¹²Peter, however, got up and ran to the tomb. Bending over, he saw the strips of linen lying by themselves, and he went away, wondering to himself what had happened.

Luke 24 not only presents the climactic event of the Resurrection, but it includes a recapitulation of the saving mission of Christ (vv.6–7, 19–27, 45–47). The Ascension, with which the chapter and the book conclude, is the final goal of Jesus' earthly ministry (cf. 9:51 and comments). It also sets the scene for the church's ministry as recorded in Acts. The first section of the narrative, concerning events at the empty tomb, contains elements that differ from those given in Matthew and Mark. Some of these are often alleged to be discrepancies that invalidate the NT records of the Resurrection as dependable history. Or they have been viewed as redactional (i.e., editorial) changes Luke made to express his own theological perspectives. It is not the purpose of the comments that follow to resolve apparent discrepancies or to deal with Luke's redaction of the resurrection narrative, except as this has clear value for the expositor. The unique features of Luke's resurrection account deserve our attention as his contribution to the reality and meaning of the event.

1–3 All four Gospels specify the first day of the week (v.1) as the day of the Resurrection. This became the day of Christian worship (cf. Acts 20:7). The change from the traditional and biblical Sabbath is in itself a strong evidence of the Resurrection because it shows the strength of the disciples' conviction about what happened on that day. Luke refers to the time of day by the general statement that it was "very early." This fits well with what the other Gospels say, though each Gospel differs from the others. All four Gospels mention the removal of the stone (v.2). While this was not, as far as the NT reports, used as an apologetic to prove the Resurrection, it could not have failed to impress those who heard of it; and its inclusion here is hardly incidental. Only Luke, who has shown particular interest in physical reality —e.g., he is the only synoptic writer to use the phrase "in bodily form" (*sōmatikos*) to describe the Spirit's descent on Jesus at his baptism (3:22)—specifically says that the "body" (*sōma*) of Jesus was gone (v.3).

4–5 Here (v.4), as elsewhere (e.g., 1:29, 66; 2:19), Luke describes someone pondering a remarkable event. Luke speaks of "two men" rather than "an angel" (Matt 28:2) or "a young man" (Mark 16:5). For a writer to focus on just one person when another is also present is not unusual (both Mark and Luke single out one of the blind men at Jericho, Mark 10:46; Luke 18:35; cf. Matt 20:30). Luke's mention of two men at the tomb seems consistent with his other references to witnesses to Jesus (cf. Simeon and Anna, 2:25–38; and esp. 24:48; cf. also the prominence of witnesses in Acts). Two witnesses are the minimum number for validation (Deut 17:6; 19:15; cf. E.G. Bode, *The First Easter Morning*, p. 60, who draws on Morgenthaler, *Die lukanische Geschichtsschreibung*, 1:97–99; 2:7–11). That Luke understands that the two "men" were angels is evident from what he says of them in v.23. Moreover, he describes their clothes as gleaming like lightning (*astraptousē*, v.4), terminology he applies to Jesus' clothes at his transfiguration (9:29; cf. also Acts 1:10—"two men dressed in white"). Luke alone tells us that not only were the women frightened (v.5) but in their fear they bowed face down to the ground. The response of fear in the presence of supernatural visitation occurs elsewhere in Luke (e.g., 1:12, 29 [though in Mary's case not at the angel but at his message]; 2:9; 9:34). "The living" (*ton zōnta*), only in Luke, stresses the factual aspect of the Resurrection Luke also refers to in Acts 2:24: "It was impossible for death to keep its hold on him."

6–8 What Luke gives us here is not in the other Gospels: The angels show the meaning of the empty tomb by repeating the essence of the three passion predictions (9:22, 43–45; 18:31–33, and parallel passages in Matthew and Mark). They begin with the words "Remember how he told you" (v.6), perhaps implying that what the women should have understood earlier the Resurrection has now clarified. The third prediction (18:31–33) was followed by Luke's statement that the saying was obscure, hidden from them (18:34; cf. also 24:16). The Resurrection is the time for revelation and understanding (v.8). Some think the reference to Galilee (v.6) is an alteration of the saying in Matthew 28:7 and Mark 16:7. There Galilee is the place where Jesus would later meet with the disciples; here it is where Jesus had given his passion predictions. Luke obviously centers attention on Jesus' appearances in the vicinity of Jerusalem, the city of destiny in Luke (e.g., 9:51; 13:32–35). His selective focus on Jerusalem is not, however, a major disagreement with the other Synoptics; nor does his different use of the word Galilee contradict theirs.

Luke's frequent use of *dei* ("must," v.7) and other expressions of divine purpose have already been noted throughout this commentary (e.g., 2:49; 4:43; 19:5). It occurs in the first passion prediction (9:22), as it does in the other Synoptics, but then reappears only in Luke in 13:33; 17:25; 22:37. Chapter 24 contains two more references to the inevitable sequence of Jesus' death and resurrection (vv.25–27, 44–46). Luke's stress on God's plan and providence continues throughout Acts, often with *dei*, but also without it (Acts 2:23–24; see Bode, *First Easter*, pp. 65–67). The term "sinful men" (*anthrōpōn hamartōlōn*) occurs in Jesus' saying at Gethsemane about his impending betrayal (Matt 26:45; Mark 14:41)—a saying Luke does not have. The idea appears again in Acts 2:23 in the term "wicked men" (*anomōn*). Luke often speaks of "sinners," but usually he does so when referring to notorious people Jesus had compassion on. Here, in contrast, the "sinners" are those who opposed him and brought about his death. Only Luke has "on the third day."

9–12 Luke postpones naming the women till this point (v.10), whereas Matthew and Mark name them at the beginning of their resurrection narratives. Luke has already (8:1–3) told of the women who accompanied and supported Jesus in his ministry. (He also mentions the women at prayer with the apostles in Acts 1:14.) While the witness of women was not acceptable in those days, nevertheless Luke records their testimony (v.9). The apostles, in their incredulity, were unable to comprehend the reality the women were trying to convey (v.11). We see this incredulity again in Peter (v.12) and in the disciples on the road to Emmaus (vv.22–24). This reluctance to believe has an important relation to the evidences for the Resurrection. The disciples were not expecting that event (cf. v.25). Thus they cannot be called fit subjects for hallucination as some would have them be.

Verse 12, though omitted by the Western text (cf. Notes), is probably authentic. It is similar, but not identical, to John 20:6–7. Luke does not mention the "other disciple" (John 20:3), probably focusing on Peter as he did in 5:1–11. The strips of linen used in the burial bear their silent but eloquent testimony to the absence of Jesus' body. Peter leaves, "wondering" (*thaumazōn*) to himself about this. In Luke people "wonder" about things that are hard to understand. The word does not in itself imply either belief or unbelief. We conclude that Peter is still incredulous at this point, not because the verb implies it, but because his visit to the empty tomb fails, in spite of the evidence, to evoke a statement of belief from him (cf. John 20:8).

Notes

3 The MSS representing the so-called Western text omit the following: (1) v.3, τοῦ κυρίου Ἰησοῦ (*tou kyriou Iēsou*, "of the Lord Jesus"); (2) v.6, οὐκ ἔστιν ὧδε ἀλλα ἠγέρθη (*ouk estin hōde, alla ēgerthē*, "he is not here; he has risen"); (3) all of v.12; (4) v.36, καὶ λέγει αὐτοῖς, Εἰρήνη ὑμῖν (*kai legei autois, Eirēnē hymin*, "and said to them, 'Peace be with you'"); (5) all of v.40; (6) v.51, καὶ ἀνεφέρετο εἰς τὸν οὐρανόν (*kai anephereto eis ton ouranon*, "and was taken up into heaven"); and (7) v.52, προσκυνήσαντες αὐτόν (*proskynēsantes auton*, "worshiped him"). Because Westcott and Hort concluded that the Western text tended to add words not in the original, they thought that in the opposite circumstance, i.e., when instead of *interpolating* words the Western text *omitted* words found in other MS traditions, such omissions (or "noninterpolations") should be given much weight. In the instances mentioned here, there has been a reluctance on the part of some scholars to reject that reasoning. More recently, however, the tendency has been to examine each case on its own merits, using standard textual principles in making decisions. Verses 23 and 40 present special considerations because they are similar to John's account of the Resurrection. But in these verses, as in the other instances just cited, there are sound reasons for considering each verse a part of Luke's original text. (See Snodgrass, "Western Non-Interpolations," pp. 369–79; cf. Metzger, *Textual Commentary*, on each verse and on the issue of "Western Non-Interpolations," pp. 191–93.)

4 Καὶ ἐγένετο (*kai egeneto*), a familiar expression, properly left untranslated in NIV, is a

Semitic transitional term that generally contributes little to the meaning (cf. KJV, "and it came to pass"). Its significance relates to the reason for Luke's frequent use of Semitic idioms, a matter of slight relevance to preachers and other Bible teachers and therefore not stressed in this commentary. But in this crucial resurrection passage, it cannot be over-looked. The question is the source of Luke's information. Luke's use of Semitisms may, at least in some places, show that he is following early traditions containing Aramaic idioms. On the other hand, he may, whether using such sources directly or adapting material from Mark or non-Semitic sources, introduce Semitic terminology naturally because of his familiarity with the LXX and his desire to represent the ambience of the events he is reporting. This passage contains a number of characteristically Lukan terms and themes, some of which we have already noted. These, along with Luke's use of Semitisms, seem to indicate a mixture of Markan material, early traditions, and original touches of Luke's own editorial skill.

2. On the Emmaus road

24:13–35

13Now that same day two of them were going to a village called Emmaus, about seven miles from Jerusalem. 14They were talking with each other about every-thing that had happened. 15As they talked and discussed these things with each other, Jesus himself came up and walked along with them; 16but they were kept from recognizing him.

17He asked them, "What are you discussing together as you walk along?"

They stood still, their faces downcast. 18One of them, named Cleopas, asked him, "Are you only a visitor to Jerusalem and do not know the things that have happened there in these days?"

19"What things?" he asked.

"About Jesus of Nazareth," they replied. "He was a prophet, powerful in word and deed before God and all the people. 20The chief priests and our rulers hand-ed him over to be sentenced to death, and they crucified him; 21but we had hoped that he was the one who was going to redeem Israel. And what is more, it is the third day since all this took place. 22In addition, some of our women amazed us. They went to the tomb early this morning, 23but didn't find his body. They came and told us that they had seen a vision of angels, who said he was alive. 24Then some of our companions went to the tomb and found it just as the women had said, but him they did not see."

25He said to them, "How foolish you are, and how slow of heart to believe all that the prophets have spoken! 26Did not the Christ have to suffer these things and then enter his glory?" 27And beginning with Moses and all the Prophets, he explained to them what was said in all the Scriptures concerning himself.

28As they approached the village to which they were going, Jesus acted as if he were going farther. 29But they urged him strongly, "Stay with us, for it is nearly evening; the day is almost over." So he went in to stay with them.

30When he was at the table with them, he took bread, gave thanks, broke it and began to give it to them. 31Then their eyes were opened and they recognized him, and he disappeared from their sight. 32They asked each other, "Were not our hearts burning within us while he talked with us on the road and opened the Scriptures to us?"

33They got up and returned at once to Jerusalem. There they found the Eleven and those with them, assembled together 34and saying, "It is true! The Lord has risen and has appeared to Simon." 35Then the two told what had happened on the way, and how Jesus was recognized by them when he broke the bread.

The Emmaus story is a literary and spiritual jewel. It is at once a moving story, a testimony to the Resurrection, an explanation of the empty tomb, and an occasion for Luke to summarize several of his major themes. Despite the fact that it has to a superlative degree the ring of truth—what literary scholars call "verisimilitude"—some have considered it legendary (cf. Notes).

13–16 The opening words of v.13 link this story with the entire Easter event. "Now" (*kai idou*) moves the reader's attention to a new and important phase of Luke's narrative. "That same day" ties the narrative to Jesus' death and resurrection (cf. the sequence in 23:54, 56; 24:1). Two travelers are speaking together (vv.14–15); so a valid witness is provided. A twofold witness is necessary according to Jewish law. Furthermore, the concept of witness is, as we have seen, important to Luke. Two witnesses (Simeon and Anna) bore testimony to the Messiah's arrival (2:25–38); now the two travelers testify to a particular resurrection appearance of Jesus (24:35). The words "of them" (*ex autōn*, v.13) do not clearly identify who the two are. They are not two of the Eleven (v.9; cf. v.33). Probably they are two of the followers of Jesus who had come to Jerusalem for the Passover. So they had been among the "disciples" who lauded Jesus on his triumphal entry to the city (19:39) and were now returning home. At any rate, the phrase "of them," like the opening words of v.13, establishes a continuity with the foregoing events.

The fact that this event occurs when the two disciples "were going" (*ēsan poreuomenoi*, v.13) and "walked along" (*syneporeueto*, v.15) continues the travel theme prominent in Luke, especially in his unique central section (9:51–19:44). That section begins as Jesus "resolutely set out" (*to prosōpon estērisen tou poreuesthai*) for Jerusalem (9:51). Now these two are leaving that same city. Shortly after the earlier journey to Jerusalem began, a man had approached Jesus regarding discipleship "as they were walking" (*poreuomenōn autōn*, 9:57). Now, after the Resurrection, Jesus approaches two disheartened followers as they are walking. Acts continues the theme of Jesus' disciples traveling, going from Jerusalem to Rome (Paul, in ch. 28) and ultimately to the ends of the earth as "witnesses" (1:8). As for the identity of Emmaus, this is uncertain (cf. Notes). It is enough to know that it is a village near Jerusalem.

The two were talking about events surrounding Jesus' resurrection. Between the lines of their dialogue, Luke shows their bewilderment. He uses two different verbs, one of them repeated: "they were talking" (*hōmiloun*, v.14), "as they talked" (*en tō homilein*, v.15), and "discussed" (*syzētein*). So the tension mounts in preparation for Jesus' appearance. Luke introduces Jesus into the story with the emphatic "Jesus himself" (*autos Iēsous*); and his comment that Jesus "walked along with" (*syneporeueto*) them suggests to us, whether or not Luke intended it, Jesus' presence with his disciples in the church age. The passive form in "were kept [*ekratounto*] from recognizing him" (v.16) may be a "divine passive," i.e., a means of connoting that an action, the subject of which is not mentioned, is actually the work of God. This device introduces the structural pattern of nonrecognition and recognition, which is central in this beautiful narrative.

17–18 Still another verb describes their discussion; *antiballete* ("discussed") reflects the exchange of ideas (lit., "throwing back and forth"). The scene in vv.14–17 is of a persistent but rather baffled attempt to understand the meaning of this most momentous weekend in history. Luke now uses a different word for walking (*peripateō*; cf. comments on vv.13–16). Another mention of walking is certainly not necessary merely to convey that fact, and we may assume that there is a deliberate

1051

emphasis on that movement. Therefore it is striking that when Jesus addressed them, the two travelers stopped short and "stood still" (*estathēsan*). Their attitude at that point was gloomy, perhaps even sullen. Only one of the two (Cleopas) is named (v.18), probably because he was known to at least some of Luke's readers. One tradition identifies him as an uncle of Jesus, brother of Joseph, and father of Simeon, who became a leader of the Jerusalem church (Eusebius, *Ecclesiastical History* 3.11; cf. Ellis, *Gospel of Luke*, p. 894). This is not the same man as Clopas (John 19:25), though the two names are variant spellings of each other.

19–24 What follows constitutes an affirmation about the person and work of Christ that is of great significance for our understanding of Jesus and of Luke's perception of him. Concerning the opening words, R.J. Dillon (*From Eyewitnesses to Ministers of the Word*, p.114) observes, "This characterization, together with the assertion of full publicity amongst the people, contains pointed echoes of Luke's introductory summary of Jesus' ministry [in the power of the] Spirit (Lk 4, 14; cp. Acts 10, 38)." See comments above at 4:14 on the popular response to Jesus. The statement there about his reputation and power precedes the progammatic statement about his ministry under the impetus of the Spirit in 4:18–19. Acts 10:38 is Peter's summary of Jesus' powerful, Spirit-filled ministry (cf. Acts 2:22) and includes the statement "he went around doing good." Peter then tells Cornelius, "We are witnesses of everything" (Acts 10:39), calling to mind Luke 1:2—"eyewitnesses and servants of the word." The importance of the affirmation of the two disciples here in 24:19 must not in any way be underestimated. It is integral to Luke's theology and purpose.

"He was a prophet" recalls the passage in chapter 4 just mentioned, where Jesus clearly identified himself with the prophets (4:24). While in Luke's narrative Jesus is perceived as a prophet (e.g., 7:16; cf. Minear, *Heal and Reveal*, pp. 102–21), the Resurrection affirmed him to be much more, as the two on the Emmaus road are to learn (e.g., v.26, "the Christ . . . glory"). The word "prophet" does not appear in what Peter told Cornelius about Jesus (Acts 10:36–43). This is probably not because Cornelius was not Jewish, for Jesus was "Lord of all" (Acts 10:36), but because the word "prophet" was inadequate to comprehend all Jesus is. The term "prophet" is then not so much an invalid as an incomplete characterization of Jesus. Another of Luke's favorite terms is "people" (*laos*), used throughout his Gospel for the responsive hearers in Israel (cf. 1:17, 68, 77; 2:10, 31–32). Later Luke will use *laos* of believing Gentiles (Acts 18:10).

The "chief priests and our rulers" (v.20) stand in contrast to the "people" (v.21) as elsewhere in Luke. It was they who "handed him over" for crucifixion. In v.21 the words "but we" (*hemēis de*, emphatic) of the two disciples provide still another contrast. Unlike the rulers, they "hoped" that Jesus would bring deliverance. Observe that the verb is "hoped," not "trusted" (as in KJV); there is a big difference between trusting Jesus as our Deliverer and Savior and hoping that he will prove to be our Deliverer and Savior. The past tense of "hoped" is, under the present circumstances, a pathetic reminder of their inability to recognize Jesus or to believe the report of the empty tomb. Their expectation that he would "redeem Israel" recalls the words of Zechariah in 1:68 (cf. 2:38; 21:28). In view of v.46 and the passion predictions, the term "third day" had a significance to Luke's readers. What should have been the day of hope realized was for them the day of hope extinguished.

The final ("in addition," *alla kai*) incomprehensible element in the travelers' report was the report of the empty tomb (v.22). This looks back to vv.1–12. Again Luke used the word "body" (v.23; see comment above on v.3). The mention of "angels" shows that this is what Luke meant by "men" in v.4, which is in harmony with the other Gospels. Verse 24 recalls v.12. In the last words in the report, "him they did not see," the word "him" (*auton*) is placed in an emphatic position. The empty tomb without the appearance of Jesus himself was inadequate. It ironically becomes the last sad part of their confused response to Jesus' question, "What things?" (v.19).

25–27 The reader of the Greek text will immediately observe following the pronoun *auton* ("him") in its emphatic position in v.24 that it occurs in v.25 (*kai autos*, "and he"; NIV, "he") to refer (still emphatically) to the same person, though he remains unrecognized. "The Stranger seizes the platform from the confused disciple" (Dillon, *Eyewitnesses*, p. 132). Jesus, who in his transfiguration was superior to Moses and Elijah (9:28–36), now invokes Moses and the Prophets to substantiate the divine plan of his path from suffering to glory (v.27). The word "all" (v.25) is a warning not to treat the Scriptures selectively. Such selectivity could lead to the omission of the Messiah's suffering (v.26). But "the Christ" (Messiah) did "have to" (*edei*) suffer. The verb *dei*, meaning "it is necessary," is one of Luke's key words (cf. 2:49; 4:43; 13:16, 33; 15:32; 18:1; 19:5; 21:9; 22:7, 37; 24:7, 44, along with the basic passion prediction of 9:22 that occurs also in Matthew and Mark; cf. comments on those verses). The future glory of the Christ (v.26) was mentioned in the context of the passion prediction, ascribed there to the "Son of Man" (9:26; cf. 21:27). Some have argued that here "glory" is to be understood as a substitute expression for "was raised from the dead" (cf. Dillon, *Eyewitnesses*, pp. 141ff.). More likely it refers to the honor anticipated in the OT for the Messiah and attributed to the Son of Man in the verses just referred to. The unexpected element in Christ's messiahship was his suffering. On the other hand, one could hardly argue that Christ's glory excludes the Resurrection. Paul quoted the OT to prove the necessity of both the suffering and the resurrection of the Messiah (Acts 17:2–3). "Beginning with" (v.27) probably implies that Jesus drew on all the Scriptures but principally on the Law (Gen-Deut) and the Prophets (Marshall, *Gospel of Luke*, p. 897). The central subject of these OT passages is "himself."

For several reasons vv.25–27 are vitally important. With great clarity they show that the sufferings of Christ, as well as his glory, were predicted in the OT and that all the OT Scriptures are important. They also show that the way the writers of the NT used the OT had its origin, not in their own creativity, but in the postresurrection teachings of Jesus, of which this passage is a paradigm. The passage also exemplifies the role of the OT in Luke's own theology. Although he does not directly quote the OT Scriptures as many times as Matthew does, nevertheless he alludes frequently to the OT, demonstrating that what God has promised must take place and employing a "proof-from-prophecy" apologetic for the truth of the gospel.

28–32 The invitation for Jesus to stay with the two follows the ancient custom of hospitality. As the afternoon drew on and suppertime approached, the stranger would need food and lodging. Jesus had "acted as if" (*prosepoiēsato*) he were going to continue his journey (v.28). The verb *prospoieō*, in spite of well-meaning efforts to weaken it to avoid any thought of deceit on Jesus' part (e.g., Plummer, in loc.), often means "pretend" (BAG, LSJ, MM, s.v.). Such a gesture would, like the invitation itself, be appropriate in the custom of those days. While it is probably true, as Plummer says, that Jesus would have gone on, had he not been invited to stay, this polite action seems intended to draw out a very strong response from Cleopas and his companion, who indeed then "urged him strongly" (*parebiasanto*) to stay (v.29). In other contexts this verb can mean to force someone to do something.

The recognition scene is the third high point in this narrative, the first two being the long reply of Cleopas and his companion to Jesus' question and Jesus' exposition of the OT's teaching about himself. While from a church perspective some have wrongly seen the Lord's Supper in the breaking of the bread, we must also realize that a table scene is characteristic of Luke and probably of his special source material (cf. 5:29; 7:36; 14:1, 7, 12, 15–16; and, less obviously, 10:38–40). What is remarkable is that Jesus took the role of the host and broke the bread, giving thanks (v.30). Of course this recalls the feeding of the five thousand (9:10–17, N.B. v.16) as well as the Last Supper (22:19), though it was not a celebration of the latter.

As to whether it was through the actual breaking of bread or through divine intervention that the moment of truth came and the two disciples recognized Jesus, the answer must be that it was through both. Whether the two noticed the nail scars (Luke does not say they did), Jesus' acting as host led to the recognition. At the same time, the passive verb *diēnoichthēsan* ("were opened") implies divine action (v.31), as was the case when Jesus' identity was hidden from them (v.16). This provides uniformity in the structure and theological meaning, as God is the revealer of the risen Christ. Note the repetition of Jesus' opening "the Scriptures" (v.32) and "their minds" (v.45).

The narrative ends abruptly as Jesus disappeared and Cleopas and his companion reflected on their feelings of intense inner warmth (cf. Ps 39:3; Jer 20:9; the vocabulary differs but something similar may be in mind). (For a survey of interpretations of *kaiomenē* ["burning"], see Marshall, *Gospel of Luke*, pp. 898–99.) The specific occasion of these feelings is the presence of the Lord and his expounding the OT.

33–35 The words "at once" (*autē tē hōra*, lit., "in the same hour," v.33) continue the chronology of the resurrection day (cf. comment at v.13). The reunion with the Eleven brought assurance to all, as the two disciples fulfilled their role as witnesses (vv.34–35). They especially spoke of recognizing Jesus when he broke bread with them (v.35).

Notes

The historicity of the Emmaus story has often been challenged (e.g., H.D. Betz, "The Origin and Nature of Christian Faith According to the Emmaus Legend," Int 23 [1969]: 32–46). There are, indeed, elements of the story many find difficult to accept—not merely the inability of the two to recognize Jesus, but the very appearance of Jesus after his death. But this difficulty relates to the concept one has of the Resurrection itself and of the possibility of a supernatural work of God in the nonrecognition and recognition sequence. There are also similarities to elements in other ancient narratives. We must, however, be careful about drawing conclusions from works written after Luke was. Also, we "must not invoke such parallels prematurely, on the basis of mere resemblance, as instruments of interpretation" (Dillon, *Eyewitnesses*, pp. 73f.). It is impossible to prove or disprove the historicity of a story such as this that exists in no other literature and that, unlike the Resurrection, has produced no effect capable of investigation. Apart from the consideration of alleged legendary elements (remembering that issues of form do not settle issues of historicity, cf. Marshall, *Gospel of Luke*, p. 891), such issues will be decided on the basis of the setting of the story, both in the resurrection narrative and within Luke's carefully researched work, with care not to reject what one may consider, a priori, difficult to accept.

13 The location of Emmaus, "about seven miles from Jerusalem," is of minor concern to the expositor but of historical interest. Attention centers on several possible sites, but certainty is not possible at this time. Two sites are located at an approximately correct distance (one about nine miles away, the other is even closer to Luke's "sixty stadia"— approximately seven miles). They are Abu-Ghosh and El-Qubeibeh. There is little evidence, however, that either is the site.

Another place, Motza-Illit, is only three and one-half miles from Jerusalem. To identify this with the village in Luke, one has to assume that Luke's figure of sixty stadia applied to a round trip. In Jesus' day it was only a "village" (κώμη, *kōmē*), precisely Luke's word. Both Josephus and the Talmud mention it, the first as Emmaus and the second as Motza. It is very possible that the Semitic sound of Ha-Motza became Ammaous or Emmaus. A Roman colony was established there later in the first century, and so it is now also known as Qaloniya or Colonia. Evidence has come to light of a Byzantine church there, indicating that the site was reverenced. This may well be the true location.

There is still another site, much better known: Imwas (by Latrun), known also as Nicopolis probably since the time of Elagabulus (A.D. 218–22). It was prominent as the place of a great victory of Judas Maccabeus in the second century B.C., described in 1 Macc 3–4. The site continued to be well known throughout Christian history, and it naturally has been favored by many as the NT Emmaus. One serious problem is that it is not 60 but 160 stadia away (a problem Sinaiticus and other MSS seem to have addressed by changing the number to 160). This distance, however, seems long, though not impossible, for the two disciples to have traveled in both directions (cf. v.33). It would have meant a round trip total of 30 miles in one busy day, with the return trip started no later than early evening. It is possible that there were actually two places known as Emmaus in Jesus' day: the *village*, hardly known, 3½ miles or 30 stadia away, and the *city*, 160 stadia or 19 miles away. It was perhaps the former to which the disciples went on the Resurrection day. See J. Monson, *A Survey of the Geographical and Historical Setting of the Bible* (Jerusalem: Institute for Holy Land Studies, 1977), pp. 3f., of Benjamin Field Study section; R.M. Mackowski, "Where Is Biblical Emmaus?" *Science et Esprit* 32 (1980): 93–103.

3. The appearance to the disciples

24:36–49

36While they were still talking about this, Jesus himself stood among them and said to them, "Peace be with you."

37They were startled and frightened, thinking they saw a ghost. 38He said to them, "Why are you troubled, and why do doubts rise in your minds? 39Look at my hands and my feet. It is I myself! Touch me and see; a ghost does not have flesh and bones, as you see I have."

40When he had said this, he showed them his hands and feet. 41And while they still did not believe it because of joy and amazement, he asked them, "Do you have anything here to eat?" [42]They gave him a piece of broiled fish, [43]and he took it and ate it in their presence.

[44]He said to them, "This is what I told you while I was still with you: Everything must be fulfilled that is written about me in the Law of Moses, the Prophets and the Psalms."

[45]Then he opened their minds so they could understand the Scriptures. [46]He told them, "This is what is written: The Christ will suffer and rise from the dead on the third day, [47]and repentance and forgiveness of sins will be preached in his name to all nations, beginning at Jerusalem. [48]You are witnesses of these things. [49]I am going to send you what my Father has promised; but stay in the city until you have been clothed with power from on high."

This is the third Easter narrative in Luke. In the first Jesus is not seen; in the second he appears to two disciples; this time he appears to the Eleven. The narrative probably goes back to an older source that also lies behind John 20:19–23. It does not have as many distinctively Lukan touches as the Emmaus story. The events Luke tells us of here also provide the substance for his apologetic for Jesus' bodily resurrection in Acts 1:3–4 and Peter's witness to Cornelius (Acts 10:40–43). Here it is not Jesus' resurrection as such that is being proved but the fact that the sudden visitor was indeed Jesus, present in a tangible body.

36 The care with which Luke connects the events after the Crucifixion chronologically (23:54, 56; 24:1, 9, 13, 33) is again apparent in the words "While they were still talking about this." Once more Luke focuses attention on Jesus by the reflexive pronoun *autos* (i.e., "Jesus himself"; cf. comment on v.25). The next words, "stood among them" (*estē en mesō*), are almost identical to those in John 20:19 (*estē eis to meson*). A sudden appearance is implied (cf. the sudden disappearance in v.31), but Luke does not include the reference to closed doors found in John. "Peace be with you" may not have been in the original but added by a copyist who knew John 20:19. Yet the words may belong to the same tradition John and Luke used (cf. Notes). The characteristically Semitic "peace" (Heb. *šalôm*) would be a striking greeting, if one were expecting the more familiar Greek *chaire* (cf. 1:28).

37–39 Luke's Gospel opened with a terrified Zechariah in the unexpected presence of an angel (1:12). Now, near its end, Luke describes the fright of the disciples at the unexpected appearance of the risen Christ (v.37). One might have thought they would not respond this way, since they had just been hearing about Jesus' appearance on the Emmaus road. But whereas in that case Jesus had walked up to Cleopas and his companion as any traveler might, this time he appeared suddenly. Equally surprising to the reader are their doubts (v.38). These are significant for any who think that the disciples were expecting the Resurrection and projected their hopes into a hallucination. Jesus identified himself very emphatically (v.39): "It is I myself" (*egō eimi autos*, cf. the *egō eimi*, "I am," frequent in John). The methods of crucifixion varied slightly, but Jesus apparently had nails in his hands (the Greek word can include wrists) and feet. Seeing and touching would convince the disciples. Later on John wrote of touching Jesus, not specifically with respect to the Resurrection, but as an argument against docetism (1 John 1:1). As in vv.3, 23, where he mentioned the body of Jesus, Luke drew attention to the physical aspect of the Resurrection.

The argument one sometimes hears that Jesus' appearance in "flesh and bones" here contradicts Paul's statement in 1 Corinthians 15:50 that "flesh and blood cannot inherit the kingdom of God" misses Paul's idomatic meaning; the human body cannot develop into a resurrection body without the change only God can bring.

40–43 Verse 40 is lacking in some MSS, but it is more likely genuine and is certainly appropriate (cf. Notes). Verse 41a is a beautifully human touch. Jesus provides further evidence of his physical presence by eating (vv.42–43). Commentators refer to instances such as Genesis 18:8 and 19:3 as examples of eating by supernatural visitors, though in these two instances the reason was not, as here, to show that they were not ghosts.

44–49 From time to time Luke has taken care to show that whatever the Lord has said unfailingly takes place (e.g., 2:20, last phrase; 2:26; 19:32; 22:13, 37). That implication is perhaps present in the words "This is what I told you" (*houtoi hoi logoi mou*, lit., "these are my words," v.44). Luke has a double emphasis in these verses, that which the OT predicted (notice the words "must be fulfilled"), and that which Jesus had taught during his ministry. The clause "while I was still with you" is a way of distinguishing between the days of Jesus' earthly ministry and his temporary postresurrection ministry before the Ascension. "Everything" (*panta*, v.44) recalls "all" (*pasin*, v.25); "must" (*dei*) corresponds to "have to" (*edei*) in v.26 (see comment there); "Law . . . Prophets . . . Psalms" expands "Moses and all the Prophets" in v.27 by adding the Psalms as a major component of the third division of the OT, the so-called Writings.

In v.31 the eyes of the two were "opened" (*diēnoichthēsan*). Now Jesus has "opened" (*diēnoixen*) the disciples' minds (v.45). Again Luke emphasizes the "Scriptures." The reader of the Greek text will see this emphasis in the pattern of related words: *gegrammena* ("written," v.44) . . . *graphas* ("Scriptures," v.45) . . . *gegraptai* ("written," v.46). The formula "on the third day" (cf. v.7) goes back to the first passion prediction (9:22). Even the widespread preaching of repentance and forgiveness was predicted in the OT (cf. Acts 26:23). Rabbis in the first centuries of our era debated whether or not they should engage in active proselytization; and some cited OT passages, especially in Isaiah, which referred to the coming of the Gentiles to the Lord. Such Scriptures as Isaiah 42:6; 49:6; 60:3 may underlie v.47 here (cf. Acts 13:47). The fulfillment began in Acts 2:38: "Repent . . . forgiven." Gentiles heard these words in Acts 10:43 and 17:30 (cf. Paul's commission, Acts 26:17–18). The idea of reaching the Gentiles is certainly prominent in Luke (e.g., the mission to the seventy or seventy-two, probably representing the nations of the world [10:1]; see comments). Also, the place of Jerusalem as the base of the mission accords with Luke's constant featuring of that city. Likewise Luke has stressed the place of "witnesses" and will continue to do so in Acts (e.g., 1:8). Therefore, v.48 supports his emphasis. The pronouns *hymeis* ("you") in v.48, *ego* ("I") in v.49, and *hymeis* ("you") again as the subject of "stay" in v.49 (omitted by NIV) are emphatic and in contrast to one another. What the Father "promised" (v.49) is the Holy Spirit (Acts 1:4–5; 2:16–17), who was indeed the promised "power" (Acts 1:8). This "power from on high" (*ex hypsous dynamin*) has been known in Luke from the very beginning of his narrative. The Son of God was conceived in Mary when she was overshadowed by the "power of the Most High" (*dynamis hypsistou*, 1:35).

Notes

36, 40 See Notes on v.3 for the textual issue in these verses.

4. The Ascension

24:50–53

> 50When he had led them out to the vicinity of Bethany, he lifted up his hands and blessed them. 51While he was blessing them, he left them and was taken up into heaven. 52Then they worshiped him and returned to Jerusalem with great joy. 53And they stayed continually at the temple, praising God.

The Ascension is more than the last event in Luke's narrative sequence or a postscript to the Resurrection. He had already mentioned it in 9:51 as Jesus' ultimate goal in his great journey toward Jerusalem (cf. comment on 9:51). The Ascension also has significance in the opening verses of Acts. The brevity of the account here at the close of Luke's Gospel is not the measure of Luke's estimate of its importance. Perhaps he already had in mind an expanded version of the Ascension at the beginning of Acts; perhaps he was simply near the end of an already long scroll (Morris, *Luke*, p. 344). This brevity may also imply a telescoping of the entire closing narrative, thus explaining why Luke did not include sufficient chronological data to indicate how much time had elapsed since Resurrection Day. Nevertheless his words here, though few, are weighty with theological significance and very much in character with the entire book. Of the Gospel authors, only Luke records the Ascension.

50–51 NIV's "to the vicinity of" (v.50) translates *pros* ("toward") and guards against the supposition that they had already arrived at Bethany and so were not actually on the Mount of Olives (Acts 1:12). Bethany was on the other side of the mount to the south. Jesus' action in lifting up his hands and blessing the disciples (v.51) was priestly. The word "bless" (*eulogeō*) was significant at the opening of Luke. Zechariah the priest was rendered speechless in the temple, so that he was unable to pronounce the priestly blessing on the people when he came out (1:22). Such a blessing now concludes the book. Elizabeth blessed Mary and her child (1:42); Zechariah blessed God (NIV, "praising") when, on his declaration of John's name, his speech was restored (1:64); he then blessed (NIV, "praise") God again in his song (1:68); Simeon blessed (NIV, "praised") God in the temple on seeing Jesus (2:28) and then blessed his parents (2:34). This word does not appear again in Luke till Jesus blessed the bread at Emmaus (24:30). Luke immediately uses the word again in v.51 and again in v.53. Thus he places Jesus clearly within the spiritual setting of the temple and priesthood. As resurrected Messiah, Jesus has the authority to bless. This imagery forms an important part of the Letter to the Hebrews, which describes the high priestly intercession of Christ after his ascension into heaven (e.g., Heb 1:3; 4:14; 6:19–20; 7:23–25; cf. Rom 8:34; Eph 1:20). Jesus is also the Prophet of God, and we are again reminded of the prophet Elijah (cf. 4:26). That prophet was "taken up" to heaven (2 Kings 2:11; LXX, *anelēmphthē*; NIV, "went up"; observe the same verb in Acts 1:2 and in Acts 1:11 and the cognate noun in Luke 9:51, though here in 24:51 the verb is *anephereto*). Luke's conclusion points to Jesus as prophet, priest, and Messiah.

52–53 Jesus is also the Son of God, and so "they worshiped him" (v.52). Luke's beautiful Gospel closes with the theme of "joy" restated in v.52 and with the city of Jerusalem and its temple again presented as the true home of Christianity—the origin of the Christian gospel and the Christian church (cf. remarks on Jerusalem throughout this commentary, e.g., 13:31–35; 19:28–44; cf. Acts 1:8). Luke's theme of doxology reappears at the very end, as the disciples are last seen "blessing" (NIV, "praising") God (v.53; cf. note on text), a response to Christ's blessing them in vv.50–51. This is both an appropriate conclusion to Luke's Gospel and a reminder to us to live a life of praise as we wait for the return of the ascended Lord.

Notes

51–52 See Note on v.3 for the textual issue in these verses.

53 There is also a textual issue here. The Byzantine texts have αἰνοῦντες καὶ εὐλογοῦντες (*ainountes kai eulogountes,* "praising and blessing"), a reading that goes back to A f¹ f¹³ 33 and other texts. If this is, as most assume, a conflation, one must choose between the highly attested *eulogountes* (P⁷⁵ ℵ B, among others) and *ainountes* (supported by the Western text). Internal considerations are somewhat in balance (see Metzger, *Textual Commentary*, pp. 190–91), but the external witnesses give the preference to *eulogountes*. It is possible that the significant use of εὐλογέω (*eulogeō,* "bless") in vv.50–51 may have caused copyists to introduce that reading here. But if, as other considerations make likely, it is the original reading here, it fits in beautifully with Luke's choice of the verb in vv.50–51. Having been blessed by God, the disciples now bless him in return (cf. Eph 1:3 for the same reciprocity). NIV's "praising" may be a nice compromise, representing both verbs, though "blessing" might be preferable and more consistent with vv.50–51.